A TEXT BOOK OF OPERATING SYSTEM

Dr. Lakhwinder Kaur
(Reader)
Dept. of Comp. Engg.
University of College of Engg.
Punjabi University, Patiala (PB)

Dr. Savita Gupta
(Asst. Professor)
Dept. Professor
Dept. of Comp. Engg.
SLIET, Longowal (PB)

Er. Jatinder Singh
(Asst. Professor)
Dept. of I.T.
Sukhvinder College of Engg. and Tech.
Gurdaspur (PB)

KHANNA BOOK PUBLISHING CO. (P) LTD.

Publisher of Engineering and Computer Books

4C/4344, Ansari Road, Darya Ganj, New Delhi-110002
Phone : 011-23244447-48 **Mobile:** +91-9910909320
E-mail : contact@khannabooks.com
Website : www.khannabooks.com

Price: ₹ 998.00

ISBN: 978-81-907448-12

A Textbook of Operating Systems
by Jatinder Singh,
Lakhwinder Kaur, Savita Gupta

First Edition: 2008
Reprint: 2025

Published by:
Khanna Book Publishing Co. (P) Ltd.
CIN: U22110DL1998PTC095547

Visit us at: **www.khannabooks.com**
Write us at: **contact@khannabooks.com**

Printed in India.

PREFACE TO THE FIRST EDITION

An Operating System is a complex software package that manages the resources of a computer system, and provides the base upon which applications can be written. The operating system thus needs a mechanism to reliably juggle the various needs of the underlining platform. This is provided through a driver mechanism, and through this the operating system can keep the hardware in check. This implies that extensive study and research is mandatory to study the operating system concepts. Our major goal is to throw light on the world of operating systems in details. In this book we will study the basic components of an operating system, their functions, mechanisms, policies and techniques used in their implementation and several examples from popular operating systems. The purpose of the book is to make the students understand the fundamentals of operating systems conveniently. The book you hold in your hands is organized systematically into seventeen chapters and four case studies in seven units.

Unit 1 : INTRODUCTION TO OPERATING SYSTEMS

This unit contains first two most basic chapters for getting a feel of the subject.

Chapter 1. The first chapter deals with the basics of operating system. Almost every kind of operating system is introduced in this chapter and it provides a convenient environment for the reader to grasp concept of operating systems before reading the whole book.

Chapter 2. The second chapter provides the view of different structures of operating system as a whole. This chapter firstly provides the basics of computer structure and then explains the concepts and frameworks for operating systems.

Unit 2 : PROCESS MANAGEMENT

This unit deals with process description and control. The detail of process concept is considered from a number of points of view with emphasis on implementation of processes.

Chapter 3. In the third chapter, the process states, PCB, process creation, process deletion and everything that can happen to a process are discussed in details.

Chapter 4. In the fourth chapter, the implementation of process is discussed with the intent of providing in-depth view of algorithms used to prevent race condition. This chapter is full of examples that highlight the practical approach of the book.

Chapter 5. The fifth chapter discusses the process scheduling in great details, all the scheduling algorithms are discussed using large number of examples. This chapter is written by taking special care of the fact that every tit-bit of the algorithms should be clear to the readers.

Chapter 6. The sixth chapter discloses the concept of deadlock. A systematic approach has been adopted to clarify the concept of preemptive, non-preemptive scheduling, deadline and other types of scheduling. The large number of illustrations and elaborated study is the most salient feature of this chapter.

Unit 3 : MEMORY MANAGEMENT

This unit deals with memory management and virtual memory. This portion is blend of fundamentals and recent concepts of memory management

Chapter 7. The seventh chapter discusses the memory management in great details; all the techniques are discussed using large number of examples.

Chapter 8. In chapter eight the reader can find an explanation of virtual memory and large number of examples for page replacement algorithms.

Unit 4 : FILE AND DEVICE MANAGEMENT

This unit deals with file, device and storage management. This portion elaborates everything about file, directories, file and directory structure, input/output device management, working of I/O subsystem and how secondary storage is organized and managed.

Chapter 9. Chapter nine addresses the basics of file management and provide the coverage of file and directory structure.

Chapter 10. Chapter ten provides the knowledge about the implementation of file, like space allocation for directories, protection mechanism for files and how files are accessed from storage.

Chapter 11. The chapter eleven discusses the methods for accessing the auxiliary memory. By storage management we mean the manner in which the main storage is managed and viewed.

The RAID that introduce the idea of redundancy which improves the overall reliability of the system, are discussed in great details.

Chapter 12. Chapter twelve present everything about the devices starting from types of devices, types of device access to the working of I/O traffic controller, I/O scheduler and I/O device handlers.

Unit 5 : SECURITY AND PROTECTION

This unit introduces the security and protection mechanisms. Security refers to the policy of authorizing accesses whereas protection refers to the actual mechanisms implemented to enforce the specified policy.

Chapter 13. The chapter thirteen discusses important security related policies like authentication and authorization and Integrity are discussed. Public and private key algorithms are also elaborated in this chapter.

Chapter 14. The chapter fourteen provides an overview of system protection. Protection must ensure that only those processes that have gained proper authorization from the OS can operate on memory segments. The access control using passwords and access matrix etc is discussed with help of examples.

Unit 6 : NETWORK AND DISTRIBUTED SYSTEMS

This unit contains first three introductory chapters for getting a feel of the multiprocessing, distributed and network systems.

Chapter 15. The fifteenth chapter introduces the concept of computer networks. Networking is the connecting together of several computers and peripheral devices. After reading this chapter the reader can easily grasp the concepts of communication media, transmission modes, topologies and every other topic that a reader requires to get the feel of the subject.

Chapter 16. The sixteenth chapter deals with the basic of distributed processing. Distributed computing deals with hardware and software systems containing more than one processing element or storage element, concurrent processes, or multiple programs, running under a loosely or tightly controlled regime.

Chapter 17. The last chapter seventeen introduces multiprocessing concepts like hardware organization, tightly and loosely coupled multiprocessors etc.

Unit 7 : CASE STUDIES OF OPERATING SYSTEMS

This last unit provides the in-depth coverage of the most popular operating systems like DOS, UNIX and windows NT-2000.

The book is predominantly addressed to students of computer science, science, and engineering. In addition, it intends to reach computational scientists already on the job who wish to get acquainted with established modern concepts of Operating Systems on an elementary level via personal studies.

Most of these examples are taken from the technical and practical point of view keeping in tune the nature of subject. The summary, keywords and the exercises given at the end of each chapter are for the quick revision of what is discussed in the chapter which will be helpful for students to prepare for the exams too. Sincere attempts have been made to make the book simple by keeping lucid style that will be appreciated by the teachers as well as students. We are confident that the book will prove of great utility to readers. Although we had tried our level best to bring the best on 'Operating Systems" yet we admit that it has wide scope for further improvement so we crave the indulgence of students and teachers to make suggestions for the improvement of the book which will be most welcome.

DR. LAKHWINDER KAUR
DR. SAVITA GUPTA
ER. JATINDER SINGH

ACKNOWLEDGEMENTS

First and foremost, we feel immense pleasure in expressing our deep sense of gratitude and indebtedness to Waheguru, the almighty God, who mercifully felt us worthy of his blessings.

We extend our deep gratitude to Er. S.S. Gill Chairman Sukhjinder Group of Institute, Dr.Manjeet Singh Patterh, Head University college of Engineering, Punjabi university, Patiala and Dr. Harmesh Kansal, Asst. Professor Dept of Mechanical Engineering SLIET Longowal.

We would like to thank Prof. Nirmaljeet Singh for unwittingly providing us with the idea for this book . We are extremely grateful to Mrs Parmjit Kaur not only for accompanying us to the author events, but also for regularly listening to our ideas. Thanks are also due to all our colleagues, for their support and encouragement.

We would also like to thank our families who encouraged and inspirited us at every instant.

We are also indebted to all those learned writers whose writing we have consulted in authoring the book of this nature.

Last but not the least very special thanks goes to Khanna Book Publishing Co. Pvt. Ltd. for being the catalyst that made all this happen.

CONTENTS

UNIT 1 : INTRODUCTION TO OPERATING SYSTEMS

UNIT 2 : PROCESS MANAGEMENT UNIT

UNIT 4 : FILE AND DEVICE MANAGEMENT UNIT

UNIT 5 : SYSTEM SECURITY AND PROTECTION

UNIT 6 : NETWORK AND DISTRIBUTED SYSTEMS

UNIT-1

INTRODUCTION TO OPERATING SYSTEMS

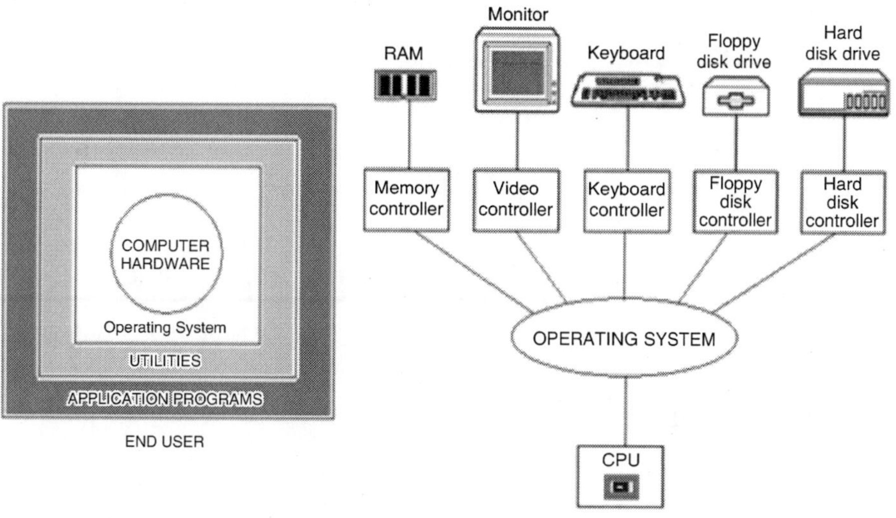

CHAPTER 1 : Operating System Fundamentals
CHAPTER 2 : Operating System Architecture

"There is no subject so old that something new cannot be said about it".

Fyodor Mikhailovich Dostoyevsky

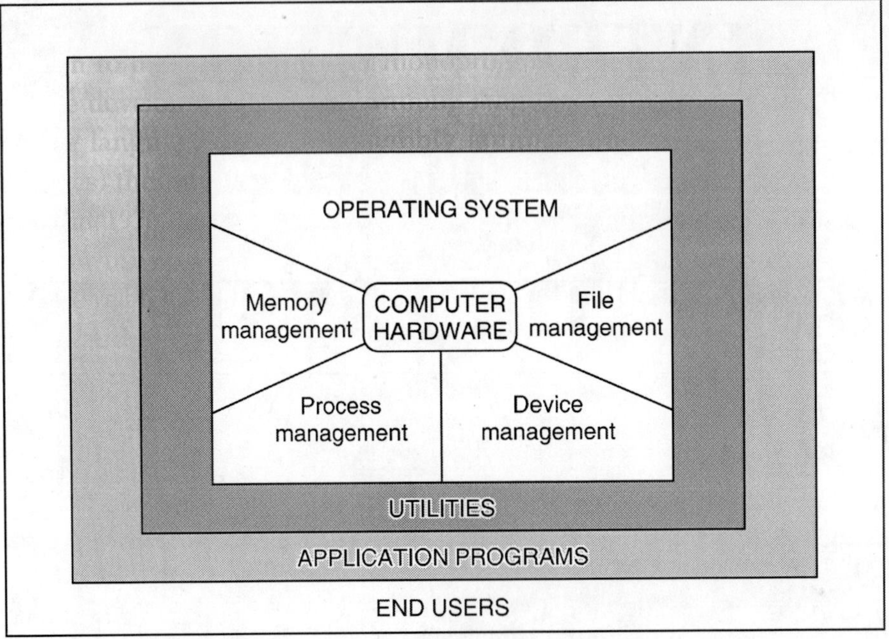

OPERATING SYSTEM FUNDAMENTALS

INTRODUCTION

Computers now play a critical role in virtually all aspects of modern life. When a computer is devoid of any software it is just like dead bodies. In a computer system the hardware provides the basic computing resources. The applications programs define the way in which these resources are used to solve the computing problems of the users. The computer software and hardware have been intrinsically linked with each other. One of them cannot do anything useful by itself without help from the other. The operating system controls and coordinates the use of the hardware among the various systems programs and application programs for the various users. The basic resources of a computer system are provided by its hardware, software and data. The operating system provides the means for the proper use of these resources in the operation of the computer system. It simply provides an environment within which other programs can do useful work. The operating system is the system software that is in charge of all the computer operations. The 1960's definition of an operating system is "the software that controls the hardware".

The operating system is the most important program that runs on a computer. Every general-purpose computer must have an operating system to run other programs. It perform basic tasks, such as recognizing input from the keyboard, sending output to the display screen, keeping track of files and directories on the disk, and controlling peripheral devices such as disk drives and printers. Basically, the operating system is the first piece of software to run on a computer when it is booted. Its job is to coordinate the execution of all other software, mainly user applications. It also provides various common services that are needed by users and applications.

An operating system is system software that controls the overall working of the computer system. It manages hardware, runs applications, provides an interface for users, and stores, retrieves, and manipulates files. An operating system is responsible for communicating with hardware of the computer system. Several applications might be installed on a computer to meet various user needs, but without the operating system even a single program can not be executed on the computer system. The most popular operating systems for personal computers today are Microsoft Windows XP, Windows 2000, and Windows 98/Me.

The operating system not only provides a basis for application programs but also act as an intermediary between a user of a computer and the computer hardware. Every general-purpose computer must have an operating system to provide a software platform on top of which other programs can run.

What is an Operating System?

The operating system is an organized set of programs that controls and coordinates the use of the computer resources among the various users and tasks. It acts as an interface between the user and the hardware. The operating system schedules tasks, manages storage, and handles communication with peripherals.

Other definitions of Operating System:

"The low-level software which schedules tasks, allocates storage, handles the interface to peripheral hardware and presents a default interface to the user when no application program is running."

"The facilities an operating system provides and its general design philosophy exert an extremely strong influence on programming style and on the technical cultures that grow up around the machines on which it runs."

"The OS may be split into a kernel which is always present and various system programs which use facilities provided by the kernel to perform higher-level house- keeping tasks, often acting as servers in a client-server relationship."

The operating system is the system software responsible for the direct control and management of hardware and basic system operations. Additionally, it provides a foundation upon which to run application software such as word processing programs and web browsers.

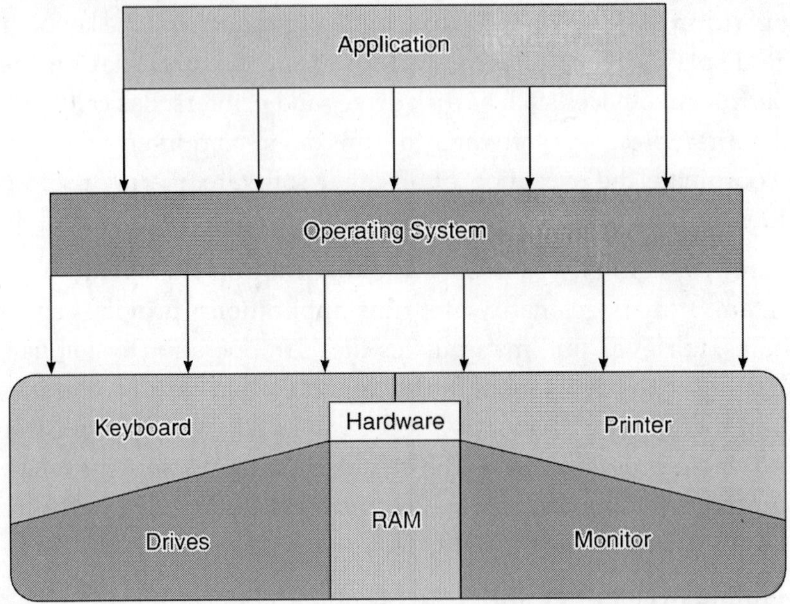

Operating System in a Hierarchy

As shown in Figure, between the applications software and the hardware is a software interface known as *operating system.* An operating system is a set of programs that lies between applications software and the computer hardware. Conceptually the operating system software is an intermediary between the hardware and the applications software. Incidentally, the term system software is sometimes used interchangeably with operating system, but system software means all programs related to coordinating computer operations.

Operating systems for mainframe and other large computers are even more complex because they must keep track of several programs from several users all running in the same time frame. Although some personal computer operating systems-most often found in business or learning environments-can support multiple programs and users, most are concerned only with a single user. We begin by focusing on the interaction between a single user and a personal computer operating system.

Where user stands?

The users of the computer system are at the top of the hierarchy. The most frequently used instructions in the operating system must be stored in main memory and remain there whilst other programs such as application programs are being executed. This portion of the operating system is called by many different names such as control program, nucleus, monitor, supervisor, or executive.

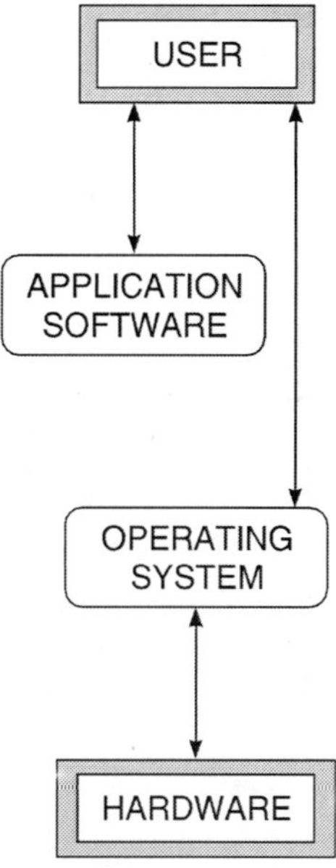

User is at the top

Hardware – provides basic computing resources (CPU, memory, I/O devices).

- CPU: Controls the operation of the computer and performs its data progressing functions. If there is only one processor it is often referred to as central processing unit (CPU).
- **Memory:** Stores data and programs.
- I/O **Devices:** Move data between the computer and its external environment.

ii. **Operating system** – controls and coordinates the use of the hardware among the various programs/processes for the various users.

iii. **Applications programs** – define the ways in which the system resources are used to solve the computing problems of the users (compilers, database systems, video games, business programs).

iv. **Users** (people, machines, other computers).

On all large computers and most micros, the operating system is held on disk and has to be loaded into main memory once the computer has been switched on, before any other programs can be run. The process of loading the operating system is called booting the system.

On a microcomputer system, the operating system is usually held on the hard disk if the system has one. Otherwise, it will be held on a floppy disk, which will be known as a system disk. On all computers a small program held in ROM (the 'loader') will tell the computer where to look for the operating system, and give instructions for loading at least part of it into memory. Once part of the operating system has been loaded, more instructions can be executed to load the rest of the nucleus. This method of 'pulling itself up by its own bootstraps' is where the expression 'booting' comes from.

Operating system is the master control program that runs the computer. The first program loaded when the computer is turned on, its main part, the "kernel," resides in memory at all times. The operating system sets the standards for all application programs that run in the computer. Applications "talk to" the operating system for all user interfaces and file management operations also called an "executive" or "supervisor" In smaller hand-held computers the control program is permanently held in ROM. The advantage is that the system boots automatically, no need for system disk and the disadvantage is that one cannot easily upgrade the OS.

What an operating system does?

The operating system works like an air traffic controller to coordinate the activities within the computer.

Air Traffic Controller	Operating System
1. Clear aircraft for takeoff	Launches programs
2. Monitors planes in the air	Monitors programs that are running
3. Keeps track of airspace and runways	Keeps track of RAM and disk space
4. Keeps track of planes on the ground	Keeps track of programs stored on disk
5. Takes care of emergency landings	Detects equipment failure

***Example:* Operating system for a security control system**

An operating system for a security control system (such as a home alarm system) would consist of a number of programs. One of these programs would gain control of the computer system when it is powered on, and initialize the system.

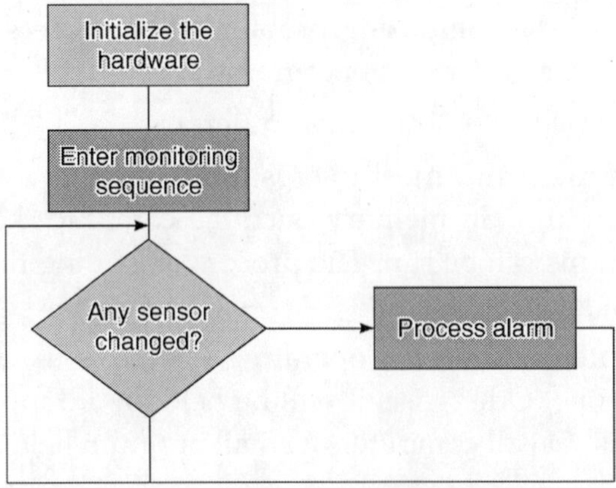

The first task of this initialize program would be to reset (and probably test) the hardware sensors and alarms. Once the hardware initialization was complete, the operating system would enter a continual monitoring routine of all the input sensors. If the state of any input sensor changed, it would branch to an alarm generation routine.

The following charts emphasize the unique features of the different types of operating systems available and there outstanding features.

DESKTOP OS	OUTSTANDING FEATURES
DOS	One of the first operating systems; command-line user interface
Mac OS	Designed by Apple computer; graphical user interface
Windows 95	Features multitasking and networking capabilities
Windows 98	Similar to Windows 95, but with increased disk and memory management
Windows Me	Similar to Windows 98, but with more features for the home user, including multimedia support
Windows 2000	Increased security features; ability to support specialized applications
Windows XP	Redesigned structure and interface, improved safety and recovery tools, greater support for multimedia and networking

SERVER OS	OUTSTANDING FEATURES
UNIX	Designed as a minicomputer OS, now popular for all sizes of network and Web servers; makes use of both command-line and graphical interfaces.
Linux	Variation of UNIX; used as a server OS for microcomputers and minicomputers; available as freeware
Novell	Developed for microcomputer networks; typically used by network managers

VIEWS OF OPERATING SYSTEM

The three views of the operating system are:

i. User View

User's view-The operating system provides an environment in which application programs can be run. It provides services to applications, like file management and I/O. The user views the OS+ hardware as a single unit, the "computer system".

From the user point of view the primary consideration is always the convenience. It should be easy to use an application. In launching an application, it helps to have an icon which gives a clue which application it is. We have seen some helpful clues for launching a browser, e-mail or even a document preparation application. In other words, the human computer interface which helps to identify an application and its launch is very useful. This hides a lot of details of the more elementary instructions that help in selecting the application. Similarly, if we examine the programs that help us in using input devices like

a key board – all the complex details of character reading program are hidden from the user.

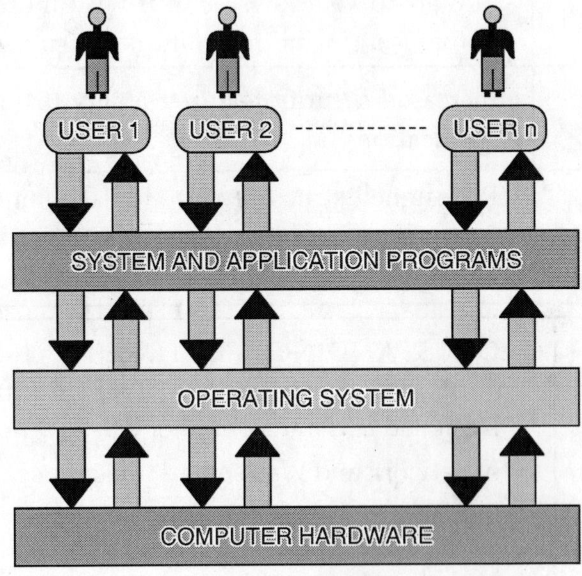

User View

The same is true when we write a program. For instance, when we use a programming language like C, a prints command helps to generate the desired form of output. The following figure essentially depicts the basic schema of the use of OS from a user stand point. However, when it comes to the view point of a system, the OS needs to ensure that all the system users and applications get to use the facilities that they need.

ii. Extended machine/virtual machine view or Programmers' view

Programmers' view- "extended machine". An operating system implements a virtual machine which is easier to program than the raw machine.

A floppy disk is used for reading and writing stored data. However, for the process of reading and writing requires the read/write head to be moved, tracks must be formatted, tracks must be initialized and so on. For example, a READ operation specifies the address of the disk block, the intersection gap spacing and so on. This is a complex process that a user will not want to program and control. Furthermore, the user would have to switch the disk motor on/off as required, since leaving a motor running constantly reduces the life of the device.

The requirements of a user is for a program that provides a simple high-level abstraction that deals with the complexities, and the user then only has to specify the operation, that is READ or WRITE to or from a file. The program would then control the physical operation of the floppy disk, open the specified file for reading or writing, permit the operation on the file, and finally close the file with minimal user intervention.

In such a case the operating system presents the user an **extended** or **virtual machine** that is easier to program and use than the underlying hardware.

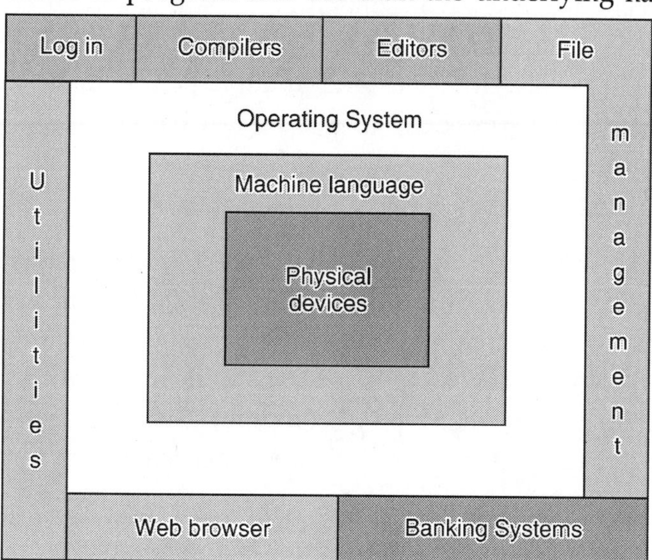

Operating system 'hides' the hardware from the user

As shown in the diagram the operating system is a software environment which 'hides' the hardware from the user environment. Programming the hardware directly is a tedious exercise, which requires a lot of low-level knowledge of the hardware architecture and the various interfaces. The operating system provides the programmer with a simpler environment where the hardware detail becomes more abstract and easier to use. For example, consider the concept of a simple file. A file is an abstraction to represent a collection of bytes stored on a physical disk (usually).

To access these data bytes directly through the hardware, knowledge of the disk drive controller design and knowledge of the low-level format details of the disk drive is required. However, the operating system provides the file concept so that a user can simply open a file by using the file name and read and write the file in a simple fashion. The operating system provides the necessary device driver to interface to the disk drive's hardware and provides the filing system to manage the various files. The programmer accesses the operating system via the API (application programmer's interface). The API provides a library of system calls which can be used by the high-level language compiler or interpreter. Thus the programmer is 'talking' to the API and not to the underlying hardware; we say that a virtual machine is created which abstracts the underlying hardware.

Users do not interact with the hardware of a computer directly but through the services offered by operating system. This is because the language that users employ is different from that of the hardware. Whereas users prefer to use natural language or near natural language for interaction, the hardware uses machine language. It is the operating system that does the necessary translation back and forth and lets the user interact with the hardware. The operating system speaks users' language one hand and machine language on the other. It takes instructions in form of commands from the user and translates into machine understandable instructions, gets these instructions executed by the CPU and translates the result back into user-understandable form.

Example of extended machine view using UNIX

A user can interact with a computer if only he/she understands the language of the resident operating system. You cannot interact with a computer running UNIX operating system, for instance, if you do not know 'UNIX language' or UNIX commands. A UNIX user can always interact with a computer running UNIX operating system, no matter what type of computer it is. Thus, for a user operating system itself is the machine – an extended machine as shown in figure as follows:

In order to interact with the computer hardware and get a computational job executed by it, the job needs to be translated in this binary form called machine language. Thus, the instructions and data of the job must be converted into some binary form, which then must be stored into the computer's main memory. The CPU must be directed at this point, to execute the instructions loaded in the memory. A computer, being a machine after all, does not do anything by itself. Which resource is to be allocated to which program, when and how, is decided by the operating system in such a way that the resources are utilized optimally and efficiently.

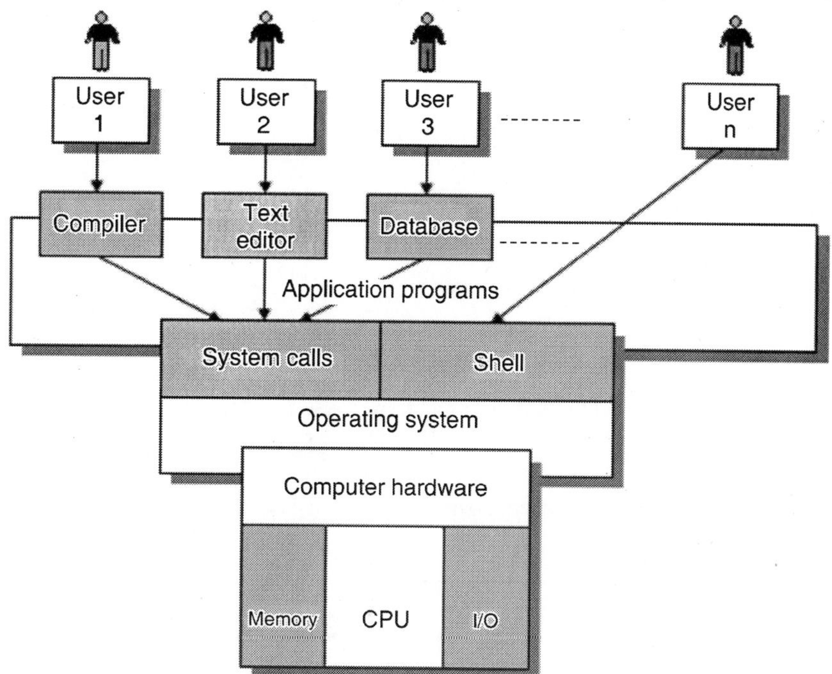

Extended-machine view of operating system.

The major role of OS is to provide hardware/software interface as an operating system shields its users from the complexities of the hardware. The way that operating systems have evolved is to put a layer of software on top of the bare hardware.

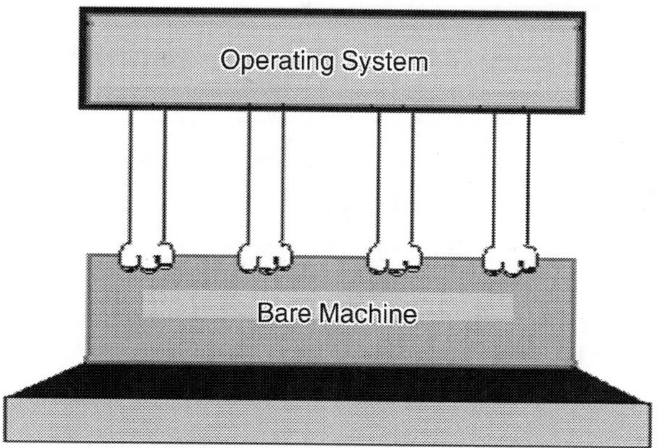

Operating system over a bare machine

This hardware/software interface provides the user with a **virtual machine** that is easier to understand, program and use as shown in the fig below.

The lowest layer consists of Physical devices such as integrated circuits, lines, cables, buses, the CPU, caches, hard-disks and so on. The layer above is **primitive software** that directly controls the physical devices and provides a cleaner interface to the next layer. This layer of software is called Microprogramming, which is used to fetch machine language instructions, and is usually stored in the physical device ROM.

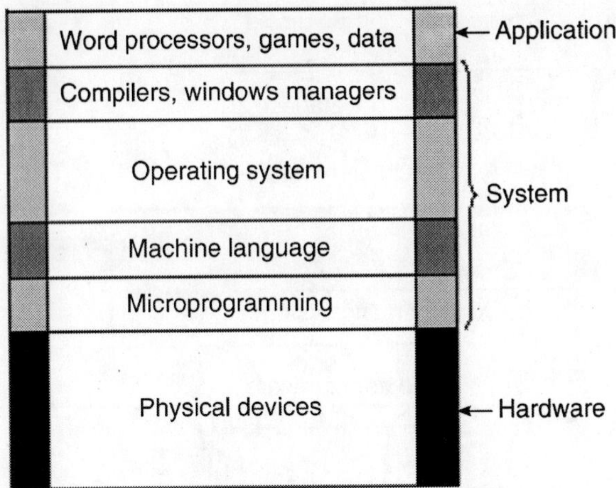

Software/Hardware Interfaces

Above the Microprogramming layer is the Machine language layer. Machine language is mainly used to move data around the computer machine itself. The machine language layer controls I/O devices. The operating system resides above the Machine language layer. A major function of an operating system is to hide the above complexities and to provide the user with a convenient set of instructions to work with. Above the operating system is the rest of the system programs, such as the command interpreter (shell), compilers, editors and so on. These programs are distinct from the operating system, even though a systems manufacturer usually provides them.

iii. Resource manager view or system view

The overall system view: The problem is to match resources with users/ applications. Resources (CPU time, memory, disk space, files, I/O devices, network bandwidth) are finite and must be shared among users. The OS is responsible for allocating these resources.

A computer is a set of resources; the operating system is responsible for managing these resources. Operating System controls the movement, storage and processing of data. Operating system functions in the same way as ordinary computer software. i.e., it is a program executed by the processor. This frequently relinquishes control and must depend on processor to allow it to regain control. Operating System is nothing more than the computer program. It provides instructions to processor like other programs do. The main difference between Operating System and other programs is that Operating System directs the processor in the use of the other system resources and in the timing of its execution of other programs.

The operating system manages t*he hardware resources* in order to provide for an orderly and controlled allocation of the processors, memories and I/O devices among the various programs competing for them. It can be considered that an operating system provides its users with a convenient top down interface. An alternative view is a bottom up interface, where the operating system manages all of the pieces of a complex system. Modern computers are comprised of many physical devices including modems, scanners, printers and so on. Such physical devices require managing, and an ideal manner to provide such management is by use of the operating system.

For example if two processes attempt to access a printer at the same times then the printed output may be garbled with mixed text from both processes. Hence the operating system needs to provide special synchronisation support to help manage the various system resources.

The operating system would manage the order in which processes are executed. Similarly, multi-user computers require management and protection of many physical devices such that resources can be shared evenly between the users. Consequently, it could be considered that the primary task of an operating system is to keep track of which user is using which resource, to grant resource requests, account for usage and to manage conflicting requests from different programs and users.

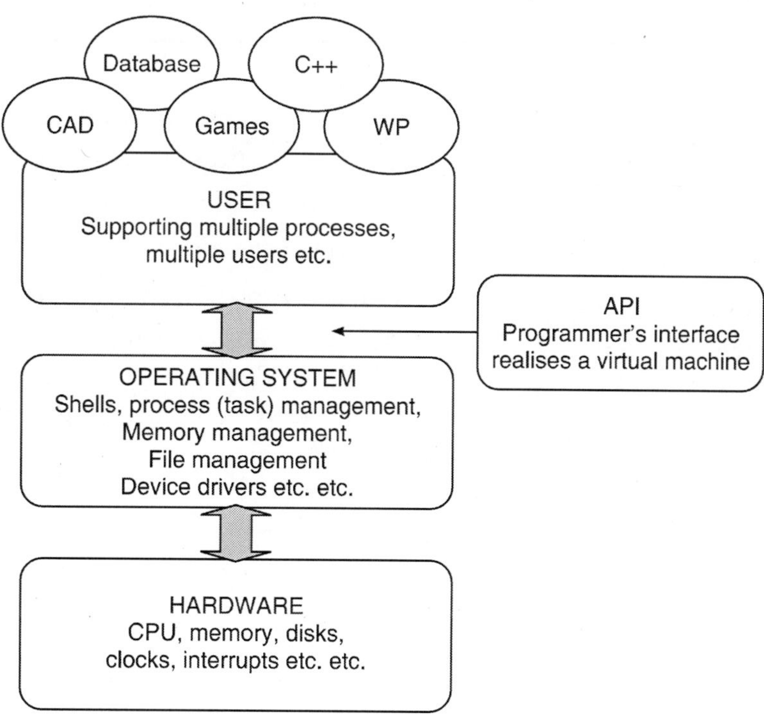

CHARACTERISTICS OF OPERATING SYSTEMS

The major characteristics of operating system are:

1. *An Operating System is a Program*

   The operating system is a set of one or more instruction called program. When you switch on a computer, the hardware ensures that the operating system program is read into the memory and than control is transferred to the OS.

2. *The Operating System Executes all the Time*

   The operating system (program) runs all the time until the computer is switched off. However, we all know that only one program can be running on a single processor at any time; and most computers operate with just one processor.

3. *The Operating System is in charge of the computer*

   We can revise that statement to say that the operating system is in charge of the computer all of the time because it controls and coordinates all the functions provided by he computer system.

4. *The Operating System as a platform for executing software*

   The operating system is that it provides a platform or environment upon which to run your application software and provides an interface with which you the user interact with the machine. In this view, the operating system provides a layer that separates the application software and the user from the hardware.

5. *The Operating System provides services*

   When an operating system is viewed as a platform for executing software (and for interfacing with humans), we can see that it provides services. For example: reading from, and saving to disks; sending data to a printer, etc.

6. *The Operating System acts as police or government*

   When modern operating systems (Windows 2000, XP, UNIX, Linux) go to the trouble of providing services they also force application programs to avail of these services. For example, unlike on MS-DOS and early versions of Windows, application programs are barred from directly accessing hardware like disks, network cards, etc., they must use the appropriate operating system service. Since accessing hardware directly is difficult and some application programs are written by less skilled programmers, directly accessing hardware was a common source of errors and frequently resulted in the systems crashing.

PRINCIPLES OF OPERATING SYSTEMS

The major principles of operating systems are as follows:

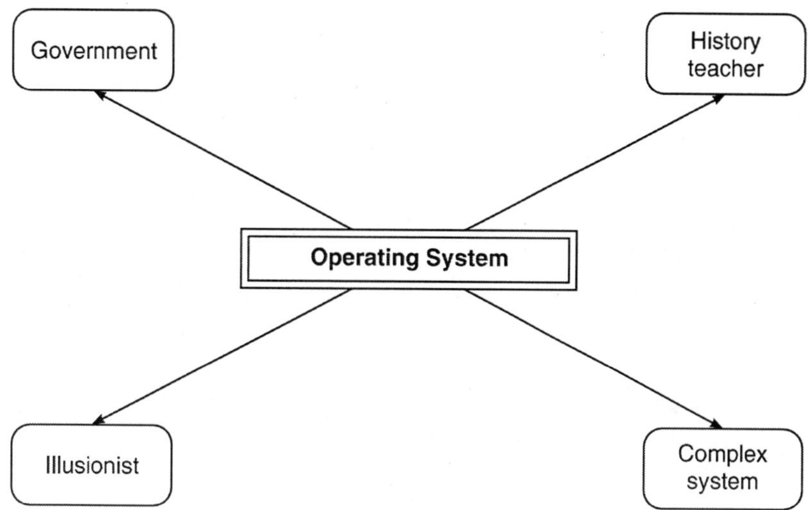

Principles of operating systems

1. **OS as government**

   The operating system protects users from each other and allocates resources efficiently and fairly.

2. **OS as illusionist**

   The operating system makes hardware limitations go away.

3. **OS as history teacher**

   The operating system is that kind of self learning system software that learns from past to predict the future.

4. **OS as complex system**

   The operating system is a complex system that believes in the fact that keeping things simple is key to getting it to work.

GOALS OF OPERATING SYSTEM

The fundamental goal of a computer system is to execute user programs and solve user problems. The two most important goals of the operating systems are stated as follows:

1. *The primary goal of an operating system is convenience for the user*

The operating system is to "hide' ' the complexity of the underlying hardware and give the user a better view of the computer system that is why an operating system can also be viewed as a special **system software** which provides a more *user-friendly* environment to computer users. The Applications "talk to" the operating system for all user interfaces and file management operations.

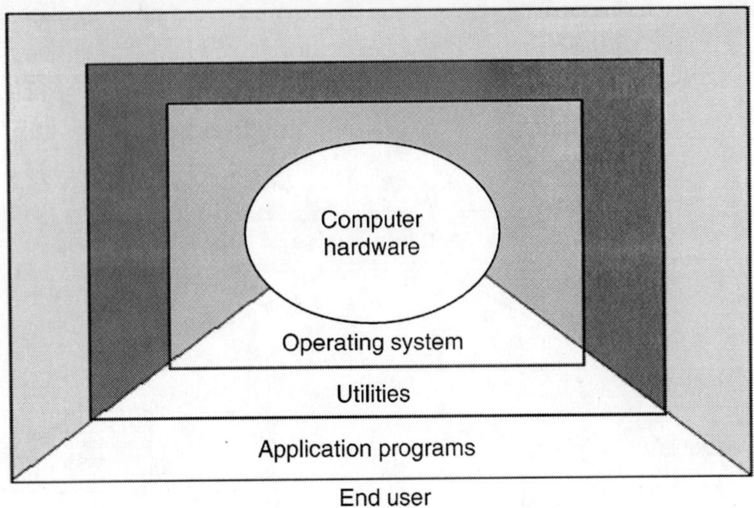

OS as a User- Computer interface for the convenience for the user

The desirable features of the user computer interface of an operating system are as follows:

1) Interface should be designed in such a manner as to master the interface. As already stated, people are hard pressed for time.
2) The speed of response should play a vital role in designing the user interface. The speed of response is nothing but the time taken to execute a particular task.
3) The user interface should reduce the number of errors committed by the user. With little practice, the user should be in a position to avoid errors.
4) The user interface should be pleasing to the senses. Vivid colours, enchanting music may achieve this.
5) The user interface should enable the people to retain this expertise for a longer time.
6) The ultimate aim of any product is to satisfy the customer. The user interface should also satisfy the customer.

2. ***The second goal is efficient operation the computer system***

The basic resources of a computer system are provided by its hardware, software and data. The operating system provides the means for the proper use of these resources in the operation of the computer system. It simply provides an environment within which other programs can do useful work.

The primary resources managed by Operating System are

i. CPU

ii. Main Memory.

iii. I/O Device

iv. Secondary Storage Devices

v. Data and Program.

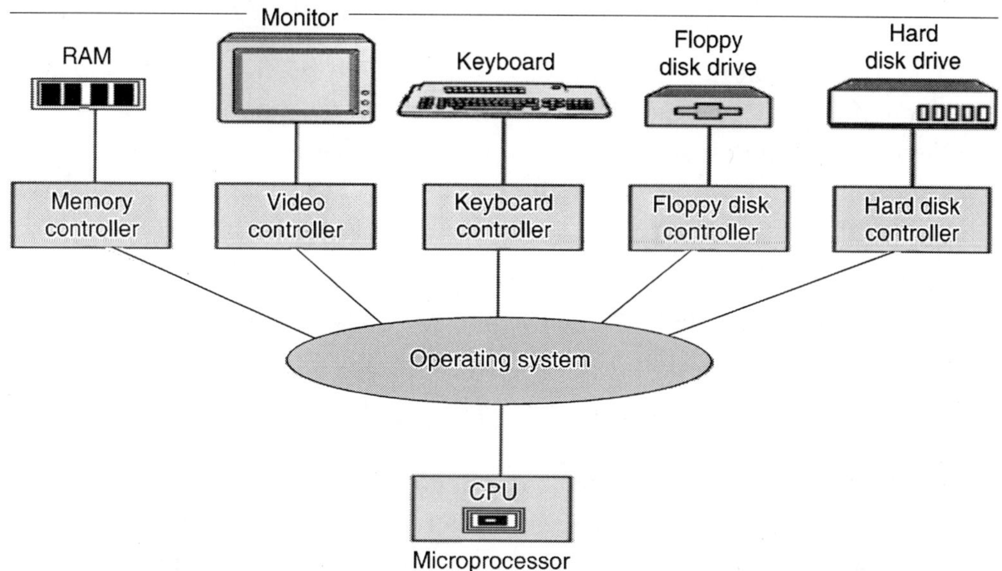

Operating system as a resource manager

An operating system provides orderly and controlled allocation and use of the resources by the jobs that compete for them.

The Operating system typically provides services in the following areas:

1. **Program Creation**

   Operating system services editors and debuggers, to assist programmer in creating programs. These services are in the form of utility programs that are accessible through the Operating System.

2. **Program Execution**

   Program execution needs instructions and data to be loaded in to main menu, Input / Output devices and files to be initialized and other resources to be prepared. The operating system handles all these tasks for the user.

3. **Access to Input / Output devices:**

   Each Input / Output device requires its own peculiar set of instructions of control signals for operation. Operating system takes care of details so, the programmers can think in terms of simple read and writes.

4. **Controlled access to files:** Operating system provides protection mechanisms to controlled access to files

5. **System Access:** Operating System controls access to the system as a whole and to specific system resources.

6. **Error detection and response:** Variety of errors can occur which a computer system is running, i.e., internal and external hardware errors, such as memory error, device failure error, various software errors, inability of Operating System to grant request of an application errors and so on. In each case, Operating System must make the response that clears the error condition. The response may range from ending the program that caused the error, to retrying the operation to simply reporting the error to the application.

7. **Accounting:** A good Operating System collects usage statistics for various resources and monitors performance parameters such as response time, which can be used for billing purposes on a multi-user system.

HISTORY AND EVOLUTION OF OPERATING SYSTEMS

The earliest operating systems were developed in the late 1950s to manage tape storage, but programmers mostly wrote their own I/O routines. In the mid-1960s, operating systems became essential to manage disks, complex timesharing and multitasking systems. Today, all multi-purpose computers from desktop to mainframe use an operating system. Special-purpose devices (appliances, games, toys, etc.) may or may not. Instead, they may employ a single program that performs all the required I/O and processing tasks.

THE OPERATING SYSTEM GENERATIONS

Because the history of computer operating systems parallels that of computer hardware, it can be generally divided into five distinct time periods, called generations, that are characterized by hardware component technology, software development, and mode of delivery of computer services.

The Zeroth Generation, mid 1800s-1951

The term zeroth generation is used to refer to the period of development of computing, which predated the commercial production and sale of computer equipment. The period might be dated as extending from the mid-1800s, and Charles

Babbage's Analytical Engine, to the development of the fist commercial computer in 1951. In particular, this period witnessed the emergence of the first electronics digital computers on the ABC, designed by John Atanasoff in 1940; the Mark I, built by Howard Aiken and a group of IBM engineers at Harvard in 1944; and the ENIAC, designed and constructed at the University of Pennsylvania by Wallace Eckert and John Mauchly. Perhaps the most significant of these early computers was the EDVAC, developed in 1944-46 by John von Neumann, Arthur Burks, and Herman Goldstine, since it was the first to fully implement the idea of the stored program and serial execution of instructions. The development of EDVAC set the stage for the evolution of commercial computing and operating system software. The hardware component technology of this period was electronic vacuum tubes.

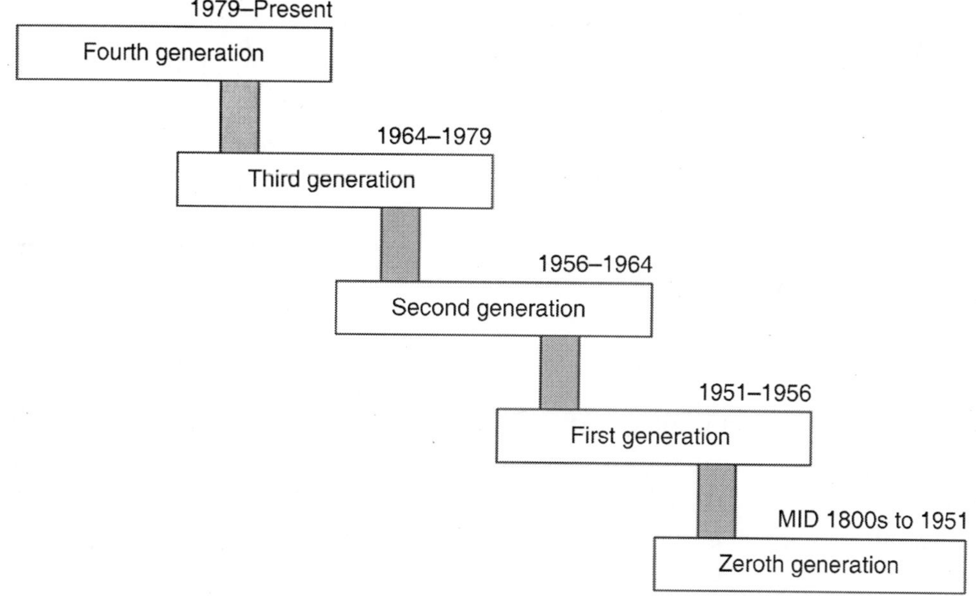

Operating system generations

The actual operation of these early computers took place without be benefit of an operating system. Early programs were written in machine language and each contained code for initiating operation of the computer itself.

The mode of operation was called "open-shop" and this meant that users signed up for computer time and when a user's time arrived, the entire (in those days quite large) computer system was turned over to the user. The individual user (programmer) was responsible for all machine set up and operation, and subsequent clean-up and preparation for the next user. This system was clearly inefficient and depended on the varying competencies of the individual programmer as operators.

The First Generation, 1951-1956

The first generation marked the beginning of commercial computing, including the introduction of Eckert and Mauchly's UNIVAC I in early 1951, and a bit later, The IBM 701 which was also known as the Defense Calculator. The first generation was characterized again by the vacuum tube as the active component technology.

Soon computers became enough reliable that they could be manufactured and sold to customers with the expectation to function enough long time without trouble. Computers were still very expensive and only big corporations, major government agencies or universities could pay the multimillion-dollar price. The cost of one machine hour was $ 150-300. Nevertheless, the number of users-programmers had increased and the problem appeared how to organize the efficient computer's utilization.

The new group of personal was appeared: operators. They were technicians on computer unit with the main task – to execute all operations faster than programmer could. A programmer first wrote the program on paper, then punch it on cards (for the second generation computers it existed special room and technicians). After this he brought the cards to the input room and hands it to one of the operators.

An operator executed all technical operations, went over to the printer and teared off the output and carried it to the output room, so that the programmer could collect it later.

PROGRAMMER ⟷ OPERATOR ⟷ COMPUTER

In this chain much of the computer time was wasted in the interaction between operator and computer. To speed up processing two points were developed – magnetic tapes were used instead of cards, jobs with similar needs were batched together and were run through the computer as a group.

The very simple "batch operating system" was always resident in memory, then normally reads a steam of separate jobs, each with own control cards that predefine what the job does. For the purpose of automatic job sequencing a small program was designed, called a resident monitor. The resident monitor is always (resident) in memory.

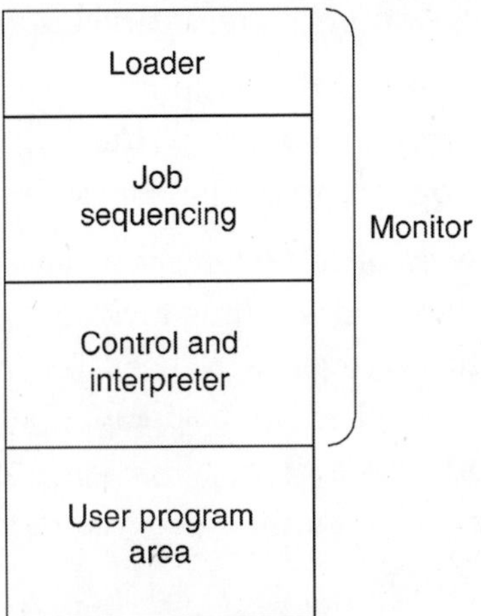

Memory layout for a resident monitor

Control-card interpreter is responsible for reading and carrying out the instructions on the cards. Loader loads system programs and application programs into memory.

The first generation saw the evolution from hands-on operation to closed shop operation to the development of monoprogrammed operating systems. At the same time, the development of programming languages was moving away from the basic machine languages; first to assembly language, and later to procedure oriented languages, the most significant being the development of FORTRAN by John W. Backus in 1956. Serveral problems remained, however. The most obvious was the inefficient use of system resources, which was most evident when the CPU waited while the relatively slower, mechanical I/O devices were reading or writing program data. In addition, system protection was a problem because the operating system kernel was not protected from being overwritten by an erroneous application program. Moreover, other user programs in the queue were not protected from destruction by executing programs.

The second Generation, 1956-1964

The second generation of computer hardware was most notably characterized by transistors replacing vacuum tubes as the hardware component technology. In addition, some very important changes in hardware and software architectures occurred during this period. For the most part, computer systems remained card and tape-oriented systems. Significant use of random access devices, that is, disks, did not appear until towards the end of the second generation. Program processing was, for the most part, provided by large centralized computers operated under monoprogrammed batch processing operating systems.

Toward the end of this period, as random access devices became available, tape-oriented operating system began to be replaced by disk-oriented systems. With the more sophisticated disk hardware and the operating system supporting a greater portion of the programmer's work, the computer system that users saw was more and more removed from the actual hardware - users saw a virtual machine.

The second generation was a period of intense operating system development. Also it was the period for sequential batch processing. But the sequential processing of one job at a time remained a significant limitation. Thus, there continued to be low CPU utilization for I/O bound jobs and low I/O device utilization for CPU bound jobs. This was a major concern, since computers were still very large (room-size) and expensive machines. Researchers began to experiment with multiprogramming and multiprocessing in their computing services called the time-sharing system. A noteworthy example is the compatible Time Sharing System (CTSS), developed at MIT during the early 1960s.

The Third Generation, 1964-1979

The third generation officially began in April 1964 with IBM's announcement of its System/360 family of computers. Hardware technology began to use integrated circuits (ICs) which yielded significant advantages in both speed and economy.

Operating system development continued with the introduction and widespread adoption of multiprogramming. This marked first by the appearance of more sophisticated I/O buffering in the form of spooling operating systems, such as the HASP (Houston Automatic Spooling) system that accompanied the IBM OS/360 system. These systems worked by introducing two new systems programs, a system reader to move input jobs from cards to disk, and a system writer to move job output from disk to printer, tape, or cards. Operation of spooling system was, as before, transparent to the computer user who perceived input as coming directly from the cards and output going directly to the printer.

Successful implementation of multiprogramming opened the way for the development of a new way of delivering computing services-time-sharing. In this environment, several terminals, sometimes up to 200 of them, were attached (hard wired or via telephone lines) to a central computer. Users at their terminals, "logged in" to the central system, and worked interactively with the system. The system's apparent concurrency was enabled by the multiprogramming operating system. Users shared not only the system' hardware but also its software resources and file system disk space.

The third generation was an exciting time, indeed, for the development of both computer hardware and the accompanying operating system. During this period, the topic of operating systems became, in reality, a major element of the discipline of computing.

The Fourth Generation, 1979 - Present

The fourth generation is characterized by the appearance of the personal computer and the workstation. Miniaturization of electronic circuits and components continued and large scale integration (LSI), the component technology of the third generation, was replaced by very large scale integration (VLSI), which characterizes the fourth generation. VLSI with its capacity for containing thousands of transistors on a small chip, made possible the development of desktop computers with capabilities exceeding those that filled entire rooms and floors of building just twenty years earlier. Examples are Microsoft's DOS for IBM-compatible personal computers and UNIX for workstation.

FUNCTIONS OF OPERATING SYSTEM

The major functions of operating system are as follows:

1. Process Management

The CPU executes a large number of programs. While its main concern is the execution of user programs, the CPU is also needed for other system activities. These activities are called processes. A process is a program in execution. Typically, a batch job is a process. A time-shared user program is a process. A system task, such as spooling, is also a process. For now, a process may be considered as a job or a time-shared program, but the concept is actually more general.

Process management is a set of functions supporting the definition of inter- related process steps and the management of their execution across a variety of hardware.

In general, a process will need certain resources such as CPU time, memory, files, I/O devices, etc., to accomplish its task. These resources are given to the process when it is created. In addition to the various physical and logical resources that a process obtains when it is created, some initialization data (input) may be passed along. For example, a process whose function is to display on the screen of a terminal the status of a file, say F1, will get as an input the name of the file F1 and execute the appropriate program to obtain the desired information.

Remember that a program by itself is not a process; a program is a passive entity, while a process is an active entity. It is known that two processes may be associated with the same program; they are nevertheless considered two separate execution sequences.

A process is the unit of work in a system. Such a system consists of a collection of processes, some of which are operating system processes, those that execute system code, and the rest being user processes, those that execute user code. All of those processes can potentially execute concurrently.

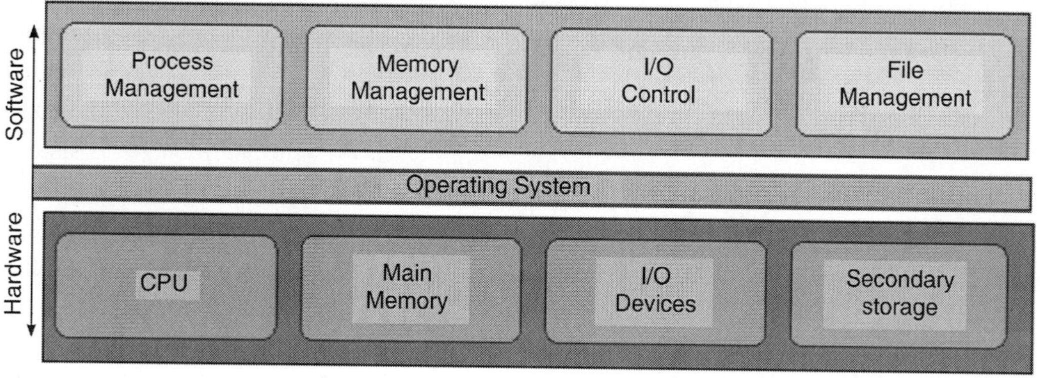

OS manages processes, memory, I/O and files

The operating system is responsible for the following activities in connection with processes managed.

- The creation and deletion of both user and system processes
- The suspension and resumption of processes.
- The provision of mechanisms for process synchronization
- The provision of mechanisms for deadlock handling.

2. Memory Management

Memory is central to the operation of a modern computer system. Memory is a large array of words or bytes, each with its own address. Interaction is achieved through a sequence of reads or writes of specific memory address. The CPU fetches from and stores in memory.

Memory management is the act of managing computer memory. In its simpler forms, this involves providing ways to allocate portions of memory to programs at their request, and freeing it for reuse when no longer needed.

In order for a program to be executed it must be mapped to absolute addresses and loaded in to memory. As the program executes, it accesses program instructions and data from memory by generating these absolute is declared available, and the next program may be loaded and executed.

In order to improve both the utilization of CPU and the speed of the computer's response to its users, several processes must be kept in memory. There are many different algorithms depends on the particular situation. Selection of a memory management scheme for a specific system depends upon many factor, but especially upon the hardware design of the system. Each algorithm requires its own hardware support.

The operating system is responsible for the following activities in connection with memory management.

- Keep track of which parts of memory are currently being used and by whom.
- Decide which processes are to be loaded into memory when memory space becomes available.
- Allocate and de-allocate memory space as needed.

3. File Management

File management is one of the most visible services of an operating system. Computers can store information in several different physical forms; magnetic tape, disk, and drum are the most common forms. Each of these devices has it own characteristics and physical organization.

File management is the software used to manage files on a disk. It provides functions to delete, copy, move, rename and view files as well as create and manage directory.

For convenient use of the computer system, the operating system provides a uniform logical view of information storage. The operating system abstracts from the physical properties of its storage devices to define a logical storage unit, the file. Files are mapped, by the operating system, onto physical devices.

A file is a collection of related information defined by its creator. Commonly, files represent programs (both source and object forms) and data. Data files may be numeric, alphabetic or alphanumeric. Files may be free-form, such as text files, or may be rigidly formatted. In general a files is a sequence of bits, bytes, lines or records whose meaning is defined by its creator and user. It is a very general concept.

The operating system implements the abstract concept of the file by managing mass storage device, such as types and disks. Also files are normally organized into directories to ease their use. Finally, when multiple users have access to files, it may be desirable to control by whom and in what ways files may be accessed.

The operating system is responsible for the following activities in connection with file management:

- The creation and deletion of files
- The creation and deletion of directory
- The support of primitives for manipulating files and directories
- The mapping of files onto disk storage.
- Backup of files on stable (non volatile) storage.

4. Secondary Storage Management

The main purpose of a computer system is to execute programs. These programs, together with the data they access, must be in main memory during execution. Since the main memory is too small to permanently accommodate all data and program, the computer system must provide secondary storage to backup main memory.

Storage management is the act of managing computer secondary memory like hard disks, floppy disks etc for efficient storage and retrieval of data.

Most modem computer systems use disks as the primary on-line storage of information, of both programs and data. Most programs, like compilers, assemblers, sort routines, editors, formatters, and so on, are stored on the disk until loaded into memory, and then use the disk as both the source and destination of their processing. Hence the proper management of disk storage is of central importance to a computer system.

There are few alternatives. Magnetic tape systems are generally too slow. In addition, they are limited to sequential access. Thus tapes are more suited for storing infrequently used files, where speed is not a primary concern. The operating system is responsible for the following activities in connection with disk management

- Free space management
- Storage allocation
- Disk scheduling.

The Information is collected from one or more sources and stored onto storage devices for later retrieval or communication.

5. Device or I/O management

One of the purposes of an operating system is to hide the peculiarities of specific hardware devices from the user.

Device management consists of the policies and procedures for handling I/O devices and the efficient working of the computer peripherals.

For example, in UNIX, the peculiarities of I/O devices are hidden from the bulk of the operating system itself by the I/O system. The I/O system consists of:

- A buffer caching system
- A general device driver code
- Drivers for specific hardware devices.

Only the device driver knows the peculiarities of a specific device.

6. Protection System

The various processes in an operating system must be protected from each other's activities. For that purpose, various mechanisms which can be used to ensure that the files, memory segment, CPU and other resources can be operated on only by those processes that have gained proper authorization from the operating system.

Protection means the prevention of unauthorized users from reading or writing a particular piece of data.

For example, memory addressing hardware ensures that a process can only execute within its own address space. The timer ensures that no process can gain control of the CPU without relinquishing it. Finally, no process is allowed to do its own I/O, to protect the integrity of the various peripheral devices.

Protection refers to a mechanism for controlling the access of programs, processes, or users to the resources defined by a computer controls to be imposed, together with some means of enforcement.

Protection can improve reliability by detecting latent errors at the interfaces between component subsystems. Early detection of interface errors can often prevent contamination of a healthy subsystem by a subsystem that is malfunctioning. An unprotected resource cannot defend against use (or misuse) by an unauthorized or incompetent user.

The major functions of the operating system are shown in tabular form as follows:

PROCESS MANAGEMENT

- Process creation and termination
- Process scheduling and dispatching
- Process switching
- Process synchronisation and interprocess communication
- Management of process control blocks

MEMORY MANAGEMENT

- Pllocation of address space to processes
- Memory swapping
- Page and segment management

I/O MANAGEMENT

- Buffer management
- Allocation of I/O channels and devices to processes

SUPPORT FUNCTIONS

- Interrupt handling
- Accounting
- Monitoring

Main operating system functions

7. Networking

A distributed system is a collection of processors that do not share memory or a clock. Instead, each processor has its own local memory, and the processors communicative with each other through various communication lines, such as high speed buses or telephone lines. Distributed systems vary in size and function. They may involve microprocessors, workstations, minicomputers, and large general purpose computer systems.

A network is comprised of two or more PCs connected so that they can communicate and share resources. Networked computers can share printers, scanners, CD-ROM drives, and files.

The processors in the system are connected through a communication network, which can be configured in the number of different ways. The network may be fully or partially connected. The communication network design must consider routing and connection strategies, and the problems of connection and security.

A distributed system provides the user with access to the various resources the system maintains. Access to a shared resource allows computation speed-up, data availability, and reliability.

8. Multithreading

A thread, sometimes called a lightweight process (LWP), is a basic unit of CPU utilization, and consists of a program counter, a register set, and a stack space. It shares with peer threads its code section, data section, and operating-system resource such as open files and signals, collectively know as a task.

Multithreading, like multitasking, is the simultaneous operation of two or more tasks by a single computer. The difference is that here, the tasks are components or "threads" of a single application rather than being separate programs. It is the capability of a processor to switch from one to another processing thread, i.e., a set of logically connected instructions that make up a part of a process.

A traditional or heavyweight process is equal to a task with one thread. A task does nothing if no threads are in it, and a thread must be in exactly one task. The extensive sharing makes CPU switching among peer threads and thread creation inexpensive, compared with context switches among heavyweight processes. Although a thread context switch still requires a register set switch, no memory-management-related work need be done.

The terms foreground and background often are used to explain a process's priority in a multitasking operating system. A process is in the *foreground* if it is the currently active process or the process with the highest priority. A process is in the *background* if it has been suspended or has a lower priority.

9. Command Interpreter System

One of the most important components of an operating system is its command interpreter. The command interpreter is the primary interface between the user and the rest of the system.

A command interpreter is the part of a computer operating system that understands and executes commands that are entered interactively by a human being or from a program. In some operating systems, the command interpreter is called the shell.

Many commands are given to the operating system by control statements. When a new job is started in a batch system or when a user logs-in to a time-shared system, a program which reads and interprets control statements is automatically executed. This program is variously called (1) the control card interpreter, (2) the command line interpreter, (3) the shell (in UNIX), and so on. Its function is quite simple: get the next command statement, and execute it.

The command statement themselves deal with process management, I/O handling, secondary storage management, main memory management, file system access, protection, and networking. A command interpreter is an interface of the operating system with the user. The user gives commands with are executed by operating system (usually by turning them into system calls). The main function of a command interpreter is to get and execute the next user specified command. Command-Interpreter is usually not part of the kernel, since multiple command interpreters (shell, in UNIX terminology) may be support by an operating system, and they do not really need to run in kernel mode. There are two main advantages to separating the command interpreter from the kernel.

- If we want to change the way the command interpreter looks, i.e., I want to change the interface of command interpreter, I am able to do that if the command interpreter is separate from the kernel. I cannot change the code of the kernel so I cannot modify the interface.
- If the command interpreter is a part of the kernel it is possible for a malicious process to gain access to certain part of the kernel that it showed not have to avoid this ugly scenario it is advantageous to have the command interpreter separate from kernel

Other functions of the OS

Some other related functions of Operating system are:

1. **Program development:**

   Operating system provides a number of facilities & services to assist the programmer during development of a program like "editor & debugger". These programs normally exist in the form of a utility program. Such programs are not part of the OS rather they are accessible through the OS.

2. **Program execution:**

   When a program is to be executed, a number of tasks like instructions & data loading into memory, I/O operation & file initialization are to be executed. The OS performs all these jobs for the user.

3. **Access to I/O devices:**

   Each I/O device requires its own set of instructions or control signals for operations. The OS takes care of all these requirements and the user only thinks in terms of reading/writing, all those details are hidden from the user.

4. **Controlled access to files:**

   In the case of files, control must include to understand the nature of the I/O devices like FD, HD & CD and also the format on the storage medium. Again

OS provides all such controls but these are transparent to the user. Furthermore in a multi-user system OS provides a protection mechanism to control access to any file.

5. **System access/protection:**

In the case of a shared or public system the OS takes control of the whole system as well as the system resources. The reason being OS has to provide protection to the data & resources from any unauthorized user and also to resolve conflicts when more than one user is competing for a resource.

6. **Error detection:**

During the execution of a program different errors can occur e.g., insufficient memory, device failure, arithmetic overflow & a program accessing a protected area etc. Typical OS takes care of all these problems and responds to clear these errors without disturbing normal functioning of the system. But in some cases it may have to terminate the application.

7. **Accounting:**

A good operating system keeps usage statistics for various resources and monitor performance parameters such as response time. For example in windows it gives you information about performance, disk usage or job queues for printing. This kind of information is useful for the user but it is more useful in multi-user system where user log-on time can be used for billing.

8. **Concurrency:**

Concurrency means the existence of several simultaneous or parallel activities. The operating system should insure that one process would not change data that another is using. All work must be done in parallel without affecting another work. For example; when a system has I/O operations with computation and the several programs in the memory, all task should be done in parallel without affecting the other. Switching

TYPES OF OPERATING SYSTEMS

Different systems enable different types of computer operations. The type of system depends on the way the system handles various data processing jobs. The types of operating systems are:

Single User - Single Processing System

The simplest of all the computer systems is a single use-single processor system.

The single user- single processing system has a single processor, runs a single program and interacts with a single user at a time.

The operating system for this system is very simple to design and implement. However, the CPU is not utilized to its full potential, because it sits idle for most of the time. Figure

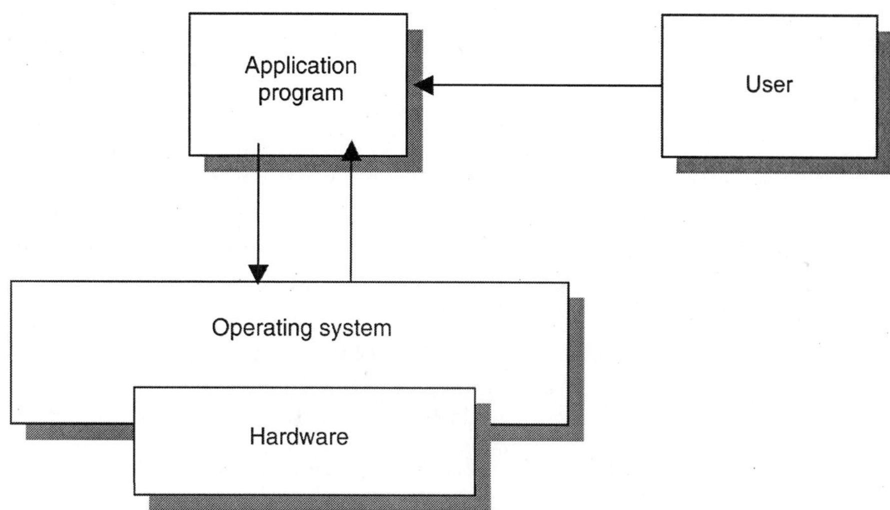

Single user – single processor system

In this configuration, all the computing resources are available to the user all the time. Therefore, operating system has very simple responsibility. A representative example of this category of operating system is MS-DOS.

Batch Processing

This type of operating system is also known as mainframes. Jobs like data processing were carried out in a batch. Data was punched in a punch card; job control cards that carried the instructions were also used.

Batch processing systems are systems in which jobs were gathered in groups or batches and than executed collectively.

The CPU and the peripherals remained unchanged most of the time in this operating system. The cards were useful here and the printer was not used. Utilization of the system resources was very low.

A batch system is one in which jobs are bundled together with the instructions necessary to allow them to be processed without intervention. It is the job of the operator to make sure that the batch of programs along with any data, usually submitted on the old punched card are put into the computer system in the right order, and other cards (job control cards) containing instructions (job control language instructions) to the operating system are placed in-between the jobs.

The basic physical layout of the memory of a batch job computer is shown below:

Operating system (memory resident)
User Space (compilers, programs, data, etc)

The operating system (called the monitor) is responsible for interpreting and carrying out the instructions in the batch jobs. Its major task is to transfer control automatically from one job to the next. To speed up processing, jobs with similar needs are batched together and are run through the computer as a group.

Advantages of these simple batch systems are:

1. much of the work of the operator is moved to the computer
2. performance increases since it is possible for job to start as soon as the previous job finished

Disadvantages are:

1. turn-around time can be large from user standpoint
2. more difficult to debug program
3. a job could enter an infinite loop (e.g. program error— To prevent an infinite loop, a timer is added to the system and the $JOB card was modified so that a maximum execution time for the job was passed to the monitor. The computer would interrupt the job and return control to the monitor when this time is exceeded.)

In early systems, there could be a significant amount of *set-up time* involved in the running of a job. In addition, the cost of computers are expensive and computer time was extremely valuable, the owners wanted their computers to be used as mush as possible. They needed high *utilization.*

Jobs with similar needs were *batched* together and run through the computer as a group so as to reduce the system set-up time. For example, suppose the operator received one FORTRAN job, one COBOL job, and another FORTRAN job. If she ran them in that order, she would have to set up for FORTRAN (load the compiler tapes, and so on), then set up for COBOL, and then set up for FORTRAN again.

It is certainly NOT a problem nowadays. There exists idle time when loading the appropriate device with the next job. To overcome this idle time, people developed *automatic job sequencing.* With this technique, the first immature operating systems were created. What was desired was a procedure for automatically transferring control from one job to the next. A small program, called a *resident monitor*, was created for this purpose. The *resident monitor* is always resident in memory: When the computer is turned on, it was invoked and transfer control to a program; when the program terminated, it would return control to the resident monitor, which would then go on to the next program.

The operator gives a short description of what programs were to be run on what data in a control card. A special character or pattern on the control card is used to distinguish them from *data cards* or *program cards*. Several system used '$' in the first column to identify a control card. IBM's Job Control Language (JCL) used slash marks '//' in the first two columns. A resident monitor thus has several identifiable parts:

(1) A control-card interpreter that is responsible for reading and carrying out the instructions on the cards at the point of execution.

(2) A loader to load system programs and application programs into memory.

(3) A set of device drivers for the system's I/O devices (such as card reader, line printer)

(4) An automatic job sequencing unit (former job scheduler) to switch control to another job.

A batch operating system, thus, normally reads a stream of separate jobs (from a card reader, for example) and output results (on a line printer, for example) when the job is complete. The definitive feature of a *batch* system is the *lack* of interaction between the user and the job while the job is executing (unlike *interactive* system).

Overlapped CPU and I/O operations

Even with automatic job sequencing, however, the CPU is often idle since the speed of the mechanical I/O devices,, which are intrinsically slower than electronic devices. Nowadays, improvements in technology resulted in faster I/O devices. Unfortunately, CPU speeds increased even faster, so that the problem was not only unsolved, but also exacerbated.

Off-line processing

Rather than have the CPU read directly from cards, however, the cards were first copied onto a magnetic tape (the 'fastest' device at the moment) via a separate device. When the tape was full, it was taken down and carried over to the computer. Similarly, output was written to the tape and the tape will be printed later. The card readers and line printers were operated off-line, rather than by the main computer.

The real gain in off-line operations comes from the possibility of using multiple reader-to-tape and tape-to-printer systems for one CPU. This can be considered as former parallel processing and multi-programming.

Buffering and Spooling

Buffering is the method of overlapping the I/O of a job with its own computation. The idea is quite simple. After data have been read and the CPU is about to start operating on them, the input device is instructed to begin the next input immediately. The CPU and the input device are then both busy. With luck, by the time that the CPU is ready for the next data item (record), the input device will have finished reading it. The CPU can then begin processing the newly read data, while the input device starts to read the following data. Similarly, this can be done for output. In this case, the CPU creates data that are put into a buffer until an output device can accept them.

Although off-line preparation of jobs continued for some time, it was quickly replaced in most systems. Disk systems became widely available and greatly improved on off-line operation. The problem with tape systems was that the card reader could not write onto one end of the tape while the CPU read from another. The entire tape had to be written before it was rewound and read. Disk systems eliminated this problem. Because the head is moved from one area of the disk to another, a disk can rapidly switch from the area of the disk being used by the card reader to store new cards to the position needed by the CPU to read the 'next' card.

In a disk system, cards are read directly from the card reader onto the disk. The location of card images is recorded in a table kept by the operating system. When a job is executed, the operating system satisfies its requests for card reader input by reading from the disk. Similarly, when the job requests the printer to ouput a line, that line is copied into a system buffer and is written to the disk. When the job is completed, the output is actually printed.

This form of processing is called *spooling*. The name is an acronym for simultaneous peripheral operation on-line. Spooling essentially uses the disk as a very large buffer, for reading as far ahead as possible on input devices and for storing output files until the output devices are able to accept them.

In addition, spooling provides a very important data structure: a *job pool*. Spooling will generally result in several jobs that have already been read waiting on disk, ready to run. A pool of these jobs on disk allows the operating system to select which job to run next, in order to increase CPU utilization. When jobs come in directly from tape, it is not possible to skip around and to run jobs in a different order. Jobs must be run sequentially, on a first-come, first-served basis. However, when several jobs are on a direct access device, such as a disk, job scheduling becomes possible.

Difference between Off-lining and Spooling

Off-lining

A job that output data, to a printer for example, places the output data onto backing store instead, and is therefore able to complete processing quickly. Later, either

i. he tape or disk is ***physically moved*** to a separate processor, which outputs the data onto a printer, or

ii. The tape or disk drive is ***reassigned*** to another front-end communications processor, which outputs the data to a line printer.

Spooling (Simultaneous Peripheral Operating On Line)

i. It can be refer to ***pseudo*** off-lining using disk (direct access storage).

ii. It is a technique used to speed up communication between devices that operate at ***different speeds***.

iii. E.g. Output to printer may be ***spooled*** (written) to disk, which is a high speed device. When the printer becomes free, the output will be printed.

iv. This technique enables several users who are using a system to share the same printer simultaneously without getting their output muddled up.

v. The program that transfers data from the disk to the output device is called ***despooling program***.

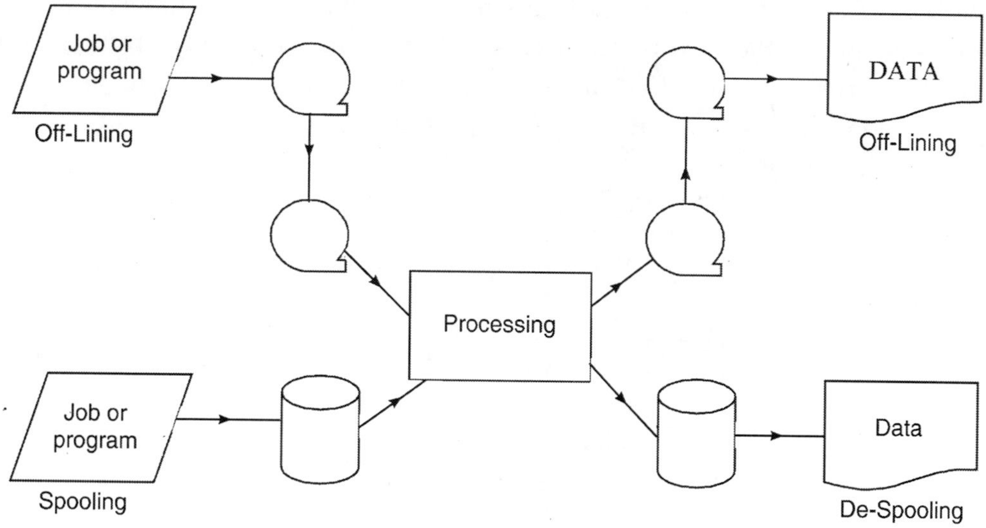

Spooling and de-spooling

Buffering and spooling are the most important techniques to reduce the speed mismatch between input/output devices and the CPU.

Multiprogramming

The most important aspect of job scheduling is the ability to *multiprogram*. Off-line operation, buffering, and spooling for overlapped I/O have their limitations. A single user cannot, in general, keep either the CPU or the I/O devices busy at all times. Multiprogramming increases CPU utilization by organizing jobs so that the CPU always has something to execute.

The execution of two or more computer programs by a single computer is called multiprogramming .It is a form of processing in which a computer holds more than one program in memory and works on them in round-robin fashion.

The idea is as follows. The operating system picks and begins to execute one of the jobs in the job pool. Eventually, the job may have to wait for some task, such as a tape to be mounted, a command to be typed on a keyboard, or an I/O operation to complete. In a non-multiprogrammed system, the CPU would sit idle. In a multiprogramming system, the operating system simply switches to and executes another job. When *that* job needs to wait, the CPU is switched to another job, and so on. Eventually, the first job finishes waiting and gets the CPU back. As long as there is always some job to execute, the CPU will never be idle.

Multiprogrammed operating systems are fairly sophisticated. To have several jobs ready to run, the system must keep all of them in memory simultaneously. Having several programs in memory at the same time requires some form of memory management. In addition, if several jobs are ready to run at the same time, the system must choose among them. This decision is *CPU Scheduling*. Finally, multiple jobs running concurrently require that their ability to affect one another be limited in all phases of the operating system, including process scheduling, disk storage, and memory management.

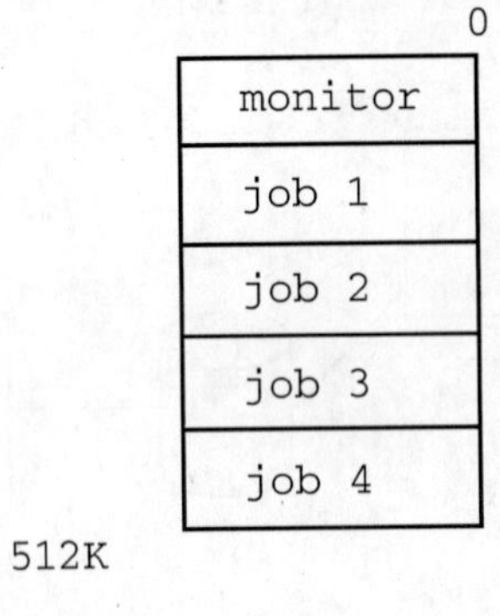

0

monitor
job 1
job 2
job 3
job 4

512K

In a multiprogrammed batch system, several jobs are kept in main memory at the same time. The idea of multiprogramming is to allow many users to use a single computer simultaneously. The goal was to make an efficient use of time. For instance, not to have the CPU do active waits on I/O operations, etc.

It is known that I/O is still the bottleneck of computational devices. To avoid a large part of this overhead, OS designers decided to have more than one job resident on the computer. When a job would do an I/O with the CPU waiting for the result, the other job would start executing and the fist job would return only when with its I/O completed. In this way, active waits were eliminated. This is how the concept of multiprogramming appeared.

It is the technique of having more than one job in the computer's main memory at any one time. When a program is being executed the CPU may be idle from time to time (e.g. I/O operation taking place).Therefore, during the time when the CPU is idled, it could easily be doing operations for other jobs.

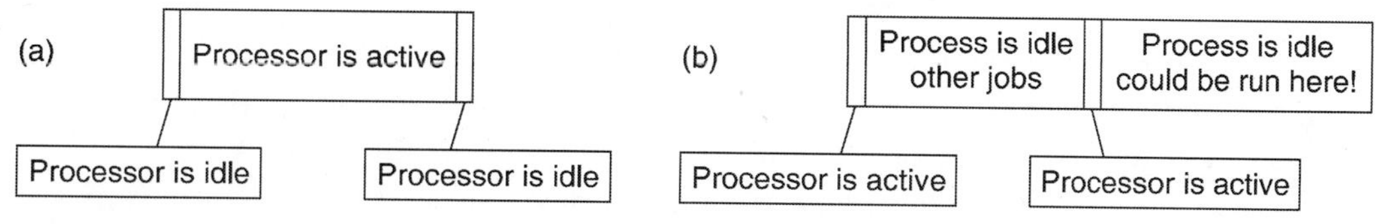

Multiprogramming

An operating system organizes the system such that the CPU is able to do multi-programming. The processes involve both memory management and management of CPU time (process scheduling). This can be achieved with the implementation of concepts such as processes, virtual memory management, and the like. Interrupts are absolutely necessary to the adequate implementation of multiprogramming.

OS features needed for multiprogramming:

1. I/O routine supplied by the system.
2. Memory management — the system must allocate the memory to several jobs.
3. CPU Scheduling — the system must choose among several jobs ready to run.
4. Allocation of devices.

Multitasking

Depending on the volume of transactions, here the card reader reads one job after another, and this is stored in the main memory. The processed output of various jobs are stored in the main or auxiliary memory, and printed one by one, on the printer. For reading, processing and outputting the CPU switches from one task to another. This saves the idle time of the peripherals.

Multitasking is the ability to execute several parts of a program in parallel. It is the ability to execute more than one task at the same time, a task being a program or a part of a program.

It is the capability of a computer with a single CPU to simulate the processing of more than one task at a time. Multitasking is effective when one (or more) of the applications spends most of its time in an idle state, waiting for a user-initiated event such as a keystroke or mouse click. More programs can reside in the central memory at the same time, and instructions can be executed by the CPU because the main memory is partitioned, and many jobs are handled simultaneously. The possible tasks of many programs can reside in the memory simultaneously because Multiprogramming and multitasking can execute multiple programs, and CPU can switch from one portion of a program to another. Many users and user terminals can also be connected and facilitated by these operating systems.

Cooperative multitasking

The concurrent processes executing in the operating system may be either independent processes or cooperating processes. A process is independent if it cannot affect or be affected by the other pr4ocesses executing in the system. Clearly, any process that does not share any data (temporary or persistent) with any other process is independent. On the other hand, a process is cooperating if it can affect or be affected by the other processes executing in the system. Clearly, any process that shares data with other processes is a cooperative process. A cooperative multitasking operating system supports cooperative process by providing extra memory and programs. The reasons for providing cooperative environment are because it can provide information sharing, computation speedup, modularity and convenience. However, concurrent execution that requires cooperation among the processes requires mechanisms to allow processes to communicate with each other, and to synchronize their actions.

Preemptive multitasking

With preemptive multitasking, the operating system prioritizes the processes to be performed and assigns a set amount of CPU time for the execution of each process. Certain processes, such as keyboard input or mouse movement, are given higher priority than other processes, such as sending data to the printer. Every few milliseconds, the CPU evaluates the processes waiting to be executed and chooses the one with the highest priority. This process then is assigned one or more increments of CPU time called a time slice.

	Process	*Priority*	*Time allocation*
	1	High	3 time slices
one time	2	Low	1 time slice
slice	3	Medium	2 time slices

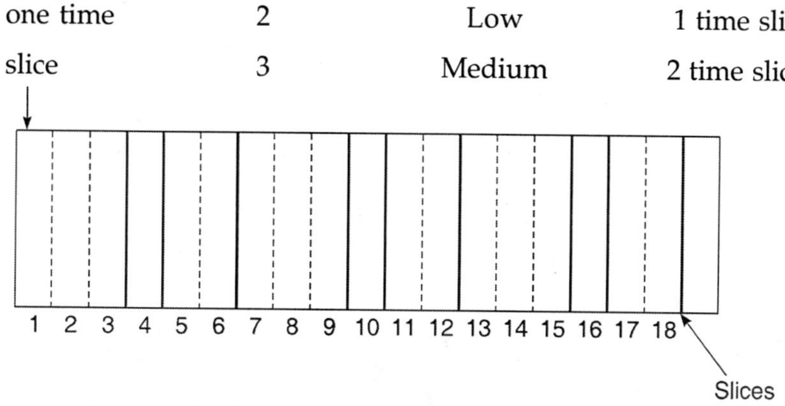

When the process finishes its work or the assigned time slice expires, the CPU executes the next highest priority process. If two or more processes have the same priority such as two users inputting data at the same time, the CPU executes the process that was least recently worked on. Eventually, each process receives a time slice and is executed. Unless the system has a heavy workload, you may not even be aware that your program process was set aside temporarily. Before you notice a delay, the operating system has allocated your program process another time slice and processing continues. A time slice is a brief amount of CPU time given to a process by the operating system. Higher priority processes receive more consecutive slices than lower priority process. In this example, process 2 is the lowest priority process.

Multi-user Systems

A multi-user operating system lets more than one user access the computer system at one time. Access to the computer system is normally provided via a network, so that users access the computer remotely using a terminal or other computer.

Multi-user is a term that defines an operating system that allows concurrent access by multiple users of a computer i.e. the ability of a computer to support multiple users while providing a full range of capability to each one.

Today, these terminals are generally personal computers and use a network to send and receive information to the multi-user computer system. Examples of multi-user operating systems are UNIX, Linux (a UNIX clone) and mainframes such as the IBM AS400.

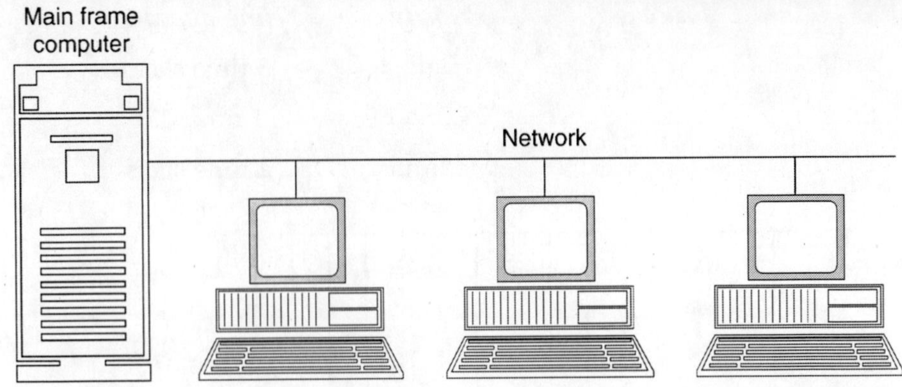

The operating system for a large multi-user computer system with many terminals is much more complex than a single-user operating system. It must manage and run all user requests, ensuring they do not interfere with each other. Devices that are serial in nature (devices which can only be used by one user at a time, like printers and disks) must be shared amongst all those requesting them (so that all the output documents are not jumbled up). If each user tried to send their document to the printer at the same time, the end result would be garbage. Instead, documents are sent to a queue, and each document is printed in its entirety before the next document to be printed is retrieved from the queue. When you wait inline at the cafeteria to be served you are in a queue. Imagine that all the people in the queue are documents waiting to be printed and the cashier at the end of the queue is the printer.

The need for multitasking and multiprogramming for interactive processing indicates the need for the development of multi-user systems. The systems like mainframes, super minis and mini systems were designed to serve the needs of multiple users incorporating the concepts of multiprogramming and time-sharing. These systems provide each user a terminal consisting of a monitor and a keyboard. The size, configuration and cost of the computer is decided not only based on the software needed, but also on the number of users, and the speed with which the processing is to be carried out.

The development of communication technologies, satellite communication, and optical fiber systems, enable large computers and terminals connected to a computer in a particular location, to download files, programs and data from a computer located thousands of kilometers away, send mail to another user, even if he is not logged on to the system when the mail is sent. Such developments in computer and communication technologies demand standardization of operating systems, communication protocols, networking software and interfaces.

The advantage of having a multi-user operating system is that normally the hardware is very expensive, and it lets a number of users share this expensive resource.

This means the cost is divided amongst the users. It also makes better use of the resources. Since the resources are shared, they are more likely to be in use than sitting idle being unproductive.

One problem with multi-user computer systems is that as more users access it, the performance becomes slower and slower. Another disadvantage is the cost of hardware, as a multi-user operating system requires a lot of disk space and memory. In addition, the actual software for multi-user operating systems tend to cost more than single-user operating systems.

Time Sharing

When many users are connected to the computer using an operating system, it is called "time sharing". In time sharing, the CPU switches from one user's job to another user at a fast rate.

A way of sharing out computer facilities between a number of people who want to use the computer at the same time. Each has a separate terminal and gets the impression that they have sole use of the computer.

After processing a user's job, the operating system proceeds to the second, third, fourth user and so on; processing each user's job within a short interval of time and this goes on in a cycle continuously. The CPU works for 1m sec for a user for every sec. For a thousand users, and in this 1m sec, the CPU can execute more than 2,50,000 instructions of every user with an average speed of 250 MHz.

Online Operating System /Real Time

Online processing consists of entering transaction data and viewing the results immediately. All the resources can be accessed immediately then it is called online system whereas in real time systems the resources are accessed in a prescribed deadline of milliseconds.

The computer starts the process immediately, takes one or all the inputs, and delivers the outputs instantaneously then it is called online processing.

Real time processing is a form of transaction processing in which each transaction is executed as soon as complete data becomes available for the transaction.

Process control, airline reservations, railway reservations and banking are some of the other examples of real time/online operating systems. Users cannot update or modify the program because these operating systems supports single application orientation, but users are allowed only to input data, make inquiries and get reports.

A real time system has well defined, fixed time constraints. Processing must be done within the defined constraints, or the system will fail. It is often used as a control device in a dedicated application. A real time system functions correctly only if it returns the correct result within its time constraints. The two types of real time systems are:

i. Hard real time system- failure results in drastic and unforeseen damage

ii. Soft real time system-failures does not result in drastic damage

HARD RTOS	SOFT RTOS
1. Time delays are not allowed 2. It assures critical tasks must completed on time	1. Time delays are allowed 2. Very critical tasks get more priority ever other tasks and retains it until it completes.

A hard real time system guarantees that critical tasks complete on time. In a soft real time system, a critical real-time task gets priority over the other tasks, and retains that priority until it completes. Soft real time systems have more limited utility than do hard real-time systems

Multiprocessing and Parallel Processing

In multiprocessing system more than one processor are used for processing data. The speed of the computer had to be enhanced, by adding few more processors, as the number of users increased, the response time had to be kept up, and when the volume of data to be processed increased, just one processor, or increasing the clock speed of the processor did not suffice.

Sharing the execution process by interconnecting more than one microprocessors is called as multi Processing.

Parallel systems employ many processors, perhaps hundreds or thousands, all working together on the same problem. The problem thus has to be able to be broken down into a number of parts which can be worked on simultaneously

Parallel processing is the ability to process "chunks" or blocks of a program simultaneously. To do this, the computer has to have several CPU units and the software to coordinate them, or it must be able to simulate such a situation.

A computer or workstation configured with multiple microcircuits, each functioning as a separate computer but usable in tandem. Either each computer can handle a separate task or each computer can hold data to which a uniform process is applied. There are two types of multiprocessing systems:

1. Symmetric multiprocessing

Each processor of symmetric multiprocessing systems runs an identical copy of the operating system, and these copies communicate with one another as needed.

An example of the multiprocessing system is Encore's version of UNIX for the Multimax computer which can be configured to employ dozens of processors, all running a copy of UNIX. The benefit of this model is that many processors can run at once without causing a *deterioration of performance.*

2. Asymmetric multiprocessing

Asymmetric multiprocessing is more common in extremely large systems. For example, a banking system might use an IBM series/1 minicomputer as a front-end. The front end acts as a buffer between the terminals and the main CPU of a mainframe at headquarters.

Symmetric multiprocessing vs. Asymmetric multiprocessing

ASYMMETRIC	SYMMETRIC
1. Working of OS is based on Master-Slave relationship	1. Each processor concurrently runs a copy of the OS
2. Each processor is assigned with a specific task. Master processor controls the system , schedules and allocates work to the slave processors.	2. Many processes can run simultaneously
3. Example : Sun OS version 4	3. Example : Windows NT , OS/2, UNIX , Solaris

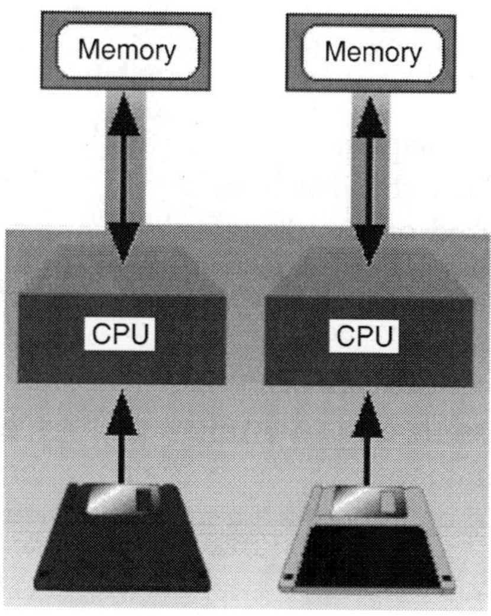

Application process

Application process

Symmetric multiprocessing

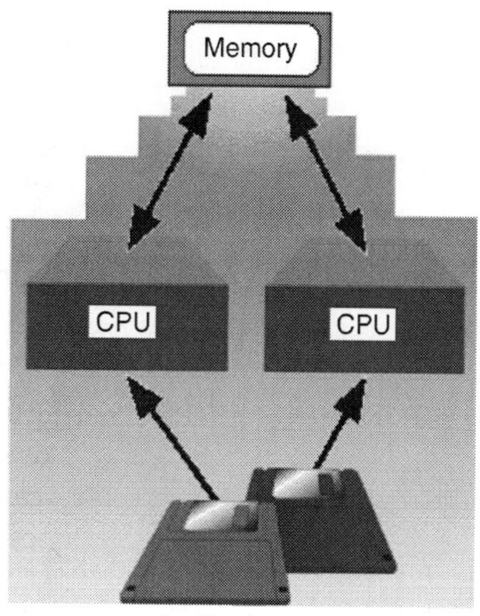

Application process

Symmetric multiprocessing

In asymmetric multiprocessing, application processes are assigned to a specific CPU that has its own memory. In symmetric multiprocessing, application processes are assigned to the first available CPU. Memory is shared by all of the CPUs.

In these cases the function of an operating system, and design in such environments became more complex. Efficient processors, interfaces and peripherals had also to be built into such operating systems, like disk mirroring and replication. One processor was to complete different jobs to different processors, and another was to complete each statement in the program to different processors. This was called parallel programming. These operating systems and techniques are associated with super mini and super computers.

Multiprogramming Vs Multiprocessing

Differences between multiprogramming and multiprocessing are explained in the table as follows:

Multiprogramming	Multiprocessing
1. Only one Processor is there.	1. More than one processor will be there
2. Programs which are ready to be executed are in main memory.	2. It increases throughput, reliability
3. It executes only one process at any time	3. It executes more than one process at any given time.
4. It increases CPU utilization.	4. It also increases CPU utilization. More than one processors shares computer memory, computer bus, clock , peripheral devices

Distributed Data Processing and Networking

The surrounding resources, such as the hard disc and printers are not fully correlated in a single user system. The printer remains inactive, when the computer is used for data entry. An application package used by different users, have to be copied to various PCs. Data modification, updating and editing becomes difficult with single user systems, since the data in the system is to be corrected continuously one by one.

Distributed processing and networking is the ability to have several computers working together in a network, where each processor runs different activities for a user, as required .A network is a collection of connected computers that can share data as well as resources.

An application package on inventory, for example, can be used by stores, accounts, purchase sections, etc. In such situations, the best choice would be for the application package to be shareable and data updateable from any computer with record locking. To meet this need, PCs in an organization are networked, enabling the sharing of resources such as the disc, printers, data and application packages. Thus, the data is made available for the entire organization. Networking also enables communication and internal mail access between various users.

Reasons for building distributed systems are:

- **Resource sharing**: sharing data, program and hardware.
- **Computation speedup**: partition a particular computation into segments.
- **Reliability**: if one site breaks down, the remaining sites can continue operating.
- **Communication**: electronic mail, teleconferencing, etc.

Client-Server Systems

The network will host a main server which is providing a service to a number of network terminals. The client software will make a request to the server for some service/processing, and the results of this request are then returned to the client computer.

The client server system is a data processing interaction in which a program at one site (the client) sends a request to a program at another site (the server) for performing some task or operation.

The fact that the processing is done on the server is transparent to the client machine. In this way, server files and application programs resident on the server are available to the client user exactly as if they were resident on that user's terminal.

Client – Server Examples

Printing work from an application program running on a client computer. The work to be printed is sent over the network to a print server to which are connected one or more printers. The print server is responsible for carrying out the printing of all clients' work.

File Server

The files available to the user at the client computer - i.e. a 'file server'

E-Mail server

The e-mails sent and received by the client are managed on a server - i.e. a 'mail server'

Web server

At the client browser software, the user keys in a URL. The request for this page is sent to the server. The web server locates the page and sends to the client computer The request could be for Active Server Pages (ASP). These pages require processing of code statements within the page to be processed at the server before the page is sent and displayed with the client browser software

Database server

Access to a centrally held database i.e. a 'database server', when a user creates a query, the query is sent to the server ,processed on the server, the query results are returned to the client workstation. The DBMS software will control all aspects of the management of the data and the various user's access to it – backup – security.

Personal-Computer Systems

A small (desktop) microcomputer designed for use by a single user. As an acronym, 'PC,' the term frequently refers to a personal computer that runs Microsoft's MS-DOS (disk operating system) or Microsoft's Windows GUI. cf. network computer, multi-user system.

The PC-based operating systems, such as MS-DOS, windows 3.1, OS/2, Windows 95,

Are used for personal computers

As hardware costs have decreased, it has once again become feasible to have a computer system dedicated to a single user. The I/O devices have certainly changed, with panels of switched and card readers replaced with typewriter-like keyboards and mouse. Line printers and card punches have succumbed to display screens and ink-jet/laser printers.

Some design concepts of mainframes may not be appropriate for smaller systems. For example, file protection may not seem necessary on a PC since there are only one *"possible" user.* Unfortunately, computers nowadays are often connected to each other computers over telephone lines or local area networks. When other computers and other users can access the files on a personal computer, file protection again becomes a necessary feature of an operating system. Moreover, the lack of such protection enables computer *worm* or *virus* to disrupt entire companies or even worldwide networks.

At the same time that features of large operating systems were being scaled down to fit personal computers, more powerful, faster, and more sophisticated hardware systems were being developed. The *personal workstation* is a large/powerful personal computer, such as the SUN/sparc, HP/decstation, or IBM/RS6000 series. Many university and business have large numbers of workstations tied together with local-area networks. The line dividing PCs and workstations become blurry. In the future, the two may merge into one category.

Interactive Processing

Now the computer is completely at the disposal of and dedicated to the single user. In this case, the operating systems like, MS-DOS, WINDOWS, etc. enables direct interaction with the compilation, and errors are displayed on the screen that helps to achieve the output.

Interactive Processing is a processing method in which each operator action causes a response from the program or system. In interactive processing computer, a person can communicate directly with the machine by means of a terminal. The user enters commands which are immediately executed by the computer which sends the results of the command back to the user's terminal.

Modern computer systems are interactive. The user asks for OS services directly and receives an immediate response. The user can easily experiment and do fast debugging.

Interactive computation + Multiprogramming = Time Sharing

Each user will have a separate program in memory and the CPU is switched rapidly from one user program to the other giving service to all user programs. So, users can share a computer system. As the CPU is switched rapidly between user programs, each user is given the impression that he/she has his/her own computer.

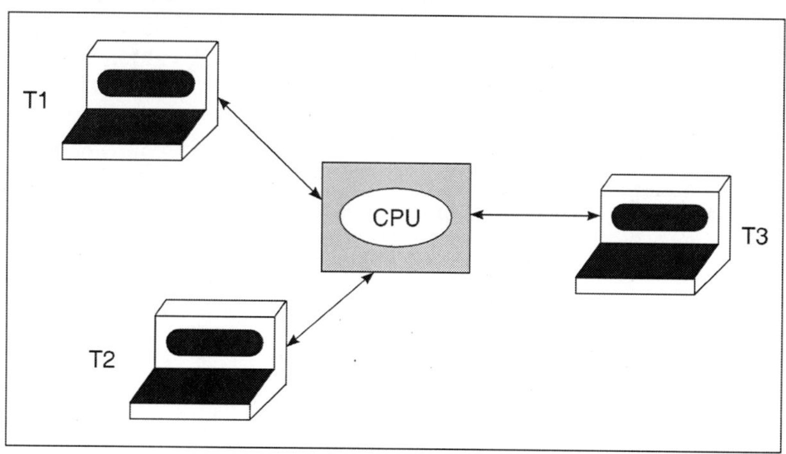

Even non- programmers can load application packages through simple commands. Interactive processing is also facilitated in multi-user systems, using dumb or intelligent terminals.

Major types of operating systems and their uses

Type	Definition	Example of Use
Batch Processing System	Data or programs are collected grouped and processed at a later date.	Payroll, stock control and billing systems.
Real-time Systems	**Inputs immediately affect the outputs. Timing is critical** i.e. they are capable of influencing the source of the data e.g. control where data from sensors is processed immediately and affect the outputs – controlling some device. **Timing is critical** and the term real-time control system.	e.g. control of nuclear power plants, oil refining, chemical processing and air traffic control systems.
Real-time transaction	**Inputs immediately affect the outputs but timing is not critical.** Each transaction is completed online as it arises e.g. booking systems – each booking is online and a database of bookings can be amended interactively and very quickly whilst another user is **locked out** so **cannot double book** or alter that record at the same time.	**Holiday and airline booking system.** **Difference between real-time and real-time transactions**. In real time, ***time is critical*** and delays can be catastrophic but in real-time transactions systems there is no time criticality. E.g. poor speeds in airline control would be dangerous but poor booking speeds would not be so crucial.
Online processing	**Processing performed under the direct control of the CPU** whilst the user remains in communication with the computer.	
Offline processing	**Processing which is done away from CPU.**	e.g. batching together of clock cards, filling in OMR forms.

Type	Definition	Example of Use
	Such systems may be single-user (e.g. a personal computer).	
Multi-access on-line	**Any users linked by workstations to a central computer such as in a network.**	Holiday or airline booking system. One person must be locked out when another is updating the file. This helps to prevent Double booking
Interactive processing	**The user has to be present and program cannot proceed until there is some input from the user**	Select from a menu at ATM.
Distributed system	**Processing is carried out independently in more than one location, but with shared and controlled access to some common facilities.**	Databases e.g. libraries.
Multiprogramming:	**Ability to run many programs apparently at the same time.**	Mainframe systems. Each job is allocated a small amount of processing time (*time slice*) in turn.
Multi tasking	**The ability to hold several programs in RAM at one time but the user switches between them.**	Usually uses GUI's. Facilitates import and export of data.

POPULAR OPERATING SYSTEMS

There are many different types of operating systems. They are designed to meet the requirements of different computing environments.. Several of the most popular Operating systems are discussed below:

DOS

DOS *(Disk Operating System)* is for single-user IBM-compatible computers. Microsoft Corporation sells this product under the name MS-DOS (Microsoft Disk Operating System) and licenses another version, called PC-DOS, to IBM for use in its personal computers. DOS was written for the microcomputer technology of the early 1980s. An enormous number of microcomputers still run under DOS. Even though there have been numerous improvements to the software since its introduction, limitations still exist. It is not GUI-capable. Nor can it take full advantage of today's 32-bit processors (e.g., Intel's Pentium® series). That is, application programs running on DOS computers have direct access to only 640,000 bytes of primary memory.

Mac OS

Macintosh Operating Systems *(Mac OS)* was introduced in the 1984 and was the first commercial GUI platform. The latest version supports multitasking, includes multiple Web browsers, and has built-in networking capability. It also is able to open, edit, and save files created in DOS and Windows platforms.

Microsoft Windows 95 and 98

Microsoft Windows 95 and 98 are GUI-capable, multitasking operating systems. Unlike the earlier Windows 3.x series, Windows 95 and 98 are true operating systems, and do not require DOS to run. Windows 95 and 98 have broken the 640,000-byte barrier, providing direct access to millions of bytes of memory. These operating systems take advantage of today's more powerful microprocessor chips, such as the Intel Pentium®, which address more memory and run faster than the older microprocessors. Windows 98 is an upgraded version of Windows 95. Windows 98 is user-friendlier than Windows 95 and has more Internet features; e.g., Windows 98 includes Microsoft Internet Explorer.

UNIX

UNIX was developed by Bell Laboratories in the 1970's, and is one of the few small-scale operating systems that are both multi-user and multiprocessing capable. This allows computers running on UNIX to process a high volume of inputs from multiple users by using multiple CPUs simultaneously.

Linux

Linux is an interesting operating system because it is not proprietary software. Its code has been made publicly available (called *open-source software*). This allows users to customize the software to meet their personal needs and to share improvements made with others. Applications that run on Linux are commercially available; for example, from Red Hat Software and Corel Corporation.

Microsoft Windows NT

Microsoft Windows NT is designed for client-server networks. It provides the user with the other features of Windows 98.

Windows XP

Windows XP is built primarily on Windows 2000 technology which includes the best attributes of previous Windows versions. People who already know and have used previous versions of Windows should have no problems using Windows XP.

One major difference will be in the logging in and logging out procedures. Windows XP offers several benefits over other versions, namely, its built-in file encryption and password control capabilities provide basic data and access security, increased reliability and performance ability, friendly graphical user interface (GUI), and its Web communication features.

Command Line Interpreter Vs Graphical User Interface

The CLI and GUI operating systems are discussed below:

CLI (Command Line Interpreter)

In the old days, under CLI – MS-DOS – one command at a time, scripts or BAT files could be written to stack up multiple commands, or to perform sub BAT files iteratively. When we migrated to Windows, we could invoke the COMMAND to get to 'DOS' screen, but NOW, we invoke the CMD –or- COMMAND

Here is the fundamental syntax for a CLI Command.

<DO SOMETHING> <HOW TO> <AN INPUT FILE> <OUTPUT FILE>

The examples of CLI based commands are:

- FORMAT
- COPY and MOVE
- DEL
- RENAME
- DIR
- CD, MD, RD

CLI offers the following advantages:

1. CLI commands are consistent, unlike in GUI where menu options may vary with different menus and applications.
2. CLI is suitable for visually impaired users.
3. It is easier for advanced users to use CLI commands rather than open windows and menus to execute commands.
4. CLI enables users to save a list of commands as a script. Executing this script will execute all the commands in the script. This is not possible in GUI where the user has to perform all the tasks required to execute the command every time.
5. All commands and options of the CLI are documented. Therefore, a rare operation can be performed as easily as a common one.

6. SOME commands do NOT have a GUI equivalent. – Like Ping, IPCONFIG, TRACERT, FDISK

To get 'HELP' for CLI – just type 'HELP' from a DOS Prompt.

However, it is not very easy for beginners to remember all the CLI commands.

GUI (Graphical User Interface)

In CLI, the user has to remember commands and their syntax to perform tasks such as creating, renaming, copying, or deleting a file or folder. New computer users may find it difficult to remember a list of commands and their syntax. This limitation of CLI led to the development of GUI which took advantage of the use of graphics in computer systems for interacting with applications. Graphical User Interface (GUI), pronounced *goo-ee,* was first designed in the 1970s by Xerox Corporation and later incorporated by Apple Macintosh computers.

However, GUIs require a very powerful CPU and a high quality terminal for viewing the graphics. This was a prohibitive factor for the popularity of GUI. Later, however, the easy availability of powerful CPUs and high-quality terminals led to the use of GUI in all the new operating systems that were being developed. Microsoft introduced GUI with the Windows 1.0 (mid to late 80's)

The basic components of a GUI are:

1. Pointer: A symbol, typically an arrow or a cursor, which helps select objects on the screen.
2. Pointing Device: A mouse or joystick that helps moves the pointer on the screen.
3. Windows: Separate instances of the GUI that can concurrently run separate programs.
4. Menus: Lists of commands that can be selected and executed.
5. Icons: Graphics that are used to represent a file or an application. The user can move the pointer on to the icon, and click the icon to invoke the application or file.

Advantages	Limitations
It has easy-to-understand graphical icons for interacting with applications and hardware	Not suitable for visually impaired users
The user does not have to remember the commands to interact with an operating system	Advanced users, who are familiar with commands, may find it tedious to select graphical options
It is easy and convenient to use for new users	Graphical options are not consistent across applications

Advantages and Limitations of GUI

WYSIWYG – from the older days when it was uncommon to actually see on your screen what was to be printed as output.

OTHER SYSTEM SOFTWARE

The system software is powerful and efficient as it deals directly with the system or hardware. System software includes the following:

Assemblers:

Hardware generally applies a rule of 'ON' or 'OFF'. Instructions are designed by the processor to execute in binary form only. The entire coding is a combination of '0' ('OFF') and '1' ('ON').Therefore it is hard coding instruction for a CPU. This is also known as machine code/language, which is converted to machine code by the assembler.

Compilers and Interpreters:

High level languages, such as COBOL BASIC, C etc. are interpreted into machine languages/codes by the concerned compiler or interpreter, which creates executable files (for compilers), or executes each statement one by one (for interpreters).

Utilities:

With the help of certain utilities designed for specific purposes, specific jobs such as sorting, merging, setting up databases, creating tabular form of data, word processing, etc. can be carried out straight away in the computer without any programming,. Utilities, also called service programs, are system programs that provide a useful service to the user of the computer by providing facilities for performing common tasks of a routine nature. Common types of utility programs are:

i. Tracing and Debugging

- Tracing involves dumping internal storage after obeying specific instructions so that the cycle of operations can be traced and errors located.
- Debugging is the term given to the process of locating and eliminating *errors* from a program.

ii. File and Directories commands

Most OS contains commands or applications to handle various file and directory operations, like copying, moving, deleting and renaming files or directories, formatting disks, etc.

iii. Object Program Libraries

The object program after compilation may use library routines provided by OS. An object program is a collection of routines stored in such a way that any routine can be selectively library is a collection of routines stored in such a way that any routine can be selectively extracted for use in another object module. Object program libraries can be classified by:

a. *system.* a collection of built-in language-defined routines, e.g. in Pascal writeln and readln.

b. *public.* a collection of generally useful routines which are not standard to the language but likely to be required by many programmers, e.g. graphics routines;

c. *private.* a collection of routines written and stored in library form for a programmer's own use.

iv. Loader and Linker

A loader is a program that takes the object codes (i.e. the machine codes produced by the assembler) and loads it into the computer's main memory in the correct place.

The function of the linker is to link all the modules, including the libraries, together by putting the appropriate machine addresses into all external call and return addresses before executing the program.

v. Editors:

Normally editors create programs and data. Editors store the data and programs in the form of files in permanent storage media, such as tapes or discs. There are various editors—simple and complex, and the types of editors, depends on the operating system.

POPULAR OPERATING SYSTEMS

Windows NT

Windows NT is a Microsoft Windows personal computer operating system designed for users and businesses needing advanced capability. NT's technology is the base for the Microsoft successor operating system, Windows 2000. Windows NT (which may originally have stood for "New Technology," although Microsoft doesn't say) is actually two products: Microsoft NT Workstation and Microsoft NT Server. The Workstation is designed for users, especially business users, who need faster performance and a system a little more fail-safe than Windows 95 and Windows 98.

The Server is designed for business machines that need to provide services for network-attached computers.

- **Windows NT Workstation**: Microsoft says that 32-bit applications run 20% faster on this system than on Windows 95 (assuming both have 32 megabytes of RAM). Since older 16-bit applications run in a separate address space, one can crash without crashing other applications or the operating system. Security and management features not available on Windows 95 are provided. The Workstation has the same desktop user interface as Windows 95.
- **Windows NT Server**: The NT Server is probably the second most installed network server operating system after Novell's NetWare operating system. Microsoft claims that its NT servers are beginning to replace both NetWare and the various UNIX-based systems such as those of Sun Microsystems and Hewlett-Packard. NT Server 5.0., essentially became what was renamed Windows 2000. Host Configuration Protocol (DHCP), and the Windows Internet Naming Service (WINS) whenever a client is reconfigured.

Windows 2000

Windows 2000 (W2K) is a commercial version of Microsoft's evolving Windows operating system. Previously called Windows NT 5.0, Microsoft emphasizes that Windows 2000 is evolutionary and "Built on NT Technology." Windows 2000 is designed to appeal to small business and professional users as well as to the more technical and larger business market for which the NT was designed.

The Windows 2000 product line consists of four products:

1. Windows 2000 Professional, aimed at individuals and businesses of all sizes. It includes security and mobile use enhancements. It is the most economical choice.
2. Windows 2000 Server, aimed at small-to-medium size businesses. It can function as a Web server and/or a workgroup (or branch office) server. It can be part of a two-way symmetric multiprocessing system. NT 4.0 servers can be upgraded to this server.
3. Windows 2000 Advanced Server, aimed at being a network operating system server and/or an application server, including those involving large databases. This server facilitates clustering and load-balancing. NT 4.0 servers with up to eight-way SMP can upgrade to this product.
4. Windows 2000 Datacenter Server designed for large data warehouses, online transaction processing (OLTP), econometric analysis, and other applications requiring high-speed computation and large databases. The Datacenter Server supports up to 16-way SMP and up to 64 gigabytes of physical memory.

Windows XP

Windows XP (code named Whistler by Microsoft) is the latest and as-yet officially unreleased version of the Windows desktop operating system for the PC. Microsoft and trade publication writers view Windows XP as the most important version of Windows since Windows 95. Windows XP is built on the Windows 2000 kernel but brings a new, more personalized look to the desktop that will also make it easier for users to scan or import images and to acquire music files on the Web and transfer them to portable devices. The new Windows will allow different family members to use their own desktop and personal sets of files. In addition to the "My Computer" and "My Documents" views provided in Windows 2000, Windows XP users see "My Music" and "My Pictures." The Start Menu has been redesigned to make the most-used programs easiest to find. Windows XP will come in a Professional version and a Home Edition version.

Windows CE

Windows CE is based on the Microsoft Windows operating system but is designed for including or embedding in mobile and other space-constrained devices. Although Microsoft does not explain the "CE," it is reported to have originally stood for "Consumer Electronics." Windows CE is used in several brands of handheld computers and as part of cable TV set-top boxes built for TCI. It competes with EPOC and also with similar operating systems from 3Com (for its PalmPilot) and other companies. Like the full-scale Windows systems, Windows CE is a 32-bit multitasking, multithreading operating system. Microsoft emphasizes that the system was "built from scratch" while taking advantage of Windows architectural concepts and interfaces. Microsoft argues that Windows desktop system users will find that products with Windows CE provide a familiar user interface.

In addition to handheld computers and cable TV boxes, Windows CE is also offered as the operating system for the Auto PC, Microsoft's concept of controlling applications (such as selecting radio channels) while driving, using interactive speech technology.

Linux

Linux (often pronounced LIH-nuhks with a short "i") is a UNIX-like operating system that was designed to provide personal computer users a free or very low-cost operating system comparable to traditional and usually more expensive UNIX systems. Linux has a reputation as a very efficient and fast-performing system. Linux's kernel (the central part of the operating system) was developed by Linus Torvalds at the University of Helsinki in Finland. To complete the operating system, Torvalds and other team members made use of system components developed by members of the Free Software Foundation for the GNU project.

Linux is a remarkably complete operating system, including a graphical user interface, an X Window System, TCP/IP, the Emacs editor, and other components usually found in a comprehensive UNIX system. Although copyrights are held by various creators of Linux's components, Linux is distributed using the Free Software Foundation's copyleft stipulations that mean any modified version that is redistributed must in turn be freely available.

Unlike Windows and other proprietary systems, Linux is publicly open and extendible by contributors. Because it conforms to the Portable Operating System Interface standard user and programming interfaces, developers can write programs that can be ported to other operating systems. Linux comes in versions for all the major microprocessor platforms including the Intel, PowerPC, Sparc, and Alpha platforms. It's also available on IBM's S/390. Linux is distributed commercially by a number of companies. A magazine, Linux Journal, is published as well as a number of books and pocket references.

Linux is sometimes suggested as a possible publicly-developed alternative to the desktop predominance of Microsoft Windows. Although Linux is popular among users already familiar with UNIX, it remains far behind Windows in numbers of users.

Mac OS

Mac OS is the computer operating system for Apple Computer's Macintosh line of personal computers and workstations. A popular feature of its latest version, Mac OS X, is a desktop interface with some 3-D appearance characteristics. OS X has a modular design intended to make it easier to add new features to the operating system in the future. It runs UNIX applications as well as older Mac applications.

Release Dates for Recent Operating Systems

UNIX	1973
DOS 1.0	1981
MacOS	1984
MacOS, System 5	1986
OS/2 1.0	1987
Windows3.0	1990
Windows3.1	1991

Windows95	1995
WindowsNT	1993
WindowsNT v.4	1996
Windows98	1998
Windows 2000, Windows ME	2000
Windows XP	2003

THE FUTURE OF OPERATING SYSTEMS

One question concerning the future of operating systems revolves around the ability of a particular philosophy of software distribution to create an operating system useable by corporations and consumers together.

Linux, the operating system created and distributed according to the principles of open source, could have a significant impact on the operating system in general. Most operating systems, drivers and utility programs are written by commercial organizations that distribute executable versions of their software -versions that can't be studied or altered. Open source requires the distribution of original source materials that can be studied, altered and built upon, with the results once again freely distributed.

The continuing growth of the Internet and the proliferation of computers that aren't standard desktop or laptop machines mean that operating systems will change to keep pace, but the core management and interface functions will continue, even as they evolve.

The next-generation operating system starts with the user. It ignores the underlying hardware — and as a result, such systems are inherently less efficient than today's primitive, machine-centered ones. Instead, it reflects the shape of your life. Its role is to track your life event by event, moment by moment, and thought by thought.

The final words

The ideal OS is one that we never have to think about, an obedient servant, who knows our wishes better than we do, takes care of all the petty details, never demands anything of us, and recedes transparently into the background except when called upon. In recent years, we've made great progress toward that goal. Wizards, platform-independent file handling, network access, intelligent agents, and multimedia capabilities will bring the OS of the future closer to that ideal.

KEYWORDS

OPERATING SYSTEM	MULTIPROGRAMMING
USER'S VIEW	MULTITASKING
EXTENDED MACHINE	MULTI-USER
RESOURCE MANAGER	ONLINE PROCESSING
PROCESS MANAGEMENT	REAL TIME PROCESSING
MEMORY MANAGEMENT	MULTI PROCESSING
FILE MANAGEMENT	NETWORKING
STORAGE MANAGEMENT	DISTRIBUTED PROCESSING
DEVICE MANAGEMENT	CLIENT SERVER SYSTEM
BATCH PROCESSING	PC OPERATING SYSTEMS

SUMMARY

The operating system is an organized set of programs that controls and coordinates the use of the computer resources among the various users and tasks. It acts as an interface between the user and the hardware. The three views of the operating system are:

- User's view-The operating system provides an environment in which application programs can be run. It provides services to applications, like file management and I/O. The user views the OS+ hardware as a single unit, the "computer system".
- Programmers' view- "extended machine". An operating system implements a virtual machine which is easier to program than the raw machine
- Resources managers view: The overall system view: The problem is to match resources with users/applications. Resources (CPU time, memory, disk space, files, I/O devices, network bandwidth) are finite and must be shared among users. The OS is responsible for allocating these resources.

Major functions of operating systems:

- Process management is a set of functions supporting the definition of inter-related process steps and the management of their execution across a variety of hardware.

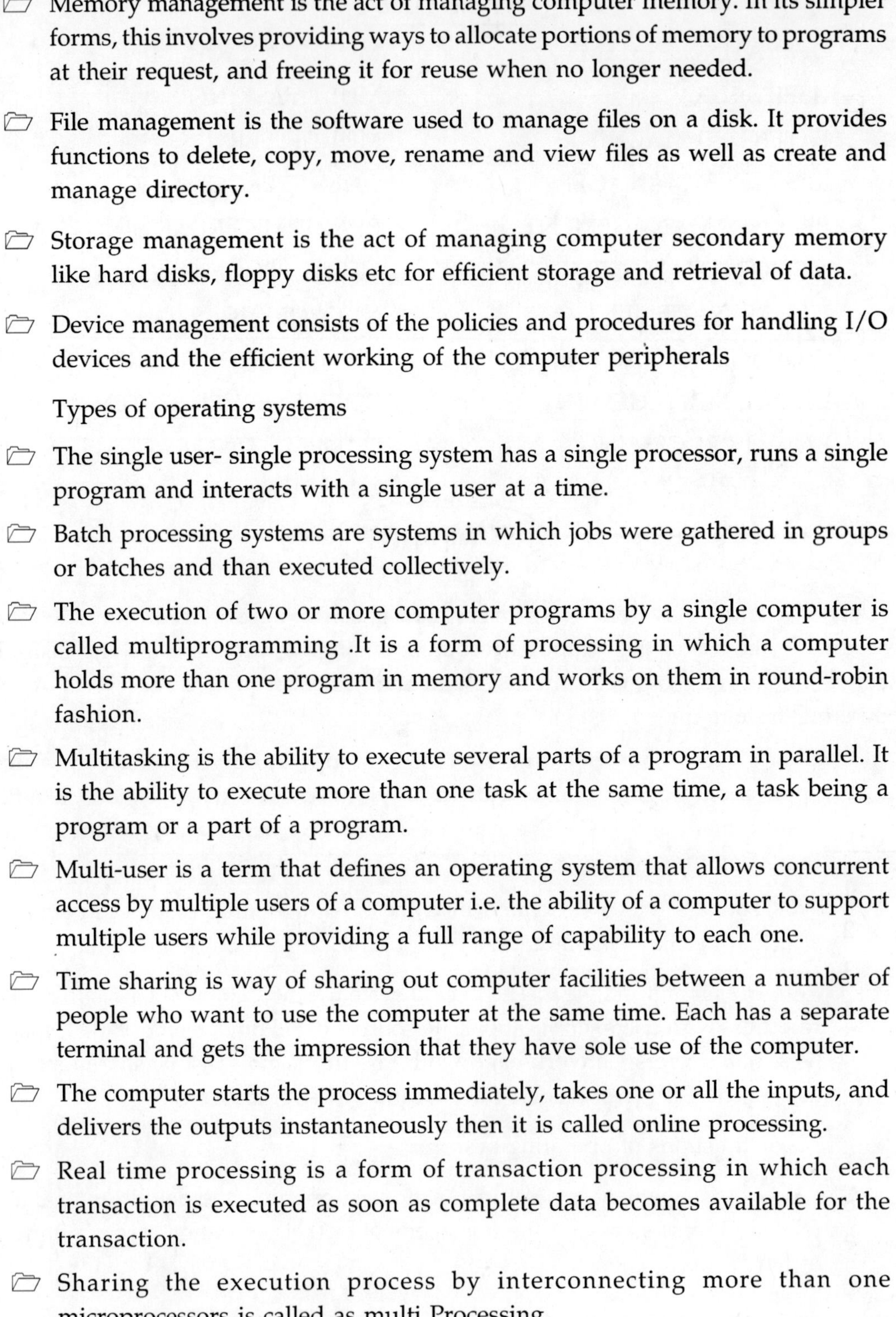

- Memory management is the act of managing computer memory. In its simpler forms, this involves providing ways to allocate portions of memory to programs at their request, and freeing it for reuse when no longer needed.
- File management is the software used to manage files on a disk. It provides functions to delete, copy, move, rename and view files as well as create and manage directory.
- Storage management is the act of managing computer secondary memory like hard disks, floppy disks etc for efficient storage and retrieval of data.
- Device management consists of the policies and procedures for handling I/O devices and the efficient working of the computer peripherals

Types of operating systems

- The single user- single processing system has a single processor, runs a single program and interacts with a single user at a time.
- Batch processing systems are systems in which jobs were gathered in groups or batches and than executed collectively.
- The execution of two or more computer programs by a single computer is called multiprogramming .It is a form of processing in which a computer holds more than one program in memory and works on them in round-robin fashion.
- Multitasking is the ability to execute several parts of a program in parallel. It is the ability to execute more than one task at the same time, a task being a program or a part of a program.
- Multi-user is a term that defines an operating system that allows concurrent access by multiple users of a computer i.e. the ability of a computer to support multiple users while providing a full range of capability to each one.
- Time sharing is way of sharing out computer facilities between a number of people who want to use the computer at the same time. Each has a separate terminal and gets the impression that they have sole use of the computer.
- The computer starts the process immediately, takes one or all the inputs, and delivers the outputs instantaneously then it is called online processing.
- Real time processing is a form of transaction processing in which each transaction is executed as soon as complete data becomes available for the transaction.
- Sharing the execution process by interconnecting more than one microprocessors is called as multi Processing.

- Parallel processing is the ability to process "chunks" or blocks of a program simultaneously. To do this, the computer has to have several CPU units and the software to coordinate them, or it must be able to simulate such a situation.
- Distributed processing and networking is the ability to have several computers working together in a network, where each processor runs different activities for a user, as required .A network is a collection of connected computers that can share data as well as resources.
- The client server system is a data processing interaction in which a program at one site (the client) sends a request to a program at another site (the server) for performing some task or operation.
- The PC-based operating systems, such as MS-DOS, windows 3.1, OS/2, Windows 95, Are used for personal computers
- Interactive Processing is a processing method in which each operator action causes a response from the program or system. In interactive processing computer, a person can communicate directly with the machine by means of a terminal. The user enters commands which are immediately executed by the computer which sends the results of the command back to the user's terminal.
- The next-generation operating system starts with the user. It reflects the shape of your life. Its role is to track your life event by event, moment by moment, and thought by thought. The ideal OS is one that we never have to think about, an obedient servant, who knows our wishes better than we do, takes care of all the petty details, never demands anything of us, and recedes transparently into the background except when called upon.

REVIEW QUESTIONS

1. What is operating system? What are the various views of operating systems?
2. What are the goals and principles of an Operating System?
3. Operating system acts as resource manager. What resources does it manage?
4. Discuss the inconveniences faced by a user interacting with a computer system without an operating system.
5. Explain in brief the Evolution of operating system?
6. Explain in brief the functions of operating system?
7. Explain the different services provided by operating system?
8. Explain the following major functions of operating system:

   (a) Process management (b) File management

   (c) Memory management (d) I/O management

9. What is buffering? What is spooling? Elaborate the differences between buffering and spooling.
10. Explain different layers of operating system?
11. Explain single process operating system?
12. Explain batch operating system?
13. Explain multiprogramming operating system?
14. Explain multitasking operating system? What is cooperative and preemptive multitasking?
15. Explain distributed operating system?
16. What are the characteristics of online and real time operating system?
17. Explain multiprocessor operating system? What is the difference between symmetric and asymmetric multiprocessing?
18. Explain time sharing operating system?
19. Explain in brief the system programs? Explain briefly about processor, assembler, compiler, loader, linker and the functions executed by them.
20. Write a note on the future of operating systems

FILL IN THE BLANKS

1. ________is software that controls the hardware.
2. ________deals with the ways to allocate portions of memory to programs at their request, and freeing it for reuse when no longer needed.
3. The execution of two or more computer programs by a single computer is called ________
4. ________is not a multiprogramming operating system.
5. Spool stands for________.
6. In ________________multitasking, the operating system prioritizes the processes to be performed and assigns a set amount of CPU time for the execution of each process.
7. In ________real time systems time delays are allowed
8. In ________multiprocessing, application processes are assigned to a specific CPU that has its own memory.
9. ________is based on the Microsoft Windows operating system designed for including or embedding in mobile and other space-constrained devices
10. A ________real time system guarantees that critical tasks complete on time.

TRUE OR FALSE

1. Memory management is the act of managing computer secondary memory like hard disks, floppy disks etc for efficient storage and retrieval of data.
2. The single user- single processing system has a single processor, runs a single program and interacts with a single user at a time.
3. A multiprogramming system necessarily has multiple processors.
4. Multitasking can be achieved only through time sharing.
5. Real-time systems are time critical systems.
6. Sharing the execution process by interconnecting more than one microprocessors is called as multi Processing.
7. Speed of computer operation does not depend on the operating system.
8. Device drives are extension to the operating system.
9. The client server system is a data processing interaction in which a program at one site (the server) sends a request to a program at another site (the client) for performing some task or operation.
10. In CLI, the user has to remember commands and their syntax to perform tasks such as creating, renaming, copying, or deleting a file or folder

ANSWERS

FILL IN THE BLANKS

1. operating system
2. Memory management
3. Multiprogramming
4. DOS
5. simultaneous peripheral operation on-line
6. preemptive
7. soft
8. symmetric
9. Windows CE
10. hard

TRUE OR FALSE

1. FALSE
2. TRUE
3. FALSE
4. FALSE
5. TRUE
6. TRUE
7. FALSE
8. TRUE
9. FALSE
10. TRUE

"The structure of a system reflects the structure of the organization that built it."

—R. Fairley

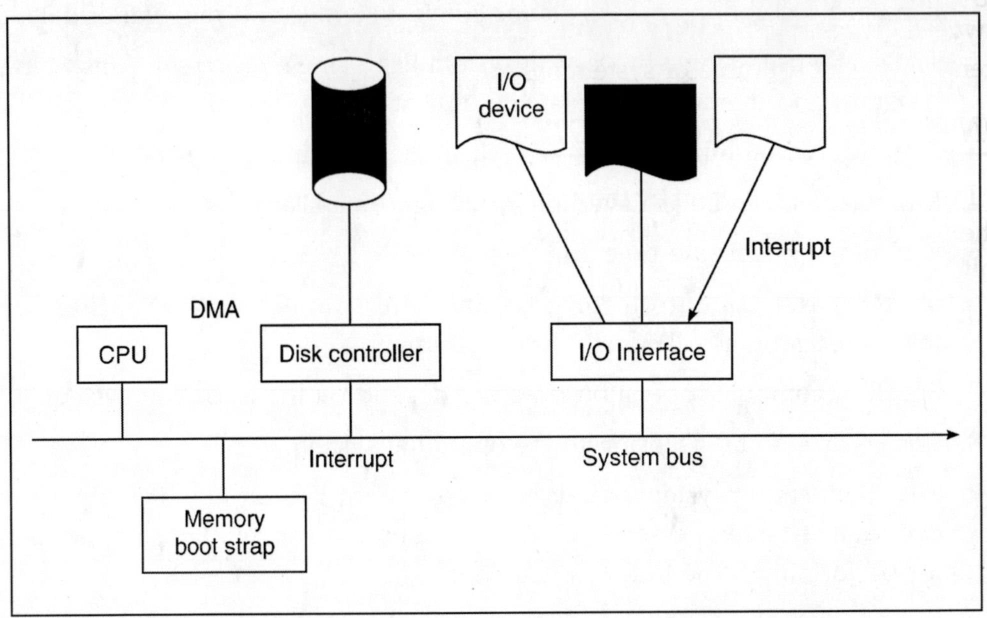

OPERATING SYSTEM ARCHITECTURE

INTRODUCTION

A computer system can be divided into two main parts: hardware and software. Hardware consists of physical components such as the keyboard, mouse, printer, monitor, modem and so on. It also includes all the advanced electronic circuitry found within the casing of your PC.

Software is the set of programs that coordinate the operation of the hardware. Without software, the hardware is as useful as a pile of metal junk. Programs take the form of a series of instructions (which may be very long and complicated) that instruct the hardware on the sequence of operations that it needs to undertake. The operating system (such as Windows 98, NT, etc) is a program.

Software can be divided into two main categories: application software and system software. Application software is designed to solve a specific problem – for example, Microsoft Word is used to process word documents and Internet Explorer is used for browsing the web. System software provides an environment in which programmers can create specific application software to meet their needs. Application software requires system software in order to be able to operate properly. The operating system (OS) is an example of system software.

VON NEUMANN ARCHITECTURE

In 1945, a mathematician by the name of Von Neumann came up with the concept of the 'stored program computer' which forms the conceptual basis for the hardware architecture of all computers up to the present day.

The von Neumann architecture is a computer design model that uses a single storage structure to hold both instructions and data.

In the Von Neumann architecture, a computer has the following components: - a central processing unit (CPU), memory and input/output (I/O) devices.

a) The CPU is essentially the 'brain' of the computer. All processing of data in the computer takes place here. It does this by undertaking the instructions in a program. This is called running or executing the program. The operating system is the first program to be executed when a PC is powered on. In a PC, the CPU takes the form of a microprocessor which contains is a very advanced form of an integrated circuit (IC). Pentium, Athlon and PowerPC are very well known processors found in a lot of modern PCs.

b) Memory (the word storage is sometimes used) is the means by which the computer stores data and programs. It can refer to the memory chips within the PC, or the hard disk, or floppy diskettes, or CD-ROMs.

c) I/O devices are hardware components which allow the computer to interact with its environment during the execution of a program. A computer that does not interact with its environment has extremely limited use. Examples of input devices include the keyboard, mouse and scanner while examples of output devices are the monitor and printer. A hard disk, which is a form of memory, can be considered as both an input and output device.

We shall illustrate this conceptual architecture with a simple example of how a program (say Internet Explorer) is used on a PC.

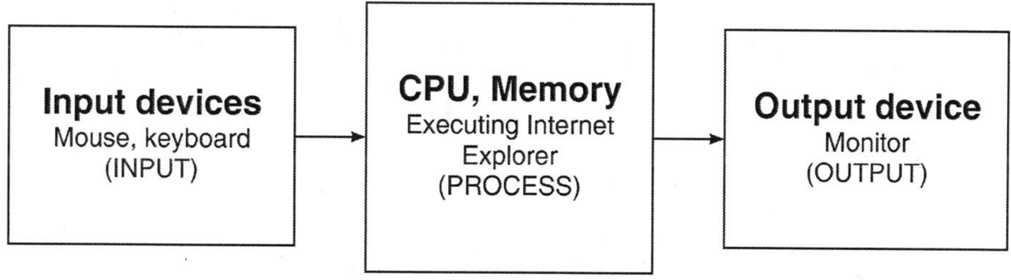

Here, the computer works in a typical Input-Process-Output (IPO) model. The program (Internet Explorer) is stored in the memory, and its instructions are executed by the CPU. This program requires input from the user (for example you need to type in the name of website or you may click on a link on a web page). This is provided via the input devices. The input is then processed by the CPU according to the instructions in the program. The results or information from this processing is directed to the monitor (output), where the user gets feedback on the results of his action.

CENTRAL PROCESSING UNIT (CPU)

This can be divided into two main parts which is the Arithmetic-Logic Unit (ALU) and the Control Unit (CU).

The ALU undertakes arithmetic operations (such as addition, division, multiplication) and logical operations (see later). The CU is the 'brain' of the CPU, is the part of the CPU that actually executes the instructions in a program and on the basis of these instructions, will control the operation of the ALU as well as the operations of all other electronic components in the computer (including the I/O devices).

When the CU executes instructions, it needs a place in the CPU to store these instructions as well as a place to store any results or data produced. There is a special type of memory within the CPU for this purpose called registers. There are many types of registers in the CPU which are used for various functions.

Memory

Memory is a very general term used to describe anything that can be used to store data or programs in a computer. In general, we can distinguish between primary memory (or main memory) and secondary memory (or backup/auxiliary memory).

Primary memory is used to store programs and data while the computer is running. It is sometimes known as volatile memory, because the data in it is lost the moment the power supply is turned off. The most common form of primary memory is Random Access Memory (RAM), which are normally found in the form of chips on the motherboard (the main circuit board holding the microprocessor inside a PC).

When data is stored in memory, we say a write (store) operation is performed; when data is retrieved from memory, we say a read (load) operation is performed. RAM allows both read and write operations.

Secondary memory, also known as non-volatile memory, retains the data stored in it when power supply is removed from the computer. Examples of this are the hard disk, floppy diskettes, CD-ROMs, etc. In addition to secondary and primary memory, we also have special types of memory such as registers and cache (which we talk about later). Why so many types of memory? This is because of what is termed the memory hierarchy.

Memory (regardless of type) is used to store and retrieve programs and data. Therefore the characteristics that we would like from memory are:

a) the ability to store and retrieve data quickly (speed)

b) the ability to store a large amount of data (capacity)

c) the ability to be manufactured cheaply (cost)

Unfortunately all criteria cannot be fulfilled simultaneously in the real world. To improve on one criterion will mean compromising on another one. Certain types of memory have high capacity and low cost, but are very slow. Other types are very fast, but have low capacity and are very expensive. We thus have the memory hierarchy as shown in the figure.

At the top of the hierarchy (registers), the speed is the fastest, but the capacity is low and the cost is high. At the opposite end (magnetic tape), the speed is the slowest, but the capacity is high and the cost is low. Each type of memory is suited for its particular use.

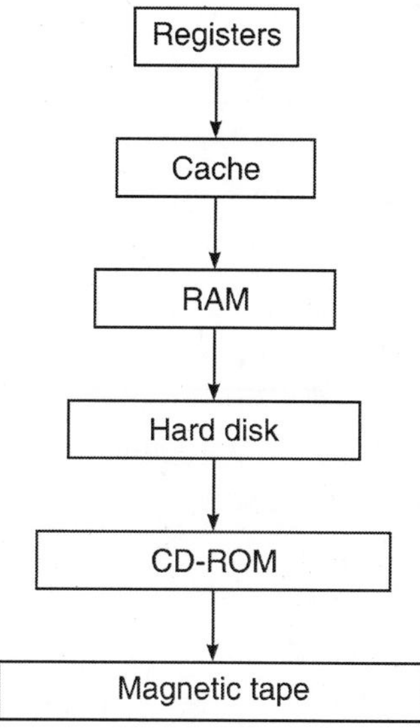

Registers are very fast because they are used by the CPU, which is the fastest electronic component in the computer. If they were slow, they would bog down the overall computer speed. On the other hand, magnetic tape is mainly used to back up data, and is rarely used except to restore lost data. Therefore the most important requirement would be to have large storage capacity, rather than speed.

As specified earlier, many modern computer architectures are based on the "von Neumann model". A central plank in this model is that a both the data to be processed and the coded instructions that define the processing algorithm (or program), are placed within the same memory unit. There is no marker to distinguish a data code from an instruction code so the two groups of codes are kept in separate regions of the memory which are distinguishable by their addresses. The CPU is equipped with a special register that holds the memory address of the next byte of the program code that needs to be fetched. In many machines this CPU register is called the program counter (PC). In CPU designs produced by the Intel Corporation it is known as the instruction pointer, a name which more accurately reflects its role.

The wires that convey the binary instruction and data codes between the memory and the CPU are known as a bus. Sometimes the term data bus is used even though of the majority of the codes being carried by this bus will be instruction codes rather than data codes. Never the less, this name distinguishes this bus from another group of wires known as the address bus. This bus is used by the CPU to signal the memory unit precisely which memory location it wishes to access. A third group of wires, known as the control bus, carries various signals to control different parts of the computer. Included here is a signal to inform the memory unit whether the addressed location is being read from or written to.

A CPU "runs" a program by repeatedly cycling through a process known as the "fetch-decode-execute" cycle. In the fetch phase, the CPU uses the value in its program counter to address a new instruction in memory and then perform a memory read. The program counter value is then incremented. The fetched information is placed in the CPU's instruction register (IR). Some CPUs will fetch the entire instruction while others may only fetch the first part of it.

The decode phase uses digital logic circuits to analyse the bit pattern in the instruction register into different fields. Typically the bit pattern in one field might identify the operation to be performed while the bit patterns of the remaining fields will identify how the CPU is to obtain the values to be operated on. These values are called operands. An operand might be held within the instruction itself, or held in a specified register, or held in a specified memory location, or its value may be inherently known for that operation type.

The execution phase is responsible for collecting the operands and delivering them to the ALU so the coded operation may occur. This phase may involve addressing memory to locate an operand. Where this occurs, the CPU may either use an address included in the later part of the instruction, or it may compute the address using a hardware algorithm identified by some bits in the instruction. The result of the operation may be returned to a specified register, or be written to a location in main memory, or perhaps an output device.

At the end of the execution phase the program counter will normally be holding the address of the next instruction in the program. An exception to this is if the instruction itself has modified the value in the program counter. Instructions that either modify the program counter's value, or install a completely new value, are called branches and jumps. They are used for program flow control.

One unfortunate consequence of the von Neumann architecture is that a serious bottleneck is created at the data bus because all the instructions and data must flow through that "pipe". Although bus speeds have increased significantly over the years, so have CPU and memory speeds so the "von Neumann bottleneck" problem remains an issue. The use of wide data buses and small but high speed cache memories is a common approach to alleviating this problem.

An alternate architecture known as the Harvard architecture is used in some systems. It keeps the instructions and data in totally separate memories and allows simultaneous access to instructions and data through separate buses. While this arrangement does allow some performance gains, the convenience of a single mechanism for loading programs and data from secondary storage has kept the von Neumann approach popular.

Basic Elements of a Computer

Processor: This is the heart of the computer, consisting of an arithmetic and logic unit (ALU), registers, and various other hardware elements.

Main Memory: This is where the running programs and their data reside. The processor directly interacts with the main memory by reading from and writing on it.

System Bus: This is the interface that connects the various elements of a computer together.

Processor Registers

➢ **User-visible registers:**

Registers that are accessible by users generally contain data, addresses, pointers to memory locations, etc. Data registers are referred to as accumulators while those that contain addresses are the stack pointers, memory segment base pointer, and the like.

➢ **Control and Status registers:**

These registers are not visible by users. Only the operating system can gain access to them. They are made up of a program counter (PC), instruction register (IR), program status word (PSW) and many others.

Instruction Execution

The execution of program instructions by the processor follows a cycle. The most basic cycle is the following:

- Fetch next instruction from main memory using the Program Counter register (PC) and place it in the Instruction Register (IR)
  - Increment the PC register
  - Execute instruction in IR
  - Verify interrupt lines
  - go to beginning

There are four different types of instructions:

- **Processor-memory:** These instructions perform the data transfers from the memory towards the CPU registers and back. They read like LOAD A6, WRITE 0x56de2, etc.
- **Processor-I/O:** These instructions perform the transfers from the CPU towards I/O controllers and back.
- **Data processing:** These instructions perform arithmetic and logic operations on the contents of registers.
- **Control:** These instructions control the flow of execution of a program. They may specify to what address the PC must jump, and they are used in the implementation of loop and conditional statement structures.

INTERRUPTS

The purpose of having interrupts is to stop the CPU's current executing of a task (process) to attend a more pressing event right away. In modern computers, interrupts are essential. Without them, there is a number of Operating System Concepts we would not be able to implement.

Interrupt is a signal from a device to a computer's processor requesting the processor's attention. Interrupts are generated for many reasons, including software errors and the signalling of the presence of data to be processed.

There are different events in a computer that will trigger an interruption and that is why we may speak of classes of interrupts and types of interrupts. Here is a short and incomplete list of events giving rise to interruptions of the CPU:

- Program: Generated by an instruction that cannot be completed
- Timer: Scheduled interrupts, required for process management
- I/O: I/O controller to signal completion of a data transfer
- Hardware failure: Component unable to satisfy requests

The internals of the interrupts mechanism can be a little tricky. Here's a simplified example of how an interrupt may be generated and then serviced:

- A device raises the processor interrupt line, and dumps the memory address of the interrupt handling code on the address bus for the processor
- The processor saves all its register values on the current stack (a special purpose location in memory)
- The processor attends to the interruption by executing code that is located at the address provided by the device (on the address bus)
- When the interrupt handling code returns, it does it in the scheduler, which resets the CPU registers to the values they contained just before the interruption, including the PC, therefore resuming the execution of the process that was interrupted.

Now, an interesting question is: *Since interrupts can happen at any time, how do we deal with interruptions that occur when the processor is already servicing a first interruption?* There are two ways of answering this question:

- We may, when servicing an interrupt, disable the processor's capability for being interrupted until it completes the first interruption. Any device that would raise the INT line would then have to wait for the CPU to be coming back from being interrupted for this new interruption to get serviced.
- Another way of dealing with the problem is to prioritize interruptions. This allows a CPU servicing an interruption to be interrupted if the new interruption has a higher priority than the one currently serviced.

The second method is better for systems in which interruptions must be serviced *right away*. If that is not the case, then the first solution is simpler to implement in hardware and in software.

SYSTEM PROGRAMS

Another aspect of a modern system is its collection of systems programs. While we could write a program to copy one file to another, as shown above, it is unlikely that we would want to.

System programs are the programs that control the working of the computer system.

In addition to the actual operating system monitor code, most system supplies a large collection of systems programs to solve common problems and provide a more convenient environment for program development and execution.

Systems programs can be divided into several categories.

- File Manipulation. These program create, delete, copy, rename, print, dump, list, and generally manipulate files and directories.
- Status Information. Some program simply ask the system for the date, time, amount of available memory or disk space, number of users, or similar status information. That information is then formatted and printed to the terminal or other output device or file.
- File Modification. Several text editors may be available to create and modify the content of files stored on disk.
- Programming Language Support. Compilers, assemblers, and interpreters for common programming language (such as for Pascal, Basic and so on) are often provided with the operating system. Recently many of these programs are being priced and provided separately.
- Program Loading and Execution. Once a program is assembled or compiled, it must be loaded into memory to be executed. The system may provide absolute loaders, relocatable loaders, linkage editors, and overlay loaders. Debugging systems for either higher level language or machine language are also needed.

BOOTSTRAP LOADER

For a computer to start running - for instance, when it is powered up or rebooted - it needs to have an initial program to run. This initial program, or *bootstrap loader*, tends to be simple (In MS-DOS, the *bootstrap loader* is placed at the ROM-BIOS). It initializes all aspects of the system, from *CPU registers* to *device controllers* to *memory contents*.

In computing, booting (booting up) is a bootstrapping process that starts operating systems when the user turns on a computer system.

The *bootstrap loader* must know how to load the operating system and to start it executing. To accomplish this goal, the *bootstrap loader* program must locate the operating system's main part called kernel (*The essential part or kernel of the operating system is composed of code and data that is shared between all processes and devices connected to the computer.)* and load it into memory. The operating system then starts executing the first process, such as 'init', and waits for some event to occur.

How does an Operating System load itself?

The operating system may be loaded into the computers memory in two ways.

- it is already present in ROM (so is permanent, immediately accessible and difficult to update)
- it is loaded from disk when the computer is turned on.

If the operating system is already present in ROM (for systems like industrial controllers, petrol pumps etc), it will gain control immediately the processor is powered on. This method is best suited for small appliances and hand held devices where the operating system is relatively simple and small.

For more complex systems, the operating system is usually stored on secondary media (such as disk), and is loaded into the computer memory (RAM) when the computer is powered on. Advantages of this type of system are that changes to the operating system are easier to make and implement.

What is the BOOTSTRAP PROCESS?

The bootstrap process describes the task of initially loading the operating system from disk into RAM. A small routine stored in ROM, called the BOOTSTRAP LOADER or IPL (Initial Program Loader), reads a special load routine from the diskette.

1. In floppy based system, this routine is normally located on Track 00, sector 00 (or 01), and is called the **boot sector**.
2. The code contained in the sector is transferred into RAM and then executed.
3. It has the sole responsibility for loading the rest of the operating system into memory.

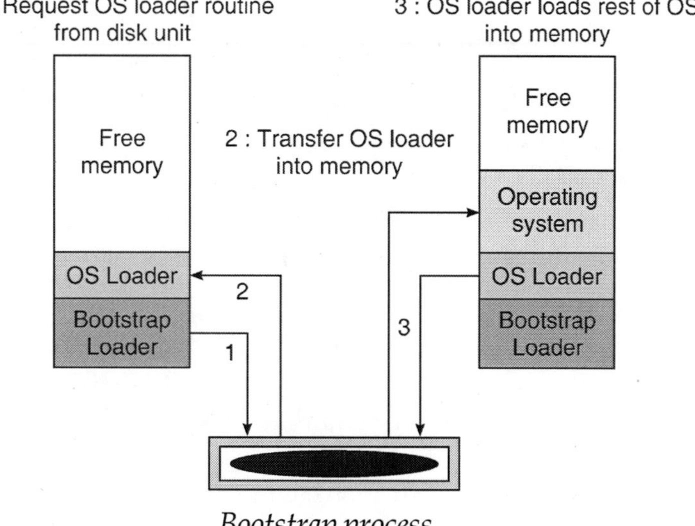

Bootstrap process

INTRODUCTION TO INPUT/OUTPUT

One of the main functions of operating systems is to control all the computer's input/output (I/O) devices. It must issue commands to the devices, catch interrupts

(I/O), and handle errors. It should also provide an interface between the devices and the rest of the system that is simple and easy to use. In this section we will look briefly at some of the principles of I/O hardware, and then we will look at I/O software in general.

Traditionally, I/O controllers would exchange data directly with the CPU. This, however, is a bit inefficient and other techniques have been developed. For instance, modern I/O controllers now perform data exchanges directly to and from memory, preventing the CPU to be in an active waiting loop. This technique is called DMA (Direct Memory Access) and is implemented with a dedicated processor for this type of data transport.

PRINCIPLES OF I/O HARDWARE

Different people look at I/O hardware in different ways. Electrical engineers look at it in term of chips, wires, power supplies, motors and all the other physical components that make up the hardware. Programmers look at the interface presented to the software the commands the hardware accepts, the functions it carries out, and the errors that can be reported back. In the next two parts we will provide a little general background on I/O hardware as it relates to programming.

I/O Devices

I/O devices can be roughly divided into two categories: Block devices and character devices. A block device is one that stores information in fixes-size blocks, each one with its own address. Common block sizes range from 128 bytes to 1024 bytes. The essential property of a block device is that it is possible to read or write each block independently of all the other ones. In other words, at any instant, the program can read or write any of the blocks. Disks are block devices.

If you look closely, the boundary between device that are block addressable and those that are not is not well defined. Everyone agrees that a disk is a block addressable device because no matter where the arm currently is, it is always possible to seek t another cylinder and then wait for the required block to rotate under the head. Now consider a magnetic tape containing blocks of 1K bytes. If the tape drive is given a command to read block N, it can always rewind the tape and go forward until it comes to block N. This operation is analogous to a disk doing a seek, except that it take much longer.

Also, it may or may not be possible to rewrite one block in the middle of a tape. Even if in were possible to use magnetic tapes as block devices, that is stretching the point somewhat: they are normally not used that way.

The other type of I/O device is the character device. A character device delivers or accepts a stream of character, without regard to any block structure. It is not addressable and does not have any seek operation. Terminals, line printers, paper tapes, punched cards, network interface, mice (for pointing), and most other devices that are not disk like can be seen as character devices.

This classification scheme is not perfect. Some devices just do not fit in. However, the model of block and character devices is general enough that it can be used as a basis for making the I/O system device independent.

Device Controllers

I/O units typically consist of a mechanical component and an electronic component. It is often possible to separate the two portions to provide a more modular and general design. The electronic component is called the device controller or adapter. On mini and microcomputer, it often takes the form of a printed circuit card that can be inserted into the parent card. The mechanical component is the device itself.

The device controller is the hardware that controls the communication between the system and the peripheral drive unit. It takes care of low level operations such as error checking, moving disk heads, data transfer, and location of data on the device.

The controller card usually has a connector on it, into which a cable leading to the device itself can be plugged. Many controllers can handle two, four, or even eight identical device. If the interface between the controller and device is a standard interface, either an official standard such as ANSI, IEEE or ISO, or de facto one, then companies can make controllers or devices that fit that interface. Many companies, for example, make disk drives that match the IBM disk controls interface.

We mention this distinction between controller and device because the operating systems nearly always deal with the controller, not the device. Nearly all microcomputer and minicomputers use the single bus model of Figure for communication between the CPU and the controllers. Large mainframes often use a different model, with multiple buses and specialized I/O computers called I/O channels taking some of the load off the main CPU.

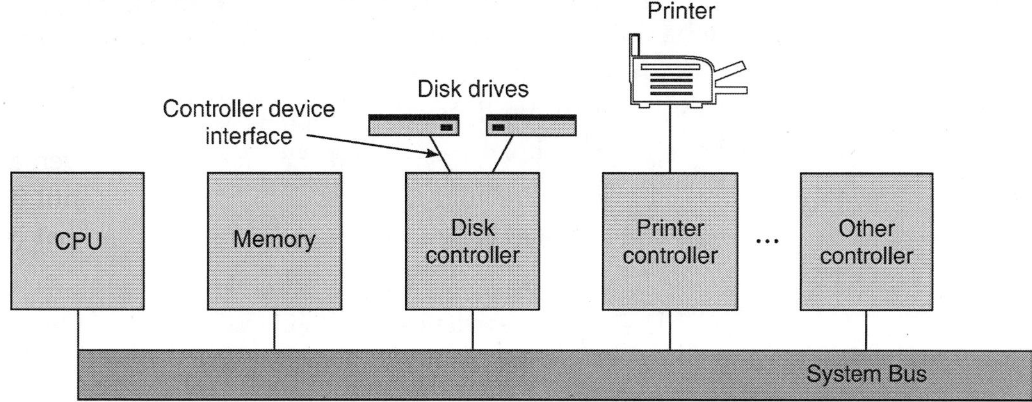

Bus Model for CPU, memory, controller, and I/O device

The operating system performs I/O by writing commands into the controllers' registers. The IBM PC floppy disk controller, for example, accepts 15 different commands, such as READ, WRITE, SEEK, FORMAT, and RECALIBRATE. many of the commands have parameters, which are also loaded into the controller's registers. When a command has been accepted, the CPU can leave the control alone, and go off to do other work. When the command has been completed, the controller causes an interrupt in order to allow the operating system to again control of the CPU, and test the results of the operation. The CPU gets the results and the device status by reading one or more bytes of information form the controller's registers.

Direct Memory Access (DMA)

A high speed device, such as tape, fixed disk, or communication network, may be able to transmit information at close to memory speeds; this would not leave much time for CPU computation and servicing of other interrupts. To solve this problem, DMA is used for *high-speed I/O devices.* After setting up buffers, pointers, and counters for the I/O device, the device controller transfers an entire block of data to or from its own buffer storage to memory directly, with no intervention by the CPU. Only one interrupt is generated per block, rather than the one interrupt per byte/word generated for *low-speed I/O devices.*

DMA is the capability provided by some computer bus architectures that allows data to be sent directly from an attached device (such as a disk drive) to the memory on the computer's motherboard. The microprocessor is freed from involvement with the data transfer, thus speeding up overall computer operation.

Many controllers, especially those for block devices, support direct memory access (DMA). To explain how DMA works, let us first look at how disk reads occur when DMA is not used. First the controller reads the block (one or more sectors) form the drive serially, bit by bit, until the entire block is in the controller's internal buffer. Next, it performs the checksum computation to verify that no read errors have occurred. (The checksum can be computed only after the entire block has been read). Then the control causes an interrupt. When the operating system starts processing the interrupt, it can read the disk block from the controller's buffer a byte or a word at a time by executing a loop, with each iteration, reading one byte or word from a controller device register and storing it in memory.

Naturally, a programmed CPU loop to read the bytes one at a time form the controller wastes CPU time. DMA was invented to free the CPU from this low-level work. When it is used, the CPU gives the controller two items of information, in addition to the disk address of the block: the memory address where the block is to go, and the number of bytes to transfer, as shown in Fig.

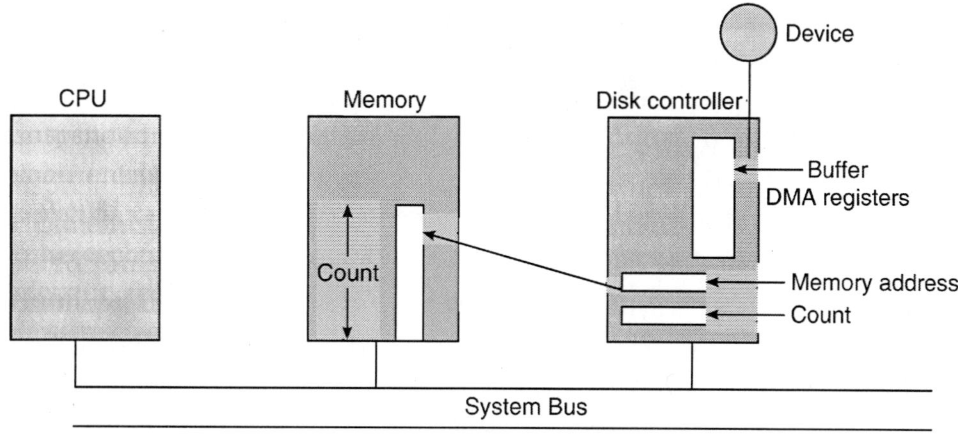

DMA transfer by the controller

After the controller has read the entire block from the device into its buffer and verified the checksum, it copies the first byte or word into the main memory at the address specified by the DMA memory address. Then it increment the DMA address and decrement the DMA count by the number of bytes just transferred. This process is repeated until the DMA count becomes zero, at which time the controller causes an interrupt. When the operating system starts up, it does not have to copy the block to memory: it is already there.

PRINCIPLES OF I/O SOFTWARE

Let's turn away from the hardware and now look at how the I/O software is structured. The general goals of the I/O software are easy to state. the basic idea is to organize the software as a series of layers, with the lower ones concerned with hiding the peculiarities of the hardware from the upper ones, and the upper ones concerned with presenting a nice, clean, regulate interface to the users. In the following we will look at these goals.

A key concept in the design of I/O software is device independence. It should be possible to write programs that can be used with files on a floppy disk or a hard disk, without having to modify the programs for each device type. In fact, it should be possible to move the program without recompiling it.

Closely related to device independence is the goal of uniform naming. The name of a file or a device should simply be a string or a integer and not depend on the device in any way. In some operating systems, floppy disks, hard disks and all other block devices can be mounted in the file system hierarchy in arbitrary places, so the user need not be aware of which name corresponds to which device. All files and devices are addressed the same way: by a path name.

Another important issue for I/O software is error handling. In general, errors should be handled as close to the hardware as possible. If the controller discovers a read error, it should try to correct the error itself if it can. If it can not, then the device driver should handle it, perhaps by just trying to read the block again. Many errors are transient, such as read errors caused by specks of dust on the read head, and will go away if the operation is repeated. Only if the lower layers are not able to deal with the problem should the upper layers be told about it.

Still another key issue is synchronous (blocking) versus asynchronous (interrupt-driven) transfers. Most physical I/O is asynchronous the CPU starts the transfer and goes off to do something else until the interrupt arrives. User programs are much easier to write if the I/O operations are blocking after a READ command the program is automatically suspended until the data are avail-able in the buffer. It is up to the operating system to make operations that are actually interrupt-driven look blocking to the user programs.

The final concept that we will deal with here is sharable versus dedicated devices. Some I/O devices, such as disks, can be used by many users at the same time. No problems are caused by multiple users having open files on the same disk at the same time. other devices, such as printers, have to be dedicated to a single user until that user is finished. Having five users printing lines intermixed at random on the printer just would not work. Introducing dedicated devices also introduces a variety of problems, including deadlock. Again, the operating system must handle both shared and dedicated devices in a way that avoids problems.

OPERATING SYSTEM CONCEPTS

The interface between the operating system and user programs is defined by the set of "extended instructions" or system calls that are provided by the operating system. System calls can create, delete and use various software objects managed by the operating system. The most important software objects are processes and files.

Processes

A process consists of the executable program, the program's data and its stack, its PC, registers including status registers and all other information that is required to run the program.

A program under execution is called a process.

The operating system has to periodically stop running one process and run another instead, perhaps at the end of a time slice or because of an intervention of an interrupt. When a process is temporarily stopped, it must be restarted in exactly the same state when it was suspended. All information about the process must therefore be explicitly saved somewhere during this suspension period. In many operating systems such information is stored in a process table, which is either an array or a link list of structures, one for each process. Each process table entry holds the process registers, PC, status bits and so on. A suspended process consists of its address space called the core image, and its process table entry.

The major process management system calls are those that handle the creation and deletion of processes. For example, the command interpreter or shell reads commands from a terminal. Perhaps, the user has typed a command that a program is to be compiled, in emacs this is Esc X compile, or the make command under the Unix/Linux operating systems. Under MS Windows systems 'the lightning strike icon' tends to be popular. Once the command has been invoked, the shell creates a new process that will run the compiler. When the process of compilation is completed, it executes a system call to terminate itself.

If a process can create one or more other processes, known as child processes, and these processes in turn create further child processes, and a tree structure develops, see Figure. Other process system calls are available to request more, or release memory and overlay its program with a different program. Process hierarchies are therefore organized as tree structures, but usually they are not very deep – usually less than or equal to 3 at most. Process hierarchies tend to be short-lived, usually no more than a few minutes. You might like to refresh yourself with the computation unit on Dynamic Data Structures.

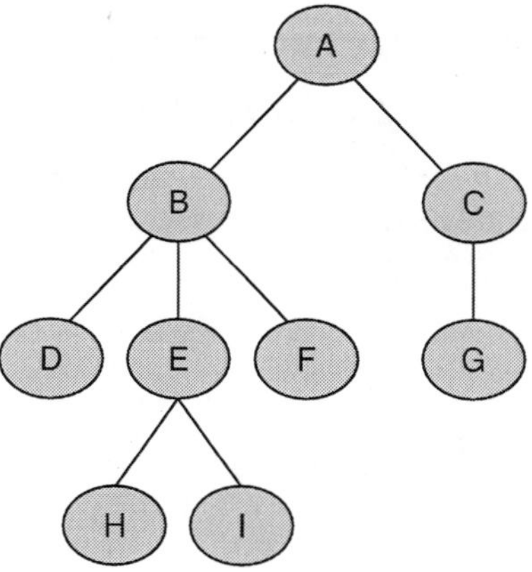

A process tree

A process that is communicating with another process on a different computer does so by sending messages over a network. To guard against the possibility that a message or its reply is lost, the sender may request that its own operating system notify it after a specified time interval, so that the message can be retransmitted if no acknowledgement is received. Consequently, once the specified time interval is reached the operating system signals the process so that the process is temporarily suspended.

When the signal handler is completed, the running process is restarted from the point that it was suspended. Signals are therefore the software equivalents to interrupts. Signals can also be used for intercommunication between processes.

In multi-user systems, it is important to manage which user owns which process. In such systems, each authorized user is assigned a **uid**, user identification, which is typically a 16-bit or 32-bit integer. When a process on a multiuser system sends a signal to another process, a check can be made to confirm that the user and receiver have a common uid. Similarly, people can be divided into groups, where each group is provided with its own **gid**, group identification. Uids and gids play an important role in protecting information in a computer system.

Files

A major function of an operating system is to hide the complexities of I/O hardware devices, and present a user with a clean independent abstract model of device-independent files. System calls are required to create, remove, read and write files in order that a file can be opened, read, written to or from and closed. To provide a place to keep these files, operating systems provide a directory structure, in the Windows operating system these are known as folders, as a way of grouping files together. As with processes, files have a tree structure hierarchy. In contrast to processes the depth of the structure can be complex and the life of the structure can be long, and is determined by the user.

Every file in a hierarchy can be specified by providing its path name from the top of the hierarchy, the root directory. Such absolute path names must be traversed through a list of directories from the root directory to get to the file, with slashes separating the components. In the UNIX operating system a / separates the component directories, whereas under the DOS and MS Windows operating systems a \ separates the component directories.

If more than one person has access to a computer, then it is important to protect the privacy of each user's files. Different systems have different approaches, in a Unix environment files and directories are protected by assigning each one with a 9-bit binary protection code.

Before a file is opened for reading or writing the permissions are checked. If the permissions are accepted a small integer the file descriptor or handle is returned, which is then used in subsequent operations. If access is prohibited, an error code is returned.

Many operating systems, including UNIX, DOS and Windows, provide an abstraction to permit users to perform I/O without having to know the detailed complexities of hardware. This abstraction represents each I/O device as a special file, which make I/O devices look like files. Using such an abstraction permits the same system calls to be used for I/O devices as well as files.

There are two types of files that exist: block special files and character special files. Block special files are used to model devices that consist of a collection of randomly addressable blocks, such as hard disks. Character special files are used to model devices that consist of character streams, such as line printers, terminals and network interfaces. In Unix and DOS, when a process is started file descriptor 0 known as standard input is usually arranged to refer to the terminal for the purpose of reading. In contrast, file descriptor 1, known as standard output refers to the terminal for writing. File descriptor 2, known as standard error, also refers to the terminal for output but is used for writing errors.

A pipe is a 'pseudo-file' that is used to connect two processes together, see Figure. When process A sends data to process B, it writes on the pipe as though it is an output file. Process B reads the data as though it is an input file. Communication between the two processes therefore appears to be the same as ordinary file reads and writes. The only way a process can determine that the output file is not really a file is by use of a system call. Pipes are supported by both UNIX and DOS.

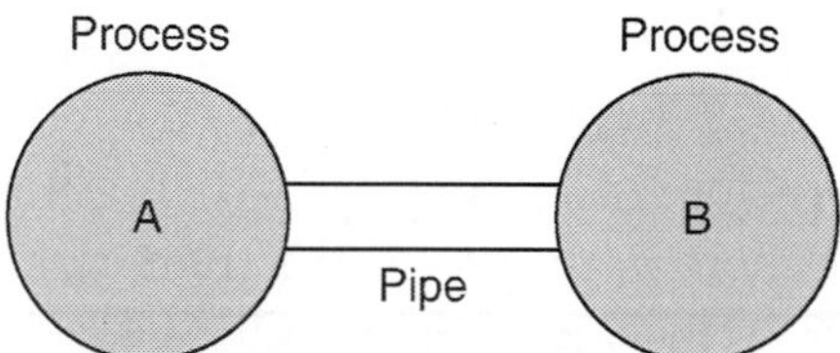

Processes connected by a pipe

System calls

User programs communicate with an operating system and request services from it by making system calls. Each system call has a library procedure that the user program calls. This procedure puts the parameters of the system call in a special place, such as a register, and then issues a TRAP instruction, a protected procedure call, to start the operating system. The library procedure hides the details of the TRAP instructions, and makes system calls appear as ordinary procedure calls.

A system call is a routine that accomplishes a system-level function on behalf of a process. It is a feature built into an application program that request service from operating systems, as when a word processing program requests the use of the printer to print a document.

Since the actual mechanics of issuing a system call are highly machine-dependent, and often must be expressed in assembly code, a procedure library is provided to make it possible to make system calls from high level language program. System calls provide the interface between a running program and the operating system.

Several languages, as C, PL/360, have been defined to replace assembly language for systems programming. These languages allow system calls to be made directly. Some Pascal systems also provide an ability to make system calls directly from Pascal program to the operating system. Most FORTRAN system provide similar capabilities, often by a set of library routines.

As an example of how system calls are used, consider writing a simple program to read data from one file and copy it to another file. The fist thing the program will need is the name of the two files: the input file and output file. These can be specified in two ways. One approach is for the program to ask the user for the names of the two files. In an interactive system, this will requite a sequence of system calls to fist write a prompting message on the terminal, and then read from the terminal the characters which define the two files. Another approach, particularly used to batch system, is to specify the names of the files with control card. In this case, there must be a mechanism for passing these parameters from the control cards to the executing program.

Once the two file names are obtained, the program must open the input file and create the output file. Each of the operations requires another system call. There are also possible error conditions for each operation. When the program tries to open the input file, it may find that there is no file of that name or that the file is protected against access. In these cases, the program should print a message on the console (another system call). If the input file exists, then we must create a new out file. We may find that there is already an output file with the same name. This situation may cause the program to abort (a system call), or we may delete the existing file (another system call) and create a new one (another system call). Another option, in an interactive system, is to ask the user (a sequence of system calls to output the prompting message and read the response from the terminal) whether to replace the existing file or abort.

Now that both files are set up, we enter a loop that reads from the input files (s system call) and writes to the output file (another system call). Each read and write must return status information regarding various possible error conditions. On input, the program may find that the end of the file has been reached, or that there was a hardware failure in the read (such as a parity error). The write operation may encounter various errors, depending upon the output device (no more disk space, physical end of tape, printer out of paper, and so on).

Finally, after the entire file is copied, the program may close both files (another system call), write a message to the console (more system calls) and finally terminate normally (the last system call). As we can see, programs may make heavy use of the operating system. All interactions between the program and its environment must occur as the result of requests from the program to the operating system.

Most users never see this level of detail, however. The run-time support system for most programming language provides a much simpler interface. For example, a write statement in Pascal or FORTRAN most likely is compiled into a call to a run-time support routine that issues the necessary system calls, check for errors, and finally returns to the user program. Thus most of the details of the operating system interface are hidden from the user programmer by the compiler and its run-time support package.

System calls occur in different ways, depending upon the computer in use. Often more information is required than simply the identity of the desired system call. The exact type and amount of information varies according to the particular operating system and call. For example, to read a card image, we may need to specify the file or device to use, and the address and length of the memory buffer into which it should be read. Of course, the device or file may be implicit in the call and, if the card images are always 80 characters, we may not need to specify the length.

Two general methods are used to pass parameters to the operating system. The simplest approach is to pass the parameters in register. However, in some cases there may be more parameters than registers. In these cases the parameters stored in a block or t able in memory and the address of the block is passed as a parameter in a register as shown in the figure below. Some operating system prefers this uniform interface, even when there are enough registers for all of the parameter for most cases.

System calls can be roughly grouped into three major categories, such as process of job control, device and the file manipulation, and information maintenance. In the following, we summarize the types of system calls that may be provided by an operating system.

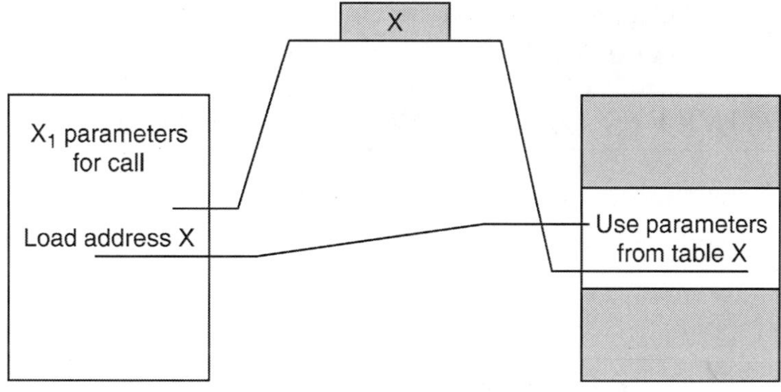

Passing parameter as a table

The figure summarizes

1. Process Control
   - End, Abort
   - Load, Execute
   - Create Process, Terminate Process
   - Get Process Attributes, Set Process Attribute
   - Wait for Time
   - Wait Event, Signal Event
2. File Manipulation
   - Create File, Delete File
   - Open/Close
   - Read, Write, Reposition
   - Get File Attributes, Set File Attribute
3. Device Manipulation
   - Request Device, Release Device
   - Read, Write, Reposition
   - Get Device Attributes, Set Device Attribute
4. Information Maintenance
   - Get Time or Date, Set Time or Date
   - Get System Data, Set System Data
   - Get Process, File, or Device Attributes, Set Process, File, or Device Attributes.

BASIC COMPONENTS OF AN OPERATING SYSTEM

The internal structure of the operating system can be best described with the help of one of its main components called kernel.

Kernel

The kernel provides the most basic interface between the machine itself and the rest of the operating system. The kernel is responsible for the management of the central processor. The kernel includes the dispatcher to allocate the central processor, to determine the cause of an interrupt and initiate its processing, and some provision for communication among the various system and user tasks currently active in the system.

The kernel is the central component of most computer operating systems. Its responsibilities include managing the system's resources and the communication between hardware and software components.

The kernel is a program that runs as the heart of an operating system. It takes control early in the boot process and manages disks, networks, and processes. It typically runs with the highest machine privileges, and is responsible for starting processes and regulating the authority of the processes that run on the system.

The operating system kernel is loaded into memory when the machine is started up, and stays there until the machine is turned off. The kernel is accessible by, and a part of, every process being executed on the machine. For example, the operating system may be permanently loaded in one area of memory, while the user part of a process may be loaded in another portion of memory, whenever that particular process is executing.

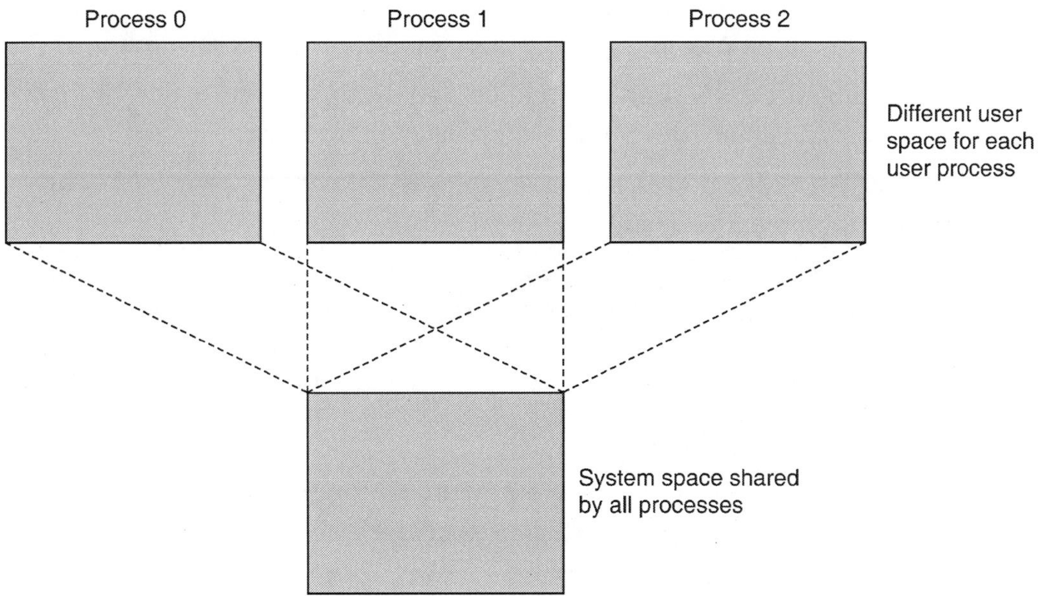

Once set up, the operating system kernel performs a completely passive role - servicing requests from threads executing user programs, and devices. If a thread executing a user program or a device requires action by the operating system, the processor stops executing the user program, and executes operating system code to handle the request that has occurred. The operating system kernel can be seen as the interface and arbiter between devices and processes.

The operating system kernel provides services such as:

1. Creation and management of processes, threads, files, etc. For example:
   - Requests can be made to the operating system kernel to create and destroy processes and threads, create, open and close files, etc.
   - Access of threads to shared data structures can be controlled by the operating system kernel. For example, a thread wanting to execute a synchronised method has to make a request to the operating system kernel, and the thread is made to block if another thread is already accessing the object. The thread is permitted to resume execution when the other thread completes its access.
2. Communication between processes and devices. For example:
   - A process can send a message to another process.
   - A disk drive can tell the operating system kernel it is ready to process another request.
   - The clock can tell the operating system kernel that it is time to schedule another thread for execution.
3. Information about objects such as processes, files, etc. For example:
   - A thread can request information about other processes and threads, the availability of resources such as disk space, etc.
4. Fair utilisation of resources, such as the processor, memory, printer, disk drive, etc. For example, the operating system:
   - Causes the processor to periodically switch from executing one thread to executing another, so that all threads get their fair share of the processor.
   - Terminates a thread or process if it has used up its total time allocation or memory allocation.
   - Periodically swaps the virtual memory for processes from physical memory to disk and back again, so that all processes get their fair share of use of computer memory.
5. Security and privacy. For example, the operating system does not usually permit a thread to:
   - Access files belonging to another user.
   - Terminate a process belonging to another user.
   - Access the virtual memory belonging to another process.
   - Directly access to the raw data on a disk drive.

KERNEL BASED OPERATING SYSTEMS

The kernel is the core of an operating system. The main functions of the kernel are as

- To provide a mechanism for the creation and deletion of process,
- To provide CPU scheduling, memory management, and device management for these process,
- To provide synchronization tools so that the processes can synchronize their actions,
- To provide communication tools so that processes can communicate with each other.

As an example, consider the UNIX operating system that has two separable parts: the kernel and the service programs. The kernel provider on the file system, CPU scheduling, memory management, and other operating system functions through system calls. System calls define the programmer interface to operating system; the set of systems programs commonly available defines the user interface. These interfaces define the context the kernel must support.

System calls provide the interface between a running program and the operating system. These calls are generally available as assembly language instructions, and are usually listed in the manuals used by assembly language programmers. Some systems may allow system calls to be made directly from a higher-level language program, in which case the calls normally resemble predefined function or subroutine calls. They may generate a call to a special run-time routine that makes the system call, or the system call may be generated directly in-line.

The C language allows system calls to be made directly. Some Pascal systems also provide an ability to make system calls directly from a Pascal program to the operating system. Scheduling is a fundamental operating system function, since almost all computer resources are scheduled before use. The CPU is, of course, one of the primary computer resources. Consequently, its scheduling is often performed in the operating system. Figure shows the various layers of software that permit an application program to access and manage resources.

Each layer uses the services of the layers below and provides a service to the layers above it. Access to a computer's resources are requested using a set of system commands. These commands call lower-level programs that in turn directly access a computer's hardware resources. The set of system commands is known as the operating system's *user interface* and the set of lower-level programs is known as the operating system's *kernel*. Some operating systems have a graphical user interface e.g. Windows; some have a command line interface e.g. UNIX.

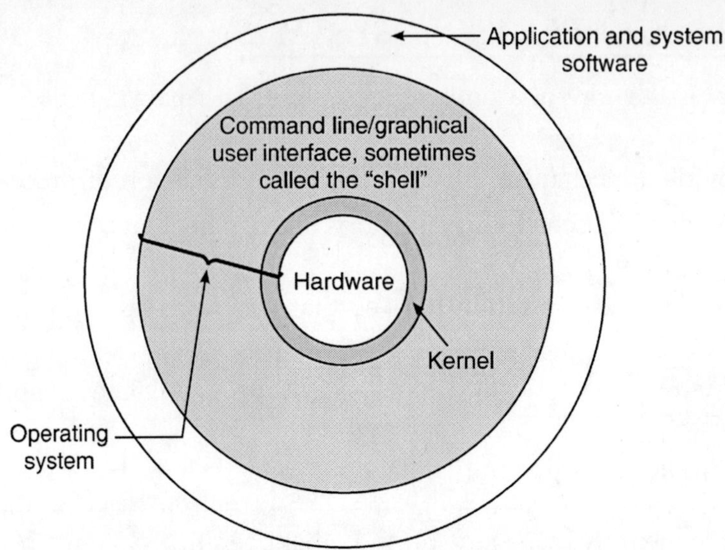

Various layers of the software

The kernel-based design often is used for designing of the operating system. The kernel (more appropriately called the nucleus) is a collection of primitive facilities over which the rest of the operating system is built, using the functions provided by the kernel (see Fig. Thus, a kernel provides an environment to build an operating system in which the designer has considerable flexibility because policy and optimization decisions are not made at the kernel level. An operating system is an orderly growth of software over the kernel, where all decisions regarding process scheduling, resource allocation, execution environment, file system, and resource protection etc. are made.

Consequently, a kernel is a fundamental set of primitives that allows the dynamic creation and control of process, as well as communication among them. Thus, the kernel only support the notion of processes and does not include the concept of a resource. However, as operating systems have matured in functionality and complexity, more functionality has been relegated to the kernel. A kernel should contain a minimal set of functionality that is adequate to build an operating system with a given set of objectives.

Shell

The operating system is the code that carries out the system calls. Command interpreters are not part of the operating system; however in this section we will discuss the UNIX command interpreter, the shell.

A shell allows a user to access the kernel. Shells are actually programs that interpret command lines and run other programs. A shell can read command lines from a terminal or from a file.

The shell makes heavy use of the operating system features and is therefore a good example of how system calls can be used. The shell is also the primary interface between a user at a terminal and the operating system.

When a user logs in, a shell is started. The shell has the terminal as standard input and standard output. It begins by typing a prompt, such as a $. This informs the user that the shell is waiting for a command.

The command program - shell or finder

The user controls the execution of programs by interacting with a **command program**. The command program can also be considered a part of the operating system, in some sort of broad sense, although it is really just the same as any other user program, and has no special privileges. Under UNIX, the command program corresponds to the **shell**. On a Macintosh, the command program corresponds to the **finder**, but since UNIX is built in to MacOS X, it is also possible to interact with the operating system via a UNIX shell. On Windows, both kinds of command program exist.

There are a vast number of other programs that are often considered a part of the operating system, in some vague sense. These include application programs, such as the compilers, editors, debuggers, programs for copying and removing files, etc., that are not a part of the operating system command program, but are just ordinary programs that can be executed.

A system as large and complex as a modern operating system must be engineered carefully if it is to function properly and to be modified easily. A common approach is to partition the task into small components, rather than have one monolithic system. Each of these modules should be a well-defined portion of the system, with carefully defined inputs, outputs, and function. We have already discussed briefly the common components of operating systems. In this section, we discuss the way that these components are interconnected and melded into a kernel.

OPERATING SYSTEM STRUCTURES

A system as large and complex as a modern operating system must be engineered carefully if it is to function properly and to be modified easily. A common approach is to partition the task into small components, rather than have one monolithic system. Each of these modules should be a well-defined portion of the system, with carefully defined inputs, outputs, and function. We have already discussed briefly the common components of operating systems. In this section, we discuss the way that these components are interconnected and melded into a kernel.

Simple Structure

There are numerous commercial systems that do not have a well-defined structure. Frequently, such operating systems started as small, simple, and limited systems, and then grew beyond their original scope. MS-DOS is an example of such a system. It was originally designed and implemented by a few people who had no idea that it would become so popular.

It was written to provide the most functionality in the least space, because of the limited hardware on which it ran, so it was not divided into modules carefully. Figure shows its structure.

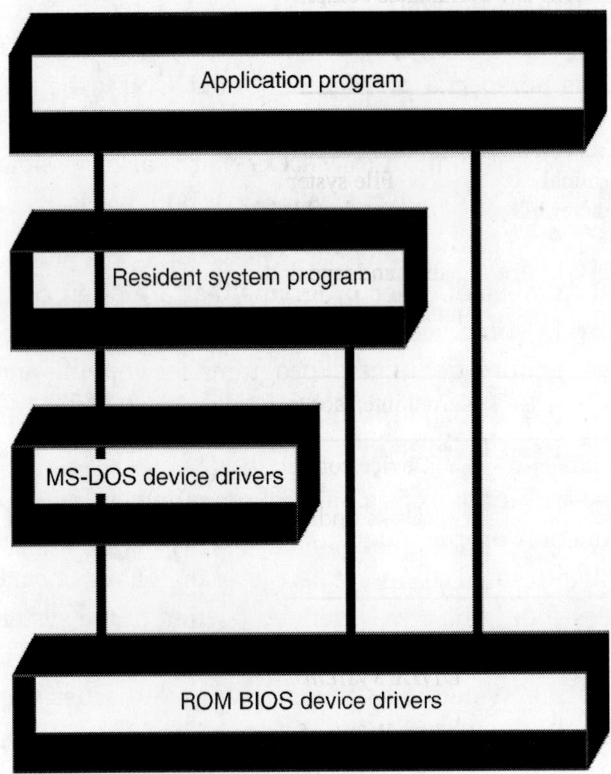

MS – DOS layer structure

In MS-DOS, the interfaces and levels of functionality are not well separated. For instance, application programs are able to access the basic I/O routines to write directly to the display and disk drives. Such freedom leaves MS-DOS vulnerable to errant (or malicious) programs, causing entire system crashes when user programs fail. Of course, MS-DOS was also limited by the hardware of its era. Because the Intel 8088 for which it was written provides no dual mode and no hardware protection, the designers of MS-DOS had no choice but to leave the base hardware accessible.

Another example of limited structuring is the original UNIX operating system. UNIX is another system that initially was limited by hardware functionality. It consists of two separable parts: the kernel and the systems programs.

The kernel is further separated into a series of interfaces and device drivers, which have been added and expanded over the years as UNIX has evolved. We can view the UNIX operating system as being layered as shown in Figure

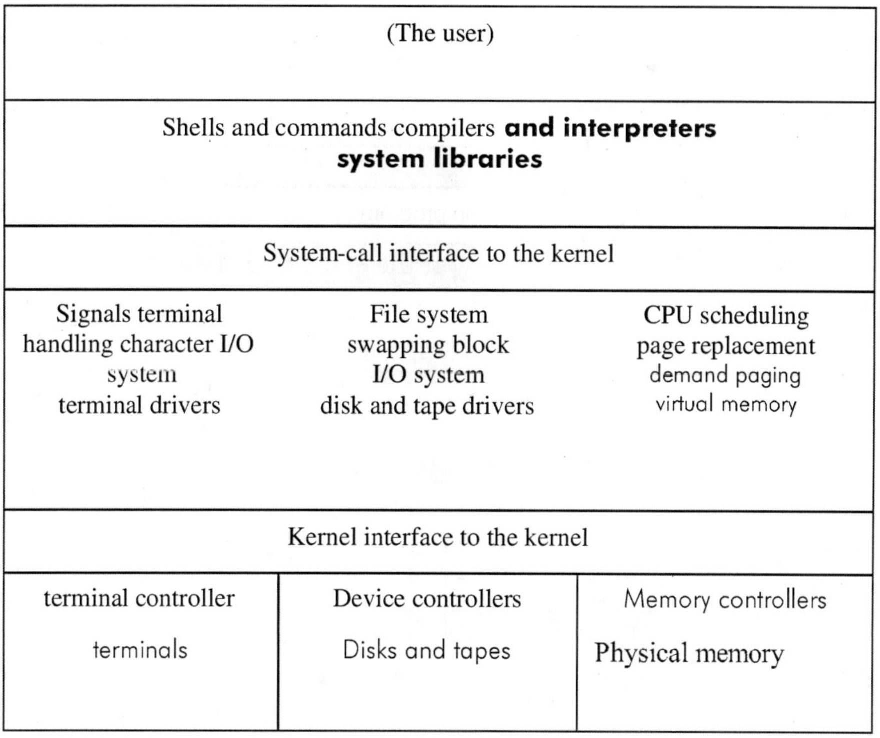

(The user)

Shells and commands compilers **and interpreters system libraries**

System-call interface to the kernel

Signals terminal handling character I/O system terminal drivers

File system swapping block I/O system disk and tape drivers

CPU scheduling page replacement demand paging virtual memory

Kernel interface to the kernel

terminal controller
terminals

Device controllers
Disks and tapes

Memory controllers
Physical memory

UNIX system structure

Everything below the system-call interface and above the physical hardware is the kernel. The kernel provides the file system, CPU scheduling, memory management, and other operating system functions through system calls.

Taken in sum, that is an enormous amount of functionality to be combined into one level. Systems programs use the kernel-supported system calls to provide useful functions, such as compilation and file manipulation.

System calls define the programmer interface to UNIX; the set of systems programs commonly available defines the user interface. The programmer and user interfaces define the context that the kernel must support. Several versions of UNIX have been developed in which the kernel is partitioned further along functional boundaries. The AIX operating system, IBM's version of UN separates the kernel into two parts. Mach, from Carnegie Mellon University, reduces the kernel to a small set of core functions by moving all nonessentials into systems and even into user-level programs. What remains is a microkernel operating system implementing only a small set of necessary primitives.

Monolithic systems

Such an operating system is written as a collection of procedures, each of which can call any of the other procedures whenever it needs to. Each procedure in the operating system has a well-defined interface in terms of parameters and results.

Some structure can be added to monolithic operating systems. The services, system calls, provided by the operating system are requested by putting the parameters in well-defined places, such as registers, or on the stack and then executing a special TRAP instruction known as the kernel call or supervisor call.

This TRAP instruction switches the computer from user mode to kernel mode, and transfers control to the operating system. The operating system then examines the parameters of the call to determine which system call is to be carried out. A table is then indexed to determine the procedure that carries out the system call. This operation identifies the service procedure, which is then called. Finally, once the system call is finished, control is returned to the user program. Such a structure can be organized:

1. A main program that invokes the requested service procedure.
2. A set of service procedures that carry out system calls.
3. A set of utility procedures that help the service procedures.

Layered systems

The monolithic system that is described above began with no structure and ended with an organized structure. That structure can in fact be layered, see Figure. This introduces a hierarchy of layers, where each layer is constructed above the one below.

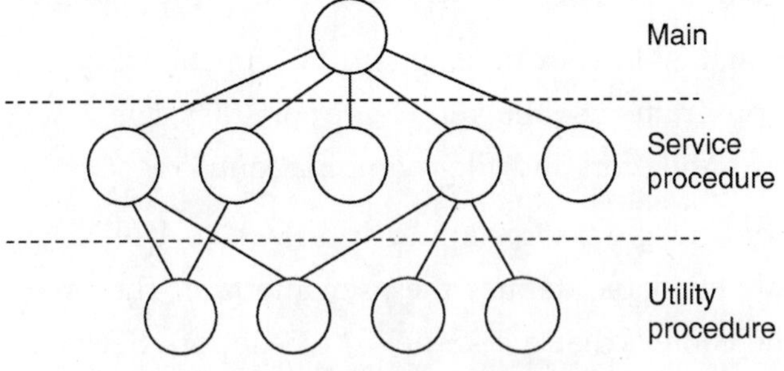

A simple layered structure

The first operating system that was based on such a layered structure was the Technische Hogeschool Eindhoven (THE), see Figure.

5	User
4	User programs
3	I/O management
2	Operator - process communication
1	Memory and drum management
0	Process allocation and multiprogramming

THE operating system

The MULTICS operating system was based on such a structure. However, MULTICS was conceptually based on a series of concentric rings, see Figure. The inner-rings have more privileges than the outer-rings.

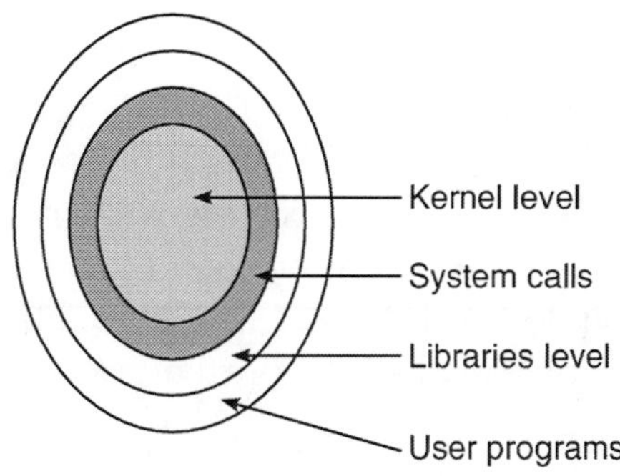

MULTICS ring structure

The UNIX operating system is also a layered structure, see the above fig.

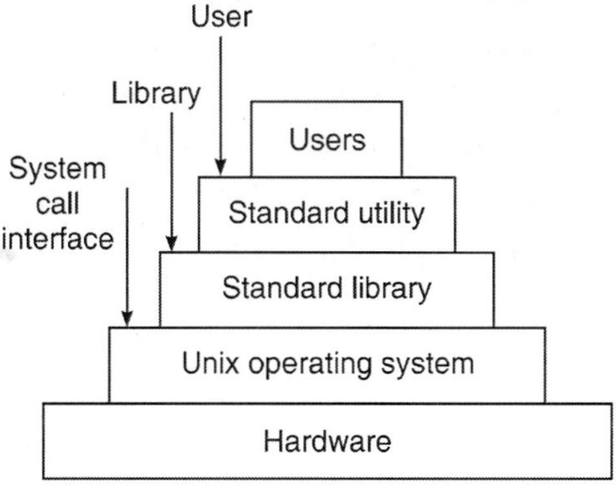

UNIX layering

Virtual Machines

Conceptually, a computer system is made up of layers. The hardware is the lowest level in all such systems. The kernel running at the next level uses the hardware instructions to create a set of system calls for use by outer layers. The systems programs above the kernel are therefore able to use either system calls or hardware instructions, and in some ways these programs do not differentiate between these two. Thus, although they are accessed differently, they both provide functionality that the program can use to create even more advanced functions. System programs, in turn, treat the hardware and the system calls as though they both are at the same level.

Some systems carry this scheme even a step further by allowing the system programs to be called easily by the application programs. As before, although the system programs are at a level higher than that of the other routines, the application programs may view everything under them in the hierarchy as though the latter were part of the machine itself. This layered approach is taken to its logical conclusion in the concept of a virtual machine. The VM operating system for IBM systems is the best example of the virtual-machine concept, because IBM pioneered the work in this area.

By using CPU scheduling and virtual-memory techniques, an operating system can create the illusion of multiple processes, each executing on its own processor with its own (virtual) memory. Of course, normally, the process has additional features, such as system calls and a file system, which are not provided by the bare hardware. The virtual-machine approach, on the other hand, does not provide any additional function, but rather provides an interface that is identical to the underlying bare hardware. Each process is provided with a (virtual) copy of the underlying computer.

The resources of the physical computer are shared to create the virtual machines. CPU scheduling can be used to share the CPU and to create the appearance that users have their own processor. Spooling and a file system can provide virtual card readers and virtual line printers. A normal user timesharing terminal provides the function of the virtual machine operator's console.

A major difficulty with the virtual-machine approach involves disk systems. Suppose that the physical machine has three disk drives but wants to support seven virtual machines. Clearly, it cannot allocate a disk drive to each virtual machine. Remember that the virtual-machine software itself will need substantial disk space to provide virtual memory and spooling. The solution is to provide virtual disks, which are identical in all respects except size; these are termed minidisks in IBM's VM operating system.

The system implements each minidisk by allocating as many tracks as the minidisk needs on the physical disks. Obviously, the sum of the sizes of all minidisks must be less than the actual amount of physical disk space available.

Users thus are given their own virtual machine. They can then run any of the operating systems or software packages that are available on the underlying machine. For the IBM VM system, a user normally runs CMS, a single-user interactive operating system. The virtual-machine software is concerned with multiprogramming multiple virtual machines onto a physical machine, but does not need to consider any user-support software. This arrangement may provide a useful partitioning of the problem of designing a multiuser interactive system into two smaller pieces.

A virtual machine is an illusion of a real machine. It is crated by a virtual machine operating system, which makes a single real machine appear to be several real machines. From the user's viewpoint, virtual machines can appear to be existing real machine or they can be dramatically different. The concept has proven valuable and many virtual machine operating systems have been developed. The most widely used of these is IBM's VM.

Conventional multiprogramming systems (figure a) share the resources of a single computer among several processes. These processes are each allocated a portion of the real machine's resources. They see a machine smaller in size and capabilities than the machine on which they run.

Virtual machine multiprogramming systems (figure b) share the resources of a single machine in a different manner. They create the illusion that one real machine is actually several machines. They create virtual processors, virtual storage, and virtual I/O devices, possibly with much larger capacities than those of the underlying real machine.

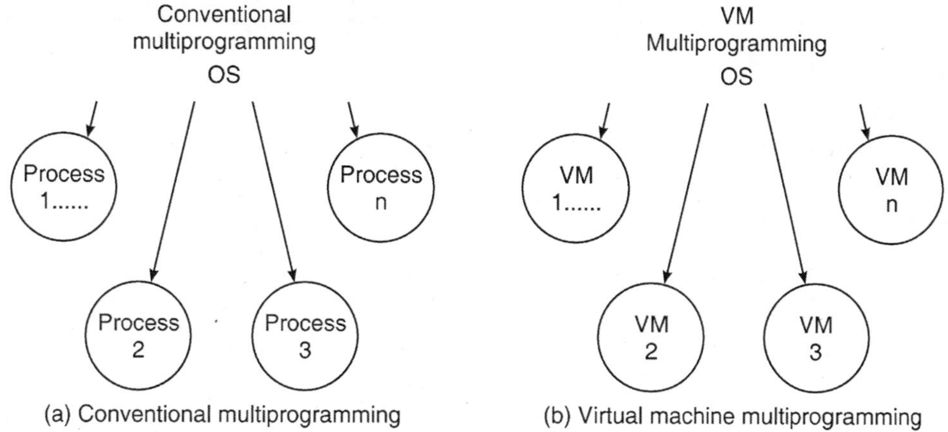

(a) Conventional multiprogramming (b) Virtual machine multiprogramming

Client server models

There has been a trend to move code up through the layers away from the operating system, leaving a minimal kernel. Usually the approach is to implement most of the operating system functions in user processes. For example, to request a service such as reading a block of a file, a user process - the client process sends the request to a server process. The server process then does the work and sends back the answer. In Figure , the kernel handles the communications between the client processes and the servers.

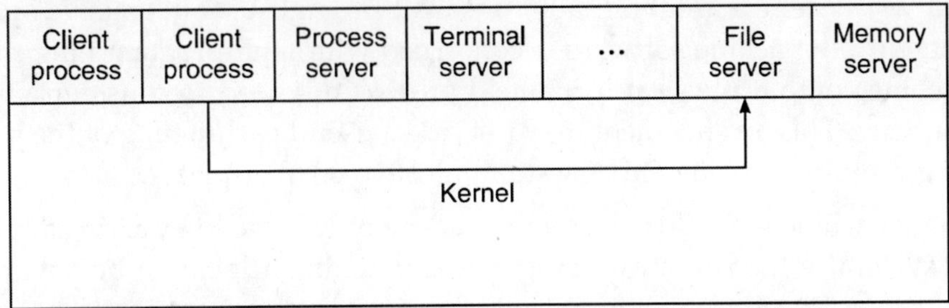

Client server model

By splitting the operating system into two parts, one that handles client processes and one that handles the services, results in an operating system becoming small and manageable. Consequently, if in the event of some failure, perhaps due to a virus, then only the affected parts of the system suffer rather than the whole machine. A further advantage of this client-server model is its adaptability for use in distributed systems, see Figure.

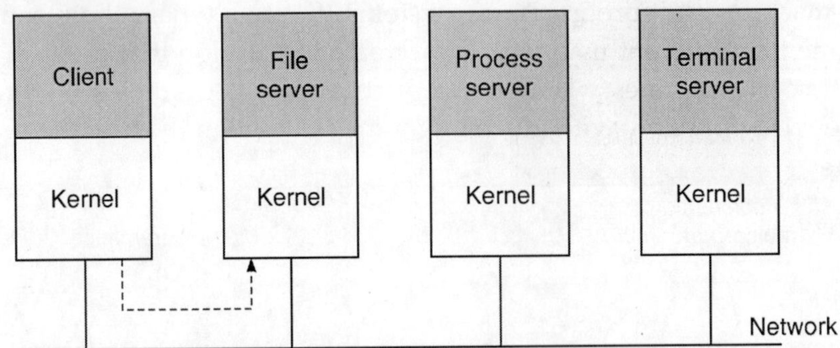

Client-server model in a distributed system

If a client communicates with a server by sending it messages, the client need not know whether the message is handled locally on its own machine, or whether it is sent across a network to a server on a remote machine. As far as the client is concerned, a request was made and an answer was returned.

TRENDS IN OPERATING SYSTEM STRUCTURES

The rate of change in the demand on operating systems requires not just modification and enhancements to existing architectures, but new ways of organizing the operating systems. A wide range of different approaches and design elements has been tried in both experimental and commercial operating systems, but much of the work fits into the following categories:

a. Microkernel architecture

Most operating systems, until recently, featured have a large **monolithic kernel**. Most of what is though of as operating-system functionality is provided in these large kernels, including scheduling, file system, networking, device drivers, memory management, and more.

Micro-kernels contain just a few essential functions. Other OS services are implemented by processes (the daemons of UNIX, for instance).

Typically, a monolithic kernel is implemented as a single process, with all elements sharing the same address space.

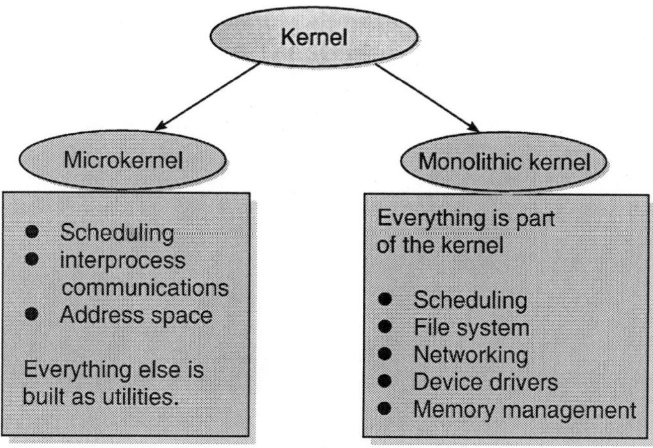

Micro-kernel structure

Microkernel **architecture** assigns only a few essential functions to the kernel, including address spaces, interprocess communication (IPC), and basic scheduling. Other OS services are provided by processes, sometimes called servers that run in user mode and are treated like any other application by the microkernel.

b. Multithreading

In Multithreading a process is created out of an existing process called thread and both can run simultaneously. It is useful for applications that perform a number of essentially independent tasks that do not need to be serialized.

In Multi-threading the processes are a collection of one or more threads and associated resources. A thread is a unit of work, including processor context, private data and stack.

Multithreading is the ability of an operating system to execute different parts of a program, called *threads*, simultaneously. The programmer must carefully design the program in such a way that all the threads can run at the same time without interfering with each other

Thread: Thread is a dispatch able unit of work; it is executed sequentially and interruptible. In programming, thread is a part of a program that can execute independently of other parts. Threads can be in one of the several states: ready, blocked, running or terminated. Like processes, threads share the CPU, and only one thread at a time is active (running). However, unlike processes, threads are not independent of one another. Threads share a single address space with other threads and each thread has its own stack and program counter.

Process: A process is:

- ➢ A program in execution
- ➢ An instance of a program running on a computer
- ➢ The entity that can be assigned to and executed on a processor

A process could be collection of threads and consists of three components

- An executable program
- Associated data needed by the program
- Execution context of the program

c. Distributed operating systems

This type of setup provides the illusion of a single main memory space and single secondary memory space.

In Distributed Operating Systems, the Operating Systems are capable of running over a network, rather than a single computer

It is a common operating system shared by a network of computers.

d. Object-oriented design

In OO Design of OS, the new ideas being brought to OS construction to minimize bugs and errors.

Object-oriented design brings the benefits of adding modular extensions to a small kernel.

Object-based structure enables programmers to customize an operating system without disrupting system integrity

e. Symmetric multiprocessing (SMP)

A symmetric multiprocessor can be defined as a standalone computer system with the following characteristics:

- ➢ There are multiple processors.
- ➢ These processors share the same main memory and I/O facilities.
- ➢ All processors can perform the same functions.

In Symmetric Multi-Processing (SMP), the Operating Systems are capable of distributing their process loads onto many processors.

SMP has a number of potential advantages over uniprocessor architecture including the followings:

➢ **Performance:** Some portions of the work can be done in parallel which improves the performance. As in Fig. 3.2. With multiprogramming only one process can execute at a time; meanwhile all other processes are waiting for the processor. With multiprocessing, more than one process can be running simultaneously, each on a different processor.

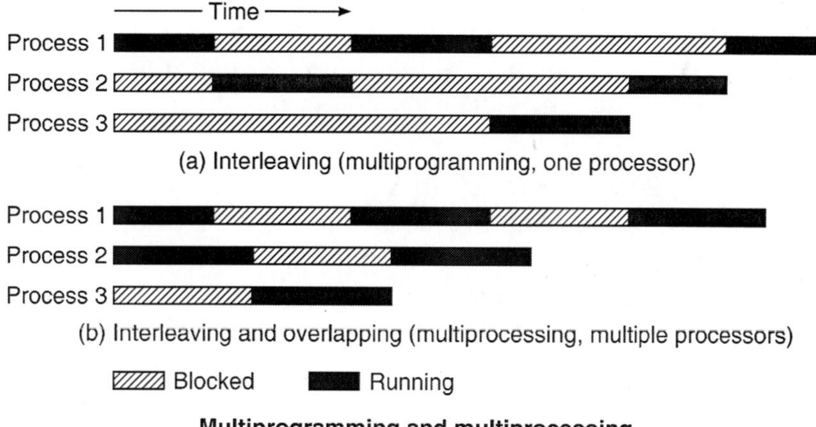

Multiprogramming and multiprocessing

- ➢ **Availability:** Because all processors can perform the same functions, the failure of a single processor does not halt the machine. Multiprocessing brings fault tolerance to the system.
- ➢ **Incremental growth:** A user can enhance the performance of a system by adding an additional processor.
- ➢ **Scaling:** Vendors can offer a range of products with different price and performance characteristics based on the number of processors configured in the system.

These concepts and their implementation represent the state-of-the-art in OS design, implementation and maintenance.

PROCESSOR MODES-SUPERVISOR MODE/USER MODE

Contemporary microprocessors incorporate a mode bit to define the execution capability of a program on the processor. This bit can be set to supervisor mode or user mode. In supervisor mode, the processor can execute every single instruction in its instruction set, while in user mode, only certain instructions can be executed. Instructions that can only be executed in supervisor mode are called supervisor, privileged or protected instructions. I/O instructions are protected instructions, so if an application program executes in user mode, it cannot perform its own I/O.

The parts of the OS that is critical to its operation execute in the supervisor mode and are known as the kernel or nucleus of the OS (could include parts from the various main components of the OS). This includes device drivers , which provides the necessary interface for the OS to the various device controllers.

In order for an application operating in user mode to perform I/O (this includes reading and writing to the hard disk), it must execute what is known as a trap instruction or a supervisor call instruction. This instruction issues an interrupt, which then alternates the CPU to supervisor mode. At the same time, the CPU will also switch execution to the device driver (or another suitable OS component) which performs the necessary I/O operations. Once the I/O operation is complete, the device driver will then switch the CPU back to user mode and return control to the user program.

The key point here is to enforce security by ensuring that the application program (user process) does not execute any instructions in the supervisor mode (this could for example, allow that program to accidentally or intentionally overwrite any part of the hard disk). This is accomplished by making sure that the only code running in supervisor mode is kernel code (the device driver or any other OS component). In essence the kernel acts as a sort of security guard. All I/O operations that wish to be performed by a user process must go through the kernel before they can be accomplished.

It may be also possible to extend the mode bit to define areas of main memory that can be accessed for either a read or write operation when the processor is in supervisor mode versus when it is in user mode. If the mode bit is set to supervisor mode, the process executing on the processor can access either the supervisor or user space of memory. If user mode is set, the process can only reference user memory space.

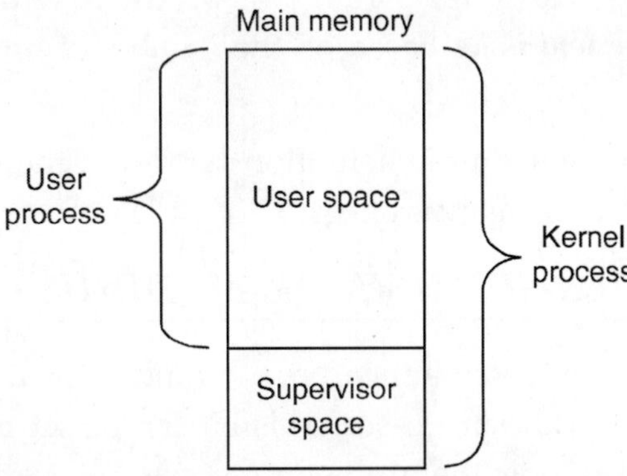

User and supervisor space

Here, we can store the kernel of the OS into the supervisor space, and all the remaining user processes into the user space. Any user process will thus be unable to access any part of main memory that belongs to the OS (the supervisor space), since all user processes will operate in user mode. Only kernel (or supervisor) processes (such as the memory manager of the OS) operate in supervisor mode and hence will be able to access any part of memory. This again prevents the user process from accidentally or intentionally corrupting any part of supervisor space which contains the OS (keep in mind the OS is the most important part of your software, if it crashes the only recourse is to reboot your system.)

CASE STUDIES - BASIC INPUT/OUTPUT SYSTEM

The BIOS is the abbreviation for Basic input/output System. The name indicates that the BIOS provide basic input and output routines for communicating between software and the hardware peripherals such as keyboard, screen and disk drive.

The BIOS itself is located in ROM, making it resident even after the computer has been turned off. It is stored in the very high processor's address space beginning at address F000:E000 (FE000 - physical address). It extends to address F000:FFFF. The BIOS routines must create, store and modify variables like any other routine. It stores these variables in the lower part of memory starting at address 0040:0000.

Outthought hardware of the IBM-PC and PC compatible are different, but input and output for each BIOS routine call are the same. These routine calls are standardized.

Programmer can develop a program on one IBM PC or compatible, and run it on another compatible PC without errors, even though neither the hardware nor the individual BIOS routines are completely compatible.

BIOS functions occur through the individual routines contained in the BIOS interrupts 10H to 17H and 1AH. Usage of the functions is also standardized, transfer data from the calling program to the interrupt and from the interrupt to the calling program.

Number	Meaning
10H	BIOS display function
11H	Testing the configuration
12H	Testing RAM
13H	BIOS disk functions
14H	Functions for asynchronous communication
15H	Cassette functions
16H	Reading the keyboard

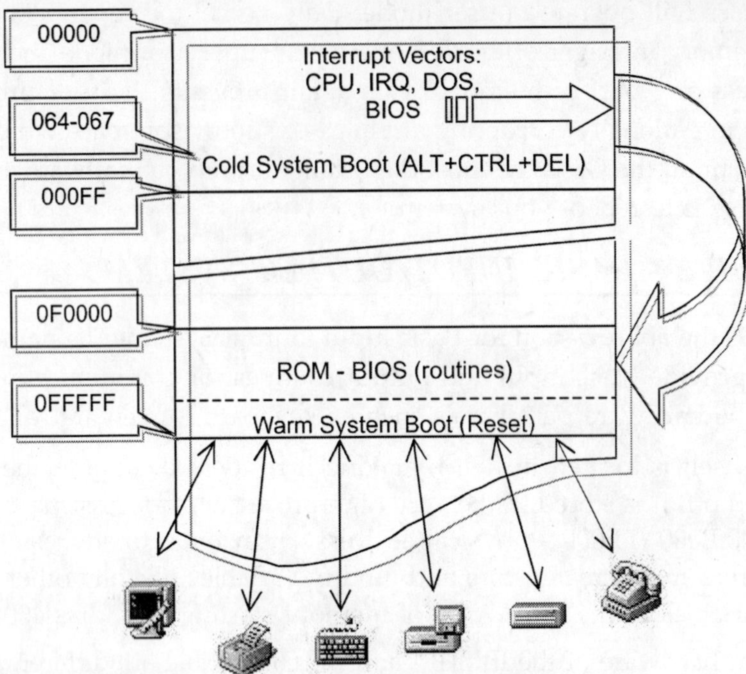

Interrupts and ROM-BIOS

Interrupts of PC

An Interrupt is a signal from a peripheral device or a request from a program to perform a specific service. When an interrupt occurs, the currently executing program is temporarily suspended and interrupt routine begins execution to handle the condition that caused the interrupt. After the interrupt routine has completed its task, it issues the return instruction to resume the program.

There are two major types of interrupts - hardware interrupts and software interrupts.

A software interrupt is an interrupt called by the INT instruction in a machine language program. A hardware device such as a disk drive, keyboard can trigger a hardware interrupt.

Booting the System

The booting process of DOS begins with examination at the point where the first sector of a diskette or hard disk is loaded into memory. From the time we switch on the computer to the booting process, a series of the following events occur.

Initialisation

Program execution starts after the computer is turned on at memory location F000:FFF0. This is part of the ROM-BIOS and contains a jump command to a BIOS routine which takes over system initialization. The location of this routine may differ from one computer to another, however the task this routine performs remains identical for nearly all PCs.

System Check

First the BIOS tests individual functions of the processor, its register and some instructions. If an error occurs during this test, the system stops without displaying an error message. If the CPU passes the test, BIOS tests the ROMs by computing checksum. Each chip on the main board goes through tests and initialization.

Peripheral testing

After determining the function of the main board, the computer tests the peripherals (keyboard, disk drive, ect.). Then computer initializes BIOS variables and interrupt vector table.

The bootstrap loader

Interrupt 19H is the bootrap loader. On startup or on system reset, this routine tries to load some form of the basic operating system from a predetermined place on the diskette.

Determining BIOS Version

Usually a 5 byte long jump instruction of the system startup can be found at the memory location F000:FFF0. After this instruction, an additional 11 bytes are available, which are normally used to store the release date of the BIOS version. We can examine the contents of these memory locations to determine which BIOS version the PC uses. Call the DEBUG program from DOS prompt:

```
C> debug
-dF000:FFF0
F000:FFF0 CD 19 E0 00 F0 31 31 2F-32 36 2F 39 36 00 FC F9   .....11/26/96...
```

Determining the PC Type

Usage of certain BIOS functions are more for model identification than for BIOS version identification. They indicate the type of PC in use. They also indicate when the BIOS has additional functions such as handle string output on the screen, real-time clock access and additional RAM beyond the 1 megabyte memory limit.

The model identification byte is located in the last memory location of the ROM-BIOS at address F000:FFFE. This byte can contain the following codes:

252 or FCH: AT

254 or FEH: XT and portable PC

255 or FFH: PC

Remember: These values aren't entirely accurate. The following rule of thumb may be used: A model identification byte of 252 (FCH) identifies an AT; any other number indicates a PC/XT.

BIOS SCREEN OUTPUT FUNCTIONS

The BIOS contains a series of routines which display data on the screen and maintain other display functions. In addition to the video mode, BIOS manages cursor positioning, text output and graphic display routines. Interrupt 10H calls all these routines. The processor registers transfer the data between the application program and the BIOS interrupt routine.

The BIOS routines offer the programmer the advantage of independence from particular video card such as IBM color, Hercules, EGA/VGA etc. The manufactures of the PC try to adapt the ROM-BIOS to new graphic cards by packaging an independent ROM-BIOS on their cards. When the system is booted, the BIOS detects this ROM expansion and allows it to redirect the BIOS video interrupt 16H to its own routines, replacing the old functions. The following table lists the routines of interrupt 10H.

Function	*Action*
00H	Set video mode
0FH	Get video mode
Text mode	
02H	Set cursor position
03H	Read cursor position
01H	Define cursor size
05H	Set active display page
09H	Write character with attribute
0AH	Write character
0EH	Teletype mode
08H	Read character/attribute
06H	Scroll window up
07H	Scroll window down

Graphic functions	
0BH	Set color palette
0DH	Read pixel
13H	Write pixel
EGA/VGA functions	
10H	Set palette
11H	Character generator
12H	Detect EGA/VGA card
13H	Write string
1AH	Query/Set Display Comb Code
1BH	Query functionality/status
1CH	Save/Restore video state

Determining System Configuration using BIOS

The system information can be obtained with the help of BIOS interrupt 11H. The system configuration can be a number of disk drives connected to the system, capacity of the RAM on main board, video mode, number of RS-232 cards attached, number of printers attached.

Determining Available RAM using BIOS

White interrupt 11h only returns the amount of RAM on main board, interrupt 12h obtains the amount of RAM available in the entire system. This is a total of the amount of RAM on main board and any memory expansion cards.

This method determines RAM below the 1 megabyte limit only. The 80286 processor or higher can manage up to 16 megabyte of memory. However, interrupt 12h cannot report on any RAM beyond 1 megabyte.

Accessing the Disk from the BIOS

Each side of a disk 3 1/2 inch consists of 80 tracks of 18 sectors each. Each sector has a capacity of 512 bytes. The tracks are numbered from 0 to 79. Track 0 is located on the outer edge and track 79 on inner edge of the disk. The disk has two sides numbered from 0 to 1. This disk has total storage capacity 1.44 megabytes.

The methods of transferring data to or from the disk are identical. First the read/ write head moves to proper track. Since the disk moves constantly, the sector to be processed eventually passes by the head, allowing data transfer. BIOS makes some functions available for disk access at the lowest level. A total of six BIOS disk functions can be accessed by calling interrupt 13h. The lists of the functions are as follows:

Function	*Action*
0	Reset disk
1	Disk status
2	Read disk data
3	Write access to the disk
4	Verify disk
5	Format part of a disk

Newer BIOS contains new disk functions which are also called through interrupt 13h. The first of these new functions, function 15h, determines the drive type in use. The next function, function 16h, detects the disk change and function 17h helps formatting disk.

Accessing the Hard Disk from the BIOS

Like the floppy disk, a hard disk consists of magnetized plates, also called disks, which can store data as magnetic impulses. Unlike the floppy disk, a hard disk contains several of these disks.

Each disk consists of platters, rings on each side of each platter called tracks, and sections within each track called sectors. A sector is the smallest physical storage unit on a disk, almost always 512 bytes in size.

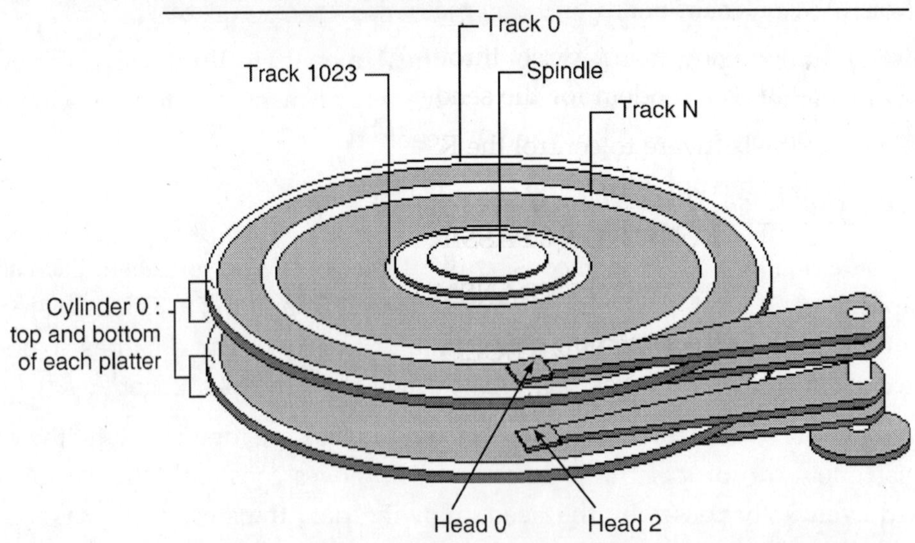

Hard disk formatting is similar to that of a floppy disk: each disk is divided into tracks which have sectors within them. A cylinder consists of all sectors which can be accessed without moving the read/write heads. Every cylinder contains the same number of sectors, which in turn contain a constant number of bytes.

BIOS accesses the hard disk through interrupt 13h - the same interrupt used for floppy disk access. The individual functions are identical for hard disk and floppy disk drives, but BIOS used different modules for controlling the hard disk and disk drives. When we call interrupt 13h, it accesses the hard disk routine first. This routine tests whether the hard disk or floppy disk drive should be addressed. If the floppy disk is involved, another module must be called by calling interrupt 40h, which points to the old disk interrupt 13h.

CMOS

The Complementary Metal Oxide Semiconductor (CMOS) chip in the computer stores information about the devices connected to the computer. When you install or change a non-SCSI disk in your computer, you need to use the BIOS setup program provided on your computer to update the information in the CMOS. (SCSI disks have their own configuration program, typically provided by the manufacturer.)

Note: It is possible for the CMOS battery to run down if you do not turn your computer on for a long time. And the CMOS chip sometimes fails.

Accessing the Serial Port from the BIOS

Computer can communicate with each other and exchange data. Data is transferred serially. Data transfer is only possible when there is an asynchronous communication port (RS-232 card, serial interface card). This card enables data transfer between two computers direct through a cable or though phone lines. The latter method requires a modem for the sender and the receiver.

BIOS offers the software to control the RS-232 card. There are 4 functions in this routine called by interrupt 14h.

FUNCTION 0 PASSING PROTOCOL

FUNCTION 1 TRANSMIT CHARACTER

FUNCTION 2 RECEIVE CHARACTER

FUNCTION 3 LINE/MODEM STATUS

Accessing the Keyboard from the BIOS

Interrupt 16h provides three functions to read the keyboard and keyboard status. No BIOS keyboard functions exist for removing characters from keyboard buffer or renaming keys.

Some key combinations can not be read by BIOS as key codes because they execute commands. The <PrtSc> or <Print> key calls BIOS interrupt 5h to send the current screen display to a printer. The <Ctrl><Num Lock> keys stop the complete system until the user hits another key. The <Ctrl><Break> keys call interrupt 1Bh to stop current program.

FUNCTION 0 OF THE INTERRUPT 16H READS THE CHARACTER IN THE KEYBOARD BUFFER AND PASSES IT TO THE CALLING PROGRAM. IF THERE IS NO CHARACTER IN THE KEYBOARD BUFFER, IT WAITS UNTIL A CHARACTER HAS BEEN INPUT AND THEN RETURNS TO THE CALLING PROGRAM.

The role of the keyboard Interrupt 9h

FUNCTION 1 OF THE INTERRUPT 16H ALSO READS THE KEYBOARD. UNLIKE FUNCTION 0, IT LEAVES THE PRECEDING CHARACTER IN THE KEYBOARD BUFFER. IN CONTRAST TO FUNCTION 0, FUNCTION 1 IMMEDIATELY INFORMS THE CALLING PROGRAM WHETHER A CHARACTER IS AVAILABLE OR NOT.

FUNCTION 2 READS THE STATUS OF CERTAIN CONTROL KEYS AND CONDITIONS.

The ROM-BIOS routine that captures keystrokes is interrupt numbered 9h. Interrupts 9h and 16h work hand in hand. INT 9h stores keystrokes into a buffer, then INT 16h gets keystroke from buffer.

Accessing the Printer from the BIOS

BIOS offers three functions, called by interrupt 17h, for communicating with one or more printers interfaced to the PC. They can specify the printer to which the output should go.

FUNCTION 0 SENDS CHARACTER TO THE PRINTER.

FUNCTION 1 INITIALIZES THE PRINTER PORTS. THIS FUNCTION SHOULD BE EXECUTED BEFORE SENDING DATA TO THE PRINTER FOR THE FIRST TIME.

FUNCTION 2 READS PRINTER STATUS.

Accessing the Date and Time from the BIOS

The 1Ch interrupt is used in the clock device to display the time on the screen. 8h updates the time of day counter and 1Ah can be used by a user program to read or set the time of day counter.

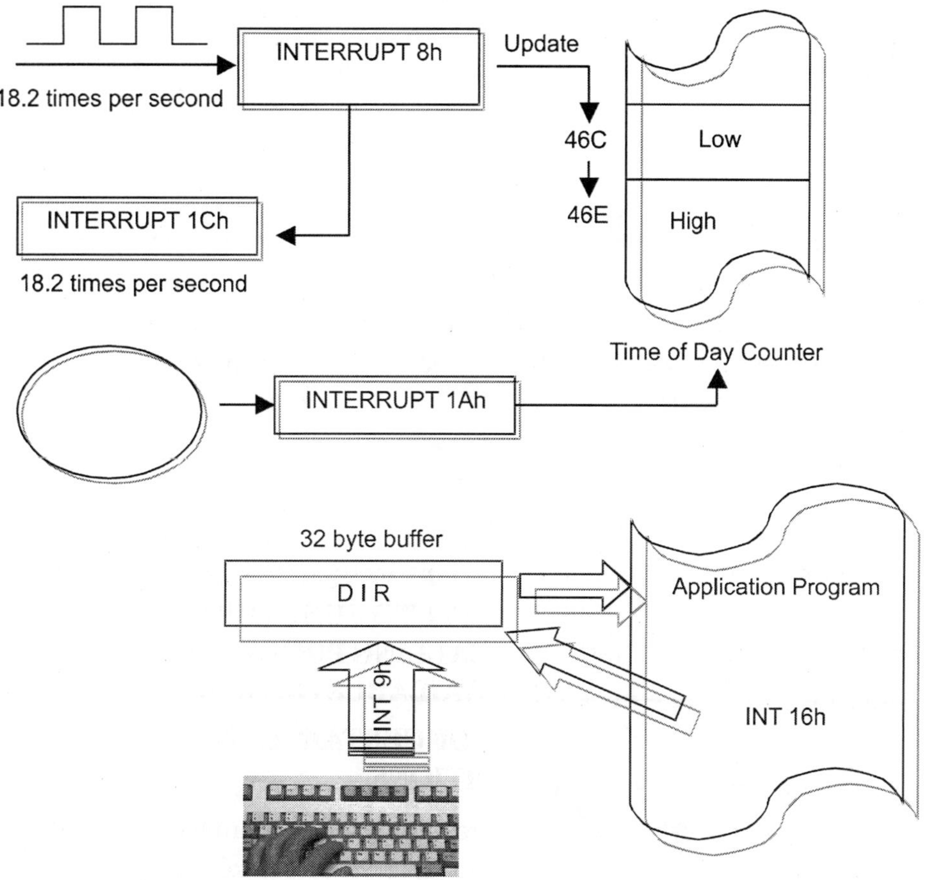

The 8h, 1Ch and 1Ah interrupts

The various time functions of the ROM-BIOS can be addressed through BIOS interrupt 1Ah.

FUNCTION NUMBER 0H GETS THE CURRENT CLOCK TIME.

FUNCTION NUMBER 01H SETS THE CURRENT CLOCK TIME.

FUNCTION NUMBER 02H READS THE CURRENT CLOCK TIME.

FUNCTION NUMBER 03H SETS THE TIME ON THE REAL-TIME CLOCK.

FUNCTION NUMBER 04H AND 05H READ AND SET THE DATE STORED IN THE REAL-TIME CLOCK.

FUNCTION NUMBER 06H SETS ALARM TIME.

FUNCTION NUMBER 07H RESETS ALARM TIME.

KEYWORDS

VON NEUMANN ARCHITECTURE	**KERNEL**
INTERRUPT	**SHELLS**
BOOTING	**THE**
DEVICE CONTROLLER	**SYMMETRIC MULTIPROCESSING**
PROCESS	**MULTI-THREADING**

SUMMARY

In 1945, a mathematician by the name of Von Neumann came up with the concept of the 'stored program computer' which forms the conceptual basis for the hardware architecture of all computers up to the present day. The von Neumann architecture is a computer design model that uses a single storage structure to hold both instructions and data.

- Interrupt is a signal from a device to a computer's processor requesting the processor's attention. Interrupts are generated for many reasons, including software errors and the signalling of the presence of data to be processed
- Booting is a bootstrapping process that starts operating systems when the user turns on a computer system.
- The device controller is the hardware that controls the communication between the system and the peripheral drive unit. It takes care of low level operations such as error checking, moving disk heads, data transfer, and location of data on the device.
- DMA is the capability provided by some computer bus architectures that allows data to be sent directly from an attached device (such as a disk drive) to the memory on the computer's motherboard. The microprocessor is freed from involvement with the data transfer, thus speeding up overall computer operation.
- A system call is a routine that accomplishes a system-level function on behalf of a process. It is a feature built into an application program that request service from operating systems, as when a word processing program requests the use of the printer to print a document.
- The kernel is the central component of most computer operating systems. Its responsibilities include managing the system's resources and the communication between hardware and software components.

- A shell allows a user to access the kernel. Shells are actually programs that interpret command lines and run other programs. A shell can read command lines from a terminal or from a file.

The various operating system structures are:

- Simple Structure: small, simple, and limited systems
- Monolithic systems: Such an operating system is written as a collection of procedures, each of which can call any of the other procedures whenever it needs to
- Layered systems: hierarchy of layers
- Virtual Machines: The resources of the physical computer are shared to create the virtual machines.
- Client server models: splitting the operating system into two parts, one that handles client processes and one that handles the services.

Trends in operating system structures

- Microkernel architecture
- Multithreading
- Distributed operating systems
- Object-oriented design
- Symmetric multiprocessing

REVIEW QUESTIONS

1. Explain the salient features of Von Neumann computers.
2. What is the difference between primary memory and secondary storage?
3. What are interrupts? Differentiate between and interrupt and an event.
4. What are system program? Explain the different types of system programs.
5. What is a bootstrap loader? Explain the bootstrap process in detail.
6. explain the function of
   a. device controllers
   b. DMA
7. What are system calls? Explain the different types of system calls in details.
8. Differentiate between a kernel and a shell
9. Explain all the types of operating system structures in details.

10. Write a short note on the recent trends in operating systems.
11. Explain the salient features of Von Neumann computers.
12. What is the difference between primary memory and secondary storage?

FILL IN THE BLANKS

1. The _________________ is a computer design model that uses a single storage structure to hold both instructions and data
2. ____________ is a signal from a device to a computer's processor requesting the processor's attention
3. __________ is a bootstrapping process that starts operating systems when the user turns on a computer system.
4. The __________ is the hardware that controls the communication between the system and the peripheral drive unit.
5. A program under execution is called a ____________.
6. _____________ manages the system's resources and the communication between hardware and software components.
7. The first operating system that was based on such a layered structure was __________.
8. _________ are the programs that interpret command lines and run other programs.
9. In_______________, the Operating Systems are capable of distributing their process loads onto many processors.
10. In ____________ the processes are a collection of one or more threads and associated resources

TRUE OR FALSE

1. The operating system kernel is loaded into memory when the machine is started up, and stays there until the machine is turned off.
2. Primary memory is generally non-volatile.
3. (In MS-DOS, the *bootstrap loader* is placed at the ROM-BIOS.
4. The major process management system calls are those that handle the creation and deletion of processes.
5. The UNIX operating system is not layered structure.

ANSWERS

FILL IN THE BLANKS

1. Von Neumann architecture
2. Interrupt
3. booting
4. device controller
5. process
6. Kernel
7. THE
8. Shells
9. Symmetric Multi-Processing
10. Multi-threading

TRUE OR FALSE

1. TRUE
2. FALSE
3. TRUE
4. TRUE
5. FALSE

❑❑❑

UNIT-2
PROCESS MANAGEMENT UNIT

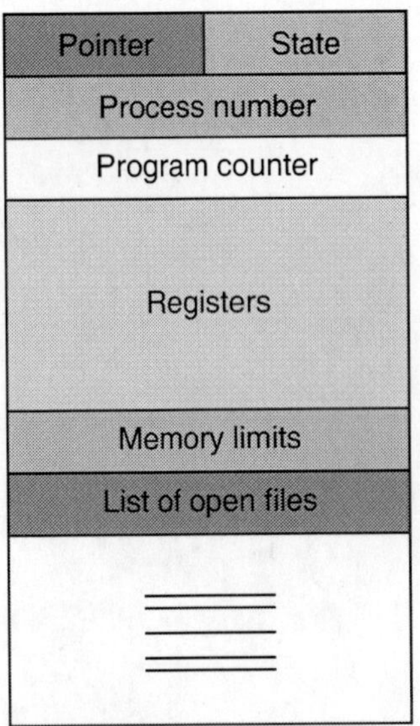

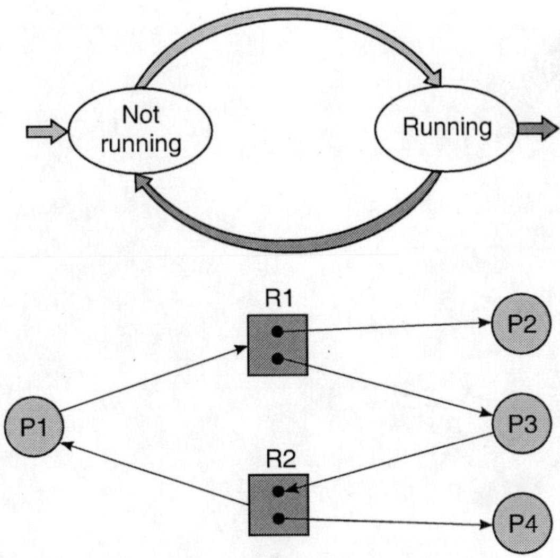

"The process of preparing programs for a digital computer is especially attractive, not only because it can be economically and scientifically rewarding, but also because it can be an aesthetic experience much like composing poetry or music." —*Donald E. Knuth*

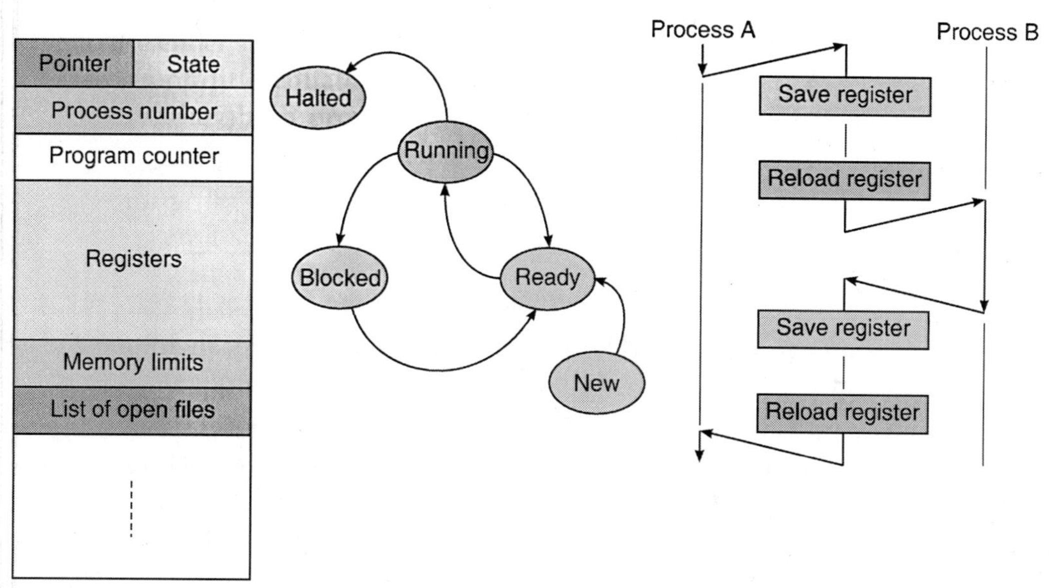

PROCESS MANAGEMENT

INTRODUCTION

The process management is an integral part of any modern day Operating System.A process is an instance of an application execution. The application may be a program written by a user, or a system application. Users may run many instances of the same application at the same time, or run many different applications. Each such running application is a process. The process only exists for the duration of executing the application.

What is a Process?

A process is an instance of a computer program that is being executed. While a program itself is just a passive collection of instructions, a process is something which actually executes those instructions.

A process is a program in execution. It also includes the value of program counter and other CPU registers, stack containing temporary data like the values of some temporary variables, and data section containing global variables. A Context for Computation a process is largely defined by:

- A program in execution
- An instance of a program running on a computer
- The entity that can be assigned to and executed on a processor
- A unit of activity characterized by the execution of a sequence of instructions, a current state, and an associated set of system resources
- Its CPU state (register values).
- Its address space (memory contents).
- Its environment (as reflected in operating system tables). Each additional level gives a wider

A process is a executing program, including the current values of the program counter, register as well as input and output values. Conceptually, each process has its own virtual CPU. In reality, the real CPU switches back and forth from process to process. To understand the system operations, it is easier to think about a collection of processes running in (pseudo) parallel than to try to keep track of how the CPU switches from process to process.

A program by itself is not a process; a program is a passive entity, while a process is an active entity. The execution of a process must progress in sequential fashion, i.e. at any point in time, one instruction is executed on behalf of process.

- A program is said to be static, i.e. it does nothing. It just sits there on disk waiting. You can think of it as a template from which processes are created.
- Processes do something, they are said to be dynamic. One can have several distinct processes running at the same time which have come from the same program. For example you can load MS Word twice and have two instances running.

In general, a process will need certain resources such as CPU time, memory, files, I/O devices etc to accomplish its tasks. These resources are allocated to the process when it is created. A single processor may be shared among several processes with some scheduling algorithm being used to determine when to stop work on one process and service a different one.

What is process management?

In processmanagement the OS must allocate resources to processes, enable processes to share and exchange information, protect the resources of each process from other processes and enable synchronisation among processes

Operating systems that support the process concept must provide some way to create all the processes needed. In simple systems, it may be possible to have all the processes that will ever be needed be present when the system comes up. In almost all systems however, some way is needed to create and destroy processes as needed during operations. In UNIX for instant, processes are created by the *fork* system call, which makes an identical copy of the calling process. In other systems, system calls exist to create a process, load its memory, and start it running. In general, processes need a way to create other processes. Each process has one parent process, but zero, one, two, or more children processes.

How does a program become a Process?

Where the Operating System is single user and single process (e.g. MS-DOS) the management of processes is really quite simple. However Operating Systems such as Windows 2003 and Linux are multi-tasking) i.e. one or more processes can be executing at the same time. Now you can begin see that things get a bit tricky.

Multiprogramming means that multiple processes are handled by the system at the same time, typically by time slicing. It is motivated by considerations of responsiveness to the users and utilization of the hardware.

"Job" and "process" are essentially synonyms. The following terms actually have slightly different meanings:

Multitasking — having multiple processes time slice on the same processor.

Multiprogramming — having multiple jobs in the system (either on the same proces- sor, or on different processors)

Multiprocessing — using multiple processors for the same job or system (i.e. parallel computing).

When there is only one CPU, multitasking and multiprogramming are the same thing. In a parallel system, you can have multiprogramming without multitasking, by running jobs on different CPUs.

Multi-tasking Operating Systems must:

1. Interleave several processes to maximise processor utilisation AND offer acceptable response times.
2. Allocate resources (memory, devices etc.) to processes equitably and yet avoid a situation where no processes can run because the resources they need are allocated elsewhere (deadlock).
3. Support inter-process communication and sharing of some resources.

4. So, how does a program become a process? Well, you, the user select a program to run (you double click on it, or you type the name of an executable file at the command line prompt). What this actually does is to invoke an Operating System routine that:
5. Checks to see if the system can cope with yet another process at present.
6. If it can it asks the resource allocator for the things this program needs e.g. memory, devices etc.
7. If the resources are available the system creates a Process Control Block (PCB) for the new process (the data structure that describes the current state of this process).
8. The new process is then marked as runnable in the PCB and put in a queue for process scheduler to give it a turn on the CPU.
9. At this point you now have a process that is waiting to get some time on the CPU. Typically the process will be on a queue with other processes that could run if they got the processor.

PROCESS STATES

The process state is defines the condition or position of a processat a perticular instance of time. As defined, a process is an independent entity with its own input values, output values, and internal state. A process often needs to interact with other processes. One process may generate some outputs that other process uses as input The process state can be defined by the two models elaborated as follows:

BASIC TWO-STATE PROCESS MODEL

The principal responsibility of the operating system is controlling the execution of processes. In the simplest process model, at any time, a process is either being executed by a processor or not. In this model, a process may be in one of two states: Running (Executing) or Not Running (Not Executing/ Idle), as shown in Figure.

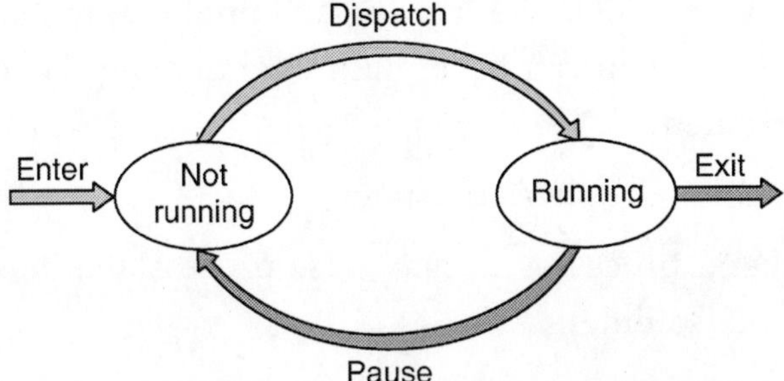

Two state process model transition diagram

When new processes enter in the system, the dispatcher schedule these processes, that is moving a non-executing process to executing state and vice versa. Therefore, the system has to keep track of the processes with their states, means when they are scheduled next time they must start executing from where they were terminated. From time to time, the currently running process will be interrupted and the dispatcher portion of the operating system will select some other process to run. If multiple processes are around, question is which process to execute; the simplest approach could be using a queue in which the suspended processes are lined up as shown in Figure. The processes that are not running should be kept in some sort of queue, waiting their turn to execute. The behavior of the dispatcher can be described in terms of queuing diagram. The process that is interrupted is transferred to the queue of waiting process. Alternatively, if the process has completed or aborted, it is discarded (exits the system). In either case, the dispatcher then selects a process form the queue to execute.

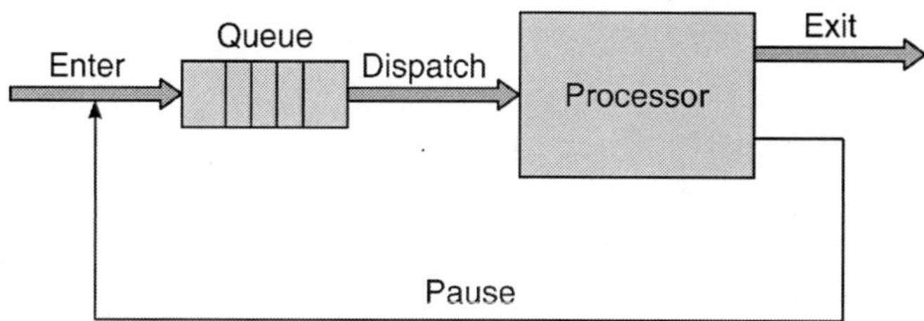

Two state process model queuing diagram

THREE-STATE PROCESS MANAGEMENT MODEL

Although the Two-State Process Management Model is a perfectly valid design for an operating system, the absence of a BLOCKED state means that the processor lies idle when the active process changes from CPU cycles to I/O cycles. This design does not make efficient use of the processor. The Three-State Process Management Model is designed to overcome this problem, by introducing a new state called the BLOCKED state. This state describes any process which is waiting for an I/O event to take place. In this case, an I/O event can mean the use of some device or a signal from another process. The three states in this model are:

- **RUNNING**: The process that is currently being executed.
- **READY**: A process that is queuing and prepared to execute when given the opportunity.
- **BLOCKED**: A process that cannot execute until some event occurs, such as the completion of an I/O operation. At any instant, a process is in one and only one of the three states. For a single processor computer, only one process can be in the RUNNING state at any one instant. There can be many processes in the READY and BLOCKED states, and each of these states will have an associated queue for processes.

Processes entering the system must go initially into the READY state, processes can only enter the RUNNING state via the READY state. Processes normally leave the system from the RUNNING state. For each of the three states, the process occupies space in main memory. While the reason for most transitions from one state to another might be obvious, some may not be so clear.

- **RUNNING-READY**

  The most common reason for this transition is that the running process has reached the maximum allowable time for uninterrupted execution; i.e. time-out occurs. Other reasons can be the imposition of priority levels as determined by the scheduling policy used for the Low Level Scheduler, and the arrival of a higher priority process into the READY state.

- **RUNNING-BLOCKED**

  A process is put into the BLOCKED state if it requests something for which it must wait. A request to the OS is usually in the form of a system call, (i.e. a call from the running process to a function that is part of the OS code). For example, requesting a file from disk or a saving a section of code or data from memory to a file on disk

- **FIVE-STATE MODEL**

  If all processes were always ready to execute, then the queuing discipline suggested by above Figure would be effective. However, even with the simple example given in the previous section, this implementation is inadequate: Some processes in the Not running state are ready to execute, while others are blocked, waiting for an I/O operation to complete. Five-state model splits the Not Running state into two states: Ready and Blocked. This model is represented in Figure as follows.

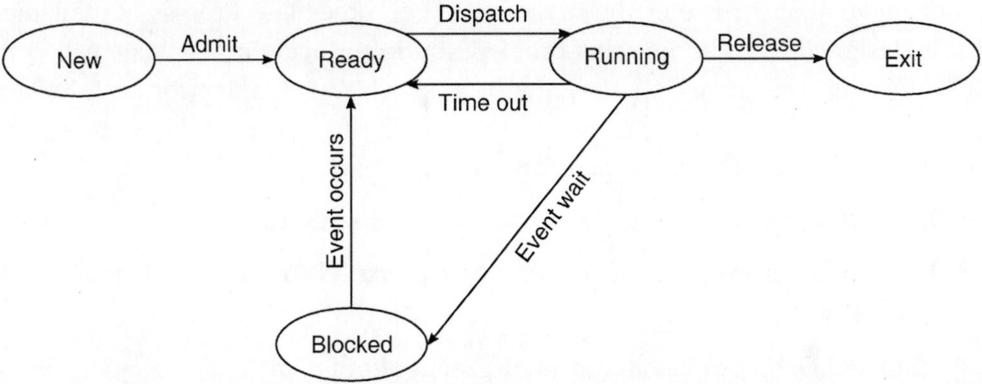

Three state process model transition diagram

The five states in this new diagram are as follows:

➢ **New:** A process that has just been created and is not admitted to the pool of executable processes by the operating system.

- **Exit:** A process that has been released from the pool of executable processes by the operating system, either because it is halted or aborted for some reason.
- **Running/Executing:** Instructions are being executed.
- **Ready:** The process is waiting its turn to go into execution by the processor.
- **Blocked/Waiting:** The process is temporarily suspended, waiting for some event to occur, e.g., an I/O function.

The possible state transitions for five-state model are:

- **NULL ? NEW:** A new process is created to execute a program. (i.e. New batch Job, Interactive logon, to provide service etc).
- **NEW ? READY:** Operating system moves a process from new state to ready state, when it is prepared to accept an additional process. There could be limit on number of processes to be admitted to the ready state.
- **READY ? RUNNING:** Any process can be moved from ready to running state. This is the job of the scheduler or dispatcher.
- **RUNNING ? EXIT:** The currently running process is terminated by the operating system if the process indicates that it has completed or if it is aborted.
- **RUNNING ? READY:** The most commonly known situation is that currently running process has reached the maximum allowable time for execution (Time out). Also, in some events a process may have to be admitted from running to ready if a high priority process has occurred.
- **RUNNING ? BLOCKED:** A process is moved to the blocked state, if it has requested some data for which it may have to wait. For example the process may have requested a resource such as data file or shared data from virtual memory[1], which is not ready at that time.
- **BLOCKED ? READY:** A process is moved to the ready state, if the event for which it has been waiting occurs.

There are two more transitions but are not shown for clarity:

- **READY ? EXIT:** In some systems, a parent may terminate a child process at any time; therefore, it will directly go to exit state.
- **BLOCKED ? EXIT:** Similarly as above, during the execution of a parent process any child process waiting for an event to occur may directly go to exit if the parent itself terminates.

Another example of process state model

In the shell command

cat chapter1 chapter2 chapter3 | grep tree

the first process, running *cat*, concatenates and outputs three files. Depending on the relative speed of the two processes, it may happen that *grep* is ready to run, but there is no input waiting for it. It must then block until some input is available. It is also possible for a process that is ready and able to run to be blocked because the operating system decided to allocate the CPU to other process for a while. There are typical three states of a process:

a) **Running** (actually using the CPU at that instant);

b) **Blocked** (unable to run until some external event happens);

c) **Ready** (runnable; temporarily stopped to let another process run).

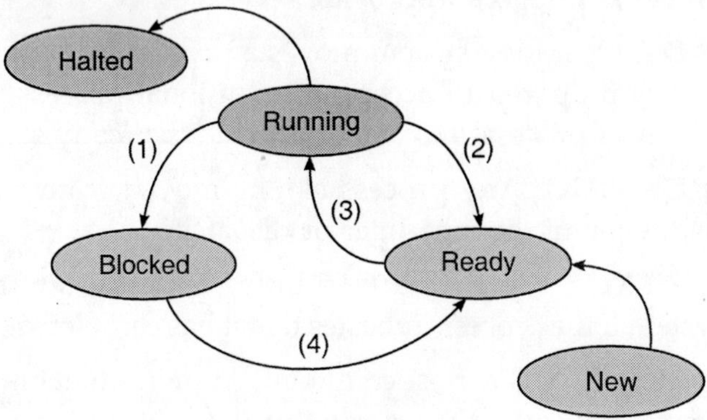

(1) Process blocks for input
(2) Scheduler picks another process
(3) Scheduler picks this process
(4) Input becomes available

Typical process states

As shown in the fig, four transitions are possible among these three states. Transition 1 appears when a process discovers that it cannot continue. In order to get into blocked state, some systems must execute a system call *block*. In other systems, when a process reads from a pipe or special file and there is no input available, the process is automatically blocked.

Transition 2 and 3 are caused by the process scheduler, a part of the operating system. Transition 2 occurs when the scheduler decides that the running process has run long enough, and it is time to let another process have some CPU time. Transition 3 occurs when all other processes have had their share and it is time for the first process to run again. Transition 4 appears when the external event for which a process was waiting happens. If no other process is running at that instant, transition 3 will be triggered immediately, and the process will start running. Otherwise it may have to wait in ready state for a little while until the CPU is available.

Using the process model, it becomes easier to think about what is going on inside the system. There are many processes like user processes, disk processes, terminal processes, and so on, which may be blocked when they are waiting for some thing happen. When the disk block has been read or the character typed, the process waiting for it is unblock and is ready to run again.

The process model, an integral part of a operating system, can be summarized as follows. The lowest level of the operating system is the scheduler with a number of processes on top of it. All the process handling, such as starting and stopping processes, are done by the scheduler.

IMPLEMENTATION OF PROCESSES

To implement the process model, the operating system maintains a table, an array of structures, called the *process table*. Each entry identifies a process with information such as process state, its program counter, stack pointer, memory allocation, the status of its open files, its accounting and scheduling information.

Each process is identified with its own process control block, PCB, which is a data block containing all information associated with this process.

What is PCB?

Process Control Blockor PCB is a dynamic structure resident in memory which stores information about each process.

Typical information may include:

- Process state, which may be new, ready, running, waiting or halted;
- Program counter, which indicates the address of the next instruction to be executed for this process;
- CPU registers, which vary in number and type, depending on the concrete microprocessor architecture;
- Memory management information, which include base and bounds registers or page table;
- I/O status information, composed I/O requests, I/O devices allocated to this process, a list of open files and so on;
- CPU scheduling information, which includes process priority, pointers to scheduling queues and any other scheduling parameters.

A PCB structure is shown as follows:

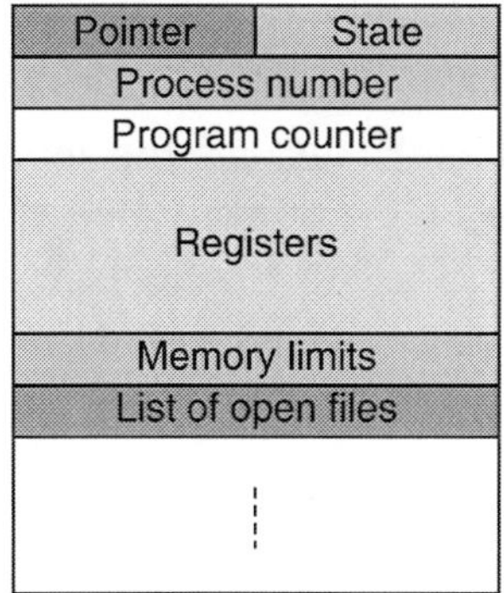

Process Control Block Structure

A process may create several new processes during its time of execution. The creating process is called parent process, while the new processes are called children processes. There are different possibilities concerning creating new processes:

- Execution: the parent process continues to execute concurrently with its children processes or it waits until all of its children processes have terminated (sequential).
- Sharing: either the parent and children processes share all resources (likes memory or files) or the children processes share only a subset of their parent's resources or the parent and children processes share no resources in common.

  A parent process can terminate the execution of one of its children for one of theses reasons:
- The child process has exceeded its usage of the resources it has been allocated. In order to do this, a mechanism must be available to allow the parent process to inspect the state of its children processes.
- The task assigned to the child process is no longer required.

  We distinguish between *independent* process and *cooperating* process. A process is independent if it cannot affect or be affected by other processes executing in the system. This type of processes has following features:
- Its state is not shared in any way by any other process.
- Its execution is deterministic, i.e. the results of execution depend only on the input values.
- Its execution is reproducible, i.e., the results of execution will always be the same for the same input.
- Its execution can be stopped and restarted without any negative effect.

In contrast to independent processes, cooperating processes can affect or be affected by other processes executing in the system. They are characterized by:

- Their states are shared by other processes;
- Its execution is not deterministic, i.e., the results of execution depend on relative execution sequence and can not be predicted in advance;
- Its execution is irreproducible, i.e., the results of execution are not always the same for the same input.

CONTEXT SWITCHING

The PCB must contain everything about the process that must be saved when the process is switched from the running state to the ready state so that it can be restarted later as if it had never been stopped. The switching between two processes is called context switching and it is illustrated by the figure.

What is context switching ?

Context switching is the process of saving an executing thread or process and transferring control to another thread or process

Associated with each I/O device is a location near the bottom of memory called the interrupt vector. It contains the address of the interrupt service procedure. Suppose a user process j is running when a network interrupt occurs. The program counter, program status word, and possibly one or more registers are pushed onto the stack by the interrupt hardware. The CPU then jumps to the address specified in the network interrupt vector. The network interrupt service procedure starts out by saving all the registers in the process table entry for the current process. The current process number and a pointer to its entry are kept in global variables, so they can be founded quickly. The information deposited by the interrupt is removed from the stack, and the stack pointer is set to a temporary stack used by the process handler.

Now the network process can be started; it is changed from blocked to ready, and the scheduler is called. Normally, different processes have different priorities. If the network process is now the highest priority runnable process, it will be scheduled to run. If the process that was interrupted is just as important or more so, then it will be scheduled to run again, and the network process will have to wait a little while.

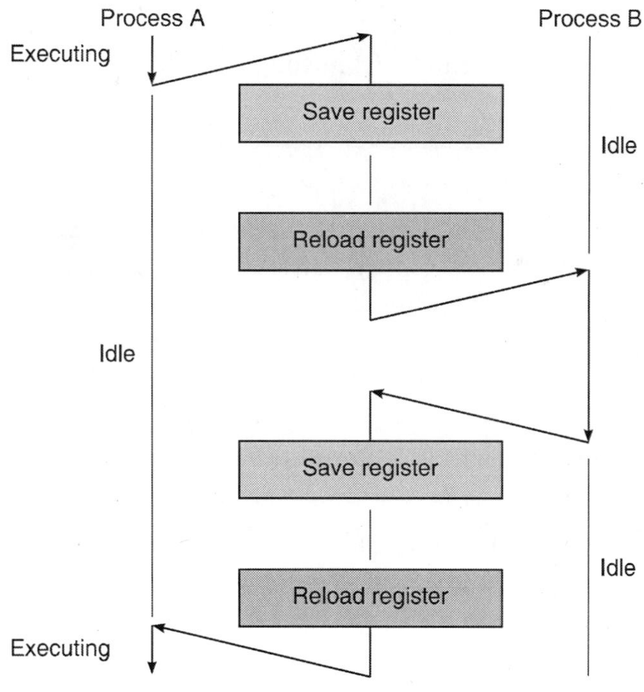

Process context switching

The CPU is said to operate in the context of a process. The context defines the environment for the CPU while it is running one particular process. When the CPU runs another process it executes in the context of the other process. The operating system must save enough status information for a process so that it can at a future time switch back to an earlier process and continue execution at the point where it left off. It does this by saving the necessary status information for a process in the context section of the process PCB.

The switching from one process to another is normally done under interrupt control. When a process is switched from the ready state to allow another process to run some specific steps are required. As an example assume that process A is running and process B is to be switched in as the running process:

1) On receipt of an interrupt the processor will save the machine status to Process A's PCB.
2) Other status information (e.g. open files) is stored to process_A's PCB.
3) The dispatcher will select the next most suitable process to run, process B in this example.
4) Process A's PCB is put to the ready queue. Process A's PCB pointers are updated to set its queue position and the PCB state field is updated. (If process A had, in fact, finished processing, its PCB would now be freed up).
5) Process B's PCB state field is set to running. The machine status and other information from process B's PCB is restored (context is switched). Process B can now continue execution from the point where it left off at its previous context switch.

PROCESS QUEUES

The operating system will maintain a list of all existing processes in a central process table, consisting of process PCB entries. Using pointers a number of separate queues can be established within this table. Only one process may be in the running state at one time. A number of processes may be in the ready state and a number of processes may be in the blocked state at any given time.

The processes in the ready state are maintained in a ready-to-run list. The processes in this list are ordered by priority so that the process at the head of the list is always the next process to run.

Where there is more than one blocked process awaiting the same event, the blocked processes may also be maintained in some priority order although it is common to queue blocked processes on a first-come-first-served basis. The can be several blocked queues, each queue corresponding to an event being waited upon.

EXAMPLE QUEUES

The number in brackets indicates process priority. This is a snap-shot of a system at some point in time.

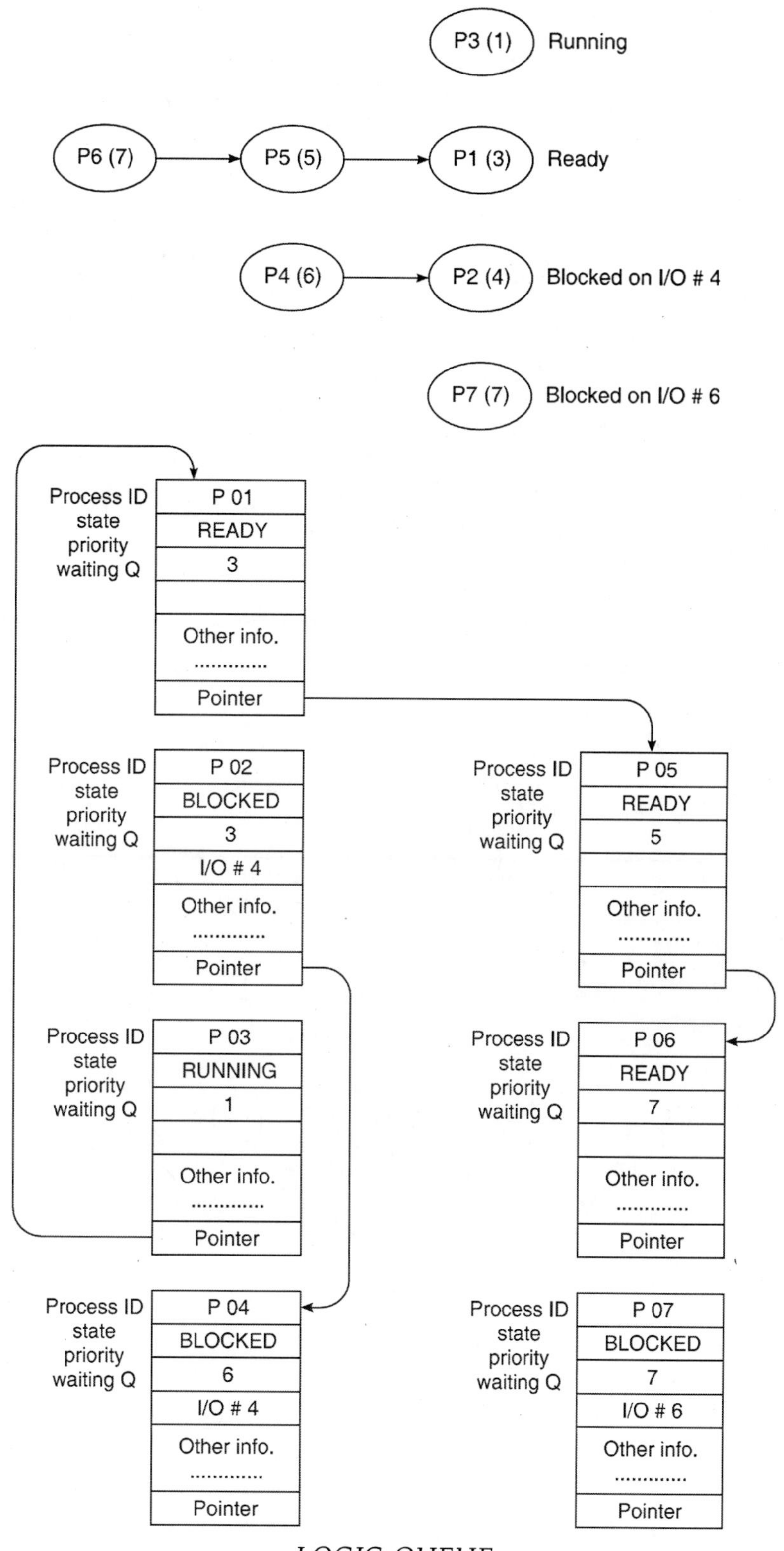
P3 (1)
Running
P6 (7)
P5 (5)
P1 (3)
Ready
P4 (6)
P2 (4)
Blocked on I/O # 4
P7 (7)
Blocked on I/O # 6
Process ID
state
priority
waiting Q
P 01
READY
3
Other info.
....
Pointer
P 02
BLOCKED
3
I/O # 4
Other info.
....
Pointer
P 03
RUNNING
1
Other info.
....
Pointer
P 04
BLOCKED
6
I/O # 4
Other info.
....
Pointer
P 05
READY
5
Other info.
....
Pointer
P 06
READY
7
Other info.
....
Pointer
P 07
BLOCKED
7
I/O # 6
Other info.
....
Pointer

LOGIC QUEUE

These queues are shown in more detail below where the PCBs are organised in logical queues to represent the system processes. Note, it is common to arrange logical queues so that the running process is at the head of the ready queue.

CREATION OF A PROCESS

A process is created with a name and an initial priority level. A **PCB** is generated and inserted in the process table. The process resources are allocated.

Processes are most often created by one process spawning another process. An identical copy of the calling process is thus created. The calling process is referred to as the **parent process** and the newly created process is referred to as the **child process**. A child process can spawn new processes. In this manner a whole tree of processes can be created. Each process will have only one parent but any process can have a number of child processes.

DESTRUCTION OF A PROCESS

When a process is destroyed it is removed from the system tables. The process' **PCB** is removed. Some operating systems destroy all of the parent's child processes when the parent process is removed. Other operating systems will allow child processes to continue to exist in the absence of the parent process.

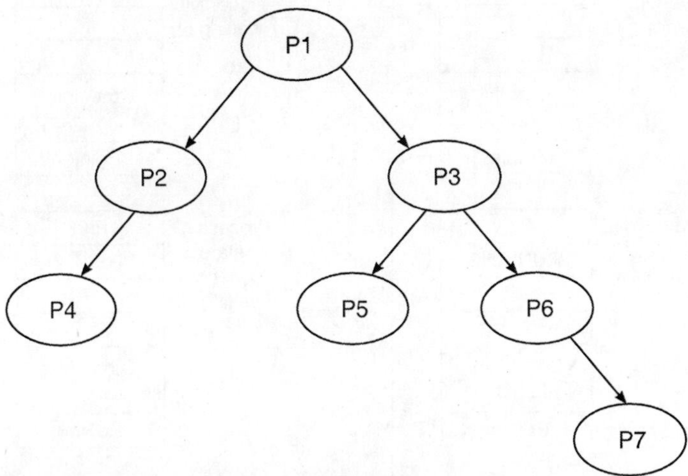

USER PROCESSES AND SYSTEM PROCESSES

System resources are managed by system processes (kernel level processes) and often referred as resource managers. These processes should not compete for system resources since they are the managers of the resources. The system processes are assigned a set of resources which they control within the system. User processes compete for system resources by making service requests (system calls). A user process cannot do any direct I/O operations. Using a system service request, a user process asks the operating system to perform a function on behalf of the process.

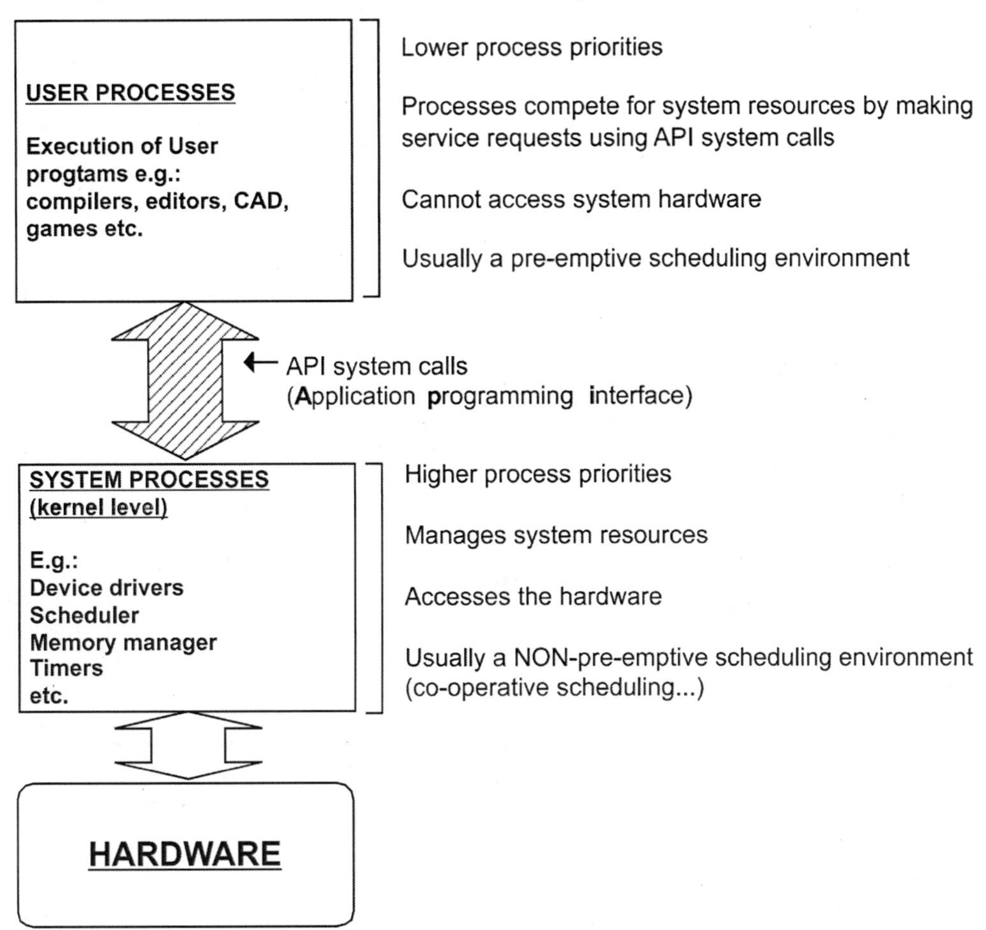

User processes and kernel processes

CONCURRENT PROCESSES

In multitasking systems several programs can be executed at the same time (or apparently at the same time). This simultaneous execution is known as **concurrency**.

To achieve such concurrency each process can run on a separate processor. However, processors are expensive devices and it is much more common to have just one processor in a system. By switching the processor from one process to another at short intervals of time an apparent concurrency is achieved on the single processor.

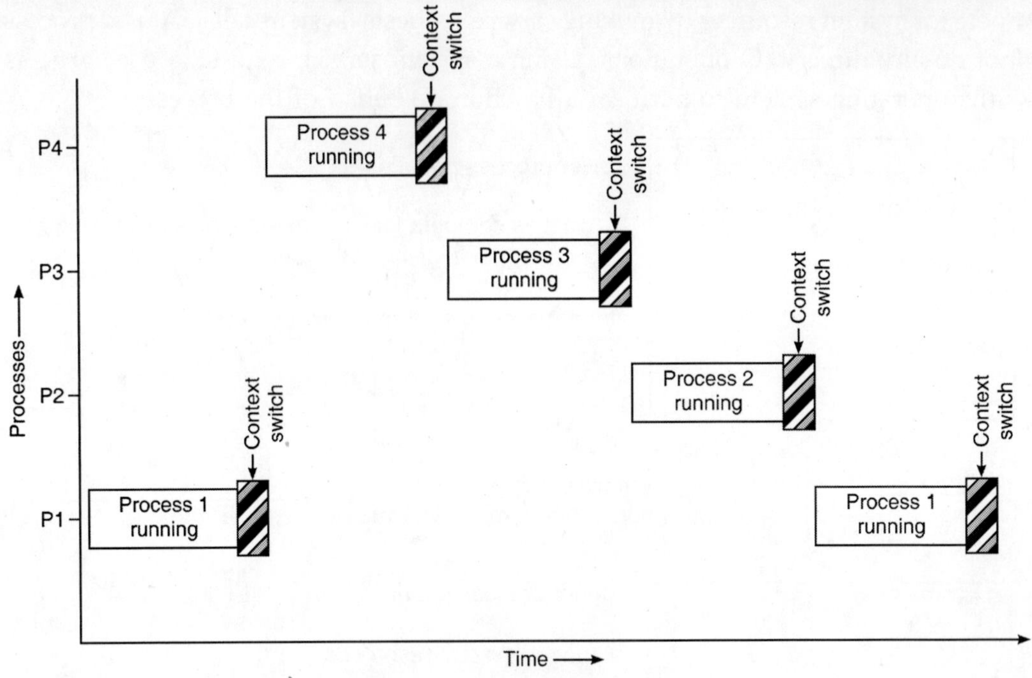

Pseudo-parallelism

Such a system gives the illusion of parallelism, sometimes referred to as pseudo-parallelism. As the CPU (the Central Processing Unit – or simply the *processor*) switches from process to process, so conceptually each process has its own CPU.

The sequence in which processes are allocated the CPU and the duration of each allocation is the subject of operating system design.

UNIPROGRAMMING AND MULTIPROGRAMMING:

The main task of an operating system is to manage a set of processes. In the simplest case (uniprogramming), there is only one process to manage. In uniprogramming processor spends a certain amount of time executing, until it reaches an I/O instructions. It must then waits until that I/O instruction concludes before proceeding (Fig. a). A mode of operation that provides interleaved execution of two ore more computer programs by a single processor is called multiprogramming. In multiprogramming; when one job needs to wait for I/O, the processor can switch to the other job (Fig b). As a result multiprogramming improves the performance.

While a job doing I/O, why should the CPU set idle? Solution of it is that to partition the memory into several pieces with a different job in each part, in other words this is called multiprogramming. On a one CPU system, there is, at any given time, at most only one current process, i.e. there is only one process that is executing for each time period. There may be many processes that wish to use CPU, on one task of the operating system kernel is scheduling, i.e. determining which processes should be current at any given time. Of course, on a system with multiple CPUs, there can be more than one current process, but at most one per CPU.

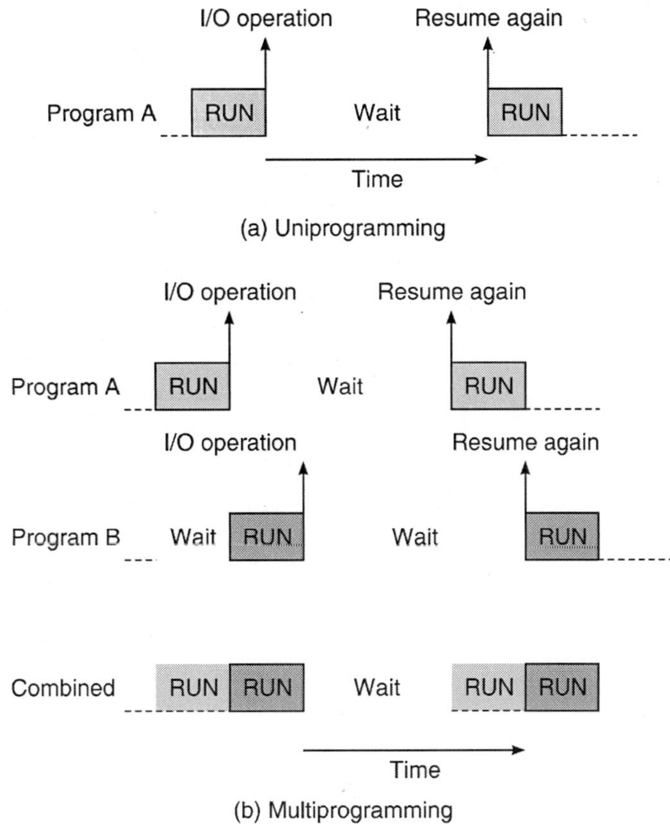

(a) Uniprogramming

(b) Multiprogramming

Example 1:

Consider a computer system with 250Mbytes of available memory (not used by OS), a disk, a terminal, and a printer. The programs JOB1, JOB2 and JOB3 are submitted for execution at the same time. Assume that; Heavy compute (JOB1) uses 70% of total processor resource and Heavy I/O (JOB2 and JOB3) uses only 10% of the total processor resource.

	JOB1	JOB2	JOB3
Type of job	Heavy compute	Heavy I/o	**Heavy I/o**
Duration	5 min	15 min	**10 min**
Memory required	50 M	100 M	**75 M**
Need disk?	NO	NO	**YES**
Need terminal?	NO	YES	**NO**
Need printer?	**NO**	**NO**	**YES**

(a) Calculate the Processor utilization with and without multiprogramming

<table>
<tr><td>

Uniprogramming:

Processor use % =

= (5×70+15×10+10×10)/30

= 20%

</td><td>

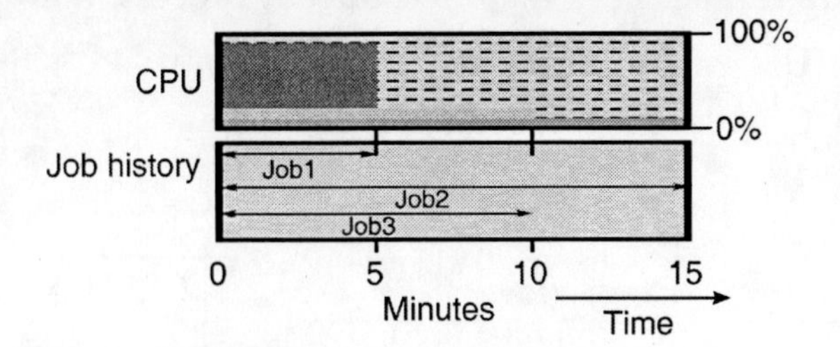

</td></tr>
<tr><td>

Multiprogramming:

0-5 mins = (70+10+10) = 90 %

5-10 mins = (10+10) = 20 %

10-15 mins = (10) = 10 %

Processor use %

=(5×90+5×20+5×10)/15

=40%

</td><td>

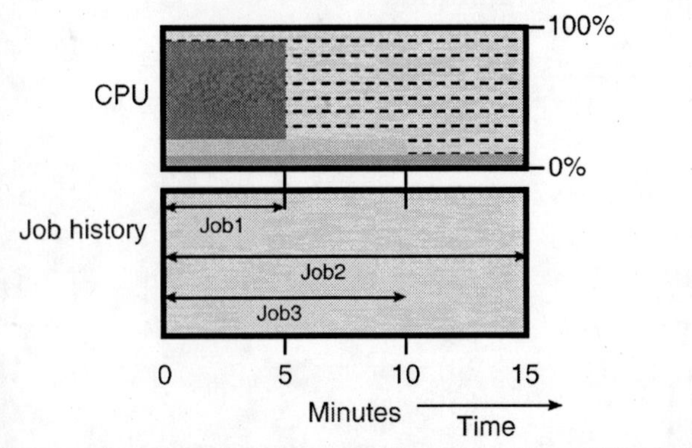

</td></tr>
</table>

Uniprogramming:

Total Memory 250 Mbytes

Job1 = 50/250 = 0.2, 20 % - for 5 min

Job2 = 100/250 = 0.4, 40 % - for 15 min

Job3 = 75/250 = 0.3, 30 % - for 10 min

Memory use % = (5×20+15×40+10×30)/30=33.3%

Multiprogramming:

Total Memory 250 Mbytes

0-5 mins = (50+100+75)/250 = 90 %

5-10 mins = (100+75)/250 = 70 %

10-15 mins = 100/250 = 40 %

Memory use % =(5×90+5×70+5×40)/15 =67%

a. Calculate the Disk utilization with and without multiprogramming.

Uniprogramming: Only a single process can use disk at a time, that's why disk usage is always 100% for a particular job. Disk use % = (5×0+15×0+10×100)/30=33.3%
Multiprogramming: Disk use % =(10×100+5×0)/15 =67%

Example 2:

Assume we have two processes A and B, each process executes for 1 millisecond and then does I/O for 2 milliseconds, and these process are repeated 5 times. Find the processor utilization without multiprogramming and with multiprogramming. Assume no contention for resources.

Solution:

Without multiprogramming (uniprogramming)

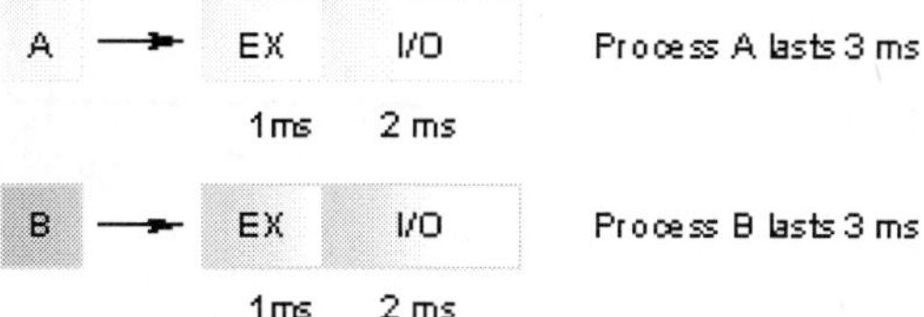

It took 30 milliseconds to run processes A and B. However, the processor was idle for 20 milliseconds (i.e. processor spends 10*2ms=20ms for I/O operations);

$$\text{Procesor utilization} = \frac{10ms}{30ms} = 0.33,\ 33\%$$

WITH MULTIPROGRAMMING

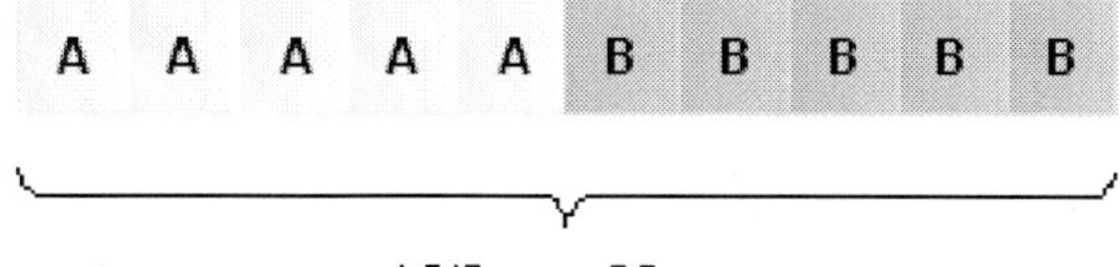

It took only 16 milliseconds to run processes A and B.

Processor executes for 10*1ms=10ms (idle for only 6 ms)

Procesor utilization = = 0.625, 62.5%

Note that: *The combined process table is;*

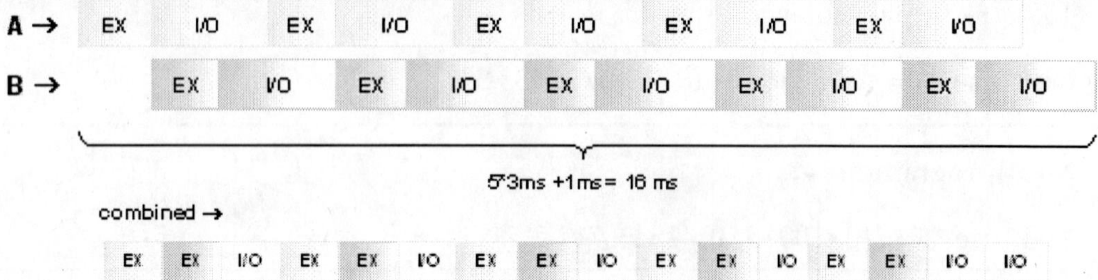

Example 3:

Assume we have two processes A and B, each process executes for 2 milliseconds and then does I/O for 2 milliseconds, and these processes are repeated 3 times. Find the processor utilization without multiprogramming and with multiprogramming. Assume no contention for resources.

Solution:

Without multiprogramming the process table can be drown as:

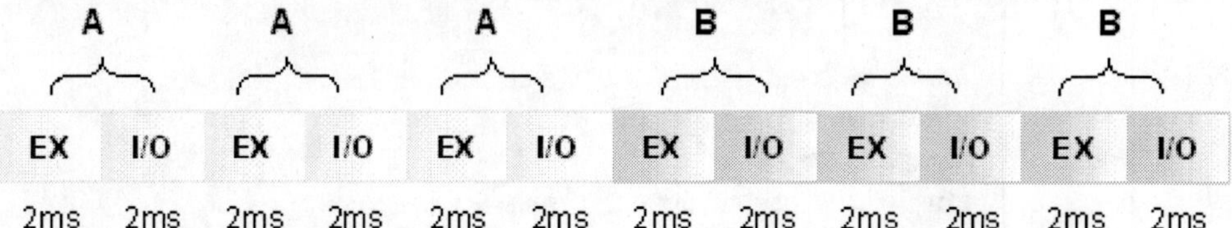

It took 24 milliseconds to run processes A and B. However, the processor was idle for 12 milliseconds.

Procesor utilization = = 0.5, 50%

With multiprogramming

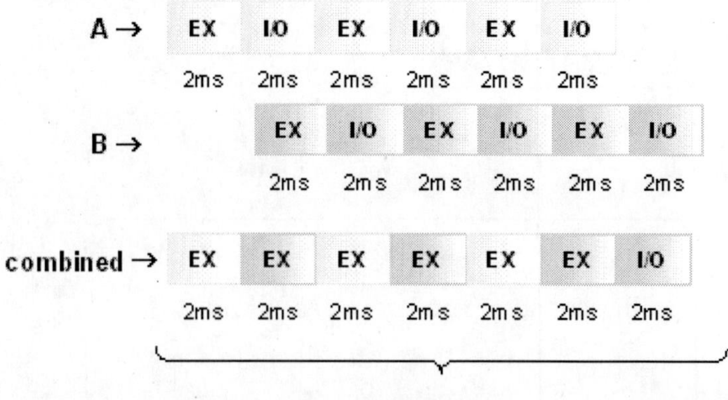

It took 14 milliseconds to run processes A and B. The processor was idle for only 2 milliseconds.

Procesor utilization = = 0.86, 86%

As seen, processor utilization is only 50% by uniprogramming, by employing multiprogramming the processor efficient is significantly improved, i.e. 86%.

Example 4:

Assume we have two processes A and B. Process A executes for 1 millisecond and then does I/O for 2 milliseconds, then executes for 2 milliseconds and does I/O for 4 milliseconds. Process B executes for 1 millisecond and then does I/O for 2 milliseconds. Assume both of the process needs to use the same resources (contention for resources). Find the processor utilization without multiprogramming and with multiprogramming.

Solution:

Without multiprogramming (uniprogramming)

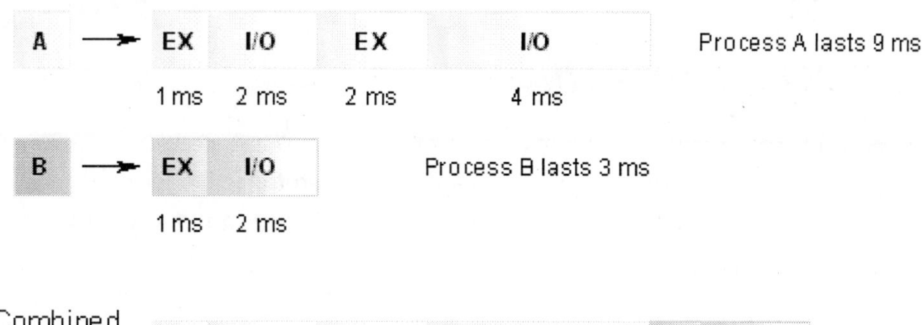

It took 12 milliseconds to run processes A and B. However, the processor was idle for 8 milliseconds.

Procesor utilization = = 0.33, 33%

With multiprogramming

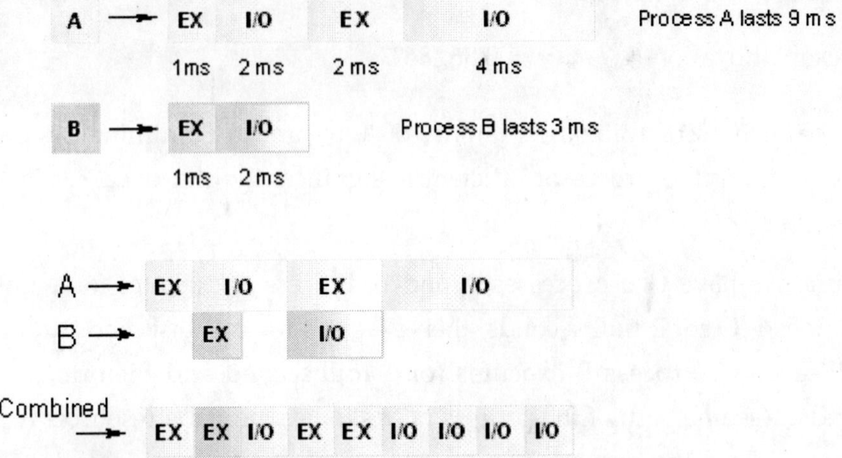

It took only 9 milliseconds to run processes A and B.

Processor executes for 4ms (idle for only 5 ms)

Procesor utilization = $\frac{4ms}{9ms}$ = 0.44, 44%

INTERPROCESS COMMUNICATION

Principally, there exist two complementary interprocess communication types: a) shared-memory system and b) message-passing system. It is clear that these two schemes are not mutually exclusive, and could be used simultaneously within a single operating system.

SHARED-MEMORY SYSTEM

Shared-memory systems require communication processes to share some variables. The processes are expected to exchange information through the use of these shared variables. In a shared-memory scheme, the responsibility for providing communication rests with the application programmers. The operating system only needs to provide shared memory.

The sharing of main memory among processes is useful to permit efficient and close interaction among processes Consider the following sequence:

1. Process P1 invokes the echo procedure and is interrupted immediately after getchar returns its value and stores it in chin. At this point, the most recently entered character, x, is stored in variable chin.

2. Process P2 is activated and invokes the echo procedure, which runs to conclusion, inputting and then displaying a single character, y, on the screen.
3. Process P1 is resumed. By this time, the value x has been overwritten in chin and therefore lost. Instead, chin contains y, which is transferred to chout and displayed.

Thus, the first character is lost and the second character is displayed twice. Because of shared global variable, chin. If one process updates the global variable and then is interrupted, another .process may alter the variable before the first process can use its value. However, if only one process at a time may be in that procedure. Then the foregoing sequence would result in the following:

1. Process P1 invokes the echo procedure and is interrupted immediately after the conclusion of the input function. At this point, the most recently entered character, x, is stored in variable chin.
2. Process P2 is activated and invokes the echo procedure. However, because P1 is still inside the echo procedure, although currently suspended, P2 is blocked from entering the procedure. Therefore, P2 is suspended awaiting the availability of the echo procedure.
3. At some later time, process PI is resumed and completes execution of echo. The proper character, x, is displayed.
4. When PI exits' echo, this removes the block on P2. When P2 is later resumed, the echo procedure is successfully invoked.

Therefore it is necessary to protect shared global variables. And that the only way to do that is to control the code that accesses the variable.

Race Condition :

A race condition occurs when multiple processes read and write data items so that the final result depends on the order of execution of instructions in the multiple processes.

A critical problem occuring in shared-memory system is that two or more processes are reading or writing some shared variables or shared data, and the final results depend on who runs precisely and when. Such situations are called ***race conditions****.*

Suppose that two processes, P1 and P2, share the global variable a. At some point in its execution, P1 updates a to the value 1, and at some point in its execution, P2 updates a to the value 2. Thus, the two tasks are in a race to write variable a. In this example the "loser" of the race (the process that updates last) determines the final value of a.

Therefore Operating System Concerns of following things

1. The operating system must be able to keep track of the various processes

2. The operating system must allocate and deallocate various resources for each active process.
3. The operating system must protect the data and physical resources of each process against unintended interference by other processes.
4. The functioning of a process, and the output it produces, must be independent of the speed at which its execution is carried out relative to the speed of other concurrent processes.

Process Interaction can be defined as:

- Processes unaware of each other
- Processes indirectly aware of each other
- Processes directly aware of each other

Concurrent processes come into conflict with each other when they are competing for the use of the same resource.

Two or more processes need to access a resource during the course of their execution. Each process is unaware of the existence of the other processes. There is noexchange of information between the competing processes. However, the execution of one process may affect the behavior of competing processes. If two processes both wish access to a single resource, then one process will be allocated that resource by the operating system, and the other will have to wait.

In the case of competing processes three control problems must be faced. First is the need for mutual exclusion.

Mutual exclusion (often abbreviated to mutex) algorithms are used in concurrent programming to avoid the simultaneous use of a common resource, such as a global variable, by pieces of computer code called critical sections

Suppose two or more processes require access to a single nonsharable resource, such as a printer. During the course of execution, each process will be sending commands to the I/O device-receiving status information, sending data, and/or receiving data. Such a resource as a critical resource, and the portion of the program that uses it a critical section of the program. It is important that only one program at a time be allowed in its critical section. In the following paragraph, we explain briefly some proposals for achieving mutual exclusion.

DISABLING INTERRUPTS

The simplest method is to have each process disable all interrupts just after entering its critical region and re-enable them just before leaving it. Because the CPU can only be switched from one process to another as a result of interrupt, disabling interrupts will prevent the CPU being switched to another process. Thus, once a process has disabled interrupts, it can examine and update the shared-memory without the fear that any other process will intervene.

Beside the mutual exclusion as an result, disabling interrupt may cause problem as well. Consider the following example. It is frequently convenient for the kernel itself to disable interrupts for a few instructions while it is updating variables or lists. If an interrupt occurred while the list of ready processes was in an inconsistent state, race conditions could occur. We see, that disabling interrupt is not appropriate as a general mutual exclusion technique for user processes.

LOCKING VARIABLES

Another mutual exclusion method is the software solution, called lock variables. Suppose having a single, shared, lock variable initialized to 0. When a process wants to enter its critical region, it first tests the lock. If the lock is 0, i.e. no process is in its critical region, the process sets it to 1 (i.e. some process is in its critical region) and enters the critical region. Otherwise, the process has to wait until the lock becomes 0.

In this case, it is not sure that race conditions will not appear. Suppose one process tests the lock and sees that it is 0. Before it can set the lock to 1, another process is scheduled, run and set the lock to 1. Thus, when the first process runs again, it will also set the lock to 1, and so two processes will be in their critical regions at the same time.

SEMAPHORES

The effective synchronization tools often used to realize mutual exclusion in more complex systems are semaphore.

Semaphore are shared variables that some operating system provide for concurrent programming

A semaphore S is an integer variable which can be accessed only through two standard atomic operation: wait and signal. The definition of the wait and signal operation are:

wait(S): while S ≤ 0 do skip;

S := S – 1;

signal(S): S := S + 1;

It should be noted that the test (S ≤ 0) and modification of the integer value of S (S := S – 1) must be executed without interruption. In general, if one process modifies the integer value of S in the wait and signal operations, no other process can simultaneously modify that same S value.

We briefly explain the usage of semaphores in the following example. Consider two currently running processes: P_1 with a statement S_1 and P_2 with a statement S_2. Suppose that we require that S_2 be executed only after S_1 has completed. This scheme can be implemented by letting P_1 and P_2 share a common semaphore *synch*, initialized to 0, and by inserting the statements:

S_1;

signal(synch);

in the process P_1 and the statements:

wait(synch);

S_2;

in the process P_2. Since *synch* is initialized to 0, P_2 will execute S_2 only after P_1 has involved signal(synch), which is after S_1.

The disadvantage of the semaphore definition given above is that it requires *busy-waiting*, i.e., while a process is in its critical region, any either process it trying to enter its critical region must continuously loop in the entry code. It's clear that through busy-waiting, CPU cycles are wasted that some other processes might use productively.

To overcome busy-waiting, we modify the definition of the wait and signal operations. When a process executes the wait operation and finds that the semaphore value is not positive, the process *blocks* itself. The block operation places the process into a waiting state. Using a scheduler the CPU then can be allocated to other processes which are ready to run.

A process that is blocked, i.e. waiting on a semaphore S, should be restarted by the execution of a signal operation by some other processes, which changes its state from blocked to ready. To implement a semaphore under this condition, we define a semaphore as a record:

```
type semaphore = record
                    value := integer;
                    L: list of processes;
                 end;
```

Each semaphore has an integer value and a list of processes. When a process must wait on a semaphore, it is added to this list. A signal operation removes one process from the list of waiting processes, and awakens it. The semaphore operation can be now defined as follows:

```
wait(S):  S.value := S.value – 1;
    if   S.value < 0
    then begin
                    add this process to S.L;
                    block;
              end;

signal(S): S.value := S.value + 1;
    if     S.value ≤ 0
    then   begin
                remove a process from S.L;
                wakeup(P);
     end;
```

The block operation suspends the process. The wakeup(P) operation resumes the execution of a blocked process P. These two operations are provided by the operating system as basic system calls.

One of the almost critical problem concerning implementing semaphore is the situation where two or more processes are waiting *indefinitely* for an event that can be only caused by one of the waiting processes: these processes are said to be *deadlocked*. To illustrate this, consider a system consisting of two processes P_1 and P_2, each accessing two semaphores S and Q, set to the value one:

```
P1              P2
wait(S);        wait(Q);
wait(Q);        wait(S);
...             ...
signal(S);   signal(Q);
signal(Q);   signal(S);
```

Suppose P_1 executes wait(S) and then P_2 executes wait(Q). When P_1 executes wait(Q), it must wait until P_2 executes signal(Q). It is no problem, P_2 executes wait(Q), then signal(Q). Similarly, when P_2 executes wait(S), it must wait until P_1 executes signal(S). Thus these signal operations can not be carried out, P_1 and P_2 are deadlocked. It is clear, that a set of processes are in a deadlocked state, when every process in the set is waiting for an event that can only be caused by another process in the set.

MESSAGE-PASSING SYSTEM

Message passing systems allow communication processes to exchange messages. In this scheme, the responsibility rests with the operating system itself.

The function of a message-passing system is to allow processes to communicate with each other without the need to resort to shared variable. An interprocess communication facility basically provides two operation: *send* (message) and *receive* (message). In order to send and to receive messages, a communication link must exist between two involved processes. This link can be implemented in different ways. The possible basic implementation questions are:

- How are links established?
- Can a link be associated with more than two processes?
- How many links can there be between every pair of process?
- What is the capacity of a link? That is, does the link have some buffer space? If so, how much?
- What is the size of the message? Can the link accommodate variable size or fixed-size message?
- Is the link unidirectional or bi-directional?

In the following we consider several methods for logically implementing a communication link and the send/receive operations. These methods can be classified into two categories: a) Naming, consisting of direct and indirect communication and b) Buffering, consisting of capacity and messages proprieties.

DIRECT COMMUNICATION

In direct communication, each process that wants to send or receive a message must explicitly name the recipient or sender of the communication. In this case, the send and receive primitives are defined as follows:

send(P, message): Send a message to process P;

receive(Q, message): Receive a message from process Q;

This scheme shows the *symmetry* in addressing, i.e. both the sender and the receiver have to name one another in order to communicate. In contrast to this, *asymmetry* in addressing can be used, i.e. only the sender has to name the recipient; the recipient is not required to name the sender. So the send and receive primitives can be defined as follows:

send(P, message): Send a message to the process P;

receive(id, message): Receive a message from any process; id is set to the name of the process with whom the communication has taken place.

INDIRECT COMMUNICATION

With indirect communication, the messages are sent to, and received from a *mailbox*. A mailbox can be abstractly viewed as an object into which messages may be placed and from which messages may be removed by processes. In order to distinguish one from each other, each mailbox owns a unique identification. A process may communicate with some other process by a number of different mailboxes. The send and receive primitives are defined as follows:

send(A, message): Send a message to the mailbox A;

receive(A, message): Receive a message from the mailbox A;

Mailboxes may be owned either by a process or by the system. If the mailbox is owned by a process, then we distinguish between the *owner* who can only receive from this mailbox and *user* who can only send message to the mailbox. When a process that owns a mailbox terminates, its mailbox disappears. Any process that sends a message to this mailbox must be notified in the form of an exception that the mailbox no longer exists.

If the mailbox is owned by the operating system, then it has an existence of its own, i.e., it is independent and not attached to any particular process. The operating system provides a mechanism that allows a process to: a) create a new mailbox, b) send and receive message through the mailbox and c) destroy a mailbox. Since all processes with access rights to a mailbox may terminate, a mailbox may no longer be accessible by any process after some time. In this case, the operating system should reclaim whatever space was used for the mailbox.

CAPACITY LINK

A link has some capacity that determines the number of messages that can temporarily reside in it. This propriety can be viewed as a queue of messages attached to the link. Basically there are three ways such a queue can be implemented:

- *Zero capacity:* the link has a message queue length of zero, i.e. no message can wait in it. The sender must wait until the recipient receives the message. The two processes must be synchronized for a message transfer to take place. The zero-capacity link is referred to as a message-passing system without buffering.
- *Bounded capacity:* the link has a limited message queue length of *n*, i.e., at most *n* messages can reside in it. If a new message is sent, and the queue is not full, it is placed in the queue either by copying the message or by keeping a pointer to the message and the sender continue execution without waiting. Otherwise, the sender must be delayed until space is available in the queue.

➢ *Unbounded capacity*: the queue has potentially infinite length, i.e. any number of messages can wait in it. That why the sender is never delayed.

Bounded and unbounded capacity link provide message-passing system with automatic buffering.

MESSAGES

Messages sent by a process may be one of three varieties: a) fixed-sized, b) variable-sized and c) typed messages. If only fixed-size messages can be sent, the physical implementation is straightforward. However, this makes the task of programming more difficult. On the other hand, variable-size messages require more complex physical implementation, but the programming becomes simpler. Typed messages, i.e., associating a type with each mailbox, are applicable only to indirect communication. The messages that can be sent to, and received from a mailbox are restricted to the designated type.

EXCEPTION CONDITIONS

In a distributed computing environment, where communication between different processes is needed, the probability that an error will occur is relative higher than in an single-machine environment. If message-passing systems are implemented in shared memory in a single-machine, the entire system fails if failure occurs. However, in a distributed environment, message-passing systems are usually handled by communication lines, and the failure of one site doesn't necessary result in the failure of the entire system.

Normally, failure events are called exception conditions and this case, some error recovery mechanism, i.e., exception condition handling, must take place. Such mechanisms are discussed briefly below.

PROCESS TERMINATES

If a sender or recipient terminates before a message is processed, it will leave a message that will never be received or processes waiting for messages that will never be sent. Two cases are possible:

➢ A recipient process P may wait for a message from a process Q that has terminated. If no action is taken, P will be blocked forever. In this case, the system should either terminate process P or inform P that process Q has terminated.

➢ Process P may send a message to a process Q that has terminated. In the automatic-buffering scheme, P simply continue its execution. If P needs to know that its message has been processed by Q, it must explicitly program for an acknowledgment. In the no-buffering scheme, P will blocked forever. As above-mentioned, the system may either terminate P or inform P that Q has terminated.

LOST MESSAGES

A message from process P to process Q may become lost somewhere in the distributed environment due to a hardware or communication line failure. There are three basic methods for dealing with this event:

- The operating system is responsible for detecting this event and for retransmitting this message; or
- The sending process is responsible for detecting this event and for retransmitting the message; and
- The combination of these two methods: the operating system is responsible for detecting this event; it informs the sending process about the message lost. Then the sending process handles the failure.

The most common mechanism for detecting lost messages is time-out. When a message is sent out, a reply message acknowledging reception of the message is always sent back. The sending process may then specify the time interval during which it expects the acknowledgment message to arrive. If this time period elapses before the acknowledgment arrives, the sending process may assume that the message is lost.

The same handling procedure described above can be applied for handling messages received with error. Checksume, parity or cyclic redundancy check CRC are commonly used to detect this type of error. In this case, the sending process is responsible for retransmitting the original message.

CONCURRENCY

On a single-processor machine, the operating system's support for ***concurrency*** allows multiple applications to share resources in such a way that applications appear to run at the same time. Since a typical application does not consume all resources at a given time, a careful coordination can make each application run as if it owns the entire machine.

An analogy is juggling. While there are only two hands, each ball thinks that it is caught and tossed with a pair of dedicated hands.

There are a number of benefits for an operating system to provide concurrency:

1. Of course, the most obvious benefit is to be able to run multiple applications at the same time.
2. Since resources that are unused by one application can be used for other applications, concurrency allows better resource utilization.
3. Without concurrency, each application has to be run to completion before the next one can be run. Therefore, concurrency allows a better average response time of individual applications.

4. Concurrency does not merely timeshare the computer; concurrency can actually achieve better performance. For example, if one application uses only the processor, while another application uses only the disk drive, the time to run both applications concurrently to completion will be shorter than the time to run each application consecutively.

Concurrency also introduces certain drawbacks:

1. Multiple applications need to be protected from one another.
2. Multiple applications may need to coordinate through additional mechanisms.
3. Switching among applications requires additional performance overheads and complexities in operating systems (e.g., deciding which application to run next.)
4. In extreme cases of running too many applications concurrently will lead to severely degraded performance.

Overall, when properly used, concurrency offers more benefits than drawbacks.

SEMAPHORE SUMMARY:

A synchronization variable that takes on positive integer values. It was invented by E. Dijkstra in the mid 60's.

- **P(semaphore)**: an atomic operation that waits for semaphore to become positive, then decrements it by 1 ("proberen" in Dutch).
- **V(semaphore)**: an atomic operation that increments semaphore by 1 ("verhogen" in Dutch).

Semaphores are simple and elegant and allow the solution of many interesting problems. They do a lot more than just mutual exclusion.

Semaphores are used in two different ways:

1. **Mutual exclusion**: to ensure that only one process is accessing shared information at a time. If there are separate groups of data that can be accessed independently, there may be separate semaphores, one for each group of data. These semaphores are always binary semaphores.
2. **Scheduling**: to permit processes to wait for certain things to happen. If there are different groups of processes waiting for different things

MONITORS

Semaphores are a big step up from low-level loads and stores. However, semaphores serve two different purposes—mutual exclusion and scheduling constraints. This design makes code development difficult.

The idea of monitors is to separate these two concerns: use locks for mutual exclusion and condition variables for scheduling constraints.

A monitor is a lock with zero or more conditional variables for managing concurrent access to shared data.

The *lock* provides mutual exclusion to the shared data. A *conditional variable* allows a queue of waiting threads while being inside a critical section. A number of textbooks present monitors as a Java or C++ class, where the lock is automatically acquired on calling any procedure inside the monitor. However, in many real-life operating systems, such as Windows NT, OS/2, or Solaris, monitors are used with explicit calls to locks and conditional variables.

LOCK

A lock provides two operations:

```
    Lock::Acquire()
    // wait until the lock is free, then grab it
    Lock::Release()
// unlock, wake up anyone waiting in Acquire
```

As a general rule of thumb, always acquire a lock before accessing a shared data structure; always release a lock after finishing with the shared data structure. A lock is initially free. The following is a simple example of using a lock on a synchronized list:

```
    AddToQueue() {
            Lock.Acquire();
    // put 1 item to the queue
    Lock.Release();
}

    RemoveFromQueue() {
            Lock.Acquire();
            // if something on the queue
    //      remove 1 item from the queue
            Lock.Release();
            return item;
    }
```

CONDITION VARIABLES

Although the example queue is synchronized, if we want to perform waiting inside locked regions, we need additional mechanisms. For example, a process may want to wait for something to be added to the queue before the removal operation.

However, holding the lock while waiting prevents other processes from entering the locked regions. Condition variables make it possible to go to sleep inside a critical section by atomically releasing the lock and going to sleep.

Associated with each condition variable is a waiting queue of threads inside a critical section, and condition variables provide the following operations:

```
    Wait();  // atomically release the lock and go to
sleep; re-acquire lock on return
    Signal();  // wake up a waiter, if any
    Broadcast();  // wake up all waiters
```

Note: These operations should always occur inside locked regions. The following is a synchronized queue with waiting inside the remove operation.

```
    AddToQueue() {
            lock.Acquire();
    // put 1 item to the queue
    condition.Signal(&lock);
    lock.Release();
}

    RemoveFromQueue() {
            lock.Acquire();
            while nothing on queue
                    condition.Wait(&lock);
    // remove 1 item from the queue
            lock.Release();
            return item;
    }
```

Mesa vs. Hoare Monitors

When using condition variables, you need to be careful about the precise definition of signal() and wait(). For the ***Hoare-style monitors***, the signaler thread directly transfers the CPU to a thread that is on the wait queue of the condition variable.

Once the waiting thread exits the critical section or waits, the CPU is transferred back to the signaler thread.

However, for the ***Mesa-style monitors*** (in most real operating systems), the waiting thread is simply put on the scheduler's ready queue. Therefore, once the waiting thread gets its turn for the CPU, the waiting condition may no longer be true and needs to be retested. In general, Mesa-style monitors use a while instead of an if to retest the condition of a reawaken thread.

COMPARISON BETWEEN SEMAPHORES AND MONITORS

Although both semaphores and monitors provide atomic operations and queueing, they have very different behaviors. For example, the following implementation has a very different behavior.

```
Wait() { semaphore→P(); }
Signal() { semaphore→V(); }
```

First, condition variables only work inside a lock. Using semaphores inside a lock may cause a deadlock. Second, condition variables have no history, but semaphores have. If a thread calls signal(), and the waiting queue is empty, the signal() call does nothing. If a thread later arrives and calls wait(), the thread will wait. However, if a thread calls V(), and no one is waiting, the semaphore increments. If a thread later calls P(), the semaphore decrements, and the thread continues.

The next example takes the lock into account. However, the behavior is still different.

```
Wait(Lock *lock) {
        lock->Acquire();  // [1]
        semaphore->P();   // [3]
        lock->Release();
}

Signal() {
        if (semaphore queue is not empty) // [2]
        semaphore→V();      // [4]
}
```

Third, semaphores cannot look at the contents of semaphore queue. Fourth, releasing the lock and going to sleep need to occur atomically. Should the semaphore queue be checked [2] right after releasing the lock [1] and before calling P() [3], the corresponding V() [4] will never be called, and the thread sleeping in P() will never wake up.

THREAD

A thread is a sequential execution stream, and it is also the smallest scheduling unit of concurrency to run on a processor. The beauty of the thread is that each thread can be programmed as if it owns the entire CPU (e.g., you can use an infinite loop within a thread without halting the entire system). In other words, a thread contains the states of its own program counter, register values, and execution stacks. Therefore, threads provide the illusion of having an infinite number of CPUs, even on a single-processor machine.

Threads simplify programming significantly, and Microsoft Word is an example. As you are typing in Word, there is a thread dedicated for checking grammar, a thread for checking spelling, a thread for reformatting the text, and many other threads for various purposes. Since the thread for grammar checking can be programmed independently from the thread for spelling check, the difficulty for programming a large application like Word is greatly simplified.

Despite of the fact that a thread must execute in process, the process and its associated threads are different concept. Processes are used to group resources together and threads are the entities scheduled for execution on the CPU.

A thread is a single sequence stream within in a process.

Because threads have some of the properties of processes, they are sometimes called *lightweight processes*. In a process, threads allow multiple executions of streams. In many respect, threads are popular way to improve application through parallelism. The CPU switches rapidly back and forth among the threads giving illusion that the threads are running in parallel. Like a traditional process i.e., process with one thread, a thread can be in any of several states (Running, Blocked, Ready or terminated).

Each thread has its own stack. Since thread will generally call different procedures and thus a different execution history. This is why thread needs its own stack. An operating system that has thread facility, the basic unit of CPU utilization is a thread. A thread has or consists of a program counter (PC), a register set, and a stack space. Threads are not independent of one other like processes as a result threads shares with other threads their code section, data section, OS resources also known as task, such as open files and signals.

Processes Vs Threads

As we mentioned earlier that in many respect threads operate in the same way as that of processes. Some of the similarities and differences are:

Similarities

1. Like processes threads share CPU and only one thread active (running) at a time.

2. Like processes, threads within a processes, threads within a processes execute sequentially.
3. Like processes, thread can create children.
4. And like process, if one thread is blocked, another thread can run.

Differences

1. Unlike processes, threads are not independent of one another.
2. Unlike processes, all threads can access every address in the task .
3. Unlike processes, thread are design to assist one other. Note that processes might or might not assist one another because processes may originate from different users.

Why Threads?

Following are some reasons why we use threads in designing operating systems.

1. A process with multiple threads make a great server for example printer server.
2. Because threads can share common data, they do not need to use interprocess communication.
3. Because of the very nature, threads can take advantage of multiprocessors.

Threads are cheap in the sense that

1. They only need a stack and storage for registers therefore, threads are cheap to create.
2. Threads use very little resources of an operating system in which they are working. That is, threads do not need new address space, global data, program code or operating system resources.
3. Context switching are fast when working with threads. The reason is that we only have to save and/or restore PC, SP and registers.

But this cheapness does not come free - the biggest drawback is that there is no protection between threads.

User-Level Threads

User-level threads implement in user-level libraries, rather than via systems calls, so thread switching does not need to call operating system and to cause interrupt to the kernel. In fact, the kernel knows nothing about user-level threads and manages them as if they were single-threaded processes.

Advantages:

The most obvious advantage of this technique is that a user-level threads package can be implemented on an Operating System that does not support threads. Some other advantages are

1. User-level threads does not require modification to operating systems.
2. Simple Representation: Each thread is represented simply by a PC, registers, stack and a small control block, all stored in the user process address space.
3. Simple Management: This simply means that creating a thread, switching between threads and synchronization between threads can all be done without intervention of the kernel.
4. Fast and Efficient: Thread switching is not much more expensive than a procedure call.

Disadvantages:

1. There is a lack of coordination between threads and operating system kernel. Therefore, process as whole gets one time slice irrespect of whether process has one thread or 1000 threads within. It is up to each thread to relinquish control to other threads.
2. User-level threads requires non-blocking systems call i.e., a multithreaded kernel. Otherwise, entire process will blocked in the kernel, even if there are runable threads left in the processes. For example, if one thread causes a page fault, the process blocks.

Kernel-Level Threads

In this method, the kernel knows about and manages the threads. No runtime system is needed in this case. Instead of thread table in each process, the kernel has a thread table that keeps track of all threads in the system. In addition, the kernel also maintains the traditional process table to keep track of processes. Operating Systems kernel provides system call to create and manage threads.

Advantages:

1. Because kernel has full knowledge of all threads, Scheduler may decide to give more time to a process having large number of threads than process having small number of threads.
2. Kernel-level threads are especially good for applications that frequently block.

Disadvantages:

1. The kernel-level threads are slow and inefficient. For instance, threads operations are hundreds of times slower than that of user-level threads.
2. Since kernel must manage and schedule threads as well as processes. It require a full thread control block (TCB) for each thread to maintain information about threads. As a result there is significant overhead and increased in kernel complexity.

MULTITHREADING MODELS

Many systems provide support for both user and kernel threads, resulting in different multithreading models. We look at three common types of threading implementation.

Many-to-One Model

The many-to-one model maps many user-level threads to one kernel thread. Thread management is done in user space, so it is effcient, but the entire process will block if a thread makes a blocking system call. Also, because only one thread can access the kernel at a time, multiple threads are unable to run in parallel on multiprocessors. Green threads Ñ a thread library available for Solaris 2 Ñ uses this model. In addition, user-level thread libraries implemented on operating systems that do not support kernel threads use the many-to-one model.

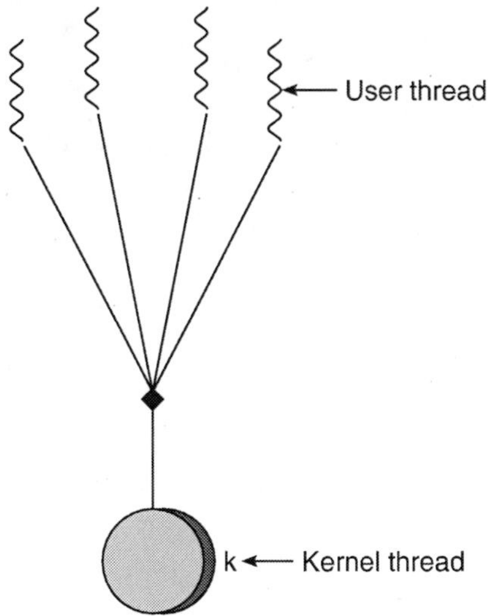

Many-to-one model.

One-to-One Model

The one-to-one model maps each user thread to a kernel thread. It provides more concurrency than the many-to-one model by allowing another thread to run when a thread makes a blocking system call; it also allows multiple threads to run in parallel on multiprocessors. The only drawback to this model is that creating a user thread requires creating the corresponding kernel thread. Because the overhead of creating kernel threads can burden the performance of an application, most implementations of this model restrict the number of threads supported by the system. Windows NT, Windows 2000, and OS/2 implement the one-to-one model.

Many-to-Many Model

The many-to-many model multiplexes many user- level threads to a smaller or equal number of kernel threads. The number of kernel threads may be speciÞc for either a particular application or a particular machine (an application may be allocated more kernel threads on a multiprocessor than on a uniprocessor). Whereas the

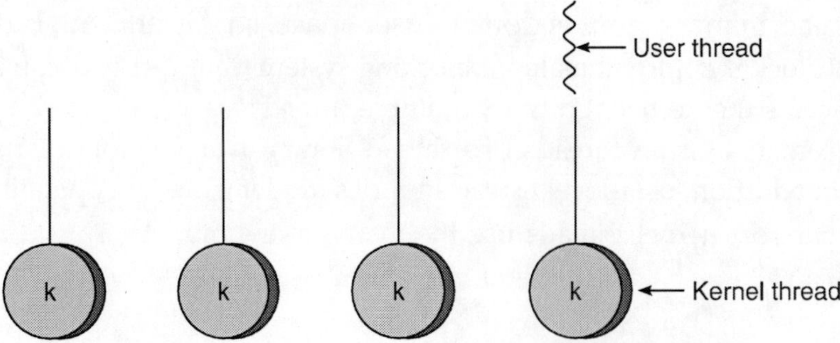

many-to-one model allows the developer to create as many user threads as she wishes, true concurrency is not gained because the kernel can schedule only one thread at a time. The one-to-one model allows for greater concurrency, but the developer has to be careful not to create too many threads within an application (and in some instances may be limited in the number of threads that she can create). The many-to-many model suffers from neither of these shortcomings: Developers can create as many user threads as necessary, and the corresponding kernel threads can run in parallel on a multiprocessor. Also, when a thread performs a blocking system call, the kernel can schedule another thread for execution. Solaris 2, IRIX, HP-UX, and Tru64 UNIX support this model.

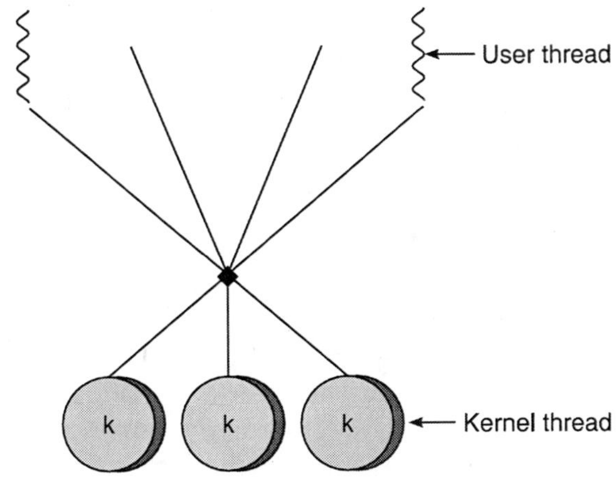

Many-to-many model

Advantages of Threads over Multiple Processes

Context Switching. Threads are very inexpensive to create and destroy, and they are inexpensive to represent. For example, they require space to store, the PC, the SP, and the general-purpose registers, but they do not require space to share memory information, Information about open files of I/O devices in use, etc. With so little context, it is much faster to switch between threads. In other words, it is relatively easier for a context switch using threads.

Sharing. Treads allow the sharing of a lot resources that cannot be shared in process, for example, sharing code section, data section, Operating System resources like open file etc.

Disadvantages of Threads over Multiprocesses

Blocking. The major disadvantage if that if the kernel is single threaded, a system call of one thread will block the whole process and CPU may be idle during the blocking period.

Security. Since there is, an extensive sharing among threads there is a potential problem of security. It is quite possible that one thread over writes the stack of another thread (or damaged shared data) although it is very unlikely since threads are meant to cooperate on a single task.

Application that Benefits from Threads

A proxy server satisfying the requests for a number of computers on a LAN would be benefited by a multi-threaded process. In general, any program that has to do more than one task at a time could benefit from multitasking. For example, a program that reads input, process it, and outputs could have three threads, one for each task.

Application that cannot Benefit from Threads

Any sequential process that cannot be divided into parallel task will not benefit from thread, as they would block until the previous one completes. For example, a program that displays the time of the day would not benefit from multiple threads.

Resources used in Thread Creation and Process Creation

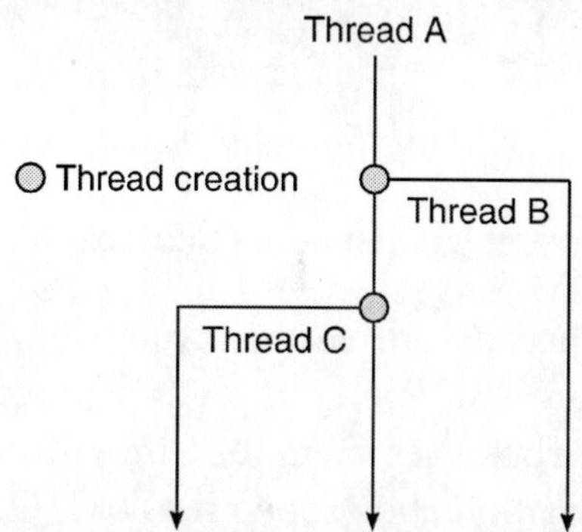

When a new thread is created it shares its code section, data section and operating system resources like open files with other threads. But it is allocated its own stack, register set and a program counter.

The creation of a new process differs from that of a thread mainly in the fact that all the shared resources of a thread are needed explicitly for each process. So though two processes may be running the same piece of code they need to have their own copy of the code in the main memory to be able to run. Two processes also do not share other resources with each other. This makes the creation of a new process very costly compared to that of a new thread.

Context Switch

To give each process on a multiprogrammed machine a fair share of the CPU, a hardware clock generates interrupts periodically. This allows the operating system to schedule all processes in main memory (using scheduling algorithm) to run on the CPU at equal intervals. Each time a clock interrupt occurs, the interrupt handler checks how much time the current running process has used. If it has used up its entire time slice, then the CPU scheduling algorithm (in kernel) picks a different process to run. Each switch of the CPU from one process to another is called a context switch.

Major Steps of Context Switching

- The values of the CPU registers are saved in the process table of the process that was running just before the clock interrupt occurred.
- The registers are loaded from the process picked by the CPU scheduler to run next.

In a multiprogrammed uniprocessor computing system, context switches occur frequently enough that all processes appear to be running concurrently. If a process has more than one thread, the Operating System can use the context switching technique to schedule the threads so they appear to execute in parallel. This is the case if threads are implemented at the kernel level. Threads can also be implemented entirely at the user level in run-time libraries. Since in this case no thread scheduling is provided by the Operating System, it is the responsibility of the programmer to yield the CPU frequently enough in each thread so all threads in the process can make progress.

Action of Kernel to Context Switch Among Threads

The threads share a lot of resources with other peer threads belonging to the same process. So a context switch among threads for the same process is easy. It involves switch of register set, the program counter and the stack. It is relatively easy for the kernel to accomplish this task.

Action of kernel to Context Switch Among Processes

Context switches among processes are expensive. Before a process can be switched its process control block (PCB) must be saved by the operating system. The PCB consists of the following information:

- The process state.
- The program counter, PC.
- The values of the different registers.
- The CPU scheduling information for the process.
- Memory management information regarding the process.
- Possible accounting information for this process.
- I/O status information of the process.

When the PCB of the currently executing process is saved the operating system loads the PCB of the next process that has to be run on CPU. This is a heavy task and it takes a lot of time

Example of threads:Solaris-2 Operating Systems

The solaris-2 Operating Systems supports:

- threads at the user-level.
- threads at the kernel-level.
- symmetric multiprocessing and
- real-time scheduling.

The entire thread system in Solaris is depicted in following figure.

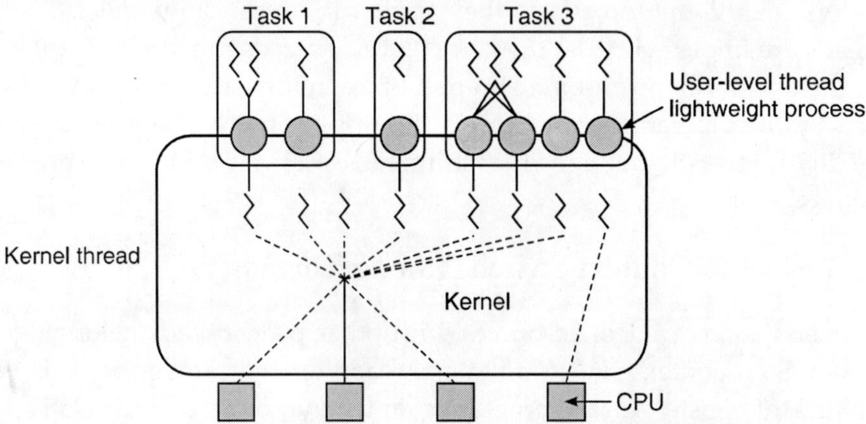

At user-level

The user-level threads are supported by a library for the creation and scheduling and kernel knows nothing of these threads.

These user-level threads are supported by lightweight processes (LWPs). Each LWP is connected to exactly one kernel-level thread is independent of the kernel.

Many user-level threads may perform one task. These threads may be scheduled and switched among LWPs without intervention of the kernel.

User-level threads are extremely efficient because no context switch is needs to block one thread another to start running.

Resource needs of User-level Threads

A user-thread needs a stack and program counter. Absolutely no kernel resource are required.

Since the kernel is not involved in scheduling these user-level threads, switching among user-level threads are fast and efficient.

At Intermediate-level

The lightweight processes (LWPs) are located between the user-level threads and kernel-level threads. These LWPs serve as a "Virtual CPUs" where user-threads can run. Each task contains at least one LWp.

The user-level threads are multiplexed on the LWPs of the process.

Resource needs of LWP

An LWP contains a process control block (PCB) with register data, accounting information and memory information. Therefore, switching between LWPs requires quite a bit of work and LWPs are relatively slow as compared to user-level threads.

At kernel-level

The standard kernel-level threads execute all operations within the kernel. There is a kernel-level thread for each LWP and there are some threads that run only on the kernels behalf and have associated LWP. For example, a thread to service disk requests. By request, a kernel-level thread can be pinned to a processor (CPU). See the rightmost thread in figure. The kernel-level threads are scheduled by the kernel's scheduler and user-level threads blocks.

In modern solaris-2 a task no longer must block just because a kernel-level threads blocks, the processor (CPU) is free to run another thread.

Resource needs of Kernel-level Thread

A kernel thread has only small data structure and stack. Switching between kernel threads does not require changing memory access information and therefore, kernel-level threads are relating fast and efficient

Classifications of Operating Systems on the basis of threads

With the vocabulary of process, thread, and address space, we can classify operating systems into four major categories.

	Single address space	Multiple address spaces
SINGLE THREAD	MS DOS, Macintosh	Traditional UNIX
MULTIPLE THREADS	Embedded systems	Windows NT, Solaris, OS/2

Threads and Dispatching Loop

Inside each thread, there is a ***thread control block***. The thread control block maintains the execution states of the thread, the status of the thread (e.g., running or sleeping), and scheduling information of the thread (e.g., priority).

Threads are run from a ***dispatching loop***.

LOOP

Run thread

Save states (into the thread control block)

Choose a new thread to run

Load states from a different thread (from the thread control block)

To run a thread, just load its states (registers, program counter, stack pointer) into the CPU, and do a jump. The process of saving the states of one thread and restoring states of another thread is often called a context switch. The decision of which thread to run next involves scheduling.

Although this dispatching loop looks simple, there are a number of questions we need to address: How does the dispatcher regain control after a thread starts running? What states should a thread save? How does the dispatcher choose the next thread?

How Does The Dispatcher Regain Control?

The dispatcher gets control back from the running thread in two ways:

1. *Internal events* (sleeping beauty—go to sleep and hope Prince Charming will wake you):

(a) A thread is waiting for I/O.

(b) A thread is waiting for some other thread.

(c) Yield—a thread gives up CPU voluntarily.

2. *External events*:

(a) Interrupts—a completed disk request wakes up the dispatcher, so the dispatcher can choose another thread to run).

(b) Timer—it's like an alarm clock.

What States Should a Thread Save?

A thread should save anything that the next thread may trash before a context switch: program counter, registers, changes in execution stack. Each thread should be treated as an independent stream of execution.

As a side note, a context switch can also occur during an interrupt. During an interrupt, hardware causes the CPU to stop what it's doing, and to run the interrupt handler. The handler saves the states of the interrupted thread, runs the handler code, and restores the states of the interrupted thread.

How Does the Dispatcher Choose the Next Thread?

The dispatcher keeps a list of threads that are ready to run.

If no threads are ready to run—the dispatcher just loops.

If one thread is ready to run—easy.

If more than one thread are ready to run, we can choose the next thread according to different scheduling policies. Some examples are FIFO (first in, first out), LIFO (last in, first out), and priority-based policies.

The dispatcher also has the control of how to share the CPU among multiple threads. Suppose that we have thread A, B, and C. At one extreme, a dispatcher can run one thread to completion before running the other.

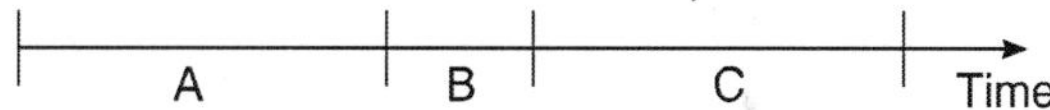

Alternatively, a dispatcher can use the timer to timeshare the CPU among three threads.

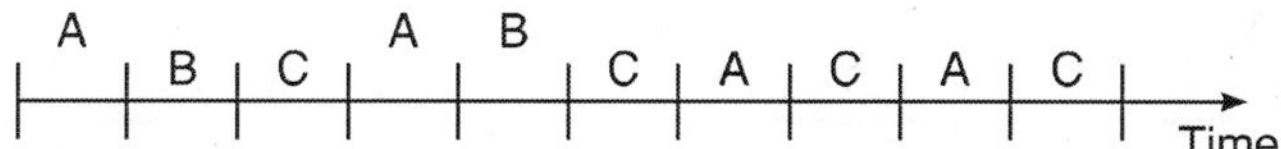

Per-Thread States

Each thread can be in one of three states:

1. Running—has the CPU
2. Blocked—waiting for I/O or another thread
3. Ready to run—on the ready list, waiting for the CPU

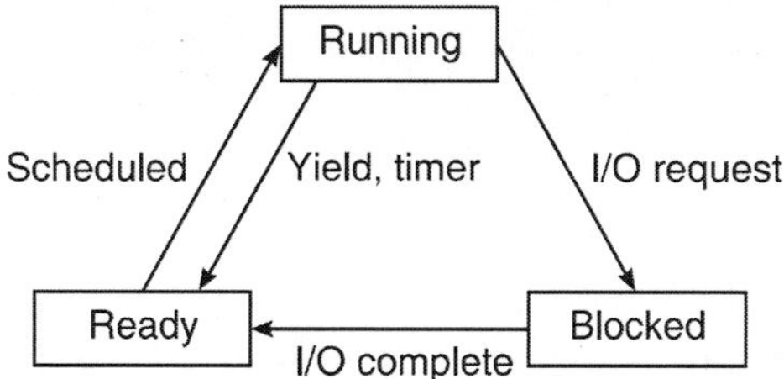

Motivation for Threads

There are tremendous benefits, from an OS point of view, to implement threads. Here is an incomplete list if these advantages:

- It is faster to create and terminate threads than processes.
- Threads share process resources and hence less security is needed between threads originating from the same process.
- If many instances of a process need to be run concurrently, only one process image is needed in memory.

  There are also some drawbacks with implementing threads. They are related to the fact that some process states apply only to processes, or only to threads or both:
- Swapping a process means that its image goes onto the swap partition of the disk and this stops all associated threads.
- In general, we can say that all process states will impact the behavior of threads. However, most process states apply to threads, exception made of *suspended* and *swapped*.

KEYWORDS

PROCESS

PROCESS CONTROL BLOCK

CONTEXT SWITCHING

RACE CONDITIONS

MUTUAL EXCLUSION

SEMAPHORE

MONITOR

THREAD

SUMMARY

A process is an instance of a computer program that is being executed. While a program itself is just a passive collection of instructions, a process is something which actually executes those instructions. The different process states are

- New: A process that has just been created and is not admitted to the pool of executable processes by the operating system.
- Exit: A process that has been released from the pool of executable processes by the operating system, either because it is halted or aborted for some reason.
- Running/Executing: Instructions are being executed.
- Ready: The process is waiting its turn to go into execution by the processor.

- Blocked/Waiting: The process is temporarily suspended, waiting for some event to occur, e.g., an I/O function.
- Process Control Block or PCB is a dynamic structure resident in memory which stores information about each process.
- The process of saving an executing thread or process and transferring control to another thread or process
- A critical problem occuring in shared-memory system is that two or more processes are reading or writing some shared variables or shared data, and the final results depend on who runs precisely and when. Such situations are called race conditions
- Mutual exclusion (often abbreviated to mutex) algorithms are used in concurrent programming to avoid the simultaneous use of a common resource, such as a global variable, by pieces of computer code called critical sections
- Semaphore are shared variables that some operating system provide for concurrent programming
- A monitor is a lock with zero or more conditional variables for managing concurrent access to shared data.
- A thread is a single sequence stream within in a process.

REVIEW QUESTIONS

1. What is process? Differentiate between a process and a program.
2. What is the role of process management unit? Explain in details
3. Explain the two state and three state models for process state transitions
4. What is context switching? Explain with examples
5. Explain the function of Process Control Block.
6. What are different state of process?
7. Sketch process state transition diagram?
8. Explain process control block ?
9. Explain and elaborate the working of semaphores and monitors with the help of examples.
10. What is thread?
11. Explain different types of thread?
12. What is kernel level thread ?
13. What is user level thread?

FILL IN THE BLANKS

1. A program under execution is called a __________.
2. A process that has been released from the pool of executable processes by the operating system, either because it is halted or aborted is in ________state.
3. ____________is the process of saving an executing thread or process and transferring control to another thread or process
4. A _________is a lock with zero or more conditional variables for managing concurrent access to shared data.
5. The ________are supported by a library for the creation and scheduling and kernel knows nothing of these threads.
6. In _________ the operating system manages only one process.

TRUE OR FALSE

1. A program is a static entity where as process is dynamic entity.
2. The switching from one process to another is normally done under interrupt control
3. PCB stores information about each program.
4. In blocked state the process is waiting its turn to go into execution by the processor
5. Mutual exclusion algorithms are used in concurrent programming to avoid the simultaneous use of a common resource.
6. In a shared-memory scheme, the responsibility for providing communication rests only with the system programmers.

ANSWERS

FILL IN THE BLANKS

1. Process
2. EXIT
3. Context switching
4. monitor
5. user-level threads
6. uniprogramming

TRUE OR FALSE

1. FALSE
2. TRUE
3. FALSE
4. TRUE
5. TRUE
6. FALSE

❑❑❑

"You can teach a user a process, but you can't make them think." —*Steve Ashley*

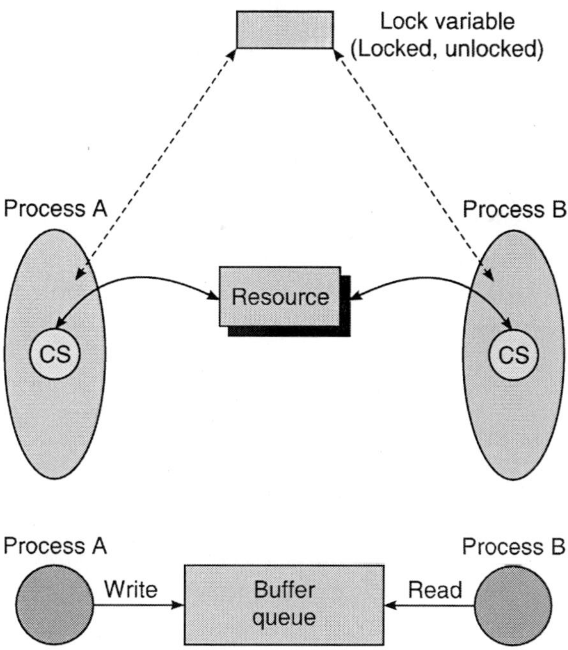

4 PROCESS SYNCHRONIZATION

INTRODUCTION

Processes frequently need to communicate with other processes. For example, in a shell pipeline, the output of the first process must be passed to the second process, and so on down the line. Thus, there is a need for communication between processes, preferably in a well-structured way not using interrupts because interrupts decrease system performance. That communication between processes in the control of the OS is called as Interprocess Communication or simply IPC.

In some operating systems, processes that are working together often share some common storage area that each can read and write. To see how IPC works in practice, let us consider a simple but common example, a print spooler. When a process wants to print a file, it enters the file name in a special spooler directory. Another process, the printer daemon, periodically checks to see if there are any files to be printed, and if there are, it sends them to printer and removes their names from the directory.

What is process synchronization?

Process synchronization implies the use of atomic operations to ensure correct cooperation between processes i.e. to eliminate race conditions.

Assume that our spooler directory has a large number of slots, numbered 0, 1, 2, ..., each one capable of holding a file name. Also suppose we have two shared variables, out, which points to the next file to be printed, and in, which points to the next free slot in the directory. These two variables might be kept on a two-word file available to all processes. Think of a certain instant, slots 0 to 3 are empty (the files have already been printed) and slots 4 to 6 are dull (with the file names to be printed). More or less frequently, processes A and B decide they want to queue a file for printing as illustrated below.

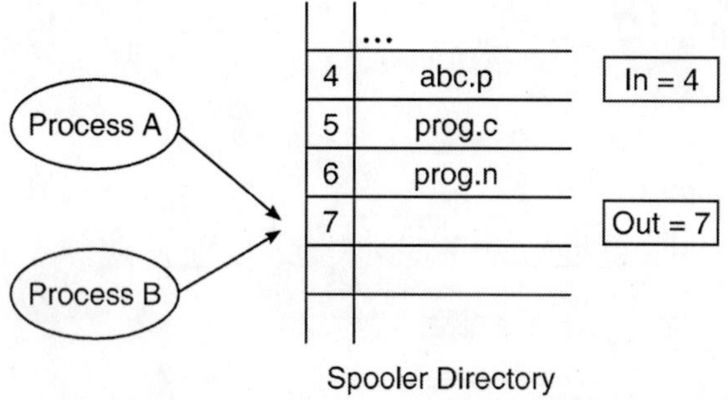

Spooler Directory

The following might happen about the printing requests of two processes. Process A reads in and stores the value, 7, in a local variable next_free_slot. Just then a clock interrupt occurs and the processor decides that process A has run long enough, so it switches to process B. Process B also reads in, and also gets a 7, so it stores the name of its file in slot 7 and updates in to be an 8. Then it goes off and does other things.

Eventually, process A runs again, starting from the place it left off. It looks at next_free_slot, in its local variable finds a 7 there, and writes its file name in slot 7, erasing the name that process B just put there. Then, it computes next_free_slot + 1, which is 8, and sets in to 8.

The spooler directory is now internally consistent, so the printer daemon will not notice anything wrong, but process B will never get an output. Situations like this, where two or more processes are reading or writing some shared data and the final result depends on who runs precisely when, are called race conditions.

The key for preventing trouble here and in many other situations involving shared memory, shared files, and shared everything else, is to find some way to prohibit more than one process from reading and writing the shared data at the same time. Put in other words, what we need is mutual exclusion (some way of making sure that if one process is using a shared variable or file, the other process will be excluded from doing the same thing. The difficulty above occurred because process B started using one of the shared variables before process A was finished with it.

Resources may be defined as **shareable** or **non-shareable**. Shareable resources can be used by several processes concurrently, e.g. **read-only** files. Non-shareable resources have their uses restricted to one process at a time, e.g. **writable** files. We can divide processes into

1. **Independent processes** - Cannot affect or be affected by other processes (no shared data)
2. **Cooperating processes** - Can affect or be affected by other processes (could shared data)

Reasons to allow cooperating processes:

- **Information sharing** - two processes using the same file
- **Computation speedup** - dividing a process into separate executing tasks to make use of multiple processors or I/O devices.
- **Modularity** - Construct a system in a modular fashion (separating system functions into separate processes.

MUTUAL EXCLUSION and RACE CONDITION revisited

MUTUAL EXCLUSION

Mutual Exclusion ensures that non-shareable resources are accessed by only one process at a time i.e. if one process is using a resource (say a variable or a file) another is excluded from accessing that resource. Some method must be implemented to achieve mutual exclusion.

RACE CONDITION

When two or more processes share some common data (or other resource) and the final result depends upon the timing of access to the data or the order in which processes are run then a race condition exists.

Example of where the action of one process interferes with another:

See program example below...

- Memory location 2000H contains the value 100D

➤ Process A wants to add 50 to this location

➤ Process B wants to subtract 30 from this location

➤ The final result should leave location 2000H with a value of **120 i.e. (100 + 50 - 30).**

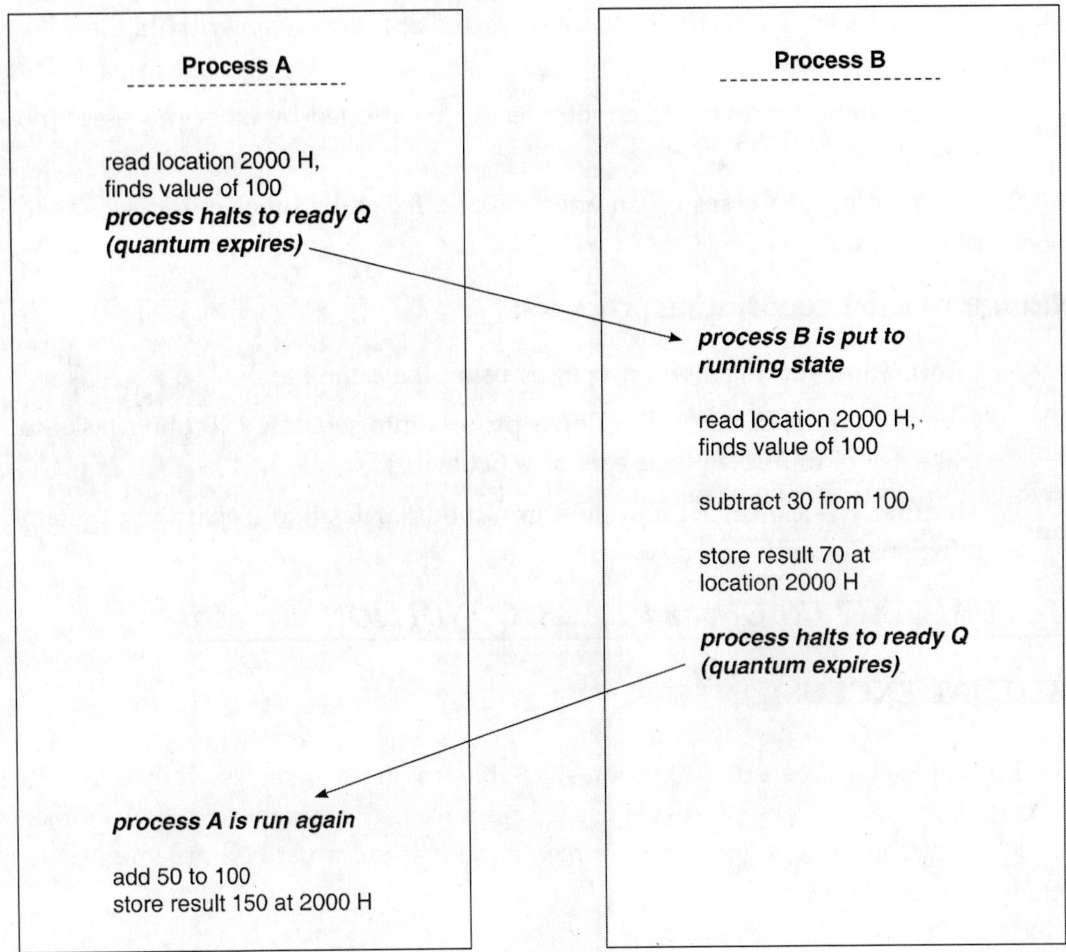

Note, **incorrect** result **150** (not 120) is now stored at location 2000H.

If some method had been used to provide ***mutual exclusion*** *for the access to location 2000H the above* ***race condition*** *could not have occurred.*

To guarantee a *good* mutual exclusion solution some specific conditions must be satisfied:

1. At any instant in time no two processes can be inside their critical sections.
2. There can be no assumptions made about the relative execution speeds of processes.

3. If any process is blocked outside its critical section it cannot affect the other processes.
4. No process should have to wait an excessively long time to enter its critical section. Design should ensure that processes about to enter their critical sections should not block each other.
5. A process should remain inside its critical section for a finite time only.

Various solutions which attempt to satisfy the above conditions will be discussed. Since only one process can be in its critical section at one time, thus inhibiting other processes from accessing the resource, it is important that the critical section is coded tightly so that it executes quickly. It is also important that a process is not allowed to block within its critical section.

PROCESS CRITICAL SECTIONS

Mutual exclusion is needed only when processes access shared write-able data. The part of the program which accesses the shareable data (or other resource) is referred to as a **critical section**. If a scheme could ensure that no two processes could be in their **critical section** at the same time then mutual exclusion could be achieved thus avoiding race conditions.

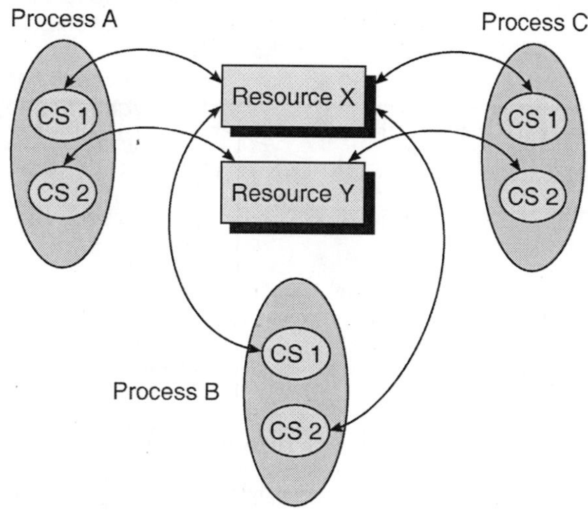

In other words, the problem of avoiding race conditions can also be formulated in an abstract way. Part of the time, a process is busy doing internal computations and other things that do not lead to race conditions. However, sometimes a process may be accessing shared memory or files, or doing other critical things that can lead to races. That part of the program where the shared memory is accessed is called the critical section (CS). If we could arrange matters such that no two processes were ever in their critical sections at the same time, we could avoid race conditions.

Solution to Critical-Section Problem

1. **Mutual Exclusion** - If process Pi is executing in its critical section, then no other processes can be executing in their critical sections
2. **Progress** - If no process is executing in its critical section and there exist some processes that wish to enter their critical section, then the selection of the processes that will enter the critical section next cannot be postponed indefinitely
3. **Bounded Waiting** - A bound must exist on the number of times that other processes are allowed to enter their critical sections after a process has made a request to enter its critical section and before that request is granted
4. **CPUs** – No assumption regarding speed and number of CPUs

MUTUAL EXCLUSION - SOFTWARE SOLUTIONS

We discuss here some attempted solutions for **two** cyclic processes where each process has a critical section. With additional complexity the solutions can be expanded to **n** processes but for simplicity only two processes are being considered here. A number of solutions are presented. Problems associated with each solution are stated. Each solution presented is an improvement on the previously presented solution.

SOLUTION A

Use a single shared lock variable, called **LOCK,** to control access to the critical section. A process must lock the variable before it can enter the critical section.

```
var LOCK: (UNLOCKED, LOCKED); (* this is a shared variable*)
    LOCK := UNLOCKED;
```

```
(* PROCESS A *)
---------------------

repeat
until LOCK = UNLOCKED;
  LOCK := LOCKED;

        critical section

LOCK := UNLOCKED;
```

```
(* PROCESS B *)
---------------------

repeat
        until LOCK = UNLOCKED;
        LOCK := LOCKED;

          critical section

        LOCK := UNLOCKED;
```

The solution does **not** guarantee mutual exclusion. On inspection of the code it can be seen that if both processes attempt to enter the critical section at the same time that they will both be successful (both will read LOCK and find its value to be UNLOCKED). Hence this is not a valid mutual exclusion solution.

Note, the conditions to provide a good mutual exclusion solution, as stated earlier, say that there can be no assumptions made about the relative execution speeds of processes. Hence, the assumption is made that two processes can run at exactly the same speed and in step. A difficult test for these mutual exclusion solutions is to ask what will happen if two processes are running at the same speed and attempt to access the resource at the same time. This test will be applied in our discussions on the various solutions. There is no discussion here suggesting how two processes might be allowed to run at the same speed and in step, i.e. there is no discussion on the background time-slicing etc., as a good solution should be valid independently of the timing conditions.

USE OF SHARED VARIABLE

The diagram shows the SOLUTION A situation. A process will test the LOCK variable before entering the critical section to access the resource.

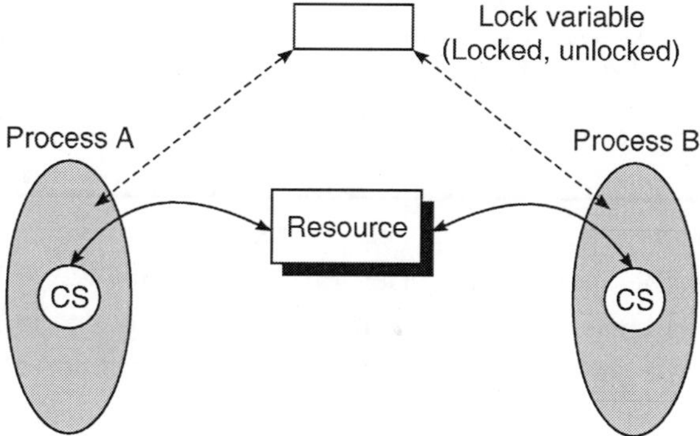

SOLUTION B

A shared variable, **TURN,** is used to control access to the critical section. This will force the processes to access the critical section in turns and hence will prevent the possibility of a simultaneous access as described in **SOLUTION A**.

In the example **TURN** is an integer variable which can have values 1 or 2. The value of the integer will define which process is allowed to enter the critical section.

```
var  TURN : 1..2;   (* this is a shared variable *)
     TURN := 1;
```

```
(* PROCESS A *)                    (* PROCESS B *)
--------------------               ------------------------

repeat                             repeat
until TURN = 1 ;                       until TURN = 2 ;

  critical section                     critical section

TURN := 2 ;                            TURN := 1 ;
```

The solution **does** guarantee mutual exclusion. However, there are two serious problems associated with the solution:

a) The processes must access the critical section in strict turns, if process A uses the critical section, it cannot use the critical section again until process B uses the critical section. This is a major constraint for each process.

b) If one process is slow it can keep the other process waiting for long periods. If one process stops the other process can be locked out of its critical section.

SOLUTION C

Each process is given its **own variable** which can have a value INSIDE or OUTSIDE, indicating whether the process is inside or outside its critical section. A process can read another process's variable but can only write to its own variable. The problems of **SOLUTION B** above are overcome. There is no requirement for process turns and if one process is slow or stops (outside the critical section) the other process is not affected.

var PROCESS_A, PROCESS_B : (INSIDE, OUTSIDE);

PROCESS_A := OUTSIDE; PROCESS_B := OUTSIDE;

```
(* PROCESS A *)                       (* PROCESS B *)
---------------------                 ----------------------

PROCESS_A := INSIDE ;                      PROCESS_B := INSIDE ;

repeat                                repeat
 until PROCESS_B = OUTSIDE;            until PROCESS_A = OUTSIDE;

   critical section                        critical section

PROCESS_A := OUTSIDE;                      PROCESS_B := OUTSIDE;
```

The solution, however, is **not** good enough. A **race condition** exists. If the processes assign the value INSIDE to their variables simultaneously, then a locked condition arises where each process will wait indefinitely for the other process to change the value of its variable to OUTSIDE.

SOLUTION D

A possible solution to the problem stated in **SOLUTION C** is to make each process test for the locked condition instead of waiting forever. Any one process can attempt to free the deadlock condition by setting its variable back to OUTSIDE thus abandoning its attempt to enter the critical section.

```
var PROCESS_A, PROCESS_B : (INSIDE, OUTSIDE);

PROCESS_A := OUTSIDE;

PROCESS_B := OUTSIDE;
```

```
(* PROCESS A*)
-------------------------

repeat

 PROCESS_A := INSIDE;

 if PROCESS_B = INSIDE then
   PROCESS_A := OUTSIDE;

   repeat
   until PROCESS_B = OUTSIDE;

until PROCESS_A = INSIDE ;

  critical section

PROCESS_A := OUTSIDE ;
```

```
(* PROCESS B *)
-------------------------

repeat

   PROCESS_B := INSIDE;

   if PROCESS_A = INSIDE then
PROCESS_B := OUTSIDE;

   repeat
until PROCESS_A = OUTSIDE;

   until PROCESS_B = INSIDE ;

   critical section

   PROCESS_B := OUTSIDE ;
```

A problem with this solution occurs if two processes happen to be cycling in step and both detect the lock condition at the same time. Both will try to give up the attempt to access the critical section at the same time and then both may retry the access at the same time, failing again and again. The use of a random time delay by each process may help avoid the problem but it adds an unwanted level of complexity and makes the system less deterministic.

SOLUTION E

DEKKER'S ALGORITHM

Dekker's solution uses a combination of the solutions proposed in **SOLUTIONs B and C** above. Each process has its own variable to indicate whether or not it wants entry to the critical section. A process can read the other process's variable. An integer variable **TURN** is used to resolve a conflict situation where two processes try to enter their critical sections simultaneously. When such a conflict arises the TURN value is used to arbitrate in favour of one process. To maintain fairness, the TURN value is set in favour of the other process each time a process leaves its critical section.

```
var TURN : 1..2; (* this is a shared variable *)
    PROCESS_A, PROCESS_B : (INSIDE, OUTSIDE);

TURN := 1 ;
PROCESS_A := OUTSIDE ;
PROCESS_B := OUTSIDE ;
```

```
(* PROCESS A *)
--------------------------

PROCESS_A := INSIDE ;

if PROCESS_B= INSIDE then

 begin
   if TURN = 2 then

   begin
   PROCESS_A := OUTSIDE ;
         repeat until TURN = 1 ;
   PROCESS_A := INSIDE;
   end ;

   repeat
   until PROCESS_B = OUTSIDE;
  end ;

          critical section

TURN := 2 ;
PROCESS_A := OUTSIDE ;
```

```
(* PROCESS B  *)
---------------------------

PROCESS_B := INSIDE ;

if PROCESS_A = INSIDE then

  begin
if TURN = 1 then

   begin
   PROCESS_B :=OUTSIDE ;
     repeat until TURN = 2 ;
PROCESS_B := INSIDE;
   end ;

   repeat
   until PROCESS_A = OUTSIDE;
  end ;

          critical section

TURN := 1 ;
PROCESS_B :=OUTSIDE ;
```

SOLUTION F

PETERSONS ALGORITHM

Dekker's solution is too complicated for general use. Peterson discovered a simpler solution to the mutual exclusion problem in 1981. The solution still uses **busy waiting** but it is simpler to implement.

A process flags its interest in entering the critical section by setting an interest flag. If the other process has previously set its own interest flag, the process will wait for the other process to clear its interest flag before entering the critical section itself.

The TURN variable is used to avoid conflicts when both processes attempt to enter their critical sections at the same time. Each process will attempt to write a number to TURN. The last process to write to the TURN variable sets the value of this variable

```
var      TURN : 1..2 ; (* this is a shared variable *)
   INTERESTED_A, INTERESTED_B : Boolean ;


TURN := 1 ;
INTERESTED_A := FALSE ;
INTERESTED_B := FALSE ;
```

```
(* PROCESS A *)
---------------------

INTERESTED_A := TRUE ;
TURN := 1 ;

while (INTERESTED_B
        AND TURN = 1)
    do ( ) ;

        critical section

INTERESTED_A := FALSE;
```

```
(* PROCESS B *)
-----------------------

INTERESTED_B := TRUE ;
TURN := 2 ;

while (INTERESTED_A
        AND TURN = 2)
    do( ) ;

        critical section

INTERESTED_B := FALSE;
```

NB: the Pascal-like **do( )** statement means to do nothing.

AND is the logical AND

MUTUAL EXCLUSION - HARDWARE SUPPORTED SOLUTIONS

Disabling Interrupts

A process could disable the processor interrupts when entering the critical section. This solution is used in some real-time systems to implement mutual exclusion. However, it is not desirable to allow the application programmer to interfere with the interrupt control logic as such action is likely to lead to other system problems.

A single processor system is assumed. If two (or more) processes attempt to disable the interrupts at the same time, then one process only can begin the execution of the *disable interrupt* instruction. Since the *disable interrupt* instruction is a machine level instruction (single assembly language level statement) it is not a divisible instruction and cannot be interrupted. Thus one process only will effect the disabling of the interrupt and can take control of the system and pre-emption activity is now stopped until the interrupt is enabled again.

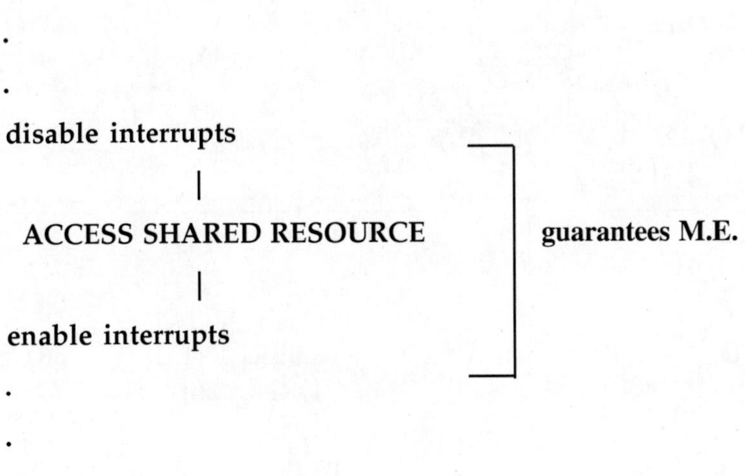

The TSL instruction

A **TEST AND SET LOCK** (TSL) instruction is useful, especially in multiprocessor systems. The TSL is a single hardware instruction which uses a shared variable (e.g. **flag**) to control access to shared memory data.

The TSL instruction reads the contents of the memory word (flag) into a machine register and writes back a non-zero value to that memory location. The operation of reading the memory, writing the register and writing back the non-zero value is guaranteed by the hardware to be a treated as a single **indivisible** operation so that no other process can access the memory while the TSL instruction is in execution.

In multiprocessor systems the CPU which is executing the TSL instruction will put a hardware lock on the memory bus so that no other CPU can access the memory until the TSL operation is done.

TSL example:

The shared variable **flag** is used to control access to the critical section.

When **flag** is 0 any process may set it to 1 using TSL and thus can be allowed access to the critical section. The process is responsible for setting **flag** back to a zero value upon return from its critical section.

```
enter_CS:                        ; label - enter critical section
    TSL register, flag.............   ; copy flag to register and write 1 to flag
    CMP register, 0.............      ; compare to zero
    JNZ enter_CS.............         ; flag indicated locked status so loop
    .
    .
    critical section code
    .
    .
leave_CS:                        ; label - leave critical section
    MOV flag, 0                  ; write zero to flag (removes lock)
```

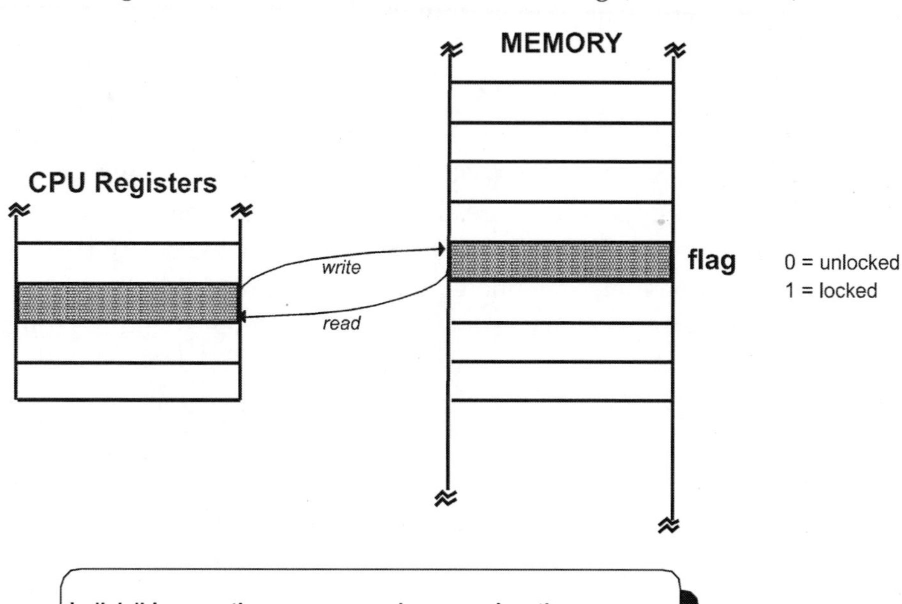

SEMAPHORES

Most of the previous techniques discussed for implementing mutual exclusion use a **busy waiting** scheme where a process loops around waiting for entry to a critical section. Such waiting is inefficient use of CPU time. Dijkstra (Dutch,1965) proposed the use of **semaphores** to support a method for implementing mutual exclusion which does not depend on the use of busy waiting. A process which is unable to enter its critical section can go to the blocked state instead of waiting, thereby freeing up the CPU for use by other processes.

The semaphore is a **non-negative** integer variable. Apart from declaring the semaphore's initial value only two operations can be performed on the semaphore:

- **Signal** (semaphore) - sometimes known as UP or V (Dutch), increases the semaphore's value by one (with some rules)
- **Wait** (semaphore) - sometimes known as DOWN or P (Dutch), decreases the semaphore value by one (with some rules)

Both operations are **indivisible** i.e. if a **signal()** or a **wait()** operation begins it will complete without interruption from any other process. Such indivisibility can ensured within the operating system by disabling the processor interrupts, or by using another suitable technique.

BINARY SEMAPHORES

A Binary (or Boolean) semaphore is an integer variable which can have a **0** or **1** value. The critical section of a program can have an associated binary semaphore, usually initiated to 1. Resources can thus be protected from simultaneous access by several processes to achieve mutual exclusion.

When a process wants to enter the critical section it performs a **wait( )** operation on the semaphore. If the semaphore already had a 0 value then the process blocks and the CPU is freed up. On exiting the critical section a process performs a **signal( )** operation which increases the semaphore value by 1. However, if there is a process or processes blocked on the semaphore, one process is awakened and the semaphore value is not increased to 1.

The **signal( )** and **wait( )** operations on binary semaphores behave as follows:

```
wait(MUTEX)   if MUTEX = 1 then            ┐
          MUTEX := 0                        │
                else                        │ Indivisible
          put process to blocked queue for  │
                    MUTEX   semaphore ;     ┘
```

```
signal(MUTEX)  if (PROCESSES EXIST IN BLOCKED QUEUE)  ┐
then              remove some process from the queue  │
                          else                        │ Indivisible
         MUTEX := 1;                                  ┘
```

It can be seen that (for the binary semaphore) at most one process can execute **wait** (MUTEX) before a **signal** (MUTEX) is executed, hence mutual exclusion can be achieved with the following code example:

```
var MUTEX : Semaphore ;
    MUTEX := 1 ; (* initialised value *)
```

```
(* PROCESS any *)
 WAIT(MUTEX) ;
        critical section
SIGNAL (MUTEX);
```

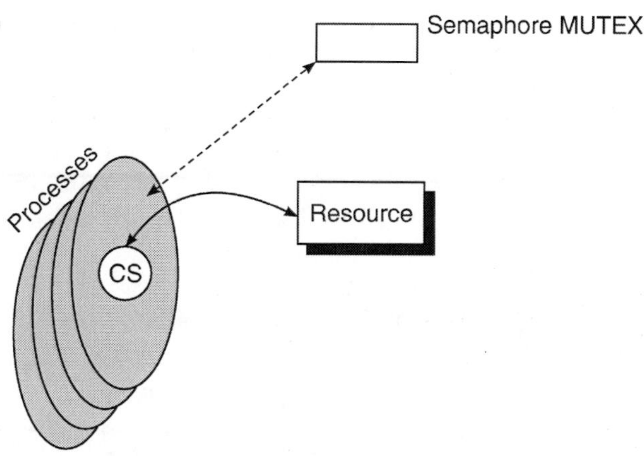

EXAMPLE: To provide mutual exclusion for a queue resource

Process A adds an item to a queue. Process B removes an item from a queue. The queue is to be accessed by only one process at a time i.e. the operation must effectively **lock** the queue until an operation is complete.

```
var     MUTEX : semaphore;
    MUTEX := 1 ; (* initialised value *)
```

(* PROCESS A *)	(* PROCESS B *)
wait(MUTEX);	wait(MUTEX) ;
add item to queue	**remove item from queue**
signal(MUTEX);	signal(MUTEX);

Any one process will be the first to execute **wait**(MUTEX) and will thus set MUTEX to 0. The other process will execute **wait**(MUTEX) and the MUTEX = 0 value will cause this process to block on MUTEX. Eventually the first process will signal(MUTEX) causing the blocked process to run and leaving MUTEX= 0 value. When this process finishes it does a **signal**(MUTEX) and since there are no other processes blocked on MUTEX, MUTEX gets a value of 1 (back to initial value).

ANOTHER SYNCHRONISATION EXAMPLE USING SEMAPHORES

Example:

```
Var     SEMAPHORE_X : semaphore;
    SEMAPHORE_X := 0 ;
```

; important to note SEMAPHORE_X has an initial value of 0

(* process A *)	**(* process B *)**
.	.
.	.
PT1: wait(SEMAPHORE_X)	**PT2: signal(SEMAPHORE_X)**
.	.
.	.

Process A cannot continue beyond PT1 until process B executes the signal operation at PT2. This is an **asymmetric** implementation as process A's progress is constrained by process B but not vice versa.

GENERAL SEMAPHORES

The General (or counting) semaphore uses an integer variable which uses only non-negative numbers. It uses the same concept as the binary semaphore - but the semaphore value is not restricted to 0 and 1 values. The general semaphore can be used to provide process synchronisation. The initial value of the semaphore will determine the maximum number of processes which can have access to the semaphore.

Value of a Semaphore

a) val(sem) = (init value) + (no. of signal(sem)) - (*no. of wait(sem))

b) val(sem) >= 0 by definition

c) no. of successful wait(sem) <= no. of signal(sem) + init value

* no. of wait(sem) means the number of **successful** wait operations

SIGNAL and WAIT OPERATIONS (GENERAL SEMAPHORE)

```
var  SEM:  Semaphore;

wait (SEM)          if  SEM >= 1                        ]
                 then  SEM := SEM - 1                   ] Indivisible

                  else
                  Process put to blocked queue on SEM semaphore ;
signal (SEM)        if   there is a process in the blocked queue   ]
                 then remove a process from the blocked queue      ] Indivisible
                  else SEM := SEM + 1 ;
```

PRODUCER/CONSUMER PROBLEM ('BOUNDED BUFFER PROBLEM')

This is a well-known example showing a symmetric implementation where two processes regulate each other. The Producer process repeats a cycle of producing items and placing the items in a buffer store. The Consumer process removes items from the buffer and consumes the items. The solution will work for multiple producer processes and multiple consumer processes as shown in the diagram below.

Assume that the buffer is of a fixed size with a capacity to hold 100 items. The following rules apply:

- The Producer cannot place any items in the buffer if the buffer is full
- The Consumer cannot remove an item from the buffer if the buffer is empty
- Only one process is allowed to access the buffer at a time (mutual exclusion)

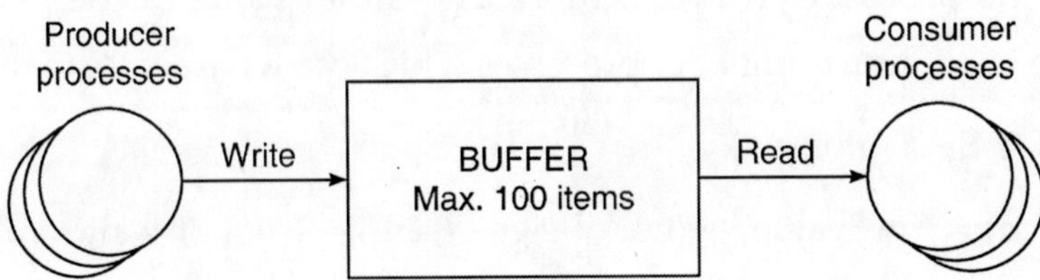

Var MUTEX, NOT_EMPTY, NOT_FULL : Semaphore;

MUTEX := 1 ;

NOT_FULL := 100 ;

NOT_EMPTY := 0 ;

```
(* producer process *)
______________________

while(true)
produce (item);
wait (NOT_FULL);
wait(MUTEX);
put_item_to_buffer();
signal(MUTEX);
signal(NOT_EMPTY);
```

```
(* consumer process *)
______________________

while(true)

wait (NOT_EMPTY);
wait(MUTEX);
take_item_from_buffer();
signal(MUTEX);
signal(NOT_FULL);
consume(item);
```

Example problems using Semaphores:

PROBLEM 1

Consider the diagram below. Two communication buffers are used to allow processes P1 and P2 to write data which is to be used by process P3. The following conditions are to be satisfied in the scheme:

- Buffer_1 has a maximum size of 1024 bytes
- Buffer_2 has a maximum size of 4096 bytes
- P1 can write a byte to Buffer_1, only when Buffer_1 is not full
- P2 can write a byte to Buffer_2, only when Buffer_2 is not full
- P3 cannot read if **any** buffer is empty
- Mutually exclusive access is to be implemented for each buffer

Using pseudo code, design programs for processes P1, P2 and P3 which will implement the defined scheme. Your solution is to be based on the use of **semaphores**. Assume a simple multi-tasking environment operating on a single processor.

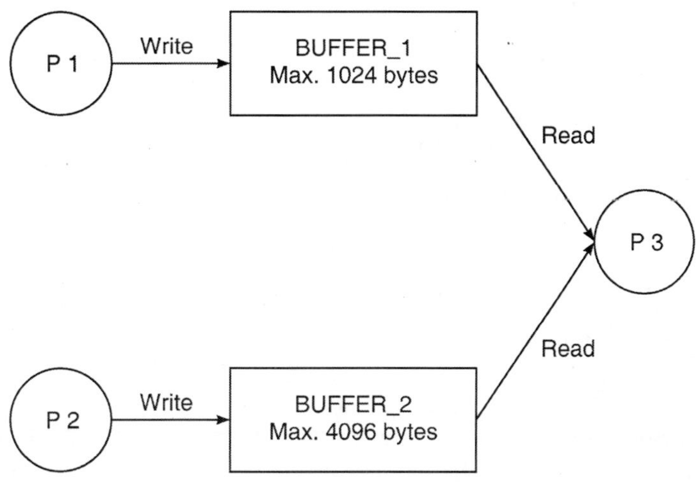

SOLUTION TO PROBLEM 1:

Var Mutex_B1, Mutex B_2, Not_full_B1,

Not_empty_B1, Not_full_B2, Not_empty_B2 **: semaphore;**

```
Mutex_B1      := 1 ;
Mutex_B2      := 1 ;
Not_full_B1   := 1024 ;
Not_empty_B1  := 0 ;
Not_full_B2   := 4096 ;
Not-empty_B2  := 0 ;
```

```
Process P1
____________
while (true) do
begin
 produce (item);
   wait (Not_full_B1);
   wait (Mutex_B1);
      write_to_Buffer_1;
   signal (Mutex_B1);
   signal (Not_Empty_B1);
end;
```

```
Process P2
____________
while (true) do
begin
 produce (item);
   wait (Not_full_B2);
   wait (Mutex_B2);
      write_to_Buffer_2;
   signal (Mutex_B2);
   signal (Not_Empty_B2);
end;
```

```
Process P3
____________

while(true) do

begin

   wait (Not_empty_B1);
   wait (Not_empty_B2);

   wait (Mutex_B1);
   wait (Mutex_B2);

   read_from_Buffer_1;
   read_from_Buffer_2;

   signal (Mutex_B2);
   signal (Mutex_B1);

   signal (Not_full_B1);
   signal (Not_full_B2);

end;
```

PROBLEM 2

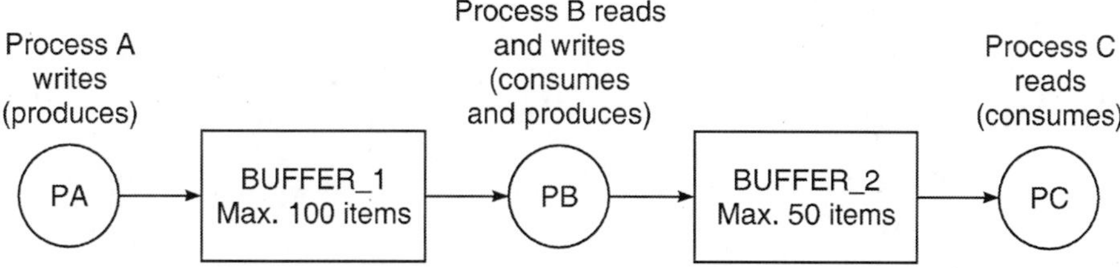

- Buff_1 has a maximum size of 100 data items
- Buff_2 has a maximum size of 50 data items
- Process A can write to Buff_1 only when Buff_1 is not full
- Process B reads from Buff_1 and writes to Buff_2. It can run only if Buff_1 is not empty and Buff_2 is not full
- Process C can read Buff_2 only when Buff_2 is not empty

- Each buffer is to be protected from simultaneous access by two processes (i.e. mutual
exclusion is to be applied).

SOLUTION TO PROBLEM 2:

```
Var  Mutex_B1, Mutex B_2, Not_full_B1,
     Not_empty_B1, Not_full_B2, Not_empty_B2 :semaphore;

Mutex_B1        := 1  ;
Mutex_B2        := 1  ;
Not_full_B1     := 100 ;
Not_empty_B1    := 0  ;
Not_full_B2     := 50  ;
Not-empty_B2    := 0 ;
```

```
Process A

while (true) do

begin
  produce (item);
     wait (Not_full_B1);

   wait (Mutex_B1);
     write_to_Buff_1;
   signal (Mutex_B1);

    signal (Not_Empty_B1);

end;
```

```
Process C

while (true) do

begin

      wait (Not_empty_B2);

    wait (Mutex_B2);
      read_from_Buff_2;
    signal (Mutex_B2);

     signal (Not_full_B2);

 consume(item);

end;
```

```
Process B

while(true) do

begin

   wait (Not_empty_B1);
   wait (Not_full_B2);

    wait (Mutex_B1);
    wait (Mutex_B2);
             read-from_Buff_1;
             write_to_Buff_2;
    signal (Mutex_B2);
    signal (Mutex_B1);

   signal (Not_full_B1);
   signal (Not_empty_B2);

end;
```

READERS AND WRITERS PROBLEM

Problem: Several processes wish to access a common **data_file**, some to **read**, some to **write**. Multiple processes are allowed to have *simultaneous* read access but *exclusive* access must be given to writers.

See a solution below. The first reading process locks the **data_file** using **wait(mutex_file).** Subsequent readers are allowed access. Readers will eventually finish with the **data_file** and the last reader frees the **data_file** using **signal (mutex_file).** The **counter** variable is used to determine the first reader and the last reader so that the **data_file** can be locked for many readers and released when all readers have finished.

Note, the variable **counter** is accessed by all readers, concurrently. The semaphore *mutex_counter* is used to provide mutual exclusion on the count variable.

If a writer process wants access to the **data_file**, it can gain exclusive access after the last reader issues **signal (mutex_file),** thereby unlocking the **data_file**.

The implementation assumes readers have priority over writers i.e. if any process needs to update (write) the **data_file** it must wait until all readers have finished. However, in many cases it may be more important to allow a writer to have priority over readers so that the most up-to-date information can be provided in the **data_file**.

A solution which provides writer priority is probably more useful – but the implementation is a little more complex.

READERS and WRITERS: A solution:

```
var mutex_file, mutex_counter : semaphore

var counter : integer

mutex_file    := 1;
mutex_counter := 1;

counter       := 0;
```

Reader Process

```
wait (mutex_counter) ;

    counter := counter +1 ;
    if counter = 1 then  wait (mutex_file) ;

signal (mutex_counter) ;

            read_the_data_file ;

wait (mutex_counter) ;

  counter := counter -1   ;
  if counter = 0 then   signal (mutex_file) ;

signal (mutex_counter) ;
```

Writer Process

```
wait (mutex_file) ;

   write_to_data_file ;   (* exclusive access ! *)

signal (mutex_file) ;
```

The Dining Philosophers Problem

There are N philosophers spending their lives thinking and eating in a room. In their round table there is a plate of infinite rice and N chopsticks. From time to time, a philosopher gets hungry. He tries to pick up the two chopsticks that are on his right and his left. A philosopher that picks both chopsticks successfully (one at a time) starts eating. A philosopher may pick one chopstick at a time. When a philosopher finishes eating, he puts down both of his chopsticks to their original position and he starts thinking again. The question is to write a program which does not let any philosopher to die due to hunger (i.e. no deadlocks.)

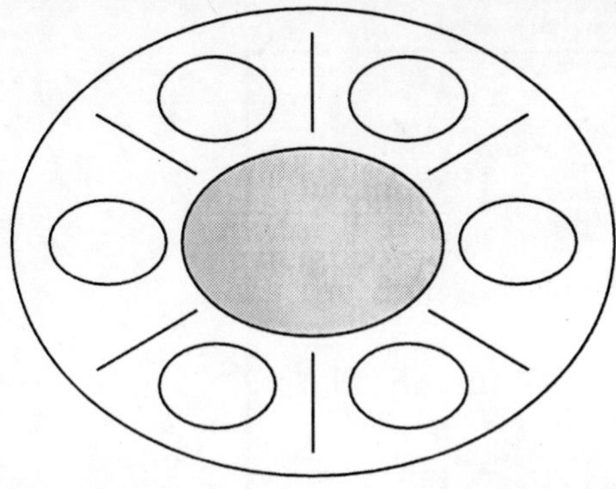

```
#define N 6                                    /* number of philosophers */
semaphore chopstick[N]                         /* a semaphore for each chopstick,
  each to be initialized to 1 */
void philosopher(int i)                        /* which philosopher (0 to N-1) ? */
{
        while (TRUE)
        {
                think();                                  /* philosopher is thinking */
                down(chopstick[i]);                     /* take left chopstick */
down(chopstick [(i+1) % N]);                   /* take right chopstick */
                eat();                                          /* yum-yum, rice */
                up(chopstick[i]);                       /* put left chopstick */
                up(chopstick [(i+1) % N]);             /* put left chopstick */
        }
}
```

Unfortunately, this program fails in the situation when all philosophers take their left chopsticks simultaneously. None will able to take their right chopsticks, there will be a deadlock, and all of them will die because of hunger.

We can modify the program so that after taking the left chopstick, the program checks whether the right chopstick is available. If it is not, the philosopher puts down the left one, waits for some time, and then repeats the whole process. This proposal too fails, although for a different reason. With a little bit of bad luck, all the philosophers could start the algorithm simultaneously, picking up their left chopsticks, seeing that their right chopsticks are not available, putting down their left chopsticks, waiting, picking up their left chopsticks again simultaneously, and so on till death. We have defined this situation in former chapters. This is the situation in which all the programs continue to run indefinitely but fail to make any progress, namely starvation.

Now, you may think, "If the philosophers would just wait a random time instead of the same time after failing to acquire the right chopstick." That is true, but in some application one would prefer a solution that always works and cannot fail due to an unlikely series of random numbers. (Think about safety control in a nuclear plant)

The following program uses an array state, to keep track of whether a philosopher is eating, thinking, or hungry (trying to acquire chopsticks). A philosopher may move into eating state only if neither neighbour is eating. The neighbors are defined by the macros LEFT and RIGHT.

```
#define N          6          /* number of philosophers */
#define LEFT       (i-1) % N  /* number i's left neighbor */
#define RIGHT      (i+1) % N  /* number i's right neighbor */
#define THINKING   0          /* mode of thinking */
#define HUNGRY     1          /* mode of hunger */
#define EATING     2          /* mode of eating */

typedef int semaphore;        /* semaphores are a special kind of int
*/ int state[N];              /* array to keep track of states */
semaphore mutex = 1;          /* mutual exclusion for CS */
semaphore s[N] ;              /* one semaphore per philosopher */

void philosopher(int i)       /* i : Which philosopher (0 to N-1) ? */
{
        while (TRUE)          /* infinite loop */
        {
                think();      /* philosopher is thinking */
take_sticks(i);               /* acquire two chopsticks or block */
                eat();        /* yum-yum, rice */
                put_sticks(i); /* put both chopsticks back */
        }
}

void take_sticks(int i)       /* i : Which philosopher (0 to N-1) ? */
{
        down(mutex);          /* enter CS */
state[i] = HUNGRY;            /* record that the philosopher is hungry*/
test(i);                      /* try to acquire 2 chopsticks */
        up(mutex);            /* leave CS */
down(s[i]) ;                  /* block if chopsticks were not acquired */
}

void put_sticks(int i)        /* i : Which philosopher (0 to N-1) ? */
{
        down(mutex);          /* enter CS */
state[i] = THINKING;          /* philosopher has finished eating */
test(LEFT);                   /* see if the left neighbor can eat now */
test(RIGHT);                  /* see if the right neighbor can eat now */
        up(mutex);            /* leave CS */
}
```

```
void test(int i)                                            /* i : Which philosopher (0 to N-1) ? */
{
if (state[i] == HUNGRY && state[LEFT] != EATING && state[RIGHT] != EATING)
  {
        state[i] = EATING;
        up(s[i]);
  }
}
```

The Sleeping Barber Problem

The barber shop has one barber, one barber chair, and N chairs for waiting customers, if any, to sit in. If there is no customer at present, the barber sits down in the barber chair and falls asleep. When a customer arrives, he has to wake up the sleeping barber. If additional customers arrive while the barber is cutting a customer's hair, they either sit down (if there is an empty chair) or leave the shop (if all chairs are full). The problem is to program the barber and the customers without getting into race conditions.

```
#define CHAIRS 5                        /* number of chairs for waiting customers */

typedef int semaphore;

semaphore customers = 0;                /* number of waiting customers */
semaphore barbers = 0;                  /* number of barbers waiting for customers */
semaphore mutex = 1;                    /* for mutual exclusion */
int waiting = 0;                        /* customers are waiting not being haircut */

void Barber(void)
{
        while (TRUE)
        {
down(customers);                        /* go to sleep if number of customers is 0 */
                down(mutex);                /* acquire access to 'waiting' */
waiting = waiting – 1;                  /* decrement count of waiting customers */
up(barbers);                            /* one barber is now ready to cut hair */
                up(mutex);              /* release 'waiting' */
                cut_hair();             /* cut hair, non-CS */
        }
}
```

```
void customer(void)
{
        down(mutex);                    /* enter CS */
if (waiting < CHAIRS)
        {
waiting = waiting + 1;                  /* increment count of waiting customers */
up(customers);                          /* wake up barber if necessary */
                up(mutex);              /* release access to 'waiting' */
down(barbers);                          /* wait if no free barbers */
                get_haircut();          /* non-CS */
        }
        else
        {
up(mutex);                              /* shop is full, do not wait */
        }
}
```

Our solution uses three semaphores: *customers*, which counts waiting customers (excluding the one being served), *barbers*, the number of idle barbers (0 or 1), and *mutex* for mutual exclusion. The variable *waiting* is essentially a copy of *customers* andit is required since there is no way to read the current value of a semaphore.

MONITORS

A monitor has the structure of an abstract data type (ADT) object. Data is encapsulated and operations are executed under mutual exclusion. Critical sections are replaced with calls to monitor procedures.

Semaphores are useful operating system primitives to support communication and synchronisation. However, with semaphores the programmer must be very careful with their use. For example if, in the producer/consumer problem, the two producer process wait ( ) functions were reversed in order, the producer process would block on a full buffer and the consumer process could not enter the critical section, resulting in a deadlock condition.

Also, in reading code which includes semaphores it can be tedious to identify all the sections which use semaphores to protect particular resources

A monitor program contains procedures, data structures, variables.

Procedures within the monitor can be called and used to access internal variables. These internal variables cannot be accessed by procedures outside the monitor. Procedures within the monitor cannot access variables external to the monitor.

Only one process can be active within the monitor at a time.

Monitors are a **programming language construct**. The compiler ensures proper handling of calls to monitor procedures, ensuring that only one process can be in the monitor at a time. The compiler will probably use a binary semaphore to implement mutual exclusion for monitor entry.

Critical sections are written as monitors to ensure mutual exclusion.

A monitor procedure is called by specifying the name of the monitor and the required procedure, separated by a dot.

E.g.: **monitorexample.proc_two (parameters)**

Skeleton monitor program

```
monitorexample: monitor
begin
 .
  declare local data;
 .
    procedure proc_one (formal parameters)
     begin
      .
      statements ..;
      .
     end;
```

```
    procedure proc_two (formal parameters)
     begin
      .
      statements ..;
      .
     end;

  main program here .......;
 .
end;
```

Condition Variables

Variables of type **condition** are declared to represent each reason that a program might need to wait. Condition variables are used within monitors to cause the calling process (the process which called the procedure within the monitor) to **block** so as to wait on some future condition to happen. Another process can then enter the monitor.

A condition variable is declared with type **condition**

E.g.: state_one, state_two : condition;

The condition variable is neither true nor false and does not have a stored value. It represents a queue (initially empty) of processes waiting on the condition.

Operations on a condition variable: **signal** and **wait**

condition_variable.**wait**;

//The calling process is caused to block waiting on the condition variable

condition_variable.**signal**;

//The process blocking on the condition variable is woken-up

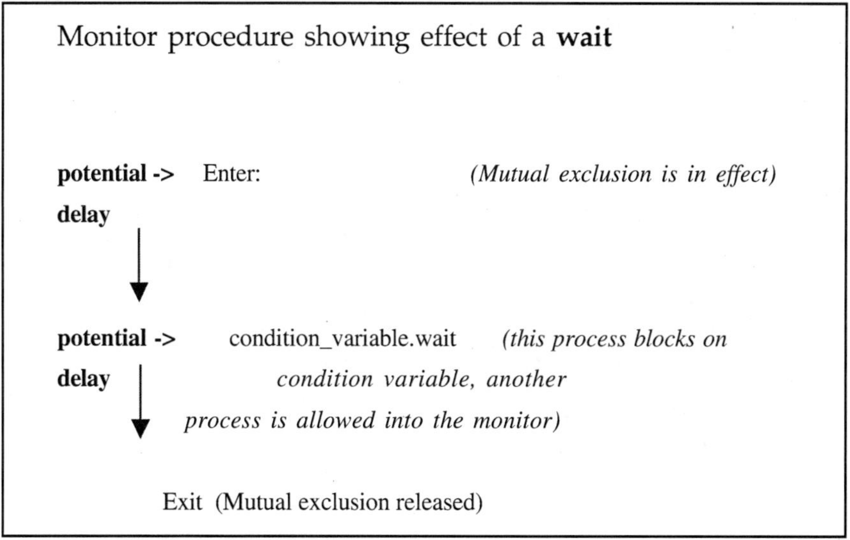

On a **signal**, what happens if there is more than one processes sleeping on the condition variable, which one should be woken-up? The newly awakened process should run and the current one should be suspended. If more than one process is blocked on the condition variable then the scheduler is responsible for queuing these in some order, probably allowing the longest waiting process to run first.

A common discipline (often imposed by the compiler) is to always make the **signal** statement the final statement in the monitor procedure so as to ensure that the current process will exit immediately the signal is executed.

A monitor process will not be pre-empted before completion, thus exclusive access is guaranteed and hence simple actions on, or testing of internal variables is safe.

Example Solve with monitors:

There is one airstrip in an airport that can be used by planes landing and taking off (but not at the same time for obvious reasons). Planes arriving (to land) must be granted permission to land as soon as possible. However, if there are three successive landings, one waiting plane (if any) is given permission to take off (to prevent indefinite postponement). Design a monitor to arrange the operations at this airport. (Each plane corresponds to a process like the ones given below. Select the one suitable for your design. Describe monitor elements thoroughly).

```
Plane ( )
{ usage = TAKEOFF  /* or LANDING */
  ...
  Airport . RequestAirstrip ( usage )
  ...
  Airport.ReleaseAirstrip( )
  /* process ends here */
}

monitor Airport
{
  int state;          /* Airstrip status   */
  int iLanded;        /* recent landings   */
  int LQueueSize;     /* Landing queue size */
  int TQueueSize;     /* Takeoff queue size */
  condition Landing;  /* Landing condition and queue*/
  condition Takeoff;  /* Takeoff condition and queue*/
```

```
entry RequestAirstrip( int usage )
{
  if ( state == BUSY )
  {
    if ( usage == 'LANDING' )      /* Adjust queue size before wait */
    {
      LQueueSize ++;
      Landing.wait ;
    }
    else
    {
      TQueueSize ++;
      Takeoff.wait ;
    }
  }
  /* Note that at this point the plane has been granted permission */
  /* to land or to take off either directly (without being queued) */
  /* or as a result of a signal operation                          */

  state = BUSY;
  if (usage == LANDING)
  {
    iLanded ++ ;     /* Count the number of landings */
  }
}
entry ReleaseAirstrip ( )
{
  state = FREE ;
  if ( iLanded > 2)       /* If 3 landings has occurred, signal */
  {                       /* a plane waiting to take off       */
    if (TQueueSize > 0)  /* Must check first to see whether a */
```

```
    {               /* plane is waiting to land          */
      TQueueSize —;   /* Adjust number of waiting planes   */
      iLanded = 0 ;   /* Restart counter                   */
      Takeoff .signal;
    }
    else (LQueueSize > 0)
    {
      LQueueSize —;   /* Adjust number of waiting planes   */
      Landing.signal;
    }
  }
  else                /* 3 landings not occurred yet.     */
  {                   /* Signal a plane queued for landing */
    if (LQueueSize > 0) /* (if any)                        */
    {
      LQueueSize— ;
      Landing .signal;
    }
    else if (TQueueSize > 0)
    {
      TQueueSize—;
      Takeoff.signal;
    }
  }
}
{ /* Initialization */
  state      = FREE ;  /* Airstrip status    */
  iLanded    = 0   ;   /* Recent landings    */
  TQueueSize = 0   ;   /* Takeoff queue size */
  LQueueSize = 0   ;   /* Landing queue size */
}
}
```

To synchronize bidirectional traffic over a narrow light-duty bridge on a public highway. Traffic may only cross the bridge in one direction at a time, and if there are ever more than 3 vehicles on the bridge at one time, it will collapse under their weight. In this

system, each car is represented by one process.

Write a monitor and the procedures ArriveBridge and ExitBridge.

Your solution must guarantee fairness and freedom from starvation (design the appropriate protocol).

```
Car(int d)  /* d - direction: is either 0 or 1 */
{
  ArriveBridge(d);
  ...
  ExitBridge(d);
}
```

The following is a simple solution that does not guarantee fairness or freedom from starvation. Change this code by introducing policies to that effect. Monitor function queue(x) returns the number of elements (waiting processes) in condition variable queue x.

```
monitor Bridge
{
   condition 0pass;  /* queue for vehicles coming from west */
   condition 1pass;  /* queue for vehicles coming from east */
   int dir;          /* Current dir -1 (not in use),0,1 */
   int count;        /* Cars on bridge */

   entry ArriveBridge (int d)
   {
     if (dir == d && count < 3)
     {
       ;
     }
     else if (dir == -1)
     {
       count = 0;
```

```
    }
    else
    {
      if (d == 0)
        0Pass.wait
      else
        1Pass.wait
    }
    count++;
    dir = d;
  }
  entry ExitBridge (int d)
  {
    count—;
    if (dir == 1)
    {
      /* Here we have cars in direction 1 already on the bridge */
      /* so we may let another car in the same direction.      */
      if queue(1Pass) > 0)
        1Pass.signal ;
      /* If no cars in direction 1
      else if (count == 0 && queue(0Pass) > 0)
        0Pass.signal ;
      else if (count == 0)
        dir = -1;
    }
    else if (dir == 0)
    {
      if queue(0Pass) > 0)
        0Pass.signal ;
      else if (count == 0 && queue(1Pass) > 0)
        1Pass.signal ;
      else if (count == 0)
```

```
            dir = -1;
        }
        { /* init */
        dir = -1;
        count = 0;
        }
    }
```

THE PRODUCER-CONSUMER PROBLEM USING MONITORS

==

```
(* ——— PRODUCER PROCEDURE ————*)

procedure producer;
begin
 while true do
     begin
       produce_an_item;
       bounded_buffer.write;
     end;
end;
```

```
(*——— CONSUMER PROCEDURE ————*)

procedure consumer;
begin
 while true do

     begin
       bounded_buffer.read;
       consume_an_item;
     end;
end
```

```
(*———— MONITOR PROGRAM ————*)

bounded_buffer: monitor
begin
 count, N    : integer;
 not_full, not_empty : condition;
 procedure write;
  begin
    if count = N then not_full.wait;
    add_to_buffer;
    count := count + 1;
    if count = 1 then not_empty.signal;
  end;
 procedure read;
  begin
    if count = 0 then not_empty.wait;
    take_from_buffer;
    count := count - 1;
    if count = N - 1  then not_full.signal;
  end;

 count := 0 ;
 N := 100;
end bounded_buffer;
```

Monitors – Some Limitations:

Monitors, semaphores and **event counters** are useful in solving Mutual Exclusion problems for single CPU systems where processes share a common memory where data structures can be easily protected by using TSL instructions or by disabling interrupts. These techniques are also useful for a multiple CPU system where the CPUs share a **common memory**.

However, distributed systems (e.g. LANs) are usually implemented with CPUs having separate, local memory. Different communication and synchronisation mechanisms are needed, usually based on **message passing** schemes.

Monitors: more on condition variable

The **.wait** operation causes a process to *block* on a condition variable whereas a **.signal** causes a process which is blocked on a condition variable to *wake up*.

SCHEDULED WAITS

The scheduled wait is a further feature of the **conditional wait**. An argument is used with the .**wait** operation to give a priority indication; so that processes blocked on a condition variable will be queued based on this priority parameter. For example the following statement causes the program to block on the condition variable *disk_ready* with a priority **n** in the blocked queue:

disk_ready.wait (**n**);

In our examples we will assume that the process which is assigned the lowest value for **n** is given the highest priority position in the blocked queue.

BOOLEAN FUNCTION OF CONDITIONS

A Boolean function of conditions implies that the value of the function is **true** if there exists any process in the queue waiting on the given conditional variable, otherwise the value is false. For example:

if (modem_ready.queue)

then PRINT "There is at least one process blocked on the modem"

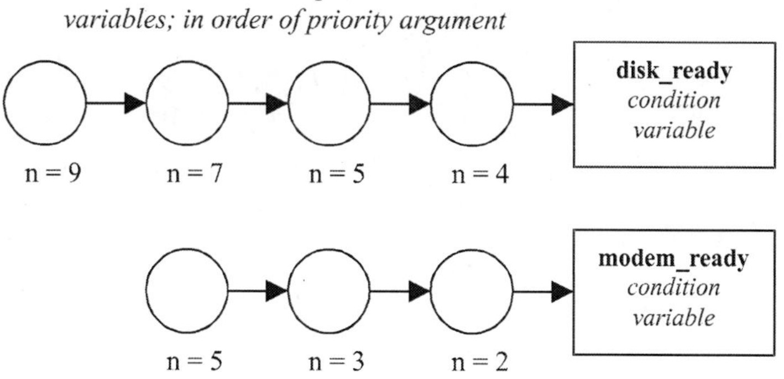

Example MONITOR program

BACKGROUND:- DESIGN APPROACH TO DISK HEAD SCHEDULING

In a multi-tasking system, when several processes are contending for disk drive access, the time to access the disk drive often becomes a system bottleneck. The time for the disk head to **seek** (move) to the desired cylinder is the most significant cause of disk latency.

A simple system will accept disk requests as they arrive, on a First Come First Served (**FCFS**) scheme.

Consider a system where multiple processes require access to the disk, and all pending seek requests (requests to move to a particular cylinder), indexed by cylinder number, will sleep in some blocked queue, awaiting their turn to wake up. This blocked queue then would hold multiple requests for access to various cylinders on the disk.

Consider a small disk with just 30 cylinders (a real hard disk will have a few thousand cylinders). Assume the disk is currently accessing cylinder number 10 and a series of pending queued requests yields a cylinder seek order of: 25, 3, 22, 5, 12. See the diagram below. Based on the **FCFS** scheme the head arm will seek over the following distances:

$$15 + 22 + 19 + 17 + 7 = \underline{80 \text{ cylinders}}$$

If instead of using the simple FCFS scheme, the Shortest Seek First (**SSF**) policy is used then the head arm would seek to the cylinders in an order where it would always go to the nearest cylinder next. See the diagram below. In our example the **SSF** scheme would access the cylinders in the sequence: 12, 5, 3, 22, 25; seeking over the following distances:

$$2 + 7 + 2 + 20 + 2 = \underline{33 \text{ cylinders}}$$

The problem with the **SSF** scheme is that on a busy disk, access the cylinders which are close to the centre of the disk would be favoured where pending seek requests to cylinders towards both extreme ends of the disk would experience delays.

The Elevator Algorithm (EA)

In practice the Elevator Algorithm (EA) is used for such disk head scheduling. The policy here is to service all seek requests in one head sweep direction until there are no more requests for cylinders in that direction, then to move in the other sweep direction and to service all requests in that direction. This is somewhat similar to way that a conventional building elevator works; and hence the name of the scheme!

Based on our example above (and assuming that we have arrived at cylinder 10 in a down sweep), the head arm seeks to cylinders in the following order: 5, 3, 12, 22 and 25. See the diagram. The use of the **EA** scheme results in seeks over the following distances:

5 + 2 + 9 + 10 + 3 = <u>29 cylinders</u>

Note, in the above example the **EA** scheme happens to provide a faster service as compared to the **SSF** scheme but statistically the **SSF** scheme might perform better. However, even if the **EA** scheme does guarantee that the maximum number of cylinders travelled is bounded to (2 x *max. no. of cylinders*).

In real life most disk servers employ the Elevator Algorithm so as to help in providing a responsive service to the multiple clients requiring access to disk files. It is also interesting to note that the Elevator Algorithm does not only save disk access time but it also saves on mechanical wear in the head drive mechanism as the amount of head movement is very much reduced, as compared to the simple **FCFS** scheme.

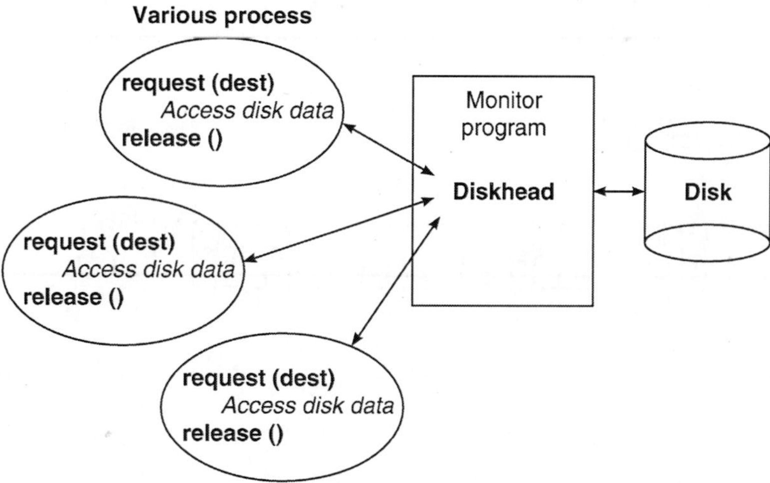

DIAGRAM - DISK HEAD SCHEDULING

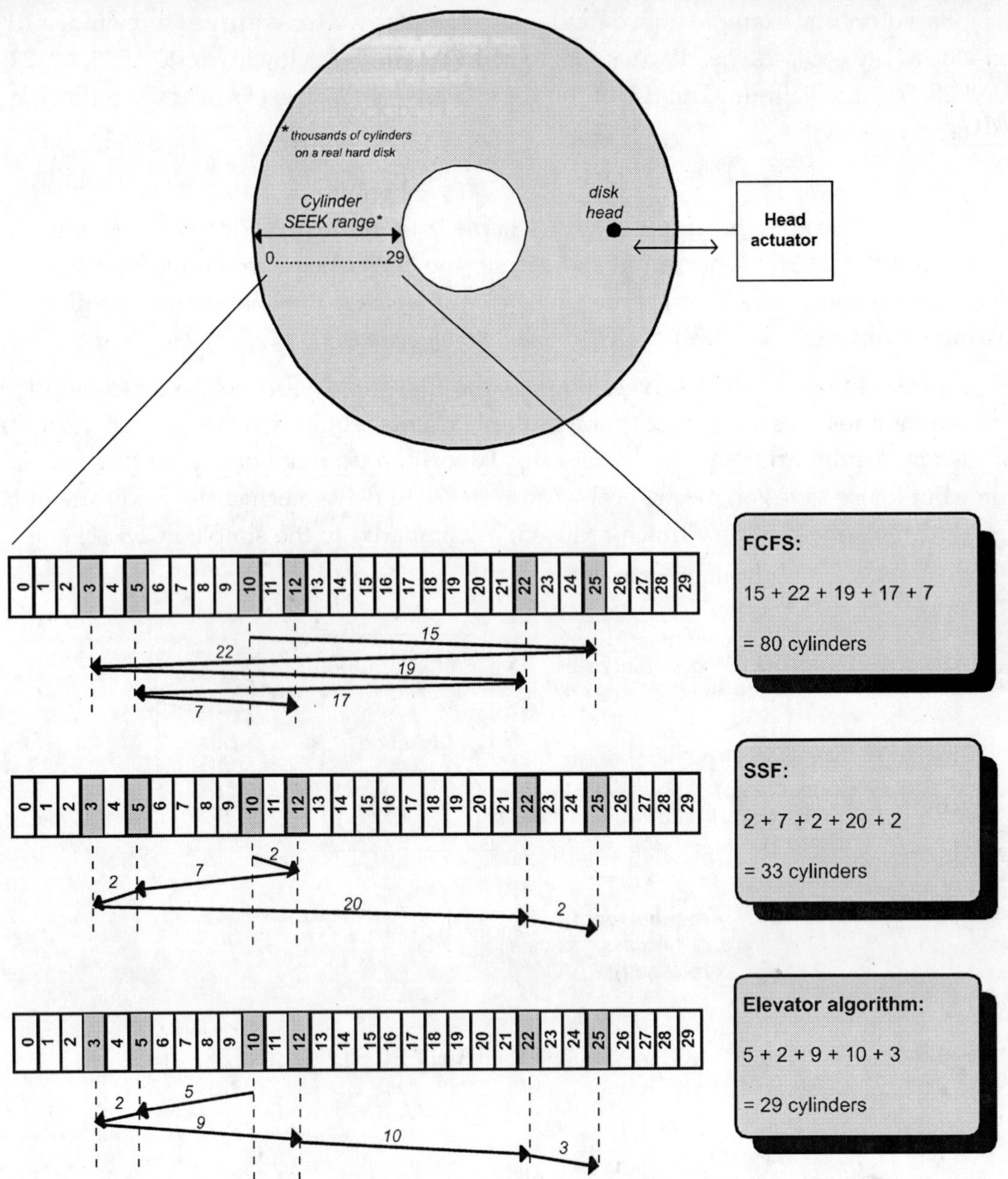

PROGRAM DESIGN FOR THE DISK HEAD SCHEDULER

THERE ARE TWO ENTRIES TO THE DISK HEAD SCHEDULER:

a) **request (dest:cylinder);**

type cylinder = 0.. topcylinder;

Entered by a program before attempting to access the disk cylinder

b) **release ( );**

Entered by a program when it has completed all transfers on the current cylinder

MONITOR LOCAL DATA AND CONDITIONS:

conditions:

The program employs two blocked queues.

going_up ..requests waiting for an up sweep

going_down ..requests waiting for a down sweep

local data:

headpos .. head position by cylinder number

direction .. sweep direction up or down

busy .. disk is busy (boolean)

THE DISK HEAD SCHEDULER - MONITOR PROGRAM

```
diskhead: monitor
begin
headpos              :cylinder;
direction            :(up, down);
busy                 :boolean;
going_up, going_down :condition;

(* this is the request ( ) procedure  ========================== *)

    procedure request (dest  :cylinder);
     begin
   if busy then
    { if (headpos < dest) OR (headpos = dest AND direction = up)
then going_up.wait (dest)
else going_down.wait (topcylinder – dest) };
  busy := true;    headpos := dest ;
```

```
    end request;
   (* ================================================ *)


  (* this is the release  procedure   ============================ *)
    procedure release;
     begin busy := false;
  if direction = up then
       { if going_up.queue   then   going_up.signal
  else {direction := down;
                      going_down.signal}
          }
  else if going_down.queue then going_down.signal
  else {direction := up;
  going_up.signal }
     end release;
  (* ================================================ *)


    headpos := 0; direction := up; busy := false


  end diskhead
```

Summary of the logic used:

When direction is up:		
if (headpos < dest)	**then**	going_up.wait
if (headpos = dest)	**then**	going_up.wait
if (headpos > dest)	**then**	going_down.wait

When direction is down:		
if (headpos < dest)	**then**	going_up.wait
if (headpos = dest)	**then**	going_down.wait
if (headpos > dest)	**then**	going_down.wait

KEYWORDS

PROCESS SYNCHRONIZATION
MUTUAL EXCLUSION
CRITICAL SECTIONS
RACE CONDITION
DEKKER'S SOLUTION
PETERSON'S SOLUTION
SEMAPHORES
MONITOR
BOUNDED BUFFER
PROCESS FLAGS

SUMMARY

Process synchronization implies the use of atomic operations to ensure correct cooperation between processes i.e. to eliminate race conditions.

- Mutual Exclusion ensures that non-shareable resources are accessed by only one process at a time i.e. if one process is using a resource (say a variable or a file) another is excluded from accessing that resource. Some method must be implemented to achieve mutual exclusion.
- When two or more processes share some common data (or other resource) and the final result depends upon the timing of access to the data or the order in which processes are run then a race condition exists
- Dekker's solution: each process has its own variable to indicate whether or not it wants entry to the critical section. A process can read the other process's variable. An integer variable TURN is used to resolve a conflict situation where two processes try to enter their critical sections simultaneously. When such a conflict arises the TURN value is used to arbitrate in favour of one process.
- Peterson's solution: A process flags its interest in entering the critical section by setting an interest flag. If the other process has previously set its own interest flag, the process will wait for the other process to clear its interest flag before entering the critical section itself.
- Dijkstra proposed the use of semaphores to support a method for implementing mutual exclusion which does not depend on the use of busy waiting. A process which is unable to enter its critical section can go to the blocked state instead of waiting, thereby freeing up the CPU for use by other processes.
- A monitor has the structure of an abstract data type (ADT) object. Data is encapsulated and operations are executed under mutual exclusion. Critical sections are replaced with calls to monitor procedures

REVIEW QUESTIONS

1) What is race condition?
2) How to avoid race condition?
3) What is mutual exclusion?
4) What are different techniques to resolve mutual exclusion ?explain briefly?
5) What is critical section?
6) What is critical region?
7) What is conditional critical region?
8) Write short note on monitor?
9) Explain dining –philosophers problem?
10) Explain producer-consumer problem?
11) Explain readers-writers problem?
12) Explain bounded buffer problem?
13) What do you mean by semaphore?
14) What are the limitations of semaphore?
15) Explain how semaphores are used to solve the critical section problem?
16) Explain how semaphores are used to solve the dining –philosophers problem?
17) What is process synchronization?
18) Explain the need for process synchronization?
19) What is inter- process synchronization?
20) Explain inter process communication?
21) Explain message –passing in case communication?

FILL IN THE BLANKS

1. __________cannot affect or be affected by other processes but there is no shared data.
2. __________can affect or be affected by other processes but there could be shared data.
3. ___________ensures that non-shareable resources are accessed by only one process at a time
4. ___________suggests that a process flags its interest in entering the critical section by setting an interest flag.
5. Monitors and __________ are useful in solving Mutual Exclusion problems.
6. A __________semaphore is an integer variable which can have a **0** or **1** value

TRUE OR FALSE

1. If a scheme could ensure that no two processes could be in their critical section at the same time then mutual exclusion could be achieved thus avoiding race conditions.
2. A TEST AND SET LOCK (TSL) instruction is useful only in uniprocessor systems.
3. Information sharing means two processes using the same file.
4. Dekker's solution is very simple for general use.
5. The critical section of a program can have an associated binary semaphore, usually initiated to 1.
6. The General semaphore uses an integer variable which uses only non-negative numbers not restricted to 0 and 1 values.

ANSWERS

FILL IN THE BLANKS

1. Mutual Exclusion
2. Peterson's solution
3. semaphores
4. binary
5. Independent processes
6. Cooperating processes

TRUE OR FALSE

1. TRUE
2. FALSE
3. TRUE
4. FALSE
5. TRUE
6. TRUE

❑❑❑

"Things that we hear pass quicker from our minds than what we read." —Ausonius

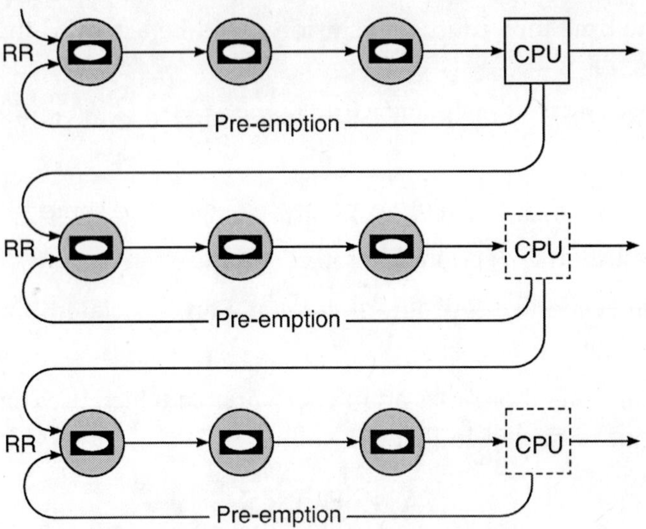

PROCESS SCHEDULING

INTRODUCTION

CPU scheduling concerns how the CPU time is allocated between the competing processes or threads. We aim for efficient CPU time use in the face of quite variable CPU time use patterns amongst different applications and different user needs e.g. interactive responsiveness. Scheduling algorithms also vary between real-time systems and general purpose computing systems.

A process is an executing program, including the current values of the program counter, registers, and variables. The subtle difference between a process and a program is that the program is a group of instructions whereas the process is the activity. A system with one CPU can only have one running process at any time. As user jobs enter the system, they are put on a queue called as the "job pool". This consists of all jobs in the system. The main objective of multiprogramming is to have some process running at all times to maximize CPU utilization. The main objective of time-sharing is to switch the CPU among different processes so frequently that users can interact with each program while it is running.

In multiprogramming systems, processes are performed in a pseudo parallelism as if each process has its own processor. In fact, there is only one processor but it switches back and forth from process to process.

Henceforth, by saying execution of a process, we mean the processor's operations on the process like changing its variables, etc. and I/O work means the interaction of the process with the I/O operations like reading something or writing to somewhere. They may also be named as "processor (CPU) burst" and "I/O burst" respectively. According to these definitions, we classify programs as CPU bound or I/O bound.

THE NATURE OF PROCESSES

Some processes are designed to act on I/O devices in a responsive fashion and other processes are not concerned with I/O activity but rather require processing time so as to operate efficiently. In general processes might be classed as being *I/O bound* or *processor bound*. Of course, many processes by their nature will require a mix of I/O activity and processor activity but it is useful to define here what is meant by *I/O bound activity* and *processor bound activity*.

Processor bound activity

Assumes that the CPU is the resource of prime importance and that when a process is assigned the CPU it will always tend to use the CPU for its full quantum time. This model does not consider the blocked state.

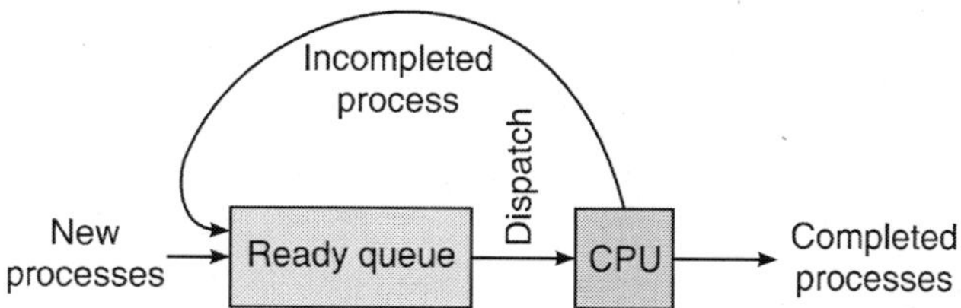

Processor-bound or CPU-bound program: A program having long processor bursts (execution instants). CPU bound processes require more CPU time than I/O time.

I/O bound activity

Assumes that the process makes frequent access to I/O and when the process gets the CPU it will make an I/O request during its quantum time and transition to the blocked state.

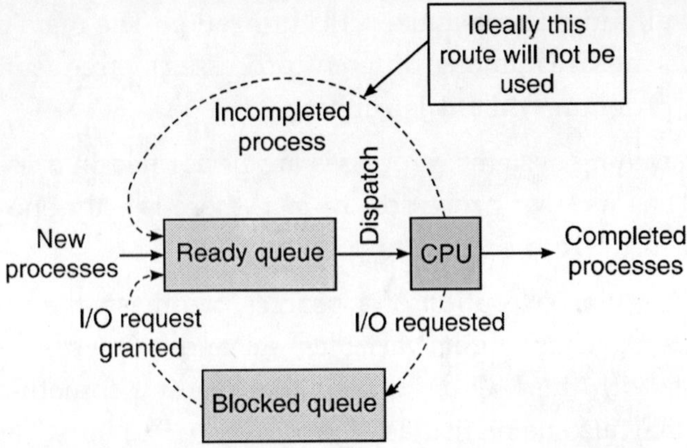

I/O-bound program: A program having short processor bursts. I/O bound processes require more I/O time than CPU time.

Assume we have two processes A and B. Both execute for 1 second and does some I/O work for 1 second. This pattern is repeated 3 times for process A and 2 times for process B.

If we have no multiprogramming, the processes are executed sequentially as below.

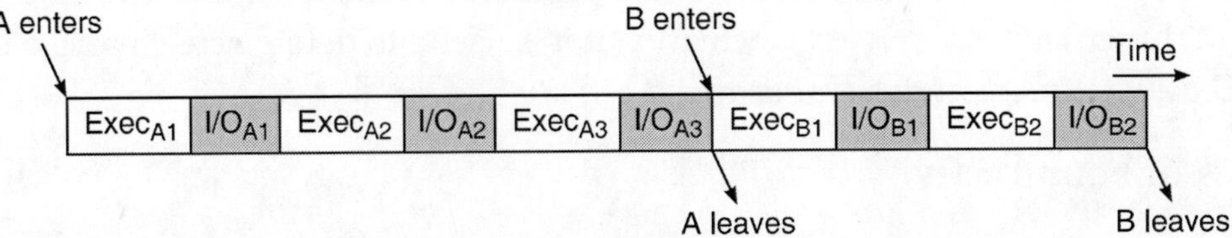

So, the processor executes these two processes in a total time of 10 seconds. However, it is idle at I/O instants of processes. So, it is idle for 5 seconds and utilized for 5 seconds.

Then the processor utilization is

$$\frac{5}{10} \times 100 = 50\%$$

Now let's consider multiprogramming case:

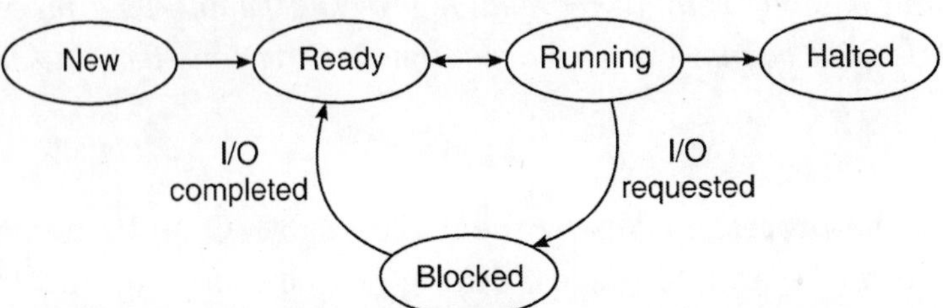

In this case, when process A passes to some I/O work (i.e. does not use the processor), processor utilizes its time to execute process B instead of being idle.

Here the processor utilization is

5 ×100 ? 8 33%

6

REMEMBER

- The main objective of multiprogramming is to have some process running at all times to maximize CPU utilization.
- The main objective of time-sharing is to switch the CPU among different processes so frequently that users can interact with each program while it is running.

PROCESS STATES AND PCB REVISITED

The process states are

New : The process has just arrived.

Ready : The process is waiting to grab the processor. Running: The process has been allocated by the processor. Blocked: The process is doing I/O work or blocked.

Halted : The process has finished and is about to leave the system.

In the OS, each process is represented by its PCB (Process Control Block). The PCB generally contains the following information:

- Process State,
- Process ID,
- Program Counter (PC) value,
- Register values
- Memory Management Information (page tables, base/bound registers etc.)
- Processor Scheduling Information (priority, last processor burst time etc.)
- I/O Status Info (outstanding I/O requests, I/O devices held, etc.)
- List of Open Files
- Accounting Info.

If we have a single processor in our system, there is only one running process at a time. Other ready processes wait for the processor. The system keeps these ready processes (their PCBs) on a list called Ready Queue which is generally implemented as a linked-list structure.

When a process is allocated by the processor, it executes and after some time it either finishes or passes to waiting state (for I/O). The list of processes waiting for a particular I/O device is called a Device Queue. Each device has its own device queue.

In multiprogramming systems, the processor can be switched from one process to another. Note that when an interrupt occurs, PC and register contents for the running process (which is being interrupted) must be saved so that the process can be continued correctly afterwards. Switching between processes occurs as depicted below.

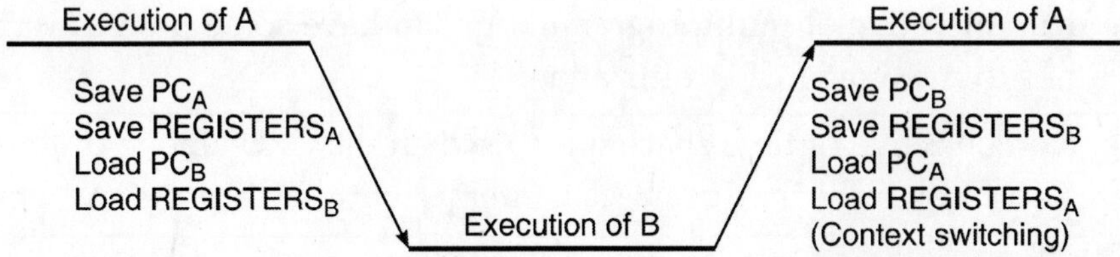

If we consider batch systems, there will often be more processes submitted than the

number of processes that can be executed immediately. So incoming processes are spooled (to a disk). The long-term scheduler selects processes from this process pool and loads selected processes into memory for execution.

LEVELS OF SCHEDULING

Three important levels of scheduling are considered.

High-level scheduling

Sometimes called job scheduling, this determines which job to be allowed to compete actively for the resources of the system. This is sometimes called admission scheduling, because it determines which jobs gain admission to the system. Once admitted, jobs become processes or group of processes.

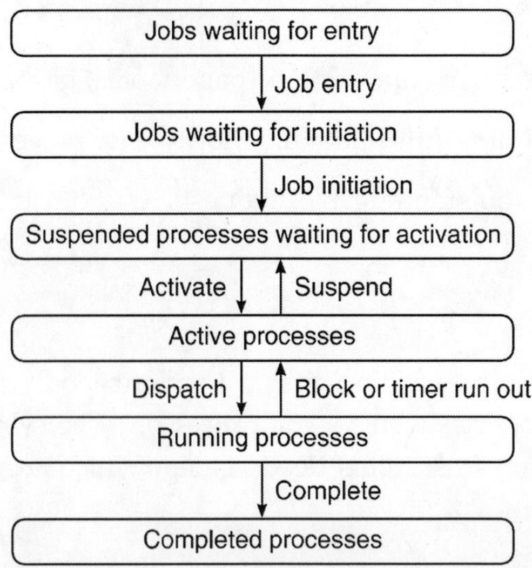

Intermediate-level scheduling

This determines which processes shall be allowed to compete for the CPU. The intermediate level scheduler responds to short-term fluctuations in system load by temporarily suspending and activating (or resuming) processes to achieve smooth system operation and to help realize certain system wide performance goals. Thus the intermediate-level scheduler acts as a buffer between the admission of jobs to the system, and the assignment of the CPU to these jobs.

Low-level scheduling

This determines which ready process will be assigned the CPU when it next become available, and actually assigns the CPU to this process (i.e., it dispatches the CPU to the process). Low-level scheduling is performed by the dispatcher that operates many times per second. The dispatcher must therefore reside at all times in primary storage.

We shall discuss now the scheduling policies that have been used in operating systems and the scheduling mechanism that implement them.

PROCESS SCHEDULERS

Process scheduler is either an algorithm or an implementation of an algorithm that multiplexes a resource among different entities that all require access to the resource.

Process schedulers are the programs that schedule priority of the processes.

At first we have a look at the number of queues present in the system as discussed in the table below:

Job Queue: Consisting of all the processes in the system

Ready Queue: Processes that are residing in the main memory and are ready and waiting to execute are kept on READY QUEUE.

Device Queue: The list of processes waiting for a particular I/O device. Each device has its own device queue.

The scheduling can be classified on the basis of time as under:

1. **Long-term scheduling**

   Concerned will the admission of a job or jobs to the system. Jobs become processes once they are admitted to the system. The concept of long-term scheduling (or job scheduling) is often used in batch systems. Multi-tasking, interactive type environments often do not include this level of scheduling.

2. **Medium-term scheduling**

   Allocates processes in priority order in the ready-to-run queue, according to some well defined strategy. Performs *load-balancing* function by temporarily suspending processes at peak activity times. In a system which does not include a long term scheduler, the medium-term scheduler is often referred to simply as the *scheduler*.

3. **Short-term scheduling**

   Selects the highest priority ready process and assigns the CPU to this process. This action of assigning the CPU to a process is known as **dispatching**.

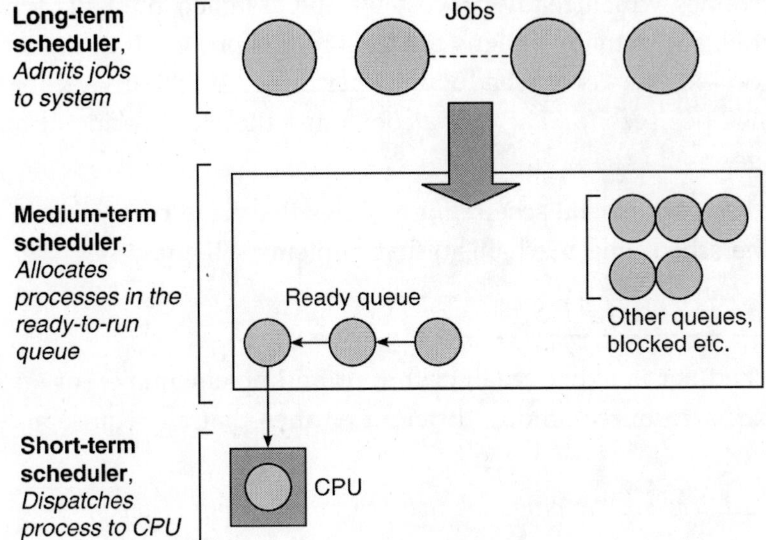

The selection of processes from the queues is managed by schedulers.

Function of the schedulers:

1. Long-term scheduler selects processes from a mass-storage (i.e., hard disk) device where they are spooled and loads them into memory for execution. Also referred to as job scheduler, it selects a job to run and creates a new process.
2. Short term Scheduler (CPU Scheduler) is responsible for scheduling ready processes that are already loaded in memory and are ready to execute.
3. Medium term scheduler controls the number of processes in memory - swaps process out to secondary storage to reduce memory load, or swaps process back into memory to increase memory usage. It is used when processes require more memory than the system can provide for them.

The long-term scheduler brings the processes into memory and hands them over to the CPU scheduler. It controls the number of processes that the CPU scheduler is handling thus maintains the degree of multiprogramming which corresponds to the number of processes in memory.

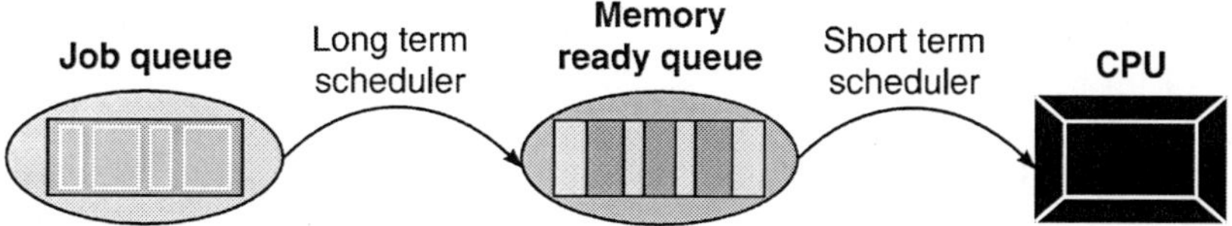

The long-term scheduler has to make careful selection among I/O-bound and CPU-bound processes. I/O bound processes spend more of their time doing I/O then computation, while CPU-bound processes spend more time on computation then I/O.

A long-term scheduler should pick a relatively good mix of I/O- and CPU-bound processes so that the system resources are better utilized. If all processes are I/O-bound, the ready queue will almost always be empty. If all processes are CPU-bound, I/O queue will be almost always empty. A balanced combination should be selected for system efficiency.

The short-term scheduler selects the process to get the processor from among the processes which are already in memory. The short-time scheduler will be executing frequently (mostly at least once every 10 milliseconds). So it has to be very fast in order to achieve better processor utilization. The short-time scheduler, like all other OS programs, has to execute on the processor. If it takes

1 millisecond to choose a process that means (1 / (10 + 1)) = 9% of the processor time is being used for short time scheduling and only 91% may be used by processes for execution.

The long-term scheduler on the other hand executes much less frequently. It controls the degree of multiprogramming (no. of processes in memory at a time). If the degree of multiprogramming is to be kept stable (say 10 processes at a time), then the long-term scheduler may only need to be invoked when a process finishes execution.

The long-term scheduler must select a good process mix of I/O-bound and processor bound processes. If most of the processes selected are I/O-bound, then the ready queue will almost be empty while the device queue(s) will be very crowded. If most of the processes are processor-bound, then the device queue(s) will almost be empty while the ready queue is very crowded and that will cause the short-term scheduler to be invoked very frequently.

Most time-sharing systems have no long-term scheduler. The stability of these systems either depends upon a physical limitation (no. of available terminals) or the self-adjusting nature of users (if you can't get response, you quit).

It can sometimes be good to reduce the degree of multiprogramming by removing processes from memory and storing them on disk. These processes can then be reintroduced into memory by the medium-term scheduler. This operation is also known as swapping. Swapping may be necessary to improve the process mix or to free memory.

Queuing diagram:

A common representation for a discussion of process scheduling is a *queuing diagram,* such as the following diagram. Each **rectangular** box represents a **queue.** The **circles** represent the **resources** that serve the queues, and the allows indicate the **flow of processes** in the system.

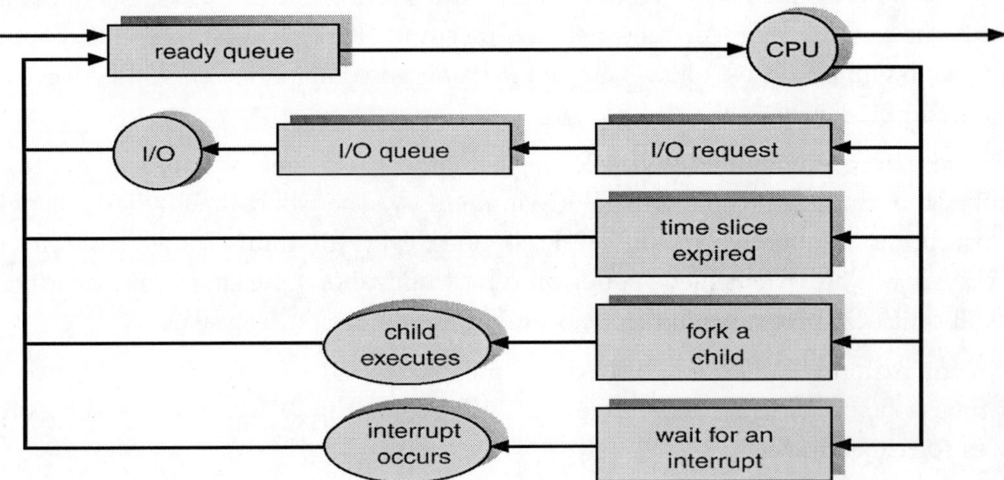

The CPU scheduler selects from among the processes that are ready to execute, and allocates the CPU to one of them. A process may execute for only a few milliseconds (say, 100 ms) in each time quantum (time slice), the scheduler should be very fast, if it takes 10 ms to decide to execute a process for each 100 ms, then 9 percent of the CPU is considered as overhead.

DISPATCHER

A dispatcher is the module that gives control of the CPU to the process selected by the short-term scheduler. This function involves:

- Switching context,
- Switching to user mode,

➢ Jumping to the proper location in the user program to restart the program.

Imagine several programs occupying memory. Some time ago, program 'A' requested data from disk (Figure ahead). Because it was unable to continue until the input operation was completed, it dropped into a wait state and processor turned to program B. Assume the input operation has just been completed.

Both programs are in now in ready state; in other words, both are ready to resume processing. Which one gets the processor? Computers are so fast that a human operator cannot effectively make such real-time choices. Instead, the processor's time is managed by an operating system routine called the dispatcher.

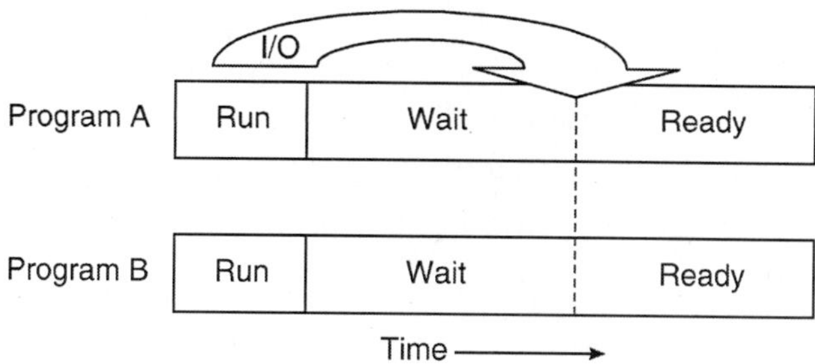

Consider a system with two partitions: foreground and background. The dispatcher checks the program in the foreground partition first; if the program is ready, it gets control. Only if the foreground program is still in a wait state does the dispatcher check the background partition. The foreground has high priority; the background has low priority.

This idea can be extended to larger systems, with the dispatcher checking partitions in a fixed order until a ready-state program is found. The first partition checked has highest priority; the last has lowest priority. The only way the low –priority program can get control is if all the higher-priority partitions are in a wait state.

The time it takes for the dispatcher to stop one process and start another running is known as the dispatch latency.

PROCESS SCHEDULING POLICIES

There are two main types of process scheduling policies. The difference between these two is in the way that **the scheduler is called to assign the CPU to a particular process** defined as follows:

PRE-EMPTIVE SCHEDULING

In a **pre-emptive** system, a process in the running state can be forcibly rescheduled at the end of its quantum time, or before it has run to the end of its quantum time. In some systems any process is allowed to run for the duration of the quantum time before pre-emption is enforced. A process can also surrender the CPU before the quantum time expires. In some real-time systems the pre-emption of the running is enforced when a process becomes ready which has a higher priority than the current running process.

In preemptive scheduling (also known as involuntary CPU sharing), a special hardware device called an interval timer is designed to produce a hardware interrupt on a periodical basis (known as a time slice). Again when this interrupt is received by the CPU, it will switch over to start running the scheduler, who will in turn decide on a new process to be run on the CPU.

For example an interrupt from an I/O device may occur which causes a high priority blocked process to go the ready state. The running process is pre-empted and positioned in the ready-to-run queue. The newly un-blocked process, now in the ready queue, is dispatched to become the running process.

Advantages of preemptive scheduling algorithms are:

1. They allow real multiprogramming.
2. Can provide somewhat more predictable response times
3. A process, or processes cannot be allowed to **hog** the system

Disadvantages of preemptive scheduling algorithms are:

1. They can lead the system to a race condition,
2. They are complex.

NON-PREEMPTIVE SCHEDULING

Some operating systems are **non-pre-emptive** where all processes are allowed to run to completion (unless they voluntarily give up the CPU). Such a non-pre-emptive scheme is sometimes referred to as **co-operative** multitasking. Some operating systems are designed to use a mix of pre-emptive and non-pre-emptive scheduling schemes. For example the UNIX operating uses pre-emptive scheduling for the *user level* processes and a non-pre-emptive scheme for the *kernel level* processes. The UNIX scheduler will be described in some detail later.

In non preemptive scheduling (also known as voluntary CPU sharing), the process is given full access to the CPU until it decides to relinquish it. This can either occur because the process becomes blocked on an I/O instruction (as we have already seen), the process executes a special yield instruction or the process completes execution. In all cases, a software interrupt is issued which in turn switches the CPU over to start running the scheduler. The scheduler can now decide the next process to be run on the CPU.

Pre-emption involves process switching overhead and additional scheduling logic which lead to increased system inefficiencies.

Advantages of non-preemptive scheduling algorithms are:

1. They cannot lead the system to a race condition.
2. They are simple i.e. they use simpler scheduler logic
3. lower switching overhead leading to more efficient operation
4. if required a process can be allowed to have control of the system

Disadvantage of non-preemptive scheduling algorithms is:

1. They do not allow real multiprogramming.
2. They lead to over aging of the processes in some situations

In both cases, the scheduler will be activated upon reception of an interrupt. For non preemptive scheduling, the interrupt is a software interrupt issued by the process, whereas in preemptive scheduling, the interrupt is a hardware interrupt issued by an external hardware device.

It is important to note that in preemptive scheduling, the process can also issue a software interrupt (through an I/O operation) which will activate the scheduler in the same way as in non-preemptive scheduling. However, in non-preemptive scheduling, if the process does not issue any I/O or yield instruction, then the CPU is effectively bound to execute that process regardless of how many other processes are waiting on the queue. This, of course, does not apply to preemptive scheduling. Non-preemptive scheduling is analogous to passive multiprogramming that we studied in Section 3.2., while preemptive scheduling is analogous to active multiprogramming

DEADLINE SCHEDULING

In deadline scheduling certain jobs are scheduled to be completed by a specific time or deadline. These jobs have very high value if delivered on time and may be worthless if delivered later than the deadline. The user is often willing to pay a premium to have the system ensure on-time completion. Deadline scheduling is complex for many reasons.

- The user must supply the precise resource requirements of the job in advance. Such information is rarely available.
- The system must run the deadline job without severely degrading service to other users.
- The system must carefully plan its resource requirements through to the deadline. This may be difficult because new jobs may arrive and place unpredictable demands on the system.

- If many deadline jobs are to be active at once, scheduling could become so complex that sophisticated optimization methods might be needed to ensure that the deadline are met.
- The intensive resource management required by deadline scheduling may generate substantial overhead. Even if deadline users are willing to pay a sufficiently high fee for the services received, the net consumption of system resources may be so high that the rest of the user community could suffer degraded service. Such conflicts must be considered carefully by operating systems designers.

The example of deadline scheduling is Real-Time Scheduling. It is of two types.

Hard real-time systems are required to complete a critical task within a guaranteed amount of time. Generally, a process is submitted along with a statement of the amount of time in witch it needs to complete or perform I/O. The scheduler then either admits the process, guaranteeing that the process will complete on time, or rejects the request as impossible. Such a guarantee, made under resource reservation, requires that the scheduler know exactly how long it takes to perform each type of operating-system function; therefore, each operation must be guaranteed to take a maximum amount of time.

Such a guarantee is impossible in a system with secondary storage or virtual memory, because these subsystems cause unavoidable and unforeseeable variation in the amount of time to execute a particular process. Therefore, hard real-time systems are composed of special-purpose software running on hardware dedicated to their critical process, and lack the full functionality of modern computers and operating systems.

Soft real-time computing is less restrictive. It requires that critical processes receive priority over less fortunate ones. Although adding soft real-time functionality to a time-sharing system may cause an unfair allocation of resources and may result in longer delays, or even starvation, for some processes, it is at least possible to achieve. The result is a general-purpose system that can also support multimedia, high-speed interactive graphics, and a variety of tasks that would not function acceptably in an environment that does not support soft real-time computing. Implementing soft real time functionality requires careful design of the scheduler and related aspects of the operating system. First, the system must have priority scheduling, and real-time processes must have the highest priority. The priority of real-time processes must not degrade over time, even though the priority of non-real-time processes may. Second, the dispatch latency must be small. The smaller the latency, the faster a real-time process can start executing once it is runnable.

It is relatively simple to ensure that the former property holds. For example, we can disallow process again on real-time processes, thereby guaranteeing that the priority of the various processes does not change. However, ensuring the latter property is much more involved. The problem is that many operating systems, including most versions of UNIX, are forced to wait either for a system call to complete or for an I/O block to take place before they can do a context switch. The dispatch latency in such systems can be long, since some system calls are complex and some I/O devices are slow.

To keep dispatch latency low, we need to allow system calls to be preemptible. There are several ways to achieve this goal. One is to insert preemption points in long-duration system calls, which check to see whether a high-priority process needs to be run. If one does, a context switch takes place; when the high-priority process terminate, the interrupted process continues with the system call. Preemption points can be placed at only safe locations in the kernel-only where kernel date structures are not being modified. Even with preemption points, dispatch latency can be large, because it is practical to add only a few preemption points to a kernel.

Another method for dealing with preemption is to make the entire kernel preemptible. So that correct operation is ensured, all kernel date structures must be protected through the use of various synchronization mechanisms. With this method, the kernel can always be preemptible, because any kernel data being updated are protected from modification by the high-priority process. This method is used in Solaris 2.

What happens if the higher-priority process needs to read or modify kernel date that is currently being accessed by another, lower-priority process? The high-priority process would be waiting for a lower-priority one to finish. This situation is known as priority inversion. In fact, there would be a chain of processes, all accessing resources that the high-priority process needs. This problem can be solved via the priority-inheritance protocol, in which all these processes (the processes that are accessing resources that the high-priority process needs) inherit the high priority until they are done with the resource in question. When they are finished, their priority reverts to its original value.

The conflict phase of dispatch latency has two components:

1. Preemption of any process running in the kernel
2. Release by low-priority processes of resources needed by the high-priority process

As an example, in Solaris 2 with preemption disable, the dispatch latency is over 100 milliseconds; with preemption enabled, it is usually reduced to 2 milliseconds.

STATIC AND DYNAMIC SCHEDULING

A static scheduler makes a one-time decision per job regarding the number of processors to be allocated. Once decided, the job is guaranteed to have exactly that number of processors whenever it is active. A static scheduler offers low runtime scheduling overhead, but it also assumes a stable parallel application. Dynamic scheduling are considered for two reasons:

Because most complex large-scale parallel applications exhibit irregular data domains or changes in domain decompositions over time, so that a static processor allocation rapidly becomes inefficient and

Large-scale parallel machines are often used in multi-user mode, so that scheduling must take into account the requirements of multiple parallel applications sharing a single machine. Dynamic scheduling performs increasingly well relative to the static scheduling as system load increases.

The dynamic policy occasionally exhibits a performance penalty when overhead values are very large. One reason for such performance condition is a possible high rate of processor reallocation. Now we will give some of the multiprocessor scheduling algorithms.

PROCESS SCHEDULING OBJECTIVES

A scheduling discipline should:

- Be fair - a scheduling discipline is fair if all processes are treated the same, and no process can suffer indefinite postponement.
- Maximize throughput - a scheduling discipline should attempt to service the largest possible number of processes per unit time.
- Maximize the number of interactive users receiving acceptable response times (i.e., at most a few seconds).
- Be predictable - a given job should run in about the same amount of time and at about the same cost, regardless of the load on the system;
- Maximize overhead - interestingly, this is not generally considered to be one of the most important objectives. Overhead is commonly viewed as wasted resources. But a certain portion of system resources invested as overhead can greatly improve overall system performance.
- Balance resource use - the scheduling mechanism should keep the resources of the system busy. Processes that will use underutilized resources should be favored.
- Achieve a balance between response and utilization - the best way to guarantee good response times is to have sufficient resources available whenever they are needed. The price to be paid for this strategy is that overall resource

utilization will be poor. In real-time systems, fast responses are essential, and resource utilization is less important. In other types of systems, the economics often makes effective resource utilization imperative.

- Avoid indefinite postponement - in many cases, indefinite postponement can be as bad as deadlock. Avoiding indefinite postponement is best accomplished by aging, i.e., as a process waits for a resource, its priority should grow. Eventually, the priority will become so high that the process will be given the resource.
- Enforce priority - in environments in which processes are given priorities, the scheduling mechanism should favor the higher-priority processes.
- Give preference to processes holding key resources - even though a low-priority process may be holding a key resource the resource may be in demand by high-priority processes. If the resource is non preemptible, then the scheduling mechanism should give the process better treatment than it would ordinarily receive so that the process will release the key resource sooner.
- Give better service to processes exhibiting desirable behavior (low paging rates, for example).
- Degrade gracefully under heavy loads - a scheduling mechanism should not collapse under the weight of a heavy system load. Either it should prevent excessive loading by not allowing new processes to be created when the load is heavy, or it should service the heavier load by providing moderately reduced level of service to all processes.

GOALS OF SCHEDULING ALGORITHMS

The following identifies some goals of a scheduling algorithm/policy according to the type of system.

All systems

1. Fairness – all processes should be treated equitably;
2. Predictability – regardless of the load on the system, it should be possible to estimate how long the job will take to complete;
3. Enforce priorities;
4. Avoid indefinite postponement – as a process waits for a resource its priority should grow
5. Degrade gracefully under heavy loads;
6. Balance – keep all parts of the system busy; processes using underutilized resources should be favoured; give preference to processes holding key resources.

Batch systems

1. Throughput – complete as many jobs as possible per unit time;
2. Turnaround – minimize time between submission of a job and its completion;

Interactive systems

1. Response times – maximize the number of interactive users receiving acceptable response times;
2. Be predictable – a given job should run in about the same amount of time regardless of the load on the system;
3. Give better service to processes exhibiting desirable behaviour, e.g. low paging rates

Real-time systems

1. Meet deadlines.
2. Be predictable and degrade gracefully, e.g. if the going is getting really tough, retreat into a safety mode.

PERFORMANCE CRITERIA

In order to achieve an efficient processor management, OS tries to select the most appropriate process from the ready queue. For selection, the relative importance of the followings may be considered as performance criteria.

Processor Utilization:

The ratio of busy time of the processor to the total time passes for processes to finish. We would like to keep the processor as busy as possible.

Processor Utilization= (Processor busy time)/(Processor busy time +Processor idle time)

We want to keep the CPU as busy as possible. CPU utilization may range from 0 to 100%. In real system, it would range from 40% to 90%.

Throughput: The measure of work done in a unit time interval.

Throughput = (Number of processes completed) / (Time Unit)

Turnaround Time (tat):

The sum of time spent waiting to get into the ready queue, execution time and I/O time.

tat = t(process completed) – t(process submitted)

From the view point of a process, the **interval** from the *time of submission* to *the time of completion* is the turnaround time. The shorter turnaround time is the better.

Waiting Time (wt):

Time spent in ready queue. Processor scheduling algorithms only affect the time spent waiting in the ready queue. So, considering only waiting time instead of turnaround time is generally sufficient.

The CPU algorithm does not affect the amount of time during which a process executes or does I/O; it affects only the *amount of time waiting* in the ready queue. The shorter, the better.

Response Time (rt): The amount of time it takes to start responding to a request. This criterion is important for interactive systems.

rt = t(first response) – t(submission of request)

We, normally, want to maximize the processor utilization and throughput, and minimize tat, wt, and rt. However, sometimes other combinations may be required depending on to processes.

In an interactive system, turnaround time may not be the best criteria. Often, a process can produce some output fairly early, and can continue computing new results while previous results are being output to the user. Thus, another measure is *the time from the submission of a request* until *the first response is produced*-The shorter the better.

CPU SCHEDULING ALGORITHMS

Now, let's discuss some processor scheduling algorithms again stating that the goal is to select the most appropriate process in the ready queue. For the sake of simplicity, we will assume that we have a single I/O server and a single device queue, and we will assume our device queue always implemented with FIFO method. We will also neglect the switching time between processors (context switching).

First-Come-First-Served (FCFS)

In this algorithm, the process to be selected is the process which requests the processor first. This is the process whose PCB is at the head of the ready queue. Contrary to its simplicity, its performance may often be poor compared to other algorithms.

In FIFO **first-in-first-out** discipline, Processes are positioned in the ready queue in the order in which they are submitted. There is no priority concept. There is no pre-emption. Processes run to completion once they get the CPU. The method is weak in that longer jobs can force short jobs to be delayed. The method is no good for interactive users. The FCFS policy is not common but the basic concept is often embedded in other schemes.

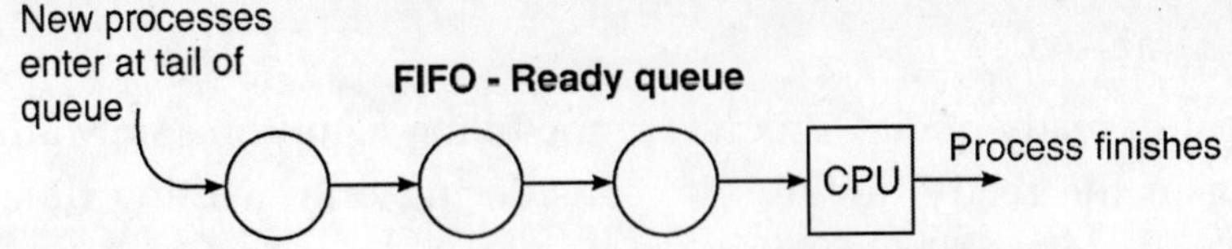

FCFS may cause processes with short processor bursts to wait for a long time. If one process with a long processor burst gets the processor, all the others will wait for it to release it and the ready queue will be filled very much. This is called the convoy effect.

Example 1:

Let processes P1, P2, and P3 arrive to the ready queue in that order and let the run times (CPU burst times) of these processes be as follows:

Process	CPU burst
P1	24
P2	3
P2	3

These processes are served by the CPU in FCFS order. The result can be shown in the following Gantt chart:

P1	P2	P3

0 24 27 30

The waiting time for P1 is: **W (P1) = 0 ms**

The waiting time for P2 is: **W (P2) = 24 ms**

The waiting time for P3 is: **W (P3) = 27 ms**

The average waiting time is: W = (0+24+27)/3 = 17 ms.

If these processes arrived in the following order: P2, P3, P1 then the Gantt chart would be as follows:

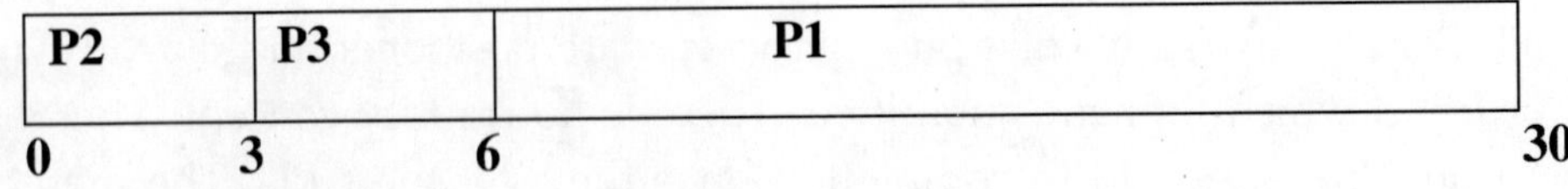

The average waiting time is now: W = (0+3+6)/3 = 3 ms

Example2 for another way of drawing gantt charts

Consider the following information and draw the timing (Gannt) chart for the processor and the I/O server using FCFS algorithm for processor scheduling.

Process	Arrival time	1st exec	1st exec	1st exec	1st exec	1st exec
A	0	4	4	4	4	4
B	2	8	1	8	–	–
D	3	2	1	2	–	–
D	7	1	1	1	1	1

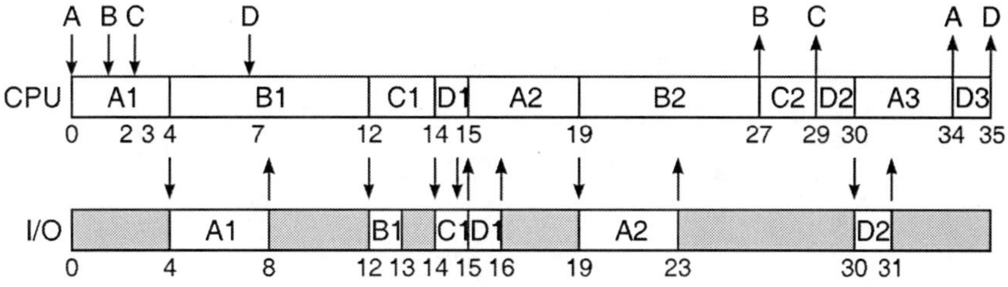

Processor utilization = (35 / 35) * 100 = 100 %

Throughput = 4 / 35=0.11

tatA = 34 – 0 = 34

tatB = 27 – 2 = 25

tatC = 29 – 3 = 26

tatD = 35 – 7 = 28

tatAVG = (34 + 25 + 26 + 28) / 4 = 28.25 wtA = (0 – 0) + (15 – 8) + (30 – 23) = 14 wtB = (4 – 2) + (19 – 13) = 12

wtC = (12 – 3) + (27 – 15) = 21

wtD = (14 – 7) + (29 – 16) + (34 – 31) = 23

wtAVG = (14 + 12 + 21 + 23) / 4 = 17.3

rtA = 0 – 0 = 0

rtB = 4 – 2 = 2

rtC = 12 – 3 = 9

tD = 14 – 7 = 7

rtAVG = (0 + 2 + 9 + 7) / 4 = 4.5

Shortest-Process-First (SPF) or SJF shortest Job First *also known as* ***STCF (Shortest Time to Completion First)***

In this method, the processor is assigned to the process with the smallest execution (processor burst) time. This requires the knowledge of execution time. In our examples, it is given as a table but actually these burst times are not known by the OS. So it makes prediction. One approach for this prediction is using the previous processor burst times for the processes in the ready queue and then the algorithm selects the shortest predicted next processor burst time.

Example:

Assume there are 4 ready processes with their next CPU burst time as follows:

Process	Next CPU burst time
P1	6
P2	8
P3	7
P4	3

Using SJF scheduling algorithm, these processes are scheduled according to the following Gantt Chart:

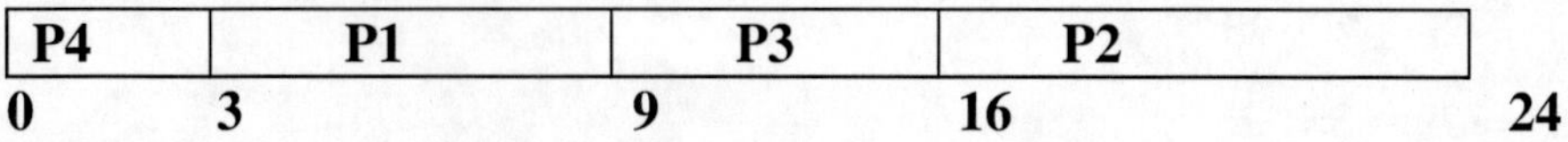

P4	P1	P3	P2

0 3 9 16 24

So, the average waiting time is (3+16+9+0) / 4 =7 ms

NOTE:

If the processes (in order P1, P2, P3, P4) are scheduled using the FCFS algorithm then the average waiting time is (0+6+14+21) /4 = 10.25 ms.

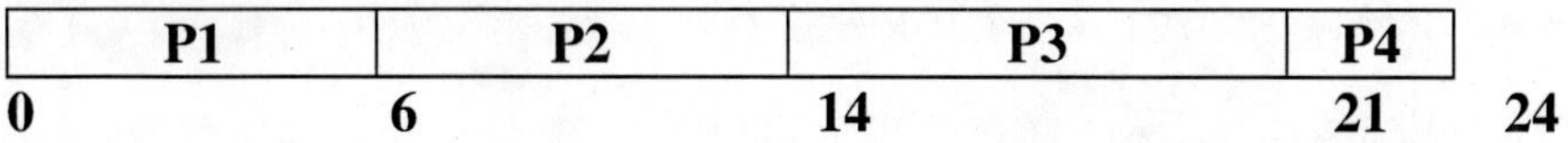

P1	P2	P3	P4

0 6 14 21 24

SJF minimizes the average wait time because it services smaller processes before large ones.

- The main problem with the SJF algorithm is to know for each process the next CPU burst time!!! However some techniques exist to predict this next CPU burst time.
- Another problem is that starvation of long processes may occur.

Another Example:

Consider the same process table in *Example2* and draw the timing charts of the processor and I/O assuming SPF is used for processor scheduling. (Assume FCFS for I/0)

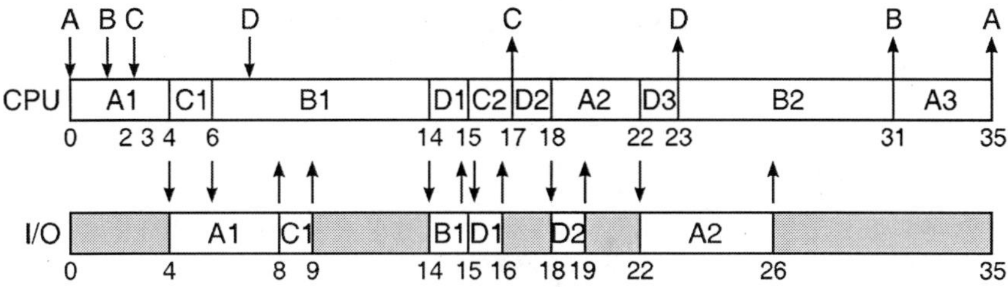

Processor utilization = (35 / 35) * 100 = 100 %

Throughput = 4 / 35 = 0.11

tatA = 35 – 0 = 35 tatB = 31 – 2 = 29 tatC = 17 – 3 =14 tatD = 23 – 7 = 16

tatAVG = (35 + 29 + 15 + 16) / 4 = 23.5 wtA = (0 – 0) + (18 – 8) + (31 – 26) = 15 wtB = (6 – 2) + (23 – 15) = 12

wtC = (4 – 3) + (15 – 9) = 7

wtD = (14 – 7) + (17 – 16) + (22 – 19) = 11

wtAVG = (15 + 12 + 7 + 11) / 4 = 11.25

rtA = 0 – 0 = 0 rtB = 6 – 2 = 4 rtC = 4 – 3 = 1 rtD = 14 – 7 = 7

rtAVG = (0 + 4 + 1 + 7) / 4 = 3

SHORTEST-REMAINING-TIME-FIRST (SRTF)

In SJF, the estimated job run time is often known in advance. The ready queue is ordered based upon the running time for each process, placing the shortest process at the head of the queue. The scheme is non-pre-emptive which means that a process will run to completion once it has been assigned to the CPU. The advantage of the scheme is that the turnaround time on short jobs is minimised.

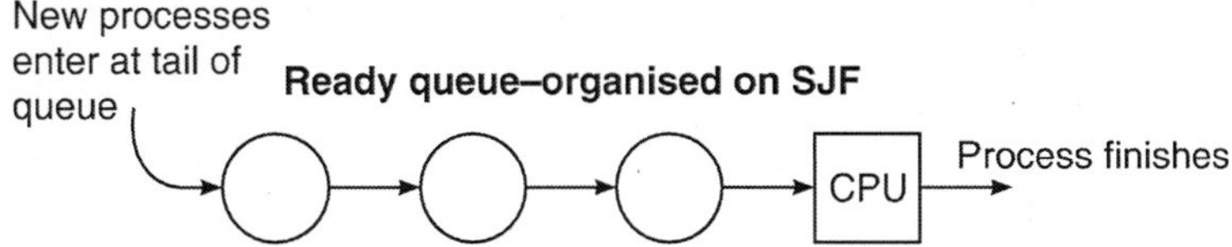

An advantage of the scheme is that the number of jobs waiting is reduced as each job is allowed to run to completion.

For the SJF algorithm to work the run time for each job must be known in advance. This is not always possible and hence must rely on a user estimate of some historical data. The scheme is of no use for interactive systems as the run to completion time for processes will cause unreasonable delays. In any case for an interactive job, the run time is not predictable.

Pre-emptive shortest job first is a modification of the algorithm where a new process which has a run time of less than the current running process causes the current process to be pre-empted in favour of the shorter job.

Assume while one process is executing on the processor, another process arrives. The new process may have a predicted next processor burst time shorter than what is left of the currently executing process. If the SPF algorithm is preemptive, the currently executing process will be preempted from the processor and the new process will start executing. The modified SPF algorithm is named as Shortest-Remaining-Time-First (SRTF)

An enhancement feature to the SJF method is to employ a priority mechanism so as to ensure that long jobs are not kept waiting indefinitely. The mechanism would periodically increase the priority of a process according its length of time in the queue.

Example:

Consider the following four processes:

Process	Arrival time	CPU burst time
P1	0	8
P2	1	4
P3	2	9
P4	3	5

P1	P2	P4	P1	P3
0	1	5	10	17

26

W (P1) = 10-1 = 9 ms
W (P2) = 0 ms
W (P3) = 17-2 = 15 ms
W (P4) = 5-3 = 2 ms

Avg. waiting time:
= (9+0+15+2) / 4
= 26/4
= 6.5 ms

tat (P1) = 17 ms
tat (P2) = 5-1 = 4 ms
tat (P3) = 26-2 = 24 ms
tat (P4) = 10-3 = 7 ms

Average tat = 13 ms

How to process preemptive scheduling:

time	P1	P2	P3	P4
0	8			
1	7	4		
2	7	3	9	
3	7	2	9	5
...				

If the SJF were used which is non-preemptive:

P1	P2	P4	P3

0 8 12 17 26

W (P1) = 0 ms **(P2) = 8-1 = 7 ms**

W (P3) = 17-2 = 15 ms **(P4) = 12-3= 9 ms**

Average waiting time = (0+7+15+9) /4 = 31/4 = 7.75 ms

Remember: SJF gives smaller wait time than FCFS since shorter processes are executed before longer ones!

Another Example

Consider the same process table in example 2 and draw the timing charts of the processor and I/O assuming SRTF is used for processor scheduling.

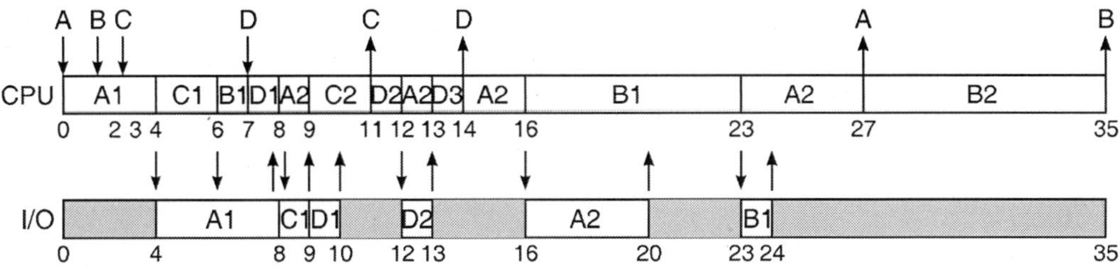

Processor utilization = (35 / 35) * 100 = 100 %

Throughput = 4 / 35 = 0.11

tatA = 27 – 0 = 27 tatB = 35 – 2 = 33 tatC = 11 – 3 = 8 tatD = 14 – 7 = 7

tatAVG = (27 + 33 + 8 + 7) / 4 = 18.75

wtA = (0 – 0) + (8 – 8) + (12 - 9) + (14 – 13) + (23 - 20) = 7

wtB = (6 – 2) + (16 – 7) + (27-24) = 16

wtC = (4 – 3) + (9 – 9) = 1

wtD = (7 – 7) + (11 – 10) + (13 – 13) = 1

wtAVG = (7 + 16 + 1 + 1) / 4 = 6.25

rtA = 0 – 0 = 0 rtB = 6 – 2 = 4 rtC = 4 – 3 = 1 rtD = 7 – 7 = 0

rtAVG = (0 + 4 + 1 + 0) / 4 = 1.25

HIGHEST-RESPONSE-RATIO-NEXT (HRN) SCHEDULING

Brinch Hansen developed the highest-response-ratio-next strategy that corrects some of the weaknesses in SJF, particularly the excessive bias against longer jobs and the excessive favoritism toward short new jobs. HRN is a non preemptive scheduling discipline in which the priority of each job is a function not only of the job's service time, but also of the amount of time the job has been waiting for service. Once a job gets the CPU, it runs to completion. Dynamic priorities in HRN are calculated according to the formula

Priority = (time waiting + service time) / service time

Because the service time appears in the denominator, shorter jobs will get preference. But because time waiting appears in the numerator, longer jobs that have been waiting will also be given favorable treatment. Remember that the sum *Time waiting + service time* is the system's response time to the job if the job were to be initiated immediately.

Highest Response Ratio Next (HRRN) chooses the next process with the largest value of Response Time Ratio (R) that is given by:

.

Where

w = Time spent in system so far (waiting + execution)

s = Total service time required by the process, including e = Time spent in execution.

If the process with this value is dispatched immediately, R is equal to the normalized turnaround time. Note that minimum value of R is 1, which occurs when process first enters the system. HRRN algorithm penalizes the longer jobs.

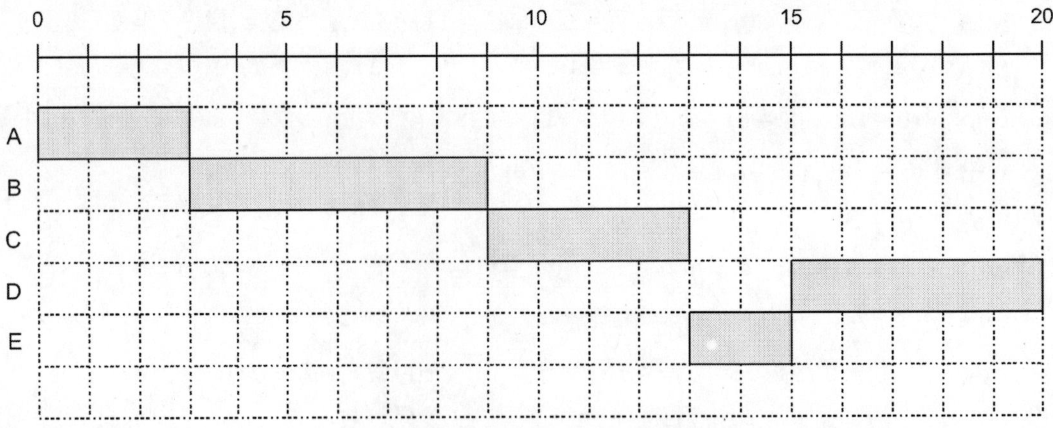

Highest Response Ration Next (HRRN)

Process	Arrival Time	Service Time (T_s)	Start Time	Finish Time	Turnaround Time (T_r)	T_r/T_s
A	0	3	0	3	3	1.00
B	2	6	3	9	7	1.17
C	4	4	9	13	9	2.25
D	6	5	13	20	14	2.80
E	8	2	18	15	7	3.5
Mean					8.00	2.14

ROUND-ROBIN SCHEDULING (RRS)

In RRS algorithm the ready queue is treated as a FIFO circular queue. The RRS traces the ready queue allocating the processor to each process for a time interval which is smaller than or equal to a predefined time called *time quantum (slice).*

In the round robin scheme, dispatching is done as with the FIFO policy but each process is allowed to run on the CPU for a fixed time slice (quantum) only. If the process does not complete within the quantum time the process is pre-empted and the processor is then given to the next process in the queue. The pre-empted process is now positioned at the back of the queue. Thus a **circular queue** which is ordered by length of time since last service is created.

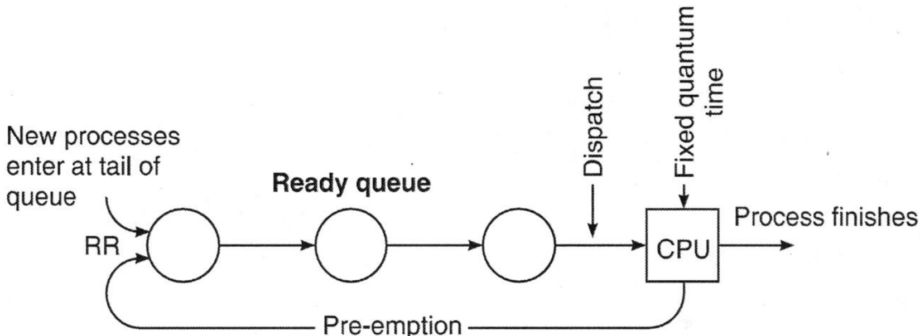

The OS using RRS, takes the first process from the ready queue, sets a timer to interrupt after one time quantum and gives the processor to that process. If the process has a processor burst time smaller than the time quantum, then it releases the processor voluntarily, either by terminating or by issuing an I/O request. The OS then proceed with the next process in the ready queue.

On the other hand, if the process has a processor burst time greater than the time quantum, then the timer will go off after one time quantum expires, and it interrupts (preempts) the current process and puts its PCB to the end of the ready queue.

Remember for RR scheduling:

- This scheduling algorithm is designed specially for time sharing systems. It is similar to FCFS scheduling, but preemption is added to switch between processes.
- A small unit of time, called a *time quantum*, or time slice, is assigned to each process. Usually a quantum is 10 to 100 ms.
- This scheduler allocates the CPU to each process in the ready queue for a time interval of up to 1 time quantum in FIFO (circular) fashion. If the process still running at the end of the quantum; it will be preempted from the CPU. A context switch will be executed, and the process will be put at the tail of the ready queue. Then the scheduler will select the next process in the ready queue. However, if the process has blocked or finished before the quantum has elapsed, the scheduler will then proceed with the next process in the ready queue.

The performance of RRS depends heavily on the selected time quantum. For an optimum time quantum, it can be selected to be greater than 80 % of processor bursts and to be greater than the context switching time.

Example

Consider the following set of process that arrive at time 0 with the order A,B,C,D and the following CPU burst time. Find the average waiting time with RR of quantum : 10 ms

Process	CPU burst time
A	20
B	40
C	14
D	6

A	B	C	D	A	B	C	B	B

0 10 20 30 36 46 56 60 70 80

W (A) = 36-10 =26 ms **W (B) = (10-0) + (46-20) + (60-56)= 40 ms**

W (C) = (20-0) + (56-30) = 46 ms **W (D) = 30-0 = 30 ms**

Average waiting time = (26+40+46+30) /4 = 142/4 = 35.5 ms

Example2 for RR scheduling:

Redo the previous example by introducing switching time of 2 ms and some I/O. i.e. A has 10 ms CPU burst – 40 ms I/O burst -10 ms CPU burst , and the others are as before.

CPU:

A1		B1		C1		D1		B2		C2		A2		B3		B4

0 10 12 22 24 34 36 42 44 54 56 60 62 72 74 84 86 96

I/O:

idle	A	idle

0 10 50

Wait (A) = 62-50 = 12 ms **Wait (B) = 12+22+20+2 = 56 ms**

Wait (C) = 24 + 22 = 46 ms **Wait (D) = 36 ms**

Average waiting time = 150/4 = 37.5 ms

Important note: smaller time quantum increases the number of context switches! So, time quantum should be large with respect to the context switching time.

Note: if time of quantum = 8, =>RR becomes FCFS.

Another Example

Consider the following information and draw the timing chart for the processor and the I/O server using RRS algorithm with time quantum of 3 for processor scheduling.

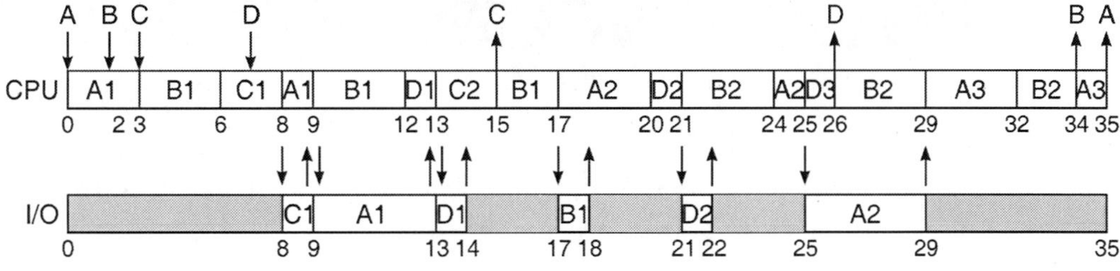

Processor utilization = (35 / 35) * 100 = 100 %

Throughput = 4 / 35 tatA = 35 – 0 = 35 tatB = 34 – 2 = 32 tatC = 15 – 3 =12 tatD = 26 – 7 = 19

tatAVG = (35 + 32 + 12 + 19) / 4 = 24.5

wtA = (0 – 0) + (8 – 3) + (17 - 13) + (24 – 20) + (29 - 29) + (34 – 32) = 15 wtB = (3 – 2) + (9 – 6) + (15 -12) + (21 – 18) + (26 – 24) + (32 – 29) = 15 wtC = (6 – 3) + (13 – 9) = 7

wtD = (12 – 7) + (20 – 14) + (25 – 22) = 14

wtAVG = (15 + 12 + 7 + 11) / 4 = 11.25

rtA = 0 – 0 = 0 rtB = 36 – 2 = 1 rtC = 6 – 3 = 3 rtD = 12 – 7 = 5

rtAVG = (0 + 1 + 3 + 5) / 4 = 2.25

	FCFS	SPF	SRT	RR
tat_{avg}	28.25	23.5	18.75	24.5
wt_{avg}	16.5	10.5	6.25	12.25
rt_{avg}	4.5	3	1.25	2.25
	Easy to implement	Not possible to know next CPU burst exactly, it can only be guessed	Not possible to know next CPU burst exactly, it can only be guessed	Implementable, rt_{max} is important for interactive systems

CHOOSING TIME SLICE

What happens if the times slice isn't chosen carefully?

For example, consider two processes, one doing 1 ms computation followed by 10 ms I/O, the other doing all computation. Suppose we use 20 ms time slice and round-robin scheduling: I/O process runs at 11/21 speed, I/O devices are only utilized 10/21 of time.

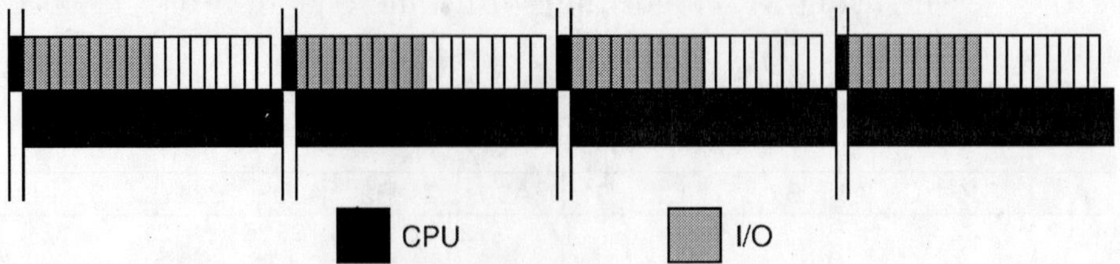

Suppose we use 1 ms time slice: then compute-bound process gets interrupted 9 times unnecessarily before I/O-bound process is runnable

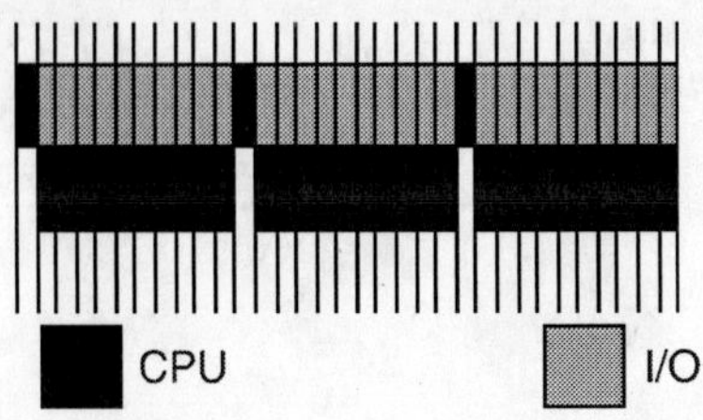

Problem: Round robin assumes that all processes are equally important; each receives an equal portion of the CPU. This sometimes produces bad results. Consider three processes that start at the same time and each requires three time slices to finish. Using FIFO how long does it take the average job to complete (what is the average response time)? How about using round robin?

Process	Arrival Time	Processing Time
A	0.000	3
B	1.001	6
C	4.001	4
D	6.001	2

* Process A finishes after 3 slices, B 6, and C 9. The average is (3+6+9)/3 = 6 slices.

* Process A finishes after 7 slices, B 8, and C 9, so the average is (7+8+9)/3 = 8 slices.

Round Robin is fair, but uniformly inefficient and the

Solution: the solution to this problem is priority based scheduling.

SOME MORE EXAMPLES:

1. For the processes listed in the following table, draw a chart illustrating their execution using:

(a) First-Come First-Served

(b) Shortest Job First

(c) Shortest Remaining Time

(d) Round Robin (quantum = 2)

(e) Round Robin (quantum =1)

Answer:

(*a*) First-Come First-Served

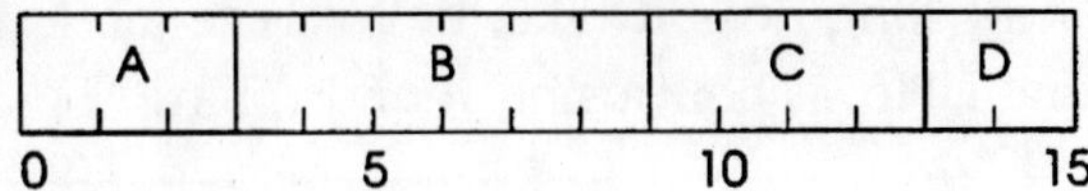

The processes are executed in the order they are received.

(*b*) Shortest Job First

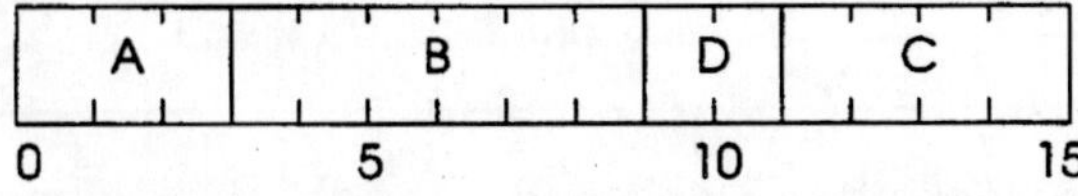

Process A starts executing; it is the only choice at time 0. At time 3, B is the only process in the queue. At time 9 when B completes, process D runs because it is shorter than process C.

(*c*) Shortest Remaining Time

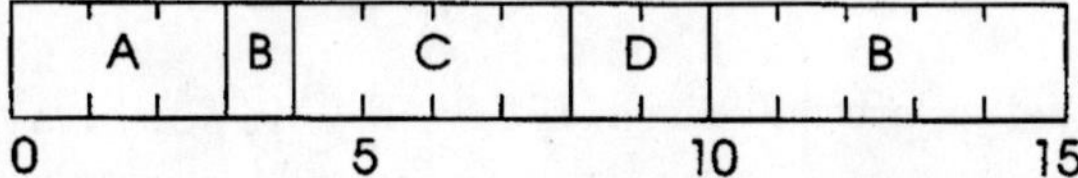

Process A starts executing; it is the only choice at time 0. It remains running when process B arrives because its remaining time is less. At time 3, process B is the only process in the queue. At time 4.001, process C arrives and starts running because its remaining time (4) is less than process B's remaining time (4.999). At time 6.001, process C remains running because its remaining time (1.999) is less than process D's remaining time (2). When process C terminates, process D runs because its remaining time is less than that of process B.

(*d*) Round Robin **(quantum = 2)**

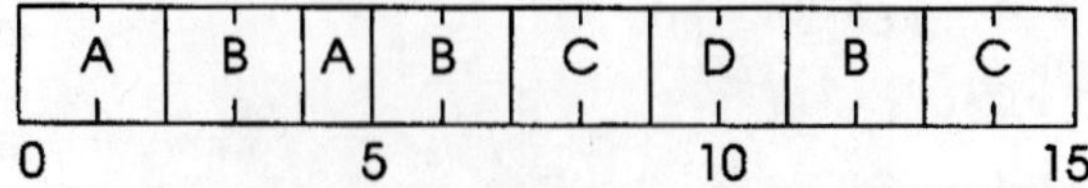

When process A's first time quantum expires, process B runs. At time 4, process A is restarted and process B returns to the ready queue. At time 4.001, process C enters the ready queue after process B. At time 5, process A terminates and process B runs. At time 6.001, process D enters the ready queue behind process C. Starting at time 7, processes C, D, B, and C run in sequence.

(*e*) Round Robin **(quantum = 1)**

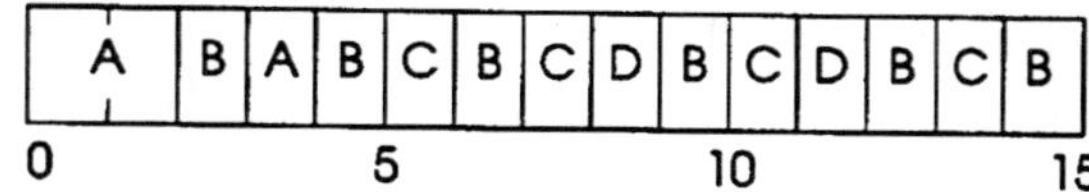

Process A runs for two time-slices since process B does not arrive until 1.001. Process B runs at time 4 since process C does not arrive until 4.001. Process B runs again at time 6 since process D does not arrive until 6.001. Process D enters the ready queue behind process C. From time 7 on, execution cycles through processes C, D, and B.

2. For the processes listed in table of Question 1, what is the average turn-around time (rounding to the nearest hundredth) using:

(a) First-Come First-Served

(b) Shortest Job First

(c) Shortest Remaining Time

(d) Round Robin (quantum = 2)

(e) Round Robin (quantum =1)

Solution:

Turnaround time is computed by subtracting the time the process entered the system from the time it terminated.

(a) ((3 - 0) + (9 - 1) + (13 - 4) + (15 - 6))/4 = 7.25

(b) ((3 - 0) + (9 - 1) + (15 - 4) + (11 - 6))/4 = 6.75

(c) ((3 -0)+ (15-1)+(8 -4)+ (10-6))/4=6.25

(d) ((5 - 0) + (13 - 1) + (15 - 4) + (11 - 6))/4 = 8.25

(e) ((4 -0)+ (15-1)+(14 -4)+ (12-6))/4=8.50

3. The following processes P1, P2, P3 arrive for execution at the times indicated. Each process will run the listed amount of time. Use non-preemptive and preemptive scheduling.

Process	Arrival Time	Burst Time
P1	0.0	8
P2	0.4	4
P3	1.0	1

FCFS algorithm:

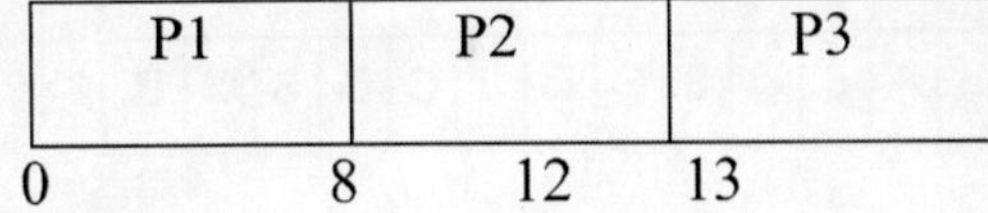

The mean (average) turnaround time =

((8.0 - 0)) + (12.0 - 0.4) + (13.0 – 1.0)) / 3 = 31.6 / 3 »10.5

SJF algorithm

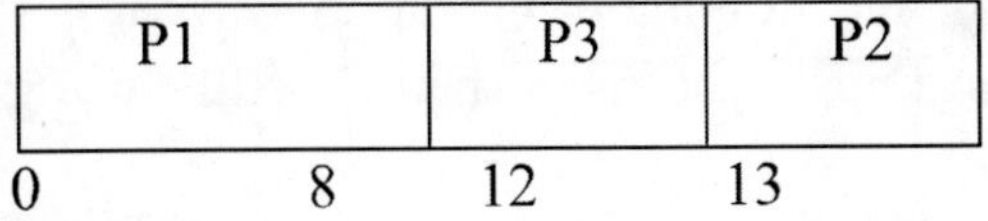

The mean turnaround time =

((8.0 – 0) + (12.0 – 1.0) + (13.0 – 0.4)) / 3 = 31.6 / 3 » 10.5

The different situation will be for the processes arriving in the same time (order will be P3, P2, P1).

Preemptive SJF

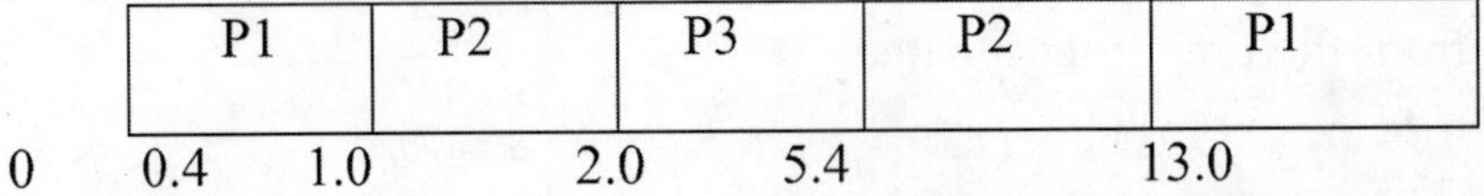

The average turnaround time =

((13.0 – 0) + (5.4 – 0.4) + (2.0 – 1.0)) / 3 = 19 / 3 » 6.3millisecond.

4. Five batch jobs A through E, arrive at a computer center at almost the same time. They have estimated running times of 10, 6, 2, 4 and 8 minutes. Their (externally determined) priorities are 3, 5, 2, 1 and 4 with 5 being the highest priority. For each of the following scheduling algorithms determine the mean process turnaround time (*and average waiting time*) Ignore process-switching overhead.

a) Round Robin

b) Priority Scheduling

c) FCFS (10, 6, 2, 4, 8)

d) Shorted Job First.

For a) assume that the system is multiprogrammed (*with time sharing*)

and that each job gets its fair share of the CPU. For

b) through d) assume that only one job at a time runs, until it finishes.

All jobs are completely CPU bound.

Process	Burst Time	Priority
A	10	3
B	6	5
C	2	2
D	4	1
E	8	4

Let's determine a time quantum as fair share:

(10 + 6 + 2 + 4 + 8) /5 = 30 / 5 = 6

a) Round Robin (with priorities)

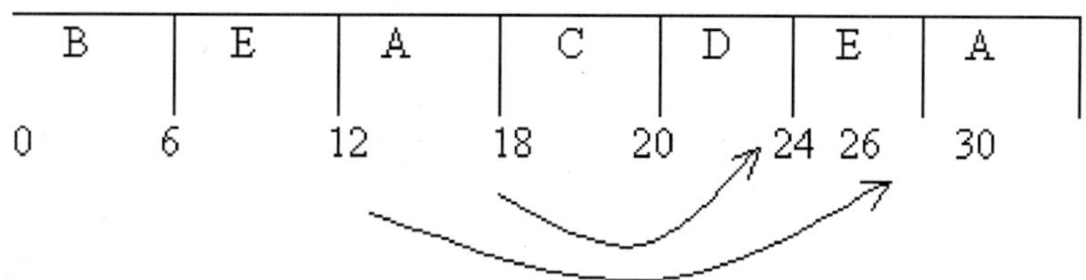

Average waiting time =

((12 + 8) + 0 + 18 + 20 + (6 + 12)) = 76 / 5 = 15.2

A B C D E

Mean turnaround time =

(30 + 6 + 20 + 24 + 26) / 5 = 106 / 5 = 21.2

A B C D E

RR without priority

A B C D E A E

0 6 12 14 18 24 28 30

Average waiting time =

((24 - 6) + 6 + 12 + 14 + (18 +4)) / 5 = 72 / 5 = 14.4

A B C D E

Mean turnaround time =

(28 + 12 + 14 + 18 + 30) / 5 = 102 / 5 = 20.4

A B C D E

b) Priority Scheduling

B	E	A	C	D

0 6 14 24 26 30

Average waiting time = (14 + 0 + 24 + 26 + 6) / 5 = 70 / 5 = 14

A B C D E

Mean turnaround time = (24 + 6 + 26 + 30 + 14) / 5 = 100 / 5 = 20

A B C D E

c) FCFS

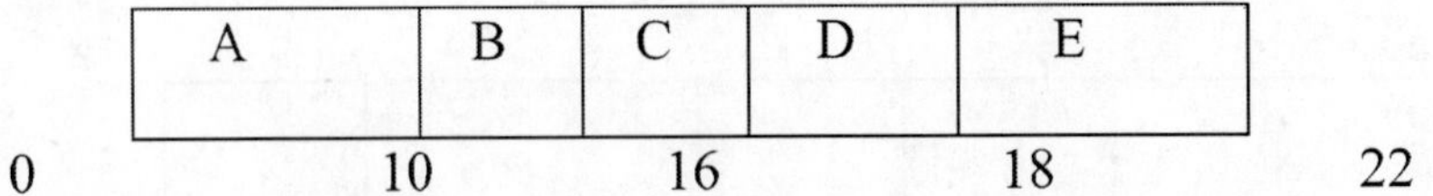

30

Average waiting time = (0 + 10 + 16 + 18 + 22) / 5 = 66 / 5 = 13.2

A B C D E

Mean turnaround time = (10 + 16 + 18 + 22 + 30) / 5 = 96 / 5 = 19.2

A B C D E

d) SJF

C	D	B	E	A

0 2 6 12 20 30

Average waiting time = (20 + 6 + 0 + 2 + 12) / 5 = 40 / 5 = 8.0

A B C D E

Mean turnaround time= (30 + 12 + 2 + 6 + 20) / 5 = 70 / 5 = 14.0

A B C D E

MULTILEVEL QUEUE SCHEDULING

The round robin scheme using a relatively short quantum size and offers good user response times, hence it is suited to interactive systems. However, for processing of long jobs, as is typical of a batch system, the use a larger quantum is more effective as it reduces the overhead of process switching and also it allows relatively short processes to clear the system faster. For example, a **two level queue** system could be used in a multimode system. Processes which do not complete within a fixed number of quanta are deemed to be long processes and are removed from the main queue into a background queue.

Hence batch type jobs tend to fall into the background queue. The background queue is serviced only if there are no processes pending in the main queue. Thus short jobs are given priority so as to maximise response times for interactive users. In most implementations, processes which are run from the background queue are given a larger quantum, so that when a processes is scheduled to run is gets a relatively long slice of CPU time.

TWO LEVEL QUEUE EXAMPLE

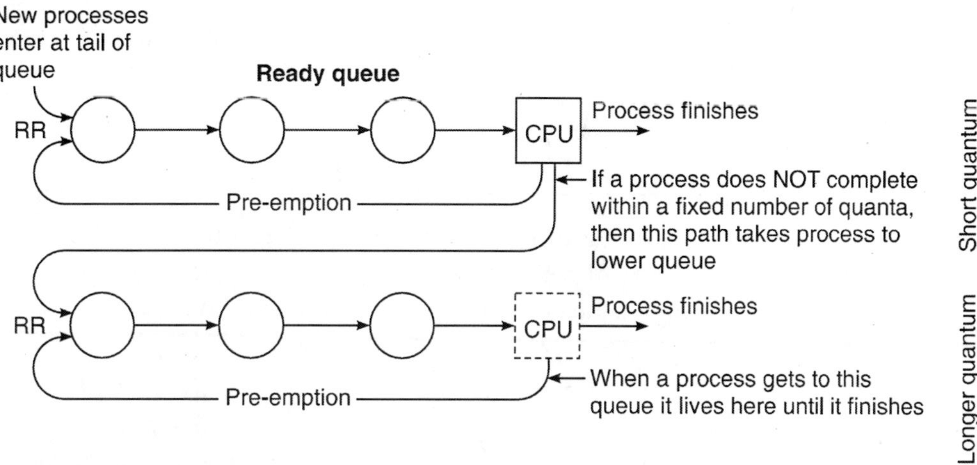

The two level scheme can be extended into a **multiple level queue**. The early DEC System-10 operating system is an example of a three level queue, as shown. Note how the quantum increases for the lower queues.

QUEUE	QUANTUM
round robin queue 1	20 msecs
round robin queue 2	250 msec
round robin queue 3	2 secs

THREE LEVEL QUEUE EXAMPLE

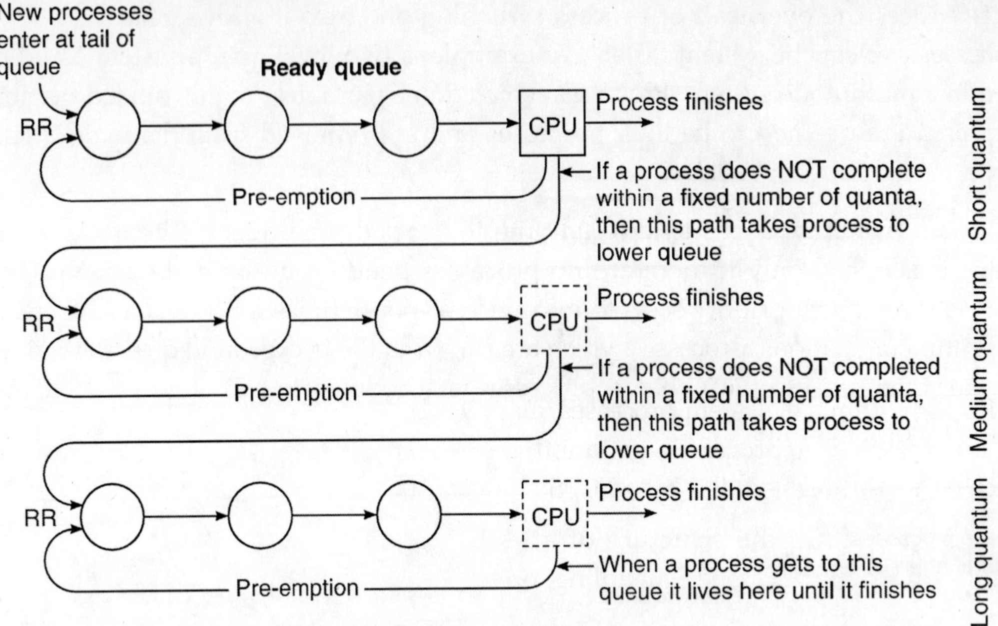

CHARACTERISTICS OF MULTILEVEL QUEUE SCHEDULING

If processes are easily classified into groups with similar resource use characteristics, then the application of multilevel queue scheduling becomes feasible. In this system, multiple ready-to-run queues operate with each one given its own scheduler algorithm and assigned to processes with certain characteristics.

If processes can easily be classified into groups we may use a multi-queue scheduling algorithm (MQS). We partition the ready queue into separate queues. Processes are assigned to one queue depending on their properties (e.g. memory size, process type). Then each queue will use a different process scheduling algorithm.

For example,

➢ Foreground processes: interactive} different response

➢ Background processes: batch} time requirements

a. schedule foreground queue by a RRS, background queue by a FCFS

b. in addition to that, there must be an interqueue scheduling policy (scheduling choice between the queues). Assume the foreground queue has an absolute priority over the background queue, or do time-slicing among the queues.

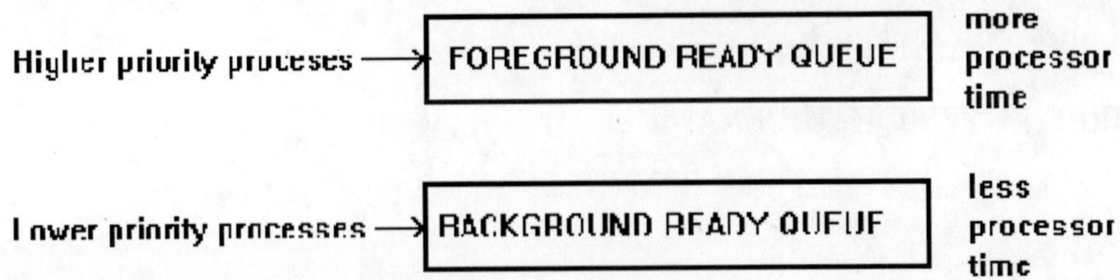

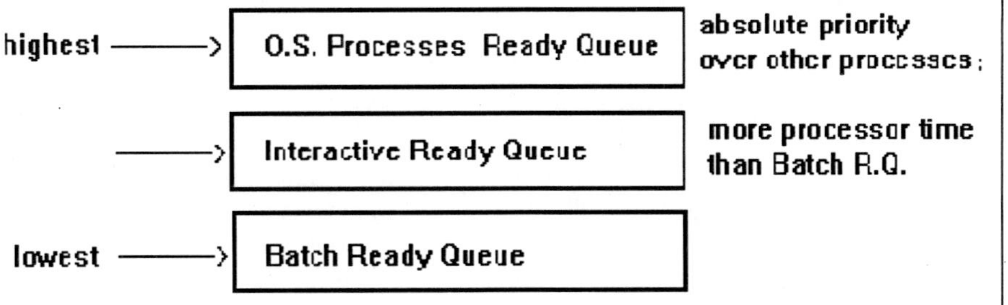

Example:

One ready-to-run queue might contain highest priority processes scheduled by an RR algorithm e.g. system processes, another might contain high priority processes for interactive user processes, yet another might contain low priority processes for batch processing scheduled by a FCFS algorithm, etc.

Figure shows the structure of a Multilevel Queue Scheduling system. In Multilevel Feedback Queue Scheduling, processes may be moved between the queues:

? *if* a process uses too much CPU time, it will be moved to a lower priority queue.

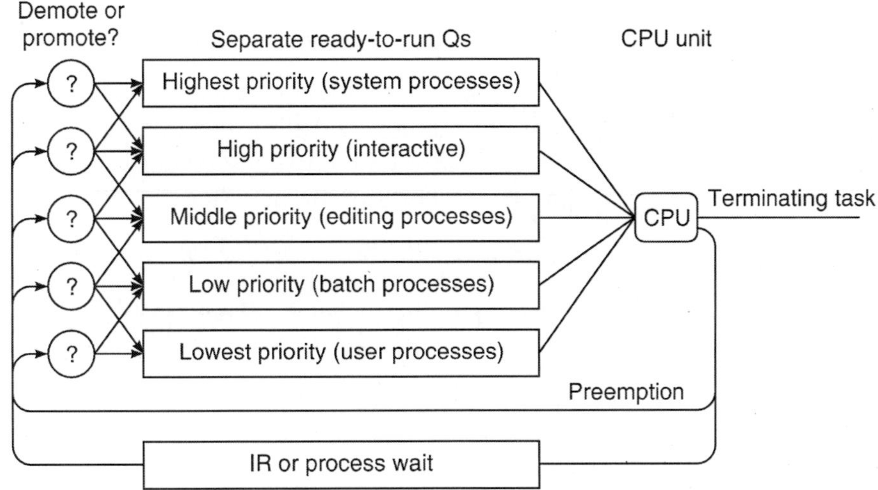

Multilevel queue scheduling

If a process spends too much time waiting in a low priority queue, it may be moved to a higher priority queue — this prevents starvation, and might better match its (bursty) CPU use to the queue since high priority queues are likely to use schedulers such as RR.? This scheme leaves IO bound and interactive processes in high priority queue Multilevel Queue Scheduling is categorized by:

- the number of queues;
- the scheduling algorithm for each queue;

- the method to promote a process to a higher priority queue;
- the method to demote a process to a lower priority queue;
- the method to select the initial queue to hold a process.
- The definition of a multilevel feedback queue scheduler makes it the most general
- CPU scheduling algorithm, and therefore the most difficult to optimally tune.

Figure shows a simple Multilevel Queue Scheduling system where processes initially enter the highest priority queue and may only be demoted:

- If the process is not complete after some time spent in an RR scheduler with time quantum = 8, it is demoted to the next queue where an RR algorithm operates with time quantum = 16;
- If the process needs further CPU time, it is moved to a low priority scheduler queue using FCFS.
- Processes in the lower priority queues may only run if the queues above are empty.

MULTILEVEL FEEDBACK QUEUE SCHEDULING

The multilevel feedback queue [Kleinrock 1970] is designed to meet the following design requirements for multimode systems:

- Give preference to short jobs
- Give preference to I/O bound processes
- Quickly establish the nature of the process and schedule the process accordingly

Multiple FIFO queues are used and the operation is as follows:

- A new process is positioned at the tail of the top-level FIFO queue.
- At some stage the process arrives at the head of the queue and is assigned the CPU.
- If the process completes it leaves the system.
- If the process voluntarily relinquishes control (e.g. blocks on I/O) it leaves the queuing network and when this process becomes ready again it enters the system on the **same** queue level.
- If the process uses all of the quantum time it is pre-empted and positioned at the end of the next lower level queue.

There is a different quantum size for each queue level, where the quantum values are larger for the lower level queues. There is normally a base level queue at the bottom where processes circulate in round robin fashion.

The dispatcher will select jobs from the top-level queue as long as there are processes in that queue. If the top-level queue is empty the dispatcher selects from the next highest level queue and so forth. In this scheme the higher level queues are favoured for process selection but the processes from the lower level queues are allowed to run for a longer time once they are assigned the CPU.

Note, that unlike the simple MULTILEVEL QUEUE system where processes at a given queue level are given access to the CPU for a fixed number of times before they are forced onto a lower level queue, in the MULTILEVEL FEEDBACK QUEUE system a process is given just one chance to complete at a given queue level before it is forced down to the next lower level. The execption is, of course, a process which does not use all of the defined time quantum and such a process can regain entry to the same queue level.

EXAMPLE: A MULTILEVEL FEEDBACK QUEUE

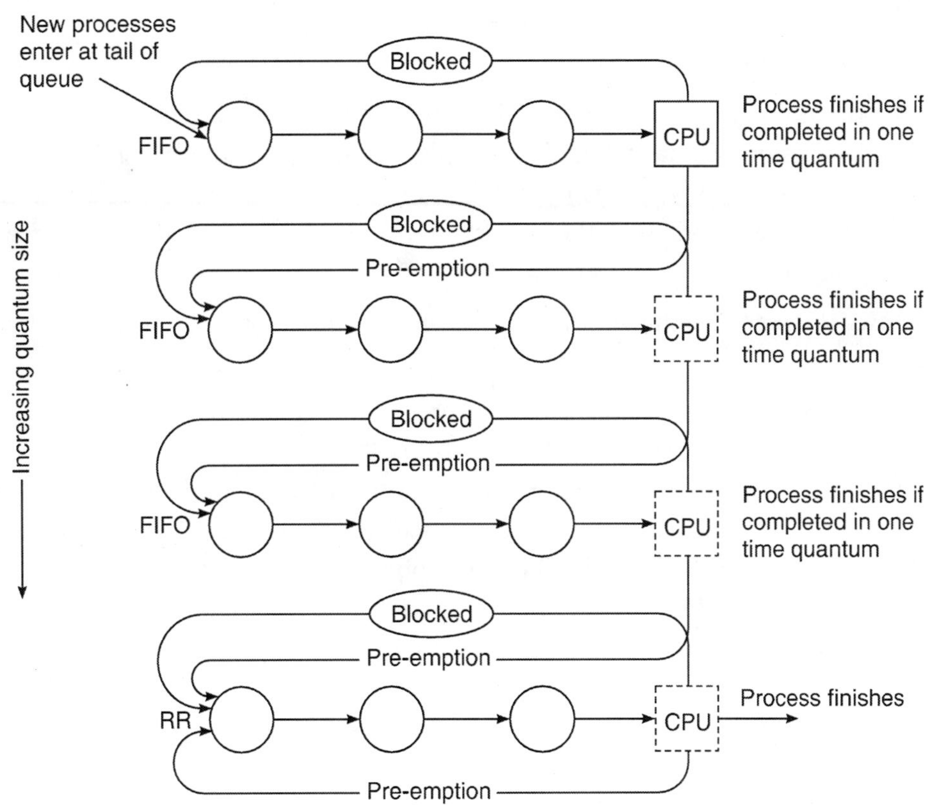

Decisions made by the scheduler for a running process:

1) If a process completes within the quantum time it exits the system
2) If a process does not complete within the quantum time it is passed to a lower level queue (or circulates to tail of bottom queue if already in this queue)
3) If a process volunteers to surrender the CPU and blocks, when awakened it will be added to the same level queue.

OBJECTIVES OF MULTI-LEVEL FEEDBACK QUEUE SCHEDULER

It can be seen that the multilevel feedback queue does meet its objectives as follows:

1) Favour short jobs

Very short jobs i.e. jobs which can complete within the quantum time for the top level queue, will be processed quickly as the top level queue is given preference. Slightly longer jobs may drop to the second or third level queues before they complete. Long jobs will fall to much lower level queues and may have to wait for long periods before they get service in a busy system. Thus the scheme inherently favours shorter jobs.

2) Favour I/O bound processes

The quantum time associated with the top level queue is chosen so that most I/O processes will have time to make the I/O request and then relinquish the CPU. This activity will keep the I/O process in the top-level queue and thus the I/O process receives the preferential treatment associated with the top level queue.

3) Quickly establish the nature of the process and schedule it accordingly

Interactive systems are associated with short processes and I/O bound processes for interactive control. Such processes will use the higher level queues as discussed. Processor bound processes will quickly drop down to the lower level queues, having spent only one quantum time running in each higher level queue. Eventually the processor bound process gets finished, even if it has to circulate in the lowest round robin queue for some time. Thus the scheme quickly separates the processor bound processes to the lower (or background) queues which have longer time quanta. Non-processor-bound processes are maintained in the top-level queues. So, effectively the scheme acts as a filter where the long processes are filtered down to the lower queues in a relatively short time.

Disadvamtage of the Multilevel Feedback Queue Scheme

In a busy interactive system processes in the lower level queues will tend to be ignored. A mechanism should be provided which would allow processes in the lower queues, which are not getting access to the CPU, to be give special attention so as to ensure that such processes are not ignored in the busy system. Later it will be seen that modern operating system schedulers do provide such priority boosting schemes for processes which do not receive CPU attention

PRIORITY BASED SCHEDULING

The multilevel feedback queue system described above sorts a process through a number of queue levels based upon the run time required by the process. Since the system always dispatches a process from the uppermost (non-empty) queue a type of priority system is realised based upon the time required for the process to run. Now we will look at priority scheduling where priorities can be pre-assigned to processes.

In this type of algorithms a priority is associated with each process and the processor is given to the process with the highest priority. Equal priority processes are scheduled with FCFS method.

To illustrate, SPF is a special case of priority scheduling algorithm where

Priority(i) = 1 / next processor burst time of process i

Priorities can be fixed externally or they may be calculated by the OS from time to time. Externally, if all users have to code time limits and maximum memory for their programs, priorities are known before execution. Internally, a next processor burst time prediction such as that of SPF can be used to determine priorities dynamically.

A priority scheduling algorithm can leave some low-priority processes in the ready queue indefinitely. If the system is heavily loaded, it is a great probability that there is a higher- priority process to grab the processor. This is called the starvation problem. One solution for the starvation problem might be to gradually increase the priority of processes that stay in the system for a long time. Priority scheduling can be of

- Non-preemptive (a process runs up to the end of its CPU burst time)
- Preemptive (a running process can be preempted can be preempted by a process with a higher priority which joined the ready queue later)

Example:

Process	Arrival time	CPU burst time	Priority
A	0	100	3
B	0	10	1
C	0	300	3
D	0	60	5
E	80	150	4

Draw the Gantt chart and compute the average waiting time in case of:

a) Non-preemptive

b) Preemptive.

a) Non-preemptive:

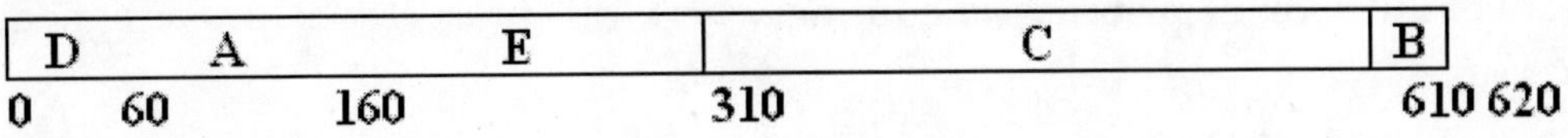

D	A	E	C	B

0 60 160 310 610 620

W (A) = 60 ms **W (B) = 610 ms**

W (C) = 310ms **W (D) = 0 ms**

W (E) = 80 ms

=> Average waiting time: 212 ms

b) Preemptive:

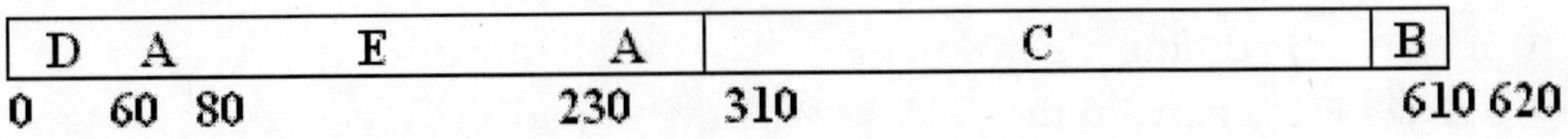

D	A	E	A	C	B

0 60 80 230 310 610 620

Wait (A) = 60+150 = 210 ms **Wait (B) = 610 ms**

Wait (C) = 310 ms **Wait (D) = 0 ms**

Wait (E) = 0 ms

=> Average waiting time: 226 ms

Note: SJF is a case of the priority scheduling where priority = 1/ (next CPU burst time).

- A major problem with the priority scheduling is **starvation**: a low priority process may wait for ever before being executed. (MIT IBM 7094 crashed in 1973. They found a ready process submitted in 1967 and still waiting for execution).

Solution: Gradually increase the priority of processes that wait for a long time (this technique is called **aging**).

- The priority scheduling algorithm may be combined with the RR algorithm. In this case, processes are grouped into priority classes:
- Among classes a priority scheduling algorithm is used.
- Inside a class a RR algorithm is used => 1 ready queue for each class.

The following shows a system with four priority classes. The scheduling algorithm is as follows: as long as there are runnable processes in priority class 4, just run each one for one quantum(i.e. round robin fashion), and never bother with lower priority classes. If priority class 4 in empty , then run the class 3 processes in round robin fashion , and so on. If priorities are not adjusted from time to time, lower priority classes may all starve.

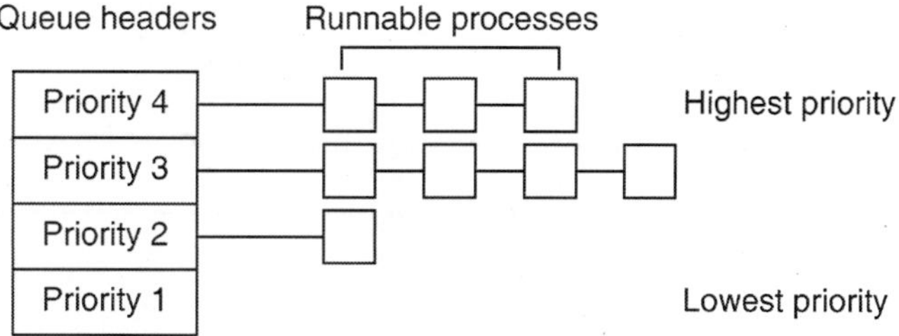

A scheduling algorithm with four priority classes.

Example:

Process	Arrival time	CPU burst time	Priority
A	0	22	1
B	0	12	2
C	0	23	2
D	0	11	3
E	0	21	5
F	0	15	3
G	30	22	3

Assume quantum =10 ms , and 0 switching time, draw the Gantt chart and compute the average waiting time in case of:

a) Non-preemptive priority scheduling

b) Preemptive priority scheduling

Queue_1 : A

Queue_2 : B, C, E

Queue_3 : D, F, G (Join the queue at time 30)

a)

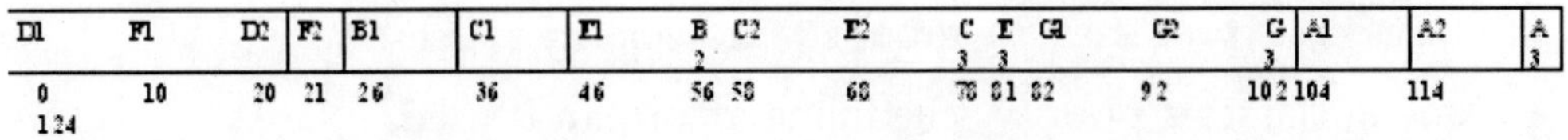

D1 F1 D2 | F2 | B1 | C1 | E1 B2 C2 E2 C3 E3 G1 G2 G3 | A1 | A2 | A3

0 10 20 21 26 36 46 56 58 68 78 81 82 92 102 104 114 124

W (A) = 104 W (B) = 46 W (C) =58 W (D) = 10

W (E) =61 W(F) =11 W (G) =52 => Average W: 48.8

b)

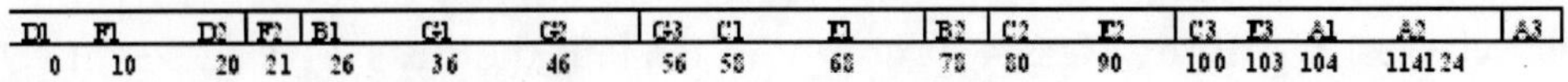

D1 F1 D2 | F2 | B1 G1 G2 | G3 C1 E1 | B2 | C2 E2 | C3 E3 A1 A2 | A3

0 10 20 21 26 36 46 56 58 68 78 80 90 100 103 104 114 124

W (A) = 104 W (B) = 68 W (C) =80 W (D) = 10

W (E) =83 W (F) =11 W (G) =6 => Average W = 51.7

Another Example 2.5

Following may be used as a priority defining function: Priority (n) = 10 + tnow – ts(n) – tr(n) – cpu(n)

where

ts(n) : the time process n is submitted to the system

tr(n) : the time process n entered to the ready queue last time cpu(n) : next processor burst length of process n

tnow : current time

The round robin system assumes that all processes are of equal priority. In practice it is important that a priority scheme is applied so that the **criticality**, or importance, of a process can be defined for appropriate treatment.

Priority based systems often have the following objectives:

a) Give preference to short jobs

b) Give preference to I/O bound activity

c) Give preference to processes which have been waiting a long time

d) Give preference to jobs which have been assigned a high priority

Let's *look at* each one of these objectives in turn.

a) **Give preference to short jobs**

It has already been seen that scheduling short jobs to run first reduces the average turnaround time and keeps long jobs from 'hogging' the CPU.

b) **Give preference to I/O bound activity**

This achieves **good device utilisation and provides good response times** for interactive users. Usually a process with I/O bound activity uses only part of the quantum and then voluntarily relinquishes control. It is therefore important that such processes are given high priority. When these processes are removed from the ready queue some system resources are usually freed up.

A common algorithm for I/O bound processes is to set the priority equal to **1/ f**, where **f** is the fraction of the quantum used by the process the previous time. Thus I/O bound processes which use only a small fraction of quantum get favourable priority. For example consider the following system which its highest priority value represented by the number100 and the lowest priority number is 1.

Process	Fraction of quantum used last time f	Priority 1 to 100 1/f
P1	50	**2** (100/50)
P2	100%	**1** (100/100)
P2	5%	**20** (100/5)
P4	2%	**50** (100/2)
P5	1%	**100** (100/1)

c) **Give preference to processes which have been waiting a long time**

To ensure that processes which have been waiting for a long time get service, a process priority could be increased as the process waiting time extends.

d) **Give preference to jobs which have been assigned a high priority**

For effective system management a mechanism should be provided so that priorities can be predefined for each process. Thus the more important, or most time-critical, processes can be assigned higher priorities. Sometimes such priority assignment is tied into the system accounting process where a user will pay more to run a high priority job.

MULTIPLE-PROCESSOR SCHEDULING

Multiple-Processor (MP) Scheduling is complex and intimately depends on the computer architecture.

The simplest situation is when all of the CPU elements and their memory systems are identically constructed i.e. the system is homogeneous. If each processor had its own ready-to-run queue, there could be instances when one CPU had many processes to run while another CPU had none — this unequal use of CPU resources can be solved by having a common ready-to-run queue sys- tem with the first free CPU taking the highest priority process available. The overheads such as scheduling processes and selecting a processor for dispatch can be handled by one of the processors, in systems called asymmetrical multiprocessor systems, or can be handled by any of the processors, in systems named sym- metrical multiprocessor systems (SMP).

The asymmetrical multiprocessor systems are also called master-slave systems. Asymmetrical MP systems sometimes have their IO and kernel code written for uniprocessor operation, and therefore require a CPU to be dedicated to IO and kernel activity. The other CPUs execute only user code.

REAL-TIME SCHEDULING

Real-Time Scheduling offers some guarantee of performance. In hard real-time, the operating system must perform an activity within some guar- anteed time.

At run-time, a process may be submitted to the scheduler with an estimate of resource requirements and the scheduler will either honour it or reject it.

At planning-time, the system designer typically chooses resources so that no pro- cess is ever rejected. In soft real-time, the guarantees are less restrictive with critical processes receiving priority over less important ones. If the soft real-time system is being implemented within a more general purpose operating system, the system must have priority scheduling with real-time pro- cesses allocated the highest priority. The priority of real-time processes must not degrade i.e. disallow priority aging on real-time processes.

HIGHEST-RESPONSE-RATIO-NEXT (HRRN) SCHEDULING

Brinch Hansen developed the highest-response-ratio-next strategy that corrects some of the weaknesses in SJF, particularly the excessive bias against longer jobs and the excessive favoritism toward short new jobs. HRN is a non preemptive scheduling discipline in which the priority of each job is a function not only of the job's service time, but also of the amount of time the job has been waiting for service. Once a job gets the CPU, it runs to completion. Dynamic priorities in HRN are calculated according to the formula

Priority = (time waiting + service time) / service time

Because the service time appears in the denominator, shorter jobs will get preference. But because time waiting appears in the numerator, longer jobs that have been waiting will also be given favorable treatment. Note that the sum

Time waiting + service time

Is the system's response time to the job if the job were to be initiated immediately.

Hand-off Scheduling:

A kernel level scheduler that accepts user hints that are stated below:

- Discouragement hints: A discouragement hint is used to discourage the scheduler to run the current thread. A discouragement hint may be either mild, strong, or weak.
- Hand-off hints: A hand-off hint is used to suggest the scheduler to run a specific thread. Using a hand-off hint, the current thread hands off the processor to another thread without intermediate scheduler interference. Such schedulers are better known as hand-off schedulers.

	FCFS	Round Robin	SJF	SRT	HRRN	Feedback
Selection Function	max(w)	Constant	min(s)	min(s-e)	max(1+w/s)	see text
Decision Mode	Nonpreemptive	Preemptive (at quantum time)	Nonpreemptive	Preemptive (at arrival)	Nonpreemptive	Preemptive (at quantum time)
Throughput	Not emphasized	May be low if quantum is too small	High	High	High	Not emphasized
Response Time	May be high, especially if there is a large variance in process execution times	Provides good response time for short processes	Provides good response time for short processes	Provides good response time	Provides good response time	Not emphasized
Overhead	Minimum	Minimum	Can be high	Can be high	Can be high	Can be high
Effect On Processes	Penalties short processes; penalties I/O bound processes	Fair treatment	Penalties long processes	Penalties long processes	Good balance	May favor I/O bound processes
Starvation	No	No	Possible	Possible	No	Possible

Other scheduling policies

FAIR-SHARE SCHEDULING

Fair-share scheduling is a scheduling strategy for computer operating systems in which the CPU usage is equally distributed among system users or groups, as opposed to equal distribution among processes.

For example, if four users (A,B,C,D) are concurrently executing one process each, the scheduler will logically divide the available CPU cycles such that each user gets 25% of the whole (100% / 4 = 25%). If user B starts a second process, each user will still receive 25% of the total cycles, but both of user B's processes will now use 12.5%. On the other hand, if a new user starts a process on the system, the scheduler will reapportion the available CPU cycles such that each user gets 20% of the whole (100% / 5 = 20%).

Another layer of abstraction allows us to partition users into groups, and apply the fair share algorithm to the groups as well. In this case, the available CPU cycles are divided first among the groups, then among the users within the groups, and then among the processes for that user. For example, if there are three groups (1,2,3) containing three, two, and four users respectively, the available CPU cycles will be distributed as follows:

- 100% / 3 groups = 33.3% per group
- Group 1: (33.3% / 3 users) = 11.1% per user
- Group 2: (33.3% / 2 users) = 16.7% per user
- Group 3: (33.3% / 4 users) = 8.3% per user

One common method of logically implementing the fair-share scheduling strategy is to recursively apply the round-robin scheduling strategy at each level of abstraction (processes, users, groups, etc.) The time quantum required by round-robin is arbitrary, as any equal division of time will produce the same results.

LOTTERY SCHEDULING

Lottery Scheduling is a probabilistic scheduling algorithm for processes in an operating system. Processes are each assigned some number of lottery tickets, and the scheduler draws a random ticket to select the next process. The distribution of tickets need not be uniform; granting a process more tickets provides it a relative higher chance of selection. This technique can be used to approximate other scheduling algorithms, such as SRTF and Fair-share scheduling.

Lottery scheduling solves the problem of starvation. Giving each process at least one lottery ticket guarantees that it has non-zero probability of being selected at each scheduling operation.

Implementations of lottery scheduling should take into consideration that there could be billions of tickets distributed among a large pool of threads. To have an array tickets with each ticket corresponding to a thread may be highly inefficient

THREAD SCHEDULING

With threads, the concept of execution is separated from the rest of the definition of a process. An application can be implemented as a set of threads, which cooperate and execute concurrently in the same address space. On a uniprocessor, threads can be used as a program structuring aid and to overlap I/O with processing, Because of the minimal penalty in doing a thread switch compared to a process switch, these benefits are realized with little cost. However, the full power of threads becomes evident in a multiprocessor system. In this environment, threads can be used to exploit true parallelism in an application. If the various threads of an application are simultaneously run on separate processors, dramatic gains in performance are possible.

SOME DEFINITIONS

- **PROGRAM:** An executable sequence of instructions which resides in the computer storage area. It is a **static** entity.
- **PROCESS:** A program in execution. It consists of the executable program, data, stack, registers and other information necessary to run the program. It is a **dynamic** entity.
- **PROCESSOR:** The agent which executes the program to realise a process. This is usually a hardware device, normally the system **CPU**.
- **JOB:** A program or a set of programs which are to be processed in a specific environment to perform a system or a user function.
- **BATCH SYSTEM:** A job or jobs are submitted to the system for processing. A user has no further contact with the process until a job has been completed.
- **INTERACTIVE SYSTEM:** Jobs or individual processes are initiated from the user console. The job may be monitored and controlled by the user in an interactive fashion.
- **MULTIPROCESSOR:** There is more than one processor in the system available for processing. This increases the overall performance of a system.
- **MULTITASKING:** Several programs can be executed on the system at the same time.
- **TASK:** Generally the same definition as a Process. In this book *a **process** and **task** will be taken as being the same thing.*

- **TASK and THREADS:** Some operating systems split the abstraction of a process into two components: **task** and **thread**. The **task** is a collection of system resources, including the address space, resource usage information etc. The **task** is like a process but has no flow of control or defined register set (hardware state). The **thread** is the basic unit of execution within the context of one **task**. Any number of **threads** may execute within a single **task.**

The final words

The FCFS algorithm is nonpreemptive. Once the CPU has been allocated to a process, that process keeps the CPU until it release the CPU, either by terminating or by requesting I/O. It is not good for time-sharing systems, where it is important that each user get a share of CPU at regular intervals, preemptive scheduling is better. Preemption may occur when the time quantum is up or a higher priority process arrives, where the running process is put back to the waiting queue.

CASE STUDY

THE MICROSOFT WINDOWS SCHEDULER

Generally, a process (or a task) is said to be a program that is in execution, within a defined processor environment. However, Microsoft Windows 2000 supports two forms of multitasking: processes and threads.

Windows Process

The process is the traditional process based multitasking scheme where the process represents the program in execution. The process environment, in terms of memory usage, registers etc., is defined for the process and the actual executing code is referred to as a *thread of execution*. Thus for any operating system's process, we could refer to the execution of code as the *thread* of execution. Thus a traditional process would have a single thread of execution.

Windows 2000 Thread

In the Microsoft Windows operating system a thread is a dispatchable unit of program execution, thus any process must have at least a single thread. However, Microsoft Windows allows a single process to have multiple threads. Windows 2000 allows the multitasking of threads so a single process can have a number of threads executing simultaneously (in a time-sliced manner).

Consider a conceptual view of three processes: Process-A, Process-B and Process-C. Process-A has a single thread shown as Thread-A1. This is just like any conventional process – just that the execution thread has been highlighted by drawing it as a separate circle. Note Process-B has three threads and Process-C has two threads. The scheduler will schedule activity at the thread level. If, for example, execution switches from Thread-A-1 to Thread-B-2 then there is a process context switch as we have switched from Process-A to Process_B. However, a thread switch from Thread B-1 to Thread B-3 does not involve a process context switch as we have switched threads within the same process. Thus thread switching within the same process does not incur the overhead of a context switch in terms of time. This is one advantage in using threads. In a sense threads are similar to *lightweight processes*, or POSIX *pthreads*, in the UNIX operating system environment.

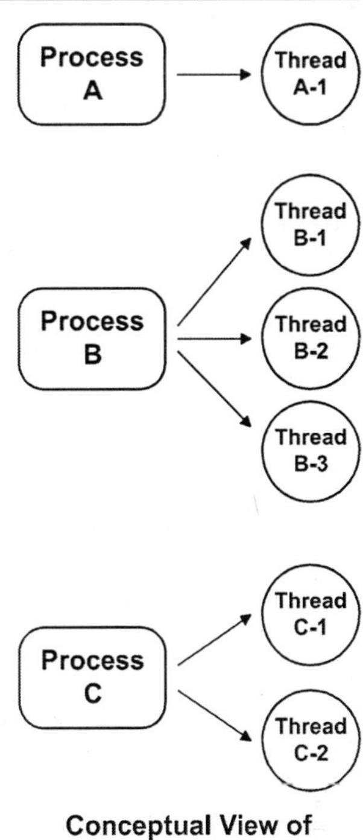

Conceptual View of Processes and Threads

Microsoft Windows Thread Scheduling

The Windows Thread Scheduler (sometimes referred to as the *dispatcher*) is responsible for the multitasking scheduling. By scheduling threads processes are inherently scheduled as threads which belong to processes. The thread scheduler is a pre-emptive scheduler supporting 32 priority levels, where 31 is the highest priority level and 0 is the lowest priority level. Some dynamism exists in the priority scheme as will be explained below.

32 Priority Levels

The priority levels 16..31 are assigned to Real-time activity and require special administrator access. Prioritiy levels 1..15 are used by normal user programs and dynamic priority is supported. Note, priority level 0 is a special system idle priority level, reserved for a system background task for zeroing memory pages.

A Process is assigned a Priority Class from one of the following:

Priority Class	Priority level
REAL-TIME	24
HIGH	13
NORMAL	8
IDLE	4

An individual thread is assigned a priority relative to its process class, where the relative priority can be within a range of +2 to –2 about the process class priority, as follows:

Highest	+2
Above normal	-1
Normal	0
Below Normal	-1
Lowest	-2

Time Quantum

The *Server* operating system configurations use a time quantum of 120 ms. The *Workstation* operating system configurations use a time quantum of 20ms., 40 ms. or 60 ms.

Dynamic Priority Operation

The dynamic priority operation applies to the priority level range 1..15. Activity requiring fast response time for users (e.g. keyboard or mouse) can use a special *priority-boosting* scheme. There is also a *starvation prevention* policy which allows low priority threads to get processor attention.

PRIORITY BOOSTING

Priority boosting applies to threads with priorities in the range 1..15. For example a blocked thread waiting for the keyboard or a mouse input will be boosted by +6 priority levels (up to but not exceeding priority level 15) when the keyboard or mouse event happens. Subsequently, the boosted priority will decay to the pre-assigned level because the thread's priority level is decreased by 1 every time the thread completes execution for one time quantum.

STARVATION PREVENTION

Windows 2000 employs an *"anti-CPU starvation"* policy within the 0..15 priority range. If a thread has not been executed in a 3 second period then that thread is boosted to priority level 15 and is allowed to run for 2 time quanta. The thread is then reverted to its assigned priority level.

SPECIAL CASE PRIORITY MODIFIERS

There are also two special case priority modifiers, as follows:

A *time critical* thread can be boosted to priority level 15 (31 for Real-time).

A thread can be put *idle* at priority level 1 (16 for Real-time).

Note on Real-time Activity

The higher priority levels, 16 .. 31, are referred to as *real-time* priority levels. Many of the system level processes/threads are executed within these priority levels while the general user level processes/threads are executed in the 1..15 priority range. The term *real-time* implies that the higher priority level environment will get favoured processor attention for the processes/threads in the 16 .. 31 range, and thus such processes/threads will be more likely to meet their various time deadlines so that any time critical requirements are satisfied. However, such deadlines are not guaranteed to be met within the operating system. A proper *real-time* operating system should be able to provide such guarantees to meet all temporal deadline requirements.

Priority Operation

PRIORITY LEVEL DIAGRAM

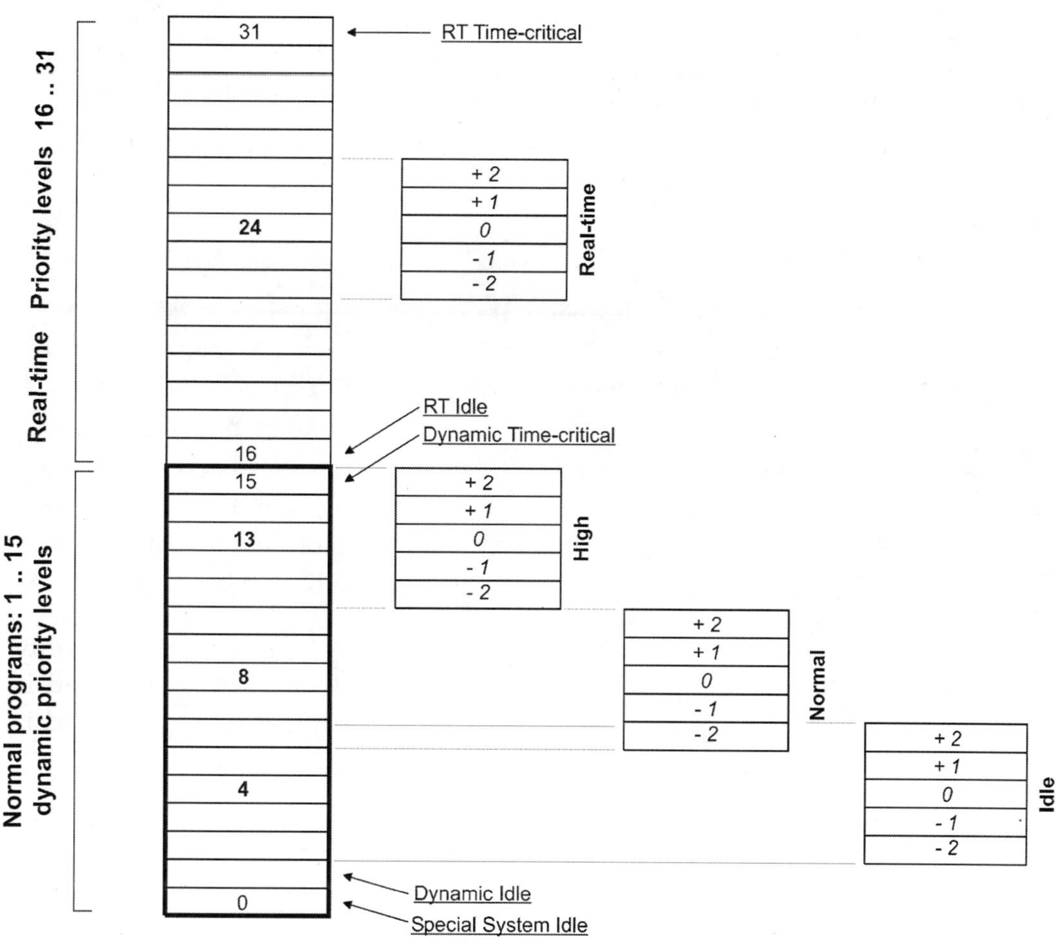

EXACT SCHEME MAY VARY WITH DIFFERENT IMPLEMENTATIONS:
E.G. Windows ME, Windows XP, etc.

The scheduler picks the next thread to run from the highest non-empty queue. If more than one thread is queued at the given priority level then the thread at the front of the queue is selected first.

If a thread is pre-empted by the scheduler before its time quantum completes then that thread is placed at the same priority level in the front of the queue.

NOTE: Multiprocessing (multiple processors) scheduling is supported within the operating system, realising a more complicated scheduling scheme. We hereare confined to single processor scheduling only.

KEYWORDS

JOB QUEUE

READY QUEUE

DEVICE QUEUE

LONG-TERSCHEDULING

MEDIUM-TERM SCHEDULING

SHORT-TERM SCHEDULING

PREEMPTIVE SCHEDULING

NON-PREEMPTIVE SCHEDULING

FIFO

SJF

SRTF

PRIORITY SCHEDULING

MULTILEVEL FEEDBACK QUEUES

SUMMARY

The program is a group of instructions whereas the process is the activity. A system with one CPU can only have one running process at any time. As user jobs enter the system, they are put on a queue called as the "job pool". This consists of all jobs in the system. The main objective of multiprogramming is to have some process running at all times to maximize CPU utilization. The main objective of time-sharing is to switch the CPU among different processes so frequently that users can interact with each program while it is running.

- *Processor-bound or CPU-bound program: A program having long processor bursts (execution instants). CPU bound processes require more CPU time than I/O time*
- *I/O-bound program: A program having short processor bursts. I/O bound processes require more I/O time than CPU time.*
- Job Queue: Consisting of all the processes in the system
- Ready Queue: Processes that are residing in the main memory and are ready and waiting to execute are kept on READY QUEUE.

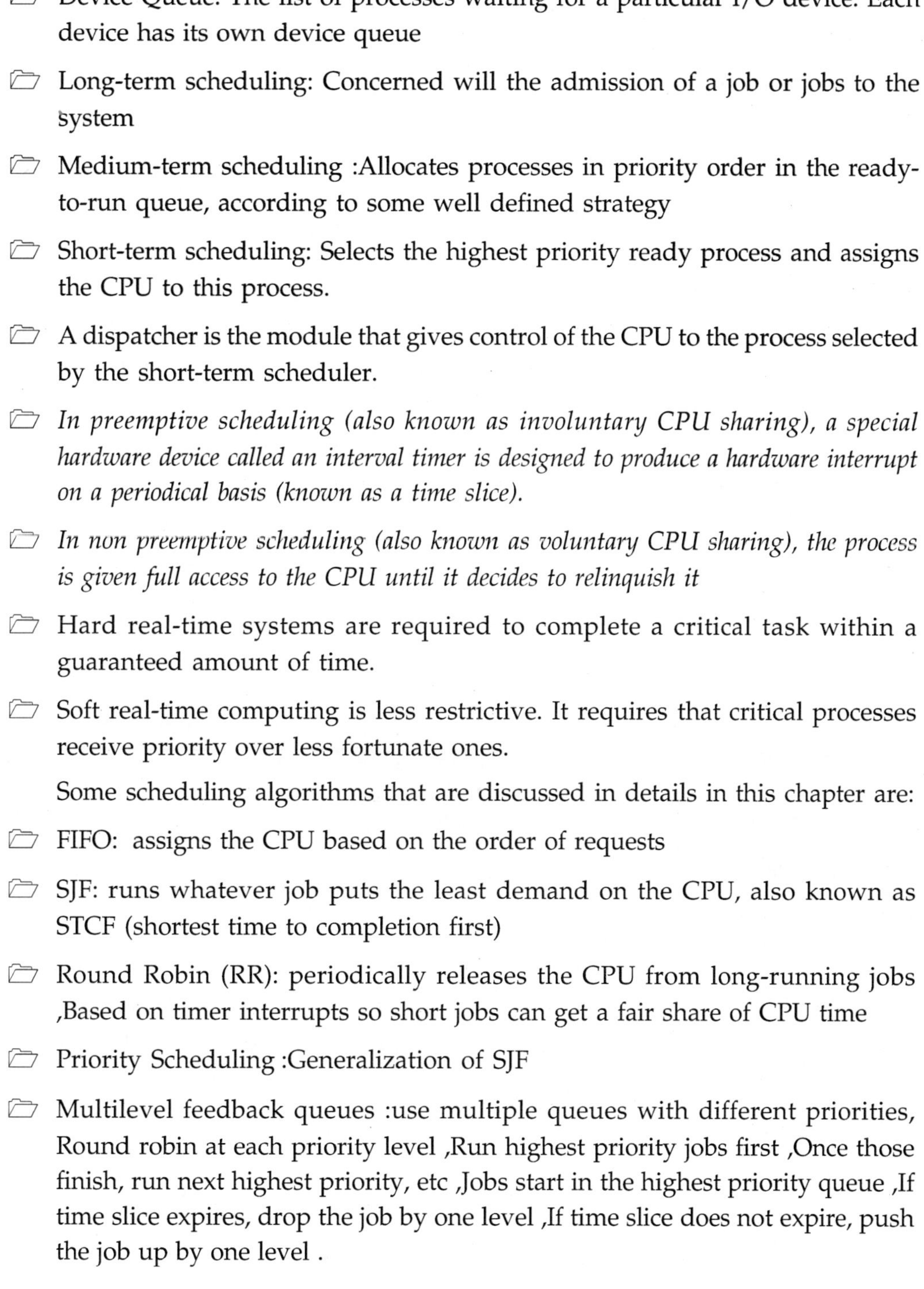

- Device Queue: The list of processes waiting for a particular I/O device. Each device has its own device queue
- Long-term scheduling: Concerned will the admission of a job or jobs to the system
- Medium-term scheduling :Allocates processes in priority order in the ready-to-run queue, according to some well defined strategy
- Short-term scheduling: Selects the highest priority ready process and assigns the CPU to this process.
- A dispatcher is the module that gives control of the CPU to the process selected by the short-term scheduler.
- *In preemptive scheduling (also known as involuntary CPU sharing), a special hardware device called an interval timer is designed to produce a hardware interrupt on a periodical basis (known as a time slice).*
- *In non preemptive scheduling (also known as voluntary CPU sharing), the process is given full access to the CPU until it decides to relinquish it*
- Hard real-time systems are required to complete a critical task within a guaranteed amount of time.
- Soft real-time computing is less restrictive. It requires that critical processes receive priority over less fortunate ones.

  Some scheduling algorithms that are discussed in details in this chapter are:

- FIFO: assigns the CPU based on the order of requests
- SJF: runs whatever job puts the least demand on the CPU, also known as STCF (shortest time to completion first)
- Round Robin (RR): periodically releases the CPU from long-running jobs ,Based on timer interrupts so short jobs can get a fair share of CPU time
- Priority Scheduling :Generalization of SJF
- Multilevel feedback queues :use multiple queues with different priorities, Round robin at each priority level ,Run highest priority jobs first ,Once those finish, run next highest priority, etc ,Jobs start in the highest priority queue ,If time slice expires, drop the job by one level ,If time slice does not expire, push the job up by one level .

REVIEW QUESTIONS

1) What is a CPU scheduler?
2) What are different types of schedulers?
3) Explain mid-term schedulers?
4) Explain short -term schedulers?
5) Explain long-term schedulers?
6) Explain performance criteria for the selection of schedulers?
7) Explain in brief evolution method for CPU scheduling algorithms?
8) Explain FCFS CPU scheduling algorithm?
9) Explain SJF CPU scheduling algorithm?
10) Explain SRTM scheduling algorithm?
11) Explain priority based non preemptive scheduling algorithm?
12) Explain priority based preemptive scheduling algorithm?
13) Explain round robin scheduling algorithm?

FILL IN THE BLANKS

1. __________periodically releases the CPU from long-running jobs ,Based on timer interrupts so short jobs can get a share of CPU time
2. __________is the list of processes waiting for a particular I/O device.
3. *A program having short processor burst and require more I/O time than CPU time is called* __________
4. ____________is concerned will the admission of a job or jobs to the system
5. The main objective of ______________is to have some process running at all times to maximize CPU utilization.
6. The main objective of ______________is to switch the CPU among different processes so frequently that users can interact with each program while it is running.

TRUE OR FALSE

1. CPU bound processes require more I/O time than CPU time
2. Long-term scheduling is concerned will the admission of a job or jobs to the system
3. A dispatcher is the module that gives control of the CPU to the process selected by the short-term scheduler.

4. In non preemptive scheduling (also known as voluntary CPU sharing), the process is given full access to the CPU until it decides to relinquish it
5. Hard real-time systems are required to complete a critical task within less restrictive amount of time.
6. Multilevel feedback queues generally use multiple queues with same priorities

ANSWERS

FILL IN THE BLANKS

1. Round Robin Scheduling
2. Device Queue
3. *I/O-bound program*
4. Long-term scheduling
5. multiprogramming
6. time-sharing

TRUE OR FALSE

1. FALSE
2. TRUE
3. TRUE
4. TRUE
5. FALSE
6. FALSE

"Besides a mathematical inclination, an exceptionally good mastery of one's native tongue is the most vital asset of a competent programmer. " —Edsger Dijkstra

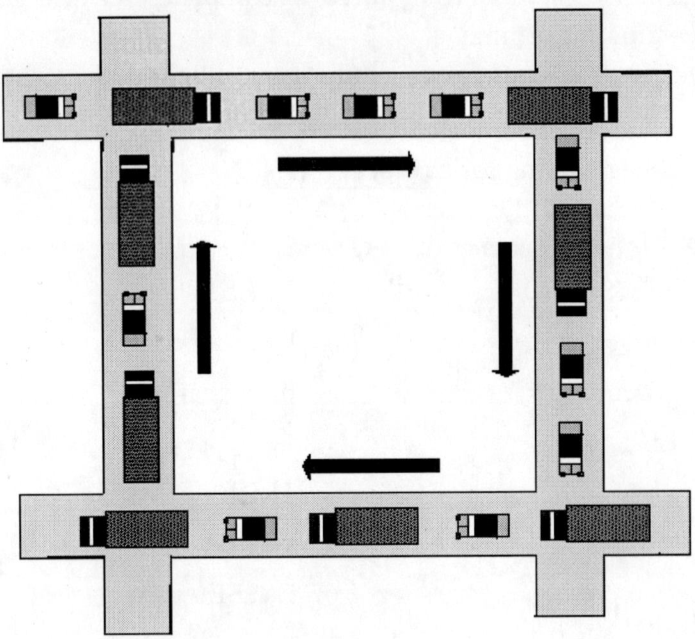

6 DEADLOCKS

INTRODUCTION

We know that one definition of an operating system is a resource allocator. There are many resources that can be allocated to only one process at a time, Sometimes a process has to reserve more than one resource. For example, a process which copies files from one tape to another generally requires two tape drives. A process which deals with databases may need to lock multiple records in a database.

In general, resources allocated to a process are not preemptable; this means that once a resource has been allocated to a process, there is no simple mechanism by which the system can take the resource back from the process unless the process voluntarily gives it up or the system administrator kills the process. This can lead to a situation called *deadlock*. A set of processes or threads is deadlocked when each process or thread is waiting for a resource to be freed which is controlled by another process.

In a multiprogramming system, processes request resources. If those resources are being used by other processes then the process enters a waiting state. However, if other processes are also in a waiting state, we have deadlock .A set of processes is in a deadlock state if every process in the set is waiting for an event (release) that can only be caused by some other process in the same set.

When several processes compete for resources deadlock can occur if each process in a set of processes is waiting for a resource that only another process in the set can make available. Since all of the processes are thus waiting for a resource which can only be freed by another process in the set, they are all blocked so that no one process can free a resource to break the lock situation.

RESOURCES

A **resource** is an object that a process makes use of. A resource can be a piece of hardware such as

- tape drive
- disk drive
- printer

  or a piece of information such as

- a file
- a record within a file
- a shared variable
- a critical section

A computer typically has many different resources. In some cases there may be many instances of a resource of a given type (e.g. buffers), all of which are equivalent. A process needing one of these resources can use any one of them. In other cases there may be only one instance of a resource (e.g. CD-ROM drive with a particular CD).

There are two classes of resources: those that are consumable and those that are not. Here is the distinction:

Classes of resources

- **Reusable resources:** They are used without being depleted after use. Examples are the CPU, I/O channels and devices, memory, etc.
- **Consumable resources:** They usually are created and then destroyed after use. Examples are: signals and messages, information in I/O buffers, etc.

Flavors of resources

Resources come in two flavors: preemptable and nonpreemptable. A **preemptable resource** is one which can be allocated to a given process for a period of time, then be allocated to another process and then be reallocated to the first process without any ill effects. Examples of preemptable resources include

- memory
- buffers
- CPU
- array processor

A **nonpreemptable resource** cannot be taken from one process and given to another without side effects. One obvious example is a printer: certainly we would not want to take the printer away from one process and give it to another in the middle of a print job. (Actually, the THE operating system treated printers as preemptable resources — the operators would have to sort the printed output to reassemble print jobs.)

As we shall see, deadlocks usually involve nonpreemptable resources. The usual sequence of events that occur as a resource is used is

1. **Request the resource.**

   One of two things can happen when a resource is requested: the request can be granted immediately (if the resource is available) or it can be postponed (or blocked) until a later time.

2. **Use the resource.**

   Once the resource has been acquired, it can be used.

3. **Release the resource.**

   When the process no longer needs the resource it releases it. Usually it is released as soon as possible but in most systems there is nothing to enforce this policy.

DEADLOCK

*A set of processes is **deadlocked** if each process in the set is waiting for an event that only another process in the set can cause.*

For Example

Process-1 requests the printer, gets it Process-2 requests the tape unit, gets it Process-1 requests the tape unit, waits Process-2 requests the printer, waits	} Process-1 and Process-2 are deadlocked!

It is possible for a single process to become deadlocked if it is waiting for an event that only it can cause. However, it is usually the case that one process is waiting for a resource that is held by another process. If the other process is itself waiting for a resource held by the first then deadlock occurs.

Example. showing how the sequence of requesting resources can lead to DEADLOCK with two processes:

It is possible for two or more programs to be hung up waiting for each other. An example is given in Figure. Two programs may each require two I/O devices to perform some operation (e.g. CD to floppy disk copy). One of the programs has taken control one of the devices and the other program has the control of the other device. Each is waiting for the other program to release the desired resource. This situation is called deadlock.

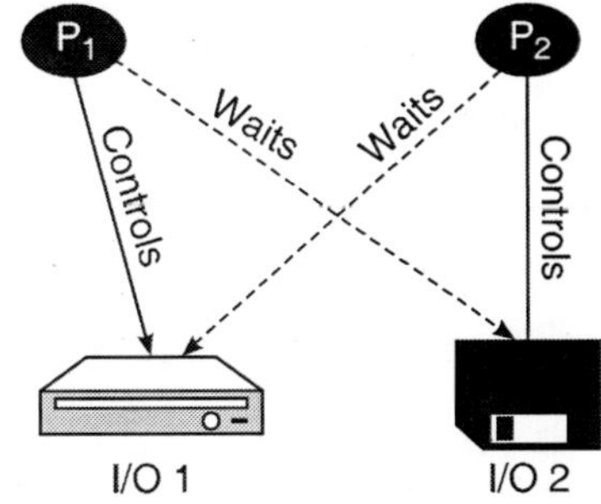

Deadlock
Process 1 waits for I/O 2 held by Process 2
Process 2 waits for I/O 1 held by Process 1

Note that deadlock is different from **starvation**. Starvation is the problem that occurs when a process is waiting for a resource that is allocated to other processes, released, and then allocated again to some process other than the one that is starving.

Bridge Crossing Example

Think of a bridge having a deadlock as:

- Traffic only in one direction.
- Each section of a bridge can be viewed as a resource.
- If a deadlock occurs, it can be resolved if one car backs up (preempt resources and rollback).
- Several cars may have to be backed up if a deadlock occurs.
- Starvation is possible.

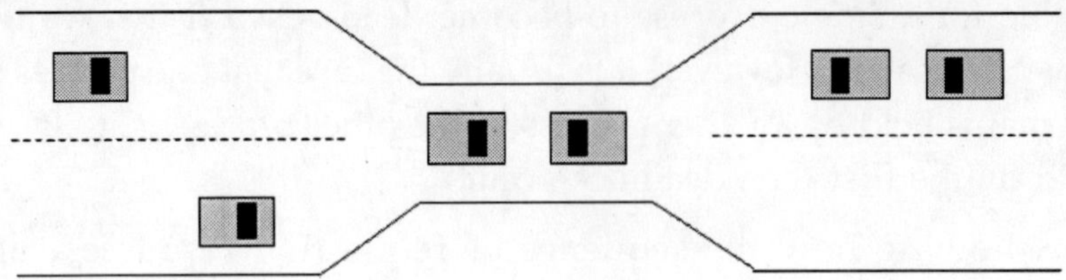

NECESSARY CONDITIONS FOR DEADLOCK

In 1971 Coffman showed that four conditions must hold in order for deadlock to occur:

1. **Mutual exclusions**:

   Each resource can be assigned to only one process at a time and is either assigned or available. Resources involved are non-shareable, a resource is either assigned to a process or it is free.

2. **Hold and wait**:

   Processes that currently hold resources can continue to hold those resources while waiting for new resources. The processes that currently hold resources can request and wait for additional resources.

3. **No preemption**:

   Resources previously granted cannot be taken away from the processes that hold them; they must be released by the holding process. The resources allocated to a process must be explicitly released by that process. Resources cannot be otherwise forcibly removed from the process

4. **Circular wait**:

   There must exist a circular chain of two or more processes, where each process holds one or more resources that are requested by the next process in the chain. In this condition each process is waiting for a resource held by the previous member of the chain.

All four of these conditions must hold in order for deadlock to occur.

RAG (RESOURCE ALLOCATION GRAPH)

We can use a directed graph called a **resource-allocation graph** to characterize a deadlock situation. It is a very useful tool in characterizing the allocation of resources to processes is the resource allocation graph . The resource allocation graph is a directed path that depicts a state of the system of resources and processes, with each process and each resource represented by a node. It provides a way to model how processes and resources are connected. The basic symbols of RAG representation are as follows

- Process

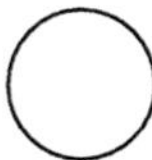

- Resource Type with 4 instances

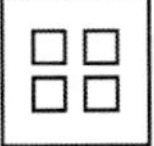

- *Pi* requests instance of *Rj*

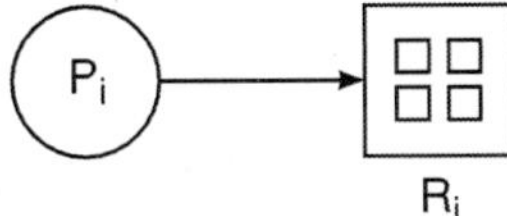

- *Pi* is holding an instance of *Rj*

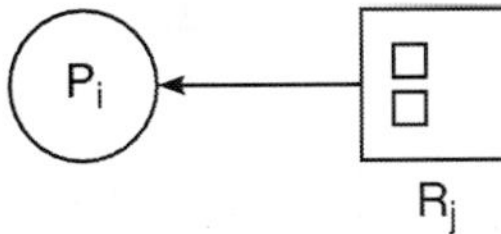

1. Vertices represent resources and processes. Generally used symbols are the **rectangular vertices** to represent **resource classes**, with dots within the vertex to represent instances of the resource. **Circular vertices** will be used for **processes**.
2. A directed edge from a process vertex to a resource vertex indicates that the process has requested an instance of the resource. This is called a **request edge**.
3. A directed edge from a dot within a resource vertex (an instance of the resource) to a process vertex indicates that the resource has been allocated to the process. This is called a **assignment edge**

   A graph edge directed form a process to a resource indicates a resource that has been requested by the process but not yet granted (Figure a). Within a resource node, a dot is shown for each instance of that resource. Examples of resource types that may have multiple instances are I/O devices that are allocated by a resource management module in the operating system.

   A graph edge directed form a reusable resource node dot to a process indicates a request that has been granted (Figure b); that is, the process has been assigned one unit of that resource. Figure c shows an example deadlock. There is only one unit each of resources Ra and Rb. Process P1 holds Rb and requests Ra, while P2 holds Ra but requests Rb. Figure d has the same topology as Figure c, but there is no deadlock because multiple units of each resource are available.

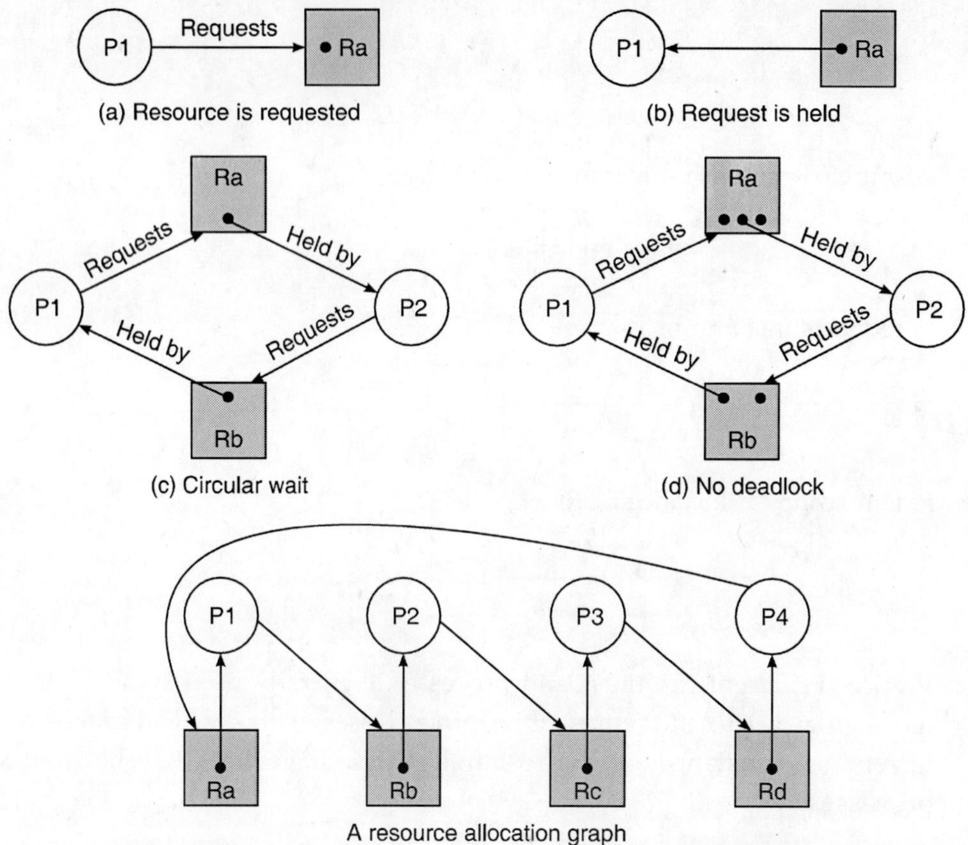

(a) Resource is requested

(b) Request is held

(c) Circular wait

(d) No deadlock

A resource allocation graph

The resource allocation graph of above Figure corresponds to the deadlock situation. Note that in this case, we do not have a simple situation which two processes each have one resource the other needs. Rather, in this case, there is a circular chain of processes and resources that result in deadlock.

REMEMBER

1. If the resource allocation graph contains no cycles then there is no deadlock in the system at that instance.
2. If the resource allocation graph contains a cycle then a deadlock may exist.
3. If there is a cycle, and the cycle involves only resources which have a single instance, then a deadlock has occurred.

A cycle in the graph indicates a DEADLOCK condition

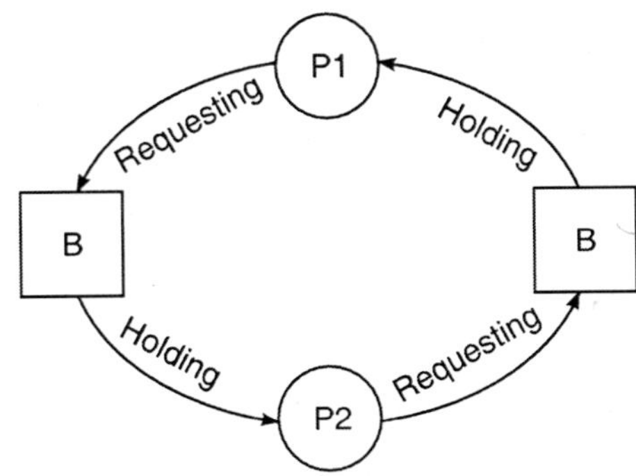

For example, consider the following graph:

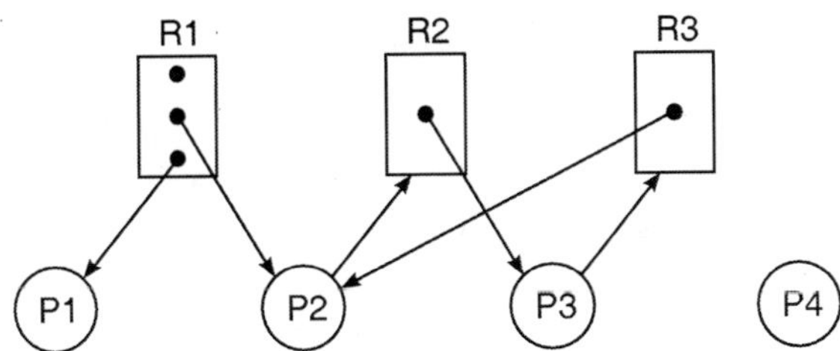

In this example the class represented by R1 has three instances of the resource associated with it. P1 and P2 each have allocated an instance of a resource of type R1. P2 has requested an instance of resource type R2, but is waiting since the only instance is held by P3. P3 is in turn requesting a resource of type R3 but the only instance of that type is held by P2. The situation depicted in this graph is deadlocked. P2 is waiting for a resource held by P3, and P3 is waiting for a resource held by P2. This can be shown to be a cycle with

P2 -> R2 -> P3 -> R3 -> P2

Now consider the graph

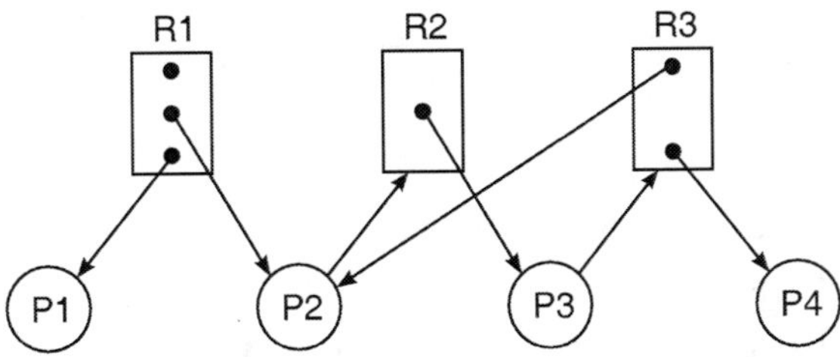

This is just the same as the case before except now there are two instances of resource type R3. Both are currently allocated so that P2 and P3 are waiting just as before. This graph also has the cycle

P2 -> R2 -> P3 -> R3 -> P2

However, this is not a deadlock situation. As soon as P4 finishes with it's instance of R3 it will release it and P3 can allocate it. Even though there is a cycle, this situation does not meet the circular wait criterion for deadlock to occur: there is an instance of a requested resource that is not held by a process in the cycle (P4 holding an instance of R3).

Some other Resource Allocation Graphs:

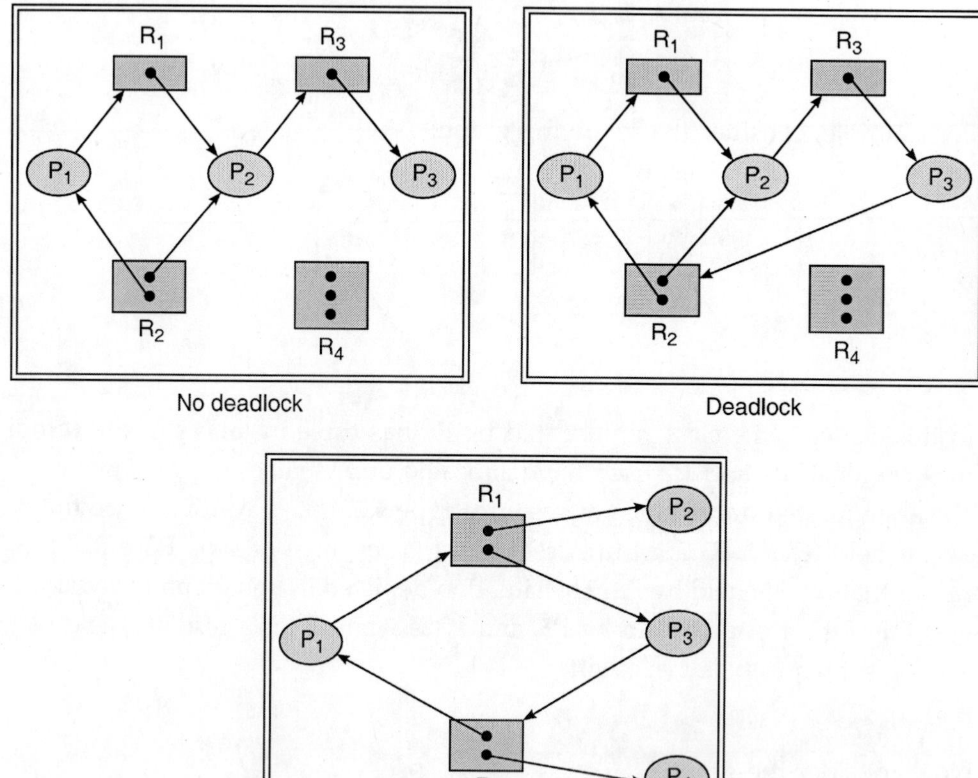

No deadlock

Deadlock

Cycle–but no deadlock

The diagram below shows a traffic deadlock example. The space at each junction can accommodate the width of just one traffic line so each junction can be considered to be a non-shareable resource. Each line of traffic can be considered a process. A line of traffic can hold one junction while waiting for access to another junction. There is nothing to pre-empt a line of traffic so that it can escape the lock up. If this situation was drawn in directed graph representation then a clear cycle would exist in the graph. Note, the four necessary conditions for deadlock do actually apply to this example so the deadlock is in effect.

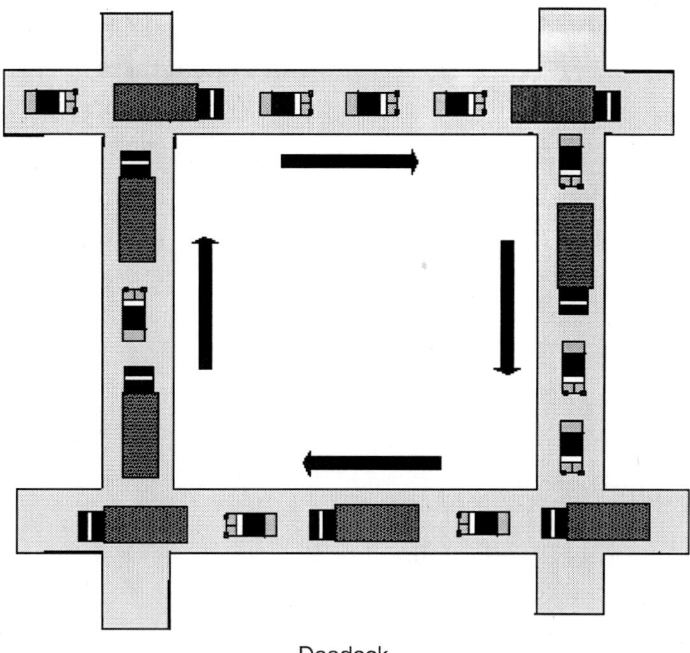

Deadock

Example showing how the sequence of requesting resources can lead to DEADLOCK with two processes:

It is possible for two or more programs to be hung up waiting for each other. An example is given in Figure. Two programs may each require two I/O devices to perform some operation (e.g. CD to floppy disk copy). One of the programs has taken control one of the devices and the other program has the control of the other device. Each is waiting for the other program to release the desired resource. This situation is called deadlock.

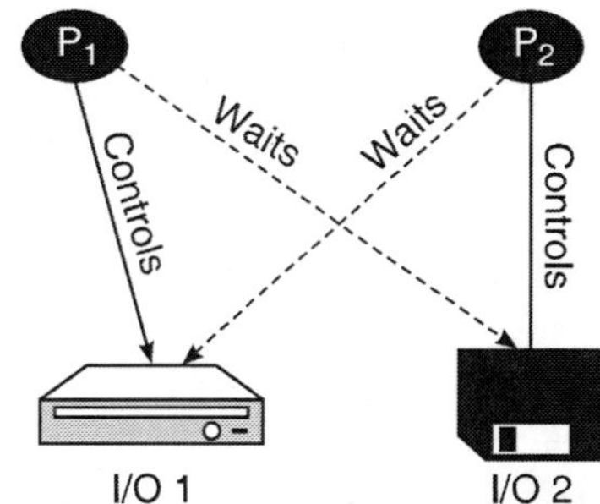

Deadlock
Process 1 waits for I/O 2 held by Process 2
Process 2 waits for I/O 1 held by Process 1

Example showing how the sequence of requesting resources can lead to DEADLOCK with three processes:

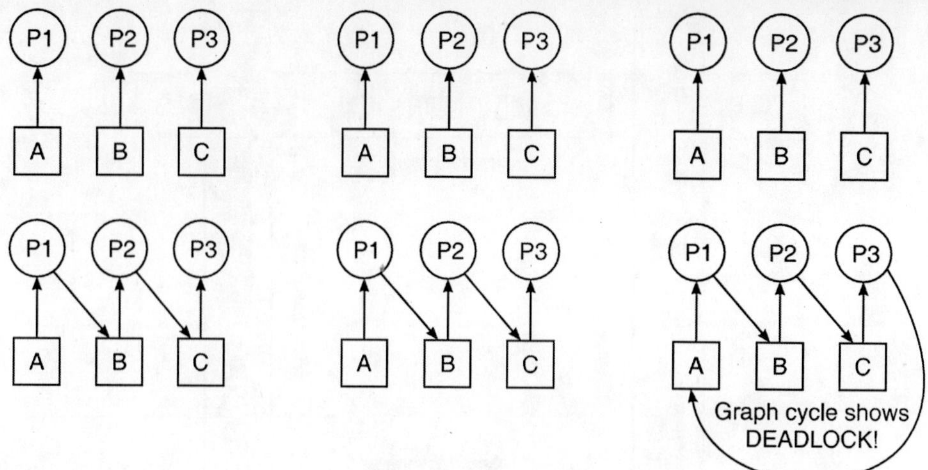

Some more Examples

Is there any deadlock in the following situation?

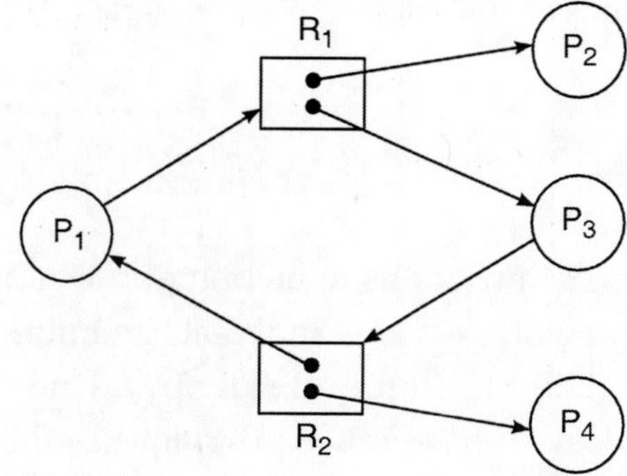

Solution:

In this situation, both P2 and P4 have all of their requests so they can run to completion. When P2 and P4 end, one unit of R1 and R2 are free and can be assigned to P1 and P3. Since then, both P2 and P3 can be assigmed all of their requests, they can now run to completion too. Hence there is no deadlock in this situation.

Example:

P is a set of processes. R is a set of resources. E is a set of request or assignment edges. The sets P, R, and E are as follows:

P = {P1, P2, P3}, **R** = {R1,R2,R3}

E = {P1→R1, P2→R3, P3→R2, R1→P2, R2→P2, R2→P1, R3→P3}

R1 has one instance. R2 has two instances. R3 has one instance.

(a) Draw the resource-allocation graph.

(b) Is there any deadlock in this situation? Briefly Explain.

Solution:

(a) the resource allocation grap is:

(b)

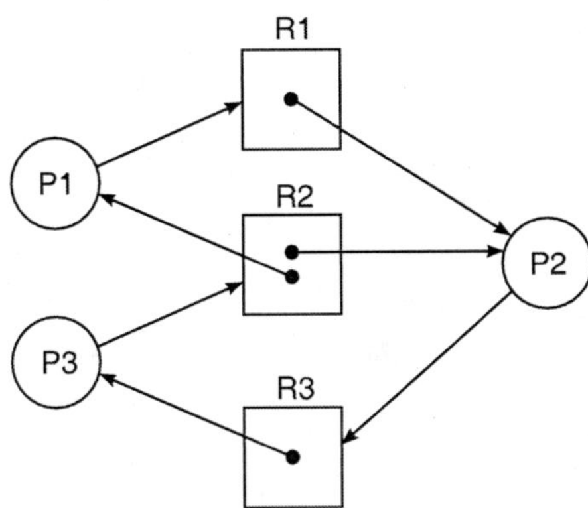

(b) Consider the resource-allocation graph. One cycle exist in the system.

P1 → R1 → P2 → R3 → P3 → R2 → P1

Hence, P1, P2, and P3 are deadlocked.

DEADLOCK SITUATIONS

The following are situations where deadlock can occur:

- Deadlock on file requests: Only one process can write to a file at any one time. If two processes require access to two files and each has claimed one, there is deadlock.
- Deadlock in databases: As for files, but databases can give exclusive access to tables.
- Deadlocks in device allocation: Devices such as printers, web-cameras etc.
- Deadlocks in a Network.

What is the difference between a deadlock and starvation?

- Deadlocks occur when resources needed by jobs to run to completion are held by other jobs which are waiting for some other resources.
- Starvation is the result of conservative allocations where a single job is prevented from execution because it's kept waiting for resources that never become available.

STRATEGIES FOR HANDLING DEADLOCK

1) **Deadlock Avoidance** - uses strategic resource allocation

2) **Deadlock Prevention** - ensures that at least one of the necessary deadlock conditions cannot occur.

3) **Deadlock Detection and Recovery** - A deadlock situation is allowed to occur and the system initiates a recovery procedure.

4) **Ignore the problem** – Some systems do not attempt to manage deadlock conditions. It is left to the users to resolve any potential locked process conditions

DEALING WITH DEADLOCK

There are four different approaches to dealing with the deadlock problem:

1. Ignore the problem
2. Detect deadlock when it occurs, and recover from it
3. Prevent deadlock from occurring
4. Dynamically avoiding deadlock

Ignoring the problem is the approach taken by most operating systems. In fact, this is really an instance of the second approach: deadlock detection and recovery. This is because a human operator will often notice the deadlocked condition (detection) and kill the offending process (es) or restart the system (recovery). The implicit assumption here is that deadlock is unlikely to occur, and when it does it is relatively easy (and inexpensive) to recover from.

This is not quite as bad as it sounds. As we will see, handing the deadlock problem is complicated and is often inconvenient. If it is the case that a given system is likely to suffer from deadlock infrequently (once a week, once a month, etc.) but for other reasons it is restarted at least that frequently (e.g., it is restarted every morning) then it's probably not worth much effort to worry about deadlock.

Another consideration is exactly what types of processes are suffering from deadlock. If user processes are likely to be the only processes that become deadlocked, and they can be killed and restarted easily, then deadlock detection, avoidance or prevention is not mandatory. However, if it is kernel processes that are becoming deadlocked, so that the system is unusable, then it is probably worth some effort to eliminate the deadlock problem.

DEADLOCK AVOIDANCE

The deadlock avoidance algorithms that recognize "symptoms" of deadlock and through careful allocation avoid it. Simplest and most useful model requires that each process declare the *maximum number* of resources of each type that it may need. The deadlock-avoidance algorithm dynamically examines the resource-allocation state to ensure that there can never be a circular-wait condition. Resource-allocation *state* is defined by the number of available and allocated resources, and the maximum demands of the processes.

The most important and widely used deadlock avoidance algorithm is *BANKERS* algorithm.

BANKER'S ALGORITHM *by Dijkstra*

The analogy here is a small-town banker with a limited amount of capital to loan (resources). Each one of a fixed number of customers (processes) has a pre-assigned credit limit (maximum number of resources, referred to as a **claim**).

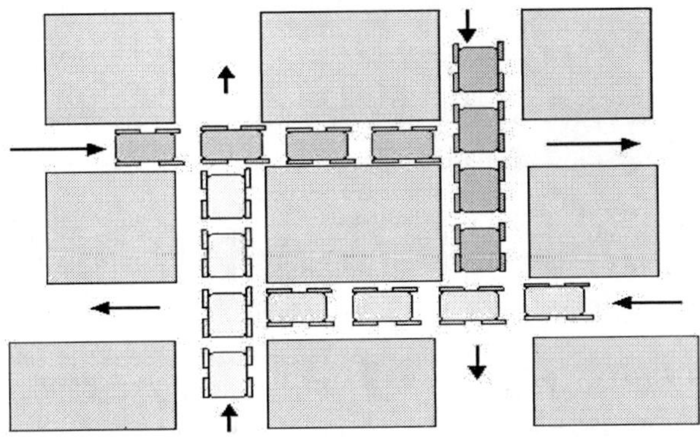

Deadlock

The following explanation relates to a single resource type, so as to provide a simple introduction. The explanation is extended to pools of different type resources later. The system has a fixed number of resources of type **R** which are shareable among **n** processes. Each process must specify in advance how many **R** type resources are required. A process will not request more than its own maximum number of allowable resources (**claim** on resources).

A process may have to wait for resources to become available but the scheme guarantees a finite wait. Once a process gets its resources it must guarantee to release the resources within a finite time.

A STATE represents a list of processes showing the resources already obtained by each process and the **claim** (max. number of resources) for each process.

A **SAFE** state is defined where all processes can obtain their resources and complete in some sequence of states, otherwise the state is defined as being **UNSAFE**.

Banker's Algorithm (Dijkstra and Habermann)

It is a deadlock avoidance algorithm. The following data structures are used in the algorithm:

m = number of resources
n = number of processes

Available [m] : One dimensional array of size m. It indicates the number of available resources of each type. For example, if Available [i] is k, there are k instances of resource r_i.

Max [n,m] : Two dimensional array of size n*m. It defines the maximum demand of each process from each resource type. For example, if Max [i,j] is k, process p_i may request at most k instances of resource type r_j.

Allocation [n,m] : Two dimensional array of size n*m. It defines the number of resources of each type currently allocated to each process.

Need [n,m] : Two dimensional array of size n*m. It indicates the remaining need of each process, of each resource type. If Need [i,j] is k, process pi may need k more instances of resource type r_j. Note that Need [i,j] = Max [i,j] - Allocation [i,j].

Request [n,m] : Two dimensional array of size n*m. It indicates the pending requests of each process, of each resource type.

Now, take each row vector in Allocation and Need as Allocation(i) and Need(i). (Allocation(i) specifies the resources currently allocated to process p_i.)

Define the ≤ relation between two vectors X and Y , of equal size = n as :

X ≤ Y ⇔ X [i] ≤ Y [i] , i = 1,2, ..., n
X !≤ Y ⇔ X [i] > Y [i] for some i

The algorithm is as follows:

1. Process pi makes requests for resources. Let Request(i) be the corresponding request vector. So, if p_i wants k instances of resource type r_j, then Request(i)[j] = k.

2. If Request(i) !≤ Need(i), there is an error.

3. Otherwise, if Request(i) !≤ Available, then p_i must wait.

4. Otherwise, Modify the data structures as follows :

Available = Available - Request(i)
Allocation(i) = Allocation(i) + Request(i)
Need(i) = Need(i) - Request(i)

5. Check whether the resulting state is safe. (Use the safety algorithm presented below.)

6. If the state is safe, do the allocation. Otherwise, p_i must wait for Request(i).

Safety Algorithm to perform Step 5:

Let Work and Finish be vectors of length m and n, respectively.

1. Initialize Work = Available, Finish [j] = false, for all j.

2. Find an i such that Finish [i] = false and Need(i) ≤ Work

If no such i is found, go to step **4.**

3. If an i is found, then for that i, do :

Work = Work + Allocation(i)
Finish [i] = true

Go to step **2.**

4. If Finish [j] = true for all j, then the system is in a safe state.

Given

Available = $\begin{bmatrix} 1 & 4 & 1 \end{bmatrix}$

Max $= \begin{bmatrix} 1 & 3 & 1 \\ 1 & 4 & 1 \end{bmatrix}$

Allocation= $\begin{bmatrix} 0 & 0 & 0 \\ 0 & 0 & 0 \end{bmatrix}$

Need $= \begin{bmatrix} 1 & 3 & 1 \\ 1 & 4 & 1 \end{bmatrix}$

Request $= \begin{bmatrix} 1 & 2 & 0 \\ 0 & 2 & 1 \end{bmatrix}$

Request(1) is to be processed. If it is satisfied data would become:

Available = $\begin{bmatrix} 0 & 2 & 1 \end{bmatrix}$

Allocation= $\begin{bmatrix} 1 & 2 & 0 \\ 0 & 0 & 0 \end{bmatrix}$

Need $= \begin{bmatrix} 0 & 1 & 1 \\ 1 & 4 & 1 \end{bmatrix}$

Now, apply the safety algorithm:

Work = [0 2 1]

Finish $= \begin{bmatrix} false \\ false \end{bmatrix}$

i = 1 :

Need(1) = [0 1 1] ≤ Work ? Yes.
Work = Work + Allocation(1) = [1 4 1]
Finish (1) = true

i = 2 :

Need(2) = [1 4 1] ≤ Work ? Yes.
Work = Work + Allocation(2) = [1 4 1]
Finish (2)= true

System is in a safe state, so do the allocation. If the algorithm is repeated for Request (2), the system will end up in an unsafe state.

If a system has no deadlock prevention and no deadlock avoidance scheme, then it needs a deadlock detection scheme with recovery from deadlock capability. For this, information should be kept on the allocation of resources to processes, and on outstanding allocation requests. Then, an algorithm is needed which will determine whether the system has entered a deadlock state. This algorithm must be invoked periodically.

Deadlock Detection Algorithm (Shoshani and Coffman)

Data Structure is as:

Available [m]
Allocation [n,m] as in Banker's Algorithm
Request [n,m] indicates the current requests of each process.

Let Work and Finish be vectors of length m and n, as in the safety algorithm.

The algorithm is as follows:

1. Initialize Work = Available
  For i = 1 to n do
    If Allocation(i) = 0 then Finish[i] = true else Finish[i] = false

2. Search an i such that

Finish[i] = false and Request(i) ≤ Work

If no such i can be found, go to step 4.

3. For that i found in step 2 do:

Work = Work + Allocation(i)
Finish[i] = true

Go to step 2.

4. If Finish[i] ≠ true for a some i then the system is in deadlock state else the system is safe

Example:

Examine whether the system whose resource allocation graph is given below is deadlocked or not.

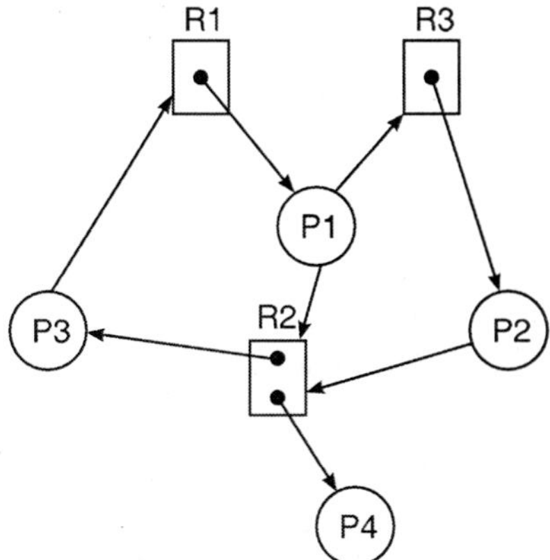

First, let's form the required structures:

Available = [0 0 0]

$$\text{Allocation} = \begin{bmatrix} 1 & 0 & 0 \\ 0 & 1 & 0 \\ 0 & 0 & 1 \\ 0 & 0 & 1 \end{bmatrix}$$

$$\text{Request} = \begin{bmatrix} 0 & 1 & 1 \\ 0 & 0 & 1 \\ 1 & 0 & 0 \\ 0 & 0 & 0 \end{bmatrix}$$

$$\text{Finish} = \begin{bmatrix} False \\ False \\ False \\ False \end{bmatrix}$$

Work = [0 0 0]

Request(4) ≤ Work → i = 4:

Work = Work + Allocation(4) = [0 0 0] + [0 0 1] = [0 0 1];
Finish[4] = True

Request(2) ≤ Work → i = 2:

Work = Work + Allocation(2) = [0 0 1] + [0 1 0] = [0 1 1] ;
Finish[2] = True

Request(1) ≤ Work→ i = 1:

Work = Work + Allocation(1) = [0 1 1] + [1 0 0] = [1 1 1] ;
Finish[1] = True

Request(3) ≤ Work → i = 3:

Work = Work + Allocation(3) = [1 1 1] + [0 0 1] = [1 1 2] ;
Finish[3] = True

Since Finish[i] = true for all i, there is no deadlock in the system .

FLOWCHART FOR BANKER'S ALGORITHM

A process request will not be granted until the system establishes that the current state is SAFE. It establishes this using the following algorithm:

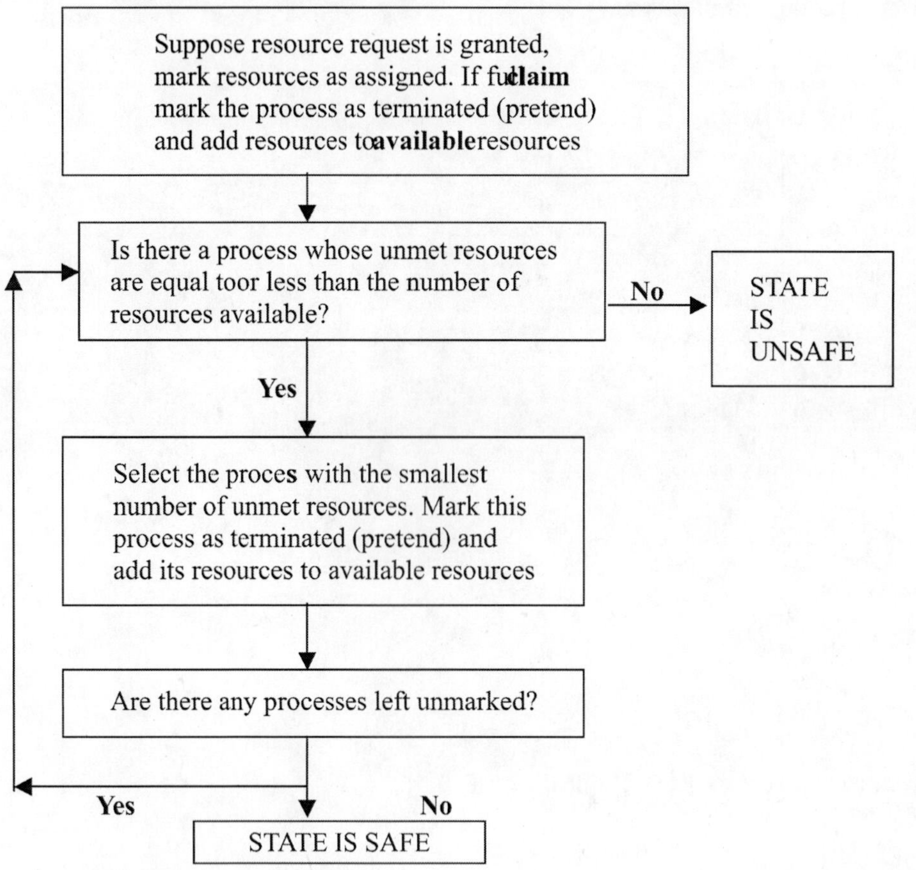

FEATURES OF BANKER'S ALGORITHM

1 Each new request for a resource requires checking current allocation with maximum needs and determines state of system.

2 Safe State - There exist a sequence of allocations so that each process can acquire its resources and terminate, thus avoiding deadlock.

3 Unsafe State - State that could lead to deadlock (may not, but *could*).

4 Avoidance – Only grant requests that lead to a safe state.

EXAMPLES:

Assume total resources (bank's total credit) are 10 resources.

Resource state model:

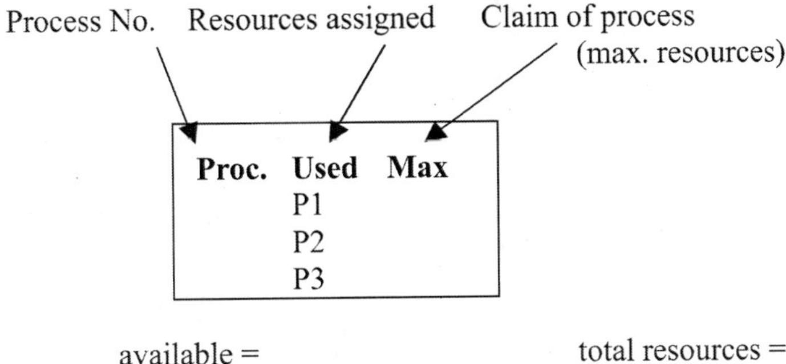

available = (total resources)-(total resources assigned)

CASE 1:

Assume a state as given in the left-most resource state representation. Assume:

process P2 requests 2 resources.

Granting this request is simulated using the Banker's algorithm. Note, when the process is granted all of its resources, it returns the resources within a finite time.

Proc.	Used	Max
P1	1	9
P2	2	4
P3	4	6
available 3 (10-7)		

Proc.	Used	Max
P1	1	9
--		
P3	4	6
available 5 (10-5)		

Proc.	Used	Max
P1	1	9
--		
--		
available 9 (10-1)		

Proc.	Used	Max
--		
--		
--		
available 10 (10-0)		

Conclusion CASE 1 - Simulation shows this to be a SAFE state so P2's request for two resources is granted.

CASE 2 :

Now, for the same state as given in CASE 1 above, suppose:

Process P1 requests 2 resources.

Proc.	Used	Max	Proc.	Used	Max	Proc.	Used	Max	Proc.	Used	Max
P1	1	9	P1	3	9	P1		9	P1		9
P2	2	4	P2	2	4	P2		4	P2		4
P3	4	6	P3	4	6	P3		6	P3		6
available 3 (10-7)			available 1 (10-9)			available			available		

POSSIBLE DEADLOCK

Conclusion CASE 2 - Simulation shows this to be an UNSAFE state since it leads to possible DEADLOCK so P1's request for two resources is not allowed.

BANKER'S ALGORITHM - SOME WEAKNESSES

1. A fixed number of available resources are assumed. This does not allow for out-of-service resource conditions.
2. Forcing a process to define its resource requirements in advance is a very restrictive requirement.
3. Assumes a fixed number of processes, this is not usually practical.
4. Guarantees resource allocation within a finite time, but this may not be good enough for a real-time system.
5. Processes must release all resources within a finite time. This is not a practical requirement.

RESOURCE TRAJECTORIES

One way to avoid deadlock in certain simple circumstances is by using **resource trajectories** (transparency). Assume that there are two processes P1 and P2 and they both need to use the printer and the plotter (a single instance of each resource is available).

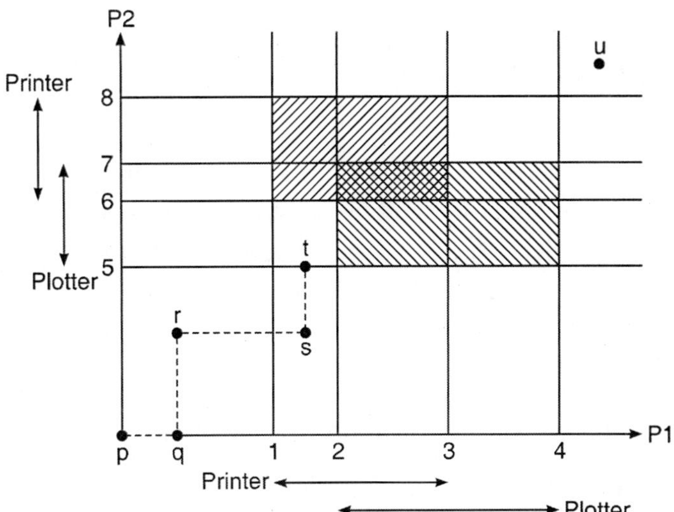

The horizontal and vertical axes represent the number of instructions executed by P1 and P2 respectively. The dashed line is a *resource trajectory*; it shows when the scheduler ran each process P1 and P2. Suppose that **p** is the initial situation and the **u** is the final point. Process P1 must pass lines 1, 2, 3, and 4 and process P2 must pass lines 5, 6, 7, and 8.

The shaded areas represent "impossible" regions; areas in which both processes hold one or both of the non-shareable resources. Notice that the trajectory must either move right or up. To avoid deadlock, once the trajectory is at **t** the scheduler must schedule process P1 to run until it passes line 4 before it lets process P2 run again. This is because if we enter the box bounded by lines 1, 4, 5 and 8 the trajectory must pass through one of the shaded "impossible" areas.

DEADLOCK PREVENTION

Research [Hanvender] showed that if any of the four necessary conditions for deadlock can be avoided then deadlock cannot occur.

DEADLOCK PREVENTION

1) **Mutual Exclusion**

   Since we do want to allow processes exclusive access to resources we do not want to avoid this condition for deadlock.

2) **Hold and Wait For**

   This condition can be avoided by stipulating that all processes must request all of their resources before execution starts. If some resources are busy then a process will wait, without holding any resources, until the resources become free. This solution ties up resources unnecessarily and it is not desirable to force a process to specify its resource requirement in advance of running.

3) **No Preemption**

If a process is denied a request for more resources it releases its already held resources and then makes a fresh request for its full requirement of resources. This is not a practical solution, e.g. a process with a printer resource cannot release the printer at an arbitrary moment.

4) **Circular Wait**

A method can be used to avoid a circular wait condition, i.e. to ensure that the resource allocation graph cannot have cycles.

For a deadlock to occur in a system, all four of the conditions listed before – mutual exclusion, hold and wait, no preemption, circular wait – must hold at the same time. Prevention strategies ensure that at least one of the conditions is always false.

1) Attacking the mutual exclusion condition –

Sharable resources do not require mutually exclusive access, and thus cannot be involved in a deadlock. Read-only files are a good example of a sharable resource: if several processes attempt to open a read-only file at the same time, they can be granted simultaneous access to the file. Nonsharable resources (for example, printer) – the mutual exclusion condition must hold for these resources. A printer cannot be simultaneously shared by several processes. In general, the mutual exclusion condition cannot be invalidated.

2) Attacking the hold and wait condition –

To negate the hold-and-wait condition, we must guarantee that, whenever a process requests a resource, it does not hold any other resources. There are two ways to make this: a) a process may be required to request all of its resources when it is created, or b) by requiring the process to release all currently held resources prior to requesting any new one. These protocols have two main disadvantages. First, resource utilization may be low, since many of the resources may be allocated but unused for a long period. Second, starvation is possible. A process that needs several popular resources may have to wait indefinitely (because at least one of the needed resources is always allocated to some other processes).

3) Attacking the no preemption condition –

This condition is that there be no preemption of resources that have already been allocated. Allowing preemption can be applied to CPU registers and memory space, it cannot generally be applied to printers. We can use the following protocol. If a process that is holding some resources requests another resource that cannot be immediately allocated to it (that is, the process must wait) then all resources currently being held are preempted. The preempted resources are added to the list of resources for which the process is waiting. The process will be restarted only when it can regain its old resources, as well as the new ones that is requesting. Alternatively, if a process requests some resources and they are not available, we check whether they are allocated to some other process that is waiting for additional resources. If so, we preempt the desired resources from the waiting process and allocate them to the requesting process. These protocols cannot be applied to such resource as printers.

4) Attacking the circular wait condition –

The circular wait can be eliminated in several ways. One way to avoid the circular wait is to impose a total ordering of all resource types, and to require that each process requests resources in an increasing order of enumeration.

Let $R = \{ R_1 , R_2 ,..., R_m \}$ be set of resource types. We define a one-to-one function $F : R \rightarrow N$, where N is the set of natural numbers. For example:

1. Imagesetter
2. Scanner
3. Plotter
4. Tape driver
5. CD ROM drive

A process may request first a plotter and then a tape driver, but it may not request first a plotter and then a scanner. If several instances of the same resource type are needed, a single request for all them must be issued. Alternatively, we can require that whenever aprocess requests an instance of resource type R_j , it has released any resources R_i such that $F(R_i) \geq F(R_j)$. In this situation the resource allocation graphs never have cycles. It is easy to check this fact. At every instant, one of the assigned resources will be highest. The process holding that resource will never ask for a resource already assigned, and the circular-wait condition will be broken.

LINEAR ASCENDING ORDER REQUEST SCHEME FOR DEADLOCK PREVENTION

The *linear ascending order request* scheme provides a solution to deadlock prevention by denying the circular wait condition.

Resources are uniquely numbered. Processes are only allowed to request resources in a linear ascending order only - thus avoiding a circular wait condition.

EXAMPLE

Resource	**No**
Modem	R1
line printer	R2
hard disk	R3
floppy	R4
tape unit	R5
laser printer	R6

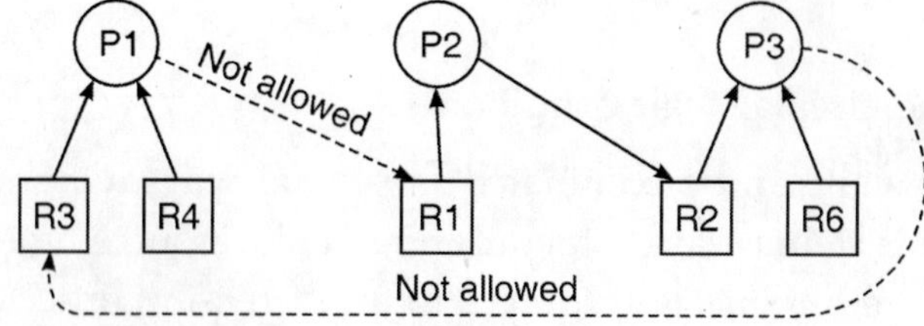

A cycle cannot now occur in the graph.

- valid resource request: **R3 R5 R6**

- invalid resource request: **R2 R4 R1** (requesting R1 violates the *linear ascending order* rule)

Imposing an order in which a process may request resources is restrictive and is not always practical for general-purpose interactive computers. However, the scheme is useful in certain embedded system solutions where the resource ordering can be tolerated in the interest of guaranteeing the prevention of deadlock.

DEADLOCK DETECTION AND RECOVERY

Deadlock detection can be implemented by using a method to reduce the graph or a method to detect the circular wait condition.

Detect the Circular Wait Condition

Each time a resource is requested the resource graph is 'inspected' to test for a **circular wait** condition. The technique must identify the processes and resources involved in the deadlock. One process at a time is terminated until the cycle is broken. The terminated processes must somehow be restarted. A method for deadlock detection and recovery has been defined by **Murphy and Bensoussan ('68)**.

MURPHY/BENSOUSSAN METHOD FOR DEADLOCK DETECTION

A deadlock detection method which detects the circular-wait condition was published by Murphy and Bensoussan in **1968**.

All processes and all resources are arbitrarily assigned unique numbers.

A process will apply a software lock (locks resource) on seizing a resource.

Two tables are used, an RA (Resource Assigned) table to keep track of assigned resources and a PW (Process Waiting) table to keep track of processes which are waiting on resources.

RA TABLE (index I ↓)

Resource number	Assigned to process no.

PW TABLE (index K ↓)

Process number	Resource waited for

The deadlock detection algorithm is applied each time that a **resource which is locked** is requested. It is assumed that a process will request just one resource at a time. If the algorithm detects that a deadlock condition exists, the deadlock condition must be broken by forcing one of the processes to release one or more of the resources. This is called **backtracking** or **backout** and separate policies must be implemented to handle this situation.

Algorithm to detect deadlock by establishing if a graph cycle exists.

The RA and PW tables are locked while the algorithm is run.

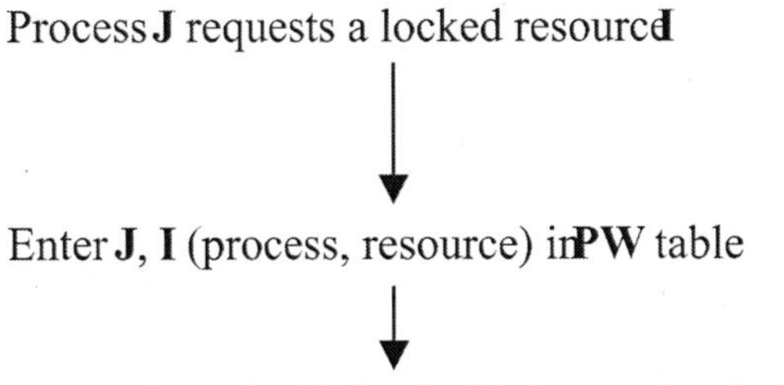

Determine who, **K**, locked **I** (.. uses **I** to index **RA** table)

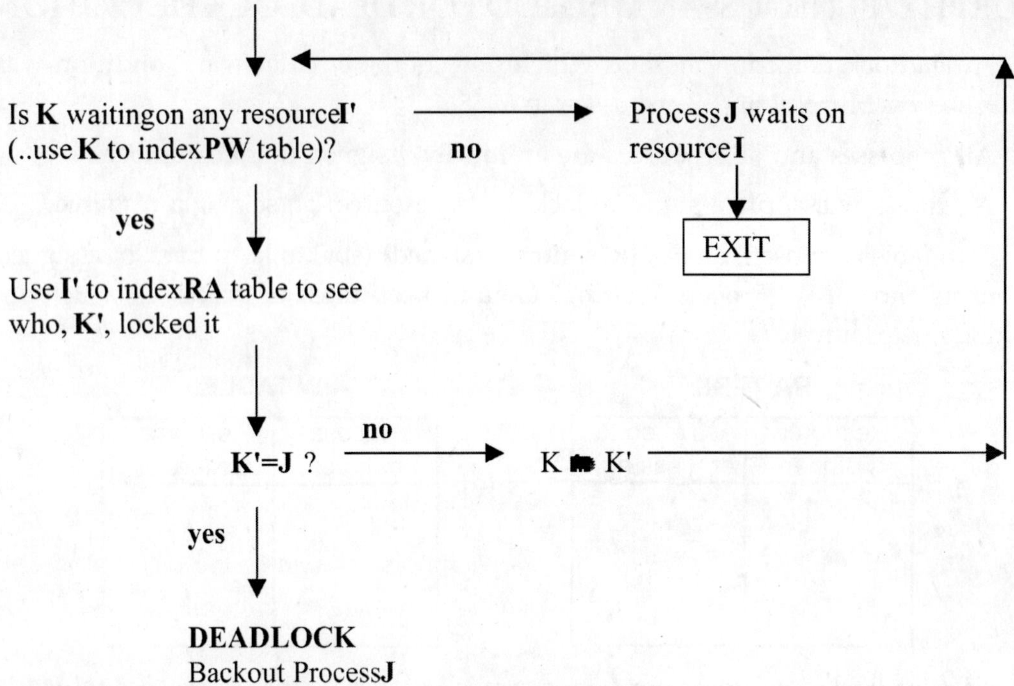

EXAMPLE to illustrate the deadlock detection process:

Consider a system with three processes P_1 ..P_3 and four resources I_1 ..I_4. Assume some sequence of processes requiring resources as follows:

Sequence

1 P_2 requests I_2 and locks it

2 P_2 requests I_1 and locks it

3 P_1 requests I_3 and locks it

4 P_3 requests I_4 and locks it

Status of RA table is now:

RA TABLE

Resource number	Assigned to process no.
2	2
1	2
3	1
4	3

5 P_2 requests I_3 and finds it locked so apply the M/B algorithm :-

J=2 I=3

from RA K = 1

but P_1 is **not** waiting on a resource so P_2 waits on I_3

PW TABLE

K ↓

Process number	Resource waited for
2	**3**

6 P_3 requests I_3 and finds it lockedso apply the M/B algorithm :-

J = 3 I = 2

from RA K = 2

from PW I′ =3

from RA K′ =1

but 1 $\neq$ J so K ← K′ (i.e. K = 1)

P_1 is **not** waiting on a resource so P_3 waits on I_2

PW TABLE

K ↓

Process number	Resource waited for
2	**3**
3	**2**

7 P_1 requests I_4 and finds it locked so apply the M/B algorithm :-

J = 1 I= 4

from RA K = 3

from PW I′ = 2

from RA K′ = 2, but 2 = J so K <-K′(i.e. K =2)

from PW I′ =3

from RA K′ =1

K′ = J so **DEADLOCK** condition exists

RESOURCE ALLOCATION GRAPH REPRESENTATION FOR THIS EXAMPLE:

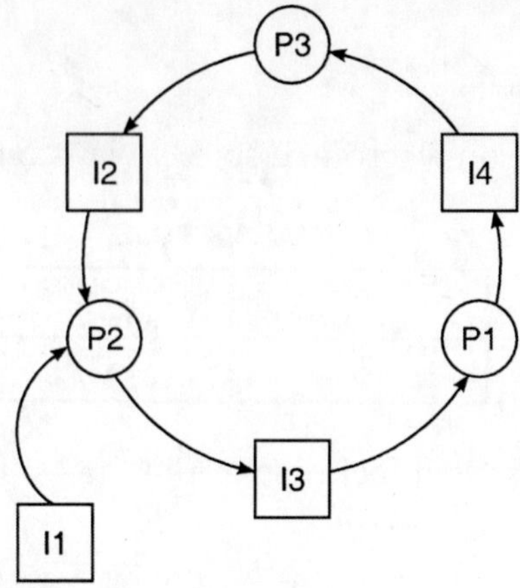

DETECTION ALGORITHM USAGE

When should we invoke the deadlock detection algorithm? The answer depends n two factors:

- How often is a deadlock likely to occur?
- How many processes will be affected by deadlock when it happens?

  Hence the options are:
- Every time a request for allocation cannot be granted immediately—expensive but process causing the deadlock is identified, along with processes involved in deadlock
- Periodically, or based on CPU utilization
- Arbitrarily—there may be many cycles in the resource graph and we would not be able to tell which of the many deadlocked processes "caused" the deadlock.

RECOVERY FROM DEADLOCK

Once detected, deadlock must be untangled. There are several recovery algorithms

1. Method 1 : Most Drastic, Terminate all jobs active in the system and restart from the beginning
2. Method 2: Terminate only jobs involved in the deadlock.
3. Method 3: Identify all jobs involved in the deadlock, and terminate them one at a time. Checking after each removal to see if deadlock eliminated.

4. Method 4: Can only be implemented if each job keeps a snapshot of its progress from beginning of execution to end. Instead of terminating job, wind it back to a previous snapshot and see if deadlock removed, if not keep rewinding.
5. Method 5: pre-empt a non-deadlocked job, deallocate its resources and allocate them to a deadlocked job so it can resume.
6. Method 6: Stop new jobs from entering the system, so non-deadlocked jobs run to completion and release their resources. Eventually with fewer jobs in the system deadlocked jobs may get the resources they need to resume

All the algorithms just considered (except the last one) have one thing in common: they require a victim. An expendable job, which when removed from the deadlock will free the system.

Two basic strategies

When a deadlock detection algorithm determines that a deadlock exists, several alternatives exist. One possibility is to inform the operator that a deadlock has occurred, and to let the operator deal with the deadlock manually. The other possibility is to let the system recover from the deadlock automatically. There are two options for breaking a deadlock. One solution is simply to abort one or more processes to break the circular wait. The second option is to preempt some resources from one or more of the deadlocked processes.

Process Termination

To eliminate deadlocks by aborting a process, we use one of two methods. In both methods the system reclaims all resources allocated to the terminated process.

- Abort all deadlocked processes: This method clearly will break the deadlock cycle, but at a great expense; these processes may have computed for a long time, and the results of these partial computations must be discarded and probably recomputed later.
- Abort one process at a time until the deadlock cycle is eliminated: This method incurs considerable overhead since after each process is aborted, a deadlock detection algorithm must be invoked to determine whether any processes are still deadlocked.

Aborting a process may not be so easy. If a process was in the midst of updating a file, terminating it will leave the system in an inconsistent state. If the partial termination method is used, then given a set of deadlocked processes, we must determine which process should be terminated in an attempt to break the deadlock. This determination is a policy decision similar to CPU scheduling problems. The question is basically an economic one, we should abort those processes the termination of which will incur the minimum cost.

Unfortunately, the term minimum cost is not a precise one. Many factors determine which process is chosen, including:

1. What the priority of the process is
2. How long the process has computed, and how much longer the process will compute before completing its designated task.
3. How many and what type of resources the process has used
4. How many resources the process needs in order to complete
5. How many processes will need to be terminated
6. Whether the process is interactive or batch

Resource Preemption

To eliminate deadlocks using resource preemption, we successively preempt some resources from processes and give these to other processes until the deadlock cycle is broken. If preemption is required to deal with deadlocks, then three issues need to be addressed:

1. **Selecting a victim:**

   Which resources and which processes are to be preempted? As in process termination, we must determine the order of preemption to minimize cost. Cost factors may include such parameters as the number of resources a deadlock process is holding, and the amount of time a deadlocked process has thus far consumed during its execution.

2. **Rollback:**

   If we preempt a resource from a process, what should be done with that process? Clearly, it cannot continue with its normal execution; it is missing some needed resource. We must roll back the process to some safe state and restart it from that state. Since, in general it is difficult to determine what a safe state is, the simplest solution is a total rollback: Abort the process and then restart it. However it is more effective to roll back the process only as far as necessary to break the deadlock. On the other hand, this method requires the system to keep more information about the state of all the running processes.

4. **Starvation:**

   In a system where victim selection is based primarily on cost factors, it may happen that the same process is always picked as the victim. As a result this process never completes its designated task, a starvation situation that needs to be dealt with in any practical system. Clearly, we must ensure that a process is picked as a victim only a finite number of times. The most common solution is to include the number of rollbacks in the cost factor.

The final words

Handling deadlocks can combine the three basic approaches of prevention, avoidance, and detection, and allow the use of the optimal approach for each resource in the system.

1. Partition resources into hierarchically ordered classes.
2. Use the most appropriate technique for handling deadlocks within each class.
3. Recall that there are 4 conditions necessary for deadlock: mutual exclusion, hold and wait, no preemption, and circular wait.
4. Resource use graphs allow people to understand dependencies.

CASE STUDY

DEADLOCK IN REAL-TIME OPERATING SYSTEMS

Simple priority assignment for processes does not guarantee the deterministic timing behaviour of operating system processes. Many real-time scheduling environments are statically scheduled based on pre-define time slots so that the scheduling activity can be verified at pre-run time. However, it is often required to use a pre-emptive multi-tasking operating system to schedule tasks in a real-time environment. It often becomes difficult to guarantee the deterministic behavior of such a system because of some inherent problems. A classical problem here is the one of *priority inversion* where lower priority processes can delay higher priority processes from running under certain circumstances.

The priority inversion problem

Priority inversion is a significant problem associated with running processes which interact with shared data or otherwise synchronise with other processes. We say that such processes are *non-independent* processes since their progression depends on the activity of other processes. The *priority inversion* problem occurs where a high priority process can be blocked by a lower priority process for an unbounded number of times.

Consider a situation where three processes P1..P3 are running on a single processor in a pre-emptive operating environment. P1 is the highest priority process and P3 is the lowest priority process, giving a priority assignment such that:

$$priority\ (P1) > priority\ (P2) > priority\ (P3)$$

Assume that a processes can be pre-empted by higher priority process but otherwise a process will run to completion. Assume Resource_X is a mutually exclusive resource which can be accessed via semaphore_X. Referring to the diagram below, Process P3 requires access to Resource_X so it locks this resource using a successful *wait (semaphore_X)* operation. P3 then enters the critical section to access Resource_X. Process P2 now needs to run so P2 pre-empts P3 and runs. Now P1, the highest priority process, needs to run so P1 pre-empts P2 and runs. Now P1 wants to access Resource_X so it performs a *wait (semaphore_X)* operation. But Resource_X is locked by process P3. Process P1 must now block, waiting on Resource_X, and P2 is allowed to run. Process P3 cannot release the Resource_X until P2 relinquishes the CPU so the high priority process P1 is blocked by a lower priority process P2. This is **priority inversion**, P1 is blocked while the lower priority processe P2 can continue.

The three processes P1..P3 have behaved in a legal manner based on the defined priority scheme. The need to give mutually exclusive access to Resource_X gave rise to the priority inversion problem. However, such a priority model is dangerous in the context of a *hard* real time system. Here we will consider the following techniques to ensure that the *priority inversion* problem cannot happen:

1) Prohibit pre-emption of a process while in its critical section
2) Priority inheritance protocol
3) Priority ceiling protocol

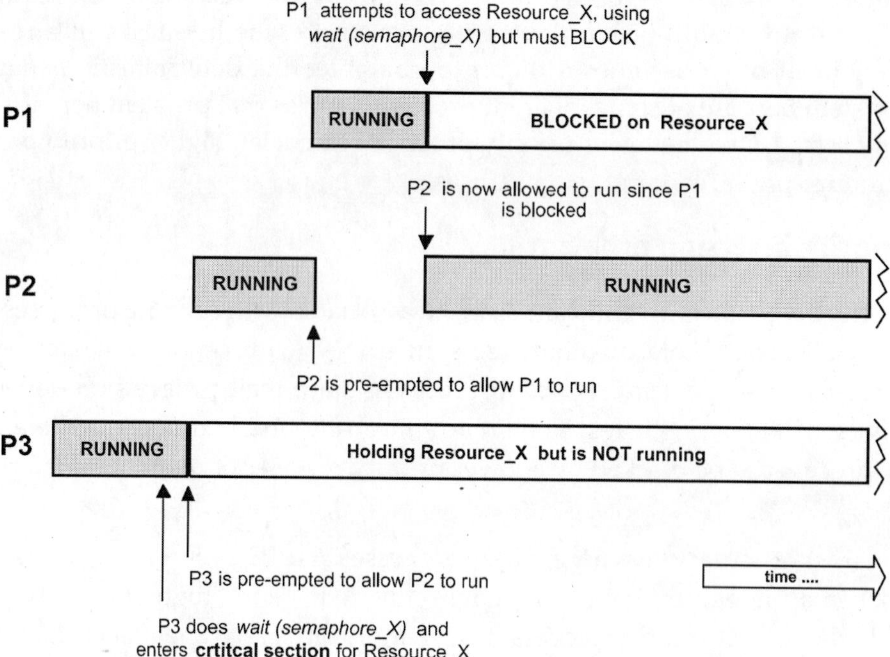

Priority inversion example

1) Prohibit pre-emption of a process while in its critical section

If a process is not allowed to be pre-empted while in its critical section, this will prevent the priority inversion scenario. However, this has the effect of allowing a lower priority process to delay a higher priority process while the lower priority process operates in its critical section. By bounding the length of time that a process spends in its critical section the effect of the delay can be reduced and the system may still be deterministic. However, there are better solutions to the problem.

2) The Priority Inheritance protocol

By allowing a temporary increase in the priority of the process which is causing blocking, to the level of the blocked process, we can prevent intermediate priority level processes from executing. In the example above if P3 was raised to P1's priority level when P1 blocked then P2 would not have been run, instead P3 would have finished and then P1 would have been run, hence P2 would not have run whilst P1 was blocked. The *priority inheritance* protocol limits the number of times that a process can be blocked by lower priority processes. A process with **n** calls to critical sections which can lead to blocking can be blocked a maximum of **n** times during a single execution, i.e. in the worst case each critical section is blocked by a lower priority process. See the example operation for the *priority inheritance* protocol in the diagram below.

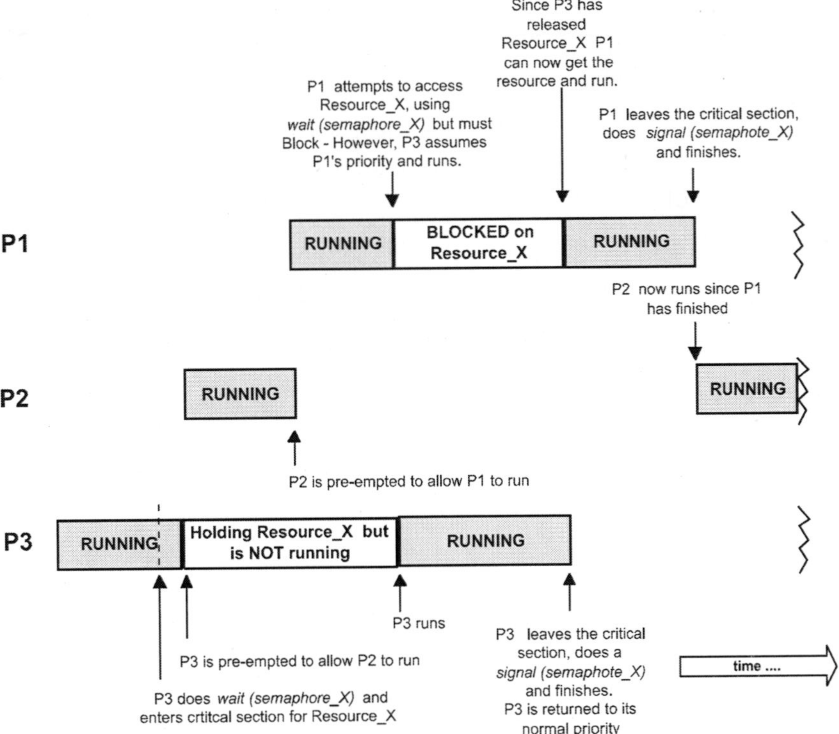

Priority inheritance example

3) Priority ceiling protocol

For the *priority inheritance* protocol – a limit can be defined for the number of times a high priority process can be blocked. In many applications this limit is too high, incurring unacceptably high worst-case calculations. The *priority inheritance* scheme can lead to chains of blocks occurring - where a high priority process is blocked by a lower priority process which is effectively blocked by a lower priority process etc. The possibility for deadlock exists in the scheme.

The *ceiling protocol* is an enhancement on the priority inheritance protocol and ensures that a high priority process cannot be blocked **more than once** by a lower priority process during an execution run. Deadlocks are prevented in the scheme. However, the solution imposes restrictions on lower priority processes accessing resources. The disadvantage here is that a process can be delayed, waiting for a semaphore which is free but cannot be locked as a lock could lead to multiple blocking of a high priority process.

There are variations on the scheme for implementing the priority ceiling protocol but a common workable solution is as follows:

- All processes are assigned a priority
- All non-sharable resources are assigned a *ceiling priority* which is defined as the maximum priority of all the processes which access the resource.
- Whenever a process accesses a resource (e.g. using *wait (sem))* the priority of that process is immediately elevated to the *ceiling priority* for that resource and when the process releases that resource the process priority is returned to its assigned normal value.

Deadlock is prevented in this scheme as it can be formally shown that the circular wait condition in the process-resource chain cannot occur - therefore denying one of the four necessary and sufficient conditions for deadlock.

In summary, if there are no locked system semaphores, then any process can lock a system semaphore. Then a process is allowed to lock a semaphore only if its priority is higher than the ceiling of any currently locked semaphore.

KEYWORDS

PROCESSES	NO PREEMPTION
REUSABLE RESOURCES:	CIRCULAR WAIT
CONSUMABLE RESOURCES	DEADLOCK AVOIDANCE
DEADLOCK	DEADLOCK PREVENTION
MUTUAL EXCLUSIONS	DEADLOCK DETECTION
HOLD AND WAIT	DEADLOCK RECOVERY

SUMMARY

A resource is an object that a process makes use of or a piece of information.

- Reusable resources: They are used without being depleted after use. Examples are the CPU, I/O channels and devices, memory, etc.
- Consumable resources: They usually are created and then destroyed after use. Examples are: signals and messages, information in I/O buffers, etc
- A preemptable resource is one which can be allocated to a given process for a period of time, then be allocated to another process and then be reallocated to the first process without any ill effects.
- A nonpreemptable resource cannot be taken from one process and given to another without side effects.

A set of processes is deadlocked if each process in the set is waiting for an event that only another process in the set can cause. The conditions for Deadlock are

- Mutual exclusions: Each resource can be assigned to only one process at a time and is either assigned or available.
- Hold and wait: Processes that currently hold resources can request and wait for additional resources.
- No preemption: Resources previously granted cannot be taken away from the processes that hold them; they must be released by the holding process.
- Circular wait: There must be a circular chain of two or more processes, each waiting for a resource held by the previous member of the chain.

Strategies for handling deadlock

- Deadlock Avoidance - uses strategic resource allocation
- Deadlock Prevention - ensures that at least one of the necessary deadlock conditions cannot occur.
- Deadlock Detection and Recovery - A deadlock situation is allowed to occur and the system initiates a recovery procedure.
- Ignore the problem – Some systems do not attempt to manage deadlock conditions. It is left to the users to resolve any potential locked process conditions

The deadlock avoidance algorithms like Banker's Algorithm by Dijkstra

that recognize "symptoms" of deadlock and through careful allocation avoid it.

The deadlock can be prevented by

- Mutual Exclusion: Since we do want to allow processes exclusive access to resources we do not want to avoid this condition for deadlock.

- Hold and Wait For: This condition can be avoided by stipulating that all processes must request all of their resources before execution starts.
- No Preemption: If a process is denied a request for more resources it releases its already held resources and then makes a fresh request for its full requirement of resources.
- Circular Wait: A method can be used to avoid a circular wait condition, i.e. to ensure that the resource allocation graph cannot have cycles.
- Deadlock detection: Can be implemented by using a method to reduce the graph or a method to detect the circular wait condition.
- Recovery from Deadlock: Once detected, deadlock must be untangled using recovery algorithms.

REVIEW QUESTIONS

1) What is deadlock?
2) What are the necessary conditions for deadlock?
3) Explain various methods for handling deadlock?
4) Explain various methods for deadlock prevention?
5) Explain various methods for avoidance of deadlock?
6) Explain banker's algorithm for deadlock avoidance?
7) Explain various methods for occurrence deadlock?
8) What is resource allocation graph?
9) Define safe state for several instance of resource type:
10) Explain in brief Bankers algorithm?
11) Explain in brief Safety algorithm?
12) Explain the methods of deadlock prevention, detection and recovery.

FILL IN THE BLANKS

1) A set of processes is in a if each process in the set is waiting for an event that only another process in the set can cause.
2) If each resource can be assigned to only one process at a time it is called __________.
3) In __________resources previously granted cannot be taken away from the processes that hold them.

4) They usually are created and then destroyed after use are called ___________.

5) The analogy of a small-town banker with a limited amount of capital to loan i.e. resources is used by __________ algorithm.

6) __________is the result of conservative allocations where a single job is prevented from execution because it's kept waiting for resources that never become available

TRUE OR FALSE

1. For circular wait, there must be a circular chain of two or more processes, each waiting for a resource held by the previous member of the chain.
2. A variable number of available resources are assumed in Banker's Algorithm
3. A deadlock cannot occur with two resources.
4. In Banker's Algorithm processes must release all resources within a finite time.
5. One method for deadlock recovery is to terminate all jobs active in the system and restart from the beginning
6. Linear ascending order request scheme is used for deadlock prevention

ANSWERS

FILL IN THE BLANKS

1. Deadlock
2. Mutual exclusions
3. No preemption
4. Consumable resources:
5. Banker's
6. Starvation

TRUE OR FALSE

1. TRUE
2. FALSE
3. FALSE
4. TRUE
5. TRUE
6. TRUE

UNIT-3

MEMORY MANAGEMENT UNIT

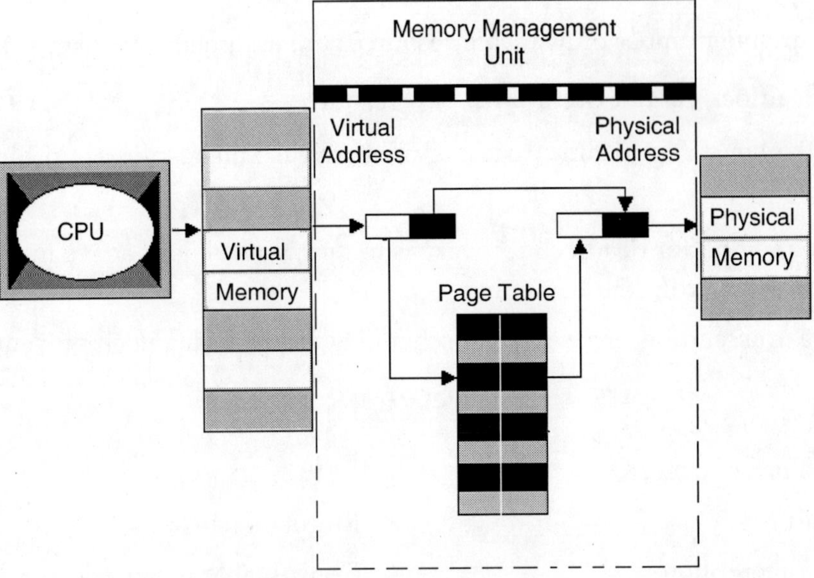

CHAPTER 7 : Memory Management

CHAPTER 8 : Virtual Memory

"Progress is possible only if we train ourselves to think about programs without thinking of them as pieces of executable code". —*E. Dijkstra*

MEMORY MANAGEMENT

INTRODUCTION

Memory systems of a typical computer system are implemented using a number of different storage components. It forms a major part of hardware and the system software in the form of memory management. In a multiprogramming system, in order to share the processor, a number of processes must be kept in memory. Memory management is concerned with managing the computer's available pool of memory, allocating space to application routines and making sure that they do not interfere with each other. Some operating system routines directly support application programs as they run and thus must be resident. Other transient routines are stored on disk and read into memory only when needed. Generally, the operating system occupies low memory. The remaining memory, called the transient area, is where application programs and transient operating system routines are loaded.

What is memory?

Memory is the electronic holding place for instructions and data. It is the place where data is recorded and stored, either permanently or temporarily. It is usually measured in kilobytes, megabytes, or gigabytes.

On many modern systems, two or more programs are loaded into memory and execute concurrently. Fixed-partition memory management divides memory into fixed-length partitions and loads one program into each one. Greater efficiency can be achieved by using dynamic memory management and dividing the transient area into variable-length regions, but the inability to fully utilize available space can lead to fragmentation.

Under segmentation, a program is broken into variable-length segments that are independently loaded into noncontiguous memory. Segmented addresses are converted to absolute form by using a segment table through a process called dynamic address translation. Paging is similar to segmentation except that pages are fixed in length and dynamic address translation uses a page table. With segmentation and paging, programs are broken into logical segments and the segments subdivided into pages.

Most operating systems incorporate memory protection features that prevent one program from destroying the contents of another's memory space. With overlay structures, a program is broken into logically independent modules, and only those modules that are actually active are loaded into memory.

Memory management is achieved through memory management algorithms. Each memory management algorithm requires its own hardware support. In this chapter, we shall see the partitioning, paging and segmentation methods. In order to be able to load programs at anywhere in memory, the compiler must generate relocatable object code. Also we must make it sure that a program in memory, addresses only its own area, and no other program's area. Therefore, some protection mechanism is also needed. At first we will discuss memory hierarchy.

Memory hierarchy

The main memory is usually located on chips inside the system unit. There are two kinds of memory: random-access memory (RAM) and read-only memory (ROM). The instructions that the computer gets and the data the processes are kept in RAM during computer works. RAM is not a permanent storage place for information. It is active only when computer is on. If computer is switched off, the information is deleted from RAM. ROM is the memory where information is only read. When the computer is is turned a off, information is not deleted from ROM. Writing information to ROM is made by vendor. The size of the main memory is measured in megabytes.

What is memory hierarchy?

The hierarchical arrangement of storage in current computer architectures is called the memory hierarchy

The external memory is disk. Unlike information stored in RAM, information stored on a disk is not deleted when the computer turned off. Information stored on the disks is moved in is and out of RAM. The amount of space on a disk is measured in give bytes. There are two kinds of disks: hard disk and floppy disk. The main memory and the floppy disk have less storage capacity than the hard disk. The hard disk can write and read information to and from the main memory much faster than a floppy disk. The access speed of main memory is also much faster than a hard disk.

Disk-based systems provide the primary on-line storage of information, both program and data. Most programs, like assemblers, sort routines, editors, formatters, and so on, are stored on a disk until loaded into memory, and then use the disk as both the source and destination of the information for their processing. Hence, the proper management of disk storage is of central importance to a computer system.

In a larger sense, however, disks systems are only one of many possible storage systems: registers, caches, main memory, disks, tapes and so on. Each storage system provides the basic functions of storing a piece of data, holding the data until it is retrieved at a later time. The main differences between the various storage systems are their speed, cost, size, and volatility.

We can see a wide variety of storage in a computer system, which can be organized in a hierarchy according to either their speed or their cost. The higher levels are expensive, but very fast. As we move down the hierarchy, the cost per bit decreases, while the access time increases and the amount of storage at each level increases. This is reasonable, since if a given storage system was both faster and cheaper than another, with other properties being the same, there would be no reason to use the slower, more expensive memory.

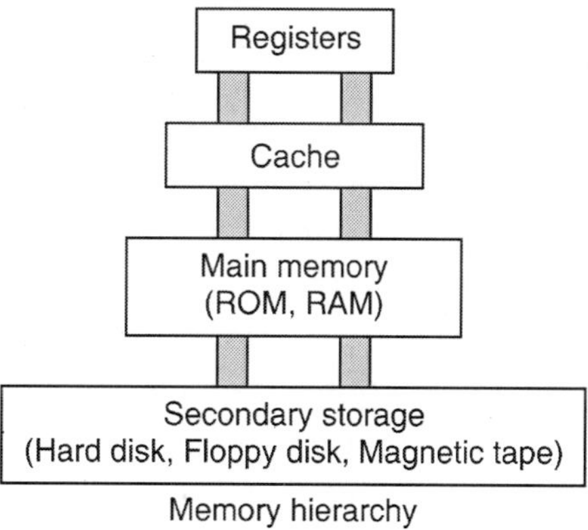

Memory hierarchy

The design of a computer memory system attempts to balance these factors: using only as much expensive memory as absolutely necessary while trying to provide as much cheap memory as possible. Demand paging is an example of such a system design: a limited amount of expensive, fast main memory is used to provide fast access to a much larger virtual memory which is actually stored on cheaper, slower secondary memory. Main memory can be viewed as a fast cache for secondary memory.

Caching is an important principle of computer systems, both in hardware and software. Information is normally stored in some storage system (like main memory). As it is used, it is copied into a faster storage system (the cache) on a temporary basis. When a particular piece of information is needed, we first check if it is in the cache. If it is, we use the information directly from the cache. If not, we use the information from the main storage system, putting a copy in the cache in the hope that it will be needed again.

Since caches have limited size, cache management is an important design problem. Careful selection of cache size and a replacement policy can mean that 80 to 90 percent of all accesses are in the cache, resulting in very high performance.

Extending this view, internal programmable registers, such as index registers and accumulators, are a high-speed cache for main memory. The programmer (or compiler) implements the register allocation and replacement algorithms to decide what information to keep in registers, and what to keep in main memory. The movement of information between levels of a storage hierarchy may be either explicit or implicit.

Memory management

The main memory is after CPU time the second most important resource in a computer system. It is one of the most limited resources in the hardware and is still compared to Hard Drives much more expensive. But the main memory offers the fastest access time (behind the registers) and therefore is the only source of data for the CPU.

In the very early Computer days memory management consisted of nothing more than allocating all memory to the next job/process. All included the part of memory containing the operating system. This was the cause of run time errors (crash of the operating system). As computers evolved it became necessary to guard the parts of main memory where the operating system was loaded. Those parts were separated from those which processes could use. Later on the operating system split up the main memory into different regions (this is called partitioning) which was the first step to modern memory management.

What is memory management?

Memory management means the observation and bookkeeping of which processes are using which parts of the memory.

During the booting process parts of the operating System are loaded into the main memory which enables the operating system to work. Every process which is executed needs to be allocated memory by the operating system. The Task of the operating system's Memory Management is:

1. to distribute memory resources to the processes
2. share memory between processes
3. secure allocated memory of a process from access of other processes
4. prevention of double usage of the same memory allocation

Therefore the operating system divides the main memory into parts and distributes resources for the programs

A program's machine language code must be in the computer's main memory in order to execute. Assuring that at least the portion of code to be executed is in memory when a processor is assigned to a process is the job of the memory manager of the operating system. This task is complicated by two other aspects os modern computing systems.

The first is multiprogramming. From its definition, we know that multiprogramming mean that several (at least two) processes can be active within the system during any particular time interval. But these multiple active processes result from various jobs entering and leaving the system in an unpredictable manner. Pieces, or blocks, of memory are allocated to these processes when they enter the system, and are subsequently freed when the process leaves the system. Therefore, at any given moment, the computer's memory, viewed as a whole, consists of a partn of blocks, some allocated to processes active at that moment, and others free ans available to a new process which may, at any time, enter the system.

In general, then, programs designed to execute in this multiprogramming environment must be compiled so that they can execute from any block of storage available at the time of the program's execution. Such programs are called relocatable programs, and the idea of placing them into any currently available block of storage is called relocation.

Resident and Transient Routines

The operating system is a collection of software routines. Some routines, such as the ones that control physical I/O, directly support application programs as they run and thus must be resident. Others, such as the routine that formats disks, are used only occasionally. These transient routines are stored on disk and read into memory only when needed.

Generally, the operating system occupies low memory beginning with address

Key control information comes first (Figure a), followed by the various resident operating system routines. The remaining memory, called the transient area, is where application programs and transient operating system routines are loaded.

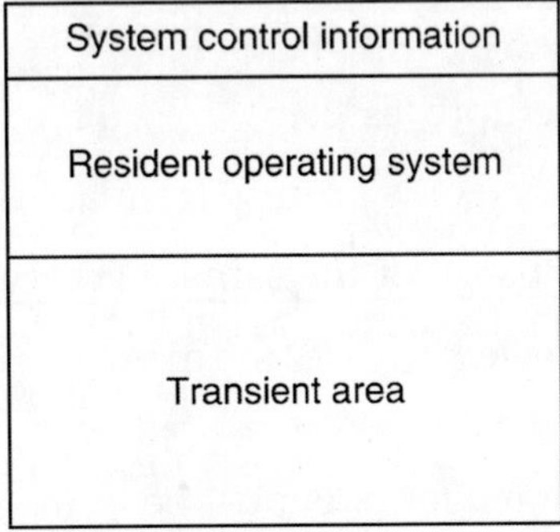

Fig. (a) Genrally, the operating system occupies low memory. The remaining memory, called the transient area, is where application programs and transient operating system routines are loaded.

Concurrency

Given the speed disparity between a computer and its peripherals, input and out- put operations significantly impact efficiency. For example, picture a computer with a single program in memory. The program cannot process data it does not yet have, and success cannot be assumed until an output operation is finished, so the pro- gram waits for input or output. Since the program controls the computer, the computer waits, too. Typically, given the speed disparity between the processor and its peripheral devices, a program spends far more time waiting for I/O than processing data.

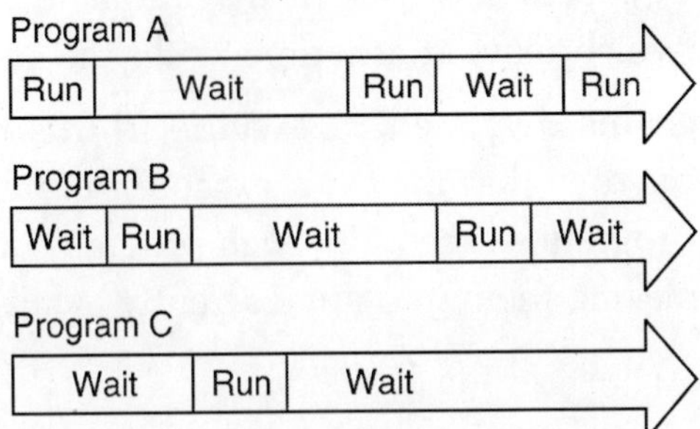

Fig. (b) On many systems, multiple programs are loaded into memory and executed concurrently.

Why not put two programs in memory? Then, when program A is waiting for data, the processor can turn its attention to program B. And why stop at two programs? With three, even more otherwise wasted time is utilized (Figure b). Generally, the more programs in memory, the greater the utilization of the processor. The processor fetches and executes a single instruction during each machine cycle. If the processor can execute only one instruction at a time, it cannot possibly execute two or more programs at a time. Consequently, although multiple programs can share memory, only one can be active. Simultaneous means "at the same instant." No single processor can execute two or more programs simultaneously. Concurrent means "over the same time period" A processor can certainly execute two or more programs concurrently.

Aims of Memory Management

The followings are the main aims that memory management is intended to satisfy.

***(i)* Relocation.** In a multiprogramming system, the available memory is generally shared among a number of processes. The operating system is managing memory and is responsible for bringing this process into main memory. Typically, programmer does not know where the program will be placed in memory when it is executed. In addition, while the program is executing, it may be swapped to disk and returned to main memory at a different location (relocation).

***(ii)* Protection.** Data integrity is essential; therefore, each process area should be protected against any undesired interferences. Processes should not be able to reference memory locations in another process for reading or writing purpose without permission.

Normally, a user process cannot access any point of the operating system, neither program nor data. Again, usually a program in one process cannot branch to an instruction in another process. Without a special arrangement, a program in one process cannot access the date area of another process. The processor must be able to abort such instructions at the point of execution.

Note that the memory protection requirement must be satisfied by the processor (hardware) rather than the operating system (software). This is because the operating system cannot anticipate (predict) all of the memory references that a program will make.

***(iii)* Sharing.** Protection does not mean that when necessary two or more processes should not be able to access a common area. Any protection mechanism must have the flexibility to allow several processes to access the same portion of main memory. For example, if a number of processes are executing the same program, it is better to allow each process access to the same copy of the program rather than have its own separate copy.

***(iv)* Logical organization.** Physical main memory is a sequence of bytes. Memory division should be such that it should reflect logic. Most programs are written in modules. If the operating system and computer hardware can effectively deal with user programs and date in the form of modules, that a number of advantages can be realized:

- Modules can be written and compiled independently
- Different degrees of protection given to modules (read-only, execute-only)
- It is possible to introduce a mechanism to share modules among processes.

***(v)* Physical organization.** Computer memory is organized into at least two levels, referred to as main memory and secondary memory. In this two-level scheme, the organization of the flow of information between main and secondary memory is a major system concern and brings several problems:

- Available space may not be enough for a process; overlaying.
- At the time of construction of programs it is not possible to predict the amount of space required at run time.

Memory management functionalities

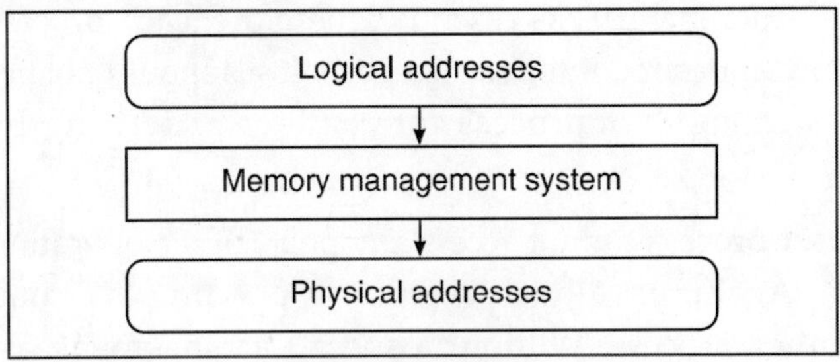

Memory management

Generally, memory management is a collective name for a whole set of hardware and software techniques which translate the addresses used by the application programs, called "logical addresses" into physical addresses meaningful to the computer hardware.

The user program deals with ***logical addresses*** whereas the actual address where the data as well as instructions are stored is called ***physical address.***

Just like the processor, memory is a precious resource and the operating system ensures the best use of this resource. Memory management is an operating system entity that provides the following functionalities.

1. Better resource usage. Since the memory is a precious resource, it is best to allocate it on demand. For example, even though the memory footprint of the program includes the heap there is no need to allocate this to a program at startup. It is sufficient to make the allocation (if and) when the program dynamically requests it. Further, if a process is not actively using memory allocated to it, then perhaps it is best to release it from that process and use it for some of other process. Both these ideas will lead to better resource utilization of the memory resource.

2. Independence and Protection. We mentioned that several processes are co-resident in memory at any point of time. A program may have a bug causing it to run amok writing into areas of memory that is not part of its footprint. How do we protect a buggy process from itself and from other processes? Further, in these days of computer viruses and worms, a malicious program could be intentionally trying to corrupt the memories of other genuine programs. Therefore, the memory manager provides independence for each process, and memory protection from one another.

3. Liberation from resource limitations. It is ideal for the programmer not to worry about the amount of physical memory while developing his/her program. The memory manager provides to the programmer an illusion of memory that is larger than the physical memory size.

4. Sharing. While memory protection among processes is necessary, sometimes processes may want to share memory either implicitly or explicitly. For example, you may have several terminal sessions opened on your desktop. Each of them may be running the same shell program but with different data (for example, location of the terminal on your desktop screen). This is an example of implicit sharing among processes. An instant messaging program between two users who are on the same time-shared computer is an instance of explicit data sharing. The memory manager facilitates memory sharing when needed among processes.

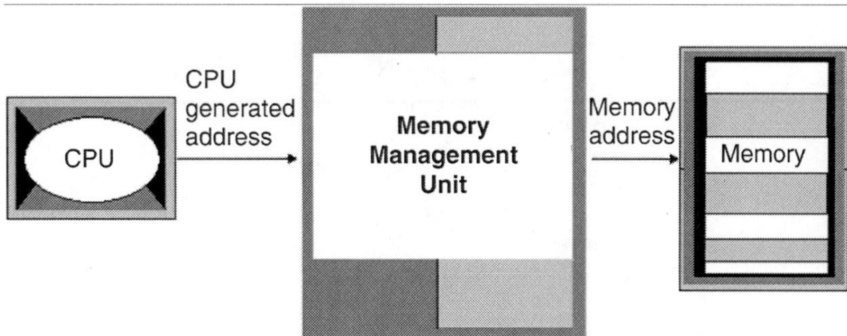

As should be evident to the absolute reader, all of the above functionalities come at a price. In particular, we are introducing a broker (Memory Management Unit) between the CPU and the memory as shown in Figure. The broker (MMU) is a piece of hardware that provides the mechanisms needed for implementing the memory management policies. In principle, it maps a CPU generated memory address to the real memory address for accessing the memory. The sophistication of the broker depends on the functionalities provided by the memory manager.

The overall goals of a good memory manager are three-fold:

1. Require minimal hardware support
2. Keep the impact on memory accesses low

3. Keep the memory management overhead low (for allocation and de-allocation of memory)

Since we must keep several processes in memory; we must *share* memory. Most systems allow a user process to reside in any part of the physical memory. Thus, although the address space of the computer starts at 00000 (hex), the first address of the user process does NOT need to be 00000.

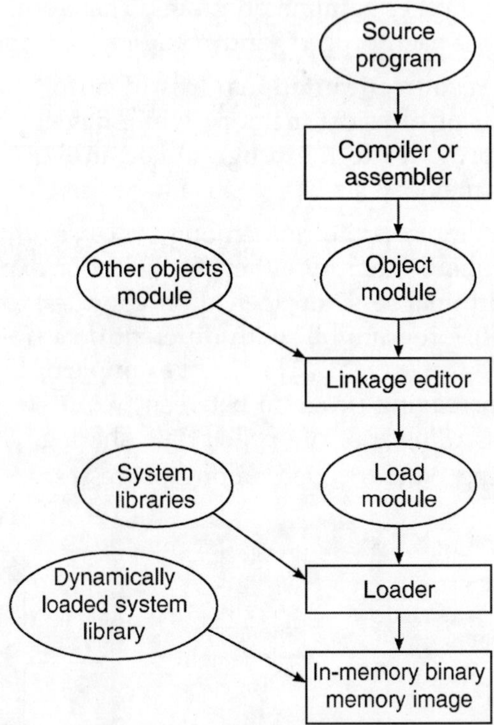

Memory addresses may be represented in different ways during these steps. Addresses in the source program are generally symbolic addresses. A compiler will typically *bind* these symbolic addresses to relocatable addresses *(such as 14 bytes from the beginning of this module)*. The linker (linkage editor) or loader will in turn *bind* these relocatable addresses to absolute *(physical)* addresses (such as 7A12D). Each binding is a mapping from one address space to another.

Address Binding

To reference any particular memory address, one needs a location of that memory address. These are physical addresses. In programs, the memory locations that are referenced are called logical addresses because an address specified by a program may or may not be the correct physical address. There are basically three different ways that logical addresses are a mapped to physical address, which is called address binding. These address binding techniques depend on the memory management methods that the OS of your computer uses. Binding of instruction/data to memory addresses can be done at:

Compile-time address binding

Generates absolute code, in other words, the addresses are already in place, and when the program is run, the logical addresses or either absolute where logical locations 000 - 999 actually correspond to physical locations 000 - 999, or where an offset is added to the logical locations to generate the physical locations. For example, in a simple system, the OS resides in physical locations 000 - 500. Any program would have to start at location 501. A program that has the logical address space of 000 - 999 would be modified so that logical locations 000 - 999 would be changed to correspond to physical locations 501 - 1500.

It is known at compile-time where the program will reside in memory. If the program had to be loaded into a different starting location, then the program would have to be re-compiled. Modern computer systems do not use this method because it isn't very flexible.

Load-time address binding

If the starting location of the program isn't known at compile time of the program, then the compiler will generate re-locatable code, i.e. the locations would be changed during the loading of the program Using the above example, at load-time, when the system does know where the program will be put at, then the load-time binding would map logical locations 000 - 999 to physical locations 501 - 1500 , or 1000 - 1999, depending on the circumstances at load-time. DOS programs are run in this fashion.

Run-time address binding

If the starting location of the program is to be moved during execution of the program, then the binding must be delayed until run-time. Physical addresses are generated during execution by adding the value of logical addresses to an offset register. Using the above example, the program would have logical locations 000 - 999, but then at run-time, the value of the logical address would be added with the value of an offset register, in this case 501, to reference the physical locations 501 - 1500. When the base location of the program is moved from501 to, say 1001, then the value of the offset register is changed from 501 to 1001.

When is address translation performed?

1. At compile time

- Compiler generates *physical* addresses.
- Requires knowledge of where the compilation unit will be loaded.
- No linker.
- Loader is trivial.
- Primitive.
- Rarely used (MSDOS .COM files).

2. At load time

- Similar to at link-edit time, but do **not** fix the starting address.
- Program can be loaded anywhere.
- Program can move but cannot be split.
- Need modest hardware: base/limit registers.
- Loader sets the base/limit registers.

3. At execution time

- Addresses translated dynamically during execution.
- Hardware needed to perform the virtual to physical address translation quickly.
- Currently dominates.
- Much more information later.

In our discussion so far, the **entire** program and data of a process must be in physical memory for the process to execute. The size of a process is limited to the size of the physical memory.

Relocation

Relocation of currently active programs is called dynamic relocation. If a currently executing process could be relocated, both the computer's response time and resource utilization could be improved.

What is a relocation register?

Relocation Register allows programs to be relocated dynamically.

The base address of the program in primary storage is placed in the relocation register. The contents of the relocation Register are added to each address developed by a running program. The user is able to program as if the user's program begins at location zero.

At execution time, as the program runs, all address references involve the relocation register; this allows the program to reside in locations other than those which it was translated to occupy.

The second aspect of modern computing systems affecting memory management is the need to allow the programmer to use a range of program addresses which may be larger, perhaps significantly larger than the range of memory locations actually available. That is, we want to provide the programmer with a virtual memory, with characteristics (especially size) different from actual memory, and provide it in a way that is invisible to the programmer. This is accomplished by extending the actual memory with secondary memory such as disk. Providing an efficiently operating virtual memory is another task for the memory management facility.

Actual implementation of dynamic relocation is not trivial. The complier can not possibly assign the correct addresses because a program must be compiled before it can be loaded and executed. Thus, program relocation, especially dynamic relocation the moving around of currently active processes must be done by the operating system's memory management facility.

Given the needs for multiprogramming and virtual memory, and having the mechanism of dynamic relocation, it is time to take a serious look at how one might design the actual memory manger.

Creating and marinating an environment which will sustain both multiprogramming and virtual memory consists basically of designing a memory management program which will facilitate the timely movement of blocks of program code into portions of main memory when they are about to be executed, and out of main memory to secondary memory (disk) when they are no longer needed. There are basically three approaches to this problem. In the fist approach, called swapping, all of the code for a particular process is transferred into main storage prior to dispatching the processor to the process.

When the process becomes blocked or its time slice used up, the entire block of code is again swapped out to secondary storage to be replated by the block of code representing the next process to assume control of the processor, and so on. This approach, while reasonable when the size of main memory is limited, obviously causes a substantial execution delay overhead during the swapping itself. This overhead cost can sometimes be ameliorated by alternative approaches, which move parts of the code for processes rather than code for entire processes.

The other two approaches are segmentation and paging. Both recognize the fact that only that portion os, a process code which is about to execute actually needs to be in main storage at any particular time. These approaches have two major advantages over swapping. Fist, if just a part of a currently executing process needs to be in main memory at a given time, then it follows that parts of more process can be simultaneously in main store, and thus a greater degree of multiprogramming can be facilitated in the system. The term degree of multiprogramming refers to the number of processes currently active within the system.

The second advantage of segmentation or paging is that the capability to move just part of programs allows part of a program to be loaded into memory and executed, and then be replaced by another part to be requiring a very large amount of memory, perhaps in total, more than the capacity of the computer's main store. But this would be, then, an implementation os virtual memory, as it has been described above.

These approaches would argue that perhaps swapping does too much. Both segmentation and paging move part of programs back and forth between secondary storage and main memory as needed. Segmentation and paging differ from one another primarily in the way the code for a particular process is divided. In segmentation, a program code is divided into number of variable sized blocks corresponding to the logical structure of the program, such as procedures, functions and data segments. Paging, on the other hand, divides the program code into fixed blocks, called pages. It is evident that the more logical subdivision of segmentation makes program linking easier, while the fixed blocks of paging, being each interchangeable with the other, makes memory management easier. In either case, since portions of program's code are being moved around during a program's execution, something like a hardware relocation register will be needed to compute actual addresses in order to avoid unacceptable slowdown in program execution times.

Overlays

A problem that many computer systems were getting in the past was that the logical address spaces of programs had to be less than the physical address spaces of the computers they were running on. To overcome this, **overlay** techniques were introduced so that only a necessary part of a program could be brought into memory. time. When the next part of the program is needed, it is brought into the address space occupied by a part of the program that is no longer necessary. In other words, it replaces the previous part of the program.

Overlays technique is used to execute a process with size larger than the amount of memory allocated to it. The idea of **overlays** is to keep in memory only those instruction and data that are needed at any given time. When other instructions are needed, they are loaded into space that was occupied previously by instructions that are no longer needed.

For example, consider a two-pass assembler requires 200K of memory but only 150K is available:

Pass 1 module	70K
Pass 2 module	80K
Symbol table	20K
Common routines	30K
Overlay driver*	10K

As a result:

ASM.exe *(overlay A)* 20K + 30K + 70K + 10K = 130K

ASM.ovl *(overlay B)* 20K + 30K + 80K + 10K = 140K

The old version of dBASE program (such as version 3plus) uses overlays technique.

Overlay techniques did not need any special support from the OS. The trouble with overlays, however, was that special relocation and linking algorithms were needed. The programmer, in essence, had the burden of managing memory for the system. In 1961, a method was proposed for performing the overlay process automatically without the programmer even knowing it was happening. This method, now called Virtual Memory, had the obvious advantage of freeing the programmer from a lot of annoying bookeeping.

Swapping

A process needs to be in memory to be executed. A process, however, can be *swapped* temporarily out of memory to a backing store (disk), and then brought back into memory for continued execution. For example, assume a multiprogramming environment with a round-robin CPU scheduling algorithm. When a quantum expires, the memory manager will start to swap out the process that just finished, and to swap in another process to the memory space that has been freed.

It should be clear that the context-switch time in such a swapping system is fairly high. To get an idea of the context-switch time, let us assume that the user process is of size 100K and the backing store is a standard hard disk with a transfer rate of 1M byte per second. The actual transfer of the 100K process to or from memory takes 100K / 1000K per second ? 100 ms. Plus the *seek time* and *rotational latency*, the total context-switch time exceeds 0.2 second. The time quantum should be substantially larger than 0.2 second.

Personal computers lack sophisticated hardware or operating system that takes advantage of the hardware to implement more advanced memory-management methods. An example is MS-windows, which supports concurrent execution or processes in memory. This OS does not provide full swapping, because the user, rather than the scheduler, decides when it is time to swap one process for another (manual swapping).

Logical address and Physical address space

An address generated by the CPU is commonly referred to as a *logical address* (or sometimes *virtual address*), whereas an address seen by the memory unit is commonly referred to as a *physical address*.

Logical address is an address used by software. The logical address might be translated into a physical address by the memory management unit.

Physical Address is the address presented to a computer's main memory.

The run-time mapping from virtual to physical addresses is done by the memory-management unit (MMU), which is a hardware device. There are a number of different schemes for accomplishing such a mapping, for example, *single-partition allocation*, *paging*, *segmentation* and *segmentation with paging*.

A simple memory-management unit scheme is:

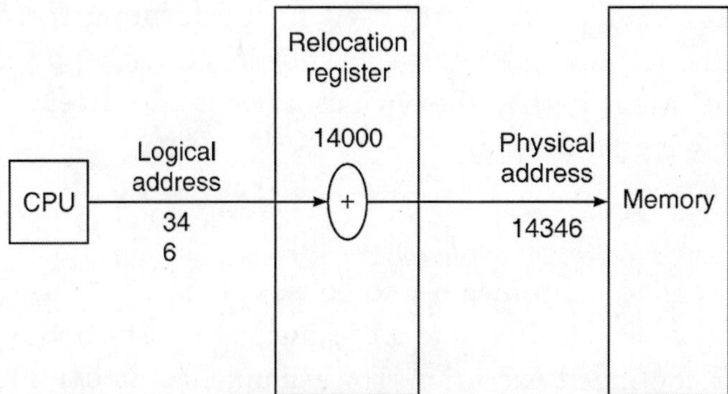

The user program deals with logical addresses. The memory-mapping hardware converts logical addresses into physical addresses by adding the content of the relocation register (for example, the CS, DS in 80x86). The "conversion" process need not be a simple "add", it may be as complex as "shift-add-shift-subtract".

If the above MMU scheme, we have two different types of addresses: logical addresses (in the range 0 to max) and physical addresses (in the range R+0 to R+max for a base value R). The user generates only logical addresses and thinks that the process runs in location 0 to max.

Memory Management Schemes

The various memory management schemes are described as follows:

1. Contiguous Allocation - Fixed Partition Allocation. In contiguous allocation the process is stored in continuous memory locations i.e. the program is stored as a whole. The contiguous fixed partition can be either for single process or multiple processes described as follows:

Single Process Contiguous

In the days of single-tasking, when one process ran in a computer at any one time. A program to be processed was loaded entirely into memory and given as much contiguous space in memory as needed. This is similar to MS-DOS approach. The following diagram shows the layout of memory in this case.

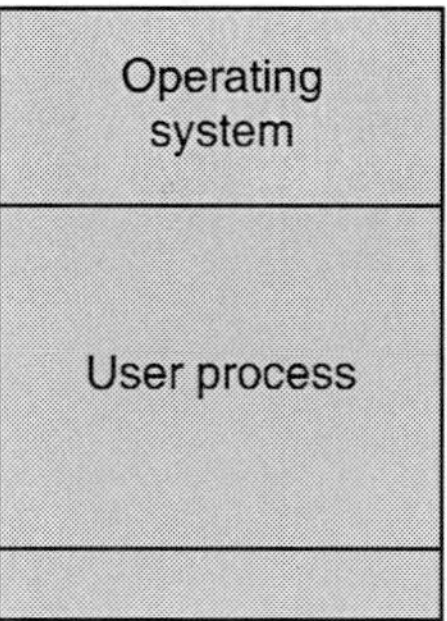

Single process contiguous memory

In these schemes, the Operating System is usually allocated a fixed area of the memory, and the user's process can use the rest. This scheme demonstrates a severely limiting factor. Suppose your process needs more memory than is physically available. If the program does not fit, then either the size of main memory must be increased, or the program modified to be made smaller or divided into segments to be **overlayed** .

Multiple processes contiguous

It is of two types as elaborated below:

(*a*) Equal-size partitions

Because all partitions are of equal size, it does not matter which partition is used.

(*b*) Unequal-size partitions

With unequal-size partitions the placement algorithm can assign each process to the smallest partition within which it will fit Processes are assigned in such a way as to minimize wasted memory within a partition (internal fragmentation).

Reference string

7	0	1	2	0	3	0	4	2	3	0	3	2	1	2	0	1	7	0	1
7	7	7	2		2		4	4	4	0			1		1		1		
	0	0	0		0		0	0	3	3			3		0		0		
		1	1		3		3	2	2	2			2		2		7		

Page frames

Operating system 8 M	Operating system 8 M
8 M	2 M
8 M	4 M
8 M	6 M
8 M	8 M
8 M	12 M
8 M	16 M

(a) Equal-size partitions (a) Unequal-size partition

Example of fixed portioning of a 64-Mbytes memory

If the operating system is residing in low memory and the user processes are executing in high memory, we need to protect the operating-system code and data from changes (accidental or malicious) by user processes. We also need to protect the user processes from one another. We can provide this protection by using a relocation register and a limit register. The limit registers contains the range of logical addresses.

When the CPU scheduler selects a process for execution, the dispatcher loads the relocation and limit registers as part of the context switch. Because every address generated by the CPU is checked against these registers, we can protect both the operating system and the other users' programs and data from being modified by this running process.

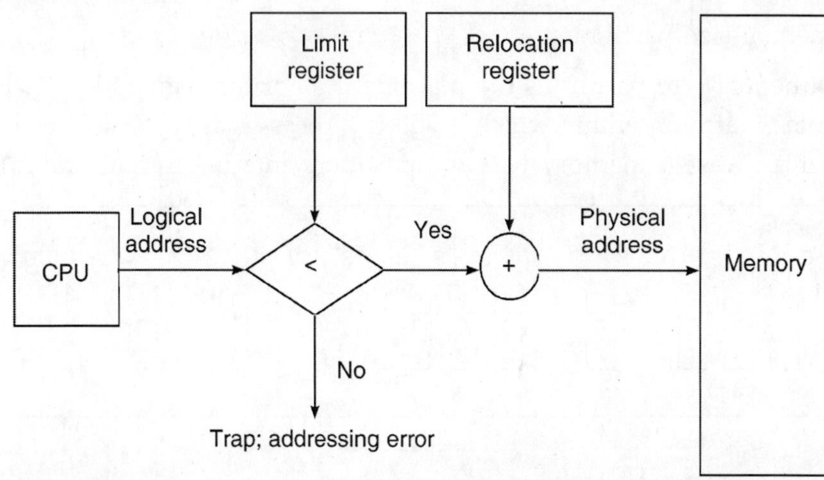

Note that the relocation-register scheme provides an effective way to allow the operating-system size to change dynamically.

2. Contiguous Allocation – Dynamic Partition Allocation. To overcome the inefficient usage of memory dynamic partitioning scheme was developed; meaning use as much as you required. With dynamic portioning, Partitions are of variable length and number. When a process brought into main memory, it is allocated exactly as much memory as required.

In a multiprogramming environment, there are several user processes residing in memory at the same time. The operating system keeps a ***table*** indicating which parts of memory are available and which are occupied.

Initially, all memory, except occupied by the residing operating system, is available for user processes. When a process arrives and needs memory, we search for a **free memory block** large enough for this process. If we find one, we allocate only as much memory as is needed, keeping the rest available to satisfy future requests.

For example, if there are 5 processes in the job queue:

	Memory	Run-time
P1	600K	10
P2	1000K	5
P3	300K	20
P4	700K	8
P5	500K	15

- Assume FCFS job scheduling is used;
- Round-robin CPU-scheduling with quantum=1;
- When a process is allocated memory, it is loaded and it can then compete for the CPU
- P1, P2 and P3 is loaded first;
- P2 terminates at time 14, releasing its memory...

After memory block is released, it is then placed back in the set of free blocks. If the new free block is adjacent to other free blocks, we merge these adjacent blocks to form one larger free block.

There are 3 strategies to select a free block from the set of available free blocks:

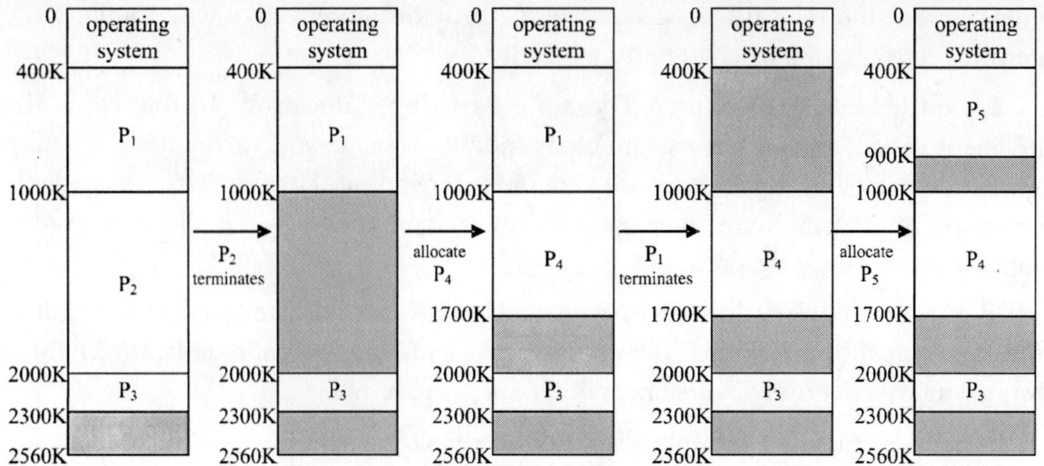

➢ **First-fit** : allocate the *first* free block that is big enough. Searching can be start either at the ***beginning of the free list*** or where the ***previous first-fit search ended.***

➢ **Best-fit** : allocate the smallest free block that is big enough. This strategy produces the smallest leftover holes.

➢ **Worst-fit** : allocate the largest free block. This strategy produces the largest leftover hole.

Simulations have shown that both first-fit and best-fit are better than worst-fit in terms of decreasing both time and storage utilization. Neither first-fit nor best-fit is clearly better in terms of storage utilization, but **first-fit** is generally faster.

Fragmentation

The fragmentation exists when enough total memory space exists to satisfy a request, but it is not contiguous; storage is fragmented into lots of small blocks.

Fragmentation is a phenomenon that leads to inefficiency in many forms of computer storage. There are three different but related uses of the term: external fragmentation, internal fragmentation, and data fragmentation

Internal fragmentation occurs when storage is allocated without ever intending to use it. This space is wasted. While this seems foolish, it is often accepted in return for increased efficiency or simplicity. The term "internal" refers to the fact that the unusable storage is inside the allocated region but is not being used.

For example, in many file systems, each file always starts at the beginning of a cluster, because this simplifies organization and makes it easier to grow files. Any space left over between the last byte of the file and the first byte of the next cluster is a form of internal fragmentation called file slack or slack space. Similarly, a program which allocates a single byte of data is often allocated many additional bytes for metadata and alignment. This extra space is also internal fragmentation.

External fragmentation is the phenomenon in which free storage becomes divided into many small pieces over time. It is a weakness of certain storage allocation algorithms, occurring when an application allocates and deallocates ("frees") regions of storage of varying sizes, and the allocation algorithm responds by leaving the allocated and deallocated regions interspersed. The result is that, although free storage is available, it is effectively unusable because it is divided into pieces that are too small to satisfy the demands of the application. The term "external" refers to the fact that the unusable storage is outside the allocated regions.

For example, in dynamic memory allocation, a block of 1000 bytes might be requested, but the largest contiguous block of free space has only 300 bytes. Even if there are ten blocks of 300 bytes of free space, separated by allocated regions, one still cannot allocate the requested block of 1000 bytes, and the allocation request will fail.

Data fragmentation occurs when a piece of data in memory is broken up into many pieces that are not close together. It is typically the result of attempting to insert a large object into storage that has already suffered external fragmentation.

For example, files in a file system are usually managed in units called blocks or clusters. When a file system is created, there is free space to store file blocks together contiguously. This allows for rapid sequential file reads and writes. However, as files are added, removed, and changed in size, the free space becomes externally fragmented, leaving only small holes in which to place new data. When a new file is written, or when an existing file is extended, the new data blocks are necessarily scattered, slowing access due to seek time and rotational delay of the read/write head, and incurring additional overhead to manage additional locations. This is called file system fragmentation.

Compaction

One of the solutions to fragmentation is compaction (or defragmentation) - to shuffle the memory contents to place all free memory together in one large block. The cost is expensive. Some intelligent compaction algorithms help to reduce the cost.

What is compaction?

Compaction is a method to overcome the external fragmentation problem. All free blocks are brought together as one large block of free space.

Compaction requires dynamic relocation. Certainly, compaction has a cost and selection of an optimal compaction strategy is difficult. One method for compaction is swapping out those processes that are to be moved within the memory, and swapping them into different memory locations.

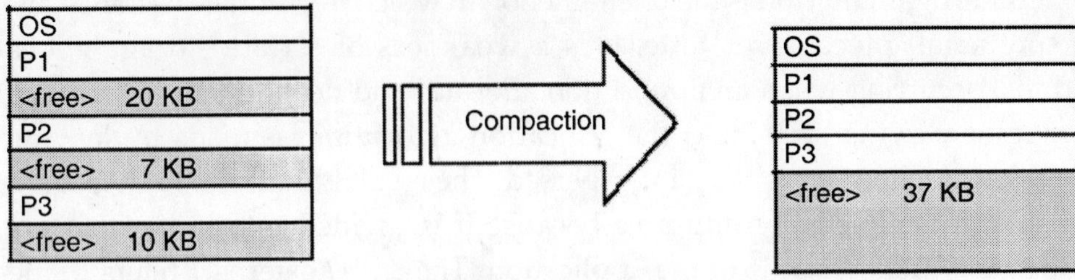

Compaction is a solution to external fragmentation. The memory contents are shuffled to place all free memory together in one large block. It is possible only if relocation is dynamic, and is done at execution time.

Example

Consider the following memory map and assume a new process P4 comes with a memory requirement of 3 KB. Locate this process.

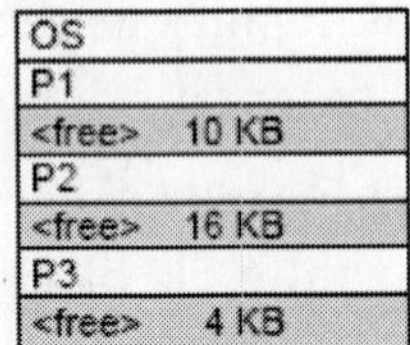

a. First fit algorithm allocates from the 10 KB block.
b. Best fit algorithm allocates from the 4 KB block.
c. Worst fit algorithm allocates from the 16 KB block.

New memory arrangements with respect to each algorithms will be as follows:

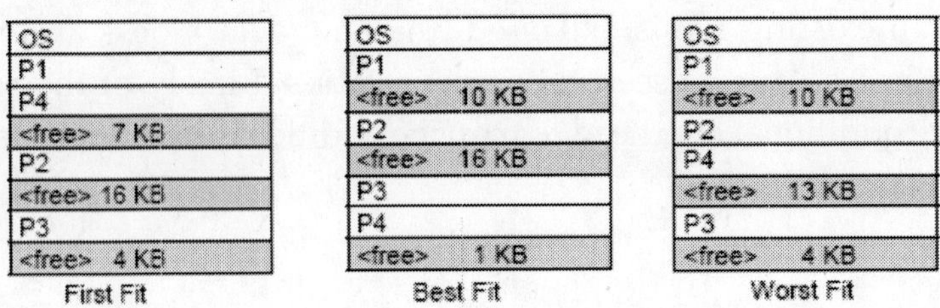

At this point, if a new process, P5 of 14K arrives, then it would wait if we used worst fit algorithm, whereas it would be located in cases of the others.

Another example

Assume that we have 2560K of memory available and a resident OS of 400K. This situation leaves 2160K for user processes. Given the input queue and FCFS job scheduling, we can immediately allocate memory to processes P1, P2, and P3.

Job Queue

Process	Memory	Time
P1	600K	10
P2	1000K	5
P3	300K	20
P4	700K	8
P5	500K	15

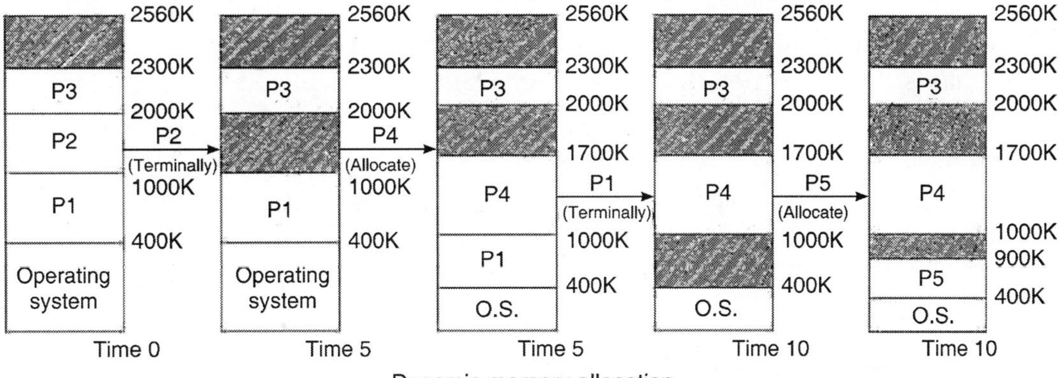

Dynamic memory allocation

We have a hole of size 260K that cannot be used by any of the remaining processes in the input queue. After 3 sec P4 will be completed after 10 sec. (7 after P4) P3 will be completed. After 15 sec P5 will be completed.

The collection of process on the disk that is waiting to be brought into memory for execution forms the input queue (with the help of long-term scheduler). The OS takes into account the memory requirements of each process and the amount of available memory space. When a process is allocated space, it is loaded into memory and it can then compete for the CPU. When a process terminates, it releases its memory, which the OS may then fill with another process from the input queue.

In general, there is at any time a set of holes, of various sizes, scattered throughout the memory. When a process arrives and needs memory, we search this set for a hole that is large enough for this process. The scheme describes before is the generalization of the MFT and called MVT (Multiprogramming with a Variable number of Tasks).

In this scheme the free memory space is broken in the little pieces; that are not contiguous, and storage is fragmented into a large number of small holes. This form of wasted memory is called external fragmentation.

One solution to the problem is compaction.

Three holes of sizes 100K, 300K and 260K can be compacted into one hole of size 660K. Usually compaction requires a lot of CPU time. Compaction attacks the problem of fragmentation by moving all the allocated blocks to one end of memory, thus combining all the holes. Aside from the obvious cost of all that copying, there is an important limitation to compaction: Any pointers to a block need to be updated when the block is moved. Unless it is possible to find all such pointers, compaction is not possible. Pointers can stored in the allocated blocks themselves as well as other places in the client of the memory manager.

In some situations, pointers can point not only to the start of blocks but also into their bodies. For example, if a block contains executable code, a branch instruction might be a pointer to another location in the same block. Compaction is performed in three phases. First, the new location of each block is calculated to determine the distance the block will be moved. Then each pointer is updated by adding to it the amount that the block it is pointing (in) to will be moved. Finally, the data is actually moved. There are various clever tricks possible to combine these operations.

Another solution to fragmentation *Paging*.

Paging

The paging scheme permits the physical address space of a process to be noncontiguous, thus allowing a process to be allocated physical memory wherever the latter is available, no compaction is required.

Paging is a mechanism by which a process can occupy less physical memory than is allocated in the logical address space. Performed through the division of memory into pages that can be paged in from or out to the swap area on disk.

It is a development from partitioning of memory. One of the characteristics of partitioning is that the whole process fits contiguously into one partition. One of the disadvantages of dynamic partitioning is that you get external fragmentation.

Paging is a method of reducing fragmentation by chopping the process up into fixed size chunks (pages) and fitting them into fixed size slots (page frames) in RAM. For example: Incoming process A is divided into pages of equal size. Only the last page of a program may not be the same size as the others because of the program size itself

The size of the page is determined by the Operating System. Some Operating Systems choose a page size that is the same as a memory block or disk sector. Windows 2003 and Linux both use a page size of 4kB on PCs.

Main Memory is also divided into equal size sections called **Page Frames**

0	
1	
2	
3	
4	
5	
6	
7	
8	
9	
10 page frames available	

The size of a Memory Page Frame is exactly the same size as a program's Page, so a Page Frame is capable of holding 1 program Page

The following diagrams show how pages for four processes are successively loaded into RAM. Process A requires 3 pages, Process B 4 pages, Process C 2 pages and process D 5 pages. At first, empty memory is filled sequentially with processes A,B and C.

Frame	10 pages available	7 pages available	3 pages available
0		A0	A0
1		A1	A1
2		A2	A2
3			B0
4			B1
5			B2
6			B3
7			
8			
9			

Process D cannot run because there is insufficient memory available. However, when process B finishes, Process D can be fitted in, as shown below. This is because the pages do not have to be contiguous. Therefore, space is not wasted as in the case of dynamic partitioning.

Frame		Frame		Frame	
0	A0	0	A0	0	A0
1	A1	1	A1	1	A1
2	A2	2	A2	2	A2
3	B0	3		3	D0
4	B1	4		4	D1
5	B2	5		5	D2
6	B3	6		6	D3
7	C0	7	C0	7	C0
8	C1	8	C1	8	C1
9		9		9	D4
1 pages available		5 pages available		0 pages available	

During the loading process, a program's pages may be placed in any available Page Frame.

Because a job's pages can be anywhere in main memory, the memory manager needs a mechanism to keep track of them. This involves increasing the size and complexity of the Operating System. Memory Manager uses three tables to keep track of Job/Page allocation.

In a multiprogramming system memory is divided into a number of fixed size or variable sized partitions or regions which are allocated to running processes. For example: a process needs m words of memory may run in a partition of n words where $n\ ^{3}\ m$. The variable size partition scheme may result in a situation where available memory is not contiguous, but fragmented into many scattered blocks.

We distinguish between *internal fragmentation* and *external fragmentation*. The difference $(n - m)$ is called internal fragmentation, memory which is internal to a partition but is not being used. If a partition is unused and available, but too small to be used by any waiting process, then it is accounted for external fragmentation. These memory fragments can not be used.

In order to solve this problem, we can either compact the memory making large free memory blocks, or implement paging scheme which allows a program's memory to be noncontiguous, thus permitting a program to be allocated physical memory wherever it is available.

Base and Displacement addressing

The CPU accesses parts of the process by using numeric addresses. Conceptually, for every process, the address starts at zero and works upwards.

When the entire process is relocated, or doesn't start at physical address 0 in main memory, then it is relatively simple to translate the process' address onto the physical address where it lives. A ***Base Register*** can be used to achieve this: it holds the address of the base of the process. All you have to do is add this value to an address for a piece of data / code within the process, and you have the physical address of that piece of data / code.

Eg: Suppose we want to access a byte of data at address 1056 within the process.

This process may be located in main memory starting at address 40000. Thus the real location of the data at process address 1056 is at 40000+1056 = 41056.

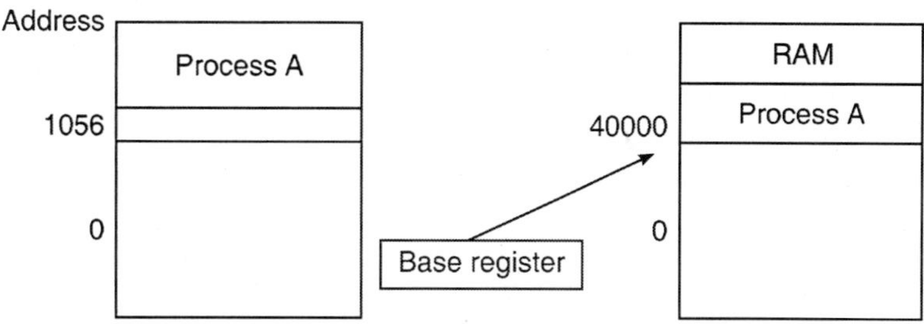

The base register is set to hold 40000. All references to anything within the process are adjusted by adding on this base address. We say that the base register points to the base of the process. This mechanism goes by the name of Base and Displacement addressing.

How paging is achieved?

Physical memory is divided into fixed size blocks called *frames* or page frames. Logical memory is also divided into blocks of the same, fixed size called *pages*. When a program is to be executed, its pages are loaded into any available memory frames from the disk. The disk is also divided into fixed sizes which are the same size as the memory frames.

A very important aspect of paging is the clear separation between the user's view of memory and the actual physical memory. Normally, a user believes that memory is one contiguous space containing only his program. In fact, the logical memory is scattered through the physical memory which also contains other programs. Thus, the user can work correctly with his own view of memory because of the address translation or address mapping. The address mapping, which is controlled by the operating system, and transparent to users, translates logical memory addresses into physical addresses.

Because the operating system is managing the memory, it must be sure about the nature of physical memory, for example: which frames are available, which are allocated; how many total frames there are, and so on. All these parameters are kept in a data structure called *frame table* that has one entry for each physical frame of memory indicating whether it is free or allocated, and if allocated, to which page of which process.

Hardware Implementation of paging

The principal mapping of logical addresses into physical addresses is illustrated in Figure -a. Every logical address generated by the CPU composes of two part: a *page number p* and a *page offset d*. The page number is used as an index into a page table. Each entry in the page table contains the base address r of each page in the physical memory. This base address is added to the page offset d to provide the required physical memory address.

The frame size and page size are specified by the concrete microprocessor architecture. Typically, the page size is a power of two, varied between 512 and 2048 words per page. The selection of a power of two as the page size makes the translation of a logical address into a physical address composed of page number and page offset much easier.

Consider an example showing how a logical address is mapped into a physical address (Figure -b). Logical address 0 is page 0, offset 0. According to the page table we find that page 0 is in frame 5. Thus, the logical address 0 is mapped into the physical address 5 * 4 + 0 = 20. So we can calculate other physical addresses mapped to each given logical addresses, such as logical address 3 maps to physical address 23, 4 maps to 24, 13 maps to 9 and so on. As shown, paging itself is a form of dynamic relocation: each logical address is mapped to some physical addresses.

Paging scheme influences process scheduling. When a process is to be executed, the scheduler checks its size expressed in pages. Available memory is looked for that process. If the process requires n pages, there must be n frames available in memory which must be allocated to this process before it can be executed.

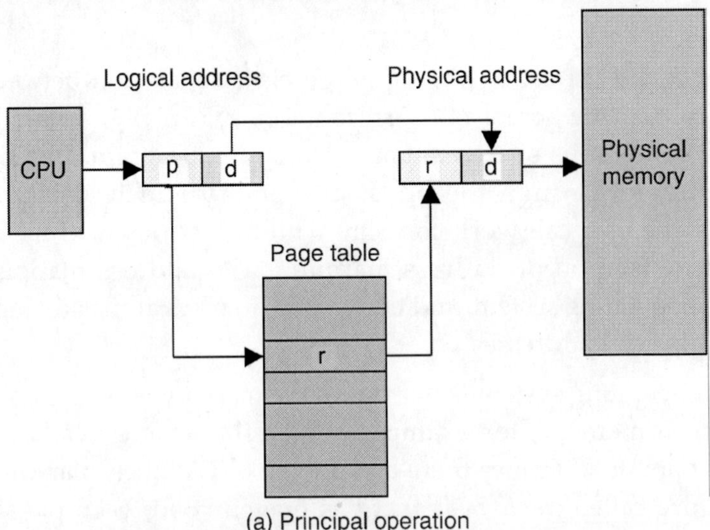

(a) Principal operation

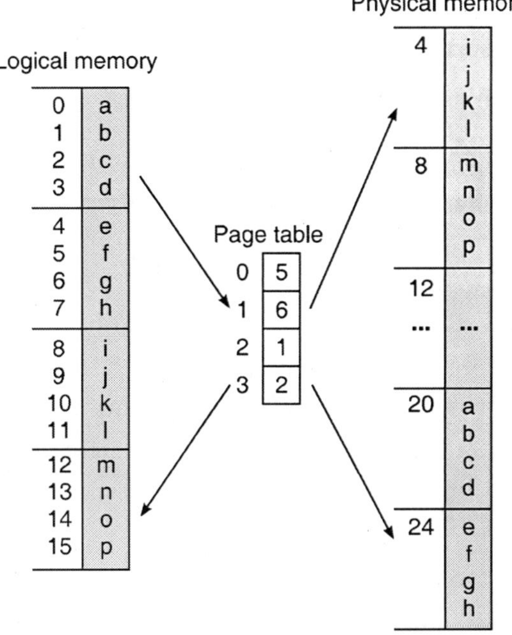

(b) Paging example
Mapping logical address into physical address

Implementation of page table

In the simplest case, the page table is implemented as a set of dedicated registers which should be built from very high-speed logic in order to allow the address translation to be carried out very fast. It is very important, because every access to system memory requires the address translation. The operating system is the only one entity which can reload or modify the page table registers.

In some systems, it is not feasible to use fast registers to implement the page table, hence it must be kept in system memory. A Page Table Base Register PTBR is used to point to the page table in memory. Thus, changing page table requires changing only this one register; the context switching time can be reduced considerably.

Keeping page table in memory may cause unacceptable problem with the duration of access time. As described above, we need two memory accesses to access the required word, one for the page table and one for the word itself. Thus system memory is slowed by a factor of two and this would be intolerable under most circumstances.

To solve this problem associative registers or content-addressable memory can be used in the following way. The page numbers are used to address locations of associative registers whose contents are base addresses of corresponding memory frames. The search can be carried out very fast, but the hardware component is quite expensive.

Associative registers contain only few of the page table entries. When a logical address is generated, its page number is used to address that location of associative registers which contains the corresponding frame number. If the page number is found in the associative registers, i.e. a "match" occurs, its frame number is immediately available, and used to access memory. Otherwise, a memory reference to the page table must be performed and the obtained frame number is used to access memory. Now, these new page number and frame number can be added into the associative registers so that they can be found very quickly on the next reference.

Protection and sharing

Let's take a look at protection first:

Protection

Memory protection in a paged environment is realized by protection bits associated with each page, which are normally stored in the page table. Each bit determines a page to be read-only or read/write. At the same time the physical address is calculated with the help of the page table, the protection bits are checked to verify whether the memory access type is correct or not. For example, an attempt to write to a read-only memory page generates a trap to the operating system indicating a memory protection violation.

We can define one more protection bit added to each entry in the page table to determine an invalid program-generated address. This bit is called valid/invalid bit, and is used to generate a trap to the operating system. Valid/invalid bits are also used to allow and disallow access to the corresponding page. We illustrate this with the following example. Consider a system with 14 bit address space, i.e. these addresses may vary from 0 to 16,383. We may have a program that should use only address 0 to 10,468. If we have a page size of 2K, then we get the situation described in Figure 3-35. Normally, addresses in pages 0, 1, 2, 3, 4 and 5 are mapped through the page table; the corresponding valid/invalid bits are set to "valid". Any access to the page 6 and 7 will generate a trap to the operating system because the valid/invalid bits are set to "invalid".

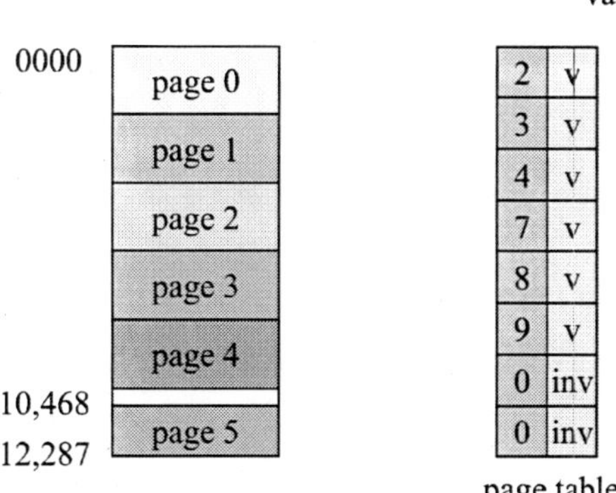

Protection bit in the page table

Function of bits

Protection

At a minimum one bit to flag the page as read-only or read/write. Sometimes more bits to indicate whether the page may be executed as instructions, etc.

Modified

This bit, usually called the *dirty bit,* is set whenever the page is referenced by a write (store) operation.

Referenced

This bit is set whenever the page is referenced for any reason, whether load or store.

Shared pages

The paging scheme supports the possibility of sharing common program code. For example, a system which supports 40 users, each of them executes a text editor. If the text editor consists of 30 KB of code and 5 KB of data, we need 1400 KB. If the code is *reentrant,* i.e., it never changes by any write operation during execution (non-self-modifying code), it could be shared as presented in Figure.

Only one copy of the editor needs to be stored in the physical memory. In each page table, the included editor page is mapped onto the same physical copy of the editor, but the data pages are mapped onto different frames. So, to support 40 users, we only need one copy of the editor, i.e., 30 KB, plus 40 copies of the 5 KB of data pages per user; the total required space is now 230 KB instead of 1400 KB.

Other heavily used programs such as assembler, compiler, data base systems and so on can also be shared among different users. The only condition for it is the code must be reentrant. It is crucial the correct functionality of shared paging scheme that the pages are unchanged. If one user were to change a location, it would be changed for all other users.

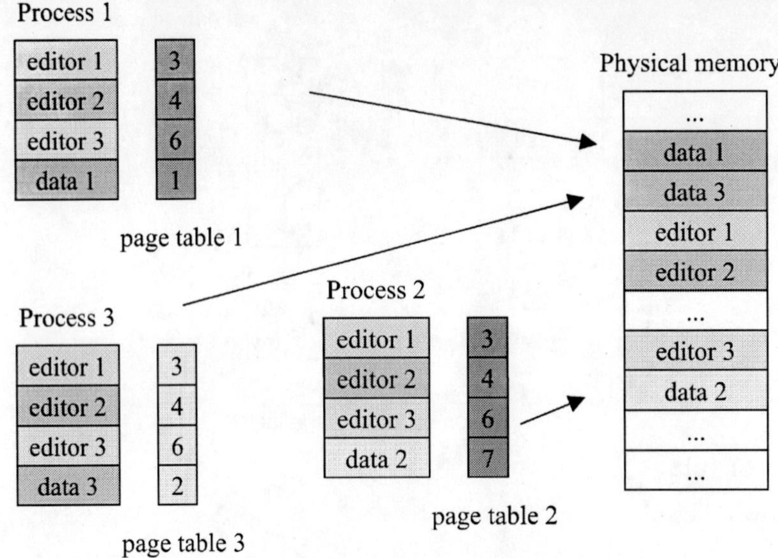

Sharing code in a paging environment

Segmentation

In general, a user or a programmer prefers to view system memory as a collection of variable-sized segments rather than as a linear array of words. Segmentation is a memory management scheme that supports this view of memory.

Segmentation allows program text and data to be broken up into logically independent address spaces and to aid sharing and protection.

A logical address space is a collection of segments. Each segment has a name and a length. The addresses specify not only the name, but also the offset within the segment, so users specify addresses by a segment name and an offset. For simple implementation, segments are numbered and referred to by a segment number (rather than a segment name).

Consider how you think of a program when you are writing it. You think of it as a main program with a set of subroutines, procedures, functions, or modules. There may also be various data structures: tables, arrays, stacks, variables, and so on. Each of these modules or data elements is referred to by name. You are not concerned with whether the symbol table is stored before or after the *Sqrt* function.

Each of these segments is of variable length; the length is intrinsically defined by the purpose of the segment in the program. Elements within a segment are defined by their offset from the beginning of the segment.

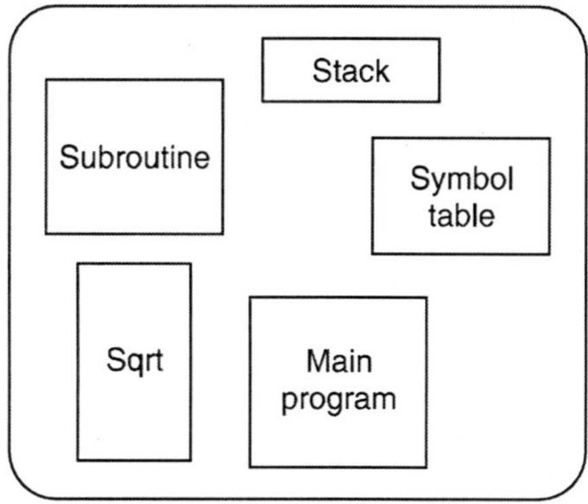

Logical address space

Segmentation is a memory-management scheme that supports this user view of memory. A logical address space is a collection of segments. Each segment has a name and a length. The addresses specify both the segment name and the offset within the segment. The user therefore specifies each address by two quantities: a segment name and an offset.

Hardware components

Because the user specifies objects in his program by two-dimensional addresses (segment number and offset) and the physical memory address is still one-dimensional, we must define a mechanism to map two-dimensional user-defined addresses into one-dimensional physical addresses. This mechanism is realized in form of the *segment table*. The operation of the segment table is illustrated by Figure.

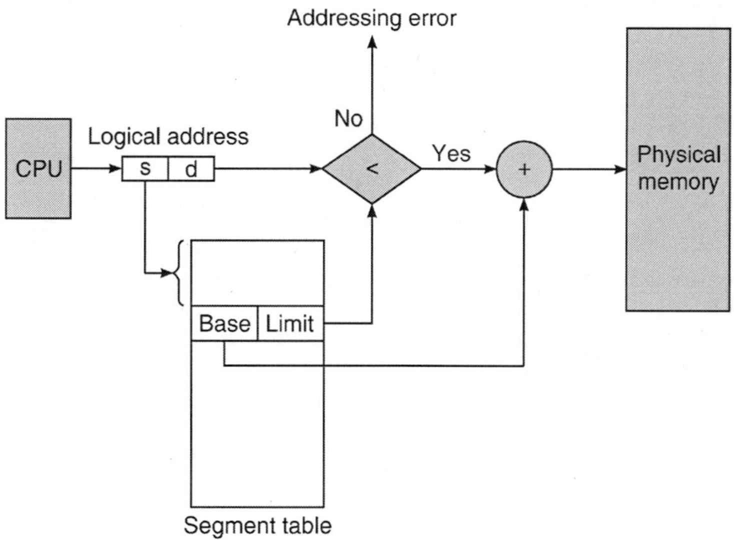

Principal operation for paging

A logical address consists of a segment number s and an offset d. The segment number s is used as an index into the segment table. Each entry in the segment table has a *segment base,* which points where the physical memory begins and a *segment limit* which points where physical memory ends. Therefore, the offset d must be between 0 and the limit; otherwise we trap to the operating system indicating that the logical addressing attempts beyond the end of the physical memory segment.

We illustrate this in the following example. We have five segments numbered from 0 through 4. Segment 2 is 400 words long, beginning at location 4300. Thus, a reference to word 53 of segment 2 is mapped into location 4300 + 53 = 4353. A reference to word 1222 of segment 0 would result in a trap to the operating system indicating a illegal access, because the required address is beyond the end of segment 0 which is only 1000 words long.

Implementation of segment tables

The segment table can be put either in fast registers or in system memory. A segment table kept in registers can be very quickly referenced: the addition to the base and the comparison with the limit can be carried out simultaneously.

Otherwise, because a program may consist of a large number of segments, the segment table must be kept in system memory. A Segment Table Base Register STBR which points to the segment table in memory, and a Segment Table Length Register STLR which limits the possible manageable number of segment are implemented. The mapping procedure is clearly: for a logical address *(s,d)*, we first check that the segment number *s* is legal, i.e. *s* < STBR; then we calculate the address in memory of the segment table entry by performing (STBR + *s*). This entry is read from memory and the physical address of the desired word is computed according to scheme illustrated in Figure.

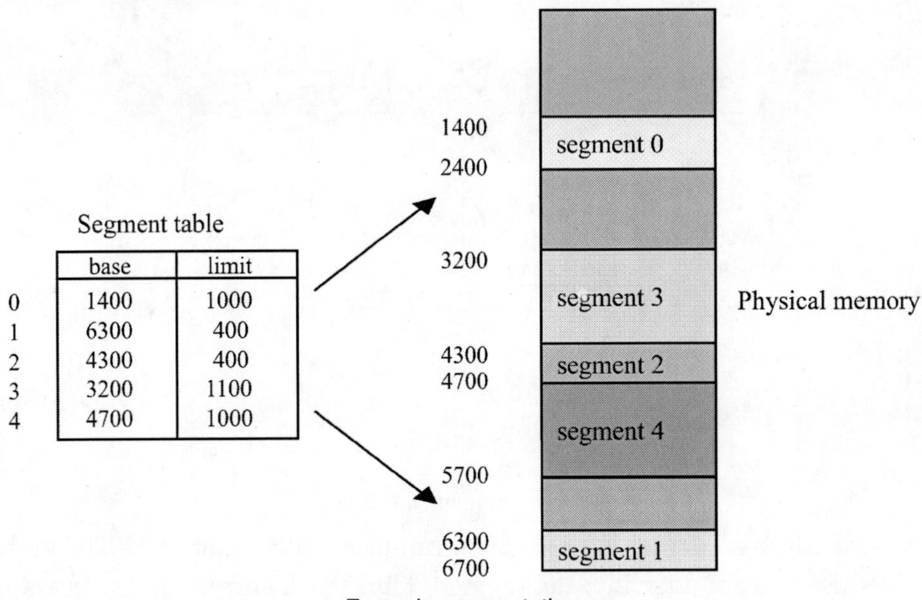

Example segmentation

The disadvantage of this implementation is that two memory references per logical address are required, so that the CPU utilization is low. A small set of associative registers can be used to cache the most recently used segment table entries.

Protection and sharing

One of the advantages of segmentation is the association of protection with the segments. Normally, a program consists of an instruction part and an data part. With segmentation we can put instruction into one segment and data into another segment. Because instructions are non-self-modifying, so instruction segment can be defined as read-only or execute-only segment. The memory-mapping hardware will check the protection bit associated with each segment table entry to prevent illegal access to memory, for example, attempts to write into a read-only segment.

Another advantage of segmentation involves the sharing of code or data. Each job has a segment table associated with its process control block, which the dispatcher uses to define the hardware segment table when this job is given to the CPU. Segments are shared when entries in the segment table of two different processes point to the same physical locations. The sharing occurs at segment level, i.e., information can be shared by defining it to be a segment. Because different segments can be shared, a program composed of several segments can also be shared. Example of sharing segments is as follows:

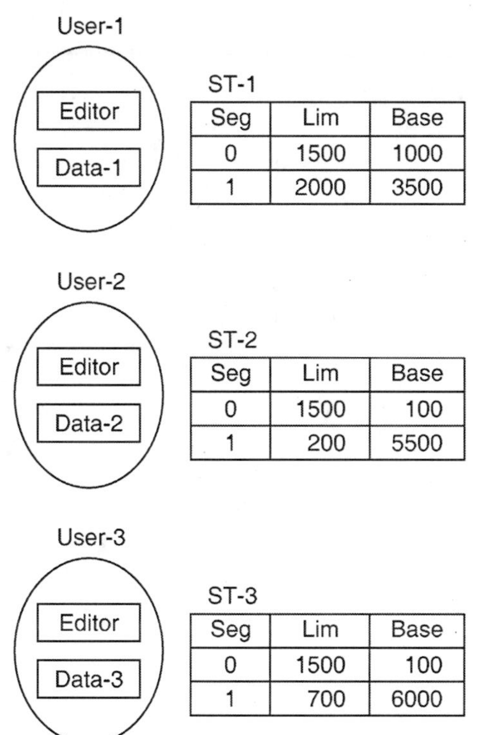

ST-1

Seg	Lim	Base
0	1500	1000
1	2000	3500

ST-2

Seg	Lim	Base
0	1500	100
1	200	5500

ST-3

Seg	Lim	Base
0	1500	100
1	700	6000

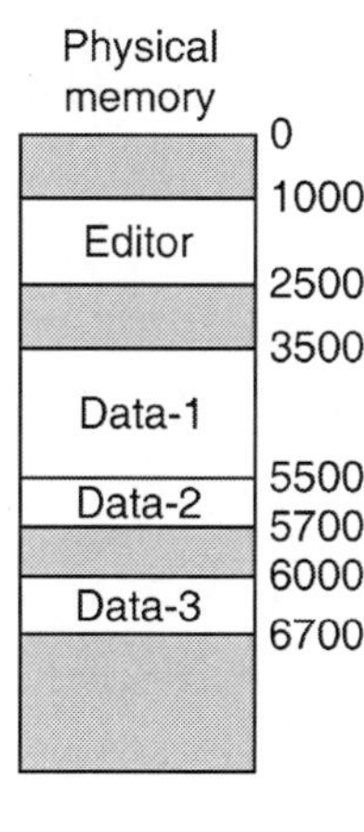

Consider the use of a text editor in a time-sharing system as an example. A complete editor may compose of many segments which can be shared among all users. So rather than n copies of the editor, we need only one copy. To store the local variables we still need separate, unique segments which could not be shared.

Fragmentation problem

Segmentation can cause *external fragmentation*, i.e., there are many blocks of free memory which are too small to accommodate a segment. If this occurs, the process has to wait until more memory becomes available or compaction may be carried out to create larger block of free memory. Another possibility to prevent processes from waiting due to memory allocation is to allow the scheduler looking through the ready queue for a smaller, lower-priority process to execute.

We know that systems with fixed-sized allocation units, such as the single-partition scheme and paging, suffer from internal fragmentation. System with variable-sized allocation units, such as the multiple-partition scheme and segmentation, suffer from external fragmentation. Segmentation may then cause external fragmentation, when all blocks of free memory are too small to accommodate a segment. Compaction may help to solve the problem.

How serious a problem is external fragmentation for a segmentation scheme? Would long-term scheduling with compaction help? The answers depend mainly on the average segment size. At one extreme, we could define each process to be one segment. This approach reduces to the variable-sized partition scheme. At the other extreme, every byte could be put in its own segment and relocated separately. This arrangement eliminates external fragmentation altogether; however, every byte would need a base register for its relocation, doubling memory use! Of course, the next logical step – fixed-sized, small segments – is paging.

Generally, if the average segment size is small, external fragmentation will also be small. (By analogy, consider putting suitcases in the trunk of a car; they never quite seem to fit. However, if you open the suitcases and put the individual items in the trunk, everything is more likely to fit.)

Remember:

In segmentation

A job may be divided into convenient storage units called segments. (A segment may well correspond to a task.) These segments may be organized so that only those segments currently requiring processing are held in main storage.

When segments of different programs are multi-programmed, the method is called interleaving.

Overlaying

While segmenting in the multi-programming environment, only those segments currently requiring processing are held in main storage. The rest are held on direct-access secondary storage.

As each new segment is brought into main store, it is said to overlay the segment it replaces.

Swapping

Moving processes from main memory to disk and back is called swapping. Generally swap space is allocated as a separate place on disk (separate from the file system) to be as fast as possible.

Assume a multiprogramming environment with a round-robin CPU scheduling algorithm. When each process finishes its quantum, the memory manager starts to swap out this process and to swap in another process to the memory space that has been freed. A variant of this swapping-based policy is used for priority scheduling algorithms: if a higher priority process arrives and wants service, the memory manager can swap out the lower-priority process so that it can load and execute the higher-priority process. Swapping area is also called a backing store.

Logical basis for swapping looks as following:

CPU utilization is a function

U = 1 – pn of the number of process n.

p – is the fraction of time that process spending in I/O wait state.

The total memory demand from processes every time exceeds the main memory size (tendency of increasing main memory size is compensated with the same tendency of process sizes increasing).

Input queue of processes is located partially in main memory and partially on disk, advanced scheduling algorithms go around the all ready queue each specified time quantum. And each quantum dispatcher (short-term scheduler) sees the next process in queue. If the process is not, and there is no free memory available, dispatcher asks for swapping.

Swapping time in such a system is fairly high. Let us assume that the user process is of size 100K and the backing store is a standard hard disk with a transfer rate of 1 megabyte per second.

Transfer of 100K processes to or from memory takes 100 milliseconds. Assuming that no head seeks are necessary and an average latency of 8 milliseconds, the swap out and swap in time 2*108 = 216 milliseconds. For efficient CPU utilization execution time for each process to be long relative to the swap time, larger than 0.216 seconds.

There are three methods that OS use to keep track of the memory usage: bit maps, lists, and buddy systems.

These three methods could be used as management tools both for main memory and disk free-space. Especially, buddy system has found application in parallel systems as an efficient means of allocation and release for parallel programs (see Johnson, T., and Davis, T. "Space efficient Parallel Buddy Memory Management".

Proceedings, Third International Conference on Computers and Information, May 1992).

A modified form of the buddy system is used for UNIX kernel memory allocation.

Fifty percent rule

From the first point of view (if you have some simulator that generates segments and holes) the number of segments and the number of holes is approximately the same. However, if adjacent holes were then merged, the number of holes would become smaller than the number of segments. If you consider the process in the middle of memory, half of the operations on segments just above it will be process allocation, and half will be process deallocation. Thus, half the time it has another process as upper neighbor, and half the time it has a hole as upper neighbor. Averaged over time, there must be half as many holes as processes. In other words, if the mean number of processes in memory is n, the mean number of holes is $n/2$.

Unused memory rule

Let f be the fraction of memory occupied by holes, s be the average size of the n processes, and $k*s$ be the average hole size for $k > 0$.

With a total memory of m bytes, the $n/2$ occupy $m - n*s$ bytes.

$$(n/2)*k*s = m - n*s \text{ ® } m = n*s\,(1 + k/2)$$

Practical result: if the mean number of processes in memory is n, the mean number of holes is $n/2$.

$$F = (n*k*s/2)/m = (n*k*s/2)/(n*s(1+k/2)) = k/(k+2)$$

As an example, if $k = ½$, 20 percent of the memory is wasted in holes.

If $k = ¼$, (as a result of using best fit instead of first fit), the wasted memory will drop to about 11 percent.

Segmentation with Paging

Paging eliminates external fragmentation and makes the allocation problem trivial since any empty page can be used for a desired logical page. Additionally, we may have a better protection controls. Segmentation with paging means there are a number of segments in a process and each segment is then paged.

The difference between this solution and pure segmentation is that the segment-table entry contains not the base address of the segment, but rather the base address of a page table for this segment.

The idea is to page the segments and eliminate the external fragmentation problem in paged segmentation the logical address is made of <s,p,d> triplet. The ST entry for segment S now, contains

- the length of semgnt S
- the base address of the PT for segment S.

There is a separate PT for every segment. On the average, now there is half a page of internal fragmentation per segment. However, more table space is needed. In the worst case, again three memory accesses are needed for each memory reference.

The flowchart for accessing a word with logical address <s,p,d> is shown below.

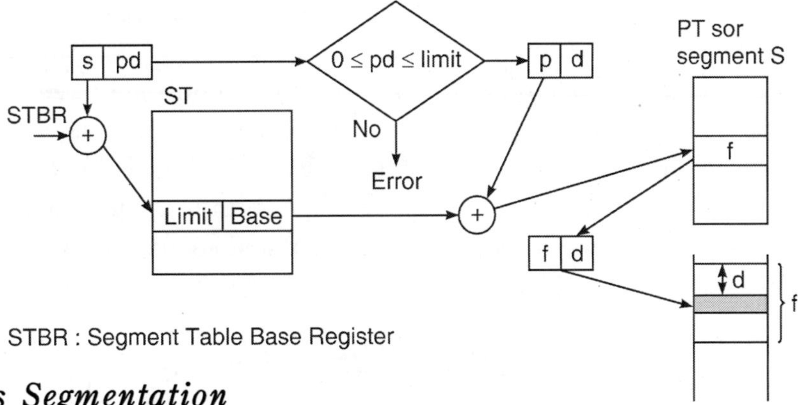

Paging Vs Segmentation

The comparison between paging and segmentation is shown in a table below:

Comparison of paging and segmentation.

Consideration	Paging	Segmentation
Need the programmer be aware that this technique is being used?	No	Yes

How many linear address spaces are there?	1	Many
Can the total address space exceed the size of physical memory?	Yes	Yes
Can procedures and data be distinguished and separately protected?	No	Yes
Can tables whose size fluctuates be accommodated easily?	No	Yes
Is sharing of procedures between users facilitated?	No	Yes
Why was this technique invented?	To get a large linear address space without having to buy more physical memory	To allow programs and data to be broken up into logically independent address spaces and to aid sharing and protection

By far, the memory system is the most important entity in a computer system. The performance of the system as a whole crucially depends on the efficiency of the memory system. The interplay between the hardware and the software of a memory system makes the study of memory systems fascinating. The memory subsystem comprises the paging, swapper, page fault handler, and so on. The subsystem works in close concert with the CPU scheduler and the I/O subsystem.

KEYWORDS

LINEAR LIST	**INDEXED ALLOCATION**
MEMORY	**MEMORY HIERARCHY**
LOGICAL ADDRESSES	**PHYSICAL ADDRESS**
COMPILE-TIME BINDING	**LOAD-TIME ADDRESS BINDING**
RUN TIME BINDING	**FIRST-FIT**
BEST-FIT	**WORST-FIT**
FRAGMENTATION	**COMPACTION**
PAGING	**SEGMENTATION**

SUMMARY

Memory is the electronic holding place for instructions and data Memory systems of a typical computer system are implemented using a number of different storage components. It forms a major part of hardware and the system software in the form of memory management. Memory management means the observation and bookkeeping of which processes are using which parts of the memory.

- The hierarchical arrangement of storage in current computer architectures is called the memory hierarchy
- The user program deals with logical addresses whereas the actual address where the data as well as instructions are stored is called physical address.
- Compile-time address binding generates absolute code, in other words, the addresses are already in place, and when the program is run.
- Load-time address binding: If the starting location of the program isn't known at compile time of the program, then the compiler will generate re-locatable code, i.e. the locations would be changed during the loading of the program called load time address binding.
- If the starting location of the program is to be moved during execution of the program, then the binding must be delayed until run-time. Physical addresses are generated during execution by adding the value of logical addresses to an offset register, this technique is called run time binding.
- Relocation Register allows programs to be relocated dynamically.
- Overlay techniques were introduced so that only a necessary part of a program could be brought into memory at a time. When the next part of the program is needed, it is brought into the address space occupied by a part of the program that is no longer necessary.
- First-fit: allocate the first free block that is big enough. Searching can be start either at the beginning of the free list or where the previous first-fit search ended.
- Best-fit: allocate the smallest free block that is big enough. This strategy produces the smallest leftover holes.
- Worst-fit: allocate the largest free block. This strategy produces the largest leftover hole.
- Fragmentation exists when enough total memory space exists to satisfy a request, but it is not contiguous; storage is fragmented into lots of small blocks. Solution to fragmentation is

- Compaction (or defragmentation) - to shuffle the memory contents to place all free memory together in one large block.
- Paging scheme permits the physical address space of a process to be noncontiguous, thus allowing a process to be allocated physical memory wherever the latter is available, no compaction is required.
- Segmentation allows program text and data to be broken up into logically independent address spaces and to aid sharing and protection

REVIEW QUESTIONS

1) What is memory management?
2) What is logical address space?
3) What is physical address space?
4) What do you mean by swapping?
5) Explain single continuous memory management techniques?
6) Explain partition memory management techniques?
7) Explain relocation memory management techniques?
8) Explain paged memory management techniques?
9) What is fragmentation? How it can be removed?
10) What is compaction? Explain compaction with the help of an example.
11) Differentiate between paging and segmentation

FILL IN THE BLANKS

1. Memory is the electronic holding place for __________.
2. Compile-time address binding generates __________
3. Physical addresses are generated during execution by adding the value of logical addresses to an offset register in __________.
4. Best-fit allocates the __________ free block that is big enough.
5. Worst-fit allocates the __________free block.
6. __________means to shuffle the memory contents to place all free memory together in one large block.

TRUE OR FALSE

1. Memory management means the observation and bookkeeping of which processes are using which parts of the secondary memory.
2. Overlay techniques were introduced so that only a necessary part of a program could be brought into memory at a time.

3. First-fit allocates the last free block that is big enough
4. Fragmentation exists when enough total memory space exists to satisfy a request, but it is not contiguous
5. Paging scheme permits the physical address space of a process to be noncontiguous.
6. Segmentation allows program text and data to be broken up into logically dependent address spaces

ANSWERS

FILL IN THE BLANKS

1. data
2. absolute code
3. run time binding
4. smallest
5. largest
6. Compaction

TRUE OR FALSE

1. FALSE
2. TRUE
3. FALSE
4. TRUE
5. TRUE
6. FALSE

"Programs must be written for people to read, and only incidentally for machines to execute."

—E. Dijkstra

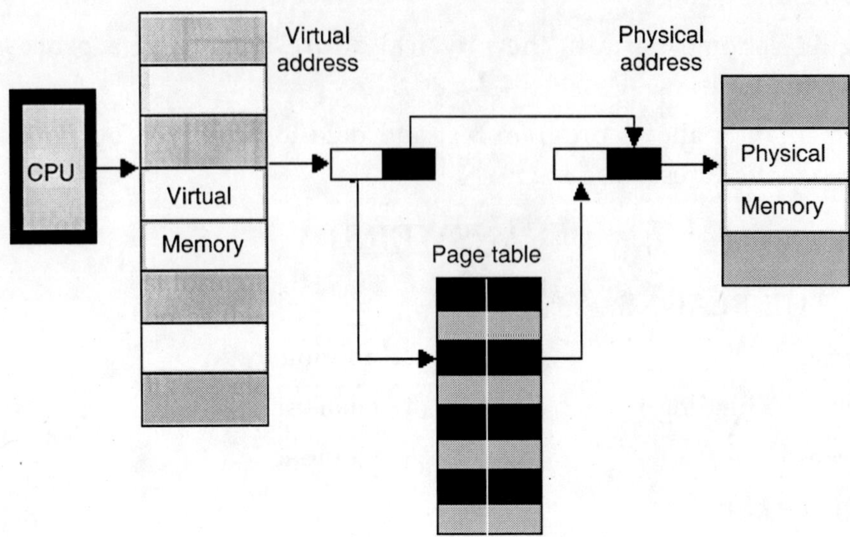

VIRTUAL MANAGEMENT

INTRODUCTION

All memory management algorithms have the same requirement that the process must be completely in system memory before it can execute. So they limit the maximal user program size to the size of the physical memory.

In general, real user programs don't need to be completely in system memory while they execute. For example: programs often have code to handle unusual error events which very rarely occur in practice. This code is almost never executed. Even in those cases where the entire program is needed, it's not necessary for all parts of the program to be in memory at the same time.

Executing a program that is partially in memory can have many benefits, not only for users but also for the system:

A program is no longer limited by the size of physical memory that is available. Writing a program in a large virtual address space is more convenient.

Because each user may take less physical memory, more user can be run at the same time. The CPU utilization and the system throughput may increase.

Less I/O operation would be needed to load users into memory, so each user could run faster.

What is virtual memory?

Virtual memory is a technique that solves the problem of limited memory by providing each process with a virtual address space, potentially larger than the system's physical address space, which the process uses to access data and instructions.

Virtual memory makes use of a phenomenon known as locality of reference in which memory references of both instructions and data tend to cluster. Over short periods of time a significant amount of:

(a) Instruction execution is localized either within loops or heavily used subroutines,

(b) Data manipulation is on local variables or upon tables or arrays of information.

Most virtual memory systems use a technique called paging in which the program and data is broken down into 'pages' (typical size 4Kbytes) which are held on disk. Pages are then brought into main memory as required and 'swapped' out when main memory is full. This technique allows program size to be much larger than the physical main memory size (typically a modern professional workstation may have 16 to 64Mbytes of main memory but a virtual memory size of 4Gbyte).

Virtual memory uses an address translation mechanism or an *address map* to relate the logical addresses allowable within the virtual memory to the actual physical addresses in hardware. Thereby, once again, freeing the programmer from having to consider the hardware. The crucial point is the distinction between *program addresses* (addresses used by the programmer) and the physical addresses of the locations within main memory. Therefore, the way to look at the address map is to regard it as a means of allowing the programmer to use a range of program addresses which may be quite different from the range of memory locations that are actually available. Thus the programmer "sees" – and writes programs within the context of – a virtual memory whose characteristics differ from those of real memory. The address map is then designed so as to produce a virtual memory convenient to the programmer, thus achieving the objectives of protection and logical organization of programs.

In a virtual memory system, the program and data are stored in secondary storage (disk) and only the parts in use at any given moment are brought into real memory. This works because of *locality of reference.*

Principle of Locality of Reference

VM only works because of the principle of locality. By observing the behaviour of running processes, it was discovered that processes tend to spend most of their time executing code (and accessing data) in a limited (local) region of the process. In other words, the process would not randomly jump all over the process' address space, but would stay, for periods of time, in a local area. As the time progressed, this local area might change, but at all times only a small proportion of the process' memory was being used. This is the principle of Locality.

This makes sense if you think about how we use applications such as Excel. You might spend a lot of time inputting data to a spreadsheet, and then move on to create a chart. The code for these functions will be in different parts (modules) of the Excel application.

This is very analogous to the behaviour of people. If you examine your lifestyle, you'll probably find that you spend a lot of time in a few places. It is in the nature of von Neumann architecture computer systems that if a word from memory has been used recently, it is likely to be used again in the near future. Similarly if a word has been used recently, words near it are likely to be used in the relatively near future.

Virtual memory is implemented by dividing the portion of the address space used by a program into fixed-size pieces called *pages.* The size of the pages is a power of two, typically from 512 bytes to about 64 K bytes. We will use a page size of 4 K in the example, and discuss the trade-offs in selecting a page size later.

Real memory is divided into *page frames* which are the same size as the virtual pages. When a page is needed during the running of a program, it is copied into a page frame in real memory. The amount of real memory available is called the *physical address space.* The area available for the programmer to use (determined by the size of an address) is called the *virtual address space.*

The process of moving program pages to and from real memory is called *paging.* Paging is transparent to the writer of the program. Remember our two definitions:

- *Transparent:* It's there, but you can't see it.
- *Virtual:* You can see it, but it's not there.

We have skipped over some details up to now, and one of them is the need for address translation, or mapping. Address translation is made necessary by the following facts:

- Programs generate virtual addresses,
- The memory subsystem hardware only understands physical addresses, and
- Any page can go into any page frame.

Address translation is accomplished by a memory management unit, or MMU. The MMU may be a part of the CPU or a separate unit. The MMU and the operating system work together to implement virtual memory. The process of reading pages in from disk only when they are needed is called *demand paging.* Pages are not loaded into page frames until there is a demand for them.

A program typically starts with none of its pages in real memory. The first reference causes a page fault. Soon, however, all the pages needed for a given part of the program are in memory. This set of pages is called the *working set*. The composition of the working set changes over time as the program runs.

As long as the working set of a program is smaller than the available physical memory, the program runs nearly as fast as it would if it had free access to enough real memory for the entire program. If there is not enough real memory to hold the working set, page faults occur frequently and the CPU spends more time moving pages around than it does running the program. This condition is called *thrashing*.

Virtual Address Space

Address generated by CPU are commonly referred to as logical addresses (virtual address), whereas addresses loaded into memory address register are commonly referred to as physical addresses.

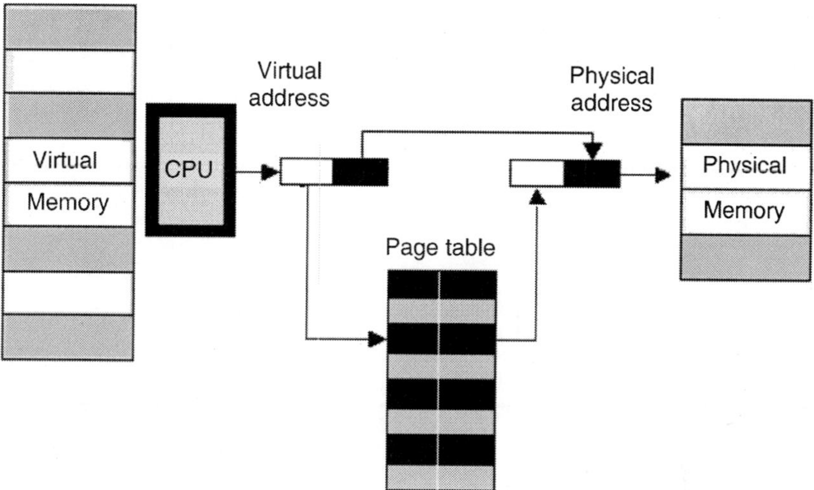

The set of all logical addresses (virtual addresses are the same) generated by a program is referred to as a logical address space. The set of all physical addresses corresponding to these logical addresses is referred to as a physical address space.

Let's take the example of a computer with a 32-bit address, 16 MB of real memory, and a virtual memory system that uses 4 K pages. The memory management process translates a 32-bit virtual address into a 24-bit physical address. This is done with the aid of a *page table*. If there are 32 bits in an address, and a page is 4 K, there are 2 20 or one M pages in the virtual address space. (How do you know that's true?) These pages are represented by a *page table* with 220 entries. Each entry contains a valid bit that indicates whether the page is currently in main memory, a dirty bit indicating whether the page has been modified, and a frame number pointing to a page frame in real memory. Since there are 4,096 4 K frames in a real memory of 16 M cells, (why?) the frame number in our example page table will be 12 bits.

Consider the figure below. The CPU has generated a 32-bit address as shown in the upper right of the figure. As far as the CPU is concerned, this is just a 32-bit number. For purposes of address translation, it is useful to think of the address as a 20-bit page number and a 12-bit "offset" that identifies a cell within a page. We will think of a physical address as a page frame number and an offset. Since the pages and page frames are the same size, the offset from the virtual address can simply be copied into the offset part of the physical address.

However, we have some work to do to translate the 20-bit page number into a 12-bit page frame number. In the example, the virtual page number is three. We look in entry three of the page table and find that the valid bit is a one, indicating that the page is already in real memory. We check the frame number from the page table and find that it is six. Virtual page three is stored in page frame six. We copy this number into the frame part of the physical address, and we have mapped a 32-bit virtual address onto a 24-bit physical address. The memory hardware can now retrieve the desired cell.

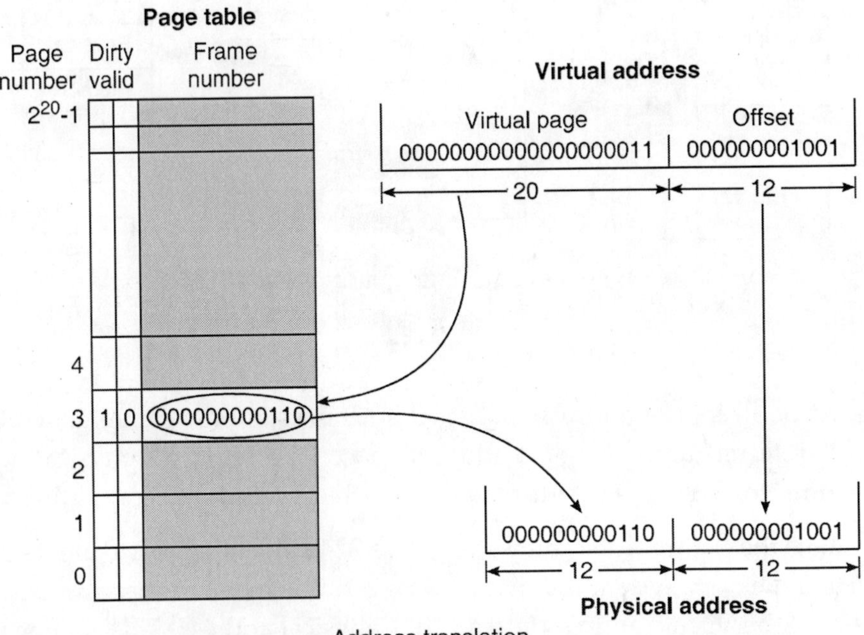

Address translation

In the example, we assumed that the page containing the needed cell was already in main memory. That doesn't always happen. A reference to a cell that's not in mail memory is called a *page fault*. In case of a page fault, the MMU would have signalled an interrupt upon finding a zero valid bit. The operating system would have read the page from disk into a free page frame, updated the page table, and restarted the instruction that caused the page fault.

Virtual memory is the mechanism to make available execution of program that is only partially in memory. All memory references within a process (that are logical addresses) are dynamically translated into physical addresses (so called run-time mapping) by memory management unit MMU (in hardware).

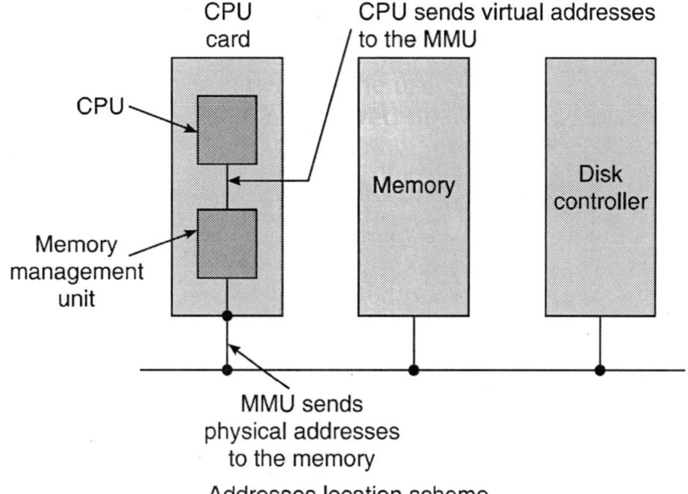

Addresses location scheme

In this environment a program (process) may be larger than all of main memory and must be broken up into number pieces (pages or segments). These pieces need not be contiguously located in main memory during execution.

This also means that a process may be swapped in and out of main memory at different regions of main memory at different times during the execution. For this purpose a page or segment table is used.

Most of virtual memory systems use a technique called paging.

Overlays

In the earliest computers, memory was a scarce and expensive resource. Computers with 2K words were not uncommon. Programmers spent significant time making their programs fit into the available memory. Careful selection of algorithms and really tight coding helped, but sometimes a program was just too big to fit. In such situations the virtual memory helped a great deal during the early days of computing. In a virtual memory system, the program and data are stored in secondary storage (disk) and only the parts in use at any given moment are brought into real memory. One technique of implementing virtual memory is overlays. The overlay is the technique of dividing a program into pieces that were used at different times during the course of executing the program.

Use of Overlays

Consider an assembler program, the language translator that turns symbolic programs in assembly language into binary programs. Earlier we learned that assemblers make two passes through the source code. In the first pass the size of each item is determined, the location counter is stepped through the program, and symbols and their locations are saved in a symbol table. On the second pass, binary values for instructions and data are generated and the addresses are looked up in the symbol table. Pass 2 generates the binary program.

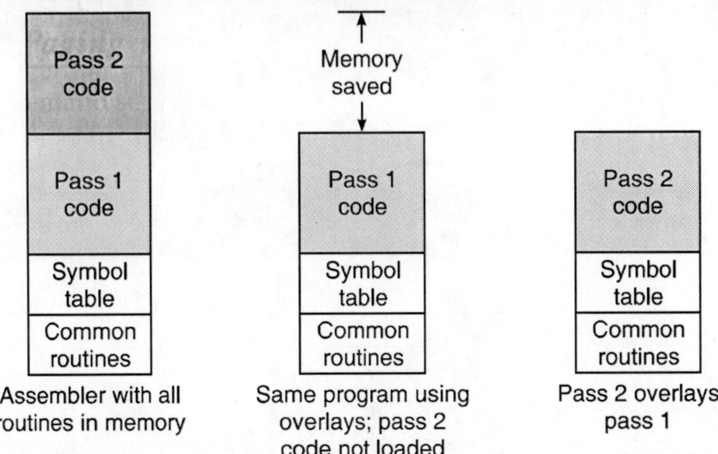

The memory map of the assembler might look like the first part of the figure, with routines common to both passes, an area for the symbol table, and the code for the two passes. If that program were too big to fit in memory, the programmer might write it so that when it starts its memory map looks like the second part of the figure. The common routines, symbol table, and pass 1 code are in memory, but the pass 2 code is not. At the end of pass 1, when that code is no longer needed, the pass 2 code is loaded in its place. This technique is called overlaying. The third part of the figure shows the memory map after the pass 2 code overlays the pass 1 code.

Dividing a program into overlays and loading them was the responsibility of the programmer. It was a difficult and error-prone task. In 1961, a group of researchers at Manchester, England set out to find a way to automate the process of managing overlays.

The key idea of the Manchester group, and the idea that makes virtual memory possible, is to separate the concept of the address space from the physical memory locations.

To understand what that means, we must examine the way we think about address space and memory in a computer without virtual memory. Consider a computer capable of generating 32-bit addresses. Such a computer has an address space of four gigabytes. However, it would be unusual for a computer actually to have 4 GB of memory. It would be much more likely for the computer to have from a few megabytes to a few hundred megabytes of actual memory.

Useful and Useless Address Spaces

The next figure shows the address space of a computer with 32-bit addresses and 16 MB of actual memory. The address *space* is still 4 GB, but only 16 MB of it is useful. If we have a program that requires more than 16 MB, it can't be run on this computer.

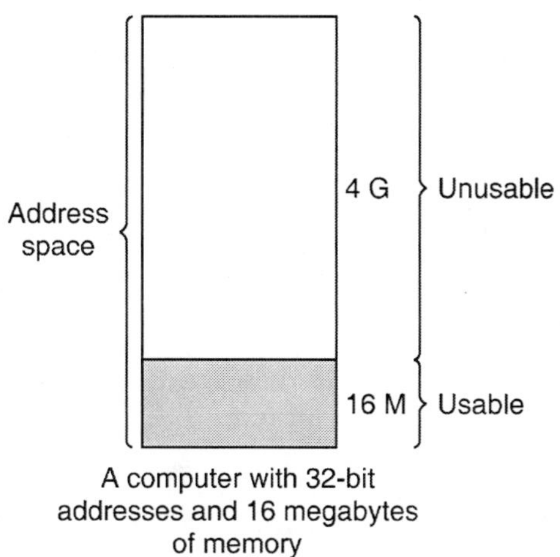

A computer with 32-bit addresses and 16 megabytes of memory

Remember, the idea that the researchers had was to separate the concepts of address space and physical memory. Virtual memory allows programmers to use the entire address space defined by the size of an address, regardless of the amount of physical memory present.

Demand paging

Demand paging is the most common virtual memory management system. It is based on the locality model of program execution. As a program executes, it moves from locality to locality.

Demand paging introduces the concept of loading only a part of the program into memory for processing. When a process begins to run, pages are brought into memory only as they are needed.

Locality is defined as a set of pages actively used together. A program is composed of several different localities which may overlap. For example, a small procedure when called, defines a new locality. A while-do loop when being executed defines a new locality.

As a program executes, it moves from locality to locality. Procedural languages with while-do, repeat-until, for-do structures (i.e. Pascal, Algol, C, etc.) have less frequently changing localities than other high-level languages with go-to structure (i.e. Basic, Fortran).

In demand paging, programs reside on a swapping device commonly known as the backing store. The backing store, for most of today's operating systems is a disk.

When the operating system decides to start a new process, it swaps only a small part of this new process (a few pages) into memory. The page table of this new process is prepared and loaded into memory, and the valid/invalid bits of all pages that are brought into memory are set to "valid". All the other valid/invalid bits are set to "invalid" showing that those pages are not brought into memory.

If the process currently executing tries to access a page which is not in the memory, a page fault occurs, and the OS brings that page into the memory. If a process causes page fault then the following procedure is applied:

1. Trap the OS.
2. Save registers and process state for the current process.
3. Check if the trap was caused because of a page fault and whether the page reference is legal.
4. If yes, determine the location of the required page on the backing store
5. Find a free frame.
6. Read (swap in) the required page from the backing store into the free frame. (During this I/O, the processor may be scheduled to some other process)
7. When I/O is completed, restore registers and process state for the process which caused the page fault and save state of the currently executing process.
8. Modify the corresponding page table entry to show that the recently copied page is now in memory.
9. Resume execution with the instruction that caused the page fault.

While executing a process, in the case of a page fault, the OS finds the desired page on the backing store and if there is no free frame, the OS must choose a page in the memory

(which is not the one being used) as a victim, and must swap it out (slow) to the backing store.

Then, the OS changes the valid/invalid bit for the victim page in the page table to indicate that it is no longer in memory. It swaps the desired page into newly freed frame, modifies the frame table, and sets the valid/invalid bit of the new page to valid. The executing process may now go on.

This operation can be summarized as:

1. Checking the address and finding a free frame or victim page (fast)
2. Swap out the victim page to secondary storage (slow)
3. Swap in the page from secondary storage (slow)
4. Context switch for the process and resume its execution (fast)

In servicing a page fault, the time is spent mainly for swap-out and swap-in. The time required for other operations are negligible.

REMEMBER: Virtual memory can be implemented in:

- paging systems
- paged segmentation systems
- segmentation systems (However, segment replacement is much more sophisticated than page replacement since segments are of variable size.)

Demand paging is in principal similar to a paging system with *swapping*. Normally, user programs are kept in secondary memory, usually on a disk. When a program is to be executed, it is swapped into system memory in the following way: only those pages that will be used before the program will swapped out again are swapped in. Through this, swapping time and amount of physical memory needed can be decreased.

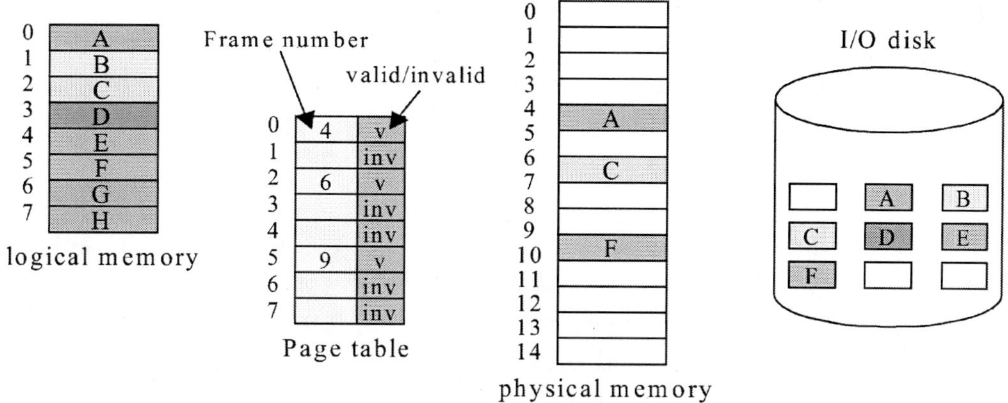

Principal operation of demand paging

The valid/invalid bit of the page table entry for a page which is swapped in is set as valid. Otherwise it is set as invalid which will have no effect as long as the program never attempts to access this page. If all and only those pages actually needed are swapped in, the process will execute exactly as if all pages were brought in.

If the process tries to access a page which was not swapped in, i.e. the valid/invalid bit of this page table entry is set to invalid, then a page fault trap will occur. Instead of showing the "invalid address error" as usually, it indicates the operating system's failure to bring a valid part of the program into memory at the right time in order to minimize swapping overhead.

In order to continue the execution of process, the operating system schedules a disk read operation to bring the desired page into a newly allocated frame. After that, the corresponding page table entry will be modified to indicate that the page is now in memory. Because the state (program counter, registers etc.) of the interrupted process was saved when the page fault trap occurred, the interrupted process can be restarted at the same place and state. As shown, it is possible to execute programs even though parts of it are not (yet) in memory.

In the extreme case, a process without pages in memory could be executed. Page fault trap would occur with the first instruction. After this page was brought into memory, the process would continue to execute. In this way, page fault trap would occur further until every page that is needed was in memory. This kind of paging is called pure demand paging: never bring a page into memory until it is required.

Performance

Demand paging has a significant effect on the system performance of a computer system. We can calculate the *effective access time Teff* for a demand paged memory to show this effect.

Let p be the probability of a page fault: 0 £ p £ 1. We would expect p to be very close to 0. Clearly (1 – p) is the probability that a page which is already in memory. Let Ta be the memory access time, Tfault be the page fault processing time. The effective access time is calculated as follows:

Teff = (1 – p) * Ta + p * Tfault

We need to determine the page fault processing time first. If a page fault trap occurs, some work has to be carried out in the following sequence:

- Serving the page fault interrupt, including: a) trap to the operating system, b) save user registers and program state, c) check the page reference and determine the location of the page on the disk.
- Swapping in the required page: a) read from disk to a free frame, b) serve interrupt from disk, c) correct the page table to indicate that the desired page is now in memory.
- Restart the process: wait for the CPU to be allocated to this process again, b) restore the user registers and program state, c) resume the interrupted instruction.

Suppose an average page fault processing time of 10 ms and a memory access time of 1 msec, then we have :

Teff = (1 – p) * Ta + p * Tfault

Teff = (1 – p) * (1 msec) + p * (10 msec)

Teff = 1 + 9999 * p msec

It is easy to see that the effective access time is directly proportional to the page fault rate p. If no page fault occurs, the effective access time is equal the memory access time. If one access out of 1000 generates a page fault, then the effective access time is 11 msec. This means that the computer would be slowed down by a factor of 11 because of demand paging. If we want less than 10% performance degradation, we need p < 0,00001.

What should be the size of a page?

Earlier we glossed over the problem of how big to make a page. No matter what we choose for a page size, most programs won't be an exact multiple of the page size. On the average, half of the last page in a program will be wasted. Since the unused bytes in a page occupy space in a page frame when the page is loaded, we would like to minimize the waste, and this drives us toward smaller page sizes. Similarly, we find that the first and last pages in each part of the working set generate some waste, driving us to smaller pages. Smaller pages waste less main memory.

However, each page requires a page table entry. Smaller pages mean more pages, and so more page table entries. Further, larger pages use I-O more effectively than smaller pages. As with much of the rest of computer architecture, the designer is faced with a set of trade-offs.

Demand Paging vs. demand segmentation

In the demand segmentation technique the same idea as demand paging is applied to segments. The major differences between demand paging and demand segmentation are as follows:

Consideration	Demand Paging	Demand Segmentation
Programmer aware	No	Yes
How many addr spaces	1	Many
VA size > PA size	Yes	Yes
Protect individual procedures separately	No	Yes
Accommodate elements with changing sizes	No	Yes
Ease user sharing	No	Yes
Why invented	let the VA size exceed the PA size	Sharing, Protection, independent address spaces

Consideration	Demand Paging	Demand Segmentation
Internal fragmentation	Yes	No, in principle
External fragmentation	Yes	Yes
Placement question	No	Yes
Replacement question	No	Yes

Page replacement algorithms

When a page fault occurs and there's no free page frame, the operating system must make room for the new page by replacing a page already in main memory. The designer of a virtual memory system must decide on a *page replacement policy* to determine which page will get evicted from its page frame when there's no free frame.

The main advantage of this virtual memory scheme is that programs can be larger than physical memory. Moreover, users would be able to write programs for an extremely large virtual addressing space, simplifying the programming task. Furthermore, because each user program could take less physical memory, more programs could be run at the same time, with a corresponding increase in CPU utilization and throughput

Virtual memory management allows the execution of processes that are partially in system memory. So programming with very large virtual memory is possible.

Using virtual memory technique, the memory is multiplexed spacially by dividing it into pieces, which are assigned to different processes.

	Real Memory	OS	Process 1	Process 2
S P	Partition 0	Real Memory		
A C	Partition	→	Virtual Memory	
E	Partition 2	→		Virtual Memory

Virtual Memory

A page replacement algorithm determines how the victim page (the page to be replaced) is selected when a page fault occurs. The aim is to minimize the page fault rate. The efficiency of a page replacement algorithm is evaluated by running it on a particular string of memory references and computing the number of page faults.

Reference strings are either generated randomly, or by tracing the paging behavior of a system and recording the page number for each logical memory reference. The performance of a page replacement algorithm is evaluated by running it on a particular string of memory references and computing the number of page faults.

In general we want a page replacement algorithm with the lowest page-fault rate. We evaluate an algorithm by running it on a particular string of memory references (reference string) and computing the number of page faults on that string.

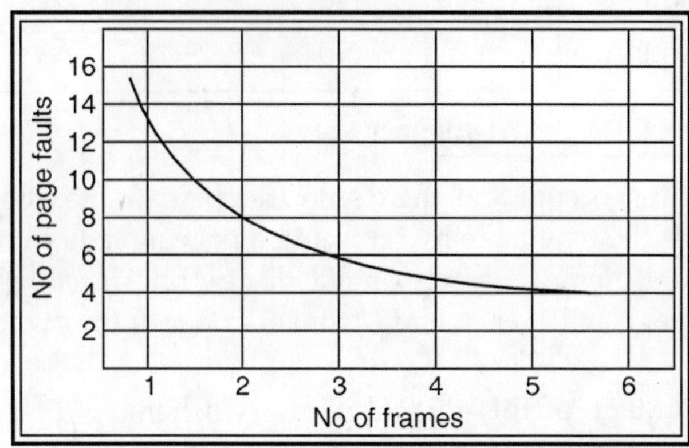

To determine the number of page faults for a particular reference string and page replacement algorithm, we also need to know the number of page frames available. Obviously as the number of frames available increases, the number of page faults decreases.

Expected relationship between number of free frames allocated to a process and the number of page faults caused by it

FIFO Page Replacement

The simplest page-replacement algorithm is a FIFO algorithm. A FIFO replacement algorithm associates with each page the time when that page was brought into memory. When a page must be replaced, the oldest page is chosen. Notice that it is not strictly necessary to record the time when a page is brought in. We can create a FIFO queue to hold all pages in memory. We replace the page at the head of the queue. When a page is brought into memory we insert t at the tail of the queue.

1, 2, 3, 4, 5, 3, 4, 1, 6, 7, 8, 7, 8, 9, 5, 4, 5, 4, 4

1	5	5	5	5	8	8	8	8
2	2	1	1	1	1	9	9	9
3	3	3	6	6	6	6	5	5
3	4	4	4	7	7	7	7	4

Consider the following example, in which the number of frames allocated is 4, and the reference string is 1, 2, 3, 4, 5, 1, 6, 7, 8, 7, 8, 9, 5, 4, 5, 4, 4. The number of page faults caused by the process is nine, as shown below.

Example for the FIFO page replacement algorithm

The problem with this algorithm is that it suffers from Belady's anomaly: For some page replacement algorithms the page fault rate may increase as the number of allocated frames increases, whereas we would expect that giving more memory to a process would improve its performance.

Belady's Anomaly

Consider the following example of the FIFO algorithm.

- Number of frames allocated = 3
- Reference string: 1, 2, 3, 4, 1, 2, 5, 1, 2, 3, 4, 5
- Number of page faults = 9

1	1	1	4	4	4	5	5	5
	2	2	2	1	1	1	3	3
		3	3	3	2	2	2	4

Now an intuitive idea is that if we increase the number of frames allocated to 4 from 3, the page faults should decrease, but the following example demonstrates otherwise.

- Number of frames allocated = 4
- Reference string: 1, 2, 3, 4, 1, 2, 5, 1, 2, 3, 4, 5
- Number of page faults = 10

1	1	1	1	5	5	5	5	4	4
	2	2	2	2	1	1	1	1	5
		3	3	3	3	2	2	2	2
			4	4	4	4	3	3	3

This is due to the **Belady's Anomaly** which states that "For some page replacement algorithms, the page fault rate may increase as the number of allocated frames increases.'

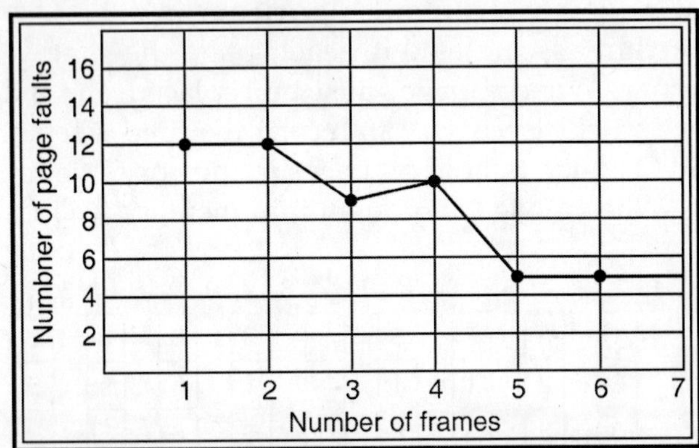

The Second Chance Page Replacement Algorithm

A simple modification to FIFO that avoids the problem of throwing out a heavily used page is to inspect the R bit of the oldest page. If it is 0, the page is both old and unused, so it is replaced immediately. If the R bit is 1, the bit is cleared, the page is put onto the end of the list of pages, and its load time is updated as though it had just arrived in memory. Then the search continues. The operation of this algorithm, called second chance, is shown in Fig. In Fig. (a) We see pages A through H kept on a linked list and sorted by the time they arrived in memory.

Suppose that a page fault occurs at time 20. The oldest page is A, which arrived at time 0, when the process started. If A has the R bit cleared, it is evicted from memory, either by being written to the disk (if it is dirty), or just abandoned(if it is clean). On the other hand, if the R bit is set, A is put onto the end of the list and its "load time" is reset to the current time (20). The R bit is also cleared. The search for a suitable page continues with B.

What second chance is doing is looking for an old page that has not been referenced in the previous clock interval. If all the pages have been referenced, second chance degenerates into pure FIFO. Specifically, imagine that all the pages in Fig. (a) have their R bits set. One by one, the operating system moves the pages to the end of the list, clearing the R bit each time it appends a page to the end of the list. Eventually, it comes back to page A, which now has its R bit cleared. At this point A is evicted. Thus the algorithm always terminates.

The Clock Page Replacement Algorithm

Although second chance is a reasonable algorithm, it is unnecessarily inefficient because it is constantly moving pages around on its list. A better approach is to keep all the page frames on a circular list in the form of a clock, as shown in Fig... A hand points to the oldest page.

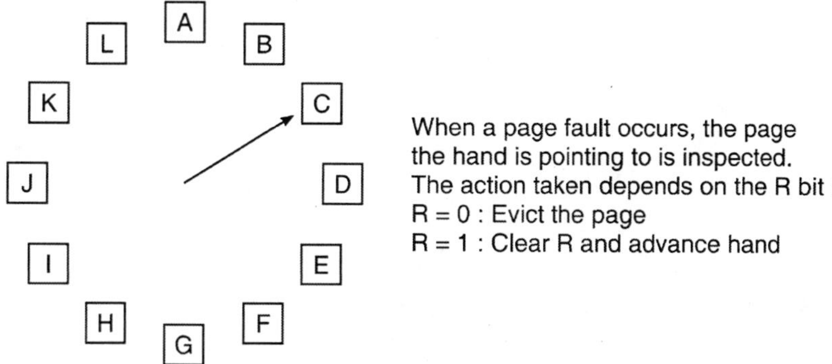

Figure : The clock page replacement algorithm.

When a page fault occurs, the page being pointed to by the hand is inspected. If its R bit is 0, the page is evicted, the new page is inserted into the clock in its place, and the hand is advanced one position. If R is 1, it is cleared and the hand is advanced to the next page. This process is repeated until a page is found with R = 0. Not surprisingly, this algorithm is called clock. It differs from second chance only in the implementation, not in the page selected.

Optimal Algorithm

An optimal page-replacement algorithm has the lowest page fault rate of all algorithms, and will never suffer from the Belay's algorithm. This algorithm is simply to replace the page that will not be used for the longest period of time. Use of this algorithm guarantees the lowest possible page-fault rate for a fixed number of frames. In case of the following example (which uses the same replacement string as the example for the FIFO algorithm), the number of page faults caused by the process is seven.

1, 2, 3, 4, 5, 3, 4, 1, 6, 7, 8, 7, 8, 9, 5, 4, 5, 4, 4

1	1	6	6	8	9	9
2	5	5	5	5	5	5
3	3	3	7	7	7	7
4	4	4	4	4	4	4

Example for the optimal page replacement algorithm

Unfortunately this algorithm is difficult to implement because it requires future knowledge of the reference string. As a result this algorithm is used mainly for comparison.

LRU Page Replacement

If we use the recent past as an approximation of the near future, then we will replace the page that has not been used for the longest period of time. This approach is the least recently used algorithms. The following example illustrates the working of LRU algorithm.

Reference string

7 0 1 2 0 3 0 4 2 3 0 3 2 1 2 0 1 7 0 1

7	7	7	2	2	4	4	4	0	1	1	1
	0	0	0	0	0	0	3	3	3	0	0
		1	1	3	3	2	2	2	2	2	7

Page frames

Example for the LRU page replacement algorithm

Here is another example, which uses the same reference string as used in the examples for the FIFO and optimal replacement algorithms. The number of page faults in this case is nine.

1, 2, 3, 4, 5, 3, 4, 1, 6, 7, 8, 7, 8, 9, 5, 4, 5, 4, 4

1	5	5	6	6	6	6	5	5
2	2	1	1	1	1	9	9	9
3	3	3	3	7	7	7	7	4
4	4	4	4	4	8	8	8	8

Another example for the LRU algorithm

An LRU page replacement may require substantial hardware assistance. The problem is to determine an order for the frames defined by the time of last use. Two implementations are feasible:

Counter-based Implementation of LRU

In the simplest case we associate with each page table entry a time-of-use field and add to the CPU a logical clock or counter. The clock is incremented for every memory reference. Whenever a reference to a page is made, the contents of the clock register are copied to the time-of-use field in the page entry for that page. In that way we always have the time of the last reference to each page. We replace the page that has the smallest time value. This scheme requires a search of the page table to find the LRU page and a write

to memory for each memory access. The times must also be maintained when page tables are changed. Overflow of the clock must be considered.

Stack-based Implementation of LRU

Another approach to implementing the LRU algorithm is to keep a stack of page numbers. Whenever a page is referenced, it is removed from the stack and put on top. In this way, the top of the stack is always the most recently used page and the bottom is the LRU page. Because entities must be removed from the middle of the stack, it is best implementing by a doubly linked list with a head and tail pointer. Removing a page and putting it on the top of the stack then requires changing six pointers at worst. Each update is a little more expensive, but there is no search for a replacement the tail pointer points

to the bottom of the stack which is the LRU page. The following diagram shows the working of stack-based implementation of the LRU algorithm.

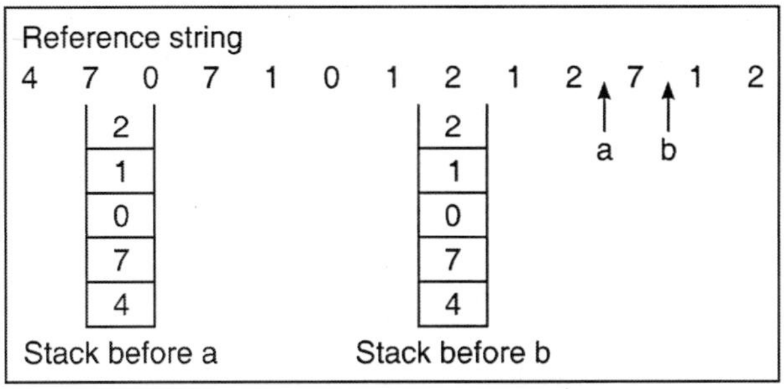

Reference string

4 7 0 7 1 0 1 2 1 2 7 1 2

Stack before a
2
1
0
7
4

Stack before b
2
1
0
7
4

a b

Stack based implementation of the LRU page replacement algorithm

LRU Approximation Algorithm

Few computer systems provide sufficient hardware support for true LRU page replacement. Some systems provide no hardware support and other page replacement algorithms must be used. Many systems provide some help however, in the form of a reference bit. The reference bit for a page is set by the hardware whenever that page is referenced. Reference bits are associated with each entry in the page table.

Initially all bits are cleared by the operating system. As a user process executes the bit associated with each page referenced is set to 1 by the hardware. After some time we can determine which pages have been used and which have not been used by examining the reference bits. We do not know the order of use however, but we know which pages were used and which were not used.

Least frequently used algorithm

This algorithm is based on the locality of reference concept— the least frequently used page is not in the current locality. LFU requires that the page with the smallest count be replaced. The reason for this selection is that an actively used page should have a large reference count. This algorithm suffers from the situation in which a page is used heavily during the initial phase of a process, but then is never used again. Since it was used heavily it has a large count and remains in memory even though it is no longer needed. One solution is to shift the counts right by 1 bit at regular intervals, forming an exponentially decaying average user count.

Most Frequently Used

The MFU page replacement algorithm is based on the argument that the page with the smallest count was probably just brought in and has yet to be used; it will be in the locality that has just started.

Page Buffering Algorithm

The OS may keep a pool of free frames. When a page fault occurs a victim page is chosen as before. However the desired page is read into a free frame from the pool before the victim is written out. This allows the process to restart as soon as possible, without waiting for the victim to be written out. When the victim is later written out, its frame is added to the free frame pool. Thus a process in need can be given a frame quickly and while victims are selected, free frames are added to the pool in the background

An expansion of this idea is to maintain a list of modified pages. Whenever the paging device is idle, a modified page is selected and is written to disk. Its modify bit is then reset. This scheme increases the probability that a page will be clean when it is selected for replacement and will not need to be written out.

Another modification is to keep a pool of free frames, but to remember which page was in which frame. Since the frame contents are not modified when a frame is written to disk, the old page can be reused directly from the free-frame pool if it is needed before that frame is reused. No I/O is needed in this case. When a page fault occurs we check whether the desired page is in the free-frame pool. If it is not we must select a free frame and read into it. This method is used together with FIFO replacement in the VAX/VMS operating system.

Stack Replacement Algorithms

These are a class of page replacement algorithms with the following property:

Set of pages in the main memory with n frames is a subset of the set of pages in memory with n+1 frames.

These algorithms do not suffer from Belady's Anomaly. An example is the LRU algorithm.

Consider the following example which shows that LRU does not suffer from Belady's anomaly for the given reference string.

- Number of frames allocated = 3
- Reference string: 1, 2, 3, 4, 1, 2, 5, 1, 2, 3, 4, 5
- Number of page faults = 10

1	1	1	4	4	4	5	3	3	3
	2	2	2	1	1	1	1	4	4
		3	3	3	2	2	2	2	5

- Number of frames allocated = 4
- Reference string: 1, 2, 3, 4, 1, 2, 5, 1, 2, 3, 4, 5
- Number of page faults = 8

1	1	1	1	1	1	1	5
	2	2	2	2	2	2	2
		3	3	5	5	4	4
			4	4	3	3	3

The Working Set Model

In the purest form of paging, processes are started up with none of their pages in memory. As soon as the CPU tries to fetch the first instruction, it gets a page fault, causing the operating system to bring in the page containing the first instruction. Other page faults for global variables and the stack usually follow quickly. After a while, the process has most of the pages it needs and settles down to run with relatively few page faults. This strategy is called demand paging because pages are loaded only on demand, not in advance.

Of course, it is easy enough to write a test program that systematically reads all the pages in a large address space, causing so many page faults that there is not enough memory to hold them all. Fortunately, most processes do not work this way. They exhibit a locality of reference, meaning that during any phase of execution, the process references only a relatively small fraction of its pages. Each pass of a multipass compiler, for example, references only a fraction of the pages, and a different fraction at that.

The set of pages that a process is currently using is called its working. If the entire working set is in memory, the process will run without causing many faults until it moves into another execution phase (e.g., the next pass of the compiler). If the available memory is too small to hold the entire working set, the process will cause numerous page faults and run slowly since executing an instruction takes a few nanoseconds and reading in a page from the disk typically takes 10 milliseconds. At a rate of one or two instructions per 10 milliseconds, it will take ages to finish. A program causing page faults every few instructions is said to be thrashing.

In a multiprogramming system, processes are frequently moved to disk (i.e., all their pages are removed from memory) to let other processes have a turn at the CPU. The question arises of what to do when a process is brought back in again. Technically, nothing need be done. The process will just cause page faults until its working set has been loaded. The problem is that having 20, 100, or even 1000 page faults every time a process is loaded is slow, and it also wastes considerable CPU time, since it takes the operating system a few milliseconds of CPU time to process a page fault, not to mention a fair amount of disk I/O.

Therefore, many paging systems try to keep track of each process' working set and make sure that it is in memory before letting the process run. This approach is called the working set model (Denning, 1970). It is designed to greatly reduce the page fault rate. Loading the pages before letting processes run is also called prepaging. Note that the working set changes over time.

It has long been known that most programs do not reference their address space uniformly Instead the references tend to cluster on a small number of pages. A memory reference may fetch an instruction, it may fetch data, or it may store data. At any instant of time, t, there exists a set consisting of all the pages used by the k most recent memory references. This set, w(k, t), is the working set. Because a larger value of k means looking further into the past, the number of pages counted as part of the working set cannot decrease as k is made larger. So w(k, t) is a monotonically nondecreasing function of k. The limit of w(k, t) as k becomes large is finite because a program cannot reference more pages than its address space contains, and few programs will use every single page. Figure depicts the size of the working set as a function of k.

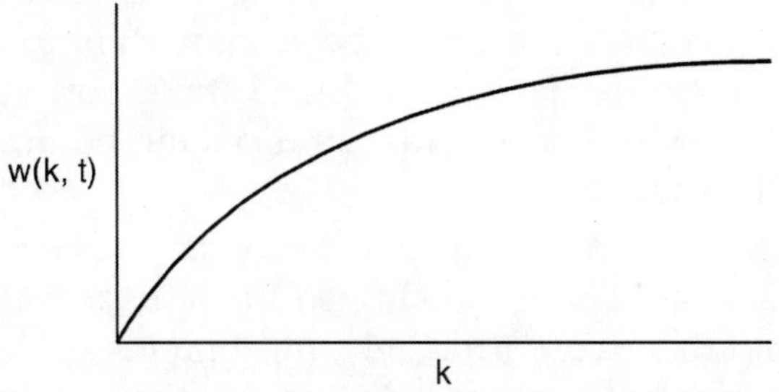

Figure : The working set is the set of pages used by the k most recent memory references. The function w(k, t) is the size of the working set at time t.

Figure. The working set is the set of pages used by the k most recent memory references. The function w(k, t) is the size of the working set at time t.

The fact that most programs randomly access a small number of pages, but that this set changes slowly in time explains the initial rapid rise of the curve and then the slow rise for large k. For example, a program that is executing a loop occupying two pages using data on four pages, may reference all six pages every 1000 instructions, but the most recent reference to some other page may be a million instructions earlier, during the initialization phase.

Due to this asymptotic behavior, the content of the working set is not sensitive to the value of k chosen. To put it differently, there exists a wide range of k values for which the working set is unchanged. Because the working set varies slowly with time, it is possible to make a reasonable guess as to which pages will be needed when the program is restarted on the basis of its working set when it was last stopped. Prepaging consists of loading these pages before the process is allowed to run again.

To implement the working set model, it is necessary for the operating system to keep track of which pages are in the working set. Having this information also immediately leads to a possible page replacement algorithm: when a page fault occurs, find a page not in the working set and evict it. To implement such an algorithm, we need a precise way of determining which pages are in the working set and which are not at any given moment in time.

As we mentioned above, the working set is the set of pages used in the k most recent memory references (some authors use the k most recent page references, but the choice is arbitrary). To implement any working set algorithm, some value of k must be chosen in advance. Once some value has been selected, after every memory reference, the set of pages used by the previous k memory references is uniquely determined.

Of course, having an operational definition of the working set does not mean that there is an efficient way to monitor it in real time, during program execution. One could imagine a shift register of length k, with every memory reference shifting the register left one position and inserting the most recently referenced page number on the right. The set of all k page numbers in the shift register would be the working set. In theory, at a page fault, the contents of the shift register could be read out and sorted. Duplicate pages could then be removed. The result would be the working set. However, maintaining the shift register and processing it at a page fault would both be prohibitively expensive, so this technique is never used. Instead, various approximations are used. One commonly used approximation is to drop the idea of counting back k memory references and use execution time instead.

For example, instead of defining the working set as those pages used dur- ing the previous 10 million memory references, we can define it as the set of pages used during the past 100 msec of execution time. In practice, such a defini- tion is just as good and much easier to use. Note that for each process, only its own execution time counts. Thus if a process starts running at time T and has had

40 msec of CPU time at real time T + 100 msec, for working set purposes, its time is 40 msec. The amount of CPU time a process has actually used has since it started is often called its current virtual time. With this approximation, the working set of a process is the set of pages it has referenced during the past ô seconds of virtual time.

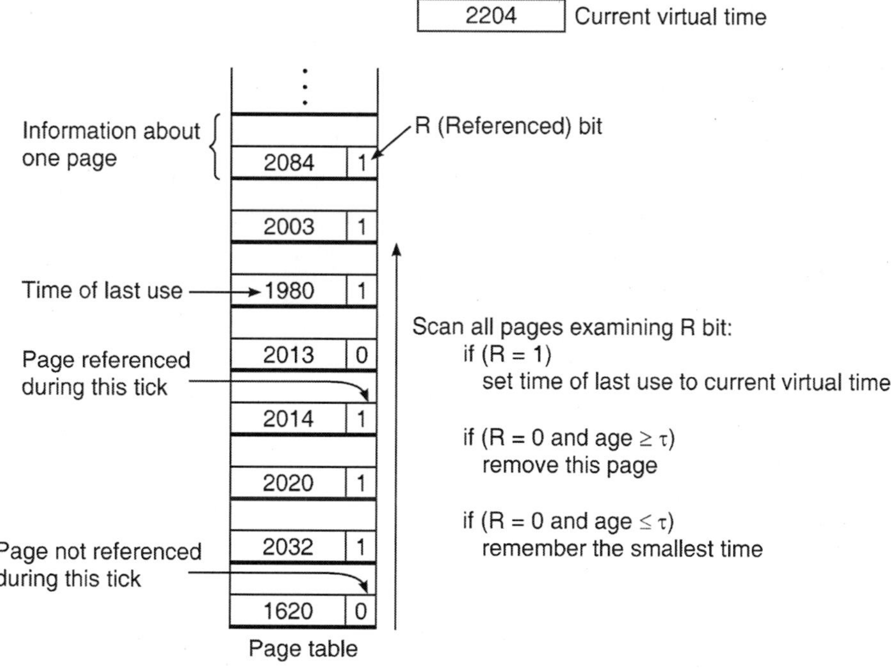

Now let us look at a page replacement algorithm based on the working set. The basic idea is to find a page that is not in the working set and evict it. In Fig-6 we see a portion of a page table for some machine. Because only pages that are in memory are considered as candidates for eviction, pages that are absent from memory are ignored by this algorithm. Each entry contains (at least) two items of information: the approximate time the page was last used and the R (Referenced) bit. The empty white rectangle symbolizes the other fields not needed for this algorithm, such as the page frame number, the protection bits, and the M (Modified) bit.

The working set algorithm

The algorithm works as follows. The hardware is assumed to set the R and M bits, as we have discussed before. Similarly, a periodic clock interrupt is assumed to cause software to run that clears the Referenced bit on every clock tick. On every page fault, the page table is scanned to look for a suitable page to evict.

As each entry is processed, the R bit is examined. If it is 1, the current virtual time is written into the Time of last use field in the page table, indicating that the page was in use at the time the fault occurred. Since the page has been referenced during the current clock tick, it is clearly in the working set and is not a candidate for removal (ô is assumed to span multiple clock ticks).

If R is 0, the page has not been referenced during the current clock tick and may be a candidate for removal. To see whether or not it should be removed, its age, that is, the current virtual time minus its Time of last use is computed and compared to ô. If the age is greater than ô, the page is no longer in the working set. It is reclaimed and the new page loaded here. The scan continues updating the remaining entries, however.

However, if R is 0 but the age is less than or equal to ô, the page is still in the working set. The page is temporarily spared, but the page with the greatest age (smallest value of Time of last use) is noted. If the entire table is scanned without finding a candidate to evict, that means that all pages are in the working set. In that case, if one or more pages with R = 0 were found, the one with the greatest age is evicted. In the worst case, all pages have been referenced during the current clock tick (and thus all have R = 1), so one is chosen at random for removal, preferably a clean page, if one exists.

The WSClock Page Replacement Algorithm

The basic working set algorithm is cumbersome since the entire page table has to be scanned at each page fault until a suitable candidate is located. An improved algorithm, that is based on the clock algorithm but also uses the work- ing set information is called WSClock (Carr and Hennessey, 1981). Due to its simplicity of implementation and good performance, it is widely used in practice. The data structure needed is a circular list of page frames, as in the clock algorithm, and as shown in Fig. (a). Initially, this list is empty. When the first page is loaded, it is added to the list. As more pages are added, they go into the list to form a ring. Each entry contains the Time of last use field from the basic working set algorithm, as well as the R bit (shown) and the M bit (not shown).

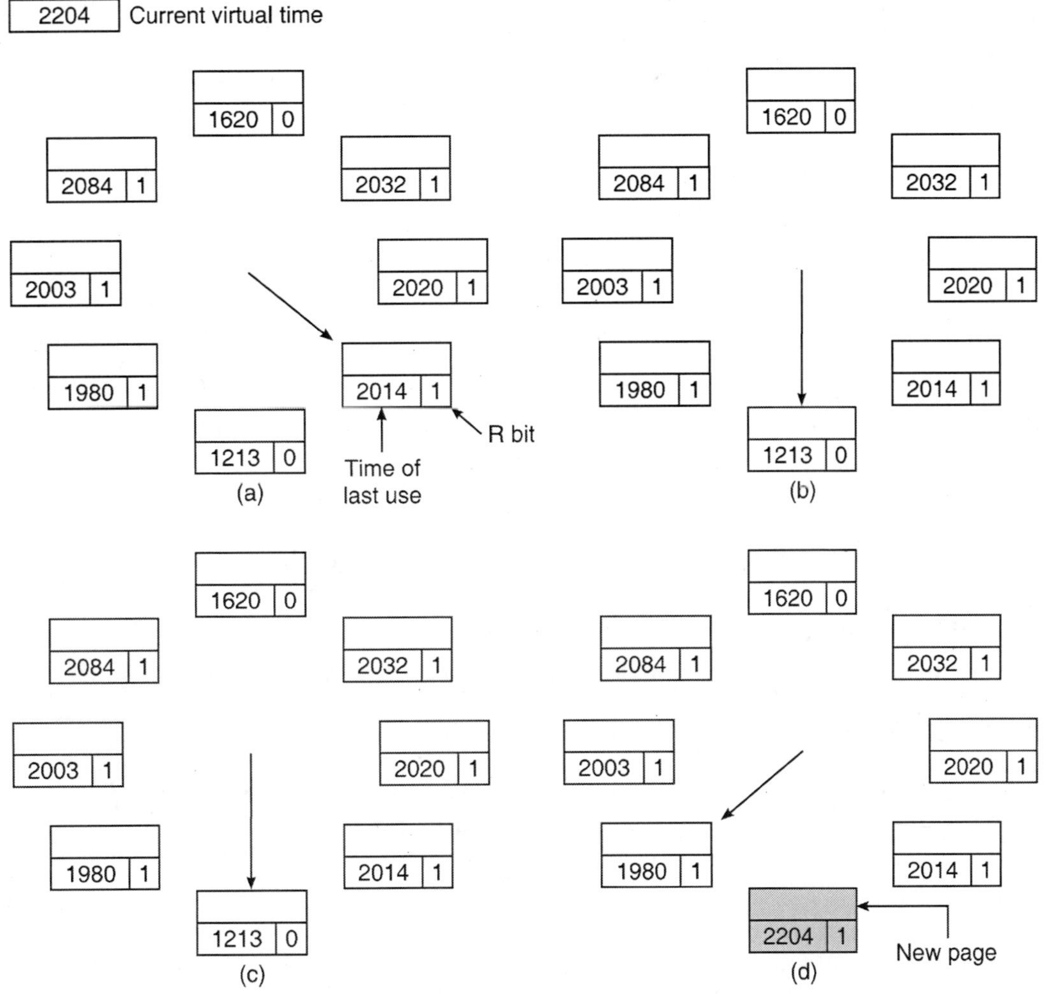

Figure : Operation of the WS Clock algorithm. (a) and (b) give an example of what happens when R = 1. (c) and (d) given an example of R = 0.

As with the clock algorithm, at each page fault the page pointed to by the hand is examined first. If the R bit is set to 1, the page has been used during the current tick so it is not an ideal candidate to remove. The R bit is then set to 0, the hand advanced to the next page, and the algorithm repeated for that page. The state after this sequence of events is shown in Fig (b).

Now consider what happens if the page pointed to has R = 0, as shown in Fig. If the age is greater than ? and the page is clean, it is not in the work- ing set and a valid copy exists on the disk. The page frame is simply claimed and the new page put there, as shown in Fig (d). On the other hand, if the page is dirty, it cannot be claimed immediately since no valid copy is present on disk. To avoid a process switch, the write to disk is scheduled, but the hand is advanced and the algorithm continues with the next page. After all, there might be an old, clean page further down the line that can be used immediately.

In principle, all pages might be scheduled for disk I/O on one cycle around the clock. To reduce disk traffic, a limit might be set, allowing a maximum of n pages to be written back. Once this limit has been reached, no new writes are scheduled.

What happens if the hand comes all the way around to its starting point? There are two cases to distinguish:

1. At least one write has been scheduled.
2. No writes have been scheduled.

In the former case, the hand just keeps moving, looking for a clean page. Since one or more writes have been scheduled, eventually some write will complete and its page will be marked as clean. The first clean page encountered is evicted. This page is not necessarily the first write scheduled because the disk driver may reorder writes in order to optimize disk performance.

In the latter case, all pages are in the working set, otherwise at least one write would have been scheduled. Lacking additional information, the simplest thing to do is claim any clean page and use it. The location of a clean page could be kept track of during the sweep. If no clean pages exist, then the current page is chosen and written back to disk.

Local vs. Global Replacement

If process P generates a page fault, page can be selected in two ways:

- Select for replacement one of its frames.
- Select for replacement a frame from a process with lower priority number.

Global replacement allows a process to select a replacement frame from the set of all frames, even if that frame belongs to some other process; one process can take a frame from another. Local replacement requires that each process select from only its allocated frames.

Consider an allocation scheme where we allow high priority processes to select frames from low priority processes for replacement. A process can select a replacement from among its own frames or the frames of any lower priority process. This approach allows a high priority process to increase its frame allocation at the expense of the low priority process.

Summary of Page Replacement Algorithms

Algorithm	Comment
Optimal	Not implementable, but useful as a benchmark
NRU (Not Recently Used)	Very crude
FIFO (First-In, First-Out)	Might throw out important pages
Second chance	Big improvement over FIFO
Clock	Realistic
LRU (Least Recently Used)	Excellent, but difficult to implement exactly
NFU (Not Frequently Used)	Fairly crude approximation to LRU
Aging	Efficient algorithm that approximates LRU well
Working set	Somewhat expensive to implement
WSColock	Good efficient algorithm

More on Page replacement

In a multiprogramming environment, almost all programs use probably half of their size. For example, a program of 10 pages actually uses only 5 pages. The demand paging mechanism saves the I/O time necessary to load the fives pages which are never used. In this case, the degree of multiprogramming should be increased.

Increasing the degree of multiprogramming may lead to the situation where *over allocation* memory could occur. This can be explained as follow. If a page fault trap occurs, the operating system checks the internal page table and determines where the desired page is on the disk, but finds there are no more free frames for these required pages which should be swapped in.

To solve this problem, the operating system has some options:

- either it terminates the user program immediately; or
- it swaps out one program, frees all of its frames and by that way reduces the degree of multiprogramming.

Page replacement is another possibility which can be explained in the following. It frees one frame which is not currently used by writing its content to the disk, changing the page table to indicate this page is no longer in memory. The freed frame can now be used to hold the page for which the program faulted. The page fault processing procedure can be modified to include the page replacement mechanism:

- Find the location of the desired page on the disk;
- Find a free frame: if there is a free frame, uses it; otherwise uses a page-replacement algorithm to select a frame; writes the selected page to the disk and changes the page and frame tables accordingly;
- Read the desired page into the newly free frame; change the page and frame tables;
- Restart the user process.

If there is no free frame, i.e., the page replacement mechanism takes place, two page transfers are carried out. This doubles the page fault processing time and therefor increases the effective access time.

In order to reduce this overhead, the *modify* bit can be used. Each page or frame owns a modify bit. Setting this bit to 1 indicates that the associated page has been modified since it was read from the disk. So, when we select a page for replacement, we check its modify bit first. If this bit is set, we must write this page to the disk before use it for swapping in the desired page. Otherwise, we can avoid writing this page to the disk (if the copy of the page on the disk has not been overwritten by some other pages).

Allocation of frames

Normally, there are fixed amounts of free memory with various processes at different time in a system. The question is how this fixed amount of free memory is allocated among the different processes.

The simplest case is the single process system. All available memory for user programs can initially be put on the free frame list (pure demand paging). When the user program starts its execution, it will generate a sequence of page faults. The user program would get all free frames from the free frame list. As soon as this list was exhausted and the more free frames are required, the page replacement algorithm can be used to select one of the in-used pages to be replaced with the next required page, and so on. After the program was terminated, all used pages are put on the free frame list again.

The frame allocation procedure is more complicated when there are two or more programs in memory at the same time.

Minimum Number of Frames

Of course, we can not allocate more than the total number of available frames in the system. On the other hand, there is a minimum number of frames which must be allocated. This minimum number is determined by the instruction architecture. It is obvious, that we must provide enough frames to hold all the different pages that any single instruction can reference. For example, all memory reference instructions of a machine have only one memory address. So we need at least one frame for the instruction code and one frame for the memory reference. If one level indirect addressing is allowed, for example, a load instruction on page m can refer to an address on page j which is an indirect reference to page k, then we need three pages.

Algorithms

The simplest way is to divide m available frames among n processes to give everyone an equal share, m/n frames. This is called *equal allocation*. Various processes will need different amounts of memory. If the equal allocation is applied, there can be some frames wasted. Therefore, other allocation scheme can be used to give available memory to each process according to its size. This is called *proportional allocation*. Let the size of the virtual memory for process *pi* be *si*, the number of frames allocated to the process *pi* be *ai*, and define

$$S = S \ si$$

If the total number of available frames is *m*, then *ai* can be approximately calculated:

$$ai = (si/S) * m.$$

Of course *ai* must be adjust to be a integer, greater than the minimum number of frames required by the instruction set with a sum not exceeding *m*.

In both of theses cases, the number of frames allocated to each process may vary according to the multiprogramming level, say *l*. If *l* increases, each process will lose some of the allocated frames to provide memory needed for the new process. Otherwise, the frames allocated to the departed process can be now spread over the remaining processes.

Within these two allocation schemes, a high-priority process is treated the same as low-priority process. By its definition, it's desirable to give the high-priority process more memory to speed up its execution, to the detriment of low-priority processes.

Thrashing

If the number of frames allocated to a low-priority process falls below the minimum number defined by the computer architecture, the operating system must suspend it's execution by swapping all of its pages, freeing all of its allocated frames.

If a process does not have enough frames, it will very quickly have page fault. At this point, it must replace some page. Since all of its pages are in use, it must replace a page which will be needed again. Consequently, it very quickly faults again and again and so on. This very high paging activity is called *thrashing*. A process is thrashing if it spends more time for paging than for executing. Thrashing phenomena may cause several performance problems. We explain it in the following example.

The operating system monitors the CPU utilization: if it is low, the degree of multiprogramming is increased by introducing a new process to the system. Suppose a process needs more frames for its execution. It starts to page fault and to take pages from other processes. These processes need those pages, so they also start to fault and to take pages from other processes, and so on. The faulting processes must use the paging device for swapping in and out, so they are queued for the paging device. As result, the ready queue is empty, i.e., the CPU utilization decreases further.

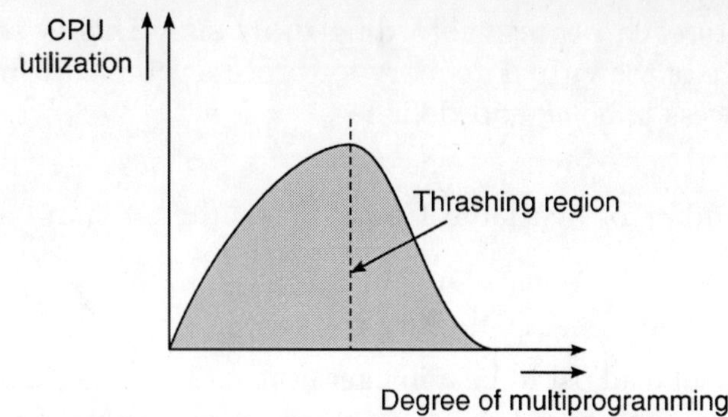

Thrashing and its impact on the system performance

The process scheduler finds the decreasing CPU utilization, and increases the degree multiprogramming. The new process tries to take pages from running processes, causing more page faults, and longer queue for the paging device. The CPU utilization drops further, so that the scheduler tries to increase the degree of multiprogramming even more: thrashing occurs and the system "breaks down" as shown in the Figure.

The thrashing effect can be limited by a *local replacement scheme*. Within the local replacement, if a process starts thrashing, it can not take frames from another process and so cause it to thrash also. Because thrashing processes are in waiting queue for paging device most of the time, the average processing time for a page fault increases. By this way, the effective access time will increase even for processes that are not thrashing.

The thrashing effect can be prevented if a process is allocated as many frames as it needs. The question is how to determine the number of frames a process really needs. One of the possible techniques is the *working set strategy* which is looking at what a process is actually using and then deciding how many frames should be allocated. The main goal of this approach is greatly to reduce the page fault rate.

Controlled thrashing

If the total memory pressure exerted on the system is greater than the total available physical memory then the memory manager decreases the degree of multiprogramming. If the total memory pressure is less than the total available physical memory then the memory manager increases the degree of multiprogramming.

How can we measure the WSS of a process? One approximate method uses the reference bits associated with the physical frames. Periodically say every Ä time units, a daemon wakes up and samples the reference bits of the physical frames assigned to a process. The daemon records the pages with the reference bits turned on and clears the reference bits. This recoding of the reference bits allows the memory manager to determine the working set and the WSS for a given process for any interval *t* and *t* + Ä.

Another simple method of controlling thrashing is to use the observed page fault rate as a measure of thrashing. The memory manager sets two markers, a *low water mark*, and a *high water mark* for page faults (See Figure). An observed page fault rate that exceeds the high water mark implies excessive paging. In this case, the memory manager reduces the degree of multiprogramming. On the other hand, an observed page fault rate that is lower than the low water mark presents an opportunity for the memory manager to increase the degree of multiprogramming.

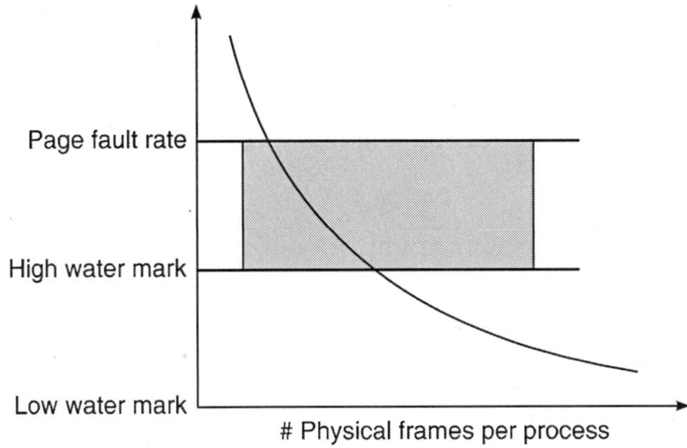

The shaded region in Figure shows the preferred sweet spot of operation for the memory manager. The paging daemon kicks in to increase the pool of free physical frames when the page fault rate goes higher than the high water mark, decreasing the degree of multiprogramming, if necessary.

Inverted page tables

Since the virtual memory is usually much larger than physical memory, some architectures (such as the IBM Power processors) use an *inverted page table*, essentially a frame table. The inverted page table alleviates the need for a per-process page table. Further, the size of the table is equal to the size of the physical memory (in frames) rather than virtual memory. Unfortunately, inverted page tables complicate the logical to physical address translation done by the hardware.

Therefore, in such processors the hardware handles address translations through the TLB mechanism. Upon a TLB miss, the hardware hands over control (through a trap) to the operating system to resolve the translation in software. The operating system is responsible for updating the TLB as well. The architecture usually provides special instructions for reading, writing, and flushing the TLB entries in privileged mode.

MEMORY PROTECTION

This unit of memory management addresses the topics related to memory like protected memory, infinite amount of memory, and transparent sharing.

Perhaps the simplest model for using memory is to provide ***uniprogramming without memory protection***, where each application runs with a hardwired range of physical memory addresses. Given that a uniprogramming environment allows only one application to run at a time, an application can use the same physical addresses every time, even across reboots. Typically, applications use the lower memory addresses (***low memory***), and an operating system uses the higher memory addresses (***high memory***). An application can address any physical memory location.

Application	Operating System
000000	ffffff

Physical memory

One step beyond the uniprogramming model is to provide ***multiprogramming without memory protection***. When a program is copied into memory, a ***linker-loader*** alters the code of the program (loads, stores, jumps) to use the address of where the program lands in memory. In this environment, bugs in any program can cause other programs to crash, even the operating system.

Application1	**Application2**	Operating System
000000	200000	ffffff

Physical memory

The third model is to have a *multiprogrammed operating system with memory protection*. *Memory protection* keeps user programs from crashing one another and the operating system. Typical memory protection is achieved by two hardware-supported mechanisms: (1) address translation and (2) dual mode operation.

Address Translation

Recall that each process is associated with an ***address space***, or all the *physical* addresses a process can touch. However, from the viewpoint of each process, it believes that it owns the entire memory, with the starting *virtual* address of 0. The missing piece is a translation table that translates every memory reference from virtual addresses to physical addresses.

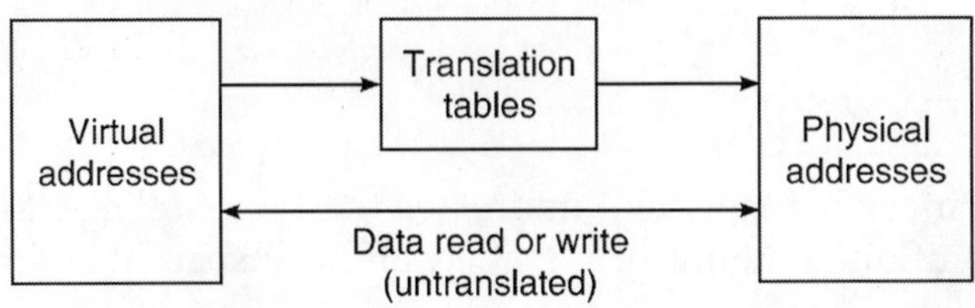

Translation provides protection because there is no way for a process to talk about other processes' addresses. Also, a process has no way of touching the code or data under the operating system. The operating system uses physical addresses directly, and involves no translation.

Dual-Mode Operation Revisited

Translation tables can offer protection only if an application cannot alter their content. Therefore, a user application is restricted to only touching its address space under the user mode. Hardware requires the CPU to be in the kernel mode to modify the address translation tables.

Although we have mentioned this dual-mode operation previously, we have not addressed two details: (1) how the CPU is shared between the kernel and user programs, and (2) how programs interact among themselves.

Switching from the Kernel to User Mode

A CPU changes from the kernel to the user mode when starting a program. To run a user program, the kernel performs the following steps:

(1) Creates a process
(2) Initializes the address space
(3) Loads the program into the memory
(4) Initializes translation tables
(5) Sets the hardware pointer to the translation table
(6) Sets the CPU to user mode
(7) Jumps to the entry point of the program.

Switching from the User to Kernel Mode

A CPU can change from the user to kernel mode either through voluntary or involuntary mechanisms. The voluntary mechanism is through the use of *system calls*, where a user application asks the operating system to do something on the user's behalf. A system call passes arguments to an operating system either through registers or copying from the user memory to the kernel memory.

A CPU can also be switched from the user to kernel mode involuntarily by *hardware interrupts* (e.g., I/O) and *program exceptions* (e.g., segmentation fault).

On system calls, interrupts, or exceptions, hardware atomically performs the following steps:

(1) Sets the CPU to kernel mode
(2) Saves the current program counter
(3) Jumps to the handler in the kernel (the handler saves old register values)

Unlike threads, context switching among processes also involves saving and restoring pointers to translation tables. To resume the process execution, the kernel reloads old register values, sets the CPU to user mode, and jumps to the old program counter.

Communication among Address Spaces

Since address spaces do not share memory, processes have to perform *inter-process communication* (*IPC*) through the kernel. Common IPC mechanisms include the followings:

- Byte stream (e.g., communicate through pipes connecting stdin/stdout)
- Message passing (send/receive)
- File system (e.g., read and write files)

Alternatively, on most UNIX platforms, a process can ask the kernel to set up an address space to be shared among processes. This invention also provides a cheap way to simulate threads on systems that do not support them.

In all cases, once you allow communication, bugs can propagate from one program to another.

Protection without Hardware Support

Hardware-supported protection can be prohibitively slow, since applications have to be structured to run in separate address spaces to achieve fault isolation. In the cases of complex applications built by multiple vendors (e.g., Netscape plug-ins), it may be desirable for two different programs to run in the same address space, with guarantees that they can't trash each other's code or data. Two approaches are strong typing and software fault isolation.

Protection via Strong Typing

If a programming language disallows the misuse of data structures, one cannot express a program that would trash another program, even in the same address space. Some examples are LISP and Java.

In Java, programs can be downloaded over the net and run safely because the language, compiler, and runtime system prevents the program from doing bad things (e.g., make system calls). Java also defines a separate virtual machine layer, so a Java program can run on different hardware and operating systems. The downside of this protection mechanism is the requirement to learn a new language.

Protection via Software Fault Isolation

A language-independent approach is to have compilers generate code that is provenly safe (e.g., a pointer cannot reference illegal addresses).

For example, a pointer can be checked before it is used.

Original instruction	Compiler-modified version
st r2, (r1)	Assert safe is a legal address Copy r1 into safe Check safe is still legal st r2, (safe)

By adding the extra checking code, a malicious user cannot just jump to the st r2, (safe) to bypass the check, since safe always holds a legal address. With aggressive compiler optimizations, this approach may induce performance overhead as low as 5%.

CASE STUDIES: Windows Memory Management

The Windows virtual memory manager control shows how memory is allocated and how paging is performed. The memory manager is designed to operate a variety of platforms and use page sizes ranging form 4 Kbytes to 64 Kbytes.

Windows Virtual Address Map

Each windows user process sees a separate 32-bit address space, allowing 4 Gbytes of memory per process. Each user process can have 4 G Byte of memory, but by default it is divided and each user has 2 GByte and the remaining 2 GByte is reserved for operating system. All the processes share the same 2 Gbytes of system space.

Windows Paging

When a process is created it can make use of the whole space (2 Gbytes). This space is divided into fixed-sizes pages any of which can be brought into main memory. In practice, a page can be in any of the following states:

- **Available:** Pages not currently used by any process.
- **Reserved:** A set of contiguous pages that virtual memory manager set aside for a process but dose not count against its quota of allocation until it is used. Therefore, when a process needs to write to memory some of it can be committed to the process.
- **Committed:** Pages for which the virtual memory manager has set aside space in its paging file.

  Reserved and committed memory concept is useful as firstly it minimizes the amount of disk space set aside for a particular process, keeping that disk space free for others and secondly enables a thread or process to declare an amount of memory that can quickly be allocated as desired.

EXAMPLE: A process has four page frames allocated to it. (All the following numbers are decimal, and everything is numbered starting form zero). The time of the last loading of a page into each page frame, the time of last access to the page in each page frame, the virtual page number in each page frame, and the modified (M) bit (use bit) for each page frame are as shown in the following table (the times are in clock ticks from the process start time 0 to the event – not the number of ticks since the event to the present).

Virtual page number	Page frame	Time loaded	Time last referenced	M bit
2	0	60	161	1
1	1	130	160	0
0	2	26	162	0
3	3	20	163	1

A page fault to virtual page 4 has occurred. Which page frame will have its contents replaced for each of the following memory management policies?

a) FIFO (first-in-first-out).

b) LRU (least recently used).

c) Clock.

Solution:

a. FIFO: In this scheme, the page that has been in memory the longest is replaced. In the given example virtual page 3 has been in the memory longest (loaded at time 20), and the content of page frame 3 should be replaced.

b. LRU: This policy replaces the page in memory that has not been referenced recently (longest time). In the given example virtual page number 1 has been referenced at time 160 that is the lowest referenced time. Hence, the content of page frame 1 should be replaced.

c. CLOCK: Last loaded page frame is 1, so pointer is set to next page frame, that is page frame 2 in that case. Since reference bit (R) is one, it is set to zero and pointer moves to the next page frame. When pointer is on page frame 0, the content of page frame 0 should be replaced since the use bit (R) is 0.

Windows NT

This microsoft OS uses demand paging with clustering. Clustering brings in pages surrounding the faulting page, in much the same way as a cache controller loads in memory lines surrounding a cache miss.

- Each process is assigned a working set minimum and maximum.
- The minimum number of pages appears to be a firm minimum and, as Silberschatz does not mention any process swap out option when this lower bound is passed, it appears possible that the process launch algorithm must be conservative (e.g. no over committing).
- Processes may be allowed to exceed their maximum number of pages if memory is available. Any excess will be reclaimed if needed.

Solaris 2

Solaris 2 maintains a reserve of free pages so that threads with page faults can obtain extra memory quickly.

- It also has a pageout process that is triggered whenever free memory falls below a threshold called lotsfree (default value = 1/64 of the physical memory).
- The pageout process scans memory searching for pages to copy out to backing store.

A two-handed-clock algorithm is employed to detect memory that is not currently in used. The "first hand" of the clock scans all pages in memory setting a reference bit to 0. At a later time, the "second hand" of the clock examines the reference bit, returning any page with its reference bit still =0 to the free page list.

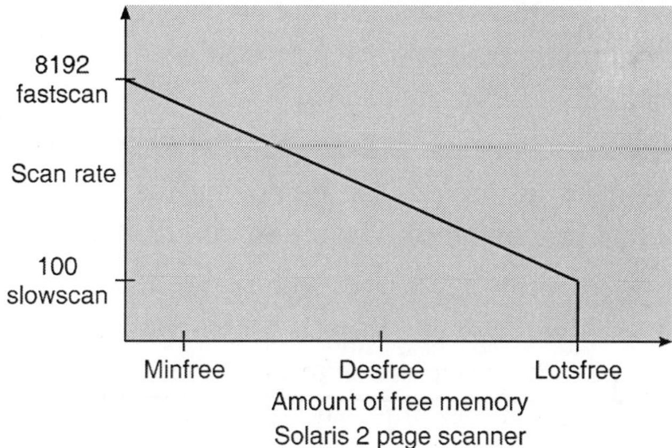

Solaris 2 page scanner

Scanrate is the rate at which pages are scanned by the two "hand clocks". The minimum scan rate is slowscan = 100 pages/second and the maximum scan rate is fastscan = 8192 pages/second. Figure 51 shows how scanrate is related linearly to free memory. The handspread is the number of pages that the inspection (second) scan trails the reference bit set (first) scan.

Pageout is called more frequently depending upon the amount of free memory available. If the pageout process cannot maintain a minimum desired free memory desfree for a period of 30 seconds, the kernel commences swapping out processes.

KEYWORDS

VIRTUAL MEMORY	SECOND CHANCE
OVERLAY	CLOCK
DEMAND PAGING	LRU
FIFO	NFU
OPTIMAL	WORKING SET
NRU	WSCLOCK

SUMMARY

Virtual memory is a technique that solves the problem of limited memory by providing each process with a virtual address space, potentially larger than the system's physical address space, which the process uses to access data and instructions

- Address generated by CPU are commonly referred to as logical addresses (virtual address), whereas addresses loaded into memory address register are commonly referred to as physical addresses.
- The overlay is the technique of dividing a program into pieces that were used at different times during the course of executing the program.
- Demand paging introduces the concept of loading only a part of the program into memory for processing. When a process begins to run, pages are brought into memory only as they are needed
- FIFO keeps track of the order pages were loaded into memory by keeping them in a linked list. Removing the oldest page then becomes trivial, but that page might still be in use, so FIFO is a bad choice.
- The optimal algorithm replaces the page referenced last among the current pages. Unfortunately, there is no way to determine which page will be last, so in practice this algorithm cannot be used. It is useful as a benchmark against which other algorithms can be measured, however.
- The NRU algorithm divides pages into four classes depending on the state of the R and M bits. A random page from the lowest numbered class is chosen. This algorithm is easy to implement, but it is very crude. Better ones exist.
- Second chance is a modification to FIFO that checks if a page is in use before removing it. If it is, the page is spared. This modification greatly improves the performance.
- Clock is simply a different implementation of second chance. It has the same performance properties, but takes a little less time to execute the algorithm.
- LRU is an excellent algorithm, but it cannot be implemented without special hardware. If this hardware is not available, it cannot be used.
- NFU is a crude attempt to approximate LRU. It is not very good. However, aging is a much better approximation to LRU and can be implemented efficiently. It is a good choice.

- The working set algorithm is reasonable performance, but it is somewhat expensive to implement.
- WSClock is a variant that not only gives good performance but is also efficient to implement.

REVIEW QUESTIONS

1) Explain segmentation memory management techniques?
2) Explain demand paged memory management techniques?
3) Explain segmentation with paging memory management techniques?
4) Explain virtual memory management techniques?
5) Explain following memory allocation strategies with example
   (a) First- fit
   (b) Best- fit
   (c) Worst- fit
6) Explain how address calculation is done segmentation?
7) Explain how to reduce memory overhead in paged system?
8) Explain how virtual memory is implemented using demand paging?
9) What is page fault and instruction restart?
10) Explain FIFO page replacement algorithm?
11) Explain LRU(least recently used)page replacement algorithm?
12) Explain OPTIMAL page replacement algorithm?
13) Explain CLOCK page replacement algorithm?
14) What is belady's anomaly which page replacement algorithm suffer from this?
15) Write short note on working set?
16) Write short note on translation look-aside buffer?
17) Write short note on memory overhead?

FILL IN THE BLANKS

1. ________________is a technique that solves the problem of limited memory by providing each process with a virtual address space, potentially larger than the system's physical address space

2. The ____________ is the technique of dividing a program into pieces that were used at different times during the course of executing the program.
3. ___________ introduces the concept of loading only a part of the program into memory for processing on demand.
4. Second chance is a modification to __________ that checks if a page is in use before removing it.
5. NFU is a crude attempt to approximate __________.
6. The ________ page replacement algorithm is based on the argument that the page with the smallest count was probably just brought in and has yet to be used.

TRUE OR FALSE

1. Clock is simply a different implementation of second chance.
2. Virtual memory is implemented with the help of demand paging.
3. FIFO is algorithm is based on the locality of reference concept
4. A *page replacement policy* determines which page will get evicted from its page frame when there's no free frame.
5. In demand paging, programs reside on a swapping device commonly known as the backing store.
6. Most of virtual memory systems use a technique called fragmentation.

ANSWERS

FILL IN THE BLANKS

1. Virtual memory
2. overlay
3. Demand paging
4. FIFO
5. LRU
6. MFU

TRUE OR FALSE

1. TRUE
2. TRUE
3. FALSE
4. FALSE
5. TRUE
6. FALSE

❑❑❑

UNIT-4
FILE AND DEVICE MANAGEMENT UNIT

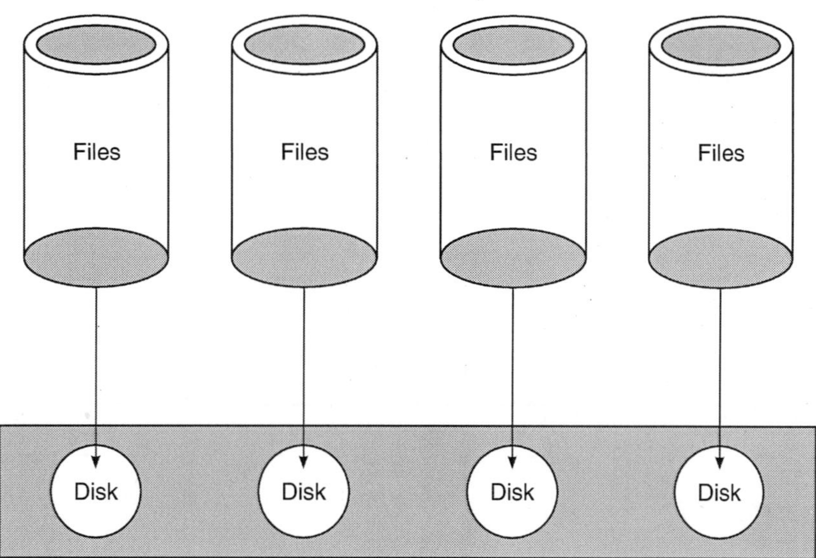

"Data is not information, Information is not knowledge, Knowledge is not understanding, Understanding is not wisdom"
—*Gary Schubert*

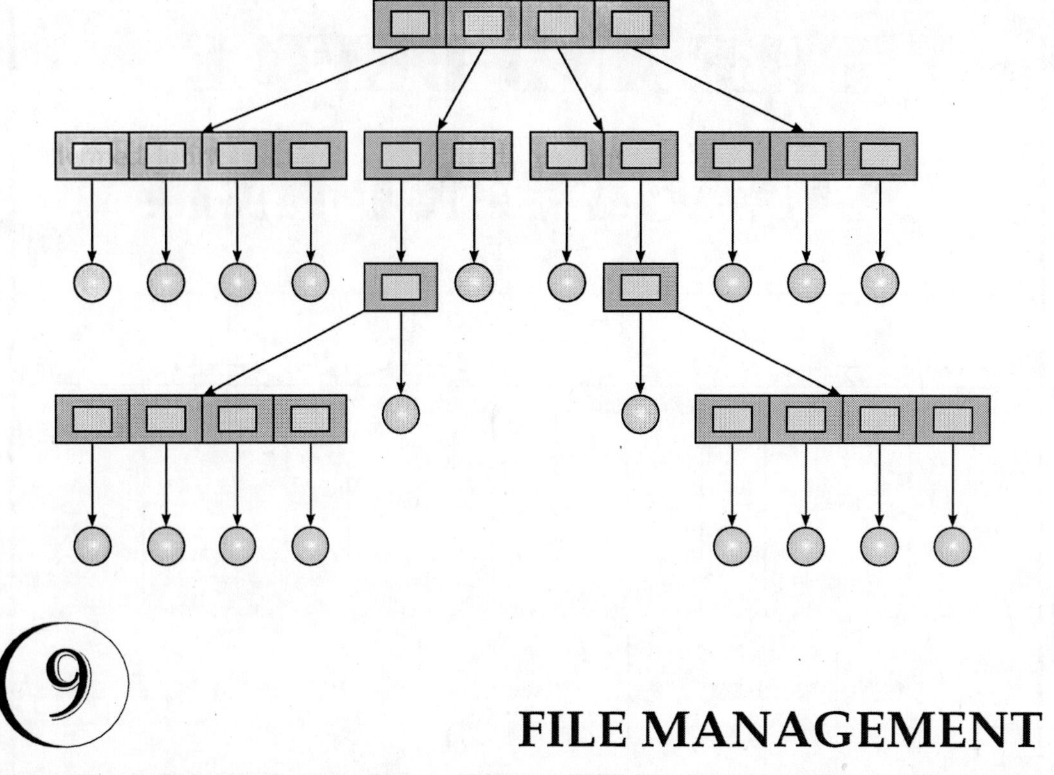

9 FILE MANAGEMENT

INTRODUCTION

Computers can store information on several different storage media, such as magnetic disks, magnetic tapes, and optical disks. So that the computer system will be convenient to use, the operating system provides a uniform logical view of information storage. The operating system abstracts from the physical properties of its storage devices to define a logical storage unit (the file). Files are mapped, by the operating system, onto physical devices. These storage devices are usually nonvolatile, so the contents are persistent through power failures and system reboots.

For most users, the file system is the most visible aspect of an operating system. Files store data and programs. The operating system implements the abstract concept of a file by managing mass storage devices, such as tapes and disks. In this chapter we consider the various ways to map files onto devices. Also files are normally organized into directories to ease their use, so we look at a variety of directory structures. Finally, when multiple users have access to files, it may be desirable to control by whom and in what ways files may be accessed. This control is known as file protection. Files are managed by the operating system. How they are structured, named, accessed, used, protected, and implemented are major topics in operating system design. As a whole, that part of the operating system dealing with files is known as the file system and is the subject of this chapter.

From the users' standpoint, the most important aspect of a file system is how it appears to them, that is, what constitutes a file, how files are named and protected, what operations are allowed on files, and so on. The details of whether linked lists or bitmaps are used to keep track of free storage and how many sectors there are in a logical block are of less interest, although they are of great importance to the designers of the file system.

What is file management?

A file management system is that set of system software that provides services to users and applications to support access to files.

This relieves the user or programmer of the need to develop special software for each application in order to control, manipulate and store data.

It is suggested that a file system should:

- Guarantee, as far as possible that data in files is valid and minimise potential for lost or corrupt data.
- optimise access and response times
- provide a standard set of interface routines for these devices and provide I/O support for a variety of storage devices (discs, CDs etc)
- support multiple user I/O (in multi-user systems
- In user terms this should mean something like the following:
- allow users to create delete, and modify files
- allow users controlled access to other users' files
- users should be able to control the access they allow to their files
- users should be able to structure and restructure their file store
- files should be able to be backed up and restored
- symbolic names should be used to access files.

In general files are sequential (one element of the file is accessible only after reading the previous element) or random (any element of the file can be accessed in any order) in organisation. In many ways their internal organisation reflects the type of processing that will be carried out on them. Data held as tables in a database will be held in some indexed way to improve access to all tables. Data for a word processing document may be organised in a sequential fashion.

However data is organized within a file the view that a user may have of their data and that of the file system may be different in several ways. For example users may see data as words, sentences and paragraphs whereas the system will see that data as streams of characters, blocks of data, and blocks on backing store. This view may go further and see the backing store as cylinders and sectors. The file management system's job is to see that data is stored safely, securely and is delivered to main memory in the most efficient way possible and written back to store when it is no longer being used. The File systems are usually built as a layer on top of the physical device drivers

For example: MS/DOS

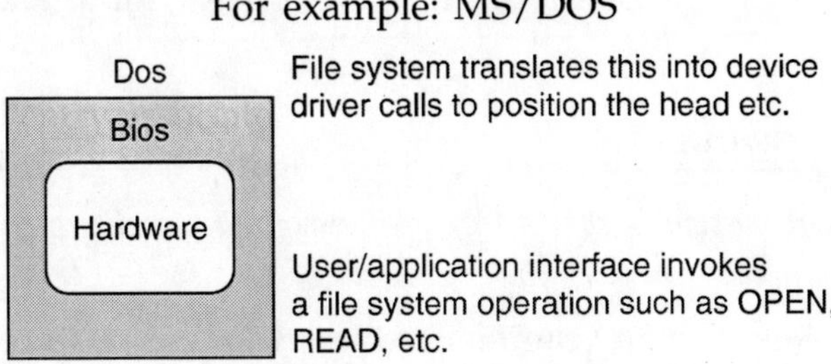

File Concept

File management is one of the most visible services of an operating system. Computers can store information in several different physical forms; magnetic tape, disk, and are the most common forms. Each of these devices has its own characteristics and physical organization.

For convenient use of the computer system, the operating system provides a uniform logical view of information storage. The operating system abstracts from the physical properties of its storage devices to define a logical storage unit, the file. Files are mapped by the operating system onto physical devices.

Consequently, a file is a collection of related information defined by its creator. Commonly, files represent programs (both source and object forms) and data. Data files may be numeric, alphabetic or alphanumeric. Files may be free form, such as text files, or may be rigidly formatted. In general, a file is a sequence of bits, bytes, lines or records whose meaning is defined by its creator and user. It is a very general concept.

File

The file is a **logical** unit of information storage. Usually, a given volume will contain many files; but it is possible to dedicate a single volume to a single large file or even to have one file spread out over multiple volumes. On a disk, a file is allocated some number of sectors when it is created, and there is generally provision to allow it to grow bigger or (more rarely) to grow smaller.

Records

A record is the **logical** subdivisions of a file. Files are typically structured into smaller units called records - e.g. lines of text, data on one employee, etc. Various record structures are possible:

1. **Fixed length records:**

   All the records of the file are of the same fixed size. This is common in many data processing applications.

2. **Variable length records:**

   Each record includes an indication of its actual size - frequently stored in the first few bytes of the record. This is useful for applications where the amount of information stored on an entity may vary widely - e.g. in a medical records system, one patient may have only been seen once, while another may have been seen several times per week for a long time.

3. **Stream records:**

   A variant of variable length records used with text files. Instead of beginning with a length indicator, each record ends with a special delimiter such as CR or LF. Word processing applications typically work with stream files.

Files may contain special information outside of the regular record structure - e.g. indexes, headers etc. We have seen that the disk is physically organized into sectors which are in turn grouped into tracks (cylinders). A file is logically organized into records. Rarely is it the case that the logical record size bears any direct relationship to the physical sector size. Thus, a single logical record may correspond to a single physical sector or block - possibly with significant wasted space (but access is convenient). Be one of several packed into a sector or block. If the logical record size does not divide equally into the sector/block size, then there may be wasted space at the end, or the last logical record may span into the next sector/block. It occupies two or more sectors, in whole or in part.

A file is named and is referred to by its name. It has certain other properties such as its type, the time of its creation, the name (or account number) of its creator, its length, and so on.

The information in a file is defined by its creator. Many different types of information may be stored in a file: source programs, object programs, numeric data, text, payroll records, and so on. A file has a certain defined *structure* according to its use. A text file is a sequence of characters organized into lines (and possibly pages); a source file is a sequence of subroutines and functions, each of which is further organized as declarations followed by executable statement; an object file is a sequence of words organized into loader record blocks.

One major consideration is how much of this structure should be known and supported by the operating system. If an operating system known the structure of a file, it can then operate on the file in reasonable ways. For example, a common mistake occurs when a use tries to print the binary object form of a program. This attempt normally produces garbage, but can be prevented if the operating system has been told that the file is a binary object program.

Often when the user attempts to execute an object program whose source file has been modified (edited) since the object file was produced; the source file will be recompiled automatically. This function ensures that the user always runs an up-to-date object file. Otherwise, the user could waste a significant amount of time executing the old object file. Notice that in order for this function to be possible, the operating system must be able to identify the source file from the object file, check the time that each file was last modified or created, and determine the language of the source program (in order to use the correct compiler).

A directory is a file (file system object) that groups together regular files, directories, and other files. Directories do not have any restriction on the amount of depletion they can contain, except that the total space on the volume cannot be exceeded. Space not used in the directory is available for use by other files and directories in the same volume.

Features of file

A file is a named collection of related information that is recorded on secondary storage. From a user's perspective, a file is the smallest allotment of logical secondary storage; that is, data cannot be written to secondary storage unless they are within a file.

1. Files represent programs (both source and object forms) and data. Data file may be numeric, alphabetic, alphanumeric, or binary. Files may be free form, such as text files, or may be formatted rigidly. In general, a file is a sequence of bits, bytes, lines, or records, the meaning of which is defined by the file's creator and user. The concept of a file is thus extremely general.
2. The information in a file is defined by its creator. Many different types of information may be stored in a file – source programs, object programs, executable programs, numeric data, text, payroll records, graphic images, sound recordings, and so on.
3. A file has a certain defined structure according to its type.

- A *text file* is a sequence of subroutines and functions, each of which is further organized as declaration followed by executable statements.

- An *object file* is a sequence of bytes organized into blocks understandable by the system's linker.
- An *executable file* is a series of code sections that the loader can bring into memory and execute.

There are disadvantages to having the operating system know the structure of a file. One problem is the resulting size of the operating system. If the operating system defined fourteen different file structures, it must then contain the code to support these file structures correctly. In addition, every file must be definable as one of the file types supported by the operating system. Severe problems may result from new applications that require information structured in ways not supported by the operating system.

For example, assume that a system supports two types of files: text files (composed of ASCII characters separated by a carriage return and line feed) and executable binary files. Now if we want to define an encrypted file to protect our files from being read by unauthorized people, we may find neither file type to be appropriate. The encrypted file is not ASCII text lines but (apparently) random bits. But though it may appear to be a binary file, it is not executable. As a result we may have so circumvent or misuse the operating system's file types mechanics, or modify or to impose (and support) no file type in the operating system.

This approach has been adopted in UNIX, among others. UNIX considers each file to be a sequence of 8-bit bytes; no interpretation of these bits is made by the operating system. This scheme provides maximum flexibility, but minimal support. Each application program must include its own code to interpret an input file into the appropriate structure.

Files are usually kept on disks. Disk systems typically have a well defined block size determined by the size of a sector. All disk I/O is in units of one block (physical record), and all blocks are the same size. It is unlikely that the physical record size will exactly match the length of the desired logical record. Logical records may even vary in length packing a number of logical records into physical blocks is a common solution to this problem.

The operating system often defined all files to be simply a stream of bytes. Each byte is individually addressable by its offset from the beginning (or end) of the file. In this case, the logical record is one byte. The file system automatically packs and unpacks bytes into physical disk blocks as necessary.

Knowledge of the logical record size, physical block size and packing technique determine how many logical records are packed into each physical block. The packing can be done either by the user's application program or by the operating system. In either case, the file may be considered to be a sequence of blocks. All of the basic I/O function operates in terms of blocks. The conversion from logical records to physical blocks is a relatively simple software problem.

Remember that allocating disk space in blocks means that, in general, some portion of the last block of each file may be wasted. If each block is 512 bytes, then a file of 1949 bytes would be allocated 4 blocks (2048bytes); the last 99 bytes would be wasted. The wasted bytes allocated to keep everything in units of blocks (instead of bytes) are internal fragmentation. All file systems suffer from internal fragmentation. In general, large block sizes cause more internal fragmentation.

File Operations

A file is an abstract data type. To define a file properly, we need to consider the operations which can be performed on files. System calls are provided to create, write, read, rewind, and delete files. To understand how file systems are supported, let us look at these five file operations in more detail.

For convenience, assume the file system is disk-based. Let us consider what the operating system must do for each of the five basic file operations. It should then be easy to see how similar operations, such as renaming a file, would be implemented.

- Creating a file.

  Two steps are necessary to create a file. First, space in the file system must be found for the file. Second, an entry for the new file must be made in the directory. The directory entry records the name of the file and its location in the file system.

- Writing a file.

  To write a file, a system call is made specifying both the name of the file and the information to be written to the file. Given the name of the file, the system searches the directory to find the location of the file. The directory entry will need to store a pointer to the current end of the file. Using this pointer, the address of the next block can be computed and the information can be written. The write pointer must be updated. In this way successive writes can be used to write a sequence of block to the file.

- Reading a File.

  To read from file, a system call specifies the name of the file and where in memory the next block of the file should be put. Again, the directory is searched for the associated directory entry. And again, the directory will need a pointer to the next block to be read. Once that block is read, the pointer is updated. In general, a file is either being read or written, thus although it would be possible to have two pointers, a read pointer and a write pointer, most systems have only one, a current file position. Both the read and write operations use this same pointer, saving space in the directory entry, and reducing the system complexity.

- Rewind a file.

  Rewinding a file need not involve any actual I/O rather the directory is searched for the appropriate entry, and the current file position is simply reset to the beginning of the file.

- Delete a file.

  To delete a file, we search the directory for the named file. Having found the associated directory entry, we release all file space (so it can be reused by other files) and invalidate the directory entry.

  It is known that all of the operations mentioned involve searching the directory for the entry associated with the named file. The directory entry contains all of the important information needed to operate on the file. To avoid this constant searching, many systems will open a file when it first becomes actively used. The operating system keeps a small table containing information about all open files. When a file operation is requested, only this small table is sorted, not the entire directory. When the file is no longer actively used, it is closed and removed from the table of open files.

  Some systems implicitly open a file when the first reference is made to it. The file is automatically closed when the job or program that opened the file terminates. Most systems, however, require that a file be opened explicitly by the programmer with a system call (open) before it can be used.

  The open operation takes a file name and searches the directory, copying the directory entry into the table of open files. The (open) system call will typically return a pointer to the entry in the table of open files. This pointer, not the actual file name, is used in all I/O operations, avoiding any further searching.

  The five operations described above are certainly the minimal required file operations. More commonly, we will also want to edit the file and modify its contents. A common modification is appending new information to the end of an existing file. We may want to create a copy of a file, or copy it to an I/O device, such as a printer or a display. Since files are named objects, we may want to rename an existing file.

Basic file operations

A file is an **Abstract Data Type**. To define a file properly, we need to consider the operations that can be performed on files.

- **Create**
- **Write**
- **Read**
- **Reposition within File** (or **File Seek**)

- **Delete**
- **Truncate**
- **Open (Fi)** – search the directory structure on disk for entry Fi , and move the content of entry to memory.
- **Close (Fi)** – move the content of entry Fi in memory to directory structure on disk.

File Attributes

A file has certain attributes, which vary from one operating system to another, but typically consist of these:

Name – only information kept in human- readable form.

Type – needed for systems that support different types.

Location – pointer to file location on device.

Size – current file size.

Protection – controls who can do reading, writing, executing.

Time, date, and user identification – data for protection, security, and usage monitoring.

The detailed list of file attributes is as follows:

Attribute	Meaning
Protection	Who can access the file and in what way
Password	Password needed to access the file
Creator	ID of the person who created the file
Owner	Current owner
Read-only flag	0 for read/write; 1 for read only
Hidden flag	0 for normal; 1 for do not display in listings
System flag	0 for normal files; 1 for system file
Archive flag	0 for has been backed up; 1 for needs to be backed up
ASCII/binary flag	0 for ASCII file; 1 for binary file
Random access flag	0 for sequential access only; 1 for random access
Temporary flag	0 for normal; 1 for delete file on process exit
Lock flags	0 for unlocked; nonzero for locked
Record length	Number of bytes in a record .
Key position	Offset of the key within each record
Key length	Number of bytes in the key field
Creation time	Date and time the file was created
Time of last access	Date and time the file was last accessed
Time of last change	Date and time the file has last changed
Current size	Number of bytes in the file
Maximum size	Number of bytes the file may grow to

Information about all files is kept in the directory structure, which is maintained on the disk.

File Types

A common technique for implementing file types is to include the type as part of the file name (a name and an **extension**, usually separated by a period character).

File type	Usual extension	Function
Executable	exe, com, bin or none	ready-to-run machine-language program
Object	obj, o	compiled, not linked, machine -language
Source code	c, cpp, p, pas, f77, asm, ai	source code in various languages
Batch	bat, sh	commands to the command interpreter
Text	txt, doc	textual data, documents
Word processor	wp, tex, rrf, etc	various word -processor formats
Library	lib, a	libraries of routines for programmers

File-System Structure

To provide an efficient and convenient access to the disk, the operating system imposes one or more file system to allow the data to be stored, located and retrieved easily. A file system poses two quite different design problems.

1. The first problem is defining how the file system should look to the user. This task involves defining a file and its attributes, the operations allowed on a file, and the directory structure for organizing files.
2. The second problem is creating algorithms and data structures to map the logical file system onto the physical secondary-storage devices.

   The disks major portion of secondary storage on which a file system is maintained. To improve I/O efficiency, I/O transfer between memory and disk are performed in units of blocks. Each block is one or more sectors. Depending on the disk drive, sectors vary from 32 bytes to 4096 bytes; usually, they are 512 bytes. Disks have two important characteristics that make them a convenient medium for storing multiple files:

1. They can be rewritten in place; it is possible to read a block from the disk, to modify the block, and to write it back into the same place.
2. One can access directly any given block of information on the disk. Thus, it is simple to access any file either sequentially or randomly, and switching from one file to another requires only moving the read-write heads and waiting for the disk to rotate.

The file system is generally composed of many different levels as shown in the fig as follows. Each level in the design uses the features of lower levels to create new features for higher levels.

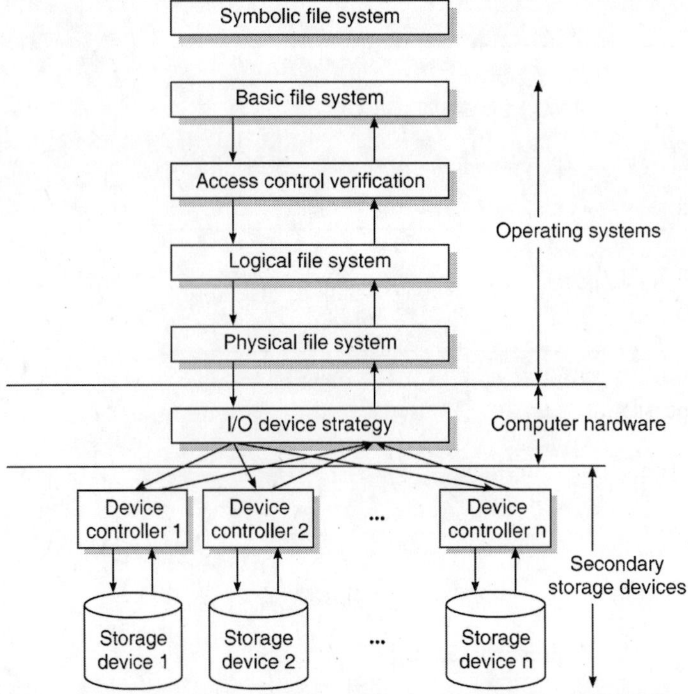

Simple File System

Disks provide the bulk of secondary storage on which a file system is maintained. The components of a file system are invoked whenever there is a command for reading or writing records in a file. A file is stored on a disk. Disk is divided into blocks. Each block may contain one or more record. At this time we assume that the records within a file are of the same length.

The information on each existing file status is kept in a table called file directory or volume table of contents. Each entry in this table contains information necessary to find and access file. Structure of the table includes.

- **Entry Number**: just like serial number used to count the entry.
- **Name**: Name of each file entered.
- **Logical record size**: Length of the record in programmer's view.
- **Number of Logical Records**: Records in each file.
- **Address of first physical block**: this can determine physical location of the file on storage device.
- **Protection and Access Control**: To protect from unauthorized users.

Let us consider a request is issued to read the 4th record of a file named abc into memory location 12000. Suppose the file abc is stored physically as in fig as follows. The steps needed to process a read statement are:

Step i: File directory is searched to find the entry for the file abc.

Step ii: Information about the file abc is retrieved and extracted from the file directory entry.

Step iii: Based on the information extracted, a decision is made whether to allow the requesting process to access abc.

Step iv: The Logical Record Address specified is transformed into a Logical Byte Address.

Logical Byte Address= (record number – 1) X Record Size.

To Logical byte address of 4th record is (4-1) X 500 = 1500.

Stepv: The Logical Byte Address is then transformed into a Physical Byte Address. Logical Byte Address 1500 corresponds to byte 500 within the second 1000-byte physical block of abc, which corresponds to physical block 7.

Step vi: Physical block 7 is read into a 1000-byte buffer area in main memory.

Step vii: Record 4 is extracted from the buffer area and moved into the 'user's area at location 12000.

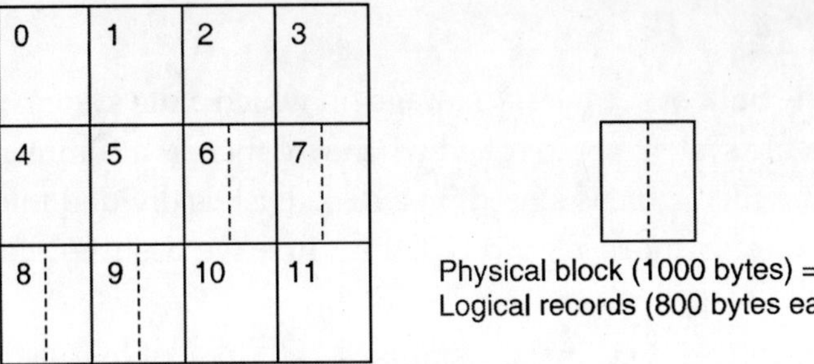

The major characteristics of the simple file system design are:

i. The records are can only be of fixed length which poses a great problem to storage efficiency i.e. there is inefficient use of secondary storage.

ii. The simple file system allows only a single unique name for each file.

iii. The files are structured sequentially.

SYMBOLIC FILE SYSTEM

It is one of the most important layers of the file system. The symbolic file system (SFS) function is to map the user's symbolic reference to an ID. Some features of SFS are:

- A file can be given multiple names called aliases. It is useful if several different programs use different names for the same file.
- Buffers in main memory as well as secondary storage space can be shared. Shared files are called linked files and give multiple users access to the same physical file.
- Maintains manual file name registry to avoid duplicate file names.
- Better file organization as related files can be subdivided into groups.

The components of file directory are:

1. Symbolic file directory (SDF)
2. Basic file directory (BFD)

These two have different functions; The SFD is concerned with file naming whereas the BFD is concerned with the physical file. There may be multiple symbolic directories and each symbolic directory is treated as file. To eliminate or minimize naming conflicts, each programmer can be assigned a separate SFD. Therefore a Master Directory (MD) that specifies the BFD entry for each programmer's private SFD is required. Master directory has unique ID. Some particular entry is fixed for it in BFD. This allows the SFS to access the MD via BFD. This concept is shown below.

SYMBOLIC FILE DIRECTORY

	File Name	ID
1	xyz	3
2	abc	5
3	....	

BASIC FILE DIRECTORY

ID	Logical Record Size	Number Logical Records	Address of First Physical Block	Protection Control and Access
1	—	—	0	Basic FD
2	20	3	1	Symbolic FD
3	80	10	2	Access by everyone
4	1000	3	3	{free}
5	500	7	6	Read Only
6	100	30	12	Read for user 1

Symbolic File System

Let us again consider a request is issued to read the 4th record of a file named abc into memory location 12000. The SFS uses the file name to locate file's unique file directory entry. Entry depicts ID for abc is 5. Now the entry number 5 of BFS is accessed. The concept can be extended to give a hierarchical structure to SFD.

LOGICAL FILE SYSTEM

Logical file system is concerned with mapping the structure of the logical records onto the linear byte string view of a file provided by the physical file system. In particular it must convert a request for a record into a request for a byte string. The logical file system manages metadata information. Metadata includes all of the file-system structure, excluding the actual data (or contents of the files).

Logical file system provides the facility for direct access based on record numbers all of which are the same length. Some of the access methods are:

(a) Sequentially structured fixed length records: For this record organization, the user views his file as a sequence of fixed-length records as shown in the figure (a). Sequential access means all the records are stored in a sequence one after another. If x is the length of each record and current logical byte address is clba, then after processing each request the clba is updated by

clba = clba + x

(b) Sequentially structured variable length records: For this record organization, the user views his file as a sequence of variable-length records as shown in the figure (b).

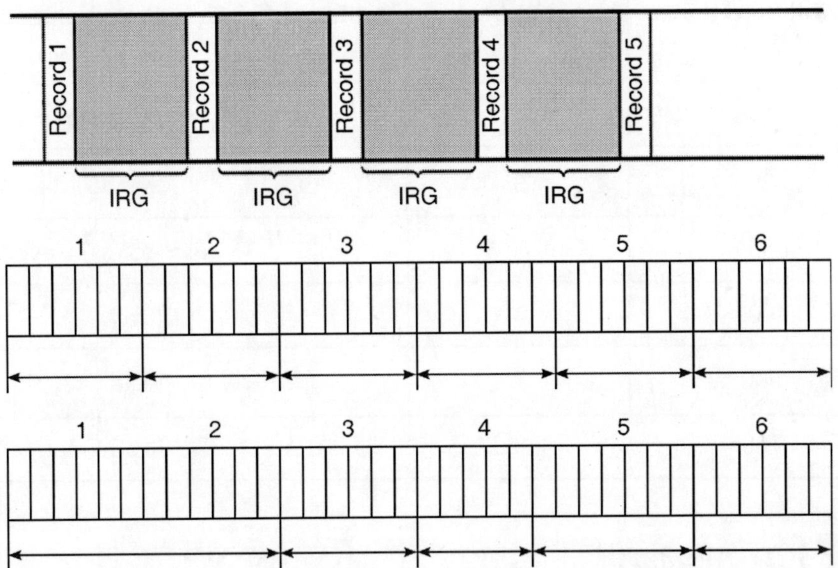

Sequential Structured (a) Fixed Length (b) Variable Length

(a) Sequentially structured keyed records: The access is based on content rather than record number or address. All records are kept in ascending order based on the keys i.e. Kl, K2, K3, etc. The logical byte addressor sequential access may be computed by searching all records for the one with correct key. A symbol table or index table is used to indicate correspondence between keys and logical byte address of the record. Index table may be divided into levels :

K1	1	K2	2	K3	3	K4	4

K1 < K2 < K3 < K4

(i) Multiple keyed records: Several keys can reference the data. To implement this multiple indexes exist. This is similar to library indexing of books by title, by author, and subject.

(ii) Chained structured records: It provides facilities for more complex record structure. It is not usually offered as a part of basic file system, but rather is built on top of one.

PHYSICAL FILE SYSTEM

The physical file system is the lower level that deals with the I/O devices. The primary function of the Physical File System (PFS) is to perform the mapping of Logical Byte Address into Physical Block Address. In this organization, the logical file system calls the physical file system, passing to it the logical byte address and length of the information request. The PFS may first call the Allocation Strategy Module and then the Device Strategy Module. The PFS keeps track of the mapping from Logical Byte Address to the blocks of physical storage.

Physical Block Address = first physical block of file +

(Logical Byte Address) / block size

The physical file system uses this is simple mapping function used in simple physical storage structure of the file. All blocks are stored sequentially on secondary storage. The objective is to

- Minimize 11/0 operations
- Allow logical record size independent of physical block size.
- Allow noncontiguous allocation of file space.

Minimizing 1/0 operations:

The number of 1/0 operations can be reduces by eliminating redundant operations. Keeping track of which physical blocks are in core can reduce the VO operation. For each 1/0 read operation, a physical block is copied into the buffer in main memory. If we keep track of' which physical block is presently in the buffer, we can test whether the desired block has already been. If the block is already in the buffer, I/0 read operations could be skipped. This technique is called file buffering.

Allowing logical record size independent of physical block size:

A physical record must hold some integral number of logical records, with no space left over. There are situations in practice in which the programmer desires to process logical records of lengths that are not an even factor of block length. There are various ways to solve this problem. For example, we can effectively store fifty 13-byte logical records in the 1000- byte blocks by using 20-byte logical records, which are really 13-byte records each with 7 bytes of wasted space. This strategy, though effective, is not efficient in the use of secondary storage space. Many storage devices allow a certain amount of flexibility in the format of the individual tracks.

Allowing noncontiguous allocation of file space: If the physical blocks of a file are not contiguous, a different algorithm is needed to map from logical byte address to physical block number. Two popular techniques are.

Chained Blocks:

In this technique, each physical block contains the address of the next "logically continuous" block. The basic file directory entries contain the address of the first physical block, as before, but subsequent block addresses are found by means of the address pointers (called chains) as shown in the figure . This approach is efficient for sequential access but quite inefficient for direct access.

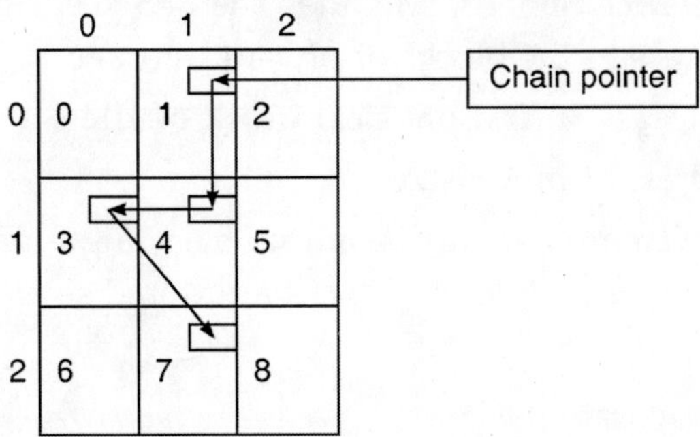

File Maps: one different approach is to use a File Map Table to map each Logical Block Address to its physical block address as shown in figure. This file map may be stored as part of the entry in Basic File Directory or in a separate block.

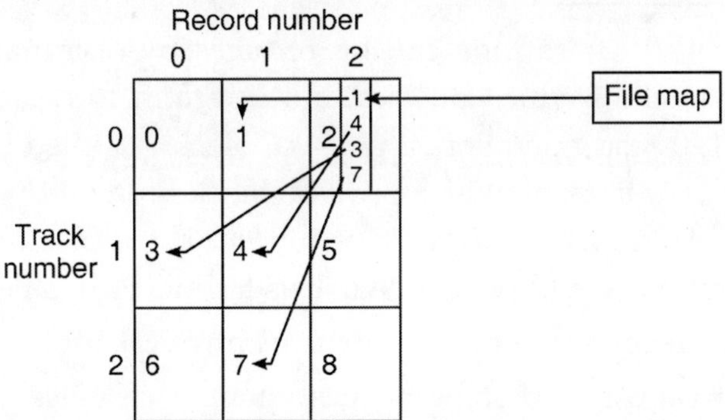

When the file is opened, all or part of the file map is copied into memory as part of the Active File Table information. In this way mapping can be done as efficiently as the contiguous allocation mapping. The mapping function becomes

Physical Block Address = file map + (Logical Byte Address/ block size)

Which is just an indexed table access. If the file map is very large, it may require several physical blocks. In this case, it may be necessary to have file maps for the file maps.

DEVICE STRATEGY

The lowest level, the I/O device strategy, consists of device drivers and interrupts handlers to transfer information between the memory and the disk system.

A device driver can be thought of as a translator. Its input consists of high level commands such as "retrieve block 123." Its output consists of low-level, hardware-specific instructions that are used by the hardware controller, which interfaces the I/O device to the rest of the system.

The device driver usually writes specific bit pattern to special locations in the I/O controller's memory to tell the controller on which device location to act and what actions to take, which interfaces the I/O device to the rest of the system. The device driver usually writes specific bit patterns to special locations in the I/O controller's memory to tell the controller on which device location to act and what actions to take.

FILE ACCESS METHODS

Files store information. This information must be accessed and read into computer memory before it is used. There are several ways the information in the file can be accessed. Some systems provide only one access method for files, and so the concept is less important. On other systems, such as those of IBM, many different access methods are supported, and choosing the right one for a particular application is a major design problem. The basic methods for accessing files are described as follows:

1. **Sequential Access**

   Information in the file is processed in order, one record after the other. This is by far the most common mode of access of files. For example, editors programs usually access files in this fashion.

Sequential access means that a group of elements (e.g. data in a memory array or a disk file or on a tape) is accessed in a predetermined, ordered sequence. The writing or reading of data in a sequential order such as reading data blocks stored one after the other on magnetic tape

The read operation on a file automatically advances the file pointer. Similarly a write appends the new information to the end of the file, and advances the file pointer to the new end. Such a file can be rewound, and on some systems, a program may be able to skip forward or back n record, for some integer n (perhaps only for n = 1). This scheme is known as sequential access to a file. Sequential access is based upon a tape model of a file.

The major characteristics of sequential access are:

- Implemented by the file system.

- Data is accessed one record right after the last.
- Reads cause a pointer to be moved ahead by one.
- Writes allocate space for the record and move the pointer to the new End Of File.
- Such a method is reasonable for tape.

2. Direct Access

An alternative access method is direct access, which is based upon a disk model of a file. For direct access, the file is viewed as a numbered sequence of blocks or records. A direct access file allows arbitrary blocks to be read of written. Thus we may read block 14, then red block 53, and then write block 7. There are no restrictions on the order of reading or writing for a direct access file.

Direct access is a means of accessing a point within a storage system without a sequential search. It goes straight to the required point of information.

Direct access files are of great use for immediate access to large amounts of information. They are often used in accessing large data bases. When a query concerning a particular subject arrives, we compute which block contains the answer and then read that block directly to provide the desired information.

The file operations must be modified to include the block number as a parameter. Thus we have to read block n, where n is the block number, rather than read the next, and write block n rather than write the next. An alternative approach is to retain read next and write next, as with sequential access, and to add an operation, postion file to n, where n is the block number. Then to perform a read block n, we would position to block n and then read next.

The block number provided by the user to the operating system is normally a relative block number. A relative block number is an index relative to the beginning of the file. Thus the first relative block of the file is 0, the next is 1, and so on, even through the actual absolute disk address of the block may be 14703 for the first block, and 14704 for the second.

The use of relative block numbers allows the operating system to decide where the file should be placed, and prevents the user from accessing portions of the file system which may not be part of his file. Some systems start their relative block number at 0; others start at 1.

The major characteristics of sequential access are:

- Method useful for disks.
- The file is viewed as a numbered sequence of blocks or records.

- There are no restrictions on which blocks are read / written in any order.
- User now says "Read N" rather than "Read Next".
- "N " is a number relative to the beginning of file, not relative to an absolute physical disk location.

Not all operating systems support both sequential and direct access for files. Some systems allow only that a file is defined as sequential or direct when it is created; such a file can only be accessed in a manner consistent with its declaration.

3. Other Access Methods

Other access method can be built on top of a direct access method. These additional methods generally involve the construction of an index for the file. The index, like an index in the back of a book, contains pointers to the various blocks. To find an entry in the file the index is consulted first i.e. to find a record in the file, we first search the index, and then use the pointer to access the file directly and to find the desired record.

Example 1: Index contains the name appearing as the first record in each block. There are as many index entries as there are blocks.

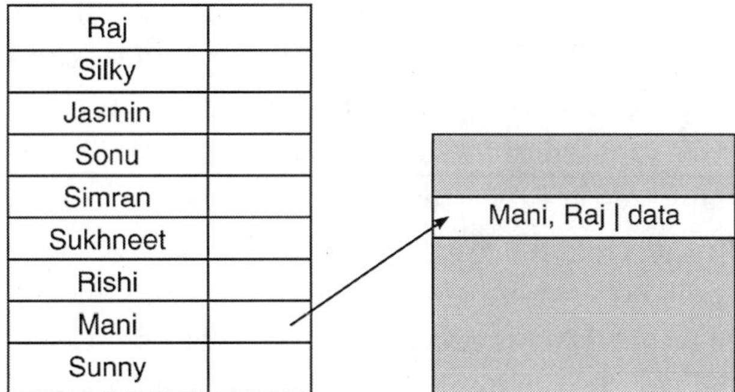

Example 2: Index contains the block number where "A" begins, where "B" begins, etc. Here there are only 26 index entries.

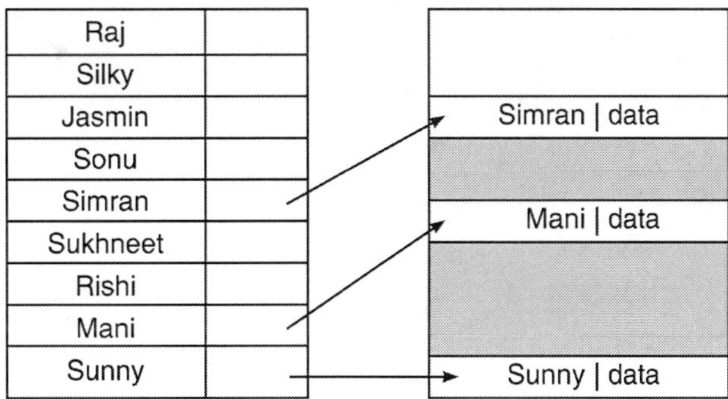

File Symbolic Link

A link is effectively a pointer or an alias to another file or subdirectory. For example, a link may be implemented as an absolute or relative path name (a symbolic link). When a reference to a file is made, we search the directory. The directory entry is marked as a link and the name of the real file (or directory) is given. We resolve the link by using the path name to locate the real file. Links are easily identified by their format in the directory entry (or by their having a special type on systems that support types), and are effectively named indirect pointers.

A symbolic link can be deleted without deleting the actual file it links. There can be any number of symbolic links attach to a single file.

Symbolic links are helpful in sharing a single file called by different names. Each time a link is created, the reference count in its inode is incremented by one. Whereas deletion of link decreases the count by one. The operating system denies deletion of such files whose reference count is not 0, meaning that the file is in use.

In a system where sharing is implemented by symbolic links, this situation is somewhat easier to handle. The deletion of a link does not need to affect the original file; only the link is removed. If the file entry itself is deleted, the space for the file is deallocated, leaving the links dangling. We can search for these links and remove them also, but unless a list of the associated link is kept with each file, this search can be expensive. Alternatively, we can leave the links until an attempt is made to use them. At that time, we can determine that the file of the name given by the link does not exist, and can fail to resolve the link name; the access is treated just like any other illegal file name. (In this case, the system designer should consider carefully what to do when a file is deleted and another file of the same name is created, before a symbolic link to the original file is used.) In the case of UNIX, symbolic links are left when a file is deleted, and it is up to the user to realize that the original file is gone or has been replaced.

Another approach to deletion is to preserve the file until all references to it are deleted. To implement this approach, we must have some mechanism for determining that the last reference to the file has been deleted. We could keep a list of all references to a file (directory entries or symbolic links). When a link or a copy of the directory entry is established, a new entry is added to the file-reference list. When a link or directory entry is deleted, we remove its entry on the list. The file is deleted when its file-reference list is empty.

The trouble with this approach is the variable and potentially large size of the file-reference list. However, we really do not need to keep the entire list - we need to keep only a count of the number of references. A new link or directory entry increments the reference counts; deleting a link or entry decrements the count. When the count is 0, the file can be deleted; there are no remaining references to it. The UNIX operating system uses this approach for non-symbolic links, or hard links, keeping a reference count in the file information block or inode). By effectively prohibiting multiple references to directories, we maintain an acyclic-graph structure.

To avoid these problems, some systems do not allow shared directories links. For example, in MS-DOS, the directory structure is a tree structure.

File Sharing and Locking

In a multi-user environment a file is required to be shared among more than one users. There are several techniques and approaches to effects this operation. Simple approach is to copy the file at the user's local hard disk. This approach essentially creates to different files, in therefore cannot be treated as file sharing.

A file can be shared in three different modes:

1. Read only: In this mode the user can only read or copy the file.
2. Linked shared: In this mode all the users sharing the file can make changes in this file but the changes are reflected in the order determined by the operating systems.
3. Exclusive mode: In this mode the file is acquired by one single user who can make the changes while others can only read or copy it.

Another approach is to share a file through symbolic links. This approach poses a couple of problems – concurrent updation problem, deletion problem. If two users try to update the same file, the updation of one of them will be reflected at a time. Besides, a file must not be deleted while it is in use by another user.

Locking is mechanism through which operating systems insures that the user making changes in the file is the one who has the lock on the file. As long as the lock remains with this user, no other user can alter the file.

Directory Systems

As particular case of indexing, to the file system of any file management system is associated a file index consisting of a directory or set of directories. Obviously, the files are represented by entries in a device directory or volume table of contents. The device directory records information, such as name, location, size, and type, for all files on that device.

The directories themselves are simply files indexing other files, which may in turn be directories if a hierarchical indexing scheme is used. In order to protect the integrity of the file system in spite of user of program error, all modifications to these particular directory files are commonly restricted to the file management system.

It may take from 16 to over 100 bytes to record this information for the each file. In a system with a large number of files, the size of the directory itself may be hundreds of thousands of bytes. Thus the device directory may need to be stored on the device and brought into memory piecemeal, as needed. More specifically, when a file is open, the directory information about this file is brought into main memory. This information remains there until the file is closed.

A device directory may be sufficient for a single-user system with limited storage space. As the amount of storage and the number of users increase, however, it becomes increasingly difficult for the users to organize and keep track of all of the files on the file system. A directory structure provides a mechanism for organizing the many files in the file system. It may span device boundaries and include several different disk units. In this way, the user need be concerned only with the logical directory and file structure, and can completely ignore the problems of physically allocating space for files.

In fact, many systems actually have two separate directory structures: the device directory and the file directories. The device directory is stored on each physical device and describes all files on that device. The device directory entry mainly concentrates on describing the physical properties of the files: where it is, how long it is, how it is allocated, and so on. The file directories are a logical organization of the files on all devices. The file directory entry concentrates on logical properties of each name: file, file type, owing user, accounting information, protection access code, and so on. A file directory entry may simply point to the device directory entry to provide physical properties or may duplicate this information. Our main interest now is with the file directory structure; device directories should be well understood.

The particular information kept for each file in the directory varies from operating system to operating system. The following is a list of some of the information which may be kept in a directory entry. Not all systems keep all this information, of course.

- File name. The symbolic file name.
- File type. For those systems that support different types.
- Location. A pointer to the device and location on that devices of the file.
- Size. The current size of the file (in bytes, words of blocks) and the maximum allowed size.
- Current Position. Pointers to the current read or write position in the file.
- Protection. Access control information the number of process that are currently using (have opened) this file.
- Time, date and process identification. This information may be kept for (a) creation, (b) last modification, and (c) last use. These can be useful for protection and usage monitoring. If we think of the directory as a symbol table

that translates file names into their directory entries, it becomes apparent that the directory itself can be organized in many ways. We want to be able to insert entries, delete entries, search for a named entry and list all the entries in the directory. Next we consider what data structure is used for the directory.

DIRECTORY STRUCTURE

Many different file directory structures have been proposed, and are in use. The directory is essentially a symbol table. The operating system takes the symbolic file name and finds the named file. We examine some directory structures here. When considering a particular directory structure, we need to keep in mind the operations which are to be performed on a directory.

- Search. We need to be able to search a directory structure to find the entry for a particular file. Since files have symbolic names, and similar names may indicate a relationship between the files, we may want to be able to find all files that match a particular pattern.
- Create File. New files need to be created and added to the directory.
- Delete File. When a file is no longer needed, we want to remove it from the directory.
- List Directory. We need to be able to list the files in a directory ans the contents of the directory entry for each file in the list.
- Backup. For reliability, it is generally a good idea to save the contents and structure of the file system at regular intervals. This often consists of copying all files to magnetic tape. This provides a backup copy in use. In this case, the file can be copied to tape and the disk space of that file released for reuse by another file.

The most common schemes for defining the logical structure of a directory are described below.

Single-Level Directory

The simplest directory structure is the single-level directory. All files are contained in the same directory, which is easy to support and understand.

A single-level directory has significant limitations, however, when the number of files increases or when the system has more than one user. Since all files are in the same directory, they must have unique names. If two users call their data file test, then the unique-name rule is violated. For example, in one programming class, 23 students called the program for their second similar assignment prog2; another 11 called it assign2. Although file names are generally selected to reflect the content of the file, they are often limited in length. The MS-DOS operating system allows only 11-character file names; UNIX allows 255 characters.

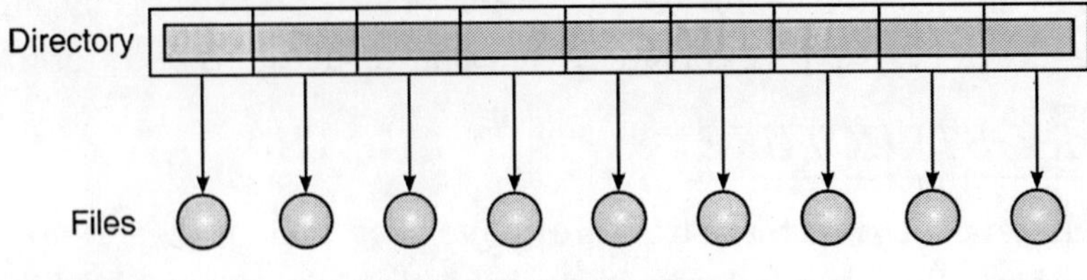

Single-Level Directory

Even a single user on a single-level directory may find it difficult to remember the names of all the files, as the number of files increases. It is not uncommon for a user to have hundreds of files on one computer system and an equal number of additional files on another system. In such an environment, keeping track of so many files is a daunting task.

Two-Level Directory

A single-level directory often leads to confusion of file names between different users. The standard solution is to create a separate directory for each user.

In the two-level directory structure, each user has its own user file directory (UFD). Each UFD has a similar structure, but lists only the files of a single user. When a user job starts or a user logs in, the system's master file directory (MFD) is searched. User name or account number, and each entry points to the UFD for that user index the MFD.

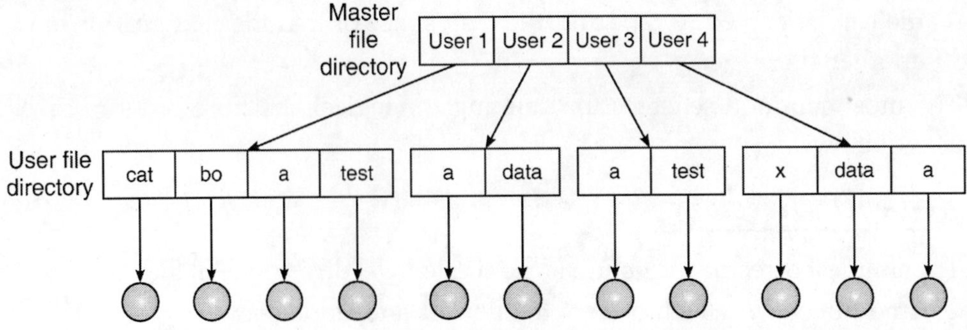

Two-Level Directory

When a user refers to a particular file, only his own UFD is searched. Thus, different users may have files with the same name, as long as all the file names within each UFD are unique.

To create a file for a user, the operating system searches only that user's UFD to ascertain whether another file of that name exists. To delete a file, the operating system confines its search to the local UFD; thus, it cannot accidentally delete another user's file that has the same name.

The user directories themselves must be created and deleted as necessary. A special system program is run with the appropriate user name and account information. The program creates a new UFD and adds an entry for it to the MFD. The execution of this program might be restricted to system administrators. The allocation of disk space for user directories can be handled with the techniques discussed later for files themselves.

Although the two-level directory structure solves the name-collision problem, it still has disadvantages. This structure effectively isolates one user from another. This isolation is an advantage when the users are completely independent, but is a disadvantage when the users want to cooperate on some task and to access one another's files. Some systems simply do not allow local user files to be accessed by other users.

If access is to be permitted, one user must have the ability to name a file in another user's directory. To name a particular file uniquely in a two-level directory, we must give both the user name and the file name. A two-level directory can be thought of as a tree, or at least an inverted tree, of height 2.

The root of the tree is the MFD. Its direct descendants are the UFDs. The descendants of the UFDs are the files themselves. The files are the leaves of the tree. Specifying a user name and a file name defines a path in the tree from the root (the MFD) to a leaf (the specified file). Thus, a user name and a file name define a path name. Every file in the system has a path name. To name a file uniquely, a user must know the path name of the file desired.

For example, if user A wishes to access her own test file named test, she can simply refer to test. To access the file named test of user B (with directory-entry name userb), however, she might have to refer to /userb/test. Every system has its own syntax for naming files in directories other than the user's own.

Additional syntax is needed to specify the partition of a file. For instance, in MS-DOS a letter followed by a colon specifies a partition. Thus, a file specification might be C:\userb\test. Some systems go even further and separate the partition, directory name, and file name parts of the specification. For instance, in VMS, the file login.com might be specified as: u:[sst.jdeck]login.com;1, where U is the name of the partition, sst is the name of the directory, jdeck is the name of subdirectory, and 1 is the version number. Other systems simply treat the partition name as part of the directory name. The first name given is that of the partition, and the rest is the directory and file. For instance, /u/pbg/test might specify partition U, directory pbg, and file test.

A special case of this situation occurs in regard to the system files. Those programs provided as a part of the system-loaders, assemblers, compilers, utility routines, libraries, and so on - are generally defined as files. When the appropriate commands are given to the operating system, these files are read by the loader and executed. Many command interpreters act by simply treating the command as the name of a file to load and execute. As the directory system is defined presently, this file name would be searched for in the current UFD. One solution would be to copy the system files into each UFD. However, copying all the system files would waste an enormous amount of space. (If the system files require 5 MB, then supporting 12 users would require 5 x 12 = 60 MB just for copies of the system files.)

The standard solution is to complicate the search procedure slightly. A special user directory is defined to contain the system files (for example, user 0). Whenever a file name is given to be loaded, the operating system first searches the local UFD. If the file is found, it is used. If it is not found, the system automatically searches the special user directory that contains the system files. The sequence of directories searched when a file is named is called the search path. This idea can be extended, such that the search path contains an unlimited list of directories to search when a command name is given. This method is the one most used in UNIX and MS-DOS.

Tree-Structured Directories

Once we have seen how to view a two-level directory as a two-level tree, the natural generalization is to extend the directory structure to a tree of arbitrary height. This generalization allows users to create their own subdirectories and to organize their files accordingly. The MS-DOS system, for instance, is structured as a tree. In fact, a tree is the most common directory structure. The tree has a root directory. Every file in the system has a unique path name. A path name is the path from the root, through all the subdirectories, to a specified file.

A directory (or subdirectory) contains a set of files or subdirectories. A directory is simply another file, but it is treated in a special way. All directories have the same internal format. One bit in each directory entry defines the entry as a file (0) or as a subdirectory (1). Special system calls are used to create and delete directories.

In normal use, each user has a current directory. The current directory should contain most of the files that are of current interest to the user. When reference is made to a file, the current directory is searched. If a file is needed that is not in the current directory, then the user must either specify a path name or change the current directory to be the directory holding that file. To change directories, a system call is provided that takes a directory name as a parameter and uses it to redefine the current directory. Thus, the user can change his current directory whenever he desires. From one change directory system call to the next, all open system calls search the current directory for the specified file.

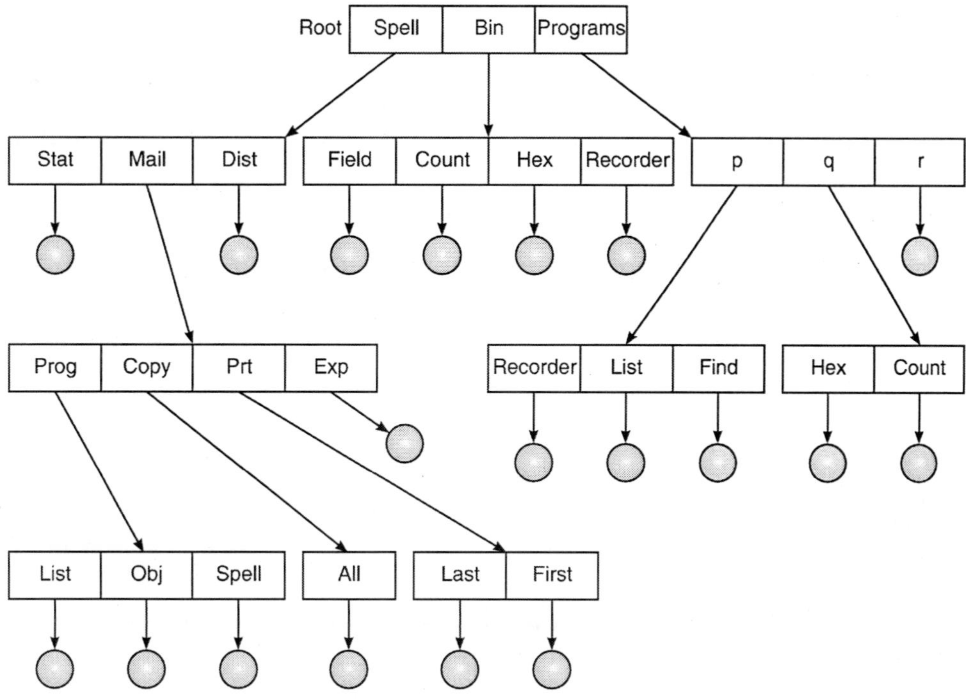

Tree-Structured Directories

The initial current directory of a user is designated when the user job starts or the user logs in. The operating system searches the accounting file (or some other predefined location) to find an entry for this user (for accounting purposes). In the accounting file is a pointer to (or the name of) the user's initial directory. This pointer is copied to a local variable for this user that specifies the user's initial current directory.

Path names can be of two types: absolute path names or relative path names. An absolute path name begins at the root and follows a path down to the specified file, giving the directory names on the path. A relative path name defines a path from the current directory.

Allowing the user to define his own subdirectories permits him to impose a structure on his files. This structure might result in separate directories for files associated with different topics or different forms of information (for example, the directory programs may contain source programs; the directory bin may store all the binaries).

An interesting policy decision in a tree-structured directory structure is how to handle the deletion of a directory. If a directory is empty, its entry in its containing directory can simply be deleted. However, suppose the directory to be deleted is not empty, but contains several files or subdirectories: One of two approaches can be taken. Some systems, such as MS-DOS, will not delete a directory unless it is empty.

Thus, to delete a directory, the user must first delete all the files in that directory If any subdirectories exist, this procedure must be applied recursively to them, so that they can be deleted also. This approach may result in a substantial amount of work.

An alternative approach, such as that taken by the UNIX rm command, is to provide the option that, when a request is made to delete a directory, all that directory's files and subdirectories are also to be deleted. Either approach is fairly easy to implement; the choice is one of policy. The latter policy is more convenient, but more dangerous, because an entire directory structure may be removed with one command. If that command were issued in error, a large number of files and directories would need to be restored from backup tapes.

With a tree-structured directory system, users can access, in addition to their files, the files of other users. For example, user B can access files of user A by specifying their path names. User B can specify either an absolute or a relative path name. Alternatively, user B could change her current directory to be user A's directory, and access the files by their file names. Some systems also allow users to define their own search paths. In this case, user B could define her search path to be

i. her local directory

ii. the system file directory

iii. user A's directory, in that order.

As long as the name of a file of user A did not conflict with the name of a local file or system file, it could be referred to simply by its name.

A path to a file in a tree-structured directory can be longer than that in a two-level directory. To allow users to access programs without having to remember these long paths, the Macintosh operating system automates the search for executable programs. It maintains a file, called the Desktop File, containing the name and location of all executable programs it has seen. When a new hard disk or floppy disk is added to the system, or the network is accessed, the operating system traverses the directory structure, searching for executable programs on the device and recording the pertinent information. This mechanism supports the double-click execution functionality described previously. A double-click on a file causes its creator attribute to be read, and the Desktop File to be searched for a match. Once the match is found, the appropriate executable program is started with the clicked-on file as its input. The Microsoft Windows family of operating systems (95, 95, NT, 2000) maintains an extended two-level directory structure, with devices and partitions assigned a drive letter.

Acyclic-Graph Directories

Consider two programmers who are working on a joint project. The files associated with that project can be stored in a subdirectory separating them from other projects and files of the two programmers. But since both programmers are equally responsible for the project, both want the subdirectory to be in their own directories. The common subdirectory should be shared. A shared directory or file will exist in the file system in two (or more) places at once.

A tree structure prohibits the sharing of files or directories. An acyclic graph allows directories to have shared subdirectories and files. The same file or subdirectory may be in two different directories. An acyclic graph, that is, a graph with no cycles, is a natural generalization of the tree-structured directory scheme.

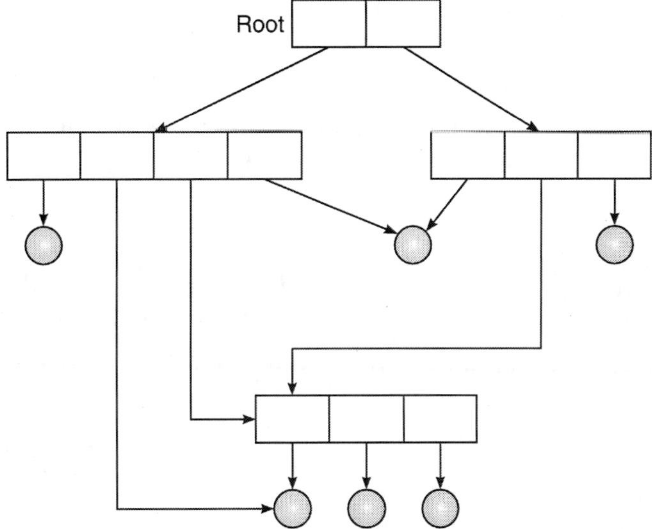

Acyclic-Graph Directories

A shared file (or directory) is not the same as two copies of the file. With two copies, each programmer can view the copy rather than the original, but if one programmer changes the file, the changes will not appear in the other's copy. With a shared file, only one actual file exists, so any changes made by one person are immediately visible to the other. Sharing is particularly important for subdirectories; a new file created by one person will automatically appear in all the shared subdirectories.

When people are working as a team, all the files they want to share may be put into one directory. The UFDs of all the team members would each contain this directory of shared files as a subdirectory. Even when there is a single user, his file organization may require that some files be put into different subdirectories. For example, a program written for a particular project should be both in the directory of all programs and in the directory for that project.

Shared files and subdirectories can be implemented in several ways. A common way, exemplified by many of the UNIX systems, is to create a new directory entry called a link. A link is effectively a pointer to another file or subdirectory. For example, a link may be implemented as an absolute or relative path name. When a reference to a file is made, we search the directory. If the directory entry is marked as a link, then the name of the real file (or directory) is given. We resolve the link by using the path name to locate the real file. Links are easily identified by their format in the directory entry (or by their having a special type on systems that support types), and are effectively named indirect pointers. The operating system ignores these links when traversing directory trees to preserve the acyclic structure of the system.

Another common approach to implementing shared files is simply to duplicate all information about them in both sharing directories. Thus, both entries are identical and equal. A link is clearly different from the original directory entry; thus, the two are not equal. Duplicate directory entries, however, make the original and the copy indistinguishable. A major problem with duplicate directory entries is maintaining consistency if the file is modified.

An acyclic-graph directory structure is more flexible than is a simple tree structure, but it is also more complex. Several problems must be considered carefully. A file may now have multiple absolute path names. Consequently, distinct file names may refer to the same file. This situation is similar to the aliasing problem for programming languages. If we are trying to traverse the entire file system-to find a file, to accumulate statistics on all files, or to copy all files to backup storage-this problem becomes significant, since we do not want to traverse shared structures more than once.

Another problem involves deletion. When can the space allocated to a shared file be deallocated and reused? One possibility is to remove the file whenever anyone deletes it, but this action may leave dangling pointers to the now-nonexistent file. Worse, if the remaining file pointers contain actual disk addresses, and the space is subsequently reused for other files, these dangling pointers may point into the middle of other files.

In a system where sharing is implemented by symbolic links, this situation is somewhat easier to handle. The deletion of a link does not need to affect the original file; only the link is removed. If the file entry itself is deleted, the space for the file is deallocated, leaving the links dangling. We can search for these links and remove them also, but unless a list of the associated links is kept with each file, this search can be expensive. Alternatively, we can leave the links until an attempt is made to use them. At that time, we can determine that the file of the name given by the link does not exist, and can fail to resolve the link name; the access is treated just like any other illegal file name. (In this case, the system designer should consider carefully what to do when a file is deleted and another file of the same name is created, before a symbolic link to the original file is used.) In the case of UNIX, symbolic links are left when a file is deleted, and it is up to the user to realize that the original file is gone or has been replaced. Microsoft Windows uses the same approach.

Another approach to deletion is to preserve the file until all references to it are deleted. To implement this approach, we must have some mechanism for determining that the last reference to the file has been deleted. We could keep a list of all references to a file (directory entries or symbolic links). When a link or a copy of the directory entry is established, a new entry is added to the file-reference list. When a link or directory entry is deleted, we remove its entry on the list. The file is deleted when its file-reference list is empty. The trouble with this approach is the variable and potentially large size of the file-reference list. However, we really do not need to keep the entire list-we need to keep only a count of the number of references. A new link or directory entry increments the reference count; deleting a link or entry decrements the count. When the count is 0, the file can be deleted; there are no remaining references to it. The UNIX operating system uses this approach for non-symbolic links (or hard links), keeping a reference count in the file information block. By effectively prohibiting multiple references to directories, we maintain an acyclic-graph structure. To avoid these problems, some systems do not allow shared directories or links. For example, in MS-DOS, the directory structure is a tree structure, rather than an acyclic graph.

General Graph Directory

One serious problem with using an acyclic-graph structure is ensuring that there are no cycles. If we start with a two-level directory and allow users to create subdirectories, a tree-structured directory results. It should be fairly easy to see that simply adding new files and subdirectories to an existing tree-structured directory preserves the tree-structured nature. However, when we add links to an existing tree-structured directory, the tree structure is destroyed, resulting in a simple graph structure.

The primary advantage of an acyclic graph is the relative simplicity of the algorithms to traverse the graph and to determine when there are no more references to a file. We want to avoid traversing shared sections of an acyclic graph twice, mainly for performance reasons. If we have just searched a major shared subdirectory for a particular file, without finding it, we want to avoid searching that subdirectory again; the second search would be a waste of time. If cycles are allowed to exist in the directory, we likewise want to avoid searching any component twice, for reasons of correctness as well as performance. A poorly designed algorithm might result in an infinite loop continually searching through the cycle and never terminating. One solution is arbitrarily to limit the number of directories that will be accessed during a search.

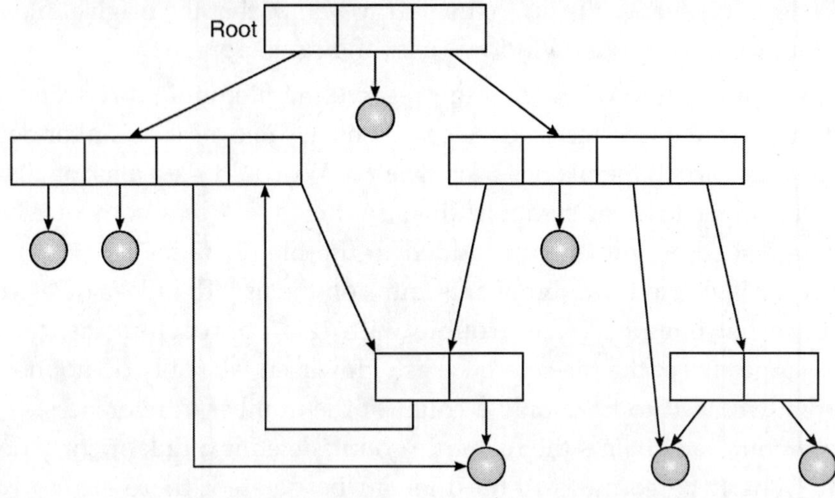

General Graph Directory

A similar problem exists when we are trying to determine when a file can be deleted. As with acyclic-graph directory structures, a zero value in the reference count means that there are no more references to the file or directory and the file can be deleted. However, when cycles exist, the reference count may be nonzero, even when it is no longer possible to refer to a directory or file. This anomaly results from the possibility of self-referencing (or a cycle) in the directory structure. In this case, we generally need to use a garbage-collection scheme to determine when the last reference has been deleted and the disk space can be reallocated. Garbage collection involves traversing the entire file system, marking everything that can be accessed. Then, a second pass collects everything that is not marked onto a list of free space. (A similar marking procedure can be used to ensure that a traversal or search will cover everything in the file system once and only once.) Garbage collection for a disk-based file system, however, is extremely time-consuming and is thus seldom attempted.

Garbage collection is necessary only because of possible cycles in the graph. Thus, an acyclic-graph structure is much easier to work with. The difficulty is to avoid cycles as new links are added to the structure. How do we know when a new link will complete a cycle? There are algorithms to detect cycles in graphs; however, they are computationally expensive, especially when the graph is on disk storage. A simpler algorithm in the special case of directories and links is to bypass links during directory traversal. Cycles are avoided and no extra overhead is incurred.

GENERAL file systems

File system types can be classified into disk file systems, network file systems and special purpose file systems.

Disk file systems

A disk file system is a file system designed for the storage of files on a data storage device, most commonly a disk drive, which might be directly or indirectly connected to the computer. Examples of disk file systems include FAT, FAT32, NTFS, HFS and HFS+, ext2, ext3, ISO 9660, ODS-5, and UDF. Some disk file systems are journaling file systems or versioning file systems.

Flash file systems

A flash file system is a file system designed for storing files on flash memory devices. These are becoming more prevalent as the number of mobile devices is increasing, and the capacity of flash memories catches up with hard drives.

Database file systems

A new concept for file management is the concept of a database-based file system. Instead of, or in addition to, hierarchical structured management, files are identified by their characteristics, like type of file, topic, author, or similar metadata. Example: dbfs.

Transactional file systems

Each disk operation may involve changes to a number of different files and disk structures. In many cases, these changes are related, meaning that it is important that they all be executed at the same time. Take for example a bank sending another bank some money electronically. The bank's computer will "send" the transfer instruction to the other bank and also update its own records to indicate the transfer has occurred. If for some reason the computer crashes before it has had a chance to update its own records, then on reset, there will be no record of the transfer but the bank will be missing some money.

Transaction processing introduces the guarantee that at any point while it is running, a transaction can either be finished completely or reverted completely (though not necessarily both at any given point). This means that if there is a crash or power failure, after recovery, the stored state will be consistent.

Network file systems

A network file system is a file system that acts as a client for a remote file access protocol, providing access to files on a server. Examples of network file systems include clients for the NFS, SMB protocols, and file-system-like clients for FTP and WebDAV.

Special purpose file systems

A special purpose file system is basically any file system that is not a disk file system or network file system. This includes systems where the files are arranged dynamically by software, intended for such purposes as communication between computer processes or temporary file space.

Special purpose file systems are most commonly used by file-centric operating systems such as Unix. Examples include the procfs (/proc) file system used by some Unix variants, which grants access to information about processes and other operating system features.

Deep space science exploration craft, like Voyager I & II used digital tape based special file systems. Most modern space exploration craft like Cassini-Huygens used Real-time operating system file systems or RTOS influenced file systems. The Mars Rovers are one such example of an RTOS file system, important in this case because they are implemented in flash memory.

File management system

The File Management System, *FMS* is the subsystem of an operating system that manages the data storage organization on disk, and provides services to processes related to file access. In this sense, it interfaces the application programs with the low-level media-I/O (e.g. disk I/O) subsystem, freeing on the application programmers from having to deal with low-level intricacies and allowing them to implement I/O using convenient data-organizational abstractions like files and records.

On the other end, the FMS services often is the only way thorough which applications can access the data stored in the files, thus achieving an encapsulation of the data themselves which can be usefully exploited for the purposes of data protection, maintenance and control.

We can summarize the aims of a FMS as follows:

- *Data Management.*

  An FMS should provide data management services to the applications through convenient abstractions, simplifying and making device-independant the common operations involved in data access and modification.

- *Generality with respect to storage devices.*

  The FMS data abstractions and access methods should remain unchanged irrespective of the devices involved in data storage.

- *Validity.*

  An FMS should guarantee that at any given moment the stored data reflect the operations performed on them, regardless of the time delays involved in actually performing those operations. Appropriate access synchronization mechanism should be used to enforce validity when multiple accesses from independent processes are possible.

- *Protection.*

  Illegal or potentially dangerous operations on the data should be controlled by the FMS, by enforcing a well defined data protection policy.

- *Concurrency.*

  In multiprogramming systems, concurrent access to the data should be allowed with minimal differences with respect to single-process access, save for access synchronization enforcement.

- *Performance.*

  The above functionalities should be offered achieving at the same a good compromise in terms of data access speed and data transferring rate.

  From the point of view of an end user (or application) an FMS typically provides the following functionalities:

- File creation, modification and deletion.
- User's (or user groups') ownership of files, and access control on the basis of ownership permissions.
- Facilities to structure data within files (predefined record formats, etc).
- Facilities for maintaining data redundancy against technical failure (back-ups, disk mirroring, etc.).
- Logical identification and structuring of the data, via file names and hyerarchical directory structures.

These functionalities are provided through sophisticated FMS techniques.

One important issue in designing a file system is the question of how much support the file system should provide for various record organizations. The UNIX file system presents a file to the user as a sequence of bytes. The user may position him at any byte position in the file prior to a read or write. But any division of the bytes into records is entirely the responsibility of the programmer - though there are some standard library routines for dealing with stream files.

FMS Architecture

A general scheme of the architecture of an FMS is depicted in fig. as follows:

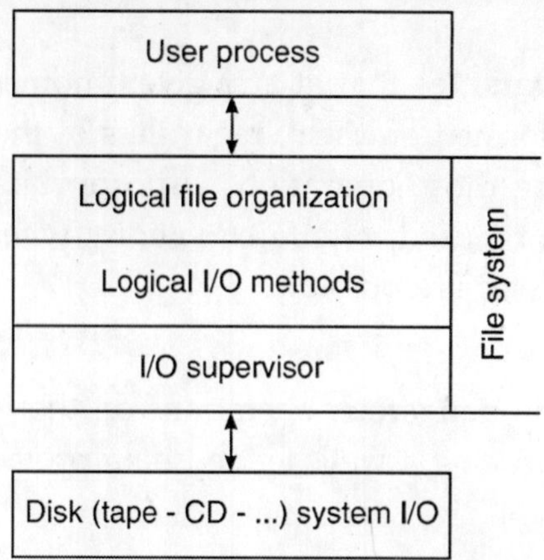

General File Management System architecture

The file system provides a unified data structure containing the data along with the necessary management information for the use of the FMS.

The user application "sees" and/or internally organizes the files according to a certain logical scheme.

A logical I/O module provides the necessary translation from this logical data organization into a physical one, suited for the low-level storage management subsystem. Record management is performed at this level, in the sense that it maps a physical (vlock-oriented) data structure into and from a record-oriented one, which is organized into some logical scheme at the upper level.

The I/O supervisor is responsible for I/O initialization, termination and data validity through multiple accesses. It also provides device independence, managing the communication between so to offer to the upper layers a uniform service structure across the various possible storage I/O devices managed by the disk (tape, cdrom ...) I/O subsystem.

Case study: SOFTWARE File manager

A file manager or file browser is a computer program that provides a user interface to work with file systems. They are very useful for speeding up interaction with files. The most common operations on files are create, open, edit, view, print, play, rename, move, copy, delete, attributes, properties, search/find, and permissions.

Typically files are displayed in a hierarchy. File managers may contain features inspired by web browsers, including forward and back navigational buttons.

Some browsers may also provide network connectivity, e.g. via FTP, NFS, SMB or WebDAV, either by allowing the user to browse for servers and connect to them and then accessing the file system from the server the same way it accesses local file systems, or by providing its own full client implementations for file server protocols.

Some file managers also provide the ability to extend operations using user written scripts. This is a typical feature of Orthodox file managers.

Orthodox file managers

Orthodox file managers or "Commander-like" file managers have three windows (two panels and one command line window).They are one of the older families of file managers. They develop and further extend the interface introduced by John Socha's famous Norton Commander for DOS. That concept is more than twenty years old as Norton Commander version 1.0 was released in 1986. Despite their age they are actively developed and dozens of implementations exist for DOS, Unix and Microsoft Windows. A public standard (version 1.2 dated June 1997) is available from Nikolai Bezroukov's website.

The following features define the class of Orthodox file managers:

- They present the user with a two-panel directory view consisting of one active and one passive panel. The latter always serves as a target for file operations. Panels are shrinkable and if shrunk they expose the terminal window hidden behind them. Normally only the last line of the terminal window (the command line) is visible.
- They provide close integration with an underlying OS shell via command line and associated terminal window that permits viewing the results of executing the shell command entered on the command line (e.g., via Ctrl-O shortcut in Norton Commander).
- They provide the user with extensive keyboard shortcuts.
- The file manager can be used without or with minimal use of the mouse.
- Users can create their own file associations and scripts that are invoked for certain file types and organize these scripts into a hierarchical tree (e.g., as a user script library or user menu).
- Users can extend the functionality of the manager via so called *User menu* or *Start menu* and extensions menu. Norton Commander introduced the concept of user-defined file associations that is now used in all modern file managers.

Other common features include:

- Information on the "active" and "passive" panels may be used for constructing commands on the command line. Examples include current file, path to left panel, path to right panel, etc.
- They provide a built-in viewer for (at least) the most basic file types.
- They have a built-in editor. In many cases, the editor can extract certain elements of the panels into the text being edited.

- Many support virtual file systems (VFS) such as viewing compressed archives, or via an FTP connection.
- They often have the word *commander* in the name.

An orthodox file manager typically has three windows. Two of the windows are called panels and are symmetrically positioned at the top of the screen. The third is the command line which is essentially a minimized command (shell) window that can be expanded to full screen. Only one of the panels is active at a given time. The active panel contains the "file cursor". Panels are resizable. Each panel can be hidden. Files in the active panel serve as the source of file operations performed by the manager. For example, files can be copied or moved to the passive panel. This gives the user the ability to use only the keyboard with the convenience of the mouse interface. The active panel shows information about the current working directory and the files that it contains. The passive (inactive) panel shows the content of the same or other directory (the default target for file operations). Users may customize the display of columns that show relevant file information. The active panel and passive panel can be switched (often by pressing the tab key). Other user interface elements include:

1. path: shows the source/destination location of the directory in use
2. information about directory size, disk usage and disk name (usually at the bottom of the panels)
3. panel with information about file name, extension, date and time of creation, last modification, permissions (attributes) and other
4. info panel with number of files in directory, sum of size of selected files..
5. tabbed interface (usually GUI file managers)
6. function keys: F1–F10 have all the same functions under all orthodox file managers: Example F5 always copies file(s) from active to inactive panel, while F6 moves the file.

The introduction of tabbed panels in some file managers (for example Total Commander) made it possible to manipulate more than one active and passive directory at the time.

Orthodox file managers are among the most portable file managers. Examples are available on almost any platform both with command-line interface and GUI interface. This is the only type of command line managers that have a published standard of the interface (and actively supported by developers). This makes possible to do the same work on different platforms without much relearning of the interface.

Sometimes they are called dual-pane managers, a term that is typically used for programs such as the Windows File Explorer. It is technically incorrect since they have three windows including a command line window below (or hidden behind) two symmetric panels. Command line windows play a very prominent role in the functionality of this type of file manager.

Furthermore, most of these programs allow using just one pane with the second one hidden. Focusing on 'dual panes' may be misleading; it is the combination of all of these features which is important.

In summary, a chief distinguishing feature is the presence of the command line window and direct access to shell via this window - not the presence of two symmetric panes which is relatively superficial.'

Examples:

- Norton Commander
- Krusader for Linux and other Unix-like systems
- Dos Navigator
- File Commander
- Total Commander
- FreeCommander, Alt Commander
- PowerDesk (latest v.6.04)
- FAR Manager
- 7-Zip file manager
- Midnight Commander (Unix example)
- muCommander
- Double Commander

File-List file manager

Less well-known, but older are the so-called *file-list* file managers. Examples include **flist** which was in use since 1981 on the Conversational Monitor System. This is a variant of **fulist** which originated before late 1978 according to comments by its author Theo Alkema. The **flist** program provided a list of files in the user's minidisk., allowed sorting by any of the file attributes. The file attributes could be passed to scripts or function-key definitions, making it simple to use flist as part of CMS EXEC, EXEC 2 or xedit scripts.

This program ran only on IBM VM/SP CMS, but was the inspiration for other programs, for example **filelist** (a script run via the Xedit editor), and programs running on other operating systems. These include a program also called **flist** running on OpenVMS[9] and **fulist** (from the name of the corresponding internal IBM program[10]) on Unix.

Directory editors

While this category is known as file managers, an older term is *directory editor*, which dates back at least to 1978. There was a directory editor written for EXEC 8 at the University of Maryland, available to other users at that time. The term was used by other developers, e.g., the **dired** program written by Jay Lepreau in 1980, which ran on BSD, which was in turn inspired by an older program with the same name running on TOPS-20. **Dired** inspired other programs, e.g., dired the editor script (for emacs and similar editors) as well as **ded**.

Navigational file manager

A **navigational file manager** is a newer type of file managers which became prominent due to the popularity of Microsoft Windows. It uses a "navigational" metaphor to represent filesystem locations and also often called "Explorer" type of file managers. The Windows Explorer is a classic representative of the type. Since the advent of GUIs it has become the dominant type of file manager for desktop computers, being used, for example, in all Microsoft Windows products.

Typically it has two panes, one with the current directory and one with the filesystem tree. For Mac OS X, the Finder is an example of a navigational file manager.The Miller Column browser from GNUstep is a type of Navigational file manager.

- The window displays the location currently being viewed.
- The location being viewed (the current directory) can be changed by the user, by opening folders, pressing a *back button*, typing a location, or using additional pane with the navigation tree representing part or all the filesystem.
- Icons represent files, programs, and directories.

The interface in a navigational file manager often resembles a web browser, complete with *back*, *forward* buttons that work with history, and maybe even *reload* buttons. Sometimes there is also an address bar where the file or directory path (or URI) can be typed.

Moving from one location to another need not open a new window. At the same time several instances of manager can be opened and they can communicate with each other via drag and drop and clipboard so it is possible to view several directories simultaneously and perform cut-and paste operations between instances.

Most navigational managers have two panes with the second pane with the tree view of the filesystem. The latter serves as the most common instrument for filesystem navigation. That means that unlike orthodox managers two panes are asymmetrical: the first (usually left) provides the tree view of filesystem and the second (usually right) file view of the current directory.

When a directory of the tree is selected it becomes current and the content of the second (right) pane changes to the files in the current directory.

File operations are based on drag-and-drop and editor metaphors: users can select and copy files or directories into the clipboard and then paste them in a different place in the filesystem or even in a different instance of file manager.

Examples:

- Windows Explorer
- Mac OS Finder
- XTree

Spatial file manager

The Nautilus file manager has a spatial mode. Each of these windows displays an open folder. **Spatial file managers** use a spatial metaphor to represent files and folders as if they were real physical objects. A spatial file manager imitates the way people interact with physical objects.

Some ideas behind the concept of a spatial file manager are:

1. A single window represents each opened folder.
2. Each window is unambiguously and irrevocably tied to a particular folder.
3. Stability: files, folders, and windows go where the user moves them, stay where the user puts them ("preserve their spatial state"), and retain all their other "physical" characteristics (such as size, shape, color and location).
4. The same item can only be viewed in one window at a time.

As in navigational managers, when a folder is opened, the icon representing the folder changes—perhaps from an image showing a closed drawer to an opened one, perhaps the folder's icon turns into a silhouette filled with a pattern—and a new window is opened.

Examples of file managers that to some extent use a spatial metaphor include:

- Apple's Finder 5 to 9 (versions up to Mac OS X)
- the RISC OS Filer
- Amiga's Workbench
- GNOME's Nautilus from version 2.6 onwards
- BeOS's Tracker
- OS/2's Workplace Shell
- Digital Research's GEM (implemented in Atari TOS and as a somewhat reduced version for PCs)

- ZDESKTOP and FILEMAGE Zoomable File-System Viewers (spatial view of hierarchical data)
- Dysfunctional spatial file managers:
- Windows Explorer in Windows 95 was set as a spatial file manager model by default; but because it also worked as a navigational file manager, folders could be opened in multiple windows, which made in fail all the above criteria. Later versions gradually abandoned the spatial model.
- Apple's Finder in Mac OS X — much like in Explorer, the integration of spatial and navigational mode means that the spatial mode does not actually work.

3D file managers

File System Visualizer, one example of a 3D file manager. Some projects have attempted to implement a three-dimensional method of displaying files and directory structures. The exact implementation tends to differ between projects, as three-dimensional file browsing has not yet become popular and thus there are no common standards to follow.

Examples of three-dimensional file managers include:

- fsn, for Silicon Graphics' IRIX systems, notably featured prominently in one scene from the film Jurassic Park, as a representation of Unix systems.
- File System Visualizer, or fsv, an open source clone of fsn for modern Unix-like systems.
- BumpTop, a file manager using a three dimensional representation of a desktop with realistic physics, intended for use with a stylus and touchscreen.
- Real Desktop, a desktop replacement with similarities to BumpTop.

Web based file managers

Web based file managers are typically scripts written in PHP, Perl, Asp or AJAX. When installed on a local server or on a remotely hosted server they allow files and folders located there to be managed and edited without the need for FTP Access. More advanced, and usually commercially distributed, web based file management scripts allow the administrator of the file manager to configure secure, individual user accounts, each with individual account permissions.

Authorized users have access to documents stored on the server or in their individual user folders anytime from anywhere via a web browser.

A web based file manager can serve as an organization's digital repository. For example, documents, digital media, publishing layouts, and presentations can be stored, managed, and shared between customers, suppliers, remote workers or just internally.

KEYWORDS

FILE	FILE MANAGEMENT
RECORD	SIMPLE FILE SYSTEMS
FILE SYSTEM	SYMBOLIC FILE SYSTEM
DEVICE DRIVER	LOGICAL FILE SYSTEM
SEQUENTIAL ACCESS	PHYSICAL FILE SYSTEMS
DIRECT ACCESS	DIRECTORY SYSTEMS

SUMMARY

The file is a logical unit of information storage. A record is the logical subdivisions of a file. A file management system is that set of system software that provides services to users and applications to support access to files.

- To provide an efficient and convenient access to the disk, the operating system imposes one or more file system to allow the data to be stored, located and retrieved easily.
- A device driver can be thought of as a translator. Its input consists of high level commands such as "retrieve block 123." Its output consists of low-level, hardware-specific instructions that are used by the hardware controller, which interfaces the I/O device to the rest of the system.
- Sequential access means that a group of elements (e.g. data in a memory array or a disk file or on a tape) is accessed in a predetermined, ordered sequence. The writing or reading of data in a sequential order such as reading data blocks stored one after the other on magnetic tape
- Direct access is a means of accessing a point within a storage system without a sequential search. It goes straight to the required point of information.
- The File Management System, *FMS* is the subsystem of an operating system that manages the data storage organization on disk, and provides services to processes related to file access.

REVIEW QUESTIONS

1) Explain file system? What are components of file system?
2) Describe the different scheme for defining the logical structure of directory?
3) Explain different file access method with their advantages and disadvantage?
4) Draw and explain layered file system?

5) Explain different directory structure of OS?
6) Compare flat and hierarchical directory structure
7) Explain different directory structure of DOS, UNIX, and WINDOWS?
8) Explain all the types of file systems in details.
9) Differentiate between
   a) Files and records
   b) Direct and sequential access
10) Write short note on
   (a) Device drivers
   (b) Fixed length records

FILL IN THE BLANKS

1. The ________ is a logical unit of information storage
2. A____________ is that set of system software that provides services to users and applications to support access to files.
3. ___________is a means of accessing a point within a storage system without a sequential search.
4. The ____________manages the data storage organization on disk, and provides services to processes related to file access
5. An ____________is a series of code sections that the loader can bring into memory and execute.
6. ____________is a variant of variable length records in which each record ends with a special delimiter such as CR or LF.

TRUE OR FALSE

1. A record is the logical subdivisions of a file.
2. Sequential access means that a group of elements are accessed in a predetermined, ordered sequence
3. Direct access goes sequentially to the required point of information
4. Logical file system is concerned with mapping the structure of the logical records onto the linear byte string view of a file provided by the symbolic file system.
5. To read from file, a system call specifies the name of the file and where in memory the next block of the file should be put.
6. An object file is a sequence of bytes organized into blocks understandable by the system's linker.

ANSWERS

FILL IN THE BLANKS

1. file
2. file management system
3. Direct access
4. File Management System
5. executable file
6. Stream records

TRUE OR FALSE

1. TRUE
2. TRUE
3. FALSE
4. FALSE
5. TRUE
6. TRUE

"Teachers open the door, but you must enter by yourself." —*Chinese Proverb*

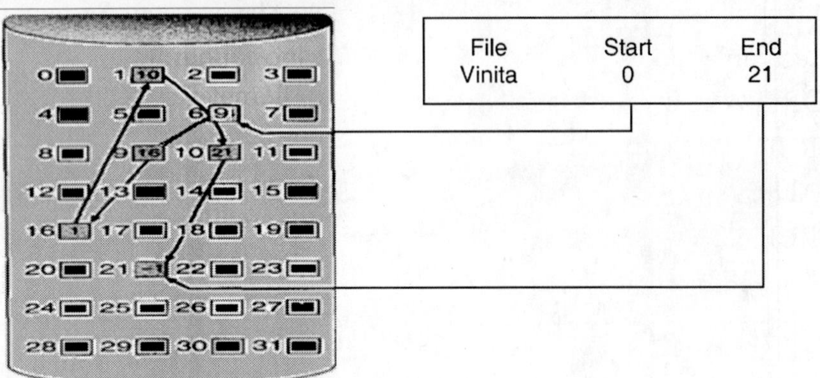

FILE IMPLEMENTATION

INTRODUCTION

Given that a file consists, generally speaking, of a collection of records, a key element in file management is the way in which the records themselves are organized inside the file, since this heavily affects system performances ad far as record finding and access. By "organization" we refer here to the *logical* arrangement of the records in the file (their ordering or, more generally, the presence of "closeness" relations between them based on their content), and not instead to the physical layout of the file as stored on a storage media, To prevent confusion, the latter is referred to by the expression "record blocking", and will be treated later on.

Choosing a file organization is a design decision, hence it must be done having in mind the achievement of good performance with respect to the most likely usage of the file. The criteria usually considered important are:

1. Fast access to single record or collection of related records.
2. Easy record adding/update/removal.

3. Storage efficiency.

4. Redundancy as a warranty against data corruption.

Needless to say, these requirements are in contrast with each other for all but the most trivial situations, and it's the designer job to find a good compromise among them, yielding and adequate solution to the problem at hand. For example, easiness of adding/etc. is not an issue when defining the data organization of a CD-ROM product, whereas fast access is, given the huge amount of data that this media can store. However, as it will become apparent shortly, fast access techniques are based on the use of additional information about the records, which in turn competes with the high volumes of data to be stored.

Logical data organization is indeed the subject of whole shelves of books, in the "Database" section of your library. Here we'll briefly address some of the simpler used techniques, mainly because of their relevance to data management from the lower-level (with respect to a database's) point of view of an OS

Operating systems implement open and close systems calls for processes to request access to file contents. In this section, we delve into the structures and operations used to implement file-system operations.

Several on-disk and in-memory structures are used to implement a file system. These vary depending on the operating system and the file system, but some general principles apply. On-disk, the file system may contain information about how to boot an operating system stored there, the total number of blocks, the number and location of free blocks, the directory structure, and individual files.

The on-disk structures include:

- A boot control block can contain information needed by the system to boot an operating from that partition. If the disk does not contain an operating system, this block can be empty. It is typically the first block of a partition. In UFS, this is called the boot block; in NTFS, it is the partition boot sector.
- partition control block contains partition details, such as the number of blocks in the partition, size of the blocks, free-block count and free-block pointers, and free FCB count and FCB pointers. In UFS this is called a superblock; in NTFS, it is the Master File Table.
- A directory structure is used to organize the files
- An FCB contains many of the file's details, including file permissions, ownership, size, and location of the data blocks. In UFS this is called the mode. In NTFS, this information is actually stored within the Master File Table, which uses a relational database structure, with a row per file.

The in-memory information is used for both file-system management and performance improvement via caching. The structures can include:

- An in memory partition table containing information about each mounted partition.
- An in-memory directory structure that holds the directory information of recently accessed directories. (For directories at which partitions are mounted, it can contain a pointer to the partition table.)
- The system-wide open-file table contains a copy of the FCB of each open file, as well as other information.

Some operating systems, including UNIX, treat a directory exactly as a file-one with a type field indicating that it is a directory. Other operating systems, including Windows NT, implement separate system calls for files and directories and treat directories as entities separate from files.

Partitions and Mounting

The layout of a disk can have many variations, depending on the operating system. A disk can be sliced into multiple partitions, or a partition can span multiple disks. The former is discussed here, while the latter is more appropriately considered a form of RAID.

Each partition can either be "raw," containing no file system, or "cooked," containing a file system. Raw disk is used where no file system is appropriate. UNIX swap space can use a raw partition, as it uses its own format on disk and does not use a file system. Likewise, some databases use raw disk and format the data to suit their needs. Raw disk can also hold information needed by disk RAID systems, such as bit maps indicating which blocks are mirrored and which have changed and need to be mirrored. Similarly, raw disk can contain a miniature database holding RAID configuration information, such as which disks are members of each RAID set.

Boot information can be stored in a separate partition. Again, it has its own format, because at boot time the system does not have file-system device drivers loaded and therefore cannot interpret the file-system format. Rather~ it is usually a sequential series of blocks, loaded as an image into memory. Execution of the image starts at a predefined location, such as the first byte. This boot image can contain more than the instructions for how to boot a specific operating system.

For instance, PCs and other systems can be dual-booted. Multiple operating systems can be installed on such a system. How does the system know which one to boot? A boot loader that understands multiple file systems and multiple operating systems can occupy the boot space. Once loaded, it can boot one of the operating systems available on the disk. The disk can have multiple partitions, each containing a different type of file system and a different operating system.

The root partition, which contains the operating-system kernel and potentially other system files, is mounted at boot time. Other partitions can be automatically mounted at boot or manually mounted later, depending on the operating system. As part of a successful mount operation, the operating sys tern verifies that the device contains a valid file system. It does so by asking the device driver to read the device directory and verifying that the directory has the expected format. If the format is invalid, the partition must have its consistency checked and possibly corrected, either with or without user intervention.

Finally, the operating system notes in its in-memory mount table structure that a file system is mounted, and the type of the file system. The details of this function depend on the operating system. Microsoft Windows-based systems mount each partition in a separate name space, denoted by a letter and a colon. To record that a file system is mounted at *f:* for example, the operating system places a pointer to the file system in a field of the device structure corresponding to f:. When a process specifies the driver letter, the operating system finds the appropriate file-system pointer and traverses the directory structures on that device to find the specified file or directory.

On UNIX, file systems can be mounted at any directory. This is implemented by setting a flag in the in-memory copy of the mode for that directory. The flag indicates that the directory is a mount point. A field then points to an entry in the mount table, indicating which device is mounted there. The mount table entry contains a pointer to the superblock of the file system on that device. This scheme enables the operating system to traverse its directory structure, switching among file systems as appropriate.

Virtual File Systems

An obvious but sub-optimal method of implementing multiple types of file systems is to write directory and file routines for each type. Rather, most operating systems, including UNIX, use object-oriented techniques to simplify, and organize the implementation. The use of these methods allows very dissimilar file-system types to be implemented within the same structure, including network file systems, such as NFS. Users can access files that are contained within multiple file systems on the local disk, or even on file systems available across the network.

Data structures and procedures are used to isolate the basic system call functionality from the implementation details. Thus, the VFS distinguishes local files from remote ones, and local files are further distinguished according to their file-system types.

The VFS activates file-system-specific operations to handle local requests according to their file-system types, and even calls the NFS protocol procedures for remote requests. File handles are constructed from the relevant nodes and are passed as arguments to these procedures. The layer implementing the file-system type, or remote file system protocol, is the bottom layer of the architecture.

Directory Implementation algorithms

The selection of directory-allocation and directory-management algorithms has a large effect on the efficiency, performance, and reliability of the file system. Therefore, you need to understand the tradeoffs involved in these algorithms.

Linear List

The simplest method of implementing a directory is to use a linear list of file names with pointers to the data blocks. A linear list of directory entries requires a linear search to find a particular entry. This method is simple to program but time-consuming to execute. To create a new file, we must first search the directory to be sure that no existing file has the same name. Then, we add a new entry at the end of the directory. To delete a file, we search the directory for the named file, then release the space allocated to it. To reuse the directory entry, we can do one of several things. We can mark the entry as unused (by assigning it a special name, such as an all-blank name, or with a used-unused bit in each entry), or we can attach it to a list of free directory entries. A third alternative is to copy the last entry in the directory into the freed location, and to decrease the length of the directory. A linked list can also be used to decrease the time to delete a file.

The real disadvantage of a linear list of directory entries is the linear search to find a file. Directory information is used frequently, and users would notice a slow implementation of access to it. In fact, many operating systems implement a software cache to store the most recently used directory information. A cache hit avoids constantly rereading the information from disk. A sorted list allows a binary search and decreases the average search time. However, the requirement that the list must be kept sorted may complicate creating and deleting files, since we may have to move substantial amounts of directory information to maintain a sorted directory. A more sophisticated tree data structure, such as a B-tree, might help here. An advantage of the sorted list is that a sorted directory listing can be produced without a separate sort step.

Hash Table

Another data structure that has been used for a file directory is a hash table. In this method, a linear list stores the directory entries, but a hash data structure is also used. The hash table takes a value computed from the file name and returns a pointer to the file name in the linear list. Therefore, it can greatly decrease the directory search time. Insertion and deletion are also fairly straightforward, although some provision must be made for collisions-situations where two file names hash to the same location. The major difficulties with a hash table are its generally fixed size and the dependence of the hash function on that size.

For example, assume that we make a linear-probing hash table that holds 64 entries. The hash function converts file names into integers from 0 to 63, for instance, by using the remainder of a division by 64. If we later try to create a 65th file, we must enlarge the directory hash table-say, to 128 entries. As a result, we need a new hash function that must map file names to the range o to 127, and we must reorganize the existing directory entries to reflect their new hash-function values. Alternately, a chained-overflow hash table can be used. Each hash entry can be a linked list instead of an individual value, and we can resolve collisions by adding the new entry to the linked list. Lookups may be somewhat slowed, because searching for a name might require stepping through a linked list of colliding table entries, but this is likely to be much faster than a linear search through the entire directory.

File Allocation Methods

The direct-access nature of disks allows us flexibility in the implementation of files. In almost every case, many files will be stored on the same disk. The main problem is how to allocate space to these files so that disk space is utilized effectively and files can be accessed quickly. Three major methods of allocating disk space are in wide use: contiguous, linked, and indexed. Each method has advantages and disadvantages. Some systems (such as Data General's RDOS for its Nova line of computers) support all three. More commonly, a system will use one particular method for all files.

Contiguous Allocation

The contiguous-allocation method requires each file to occupy a set of contiguous blocks on the disk. Disk addresses define a linear ordering on the disk. With this ordering, assuming that only one job is accessing the disk, accessing block $b + 1$ after block b normally requires no head movement. When head movement is needed (from the last sector of one cylinder to the first sector of the next cylinder), it is only one track. Thus, the number of disk seeks required for accessing contiguously allocated files is minimal, as is seek time when seek is finally needed. The IBM VM/CMS operating system uses contiguous allocation because it provides such good performance.

Contiguous allocation of a file is defined by the disk address and length (in block units) of the first block. If the file is n blocks long and starts at location b, then it occupies blocks $b, b + 1, b + 2,..., b + n - 1$. The directory entry for each file indicates the address of the starting block and the length of the area allocated for this file.

Accessing a file that has been allocated contiguously is easy. For sequential access, the file system remembers the disk address of the last block referenced and, when necessary, reads the next block. For direct access to block i of a file that starts at block *b,* we can immediately access block *b* + i. Thus, both sequential and direct access can be supported by contiguous allocation.

The contiguous-allocation method requires each file to occupy a set of contiguous blocks on the disk. Define by a pair <first block location, length >.

1. Accessing the file requires a minimum of head movement.
2. Easy to calculate block location: block **i** of a file, starting at disk address b, is **b + i**.
3. Difficulty is in finding the contiguous space, especially for a large file. Problem is one of dynamic allocation (first fit, best fit, etc.) which has external fragmentation.
4. If many files are created /deleted, compaction will be necessary.
5. It's hard to estimate at create time what the size of the file will ultimately be. What happens when we want to extend the file - we must either terminate the owner of the file, or try to find a bigger hole.

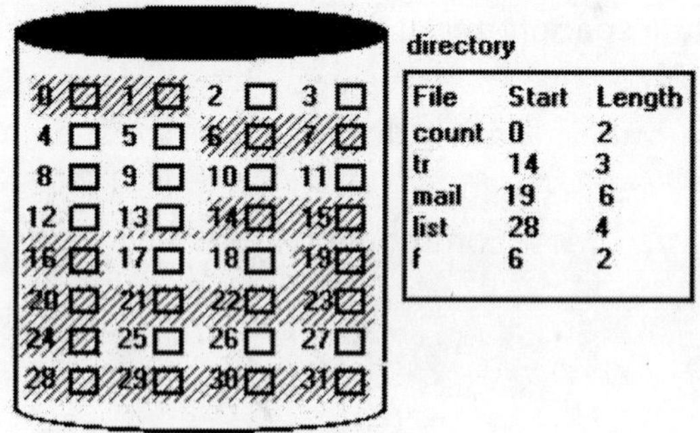

Contiguous allocation has some problems, however. One difficulty is finding space for a new file. The implementation of the free-space-management system, discussed in Section 12.5, determines how this task is accomplished. Any management system can be used, but some are slower than others.

The contiguous disk-space-allocation problem can be seen to be a particular application of the general dynamic storage-allocation problem, which is how to satisfy a request of size *n* from a list of free holes. First fit and best fit are the most common strategies used to select a free hole from the set of available holes. Simulations have shown that both first fit and best fit are more efficient than worst fit in terms of both time and storage utilization. Neither first fit nor best fit is clearly best in terms of storage utilization, but first fit is generally faster.

These algorithms suffer from the problem of external fragmentation. As files are allocated and deleted, the free disk space is broken into little pieces. External fragmentation exists whenever free space is broken into chunks. It becomes a problem when the largest contiguous chunk is insufficient for a request; storage is fragmented into a number of holes, no one of which is large enough to store the data. Depending on the total amount of disk storage and the average file size, external fragmentation may be a minor or a major problem.

Some older microcomputer systems used contiguous allocation on floppy disks. To prevent loss of significant amounts of disk space to external fragmentation, the user had to run a repacking routine that copied the entire file system onto another floppy disk or onto a tape. The original floppy disk was then freed completely, creating one large contiguous free space. The routine then copied the files back onto the floppy disk by allocating contiguous space from this one large hole. This scheme effectively compacts all free space into one contiguous space, solving the fragmentation problem. The cost of this compaction is time. The time cost is particularly severe for large hard disks that use contiguous allocation, where compacting all the space may take hours and may be necessary on a weekly basis. During this **down time,** normal system operation generally cannot be permitted, so such compaction is avoided at all costs on production machines.

Another problem with contiguous allocation is determining how much space is needed for a file. When the file is created, the total amount of space it will *need* must be *found and allocated. How does the creator* (program *or* person) know the size of the file to be created? In some cases, this determination may be fairly simple (copying an existing files, for example); in general, however, the size of an output file may be difficult to estimate.

If we allocate too little space to a file, we may find that the file cannot be extended. Especially with a best-fit allocation strategy, the space on both sides of the file may be in use. Hence, we cannot make the file larger in place. Two possibilities then exist. First, the user program can be terminated, with an appropriate error message. The user must then allocate more space and run the program again. These repeated runs may be costly. To prevent them, the user will normally overestimate the amount of space needed, resulting in considerable wasted space.

The other possibility is to find a larger hole, copy the contents of the file to the new space, and release the previous space. This series of actions may be repeated as long as space exists, although it can be time-consuming. However, in this case, the user never needs to be informed explicitly about what is happening; the system continues despite the problem, although more and more slowly.

Even if the total amount of space needed for a file is known in advance, pre-allocation may be inefficient. A file that grows slowly over a long period (months or years) must be allocated enough space for its final size, even though much of that space may be unused for a long time. The file, therefore, has a large amount of internal fragmentation.

To minimize these drawbacks, some operating systems use a modified contiguous-allocation scheme, in which a contiguous chunk of space is allocated initially, and then, when that amount is not large enough, another chunk of contiguous space, an extent, is added to the initial allocation. The location of a file's blocks is then recorded as a location and a block count, plus a link to the first block of the next extent. On some systems, the owner of the file can set the extent size, but this setting results in inefficiencies if the owner is incorrect. Internal fragmentation can still be a problem if the extents are too large, and external fragmentation can be a problem as extents of varying sizes are allocated and de-allocated. The commercial Veritas File System uses extents to optimise performance. It is a high-performance replacement for the standard UFS.

Advantages

- Easy to implement and manage
- Efficient access because of minimal head movement

Disadvantages

- Finding space for a new file i.e. a contiguous space that is big enough. If there are holes to fit, which one to use? This raises the issues of first-fit Vs best-fit Vs worst fit once again, and of course, (external) Fragmentation and the corresponding need for compaction.
- Expanding an existing file can be a problem.

Linked Allocation

The problems discussed with contiguous allocation can be traced directly to the requirement that space be allocated contiguously. *Linked allocation* solves these problems. With linked allocation, each file is a linked list of disk blocks; the disk blocks may be scattered anywhere on the disk. The directory contains a pointer to the first and last blocks of the file. For example, a file of five blocks might start at block 9, continue at block 16, then block 1, block 10, and finally, block 25(see below).

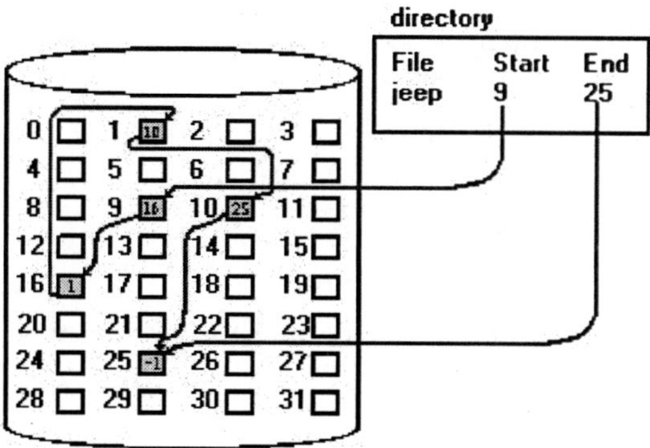

Each block contains a pointer to the next block. These pointers are not made available to the user. Thus, if each sector is 512 words, and a disk address (the pointer) requires two words, then the user sees blocks of 510 words.

Creating a file is easy. We simply create a new entry in the device directory. With linked allocation, each directory entry has a pointer to the first disk block of the file. This pointer is initialized to *nil*(the end-of-the-list pointer value) to signify an empty file. The size field is also set to zero. A write to a file removes the first free block from the free-space list, and writes to that block. This new block is then linked to the end of the file. To read a file, we simply read blocks by following the pointers from block to block.

There is no external fragmentation with linked allocation. Any free block on the free-space list can be used to satisfy a request, since all blocks are linked together. Notice also, that there is no need to declare the size of the file when that file is created. A file can continue to grow as long as there are free blocks. Consequently, it is never necessary to compact free disk space.

Linked allocation does have its disadvantages, however. The major problem is that it can be used effectively for only sequential access files. To find a block of the file, we must start at the beginning of that file and follow the pointers till we get to the *i*th block. Each access to a pointer requires a disk read. Hence, it is inefficient to support a direct-access capability for linked allocation files.

Another disadvantage is reliability. Since the files are linked together by pointers that are scattered all over the disk, consider what would happen if a pointer were lost or damaged. A bug in the operating system software or a disk hardware failure might result in picking up the wrong pointer. This error could result in linking into the free-space list or into another file. One partial solution is to use doubly linked lists or to store the file name and relative block number in each block; these schemes require even more overhead for each file.

An important variation on the linked allocation method is the use of a *file allocation table (FAT)*. A section of disk that contains a table is set aside. The table has one entry for each disk block, and is indexed by block number. The table is used much as is a linked list. The directory contains the block number of the first block of the file. The table entry indexed by that block number then contains the block number of the next block in the file. This chain continues until the last block, which has a special end-of-file value. Allocating a new block to a file is a simple matter of finding the first zero-valued table entry, and replacing the previous end-of-file value of the file's table entry with the address of the new block. The zero of this new block is then replaced with the end-of-file value. This simple but efficient method is used by the DOS and OS/2 operating systems.

Indexed Allocation

Linked allocation solves the external-fragmentation and size-declaration problems of contiguous allocation. However, in the absence of a FAT, linked allocation cannot support efficient direct access, since the pointers to the blocks are scattered with the blocks themselves all over the disk and need to be retrieved in order. Indexed allocation solves this problem by bringing all the pointers together into one location: the index block.

Each file has its own index block, which is an array of disk-block addresses. The *i*th entry in the index block points to the *i*th block of the file. The directory contains the address of the index block. To read the *i*th block, we use the pointer in the *i*th index-block entry to find and read the desired block.

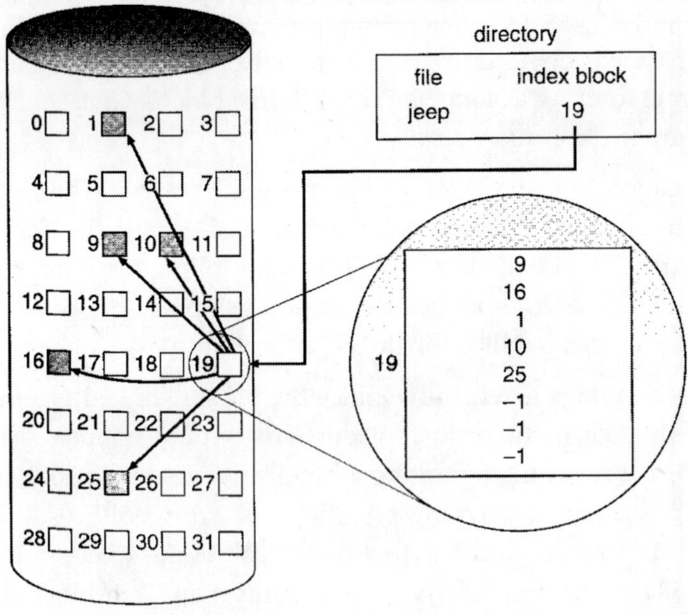

When the file is created, all pointers in the index block are set to *nil*. When the *i*th block is first written, a block is obtained from the free-space manager, and its address is put in the *i*th index-block entry.

Indexed allocation supports direct access, without suffering from external fragmentation, because any free block on the disk may satisfy a request for more space.

Each file uses an index block on disk to contain addresses of other disk blocks used by the file.

1. When the i th block is written, the address of a free block is placed at the i th position in the index block.
2. Method suffers from wasted space since, for small files, most of the index block is wasted. What is the optimum size of an index block?
3. If the index block is too small, we can:
   a. Link several together
   b. Use a multilevel index

Advantages

- No Fragmentation of Disk Space. Any file can use any free block of disk space.
- All pointers are brought together in one place
- Supports direct access readily

Disadvantages

- Suffers from wasted space. Pointer overhead is generally greater than in linked allocation. (but the benefits outweigh this, especially since disk space is now very cheap)

Indexed allocation does suffer from wasted space. The pointer overhead of the index block is generally greater than the pointer overhead of linked allocation. Consider a common case in which we have a file of only one or two blocks. With linked allocation, we lose the space of only one pointer per block (one or two pointers). With indexed allocation, an entire index block must be allocated, even if only one or two pointers will be non-varnil.

This point raises the question of how large the index block should be. Every file must have an index block, so we want the index block to be as small as possible. If the index block is too small, however, it will not be able to hold enough pointers for a large file, and a mechanism will have to be available to deal with this issue:

➾ ***Linked scheme***: An index block is normally one disk block. Thus, it can be read and written directly by itself. To allow for large files, we may link together several index blocks. For example, an index block might contain a small header giving the name of the file, and a set of the first 100 disk-block addresses. The next address (the last word in the index block) is *nil* (for a small file) or is a pointer to another index block (for a large file).

Advantages

- There is no fragmentation of disk space since any file can use any free block.
- No need to declare file size when creating and a file can grow as long as there are free blocks

Disadvantages

- It can be used effectively only for sequential access files since you cannot find one block without reading the previous block.
- Reliability as the files are linked by pointers scattered over disk and if the chain breaks there will be problems.

There is no parallel for this method in memory management

- ***Multilevel index***: A variant of the linked representation is to use a first-level index block to point to a set of second-level index blocks, which in turn point to the file blocks. To access a block, the operating system uses the first-level index to find a second-level index block, and that block to find the desired data block. This approach could be continued to a third or fourth level, depending on the desired maximum file size. With 4,096-byte blocks, we could store 1,024 4-byte pointers in an index block. Two levels of indexes allow 1,048,576 data blocks, which allows a file of up to 4 GB.

Other common scheme is the hierarchical one: a multi-level indexing scheme is used, in which a top-level directory indexes both files and other directories, which in turn index files and directories, and so on. Usually this scheme is represented in the form of a tree, see fig.

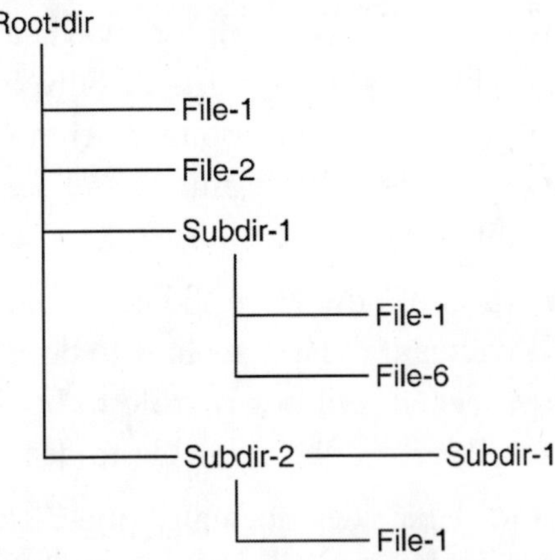

Tree representation of a hierarchical directory structure

The hierarchical architecture has distinct advantages over a simple, one-level indexing one: the tree structure can be effectively used to reflect a logical organization of the data stored in the files; names can be reused (they must uniquely identify files within each directory, not across the whole fle system); in a multi-user system, name conflicts between files owned by different users can be solved by assigning to each user a directory for her own files and sub-directories, the so called user's "home" directory.

A complete indexing of a file is obtained by navigating the tree starting from the top-level, "root", directory, and walking along a path to the tree leaf coresponding to the file. A "pathname" is thus obtained, which uniquely identifies the file within the whole file system. For example, the pathname for file "File-6" in figure is ":Root-dir:Subdir-1:File-6", where a colon is used to separate tree nodes.

A complete pathname is not the only way to identify a file in the directory tree structure: a "relative" pathname, starting from a parent directory is suited just as well, provided that the FMS already knows about that directory. This addressing methods can be usefully exploited by making the FMS assign to all processes a "current working directory" (CWD) attribute, i.e. the complete pathname of a directory of interest, and defining a way for the process to identify files by just specifying a "relative" pathname starting from that directory. In the same example, if ": Root-dir: Subdir-1" is the CWD of a process, the above file might be identified simply as "File-6", using the convention that pathnames not starting with a color are relative to the CWD.

The advantage is twofold: the entire file system structure up to the CWD need not be known by a program (hence its data can be safely moved in other directories without having to rewrite the program), and file access time is decreased, since it's no longer necessary to navigate the whole tree in order to find the address of a file.

➻ *Combined scheme*: Another alternative, used in the UFS, is to keep the first, say, 15 pointers of the index block in the file's mode. The first 12 of these pointers point to direct blocks; that is, they contain addresses of blocks that contain data of the file. Thus, the data for small (no more than 12 blocks) files do not need a separate index block. If the block size is 4 KB, then up to 48 KB of data may be accessed directly. The next 3 pointers point to indirect blocks. The first indirect block pointer is the address of a single indirect block. The single indirect block is an index block, containing not data, but rather the addresses of blocks that do contain data.

Then there is a double indirect block pointer, which contains the address of a block that contains the addresses of blocks that contain pointers to the actual data blocks. The last pointer would contain the address of a triple indirect block. Under this method, the number of blocks that can be allocated to a file exceeds the amount of space addressable by the 4-byte file pointers used by many operating systems. A 32-bit file pointer reaches only 232 bytes, or 4 GB. Many UNIX implementations, including Solaris and IBM's AIX, now support up to 64-bit file pointers. Pointers of this size allow files and file systems to be terabytes in size.

Indexed-allocation schemes suffer from some of the same performance problems, as does linked allocation. Specifically, the index blocks can be cached in memory, but the data blocks may be spread all over a partition.

Inverted Allocation

If we use a disk as a device for backups (e.g., tape), the storage capacity may be the primary concern, and the speed of disk may not matter (as long as it is faster than tape). Since backup storage keeps track of all modifications, a small modification to a large file results in storing the entire modified file,. ***Inverted allocation*** allocates a disk block by hashing the file block content to a disk block location. By doing so, different file blocks of the same content (e.g., empty blocks) can share the same disk block for storage. For example, if one block is modified in a N-block file, the storage requirement for both files is N + 1 blocks.

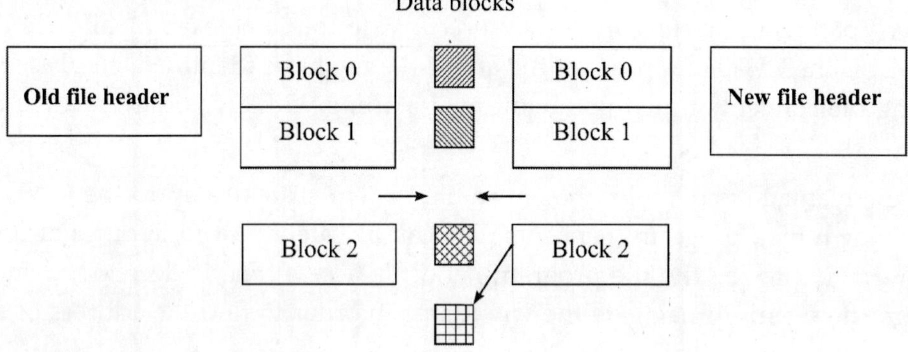

UNIX Disk Space Allocation

UNIX allocates disk space using an indexed method. Unix views all files as streams of bytes – internal logical structure is application specific. All Unix files are administered through ***inodes*** (i.e. information node). The i-node is the unique block of descriptor information for that file (containing, for example, the file's block numbers on disk). Each file has an i-node.

File allocation is done on a block basis and is dynamic (i.e. space is allocated as needed). Allocation is thus non-contiguous and UNIX uses a variation on the indexed method. Each i-node contains a 39-byte file address made up of thirteen 3-byte addresses. The first 10 point to the first 10 blocks of the file. If the file is longer than 10 blocks then the remaining 3 addresses are used to implement one or more levels of indirection as needed in the following order:

- **Single indirection**

  11th address points to a block containing an index. Each entry in the index block points to the succeeding blocks of the file.

- **Double indirection**

  12th address points to a block containing an index to indexes. Each entry in the first index block points to another index block which itself points to the succeeding blocks of the file.

- **Triple indirection**

  13th address points to a block containing an index to indexes to indexes. Each entry in the first index block points to a second set of index blocks. Each entry in the index blocks of the second level of indexes points to a third set of index blocks which themselves point to the succeeding blocks of the file.

The total no. of data blocks that a UNIX file can contain depends then on the capacity of the fixed-sized blocks. In UNIX System V, the length of a block is 1Kbyte and each block that acts as an index block can hold 256 block addresses. So the maximum file size is over 16Gbytes.

Advantages of the scheme

1. The i-node is of a small fixed size and so can be kept in memory for long periods.
2. Smaller files (most common) can be accessed with no indirection which reduces access time.
3. The upper limit of 16Gbytes is large enough to cope with virtually all files.

Performance of allocation methods

The allocation methods that we have discussed vary in their storage efficiency and data-block access times. Both are important criteria in selecting the proper method or methods for an operating system to implement.

Before selecting an allocation method, we need to determine how the systems will be used. A system with mostly sequential access should use a method different from that for a system with mostly random access. For any type of access, contiguous allocation requires only one access to get a disk block. Since we can easily keep the initial address of the file in memory, we can calculate immediately the disk address of the ith block (or the next block) and read it directly.

For linked allocation, we can also keep the address of the next block in memory and read it directly. This method is fine for sequential access; for direct access, however, an access to the ith block might require i disk reads. This problem indicates why linked allocation should not be used for an application requiring direct access.

As a result, some systems support direct-access files by using contiguous allocation and sequential access by linked allocation. For these systems, the type of access to be made must be declared when the file is created. A file created for sequential access will be linked and cannot be used for direct access. A file created for direct access will be contiguous and can support both direct access and sequential access, but its maximum length must be declared when it is created. In this case, the operating system must have appropriate data structures and algorithms to support *both* allocation methods. Files can be converted from one type to another by the creation of a new file of the desired type, into which the contents of the old file are copied. The old file may then be deleted, and the new file renamed.

Indexed allocation is more complex. If the index block is already in memory, then the access can be made directly. However, keeping the index block in memory requires considerable space. If this memory space is not available, then we may have to read first the index block and then the desired data block. For a two-level index, two index-block reads might be necessary. For an extremely large file, accessing a block near the end of the file would require reading in all the index blocks to follow the pointer chain before the needed data block finally could be read. Thus, the performance of indexed allocation depends on the index structure, on the size of the file, and on the position of the block desired.

Some systems combine contiguous allocation with indexed allocation by using contiguous allocation for small files (up to three or four blocks), and automatically switching to an indexed allocation if the file grows large. Since most files are small, and contiguous allocation is efficient for small files, average performance can be quite good.

For instance, the version of the UNIX operating system from Sun Microsystems was changed in 1991 to improve performance in the file-system allocation algorithm. The performance measurements indicated that the maximum disk throughput on a typical workstation (12-MIPS SpARCstation) took 50 percent of the CPU and produced a disk bandwidth of only 1.5 MB per second. To improve performance, Sun made changes to allocate space in clusters of size 56 KB whenever possible. (56 KB was the maximum size of a DMA transfer on Suns at that time.) This allocation reduced external fragmentation, and thus seek and latency times. In addition, the disk-reading routines were optimised to read in these large clusters. The mode structure was left unchanged. These changes, plus the use of read-ahead and free-behind, resulted in 25 percent less CPU being used for substantially improved throughput.

Many other optimisations are possible and are in use. Given the disparity between CPU and disk speed, it is not unreasonable to add thousands of extra instructions to the operating system to save just a few disk-head movements. Furthermore, this disparity is increasing over time, to the point where hundreds of thousands of instructions reasonably could be used to optimise head movements.

Free-Space Management

Since disk space is limited, we need to reuse the space from deleted files for new files, if possible. (Write-once optical disks only allow one write to any given sector, and thus such reuse is not physically possible.) To keep track of free disk space, the system maintains a free-space list. The free-space list records all *free* disk blocks-those not allocated to some file or directory. To create a file, we search the free-space list for the required amount of space, and allocate that space to the new file. This space is then removed from the free-space list. When a file is deleted, its disk space is added to the free-space list. The free-space list, despite its name, might not be implemented as a list, as we shall discuss.

Bit Vector

Frequently, the free-space list is implemented as a bit map or bit vector. Each block is represented by I bit. If the block is free, the bit is 1; if the block is allocated, the bit is 0.

For example, consider a disk where blocks 2, 3, 4, 5, 8, 9, 10, 11, 12, 13, 17, 18, 25, 26, and 27 are free, and the rest of the blocks are allocated. The free-space bit map would be

001111001111110001100000011100000...

The main advantage of this approach is it's relatively simplicity and efficiency in finding the first free block, or H consecutive free blocks on the disk. Indeed, many computers supply bit-manipulation instructions that can be used effectively for that purpose. For example, the Intel family starting with the 80386 and the Motorola family starting with the 68020 (processors that have powered PCs and Macintosh systems, respectively) have instructions that return the offset in a word of the first bit with the value 1. In fact, the Apple Macintosh operating system uses the bit-vector method to allocate disk space. To find the first free block, the Macintosh operating system checks sequentially each word in the bit map to see whether that value is not 0, since a 0-valued word has all 0 bits and represents a set of allocated blocks. The first non-0 word is scanned for the first 1 bit, which is the location of the first free block. The calculation of the block number is

(number of bits per word) x (number of 0-value words) + offset of first 1 bit.

Again, we see hardware features driving software functionality. Unfortunately, bit vectors are inefficient unless the entire vector is kept in main memory (and is written to disk occasionally for recovery needs). Keeping it in main memory is possible for smaller disks, such as on microcomputers, but not for larger ones. A 1.3-GB disk with –2-byte blocks would need a bit map of over 332 KB to track its free blocks. Clustering the blocks in groups of four reduces this number to over 83 KB per disk.

Linked List

Another approach to free-space management is to link together all the free disk blocks, keeping a pointer to the first free block in a special location on the disk and caching it in memory. This first block contains a pointer to the next free disk block, and so on. In our example, we would keep a pointer to block 2, as the first free block. Block 2 would contain a pointer to block 3, which would point to block 4, which would point to block 5, which would point to block 8, and so on. However, this scheme is not efficient; to traverse the list, we must read each block, which requires substantial I/O time. Fortunately, traversing the free list is not a frequent action. Usually, the operating system simply needs a free block so that it can allocate that block to a file, so the first block in the free list is used. The FAT method incorporates free-block accounting into the allocation data structure. No separate method is needed.

In linked allocation, each file is a linked list of disk blocks, scattered anywhere on the disk.

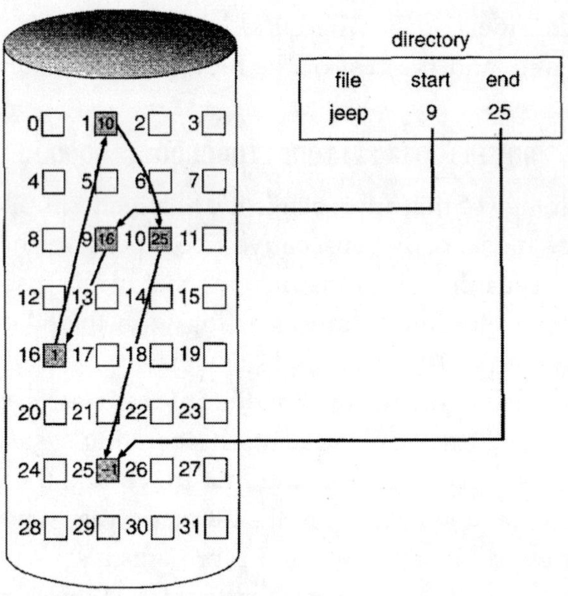

1. At file creation time, simply tell the directory about the file. When writing, get a free block and write to it, en-queuing it to the file header.

2. There's no external fragmentation since each request is for one block.
3. Method can only be effectively used for sequential files. Pointers use up space in each block.

- Reliability is not high because any loss of a pointer loses the rest of the file.
- A File Allocation Table is a variation of this. It uses a separate disk area to hold the links.
- This method doesn't use space in data blocks. Many pointers may remain in memory.
- A FAT file system is used by MS-DOS.

Grouping

A modification of the free-list approach is to store the addresses of n free blocks in the first free block. The first *n* 1 of these blocks are actually free. The last block contains the addresses of another n free block, and so on. The importance of this implementation is that the addresses of a large number of free blocks can be found quickly, unlike in the standard linked-list approach.

Counting

Another approach is to take advantage of the fact that generally, several contiguous blocks may be allocated or freed simultaneously, particularly when space is allocated with the contiguous-allocation algorithm or through clustering. Thus, rather than keeping a list of n free disk addresses, we can keep the address of the first free block and the number *n* of free contiguous blocks that follow the first block. Each entry in the free-space list then consists of a disk address and a count. Although each entry requires more space than would a simple disk address, the overall list will be shorter as long as the count is generally greater than 1.

Efficiency and Performance

Now that we have discussed the block-allocation and directory-management options, we can further consider their effect on performance and efficient disk use Disks tend to be a major bottleneck in system performance, since they are the slowest main computer component. In this section, we discuss a variety of techniques used to improve the efficiency and performance of secondary storage.

Efficiency

The efficient use of disk space is heavily dependent on the disk allocation and directory algorithms in use. For instance, UNIX modes are pre-allocated on a partition. Even an "empty" disk has a percentage of its space lost to modes. However, by pre-allocating the modes and spreading them across the partition, we improve the file system's performance. This improved performance is a result of the UNIX allocation and free-space algorithms, which try to keep a file's data blocks near that file's mode block to reduce seek time.

The types of data normally kept in a file's directory (or mode) entry also require consideration. Commonly, a "last write date" is recorded to supply information to the user and to determine whether the file needs to be backed up. Some Systems also keep a "last access date," so that a user can determine when the file was last read. The result of keeping this information is that, whenever the file is read, a field in the directory structure must be written to. This change requires the block to be read into memory, a section changed, and the block written back out to disk, because operations on disks occur only in block (or cluster) chunks.

So, any time a file is opened for reading, its directory entry must be read and written as well. This requirement can be inefficient for frequently accessed files, so we must weigh its benefit against its performance cost when designing a file system. Generally, *every* data item associated with a file needs to be considered for its effect on efficiency and performance.

As an example, consider how efficiency is affected by the size of the pointers used to access data. Most Systems use either 16- or 32-bit pointers throughout the operating system. These pointer sizes limit the length of a file to either 216 (64 KB) or 232 bytes (4 GB). Some Systems implement 64-bit pointers to increase this limit to 264 bytes, which is a very large number indeed. However, 64-bit pointers take more space to store, and in turn make the allocation and free-space-management methods (linked lists, indexes, and so on) use more disk space.

One of the difficulties in choosing a pointer size, or indeed any fixed allocation size within an operating system, is planning for the effects of changing technology. Consider that the IBM PC XT had a 10-MB hard drive and an MS-DOS file system that could support only 32 MB. (Each FAT entry was 12 bits, pointing to an 8-KB cluster.) As disk capacities increased, larger disks had to be split into 32-MB partitions, because the file system could not track blocks beyond 32 MB. As hard disks of over 100-MB capacities became common, the disk data structures and algorithms in MS-DOS had to be modified to allow larger file systems. (Each FAT entry was expanded to 16 bits, and later to 32 bits.) The initial file-system decisions were made for efficiency reasons; however, with the advent of MS-DOS Version 4, millions of computer users were inconvenienced when they had to switch to the new, larger file system.

As another example, consider the evolution of Sun's Solaris operating system. Originally, many data structures were of fixed lengths, allocated at system startup. These structures included the process table and the open-file table. When the process table became full, no more processes could be created. When the file table became full, no more files could be opened. The system would fail to provide services to the users. Only recompiling the kernel and rebooting the system could increase these table sizes. Since the release of Solaris 2, almost all kernel structures are allocated dynamically, eliminating these artificial limits on system performance. Of course, the algorithms that manipulate these tables are more complicated, and the operating system is a little slower because it must dynamically allocate and de-allocate table entries, but that price is the usual one for more functional generality.

Performance

Once the basic file-system algorithms are selected, we can still improve performance in several ways. Most disk controllers include local memory to form an on-board cache that is sufficiently large to store entire tracks at a time. Once a seek is performed, the track is read into the disk cache starting at the sector under the disk head (alleviating latency time). The disk controller then transfers any sector requests to the operating system. Once blocks make it from the disk controller into main memory, the operating system may cache the blocks there.

Some systems maintain a separate section of main memory for a disk cache, where blocks are kept under the assumption that they will be used again shortly. Other systems cache file data using a page cache. The page cache uses virtual-memory techniques to cache file data as pages rather than as file-system-oriented blocks. Caching file data using virtual addresses is far more efficient than caching through physical disk blocks. Several systems, including Solaris, some new Linux releases, and Windows NT and 2000, use page caching to cache both process pages and file data. This is known as unified virtual memory. Solaris uses both a block cache and a page cache. The block cache is used for file-system metadata (such as modes) and the page cache is used for all file-system data.

Some versions of UNIX provide a unified buffer cache. Consider the two alternatives of opening and accessing a file. One approach is to use memory mapping, the second is to use the standard system calls read and write.

A memory mapping proceeds by reading in disk blocks from the file system and storing them in the buffer cache. Because the virtual memory system cannot interface with the buffer cache, the contents of the file in the buffer cache must be copied into the page cache. This situation is known as double caching and requires caching file-system data twice. Not only is it wasteful of memory, but it wastes significant CPU and I/O cycles due to the extra data movement within system memory. Also, inconsistencies between the two caches can result in corrupt files. By providing a unified buffer cache, both memory mapping and the read and write system calls use the same page cache. This has the benefit of avoiding double caching and it allows the virtual memory system to manage file-system data.

Regardless of whether we are caching disk blocks or pages, LRU seems a reasonable general-purpose algorithm for block or page replacement. However, the evolution of the Solaris page-caching algorithms reveals the difficulty in choosing an algorithm. Solaris allows processes and the page cache to share unused memory. Prior to Solaris 2.5.1, there was no distinction between allocating pages to a process or the page cache. As a result, a system performing many I/O operations uses most of the available memory for caching pages. Because of the high rates of I/O, the page scanner reclaims pages from processes-rather than the page cache-when free memory runs low.

Solaris 2.6 and Solaris 7 optionally implemented *priority paging,* in which the page scanner gives priority to process pages over the page cache. Solaris 8 added a fixed limit between process pages and file-system page cache, preventing either from forcing the other out of memory.

The page cache, the file system, and the disk drivers have some interesting interactions. When data are written to a disk file, the pages are buffered in the cache, and the disk driver sorts its output queue according to disk address. These two actions allow the disk driver to minimize disk-head seeks and to write data at times optimised for disk rotation. Unless synchronous writes are required, a process writing to disk simply writes into the cache, and the system asynchronously writes the data to disk when convenient. The user process sees very fast writes. When data are read from a disk file, the block I/O system does some read-ahead; however, writes are much nearer to asynchronous than are reads. Thus, output to the disk through the file system is often faster than is input for large transfers, counter to intuition.

Synchronous writes occur in the order in which the disk subsystem receives them, and the writes are not buffered. Thus the calling routine must wait for the data to reach the disk drive before it can proceed. Asynchronous writes are done the majority of the time. In an asynchronous write the data is stored in the cache and returns control to the caller. Metadata writes, among others, can be synchronous. Operating systems frequently include a flag in the open system call to allow a process to request that writes be performed synchronously. For example, databases use this feature for atomic transactions, to assure that data reaches stable storage in the required order.

Some systems optimise their page cache by using different replacement algorithms, depending on the access type of the file. A file being read or written sequentially should not have its pages replaced in LRU order, because the most recently used page will be used last, or perhaps never again. Instead, sequential access may be optimised by techniques known as free-behind and read-ahead. Free-behind removes a page from the buffer as soon as the next page is requested. The previous pages are not likely to be used again and waste buffer space.

With read-ahead, a requested page and several subsequent pages are read and cached. These pages are likely to be requested after the current page is processed. Retrieving this data from the disk in one transfer and caching it saves a considerable amount of time. A track cache on the controller does not eliminate the need for read-ahead on a multi-programmed system, because of the high latency and overhead of many small transfers from the track cache to main memory.

Another method of using main memory to improve performance is common on PCs. A section of memory is set aside and treated as a virtual disk (or RAM disk). In this case, a RAM-disk device driver accepts all the standard disk operations but performs those operations on the memory section, instead of on a disk. All disk operations can then be executed on this RAM disk and, except for the lightning-fast speed, users will not notice a difference. Unfortunately, RAM disks are useful only for temporary storage, since a power failure or a reboot of the system will usually erase them. Commonly, temporary files such as intermediate compiler files are stored there.

The difference between a RAM disk and a disk cache is that the contents of the RAM disk are totally user controlled, whereas those of the disk cache are under the control of the operating system. For instance, a RAM disk will stay empty until the user (or programs, at a user's direction) creates files there

File Allocation Methods examples

Contiguous Allocation: In this method, each file occupies a set of contiguous blocks on the disk. If a file is n blocks long, and starts at location b, then it occupies blocks b, b+1, b+2, ... b+n-1. The directory entry for each file indicates the address of the starting block and the length of the area allocated for this file.

file	**start**	**length**
count	0	2
tr	14	3
mail	19	6
list	28	4
f	6	2

Linked Allocation: This method solves all problems of contiguous allocation. With linked allocation, each file is a linked list of disk blocks; the disk blocks may be scattered anywhere on the disk. The directory contains a pointer to the first and last blocks of the file. However, each block contains a pointer to the next block.

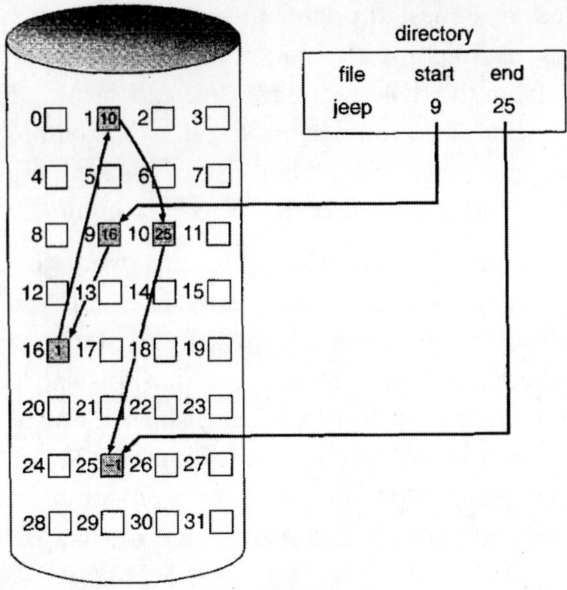

Indexed Allocation: Indexed allocation brings all the pointers together into one location — the index block. Hence, each file has its own index block, which is an array of disk-block addresses. The ith entry in the index block points to the ith block of the file (so direct access can be provided by this scheme). The Directory contains the address of the index block:

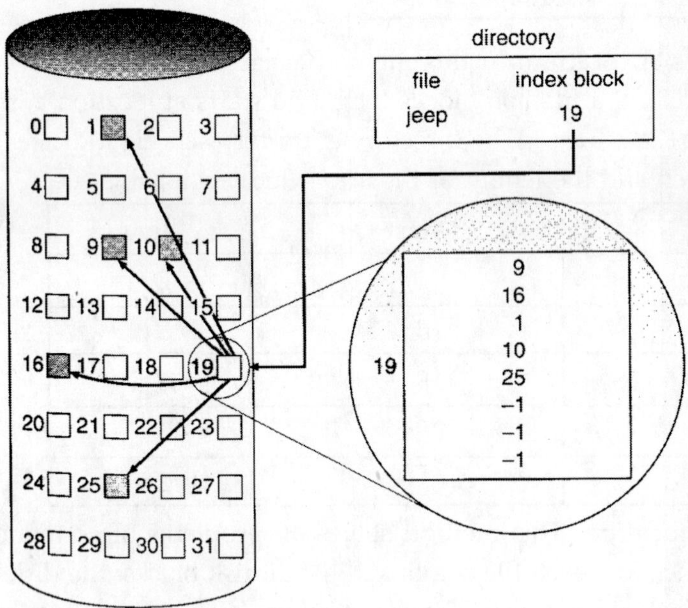

PERFORMANCE ISSUES FOR THESE METHODS

- Let's calculate, for each method, the numbers of disk accesses to read block i from a file:

Contiguous	1 access from location start + i.
Linked	(i + 1) accesses, reading each block in turn.
Index	2 accesses, 1 for index, 1 for data.

It's difficult to compare mechanisms because usage is different.

File protection

When information is kept in a computer system, we want to keep it safe from physical damage (*reliability*) and improper access (*protection*).

- Reliability is generally provided by duplicate copies of files. Many computers have system programs that automatically (or through computer-operator intervention) copy disk files to tape at regular intervals (once per day or week or month) to maintain a copy.
- Protection can be provided in many ways. For a small single-user system, we might provide protection by physically removing the floppy disks and locking them in a desk drawer of file cabinet. In a multi-user system, however, other mechanisms are needed.

When information is kept in a computer system, a major concern is its protection from both physical damage and improper access. Protection can be provided in many ways. In a multi-user system, appropriate mechanisms are needed. The need for protection files is a direct result of the ability to access file.

Protection mechanisms provide controlled access by limiting the types of file access which can be made. Several different types of operations may be controlled:

1. Read. Read from the file.
2. Write. Write or rewrite the file.
3. Execute. Load the file into memory and execute it.
4. Append. Write new information at the end of the file.
5. Delete. Delete the file and free its space for possible reuse.

Access Control

An initial sign-on procedure is normally desirable in order to establish the identity of the user for accounting purposes. It may also be necessary to control the way in which the user may use the system. There are two basic approaches to using the hierarchy of files described here. First, the file structure may be **essentially open,** with initial access unrestricted and with subsequent access permitted to all other directories unless specifically denied.

On the other hand, the file structure may be **essentially closed**, with initial access restricted for any user to a particular initial directory (assuming his ability to give a password, for example) and with subsequent access to other directories denied unless specifically permitted. There are in fact arguments for each extreme. The essentially open scheme implies that locks need be placed only where they are essential (and most effective). The essentially closed scheme provides well-defined working areas, frees the user from worrying about other users, and helps prevent the user's files from being accidentally altered. It may be observed that the scope of capabilities of the file structure described here does not depend on whether the structure is essentially open or closed. In practice, a position somewhere in between the two extremes is likely to result.

In attempting to access a file, a user may or may not be successful; depending upon what he is trying to do. The basic framework within which permissions are granted is now considered. This framework is independent of the file structure described above. Although the exact set of permissions may therefore vary from system to system, a flexible set adequate for normal usage is given here as an illustration. All permissions are logically on the branches which point to files. (In actual implementation, however, there may in some cases be permissions associated with a directory rather than repeated for each entry in that directory.)

Types of Access

Protection mechanisms provide controlled access by limiting the types of file access that can be made. Access is permitted or denied depending on several factors, one of which is the **type of access** requested. Several different types of operations may be controlled.

- Read
- Write
- Execute
- Append
- Delete
- List

The most common approach to the protection problem is to make access *dependent on the identity of the user*. Various users may need different types of access to a file or directory. The most general scheme to implement identity-dependent access is to associate with each file and directory an **access-control list (ACL)** specifying the user name and the types of access allowed for each user. When a user requests access to a particular file, the operating system checks the access list associated with that file. If that user is listed for the requested access, the access is allowed. Otherwise, a protection violation occurs, and the user job is denied access to the file.

This approach has the advantage of enabling complex access methodologies. The main problem with access lists is their length. If we want to allow everyone to read a file, we must list all users with read access. This technique has two undesirable consequences:

- Constructing such a list may be a tedious and unrewarding task, especially if we do not know in advance the list of users in the system.
- The directory entry, previously of fixed size, now needs to be of variable size, resulting in more complicated space management.

These problems can be resolved by use of a condensed version of the access list. To condense the length of the access control list, many systems recognize three classifications of users in connection with each file.

1. Owner : The user who created the file is the owner

2. Group: A set of users who are sharing the file and need similar access is a group, or work group

3. Public: All other users in the system

Mode of Access: **Read(R), Write (W), Execute(X)**

Three classes of users		R	W	X
Owner Access	7	1	1	1
Groups Access	6	1	1	0
Public Access	1	0	0	1

Ask manager to create a group (unique name), say G, and add some users to the group. The set of permissions with which a given user may access a particular branch is called the **mode** of the branch for that user. Associated with each branch is an **access control list**, which contains the list of users (or sets of users) along with the corresponding mode associated with each user. The permissions for any users on the list may be overridden (assuming permission to do so—see below) by adding subsequent users and modes to the list. The list is scanned in order of recency, and thus the addition acts as an override. (Each time the access control list is changed, a garbage collection is performed in order to keep the list nonredundant.) All access control information required for the use of a given file is contained in the list on the branch pointing to that file, and is thus independent of the way in which the file was accessed.

The mode consists of five **attributes**, named TRAP, READ, EXECUTE, WRITE and APPEND, each of which is either ON or OFF. In performing access control, the TRAP attribute is examined first. It is by itself powerful enough to accomplish the roles of the other four attributes, which are called **usage attributes**. However, the four usage attributes are included here for ease of description, as well as for ease of use of the system. The four usage attributes indicate permission to perform the given activity on the branch by the particular user only if the corresponding attribute is ON. The function of each attribute is now defined.

TRAP. When a branch has the TRAP attribute ON for a given user, a trap occurs on any reference by that user which affects the contents of the file to which that branch points. In this case, the access control module calls a procedure whose name is given as the first entry of a **trap list**. A trap list may be associated with each user in the access control list. Additional parameters may be defined in the trap list, and are passed as constants to the called procedure. Furthermore, all pertinent information regarding the branch as well as the calling sequence which caused the trap are passed to the called procedure. The traps are processed in the order specified by the trap list. The return to the access control module specifies the effective values of the four usage attributes which are to govern the access. The returned value may override the initial values of these attributes.

The user of a branch may inhibit the trap process. In this case, all references to an entry with the TRAP attribute ON cause an error return to the calling procedure. The TRAP attribute is extremely useful for monitoring of file usage, for placing additional restrictions on access (e.g., user-applied locks), for obtaining subroutines only if and when they are actually referenced, etc. A pair of commands such as LOCK and UNLOCK provide the user with a standard way of applying locks on an entry.

LOCK FILENAME,KEY

UNLOCK FILENAME

(FILENAME is the name of a branch given as a path name.) The command LOCK inserts a trap which on each attempted access may request the user to supply the designated key, and permit access only if the key is correctly supplied. UNLOCK removes the lock. (A timelock command might also be desirable, for example, to make a given branch available to a particular user only between certain times on certain days.) These commands are available to a user only if the branch pointing to the directory which contains the entry FILENAME has the WRITE attribute ON for that user (see below).

The Usage Attributes. The READ, EXECUTE, WRITE and APPEND attributes govern permission to perform operations upon files with certain intents, with an intent corresponding to each attribute. Every operation on a given branch implies one of the four intents, namely **read, execute, write or append**. The interpretation of the intent depends upon whether the accessed branch points to a directory (a **directory branch**) or to a nondirectory (a **nondirectory branch**), as seen below.

If a branch is a nondirectory branch, the meaning of each intent is quite simple. The read intent is the desire to read the contents of the file. The execute intent is the desire to execute the contents of the file as a procedure. The write intent is the desire to alter the contents of the file without adding to the end of it. The append intent is the desire to add to the end of the file without altering its original contents. The attribute on a nondirectory branch which corresponds to the particular intent of an operation on that branch indicates permission to carry out that operation only if that attribute is ON.

If a branch is a directory branch, the meaning of each intent is different. The read intent is the desire to read those contents of the directory which may be available to the user, i.e., to obtain an itemization of the directory entries. The execute intent is the desire to search the directory. The write intent is the desire to alter existing entries in the directory without adding new ones. This includes renaming entries, deleting entries, and changing the access control list for branches in that directory. The last of these includes adding traps to the trap list and changing the usage attributes. The append intent is the desire to add new entries without altering the original entries. The attribute on a directory branch which corresponds to the particular intent of an operation on that branch indicates permission to carry out that operation only if that attribute is ON.

Several additional examples of system commands are now given. Assuming the necessary WRITE attributes are ON for the appropriate directory branches, a user may by use of suitable commands change the access control list of entries or delete entries in various ways. For example, he may change (wherever permitted by the WRITE attribute of an inferior branch) the list for all inferior directory branches, or for all inferior nondirectory branches, or for all inferior nondirectory branches whose names include the parts FAP DEBUG, or for all directory branches not more than some number of levels inferior. Similarly, an elaborate delete command may be constructed. (The possibility of no one having the WRITE attribute ON for a given directory branch can be combated in various ways. One way is not to permit a change in the list to occur which brings about this circumstance, another way is to make this condition imply no restriction.)

Assuming that the necessary READ attributes are ON for the appropriate directory branches, a user may obtain an itemization of desired portions of desired inferior directories, possibly obtaining a graphical picture of the hierarchy

Putting Devices in the File System

The simple, powerful semantics of files lend themselves to controlling a variety of resources. For example, terminal input can be thought of as a sequential read-only file, and terminal output as a sequential write-only file. This means that programs can be written to take an input and output file and transparently run interactively or from disk files. Furthermore, by introducing memory-resident sequential files that are written by one process and read by another, called *pipes*, programs can be linked together in arbitrary ways. The OS has to do extra work to make a terminal look like a file, or create a pipe, but the result is a simpler programming model for developers: I/O is file I/O.

UNIX takes this to an extreme - nearly every OS resource has a file system interface. Physical disk drives are a special type of file, so are terminals, modems and printers. All of these can be accessed through the familiar file system interface. Recently, the data of running procedures has been added to the list of data accessible through the file system.

Furthermore, the access control mechanisms of files can be directly applied to prevent unauthorized manipulations of the hardware. Raw disk drives or modem devices can only be accessed by privileged users, and those accesses are controlled by the same system as file accesses. A unified access control system is easier to use and only having one to debug implies that it will be more secure.

All is not a bed of roses, though. Hardware has features that are not easily expressed as file operations. The result is the introduction of extraneous system calls to access special features. In UNIX these system calls are called ioctls, for I/O controls. Being forced to add this feature implies that the interface is not as versatile as one might like. There are various attempts to refine the interface to be more expressive without breaking the good parts.

OPERATING SYSTEM- FILE SYSTEM INTERFACE

Many Linux users have several operating systems installed, often necessitated by hardware setup systems that run under other operating systems, typically DOS or some flavour of Windows. A small section on how best to deal with this is therefore included here.

DOS

Leaving aside the debate on weather or not DOS qualifies as an operating system one can in general say that it has little sophistication with respect to disk operations. The more important result of this is that there can be severe difficulties in running various versions of DOS on large drives, and you are therefore strongly recommended in reading the Large Drives mini-HOWTO. One effect is that you are often better off placing DOS on low track numbers.

Having been designed for small drives it has a rather unsophisticated file system (fat) which when used on large drives will allocate enormous block sizes. It is also prone to block fragmentation which will after a while cause excessive seeks and slow effective transfers.

One solution to this is to use a defragmentation program regularly but it is strongly recommended to back up data and verify the disk before defragmenting. All versions of DOS have chkdsk that can do some disk checking, newer versions also have scandisk which is somewhat better. There are many defragmentation programs available, some versions have one called defrag. Norton Utilities have a large suite of disk tools and there are many others available too.

As always there are snags, and this particular snake in our drive paradise is called hidden files. Some vendors started to use these for copy protection schemes and would not take kindly to being moved to a different place on the drive, even if it remained in the same place in the directory structure. The result of this was that newer defragmentation programs will not touch any hidden file, which in turn reduces the effect of defragmentation.

Being a single tasking, single threading and single most other things operating system there is very little gains in using multiple drives unless you use a drive controller with built in RAID support of some kind.

There are a few utilities called join and subst which can do some multiple drive configurations but there is very little gains for a lot of work. Some of these commands have been removed in newer versions.

In the end there is very little you can do, but not all hope is lost. Many programs need fast, temporary storage, and the better behaved ones will look for environment variables called TMPDIR or TEMPDIR which you can set to point to another drive. This is often best done in autoexec.bat.

SET TMPDIR=E:/TMP

SET TEMPDIR=E:/TEMP

Not only will this possibly gain you some speed but also it can reduce fragmentation.

There have been reports about difficulties in removing multiple primary partitions using the fdisk program that comes with DOS. Should this happen you can instead use a Linux rescue disk with Linux fdisk to repair the system.

There are other alternatives to DOS, the most well known being DR-DOS a direct descendant from DR-DOS from Digital Research.

Another alternative which also is free is Free DOS which is a project under development. A number of free utilities are also available. Also see Club Dr-DOS and Unofficial DR-DOS Resources for more information.

Windows

Most of the above points are valid for Windows too, with the exception of Windows95 which apparently has better disk handling, which will get better performance out of SCSI drives.

A useful thing is the introduction of long filenames, to read these from Linux you will need the vfat file system for mounting these partitions.

Disk fragmentation is still a problem. Some of this can be avoided by doing a defragmentation immediately before and immediately after installing large programs or systems. I use this scheme at work and have found it to work quite well. Purging unused files and emptying the waste basket first can improve defragmentation further.

Windows also use swap drives, redirecting this to another drive can give you some performance gains. There are several mini-HOWTOs telling you how best to share swap space between various operating systems.

The trick of setting TEMPDIR can still be used but not all programs will honour this setting. Some do, though. To get a good overview of the settings in the control files you can run sysedit which will open a number of files for editing, one of which is the autoexec file where you can add the TEMPDIR settings.

Much of the temporary files are located in the /windows/temp directory and changing this is trickier. To achieve this you can use regedit which is rather powerful and quite capable of rendering your system in a state you will not enjoy, or more precisely, in a state much less enjoyable than windows in general. Registry database error is a message that means seriously bad news. Also you will see that many programs have their own private temporary directories scattered around the system.

Setting the swap file to a separate partition is a better idea and much less risky. Keep in mind that this partition cannot be used for anything else, even if there should appear to be space left there.

It is now possible to read ext2fs partitions from Windows, either by mounting the partition using FSDEXT2 or by using a file explorer like tool called Explore2fs.

OS/2

The only special note here is that you can get file system driver for OS/2 that can read an ext2fs partition. Matthieu Willm's ext2fs Installable File System for OS/2 can be found at ftp-os2.nmsu.edu, Sunsite, ftp://ftp.leo.org/pub/comp/os/os2/drivers/ifs/ext2_240.zip and ftp-os2.cdrom.com.

The IFS has read and write capabilities.

NT

This is a more serious system featuring most buzzwords known to marketing. It is well worth noting that it features software striping and other more sophisticated setups. Check out the drive manager in the control panel. I do not have easy access to NT, more details on this can take a bit of time.

One important snag was recently reported by acahalan at cs.uml.edu : (reformatted from a Usenet News posting)

NT DiskManager has a serious bug that can corrupt your disk when you have several (more than one?) extended partitions. Microsoft provides an emergency fix program at their web site. See Microsoft Help and Support for more. (This affects Linux users, because Linux users have extra partitions)

You can now read ext2fs partitions from NT using Explore2fs.

Windows 2000

Most points regarding Windows NT also applies to its descendant Windows 2000 though at the time of writing this I do not know if the aforementioned bugs have been fixed or not.

While Windows 2000, like its predecessor, features RAID, at least one company, RAID Toolbox, has found the bundled RAID somewhat lacking and made their own commercial alternative.

Windows XP

The successor to Windows 2000 is Windows XP. Allegedly XP means "experience", a good thing to have after more than 20 years in the business. This has of course not put an end to all problems such as loss of IDE DMA resulting in loss of disk speed. In the spirit of Linux generosity, this HOWTO will give a brief guide to one possible solution (short of installing Linux):

- Check cabling, connectors and jumpers. A problem here can cause XP to turn off DMA mode.
- Open "Device manager", remove all disks, CD ROMs etc. from the "Device manager"

- Remove primary and secondary IDE channel from the "Device manager"
- Remove IDE controller from the "Device manager".
- Reboot and let XP doscover and (re)install hardware
- Turn on "DMA if available" and DMA should be back.

This has worked for some but as usual there are no guarantees given.

Sun OS

There is a little bit of confusion in this area between Sun OS vs. Solaris. Strictly speaking Solaris is just Sun OS 5.x packaged with Openwindows and a few other things. If you run Solaris, just type uname -a to see your version. Parts of the reason for this confusion is that Sun Microsystems used to use an OS from the BSD family, albeight with a few bits and pieces from elsewhere as well as things made by themselves. This was the situation up to Sun OS 4.x.y when they did a "strategic roadmap decision" and decided to switch over to the official Unix, System V, Release 4 (aka SVR5), and Sun OS 5 was created. This made a lot of people unhappy. Also this was bundled with other things and marketed under the name Solaris, which currently stands at release 10. In spite of the large jump in version number this is actually a minor technical upgrade but a giant leap for marketing.

Sun OS 4

This is quite familiar to most Linux users. The last release is 4.1.4 plus various patches. Note however that the file system structure is quite different and does not conform to FSSTND so any planning must be based on the traditional structure. You can get some information by the man page on this: man hier. This is, like most man pages, rather brief but should give you a good start. If you are still confused by the structure it will at least be at a higher level.

Sun OS 5 (Solaris)

This comes with a snazzy installation system that runs under Openwindows, it will help you in partitioning and formatting the drives before installing the system from CD-ROM. It will also fail if your drive setup is too far out, and as it takes a complete installation run from a full CD-ROM in a 1x only drive this failure will dawn on you after too long time. That is the experience we had where I used to work. Instead we installed everything onto one drive and then moved directories across.

The default settings are sensible for most things, yet there remains a little oddity: swap drives. Even though the official manual recommends multiple swap drives (which are used in a similar fashion as on Linux) the default is to use only a single drive. It is recommended to change this as soon as possible.

Sun OS 5 offers also a file system especially designed for temporary files, tmpfs. It offers significant speed improvements over ufs but does not survive rebooting.

The only comment so far is: beware! Under Solaris 2.0 it seem that creating too big files in /tmp can cause an out of swap space kernel panic trap. As the evidence of what has happened is as lost as any data on a RAMdisk after powering down it can be hard to find out what has happened. What is worse, it seems that user space processes can cause this kernel panic and unless this problem is taken care of it is best not to use tmpfs in potentially hostile environments.

Trivia: There is a movie also called Solaris, a science fiction movie that is very, very long, slow and incomprehensible. This was often pointed out at the time Solaris (the OS) appeared...

BeOS

This operating system is one of the more recent one to arrive and it features a file system that has some database like features.

There is a BFS file system driver being developed for Linux and is available in alpha stage. For more information check the Linux BFS page where patches also are available.

Case studies: The File System in UNIX

Internal Structure of the file system

None of the file attributes as listed in **ls –l** are stored in the file. Every file has a **table** associated with it, which is stored in a special area of the disk. This table is called the **identification node** or **i-node.** The i-node describes the file uniquely. The list of all i-nodes is called the **i-list**.

A **file system** is a logical organization imposed on a physical data storage medium by the operating system. There may be more than one **file system** in a single machine. Every disk in the UNIX system has at least one file system, each with its own **root.** One of them is considered to be the main system. Command **df** gives file systems.

Every file system consists of a sequence of blocks, each of size 512 bytes. (An improvement in many UNIX systems is to use larger blocks, e.g., 4K bytes, and allow the last block of a file to be a smaller block called a **fragment**.) Some of these blocks are not allotted to the user, and are reserved exclusively for the use of the kernel. The file system breaks the disk in **4 segments**.

Segment 1 – Boot Block

The first block numbered 0 is the **boot block**, which is normally unused by the file system, and set aside for the booting procedure. This is true for the main file system. For the other systems this block is left unused.

Segment 2 – Super Block

The second block, numbered 1 is called the **super block** and is used to control allocation of disk blocks. The super block contains details of the active file system: the size and status of the system, the details of the free blocks and i-nodes, etc.

Segment 3 – i-nodes

The third segment includes block 2 onwards, up to a number determined during the creation of the file system. Every file in the system will have an entry in this area identified by a 64-bit structure called the i-node. The complete list of i-nodes is known as the **i-list**. Every i-node is identified by its position in the list called the **i-number** (the internal name of the file). Use **–i** option with **ls –l** to show i-number of a file.

Each i-node contains the following attributes of a file:

file mode (16-bit integer quantity specifying *file type, run and access*

number of links (total number of hard links to file)

owner (the user-id number of owner)

group (the group-id number)

size (total size in bytes of the data contained in file)

last content change (time when contents of file were last modified; displayed by **ls –l**)

last status change (time when any status item file was changed)

i-number (the index number of this i-node)

device (hardware device where file is stored)

block size (optimal block size to use for file I/O operations)

block count (total number of file blocks allocated to file)

array of 13 pointers to the file (array of 13 disk block addresses which keeps track of all disk blocks containing file segments)

The UNIX i-node structure is in sharp contrast to the system followed in MSDOS, which stores the file attributes, including the modification time, the number of bytes and the address of the starting disk cluster in the directory itself.

16 bits of file mode

4 high bits – file type

next 3 bits – manner in which executable file is run

lowest 9 bits – read, write, execute permissions of user, group or other.

The time of creation of the file is not displayed by an UNIX command, but the other two time stamps are. When **ls** is used with **-t** the files are listed in order of their modification time. Coupled with **–u**, they are listed in order of their access time. A file is **accessed** if it is executed or read by any program. When you change the contents of a file, the i-node gets updated. It also gets updated when you modify file permissions, etc. If a command such as **wc (word count)** is invoked with the file then it is accessed but not modified, e.g.,

%wc address

accesses the file address, but doesn't modify it.

User and Group ID

The password file (/etc/passwd) entry of each user contains a group affiliation. If user belongs to more than one group the additional group affiliations are specified in the file /etc/group. The group ID of a file can be set to any group name of which the owner is a member. When a file is first created, it is given by default the group ID of the directory that contains its. You can change the group ownership of a file using command:

chgrp *groupid filename*

e.g.,

% chgrp research mypaper

changes the group ID of the file *mypaper* to research.

Segment 4 – Data Blocks

The fourth and final segment contains a long chain of blocks for storing the contents of files (physical blocks of 512 bytes). These data blocks begin from the point the i-node blocks terminate. A UNIX file is a sequentially organized set of blocks scattered throughout the disk. It is the array of the 13 disk block addresses, which keeps track of all disk blocks containing the file segments (giving the illusion of a contiguous file). This array can be called the heart of the i-node.

For regular files, the first 10 pointers contain the addresses of the first 10 storage blocks of file.

For example, if the file is 5 blocks long, the first 5 pointers will contain list of the 5 disk block addresses and remaining 8 points will contain zeros.

As file grows beyond 10 blocks, an 11th data block, called the **indirect block** is allocated to specify a disk block, which contains the addresses of the next 256 blocks of the file. With the first eleven pointers, you are able to located 10+256 = 266 blocks.

As file grows beyond this size, the 12th block, called the **double indirect block** contains the addresses of 256 indirect blocks, referencing a total of 256x256 blocks for a total of

$$10 + 256 + 256^2 = 65,802 \text{ blocks.}$$

The 13th block is a **triple indirect block** referencing an additional 256x256x256 blocks for a total of $10 + 256 + 256^2 + 256^3 = 16,843,018$ blocks (around 17GB).

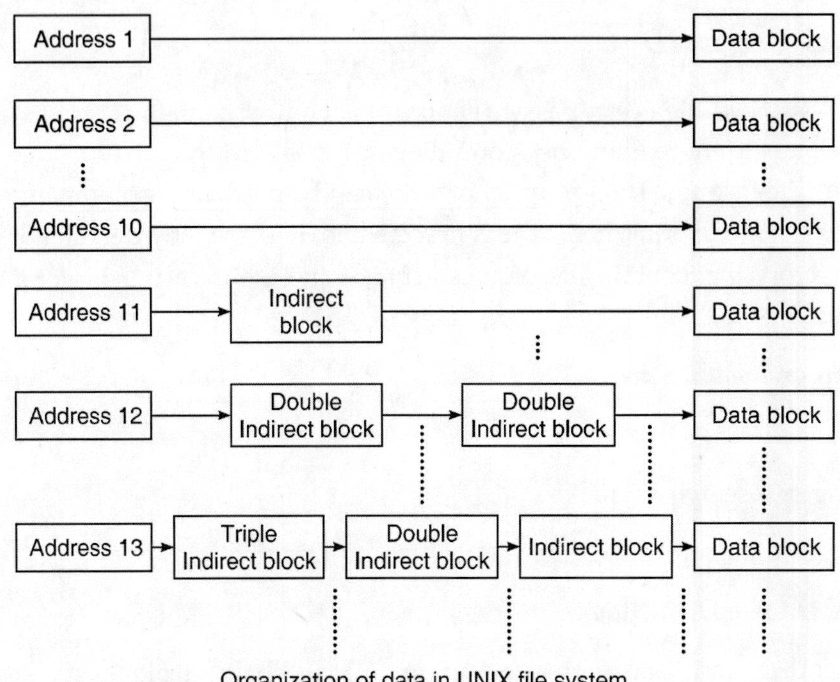

Organization of data in UNIX file system

Links

A directory entry may to a **pointer** to another file or **link**. There are two types of links: a **hard link** and a **symbolic link.**

Use command **ln** to create links. For example,

```
% ls -l
total 1
-rw———   1 bermanka faculty   7 Aug 19 19:17 coffee
% ln coffee tea
% ls -l
total 2
-rw———   2 bermanka faculty   7 Aug 19 19:17 coffee
-rw———   2 bermanka faculty   7 Aug 19 19:17 tea
```

A hard link was created between files coffee and tea. The following example establishes a **soft link** between orange and lemon, even though orange does not exist.

% ln -s orange lemon

% ls -l

total 2

-rw——— 2 bermanka faculty 7 Aug 19 19:17 coffee

lrwxrwxrwx 1 bermanka faculty 6 Aug 19 19:25 lemon -> orange

-rw——— 2 bermanka faculty 7 Aug 19 19:17 tea

File permission mask

There is a system default permission, which is inherited by all files when they are created. Normally the permission is rw-rw-rw- (octal value 666) for regular files, and rwxrwxrwx (octal value 777) for directories. To find out default value use command **umask**,

The system default can be changed by making a subtraction from it, using the command **umask**, with one octal number argument, e.g.,

%umask 022

subtract 022 from default, e.g., 666-022 = 644

System Adminstrator

System administrator's login

login: root

password: <enter>

The system administrator has enormous powers as **root** user. For example, when he/she invokes **rm**, the system will delete files even if they are write protected. The super user can change the attributes of any file. The restriction on ownership doesn't apply to him/her. He can also use the **chown** and **chgrp** commands for any file in any directory.

Super user powers can be acquired from any user directory by invoking the command**: su**

Case study2: WINDOWS 98 -Disks and File Systems

The new 32-bit, protected-mode file system support in Windows 98 allows optimal access to hard disks, CD-ROM drives, and network resources. The new file system support means faster, better performance for all file I/O operations than what was available under earlier version of MS-DOS or Windows

Because of enhancements to the file systems, there is no longer an eight-character limit on filenames that was imposed by the FAT file system under MS-DOS. You can use long filenames and directory names in Windows 98 and in any applications that support long filenames.

The enhanced FAT file system in Windows 98 also permits exclusive access to a disk device for file system utilities. File system utilities, such as ScanDisk, require exclusive access to the file system to ensure data integrity in a multitasking environment. Otherwise, if a file on the disk were to be saved while the utility was writing information to the disk at the same time, data corruption could occur.

Exclusive disk access means you can now run disk management and optimization utilities without quitting Windows. You can even complete tasks such as disk defragmentation without stopping work in other applications. The exclusive access support is used by the disk utilities provided with Windows 98 and can be used in Windows-based disk management utilities from any.

The file system also detects when Windows 98 shuts down improperly. If Windows 98 is shut down without going through the standard shutdown sequence, real mode Scandisk will be executed at the next startup. The purpose of running Scandisk is to correct potential errors in the file allocation table (FAT) before continuing the boot process. In the event that a Disk read/write error is encountered during normal Windows 98 operation, a flag will also be set to run real mode Scandisk with Surface Scan.

a. File Allocation Table

File allocation table (FAT) refers to a disk format, which is a way of organizing the storage space on a hard disk.

FAT organizes information about the files on the hard disk, representing each one as a chain of numbers that identifies where each part of a file is located. The operating system uses the FAT to look up a file and find which clusters that file is written to on the hard disk.

- FAT is probably the most widely recognized disk format, being read by most operating systems.
- A 12-bit FAT was first used by Microsoft for managing floppy disks and logical drives smaller than 16 MB.
- A 16-bit FAT was introduced in MS-DOS version 3.0 for larger drives.

FAT32

FAT32 provides the following enhancements over previous implementations of the FAT file system:

- FAT32 goes beyond the capabilities of FAT16.
- FAT32 supports drives of up to 2 terabytes in size.
- FAT32 decreases the cluster size on large drives, thus reducing the amount of unused space. For example, with FAT16, a 2 GB drive has a 32 KB cluster size. The same drive under FAT32 has 4 KB clusters.
- Programs load up to 50% faster. FAT32's smaller cluster size enables the new and improved Disk Defragmenter to optimally locate the portions of an application and its supporting files needed at the time it is loaded.

  To maintain the greatest possible compatibility with existing programs, networks, and device drivers, FAT32 was implemented with as little change as possible to existing architecture, internal data structures APIs, and on-disk format for Windows 98.
- Many internal and on-disk data structures have been revised or expanded, because 4 bytes are now required to store cluster values. Existing tools and drivers should continue to work on FAT32 drives.
- MS-DOS block device drivers (for example, Aspidisk.sys) and disk tools must be revised to support FAT32 drives.
- Note:
- A FAT32 volume cannot be compressed using Microsoft DriveSpace 3.
- You cannot dual boot Windows 98 and Windows NT 4.0 if you use FAT32. Windows NT 4.0 cannot access or boot from a FAT32 drive

FAT16 vs. FAT32

- FAT16 is still available because of its widespread compatibility with all other non-Microsoft operating systems.
- The major benefits of FAT32 are that it is more efficient than a 16-bit FAT on larger disks (sometimes by as much as 20–30 percent), and that it can support disk drives larger than 2 GB without having to use multiple partitions.
- *Note*: In real-mode MS-DOS or when running Windows 98 in safe mode, FAT32 is considerably slower than FAT16.

Some older applications that were written to FAT16 specifications may be unable to display free or total disk space over 2 GB correctly. Windows 98 provides new MS-DOS and Win32 APIs that applications can use to determine free or total disk space over 2 GB.

- The following table shows a comparison of FAT16 and FAT32.

FAT16	*FAT32*
Most operating systems (MS-DOS, Windows 98, Windows NT, OS/2, and UNIX) are designed to implement and use it.	FAT32 can be used only in Windows 98 and Windows 95 OSR2.
It is efficient, both in speed and storage, on logical drives smaller than 256 MB.	Drives smaller that 512 MB are not supported by FAT32.
Disk compression, such as Drvspace, is supported.	Disk compression is not supported with FAT32.
The largest drive is limited to 2 GB.	The largest drive can be up to 2 terabytes.
Storing files in a FAT16 system can be inefficient in larger drives as the size of the cluster increases.	FAT32 cluster sizes are 4 KB (drives less than 800 MB).

Cluster Sizes of FAT16 and FAT32

The largest possible file for a FAT32 drive is 4 GB minus 2 bytes.

- Within the file allocation table :
- The FAT32 file system includes 4 bytes per cluster
- The FAT16 file system contains 2 bytes per cluster
- The FAT12 file system contains 1.5 bytes per cluster.

Note that the high 4 bits of the 32-bit values in the file allocation table for FAT32 are reserved and are not part of the cluster number.

- The following table provides a comparison of FAT16 and FAT32 cluster sizes according to drive size.

Drive size	*FAT16 cluster size*	*FAT32 cluster size*
256 MB – 511 MB	8 KB	Not supported
512 MB – 1023 MB	16 KB	4 KB
1024 MB – 2 GB	32 KB	4 KB
2 GB – 8 GB	Not supported	4 KB
8 GB – 16 GB	Not supported	8 KB
16 GB – 32 GB	Not supported	16 KB
>32 GB	Not supported	32 KB

b. File Systems

With the Windows 98 installable file system, multiple file systems can coexist on the computer. Windows 98 includes the file systems described as follows:

- Virtual File Allocation Table

  In Windows 98, the 32-bit *virtual file allocation table* (VFAT) file system is the primary file system and cannot be disabled. VFAT can use 32-bit, protected-mode drivers or 16-bit, real-mode drivers. Although VFAT will function correctly when 16-bit disk drivers are being used by IO Supervisor (IOS), its performance is compromised. VFAT handles all hard disk drive requests, using 32-bit code for all file access for hard-disk volumes.

- Network Redirectors

  A network redirector (such as Microsoft Client for NetWare Networks or Client for Microsoft Networks) is a file system driver that accesses the network file system. Windows 98 supports multiple network redirectors simultaneously.

- UDF (Universal Disk Format system)

  DVD disks use UDF.

- CD-ROM File System

  The virtual CD-ROM file system (CDFS) has the same responsibilities for a CD-ROM device as VFAT has for a standard hard disk. If a CD-ROM device is detected, the CDFS driver loads dynamically. When CDFS is installed, the standard disk type-specific device and Disk SCSI translator are replaced with CD-ROM versions. The CDFS driver is a protected-mode version of MSCDEX.EXE, providing the interface from the CD-ROM device to the operating system.

KEYWORDS

LINEAR LIST	**INDEXED ALLOCATION**
HASH TABLE	**INVERTED ALLOCATION**
CONTIGUOUS-ALLOCATION	**BIT MAP**
LINKED ALLOCATION	**LINKED LIST**

SUMMARY

A file consist a collection of records, a key element in file management is the way in which the records themselves are organized inside the file, since this heavily affects system performances ad far as record finding and access. Most operating systems, including UNIX, use object-oriented techniques to simplify, and organize the implementation. The use of these methods allows very dissimilar file-system types to be implemented within the same structure, including network file systems, such as NFS. Users can access files that are contained within multiple file systems on the local disk, or even on file systems available across the network.

- The simplest method of implementing a directory is to use a linear list of file names with pointers to the data blocks. A linear list of directory entries requires a linear search to find a particular entry. This method is simple to program but time-consuming to execute.
- Another data structure that has been used for a file directory is a hash table. In this method, a linear list stores the directory entries, but a hash data structure is also used. The hash table takes a value computed from the file name and returns a pointer to the file name in the linear list. Therefore, it can greatly decrease the directory search time.
- The contiguous-allocation method requires each file to occupy a set of contiguous blocks on the disk. Disk addresses define a linear ordering on the disk.
- With linked allocation, each file is a linked list of disk blocks; the disk blocks may be scattered anywhere on the disk. The directory contains a pointer to the first and last blocks of the file.
- Indexed allocation brings all the pointers together into one location: the index block.
- Inverted allocation allocates a disk block by hashing the file block content to a disk block location. By doing so, different file blocks of the same content (e.g., empty blocks) can share the same disk block for storage.
- Frequently, the free-space list is implemented as a bit map or bit vector.
- Another approach to free-space management is to link together all the free disk blocks, keeping a pointer to the first free block in a special location on the disk and caching it in memory.
- Protection can be provided in many ways. For a small single-user system, we might provide protection by physically removing the floppy disks and locking them in a desk drawer of file cabinet. In a multi-user system, however, other mechanisms are needed.
- Before selecting any algorithm or method, we need to determine how the systems will be used.

REVIEW QUESTIONS

1) What are the different methods of file system implementation?
2) Explain different allocation techniques?
3) Explain advantage of contiguous allocation over linked allocation?
4) Differentiate between contiguous and indexed allocation with the help of examples.
5) What is virtual file system? Explain in detail.
6) Explain the linear list algorithm with the help of an example.
7) Explain the hash table method for directory implementation.
8) Explain all the allocation methods in details.
9) Discuss the free-space management techniques used by the various file system.
10) Differentiate between FAT 16 and FAT 32

FILL IN THE BLANKS

1. A key element in file management is the way in which the ________are organized inside the file
2. The simplest method of implementing a directory is to use a _______of file names with pointers to the data blocks.
3. The ___________takes a value computed from the file name and returns a pointer to the file name in the linear list.
4. _______________brings all the pointers together into one location i.e. the index block.
5. ___________mechanisms provide controlled access by limiting the types of file access which can be made.
6. The file structure may be_________, with initial access restricted for any user to a particular initial and with subsequent access to other directories denied unless specifically permitted

TRUE OR FALSE

1. The contiguous-allocation method requires each file to occupy a set of non-contiguous blocks on the disk.
2. With linked allocation, each file is a linked list of disk blocks; the disk blocks may be scattered anywhere on the disk.

3. Inverted allocation allocates a disk block by hashing the file block content to a disk block location
4. Frequently, the free-space list is implemented as a bit map or bit vector
5. the file structure may be **essentially closed**, with initial access unrestricted and with subsequent access permitted to all other directories unless specifically denied.
6. Reliability is generally provided by duplicate copies of files

ANSWERS

FILL IN THE BLANKS

1. records
2. linear list
3. hash table
4. Indexed allocation
5. Protection
6. essentially closed

TRUE OR FALSE

1. FALSE
2. TRUE
3. TRUE
4. TRUE
5. FALSE
6. TRUE

❑❑❑

"Teachers open the door, but you must enter by yourself." —*Chinese Proverb*

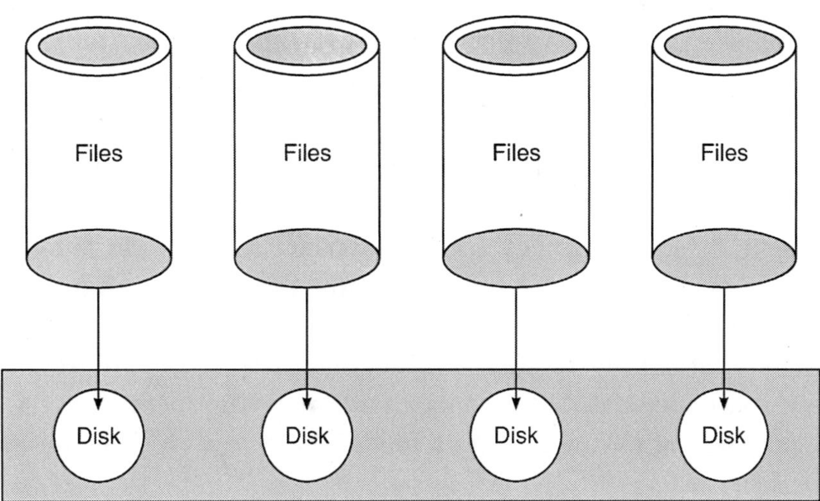

11 STORAGE MANAGEMENT

INTRODUCTION

Once a file has been created, it has to be stored in permanent memory, usually a disk. The operating system can only address storage media by dividing them into clusters, whose size may vary depending on the system used. So, it is the task of the operating system to map the logical units of the file (e.g. a letter or a word) to the physical units of the storage device, i.e. the clusters. Every logical unit is stored in one or more clusters, even if it is smaller than one cluster.

A disk is an electromechanical device that holds data. Typically there is one or more disk platters, and data is written on one or both sides, sometimes in layers, by heads that read and/or write data using electromagnets, lasers, or other technologies. From the computer's point of view, it's just a big storage area for bytes.

Before storing a file, the operating system has to find a sufficient amount of free space on the disk. There are two ways of doing so, depending on the system used. One way is to store files consecutively, which means to store them in sequential blocks or clusters. So, every time the user wants to store a file, the operating system has to find a suitable number of adjacent free clusters. Advantages of this are that in order to find the file again, only the starting cluster has to be recorded and that the file can be read again with a minimum amount of read/write head activity. Disadvantages are the difficulties that arise when the user wants to modify a file and the neighbouring clusters on the storage medium are already taken as well as the problems of finding sufficient space on a disk that is already quite full and leaves only small groups of clusters free.

The other way of storing files is called non-consecutively. In this method, the units of the file are distributed to clusters throughout the medium. Advantages of non- consecutive storage are that every cluster can be used even if the disk is almost full and that modifying files is no problem and a file can grow as long as there is free space available.Disadvantages are that the operating system has to record the numbers of all the clusters a file is stored in as well as the numbers of every single free cluster.

The organization and management of the main memory or primary memory or real memory of a computer system has been one of the most important factors influencing operating systems design. The terms memory and storage have been used interchangeably in the literature. Of the two terms, storage is more fashionable today. Programs and data must be in main storage in order to be run or referenced directly. Secondary storage, most commonly disk, drum, and tape, provides massive, inexpensive capacity for the abundance of programs and data that must be kept readily available for processing.

Storage organization

Historically, main storage has been viewed as an expensive resource. As such, it has demanded the attention of systems designers; it has been necessary to squeeze the maximum use out of this costly resource. Early systems were concerned with organizing and managing main storage for optimal use.

By storage organization we mean the manner in which the main storage is viewed. Do we place only a single user in the main storage, or do we place several users in it at the same time? If several user programs are in main storage at the same time, do we give each of them the same amount of space, or do we divide main storage into portions, called partitions, of different sizes? Do we partition the main storage in a rigid manner with partitions defined for extended periods of time, or do we provide for a more dynamic partitioning allowing the computer system to adapt quickly to changes in the needs of user jobs? Do we require that user jobs be designed to run in a specific partition, or do we allow jobs to run anywhere they will fit? Do we require that each job be placed in one contiguous block of storage locations, or do we allow jobs to be parceled up into separate blocks and placed in any available slots in main storage?

Systems have been built implementing each of these schemes.

Storage hierarchy

In the 1950s and 1960s, main storage, usually magnetic core memory, was very expensive. A decision about how much main storage to place on a computer system was made carefully. Installations couldn't buy more that it could afford, but it had to buy enough to support the operating system and a given number of users. The goal was to buy the minimum amount that could adequately support the anticipated user loads within the economic constraints of the installations.

Programs and data need to be in main storage in order to be executed or referenced. Programs and data need to be in main storage in order to be executed or referenced. Programs or data not needed immediately may be kept on secondary storage until needed and then brought into the main storage for execution or reference. Secondary storage media such as tape or disk are generally less costly than main storage and have much greater capacity. Main storage may generally be accessed much faster than secondary storage.

In systems with several levels of storage, a great deal of shuttling goes on in which programs and data are moved back and forth between the various labels. This shuttling consumer's system resource, such as CPU time that could otherwise be put to productive use.

In the 1960s it became clear that the storage hierarchy could be extended by one more level with dramatic improvements in performance and utilization. This additional level, the cache, is a high-speed storage that is much faster than the main storage. Cache storage is extremely expensive compared with storage and therefore only relatively small caches are used.

Cache storage imposes one more level of shuttling on the system. Programs in the main storage are shuttled to the very high-speed cache before being executed. In the cache, they may be executed much faster than in main storage. The hope of designers using the cache concept is that the overhead involved in shuttling programs back and forth will be much smaller than the performance increase obtained by the faster execution possible in the cache.

Storage management

Regardless of what storage organizations scheme we adopt for a particular system, we must decide what strategies to use to obtain optimal performance.

Storage management strategies determine how a particular storage organization performs under various policies:

When do we get a new program to place in the memory? Do we it when the system specifically asks for it, or do we attempt to anticipate the system's requests? Where in main storage do we place the next program to be run? Do we place program as tightly as possible into available memory slots to minimize wasted space, or do we place programs as quickly as possible to minimize execution time?

If a new program needs to placed in main storage and if main storage is currently full, which of the other programs we should displace. Should we replace the oldest programs, or should we replace those that are least frequently used, or those that are least recently used? Systems have been implemented using each of these storage management strategies.

Storage management strategies

Expensive resources are managed intensively to achieve better use. Storage management strategies are geared to obtaining the best possible use of the main storage resource. Storage management strategies are divided into the following categories.

1. Fetch strategies
   a) Demand fetch strategies
   b) Anticipatory fetch strategies
2. Placement strategies
3. Replacement strategies

1. Fetch strategies are concerned with when to obtain the next piece of program or data for insertion into main storage. For many years, the conventional wisdom has been demand fetch in which the next piece of program or data is brought in to the main storage when it is referenced by a running program. It was believed that since we cannot generally predict where program control will go next, the overhead involved in making guesses and anticipating the future would far exceed expected benefits. Today many researchers feel that anticipatory fetching will yield improved system performance.
2. Placement strategies are concerned with determining where in main storage to place an incoming program
3. Replacement strategies are concerned with determining which piece of program or data to displace to make room for incoming programs.

Contiguous vs. noncontiguous storage allocation

The earliest computing systems required contiguous storage allocations-each program had to occupy a single contiguous block of storage locations. It wasn't until variable partition multiprogramming was attempted that it became clear noncontiguous storage allocation might be useful.

In noncontiguous storage allocations, a program is divided into several blocks or segments that may be placed throughout main storage in pieces not necessarily adjacent to one another. It is more difficult for an operating system to control noncontiguous storage allocation. The benefit is that if main storage has many small holes available instead of a single large hole, then the operating system can often load and execute a program that would otherwise need to wait. Virtual storage systems involve noncontiguous storage allocation.

Single user contiguous storage allocation

The earliest computer systems allowed only a single person at a time to use the machine. All of the machine's resources were at the user's disposal. Billing for the use of the computer was straightforward-because the user had the entire machine, the user was charged for all of the resources whether or not the job used those resources. In fact, the normal billing mechanisms were based upon wall clock time. A user was given the machine for some time interval and was charged a flat hourly rate. Some of today's shared systems have far more complex billing algorithms.

Originally each user wrote all of the code necessary to implement a particular application, including the highly detailed machine level input/output instructions. Very quickly, the input/output coding needed to implement basic functions was consolidated into an input/output control system (IOCS). Users wishing to do input/output no longer had to code the instructions directly. Instead, they called IOCS routines to do the real work. This greatly simplified and speeded the coding process. The implementation of input/output control systems may have been the beginning of today's concept of operating systems.

Programs are limited in size to the amount of main storage, but it is possible to run programs larger than the main storage by using overlays.. If a particular program section is not needed for the duration of the program's execution, then another section of program may be brought in from secondary storage to occupy the storage used by the program section that is no longer needed.

Overlay gives the programmer a way to extend limited main storage. But manual overlay requires careful and time-consuming planning. A program with a sophisticated overlay structure can be difficult to modify. Virtual storage systems have obviated the need for programmer-controlled overlays.

Protection in Single User Systems

In single user contiguous allocations systems, the user has complete control over all of main storage. Storage divided into a portion holding operating system routines, a portion holding the user's program, and an unused portion. The question of protection is simple. How should the operating system be protected from destruction by the user's program?

If the user's program goes astray, it can destroy the operating system. If this is fatal and the user cannot proceed, then the user will know something is wrong, will terminate execution, fix the problem, and retry the job. In these circumstances, the need for protecting the operating system is not apparent.

But suppose the user destroys the operating system more "gently". For example, suppose certain input/output routines are accidentally changed. Then all output records might be truncated. The job could still run. If the results are not examined until it completes, then the machine resource will be wasted. Worse yet, the damage to the operating system might cause outputs to be produced that can not easily be determined to be inaccurate.

It surely is clear that the operating system should be protected from the user. Protection is implemented by the use of a single boundary register built into the CPU, as in. Each time a user program refers to a storage address, the boundary register is checked to be certain that the user is not about to destroy the operating system. The boundary register contained the address of the highest instruction used by the operating system. If the user tried to enter the operating system, then the instruction is intercepted and the job terminates with an appropriate error message.

Of course, the user needs to enter the operating systems from time to time to obtain services such as input/output. This problem is solved by giving the user a specific instruction with which to request services from the operating system (i.e., a supervisor call instruction). The user wanting to read from tape will issue an instruction asking the operating system to do so in the user's behalf. The operating system will perform the desired function, and then return control to the user program.

As operating systems have become more complex, it has been necessary to implement far more sophisticated mechanisms to protect the operating system from the users and to protect the users from one another. We shall discuss these mechanisms in detail later.

Single Stream Batch Processing

Single user systems are dedicated to one job for more than the job's execution time. Jobs generally require considerable setup time during which the operating system is loaded, tapes and disk packs are mounted, card decks are placed in the reader, appropriate forms are placed in the printer, time cards are "punched in", etc. When jobs complete, they require a considerable amount of teardown time as tapes, card decks, and disk packs are removed, forms are removed, time cards are "punched out", etc. During job setup and job teardown the computer sits idle.

Designers realized that if they could automate job-to-job transition, then they could reduce considerably the amount of time wasted between jobs. This led to the development of batch processing systems. In single stream batch processing, jobs are grouped in batches by placing their control cards back-to-back in the card reader, (or by loading the jobs consecutively onto tape or disk). A job stream processor reads the job control language statements, and facilitates the setup of the next job. It issues directives to the system operator, and performs many functions automatically that were previously performed manually.

When the current job terminates, the job stream reader automatically reads in the control language statements for the next job, and performs appropriate housekeeping chores to facilitate the transition to the next job. Batch processing systems greatly improved the use of computer systems and helped demonstrate the real value of operating systems and intensive resource management.

Because reading cards is a relatively slow operation, it was common in large computer installations to use small satellite computers to prepare the batches for the large system. Job decks would arrive at the computer center, be grouped into batches, and loaded to tape on the satellite systems. The tapes would then be brought to the large system. This was an effective way to reduce job transition time on the large system and get better use of the computer. Single stream batch processing system was the state of the art in the early 1960s.

Disk Organisation

The hard disk is a 30-year-old storage technology, and is incredibly complicated. A modern hard drive comes with 250,000 lines of micro code to govern various hard drive components. A hard disk drive generally has more than one circular disk on a spindle, each covered with magnetic material. The data is read or written using a 'head' for each surface of the disk. Thus, if there were two disks, there are four surfaces and there would be four read/write heads. The heads are connected together in a comb -like arrangement. They all move in or out at the same time. Thus, if there is a head over track 2 on side 0, there will also be a head over track 2 on sides 1,2,3,4 etc.

Each surface is divided into **concentric tracks**, and each track is divided into **sectors, like segments of a cake** (food again!). Each sector holds the same amount of data, so you can see that a sector nearer the outside edge of the disk has lower density of bits per inch.

The diagram below shows this structure. The set of corresponding tracks on each surface map out a cylindrical shape and are often referred to as a cylinder.

Any particular sector on a disk can, in principle, be accessed directly. It has an address. The address is derived from knowing the side number (surface), the track (or cylinder) number and the sector number within a track.

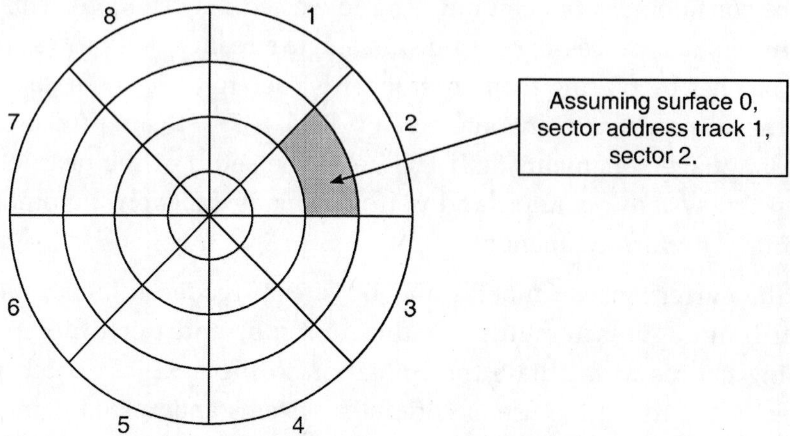

The figure shows a view of a disk surface looking down, The sector numbers are shown, starting at 1 (this is convention) the track numbers start at zero and work inwards, so the sector that is shaded would have address Track 1, sector 2.

Operating systems read data from disks in ***blocks***. A block cannot be smaller than a sector, but more than one contiguous sector could be regarded as a block. In Windows / DOS these amalgamated sectors are known as **clusters**.

Hardware Characteristics

Briefly, a hard drive consists of a disk arm and disk platters. *Disk platters* are coated with magnetic materials for recording. The *disk arm* moves a comb of disk heads, among which only one *disk head* is active for reading and writing.

One fascinating detail is that heads are aerodynamically designed to fly as close to the surface as possible. In fact, the distance is so close that there is no room for air molecules, and a hard drive is filled with special inert gas to fly disk heads. If a head touches the surface, it results in a head crash, which scrapes off magnetic information.

Each disk platter is further divided into concentric *tracks* of storage, and each track is divided into *sectors* (typically 512 bytes). Each sector is a minimum unit of disk storage. A *cylinder* consists of all tracks with a given arm position.

A modern hard drive also takes advantage of the disk geometry. Disk cylinders are further grouped into *zones*, so zones near the edge of the disk can store more information than zones near the center of the disk due to the differences in storage area (also known as *zone-bit recording*). More information stored in outer zones also means that the transfer rate (rotational speed multiplied by the information stored in a cylinder) is higher near the edge of the disk.

Since moving a disk arm from one track to the next takes time, the starting position of the next track is slightly skewed (*track skew*), so that a sequential transfer of bytes across multiple tracks can incur minimum rotational delay.

A hard drive also periodically performs *thermo-calibrations*, which adjusts the disk head positioning according to the changes in the disk radius caused by temperature changes. To account for other minor physical inaccuracies, typically 100 to 1000 bits are inserted between sectors.

Disk Performance Parameters :

When the disk drive is operating, the disk is rotating at constant speed. To read or write, the head must be positioned at the desired track and at the beginning of the desired sector on that track. Track selection involves moving the head in a movable-head system or electronically selecting one head on a fixed-head system. On a movable-head system, the time it takes to position the head at the track is known as **seek time.** When once the track is selected, the disk controller waits until the appropriate sector rotates to line up with the head. The time it takes for the beginning of the sector to reach the head is known as **rotational delay,** or rotational latency. The sum of the seek time, if any, and the rotational delay equals the **access time,** which is the time it takes to get into position to read or write. Once the head is in position, the read or write operation is then performed as the sector moves under the head; this is the data transfer portion of the operation; the time required for the transfer is the **transfer time.**

Seek Time Seek time is the time required to move the disk arm to the required track. It turns out that this is a difficult quantity to pin down. The seek time consists of two key components: the initial startup time and the time taken to traverse the tracks that have to be crossed once the access arm is up to speed.

Rotational Delay Disks, other than floppy disks, rotate at speeds ranging from

3600 rpm up to, as of this writing, 15,000 rpm; at this latter speed, there is one revolution per 4 ms. Thus, on the average, the rotational delay will be 2 ms. Floppy disks typically rotate at between 300 and 600 rpm. Thus the average delay will be between 100 and 50 ms.

Transfer Time The transfer time to or from the disk depends on the rotation speed of the disk in the following fashion:

where transfer time

b = number of bytes to be transferred

N = number of bytes on a track

r = rotation speed, in revolutions per second

Thus the total average access time can be expressed as

Ta = Ts +

where Ts is the average seek time.

For the single disk, there will be a number of I/O requests (reads and writes)- from various processe in the queue. This **random scheduling** is useful as a benchmark against which to evaluate other techniques.

Therefore the access time to read or write a disk section includes three components:

1. *Seek time*: the time to position heads over a cylinder (~8 msec on average).

2. *Rotational delay*: the time to wait for the target sector to rotate underneath the head. Assuming a speed of 7,200 rotations per minute, or 120 rotations per second, each rotation takes ~8 msec, and the average rotational delay is ~4 msec.

3. *Transfer time*: the time to transfer bytes. Assuming a peak bandwidth of 58 Mbytes/sec, transferring a disk block of 4 Kbytes takes 0.07 msec.

Thus, the overall time to perform a disk I/O = seek time + rotational delay + transfer time.

The sum of the seek time and the rotational delay is the disk ***latency***, or the time to initiate a transfer. The transfer rate is the disk ***bandwidth***.

If a disk block is randomly placed on disk, then the disk access time is roughly 12 msec to fetch 4 Kbytes of data, or a bandwidth 340 Kbytes/sec.

If a disk block is randomly located on the same disk cylinder as the current disk arm position, the access time is roughly 4 msec without the seek time, or a bandwidth of 1.4 Mbytes/sec.

If the next sector is on the same track, the access time is 58 Mbytes/sec without the seek time and the rotational delay.

Therefore, the key to using the hard drive effectively is to minimize the seek time and rotational latency.

Disk Tradeoffs

One design decision is the size of disk sector.

Sector size	Space utilization	Transfer rate
1 byte	8 bits/1008 bits (0.8%)	80 bytes/sec (1 byte / 12 msec)
4 Kbytes	4096 bytes/4221 bytes (97%)	340 Kbytes/sec (4 Kbytes / 12 msec)
1 Mbyte	(~100%)	58 Mbytes/sec (peak bandwidth)

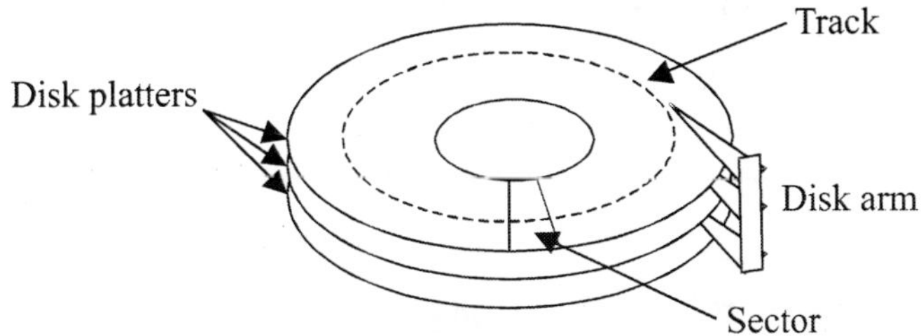

A bigger sector size seems to get a more effective transfer rate from the hard drive. However, this allocation granularity is wasteful if only 1 byte out of 1 Mbyte is needed for storage.

Disk Controller

Two popular disk controllers are SCSI (small computer systems interface), and IDE (integrated device electronics).

Disk Device Driver

The device drivers are part of the operating system directly controlling operations of devices. As they operate directly with the device they are usually written in assembly language or system programming language.

A typical device driver will contain device-dependent code supplied by hardware manufacturers. A device controller can have one or more device registers used to give them commands. The device drivers issue these commands and check that they are carried out properly. In general terms, the job of a device driver is to accept abstract requests from the device-independent software above it, and see to it that the request is executed.

A device driver can maintain a queue of requests. Some controllers accept multiple commands and some do not. The device driver knows the controller it's talking to and adjusts accordingly

For example, requests to read a disk block. This requires that one do the following:

- work out where the block is located
- make sure the drive is working properly (motor on, etc.)
- position the read head over the proper cylinder
- determine the disk rotation delay in getting to the proper sector
- read the block
- check for errors
- return status information

Depending on the device and the system the driver may be responsible for the actual data transfer to or from the device. It may also use special hardware like DMA (direct memory access) or an I/O channel to make the transfers (this would be more rapid). If the I/O transfer is finished the device driver will inform the IOCS.

The Device Management is very strongly connected to the file management of an operating system. The UNIX file system, for instance, which is structured as a tree, reserves one of its subdirectories for devices. It is called /dev. So, all devices are treated as files in the root file system. In MS-DOS, every device has its own file system, for example A:\ stands for the floppy disk drive.

One major function of the disk device driver is to reduce the seek time for disk accesses. Since disk can serve only one request at a time, the device driver can schedule the disk request in such a way to minimize disk arm movements. There are a handful of disk scheduling strategies.

The path between the operating system and virtually all hardware not on the computer's motherboard goes through a special program called a **driver**. Much of a driver's function is to be the translator between the electrical signals of the hardware subsystems and the high-level programming languages of the operating system and application programs. Drivers take data that the operating system has defined as a file and translate them into streams of bits placed in specific locations on storage devices, or a series of laser pulses in a printer.

Because there are such wide differences in the hardware controlled through drivers, there are differences in the way that the driver programs function, but most are run when the device is required, and function much the same as any other process. The operating system will frequently assign high-priority blocks to drivers so that the hardware resource can be released and readied for further use as quickly as possible.

One reason that drivers are separate from the operating system is so that new functions can be added to the driver and thus to the hardware subsystems - without requiring the operating system itself to be modified, recompiled and redistributed.

Through the development of new hardware device drivers, development often performed or paid for by the manufacturer of the subsystems rather than the publisher of the operating system, input/output capabilities of the overall system can be greatly enhanced.

Managing input and output is largely a matter of managing **queues** and **buffers**, special storage facilities that take a stream of bits from a device, perhaps a keyboard or a serial port, hold those bits, and release them to the CPU at a rate slow enough for the CPU to cope with.

This function is especially important when a number of processes are running and taking up processor time. The operating system will instruct a buffer to continue taking input from the device, but to stop sending data to the CPU while the process using the input is suspended. Then, when the process needing input is made active once again, the operating system will command the buffer to send data.

This process allows a keyboard or a modem to deal with external users or computers at a high speed even though there are times when the CPU can't use input from those sources.

Managing all the resources of the computer system is a large part of the operating system's function and, in the case of real-time operating systems, may be virtually all the functionality required. For other operating systems, though, providing a relatively simple, consistent way for applications and humans to use the power of the hardware is a crucial part of their reason for existing.

Disk Scheduling

Since most jobs depend heavily on the disk for loading of input and output files, it is important that disk service be as fast as possible. The operating system can improve on the average disk service time by scheduling the requests for disk access.

Disk speed is composed of three parts. To access a block on the disk, the system must first move the head to the appropriate track or cylinder. This head movement is called a *seek*, and the time to complete it is *seek time*. Once the head is at the right track, it must wait until the desired block rotates under the read-write head. This delay is *latency* time. Finally, the actual transfer of data between the disk and main memory can take place. This last part is *transfer* time. The total time to service a request is the sum of the seek time, latency time, and transfer time.

As discussed before, every I/O device, including each disk drive, has a queue of pending requests. Whenever a process needs I/O to or from the disk, it issues a system call to the operating system. The request specifies several pieces of necessary information:

- Whether this is an input or output operation
- What the disk address is(drive, cylinder, surface, block)
- What amount of information is to be transferred (a byte or word count)

If the desired disk drive and controller are available, the request can be serviced immediately. However, while the drive or controller is serving one request, any additional requests, normally from other processes, will need to be queued. For a multiprogramming system with many processes, the disk queue may often be not empty. Thus, when a request is complete, we must pick a new request from the queue and service it. A disk service requires that the head be moved to the desired track, then a wait for latency, and finally the transfer of data.

A seek strategy for the I/O device handler is the predetermined policy that the device handler uses to allocate access to the various processes that may make a request for it. The most popular strategies are discussed as follows:

1. FCFS(first-come-first-serve) **Scheduling**

The simplest form of disk scheduling is, of course, *first-come-first-served* (FCS) scheduling. FCFS is the simplest and easiest to program and is essentially fair to the users Requests are served in the order of arrival. This policy is fair among requesters, but requests may land on random spots on disk. Therefore, the seek time may be long and it may not provide the best (average) service. Consider, for example, an ordered disk queue with requests involving tracks

98,183,37,122,14,124,65 and 67

Listed first (98) to last (67). If the read-write head is initially at track 53, it will first move from 53 to 98, then to 183, 37, 122, 14, 124, 65, and finally, to 67, for a total head movement of 640 tracks. This schedule is diagrammed below.

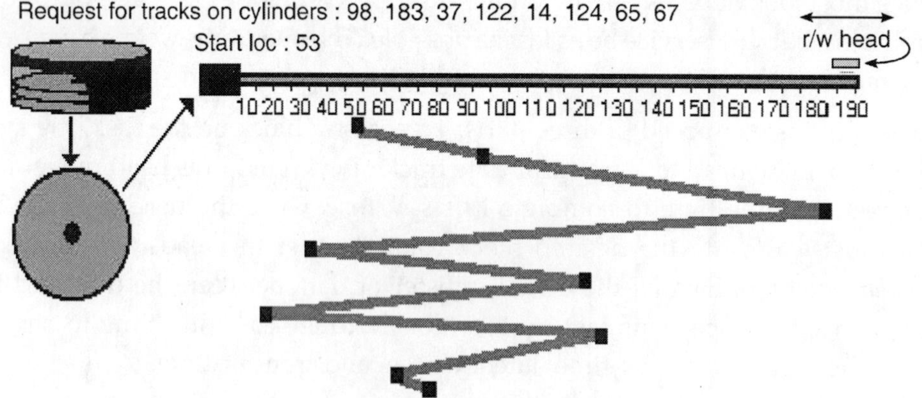

FCFS Disk Scheduler

The problem with this schedule is illustrated by the wild swing from 122 to 14 and then back again to 124. If the request for tracks 37 and 14 could be serviced together, before or after the requests at 122 and 124, the total head movement could be decreased substantially and the average time to service each request would decrease, improving disk throughput.

2. **SSTF (*Shortest Seek Time First*)Scheduling**

   The shortest seek time first approach picks the request that is closest to the current disk arm position. (Although called the shortest seek time first, this approach actually includes the rotational delay in calculation, since rotation can be as long as seek.) SSTF is good at reducing seeks, but may result in starvation. **SSTF** uses the same idea as SJN (do you recall this?), but can also correspondingly result in indefinite postponement of certain requests.

   It seems reasonable to service together all requests close to the current head position, before moving the head far away to service another head position. - Serve all requests that are closest to the current head position before moving the head far away to serve another request. note: You won't see this algorithm implemented anywhere as requests from the other side of the head direction will suffer from starvation.

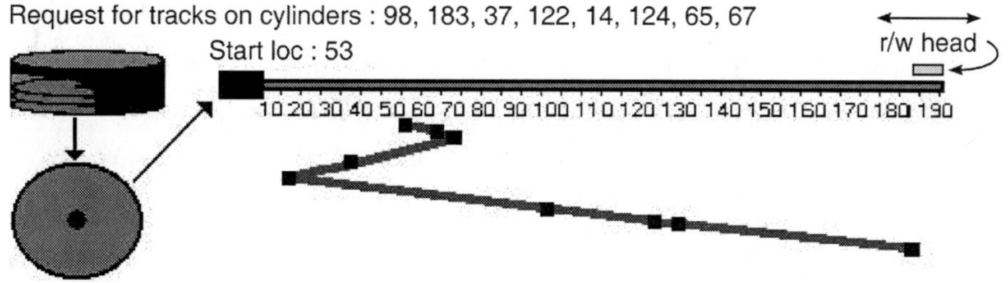

3. **Scan**

   SCAN implements an elevator algorithm. It takes the closet request in the direction of travel. It guarantees no starvation, but retains the flavor of SSTF. However, if a disk is heavily loaded with requests, a new request at a location that has been just recently scanned can wait for almost two full scans of the disk.

SCAN moves the arm from the outer to the inner track, servicing every request in its path. When it reaches the innermost track, it reverses direction and moves towards the outer tracks, again servicing every request in its path. The disk head scans from track 0 to the final track, and from the final track back to track 0 continuously. The direction of the movement of the head as it scans determines which request gets serviced next. Scan always chooses the job at the next nearest track in its direction. So it services the job which is next closest to the current track first.

Processing the requests in Scan order (assuming the head is moving toward track 0 to begin with), the sequence of tracks visited by the disk head is:

53, 37, 14, 0, 65, 67, 98, ...

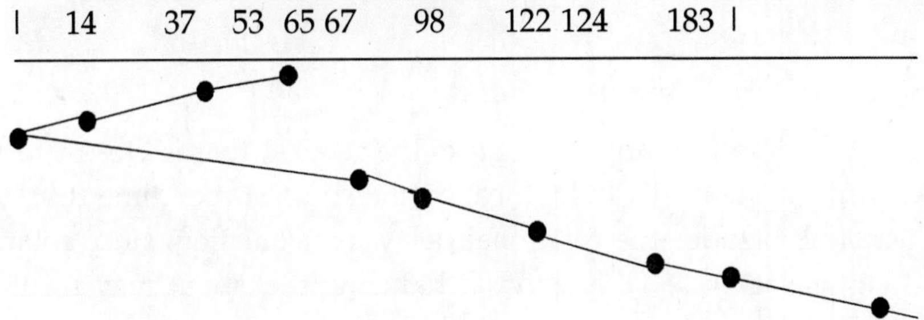

Giving a total head movement of: 234 tracks.

4. C-Scan (*Circular-Scan*)

For C-SCAN, the disk arm always serves requests by scanning in one direction. Once the arm finishes scanning for one direction, it quickly returns to the 0th track for the next round of scanning. As with Scan, the disk head scans along the disk tracks continuously. However, C-scan only scans from track 0 to the final track. When it reaches the end it skips back to 0 and recommences. C-Scan too always chooses the job at the next nearest track as it goes.

As with Scan, the disk head scans along the disk tracks continuously. However, C-scan only scans from track 0 to the final track. When it reaches the end it skips back to 0 and recommences. C-Scan too always chooses the job at the next nearest track as it goes.

Processing the requests in C-Scan order (assuming the head is moving toward the final track), the sequence of tracks visited by the disk head is:

53, 65, 67, 98, ..., 0, 14, 3

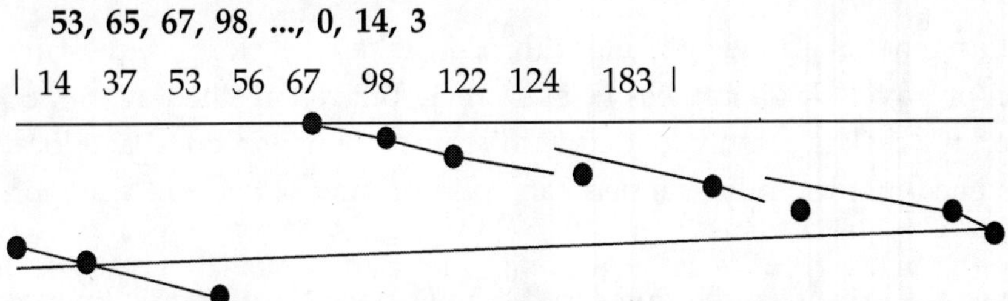

Giving a total head movement of: 147+200+37=384 tracks.

5. Look & C-Look (*Look and Circular-Look*)

These two algorithms are the more practical implementations of Scan and C-Scan. The only difference is that these algorithms do not bother going all the way to the final track and to track 0 if there are no requests in those directions.

LOOK is a variation of SCAN which does not go all the way to the innermost or outermost track unless there is a request for that track. LOOK eliminates indefinite postponement of requests found in SSTF.

6. **N-step-SCAN and FSCAN**

SSTF, SCAN and C-SCAN algorithms are subject to 'arm stickiness.' That is, the disk arm will stick around a particular track if there are a lot of requests for that track (especially on high-density multi-surface disks). This may lead to inefficient access for other requests (or starvation). To counteract this both of these algorithms divide the disk access queue into more than one sub-queue and completely process one sub-queue before beginning another. This ensures that old requests are serviced before newer ones.

N-step-SCAN divides the queue into several sub-queues each of length N. Each sub-queue is processed in turn using SCAN. While one sub-queue is being serviced new requests must join another sub-queue. For large values of N the performance approaches that of SCAN; for N=1 we get FIFO.

N-step-SCAN doesn't incorporate requests into the arm's path as it travels but holds all the requests until the arm starts on its way back. **C-SCAN** and **C-LOOK** are optimizations of SCAN and LOOK respectively, but instead of reversing direction when the innermost track is reached, the arm is brought back immediately to the outermost track and then starts sweeping inward again to service requests.

FSCAN uses only two sub-queues. While one sub-queue is being serviced new requests must join the other sub-queue.

Selection of a Disk-Scheduling Algorithm

Given so many disk-scheduling algorithms, how do we choose the best? SSTF is common and has a natural appeal. SCAN and C-SCAN perform better in systems that place a heavy load on the disk, because they are less likely to have the starvation problem described earlier. For any particular list of requests, it is possible to define an optimal order of retrieval, but the computation needed to find an optimal schedule may not justify the savings over SSTF or SCAN.

With any scheduling algorithm, however, performance depends heavily on the number and types of requests. For instance, suppose that the queue usually has just one outstanding request. Then, all scheduling algorithms are forced to behave the same, because they have only one choice for where to move the disk head. They all behave like FCFS scheduling. Notice also that the requests for disk service can be greatly influenced by the file-allocation method. A program reading a contiguously allocated file will generate several requests that: are close together on the disk, resulting in limited head movement. A linked or indexed file, on the other hand, may include blocks that are widely scattered on the disk, resulting in greater head movement.

The location of directories and index blocks also is important. Since every file must be opened to be used, and opening a file requires searching the directory structure, the directories will be accessed frequently. Suppose a directory entry is on the first cylinder and a file's data are on the final cylinder. In this case, the disk head has to move the entire width of the disk. If the directory entry were on the middle cylinder, the head has to move at most one half the widths. Caching the directories and index blocks in main memory can also help to reduce the disk-arm movement, particularly for read requests. Because of these complexities, the disk-scheduling algorithm should be written as a separate module of the operating system, so that it can be replaced with a different algorithm if necessary. Either SSTF or LOOK is a reasonable choice for the default algorithm.

Note that the scheduling algorithms described here consider only the seek distances. For modern disks, the rotational latency can be nearly as large as the average seek time. But it is difficult for the operating system to schedule for improved rotational latency because modern disks do not disclose the physical location of logical blocks. Disk manufacturers have been helping with this problem by implementing disk-scheduling algorithms in the controller hardware built into the disk drive. If the operating system, sends a batch of requests to the controller, the controller can queue them and then schedule them to improve both the seek time and the rotational latency. If I/O performance were the only consideration, the operating system would gladly turn over the responsibility of disk scheduling to the disk hardware. In practice, however, the operating system may have other constraints on the service order for requests.

For instance, demand paging may take priority over application I/O, and writes are more urgent than reads if the cache is running out of free pages. Also, it may be desirable to guarantee the order of a set of disk writes to make the file system robust in the face of system crashes; consider what could happen if the operating system allocated a disk page to a file, and the application wrote data into that page before the operating system had a chance to flush the modified inode and free-space list back to disk. To accommodate such requirements, an operating system may choose to do its own disk scheduling, and to "spoon-feed" the requests to the disk controller, one by one.

Performance

Once the basic disk methods are selected, there are still several ways to improve performance. The basic methods are discussed as under:

Caching

Far and away the most effective strategy for improving file system performance is caching. Every time a file is opened or created it requires accesses to all the directories from the root to the file itself, and many files are referenced often. Consider executables for commonly executed utilities. Accesses to the physical disk for these common cases can be avoided if the blocks that would have been read from the disk are cached in memory rather than being read from disk each time.

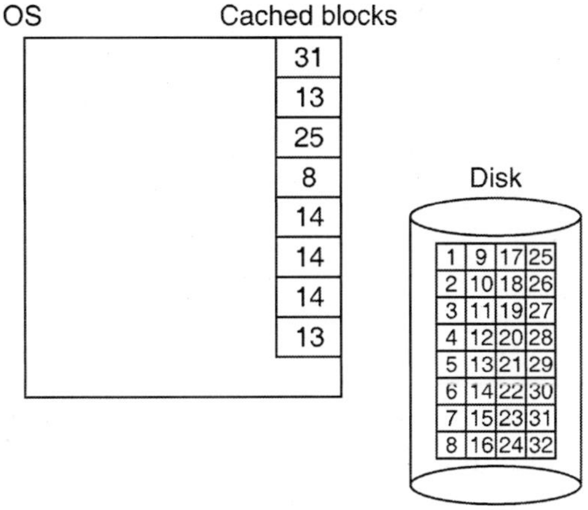

OS | Cached blocks: 31, 13, 25, 8, 14, 14, 14, 13

Disk:

1	9	17	25
2	10	18	26
3	11	19	27
4	12	20	28
5	13	21	29
6	14	22	30
7	15	23	31
8	16	24	32

Caching is accomplished by setting aside a portion of memory and using it to store blocks as they are brought into memory. Blocks are read or written into the memory if possible and written out to disk when convenient or when the block must be removed from the cache to make way for a new block.

The important issue with any caching system is the tradeoff between performance and consistency of the caching system. In this case that means the difference between the versions of file blocks that are in the cache and on the disk. During operation this distinction isn't terribly interesting - processes always read from the file cache first and only from the disk if the block is not cached. The consistency problem arises when the computer catastropically fails; for example a power outage when all the file cache blocks haven't been written out to disk. When the OS restarts, the file system may be in an inconsistent state. The issue is how writes are cached.

There are several models of consistency that can be used, each of which marks a point on the consistency/performance curve. The Linux EXT2FS file system makes no special concessions to consistency. Its goal is a blazingly fast UNIX(R) file system, and it's willing to risk the dangers of filesystem corruption if operation is interrupted at an inopportune moment. The BSD FFS systems take a more conservative approach, but not the most conservative approach. They write metadata synchronously to disk - that is any changes to the file system structures themselves are not cached. File system structures include the free block list and file allocations. Thus its possible to lose modifications to allocated blocks in a file, but not to have a block appear once on the free list and once on a file's allocation list. The slowest and most reliable choice is to write all data synchronously to disk. Thi sis the choice made by MS-DOS and Windows (for floppies anyway).

The consistency issue underscores the difference between file cache management and virtual memory management algorithms. In paging, all pages are transient and therefore equally important. In the file system some blocks contain data that is essential to the continued correct operation of the filesystem[1] and must be treated specially. Modulo these differences, paging algorithms are a good fit for managing the file cache. In general a variant of LRU is usually used, with the modifications appropriate for the level of consistency required being made.

In fact, some systems, like FreeBSD and Solaris, use only one cache for both virtual memory pages and cached file blocks. This allows the number of pages or file blocks to grow as needed.

File System Checking

Most systems have a mechanism for checking the file system integrity, even if they take great pains to maintain that integrity. Occasional bad blocks or software bugs may corrupt data, and it's worthwhile to periodically check the file systems to reduce the impact of any damage.

The checking process is basically:

- Compare the free list to the list of allocations for all the files. Each block should appear exactly once. Blocks no appearing at all should be considered free. Blocks appearing on both the free list and one file can (probably) be allocated to the file. Blocks allocated to two or more files are a complicated case that probably requires human intervention.

  - Check all directories for pointers to the files. If files exist that have no directory entries deleted them and reclaim their allocations. This can be caused by a system like UNIX that allow open files to remain on the disk while a process has them open.

The less consistency the operating system enforces, the more frequently the file system should be checked.

Disk Layout

Avoiding disk seeks is the most fruitful optimization to a file system after caching. One source of seeks is seeking from i-nodes allocated on one end of the disk to data blocks on the other. Alternatively, seeking from directory entry to data block. Consider the i-node case.

In the original UNIX file system, i-nodes were allocated at the beginning of the disk and datablocks everywhere else. The fast file system disperses in-nodes throughout the disk, and does its best to place data sectors near the i-node that owns the file to reduce seek times.

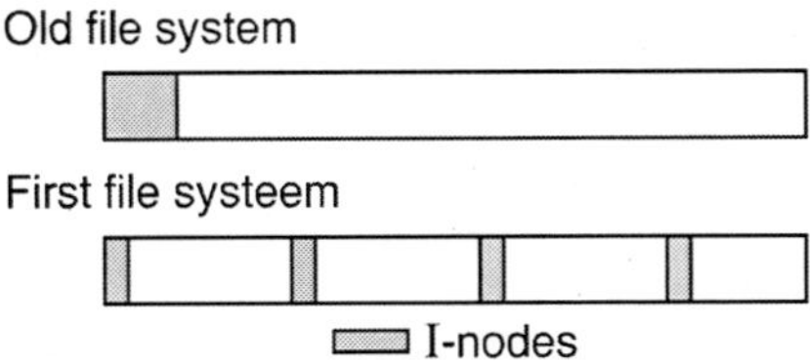

Although that example is UNIX-specific, the concept covers many operating systems. When seeks are expensive, try to place related data physically close together on the disk.

A related issue is reducing rotational latency. Files are usually read sequentially, but if file blocks are laid out contiguously on the disk, additional rotational delays can be incurred. The problem is that after the first block is read and returned, the OS issues a request for the next block, which has partially rotated past the disk head. The disk now must wait one rotation time until the beginning of the secotr appears again. By interleaving file blocks, the time to return the block and get the next request can be spend spinning over an unneeded block.

Other method

Another method of using main memory to improve performance is common on personal computers. A. section of memory is set aside and treated as a virtual disk, or RAM disk. In this case, a RAM disk device driver accepts all the standard disk operations, but performs those operations on the memory section, instead of on a disk. All disk operations can then be executed on this RAM disk and, except for the lightning-fast speed, users will not notice a difference. RAM disks are useful only for temporary storage, since a power failure or a reboot of the system will usually erase them. Commonly, temporary files such as intermediate compiler files are stored there.

The difference between a RAM disk and a disk cache is that the contents of the RAM disk are totally user controlled, whereas those of the disk cache are under the control of the operating system. A RAM disk will stay empty until the user creates files there.

Secondary Storage Backup and Retrieval

One important aspect of the file system is that the user is given the illusion that the capacity of file storage is infinite. This concept is felt to be extremely important, as it gives all responsibility for remembering files to the system rather than to the individual user. Many computer installations already find themselves in the business of providing tape and card-file storage for their users. It is intended that most of this need will be replaced by the file system in a more general and orderly manner.

That portion of the file system storage complex which is immediately accessible to the file system, i.e. disks and drums, is called the **on-line storage system**. Devices which are removable from the storage complex, such as tapes, data cells and disk packs which are used by the file system as an extension of the on-line facilities, are called the **file backup storage system**. To the user, all files appear to be on line, although access to some files may be somewhat delayed. For the purpose of discussion, a backup system consisting only of magnetic tape is considered. However, the system presented here is readily adaptable to other devices.

Incremental Dumping of New Files

Whenever a user signs off, additional copies of all files created or modified by that user are made in duplicate on a pair of magnetic tapes. At the end of every N hour period, any newly created or modified files which have not previously been dumped are also copied to these tapes. When this is done, the tapes are removed from the machine and replaced by a fresh set of tapes for the next N hour period. Typically N would be a period of between 2 and 4 hours. This procedure has the advantage that the effects of the most catastrophic machine or system failure can be confined to the N hour dumping period.

Weekly Dumping of Frequently Used Files

In the event of a catastrophe, the on-line storage system could be reloaded from these incremental dump tapes. However, since many valuable files, including system programs, may not have been modified for a year or over, this method of reloading is far too impractical. In order to minimize the time necessary to recover after a catastrophe, a weekly dump is prepared of all files which have been used within the last M weeks. This dump is also made on duplicate tapes for reliability.

Actually this weekly dump is taken in two parts. The first part consists of all files which must be present in order to start and run the basic system. The second part consists of all other files which have been used within the last M week period. Typically M would be a period of about three to five weeks. The weekly dump tapes may be released for other use after a period of about two or three months. The incremental dump tapes must be kept indefinitely. However, it may be advantageous to consolidate these tapes periodically by deleting obsolete files.

Catastrophe Reload Procedure

Should a catastrophe occur in which the entire contents of the on-line storage system is lost, the following reload procedure can be used. First reload a copy of the system files from the most recent weekly dump tapes. When this has been done the system may be started, with the rest of the reloading process continuing under the control of the system. Note that this does not necessarily represent the most recent copy of the system. If an important system change has been made since the weekly dump was taken, it may be necessary to reload the incremental tapes before starting the system.

After the system files are reloaded, the incremental dump tapes are reloaded in reverse chronological order, starting with the most recent set of incremental tapes. This process is continued until the time of the last weekly dump is reached. At this time, the second part of the weekly dump tapes is reloaded. During this process all redundant or obsolete files are ignored. The date and time a file is created or last modified is used to insure that only the most recent copy of a file remains in the on-line storage system. Since directories are dumped and reloaded in the same manner as ordinary files, the contents of the on-line storage system can be accurately restored.

It is possible to continue to load the older weekly tapes until the on-line system is totally reloaded. However, the amount of new information picked up from these tapes becomes increasingly small as one goes further back in time. In view of this, files which do not appear on the most recent set of weekly dump tapes, due to inactivity, are not reloaded at this time. Instead, a trap is added to the Appropriate directory branch so that a retrieval procedure is called when the file is first referenced. This allows these files to be reloaded as needed by the retrieval mechanism which is discussed later in this paper.

On-Line Storage Salvage Procedure

Although the catastrophe reload procedure can accurately reconstruct the contents of the on-line storage system, it is normally used only as a backstop against the most catastrophic of machine or system failures. When the milder and more common failures occur, it is often possible to salvage the contents of secondary storage without having to resort to the reload procedure. If this can be done, many files which have been created or modified since the end of the last incremental dump period can be saved. In addition, much of the time necessary to run the reload procedure can also be saved.

The usual result of a machine or system failure is that the contents of secondary storage are left in a state which is inconsistent. For example, two completely unrelated directory entries may end up pointing to the same physical location in secondary storage, while the storage assignment tables indicate that this area of storage is unused. If the system were restarted at this time, the situation might never be resolved. The usual effect is that any information subsequently assigned to that area of secondary storage is likely to be overwritten.

This situation arises when the system goes down before the file system has updated its assignment tables and directories on secondary storage. What has probably happened is that some user has deleted a file and another user created a new file which was assigned to the area of storage just vacated by the previous file. When the system goes down, the changes have not been recorded in secondary storage. This is only one example of the type of trouble which occurs when the system fails unexpectedly.

The salvage procedure is designed to read through all the directories in the hierarchy and correct inconsistent information wherever possible. The remaining erroneous files and directory entries are deleted or truncated at the point at which the error was found. Storage assignment tables are corrected so that only one branch points to the same area of secondary storage. Since it is necessary to read only the directories and the storage assignment tables, the salvage procedure can be run in a small percentage of the time necessary to run a complete reload procedure.

The salvage procedure also serves as a useful diagnostic tool, since it provides a printout of every error found and the action taken. This program can also be run in a mode in which it only detects errors but does not try to correct them.

Retrieval of Files from Backup Storage

Unless a file has been explicitly deleted by a user, the directory entry for that file remains in the file system indefinitely. If, for some reason, the file associated with this entry does not currently reside on an on-line storage device, the corresponding branch for that file contains a trap to a file retrieval procedure. When a user references a file which is in this condition, his process traps to the retrieval procedure. At this time the user may elect to wait until the file is retrieved from the backup system, to request that the file be retrieved while he works on something else, to abort the process that requested the files or to delete the directory entry.

If the user elects to retrieve the file, the date and time the file was created or last modified (which are available from the directory entry) are used to select the correct set of incremental dump tapes. The retrieval procedure requests the tape operator to find and mount these tapes. These tapes are then searched until the precise copy of the requested file is found and reloaded. At this time the original access control list of the branch is restored, and the file is now ready to be used by the user.

If a user deletes a file, both the file and the corresponding directory entry are deleted. However, if a copy of this file appears on a set of incremental dump tapes, this copy is not deleted at this time. This file can still be retrieved if the user specifies the approximate date and time when the file was created or last modified. To help the user in this situation, the incremental dump procedure provides a listing for the operations staff of the contents of each set of incremental tapes. These listings are kept in a log book which may be consulted by the operators in situations such as the above. Selected portions of this listing may be made available to the user.

The user is able to declare that he wishes a certain file to be removed from the on-line storage system without deleting the corresponding directory entry. This may be accomplished by using a system procedure which places the file in a state where it can be retrieved by the normal retrieval procedure.

General Reliability

Since the file system is designed to provide the principal information storage facility for all users of the system, the full responsibility for all considerations of reliability rests with the file system. For this reason all dumping, retrieval and reloading procedures use duplicate sets of tapes. These tapes are formatted in such a manner as to minimize the possibility of unrecoverable error conditions. When reading from these tapes during a reload or retrieval process, multiple errors on both sets of tapes can be corrected as long as the errors do not occur in the same physical record of both tapes. If an error occurs which cannot be corrected, only the information which was in error is lost. If the error is a simple parity error, the information is accepted as if no error occurred. When a user first attempts to use a file in which a parity or other error was found, he is notified of this condition through a system procedure using the trap mechanism.

Secondary Storage Allotments

The file system assigns all secondary storage dynamically as needed. In general, no areas of the on-line storage system are permanently assigned to a user. A user may keep an essentially infinite amount of information within the file system. However, it is necessary to control the amount of information which can be kept in the on-line storage system at a time.

When a user first signs on, the file system is given an account name or number. All files subsequently created by this user are labeled with his account name. When the user wishes to increase his usage of secondary storage, the file system calls upon a secondary storage accounting procedure giving the user's account name and the amount and class of storage requested.

The accounting procedure maintains records of all secondary storage usage and allotments. A storage allotment is defined as the amount of information which a particular account is allowed to keep in the on-line storage system at one time. Normally the accounting procedure allows a process to exceed the allotment after informing the file system that the account is overdrawn. However, the accounting procedure may decide to interrupt the user's process if the amount of online storage already used seems unreasonable.

Multilevel Nature of Secondary Storage

In most cases a user does not need to know how or where a file is stored by the file system. A user's primary concern is that the file be readily available to him when he needs it. In general, only the file system knows on which device a file resides.

The file system is designed to accommodate any configuration of secondary storage devices. These devices may cover a wide range of speeds and capacities. All considerations of speed and efficiency of storage devices are left to the file system. Thus all user programs and all other system programs are independent of the particular configuration of secondary storage.

All permanent secondary storage devices are assigned a level number according to the relative speed of the device. The devices which have the highest transmission and access rates are assigned the highest level numbers. As files become active, they are automatically moved to the highest-level storage device available. This process is tempered by considerations such as the size of the file and the frequency of use.

As more space is needed on a particular storage device, the least active files are moved to a lower-level storage device. Files which belong to overdrawn accounts are moved first. Files continue to be moved to lower-level storage until the desired amount of higher-level storage is freed. If a file must be moved from the lowest-level on-line storage device, the file is removed and the branch for this file is set to trap to the retrieval procedure.

RAID (Redundant Array of Independent Disks)

RAID was introduced because the increase of performance in hard disk drives was not as dramatic as the increase in the performance of processors and memory. The idea of using several hard disks together in parallel to increase performance is based on the same motivation of using several CPUs together (multiprocessing) to increase performance.

RAID also introduces the idea of redundancy which improves the overall reliability of the system (i.e. one of the biggest problems in computer systems is the threat of disk crash, which results in the partial or complete loss of all data stored on the disk. Even backups are not very useful, since any changes since the last backup will be lost).

What is RAID ?

RAID, or Redundant Array of Inexpensive Disks (or later also referred to as Redundant Array of Independent Disks) is an acronym first used in a 1988 paper by Berkeley researchers Patterson, Gibson and Katz. RAID is a technology developed to improve data protection and performance while storing large amounts of data, without necessarily requiring improvements in disk drive technology.

RAID LEVELS

As the definition and awareness of the RAID technology has grown, several RAID configurations for storing data have been devised and standardized upon. These RAID "levels" are now commonly discussed in the industry. The simplest RAID configurations either "stripe" data across two drives to increase data transfer speed, but offer no data protection; or "mirror" redundant data onto a second drive, without increasing performance. More advanced configurations involve three or more drives, and simultaneously provide fault tolerance, increased performance, and the ability to "recreate" information onto a spare drive should a drive failure occur. These more advanced RAID configurations are preferred in server environments where maximum data availability and performance is critical. The applications, advantages, and disadvantages of the different RAID configurations, or levels, are described below. The numbers assigned to each level of RAID do not indicate superiority or effectiveness; they are only used to differentiate between them.

RAID 0 - Disk Striping

With RAID 0, or a configuration known as "data striping", data is written in sequential sections across more than two drives. RAID 0 is easy to implement, and it can dramatically improve performance. Several drives can be accessed at once, minimizing the overall "seek" time of larger files. This configuration has no data redundancy and therefore no protection against data loss, however, so it should not be used for business-critical applications.

Drive 0	Drive 1	Drive 2	Drive 3	Drive 4
Block 1	Block 2	Block 3	Block 4	Block 5
Block 6	Block 7	Block 8	Block 9	Block 10
Block 11	Block 12	Block 13	Block 14	Block 15
Block 16	Block 17	Block 18	Block 19	Block 20
Block 21	Block 22	Block 23	Block 24	Block 25

RAID 1 - Mirroring

Also known as "drive mirroring", RAID 1 simultaneously copies data to a second drive. The mirroring method offers data protection and good performance in the case where a mirrored drive fails. RAID 1 is the simplest RAID configuration, requiring only a minimum of two drives with equal capacity, and also that the drives be added in pairs. The main disadvantage of RAID 1 is that it uses 100% drive overhead (the highest of all RAID levels), which can be considered an inefficient use of drive capacity.

Drive 0	Drive 1
Block 1	Block 1
Block 2	Block 2
Block 3	Block 3
Block 4	Block 4
Block 5	Block 5

RAID 2- Redundancy Using Hamming Code

A RAID 2 array stripes data to a group of drives using a byte stripe. A hamming code Error Checking and Correction (ECC) symbol for each data stripe is stored on a dedicated drive. This code provides detection and correction of data errors, allowing data to be recovered without completely duplicating the data. Since most drives now embed ECC information within each sector as standard, however, RAID 2 doesn't offer any advantages over RAID 3.

Drive 0	Drive 1		ECC Drive 6	ECC Drive 7
Block 1	Block 1		ECC 1-32	ECC 1-32
Block 2	Block 2		ECC 33-64	ECC 33-64
Block 3	Block 3	• • •	ECC 65-96	ECC 65-96
Block 4	Block 4		ECC 97-128	ECC 97-128
Block 5	Block 5		ECC 129-160	ECC 129-160

RAID 3 - Striping Plus Parity

RAID 3 stripes data across multiple drives, with an additional drive dedicated to parity for error correction/recovery. This configuration offers very high data transfer rates and only requires a small percentage of ECC (parity) to data drives. However, RAID 3 requires a complicated controller design and the configuration may be difficult to rebuild after a drive failure.

Drive 0	Drive 1	Drive 2		Parity Drive
Bit 1	Bit 2	Bit 3		Parity 1-32
Bit 33	Bit 34	Bit 35		Parity 33-64
Bit 65	Bit 66	Bit 67	• • •	Parity 65-96
Bit 97	Bit 98	Bit 99		Parity 97-128
Bit 129	Bit 130	Bit 131		Parity 129-160

RAID 4 - Independent Striping Plus Parity

RAID 4 is identical to RAID 3 except that large strips are used, so that records can be read from any individual drive in the array apart from the parity drive, allowing read operations to be overlapped. Since RAID 4 offers no significant advantages over RAID 5, the RAID 4 configuration is now rarely implemented.

Drive 0	Drive 1	Drive 2	Drive 3	Parity
Block 1	Block 2	Block 3	Block 4	Parity 1-4
Block 5	Block 6	Block 7	Block 8	Parity 5-8
Block 9	Block 10	Block 11	Block 12	Parity 9-12
Block 13	Block 14	Block 15	Block 16	Parity 13-16
Block 17	Block 18	Block 19	Block 20	Parity 17-20

RAID 5 - Independent Striping Plus Distributed Parity

With RAID 5, each block of data is written on a data drive and parity information is then striped across all drives. RAID 5 is the most popular of the RAID levels because it delivers data protection and good performance with a small overhead for parity. RAID 5 offers the most efficient use of drive capacity of all the redundant RAID levels. This configuration requires at least three drives of equal size, which can be added one at a time.

Drive 0	Drive 1	Drive 2	Drive 3	Drive 4
Block 1	Block 2	Block 3	Block 4	Parity 1-4
Block 6	Block 7	Block 8	Parity 5-8	Block 5
Block 11	Block 12	Parity 9-12	Block 9	Block 10
Block 16	Parity 13-16	Block 13	Block 14	Block 15
Parity 17-20	Block 17	Block 18	Block 19	Block 20

RAID 6 -RAID 5 With Double Parity (or "P+Q Redundancy")

RAID 6 is an extension of RAID 5 that uses a second independent distributed parity scheme. Data is striped on a block level across a set of drives, and then a second set of parity is calculated and written across all of the drives. This configuration provides extremely high fault tolerance and can sustain several simultaneous drive failures, but it requires an "n+2" number of drives and a very complicated controller design.

RAID 10 - Combination of RAID 1 and RAID 0

RAID 10 combines RAID 0 and RAID 1 by striping data across multiple drives without parity, and it mirrors the entire array to a second set of drives. This process delivers fast data access (like RAID 0) and single drive fault tolerance (like RAID 1), but cuts the usable drive space in half. RAID 10 requires a minimum of four equally sized drives, is the most expensive RAID solution and offers limited scalability.

Drive 0	Drive 1	Drive 2	Drive 3
Block 1	Block 2	Block 1	Block 2
Block 3	Block 4	Block 3	Block 4
Block 5	Block 6	Block 5	Block 6
Block 7	Block 8	Block 7	Block 8
Block 9	Block 10	Block 9	Block 10

RAID-01

Most of the discussion in the SQL Server documentation that concerns combining RAID0 and RAID-1 assumes that two stripes will be created first, and then one of the stripes will be defined as the mirror of the other. However, there is another possibility, which is to create multiple mirrored sets of disks first and then create a stripe from the mirrors. The first solution is referred to as *mirrored stripes*, and is the RAID 10 solution I discussed in the previous section. The second solution is referred to as striped mirrors and can be called RAID-01.

Both RAID-10 and RAID-01 refer to combining the capabilities of RAID-0 (striping) with RAID-1 (mirroring) so that speed and fault tolerance are achieved, without the overhead of computing a parity value. However, the terminology is not standard. As mentioned previously, some sources will refer to RAID-1&0, or RAID-1+0. Some use the term RAID-10 to refer to striping a set of mirrored volumes, and use RAID-01 to refer to mirroring a striped volume, which is the opposite of the terminology I've been using. In many cases it might not matter which is done first, striping or mirroring, at least for the discussion at hand. I hope that in situations where it does matter, the authors of whatever sources you read will define the terms they use.

RAID 53 - Combination of RAID 0 and RAID 3

The RAID 53 configuration should really be called "RAID 03". This configuration is a striped array whose segments are essentially RAID 3 arrays. It has the same fault tolerance and high data transfer rates of RAID 3, with the high I/O rates associated with RAID 0 (striping), plus some added performance. This configuration is very expensive and requires at least 5 drives to implement.

RAID Applications, Tradeoffs and Limitations

Typically, RAID is used in systems where data accessibility is critical and fault tolerance is required, such as in large file servers. However, RAID is now also more frequently seen used in desktop systems for CAD, multimedia editing and playback where higher transfer rates are needed. In general, for a given price point, the performance improvement of a particular type of RAID array "trades off" with the amount of the redundancy and data security of the array. Similarly, capacity of the array "trades off" with the price and fault tolerance. Inexpensive RAID solutions are limited in their ability to protect your data or improve performance, whereas high-end RAID implementations providing very high performance and very high data reliability are quite expensive.

Although RAID can greatly improve the reliability and performance of a storage system, it is dangerous to assume that a RAID system with redundancy provides absolute data protection. Since there are sources of failure that are still applicable to RAID systems, such as viruses, environmental disturbances and/or cases where more than one drive fails at the same time, regular system maintenance and backup remain critical practices.

By now, you should know there's no one correct answer to the RAID-level question. The appropriate decision depends on your performance characteristics and fault tolerance needs. A complete discussion of RAID and storage systems is beyond the scope of this book. But the most important point is that you shouldn't simply buy storage space—you should buy the system that gives you the appropriate level of redundancy and fault tolerance for your data

The final words

A versatile secondary storage file system is presented. Various goals which such a system should attain have been set, and the system designed in such a way as to achieve these goals. Such a system is felt to be an essential part of an effective on-line interactive computing system.

Case study: MULTICS File System Program Structure

This section describes the basic program structure of the file system presented in the last chapters, as implemented in the Multics system. A user may reference data elements in a file explicitly through read and write statements, or implicitly by means of segment addressing. It should be noted here that the word "file" is not being used in the traditional sense (i.e., to specify any input or output device). In the Multics system a file is a linear array of data which is referenced by means of a symbolic name or segment number and a linear index. In general, a user will not know how or on what device a file is stored.

A Multics file is a segment, and all segments are files.[1,3] Although a file may sometimes be referenced as an input or an output device, only a file can be referenced through segment addressing. For example, a tape or a teletype cannot be referenced as a segment, and therefore cannot be regarded as a file by this definition.

Input or output requests which are directed to I/O devices other than files (i.e. tapes, teletypes, printers, card readers, etc.) will be processed directly by a Device Interface Module (see reference 4) which is designed to handle I/O requests for that device. However, I/O requests which are directed to a file will be processed by a special procedure known as the File System Interface Module (see reference 4). This module acts as a device interface module for files within the file system. Unlike other device interface modules, this procedure does not explicitly issue I/O requests. Instead, the file system interface module accomplishes its I/O implicitly by means of segment addressing and by issuing declarative calls to the basic file system indicating how certain areas of a segment are to be overlayed.

The Basic File System

Whether a user refers to a file through the use of read and write statements or by means of segment addressing, ultimately a segment must be made available to his process. The basic file system may now be defined as that part of the central software

which manages segments. In general this package performs the following basic functions.

1. Maintain directories of existing segments (files)
2. Make segments available to a process upon request.
3. Create new segments.
4. Delete existing segments.

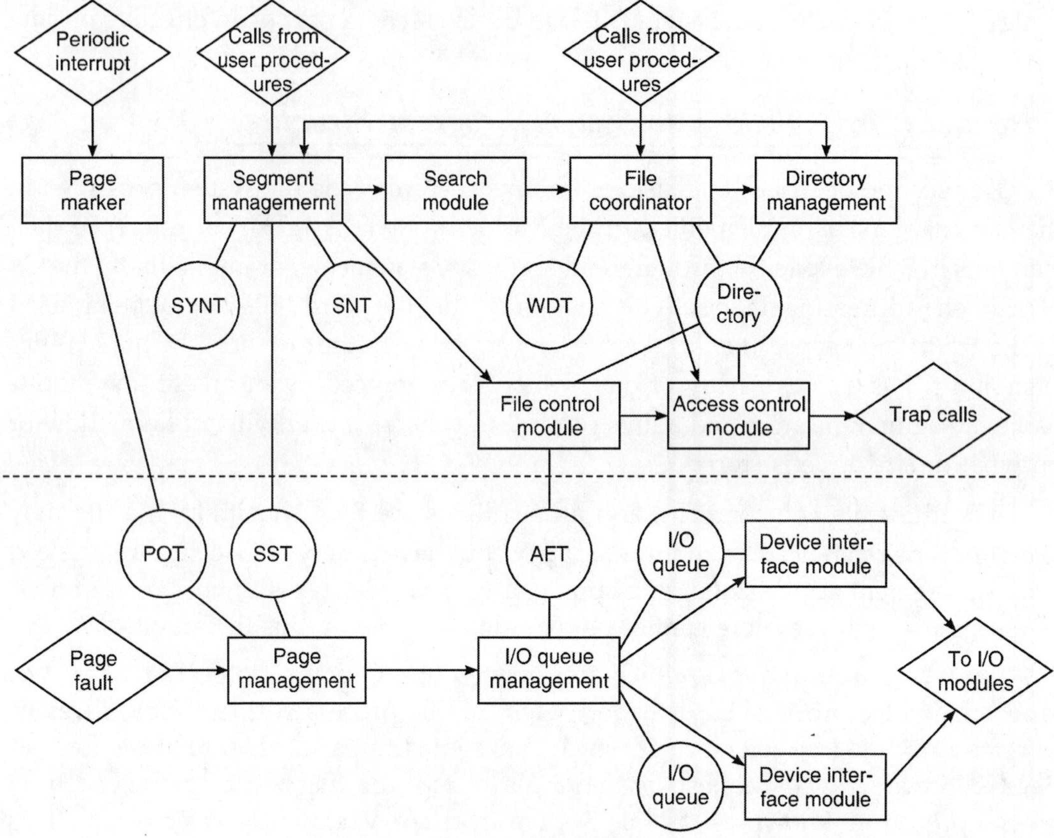

The basic file system

Figure is a rough block diagram of the modules which make up the basic file system. This diagram is by no means complete but is used here to give the reader an overall view of the basic flow. The directional lines indicate the flow of control through the use of formal calling sequences, with formal return implied. Lines with double arrowheads are used to indicate possible flow of control in either direction. The circles in the diagram indicate some of the data bases which are common to the modules indicated. The modules and data bases drawn below the dotted line must at least partially reside in core memory at all times since they will be invoked during a missing-page fault (see reference 3).

Segment Management Module

The segment management module maintains records of all segments which are known to the current process. A segment is **known to a process** once a segment number has been assigned to that segment for this process. A segment which is known to a process is **active** if the page table for that segment is currently in core. If the page table is not currently in core, that segment is **inactive.**

If a segment is known to a process, an entry will exist for that segment in the Segment Name Table (SNT). This entry contains the call name, the tree name and the segment number of the segment (file) along with other information pertinent to the segment as used by this process. The **call name** is a symbolic name used by the user to reference a segment. This name normally corresponds to an entry in the user's directory hierarchy which effectively points to the desired file. It should be noted that a different copy of the segment name table exists for each individual process.

If a segment is active, an entry for that segment exists in the Segment Status Table (SST). This table is common to all processes and contains an entry for each active segment. If a segment is inactive (no page table is in core), no entry exists for that segment in this table. Each entry in the segment status table contains information such as the number of processes to which this segment is known and a pointer which may be used to reference the file or files which are to receive all I/O resulting from paging this segment in and out of core.[3] When a user references a segment for the first time, a directed fault will occur. At this time control is passed to a procedure known as the linker.[3] This procedure picks up the symbolic segment call name from a pointer contained in the machine word causing the fault. The linker must now establish a segment number from this symbolic name. An entry to the segment management module is provided for precisely this purpose. When a call is made to the segment management module to establish a segment number from a call name, the segment name table is searched for that call name. If the call name is found in the segment name table, the segment number from this table is returned immediately to the calling procedure. However, if this is not the case, the segment management module must take the following steps.

1. Locate the segment (file) in the user's directory hierarchy via a call to the search module.
2. Assign a segment number for this segment.
3. Update the segment name table indicating that this segment is now known to this process.
4. Open the file or files which are to receive I/O resulting from paging.
5. Create or update the appropriate entry in the segment status table.
6. Establish a page table and segment descriptor for this segment if the segment was not already active for some other process.
7. Return the segment number to the calling procedure.

If a segment is known to a process but is not currently active, the descriptor for that segment will indicate a fault condition. If and when this fault occurs, the segment can be reactivated by locating the approve private entry in the segment name table and repeating steps 4 through 7. Note that the segment does not have to be located again in the directory hierarchy since the tree name is retained in the segment name table.

If a segment is to be modified during its use in a process, the user may elect to modify a copy of that segment rather than the original. When this is the case, the copying of this segment is done dynamically as a by-product of paging. However, if the copying is not complete at the time the segment becomes inactive, the copying must be completed at this time.

If a segment is to be copied, there are actually two open files involved, the original file and the copy or **execution file**. When a page table is initially constructed by the segment management module, each entry in that page table will contain a fault indication and a flag indicating what action should be taken if and when that fault occurs. This flag may indicate one of the following actions:

1. Assign a blank page.
2. Retrieve the missing page from the original file.
3. Retrieve the missing page from the execution file.

Once a page has been paged out (written) into the execution file, it must be retrieved from that file.

An entry to the segment management module is provided by which a user may declare a synonym or list of synonyms for a segment name. For example, a user may have a certain procedure which references a segment called "Gamma" and another procedure which references a segment called "Alpha." If the user wishes to operate both procedures as part of the same process using a segment called "Data" he may do so by declaring Alpha and Gamma to be synonyms for Data. This association is kept by the segment management module in a Synonym Table (SYNT). Whenever the segment management module is presented with a call name which has been defined as a synonym, the appropriate name is substituted before any further processing takes place.

In addition to the functions described above, the segment management module provides entries through which the user may ask questions or make declarations involving the use of segments known to his process. Some of these functions are listed below.

1. Declare that a segment or some specific locations within a segment are no longer needed at this time.
2. Declare that a segment or some specific locations within a segment are to be reassigned rather than paged in as needed. (The user is about to overwrite these locations.)
3. Ask if a segment or some specific locations within a segment are currently in core.
4. Declare that a certain segment is to be created when first referenced.
5. Terminate a segment, indicating that this segment is no longer to be considered as known to this process.

Search Module

The search module is called by the segment management module to find a particular segment (file) in the user's directory hierarchy. The search module directs the search of individual directories in the user's hierarchy in a predetermined pattern until the requested branch is found or the algorithm is exhausted. This module calls the file coordinator to search particular directories and to move to other directories in the hierarchy. The user is able to override this search procedure by providing his own search procedure at the initiation or during the execution of his process.

The File Coordinator

The file coordinator provides all the basic tools for manipulating entries within the user's current working directory. The functions provided by this module perform only the most primitive operations and are usually augmented by more elaborate system library procedures. The following is a list (of some of these operations.

1. Create a new directory entry.
2. Delete an existing entry.

3. Rename an entry.
4. Return status information concerning a particular entry.
5. Change the access control list for a particular branch.
6. Change working directory.

Whenever a user wishes to perform any operation through the use of the file coordinator, the access control module is consulted to determine if the operation is to be permitted.

Since most calls to the file coordinator refer to entries contained in the user's working directory, the file coordinator must maintain a pointer to this directory. This is done by keeping the tree name of the working directory in a Working Directory Table (WDT) for this process.

Directory Management Module

When the file coordinator wishes to search the user's working directory, the actual search is accomplished by use of the directory management module. This module searches a single directory specified by a tree name for a particular entry or group of entries. The actual directory search is confined to this module to isolate the recursion process which may be required to search a given directory.

The directory management module issues calls to the segment management module to obtain a segment number for the directory for which it has only a tree name. When the directory management module obtains this segment number and references the directory by means of segment addressing, a descriptor fault may occur indicating that this segment is no longer active. If this happens, the segment management module will try to reactivate this segment by attempting to find this directory in the next superior directory by means of the tree name in the segment name table. To do this the segment management module issues a direct call to the directory management module to search the next superior directory for the missing directory. After obtaining a segment number for the superior directory, the directory management module may cause another descriptor fault to occur when attempting to search this directory. This process may continue until a directory is found to be an active segment or until the root of the directory hierarchy is reached. Since the root is always known to the directory management module, the depth of recursion is finite.

File Control Module

The file control module is provided to open and close files for the segment management module. A file is said to be open, or **active**, if it has a corresponding entry in the Active File Table (AFT). If a file is active, the corresponding entry in the active file table provides sufficient information to control subsequent I/O requests for that file.

If the file is inactive, the open procedure needs only to open the file to the requested state and make the corresponding entry in the active file table. If the file is active, it may have N users reading, or 1 user reading and writing, or N users data sharing (using file as a common data base). If the requested state is incompatible with the current state of the file, the current process must be blocked.[3] For example, if the current user wishes to read a stable copy of the file and there is currently a user writing into that file, the requested state (reading) and the current state (reading and writing) are said to be incompatible.

If the requested state and the current state of the file are found to be compatible, the number of users using the file in that state is increased by one. When a file has been successfully opened by the file control module (with the permission of the access control module), the pointer to the corresponding entry in the active file table is returned to the calling procedure. This pointer is used to direct requests for subsequent input or output to the correct file.

Access Control Module

The access control module is called to evaluate the access control information for a particular branch, as defined in Section 2. This module is given a pointer to the directory entry for the branch in question and a code indicating the type of operation which is being attempted. The access control module returns a single effective mode to the calling procedure. The effective mode is the mode which governs the use of a file with respect to the current user or process. The calling procedure uses this mode to determine if the requested operation is to be permitted.

If the access control information indicates that a trap is to be effected, the procedure to which the trap is directed is passed the entry for the branch in question and the operation code. The procedure which processes the trap must return to the access control module, specifying the effective mode to be returned by the access control module to its calling procedure. The procedure which processes the trap may choose to strengthen, weaken or leave unchanged the usage attributes which define the effective mode for the branch.

Page Marker Module

The page marker periodically interrupts the current process and takes note of page usage, and resets the page use bits[2] of all pages involved in the current process. Pages which fall below a dynamically set activity threshold are listed in the Page Out Table (POT) as likely candidates for removal when space becomes needed.

Page Management Module

Control passes to the page management module by means of a missing-page fault in a page table in use by the current process. This fault may indicate that a new page should be assigned from free storage or that an existing page should be retrieved from an active file. In either case a free page must be assigned before anything else can happen. If no pages are currently available, the first page listed in the page out table is paged out. If no pages are listed in the page out table, a random page of appropriate size is removed.

If a new page is to be read in, the page table entry for the missing page contains a pointer to the appropriate entry in the segment status table and a flag indicating whether this page is to be read from the original file or the execution file. In either case a pointer to the appropriate active file may be obtained from the segment status table. This pointer is passed as a parameter to the I/ O queue management module with a read request to restore the correct page to core memory.

I/O Queue Management Module

The I/O queue management module processes input and output requests for a particular active file. The calling procedure specifies a read or a write request and a pointer to an entry in the active file table which corresponds to the desired file. This request is placed on the appropriate queue for the particular device interface module which will process the request. The queue management module then calls that device interface module indicating that a new request has been placed on its queue. When this is done, the queue management module returns to the calling procedure which must decide whether or not to block itself until the I/O request or requests are completed.

Device Interface Modules

For each type of secondary storage device used by the basic file system, a device interface module will be provided. A device interface module has the sole responsibility for the strategy to be used in dealing with the particular device for which it was written. Any special considerations pertaining to a particular storage device are invisible to all modules except the interface module for that device.

A device interface module is also responsible for assigning physical storage areas, as needed, on the device for which it was written. To accomplish this function, the interface module must maintain records of all storage already assigned on that device. These records are kept in **storage assignment tables** which reside on the device to which they refer.

Other File System Modules

The modules described below are not considered part of the basic file system. However, these modules are considered to be a necessary and integral part of the file system as a whole.

Multilevel Storage Management Module

The multilevel storage management module operates as an independent process within the Multics system. This module collects information concerning the frequency of use of files currently active in the system. In addition, this module collects information concerning overdrawn accounts from the secondary storage accounting module.

The storage management module insures that an adequate amount of secondary storage is available to the basic file system at all times. This is accomplished by moving infrequently used files downward in the multilevel storage complex. This module also moves the most frequently used files to the highest-level secondary storage device available.

Storage Backup System Modules

The storage backup system consists of five modules which operate as independent processes. These modules perform the functions described in Section 3.

1. Incremental Dump Module—The sole responsibility of this module is to prepare incremental dump tapes of all new or recently modified files.
2. Weekly Dump Module—This module is run once a week to prepare the weekly dump tapes.
3. Retrieval Module—This module retrieves files which have been removed from the on-line storage system.
4. Salvage Module—This module is run after a machine or system failure to correct any inconsistencies which may have resulted in the on-line storage system. Since the Multics system cannot safely be run until these inconsistencies are corrected, the salvage module must be capable of running on a raw machine.
5. Catastrophe Reload Module—This module is used to reload the contents of the on-line storage system from the incremental and weekly dump tapes after a machine or system failure. Normally, this module is run only when all attempts to salvage the contents of the on-line storage system have failed. This module must be capable of running on a raw machine or under the control of the Multics system.

Utility and Service Modules

A large library of utility modules is provided as part of the file system. These modules provide all the necessary functions for manipulating links, and branches using the more primitive functions provided by the file coordinator. A special group of utility modules is provided to copy information currently stored as a file to other input or output media, and vice versa. The following functions are provided as a bare minimum:

1. File to printer
2. File to cards
3. Cards to file
4. Tape to file
5. File to tape

Actually these modules merely place the user's request on a queue for subsequent processing by the appropriate service module. The service module executes the requests in its queue as an independent process. As soon as the user's request has been placed on an appropriate queue, control is returned to the calling procedure although the request has not yet been executed.

KEYWORDS

STORAGE ORGANIZATION	**FCFS**
SEEK TIME	**SSTF**
ROTATIONAL DELAY	**SCAN**
TRANSFER TIME	**C-SCAN**
DISK SCHEDULING	**RAID**

SUMMARY

By storage organization we mean the manner in which the main storage is viewed

- A disk is an electromechanical device that holds data. Typically there is one or more disk platters, and data is written on one or both sides, sometimes in layers, by heads that read and/or write data using electromagnets, lasers, or other technologies. From the computer's point of view, it's just a big storage area for bytes.

- Historically, main storage has been viewed as an expensive resource. As such, it has demanded the attention of systems designers; it has been necessary to squeeze the maximum use out of this costly resource. Early systems were concerned with organizing and managing main storage for optimal use.
- Fetch strategies are concerned with when to obtain the next piece of program or data for insertion into main storage. For many years, the conventional wisdom has been demand fetch in which the next piece of program or data is brought in to the main storage when it is referenced by a running program. It was believed that since we cannot generally predict where program control will go next, the overhead involved in making guesses and anticipating the future would far exceed expected benefits. Today many researchers feel that anticipatory fetching will yield improved system performance.
- Placement strategies are concerned with determining where in main storage to place an incoming program.
- Replacement strategies are concerned with determining which piece of program or data to displace to make room for incoming programs
- Seek Time: Seek time is the time required to move the disk arm to the required track. It turns out that this is a difficult quantity to pin down. The seek time consists of two key components: the initial startup time and the time taken to traverse the tracks that have to be crossed once the access arm is up to speed.
- Rotational Delay Disks, other than floppy disks, rotate at speeds ranging from 3600 rpm up to, as of this writing, 15,000 rpm; at this latter speed, there is one revolution per 4 ms. Thus, on the average, the rotational delay will be 2 ms. Floppy disks typically rotate at between 300 and 600 rpm. Thus the average delay will be between 100 and 50 ms.
- The transfer time to or from the disk depends on the rotation speed of the disk.
- The simplest form of disk scheduling is, of course, *first-come-first-served* (FCS) scheduling. FCFS is the simplest and easiest to program and is essentially fair to the users Requests are served in the order of arrival.
- SCAN implements an elevator algorithm. It takes the closet request in the direction of travel.
- For C-SCAN, the disk arm always serves requests by scanning in one direction. Once the arm finishes scanning for one direction, it quickly returns to the 0th track for the next round of scanning. As with Scan, the disk head scans along the disk tracks continuously.

- Look and C Look algorithms do not bother going all the way to the final track and to track 0 if there are no requests in those directions. LOOK is a variation of SCAN which does not go all the way to the innermost or outermost track unless there is a request for that track. LOOK eliminates indefinite postponement of requests found in SSTF.

REVIEW QUESTIONS

1) Explain Storage hirrarchy in details.
2) Explain in brief different disk allocation methods?
3) Discuss the issue related to selection of disk scheduling algorithm?
4) Explain first come first serve disk scheduling algorithm?
5) Explain Shortest seek time first disk scheduling algorithm?
6) Explain SCAN disk scheduling algorithm ?
7) Explain C-SCAN disk scheduling algorithm ?
8) Explain SEEK disk scheduling algorithm ?
9) Explain C-SEEK serve disk scheduling algorithm ?
10) Explain LOOK disk scheduling algorithm ?
11) Explain all the RAID methods in details.

FILL IN THE BLANKS

1. A disk is an ________________device that holds data
2. _____________are concerned with when to obtain the next piece of program or data for insertion into main storage.
3. Placement strategies are concerned with determining where in main storage to place an incoming ____________.
4. ________________are concerned with determining which piece of program or data to displace to make room for incoming programs
5. ___________is the time required to move the disk arm to the required track.
6. The ________________to or from the disk depends on the rotation speed of the disk.

TRUE OR FALSE

1. FCFS is the simplest and easiest to program and is essentially fair to the users requests are served in the order of arrival.
2. SCAN implements an elevator algorithm.
3. LOOK goes all the way to the innermost or outermost track unless there is a request for that track.
4. Main storage has been viewed as an inexpensive resource
5. RAID 0 uses mirroring.
6. RAID 2 deals with Redundancy Using Hamming Code.

ANSWERS

FILL IN THE BLANKS

1. electromechanical
2. Fetch strategies
3. program
4. Replacement strategies
5. Seek time
6. transfer time

TRUE OR FALSE

1. TRUE
2. TRUE
3. FALSE
4. FALSE
5. FALSE
6. TRUE

❑❑❑

"Computers are magnificent tools for the realization of our dreams, but no machine can replace the human spark of spirit, compassion, love, and understanding."

Louis Gerstner

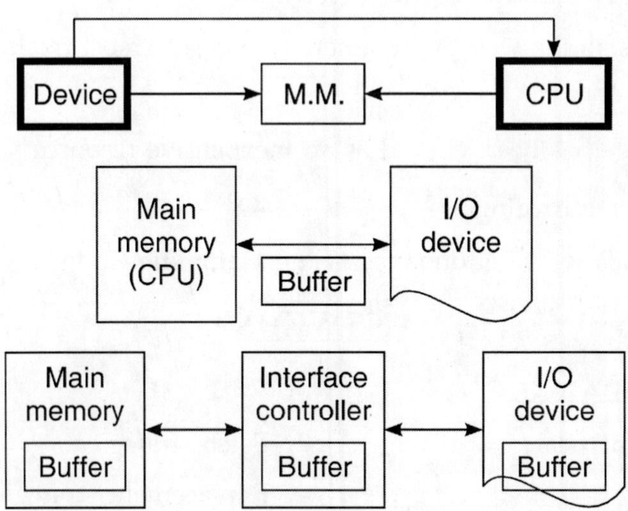

DEVICE MANAGEMENT

INTRODUCTION

The oldest parts of the operating system are the routines that control the peripheral devices. Devices are for example keyboards, printers, hard disk or the monitor. The operating system has to control these resources to be able to execute processes e.g. a printing job. Therefore an operating system has an input-output control system (IOCS) which is responsible for processing the I/O requests from executing processes. It does such things as checking to see whether the requested device is available or not. It initiates status reports of drivers and passes resource requests to the correct device drivers. Device drivers (or I/O handlers) are programs within the operating system which can communicate with the devices. In addition the IOCS offers a memory management for devices with e.g. buffering (saving data in a fast memory). Data of the I/O transfer is copied into the main memory (or out of it).

The operating system must issue commands to the devices, catch interrupts (I/O), and handle errors. It should also provide an interface between the devices and the rest of the system that is simple and easy to use. Different people look at I/O hardware in different ways. Electrical engineers look at it in term of chips, wires, power supplies, motors and all the other physical components that make up the hardware. Programmers look at the interface presented to the software the commands the hardware accepts, the functions it carries out, and the errors that can be reported back.

What is device management?

Device management is the part of the OS that manages hardware devices. The device management tries to provide a uniform interface to ease the access to devices with different physical characteristics, and optimize the performance of individual devices.

This is one of the key factors in the performance of Operating Systems because it attempts to offer ways in which data from the real world can enter a computer system. There is however a great mismatch between the speed at which computers operate and the speed at which users can type - instructions can be executed at speeds in the order of nano seconds (10^{-9} seconds) whereas most people type at rates of one or two characters per second. This means a computer can execute over 100 million instructions while you're typing a character! The I/O sub-system must find ways of coping with such differences.

Another difficulty for the I/O system is the vast range of peripherals used with computers. For example

MONITORS	KEYBOARDS	MICE
PRINTERS	PLOTTERS	SCANNERS
HARD DISKS	FLOPPY DISKS	CD-ROMs
BAR CODE SCANNERS	NETWORK CARDS	DIGITIZERS

These are a just few of the many peripherals concerned, but to make matters worse (for the operating system) each of them are manufactured by a *variety* of independent companies, each have their own individual characteristics and formats, and each have their own limitations. The I/O system needs to be able to communicate with each and provide a service between applications and peripherals that is robust, reliable and correct. The major functions of device management are:

1. Tracking the status of each device
    a. e.g., disk drives, printers, modems, etc.
2. Using preset policies to determine which process will get a device and for how long
3. Allocating the devices
4. Deallocating devices at two levels
    - At the process level
    - At the job level

The optimum device management is must for efficient operating system software.

Principles of I/O software

The general goals of the I/O software are easy to state. the basic idea is to organize the software as a series of layers, with the lower ones concerned with hiding the peculiarities of the hardware from the upper ones, and the upper ones concerned with presenting a nice, clean, regulate interface to the users.

A key concept in the design of I/O software is device independence. It should be possible to write programs that can be used with files on a floppy disk or a hard disk, without having to modify the programs for each device type. In fact, it should be possible to move the program without recompiling it.

Closely related to device independence is the goal of uniform naming. The name of a file or a device should simply be a string or a integer and not depend on the device in any way. In some operating systems, floppy disks, hard disks and all other block devices can be mounted in the file system hierarchy in arbitrary places, so the user need not be aware of which name corresponds to which device. All files and devices are addressed the same way: by a path name.

Another important issue for I/O software is error handling. In general, errors should be handled as close to the hardware as possible. If the controller discovers a read error, it should try to correct the error itself if it can. If it can not, then the device driver should handle it, perhaps by just trying to read the block again. Many errors are transient, such as read errors caused by specks of dust on the read head, and will go away if the operation is repeated. Only if the lower layers are not able to deal with the problem should the upper layers be told about it.

Still another key issue is synchronous (blocking) versus asynchronous (interrupt-driven) transfers. Most physical I/O is asynchronous the CPU starts the transfer and goes off to do something else until the interrupt arrives. User programs are much easier to write if the I/O operations are blocking after a READ command the program is automatically suspended until the data are avail-able in the buffer. It is up to the operating system to make operations that are actually interrupt-driven look blocking to the user programs.

Some I/O devices, such as disks, can be used by many users at the same time. No problems are caused by multiple users having open files on the same disk at the same time. Other devices, such as printers, have to be dedicated to a single user until that user is finished. Having five users printing lines intermixed at random on the printer just would not work. Introducing dedicated devices also introduces a variety of problems, including deadlock. Again, the operating system must handle both shared and dedicated devices in a way that avoids problems. These goals can be achieved in a comprehensible and efficient way by structuring the I/O software.

Application programs can directly interact with devices trough system call provided by kernel of the operating system. In this case, however, the responsibility of controlling the communication with the device lies completely with the programmer. So also, the error handling is responsibility of the programmer.

The availability of wide range of I/O devices makes it difficult, if not impossible for the programmer to learn specific commands and interact with the desired devices. Alternately, the operation system may implement device encapsulation, which is an abstraction of a device with no specific commands attached to it.

This concept allows applications programmers to communicate with any device in a similar manner irrespective of the make and nature of the devices. The application programmers has to input or output data to or from a logical device. This logical device presents a virtual representation of any devised attached to operating system. The user is oblivious of internal implementation and low-level communication details.

Division of I/O devices one the basis of data storage

I/O devices can be roughly divided into two types:

1. Block device

A ***block device*** (e.g., disks) stores information in fixed-size blocks, each one with its own address. They allow data to be read / written **independently** of any other block and as such each block has an address. This is analogous to using a book. Each page of a book has a page number (address), you can access information on any page without going through all the others. The block based devices are peripherals such as:

- Disks
- CD-ROMs

2. Character device

A ***character device*** (e.g., keyboards, printers, network cards) delivers or accepts a stream of characters, and individual characters are not addressable. So it offers no random access to the data. This is analogous to finding a track on a cassette tape; you have to work through all of them from the beginning. The character based devices are peripherals such as:

- Keyboards
- Printers
- Mice. etc

Diversity of I/O devices

There are all kinds of I/O devices in an operating system. Although they never play a centric role in the system, the management of these devices is absolutely the messiest aspect of operating system design.

I/O devices may differ from one another on all kinds of aspects. Some are human readable, suitable for communicating with the computer users, such as printers, monitors, speakers, keyboards, and mice. Some are machine readable, suitable for communicating with electronic equipments, such as disks and tapes. Some others are otherwise used for communicating with remote devices, such as modems and network cards.

The above categories are obtained based on the functions of I/O devices. What's more, even those that fall into one category may still be different from one another in various aspects. They may have different data transferring speed, different complexity of control, etc

Two objects are paramount in designing the I/O management facility:

1. Generality
2. Efficiency.

Generality

We always desire to manage all the I/O devices in a uniform manner; however the above differences make it difficult to achieve this goal, both from the point of view of the operating system and from the point of view of user processes.

What we can do is to use a hierarchical approach to the design of the I/O function, which is similar to the abstraction scheme in object orientation theory. That is the routines that are involved in dealing with accessing I/O devices are divided into several layers, and each layer provides a concise interface for the immediate upper-level layer, so that most of the details of the I/O devices are hidden in lower-level layers and the user processes may operate the devices in terms of general functions, such as read, write, open, close, lock, unlock.

What kind of hierarchy should be used depends on the type of I/O devices of concern. Figure shows the organization of three different types of I/O devices.

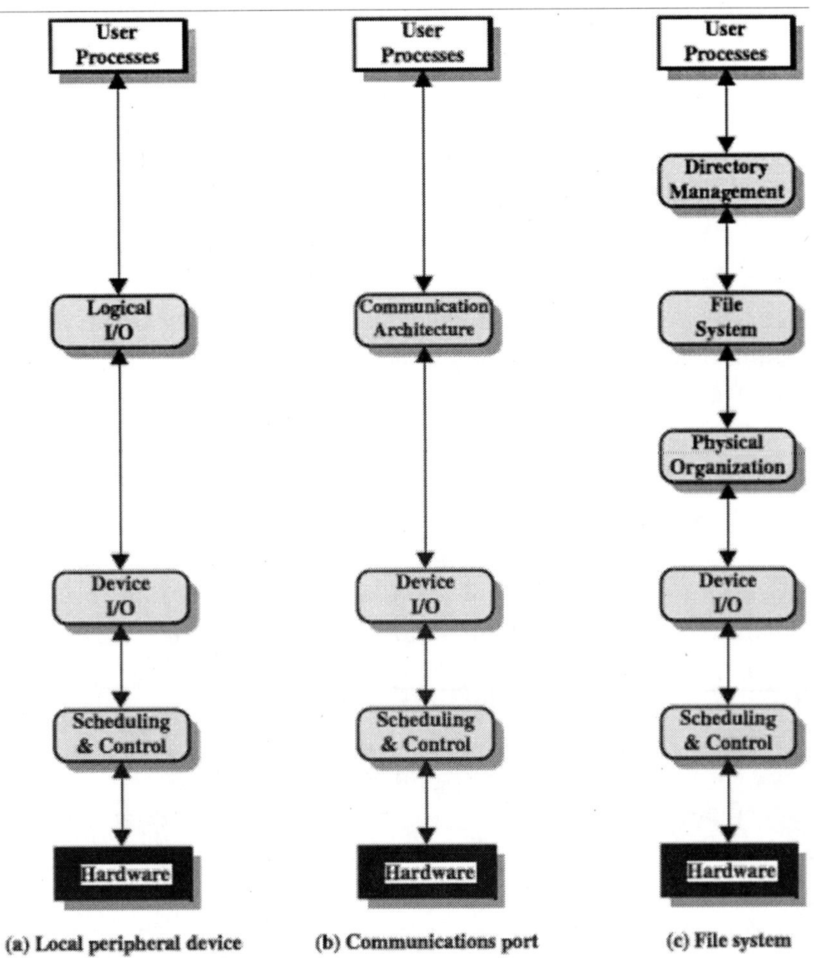

(a) Local peripheral device (b) Communications port (c) File system

Logical peripheral device

The figure (a) displays the simplest case, a local peripheral device, which may be accessed in terms of a stream of bytes or records. The layers involved are as follows:

- Logical I/O deals with the I/O device as a logical resource without concerning the de- tails of actually controlling the device. This layer provides a simple interface for user processes: specifying a unique ID to this device and simple control commands, such as open, close, read, write, etc.

- Device I/O converts the requested operation from the logical I/O layer into a series of I/O instructions. Data may be buffered in this layer and forwarded in the format that is acceptable to the destination layer.
- Scheduling and control: actually interacts with the I/O device, including queuing and scheduling of I/O operations, handling interrupts, collecting and reporting status information, etc.

Communication port

For a communication device, rather than logical I/O, a communication protocol layer is used instead as Figure (b) shows.

File system

For a storage device on which a file system is used as shown in figure (c), more complexity is involved. Besides scheduling and control layer and device I/O layer, the following layers are also used:

- *Directory management* provides user processes a hierarchical view of the collection of files stored on the device. Operations may be performed to add, or delete a directory.
- *File system* provides a flat view of a collection of files. At this layer, a directory file is treated in the same way as other regular files, although the content of this special file includes information about files under this directory. The upper level may use this interface of this layer to open, close, read, write, add, or delete a file. Access control may also be included here.
- *Physical organization* converts the logical references to files into physical addresses in terms of track, sector. Allocation and de-allocation of storage space are also treated in this layer.

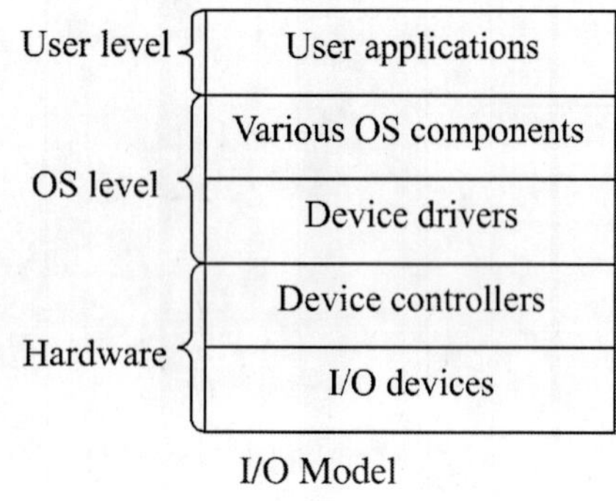

I/O Model

Efficiency

Efficiency is the other objective in I/O subsystem design. Remember, at the beginning of this course, we have discussed three popular ways to access I/O devices:

Programmed I/O means the microprocessor is involved all the way through the I/O process. The microprocessor issues command to initiate the I/O device, tell it what to do, and wait until the I/O process is finished. Almost all I/O devices are slower than the microprocessor, so the latter has to be idle for a long time, which results in inefficiency.

Interrupt-driven I/O otherwise aims to let the microprocessor and the I/O devices work simultaneously. With this scheme, the microprocessor, after issuing a command on be- half of a process to start an I/O operation, may turn to execute another process. When the I/O operation completes, an I/O interrupt will be generated to signal the microprocessor to resume the former process. Although switching between different processes involves overhead, it is still worth doing unless the context switching is too frequent.

DMA When a large amount of data needs to be transferred to/from an I/O device, it is not realistic any longer to take the interrupt-driven approach because frequent context switching is unavoidable in this case. To deal with this problem, the DMA approach is taken, in which a DMA controller is responsible to control the data exchange between main memory and an I/O device. What the microprocessor needs to do is simply to send necessary information to the DMA controller at the very beginning. An interrupt is also generated finally so that the microprocessor knows the completion of the whole DMA process.

By considering whether the processor is directly involved in the I/O process and whether interrupt schemes are used or not, we may have Table, showing the similarity and difference among the above three schemes:

	No Interrupts	**User of Interrupts**
I/O-to-memory transfer through processor	Programmed I/O	Interrupt-driven I/O
Direct I/O-to-memory transfer	–	Direct memory access (DMA)

I/O MODEL

A device is connected to a computer through an electronic component, or a *device controller*, which converts between the serial bit stream and a block of bytes and performs error correction if necessary.

Each controller has a few device registers that are used for communicating with the CPU, and a data buffer that an OS can read or write. Since the number of device registers and the natures of device instructions vary from device to device, a *device driver* OS component is responsible hiding the complexity of an I/O device, so that the OS can access various devices in a relatively uniform manner.

Categories of I/O devices

Generally peripheral (I/O) devices fall into 3 categories, **dedicated**, **shared** and **virtual**.

Dedicated devices

Dedicated devices are assigned to only one job at a time. Examples may include tape drives, printers, and plotters.

Dedicated devices are only assigned to one job at a time, they serve that job for the entire time it is active

The example of printer as a dedicated device is shown in the figure:

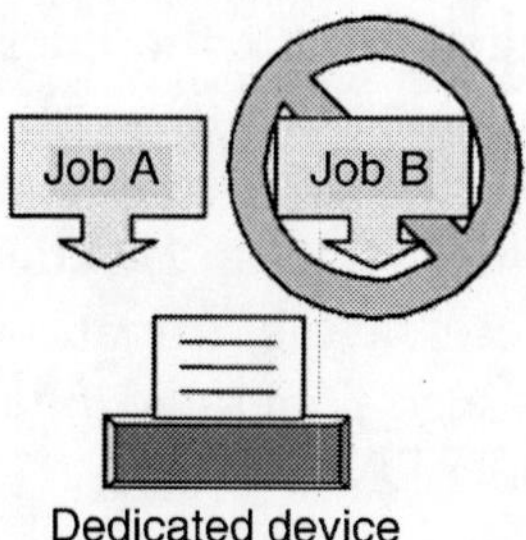

Dedicated device

The disadvantages of dedicated devices are:

1. Must be allocated to a single user for duration of a job's execution
2. Can be quite inefficient, especially when device isn't used 100% of the time

Shared devices

Shared devices can be assigned more than one processes – the resolution of multiple requests from these processes will be achieved based on predetermined policies.

Shared devices can be assigned several processes.

The example of hard disk as a shared device is shown in the figure

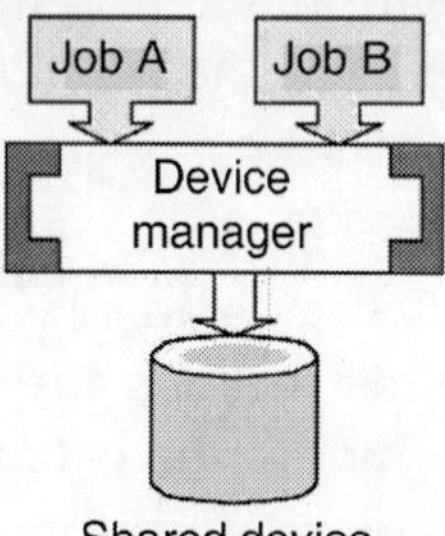

Shared device

The assigned processes are interleaved and carefully controlled by the device manager. Any conflicts are resolved based on predetermined policies.

Virtual devices

Virtual devices are a combination of the other two; that is, they are dedicated devices which have been transformed into shared devices.

Virtual devices are the combination of the dedicated and shared devices

The example of printer as a virtual device with the help of hard disk as spooler is shown in the figure

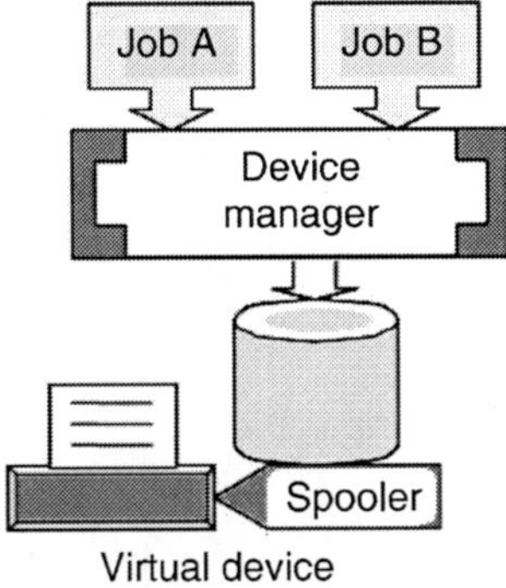

Virtual device

In this example a printer use a spooling program the reroutes all print requests to a disk. Spooling is used to speed up slow dedicated I/O devices. Another example is a USB controller, a virtual device that acts as an interface between OS, device drivers, and applications and the devices that are attached via the USB host

Sequential and direct access storage media

There are two types of access methods:

1. Sequential access storage media

It is now used for routine archiving and storing back up data. Data, or records, on magnetic tape are stored serially, one after the other. Each record is physically located at some position on the tape. Therefore the tape must forwarded, or reversed, to the physical location of the record resulting in a very time-consuming task.

Sequential access storage media (SASD) means that data or records stored must be accessed and stored serially (in a linear sequence), one at a time.

Magnetic tape was used for secondary storage on early computer systems; now used for routine archiving & storing back-up data

- Records on magnetic tapes are stored serially
- Record length determined by the application program
- Each record identified by its position on the tape
- Mounted and fast-forwarded to access a record

An inter-record gap is required to allow the moving tape time to stop under the read/write head – this is fixed in size. A more efficient use of tape space would be to group the records into blocks before recording them on tape (for which we have a corresponding inter-block gap). The tape consists of tracks; one track for each data bit, plus an additional track for parity. The number of characters that can be stored on a given length of tape is determined by the density of the tape. The nine-track magnetic tape is shown is the figure.

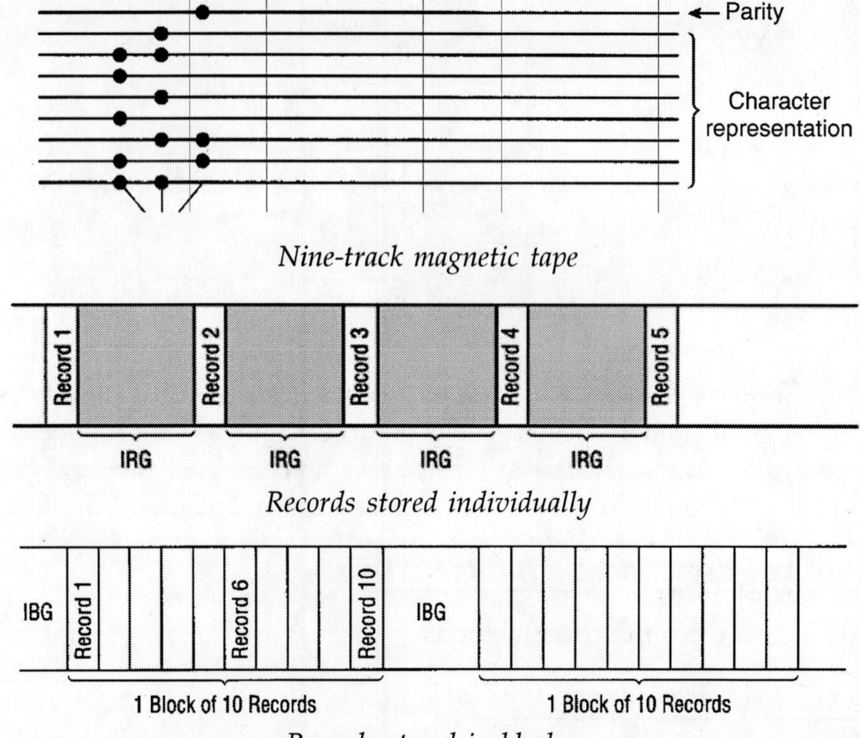

Nine-track magnetic tape

Records stored individually

Records stored in blocks

Data is recorded on 8 parallel tracks that run the length of tape. The ninth track holds parity bit for routine error checking. The density of tape determines number of characters that can be recorded per inch .Records can be stored individually or in blocks. "Blocking" records increases the speed at which records may be accessed, known as transfer rate.

Additionally, more data may be stored on a given length of tape as less "overhead" is required to manage the records. Still, magnetic tape is a poor choice for routine secondary storage as average access time is not too great.

Advantages of magnetic tapes:

- Low cost
- Compact storage capabilities: Good medium for backing up magnetic disks and for long-term archival file storage

Disadvantages of magnetic tapes:

- Access time variability: Poor medium for routine secondary storage
- Not good for interactive applications

2. Direct access storage devices

Direct access storage devices, also known as random access storage devices, are devices that can read or write to a specific place.

Direct access storage devices (DASD) can directly read or write from a specific location on the device without having to access sequentially from the first location.

The most common types are disks with movable read/write heads. Most disk drives come in the form of a disk pack, which is a stack of magnetic platters. The concept of cylinders is used to simplify the transfer of data from the fixed read/write heads to the disk surfaces. Thus to access any particular record (where one record is stored on a sector), the cylinder number, sector number and surface/head number needs to be specified. Two general categories are fixed head and movable head devices.

Fixed head drums represent an example of early types of these devices. They were very fast, but very expensive and held less data. Fixed head disks are a similar concept, just on a different plane. Tracks are comprised of concentric circles on each platter, or disk. While fixed head devices are faster than movable head devices, they store less data and are more expensive. It looks like a large CD or DVD covered with magnetic film, formatted, usually on both sides, into tracksThe data is recorded serially on each track by the fixed read/write head positioned over it

- **Applications:** Spacecraft monitoring or aircraft applications (where speed is of utmost importance)
- **Disadvantages:** High cost & reduced storage

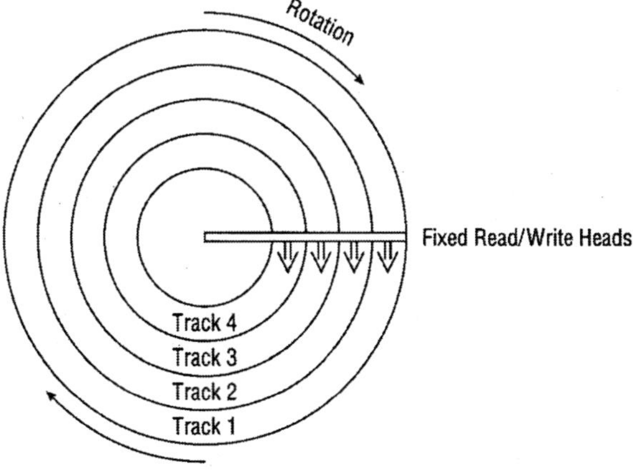

Fixed-head disk with four read/write heads, one per track

Movable head devices have one read/write head that floats over the surface of the disk. If disks are "stacked" with a read/write head for each platter, a virtual cylinder is formed. Using the same track (i.e., track zero) on each platter to store data results in faster write times, and illustrates the data cylinder, or drum, concept.

Typical hard drive from a PC

Optical disk drives use a laser beam to read and write to multilayered discs. CD-ROMs are created by using a high-intensity laser beam to burn **pits (indentations)** and **lands (flat areas)** into the disc to represent ones and zeros respectively. The read head of a CD-ROM drive directs a laser on the surface. The amount of light reflected back would depend on whether a pit or a land reflects back the laser. This is correspondingly measured to indicate either a one or zero.

Access Time

The access time for information from a DASD can be divided into seek time (time to position the read/write heads on to the proper cylinder), search time or rotational delay (time to rotate the disc surface until the correct sector (holding the desired record) is underneath the read/write head, and transfer time, where the actual reading of information off the magnetic surface is achieved by the read/write head.

Access time can be affected by as many as three important factors: seek time, search time, and transfer time.

As usual, blocking records allows a decrease in access time; but this must be balanced by a fast unblocking process in memory. For fixed head devices, access time equals search time plus transfer time. Whereas, for movable head devices, access time is seek time plus search time plus transfer time. Still, movable head devices are more common as they store more data and cost less

Device Addressing

In general, there are two approaches to addressing these device registers and data buffers. The first approach is to assign each device a dedicated range of device addresses in the physical memory, so accessing those device addresses requires special hardware instructions associated with individual devices. The second approach (***memory-mapped I/O***) is not to distinguish device addresses from normal memory addresses, so devices can be accessed the same way as normal memory, with the same set of hardware instructions.

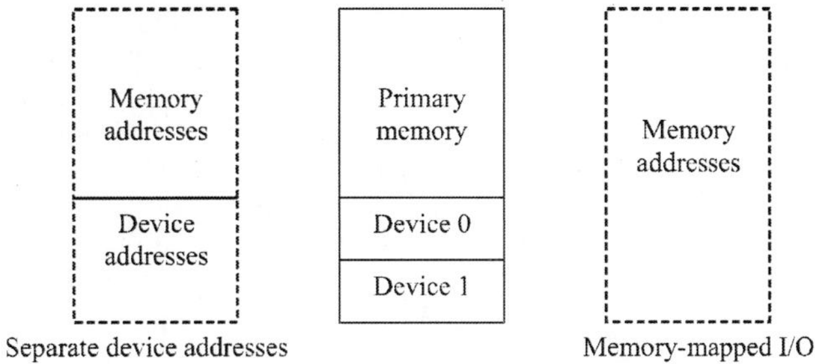

Device Accesses

Regardless of the device addressing approach, the operating system has to track the status of a device for exchanging data. The simplest approach is to use *polling*, where the CPU repeatedly checks the status of a device for exchanging data.

However, wasting CPU cycles on busy-waiting is undesirable. A better approach is to use *interrupt-driven I/Os*, where a device controller notifies the corresponding device driver when the device is available. Although the interrupt-driven approach is much more efficient than polling, the CPU is still actively involved in copying data between the device and memory. Also, interrupt-driven I/Os still impose high overheads for character devices. For example, a printer raises one interrupt per byte, so the overhead of interrupt far exceeds the cost of transmitting a single byte.

An even better approach is to use an additional ***direct memory access*** (***DMA***) controller to perform the actual movements of data, so the CPU can use the cycles for computation as opposed to copying data.

The use of DMA alone still has room for improvement. Since a process cannot access the data that is being brought into memory at the moment, due to mutual exclusion, a more efficient approach is to pipeline the data transfer. The ***double buffering*** technique uses two buffers in the following way: while one is being used, the other is being filled. Double buffering is also used extensively for graphics and smooth animation. While the screen displays an image frame from one buffer in the video controller, a separate buffer is being filled pixel-by-pixel in the background, so a viewer does not see the line-by-line scanning on the screen. Once the background buffer is filled, the video controller switches the roles of the two buffers and displays from the freshly filled buffer.

Overlapped I/O and CPU Processing

By freeing up CPU cycles while devices are serving requests, CPU-bound processes can be executed concurrently with I/O-bound processes. For example, if process A is CPU-bound, and process B is I/O-bound, the system as a whole can reach high utilization by overlapping CPU and I/O processing effectively.

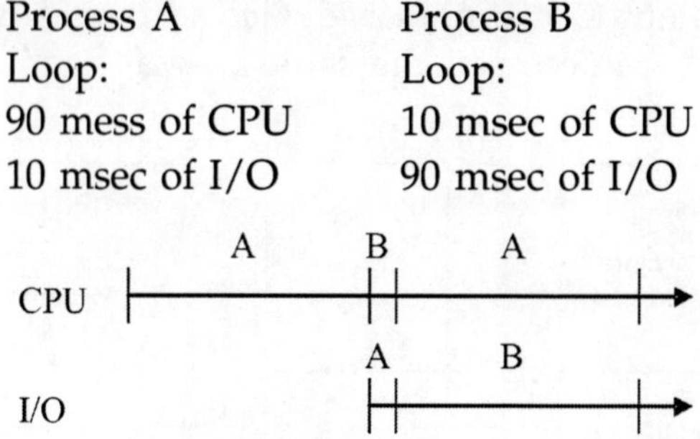

I/O buffering

Buffer is the small amount of memory used to store data. Let's begin with an example to introduce the necessity of I/O buffering. Suppose a user process wishes to read a block of data from a tape into a data area in the address space of this process at virtual location 1000. The most straightforward way to do so in the process is to execute an I/O command to the tape device, and then wait for the data to be available.

Buffers *are temporary storage areas used to synchronize the movement of data between I/O devices and the CPU. They are normally located in the main memory, as well as in channels and device controllers (control units). The idea (during an input operation) is to accumulate data into a buffer in a controller from a device until it becomes full, before transferring the entire block of data to the CPU (or main memory).*

However there are two problems with this approach. First, the process has to wait a long time before the completion of the operation due to the low speed of the tape device. Second, this data exchange may interfere with the swapping mechanism in the operation system. That is, before the whole operation is finished, the data area in the process to contain data from the tape has to remain in the main memory. Thus this section of space must be locked in some way so that it will not be swapped out to secondary memory.

To avoid the above inefficiency and inconvenience, it is possible to perform data input transfers in advance of requests being made or output transfers after the request is made, which is known as buffering. We will discuss some of buffering schemes to improve the performance of the system.

Single buffer

The simplest buffering scheme is single buffering. As illustrated in Figure (b), when a user process issues an I/O request, the operating system allocates a buffer in the system portion of main memory to the operation.

With this scheme, data is first gradually transferred into the system buffer. When the transfer is complete, the data is then moved into the user process space. Note that this is not the end of the story. The I/O facility in the operating system continues to read more data from the device, which is called reading ahead. This is performed because user processes usually access data on an I/O device sequentially.

Thus this approach wills generally speedup the I/O operations requested by a process. After a block of data becomes available and is delivered to the user process, the operation system may read ahead another block of data while the process is processing the former block. This approach also makes it possible to swap out the process that made I/O requests.

To support this mechanism, more effort needs to be made in the operating system, such as tracking the buffers allocated to user processes. What's more, the swapping of the process though is made possible, another problem arises. That is if the I/O request has been made and the process is to be swapped out to the same secondary storage device as involved in the I/O request, then the swapping will not happen until after the I/O request is finished. Nevertheless, at this moment, it may not be appropriate any more to swap out the process, since the data it has been waiting for are available and it may proceed to process them. Despite these disadvantages, it is still worth using the buffering scheme.

A similar circumstance will occur regarding outbound data transfer. When data are to be outputted to a device, they may be copied from the requesting process into a system buffer first. Then the process may simply continue or be swapped out.

Double buffer

An improvement of single buffering is to use two system buffers for a user process, called double buffering, as Figure (c) shows. In this case, moving data from one system buffer to the process and reading data from the I/O device to the other buffer may be performed simultaneously. Again, this improvement comes at the cost of increased complexity.

During an output operation, data will be accumulated in a buffer in main memory before being transferred in a single operation to a controller. Double buffering can be used to implement simultaneous read and write operations to two buffers. Double buffering can be applied at the hardware level and at the controller-driver interface level.A buffer in main memory which is used to temporarily hold data that is to be transferred to the hard disk is sometimes known as a disk cache.

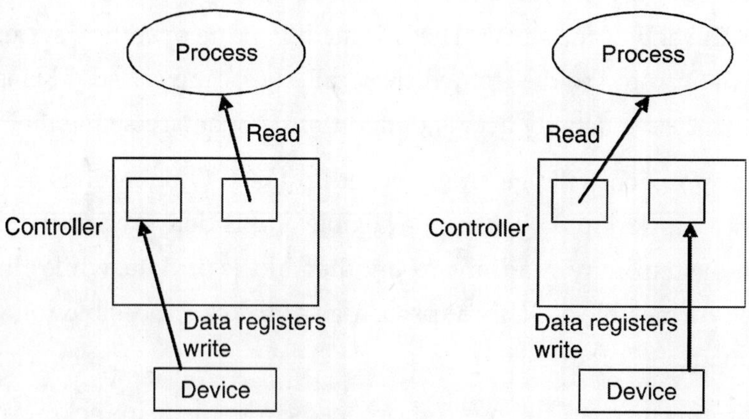

(a) Double buffering at hardware level

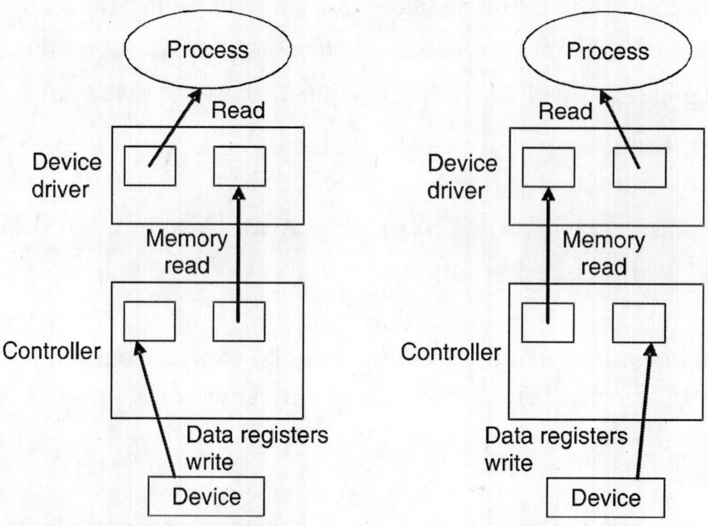

(b) Double buffering at driver controller interface

Circular buffer

The idea of double buffering may be generalized to circular buffering. That is more than two buffers are used and the collection of these buffers is referred to as a circular buffer, as illustrated in Figure (d). In this way, although the I/O device is much slower, there may be enough data in the system buffers for the process to read.

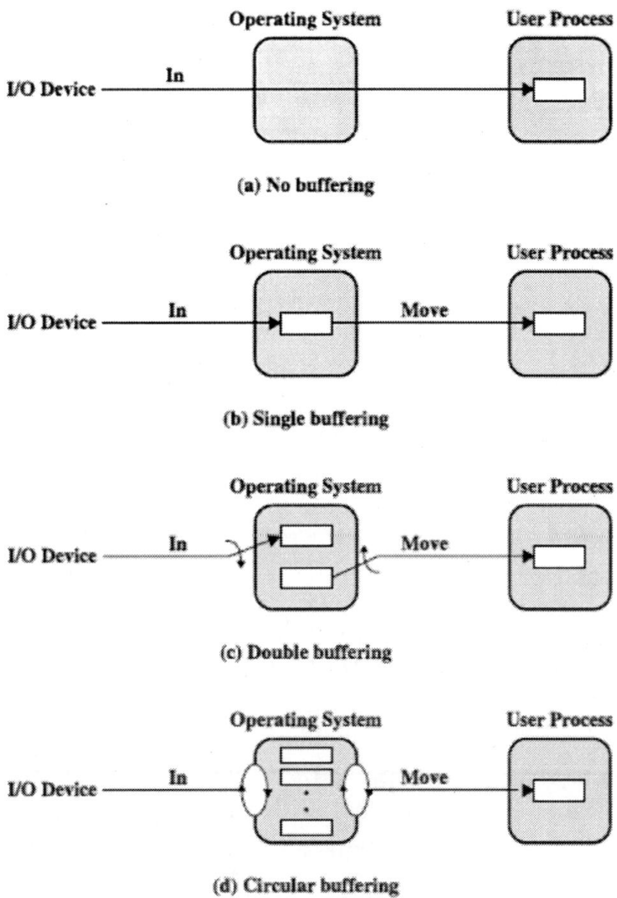

Spooling

A variation on the same theme is Spooling (Simultaneous Peripheral Operation On-Line). The idea here is to use a disk or similar device as a large buffer for reading as far ahead as possible on input devices or storing output files until the output devices (or devices) are ready for them.

SPOOLING is then an acronym for simultaneous ***p****eripheral* ***o****peration* ***o****n-line. It essentially uses the disk as a very large buffer, for reading as far ahead as possible on input devices and for storing output files until the output devices are able to accept them.*

The most common example is a printer. You are probably very familiar with the concept of a print queue, and that you can submit a job to a print queue and log out. Your process can have finished before the printout arrives.

You need to remember that if there is one printer on the system and there are twenty processes all trying to print at the same time only process can have access to that printer (WHY? What would happen if you allocated each process access to the printer in a round robin fashion?). So what do the other processes do? Well, one thing would for the other nineteen processes to suspend until that process finished printing. That would slow things up, and what if there were no other processes running, the processor would be idle.

The answer is to write the output to a file and for a special process, the spooler (called the printer daemon in UNIX), to control the printing of spooled files. This would occur as a background activity. I.e. the spooler is a low priority process that will only run when there are no other jobs on the system. Remember that spooling overlaps I/O of a job with the computation of all other jobs.

I/O SUBSYSTEM

The components of the I/O subsystem consist of the I/O channels, I/O control units, and I/O devices (e.g. disk drives, tape drives, printers, etc.).

I/O channel

It is one of the main components of the input output subsystem. Generally it Controls transmission of data between main memory and control units.

The I/O channel is a dedicated special purpose CPU found in high-end computer systems (such as workstations and mainframes), whose main purpose is to offload I/O work from the CPU.

By comparison with device controllers and DMA controllers found in small computer systems, a channel is capable of executing sophisticated programs which permit them to flexible enough to deal with different I/O activities. I/O Channels are the programmable units placed between CPU and control unit, it

- Keeps up with I/O requests from CPU and passes them down the line to appropriate control unit
- Synchronizes fast speed of CPU with slow speed of the I/O device
- Uses channel programs that specify action to be performed by devices
- Controls transmission of data between main memory and control units

I/O control unit

The I/O control unit is roughly similar to the device controller; the main difference is that a control unit can coordinate the operation of more than one I/O device, whereas a device controller is normally associated with a single device. Thus you can think of an I/O control unit as a 'higher level' controller that coordinates primitive device controllers.

The I/O controls unit Monitors device and communicates with I/O channel

Its functionality include

- Need to know who is busy and who is free
- Must be able to all requests
- Must be able to handle speed disparities
- Must be able to all requests

Polling and interrupts is accomplished in conjunction with I/O channels through the use of the Channel Status Word (**CSW**).

Channel Status Word

The I/O operation's completion is signaled by a hardware flag that is tested by the CPU. This flag is made up of three bits and resides in the Channel Status Word, a pre-defined location in main memory. Each component of the I/O subsystem, channel, control unit, and device, is represented by one of the three bits.

There are two common methods used to test the status of I/O paths: polling and interrupts.

- **Polling** uses a special machine instruction to routinely check the flag status. The disadvantage to polling is the frequency at which the flag is tested. If the flag is tested too frequently, processor time is wasted. If it is checked to seldom, the device may remain idle too long.
- **Interrupts** are more efficient for testing the flag. A hardware mechanism tests the flag during each machine cycle, instead of the CPU. Thus, status of I/O devices is continually monitored. Devices are employed using a pre-defined priority scheme.

The pieces of the I/O subsystem must work in harmony. An analogy we will use is a mythical taxicab company dispatcher. The dispatcher handles incoming calls as they arrive and finds transportation. The dispatcher organizes the calls in an order most efficient for his available resources.

Once the order is set the dispatcher communicates with the drivers who (ideally) pick up and deliver the passengers. As you might imagine, problems or "conflicts" inevitably occur. The I/O subsystem's components function similarly. The channel keeps up with I/O requests from the CPU and passes them down the line to the appropriate control unit (taxicab/driver). The I/O devices act as the vehicles.

I/O Channels

I/O channels are placed between the CPU and the control units and they synchronize the fast speed of the CPU with the slower I/O devices. They make it possible for I/O operations and processor operations to overlap so the CPU and I/O can process concurrently. Channels use channel programs which specify the action to be performed by the devices and controls data transmission between main memory and the control units. The channel sends one signal for each function, which is interpreted by the I/O control unit.

Channels are as fast as the CPU. Thus they are able to direct several control units by interleaving commands (just as several taxicab drivers can be controlled by one dispatcher). Additionally, each control unit can control several devices. The flexibility can be achieved by connecting more than one channel to a control unit or by connecting more than one control unit to a device. These multiple paths increase reliability as redundancy is built into the system. To keep the device manager running efficiently three problems must be resolved:

1. The device manager must know which components are free or busy
2. It must be able to accommodate requests that enter during heavy I/O traffic
3. It must accommodate the disparity of speeds between the CPU and the I/O devices

Device management must also take responsibility for the channels and control units. The channels are the special processors that execute the channel programs. Due to the high cost of channels, there are usually fewer channels than devices.

The channels must, therefore, be switched from one device to another. Further cost savings can be obtained by taking advantage of the fact that relatively few I/O devices are in use at one time. The electronics for several devices can be replaced by a single control unit, which can be switched from one device to another

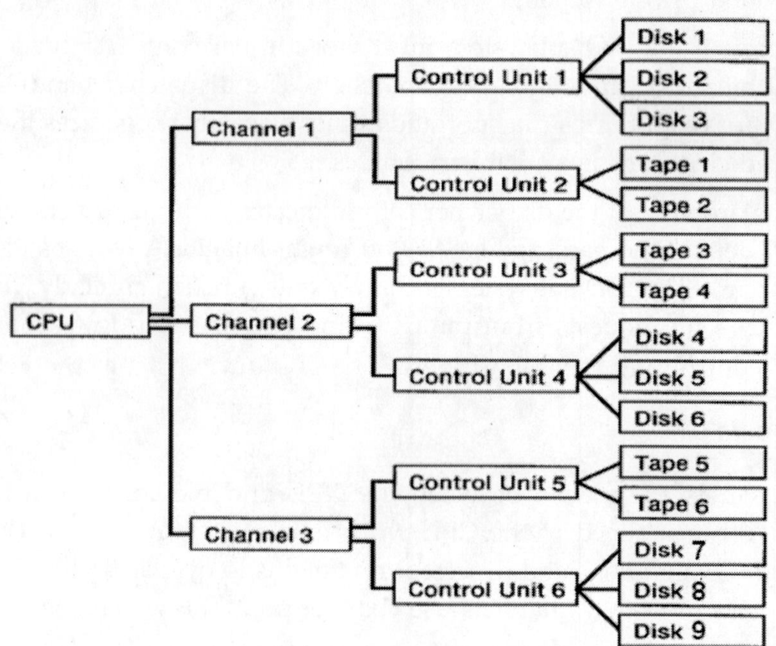

The device management routines must keep track of the status of

(*i*) channels (*ii*) control units (*iii*) devices

Since the channels and control units are usually scarce, they frequently create a serious bottleneck. Several hardware techniques can be used to lessen this problem: independent device operation, device buffering, multiple paths, and block multiplexing.

Input/output Operation

The channels and control units together are very important components of I/O subsystem but in many cases there is sufficient capability in the device to complete an I/O operation without further assistance from the channel or control unit. A disk seek operation only needs the channel long enough to transmit the seek address from memory to the disk. The seek operation can be completed by the device alone. Likewise, there are operations that may require both the device and the control unit but not the channel for completion.

When a 1/0 operation is initiated, the entire path must be available. In order to indicatc when parts of the path become available, there may be separate 1/0 completion interrupts: channel end, control unit end, and device end. The type of 1/0 completion interrupt is designated by the status bits in the Channel Status Word. If more than one part of the path becomes available at the same time, there will be only one interrupt but the status bits will indicate all available parts. If a channel end occurs, the channel is no longer busy, although the device may still be busy. An I/0 operation can then be initiated on some other device using that channel.

Track Multiplexing

The tracks are the paths that transfer data. The device engineers could reduce the channel and control unit bottlenecks by buying more channels and control units. A more economical alternative, however, is to use the channels and control units in a more flexible manner and allows multiple paths to each device.

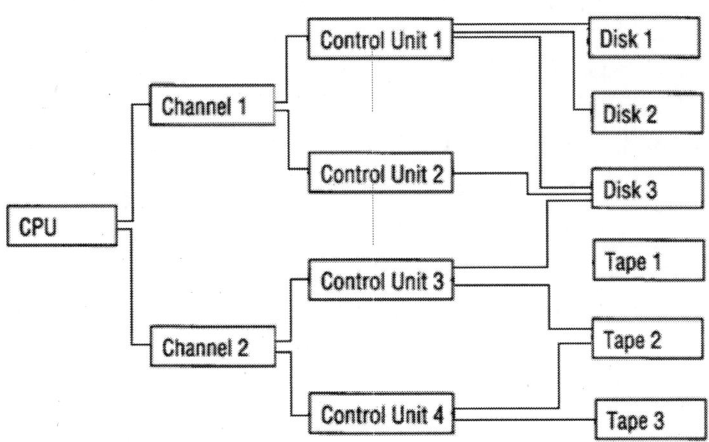

As specified in the previous section, there are many different paths from CPU to disk 3. If channel 1 and control unit 1and control unit 2 were both busy due to I/O, a path could be found through channel 2 and control unit 3 to service disk 3. In addition to providing flexibility, a multiple path 1/0 configuration is desirable for reliability. For example, if channel 1 malfunction and must be repaired, other control units and devices can still be accessed through channel 2. It is the responsibility of the device management routines to maintain status information on all paths in the 1/0 configuration and find an available route to access the desired device.

Block Multiplexing

The channels can be block multiplexed, A block multiplexer Channel can be servicing multiple channel programs at the same time, may be ten channel programs). When the channel encounters an I/O operation such as a buffered or independent device operation that does not need the channel for a while, it automatically switches to another channel program that needs immediate servicing. In essence, a block multiplex or channel represents a hardware implementation of multiprogramming for channel programs. This type of channel multiprogramming could be simulated on a selector channel by making all channel programs only one command long. The device management software routines could then reassign the channel as necessary.

Generally, this approach is not very attractive unless the central processor is extremely fast, since the channel switching must be done very frequently and very quickly and shared devices are to be assigned to the job. In general, device management tries to spread the allocation among devices so as to minimize channel and control unit bottlenecks.

DEVICE ALLOCATION CONSIDERATIONS

Due to the relative ease and speed with which a direct access device such as a magnetic drum or disk can be repositioned, it is possible to share it among several jobs running concurrently. A shared device is logically treated as if it were a group of dedicated devices. Each job using a shared device logically has a separate area to itself; the direct access property of the device makes it economical to switch back and forth among these areas. The device management routines may decide which shared device will be assigned to a job and what area of the device will be assigned. These decisions are also frequently made in conjunction with the job-scheduling routines.

For both dedicated and shared devices, static and dynamic allocation decisions must be made. The static decisions largely involve determining which dedicated and shared devices are to be assigned to the job. In general, device management tries to spread the allocation among devices so as to minimize channel and control unit bottlenecks. The static allocation decisions of device management are analogous to the job scheduling in processor management.

Management of I/O Requests

Device Manager divides task into three parts, each handled by specific software component of I/O subsystem:

1. ***I/O traffic controller*** watches status of all devices, control units, and channels
2. ***I/O scheduler*** implements policies that determine allocation of, and access to, devices, control units, and channels
3. ***I/O device handler*** performs actual transfer of data and processes the device interrupts

1. I/O traffic controller

The I/O traffic controller is involved in monitoring the status of every device, controller and channel. Its three main tasks include determining if at least one path is available, which path to select if more than one is available, and if all paths are busy, when one will be open.

The I/O traffic controller monitors the status of every device.

To achieve these tasks it uses a database containing the status and connections of each unit in the I/O subsystem. In other words, it the I/O traffic controller is in charge of the data that is coming into the computer (input by way of the keyboard or mouse) and going out of the computer (output by way of printer or screen display). It directs the flow of data to and from the external devices and also takes care of control routing information along the bus to be processed by the processor.

Three main tasks of I/O traffic controller:

- Determine if there's at least one path available
- If more than one path available, it must determine which to select
- If the paths are all busy, it must determine when one will become available

Whereas the I/O scheduler is mainly concerned with policies (e.g., who gets the device and when), the I/O traffic controller is primarily concerned with mechanics (e.g., can the device be assigned?). The traffic controller maintains all status information. The I/O traffic controller becomes complicated due to the interdependencies introduced by the scarcity of channels and control units, and the multiple paths. The traffic controller attempts to answer at least three key questions:

1. Is there a path available to service an 1/0 request?
2. Is more than one path available?
3. If no path is currently available, when will one be free?

The traffic controller maintains a database reflecting status and connections of the channels, control units and devices. This can be accomplished by means of Unit

Control Blocks (UCB), Control Unit Control Blocks (CUCB), and Channel Control Blocks (CCB) as depicted in figure. The first question can be answered by starting at the desired UCB and working back through the connected control units and channels trying to find a combination that is available. In a similar manner it is possible to determine all available paths.

Channel Control Block	Control Unit Control Block	Device Control Block
• Channel identification	• Control Unit identification	• Device identification
• Status	• Status	• Status
• List of control units connected to it	• List of channels connected to it	• List of control units connected to it
• List of processes waiting for it	• List of devices connected to it	• List of processes waiting for it
	• List of processes waiting for it	

Table 1

This second question may be important, especially when the I/O configuration is not symmetric. Since choosing one path may block out other I/O requests. Thus, one path may conflict with fewer I/O requests than another path.

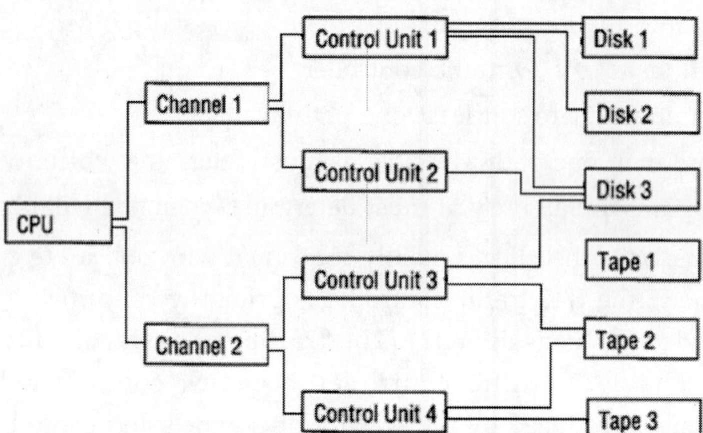

In Figure there are many different paths from CPU to disk 3. If channel 1 and control unit 1and control unit 2 were both busy due to I/O, a path could be found through channel 2 and control unit 3 to service disk 3. Under heavy I/O loads, it is quite likely that there will not be a path available at the time an I/O request is issued by a process. When I/O completions interrupt Occurs, one or more components (i.e., device, control units, and channel) become available again. We could try all 1/0 requests that are waiting to see if any can, now be satisfied; if, however, hundreds of 1/0 requests were waiting, this could be a time consuming approach. A more efficient approach would be to list all 1/0 requests that are "interested" in the component in the control block, as suggested in Table.1. Only those particular I/O requests would then have to be examined.

2. I/O scheduler

The I/O scheduler allocates the devices, control units and channels. Some systems allow the I/O scheduler to give preferential treatment to I/O requests from "high-priority" programs.

The I/O scheduler has the same task as the process scheduler and must arbitrate between I/O requests and allocate devices, channels and controllers to processes.

The I/O scheduler synchronizes its work with the traffic controller to satisfy I/O requests. If there are more I/O requests pending than available paths, it is necessary to choose which VO requests to satisfy first. Many of the same concerns discussed in process scheduling are applicable here. One important difference is that I/O requests are not normally time sliced, that is, once a channel program has been started it is not usually interrupted until it has been completed. Most channel programs are quite short and terminate within 50-100 ms; it is, however, possible to encounter channel programs that take seconds or even minutes before termination.

Many different policies may be incorporated into the 1/0 scheduler. For example, if a process has a high priority assigned by the process scheduler, it is reasonable also to assign a high priority to its I/O requests. This would help complete that job as fast as possible. Once the I/O scheduler has determined the relative orderings of the I/O requests, the I/O traffic controller must determine which, if any, of them can be satisfied. The I/O device handlers then provide another level of device-dependent I/O scheduling and optimization.

3. I/O Device handler

The I/O device handler processes I/O interrupts, handles error conditions, and provides detailed scheduling algorithms, which are extremely device dependent.

The device handler is part of the device driver and is involved in handling interrupts, completing I/O operations and correcting errors.

Each I/O device has its own algorithm for scheduling or other similar purposes.

Device handler function – *disk scheduling revisited*

In addition to setting up the channel command words, handling error conditions, and processing 1/0 interrupts, the 1/0 device handlers provide detailed scheduling algorithms that are dependent upon the peculiarities of the device type. There is usually a different device handler algorithm for each type of 1/0 device.

Disk arm motion is the greatest consumer of service time within most disk configurations. The average rotational delay—the time that it takes for the desired sector to move under the read/write head—is about 4ms for a 7200 RPM disk, and about 3ms for a 10,000 RPM disk (this delay is calculated as the time required for half a revolution). For this same class of disks, average seek time— the time required to position the read/write head over the desired track—ranges from 5 to 10ms. In many cases, this is twice the rotational latency of the disk. Furthermore, actual seek times can be much worse than the average. As much as 15 to 20ms can be consumed during a *full-stroke seek* (moving the disk arm from the innermost track to the outermost, or vice versa).

Clearly, one road to better disk performance involves finding ways to minimize disk arm motion. This can be done by optimizing the order in which requests for sectors on the disk are serviced. *Disk scheduling* can be a function of either the device handler or the host operating system, but it should not be done by both, because conflicting schedules will probably result, thus reducing throughput.

FCFS

The most naïve disk scheduling policy is *first-come, first-served* (*FCFS*). As its name implies, all I/O requests are serviced in the order in which they arrive in the disk service queue. The easiest way to see the problem with this approach is through an example. Let's say we have a disk with 100 tracks, numbered 0 through 99. Processes running in the system issue requests to read tracks from the disk in the following order:

28, 35, 52, 6, 46, 62, 19, 75, 21

With the FCFS scheduling policy, assuming we are currently servicing track 40, the disk arm traces the pattern shown in Figure . As you can see by the diagram, the disk arm changes direction six times and traverses a total of 291 tracks before completing this series of requests.

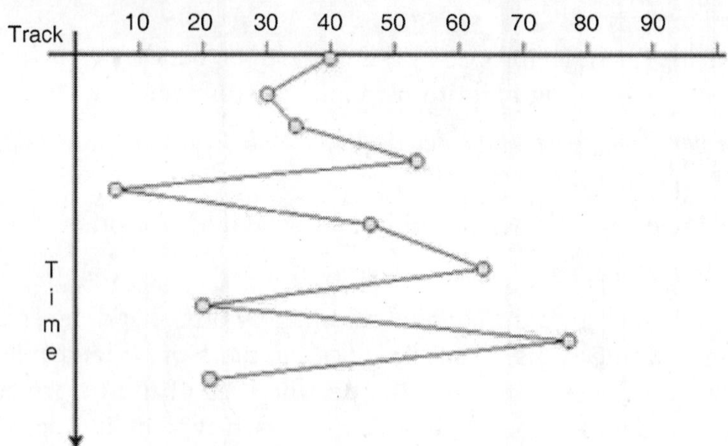

Disk Track Seeks Using the First-Come, First-Served Disk Scheduling Policy

Surely, arm motion could be reduced substantially if requests were ordered so that the disk arm moves only to the track nearest its current location. This is the idea employed by the *shortest seek time first* (*SSTF*) scheduling algorithm.

SSTF

Using the same disk track requests as listed above, assuming that the disk arm starts at track 40, the disk schedule using SSTF would be carried out as follows:

35, 28, 21, 19, 6, 46, 52, 62, 75

The pattern for this schedule is shown in Figure, as you can see, the disk arm changes direction only once and traverses a total of only 103 tracks. One shortcoming of SSTF is that *starvation* is possible: Theoretically, a track requested at a "remote" part of the disk could keep getting shoved to the back of the queue when requests for tracks closer to the present arm position arrive. Interestingly, this problem is at its worst with low disk utilization rates.

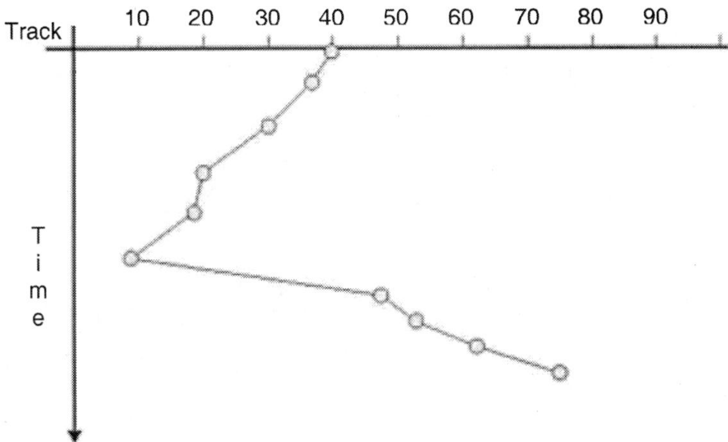

Disk Arm Motion for the Shortest Seek Time First Scheduling Algorithm

SCAN

To avoid the starvation risk of SSTF, some fairness mechanism must be designed into the system. An easy way to do this is to have the disk arm continually sweep over the surface of the disk, stopping when it reaches a track for which it has a request in its service queue. This approach is called the *elevator algorithm*, because of its similarity to how skyscraper elevators service their passengers.

In the context of disk scheduling, the elevator algorithm is known as SCAN (which is *not* an acronym). To illustrate how SCAN works, let's say that in our example, the disk arm happens to be positioned at track 40, and is in the process of sweeping toward the inner, higher-numbered tracks. With the same series of requests as before, SCAN reads the disk tracks in the following order:

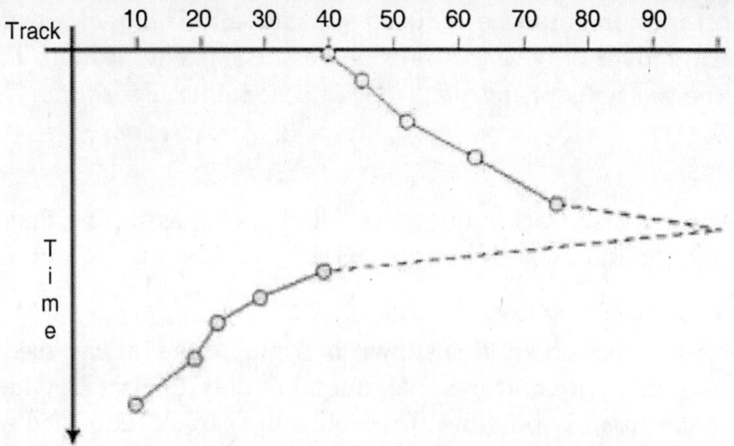

Disk Arm Motion for the SCAN Disk Scheduling Algorithm

C-SCAN

The disk arm passes over track 99 between reading tracks 75 and 35, and then travels to track zero after reading track 6, as shown in Figure. SCAN has a variant, called *C-SCAN* for circular SCAN, in which track zero is treated as if it is adjacent to track 99. In other words, the arm reads in one direction only, as shown in Figure. Once it passes track 99, it moves to track zero without stopping. Thus in our example, C-SCAN would read disk tracks as follows:

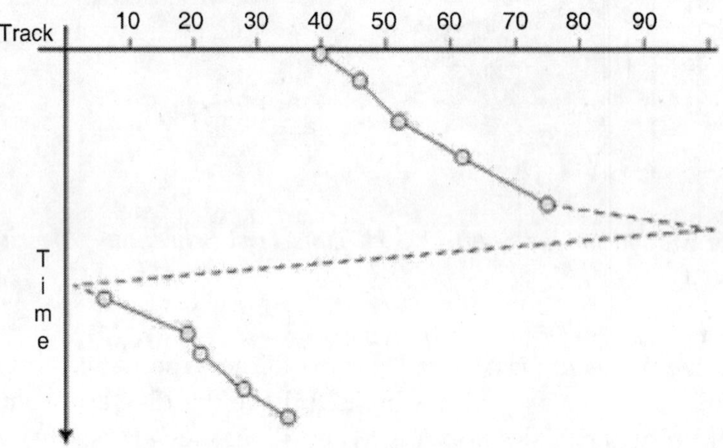

Disk Arm Motion for the C-SCAN Disk Scheduling Algorithm

46, 52, 62, 75, 6, 19, 21, 28, 35.

The disk arm motion of SCAN and C-SCAN is reduced even further through the use of the *LOOK* and *C-LOOK* algorithms. In our example, SCAN and C-SCAN continually sweep over all 100 disk tracks. But, in fact, the lowest required track is 6 and the highest is 75. Thus, if the disk arm changes direction only when the highestand lowest-numbered tracks are read, the arm will traverse only 69 tracks. This gives an arm-motion savings of about 30% over SCAN and C-SCAN.

Interestingly, at high utilization rates, SSTF performs slightly better than SCAN or LOOK. But the risk of starving an individual request persists. Under very low utilization (under 20%), the performance of any of these algorithms is acceptable.

Maximum performance is realized if the most frequently used files are placed at the center of the disk. Of particular importance are the disk directory and memory page (swap) files. A central position provides the least head motion and, hence, the best access time for both SSTF and SCAN/LOOK. A worst-case situation presents itself when files are badly fragmented, that is, when a file is located in more than one contiguous disk location. If SCAN/LOOK is the scheduling method of the disk, it is possible that several full-stroke head movements will occur before the end of the file is encountered. For this reason, disks should be *defragmented*, or reorganized, on a regular basis. Additionally, disks should not be allowed to get too full. Another rule of thumb is that when a disk is 80% full, it is time to start removing some files. If no files can be removed, it's time to get another disk.

Device drivers

Device drivers are special programs that form part of the device management component of the operating system (we will study all the remaining components of the operating system in the next chapter). They know how to communicate with a device controller (sending commands and data to the command and data register) as well as the meaning of the status register in the controller.

Drivers for different devices present a similar interface to the application program. The goal is to simplify interfaces to devices as much as possible, so that differences between controllers produced by different manufacturers and even differences between different types of devices are made as transparent as possible.

Device drivers are often written by the device manufacturers and must be installed into the operating system before the particular device can be used. Most modern operating systems (such as Windows) have a library of drivers from well-known manufacturers.

Device Controllers

I/O units typically consist of a mechanical component and an electronic component. It is often possible to separate the two portions to provide a more modular and general design. The electronic component is called the device controller or adapter. On mini and microcomputer, it often takes the form of a printed circuit card that can be inserted into the parent board. The mechanical component is the device itself.

The controller card usually has a connector on it, into which a cable leading to the device itself can be plugged. Many controllers can handle two, four, or even eight identical device. If the interface between the controller and device is a standard interface, either an official standard such as ANSI, IEEE or ISO, or de facto one, then companies can make controllers or devices that fit that interface. Many companies, for example, make disk drives that match the IBM disk controller interface.

We mention this distinction between controller and device because the operating systems nearly always deal with the controller, not the device. Nearly all microcomputer and minicomputers use the single bus model of Fig for communication between the CPU and the controllers. Large mainframes often use a different model, with multiple buses and specialized I/O computers called I/O channels taking some of the load off the main CPU.

The operating system performs I/O by writing commands into the controllers' registers. The IBM PC floppy disk controller, for example, accepts 15 different commands, such as READ, WRITE, SEEK, FORMAT, and RECALIBRATE. Many of the commands have parameters, which are also loaded into the controller's registers. When a command has been accepted, the CPU can leave the controller alone, and go off to do other work. When the command has been completed, the controller causes an interrupt in order to allow the operating system to again control of the CPU, and test the results of the operation. The CPU gets the results and the device status by reading one or more bytes of information form the controller's registers.

Direct Memory Access (DMA)

Many controllers, especially those for block devices, support direct memory access (DMA). To explain how DMA works, let us first look at how disk reads occur when DMA is not used. First the controller reads the block (one or more sectors) form the drive serially, bit by bit, until the entire block is in the controller's internal buffer. Next, it performs the checksum computation to verify that no read errors have occurred. (The checksum can be computed only after the entire block has been read). Then the controller causes an interrupt. When the operating system starts processing the interrupt, it can read the disk block from the controller's buffer a byte or a word at a time by executing a loop, with each iteration reading one byte or word from a controller device register and storing it in memory.

Naturally, a programmed CPU loop to head the bytes one at a time form the controller wastes CPU time. DMA was invented to free the CPU from this low-level work. When it is used, the CPU gives the controller two items of information, in addition to the disk address of the block: the memory address where the block is to go, and the number of bytes to transfer, as shown in Fig.

After the controller has read the entire block from the device into its buffer and veripied the checksum, it copies the first byte or word into the main memory at the address specified by the DMA memory address. Then it increment the DMA address and decrement the DMA count by the number of bytes just transferred. This process is repeated until the DMA count becomes zero, atWhich time the controller causes an interrupt. When the operating system starts up, it does not have to copy the block to memory: it is already there.

Internal working of Input/Output Devices

Let's have an introduction to about the working of input/output devices of computer system

Control/Status Registers

Access to input/output devices is via device registers that are shared between the computer and the device controller. The device registers are usually memory mapped. In other words, when the processor reads and writes what it thinks is a word of physical memory, it is actually reading and writing the device registers. The device can also read and write these registers, and hence communicate with the processor. The control/status register for a device will often have at least three flags:

1. **An interrupt enable flag** that the processor sets or clears to indicate whether it is interested in knowing when the device wants to communicate with the processor.
2. **An interrupt request flag** that the device sets when it wants to communicate with the processor (in other words, cause an interrupt). The processor clears this flag after it has dealt with the request.
3. **An error flag** that the device sets if something goes wrong. For example, if the device tries to set the interrupt request flag, when it is already set, the error flag will be set, to indicate that an interrupt has been missed.

When both the interrupt enable flag and the interrupt request flag are set, and the interrupt priority level is lower than the priority level of the device, then an interrupt occurs. The processor raises the interrupt priority level to the priority level of the device, and executes the interrupt handler. The interrupt handler accesses other device registers to read or write the device, etc. On completion, the return from trap or interrupt (rti) instruction restores the interrupt priority level back to its previous value.

The Keyboard and Mouse

Suppose we have a microcomputer with its own keyboard, mouse, and screen. Whenever a key is pressed or released, an interrupt is generated. An indication of the keys that are pressed, and the current status of special keys such as the shift, caps lock, control and option keys, will be placed in a device data register, and the interrupt request flag will be set by the keyboard controller. The interrupt handler reads this register, and copies the information into an operating system data structure.

Mouse presses, releases, and mouse motions will be dealt with in a similar manner. An interrupt will occur whenever the mouse is moved, or a button pressed or released. An indication of the change in X and Y values since the last event, and the current status of the buttons, will be placed in a device data register.

The Screen

On a modern machine, the screen is accessed as memory. For example, each pixel could be represented by three bytes of information, specifying the red, green and blue components of the color of the pixel. To alter the screen image, the processor1 just changes the values of the memory for each pixel. The screen hardware also accesses this memory, and uses it to control the intensity of the beam that scans left to right, top to bottom across the screen.

Disk Drives and DMA controllers

The central processing unit (CPU) is not the only processor in a computer. For example, there are processors for controlling input/output devices, network ports, etc.

As discussed earlier, most modern device bus controllers are able to perform what is called Direct Memory Access (DMA). Data can be copied directly between the computer memory and the disk drive without the involvement of the CPU. DMA is performed with the help of a special processor, namely the DMA controller that sits between the memory bus and device bus. (The USB controller, SCSI controller, or Ethernet controller correspond to DMA controllers.) The DMA controller takes responsibility for moving the data between the disk controller registers and memory. The only problem is that the transfer of the data makes use of the memory bus (wires) used to connect the processor to memory so may cause the CPU to wait when the bus is busy.

To perform disk input/output, the CPU supplies information to the DMA controller to specify the address of the data on disk and in memory, the amount of data to read or write, and whether to perform a read or write. The disk controller communicates with the DMA controller to perform the appropriate data transfer. The DMA controller finally sets the interrupt request flag to indicate that it has completed its action.

The information given to a modern DMA controller is often supplied by setting a register to the address of a linked list of records containing input/output requests. The DMA controller can process this list, removing requests from the head of the list. The CPU can add requests to the tail of the list.

Network Connections

Network connections work in much the same way as disk drives – the network controller performs direct memory access. The CPU provides information to specify the address of the data in memory. Incoming packets are copied from the network into memory, and the network controller then sets the interrupt request flag to indicate that input has arrived. Outgoing packets are copied from memory to the network, and the network controller then sets the interrupt request flag to indicate that the output has been sent.

Terminals and Printers

Microcomputers are often used as terminals for UNIX machines. On the microcomputer, key presses are processed by an interrupt handler. A thread in an application program "reads" the input, and sends it to the UNIX machine via the network. The UNIX machine sends requests via the network to the microcomputer to draw on the microcomputer's screen. The requests are likely to be at a similar level of abstraction to the methods in the Graphics class in Java - draw text in a specified font, draw a line, draw or fill a circle, rectangle, etc. Communication with a modern printer is at a similar level. In fact a modern personal computer is likely to have a separate processor to draw on the screen. Directives from the CPU to the graphics processor will also be fairly high level.

How Input and Output are controlled ?

One of the main problems with input is that it can arrive without notice. If the user types ahead, the operating system has to buffer the input, so that it can be consumed later by a thread. If the thread wanting to read the input executes before the input has been typed, then it has to block and wait until the input arrives.

Output can also cause a thread to block, because the thread can generate output at a faster rate than the device can consume it. Because output is often generated in bursts, throughput can be maximised by the operating system buffering output generated by the thread, but not accepted by the device.

The actions involved in input and output are distributed over library functions such as scanf and printf, library functions that pass the request over to the operating system, system call handlers, interrupt handlers, and the devices themselves.

Input

Assume the C programming language under UNIX. C is a bit old fashioned, so input is performed by a "blocking read", rather than an event handler. Moreover, by the time the information is processed by the C program, input is normally seen as a sequence of ASCII characters, rather than key presses and releases.

A thread invokes the scanf library function. This function invokes the read library function to "read" characters from the standard input and place them in an input buffer in user space. When reading numbers, scanf has to parse the text to convert the input from ASCII into internal form. Thus the main work performed by scanf is parsing of ASCII text.

The read library function does almost nothing. It just executes the callsys instruction to make a system call. The system call handler invokes an operating system function to handle the read system call. If the user has typed ahead, the characters typed will have been placed in an operating system input buffer by an interrupt handler.

The read system call handler takes the characters out of this buffer, and copies them from the system input buffer to the user buffer. If insufficient characters are available, the thread blocks.

Assume we are using a microcomputer as a terminal. Then the input will arrive from the microcomputer, over the network. The network interrupt handler on the UNIX machine will execute whenever a packet has arrived. The network interrupt handler will extract the input out of the packet, place it in the operating system input buffer, and notify a blocked thread that it can resume execution, if a thread is waiting for input.

Similar actions will happen for the terminal emulator on the microcomputer, except that the input will come from the keyboard, rather than arriving over the network. The terminal emulator on the microcomputer will pass the character on to the main computer, by sending it in a packet over the network.

Output

Assume the C programming language under UNIX. Again, C is somewhat old fashioned. Output is normally plain ASCII text, rather than directions to draw on the screen.

A thread invokes the printf library function. This function formats numbers, etc, as text, which it places in an output buffer in user space. Printf then invokes the write library function to "write" the characters to the standard output. Thus the main work performed by printf is conversion of numbers to text.

The write library function does almost nothing. It just executes the callsys instruction to make a system call.

The system call handler invokes an operating system function to handle the write system call. The write system call handler copies the data from the user output buffer to an operating system output buffer. If the operating system output buffer becomes full, the thread blocks, until space becomes available.

Assume we are using a microcomputer as a terminal. Then the output will have to be sent in packets to the microcomputer. The write system call handler sets up information to say that it wants to send the data to the microcomputer, and sets the interrupt enable flag for the network controller so that a network interrupt will occur as soon as the network is ready to transmit a packet. If the network is not busy, this will cause an almost immediate interrupt.

The network interrupt handler sets up the registers to cause the packet to be sent. Once the packet has been sent, another interrupt will occur. The network interrupt handler will send another packet, and repeat the process, until all data has been sent. When all the data has been sent, the interrupt handler will clear the interrupt flag so that network interrupts will no longer occur. Once sufficient space is available in the system output buffer, the interrupt handler will notify the blocked thread that it can resume execution.

Input/Output in Event Based Programming Languages

With the popularity of Java, performing input/output by read and write statements that block, is somewhat old fashioned, although still essential for disk input/output. The new model for input/output is event based. Also, modern systems deal with not only typing of ordinary characters, but also key and mouse presses and releases, mouse motion, etc. Output involves not only the generation of text, but also the drawing of pictures.

When a key or mouse press or release, or a mouse motion occurs, this generates an interrupt. The interrupt handler creates an operating system event object containing information about the event that has occurred, and adds this to a terminal manager event queue.

Each process has its own thread to handle events related to that process. The user level code for this thread loops, making a system call each time though the loop, to obtain an event, and handle the event in some way. It blocks when there are no events left to handle. The code for adding an event to an event queue resumes a thread waiting to obtain an event from the event queue, if there is one.

There is a terminal manager event handling thread that handles events placed on the terminal manager event queue. The terminal manager event handling thread processes the events related to key and mouse events in sequence. It collapses some frequently occurring events, such as mouse motions into a single event. It deals with some events itself. For example a mouse motion will alter the information on the position of the mouse. A mouse press over a window will be converted into higher level events to bring the window to the front, repaint part of a window, etc. High level events, and some low level events, such as key presses and releases, are added to the event queue for the process corresponding to the foreground window.

The event handling thread in a Java based process decides which object (e.g., AWT component) the event relates to, then invokes an appropriate event handler method within that object, to deal with the event. This event handler method invokes appropriate methods in the listeners associated with that object.

We can interpret the above in the conventional terminology of a thread that blocks waiting for an event. However, there is an alternative approach. We can ignore the existence of the event queue and the thread for handling the event queue, and just say that the operating system converts system interrupts into user level interrupts, that are handled by user level interrupt handlers - the methods in the listeners associated with AWT components. The event queue and thread does nevertheless serve some purpose, namely it serializes the processing of events, rather than allowing them to be processed in parallel. Whether this is good or bad is not clear. It limits multi-processing, so makes the system slower, but more reliable.

Device Management Approaches

A device manager is responsible for manipulating a hardware device and is typically structured as shown in the Figure ahead. Commonly devices are made up of a mechanical and an electrical component e.g. a hard disc and its controller e.g. IDE (integrated Drive Electronics), SCSI (Small Computer System Interface) controllers for Seagate, Fujitsu etc. hard discs. It is not unusual for one controller to service several identical devices.

One can recognise the fact that the computer I/O sub-system will be dealing with the controller and NOT the device. The controller provides the I/O sub-system with data in the expected form.

The diagram shows another sandwich. At the bottom there is hardware, the device controller, which will be connected physically to the hardware device it is controlling. The device controller receives data, together with commands (e.g. Read / Write) and it provides status information back to the operating system (e.g. Read complete, error detected).

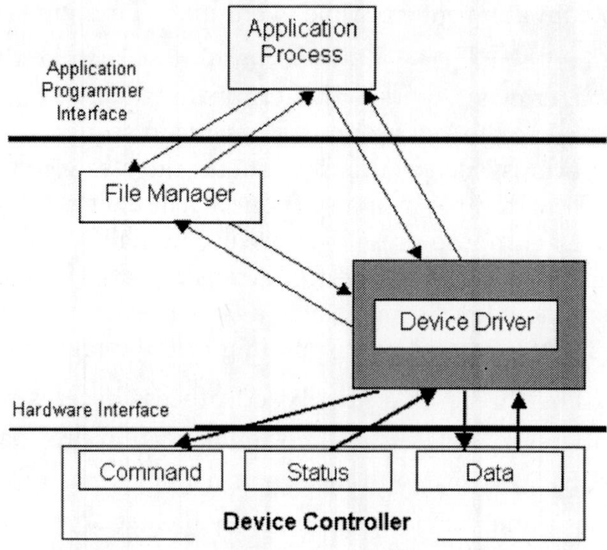

Device Management

The top part of the sandwich is the application program. You can see that it need not know about the physical characteristics of the actual device. The API enables the application to send requests/ data to the sandwich filling (O/S I/O sub-system). The device driver formats these requests into a specific format that the device controller can understand.

Given that devices are concerned with data transfer at speeds significantly slower than the processor the last thing that you want to do is to have the processor wait while the current process carries out some I/O activity. What happens is that when the current process makes an I/O request it is suspended until that I/O request has been completed. What this means is that it gives up the processor to some other process (see process management). How does the computer know when the I/O is complete? Well that's where interrupts or polling come in.

As discussed earlier, Interrupt - the device sends a signal to the CPU system to say the I/O request is complete. The CPU has to stop what it's doing, save data about the process it is executing and service the interrupt. The process waiting for that I/O is moved off the Blocked queue and placed on the Ready queue. The runnable process priorities are reviewed and one is selected according to the low level-scheduling algorithm in use.

Polling - at regular intervals all devices are checked to see if the I/O requests they were dealing with have been completed. Where this is true the same above actions occur as for interrupts. This is done at the CPUs convenience.

Performance Factors

There are several performance factors which make the PCI bus an ideal choice for handling a systems most demanding I/O requirements. Four of these factors are burst mode, bus mastering, high bandwidth, and expansion.

Burst Mode: Once an initial address is provided, the PCI bus can transfer multiple sets of data in a row (a burst of information).

Bus Mastering: The capability of devices on the PCI bus to take control of the bus and perform transfers directly. The PCI design supports full device bus mastering, in that it allows bus mastering of multiple devices on the bus simultaneously. It has arbitration circuitry that works to ensure no device on the bus locks out any other device. At the same time it allows any given device to use the full bus throughput if no other device needs to transfer anything.

High Bandwidth: Current PCI specifications call for expandability to 64 bits and 66 MHz speed which, if implemented, would quadruple bandwidth over the current design. This design does currently exist on non-PC platforms and servers; however, mainstream PCI is still limited to 32 bits and 33 MHz.16

Expansion: The PCI bus offers a great variety of expansion cards compared other system I/O buses. The most commonly found cards are video cards, SCSI host adapters, and high-speed networking cards. Hard disk drives are also on the PCI bus but are normally connected directly to the motherboard on a PCI system.

As all these factors make the PCI bus a good choice for device integration. As a result, it has become the most task saturated I/O bus on today's systems.

Interface Types

The two most common types of interfaces between the CPU and a PC's peripheral devices are SCSI and IDE. SCSI stands for "Small Computer Systems Interface" while IDE stands for "Integrated Device Electronics." Each interface requires the use of a host adapter whose job is to act as the gateway between the SCSI or IDE bus and the PC's internal I/O bus. Normally that is the PCI bus since it supports the fastest transfer rates of the PC's I/O buses. It sends and responds to commands and transfers data to and from devices on the bus and inside the computer itself.

SCSI Interface

In the SCSI interface, devices on the SCSI bus talk to the computer through a single device on the SCSI bus – called the controller or host adapter. The controller sends and responds to commands from the CPU via its interface on the PCI bus. The SCSI bus is able to manage several devices because each one has the ability to release the bus after being requested to do a time consuming job, therefore leaving the bus free for other devices to use for data transfer or receiving commands.

ATA/IDE Interface

The most popular interface used in modern PCs are ATA/IDE – Advanced Technology Attachment/Integrated Device Electronics (names are synonymous). It integrates the hard disk and other IDE devices through an IDE controller (or host adapter), which is normally built into the PC's motherboard.

There are both physical limitations and technological issues that make both interfaces ideal for certain situations.

KEYWORDS

LINEAR LIST
INDEXED ALLOCATION
DEVICE MANAGEMENT
A BLOCK DEVICE
A CHARACTER
EFFICIENCY
GENERALITY
DEDICATED DEVICES
SHARED DEVICES
VIRTUAL DEVICES
SASD
DASD
BUFFERING
SPOOLING
THE I/O CHANNEL
THE I/O CONTROLS UNIT
I/O TRAFFIC CONTROLLER
I/O SCHEDULER
I/O DEVICE HANDLER
SCSI

SUMMARY

Device management is the part of the OS that manages hardware devices. The device management tries to provide a uniform interface to ease the access to devices with different physical characteristics, and optimize the performance of individual devices.

- The general goals of the I/O software are easy to state. the basic idea is to organize the software as a series of layers, with the lower ones concerned with hiding the peculiarities of the hardware from the upper ones, and the upper ones concerned with presenting a nice, clean, regulate interface to the users.
- A block device (e.g., disks) stores information in fixed-size blocks, each one with its own address.
- A character device (e.g., keyboards, printers, network cards) delivers or accepts a stream of characters, and individual characters are not addressable.

  Efficiency is improved through approaches such as:
- buffering - reading and storing data in large chunks
- interrupts - using time and events to interrupt the current active process
- polling - checking all devices regularly to see which needs to be serviced and interrupting the current active process to provide the service
- spooling - data to be transferred is temporarily stored until there is free processor time

Generalisation is achieved through:

- device controllers - hardware interface between the Operating System and a peripheral
- device drivers - software that controls a specific type of device.
- Dedicated devices are only assigned to one job at a time, they serve that job for the entire time it is active.
- Shared devices can be assigned several processes.
- Virtual devices are the combination of the dedicated and shared devices
- Sequential access storage media (SASD) means that data or records stored must be accessed and stored serially (in a linear sequence), one at a time.
- Direct access storage devices (DASD) can directly read or write from a specific location on the device without having to access sequentially from the first location.
- Access time can be affected by as many as three important factors: seek time, search time, and transfer time.
- Buffers are temporary storage areas used to synchronize the movement of data between I/O devices and the CPU. They are normally located in the main memory, as well as in channels and device controllers (control units).
- SPOOLING is then an acronym for **s**imultaneous **p**eripheral **o**peration **o**n-line. It essentially uses the disk as a very large buffer, for reading as far ahead as possible on input devices and for storing output files until the output devices are able to accept them.
- The I/O channel is a dedicated special purpose CPU found in high-end computer systems (such as workstations and mainframes), whose main purpose is to offload I/O work from the CPU.
- The I/O controls unit Monitors device and communicates with I/O channel.
- I/O traffic controller watches status of all devices, control units, and channels
- I/O scheduler implements policies that determine allocation of, and access to, devices, control units, and channels
- I/O device handler performs actual transfer of data and processes the device interrupts

REVIEW QUESTIONS

1) What is device management? How it is important for the proper functioning of the computer systems?
2) What are block address and character address devices?
3) What are the two major goals of device management? Explain in details.
4) Differentiate between
   a. dedicated
   b. shared
   c. virtual devices
5) What are the major differences between SASD and DASD?
6) Explain
   a. seek time
   b. search time
   c. transfer time
7) Differentiate between buffering and spooling in details
8) Explain the working of
   a. I/O channels
   b. I/O control units
   c. I/O traffic controller
   d. I/O scheduler
   e. I/O device handler

FILL IN THE BLANKS

1. ____________is the part of the OS that manages hardware devices.
2. ___________watches status of all devices, control units, and channels.
3. ____________implements policies that determine allocation of and access to, devices, control units, and channels.
4. Direct access storage devices (DASD) can directly read or write from a specific location on the device without having to access ____________from the first location.

5. ____________are only assigned to one job at a time, they serve that job for the entire time it is active.

6. _____________performs actual transfer of data and processes the device interrupts

TRUE OR FALSE

1. SPOOLING is then an acronym for **s**imultaneous **p**eripheral **o**peration **o**ff-**l**ine.
2. The I/O controls unit monitors device and communicates with I/O channel.
3. A block device stores information in fixed-size blocks, each one with its own address.
4. Polling means checking all devices regularly to see which needs to be serviced and interrupting the current active process to provide the service
5. I/O traffic controller implements policies that determine allocation of, and access to, devices, control units, and channels
6. The I/O controls unit Monitors device and communicates with I/O channel.

ANSWERS

FILL IN THE BLANKS

1. Device management
2. I/O traffic controller
3. I/O scheduler
4. sequentially
5. Dedicated devices
6. I/O device handler

TRUE OR FALSE

1. FALSE
2. TRUE
3. TRUE
4. TRUE
5. FALSE
6. TRUE

❑❑❑

UNIT-5

SYSTEM SECURITY AND PROTECTION

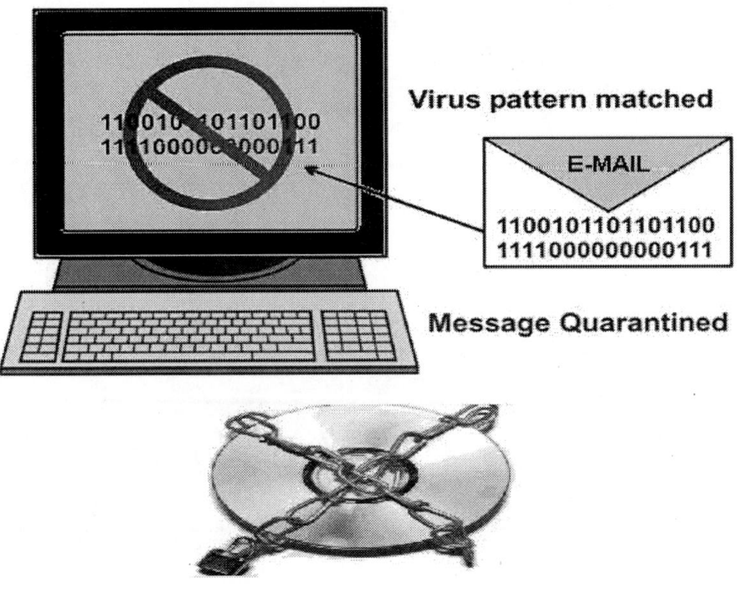

"Always secure your files; you never know who is lurking about." —**Rick Cook**

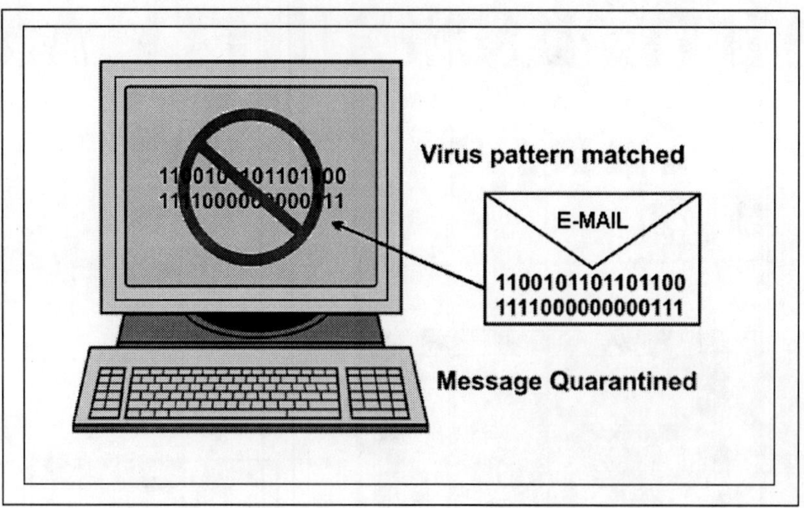

SYSTEM SECURITY

INTRODUCTION

In the current climate of viruses, hackers, electronic eavesdropping and electronic fraud computer security has become one of the central issues of Operating Systems. Given the enormous growth of computer systems and their interconnection over networks, the increasing dependence most organisations place on storing data electronically makes them very vulnerable to security shortcomings. Hence there has been a major investment in measures to counteract security threats, including the development of systems to authenticate both data and transactions on that data.

The terms *protection* and *security* are often used together, and the distinction between them is a bit blurred, but security is generally used in a broad sense to refer to all concerns about controlled access to facilities, while protection describes specific technological mechanisms that support security.

What is security and protection?

Security *refers to the policy of authorizing accesses.*

whereas

Protection *refers to the actual mechanisms implemented to enforce the specified policy.*

Security aims to prevent intentional misuses of a system, while protection aims to prevent either accidental or intentional misuses.

A secure system tries to accomplish three goals:

1. Data confidentiality: secret data remains secret.

2. Data integrity: unauthorized users should not be able to modify any data without the owner's permission.

3. System availability: nobody can disturb the system to make it unusable.

How system security is managed?

The security management by the operating system includes the following:

1. Programs protected from one another when running.
2. Multi-user operating systems provide some kind of authorization scheme. Many computers are password protected.
3. Operating system log successful and unsuccessful logon attempts and these logs can be reviewed by network administrators.
4. An operating system can also encrypt data going over the network as an additional protection mechanism.
5. Encryption: process of converting readable data into unreadable characters in order to prevent unauthorized access.
6. Versions, service packs, and automatic updating.

Components of security

There are three components of security:

1. **Authentication** determines who the user is.
2. **Authorization** determines who is allowed to do what.
3. **Enforcement** makes sure that people do only what they are supposed to do.

As you look at computer security it is helpful to specify what you mean by secure.

As you look at computer security it is helpful to specify what you mean by secure. Computer security should preserve:

1. Confidentiality:

Information held in a computer system should only be accessible for reading by authorised users. This should also be applied to printing, displaying and any other form of disclosing information. In particular it should include revealing the existence of specific 'objects'.

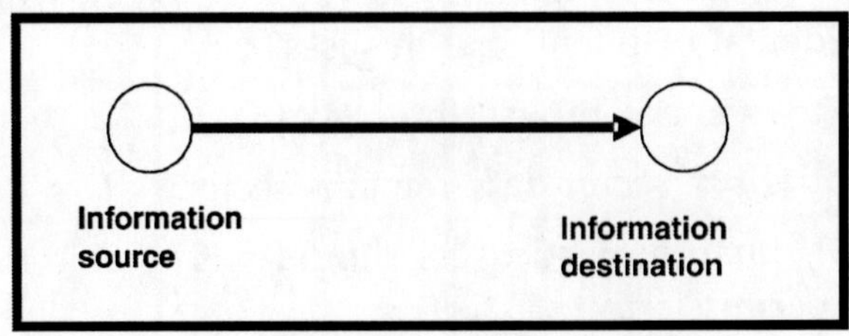

Normal Provision of Information

2. Integrity:

Computer assets should only be modified by authorised users. Modification includes writing, changing, changing the status, deleting and creating.

3. Availability:

Computer assets should only be available to authorised users.

Given these requirements you can see that threats to security are best seen as ways to breach these aims.

One such grouping of security threats is as follows:

Interruption: an asset of the system is either destroyed or becomes unavailable or

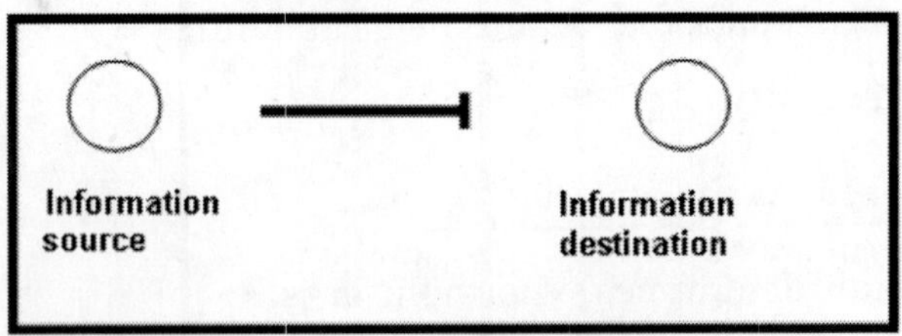

Interruption of information flow

unusable. This is an attack on availability. Examples include the destruction of hardware, cutting a communications line or disabling the file management system.

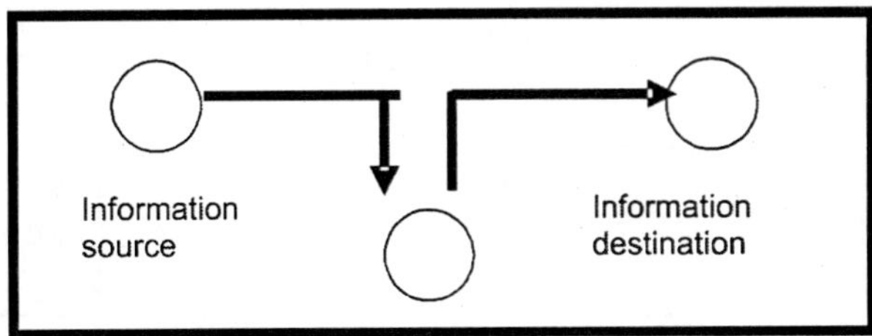

Modification of Information

Interception: Unauthorised access to a computer asset. This is an attack on confidentiality. The unauthorised user could be a person, program or another computer. Examples include wire tapping on a network, and illicit copying of files.

Modification: an unauthorised user not only gains access to but tampers with an asset. This is an attack on integrity. Examples include changing values in a data file, altering a program so that it performs differently, and modifying the content of messages being transmitted over a network.**Fabrication:** An unauthorised user inserts counterfeit objects into the system. This is an attack on authenticity. Examples include the insertion of spurious messages on a network or the addition of records to a file.

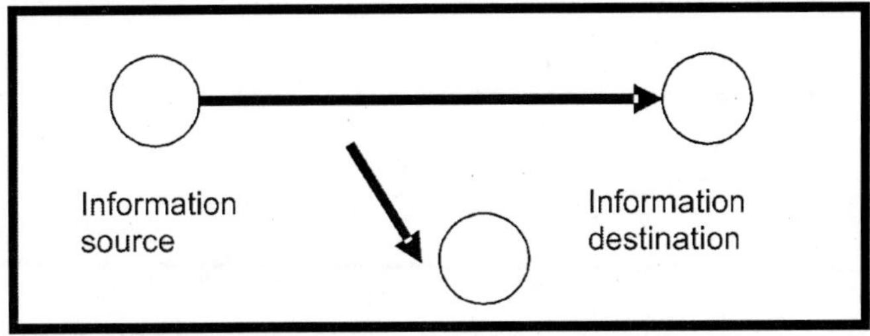

Interception of Information

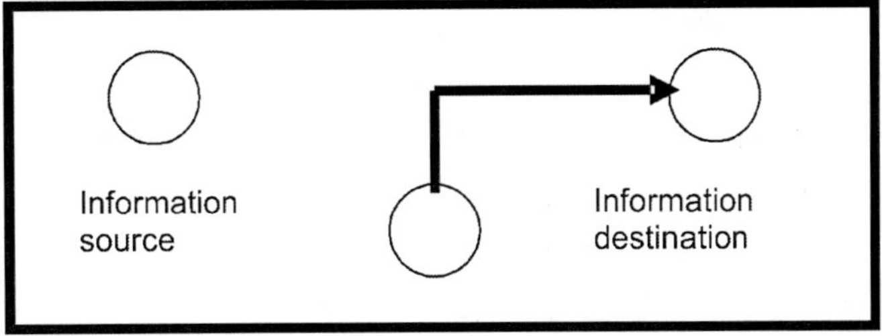

Fabrication of Information

Computer System Assets

To all intents and purposes the assets of a computer system can be categorised as its hardware, software, data, communication lines and networks. These can be individually threatened:

Category	Availability	Confidentiality	Integrity
Hardware	Equipment stolen or disabled, denial of service		
Software	Programs deleted, denial of access	Unauthorised copying of software	Program modified, causes failure or unexpected actions
Data	Files deleted, denial of access	Unauthorised data reading. Analysis of data reveals information about other data	Existing files modified, new files created
Comms. lines	Messages destroyed or deleted. Comms. unavailable	Messages are read. Traffic patterns observed	Messages modified, delayed, reordered or duplicated. False messages sent.

Classes of Security Problems

Eavesdropping

Eavesdropping is the listener approach. One can tap into the serial line on the Ethernet, and see everything typed in; almost everything goes over network unencrypted. For example, your password goes over the network unencrypted when you `rlogin` to a remote machine.

The military approach to defeat wired eavesdropping is to use pressurized cables. If the air pressure drops, someone may be trying to tap into the cable.

Abuse of Privilege

If the super user is evil, there is nothing you can do.

Imposter

An imposter breaks into the system by pretending to be someone else. For example, if a system authenticates by a person's voice or facial image, the system can be fooled. A countermeasure against the imposter attack is to use *behavioral monitoring* to look for suspicious activates (e.g., overwriting the boot block).

Trojan Horse

A Trojan horse is a seemingly innocent program that contains code that will perform an unexpected and undesirable function. A countermeasure against the Trojan horse is integrity checking. Periodically, the system should check the content of the disk against the original checksums for various files.

Salami Attack

The idea is to build up a chunk one-bit at a time. A programmer at a bank can reprogram the accounting program, so that the partial pennies go into his account. A countermeasure is for companies to have code reviews as a standard practice.

Logic Bombs

A programmer may secretly insert a piece of code into the production system. As long as the programmer feeds the system password periodically, it does nothing. However, if the programmer is suddenly fired, the logic bomb does not receive its password, so it goes off. Logic bombs can be also prevented by code reviews.

Denial-of-Service Attack

Denial-of-service attacks refer to attacks on system availability. A handful of compromised machines can flood a victim machine with network packets to disrupt its normal use. Currently, researchers are still looking for effective countermeasures.

Concrete Examples

Pentagon Traffic Analysis (eavesdropping)

Before the 1991 Persian Gulf War, foreign intelligence tried to predict the start of the war by monitoring the pizza delivery orders near Pentagon. Historically, the pizza orders increased significantly 72 hours prior to a major event....so much for the element of surprise...Now, the Pentagon has its own internal pizza huts.

Tenex

Tenex used to be the most popular system at universities before UNIX. The system was thought to be very secure. To demonstrate it, a team was hired to find loopholes. They were given all the source code and documentation, and a normal account. In 48 hours, they had every password in the system.

Here is the code for the password check:

```
for (j = 0; j < 8; j++) {
        if (userPasswd[j] != realPasswd[j]) {
                go to error;
        }
}
```

From the code, if you want to try all combinations, you need to go through 2568 combinations. However, Tenex also used virtual memory, and it interacts badly with the above code.

Therefore, by forcing page faults at inopportune times, one can break passwords quickly. For example, the array can be allocated in a way that the first character is in one page, while the remaining characters are on the next page. The first page is currently in memory, and the second page is on disk.

By timing how long the password check takes, one can figure out whether the first character is correct. A fast password check means that the first character is wrong. A slow password check means that the first character is right and causes a page fault. Therefore, by shifting the array across the page boundary, it takes only 256 * 8 checks to crack one password.

The fix is easy, the loop should not return until all characters are checked.

The Internet Worm

In 1988, a Cornell graduate student, RTM, released a worm program into the Internet. The worm used three attacks:

1. `rsh`
2. `fingerd`
3. `sendmail`

Some machines trust other machines, and the use of `rsh` was sufficient to get into a remote machine without further authentication. If this worked, the remote shell just uploaded the worm program.

The second attack involved the use of `finger` command, which allows a user to lookup another person by typing:

```
finger name@location
```

It turned out the finger daemon process did not check the parameter size, and the worm used finger with a handcrafted 536-byte string as parameter. This long stream overflowed the daemon's buffer and overwrote its stack. When the daemon returned from the procedure, it returned to the 536-byte string, which tried to execute the shell program. By gaining the access of the shell, the worm can move to the machine.

The third method depended on the bug in the mail system, `sendmail`, which allowed the worm to mail a copy of the bootstrap and get it executed.

The worm was caught because multiple worms broke into the same machine multiple times, and dragged the CPU down so much that people noticed.

Authentication

Authentication involves sharing a secret between two parties. One common approach of authentication is the use of *passwords*. The rational goes: since only I know the password, the machine can assume that I am the user. However, there are some problems with the password approach:

In computer security, verification of the identity of a user or the user's eligibility to access an object is called authentication.

First, the system must keep a copy of the secret (password). To prevent a malicious user from gaining the access to this list of passwords, a system needs to use *encryption*, which is, using a key to transform the data and make it difficult to reverse without the key. For example, the UNIX `/etc/passwd` file stores passwords that are encrypted using one-way transformations. Since the system only stores the encrypted version, a malicious user cannot read those passwords. When you type in the password, the system first encrypts your password and then compares it to the encrypted version.

The second problem with the password scheme is that it is difficult to come up with good passwords. Short passwords are easy to crack, but people tend to write down long passwords. UNIX initially required only lower-case, 5-letter passwords. Therefore, there were only 265 or 1 million combinations for exhaustive searches. In 1975, it took about 10 ms to check a password; therefore, 1 million combinations would take one day. Today, we can go through those combinations in 1 second. Many people choose very simple passwords, such as English words—it takes even less time to check all words in the dictionary.

Currently, there are some partial solutions:

1. Extend everyone's password with a unique number.
2. Require more complex passwords. For example, with 6 letters of upper, lower cases, numbers, and special characters, we can have 706 or 100 billion combinations, and it would take about one day. Unfortunately, people still pick common patterns (i.e., 5 lower case letters, plus one number).
3. Delay every remote login attempt by 1 second, so that it takes a long time to check each password.
4. Assign very long passwords. Give everyone a calculator (or ATM card) to carry around to remember the password. It then requires a physical theft to steal the password.

The third problem concerns whether we can trust the encryption algorithm. If there is a backdoor, decryption may not require exhaustive search.

Authentication in Distributed Systems

In the distributed environment, encryption is needed for authentication and guarding the secrecy of data in transit.

Private Key Encryption

The idea of ***private key*** encryption is to use an encryption algorithm that can be easily reversed, given the correct key (and hard to reverse without the key).

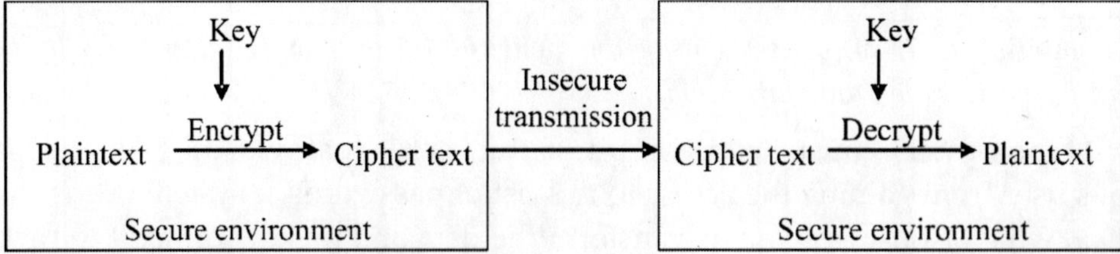

Without the key, one cannot decode the cipher text without exhaustive searches. From the plaintext and the cipher text, one cannot derive the key. As long as the key stays secret, private key encryption provides both secrecy and authentication.

The tricky part of the private key approach is to distribute keys in the first place. It usually involves an ***authentication server***, which keeps a list of keys and provides a way for two parties to talk to each other, as long as they trust the server.

Suppose Keyxy denotes the key for talking between x and y, and Keyxy[message] means to encrypt a message with Keyxy. Also, suppose we have clients A and B, and the server S. A and B already own KeyAS and KeyBS respectively, in order to talk to S. If A wants to talk to B, we go through the following steps under the Kerberos protocol.

Client A first asks S: "Yo, ring me B, and I want KeyAB"

A→ S: KeyAS[give me KeyAB]

S gives back KeyAB to A, and a message for B signed by KeyBS, containing KeyAB.

S→A: KeyAS[here is KeyAB and a message to B]

A sends the message to B

A→B: KeyBS[use KeyAB to talk to A]

There are additional details:

1. The server adds timestamps to limit how long a key can be used; this will prevent a machine from replaying messages later (e.g., "deposit $100").

2. The encrypted message also includes checksums to prevent a malicious user from inserting things into the message (e.g., "deposit $1,000").
3. To reduce the exposure of KeyAS (or KeyBS), A can periodically ask the server to give a temporary key KeyA'S that is different each time to serve the function of KeyAS.

Public Key Encryption

Public key encryption is an alternative to the private key encryption, which separates authentication from secrecy. Encryption and decryption involves a pair of public keys and private keys. With private key systems, a key is used for both encryption and decryption:

Encryption(Key, plaintext) = cipher text

Decryption(Key, cipher text) = plaintext

With the public key scheme, if the public key is used for encryption, the private key is used for decryption; if the private key is used for encryption, the public key is used for decryption:

Encryption(Keypublic, text) = cipher text

Decryption(Keyprivate, cipher text) = plaintext

Encryption(Keyprivate, text) = cipher text

Decryption(Keypublic, cipher text) = plaintext

The idea is that the private key is kept secret, while the public key is listed in the directory. So, we can have the following variations of encrypted transmissions:

- Keymy_public [Hi, Andy]: anyone can create it, but only I can read it (secrecy).
- Keymy_private [I'm Andy]: everyone can read it, but only I can send it (authentication).
- Keyyour_public [Keymy_private[I know your secret]]: only I can send it, and only you can read it.

Authorization

The authorization is implemented with the help of access matrix, access control list and capability lists.

Authorization determines who is allowed to do what.

The authorization implementation is discussed as follows:

The ***Access matrix*** is a formalization of all the permissions in the system, describing who can do what. For example, in the following matrix, it says that Bart can read Lisa's diary.

	File1	Lisa's diary	File3	...
Bart	read, write	read		
Lisa		read, write		
Maggie			read	
...				

However, due to the size and the sparse use of the matrix, almost all systems implement two alternatives: the access control list and the capability list.

The ***Access control list*** stores all permissions for all users with each object. An analogy is a guard standing in front of a door with a list of people who are allowed to enter. However, as the number of users increases, this list may become very long. Under UNIX, the permission of each file is specified according to its owner, user group, and the world (everyone). Therefore, a file may be specified as world readable, group readable and writeable, and owner executable.

The ***Capability list*** stores all objects the process has permission to touch for each process. An analogy is that each person owns a set of keys. Whoever has the key has the right to enter the door. Page tables are an example. Each process has a list of pages it has access to, *not* each page has a list of processes that have access permission.

Access control list allows an object to easily know who is allowed to access the object. However, it is difficult to know which objects a user can access. Therefore, it is more difficult to revoke a user's access rights to a set of objects. The capability list allows a user to easily know the list of objects to access. However, it is difficult to discover the list of people who can access an object. Therefore, it is more difficult to revoke capabilities of an object from a set of users. Most of the operating systems today use an access control list for most resources.

Enforcement

The enforcer checks passwords, access control lists, and so on. Any bug in enforcer means that a malicious user can gain the ability to do almost anything. In UNIX, the superuser has all the powers of the UNIX kernel. Because of the coarse-grained access control, lots of things have to run as superuser in order to work. If there is a bug is in any one of these programs, you are hosed!

To reduce the number of bugs, the enforcer should be as small as possible, which often leads to a simple protection model. Minimal-privilege-based enforcers tend to be complex and more prone to bugs.

NETWORK SECURITY

Every network presents a variety of security holes through which potential hackers and disgruntled or simply curious employees can implement random threats, such as viruses. Many of these threats are network and operating system specific. For example, Microsoft typically announces a service pack within a few weeks after the introduction of a server-based operating system to patch security holes discovered by users. The network security is one of the most important aspects of the network and therefore, defining the user's setting is your first line of defense in protecting the client/server environment. It is an ever-increasing concern in all computer system environments. The millions of personal computers that are now connected to the Internet, particularly those with "always-on" broadband connections, pose a very real threat to the critical infrastructure of this or any other computer-dependent country. All systems, whether networked or stand-alone, are subject to both malicious and accidental loss and compromise of data. The security is becoming a key priority because communication and information have become a key factor in economic and societal development. The networks and information systems are now supporting services and carrying data to an extent inconceivable only a few years ago.

Network security is the process of taking both physical and software means of protecting data from misuse by others or from a malfunction or system crash.

Before implementing security mechanisms, administrators need to understand and define just what it is they are trying to accomplish. For example, what needs to be protected? Who does it need to be protected from? What are the possible threats? All security breaches should be defined relative to a security policy, and unless it is clearly defined what is and is not allowed on a system, it is of questionable value to attempt to prevent or catch intrusions. A security policy should be written with these needs in mind. A security policy is a statement of the rules and practices that regulate how an organization manages, protects, and distributes sensitive information

Network Security challenges

The network security has become a key challenge for policy makers, finding an adequate policy response are becoming an increasingly complex task. Only a few years ago, network security was predominantly an issue for state monopolies offering specialized services based on public networks, in particular the telephone network. Security of computer systems was limited to large organizations and focused on access controls. Establishing a security policy was a relatively straightforward task. This situation has now changed considerably because of a variety of developments in the wider market context, amongst them liberalization, convergence and globalization:

- **Networks are now mainly privately owned and managed.**

  Communication services are offered on a competitive basis with security as part of the market offer. However many customers remain ignorant of the extent of the security risks they run when connecting to a network and are therefore making their decisions in a situation of incomplete information.

- **Networks and information systems are converging.**

  They are becoming increasingly interconnected, offering the same kind of seamless and personalized services and to some extent sharing the same infrastructure. End terminals like PCs and mobile phones, have become an active element in the network architecture and can be connected to different networks.

- **Networks are international.**

  A significant part of today's communication is cross border or transits through third countries, so any solution to a security risk needs to take account of this. Most networks are built using commercial products from international vendors. Security products must be compatible with international standards.

Security implementation

The implementation of network security is an important aspect of the network administrator's job. Security tasks include assigning user access privileges and monitoring network access by implementing a regular procedure to audit that accesses the system and what activities are performed.

- The network administrator must manage network services, such as printing and e-mail.
- The administrator must also plan for regular data backup so that data can be recovered in the event of minor problems, such as a server going down, or major problems, such as a natural disaster.
- The network administrator must manage network services, such as printing and e-mail.
- The administrator must also plan for regular data backup so that data can be recovered in the event of minor problems, such as a server going down, or major problems, such as a natural disaster.

Rules for network security

A security policy need not be very complex. On the contrary, it should be easy to understand, so that those who read it are not left confused and bewildered. Here are a few examples of regulations that might be included:

- The user authentication shall be employed to ensure that only authorized individuals have access to resources.
- The most important and critical files shall be protected against modification by unauthorized individuals.

- The activity logs shall be maintained and periodically scanned for evidence of suspicious activity.
- The users shall be trained in how to use security mechanisms, including file access permissions and passwords.
- Every system's files shall be backed up on a periodic basis, commensurate with the frequency of data change, relative value of the data, and risk factors which could cause a loss of data.

Security Models

There are generally two security models that network security follows. They are explained as follows.

***(i)* Share-level security model.** In this model the access to a network object (printer, drive, or directory) is defined under the properties of that object. The permissions assigned to the object are secured through the use of passwords. For example, if you wanted to print to the printer in sales, you would have to know the password to gain access to the printer after you sent the document to be printed. It is a simple model to implement and is perfect for a small network environment. However, there are some drawbacks to this model. Each user is directly responsible for the security of the resource.

***(ii)* User-level security model.** In this approach, the server validates the use of the resource against the user and group permissions. Instead of being password-based at the resource level, the server handles the access permissions for each resource. A client/server network is required for this model and handles the peer to peer network as well. All the windows operating systems (WFW, Win95, and WinNT) support user-level security.

Security threats

There are many threats to the security of our computers and networks. These range from data stealing and diddling to the accidental loss of data.

- **Data Stealing**

  The data stealing may be simply removing a diskette with important data. It may involve copying the data from a hard disk. With the increase of networks, it may involve downloading the data to a diskette. Even with the workstations secure, in a computer network, what is to prevent someone from intercepting a transmission of data via the network.

- **Data Diddling**

  This problem is well known in the large computer environments especially in the banking industry. The modification of data is called data diddling. The data diddling is hard to detect and even harder to identify and prove who the culprit is.

- **Hackers**

  The hackers are typically people who are exploring a computer system or network. Many hacker activities include modification and steal of data. Other activities might include snooping through a database or using the computer for personal use.

- **Viruses**

  It's a well known fact that biggest problem in computer security today is that of computer viruses. Anyone who has seen a computer virus ripple through a computer network in a matter of seconds can attest to the disaster that is just waiting to happen on most computer networks.

These various security threats can be grouped as follows:

- Electronic communication can be intercepted and data copied or modified. This can cause damage both through invasion of the privacy of individuals and through the exploitation of data intercepted.
- Unauthorized access into computer and computer networks is usually done with malicious intend to copy, modify or destroy data.
- Disruptive attacks on the Internet have become quite common and in future the telephone network may also become more vulnerable.
- Malicious software, such as viruses, can disable computers, delete or modify data. Some recent virus attacks have been extremely destructive and costly.
- Misrepresentation of people or entities can cause substantial damages, e.g. customers may download malicious software from a website masquerading as a trusted source, contracts may be repudiated, and confidential information may be sent to the wrong persons.
- Many security incidents are due to unforeseen and unintentional events such as natural disasters (floods, storms, and earthquakes), hardware or software failures, and human error.

Security requirements

The generic security requirements of networks and information systems can be considered to consist of the following interrelated characteristics:

***(i)* Authentication.** In network security and other operations, authentication is the process of determining the identity and legitimacy of a user, node, or process. Various authentication strategies have been developed. Among the simplest are the use of user IDs and passwords. A relatively new authentication scheme, called digital signatures, is very effective and almost impossible to fool. Basically authentication is the confirmation of an asserted identity of entities or users. The proper authentication methods are needed for many applications and services such as concluding a contract online, controlling access to certain data and services. The authentication provides the information necessary to provide tiered access to networked resources. This access can be controlled at the workstation, the server, and firewall levels to limit access to specific databases, applications, or network databases.

***(ii)* Integrity.** It is the confirmation that data which has been sent, received, or stored are complete and unchanged. This is particularly important in relation to authentication for the conclusion of contracts or where data accuracy is critical for example in medical data, industrial design, etc.

***(iii)* Authorization.** It is the permission to use a computer resource. The permission is granted, directly or indirectly, by the application or system owner. The network administrator authenticates users prior to accessing services but he authorizes users based on least privilege.

***(iv)* Availability.** It means that data is accessible and services are operational, despite possible disruptive events such as power supply cuts, natural disasters, accidents or attacks. This is particularly vital in contexts where communication network failures can cause breakdowns in other critical networks such as air transport or power supply.

***(v)* Access Rights.** The term *access* is often confused with *authorization* and *authentication*. The *access* is the *ability* to do something with a computer resource. This usually refers to a technical ability (e.g., read, create, modify, or delete a file, execute a program, or use an external connection). The access rights are properties associated with files or directories in a networking environment; also known as access privileges or *trustee rights. Access rights determine how* users and network services can access and use files and directories. All networking environments and operating systems use some type of access rights settings to control access to the network and its resources. Access rights are similar to security attributes, which specify additional properties relating to a file or directory. Security attributes can override access rights. In general, rights are assigned to a user for a specific file or directory.

Internet Security

Since we use the Internet as the communication with costumer and Internet and all shared network, we need some way of protecting the data from the other person. There are some alternative ways to protect data and our server from the other people.

1. Firewall (Packet filtering)Protection for servers
2. SSL (Security Socket Layer)Protection for data
3. PGP Authorization for the users
4. Antiviral Utilities

1. Firewall. By the definition, firewall is "Combination of Hardware and software system designed to help enforce the corporate policy" and "Gateway through which all traffic passes to and from the protected network".

2. Gateway Router. All transaction with the customers has to use the Internet. Since we have built a LAN, connection between LAN and Internet is necessary. The gateway router is the router that is the entrance to/from Internet. Therefore, it is very important device.

3. SSL (Security socket layer). SSL stands for Security socket layer. Idea of public key and encryption is important to secure the data going through shared network. By implementing SSL in our server the level security will be increased.

4. Antivirus Utilities. In addition to threats from hackers, there is a constant threat of catastrophic loss of data from viruses attached to documents from outside sources, even those from trusted collaborators. The risk of virus infection can be minimized by installing virus-scanning software on servers and locally on workstations. The downside to this often-unavoidable precaution is decreased performance of the computers running antiviral programs, as well as the maintenance of the virus-detection software to insure that the latest virus definitions are installed.

Flaws in Computer Security

Kernel Errors

The intention of having user/kernel mode, virtual memory mapping, and interrupt and exception handling, is to provide a secure environment in which to execute programs. Given a well written operating system, it is not possible for a user program to create code that is executed in kernel mode, gain direct access to IO devices, or gain access to data for other processes. Operating system kernels do have errors, so it is possible that there are ways of gaining kernel mode privileges, but operating system kernel errors usually result in the system crashing, rather than allowing privileged access. Thus, to a large extent, operating system kernel errors can only be used to cause malicious damage to files, loss of data and time, etc.

The best way of breaking security due to errors in the operating system kernel, is to look for places where system calls fail to make proper checks that addresses are in range, resources belong to the user, etc.

For example, suppose the read system call doesn't make sure that the user buffer is writeable in user mode - then it might be possible to overwrite system space with information from a file. Thus an algorithm for breaking security might be to try executing system calls with invalid parameters, or executing system calls with parameters that are only valid parameters when the program belongs to the superuser (for example, the system call to change ownership of a file).

Apparently one of the main sources of errors in the kernel relate to the size of buffers. When updates to the kernel are provided, they are usually in the form of relocatable object files. These patches have to be used to replace portions of the kernel code file. As machines get larger and faster, the constants representing the size and number of buffers are often increased. The older portions of the kernel code may have been compiled with a smaller value for the buffer size than the new patches. Thus the two end up being inconsistent. Quite possibly the checks for the size of the buffer use the wrong size. As a consequence, it may be possible to overwrite data structures within the kernel.

File Protection Errors

There needs to be a hardware mechanism for enforcing security between executing processes. However, there are other problems with providing security, that are not hardware or operating system kernel related. It is not necessary to gain kernel mode status to breach security. Files are stored on disk. Files are owned by individual users. The operating system controls access to user files. Files must have the appropriate access restrictions to stop other users from deleting or modifying them. Failure to do so may result in loss or corruption of important data.

If they do not have the appropriate access restrictions, then a user can modify another user's code file. The other user will eventually execute this code file. The program will then do whatever it has been changed to do. Many security breaches are due to errors in file protection.

Path Setup Errors

UNIX shells have a PATH variable used to specify the directory path in which to look for files corresponding to commands. The path variable is often incorrectly set up so that it first looks in the current directory, then in more normal places, such as /usr/bin, etc. If you place a file with a common name such as ls in a directory, and wait for an unsuspecting hacker to look in the directory, and type ls, then they will execute the local command instead of the system command.

The command can be made to quietly do something nasty, then execute the normal system command (but delete the information related to the local ls), so that the user is not aware that anything is wrong.

Trojan Horses

One way of infiltrating a system is to provide another user with a program that does something malicious or contains a computer virus. For example, many modern email systems will accept attachments (such as Microsoft Word documents), and will automatically open these attachments with the appropriate application. Unfortunately, documents can also include Visual Basic programs, and these are executed by the Visual Basic interpreter. Hence it is possible to mail arbitrary programs to another user and have them executed on their machine. They can delete files, mail themselves off to all other known email aliases, etc. It is possible to turn this feature off, but most users do not know they have such a feature.

A general way of dealing with untrusted programs, including viruses, is to execute the program in a restricted environment. We should be able to run a program, with options set to specify that it can only access files within a specific directory, that it cannot access data over the network, that it cannot modify files, etc. Something similar to this can be achieved under UNIX. It is possible to change the meaning of "/" to a subdirectory. The Mach microkernel provides the potential to let another program handle all system calls, and limit their effectiveness. Obviously if "computer terrorism" becomes even more prevalent than it is today, such mechanisms will have to be one of the standard features of all operating systems. However, for such features to be effective, users have to actually use them, and if too much hassle is involved, they will not do so.

Errors in Set Effective User ID Programs

Under UNIX, code files can be marked as "Set Effective User Identification" or SUID programs. When these programs are executed, the process takes on the powers of both the owner of the program and the owner of the process. If the owner of the program is the superuser, then the process acquires superuser powers. SUID programs include the login program (since it lets you change ownership of the process), the printing program lpr, the ps program to display information on all executing processes, the finger program to display information about other users, etc. Well written SUID programs do not allow the user to breach security, since the user did not write the program, and hence cannot control what the program does. However, poorly written SUID programs, especially those owned by the superuser, are a common source of security breaches. For example, one of the older mail programs on UNIX allowed the user to execute a shell from within the mailer, and this shell accidentally kept the superuser powers of the mailer.

Apparently Windows NT includes a similar notion to SUID programs, and one of the common applications is an SUID program owned by the administrator, even though it doesn't have to be. It is possible to take advantage of bugs in this program to access all files on the system, even those owned by other users.

Distributing System Software with Deliberate Loopholes

If you are responsible for generating operating system software, or SUID programs that are distributed to other installations, then you may manage to gain entry to the other installations by deliberately leaving a loophole in your code.

For example, suppose you are responsible for writing the login program. You could make it accept a specific login name and password, without checking that the login name or password is valid. You could then log on to any machine running your version of the login program.

Computer Viruses

Computer Viruses are a major problem on most microcomputers. Many microcomputers have essentially no security. On older operating systems for personal computers there is no virtual memory, no notion of kernel mode, no file protection information, no notion of users, no need to log on, etc. A process can modify the operating system code and data. Users often exchange programs. These programs may be "infected" by computer viruses. Executing an infected program may result in the virus being spread to other programs on any writeable disks inserted into a drive at the same time, and may even result in the virus being incorporated into the operating system, and then spread to every writeable disk inserted into the drive afterwards. Since the boot disk is usually required to be writeable, the boot disk also becomes infected, and hence even rebooting has no effect, since the virus starts up again on rebooting.

What is a computer virus, how does it spread, and what effect does it have? A computer virus is usually an additional piece of code appended to an existing program. Most code files start with a header that specifies the entry point. The header is modified so that the virus code is executed before the normal code. The virus copies itself into all other writeable code files, does whatever else it wants to do, then jumps to the original entry point and continues execution as normal, so that the user suspects nothing. Very occasionally, perhaps after months of quietly duplicating itself, the virus may perform some malicious act, such as deletion or modification of files. A less malicious virus may just slow down the machine, or use up disk space, or tell you that your disk is unreadable when it isn't.

Not only can viruses spread to all writeable disks placed in drives connected to the machine. If the machine is connected to a network, and writeable file servers are also connected to the network, then the virus can infect the file server as well. If there is access to other machines, then these machines may become infected as well, when they use files on the file server.

A boot disk contains special code (for example, on track 0), that is executed on startup. On many systems, even non boot disks contain code that is executed on insertion of the disk into the drive. If this code has been infected by a virus, then it is not even necessary to execute an ordinary program, for the virus to propagate itself. The virus can replace the code for the disk interrupt handler by code that looks for other disks to infect, performs the infection, then executes the standard code for the disk interrupt handler, so that the user suspects nothing.

Even if the boot code on a disk appears the same as that on an uninfected disk, there is no guarantee that the disk is not infected. The virus can keep the original boot code somewhere else on the disk. Whenever a request is made to read the boot block of the disk, the virus infected handler returns the saved boot code instead. The only detectable difference is that the disk will have a few blocks that the virus has marked as bad blocks - these blocks will contain the old boot code.

Before checking a disk for the existence of viruses, you need to reboot your machine with a "clean" version of the operating system, that doesn't run any code on any untrusted disks inserted into the drive. This guarantees that when you check data on any inserted disks, you can be sure that the data is real, and not false data provided by a virus. Virus detection programs often work by looking for known patterns or signatures on the disk (namely the code for the virus).

A way of checking any new attempt by a virus to infiltrate the system is to check for attempts to modify code files, and read-only data stored on disk.

Passwords

The superuser is a user with special powers - the ability to modify other users files, kill other users processes, change the time of day, mount and unmount disk drives, reboot the machine, etc. If you can become superuser, you can wreak havoc to the computer system. The easiest method of gaining superuser rights is to find out the password for the superuser. Passwords are often common names, so it is easy to try out a few possibilities, especially if it is done automatically, by a program attempting to login using tens of thousands of words out of a file of common login names. A dictionary of all common words in the English language, together with obscene words, common personal names, and place names will probably include passwords of half the users on a system. Because of this problem, we specifically disallow common English words as passwords on our system (but of course we don't check for other languages). We also put a time delay in, so that it takes several seconds to attempt to log in.

Networks

Another easy way of breaching security is to gain access over a network. Computers that can be connected to via the internet or telephone system are very insecure. Not only are legitimate users able to attempt to breach security, but every hacker in existence can attempt to log on by trying common passwords. At one time it was possible to alter the timing of traffic lights in Auckland by connecting to an Auckland City Council computer, which was not even password protected.

A sophisticated but very simple method of breaching security is to listen in to messages being sent over networks. If you are in control of a machine used as an internet service provider, you can read all traffic that passes through the machine. This can include passwords, VISA account numbers, personal email that could be used for blackmail or gaining inside information on companies, etc. It is also possible to send and receive packets that appear to come from another machine, and so hijack connections that have already been set up. For example, apparently it is relatively easy to hijack an existing telnet session (for example, just wait until the user attempts to log out, close the connection between the user and the intermediate machine, but continue the session between the intermediate machine and the host).

To avoid the problem of interception of data, by computers along the path that packets travel between a user and host machine, all data can be encrypted, using the password as the encryption key.

If all you want to do is make a machine unusable, then all you need to do is send lots of packets of data to it, over the network. The machine and the network will be so busy discarding these packets, that it will have no time to deal with legitimate requests. The real origin of the attack can be hidden by giving a false return address. The effectiveness of this kind of attack can be decreased by having a "firewall". A firewall is a computer or router that sits between a local network, and the outside world. It filters incoming (and possibly outgoing) packets, so that only packets from and to certain internet addresses are allowed. It can even be used to limit access to only certain ports on a computer (for example, allowing HTTP access, but disallowing FTP access).

To avoid the problem of data coming from fake addresses, all users can first be required to log on to the system (as with NetAccount). Only after the host has successfully performed an appropriate handshake with the user to verify that they really exist and are who they say they are, will any other access be allowed. This also allows the host to charge the user for any internet access that passes through the host.

Until recently, the computers in our laboratory were connected together via a shared network cable. All machines could listen in to the traffic on the network, including passwords. Passwords are now sent in encrypted form.

Cables for individual machines now go directly back to a switch, so data is now sent on a dedicated line. It is not possible to record the encrypted password, and use it for a later attempt, because the computer you wish to log into provides the client with additional data that must be encrypted along with the password, thus making the data to be sent different on each login attempt.

Physical Access to Machines and Disks

No computer is totally secure, if there is physical access to the computer and its peripheral devices. A machine can often be rebooted without a password, and may start up with a single user with superuser privileges. A disk drive may be physically moved, and read on a different machine, to gain access to the raw data on the disk. There must always be some mechanism for gaining access to files if the superuser password has been forgotten.

State of the World in Security

The security of a system can be improved by two management techniques. One is threat monitoring: The system can check for suspicious patterns of activity in an attempt to detect a security violation.

Another technique is an audit log. An audit log simply records the time, user, and type of all accesses to an object. Networked computers are much more susceptible to security attacks than are standalone systems.

One solution is the use of a firewall to separate trusted and un-trusted systems. A firewall is a computer or router that sits between the trusted and the un-trusted. It limits network access between the two security domains, and monitors and logs all connections. A firewall therefore may need to allow http to pass.

Authentication in the single-machine environment is mostly password-based, and people still use poor passwords. Authentication in distributed systems mostly depends on encryption, but almost nobody encrypts (e.g., emails).

Authorization is largely based on the access control list. However, many systems provide only very coarse-grained access control (e.g., UNIX). Therefore, often protection mechanisms are turned off to enable sharing.

Enforcement is mostly achieved through the kernel model. It is hard to write a million lines of code without bugs, and any bug is a potential security loophole.

Now you need to be able to describe the different threats to security of a computer system and explain any action that can be taken to reduce the threat.

1. The only secure system is one that is switched off.
2. A secure system should offer:
   - confidentiality - authorised users only can read data
   - integrity - authorised users only can create, modify or write data
   - availability - systems always available to authorised users
3. Security threats can be seen as:
   - interruption of service
   - interception
   - modification
   - fabrication
4. Systems can apply security by controlling what a user (or group of users) can have access to as well as specifying controls for files/resources.

5. Intruders to a system can be:
   - masqueraders - using someone else's account
   - malicious - legitimate user doing unauthorised things
   - clandestine - evading audit
6. Most intruders get into a system by getting the ID and password from an existing user.
7. User passwords are vulnerable
   - can be cracked
   - users choose simple ones, forget them write them down etc.
8. Masqueraders often detected after breaking in using history of system interactions of legitimate user.
9. Audit trails usual way of recognising hacking.
10. Viruses are a big problem - usually they remove service and also modify programs.
11. Anti-virus software is always a little way behind new viruses.

KEYWORDS

SECURITY	**PROTECTION**
AUTHENTICATION	**AUTHORIZATION**
EAVESDROPPING	**TROJAN HORSE**
SALAMI ATTACK	**LOGIC BOMBS**
PRIVATE KEY ENCRYPTION	**PUBLIC KEY ENCRYPTION**
ACCESS MATRIX	**ACCESS CONTROL LIST**
CAPABILITY LIST	**NETWORK SECURITY**

SUMMARY

Security refers to the policy of authorizing accesses whereas protection refers to the actual mechanisms implemented to enforce the specified policy.

- Data confidentiality: secret data remains secret.
- Data integrity: unauthorized users should not be able to modify any data without the owner's permission.
- System availability: nobody can disturb the system to make it unusable.
- Authentication determines who the user is.

- Authorization determines who is allowed to do what.
- Enforcement makes sure that people do only what they are supposed to do.
- Eavesdropping is the listener approach. One can tap into the serial line on the Ethernet, and see everything typed in; almost everything goes over network unencrypted.
- Abuse of Privilege means the super user is evil.
- An imposter breaks into the system by pretending to be someone else.
- A Trojan horse is a seemingly innocent program that contains code that will perform an unexpected and undesirable function.
- Salami Attack: The idea is to build up a chunk one-bit at a time. A programmer at a bank can reprogram the accounting program, so that the partial pennies go into his account
- Logic Bombs: A programmer may secretly insert a piece of code into the production system. As long as the programmer feeds the system password periodically, it does nothing.
- Denial-of-service attacks refer to attacks on system availability. A handful of compromised machines can flood a victim machine with network packets to disrupt its normal use.
- Private Key Encryption is an encryption system that uses two private keys for encrypting and decrypting messages. Both parties must have a secret key to decrypt a message
- Public Key Encryption is a strong encryption method that uses a set of two keys, one of which is made public, and one of which is kept private. Data encrypted using the public key can only be decrypted using the private key. The longer the keys, the more difficult it is to break the encryption.
- The Access matrix is a formalization of all the permissions in the system, describing who can do what.
- The Access control list stores all permissions for all users with each object.
- The Capability list stores all objects the process has permission to touch for each process.
- Network security is the process of taking both physical and software means of protecting data from misuse by others or from a malfunction or system crash.
- Share-level security model: In this model the access to a network object (printer, drive, or directory) is defined under the properties of that object.

The permissions assigned to the object are secured through the use of passwords.

- User-level security model: In this approach, the server validates the use of the resource against the user and group permissions. Instead of being password-based at the resource level, the server handles the access permissions for each resource.
- The best way of breaking security due to errors in the operating system kernel, is to look for places where system calls fail to make proper checks that addresses are in range, resources belong to the user, etc.

REVIEW QUESTIONS

1) What are the main ways of breaching security on a multi-user computer system?
2) Write short note on Goals of security?
3) How can mailing an attachment be used to breach security? Why is it not even necessary for the recipient to open the attachment?
4) Explain all the methods of computer security in details.
5) Explain the problems associated with network security.
6) What is a computer virus, and how does it work?
7) Why do passwords represent one of the easiest ways of breaching security?
8) How can you use access to a computer network to breach security?
9) What is a firewall?
10) write short note on
    a. Authentication
    b. Authorization
    c. Eavesdropping
    d. imposter
    e. Trojan horse
    f. Salami Attack
    g. Logic Bombs

FILL IN THE BLANKS

1. ____________determines who the user is.
2. ____________determines who is allowed to do what.

3. ____________makes sure that people do only what they are supposed to do.
4. In____________, one can tap into the serial line on the Ethernet, and see everything typed in; almost everything goes over network unencrypted.
5. An ___________breaks into the system by pretending to be someone else.
6. A ___________is a seemingly innocent program that contains code that will perform an unexpected and undesirable function

TRUE OR FALSE

1. Data confidentiality secret data gets public.
2. Data integrity means authorized users should not be able to modify any data without the owner's permission.
3. Private Key Encryption is an encryption system that uses one private key for encrypting and decrypting messages.
4. Public Key Encryption is a strong encryption method that uses a set of two keys, one of which is made public, and one of which is kept private.
5. The Capability list stores all objects the process has permission to touch for each process.
6. The Access matrix is a formalization of all the permissions in the system, describing who can do what.

ANSWERS

FILL IN THE BLANKS

1. Authentication
2. Authorization
3. Enforcement
4. eavesdropping
5. imposter
6. Trojan horse

TRUE OR FALSE

1. FALSE
2. FALSE
3. FALSE
4. TRUE
5. TRUE
6. TRUE

❑❑❑

"Don't worry about people stealing your ideas. If your ideas are any good, you'll have to ram them down people's throats." —*H. Aiken*

14 SYSTEM PROTECTION

INTRODUCTION

The processes in an operating system must have controls on their access to system resources, and they must be protected from each other. In addition, the actions and impact of 3rd parties such as local users and remote computers must also be controlled.

What is protection?

Protection must ensure that only those processes that have gained proper authorization from the OS can operate on memory segments, the CPU, and other resources.

When Operating Systems were set up as dealing with single users the issue of security was very much a physical one. However the introduction of multi-processing and networks has complicated matters significantly. For a start it introduced the idea that resources can be shared e.g.

- memory
- I/O devices e.g. disks, printers
- programs e.g. DLLs
- data

Levels of protection

Looking at issues involved in applying protection you should be able to see that there are various levels of protection:

1. **no protection:** all sensitive procedures are carried out when nothing else is being done
2. **Isolation:** all processes operate separately from each other with no sharing or communication. Each process has its own address space, files etc.
3. **Share all or nothing:** the owner of an object or data declares it to be either private or public. Public objects are accessible by any other object.
4. **Share via access limitations:** the Operating System checks the permissibility of each access by a specific user on a specific object. Here the Operating System acts as the guardian of access to objects.
5. **Share via dynamic capabilities:** dynamic creation of access control rights to objects.
6. **Limit the use of an object:** grant read but not write or copy access to objects.

The difficulty of achieving these various levels of protection mechanism increase as you progress down the list. Most current Operating System would offer some form of limited use of objects.

There is a need to offer some form of protection to the memory allocated to processes in a computer system. If you remember the aim is to ensure that each process has its own memory for instructions and data and it should control access to these. Virtual memory using segmentation and paging supports the separation of instructions and data for a process. This separation then allows control over data and instructions and this in turn means that access can be granted to other processes to SHARE data or instructions. The default position will always be access for the owning process only.

User-Oriented Access and Data-oriented Access Control

User-Oriented Access Control

You can control access to computer assets either by restricting the user or restricting the data, or both. User restrictions can be applied through:

- **password**: each user has a unique ID and an associated password. Both are required to logon to the system. This is not a terribly strong restriction because it is based on human memory.
- **levels of access** e.g. logon to a network, then logon on to a system.

It is common to find that individual computers are given logon facilities to protect their resources. In addition the network as a whole may provide protection to restrict network access to authorised users.

Data-oriented Access Control

Once a user has gained access to a system without any further restrictions the system is at their mercy. Some further restrictions can be applied to the user through the concept of a user 'profile' where permissible actions and accesses can be stated. The Operating System can use these to control an individual user's access. However if you consider a database, you might want to allow a user to see part of the database but not all of it. Similarly you might want to allow a user to see some of the files in a directory but not all of them, and so on.

To attain this greater level of control most Operating Systems use something called an access control list or an access matrix. The details recorded here are used to provide a much finer degree of control on access. The components of an access matrix are:

1. **Subject:** an entity (process) capable of accessing objects. Users achieve access through programs!
2. **Object:** anything to which access is controlled .g. files, parts of files, programs, memory etc
3. **Access right:** the way in which an object is accessed by a subject e.g. read, write, execute.

One axis of the matrix identifies subjects e.g. users or groups of users. The other axis lists the objects that may be accessed. One very common way that this is implemented is called an access control list. This is a list of the various aspects of access granted to users for a specific object. You will see this as the access rights that can be attributed to a file. Most systems allow the owner of files to state which other users or groups of users have what type of access to them.

Password Protection

For the vast majority of computer systems passwords are the front line defence. This requires each user to enter a specific user ID and an associated password. The user ID verifies the person and the password authenticates the ID.

- The ID must be valid
- The ID has privileges associated with it
- The ID is used to grant discretionary access control.

Password Vulnerability

The trouble with computers is that they are used by *people*. If users weren't people then we'd have a lot less trouble with passwords. Of course, I'm sure that you don't do any of the following, but you do know people who:

- forget passwords, write them down, use short, simple ones, choose family names, dates, car registrations, common phrases, films etc, use the same password on several systems, rarely change them and also eat lots of chocolate.

In one study (reported in 1990) the following strategies were used to guess user passwords and resulted in cracking 25% of user passwords:

1. try the user's name, initials, account name, and other relevant details - some 130 permutations were tried against each user
2. try words from various dictionaries - some 60,000 words were built into a dictionary
3. try various permutations from step 2 e.g. first letter as uppercase, whole word as uppercase, change letter 'o' to number '0'
4. try various permutations with more random uppercase attempts.

This resulted in a set of some 3 million words that formed a set of possible passwords. These were used against encrypted passwords stored in UNIX password files. It took about an hour to try them all against some 13,800 user passwords.

Clearly one way to limit the threat would be to ensure that only privileged users have access to the password file. However this is not foolproof:

- many systems have guest accounts with either no or just simple password protection
- once on to a system a hacker can collect passwords and Ids through simple imitation logon programs
- the password file is a resource and can be rendered visible by error
- users use the same password on several systems. Cracking a user's account on one system could make others vulnerable too!

Password Selection Strategies

Left to users, passwords would not be a very efficient protection mechanism. Hence the following strategies are available:

- **User education:** tell the users about the threats and the consequences. Offer them guidelines for selecting strong passwords.
- **Use computer generated passwords:** random selection of the character sequence for a password improves matters. Unfortunately the results are often unacceptable to users. Such passwords are difficult to remember and users tend to write them down (if they are unable to change them).
- **Proactive password checking:** check the password against a set of rules for 'strong' passwords e.g. length, mixture of letters and digits, not used previously (often last two or five), not in a list of 'bad' passwords. Force passwords to be changed at frequent intervals. Windows 2003 adopts this kind of approach. The System Administrator can activate or switch off, or modify the rules.

Intruders

One of the two most publicised threats to security are 'intruders' (the other is viruses). Generally called a hacker or a cracker, intruders can be categorised as:

- **masquerader:** an unauthorised user who gets into a legitimate user's account - usually an outsider
- **malicious:** a legitimate user who accesses data or programs which they are not authorised to access. Someone who misuses their privilege - usually an insider
- **clandestine:** someone who grabs supervisory control of a system and uses this to evade detection (by editing audit logs and suppressing audit collection) - can be either insider or outsider.

Many systems have reported frequent and widespread attacks from users attempting to logon to their systems with multiple repeated attempts to logon. Though some intruders are benign i.e. do it for the challenge, many others seek either to destroy, steal or modify information held on the systems.

Part of the growing problem with intruders arises from:

- competitors stealing commercial information. The globalisation of many organisations means that their computer systems are many and varied; often with variable levels of security
- client/server architecture. When organisations had mainframe computers centralised control meant that security was easier to impose. Client/server

architectures mean decentralisation; additionally many servers run using UNIX and this has an open systems view of itself so many people know exactly how security has been implemented. Hackers if the world rejoice.

- Hackers spreading information about system vulnerabilities. Most organisations don't want to acknowledge being hacked so loopholes may exist for some time before all systems have them closed.

Intrusion Techniques

To logon to a system an intruder needs an ID and its password. The easiest way is to get them from an existing user (disgruntled or plain naïve). Other ways are to try password cracking techniques - most systems have several 'standard' users such as administrator, root, system, admin etc. Some also have 'open' accounts such as guest which often have no password.

Once in the first port of call is the password file. In UNIX / Linux the password file is held as '/etc/password'; this contains the details of all user Ids (unencrypted) together with their respective passwords (encrypted). Now revert back to your password cracking mechanism to see if you can crack any of the passwords.

If the password file is denied you may still be able to get at it using a variety of other sophisticated techniques (but the effort is much greater). An alternate is to carry on searching for passwords:

1. try default passwords on standard accounts
2. try all short passwords - say one to three letters
3. try words in the system dictionary
4. try likely passwords - lists on hackers bulletin boards
5. collect information about users - full names, addresses, family members, addresses car registrations etc
6. try users' phone numbers, NI numbers etc
7. try all legitimate car registration numbers
8. use a trojan horse to simulate logon screens
9. Tap the line between a remote user and the host system

1 - 7 are attempts to guess passwords. An intruder needs to check and see if they have generated a valid password and this would require repeated logon attempts. Many systems allow three attempts at a logon before denying any further attempts on that userID. Where this occurred the attempt would be logged. However it only

forces the intruder to reconnect to the computer and try the next three possible passwords.

Using a Trojan horse can be difficult to counter; what would you think if you entered your user ID and password and the system reported a failure? Yes, that you had typed something incorrectly. Something more insidious could be to write a computer game as a standard user and invite other people to use it. If the systems administrator uses the game whilst logged in as systems administrator the program has system admin privileges. Lo and behold the program could check who was using the program and if it was the systems administrator you could include code in the game that accessed system resources e.g. password files; altered access privileges. This is possible under UNIX.

Intruder Detection

It is inevitable that at some point your intruder protection system will fail, so the next best thing is to recognise that an intruder has been into your system.

- early detection can lead to the identification and removal of intruders from your system. It will minimise any damage, but it won't necessarily eliminate it.
- efficient detection can serve as a deterrent
- all information about intruders can be used in the battle to improve intruder protection.

How do you detect the presence of an intruder? With difficulty! Where you are dealing with a masquerader it is possible to use the history of the way that the legitimate user interacts with the system to suggest differences between the legitimate user and the intruder. This is not infallible and can result in false detection. Such a history could be constructed by statistical analysis of user interaction with a system. This is still the area of much research.

For other types of intruder the most basic tool is the creation of audit trails for individual users. Most operating systems include accounting software that logs user activity e.g. all commands issued, when, how long, system resources used etc.

All in all the systems administrator of any computer system needs to keep their wits about them.

Viruses

There are whole plethora of malicious programs, of which viruses are probably the most well known. Malicious programs can be grouped as:

1. **Bacteria** - a program that consume system resources by replicating itself
2. **Logic Bomb**: a program that executes unauthorised actions when it detects a certain set of conditions e.g. a specified date
3. **Trapdoor:** undocumented entry point into a program; used to grant unauthorised access
4. **Trojan horse:** a program masquerading as other program.
5. **Virus:** code inserted into a program that causes a copy of itself to be inserted in other programs. In addition the virus also performs some unwanted functions.
6. **Worm:** program that can replicate itself and send copies from computer to computer across a network. In addition the worm may also perform unwanted functions.

Forms of viruses

Most viruses work in a specific way and are often both operating system and hardware specific. There is a continual race between those who create viruses and those who seek to remove viruses from systems. As effective countermeasures are developed virus writers have modified and evolved new forms of virus.

The most significant types of virus are:

1. **Parasitic:** the traditional and most common form. This attaches itself to executable files and replicates when the infected program executes. Replication occurs in other executable files.
2. **Memory-resident virus:** lives in main memory as part of a resident system program. All programs that execute while the virus is in main memory are infected.
3. **Boot sector virus:** infects a master boot record or boot record and spreads when the system is booted from the disc containing the virus
4. **Stealth virus:** specifically designed to hide itself from detection by anti-virus software
5. **Polymorphic virus:** mutates with every infection, makes the detection of the virus by its signature impossible.

You don't really want to know this but there is software available to help people create viruses (virus-creation toolkit) and there are also virus bulletin boards where people exchange ideas and offer versions of viruses.

Anti-Virus Approaches

Okay, so how do tackle the problem of viruses? Well, the ideal is not to allow viruses on the system in the first place. Unfortunately this has not proved possible so the next steps include:

1. **Detection:** recognise that a virus has infected your system and find out where it is
2. **Identification:** determine which virus it is and remove it from all infected programs
3. **Removal:** Remove all traces from the infected program and restore that program to its original state.

How do you find a virus in your system, by running anti-virus software. As viruses have become more sophisticated so has anti-virus software:

First generation used a virus signature to identify a virus. Typically a virus has essentially the same structure and bit pattern in all its copies. Signature specific software are limited to known viruses and they search trough all executable files searching for matching patterns.

A variation on this idea was to keep a record of the length of all programs and look for changes in length.

Second Generation uses signature together with rules of thumb. For example look for code fragments that are typical of viruses e.g. the start of an encryption loop used by polymorphic viruses.

Another approach is to use integrity checking. Each program has a checksum appended to it. If it is infected the checksum is highly likely to be invalid. To combat more sophisticated viruses that amend the checksum you could encrypt the checksum and store the key separately. Hashing the checksum would increase the likelihood of the success for this approach.

Third generation ant-virus software are typically memory resident programs that identify viruses by their actions rather than their signature. This does not require the large and ever changing sets of virus signatures needed by earlier generations. What is required is the recognition of the small set of actions that indicate an infection is being attempted and then to intervene.

Fourth generation packages comprise a variety of anti-virus techniques. These include signature and activity recognition approaches. In addition these packages include access control capabilities which limits the ability of viruses to update files and hence propagate themselves.

PROTECTION ISSUES

Protection has long been an issue for operating systems

From the very beginning, operating systems have been concerned with the protection of system resources from accidental or malicious corruption by users:

1. **Two-mode Systems**

   Two-mode CPU allowed early batch monitors to protect themselves from modification by one user that might cause the next user's job to run incorrectly.

2. **Monitor performs all IO operations**

   The requirement that all IO operations be done by the monitor served to protect the cards of one job from being inadvertently read as data by a preceding job.

3. **File systems need per-user protection**

   With the advent of on-line mass-storage, file systems were developed with a provision for protecting the files belonging to one user from unauthorized access by another user.

Protection is becoming increasingly important as system complexity grows.

- Additional issues are raised by networking and telecommunications.
- Protection schemes can be used to enhance program integrity

There is a concern to extend the concept of protection so as to enhance the integrity of applications programs. For example, in a large applications system, it might be desirable to require that all accesses to a common data base be done by calling library routines that have had their correctness verified, so as to minimize the harm that might be done by a buggy program. To make this work, it would be desirable to enforce this requirement on all programs in the system, perhaps through an operating system provided facility.

Protection is concerned with providing facilities that allow the "owner" of an object to constrain accesses to it.

The more specific the control that can be arranged, the better the protection system.

For example, a minimal protection system may allow the owner of a file to specify either that he be the only user allowed to access the file or that all users be allowed to access the file - the choices are totally private or totally public. A better protection system would allow the owner to grant access to selected users other than himself without granting access to the world at large.

Level of protection and level of security are not necessarily related.

A certain system might provide very little in terms of protection facilities - but the facilities it provides might be very secure. (E.g. a system with only a two-mode CPU might provide very secure protection for monitor memory; but no protection at all for files.) Conversely, a system with very rich protection facilities might be insecure due to weaknesses that penetrators might exploit.

Mechanisms and policies

In discussing protection, we distinguish between mechanisms and policies:

1. A **mechanism** is a facility the operating system provides for specifying how an object may be accessed.
2. A **policy** is a decision made by the object's owner (or system management) as to how the mechanisms are to be applied in a specific case.

Example: a particular system may allow the owner of a file to specify who may read the file. This is a mechanism. If the owner of a file decides that anyone whose last name begins with "A" may read a certain file, then he has chosen a policy which (hopefully) can be implemented using the mechanism provided.

Ideally, mechanisms should be flexible, so as to allow as broad as possible a range of policy choices. One key principle to use in making policy decisions is the **"need to know"** principle. Insofar as possible, a process ought only to be granted levels of access to resources that it needs to have. (This may not apply, though, to access rights that pose no threat of misuse - e.g. the ability to read system help files or use library subroutines.)

Access Matrices

A. An access matrix provides an abstract model of a protection mechanism

We should note that an **access matrix** is, at least at the present time, more a model to be used in describing real protection systems than a practical protection system in its own right. Actually implementing an access matrix as a protection mechanism would usually not be practical. It is an abstract model - but a helpful one.

B. Access matrix columns correspond to *objects*

In an access matrix, the columns correspond to objects - entities to be protected. These might include:

1. Regions of physical or virtual memory.
2. Individual disk files or groups of files.
3. Peripheral devices.
4. System services that affect the overall state of the system (e.g. creating new processes, modifying quotas etc.)
5. Various kinds of operations on a shared database etc.

PROTECTION Domain

In an access matrix, the individual rows correspond to domains. These are not as easily defined. At any given time, a process may be said to be executing in a protection domain.

Protection domains may be based on users.

A process runs in the protection domain of the user who is executing it. This is the case on most multi-user timeshared systems. Typically, when a user logs in the process that is created for him is placed in the protection domain specified for that user by system management.

Protection domains may be established on a per-process basis.

As we shall see, for example, it is possible for a Unix process to run in a different protection domain than that of the user on whose behalf it is being executed. (In the Unix case, this is determined by the program that the process is executing.)

Protection domains may be established on a per-procedure basis

When a process calls a given procedure it changes to a protection domain associated with that procedure (and returns to the original protection domain when the procedure exits.)

a. Some of this takes place with system services on VMS. A VMS system service call is a procedure call, but may execute with the CPU in a more privileged mode.

b. One research area is the extension of this idea to allow any procedure to be associated with its own set of access rights, which may differ from those of its caller. This would facilitate the kind of protection of data structures we talked about earlier.

Processes could even change domains during execution

Finally, a system may allow for a given process to totally change domains during the course of execution. This can be modeled by adding a column for each domain to the matrix, where an entry in one domain column for another domain indicates that a process executing in the "row" domain may switch to the "column" domain.

Temporary protection domain amplification

As a related concept, a system may allow a process's protection domain to be temporarily amplified by privileges belonging to a privileged program it is executing. For example, on most systems, ordinary users are not allowed direct access to IO devices. However, when a user executes an IO system service call, the code that is executed on behalf of the process does do physical IO. In effect, the process's domain has temporarily been amplified by the system service's right of direct access to the IO device.

Provision for rights amplification allows a protection system to be more flexible.

Suppose, for the sake of illustration, that it is desired to grant certain users access to a certain file only on their birthday. (Perhaps a certain game?) Clearly, no commercial operating system will provide a protection mechanism that includes this as a standard option. However, such a policy might be implemented as follows:

c. The access control matrix could deny access to the file to all users. Thus, no user could access the file directly.

d. A program could be written that would be granted the right to access the file. A user running this program would have his rights temporarily amplified by the right to access the file.

e. The program would include code to check to see if the user's birthday matches the current date, and would abort itself otherwise.

A trusted user is required to set things up.

Such a program (which may be a conventional stand-alone program or a utility procedure installed in a system library) assumes the status of a trusted user that mediates between the protected resource and the world at large.

Increased risk of security penetration

Rights amplification, while increasing protection flexibility, also increases the risk of system security penetration. Therefore, code that is to be installed as "trusted code" must be guarded very carefully.

Changing code of a privileged program

Suppose a trusted program is stored in a file that is accessible to a user who is allowed to run the program to gain amplified capabilities. If the user can modify the file - thus changing code that is privileged - he can make it do other things than what it was intended to do. Thus, trusted code must be protected against alteration by anyone who does not possess the same rights that the protected code possesses.

Dynamically changing parameter values

A user who can fool the code's access validation procedures can illicitly penetrate the resource it protects. For example, the user may find a way to invoke a trusted procedure with a parameter that specifies an access that he is allowed, but may then find a way to change the parameter that was passed between the time that the trusted code validates it and the time that the trusted code actually does the requested operation. The changed parameter may specify an illicit operation. This might be done, for example, by passing the parameter by reference, with the actual parameter being stored in memory that is shared by two processes both belonging to the same user. After one process requests the desired access, the second process modifies the parameter.

Need to ensure nothing privileged is left hanging around

Provision must be made to ensure that the amplified rights do not linger on after the trusted code terminates. For example, if the trusted code reads a memory location or file that ordinary users cannot read, it must be written in such a way as to ensure that no portion of what it read remains in the user's memory after termination. This can be tricky if the user aborts execution of the protected code mid-way through - before it has a chance to clean up.

Modifications to access matrices to support amplified rights

We can model rights amplification in an access matrix as a domain which has the amplified rights, which domain users in other domains can enter. (I.e. the domain appears as a row with its amplified rights and as a column for which certain domains possess the switch domain right.) However, rights amplification differs from an ordinary domain switch in that the process reverts to its original domain when the code with the amplified rights exits.

Access matrices can be changed dynamically

Note that the access matrix itself need not necessarily be static, either. We can model the ability to alter the matrix itself by means of various new kinds of right. Unfortunately, the terminology used for these is not uniform - you will sometimes find the same name used for different kinds of right.

1. The **owner right** allows a domain to set the access rights of any domain for a given object - i.e. to change any entry in the column for the object.
2. The **grant right** extends the owner rights to individuals other than the actual owner of an object. One who has the grant right for an object can grant or revoke access to that object to other domains the same way as the owner can. (Sometimes this is called the **control right**.)
3. The **copy right** allows a domain that has access to a given object to grant that same access (or a subset of it) to other domains - i.e. to copy an entry within a column. (This is more limited than grant - one can only copy what one has oneself.)
4. The **control right** (which only applies to objects that are themselves domains) allows a "row" domain to take rights away from a "column" domain. (Actually, the term control is sometimes used with another meaning. E.g. on VMS it means what we have called "grant".)

In practice access matrices would be large and sparse

The reason why access matrices are not implemented directly in practice is that, in general, the matrix is very large and contains many blank entries - i.e. it is a sparse matrix. For example, files are frequently accessible only to their owners - thus the access domain column corresponding to such a file would contain an entry in only one row, with all other rows being blank. However, the effect of an access matrix can be achieved in one of several ways:

Access control lists

We can associate a list of domains allowed to access an object with the object. Each access control list, then, contains the non-blank entries from a column of the access matrix.

ACL stands for Access Control List. A more fine-grained way to control file access than the usual conventions.

Usually, the ACL rules are added on to the usual rules. The usual rules are used for widespread, general permissions, and the ACL information is used to fine-tune.

In many cases, this will work well - the access control list will be short (perhaps only the owner) and so will consume little space and search time.

But for a resource that is made available to many or all domains, the access list could become quite long, and searching the list to see if a given domain is allowed access could be time-consuming. This can be minimized by associating with each "public" resource a default access that applies to all domains plus individual entries for domains allowed more than the minimal public access.

Where is the access-control information stored?

- If all directory information is in the directory per se, then access control information must be there too.
- If the file has a separate header, then access control information can be stored either in the directory entry pointing to the header (in which case different users can have different accesses) or in the file header. The latter approach is more secure, since the user in some sense "owns" his directory.

Capability lists

With each domain we can associate a list of the objects it is allowed to access. Each capability list, then, contains the non-blank entries from one row of the matrix.

In general, this is less workable for permanent storage of access information, since a given user domain may have potential access to hundreds of objects.

Its major usefulness is in a hybrid system, in which capabilities are used to record the rights held by a particular process, after it has acquired those rights by some other mechanism. (We will discuss this shortly.)

A typical implementation for a capability is as a "protected pointer" - i.e. it is a pointer to the object whose access it allows, and is itself stored in such a way that the user cannot alter its value (thus making it point to some other object instead.)

- One way to manage this is to store capabilities in a table in a a region of memory that belongs to the operating system, with the process that wants to use a given capability specifying it by means of an index into that table.
- As the text, some capability-based systems have been built around special hardware that treats capabilities as a special "read-only" data type. A process that owns a capability may copy it and pass it as a parameter, but may not alter it.

One significant problem with capabilities is **revocation**: to take away a capability that has been granted, it is necessary to locate and destroy all copies.

Locks and keys

With each resource, we associate a lock, and with each domain, we associate one or more keys. A domain is allowed access to an object if and only if one of its keys fits the lock. (Note that this approach only simplifies matters if a given key fits the locks of many objects - else if a process needs one key for each object it is allowed to access then its collection of keys is in fact as cumbersome as a capability list.). This can be extended by also allowing a given object to have multiple locks, so that an access is allowed if any of a domain's keys fit any of the object's locks.

Hybrid approach

When a process first requests access to a resource, its request may be checked by looking at an access list for the resource. If the access is granted, the process may be given a capability for that resource which it can present for further accesses to avoid having to re-search the access list.

Example: the "open" operation for files works like this on many systems. When a process attempts to open a file, the request is validated in terms of the protection specified for the file. If the request is valid, an entry is made in a system table. Subsequent accesses to the file (read and/or write) are allowed on the basis of the table entry, which functions as a capability. (In Unix and some other systems, the return value of an open call is an index into a table of open file descriptors maintained for each process by the kernel. This index is passed as a parameter to subsequent operations on the file, and the kernel uses it to access a pointer to the internal data structure for actually manipulating the file.

6. However implemented, an access matrix can be made less cumbersome by grouping. E.g. it may be possible to group domains in such a way as to allow a single access list entry to specify the access allowed to all the members of a given group.

The Unix approach to protection

A. Simple but elegant. Unix's protection mechanisms are much simpler than those of VMS, and do not allow nearly the same degree of fine-grained control. However, they do include one very elegant feature - so elegant that it is patented. (One of the few cases of a patent being granted for something that is strictly software.)

B. User and Group. Unix uses a two-part user identification like VMS does, with the first part being the group number and the second identifying the individual user. (On the SGI systems, ordinary users are group 20 and have individual user identifiers 1110, 1111, 1112 ...) The group and user IDs associated with a given login name are found (as on VMS) in a user authorization file (`/etc/passwd` on Unix.) There are two important differences from VMS, however.

1. User numbers are unique. The individual user numbers are unique across the system, not just within the group. Thus, the numbers 99,100 and 100,100 would both refer to the same individual.

2. User can belong to several groups . An individual can be a member of multiple groups. One group is the primary group for the individual, and is specified in the password file. Additional groups may be listed in `/etc/group`.

a. When an individual creates a file, its group ownership is set to his primary group.

b. However, an individual can access a file under group permissions if the group that owns the file is any of the groups he is a member of.

C. only one set of permissions is checked by the system. As we noted in discussing file systems, access permission for each file is established in terms of user (u), group (g) and others (o), with read, write, and execute access being capable of being granted or denied for each category. Unlike VMS, however, only one permission entry is checked for any given user.

1. For the file's owner, only the user entry is checked. Thus, it is possible for a file's owner to deny himself access to a file while granting it to his group and/or the world. (But note that the file's owner can always alter the protection on it, so this is not permanent.)
2. For a non-owner that is a member of the same group as the owner, only the g entry is checked. Thus, a file's owner could deny access to his own group while granting it to the world.
3. There is no provision for an access control list beyond this.

D. The superuser: Root. One user is above the protection system - the superuser (user ID 0 - login name **root**).

1. The superuser can access any file, regardless of protection, and may also alter the protection and/or ownership of any file.
2. Some very important system files are owned by the superuser and are alterable only by him (write access granted only to owner.) One of these is the password file (`/etc/passwd`) that lists authorized users.
3. Certain system services can only be executed by the superuser (e.g. the system service to shut down the system). Others can be used by any user, but offer more functionality to the superuser.
4. To somewhat reduce the risk of unauthorized users gaining superuser status, two special limitations apply to logging into username root.

Secure terminals

A system terminal configuration file specifies, for each terminal, whether or not it is a "secure" terminal. Root login attempts from a non-secure terminal are always denied.

The su program

Since this restriction could be too severe, it is also possible for an authorized superuser to log in under his own name and then use the `su` (switch user) command to change to superuser. (This requires the one using it to known the root password.) On some systems, mainly those based on BSD Unix, only users who are members of the special group "wheel" are allowed to use the `su` command to become superuser. All attempts at using the `su` program are recorded by the system.

Hard to apply the "need to know" principle.

Since special privilege on Unix is essentially "all or nothing" it is hard to apply the "need to known principle". This is one reason why Unix has a reputation for being weak on security - though some newer versions being developed are working on tightening this up.

E. Rights amplification: SetUID and SetGID. Some relief from this "all or nothing" problem is provided by the rights amplification mechanism.

1. Additional protection/permission codes. In addition to the nine protection code bits we mentioned earlier (r, w, and x access for each of three categories of user), there are two more bits that the owner of a file may set in the protection code of an executable file.

2. setuid (4000 octal). One of these is the "set user ID" bit. If this bit is set on an executable program, then whenever the program is run (by someone otherwise authorized to do so) the **effective** user ID of the process running it is changed to that of the file's owner. Thus, the program is able to access files according to the rights of the owner of the program, rather than the actual user. (The user ID reverts to its actual value when the program terminates.)

Note: In a long directory listing (`ls -l`), this bit shows up as an "s" where the "x" for owner execute permission would appear.

3. setgid (2000 octal). Another bit is the "set group ID" bit. It has a similar effect, but sets the group ID of the process to match the group ownership of the file. (This shows up in a long directory listing as an "s" in the slot where group execute permission would occur.)

4. Example.

a. The utility program `ps` allows anyone to look at a synopsis of all the processes currently running. The `ps` program does this by reading through a process table maintained in kernel memory.

b. Of course, ordinarily users are not permitted to directly access kernel memory, so the `ps` program needs to run with amplified access rights. This is handled as follows:

- ➢ The file system contains an entry for a pseudo-device called /dev/kmem. The kernel translates read/write requests on this "file" into accesses to addresses in kernel memory.
- ➢ The /dev/kmem "file" is owned by the user root and the group sys, and allows read/write access to owner, read access to group, and no access to others.
- ➢ The ps program is owned by the group sys, and has the set group ID bit turned on in its permissions. Thus, when any user runs it, he is temporarily made a member of the sys group and allowed to access kernel memory through the program.

5. Setuid and setgid programs can be used by normal users. A distinctive feature of this mechanism is that it can be used by ordinary users, not just by system management. (This contrasts with the provisions systems like VMS have for installing trusted images.)

Example: Suppose someone has a file of data that he wants to let only two other people read.

a. Rather than trying to talk the system manager into creating a special group for these two people, he could use the set user ID mechanism.

b. He would have to write out a program that checks to see if it is being run by one of these two people, and then simply types out the contents of the file to the screen. This program would be set up with the set user ID bit.

c. If the file was protected to allow only its owner to read it, it could still be accessed by anyone running this program. But the program itself would limit access to only the two chosen individuals.

6. setuid / setgid security problems. This mechanism, though elegant, is also the source of a number of the security problems Unix has experienced. (The Internet worm made illicit use of this feature by taking advantage of some debugging code that was left installed in running systems) To reduce the threat somewhat, the kernel automatically clears the set user ID and set group ID bits whenever a file is written to or has its ownership changed - except when these operations are done by the superuser.

Various other approaches to protection

A. Use of groups of users rather than ACLs is common

We have noted that implementing an access matrix per se is not usually practical. Likewise, access control lists and/or capability lists can become unmanageably large. Thus, most practical systems rely on less flexible mechanisms in which users are grouped into broad categories, which effectively reduces the number of rows in the access matrix to a manageable number. For example, the grouping of users into categories like owner, group, and world vis-a-vis a certain resource (as is done in

VMS with UICs) is a very common approach that allows for short access control lists to be associated with each protected resource (one entry per category).

Rings of protection

This is a special case of a more general concept known as rings of protection. For example, the UIC mechanism can be pictured this way:

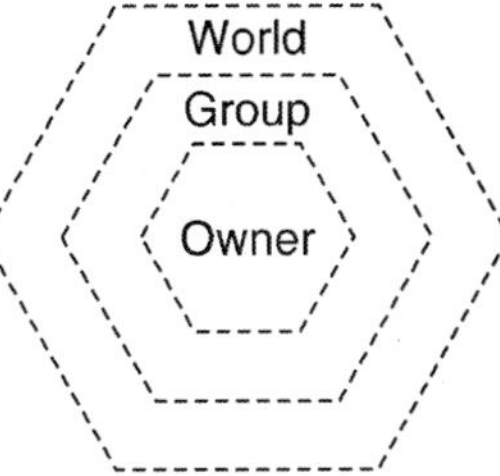

An inner ring is a subset of an outer ring, and possesses all of the privileges of the outer ring plus privileges uniquely its own.

Some systems use a ring-like approach to capabilities. For example, prior to the most recent release (version 9.0), RSTS/E had two categories of users vis-a-vis system services: ordinary users and privileged users. In the documentation for the system services, one finds that certain services are either restricted to privileged users only (such as the service that creates new user accounts) or have increased options when executed by privileged users (e.g. the system service to change the characteristics of a user terminal can be used by any process to change the characteristics of its own terminal only; but a privileged user can invoke it to change the characteristics of any terminal on the system.) This can be pictured as a ring structure like this:

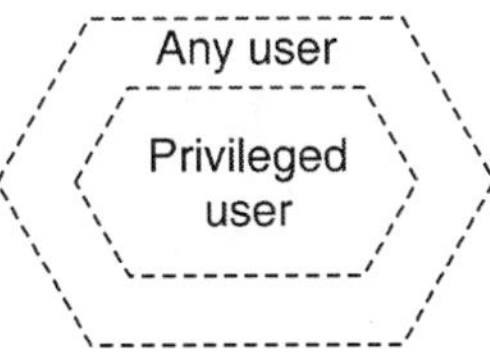

MULTICS used a similar structure, but with 8 rings of decreasing privilege (ring 0 = maximum privilege). Text - page 602.

Note that ring-like mechanisms are much less flexible. However, a UIC-type approach is more flexible than a level of privilege approach, since the rings are defined vis-a-vis each individual resource. (A given user is in the owner ring for files he owns and in either the group or world ring for other files.) Many systems combine both UIC and capability rings - e.g. UNIX, RSTS/E, and in a certain sense VMS.

Compile time access control

Another research area is the building of protection into programming languages in such a way that rights of access to resources are validated by the compiler at compile time, rather than by the operating system at run time. Of course, on such a system only code compiled by a trusted compiler could be allowed to be executed; in particular, all coding in assembly language or run-time patching of compiled programs must be forbidden.

KEYWORDS

PROTECTION	**USER-ORIENTED ACCESS CONTROL**
DATA-ORIENTED ACCESS CONTROL	**VIRUSES**
WORM	**ANTI-VIRUS**
BACTERIA	**LOGIC BOMB**
TRAPDOOR	**TROJAN HORSE**

SUMMARY

Protection must ensure that only those processes that have gained proper authorization from the OS can operate on memory segments, the CPU, and other resources.

- no protection: all sensitive procedures are carried out when nothing else is being done
- Isolation: all processes operate separately from each other with no sharing or communication. Each process has its own address space, files etc.
- Share all or nothing: the owner of an object or data declares it to be either private or public. Public objects are accessible by any other object.
- Share via access limitations: the Operating System checks the permissibility of each access by a specific user on a specific object. Here the Operating System acts as the guardian of access to objects.
- Share via dynamic capabilities: dynamic creation of access control rights to objects.
- Limit the use of an object: grant read but not write or copy access to objects

- User-Oriented Access Control

  You can control access to computer assets either by restricting the user or restricting the data, or both. User restrictions can be applied through passwords and levels of access

- Data-oriented Access Control

  Once a user has gained access to a system without any further restrictions the system is at their mercy. Some further restrictions can be applied to the user through the concept of a user 'profile' where permissible actions and accesses can be stated. The Operating System can use these to control an individual user's access. To attain this greater level of control most Operating Systems use something called an access control list or an access matrix.

- Virus: code inserted into a program that causes a copy of itself to be inserted in other programs. In addition the virus also performs some unwanted functions.

- Worm: program that can replicate itself and send copies from computer to computer across a network. In addition the worm may also perform unwanted functions.

  Malicious programs can be grouped as:

- Bacteria - a program that consume system resources by replicating itself

- Logic Bomb: a program that executes unauthorised actions when it detects a certain set of conditions e.g. a specified date

- Trapdoor: undocumented entry point into a program; used to grant unauthorised access

- Trojan horse: a program masquerading as other program.

  The antivirus approaches for generations

- First generation used a virus signature to identify a virus

- Second Generation uses signature together with rules of thumb.

- Third Generation uses signature together with rules of thumb.

- Fourth generation packages comprise a variety of anti-virus techniques. These include signature and activity recognition approaches.

REVIEW QUESTIONS

1) How can file protection errors and path setup errors be used to breach security?
2) Write short note on Cryptographic techniques?
3) Explain language based protection?
4) Write short note on Goals of protection
5) What is User-Oriented Access Control and Data-oriented Access Control?
6) Explain the following
   a. Bacteria
   b. Logic Bomb
   c. Trapdoor
   d. Trojan horse.
   e. Virus
   f. Worm

FILL IN THE BLANKS

1. __________ is code inserted into a program that causes a copy of itself to be inserted in other programs.
2. __________is a program that consume system resources by replicating itself
3. _________is a program that executes unauthorised actions when it detects a certain set of conditions e.g. a specified date
4. _________is an undocumented entry point into a program; used to grant unauthorised access
5. ___________is a program masquerading as other program.
6. _____________is program that can replicate itself and send copies from computer to computer.

TRUE OR FALSE

1. Protection must ensure that only those processes that have gained proper authorization from the OS can operate on memory segments, the CPU, and other resources.

2. User-Oriented Access Control can control access to computer assets either by restricting the user or restricting the data or both.
3. in Data-oriented Access Control, once a user has gained access to a system without any further restrictions the system is at supervisors.
4. A mechanism is a facility the operating system provides for specifying how an object may be accessed.
5. First generation used a virus activity recognition to identify a virus
6. Fourth generation packages comprise a variety of anti-virus techniques that include signature and activity recognition approaches.

ANSWERS

FILL IN THE BLANKS

1. Virus:
2. Bacteria
3. Logic Bomb
4. Trapdoor
5. Trojan horse
6. Worm:

TRUE OR FALSE

1. TRUE
2. TRUE
3. FALSE
4. TRUE
5. FALSE
6. TRUE

❑❑❑

"Be strict in what you send, and forgiving in what you receive." —*Mr Protocol*

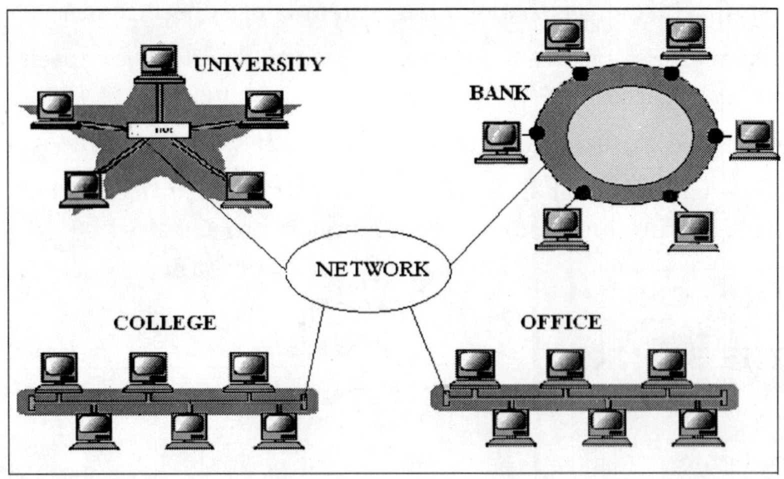

15 COMPUTER NETWORKS

INTRODUCTION

Networking is the connecting together of several computers and peripheral devices. The peripheral devices are commonly terminals, workstations and printers. Computers may connect together to share their file stores and other resources. Today's long distance communications involve the transmission and reception of a large amount of information in a short period of time. The days are gone when people relied on human messengers, radio, books, postal services, newspapers or even pigeons to send and receive information. All these methods were the evolutionary steps, which have led to today's modern technologies of long distance communication. Today's long distance communications involve the transmission and reception of a large amount of information in a short period of time. The computer has opened a variety of ways to communicate more quickly and effectively. The advent of cheap personal computers along with appropriate software provided people with very powerful productivity tools e.g. word processors, spreadsheets, email. The computer networks play an integral role in computer communication. They are also playing a dominant role in integrating technology into our lives. The networks not only connect computers in our organizations but they also can link us to other computers across the nation and around the world.

They allow people remote to the computer to access the information available to that computer within no time. A network is a way of transmitting or receiving data or information form one or various sources. Earlier, computers were isolated and largely incompatible. Today, networks support communication from computer to computer as well. The computer systems can request and receive services from other computers automatically and invisibly to the user

What is a Computer Network?

Computer network is an interconnection of a group of computers. In a network two or more autonomous computers are linked together to share information and resources.

The computer network enables us to share the resources. Here autonomous means, there is no master and slave relationship and all computers are equal and free to act independently. Basically the computer network is a collection of computers, printers and other equipment, which are connected together so that they can communicate with each other. The components in a network system are normally connected together through a cable, however the connection may be wireless. The diagram for a network system is as follows:

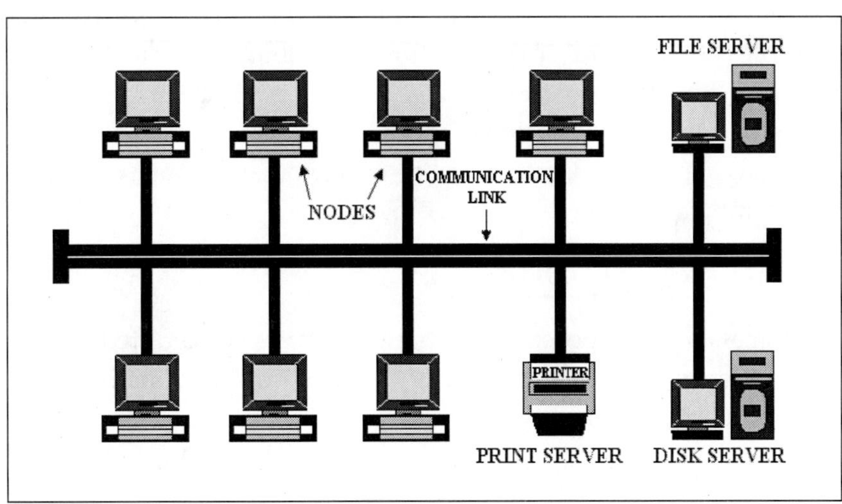

A computer network

The networks can be designed in an amazing variety of ways, from simple in-office group of three personal computers connected to a shared printer, to a global collection of networks including thousands of personal computers, minicomputers, mainframes, and other devices. If the network in place has a server, i.e., a central computer, and the appropriate software or network operating system, various levels of security can be implemented across the network. A single computing system in a network is often called a node, and its processor (computer) is called a host. A connection between two hosts is known as a link. Network computing consists of users, communications media, visible hosts, and systems not generally visible to end users as shown in the figure

The administration of the computer network involves, among other things, updating software on the computers, managing user information and accounts, and controlling network security. These functions can be performed from any location on the network. The motivation for building computer networks is:

- To provide high reliability.
- To improve communication between people.
- To increase efficiency by sharing resources e.g. printers, secondary storage etc.
- To increase responsiveness to business requirements as demand expands and contracts by permitting shared computing resources to be added/removed as appropriate.

The computer networks are very beneficial but networking needs enough skill and wisdom of the professionals involved in laying out the network and managing it. Using networks, computer systems can share resources and information. For example, employees in many organizations rely more on electronic mail than conventional mail for communication. Indeed, networks have created a new habitat, commonly called *cyberspace*. The information more readily available and it is also richer and strikingly more dynamic. In cyberspace, you are immersed in and engaged by information rather than merely possessing it.

Analog and Digital Transmission

Analog signals are composed of continuous waves transmitted over a medium at a certain frequency range. Changes in the wave transmissions reflect changes in voice and sound pitch, or tone.

Computers cannot understand data in analog form. Instead, computers use the binary number system to transform data into digital signals. Newer communications technologies generally employ digital signals.

Whenever digital data is sent from one computing device to another over an analog communications medium, such as a telephone line, both the sending and receiving devices must be equipped with a modem. A modem converts digital signals into analog form so an analog communications medium can send those signals.

Modems also convert incoming analog signals back to their digital equivalents so computers can receive those signals. Some newer modems are able to transmit and receive digital data without analog conversion, provided they are connected to the right communications media.

The term modem is derived from the words modulate and demodulate. The term modulation refers to the process of changing a digital signal into an analog signal, while demodulation refers to the process of changing an analog signal into a digital signal. Originally, personal computers used a type of modem called a dial-up modem, which can dial a telephone number, establish a connection, and close the connection when it is no longer needed.

Modems can be internal or external. An internal modem is an electronic board (card) inserted into an expansion slot on a computer's motherboard . One end of a standard telephone line is plugged into the modem port and the other end into a telephone outlet. The advantage of an internal modem is that it does not take up space on a user's desktop. An external modem operates in the same fashion as an internal modem, but is a stand-alone device connected by cable to a computer's motherboard. The advantage of an external modem is that it can easily be moved from one computer to another.

Notebook and other portable computers use a Personal Computer Memory Card International Association (PCMCIA) modem that inserts into a PCMCIA slot.

Basic Components of a Computer Network

Understanding how your computer connects to a network is only the first step in appreciating the complexity and power of networks. Networks allow for the sharing of information among devices along many different mediums as well as over great distances. There are many ways for networks to be setup and established involving various mediums, hardware, and network layout. The basic components of a computer network that are used to transmit message are:

The Sending device:

The sender is the device that sends the data message. It can be computer, workstation, telephone etc.

The Receiving device:

The receiver is the device that receives the message. It can be a computer, workstations, telephone, fax machine

Communication link:

The communication link is the physical path by which a message travels from sender to receiver. It can consist of twisted pair wire, coaxial cable, fiber optic cable or radio waves.

Modem:

A modem is a device that converts a digital signal to an analog signal and vice versa. The modem is short for **mo**dulator /**dem**odulator.

Protocols:

The systems connected to the communication link must follow a set of common communication rules for data to arrive at its intended destination and for the sending and receiving systems to understand each other; these rules governing computer communication are called protocols.

NOS:

A **N**etwork **O**perating **S**ystem (*NOS*) is required for the computer connected to the network for example; Windows 98 can be used as a NOS.

NICs:

The PCs that are not ready for use in a network; they may require **N**etwork **I**nterface **C**ards (*NICs*) to provide the connections they need.

In a computer network there are two types of communications software:

1. **Communications System Software or Network Software**

   This software controls and implements the communications protocols between DTEs and DCEs, and the transport of information between remote DCEs. In this form it provides the services required by the network users to establish the end-to-end connectivity and data transfer. The Communications System Software is distributed between the host computers and the DCEs. In the host computers it is normally an integral part of the Operating System (OS). For example in UNIX and Windows NT OSs, it is part of the Kernel.

2. **Communications Application Software**

   This is software that, using the services provided by the communications system software, implements user-oriented functions. An example of communications application software is Netscape, which allows users to access remote files download them and display them in the user's computer screen. Another example is Telnet, which emulating a terminal allows users to connect to a remote computer. One interesting inference in computer networks is that some application software can classify as DTE, for example a File Transfer program (FTP). Applications always run on the hosts.

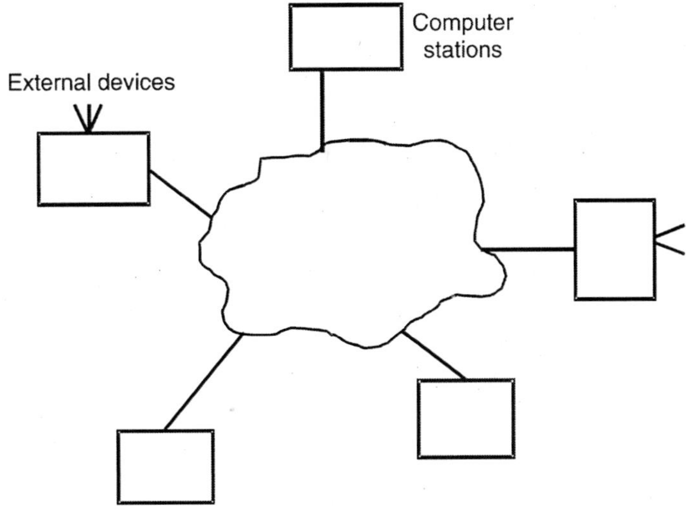

A Computer Network

Advantages of Computer Networks

The computer network acts as a very powerful communication medium. It helps the people to exchange their information easily and efficiently. The various advantages of computer networks are as follows:

Resource sharing

The computer networks make resources available to anyone on the network regardless of the physical location of the resource or the user.

- A ***Local Resource*** is any peripheral like optical drive, printer, scanner, modem, and so on, that is attached to your machine. Since the machine doesn't have to go on the network to get to the device, it is called a local device or a local resource.
- A ***Remote Resource*** is any device that must be reached through the network. Any devices attached to a server, are remote resources. This allows the companies to share software and peripherals such as printers, plotters, scanners and so on.

When compared to mainframe computers, network of computers saves money. The resource sharing is of two types:

- *File sharing*

  The files can be shared in a computer network in two ways. The one way is to transmit the file or data from your computer to the other computer directly. The other way is to send data to an intermediate place, from where the other person can pick it up later.

- *Hardware sharing*

  With the help of a computer network all the computers in an office can be connected to a single printer and scanner. It helps in using hardware efficiently as it permits various departments and people to share hardware. Sharing a device across a computer network makes maximum use of that device as it is available for use by all the users on the network. A whole range of devices can be connected to a network and shared, including:

SHAREABLE DEVICES

Printers	***DVD drives***	***Zip drives***
Scanners	***Hard disksTape drives***	
Plotters	***Floppy disks***	***Modems***
CD-ROM drives	***Certain fax machines***	***ISDN lines***

A printer is usually one of the first devices to be shared across a network. To make such sharing initiatives as cost-effective as possible, the following considerations should be borne in mind:

- As all users can print directly to a printer, only a small number of strategically located printers are required
- Reducing the number of printers produces a cost saving, which may be translated into purchasing higher quality, more powerful printers or printers with extra features
- With fewer printers, maintenance costs are lower
- With fewer printers, the time spent on maintenance is reduced

Sharing printers across a network undoubtedly makes practical and economic sense. The same is also true for other devices. For example, expensive items such as a color laser printer or a plotter should be accessible to all users so that they can be used regularly and effectively.

Job sharing

The job sharing is also one of the most important advantages of the computer networks. With the help of the computer network the job is processed on the least crowded (or busy) machine. For example if computer X has 26 jobs ,Y has 46 and Z has 6 processes to run then, a new job will be processed at the least crowded computer i.e. Z. The process sharing has two forms as explained below:

- ➢ ***Load Balancing***: Processes are distributed across the network to attempt to balance the processing load of each of the computers.
- ➢ ***Load Sharing***: Processes overflow from a computer that has reached capacity.

Communication

The computer network allows easy human-to-human communication through email, internet telephony, teleconferencing, etc. This permits the communication between various organizations, which need to cooperate with each other in performing certain task rapidly. The computer network offers the opportunity to communicate more efficiently with others that is why it is of great significance for the organization.

High reliability

The provision of alternate sources of resources lends towards high reliability of the system as there are multiple existence of same resource. For example, if there are multiple copies of same file in a network the system will not crash even if one file gets damaged by any means.

Centralized Software Management

One of the greatest benefits of installing a network is that all of the software can be loaded on one computer (the file server). This eliminates that need to spend time and energy installing updates and tracking files on independent computers throughout the building or campus

Speed

Networks provide a very rapid method for sharing and transferring files. Without a network, files are shared by copying them to floppy disks, then carrying or sending the disks from one computer to another. This method of transferring files is very time-consuming as compared to file transfer through networks.

Cost Reduction

The use of computer networks ultimately leads to the reduced equipment costs. As the networks enable computers to share their resources by offering services to other computers and users on a network, the average cost gets reduced. Also there are various aspects of technology that are likely to force the price of terminal usage drastically lower. This is important because almost all aspects of telecommunications are characterized by high price elasticity. In other words, when the price comes down, the usage goes up.

Interactive entertainment

The computer networks provide interactive entertainment in the form of online games, video on demand and live television quiz shows etc. In the days to come we will be able to choose our favorite among the latest new films and watch it live. The real time interactive games like flight simulators are also becoming increasingly popular by the day. Therefore the computer networks are providing a massive new platform to the entertainment industry.

Disadvantages of Computer Networks

The computer networks are very helpful, when it comes to share resources and saving time and money but this technology has some disadvantages too. The most common disadvantages of computer network are as follows:

Expensive:

The first and the foremost disadvantage of computer networks is that they are expensive to purchase and maintain. The cabling and installation of a large sized computer network is very costly.

Data Security:

The special security measures are needed to stop users from using programs and data that they shouldn't have access to. The proper permissions must be issued to various users according to their nature of work. The proper password validation check must be applied for the authorization and authentication of the user.

Manager dependence

The complex networks require a network manager to keep it running. The major problem with networks is that their efficiency is very dependent on the skill of the network manager. A badly managed network may operate less efficiently than non-networked computers. Also, a badly run network may allow external users into it with little protection against them causing damage.

Vulnerable to hackers and viruses

The computer networks are very vulnerable to hackers and viruses .For example, if the network is poorly implemented, improper communication may take place. This may lead to the situation in which the private or important mails can be seen by other users or hackers and this may result in loss of privacy or corrupt information system. Secondly the virus on one system in a network can affect the whole computer network and could prove fatal for the organization.

Social problems

The computer networks pose social problems when people post offensive views about sensitive issues like religion, sex and politics. The newsgroup or bulletin boards allow people to exchange messages freely on the network. This could lead to a problem because they are not restricted to post materials on any subject including deeply offensive views regarding religion, caste or creed etc.

COMMUNICATIONS MEDIA

Users must have access to communications media to communicate between computing devices. A communications medium is a link (a connection) that allows computers in different locations to be connected. When communications take place between distant computers, a combination of media may be used, some of which the user may never see. Communications media are broadly classified as either wired or wireless.

Wired Communications Media

While many computers, devices, and networks now use wireless technologies, many others continue to use wired technologies as a means of communicating. The medium chosen depends mainly on user requirements relating to availability, cost, speed, and other factors.

Twisted-Pair Cable Twisted-pair cable, one of the older types of communications media, was originally developed for telephone networks. Twisted pair cable typically consists of two parallel copper wires; each individually wrapped in plastic and bound together by another plastic casing. The pairs are often bundled in packs of hundreds or thousands.

Coaxial Cable Coaxial cable is commonly used for television connections, in telephone networks, and in some computer networks. The cable consists of an insulated center wire grounded by a shield of braided wire. **Baseband** coaxial cable is about 3/8 inch thick and has a single channel for transmitting digital signals at about 10 mbps. **Broadband** coaxial cable has several channels, each of which can carry about 10 mbps.

Fiber-Optic Cable A **fiber-optic cable** consists of hundreds of clear fiberglass or plastic fibers (threads), each approximately the thickness of a human hair. Fiber-optic cable uses a string of glass and laser technology to transmit photons (beams of light). Billions of bits can be transmitted per second. The advantages of using fiber-optic cables include:

- faster transmission speeds (up to 1 trillion bits per second)
- higher data transmission volumes
- minimal interference
- greater security
- longer cable life

Integrated Services Digital Network (ISDN) Lines In some locations a special digital telephone line, called **Integrated Services Digital Network (ISDN) line,** is available. This type of line can be used to dial into the Internet and transmit and receive information at very high speeds, ranging from 64 Kbps to 128 Kbps. Using an ISDN line requires a special ISDN modem. With the widespread adoption of high-speed cable modems and DSL lines at a relatively low cost, the growth of ISDN line usage remains flat.

Digital Subscriber Line (DSL) Digital Subscriber Line (DSL) technology uses existing copper phone lines and new optimized switched connections to achieve faster telecommunications speeds than traditional dial-up phone access. DSL separates voice and data into discrete channels so that users can still make phone calls while connected to the Internet via a DSL modem. DSL is considered a broadband technology, as connection speeds range from 144 Kbps to 1.56 Mbps.

Wireless Communications Media

Wireless media transmit information as electromagnetic signals through the air in much the same way as a battery-operated radio. Wireless technologies include:

Microwave Systems Microwave transmission involves the sending and receiving of information in the form of high-frequency radio signals. A microwave system transmits data through the atmosphere from one microwave station to another, or from a microwave station to a satellite and then back to another microwave station on earth. When data is sent between microwave stations, the stations must be positioned at relatively short line-of-sight intervals.

Satellite Systems A **communications satellite** is a solar-powered electronic device containing several small, specialized radios called transponders. A **transponder** receives signals from a transmission station on the ground, called an **earth station.** Communications satellites are positioned thousands of miles above the earth. A satellite receives transmitted signals, amplifies them, and then retransmits them to the appropriate locations on earth. Satellites orbit the earth at the same speed as the earth's rotation, making them appear stationary when viewed from the ground. This is called a **geosynchronous orbit**.

Communications satellites are capable of transmitting billions of bits per second, making them ideal for transmitting very large amounts of data. Several satellites now in orbit handle domestic and international data, video, and voice communications for owners and subscribers. For instance, banks use satellites to transmit thousands of customer transactions to other banks. Money can be transferred from an account in New York to an account in London within seconds.

Infrared Technology In recent years infrared technology has become increasingly popular for providing wireless communication links between computers and peripheral devices. **Infrared technology** transmits data as light waves instead of radio waves Television remote control units use the same technology.

Wireless keyboards, also called cordless keyboards, are a recent application of infrared technology. The battery-powered keyboards communicate with computers by transmitting data to a receiver connected to a port on the computer's system unit. A wireless mouse is another popular infrared device that works in the same way as a wireless keyboard, requiring less desktop space because there is no need for a cable.

Cellular Technology People can communicate wirelessly to and from nearly anywhere in the world using **cellular technology**. Cellular phones and devices work by maintaining contact with cellular antennae that resemble metal telephone poles positioned throughout a cellular calling area. Each area, called a cell, has its own antenna encompassing an area approximately 10 to 12 square miles in diameter. As users move from cell to cell, the closest antenna picks up the signal and relays it to the appropriate

Communications networks that support cellular communications also work well for handling business data. Using a portable computer with a cellular modem, a person can access both Internet resources and information stored on a company's intranet databases. Using a device with a wireless modem requires the services of a **wireless service provider (WSP)** to provide wireless Internet access.

Wi-Fi Technology The most commonly used wireless technology today is Wi-Fi. **Wi-Fi** is a wireless local area network (WLAN) technology based on the 802.11 standards of the Institute of Electrical and Electronics Engineers (IEEE).

A Wi-Fi device, such as a PDA or a notebook computer with a Wi-Fi card, must be in close proximity (usually within 150 feet indoors or 300 feet outdoors) to a device called a wireless access point. The **wireless access point** is a hardware device that transmits a wireless network signal to Wi-Fi–enabled devices. A Wi-Fi **hotspot** is a location that has one or more wireless access points. Many restaurants, hotels, school campuses, and airports provide Wi-Fi hotspots for a fee or at no charge.

Bluetooth Technology Bluetooth wireless connectivity is becoming increasingly common. Most PDAs, cell phones, and notebook computers have built-in Bluetooth capabilities. This technology offers short-range (usually 15 to 20 feet) connectivity with other Bluetooth devices. Devices connected with Bluetooth essentially form their own small, temporary network that can transmit both voice and data. Common uses of Bluetooth include connecting mobile headsets to cell phones and synchronizing PDA information with notebook computer or cell phone information.

Transmission mode

The transmission mode explains how data flow will occur between to connected devices. It can be set by communications software.

The term transmission mode refers to the direction of flow of information between to linked devices.

Both ends of a communication circuit must agree as to which transmission mode is being used. The transmission along a channel is possible in three modes:

1) Simplex

2) Half Duplex

3) Full Duplex

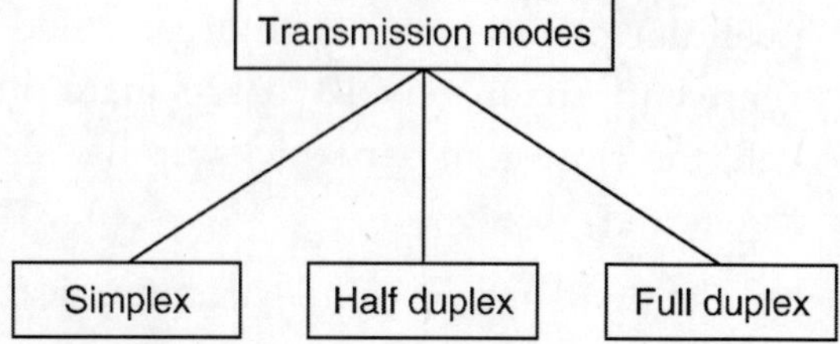

1. *Simplex* transmission sends data in one direction only for example: TV.

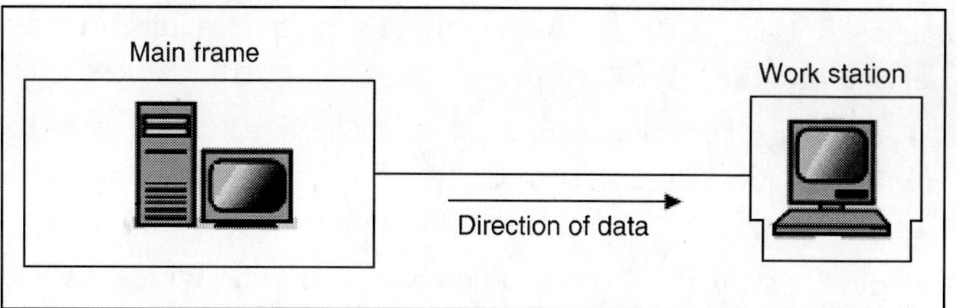

2. *Half-duplex* transmission sends data in either direction, but only one way at a time for example police wireless.

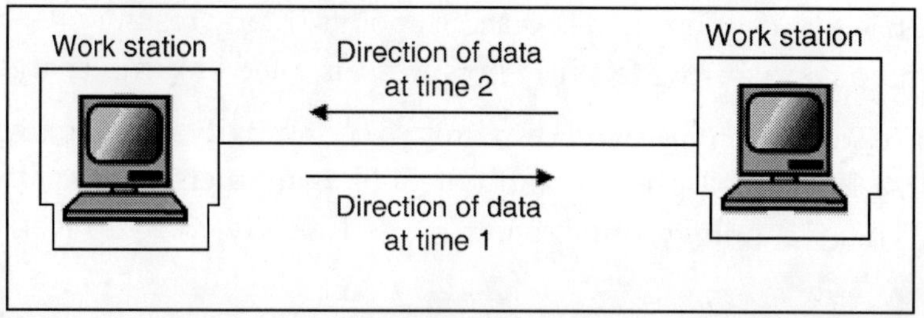

3. *Full-duplex* transmission allows transmission in both directions at once for example: telephone.

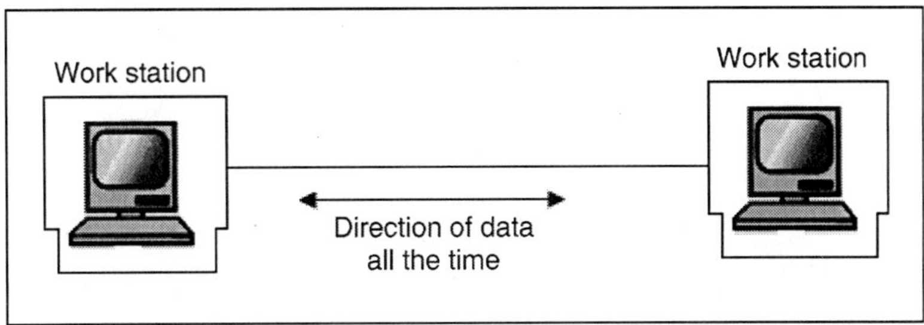

The Full Duplex requires two channels along which data can be sent. In Half duplex a single, bi-directional channel can be used, but each end must know when to change from talk to listen – creating a "turn around" delay.

NETWORK TOPOLOGIES

The term topology refers to the physical or logical layout of the network. It is determined only by the configurations of connections between nodes. A node is an active device connected to the network, such as a computer or a printer. It can also be a piece of networking equipment such as a hub, switch or a router.

A network topology is the geometric arrangement of nodes and cable links in a LAN

A given node has one or more links to others, and the links can appear in a variety of different shapes. Network topology is not concerned with the things that physically affect the network such as signal strength, distances between nodes, transmission rates etc.

There are two types of topologies

➢ ***Logical topology***

The logical topology defines how the media is accessed by the hosts. It is used to describe the arrangement of devices on a network and how they communicate with one another. It is also referred to as Signal Topology

➢ ***Physical topology***

The physical topology defines the actual layout of the wire i.e. media. It is concerned with the physical layout of the network; how the cables are arranged; and how the computers are connected. The physical topology of a network refers to the configuration of cables, computers, and other peripherals.

The physical topology should not be confused with logical topology which is the method used to pass information between workstations. The main types of Physical Topologies are as under:

I. **I. Bus topology**

II. **Ring topology**

III. **Star topology**

IV. **Tree topology**

V. **Mesh**

- **Partial connected mesh topology**
- **Fully connected mesh topology**

VI. **Hybrid topology**

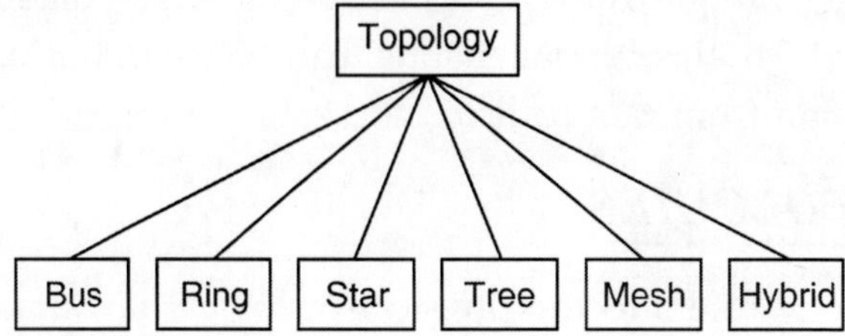

Types of physical topologies

Bus

The bus topology is the simplest network configuration. It uses a single transmission medium called a bus to connect computers together. A bus topology consists of a main run of cable with a terminator at each end. All nodes (file server, workstations, and peripherals) are connected to the linear cable. Ethernet and LocalTalk networks use a linear bus topology.

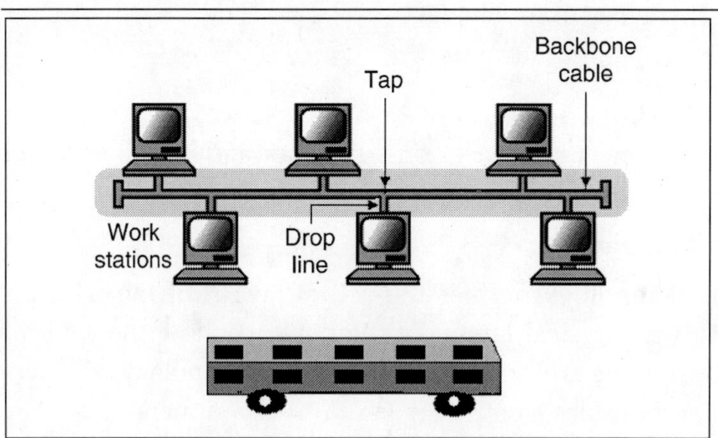

The Bus topology connects the workstations in the form of a bus

The workstations are connected to the bus cable by taps and drop lines. A drop line connects the workstations and hosts whereas the tap creates the actual contact by puncturing the main cable. The special hardware has to be used to terminate both ends of the coaxial cable such that a signal traveling to the end of the bus would come back as a repeat data transmission. The common implementation of this topology is Ethernet. A message transmitted by one workstation is heard by all the other workstations.

Advantages of a Bus Topology

1) It is quite cheap than other topologies.

2) It is easy to connect a computer or peripheral to a linear bus.

3) It requires less cable length than a star topology.

4) In the Bus topology the failure of a node does not affect others

Disadvantages of a Bus Topology

1) The performance may decrease as number of nodes is increased

2) The entire network shuts down if there is a break in the main cable.

3) The terminators are required at both ends of the backbone cable.

4) It is difficult to troubleshoot i.e. identify the problem if the entire network shuts down.

Ring

In this arrangement of components the stations are connected by point-to-point links and consequently form an unbroken circle. In a Ring, all the devices on the network are connected to a common cable which loops from machine to machine. After the last machine on the network, the cable then returns to the first device to form a closed loop. The transmissions from one node may travel through several others before reaching the targeted destination node. The transmission may occur in one direction only i.e. the rings are unidirectional and operate by passing packets of data from one station to the next until the correct destination is arrived at, thus rings are broadcast systems.

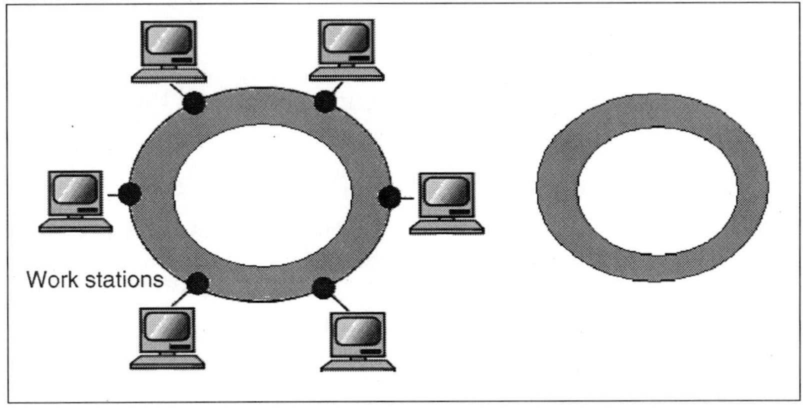

The Ring topology connects the workstations in the form of a ring.

The information travels around the ring from one workstation to the next. Each packet of data sent on the ring is prefixed by the address of the station to which it is being sent to. When a packet of data arrives, the workstation checks to see if the packet address is the same as its own. If it is, it grabs the data in the packet. If the packet does not belong to it, it sends the packet to the next workstation in the ring. Each node in the network is able to purify and amplify the data signal before sending it to the next node.

Advantages of Ring

1) The equal access is granted to all nodes

2) The Ring topology introduces less signal loss as data traveling along the path.

3) The Ring-topology network is often used to cover a larger geographic location where implementation of star topology is difficult.

4) The number of slots in any device does not limit the number of devices connected to the network

Disadvantages of Ring

1) The Ring topology is more expensive to implement than other topologies like Bus and Star.

2) A break anywhere in the ring will cause network communications to stop therefore a backup signal path may be implemented in this case to prevent the network from going down.

3) The users may access the data circulating around the ring only when it passes through his or her computer.

Star

A star topology is designed with each node is connected directly to a central network hub or concentrator. Usually the central node has the peripherals that are to be shared across the network attached to it, and often it acts as a file and printer server to the rest of the stations on the network. The data on a star network passes through the hub or concentrator before continuing to its destination. The hub or concentrator manages and controls all functions of the network.

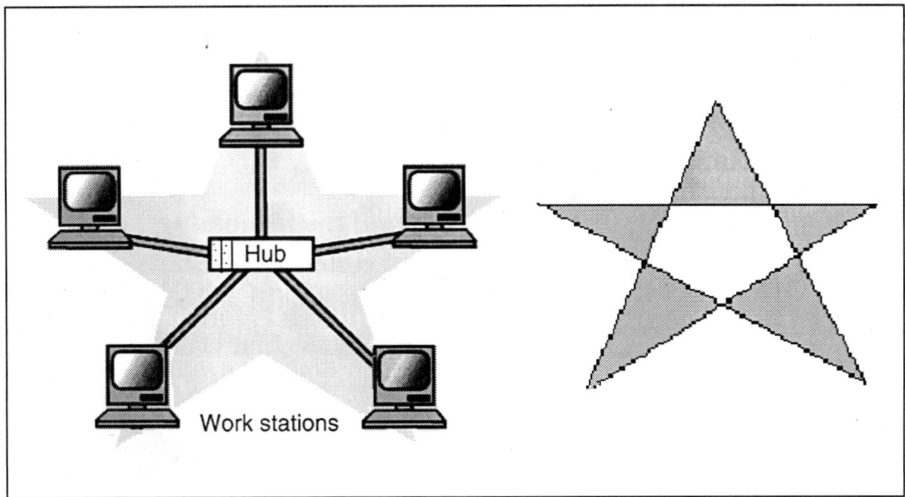

The Sing topology connects the workstations in the form of a star

A star network uses a significant amount of cable (each terminal is wired back to the central hub, even if two terminals are side by side several hundred meters away from the host). All routing decisions are made by the central hub, and all other workstations can be. The protocols used with star configurations are usually Ethernet or LocalTalk.

Advantages of a Star Topology

1) The Star topology easily and quickly installed and wired.

2) A cable break may not bring down entire network.

3) It is easy to detect faults and to remove parts.

Disadvantages of a Star Topology

1) The maintenance costs may be high

2) It requires more cable length than a linear topology.

3) If the hub or concentrator fails, nodes attached are disabled and the use of hub makes it exp ensive too.

Tree

A tree topology can be thought of as being a "Star of Stars" network. In a Tree network, each device is connected to its own port on a concentrator in the same manner as in a Star. However, concentrators are connected together in a hierarchical manner i.e. a hub will connect to a port on another hub. This tree has individual peripheral nodes (i.e. leaves) which are required to transmit to and receive from one other node only and are not required to act as repeaters or regenerators. It combines characteristics of linear bus and star topologies. It consists of groups of star-configured workstations connected to a linear bus backbone cable. The tree topologies allow for the expansion of an existing network.

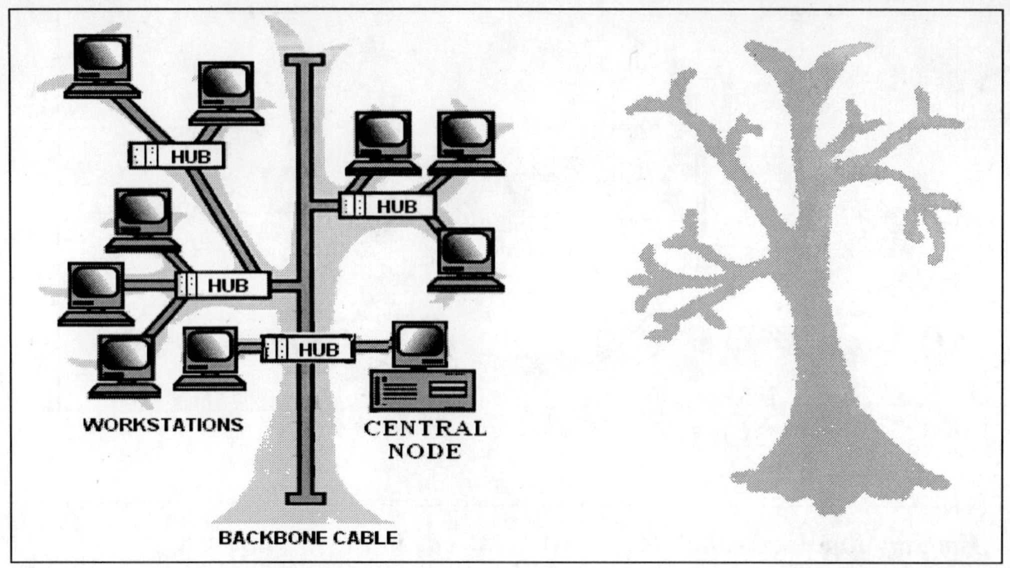

The tree topology connects the workstations in the form of a tree

Advantages of a Tree Topology

1. The new nodes can easily be added at the bottom of the tree.
2. There is point-to-point wiring for individual segments.
3. The Tree topology is supported by several hardware and software venders.

Disadvantages of a Tree Topology

1) If the top node is assigned all the tasks then quickly a bottleneck will occur and terminal traffic will increase.

2) The overall length of each segment is limited by the type of cabling used.

3) If the backbone line breaks, the entire segment goes down.

4) It is more difficult to configure and wire than other topologies.

Mesh

A Mesh topology consists of a network where every device on the network is physically connected to every other device on the network. This provides a great deal of performance and reliability, however the complexity and difficulty of creating one increases geometrically as the number of nodes on the network increases. For example, a three or four node mesh network is relatively easy to create, whereas it is impractical to set up a mesh network of even 50 nodes. The number of interconnections would be so ungainly and expensive that it would not be worth the effort. The Mesh networks are not used much in local area networks (LANs) but are used in Wide Area Networks (WANs) where reliability is important and the number of sites being connected together is fairly small. There are two types of Mesh topologies

- Partially connected Mesh or irregular topology
- Fully connected Mesh or Complete topology

Partially connected Mesh or irregular topology

The Mesh layout is used in Wide Area Networks and allows multiple routes between hosts, as shown below:

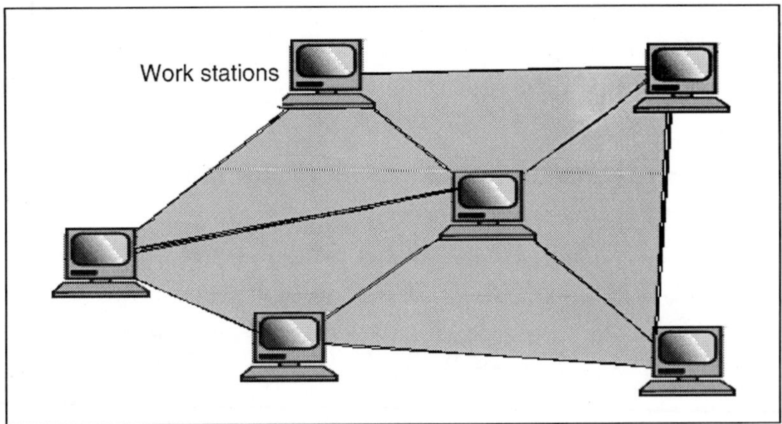

Fully connected Mesh or Complete topology

A mesh network where every node is connected to every other node is known as a fully connected network, and is shown below:

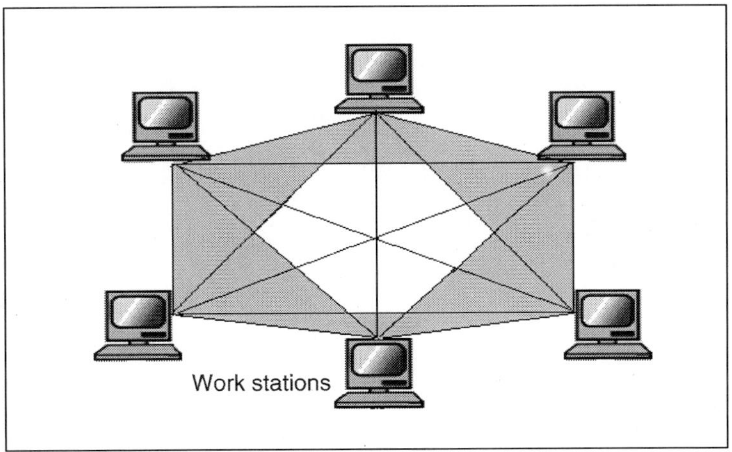

Advantages of Mesh

1) There is more than one path between the nodes.

2) Any failure of one computer allows all others to continue

3) The Mesh topology provides a great deal of performance and reliability.

4) Another advantage is privacy or security because when every message sent travels along dedicated line, only the intended recipient sees it.

5) The point-to-point links make fault identification and fault isolation easy.

Disadvantages of Mesh

1) The large amount of cable is required to implement Mesh topology.

2) The complexity and difficulty of creating one increase geometrically as the number of nodes on the network increases.

Hybrid

Hybrid topologies refer to those networks that are made of several different topologies. The hybrid topologies are becoming quite common today as corporations continue to link their internal LANs together while adding external networks to the mix via wide area networks (WANs). This topology description usually refers to a collection of networks. An example of a special or hybrid topology would be one where a star topology network is used to connect a ring, a bus topology and star topology LANs.

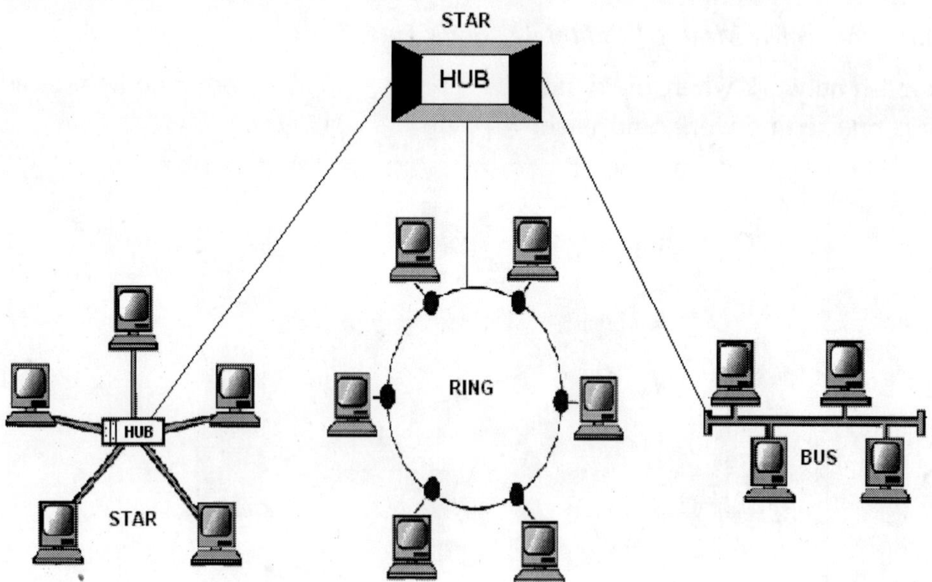

Types of Networks- LAN, WAN and MAN

Many types of networks exist today. We know that a network is a collection of communicating hosts. It is very important to understand the several types of subclasses of networks, since they commonly combine into larger networks. The networks are categorized according to size, topology, and its ownership. The three primary types of computer networks are: Local Area Network (LAN), Metropolitan Area Network (MAN), and Wide Area Network (WAN).

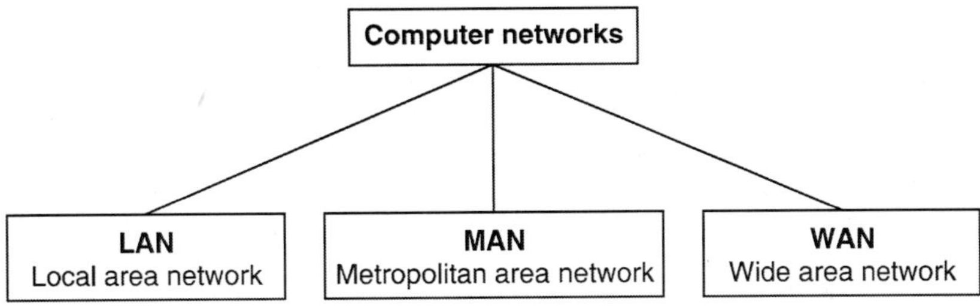

Types of Computer Networks

Local area network (LAN)

The `local area network (LAN)` is probably the most common network setup. As the name implies, LAN covers a small distance, typically within a single building or a college campus. LANs can be small, linking as few as three computers, but often link hundreds of computers used by thousands of people.

A LAN is a group of microcomputers or other workstation devices located in the same general area of less than 2kms and connected by a common cable.

The development of standard networking protocols and media has resulted in worldwide proliferation of LANs throughout business and educational organizations. Having a simple operating system such as Windows 98 or Macintosh OS on the computers in a LAN isn't enough. To share network resources, such as printers, and to route communications on a LAN requires special software called a `Network Operating System`. A LAN is used to share resources amongst a group of individuals or company employees. LANs are distinguished from other types of networks by their transmission media and topology. In general, a given LAN will use only one type of transmission medium. The most common LAN topologies are bus, ring, and star. Traditionally, LANs have data rates in the 4 to 16 Mbps range. Today, however speeds are increasing and can reach 100 Mbps with gigabit systems in development.

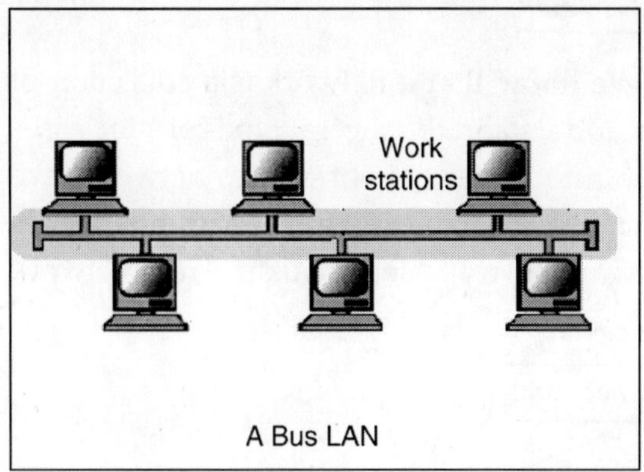

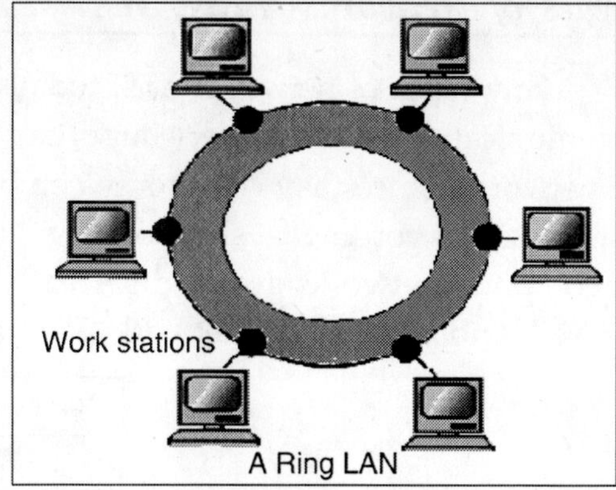

Types of LAN

Metropolitan Area Network (MAN)

A MAN often covers a city, with the communication offering of one provider in that area.

A metropolitan area network (MAN) is designed to extend over an entire city. A MAN usually consists of two or more LANs in a common geographic area.

For example, a bank with multiple branches may utilize a MAN. It may be a single network such as a cable television network, or it may be a means of connecting a number of LANs into a larger network so that resources may be shared LAN-to-LAN as well as device-to-device. The MANs, and WANs cover a wide range of possibilities; they loosely characterize everything between LANs and Internets, the two extremes of the networking spectrum.

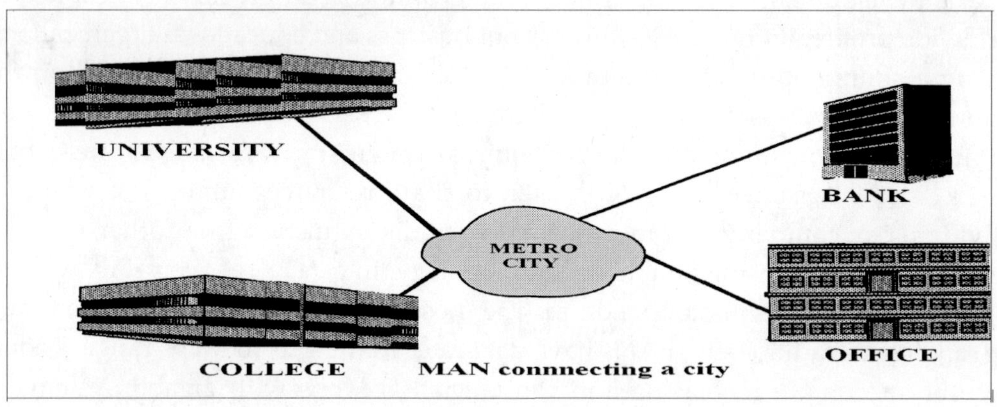

MAN connnecting a city

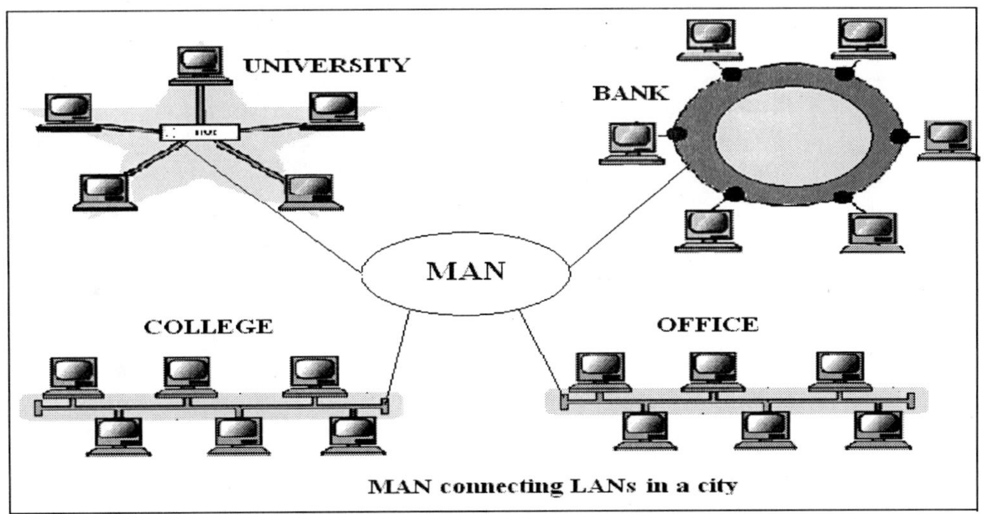

MAN connecting LANs in a city

MAN connecting a city

A MAN is a network connecting computers over a large geographical area than LAN. It is not generally owned by a single organization. The MAN, its communications links and equipment are generally owned by either a consortium of users or by a single network provider who sells the service to the users.

Wide Area Network (WAN)

A wide area network, or WAN, differs from a local area network in terms of both size and distance and control or ownership. As its name implies, it covers a wider geographic area than does a LAN.

A WAN provides long-distance transmission of data, voice, image, and video information over large geographical areas that may comprise a country, a continent, or even the whole world.

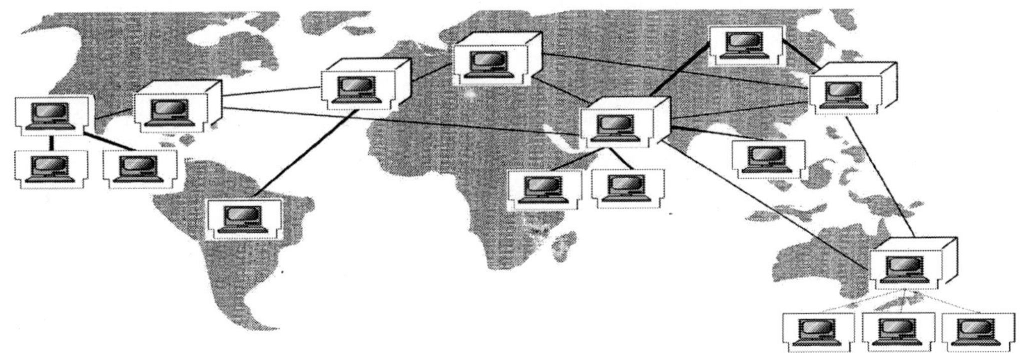

WAN connecting the world

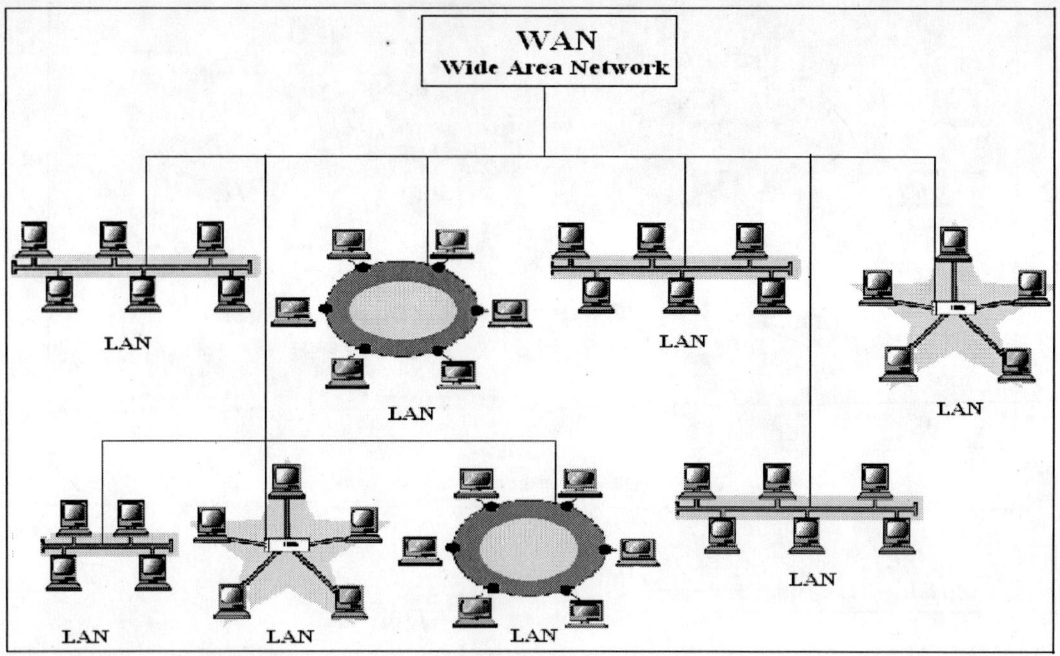

WAN connecting LANs

Network architecture

On the basis on their layout, not the physical but the imagined layout, there are two types of networks i.e. there are mainly two types of network architectures.

1. Peer-to-peer model
2. Client/server model

Peer-to-peer model

In a Peer-to-Peer networking configuration, there is no server, and computers simply connect with each other in a workgroup to share files, printers, and Internet access. The peer-to-peer networks are more commonly implemented where less then ten computers are involved and where strict security is not necessary. In a peer-to-peer network, each computer holds its files and resources. Other computers can access these resources but a computer that has a particular resource must be turned on for other computers to access the resource it has. For example, if a printer is connected to computer A and computer B wants to printer to that printer, computer A must be turned on.

A peer-to-peer network model is simply two or more computers linked together, sharing resources such as printer, scanner or Internet connection, and storing files and programs on their own hard drives.

All computers have the same status, hence the term 'peer', and they communicate with each other on an equal footing. This is most commonly found in home configurations, and is only practical for workgroups of a dozen or less computers.

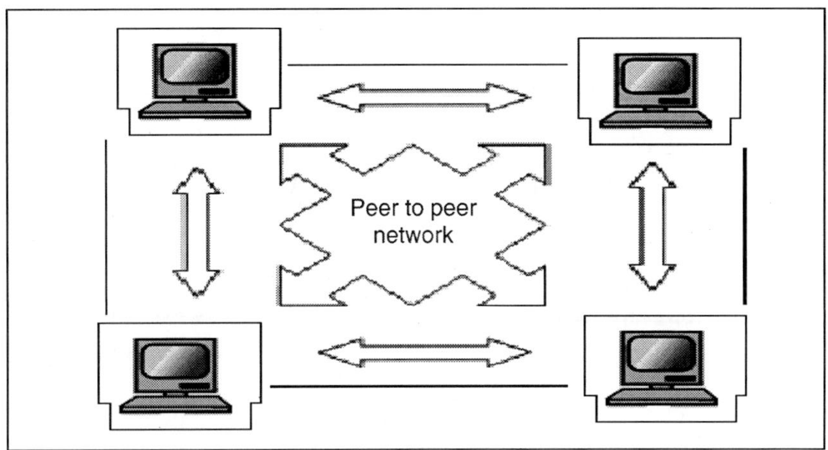

The peer-to-peer networking is the easiest and most inexpensive way to network your computer. A soon as you have more than one computer in a working environment, it becomes as asset to be able to share information and resources.

Client/server model

In the client server model, the server can provide various services, including centrally routed Internet Access, mail (including e-mail), file sharing, and printer access, as well as ensuring security across the network. Usually the server is a higher than average performance computer. The server also controls the network access of the other computers which are referred to as the 'client' computers. This is most commonly found in corporate configurations, where network security is essential.

In a client/server network, at least one computer is designated as a server; that it is a central computer in the network that provides services to clients. A client is a machine that's requesting something from another computer; a server responds to the request with the desired data or service.

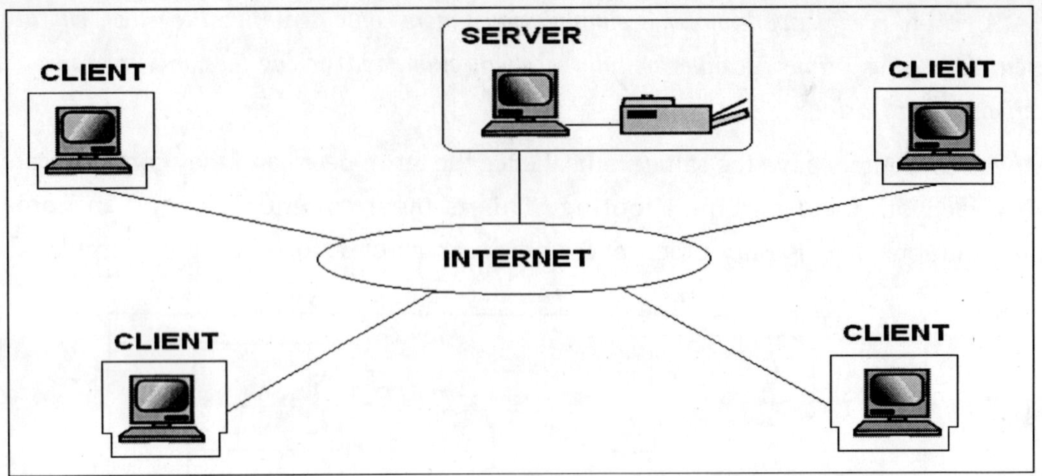

Client

A Client is any machine that requests something from a server. The server supplies files and sometimes processing power to the smaller machines connected to it. Each machine is a client in this type of network.

Server

A Server is any machine that can provide files, resources, or services to another machine. Any machine that you request a file from is a server. The server is a powerful machine that holds main files and large applications.

A client/server network involves a centralized form of networking. The other computers come to this server for a variety of purposes, for example, to access information. A file server is a computer that serves as a central repository of files that are available to other computers on the network, which are known as *clients*. Another big advantage of a client/server network is that security is created, managed, and can highly get enforced. To access the network, a person, called a user must provide some credentials, including a username and a password. If the credentials are not valid, the user can be prevented from accessing the network. The client/server type of network also provides many other advantages such as centralized backup, Intranet capability, Internet monitoring, etc.

Data Communication media

There are a variety of media that can be used for data communications. Some are useful over a few meters, while others are useful for data communication between planets.

Parallel Buses

A parallel bus is just a number of parallel wires, together with a protocol for transfer of information on the bus. The wires are connected to every device. One device can communicate with another device by the first device setting the voltages on the wires, and the second device observing the new voltages. For example, 1 could be represented by a high voltage, and 0 by a low voltage.

The bus connecting the devices and processor together has a number of lines. These include control lines, to indicate the nature of the request (e.g., read or write), and address/data lines to indicate the address to be read or written or the data to be read or written. Control lines are used for indicating the nature of the request, priority arbitration between the different devices, parity information, interrupt requests from devices, clock signals, error flags, etc.

Associated with a bus is a communication protocol. This is a convention specifying how information sent over the bus is to be interpreted, and the sequence of requests and replies necessary to transfer information over the bus.

A bus may be either synchronous (when information is placed on the bus at regular time intervals, controlled by a clock), or asynchronous (when there may be an arbitrary delay in response, and the device wishing to send information on the bus sets a wire to indicate when the data is available). The choice of clock cycle time relates to the speed at which memory and other devices can respond to requests. For example the PCI (Personal Computer Interface) bus used as the backplane bus on many modern microcomputers transfers data at 4 bytes / 30 nanosecs = 133 Mbytes/ sec ≈ 1 Gbit/sec. Outdated buses become a major bottleneck in data transfer, when components are upgraded.

A bus works on the assumption that, whenever a device places information on the bus, the information is transmitted throughout the bus, so that it can be read by all other devices. Information travels at about $2 * 10^8$ metres/sec, or 20 metres in 100 nanosecs. (The speed of light is $3 * 10^8$ metres/sec.). This provides a significant limitation on the length of the bus, in relation to the rate at which information is placed on the bus. For example, if the bus is required to settle down in 20 nanosecs, then it cannot be more than 4 metres long. There are also limitations on bus length due to the fact that information may travel at a different rate on different wires, due to physical differences in the wires. Thus it is not possible to transmit information in parallel over long distances.

The SCSI (Small Computer Systems Interface) bus is a parallel bus used to connect peripheral devices, such as disk drives, to the main computer. A typical version transfers 16 bits per clock cycle, with a 100 nanosec clock, giving a data transfer rate of 160 Mbits/sec.

There are in fact lots of buses within a computer. There is a bus within the CPU, for moving data between registers and the control unit. A system controller chip acts as a hub. The CPU, memory, and input/output buses are connected to it by the host bus, memory bus, and backplane bus. Input/output buses, such as the SCSI, USB and ethernet buses are connected to the backplane bus.

Serial transmission

To transmit information over larger distances, the information must be transmitted serially, rather than in parallel. Data is transmitted a bit at a time, in sequence. Over short distances, with low data rates, it is possible to require a transmitted bit to travel the whole length of the wire before the next bit is transmitted. However, this limits the rate at which information can be transmitted over the wire. The solution is to propagate the information along the wire as a wave of data. The data travels along the wire as a series of 0s and 1s, without waiting for the voltage to settle down.

An alternative to parallel buses for communication over short distances (up to 5 metres), is the **Universal Serial Bus** (USB), which is used for connecting peripheral devices to the main computer. A USB cable is composed of two pairs of twisted wires for data transmission, and two power wires. Each wire is about 1mm thick. The wires are twisted to stop them acting as a transmitter. Devices are connected together in a tree structure. Data rates of 480 Mbits/sec (USB 2.0), 12 Mbits/sec, and 1.5 Mbits/sec are permitted. At 480 Mbits/sec, travelling at $2 * 10^8$ metres/sec, a bit covers a distance of 0.4 metres.

Devices connected to the USB bus are required to identify themselves and satisfy various protocols, to enable "plug and play" to work - devices can be plugged in and removed, without modifying the operating system, or rebooting. Because the USB cable includes limited power, many devices do not need an independent power source. USB devices include slow devices, such as the keyboard and mouse. It is also possible to use USB with portable flash memory "drives" and compact hard drives, that fit in a shirt pocket. The fact that power is provided by the USB bus itself is very convenient.

Firewire

Firewire works on the same principle, and is a better quality product, but the marketplace chose the cheaper product. Firewire was originally intended for connecting audio visual equipment together, but can be used with computer peripherals as well.

Twisted pair can also be used for local area networks. Individual wires can be up to 90 metres long, but can be connected together by repeaters up to several kilometres. All wires connect directly to a central hub machine. Data rates of 10 - 100 Mbits/sec can be achieved.

Coaxial Cable

Coaxial cable consists of a central wire, surrounded by insulating material. The insulator is surrounded by a conducting mesh, to protect the central cable from outside interference. Each individual cable can be about 180 metres long, but they can be connected together by repeaters. Devices can be plugged into the cable at any point, by cutting the wire, and inserting a T junction. Data rates of 10 Mbits/sec are possible over a few kilometres. At 10 Mbits/sec, travelling at $2 * 10^8$ metres/sec, a bit covers a distance of 20 metres, and a 64 byte message covers a distance of 10 kilometres.

Fibre Optics

Thin glass fibres can be used to transmit light. Due to the refractive index of the glass fibre relative to air, the light will stay inside the fibre, even if the fibre is bent to go around corners. The light can propagate hundreds of kilometres in a single cable without any significant loss of power. Information can be transmitted by altering the power of a light emitting diode to represent 0 and 1. Fibre optics can be used to transmit data at the rate of about 10 Gbits/sec. Experimental designs are getting up to 100 Gbits/sec.

Radio and Microwave Transmission

For very long distances, radio and microwaves can be used as the transmission medium. If a satellite is placed 36000 km above the equator, it rotates around the earth at the same rate as the earth rotates, and so appears to stay in a fixed position. Data can be transmitted at about 500 Mbits/sec. However the time taken to reach the destination is about 270 millisecs, due to the time it takes light to travel up to the satellite and back.

Dial Up Lines

At the other end of the spectrum for data rates, it is possible to use dial up telephone lines for data communications. At present, telephone lines are still designed for use with voice, rather than high speed data transmission between computers, although this is changing. Voice transmissions will soon be sent as packets in digital form. This is already done for transmission between telephone exchanges, but not for the final link between the local exchange and user's house.

It is not possible to send digital signals represented by different voltages over voice telephone lines. The telephone hardware filters out frequencies outside the range of 330 Hz to 3000 Hz, since frequencies outside this range are considered to represent noise, and thus all high speed data is lost[1] . Instead, we must use audible frequencies to represent bits. For example, different frequencies, amplitudes, or phases can be used to represent data. Data rates of up to 56 kbits/sec[2] can be achieved, with an error rate of about 1 in 10^5, compared with a rate of about 10 Mbits/sec, with one error per day, that would be considered appropriate for a typical computer-computer connection.

A **modem**, or modulator-demodulator, is used to connect each end of the telephone line to a computer or terminal, and convert between the telephone sounds and digital information. Because of the potential for noise over modems, the data rate is adjusted to suit the conditions - your modem will transmit at a slower rate on a wet day.

ADSL (Asymmetric Digital Subscriber Line) permits a telephone line to be used for both voice and digital data at the same time. Voice is transmitted as normal, using low frequency analog signals (up to 20 kHz). Data is transmitted using high frequency signals, that would normally be filtered out as noise (25-200 kHz upstream, 250+ kHz downstream). Filters are placed between the phone or modem and the local line, to remove the portion of the incoming signal that is not intended for that device. The reason why ADSL is described as asymmetric is because the data rates are different in each direction - perhaps up to 500 kbits/sec upstream, and up to 6 Mbits/sec downstream, due to the different ranges of frequency allocated for each direction.

The big advantage of using the telephone system for data communication is its availability. It is possible to communicate almost everywhere in the world by telephone.

Transmission Protocol

Parallel Buses

With a simple parallel bus, or a system where a bit of information pervades the whole medium before the next bit is placed on the bus, it is relatively easy to determine whether there is another device wanting to use the system. On a parallel bus, devices are ranked in order, and the highest priority device takes precedence. Other devices have to wait until there are no higher priority devices waiting to use the medium.

Serial Lines

For other media, the information propagates through the medium as a wave, without waiting for each bit of information to pervade the medium. This allows us to achieve a higher data rate over long distances, even though the total transmission time for each bit may still be quite long, due to the speed at which information propagates. The rate of transmission in electrical wires and fibre optic cables is comparable to the speed of light, so the theory of relativity indicates that we cannot significantly decrease the delay between transmission from one device and reception by another device at the other end. However, as technology permits, we can increase the transmission rate by sending the bits more rapidly.

Packets

For most media other than a parallel bus, information is sent serially in the form of a packet. A packet is typically composed of:

- A **synchronisation pattern**, to allow the destination device to synchronise with the incoming data.
- A **header** indicating such things as the **source and destination address for the packet**, and perhaps such things as the packet type or length.
- **Checksum information** (basically bits that are computed by taking the exclusive or of the other bits in the packet), to allow the receiver to check whether the message has been received correctly, and discard the packet if there are any errors. In some protocols, the checksum information relates to the whole packet, and in other protocols, it only relates to the header.
- The **data to be transmitted**. Information in the body of the packet that might be mistaken for a synchronisation pattern will have to be escaped in some way, so that its purpose is not mistaken.

Ethernet

Some existing data communication protocols, such as ethernet, allow many communicating devices to share the same transmission medium, in much the same way that the devices on a single computer share the same bus. The protocol is more complex because the speed at which the data travels along the line has to be taken into account.

To transmit a packet on ethernet, the following protocol is used:

- A device wishing to transmit listens to the medium until it has detected no other transmissions for a given period of time.
- The device then starts transmitting.
- As it transmits, it listens to the medium for other transmissions.
- If it detects any other transmissions, it aborts its transmission, and waits a random period of time before trying again. If necessary it tries several times, waiting for longer periods on each occasion.

To receive a packet on ethernet, a device just listens to the medium, and waits for a packet with its destination address. Any protocol that involves several devices sending messages over the same medium only works over distances up to about 10 km. For longer distances, the delay waiting to verify that no other device is using the network becomes unacceptable.

For longer distances, or high data rates, it is necessary to have a single transmitter using the medium, although there may be several receivers using the same medium. (In other words we can have a system like a radio station, with a single transmitter, but many listeners.) For two way communication, we need two media - one in each direction. For example, this might be achieved by using two cables, or two different transmission frequencies.

Computer hardware is moving away from using shared media, since shared access limits the data transfer rate. Modern technologies tend to have a hub, with dedicated lines in each direction connecting each machine to the hub. Thus data can be sent in each direction without the possibility other devices attempting to use the medium at the same time.

Asynchronous Transfer Mode (ATM)

Even with separate lines for transmission in each direction, there are problems with contention at the network level. More than one message might need to be transmitted across the same medium. Problems occur if one packet is in the process of being transmitted over a line, and another higher priority packet arrives on another line. The higher priority packet has to wait for transmission of the lower priority packet to complete. To solve this problem, and simplify the buffering of packets waiting to be processed, modern technologies such as the **ATM protocol** used for telephone switching tend to use **small fixed size packets** (called cells) as the fundamental transmission data unit. The waiting time for high priority data is decreased, since the transmission time for a single cell is small.

If the data is divided into small cells, then the overheads of routing the data through the network increase. To avoid this problem, a **virtual path** is set up before transmission of the data. Each cell header contains a virtual path ID. Each router within the network has a table indicating the outgoing route for each path, simplifying the work of deciding where to send the cell.

Layers Associated with Data Communication Protocols

Getting computers to communicate over a worldwide network is a difficult task. The source code for doing data communications under UNIX is considerably larger than the operating system itself. To design any large computer program, we need to structure the program. A standard way of designing both operating systems and data communication systems is to develop a layered system.

Each level represents a given level of abstraction. The level hides the details of the lower level that we do not wish to see at the current level of abstraction, and provides more abstract services for the higher levels to use.

For example, consider an operating system. Suppose we start with the bare machine, with a single processor. We have no concept of multiple threads and processes. We extend our machine, by writing software to perform context switching and interrupt handling. We now have a virtual machine that appears to support multi-threading. We can now program as if we have many threads running simultaneously, even though they actually run by each taking a time slice in a round robin fashion.

We then add another layer to our virtual machine, to provide memory management, so that we can swap portions of processes out to disk, etc. We now have a virtual machine in which processes do not have to worry about whether they are resident in memory, or swapped out to disk. We add a further layer, to provide inter-process communication. We then add file management, so that we can view the file system as a directory system, with file protection, rather than disks composed of tracks and sectors. We now have the conventional system, as seen by the programmer. Above this we have the system, as seen by a non-programmer, who wishes to use the computer for word processing, etc.

For a data communication protocol, we also divide the system up into levels. In the ISO/OSI (International Standards Organisation/Open Systems Interface) model, the levels correspond to the physical layer, which deals with the transmission of bits; the data link layer, which involves the transmission of packets over a single line; the network layer which involves the transmission of packets between machines over the whole network; the transport layer, which involves the transmission of whole messages between processes over the network; the session layer, which handles a whole remote connection; the presentation layer, which handles data representation and encryption; and the application layer, which handles information in an abstract manner that is independent of the computers or terminals trying to communicate.

As we progress further up the layers, we view the data transferred in a more abstract manner. The details of the lower levels can be ignored. The data link layer does not need to know how bits are represented in the physical layer. The network layer does not need to know how packets are represented in the data link layer. The session layer does not need to know about the network topology, and so on. Similarly, the lower levels do not need to know about the higher levels. For example, the data link layer is purely concerned with sending packets over a single link, and does not need to know about the overall network topology. The network layer needs to know about the network topology, and how to connect to a remote host, but not which process or user the packet is intended for.

As data is transferred down the layers, headers are added for the lower layer. At the physical layer, the data is transferred over the medium to the next machine, and the data is then transferred back up through the layers. Each layer analyses its own header to determine what to do with the information.

The Hardware Layer

Physical Layer - Bit Transmission

The **physical layer** involves the transmission of bits across the medium. When defining the physical layer, we need to specify the physical medium. (Do we use twisted pair, coaxial cable, or microwave, etc? What is the length of the medium, etc?). We need to specify the method of encoding. (For example, we might encode 0 and 1 using different voltage levels or frequencies. We might use a change in voltage or frequency to represent the bit, rather than a voltage or frequency itself.

We might have to perform what is called "bit stuffing" (adding in an extra bit, that is ignored by the receiver) if we get long runs of binary digits that generate a constant signal, to avoid the potential for the receiver becoming confused about the boundaries between successive bits.). The physical layer is probably completely implemented in hardware. The higher level layers do not need to know how bits are represented physically.

Operating System Kernel Layers

Data Link Layer - Packet Transmission between machines connected to the same medium

The data link layer involves the unreliable transmission of packets across the medium. If the checksum disagrees with the rest of the data in the packet, the packet is discarded.

Typical data link layer protocols are the Point to Point Protocol (PPP) over dedicated lines, and the ethernet protocol over a shared medium. The Asynchronous Transfer Mode (ATM) protocol, used over fibre optic telephone cables, can also be considered to be a data link protocol. (It is a bit more complex than this, since it also involves setting up virtual circuits, etc.)

At the data link layer, addresses usually correspond to hardware addresses allocated to the machine by the manufacturer.

In the ethernet protocol, the packet is composed of a synchronisation pattern, destination address, source address, type, data from the network layer packet, followed by a checksum. The end of the packet is detected by lack of signal.

The Network Layer - Packet Routing between machines over a network

There may not be a direct link from one device to another. It may be necessary to route a packet through a number of devices and media to transfer the packet from one device to another. The **network layer** is responsible for routing packets over the network of links, determining a path from one device to another, etc. Problems involved with communication over a network include dealing with different media, protocols, and addressing methods on different paths. Sometimes packets have to be subdivided into smaller packets called frames, which are reassembled again at the other end, since different media require different sized packets.

A typical network layer protocol is the Internet Protocol (IP).

At the network layer, addresses correspond to IP addresses of machines, such as chaos.cs.auckland.ac.nz (in symbolic form) or 130.216.34.26 (in numeric form).

The network layer header is added to the front of the transport layer data. For the internet protocol, this header includes the length of the packet, the time the packet is allowed to live (the packet will be discarded if not delivered by this time), a header checksum, and a source and destination IP address. This header is followed by the data from the transport layer.

The Transport Layer - Reliable message transmission between applications

The transport layer is involved with the reliable transmission of whole messages between applications over a network. For long messages, the message must be divided up into packets, which may be sent by different routes. Short messages may be grouped together. The transport layer must then reconstitute the different parts of the message, when they arrive at the destination - possibly in a different order from the order in which they were received. The services supplied by the transport layer should be network and hardware independent. Thus although the lower level layers will be different for different media and protocols, the higher level layers do not need to know which media are being used for transmission. Nor do they need to know how the devices are networked together.

When a message is transmitted from a source to a destination, the destination should acknowledge the reception of the message. If some packets are lost, a negative acknowledgment should be returned to the source. If the source fails to receive a positive acknowledgment within a given time, the message will be retransmitted. The transport layer must also cope with congestion, and requesting the sender to stop sending. The higher level layers can assume that messages are transmitted in a reliable fashion.

The transport layer usually uses a "sliding window protocol" for acknowledgment. Rather than requiring an acknowledgment after each message, up to a specified number of messages can be sent without waiting for an acknowledgment. This decreases the frequency of delays due to waiting for acknowledgment.

A typical transport layer protocol is the Transmission Control Protocol (TCP) that provides reliable transmission of data. Another transport layer protocol is the User Datagram Protocol (UDP) that provides unreliable transmission of data (used for transmission of sound and video data, where speed is more important than completeness).

At the transport layer, addresses correspond to a port number (for example 23 for telnet, 21 for FTP, 42 for the host name server, 52 for the domain name server, etc).

The transport layer header is added to the user level data. For TCP, the header contains the source and destination port number, a sequence number (which portion of the complete message it is), and various fields relating to acknowledgment of previous messages, willingness to accept future messages, etc, and a checksum. For UDP, the header contains the source and destination port number, length and checksum.

User Level Layers

The divisions between layers at the higher level layers is a bit more hazy (at least from the point of view of data communications experts, who regard the higher levels as outside their domain), and reality does not follow the official divisions with any precision. In the TCP/IP model, all three user level layers are combined into one application layer, and implemented within a user program.

The session and higher layers are internal to protocols such as the File Transfer Protocol (FTP), Hypertext Transfer Protocol (HTTP), Remote Procedure Calls (RPC), Telnet, etc.

The user levels communicate with the operating system via calls to read and write what are called sockets. A socket is essentially a reference to a host and port on a remote machine, and from the users point of view represents a mailbox that messages can be sent to and received from. When a socket is created and bound to an endpoint (by various system calls), an IP address and port number have to be specified.

The Session Layer - Management of sessions

The session layer provides the management of a complete session, dealing with user identification, passwords, etc. The session layer also deals with the establishment of synchronisation points, when transferring large amounts of data. If a system crash occurs, then a file transfer can be restarted at its last synchronization point, rather than having to go back to the beginning again. Telnet, used for remote logins, more or less corresponds to a session layer protocol.

The Presentation Layer - Conversion of data

The presentation layer deals with the presentation of data in a machine independent way. For example, text files might need to be converted, to convert between CR/LF (IBM PC) CR (Macintosh) and LF (UNIX). One machine might represent integers in a big endian format, while another may use a low endian format. Data might need to be encrypted for security reasons, or compressed to decrease the transmission time.

The Application Layer - Machine independent abstraction of information

This layer deals with the abstraction of information about screen layout, file naming and directory lookup, electronic mail format, remote job entry, etc., in a machine independent way.

KEYWORDS

COMPUTER NETWORK	**TRANSMISSION MODE**
ANALOG SIGNALS	**LAN**
DIGITAL SIGNALS	**MAN**
NETWORK SOFTWARE	**WAN**
LOCAL RESOURCE	**PEER-TO-PEER**
REMOTE RESOURCE	**CLIENT/SERVER NETWORK**
WIRED COMMUNICATIONS MEDIA	**PARALLEL DATA TRANSMISSION**
WIRELESS COMMUNICATIONS MEDIA	**SERIAL DATA TRANSMISSION**

SUMMARY

A computer network is an interconnected collection of a group of two or more autonomous computers that are linked together to share information and resources.

- Analog signals are composed of continuous waves transmitted over a medium at a certain frequency range. Changes in the wave transmissions reflect changes in voice and sound pitch, or tone.
- Computers cannot understand data in analog form. Instead, computers use the binary number system to transform data into digital signals. Newer communications technologies generally employ digital signals.

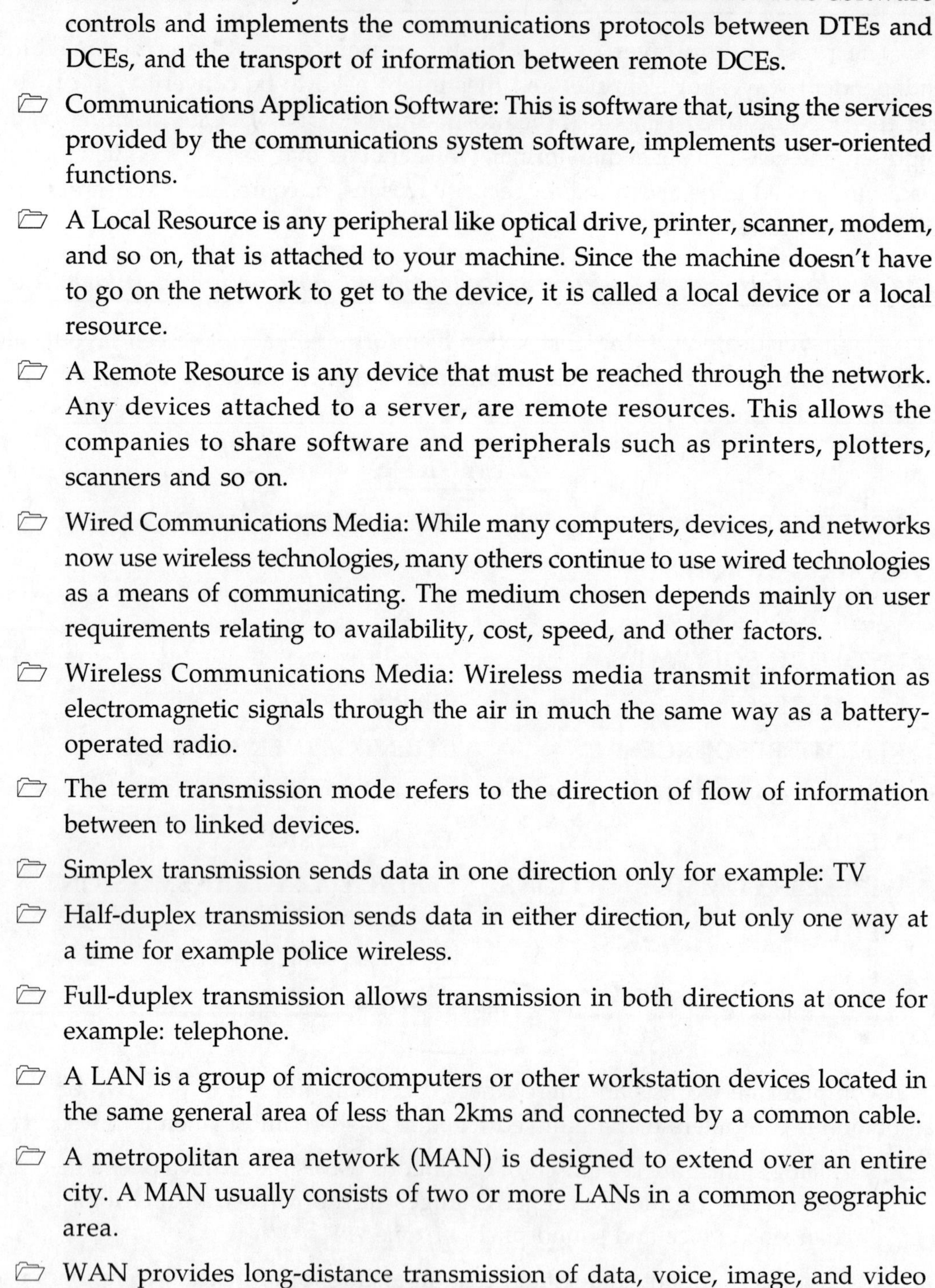

- Communications System Software or Network Software: This software controls and implements the communications protocols between DTEs and DCEs, and the transport of information between remote DCEs.
- Communications Application Software: This is software that, using the services provided by the communications system software, implements user-oriented functions.
- A Local Resource is any peripheral like optical drive, printer, scanner, modem, and so on, that is attached to your machine. Since the machine doesn't have to go on the network to get to the device, it is called a local device or a local resource.
- A Remote Resource is any device that must be reached through the network. Any devices attached to a server, are remote resources. This allows the companies to share software and peripherals such as printers, plotters, scanners and so on.
- Wired Communications Media: While many computers, devices, and networks now use wireless technologies, many others continue to use wired technologies as a means of communicating. The medium chosen depends mainly on user requirements relating to availability, cost, speed, and other factors.
- Wireless Communications Media: Wireless media transmit information as electromagnetic signals through the air in much the same way as a battery-operated radio.
- The term transmission mode refers to the direction of flow of information between to linked devices.
- Simplex transmission sends data in one direction only for example: TV
- Half-duplex transmission sends data in either direction, but only one way at a time for example police wireless.
- Full-duplex transmission allows transmission in both directions at once for example: telephone.
- A LAN is a group of microcomputers or other workstation devices located in the same general area of less than 2kms and connected by a common cable.
- A metropolitan area network (MAN) is designed to extend over an entire city. A MAN usually consists of two or more LANs in a common geographic area.
- WAN provides long-distance transmission of data, voice, image, and video information over large geographical areas that may comprise a country, a continent, or even the whole world.

- A peer-to-peer network model is simply two or more computers linked together, sharing resources such as printer, scanner or Internet connection, and storing files and programs on their own hard drives.
- In a client/server network, at least one computer is designated as a server; that it is a central computer in the network that provides services to clients. A client is a machine that's requesting something from another computer; a server responds to the request with the desired data or service.
- A parallel bus is just a number of parallel wires, together with a protocol for transfer of information on the bus.
- To transmit information over larger distances, the information must be transmitted serially, rather than in parallel. Data is transmitted a bit at a time, in sequence.

REVIEW QUESTIONS

1. What are computer networks? What are the main advantages of computer networks?
2. Explain all the principles and characteristics of computer networks.
3. What are LANs, MANs and WANs? Discuss the characteristics of each.
4. Explain the following:

   i) Transmission modes

   ii) Network topologies

   iii) Network line configuration

   iv) Network architectures
5. Explain wired communications media and wireless communication media in details.
6. Explain the Layers Associated with Data Communication Protocols in details.

FILL IN THE BLANKS

1. the machine doesn't have to go on the network to get to the device then it is called ________
2. A __________is any device that must be reached through the network.
3. The term ____________refers to the direction of flow of information between to linked devices.

4. ____________transmission sends data in either direction, but only one way at a time for example police wireless.

5. A ________is a group of microcomputers or other workstation devices located in the same general area of less than 2kms

6. __________provides long-distance transmission of data, voice, image, and video information over large geographical areas

TRUE OR FALSE

1. A computer network is an interconnected collection of only two autonomous computers that are linked together to share information and resources
2. Simplex transmission sends data in one direction only.
3. Full-duplex transmission allows transmission in both directions one at a time.
4. A metropolitan area network (MAN) is designed to extend over an entire world.
5. To transmit information over larger distances, the information must be transmitted serially, rather than in parallel.
6. Wireless media transmit information as electromagnetic signals through the air in much the same way as a battery-operated radio.

ANSWERS

FILL IN THE BLANKS

1. Local Resource
2. Remote Resource
3. transmission mode
4. Half-duplex
5. LAN
6. WAN

TRUE OR FALSE

1. FALSE
2. TRUE
3. FALSE
4. FALSE
5. TRUE
6. TRUE

❑❑❑

"A distributed system is one in which the failure of a computer you didn't even know existed can render your own computer unusable." —**Leslie Lamport**

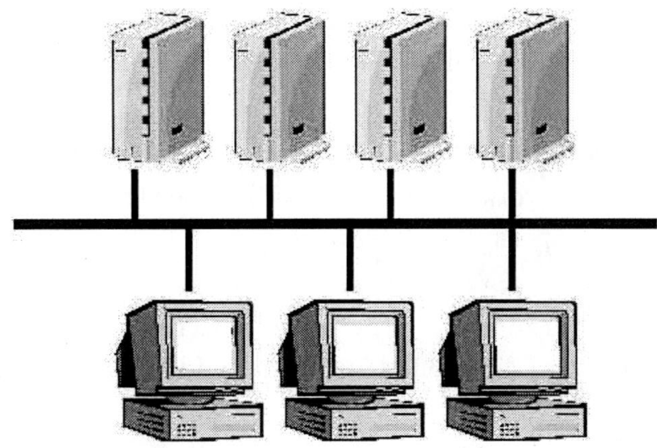

DISTRIBUTED SYSTEMS

INTRODUCTION

Distributed computing deals with hardware and software systems containing more than one processing element or storage element, concurrent processes, or multiple programs, running under a loosely or tightly controlled regime.

What us a distributed system?

A distributed system is any system involving multiple sites connected together into some kind of communication network, in which a user at any site can access data stored at any site.

In distributed computing a program is split up into parts that run simultaneously on multiple computers communicating over a network. Distributed computing is a form of parallel computing, but parallel computing is most commonly used to describe program parts running simultaneously on multiple processors in the same computer. Both types of processing require dividing a program into parts that can run simultaneously, but distributed programs often must deal with heterogeneous environments, network links of varying latencies, and unpredictable failures in the network or the computers.

It combines the efficiency of processing (The data is stored close to the point where it most frequently used) with increased accessibility (it is possible to access a LA account from san Francisco account and vice versa via the communication link)

Generally, The collections of computers working together can be classified one of two ways:

- **Networked systems** are collections of computers that are connected together by some form of network in such a way that users are aware of the different computers that comprise the network.
- **Distributed systems** are collections of computers also connected by some form of network, but in such a way that the user is not aware of the different computers. The entire distributed system should appear as a single computer system.

In practice true distributed systems are difficult to achieve.

Organization

Organizing the interaction between the computers that execute distributed computations is of prime importance. In order to be able to use the widest possible variety of computers, the protocol or communication channel should not contain or use any information that may not be understood by certain machines. Special care must also be taken that messages are indeed delivered correctly and that invalid messages, which would otherwise bring down the system and perhaps the rest of the network, are rejected.

Another important factor is the ability to send software to another computer in a portable way so that it may execute and interact with the existing network. This may not always be practical when using differing hardware and resources, in which case other methods, such as cross-compiling or manually porting this software, must be used.

Goals and advantages

There are many different types of distributed computing systems and many challenges to overcome in successfully designing one. The main goal of a distributed computing system is to connect users and resources in a transparent, open, and scalable way. Ideally this arrangement is drastically more fault tolerant and more powerful than many combinations of stand-alone computer systems. The advantages of Distributed System are as follows

a) Compared to centralized systems:

- better price/performance than mainframe
- more total computing power

- sum of the computing power of the processors in the distributed system may be greater than any single processor available (parallel processing)
- some applications are inherently distibuted
- improved reliability because system can survive crash of one processor
- incremental growth can be achieved by adding one processor at a time
- shared ownership facilitated

b) Compared to isolated PCs:

- shared management of system
- backups
- maintenance: download new software
- data sharing: many users can access a shared database
- device sharing: share expensive peripherals
- communication between users easier (e.g., electronic mail)
- flexibility: spread workload over machines (the jobs are not necessarily run on the owner's machine)

The advantages and goals are categorized as under:

1. **Local autonomy**:

   Let individual group to exercise local control over their own data.

2. **Reliability and Availability**:

It can continue to function (at a reduced level) in the face of a failure of an individual site or individual communication link between sites. And if data is replicated, availability is improved also because a given data object remains available so long as one copy of that object is available.

3. Efficiency and Flexibility:

Data can be stored close to its normal point of use thus reducing both response times and communication cost (most access is local) And if the usage pattern changes then data can be dynamically moved or replicated or deleted.

4. Openness

Openness is the property of distributed systems such that each subsystem is continually open to interaction with other systems. Web Services protocols are standards which enable distributed systems to be extended and scaled. In general, an open system that scales has an advantage over a perfectly closed and self-contained system.

Consequently, open distributed systems are required to meet the following challenges:

- **Monotonicity**

  Once something is published in an open system, it cannot be taken back.

- **Pluralism**
  Different subsystems of an open distributed system include heterogeneous, overlapping and possibly conflicting information. There is no central arbiter of truth in open distributed systems.
- **Unbounded nondeterminism**
  Asynchronously, different subsystems can come up and go down and communication links can come in and go out between subsystems of an open distributed system. Therefore the time that it will take to complete an operation cannot be bounded in advance.

Drawbacks and disadvantages

The major disadvantages of distributed systems are

1. software may not be available
2. networks can become saturated (may need additional wiring)
3. security problems protecting data (only an isolated machine is safe)
4. incremental growth is difficult in practice because of changing hardware and software

Other Technical issues

If not planned properly, a distributed system can decrease the overall reliability of computations if the unavailability of a node can cause disruption of the other nodes. Leslie Lamport famously quipped that: "A distributed system is one in which the failure of a computer you didn't even know existed can render your own computer unusable."[1]

Troubleshooting and diagnosing problems in a distributed system can also become more difficult, because the analysis may require connecting to remote nodes or inspecting communication between nodes.

Many types of computation are not well suited for distributed environments, typically owing to the amount of network communication or synchronization that would be required between nodes. If bandwidth, latency, or communication requirements are too significant, then the benefits of distributed computing may be negated and the performance may be worse than a non-distributed environment.

Architecture of distributed Systems

Various hardware and software architectures are used for distributed computing. At a lower level, it is necessary to interconnect multiple CPUs with some sort of network, regardless of whether that network is printed onto a circuit board or made up of loosely-coupled devices and cables. At a higher level, it is necessary to interconnect processes running on those CPUs with some sort of communication system.

Distributed programming typically falls into one of several basic architectures or categories: Client-server, 3-tier architecture, N-tier architecture, Distributed objects, loose coupling, or tight coupling.

- **Client-server**

  Smart client code contacts the server for data, then formats and displays it to the user. Input at the client is committed back to the server when it represents a permanent change.

- **3-tier architecture** —

  Three tier systems move the client intelligence to a middle tier so that stateless clients can be used. This simplifies application deployment. Most web applications are 3-Tier.

- **N-tier architecture**

  N-Tier refers typically to web applications which further forward their requests to other enterprise services. This type of application is the one most responsible for the success of application servers.

- **Tightly coupled** (clustered)

  refers typically to a cluster of machines that closely work together, running a shared process in parallel. The task is subdivided in parts that are made individually by each one and then put back together to make the final result.

- **Peer-to-peer**

  an architecture where there is no special machine or machines that provide a service or manage the network resources. Instead all responsibilities are uniformly divided among all machines, known as peers. Peers can serve both as clients and servers.

- **Space based**

  refers to an infrastructure that creates the illusion (virtualization) of one single address-space. Data are transparently replicated according to application needs. Decoupling in time, space and reference is achieved.

Another basic aspect of distributed computing architecture is the method of communicating and coordinating work among concurrent processes. Through various message passing protocols, processes may communicate directly with one another, typically in a master/slave relationship. Alternatively, a "database-centric" architecture can enable distributed computing to be done without any form of direct inter-process communication, by utilizing a shared database.

CHALLENGES FOR DISTRIBUTED SYSTEMS

1. Heterogeneity:
   Variety and differences in networks, computer hardware, operating systems, programming languages, and implementations by different developers

- **Middleware**: software layer that provides a programming abstraction as well as masking the heterogeneity of the underlying systems (networks, hardware, operating systems, and programming languages): e.g., CORBA and Java RMI.
- **Mobile code**: code that can be sent from one computer to another and run at the destination; e.g., Java applets.

2. Openness:
   System made extensible by publishing the specification and documentation for key software interfaces, i.e. made available to software developers.
3. Security:
   Confidentiality (protection against disclosure to unauthorized individuals), integrity (protection against alteration or corruption), and availability (protection against interference with the means to access the resource).

- **Denial of service attacks:** bombard a service with such a large number of pointless requests that serious users are unable to use it.

4. Scalability:
   System will remain effective if there is a significant increase in the number of resources and users

- Cost of physical resources should O(n) for n users, performance on lookup tasks should be no worse than O(log n) for data of size n, software resources shouldn't run out, and performance bottlenecks should be avoided.
- Techniques for avoiding bottlenecks: distributed algorithms; caching, replication, and other forms of distributed data; e.g., multiple servers.

5. Failure Handling:
   Failure may be partial in a distributed system because some components may fail while others continue processing.

- Techniques are needed for failure detection, failure masking, failure tolerance (by software and users), and recovery from failure.
- Use of redundant components is crucial to failure handling: e.g., multiple routes, Domain Name Servers, and databases.

6. Concurrency:
   Allowing requests from several clients to be processed such that they are in between starting and finishing at the same time

- Operations on any object in a distributed environment must be synchronized such that the object's data remains consistent

7. Transparency:
   Concealment from the user and application programmer of the separation of components in a distributed system , so that the system is perceived as a whole rather than as a collection of independent components.

TYPES OF TRANSPARENCY

1. **Location Transparency**
   Users can not tell where resources such as CPUs, printers, files, and database are located
   also cannot tell where other users are located
2. **Migration Transparency** (replaced by Mobility Transparency in CDK)
   Resources can be moved from one location to another without their names changing
   e.g., files or printers moving between servers
3. **Replication Transparency**
   Users don't need to know how many copies of resources are available
   e.g., files
4. **Concurrency Transparency**
   System ensures resources are accessed in a sequential manner (at some level of detail)

➢ users do not have to consider other users
➢ a more elaborate scheme than simple file locking

5. **Parallelism Transparency** (absorbed into Replication Transparency)
   Computer, runtime system and OS make use of all processors available without explicit coding by user
   e.g., same executable creates more parallel processes when more processors are available

Major features of distributed computing

Concurrency

Distributed computing implements a kind of concurrency. It interrelates tightly with concurrent programming so much that they are sometimes not taught as distinct subjects [3].

Multiprocessor systems

A multiprocessor system is simply a computer that has more than one CPU on its motherboard. If the operating system is built to take advantage of this, it can run different processes (or different threads belonging to the same process) on different CPUs.

Multicore systems

Intel CPUs from the late Pentium 4 era (Northwood and Prescott cores) employed a technology called Hyperthreading that allowed more than one thread (usually two) to run on the same CPU. The more recent Sun UltraSPARC T1, AMD Athlon 64 X2, AMD Athlon FX, AMD Opteron, Intel Pentium D, Intel Core, Intel Core 2 and Intel Xeon processors feature multiple processor cores to also increase the number of concurrent threads they can run.

Multicomputer systems

A multicomputer may be considered to be either a loosely coupled NUMA computer or a tightly coupled cluster. Multicomputers are commonly used when strong compute power is required in an environment with restricted physical space or electrical power.

Common suppliers include Mercury Computer Systems, CSPI, and SKY Computers.

Common uses include 3D medical imaging devices and mobile radar.

Computing taxonomies

The types of distributed systems are based on Flynn's taxonomy of systems; single instruction, single data (SISD), single instruction, multiple data (SIMD), multiple instruction, single data (MISD), and multiple instruction, multiple data (MIMD)..

Computer clusters

A cluster consists of multiple stand-alone machines acting in parallel across a local high speed network. Distributed computing differs from cluster computing in that computers in a distributed computing environment are typically not exclusively running "group" tasks, whereas clustered computers are usually much more tightly coupled. Distributed computing also often consists of machines which are widely separated geographically.

Grid computing

A grid uses the resources of many separate computers, loosely connected by a network (usually the Internet), to solve large-scale computation problems. Public grids may use idle time on many thousands of computers throughout the world. Such arrangements permit handling of data that would otherwise require the power of expensive supercomputers or would have been impossible to analyze.

Languages

Nearly any programming language that has access to the full hardware of the system could handle distributed programming given enough time and code. Remote procedure calls distribute operating system commands over a network connection. Systems like CORBA, Microsoft DCOM, Java RMI and others, try to map object oriented design to the network. Loosely coupled systems communicate through intermediate documents that are typically human readable (e.g. XML, HTML, SGML, X.500, and EDI).

Characteristics of distributed systems

The three significant characteristics of a Distributed System are:

1. **Concurrency**:
   In a realistic distributed system, multiple processes run at the same time. For example, while your web browser is downloading content from a web server, it may also be determining how to present the content to you on the screen. Meanwhile, the web server is loading content from disk to send across the internet to you. A key complexity with concurrency is handling shared access to resources. For example, if you want to access a file on the internet at the same time that one of your friends does, there may need to be mechanisms in place to ensure that any conflicts in accessing the file are resolved. Consider the case where both you and your friend try to edit the file at the same time.

- concurrency: several processes are in between starting and finishing at the same time
- parallelism: several processes are executing at the same time

2. **No global clock**
   The Synchronization is in time. Very often, in a realistic distributed program, components and processes must synchronize and coordinate their activities. For example, consider the SABRE system that we briefly mentioned ear- lier. It allows travel agents to find and book flights for customers. Clearly, there must be a notion of time in SABRE, so that if one travel agent say, based in London— books a ticket at 09:00 GMT, that ticket cannot be booked by a travel agent —based in Paris— at 10:05 CET. This simple example demonstrates that synchronization and coordination of activities often depends on some notion of time at which activities occur. There are, of course, limits on the accuracy of clocks (just think about how accurate your own watch is). There are also limits on the accuracy with which clocks on a network can synchronize.

- limits to how closely computers can synchronize their clocks

3. **Independent failures**
   In a distributed system that relies on independent components, it is an unhappy reality that these components can fail (e.g., due to errors in software, or hardware faults, or erroneous input from the outside world), and that the overall system has little, if any control over how and when these

components will fail. A designer of a distributed sys- tem is therefore responsible for anticipating that components will fail, and compensating for potential failures in the overall system. Having a distributed system that can cope with component failures —i.e., having a dependable distributed system— is of substantial importance in many domains, for example, the bank machine system discussed earlier.

- any component of the network can fail and software must deal with this

Reliability of a Distributed System

The three components of reliability are availability, security, and fault tolerance

1. availability
- the fraction of the time the system is usable
- try to reduce dependence between servers because this increases the chance that the user can still do something
- to improve availability, key components should be replicated
2. security
- must authenticate every message in a distributed OS
- can't trust id field in a message
- should also encrypt contents to prevent snooping on the network
- Secure Sockets Layer (SSL) provides this type of security
3. fault tolerance
- refers to the general ability of the system to tolerate errors
- most often achieved by having multiple instances of a resource
- server should be able to crash and recover without affecting service
- may want to reject the request that caused crash
- should be able to vary number by choice
- performance degrades when one crashes or is removed from service
- perhaps if one crashes, others should take over its work queue

Grid Computing, Computing on Demand, Computing as an Utility

Computing is changing both in the size of problems tackled and in the organizations and processes through which it is carried out. Grid computing is intended to address such problems that are beyond the reach of any single supercomputer. In grid computing computation takes place across totally independent computer systems, each with its own administration and control. Enormous obstacles in message passing, load balancing, reliability, and especially security need to be addressed and solved. Computer systems may participate in a way totally transparent to their users, taking advantage of unused machine-cycles and storage.

If such obstacles can be overcome, it may become possible to accomplish the vision of **Computing as a Utility** or **Computing on Demand** that some are suggesting: each user with its local limited equipment can access reliably and securely as much computing/storage power as it needs at a each moment, and pay in accordance to use.

Middleware

Distributed systems are developed on top of existing networking and operating systems software. They are not easy to build and maintain. To simplify their development and maintenance a new layer of software, called **Middleware,** is being developed, following agreed standards and protocols, to provide standard services such as naming (association of entities and identifiers, directory services (maintaining the association of attributes to entities), persistence, concurrency control, event distribution, authorization, security. Examples of such services that you may be familiar with are the Distributed Name Service (DNS) with associated protocol, the Internet Network Time service with the Network Time Protocol (NTP), transaction servers, etc. The following diagram indicates the architecture of distributed systems. Notice that the box we have called networking is itself decomposed into layers as we will see when we discuss networking issues.

Client-Server Architecture

We receive snail mail thanks to the post office **service**. But to us the service is provided by a specific mailman, a **server**. As users, our interest is in services, to identify what services are available and where are the servers that support each

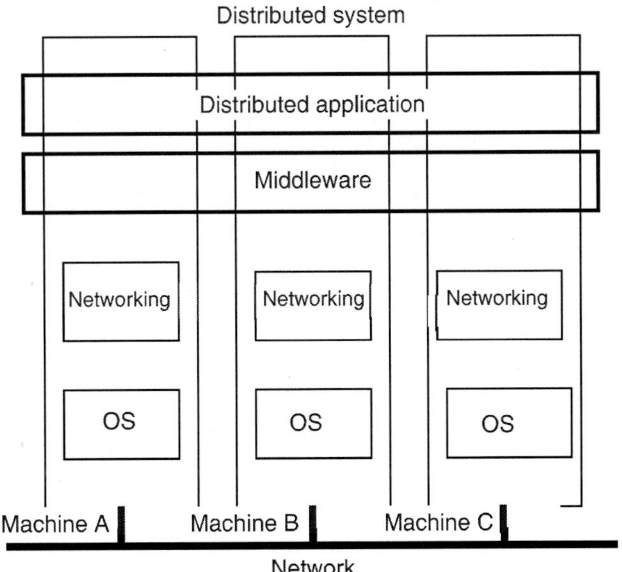

service. So usually we need an "Identification/Discovery or Naming Service" that will provide us with the identities of the available services, their properties, and their servers [and we need to know at least one server of the "identification/discovery service"]. The problem of characterizing services, in terms of who they are, what they do, and where they are accessible is of great current interest. A number of efforts address this problem.

A typical way in which people organize distributed applications is represented by the **Client-Server Model**. In this model a program at some node acts as a **Server** which provides some **Service**, things like a Name Service, a File Service, a Data Base Service, etc. The Client sends requests to the Server and receives replies from it. The Server can be **Stateful** or **Stateless**, i.e. may remember information across different requests from the same client. The Server can be **local**, i.e. on the same system as its clients, or **remote**, i.e. accessed over a network.

The Server can be **iterative** or **concurrent**. In the former case it processes one request at a time, in the latter it can service a number of requests at the same time, for example by forking a separate process to handle each requests. In a concurrent server, the processes or threads that handle the individual requests are called **slaves** of the server. These slaves may be created "on demand" when a request is received, and deleted when the request has been handled. Or they may be "preallocated" into a pool of slaves when the server is started, available to handle future requests. And the size of this pool can be made adaptive to the load on the server.

Also the Client could be **iterative** or **concurrent**, depending if it can make requests to different servers sequentially or concurrently.

Often the interaction from the client to the server is using **Remote Procedure Calls** (RPC), or using **Remote Method Invocation (RMI)**, or using CORBA, SOAP, web services... Note that the way we interact with an object, by calling one of its methods, is a typical client-server interaction, where the object is the server. Thus **distributed objects** fit within the client-server architecture. An objects, at different times, may play the role of server or the role of client. In fact an object can act at one time as a server (responding to a request) and as a client (requesting service from a third object as part of implementing its own service).

In the Client-Server Architecture the initiative lays with the client. The server is always there at a known endpoint waiting for requests, it only responds to requests

A **Peer-to-Peer Architecture** instead emphasizes that the interaction initiative may lay with any object and all objects may be fairly equivalent in terms of resources and responsibilities. In the client-server architecture usually most of the resources and responsibilities lay with the servers. The clients (if **Thin Clients**) may just be responsible for the Presentation Layer to the user and for network communications.

A few more words about Stateful vs Stateless servers. A stateless server will tend to be more reliable since, if it crashes, the next interaction will be accepted directly, not rejected , since it is not part of an interrupted session. Also, the stateless server will require less resources in the server since no state needs to be preserved across multiple requests. Hence the stateless server is both more reliable and more scalable than a stateful server. A stateful server, in turn, is usually with higher performance since the state information can be used to speed up processing of requests.

A further distinction when talking of the "state" of a server, is between **Hard-state** and **Soft-state**. Hard-state is true state, in the sense that if it is lost because of a crash, we are lost: the server interaction has to be fully re-initialized. Instead soft-state if lost it can be reconstructed. In other words, it is a **Hint** that improves the performance of a server when it is available. But, if lost, the state can be recomputed. For example, the NFS server could maintain for each recent request information on user, cursor position, etc. Then if another request arrives from that user for that file, this state information can be used to speed up access. If this 'state" information is lost or becomes stale, then it can be reconstructed because an NSF request carries all the information required to satisfy it. Note that a server with soft-state is really just a stateless server.

The stateful/stateless distinction is used also when talking of protocols used in the interaction client/server. So we talk of **Stateful or Stateless Protocols**. HTTP, the protocol used for www interactions, is stateless, since its response to requests are independent of each other, and so is the web server. Also the Network File System (NFS) protocol is stateless. It deals with accessing files made available by a server on a network. All requests are made as if no Open file command was available, thus the requests must explicitly state in the request the name of the file and the position of the cursor. Instead the File Transfer Protocol (FTP) is stateful since a session is established and requests made in context, for example, the current working directory.

Though HTTP is stateless, it can be made stateful by having the clients preserve state information and sending it to the server at the time requests are made. This is the role played by **cookies**. When the client sends a request, it can provide the state information (the cookie) with the Cookie header. When the server responds, it places in the header, with the Set-Cookie header, the state, appropriately updated [For a dark view of the role of cookies, see CookieCentral. Part of the danger is that where normally the cookie is specific to the interaction between a specific client and a specific server, **first-party cookie**, (as when I fetch a page form a specific location, say moo) it is also possible to have **third-party cookies**, that is cookies that collect information across multiple servers and give it to a hidden server. (For example, the page i fetch from moo may hide a request to a one-pixel image that is fetched from the third-party.)]. The fact that the state is kept in the client makes the server more scalable since no space has to be devoted to the clients's state. Also, if the server crashes, then the client's state is not affected. For a technical discussion of cookies and their use in state management see rfc2109 (in particular, examine the two examples of client-server interaction). Remember, cookies are manipulated at the server but stored at the client.

When servers require the power of many computer systems two architectures are common.

One architecture uses **vertical distribution**, arranging computers on a number of **tiers**, usually three. This is the **3-tier architecture**: The tier where user interactions take place, the **presentation tier**; The tier where user requests are received and analysed, the **application tier**; The tier where data is preseved and manipulated, the **data tier**. Upon receiving a user request appropriate interactions take place between the application tier and the data tier. They result in the development within the application tier of the response to be sent to the presentation tier.

The other architecture uses **horizontal distribution** between a number of equivalent, fully functional servers. User requests are routed, usually in round-robin fashion or hashed on the basis of the requesting IP address, to one of the available servers. This architecture is often used by heavily loaded web servers.

PEER-TO-PEER ARCHITECTURE

Let's start with two examples of peer-to-peer (**P2P**) systems. Napster is a system for sharing files, usually audio files, between different systems. These systems are peers of each other in that any of them may request a file hosted by another system. The system has a central service used for the discovery of desired files, i.e. for helping a peer identify peers where are available desired files.

Instant Messaging is the capability of a system to send a message to another currently running system. Again a central service may be used to determine which systems are currently present as potential targets for delivery of an instant message. Notice that in both cases we have systems, peers, that have all similar capabilities and can provide services to, or interact with, each other. And we have a central service that helps the peers find each other. This central element [which is available in the form of traditional server] improves the performance of the system as a whole, but it is not strictly necessary since the peers could find each other through a search started from neighbors and propagated as an oil spot

Now we have a general idea of what are peer-to-peer systems. They seem to use two basic ideas: a service to determine which user agents [this means any entity intended to be able to exchange messages] are currently online = a **presence** service; and a service for delivering immediately a message to a currently active user agent = an **instant message** service.

An interesting P2P system is BitTorrent. Now we are interested in downloading a movie from a server without overwhelming the server when multiple clients are downloading the same movie. So the movie is divided in segments and the clients become servers themselves for the segments they have downloaded.

Interactions

We have seen two important distictions on the interactions taking place between two interacting systems

- stateful vs stateless, and
- push vs pull.

  Here some other important distinctions
- synchronous vs asynchronous: whether the communicating entities must be both present and active (as when we talk on the phone), or they do not need to be (as with snail-mail, or on the phone with answering machine)
- time-assured vs time-insensitive: whether there are or not deadlines on the delivery of messages
- best-effort vs reliable: for example, snail-mail is best-effort, i.e. the post service does all it can to deliver the mail, but it may be lost; instead federal express type services make sure that there is delivery receipt
- message vs stream, that is the participants send and receive full messages or they send and receive sequences of characters without apriori subdivisions. "message" usually is in a connectionless interaction, where the sender and receiver interact only for the duration of the individual message. "stream" instead is in a connection oriented interaction, where sender and receiver exchange data for a time (from when the connection is set up to when it is torn down).

More on RPC

One set of primitives to build distributed applications is ***send*** and ***receive***, which can be used to synchronize cooperating threads running on different machines. Send and receive communicate messages through ***mailboxes*** (ports), which are temporary holding areas for messages. Send and receive are atomic operations. Therefore, they will either send/receive the entire message or nothing, and two receivers cannot get the same message.

To put a message to the network, a thread invokes send with a message and the destination mailbox. Receive waits until a message arrives, and copies the message into a given buffer.

```
send(message, dest_mbox);
receive(buffer, mbox);
```

Remote Procedure Call

Remote procedure call (RPC), literally, allows you to invoke a procedure on either a local or a remote machine transparently. A client's call is translated into a call on the remote machine.

Client

RemoteFileSystem→Write("yaddy yadda");

Server

FileSystem→Write("yaddy yadda");

RPC is implemented on the top of two-way messaging, with *procedure stubs* on both the client and the server. These ***procedure stubs*** merely provide the invocation interface for programmers (e.g., foo(int a)). The actual implementations of those procedures are defined remotely.

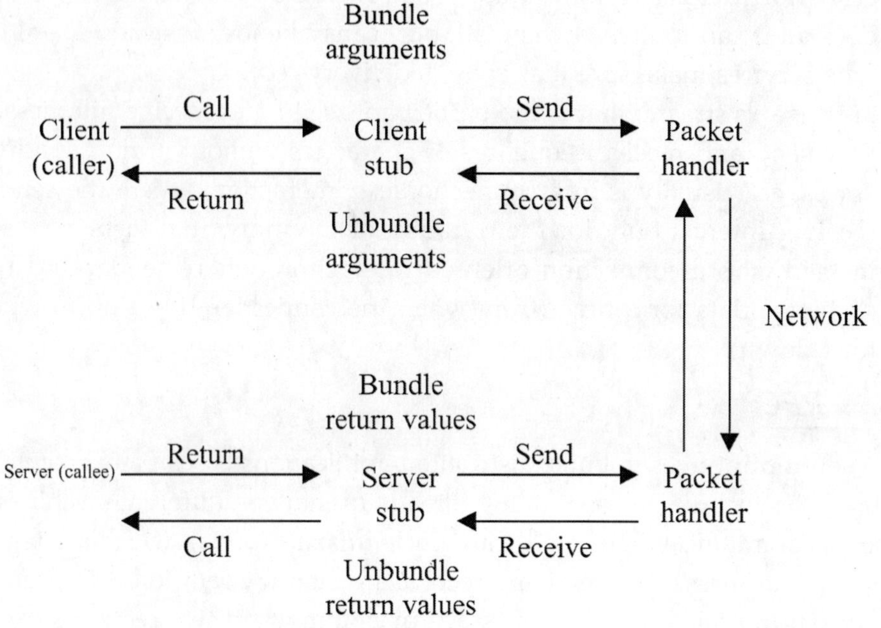

The client stub basically performs the following:

- Build messages (also known as ***marshalling***)
- Send messages
- Wait for response
- Unpack reply
- Return result

The server stub performs the following:

- Create N threads to wait for requests
- Loop:
- Wait for command
- Decode and unpack request parameters (***unmarshalling***)
- Call procedure
- Build replay message with results
- Send reply

Comparison between RPC and Procedure Call

From the programmer's viewpoint, invoking a remote procedure call should be similar to invoking a local procedure call. Parameters of a procedure call are transmitted in the request message. Results of the procedure call are in the reply message. The name of the remote procedure is passed in the requested message by the client's stub.

However, when passing pointers, since the process running on the remote machine is in a different address space, calling RPC requires copying the data structure pointed by the pointer to the remote procedure.

Implementation Issues

The stubs are automatically generated. A client does not know which port to use until the runtime. Therefore, the client needs to have a well-known port for either a server, or a procedure name server that determines which server to contact.

Since the actual implementation of a procedure is located at the server side, a server can upgrade the implementation without recompiling client applications.

Inter-Process Communication

In addition to file systems, shared memory, and pipes, RPC is another way to communicate between address spaces on different machines, or on the same machine. An example use of RPC on the local machine is the ***microkernel operating system***, which partitions the operating system into several application-level servers to minimize the kernel-level code.

By separating the operating system so that different services run in separate address spaces, we gain the following benefits:

- Fault isolation—bugs are less likely to propagate across different address spaces.
- Modularity—each piece of operating system can be upgraded independently.
- ***Location transparency***—a service can be provided either from the local or remote machines.

Another example of using RPC on the local machine is ***OLE*** (object linking and embedding), which allows you to mix and match application components.

Problems with RPC

The failure semantics of RPC in the distributed environment is different from that of local procedure calls. RPC has to handle the following kinds of failures:

- A user-level bug can cause a process failure.
- A kernel-level bug can cause multiple processes to fail.
- A network failure, server failure, or an earthquake can cause multiple machines to fail.

The second concern is the performance. Local procedure calls are faster than local RPC, which is faster than remote RPC. Therefore, a programmer cannot completely treat RPC as local procedure calls.

Software for Distributed Systems

- determines user view of system
- loosely connected software: gives view that there are many machines
- tightly coupled software: organizes system for single task

Types of Software for Distributed Systems

a) Network Operating System
- loosely connected software on loosely connected hardware (multicomputer)
- network of workstations or PC's
- each machine running an OS; the OSes may even differ
- e.g., our lab of Linux machines

b) Integrated Distributed System
- tightly coupled software on loosely coupled hardware
- runs on a collection of shared machines that do not have shared memory yet work like one computer
- we don't have one
- we had a package called Xpress that gave many of these features, but it silently disappeared because no one used it

c) Multiprocessor Timesharing System

0. tightly coupled software on tightly coupled hardware
1. e.g., UNIX machine with several processors
2. shared memory
3. one short-term scheduler queue (kept in shared memory)
4. e.g., Grendel (24 processor SGI super computer)

Performance of a Distributed System

1. measures:
   - response time
   - number of jobs per hour
   - system utilization
   - fraction of network capacity
2. strongly affected by messaging delays
   - transmission time
   - protocol handling
3. must distribute inherently distributed computations. i.e. info sharing among users
4. perhaps best addressed by grain size of computation
   - distribute computations with course-grained parallelism (large computations, low interaction rates, little data)
   - don't distribute computations with fine-grained parallelism (small computations, interact with one another)

Distributed File System

A distributed file system (DFS) is a distributed implementation of the classical time-sharing model of a file system, where multiple users share files and storage resources. The purpose of a DFS is to support the same kind of sharing when the files are physically dispersed among the various sites of a distributed system.

In the context of operating systems, a file system is the part of the operating system responsible for managing files and directory structures. Traditional file systems are local to an individual machine. T

A distributed file system is a network file system where a single file system can be distributed across several physical computer nodes.

Separate nodes have direct access to only a part of the entire file system, in contrast to shared disk file systems where all nodes have uniform direct access to the entire storage.

Distributed file systems generally include facilities for transparent replication and fault tolerance. That is, when a limited number of nodes in a file system go offline, the system continues to work without any data loss.

To explain the structure of a DFS, we need to define the terms service, saw, and client. A service is a software entity running on one or more machines and providing a particular type of function to a priori unknown clients. A server is the service software running on a single machine. A client is a process that can invoke a service using a set of operations that forms its client interface. Sometimes, a lower-level interface is defined for the actual cross-machine interaction, which we refer to as the inter-machine interface.

Using the terminology we have defined above, we say that a file system provides file services to clients. A client interface for a file service is formed by a set of primitive file operations, such as create a file, delete a file, read from a file, and write to a file. The primary hardware component that a file server controls is a set of local secondary-storage devices (usually, magnetic disks), on which files are stored, and from which they are retrieved according to the client requests.

A DFS is a file system whose clients, servers, and storage devices are dispersed among the machines of a distributed system. Accordingly, service activity has to be carried out across the network, and instead of a single centralized data repository, there are multiple and independent storage devices.

As will become evident, the concrete configuration and implementation of a DFS may vary. There are configurations where servers run on dedicated machines, as well as configurations where a machine can be both a server and a client. A DFS can be implemented as part of a distributed operating system, of alternatively by a software layer whose task is to manage the communicational between conventional operating systems and file systems. The distinctive features of a DFS are the multiplicity and autonomy of clients and servers.

Ideally, a DFS should look to its clients like a conventional, centralized file system. The multiplicity and dispersion of its servers and storage device should be made transparent. That is, the client interface of a DFS should not distinguish between local and remote files. It is up to the DFS to locate the file and to arrange for the transport of the data. A transparent DFS facilitates use mobility by bringing over the user's environment (that is, home directory) wherever a user log's in.

The most important performance measurement of a DFS is the amount of time needed to satisfy various service requests. In conventional systems, time consists of disk access time and a small amount of CPU processing time.

In a DFS, however, a remote access has the additional overhead attributed the distributed structure. This overhead includes the time needed to deliver the request to a server, as well as the time for getting the response across network back to the client. For each direction, in addition to the actual time of the information, there is the CPU overhead of running the communication protocol software. The performance of a DFS can be viewed as another dimension of the DFS's transparency.

The fact that a DFS manages a set of dispersed storage devices is the DFS's key distinguishing feature. The overall storage space managed by a DFS is composed of different, and remotely located, smaller storage spaces. Usually, there is correspondence between these constituent storage spaces and sets of files. We use the term component unit to denote the smallest set of files that I can be stored on a single machine, independently from other units. All files belonging to the same component unit must reside in the same location.

The difference between a distributed file system and a distributed data store can be vague, but DFSes are generally geared towards use on local area networks.

The file system provides an interface between the operating system and the device drivers for the disks. At this level, the file system is concerned with the following things:

1. Physical layout on the disk

The disk is logically thought of as an array of sectors or blocks, which the individual device drivers map onto the physical disks. Often some parts of the disk are reserved for super blocks or other structures that hold information required by the file system.

Another issue is the method by which space for files is allocated and addressed on the disk (contiguous, linked, indexed, etc.).

2. Structure of the directory files

Most modern file systems use the concept of directories or folders to allow user files to be organized in a logical, useful way. The file system defines the structure of these files and is responsible for maintaining them

3. How the file space is seen by the operating system

The entire file system space can be viewed by the operating system in several different ways:

a. User is aware of physical disks and/or devices

A file on these systems is usually specified by both a disk and a directory, such as DISK: DIRECTORY/FILE.

In this type of system the user knows that the file he or she wants is on a particular logical disk. For example, on MS-DOS and it's derivatives drives are referred to with A:, B:, C:, etc. Actually, in many cases its not physical disks that are being referred to, but disk partitions, which can be thought of as logical disks.

b. Physical devices are hidden from user

The Unix file system is conceptually a single tree regardless of how many physical disks comprise it. The disks are **mounted** at particular points called **mount points** in the tree. These mount points must be previously existing directories whose contents are unavailable as long as a disk is mounted over them.

It is usually possible to find out exactly where a particular file actually resides, but the user has to search this information out and is not normally required to know it.

The goal of a distributed file system (DFS) is to provide access to files on multiple computers in a way similar to how files on the local computer are accessed.

Naming and Transparency

Naming is a mapping between logical and physical objects. For instance, users deal with logical data objects represented by file names, whereas the system manipulates physical blocks of data, stored on disk tracks. Usually, a user refers to a file by a textual name. The latter is mapped to a lower-level numerical identifier that in turn is mapped to disk blocks. This multilevel mapping provides users with an abstraction of a file that hides the details of how and where on the disk the file is actually stored.

In a transparent DFS, a new dimension is added to the abstraction: that of hiding where in the network the file is located. In a conventional file system, range of the naming mapping is an address within a disk. In a DFS, this range is augmented to include the specific machine on whose disk the file is stored. Going one step further with the concept of treating files as abstractions leads to the possibility of file replication. Given a file name, the mapping returns a set of the locations of this file's replicas. In this abstraction, both the existence of multiple copies and their location are hidden.

Naming Structures

There are two related notions regarding name mappings in a DFS that need to be differentiated:

- Location transparency: The name of a file does not reveal any hint of the file's physical storage location.
- Location independence: The name of a file does not need to be changed when the file's physical storage location changes.

Both definitions are relative to the level of naming discussed previously, since files have different names at different levels (that is, user-level textual names, and system-level numerical identifiers). A location-independent naming scheme is a dynamic mapping, since it can map the same file name to different locations at two different times. Therefore, location independence is a stronger property than is location transparency.

In practice, most of the current DFSs provide a static, location-transparent mapping for user-level names. These systems, however, do not support file migration; that is, changing the location of a file automatically is impossible. Hence, the notion of location independence is quite irrelevant for these systems.

Files are associated permanently with a specific set of disk blocks. Files and disks can be moved between machines manually, but file migration implies an automatic, operating-system initiated action. r requests, without changing either the user-level names, or the low-level

There are a few aspects that can further differentiate location independence and static location transparency: Divorcing data from location, as exhibited by location independence, provides better abstraction for files. A file name should denote the files. Most significant attributes, which are its contents, rather than its location. Location-independent files can be viewed as logical data containers that are not attached to a specific storage location. If only static location transparency is supported, the file name still denotes a specific, although hidden, set of physical disk blocks.

Static location transparency provides users with a convenient way to share data. Users can share remote files by simply naming the files in a location-transparent manner, as though the files were local. Nevertheless, sharing the storage space is cumbersome, because logical names are still statically attached to physical storage devices. Location independence promotes sharing the storage space itself, as well as the data objects. When files can be mobilized, the overall, system-wide storage space looks like a single, virtual resource. A possible benefit of such a view is the ability to balance the utilization of disks across the system.

Location independence separates the naming hierarchy from the storage-devices hierarchy and from the inter-computer structure. By contrast, if static location transparency is used (although names are transparent), we can easily expose the correspondence between component units and machines. The machines are configured in a pattern similar to the naming structure. This may restrict the architecture of the system unnecessarily and conflict with other considerations. A server in charge of a root directory is an example of a structure that is dictated by the naming hierarchy and contradicts decentralization guidelines.

Once the separation of name and location has been completed, files residing on remote server systems may be accessed by various clients. In fact, these clients may be diskless and rely on servers to provide all files, including the operating-system kernel. Special protocols are needed for the boot sequence, however. Consider the problem of getting the kernel to a diskless workstation. The diskless workstation has no kernel, so it cannot use the DFS code to retrieve the kernel. Instead, a special boot protocol, stored in read-only memory (ROM) on the client, is invoked. It enables networking and retrieves only one special file (the kernel or boot code) from a fixed location.

Once the kernel is copied over the network and loaded, its DFS makes all the other operating-system files available. The advantages of diskless clients are many, including lower cost (because no disk is needed on each machine) and greater convenience when an operating-system upgrade occurs, only the server copy needs to be modified, rather than all the clients as well. The disadvantages are the added complexity of the boot protocols and the performance loss resulting from the use of a network rather than of a local disk.

The current trend is toward clients with local disks. Disk drives are increasing in capacity and decreasing in cost rapidly, with new generations appearing every year or so. The same cannot be said for networks, which evolve every 5 to 10 years. Overall, systems are growing more quickly than are networks, so extra efforts are needed to limit network access to improve system throughput.

Naming Schemes

There are three main approaches to naming schemes in a DFS. In the simple approach, files are named by some combination of their host name and local name, which guarantees a unique system wide name. In Ibis, for instance, file is identified uniquely by the name host-.local-name, where local-name is UNIX-like path. This naming scheme is neither location transparent nor location- independent. Nevertheless, the same file operations can be used for both local and remote files. The structure of the DFS is a collection of isolated component units that are entire conventional file systems. In this first approach, components remain isolated, although means are provided to refer to a remote file

Implementation Techniques

Implementation of transparent naming requires a provision for the mapping of a file name to the associated location. Keeping this mapping manageable call for aggregating sets of files into component units, and providing the mapping on a component unit basis rather than on a single file basis. This aggregation serves administrative purposes as well. UNIX-like systems use the hierarchical directory tree to provide name-to-location mapping, and to aggregate files recursively into directories.

To enhance the availability of the crucial mapping information, we can use methods such as replication, local caching, or both. As we already noted, location independence means that the mapping changes over time; hence, replicating the mapping renders a simple yet consistent update of this information impossible. A technique to overcome this obstacle is to introduce low level, location-independent file identifiers. Textual file names are mapped to lower-level file identifiers that indicate to which component unit the file belongs. These identifiers are still location independent. They can be replicated and cached freely without being invalidated by migration of component units. A second level of mapping, which maps component units to locations and needs a simple yet consistent update mechanism, is the inevitable price.

Remote File Access

Overview of the remote service mechanism

In one of the most common ways to implement distributed file systems is using the **remote service** mechanism. When a user wants to open a file that is actually on a remote machine, the following events happen:

The user attempts to open the file using the location-transparent file name.

The local file system - or the local operating system - recognizes that the file is not local.

A request is sent to the remote machine to open the file

The response to this request is processed by the local machine's file system (or operating system) and a valid file descriptor is given to the user

At this point the user can read from and/or write to the file. However, just as when the file was opened, the desired operations are actually performed on the remote machine on behalf of the user.

One way to think of this is that there is just one additional layer of abstraction between the file system and the hardware. Rather than the file system interacting directly with the device drivers, it interacts with the remote file system (with some form of network interface between them) which in turn interacts with the device drivers on the remote machine.

Remote Procedure Call (RPC)

One way (probably the most common way) to implement a remote service mechanism is with the **remote procedure call (RPC)** paradigm. This allows certain library routines to be called on a remote machine. In order to do this, the two machines need some way to establish a logical connection; this may happen for each procedure call or once for multiple procedure calls.

Caching

For performance reasons, DFSs usually use some form of caching to reduce the network traffic just as regular file systems use caching to reduce the number of physical disk accesses. Actually in the case of DFSs, caching not only reduces the network traffic but also reduces disk IO.

One major issue with regard to caching is **where is the cache stored**? There are basically two choices:

Main-memory:

In this case the cached data from the remote file is kept in volatile memory on the local machine. This has the obvious advantage of speed and the obvious disadvantage when the power goes off.

Local disk:

In this case the cached data from the remote file is kept on a local disk. This solves the volatility problem but at the expense of performance.

Regardless of where the cache is kept, care must be taken to ensure that when the cached data is changed that the remote file is updated properly and that it remains consistent in the face of all network accesses. This relates to the **cache update policy**:

Immediate update:

Whenever any cache data is modified the remote file is updated. This ensures the highest reliability of any update scheme but performance suffers due to the resulting remote file access time.

Delayed update:

Updates to the remote file are not performed immediately, but occur sometime after the cached data has been modified. There are several variations of delayed update schemes:

a. One option is to update the remote file when a modified block is about to flushed from the local cache. Since it is possible for a modified block to remain in the local cache for a relatively long time, this approach is not very reliable, even though it is efficient.

b. Another approach is the same as above but to also periodically update the remote file using modified cache blocks (which can then be marked as unmodified or flushed).

Update-on-close:

Update the remote file when it is closed. This will have performance advantages over delayed update when files are open for a relatively long time and there are frequent modifications to them.

Stateful vs. Stateless Service

Stateful service

Service begins by the establishment of a connection and the creation of an **identifier** for the connection.

All subsequent communication between the server and the client use the identifier.

It is possible that both client and server retain information regarding the status of the connection.

Stateless Service

Each request from the client to the server is self-contained and is independent from any other requests.

The server does not retain any information about the clients (e.g. a table of open files, etc.) Of course, the server may well log each request.

Since more information must be packed into each message, and since the server may have to repeatedly carry out operations on behalf of the same client (open file, read data, send to client, close file) a stateless service is generally **slower** than a Stateful service.

The big **advantage** of a stateless service is it's integrity. Even when the server is terminated and restart the client requests can still be served — no information was lost.

More on distributed file system

A distributed file system provides transparent access to files stored on a remote disk. As we go through different distributed file systems, you will see a recurrently themes of design issues: failure handling, performance optimizations, and cache consistency.

No Client Caching

A simple way to construct a distributed file system is to use RPC to forward every file system request to the remote server (e.g., `open`, `seek`, `read`, `write`, and `close`). The server implements each operation as it would for a local request, and sends back the result to the client.

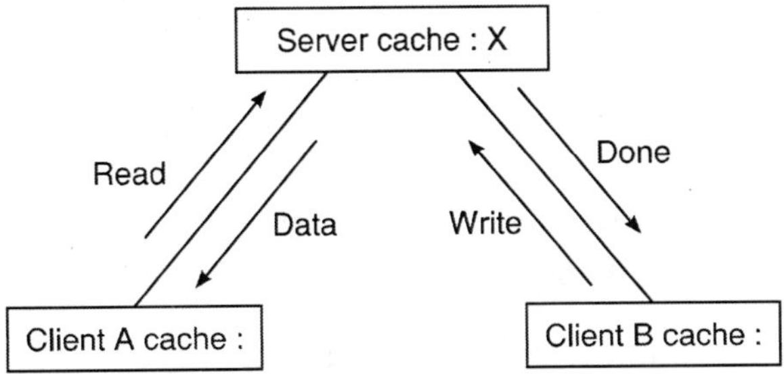

The advantage of this approach is that the server always has a consistent view of the file system. However, the performance can be slow. The server is both the performance bottleneck and the single point of failure.

Sun Network File System (NFS)

NFS uses client caching to reduce network load. NFS is built on the top of a number of protocols, as illustrated in the following alphabet soup diagram.

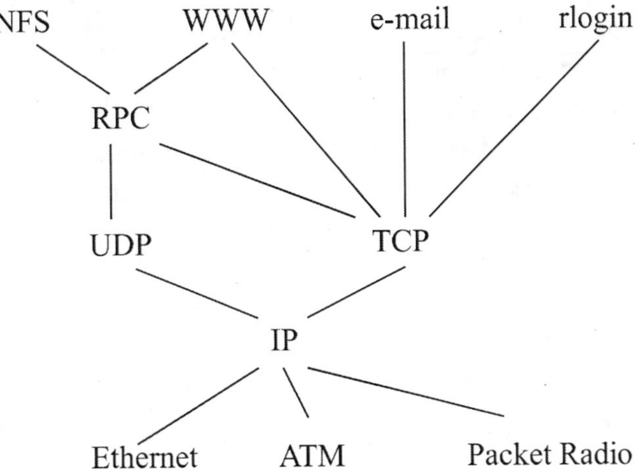

Since both clients and servers cache file blocks and metadata, the main advantage of this approach is that many file operations (e.g., `read`, and `write`) can be done locally. However, NFS has to worry about handling failures and maintaining cache consistency.

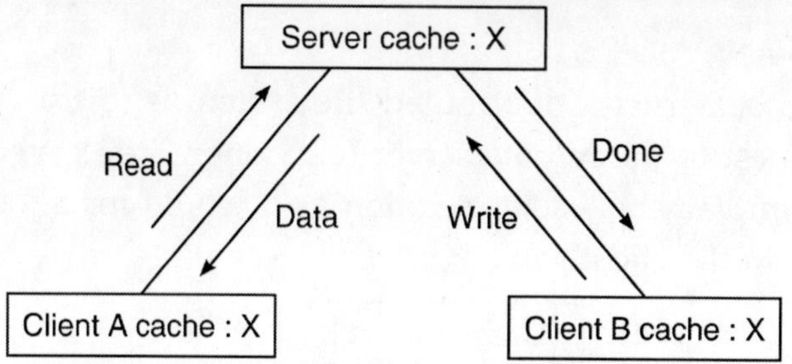

NFS Stateless Protocol

If the server crashes, a number of bad things can happen.

1. Any data in server memory that are not yet committed to disk can be lost.
2. Since state is shared across RPCs (e.g., open, seek, read, and close), if the server crashes after the seek operation, client will fail on the read operation.
3. Suppose the server fails after "rm file" but before returning an acknowledgement. The retransmitted message can confuse the server.

If a client crashes, the modified data in the client cache might be lost.

NFS uses the following design principles to handle failures.

1. Write-through caching: modified blocks are sent immediately to the server.
2. ***Stateless protocol***: the server keeps no state about the client, and each client's request contains enough information to do the entire operation. For example, instead of just reading an opened file, which contains current file location state, a read operation under NFS needs to specify the `i_node` number and the read position of the file.
3. NFS operations are ***idempotent***: Repeated operations get the same result. So, if the server crashes, a client can just resend the message and perform the operation again.
   Read and write operations are easy—a client just re-reads or re-writes a file block without side effects. For operations like file removal, NFS simply does the removal twice, with an error returned for the second call. All operations cannot not use static variables due to the idempotent requirement.
4. Transparent failures to clients: There are two options to handle server crashes. (1) The client waits until the server comes back, even if it takes a week. (2) The client can return an error to the user application. However, since user applications may not know the existence of the NFS (it's transparent) and ignore error values (e.g., `close`), some applications may crash.

NFS Weak Consistency Protocol

If multiple clients are reading the same file, each client can just get one copy. However, if multiple clients are writing the same file, we need mechanisms to propagate updates to all copies.

In NFS, a client polls the server periodically for changes. Thus, when a file is modified, the server is immediately notified via the write-through cache, but other clients still use the old version of the file until they timeout. They then check the server and get the new version. If multiple clients write to the same file, the result is completely arbitrary. A client can get either version, or parts of both versions.

NFS Summary

NFS is simple and highly portable. However, NFS sometimes gets into an inconsistent state. Also, NFS does not scale to a large number of clients. The inconsistency problem may sound worse than it is, since typically a file has a single writer, and multiple writers tend not to work on the same file at the same time. Also, we use old and inconsistent data all the time (e.g., Web browsing).

Andrew File System (AFS)

AFS was developed in the late 80s at CMU. It uses the following design principles:

1. Callbacks: The server records who has the copy of a file.
2. Write-back cache on file close: If a file is modified, the update is propagated to server when the file is closed. The server then immediately tells all clients who own an old copy.
3. Files are cached on each client's disk. NFS caches only in clients' memory.
4. Session semantics: Updates are only visible on close.

In UNIX (single machine), updates are visible immediately to other processes that have the file open. In AFS, everyone who has the file open sees the old version; anyone who opens the file again will see the new version.

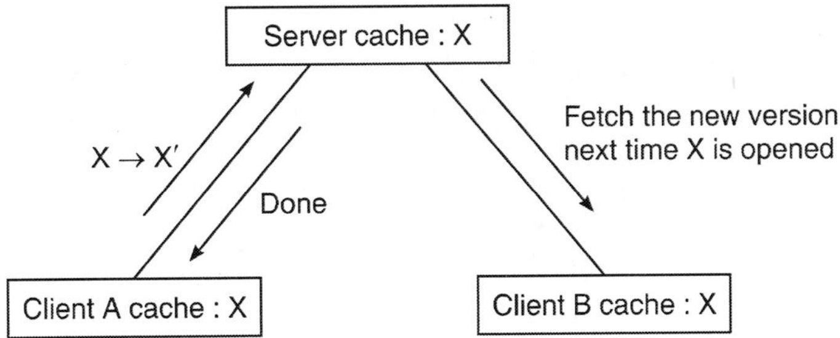

When a client opens a file and the file is not on the local disk, the client gets the file from the server and adds itself on the callback list. When a client closes a file, the client sends the updated copy back to the server and tells all clients to get the new version on the next open.

If the server crashes, the server loses all the callback states and needs to ask all clients to reconstruct the callback states.

AFS vs. NFS

Relative to NFS, AFS has a less server load due to the clients' disk caches. Also, AFS is not involved for read-only files. However, on a high-speed local area network, it is entirely likely that remote memory accesses can be faster than local disk accesses.

For both AFS and NFS, the central server is a performance bottleneck, since all updates and all cache misses have to go to the server. The server is also the single point of failure.

Serverless Network File Service (xFS)

The key idea of xFS is to construct a file system as a parallel program and to exploit the high-speed local area network. There are four innovative pieces: cooperative caching, write-ownership cache coherence, software RAID, and distributed control.

Cooperative Caching

The key observation is that remote memory accesses can be faster than local disk accesses. Therefore, ***cooperative caching*** uses remote memory to avoid going to disk.

1. On a cache miss, get the file from someone else's memory instead of from disk.
2. At replacement, if the client has the last memory copy of the file, send to a client that is idle, instead of discarding the memory content.

Therefore, active clients can use the memory of idle clients. Also, the combined cache hit-rate is higher for reads.

Write-Ownership Cache Coherence

Since a file is typically updated by one writer at a time, ***write-ownership cache coherence*** declares a client to be the owner of the file at writes, while no other clients can have a copy of the file. Therefore, in xFS, there is either one owned copy of a file that is both readable and writeable, or one or multiple copies of a read-only file.

To read a file, if the local copy is valid, the client just reads. If invalid, the client asks the remote owner to mark the file read-only as needed and copy over the file. To write a file, if the local copy is valid and read-only, the client marks all copies invalid, declares itself the owner, and writes. If the local copy is invalid, the client grabs the latest copy, marks all copies invalid, declares itself the owner, and writes.

Software RAID

In this model, pieces of file system are scattered everywhere, and the reliability is a lot worse. If any machine goes down, a part of the file system is unavailable. The xFS solution is to stripe data redundantly over multiple disks, using software RAID. Each client writes its modifications to a log stored on redundant stripe of disks. On failures, other clients can reconstruct data from remote disks to reconstruct missing data.

Distributed Control

The manager for various copies of data is also spread across all machines. If anyone fails, responsibility shifts from the failed client to someone else.

Application areas

We have mentioned several examples of distributed systems earlier. In general, today's distributed systems are pervasive, and are used in the banking industry (e.g., for transactions and accounting), e-commerce, computer games, embedded systems, bioinformatics (e.g., analysis of biological models), mobile devices (e.g., personal digital assistants, mobile phones, digital cameras) and many others.

Case study: Mach kernel

The mach microkernel is from CMU (Carnegie-Mellon University). The development started in 1985 and the kernel is considered stable. The original design goal was to:

- Retain compatibility with BSD UNIX
- Support distributed UNIX

Older versions of MACH placed the UNIX support inside the kernel. However, since mach Vs 3.0, all of this has been removed to a user-level compatibility library. (UNIX,MS-DOS, OS/2, VMS).

The kernel is found in OSF/1 (The Open Software foundation UNIX - DEC/ ALPHA), NEXT workstations and is often retro-fitted to UNIX clusters. It is common to find mach where there are large numbers of UNIX workstations.

What's not in the kernel:

- a file system - MACH file support is dependent on the user level compatibility library.
- comms - The kernel has messaging calls, but the datacomms is done by a user-level process. However, it is normal for TCP/IP to be used as a transport.

There are about 100 kernel calls in mach , for:

- Tasks & Threads - which may reside in different memory maps.
- Tasks - use heavyweight context switching.
- Ports - Anything you can communicate with is acessible through ports with associated buffering (queues).
- Memory - Both local virtual memory and support for Distributed Shared Memory (DSM).
- Devices - Just as in UNIX /NT calls to devices are made through the kernel.
- Messaging - simple calls to do messaging.

One unusual behavior of mach messaging implemented at the kernel level is that messages may contain pointers! The kernel support for DSM allows pointers to still be valid on another machine using copy-on-write semantics.

KEYWORDS

DISTRIBUTED SYSTEM
NETWORKED SYSTEMS
LOCAL AUTONOMY
LOCAL AUTONOMY
OPENNESS
MONOTONICITY
TRANSPARENCY
RPC

SUMMARY

A distributed system is any system involving multiple sites connected together into some kind of communication network, in which a user at any site can access data stored at any site.

- Networked systems are collections of computers that are connected together by some form of network in such a way that users are aware of the different computers that comprise the network.
- Distributed systems are collections of computers also connected by some form of network, but in such a way that the user is not aware of the different computers. The entire distributed system should appear as a single computer system.
- Local autonomy: Let individual group to exercise local control over their own data.
- Reliability and Availability: It can continue to function (at a reduced level) in the face of a failure of an individual site or individual communication link between sites. Efficiency and Flexibility: Data can be stored close to its normal

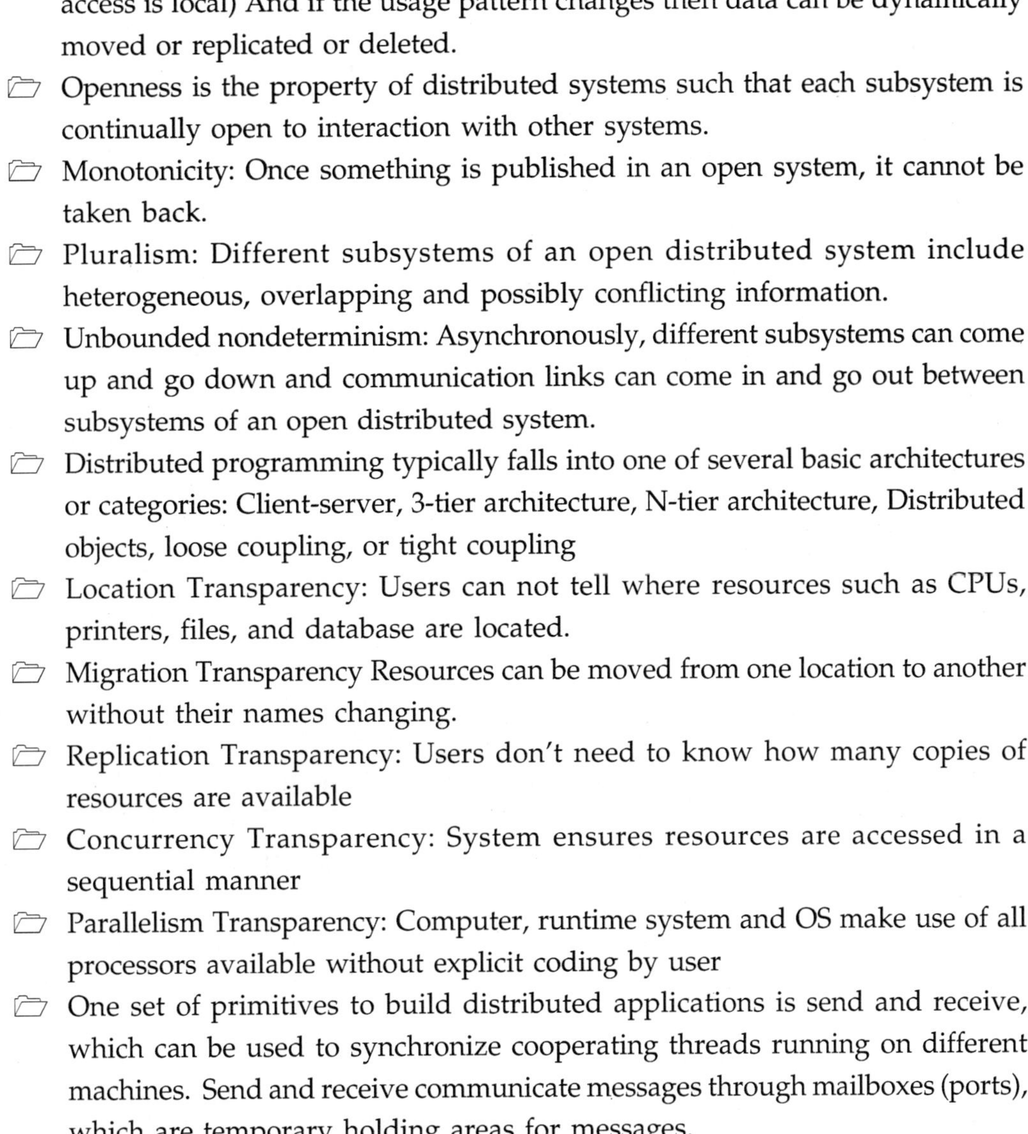

point of use thus reducing both response times and communication cost (most access is local) And if the usage pattern changes then data can be dynamically moved or replicated or deleted.

- Openness is the property of distributed systems such that each subsystem is continually open to interaction with other systems.
- Monotonicity: Once something is published in an open system, it cannot be taken back.
- Pluralism: Different subsystems of an open distributed system include heterogeneous, overlapping and possibly conflicting information.
- Unbounded nondeterminism: Asynchronously, different subsystems can come up and go down and communication links can come in and go out between subsystems of an open distributed system.
- Distributed programming typically falls into one of several basic architectures or categories: Client-server, 3-tier architecture, N-tier architecture, Distributed objects, loose coupling, or tight coupling
- Location Transparency: Users can not tell where resources such as CPUs, printers, files, and database are located.
- Migration Transparency Resources can be moved from one location to another without their names changing.
- Replication Transparency: Users don't need to know how many copies of resources are available
- Concurrency Transparency: System ensures resources are accessed in a sequential manner
- Parallelism Transparency: Computer, runtime system and OS make use of all processors available without explicit coding by user
- One set of primitives to build distributed applications is send and receive, which can be used to synchronize cooperating threads running on different machines. Send and receive communicate messages through mailboxes (ports), which are temporary holding areas for messages.
- Remote procedure call (RPC), literally, allows you to invoke a procedure on either a local or a remote machine transparently. A client's call is translated into a call on the remote machine.

A distributed file system is a network file system where a single file system can be distributed across several physical computer nodes.

REVIEW QUESTIONS

1. What are distributed systems?
2. Differentiate between distributed and networked systems.
3. What are the different goals and advantages of distributed systems?
4. What are the drawbacks and disadvantages of distributed system?
5. What are the characteristics of distributed systems?
6. What is the function of send and receive applications?
7. What are the different architectures of distributed systems?
8. Explain the working of RPC?
9. Explain the distributed file system in details.
10. Differentiate between NFS and AFS with the help of examples.

FILL IN THE BLANKS

1. ______________________are collections of computers in such a way that users are aware of the different computers that comprise the network.
2. ______________allows individual group to exercise local control over their own data.
3. ___________is the property of distributed systems such that each subsystem is continually open to interaction with other systems.
4. _________________implies that once something is published in an open system, it cannot be taken back.
5. _____________implies users can not tell where resources such as CPUs, printers, files, and database are located.
6. ___________________ensures that resources are accessed in a sequential manner

TRUE OR FALSE

1. Distributed systems are collections of computers in such a way that the user is not aware of the different computers.
2. Replication Transparency implies that users don't need to know how many copies of resources are available
3. Unbounded nondeterminism implies that users can not tell where resources such as CPUs, printers, files, and database are located.
4. Remote procedure call (RPC), literally, allows you to invoke a procedure on either a local or a remote machine transparently.

5. There is no difference between distributed and networked systems.
6. A distributed file system is a network file system where a single file system can be distributed across several physical computer nodes.

ANSWERS

FILL IN THE BLANKS

1. Networked systems
2. Local autonomy
3. Openness
4. Monotonicity
5. Location Transparency
6. Concurrency Transparency

TRUE OR FALSE

1. TRUE
2. TRUE
3. FALSE
4. TRUE
5. FALSE
6. TRUE

"Computer Science is a science of abstraction creating the right model for a problem and devising the appropriate mechanizable techniques to solve it." —*A. Aho and J. Ullman*

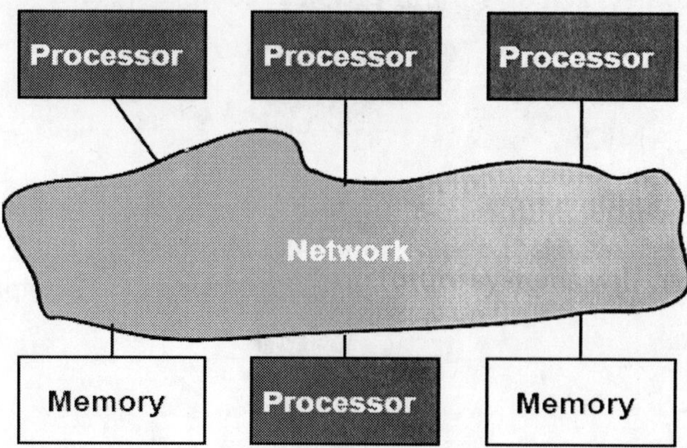

MULTIPROCESSING

INTRODUCTION

One significant trend in the computer field today is toward the greater use of multiprocessing (i.e., configuring a computing system with several processors). Multiprocessing has been used in systems for several decades, but it is again receiving intense interest because of the availability of inexpensive microprocessors. Microprocessors have made it possible to obtain processors cycles for a nominal cost, and there small size makes it reasonable to consider packing many of them in a single system. It is not unreasonable today to conceive of a system build with several hundred microprocessors. With future technologies it may be reasonable to construct systems with thousands and even millions of processors.

What is multiprocessing?

Multiprocessing is the use of two or more central processing units (CPUs) within a single computer system. The term also refers to the ability of a system to support more than one processor and/or the ability to allocate tasks between them

There are two types of multiprocessing systems:

1. *Symmetric multiprocessing*

   Each processor of symmetric multiprocessing systems runs an identical copy of the operating system, and these copies communicate with one another as needed. An example of the multiprocessing system is Encore's version of UNIX for the Multimax computer which can be configured to employ dozens of processors, all running a copy of UNIX. The benefit of this model is that many processors can run at once without causing a *deterioration of performance.*

2. *Asymmetric multiprocessing*

In asymmetric multiprocessing, application processes are assigned to a specific CPU that has its own memory. Asymmetric multiprocessing is more common in extremely large systems. For example, a banking system might use an IBM series/1 minicomputer as a front-end. The front end acts as a buffer between the terminals and the main CPU of a mainframe at headquarters.

Symmetric multiprocessing vs. Asymmetric multiprocessing

ASYMMETRIC	SYMMETRIC
1. Working of OS is based on Master-Slave relationship	1. Each processor concurrently runs a copy of the OS
2. Each processor is assigned with a specific task. Master processor controls the system , schedules and allocates work to the slave processors.	2. Many processes can run simultaneously
3. Example : Windows NT , OS/ 2, UNIX , Solaris	3. Example : Sun OS version 4

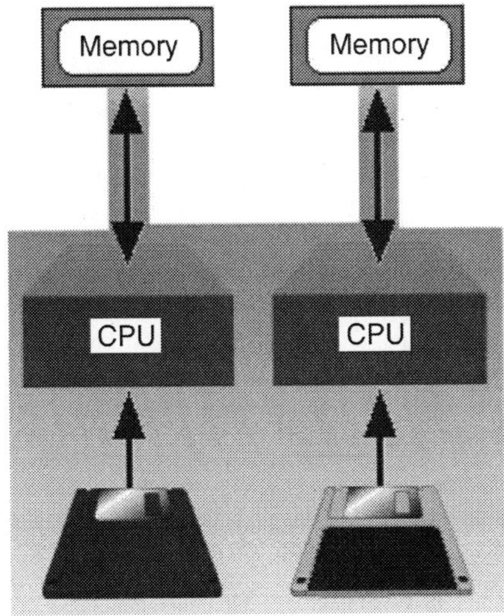

Application process
Application process
Asymmetric multiprocessing

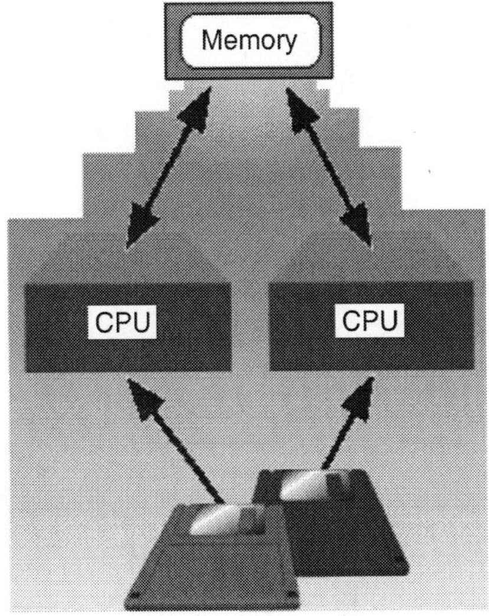

Application process
Symmetric multiprocessing

As we discussed in asymmetric multiprocessing, application processes are assigned to a specific CPU that has its own memory. In symmetric multiprocessing, application processes are assigned to the first available CPU. Memory is shared by all of the CPUs.

The view of the processors as the most precious resource on a given computer system, a view common for the first two decades of modern computing, is no longer applicable. With multiprocessing it is now more important to consider the issues of reliability, parallelism in computation, optimal connection schemes, and contention between processors attempting to access the same resources.

Reliability

One appeal of multiprocessing systems is that if a processor fails, then the remaining processors can continue operating. This is not automatic. It requires careful design. A failing processor must somehow inform the other processor that they must take over. Functioning processors must be able to detect a processor that has failed. The operating system must know that a particular processor has failed and is no longer available for allocation. Similarly, because the system now has fewer capacities, the operating system must adjust its resource allocation strategies to prevent the system from becoming over committed.

Exploiting Parallelism

It is interesting to note that most multiprocessing systems have as their central goal-increasing throughput programming remains and essentially sequential activity, and few programs are written to exploit concurrency. There are many reasons for these.

- People think sequentially. The human mind is simply not geared to think about parallelism
- No human language provides for the convenient expression of parallelism. There are several computer languages in use, such as Ada, Concurrent Pascal and Modula, but none of these has yet achieved wide acceptance.
- Because multiprocessing itself has not generally been used to exploit parallelism there is little experience with the problems of doing so.
- Computer hardware is oriented toward sequential operation.
- It is extremely difficult to debug parallel programs.
- Proving the correctness of parallel programs is far more complex than proving the correctness of sequential programs.

The hardware is available to perform operations in parallel, but it will be a long time before parallel programming is understood well enough for large numbers of parallel programs to be written. These difficulties explain why today's multiprocessors are not often used for exploiting parallelism. Real progress in this area will probably occur when compliers and operating systems can be built to detect and implement parallelism automatically.

Massive Parallelism

One key to exploiting parallelism in future systems will certainly be the availability of a sufficient number of processors so that all operations which may be performed in parallel may be assigned to separate processors.

Instead of talking about multiprocessing in today's sense, i.e., two (or perhaps a few more) processors, we now commonly talk about massive parallelism.

Massive parallelism offers us a way to run a given program to completion in the shortest possible time. The theoretical question of interest is "given the availability of massive parallelism, what is the minimum time required to execute a particular algorithm?"

GOALS OF MULTIPROCESSING SYSTEMS

By utilizing many CPU's, systems may realize many goals. Among these are very high reliability and availability, and increased computer power.

Reliability is improved because if a processor fails, the other processes may continue functioning. The system will continue to operate although with reduced capabilities. Increased computer power is made possible by combining the processing power of several processors.

With decreasing hardware costs it has become common to connect a large number of microprocessors to form a multiprocessor. In this way, large-scale computer power can be achieved without the use of costly ultra high-speed processors.

Multiprocessing can provide a means for significantly increasing the computing capacity of a single processor computer system without substantial increases in cost.

It is sometimes more attractive to convert to multiprocessing to increase capacity rather than to add additional complete systems. Multiple systems can involve significant space problems; can inquire additional labor to support them, etc.

Multiprocessing systems provide important flexibility in computer systems. Their modular design can make it easy to expand an installations capacity by adding processors as needed.

Differences between Master/Slave and Loosely Coupled multiprocessing configurations

Master/ Slave	Loosely Coupled
Easiest to implement	Each processor has its own operating system
Only master may execute operating system	Mutual exclusion techniques are used to control access to global system information
Mutual exclusion for system tables is greatly simplified	Failure of a single processor is unlikely to be catastrophic
A failure in the master causes catastrophic system failure	Each processor controls its own resources
	Utilization can be poor. It is possible for some processors to remain idle while one processor executes a lengthy process.
	A process runs to completion on the processor to which it is assigned

AUTOMATIC DETECTION OF PARALLELISM

Multiprocessors make it possible exploit parallelism. Most programs are written for sequential execution. Computer systems achieve the benefits of concurrent processing more by multiprogramming several processes than by exploiting parallelism within a single process. The detection of parallelism - by the programmer, the language translator, the hardware, or the operating system - is a complex problem of intense interest today. Regardless of how such parallelism is eventually detected, multiprocessors make it possible to exploit it by executing the parallel portions of computations simultaneously.

Parallelism in programs may be either explicit or implicit. A programmer using a concurrency construct such as COBEGIN / COEND specifically indicates explicit parallelism as follows:

```
cobegin;
  statement-1;
  statement-2;
  ...
  statement-n;
coend;
```

In a multiprocessing system designed to exploit this concurrency, separate processors might be used to execute each of the statements so that the computation could be completed more quickly than if the statements were executed sequentially.

Explicit indication of parallelism places certain responsibilities with the programmer. It is a time-consuming operation and the programmer may erroneously indicate that certain operations can be performed in parallel when in fact they cannot. The programmer may miss many situations in which parallelism may be exploited. It is likely that the programmer will detect and code explicit parallelism only for the more obvious situations. But many instances of parallelism in algorithms are hard to detect by manual inspection, so they will be missed.

One rather serious consequence of explicit expression of parallelism is that programs may become more difficult to modify. Modifying a program with a great deal of explicit parallelism could easily introduce bugs and, in fact, particularly subtle ones.

The real hope is the automatic detection of implicit parallelism, i.e., parallelism intrinsic to the algorithm, but not explicitly stated by the programmer. Detection mechanisms would be included in compilers, operating systems, and computer hardware to exploit implicit parallelism. This is more likely than explicit specification of parallelism to result in fast executing and correct programs.

Two common techniques used by compilers for exploiting implicit parallelism are loop distribution and tree height reduction.

Loop Distribution

A looping structure or repetition structure involves repeating a series of statements called the loop body until some terminating condition occurs. In certain cases, the statements within the loop body are such that parallel execution may be possible. Consider the following

for i = 1 to 4 do A(i) = B(i) + C(i)

that adds the corresponding elements of arrays B and C and places the element sums in array A. This loop causes a sequential processor to perform the following statements in sequence.

A(1) = B(1) + C(1);

A(2) = B(2) + C(2);

A(3) = B(3) + C(3);

A(4) = B(4) + C(4);

Four processors may perform these statements concurrently in a multiprocessor system, thus greatly reducing the run time of the loop. A compiler geared to automatic detection of implicit parallelism might convert the loop above into

```
cobegin;
   A(1) = B(1) + C(1);
   A(2) = B(2) + C(2);
   A(3) = A(3) + C(3);
   A(4) = A(4) + C(4);
coend;
```

thus indicating the parallelism to the computer system. This technique is called loop distribution and is relatively easy to implement. Of course, many loops involve substantially more than four iterations so it is common for the loop distribution method to indicate a greater degree of parallelism than the number of processors available. The operating system and the computer hardware would then decide which subset of the parallel computations to perform at the same time.

Tree Height Reduction

By making use of the associative, commutative, and distributive properties of arithmetic, compilers may detect implicit parallelism in algebraic expressions and produce object code for multiprocessors indicating the operations that may be performed simultaneously. Compilers must perform operations according to rules of operator precedence. Not all compilers use the same rules, but many precedence rules similar to the following:

1. Perform operations in nested parentheses first and, in particular, perform those operations first which are most deeply nested.
2. Perform operations in parentheses next.
3. Perform exponentiations next.
4. Perform multiplications and divisions next.
5. Perform additions and subtractions next.
6. Whenever an expression contains several operations to be performed next "on the same level of precedence" performs those operations in left-to-right order.

These rules of operator precedence make it possible for the compiler to assign a unique sequential ordering to the operations within an algebraic expression and the compiler may then proceed to generate machine code implementing the algebraic expression.

Often, the uniqueness and the sequential ordering is not necessary. For example, since addition and multiplication are both commutative operations, a compiler generating code to multiply p and q may generate either p * q or q * p. Similarly, adding p and q may be accomplished by either p + q or q + p.

Taking advantage of comutativity, and also associativity and distributivity, it is possible for a compiler to rearrange expressions so that they are more amenable to parallel computation.

The Never Wait Rule

It sometimes makes sense to have processors performing computations that may never be needed if indeed the possibility that they are used will speed the execution of a given computation.

The never wait rule states that it is better to give a processor a task that may or may not be used eventually than it is to let the processor sit idle. The point is that if the task is eventually needed, then it will be possible to perform computations faster. Consider the following example:

A = B * C

if A = 9 then D = 10

E = D * F

Based upon the result of the first statement, the second statement may alter the value or D, or it may leave D as is. If D is left as is, then the third statement could have been performed in parallel with the first statement. If D is altered, then the third statement needs to use this new value. The strategy of "never wait" is to perform the third statement in parallel with the first statement. If D changes, then the third statement will have to be recalculated. But if D doesn't change, then the third statement has already been performed, so the computation, in this case, may run to completion faster.

MULTIPROCESSOR HARDWARE ORGANIZATION

One of the key problems in the design of multiprocessor systems is determining the means of connecting the multiple processors and input/output processors to the storage units. Several popular schemes have evolved.

We are concerned in the next several sections only with true multiprocessors that may be characterized as follows:

- A multiprocessor contains two or more processors of approximately comparable capabilities.

- All processors share access to common storage.
- All processors share access to input/output channels, control units, and devices. The entire system is controlled by one operating system providing interaction between processors and their programs at the job, task, step, data set, and data element levels.

The most common multiprocessor system organizations are:

1. Time-shared common bus
2. Multiport memory
3. Crossbar switch
4. Multistage switching network
5. Hypercube system

Time-Shared Common Bus

A common-bus multiprocessor system consists of a number of processors connected through a common path to a memory unit. A time-shared common bus for five processors is shown in Fig. 6.46. Only one processor can communicate with the memory or another processor at any given time. Transfer operations are conducted by the processor that is in control of the bus at the time. Any other processor wishing to initiate a transfer must first determine the availability status of the bus, and only after the bus becomes available can the processor address the destination unit to initiate the transfer. A command is issued to inform the destination unit what operation is to be performed. The receiving unit recognizes its address in the bus and responds to the control signals from the sender, after which the transfer is initiated. The system may exhibit transfer conflicts since one common bus is shared by all processors. These conflicts must be resolved by incorporating a bus controller that establishes priorities among the requesting units.

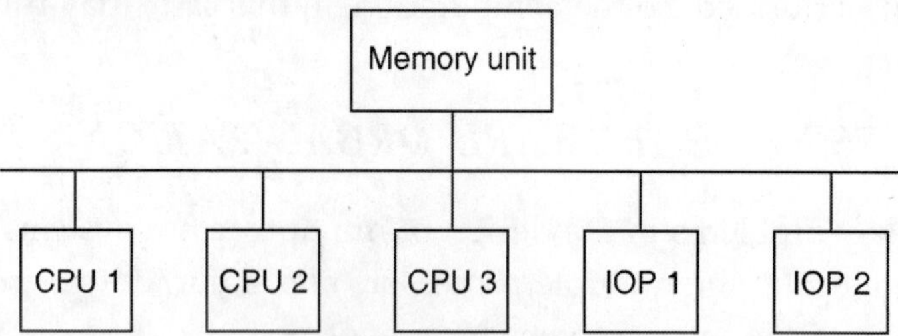

Time-shared common bus organization

A single common-bus system is restricted to one transfer at a time. This means that when one processor is communicating with the memory, all other processors are either busy with internal operations or must be idle waiting for the bus. As a consequence, the total overall transfer rate within the system is limited by the speed of the single path. The processors in the system can be kept busy more often through the implementation of two or more independent buses to permit multiple simultaneous bus transfers. However, this increases the system cost and complexity.

A more economical implementation of a dual bus structure is depicted in Fig. 6.47. Here we have a number of local buses each connected to its own local memory and to one or more processors. Each local bus may be connected to a CPU, an IOP, or any combination of processors. A system bus controller links each local bus to a common system bus. The I/O devices connected to the local IOP, as well as the local memory, are available to the local processor. The memory connected to the common system-bus is shared by all processors. If an IOP is connected directly to the system bus, the I/O devices attached to it may be made available to all processors. Only one processor can communicate with the shared memory and other common resources through the system bus of any time.

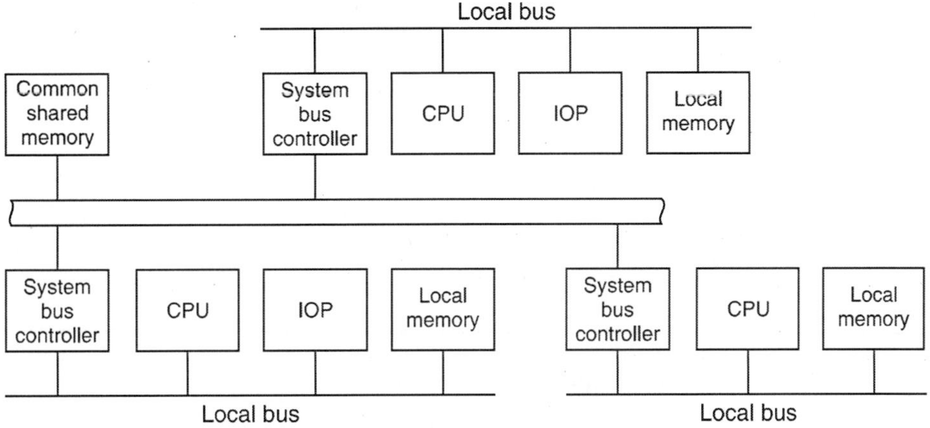

SYSTEM BUS STRUCTURE FOR MULTIPROCESSORS

Multiport Memory

A multiport memory system employs separate buses between each memory module and each CPU. This is shown in Figure 6.48 for four CPUs and four memory modules (MMs). Each processor bus is connected to each memory module. A processor bus consists of the address, data, and control lines required to communicate with memory. The memory module is said to have four ports and each port accommodates one of the buses. The module must have internal control logic to determine which port will have access to memory at any given time. Memory access conflicts are resolved by assigning fixed priorities to each memory port. The priority for memory access associated with each processor may be established by the physical port position that its bus occupies in each module. Thus CPU1 will have priority over CPU2, CPU2 will have priority over CPU3, and CPU4 will have the lowest priority. The advantage of the multiport memory organization is the high transfer rate that can be achieved because of the multiple paths between processors and memory. The disadvantage is that it requires expensive memory control logic and a large number of cables and connectors. As a consequence, this interconnection structure is usually appropriate for systems with a small number of processors.

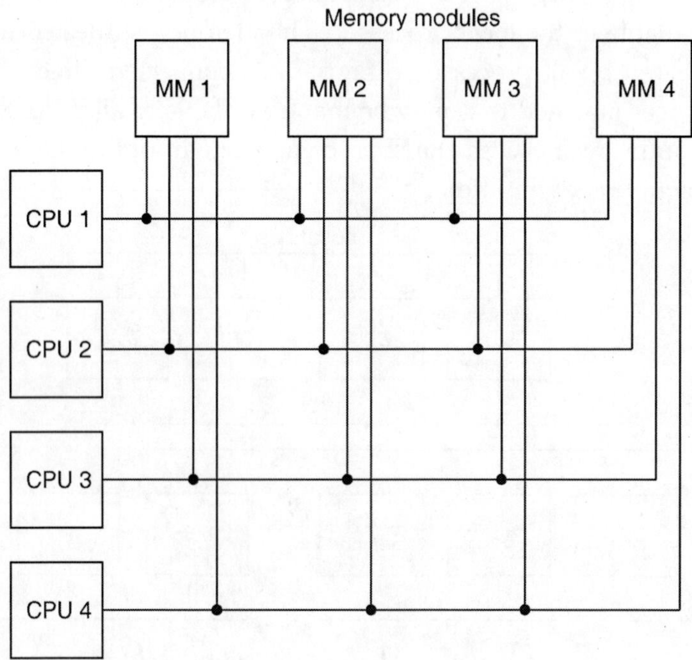

MULTIPORT MEMORY ORGANIZATION

Crossbar Switch

The crossbar switch organization consists of a number of crosspoints that are placed at intersections between processor buses and memory module paths. Figure 6.49 shows a crossbar switch interconnection between four CPUs and four memory modules. The small square in each crosspoint is a switch that determines the path from a processor to a memory module. Each switch point has control logic to set up the transfer path between a processor and memory. It examines the address that is placed in the bus to determine whether its particular module is being addressed. It also resolves multiple requests for access to the same memory module on a predetermined priority basis.

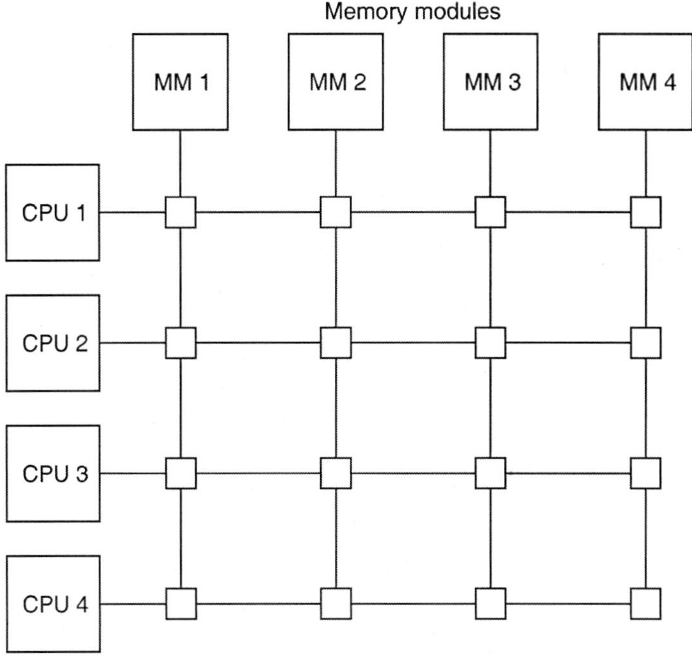

Cross Switch

Multistage Switching Network

The basic component of a multistage network is a two-input, two-output interchange switch. As shown in Figure 6.50 the 2 x 2 switch has two inputs, labeled A and B, and two outputs, labeled 0 and 1. There are control signals (not shown) associated with the switch that establish the interconnection between the input and output terminals. The switch has the capability of connecting input A to either of the outputs. Terminal B of the switch behaves in a similar fashion. The switch also has the capability to arbitrate between conflicting requests. If inputs A and B both request the same output terminal, only one of them will be connected; the other will be blocked.

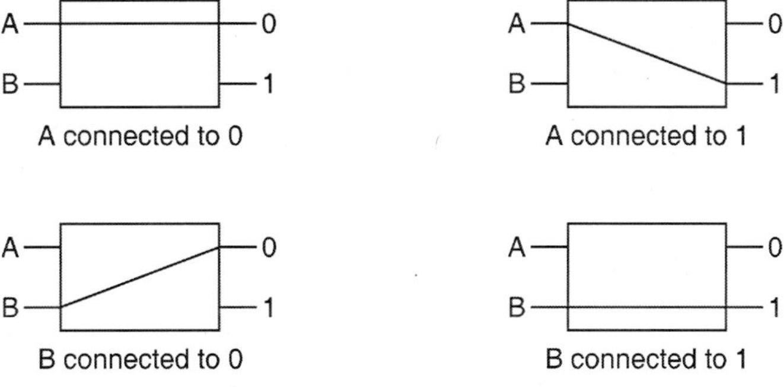

OPERATION OF 2 X 2 INTERCHANGE SWITCH

Using the 2 x 2 switch as a building block, it is possible to build a multistage network to control the communication between a number of sources and destinations. To see how this is done, consider the binary tree shown in Fig. 6.51. The two processors P_1 and P_2 are connected through switches to eight memory modules marked in binary from 000 through 111. The path from a source to a destination is determined from the binary bits of the destination number. The first bit of the destination number determines the switch output in the first level. The second bit specifies the output of the switch in the second level, and the third bit specifies the output of the switch in the third level. For example, to connect P_1 to memory 101, it is necessary to form a path from P_1 to output 1 in the first-level switch, output 0 in the second-level switch, and output 1 in the third-level switch. It is clear that either P_1 or P_2 can be connected to any one of the eight memories. Certain request patterns, however, cannot be satisfied simultaneously. For example, if P_1 is connected to one of the destinations 011 through, P_2 can be connected to only one of the destinations 100 through 111.

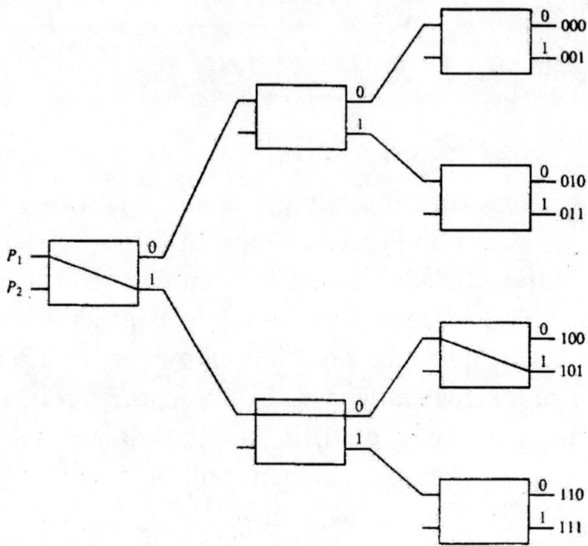

BINARY TREE WITH 2X2 SWITCHES

Many different topologies have been proposed for multistage switching networks to control processor-memory communication in a tightly coupled multiprocessor system or to control the communication between the processing elements in a loosely coupled system. One such topology is the omega-switching network shown in Fig. 6.52. In this configuration, there is exactly one path from each source to any particular destination. Some request patterns, however, cannot be connected simultaneously. For example, any two sources cannot be connected simultaneously to destinations 000 and 001.

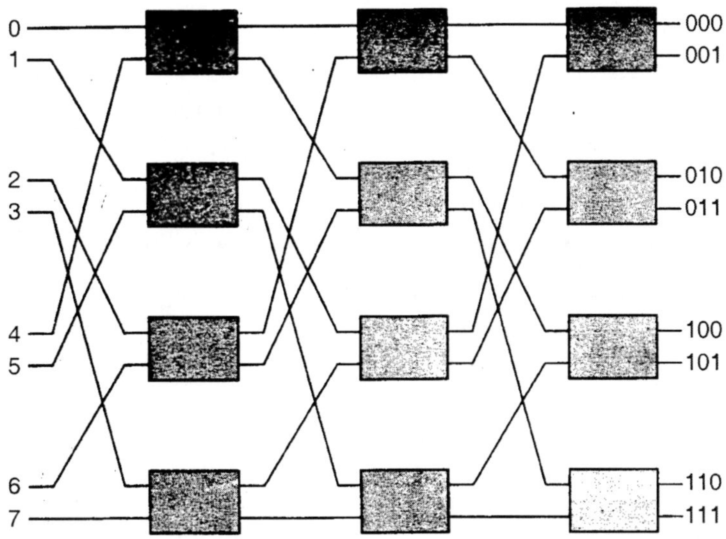

8x8 Omega Switching Network

A particular request is initiated in the switching network by the source, which sends a 3-bit pattern representing the destination number. As the binary pattern moves through the network, each level examines a different bit to determine the 2 x 2 switch setting. Level 1 inspects the most significant bit, level 2 inspects the middle bit, and level 3 inspects the least significant bit. When the request arrives on either input of the 2 x 2 switch, it is routed to the upper output if the specified bit is 0 or to the lower output if the bit is 1.

Hypercube Interconnection

The hypercube or binary n-cube multiprocessor structure is a loosely coupled system composed of $N = 2^n$ processors interconnected in an n-dimensional binary cube. Each processor forms a node of the cube. Although it is customary to refer to each node as having a processor, in effect it contains not only a CPU but also local memory and I/O interface. Each processor has direct communication paths to n other neighbor processors. These paths correspond to the edges of the cube. There are 2n distinct n-bit binary addresses that can be assigned to the processors. Each processor address differs from that of each of its n neighbors by exactly one bit position.

Figure 6.53 shows the hypercube structure for n = 1,2, and 3. A one-cube structure has n = 1 and $2^n = 2$. It contains two processors interconnected by a single path. A two-cube structure has n = 2 and $2^n = 4$. It contains four nodes interconnected as a square. A three-cube structure has eight nodes interconnected as a cube. An n-cube structure has 2^n nodes with a processor residing in each node. Each node is assigned a binary address in such a way that the addresses of two neighbors differ in exactly one bit position. For example, the three neighbors of the node with address 100 in a three-cube structure are 000, 110, and 101. Each of these binary numbers differs from address 100 by one bit value.

Routing messages through an n-cube structure may take from one to n links from a source node to a destination node. For example, in a three-cube structure, node 000 can communicate directly with node 001. It must cross at least two links to communicate with 011 (from 000 to 001 to 011 or from 000 to 010 to 011). It is necessary to go through at least three links to communicate from node 000 to node 111.

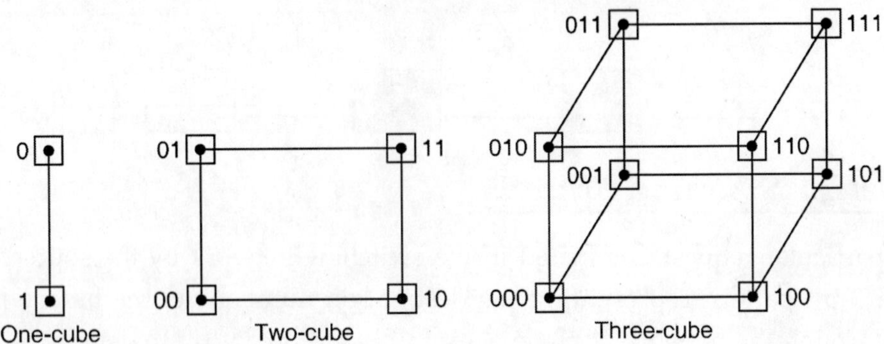

Hypercube Structures for n=1, 2, 3

Multiprocessor system organizations revisited:

Timeshared or Common Bus

The timeshared or common bus organization uses a single communication path between all of the functional units, namely the processors, the storage units, and the I/O processors. In this simple scheme, the common bus is essentially a passive unit, i.e., transfer operations between the functional units are controlled by the bus interfaces of the units themselves.

The processor or I/O processor wishing to transfer data must check the availability of the bus and the availability of the destination unit, inform the destination unit of what is to be done with the data, and initiate the actual data transfer. Receiving units must be able to recognize that messages on the bus are addressed to them, and they must follow and acknowledge the control signals received from the sending unit.

The common bus organization makes it easy to add new units by simply attaching them directly to the bus. For communications to occur, each unit must know what other units are on the bus, but this is generally handled in software.

The most serious disadvantages come from the single communication path:

- The entire system fails if the bus fails.
- The net transmission rate of the system is constrained by the net transmission rate of the bus.
- Contention for the use of the bus in a busy system can use serious performance degradation.

This system is economical, simple, and flexible, but the limitations of the common bus confine its use to smaller multiprocessing systems.

Crossbar Switch Matrix

Increasing the number of buses in a common bus system to the number of storage units creates a multiprocessor organization called the crossbar-switch matrix in which there is a separate path to every storage unit. With this scheme references to two different storage units may occur simultaneously – one cannot block the other. In fact, a crossbar-switch matrix system can support simultaneously transmissions for all storage units. Crossbar switches were first used in telephone switching systems many decades ago.

The hardware required to build a crossbar switch can become complex. For example, the switch must be capable of resolving conflicts for the same storage unit. But the complexity of the switch actually makes the interfaces at the functional units much simpler.

The multiplicity of transmission paths can yield very high transmission rates. Adding functional units in a crossbar-switch system normally results in better throughput increases than those that occur within the other schemes.

The crossbar switch can contain redundant logic to increase reliability. The multiplicity of transmission paths makes it easier to partition the system. Malfunctioning units may be removed easily while the system continues functioning.

Multiport Storage

By taking the control logic, switching logic, and priority arbitration logic out of the crossbar switch and placing all this logic at the interface to each storage unit, a multiport storage system is obtained. In this scheme, each functional unit may access each storage unit but only at a specific storage port. One storage port is supplied per functional unit.

Storage ports are normally assigned permanent priorities to resolve conflicts among the functional units attempting to access storage at the same time.

One interesting possibility with the multiport scheme is to restrict access to various storage units to certain subsets of the processors and I/O processors, thus creating certain private storage units. This is particularly attractive to designers of secure systems. But regardless of whether all processing units can access all storage units, or access is restricted, the amount of cabling involved in multiport systems to make all necessary connections is often larger than it is with the other schemes

LOOSELY COUPLED VS. TIGHTLY COUPLED SYSTEMS

Loosely coupled multiprocessing involves connecting two or more independent computer systems via a communication link. Each system has its own operating system and storage. The systems can function independently and can communicate when necessary. The separate systems can access each other's files across the communications link, and in some cases, they can switch tasks to more lightly loaded processors to achieve a degree of load balancing.

Tightly coupled multiprocessing uses a single storage shared by the various processors and a single operating system that controls all of the processors and system hardware.

Tightly-coupled systems (multiprocessors):

Many "conventional" computers are in fact asymmetric multiprocessors

As we have noted, such systems can be symmetric or asymmetric. In point of fact, many systems that are thought of as being a single computer may, in fact, be a form of asymmetric multiprocessor.

IO channels found on large mainframes are programmable and can be thought of as processors specialized for IO.

Some mainframe systems incorporate conventional minicomputers as IO processors:

a. "Front-end" processors to service the requirements of terminals (echoing, line editing etc.)

b. "Back-end" database processors.

Microprocessors in the system console that manage system startup, shutdown, and failure diagnosis. In such systems, all processors except the main CPU are dedicated to specific tasks and run software dedicated to that task, perhaps without any true operating system. Therefore, from an operating system standpoint they are relatively straight-forward; the central CPU operating system sees the dedicated processors as very smart peripherals and communicates with them as such.

Symmetric systems have some interesting features not found in asymmetric systems.

Efficiency

First, an observation about efficiency. One of the prime goals of symmetric systems is increased computational power. However, the communication overhead involved means that one cannot double computation power by simply going from one CPU to two. Experimental data indicates that 2 CPU's have roughly 1.8 times the power of 1, and 3 CPU's have roughly 2.1 times the power of 1 - though some systems have achieved better results (e.g 4 CPU's with 3.6 times the power of 1.)

The chief villain - but not the only one - is contention for access to shared memory.

There is the question of the locus of operating system kernel functions.

Master-slave: one CPU manages kernel functions such as CPU scheduling and IO. This is simpler to implement, but can lead to a bottleneck; and if the master CPU goes down then the whole system goes down (cf goal of graceful degradation.)

Totally symmetric: any CPU can execute operating system kernel code. Of course, this raises important synchronization questions: while one CPU is executing the OS kernel, other CPU's must be locked out of doing so, and probably must simply busy wait (since scheduling is a kernel function!) This argues for keeping the kernel as small as possible.

There is the question of migration of processes; a given process could be scheduled on only one CPU.

In the simplest case, once a given process starts executing on a certain CPU, it continues to run only on that CPU.

- Apportioning of workload among CPU's is an issue only when a new process is created.
- This allows each CPU to have a private memory for the processes it is currently running, plus access to a shared memory that all of the CPU's use for functions like communication and scheduling - which reduces contention for shared memory.
- This can lead to load imbalance, with one CPU very busy while others are idle.

A given process could be scheduled on more than one CPU

Alternately, a process may run on any CPU that is free to run it. This generally requires that processes reside in shared memory, and thus leads to increased memory contention problems; but it allows better use of CPU cycles. (Note: the memory contention problem can be greatly reduced if each CPU has its own private cache memory, since the majority of memory operations will then be performed in the cache rather than in shared memory.)

loosely-coupled (distributed/network) systems:

Includes a very broad family of systems

We can only make very general comments. Some key issues:

1. Communication configuration.
2. Routing of messages.
3. Message security.
4. Time-ordering of events.
5. Control of access to critical sections in a distributed environment.
6. Deadlock handling.
7. **Methods for main**taining network integrity in the face of possible failure of sites and/or links.

Communication configuration:

Types of network connections

Clearly, every site in a network must be able to communicate with each other site in the network by some means. Depending on the goals of the network, there are a number of viable options:

Fully connected is usually neither necessary nor feasible.

Partially connected is suitable for networks whose primary functions are communication and remote login. To minimize the possibility of the network being partitioned by the failure of a link, it is desirable for each site to connect to at least two others, and to ensure that no one link is on all the paths between any pair of sites. Note that techniques from graph theory (cf CS321) can be used to find minimal cost interconnection patterns etc. Networks such as the Internet use this approach.

Tree structured or **hierarchical** is suitable for distributed computation within a hierarchically structured organization. The root of the tree would be the home office, the level 2 nodes the regional offices etc. This is advantageous, since the structure of the computer system mirrors corporate organization.

The **star configuration** can be thought of as a special case of hierarchical. It can be used for distributed systems, and is also useful in LAN's where the central site may be a file server dedicated to providing shared access to files, perhaps coupled with major shared resources such as high-speed printers. Also, within a larger network, a series of stars might service a number of sites within close geographic proximity, with long distance communication service being provided only from star to star. (Networks such as Internet make use of this approach.)

Ring structures are useful for networks whose primary function is communication; but they may impose too much delay for other functions. (Note that on a one-way ring a message may have to pass through n nodes and on a two-way ring through n/2 nodes, worst case.) IBM's LAN architecture is based on this model.

Bus structures differ from the others in that a link connects several sites, rather than just two. This means that a site cannot transmit over the link whenever it wants to, but must instead wait until the link becomes free.

- Contrast CB radio with ordinary telephones.
- Such systems must deal with the possibility of collision: if two sites are both waiting for the link to become free, they might both begin transmitting at the same time when the previous user finishes. To deal with this, a site must listen for a collision when it is transmitting, and if it detects one must stop transmitting, wait for a while, then start again. To prevent repeated collisions, each site waits for a random time before restarting.
- An alternate approach to collisions, if the bus is logically (but not necessarily physically) structured as a ring, is **token passing**.

Bus structures are common for LAN's, but not for longer-distance networks.

A prime example is Ethernet, which underlies the LAN network of a number of manufacturers

Example: At Gordon, FAITH, HOPE, and the minor prophets cluster are connected to an Ethernet that also has terminal servers and our Internet connection on it.

Master/Slave Organization

In master/slave multiprocessor organization, one processor is designated as the master and the others are the slaves. The master is a general-purpose processor and performs input/output as well as computation. The slave processors perform only computation.

The slaves can run compute-bound jobs effectively, but I/O-bound jobs running on the slaves cause frequent calls for services only the master can perform, and this can be inefficient.

From a reliability standpoint, if a slave fails, some computing capability is lost, but the system can still function. If the master fails, the system cannot perform I/O. On some systems switching the I/O devices onto a slave and restarting the system with that slave re-designated as the master handle this problem.

In recent years, improvements in processor speeds have far outpaced improvements in I/O speeds. This has caused jobs that were previously compute-bound to become I/O-bound since the computations they perform between successive I/Os are now done so much faster. This has caused jobs previously well suited to master/slave multiprocessing on one model of a system to be less appropriate for such processing on newer models of the hardware. Thus the largest problem with master/slave multiprocessing is the asymmetry of the hardware. The processors are not equivalent because only the master can do I/O as well as computation. In symmetrical multiprocessing, all of the processors are functionally equivalent and can perform I/O and computation.

Multiprocessor Operating Systems

The distinction between multiprogramming operating systems and multiprocessing operating systems is not as great as one might imagine. The functional capabilities of both types of systems include:

- resource allocation and management
- table and data set protection
- prevention of system deadlock
- abnormal termination
- I/O load balancing
- processor load balancing, and
- reconfiguration

The last three of these are considerably different for multiprocessing system. The ability to exploit parallelism in the hardware and in the programs is central to multiprocessing systems, and supporting this automatically is a key aspect of multiprocessor operating systems.

Adding more processors, as well as the complex connections to storage and I/O processors, adds considerably to the cost of the hardware. The burden is upon the operating system to manage this additional hardware efficiently so that the benefits exceed the increased costs. Certainly, the additional software costs cannot be ignored - implementing multiprocessing requires more operating system cost as well as hardware.

Multiprocessor Operating Systems Organizations

The major difference between multiprocessor and uniprocessor operating systems is the organization and structure of the operating system with regard to the multiple processors. The three basic operating systems organizations for multiprocessors are:

- Master/slave
- Separate executive for each processor
- Symmetric (or anonymous) treatment of all processors

Master/Slave

Master/slave is the easiest organization to implement, and is often constructed by straightforward extension of an existing multiprogramming system. The master/slave organization does not achieve optimal utilization of the hardware.

In the master/slave organization, only one particular processor, the master, may execute the operating system. A slave processor can execute only user programs. When the process executing on a slave requires the attention of the operating system, it generates an interrupt and waits for the master processor to handle the interrupt. Depending on the number of slave processors and the interrupt activity the slaves are generating, large queues could develop at the master. Interestingly, the operating system does not have to be reentrant, since only one processor can use it at a time, and in behalf of only one user at a time.

The mutual exclusion problem for system tables is greatly simplified because of the single processor executing the operating system. The master/slave organization is less reliable than the other organizations-a failure of the master causes a catastrophic system failure.

Utilization on a slave may be poor if the master does not service slave requests efficiently enough. This type of organization is particularly appropriate for environments with well defined loads-the scheduling of the master can be precisely tuned. It is also appropriate for asymmetrical systems in which the slave processors are much less powerful than the master.

In master/slave, the operating system always runs in only one of the processors. This processor may be designed especially for running the operating system efficiently, or it may be similar to the other processors.

A slave processor that becomes available while the master is occupied must wait until the master assigns more work to it. If the slaves are running large numbers of short tasks, this can generate an excessive burden on the master. If the master cannot respond efficiently to these requests, then large portions of slave capacity will be wasted.

Separate Executives

In the separate executives' organization, each processor has its own operating system, and responds to interrupts from users running on that processor. Some tables contain information global to the entire system (for example, the list of processors known to the system), and access to these tables must be carefully controlled using mutual exclusion techniques.

The separate executives' organization is more reliable than the master/slave organization. The failure of a single processor is unlikely to cause a catastrophic system failure, but restarting the failed processor can be difficult.

Each processor controls its own dedicated resources such as files and I/O devices. Reconfiguring the I/O devices on the system may involve switching the devices to different processors with different operating systems. This can be complex and require considerable manual effort.

With separate executives' organization, each processor has its own operating system and functions like a uniprocessor with its own resources. A process assigned to run on a particular processor runs to completion on that processor.

Each processor servicing its own requirements and those of the processes it has been assigned to execute performs operating systems functions. There is a minimal amount of contention over operating systems tables because these are distributed among the individual operating systems for their own use.

Each processor has its own private set of I/O devices it manages independently of the other processors. The processor to which the process is assigned services I/O operations requested by a process strictly. I/O interrupts return directly to the processors that initiate them. Since I/O devices are directly attached to individual processors, reconfiguration requires manual intervention.

In the separate executives organization, the processors do not cooperate on the execution of ail individual process. It is possible for some of the processors to remain idle while one processor executes a lengthy process.

Symmetrical multiprocessing

Symmetrical multiprocessing is the most complex organization to implement, and the most powerful. All processors are identical. The operating system manages a pool of identical processors any one of which may be used to control any I/O device or reference any storage unit.

Because many processors may be executing the operating system at once, reentrant code and mutual exclusion are necessary. Because of the symmetry, it is possible to balance the workload more precisely than it is with the other organizations.

Conflict resolution hardware and software are important. Conflicts between processors attempting to access the same storage at the same time are ordinarily resolved by hardware. Conflicts in access to system-wide tables are ordinarily resolved by software.

Symmetrical multiprocessing systems are generally the most reliable - a failure in one processor causes the operating system to remove that processor from its pool of available processors and to notify the operator of the difficulty. The system may continue to function at reduced levels (i.e., graceful degradation) while repairs are made to the failed processor.

A process running on a symmetric multiprocessor may be run at different times by any of the equivalent processors. All of the processors may cooperate in the execution of a particular process.

The operating system floats from one processor to the next. The processor currently responsible for system tables and system functions is called the executive processor. Only one processor at a time may be the executive - this prevents conflicts over global system information.

Symmetrical multiprocessing offers better utilization. The load on the complete system may be balanced more easily because most work can be routed to any available processor.

Contention problems can become severe, especially because several processors may be in the supervisor state at once. Careful design of system tables is essential to prevent excessive lockouts. One technique that helps minimize contention is to divide the system data into a number of separate and independent entities that may be locked individually.

Cost Effectiveness of Multiprocessor Systems

Choosing a multiprocessing approach to growth rather than a multiple computer approach requires careful analysis for each different organization and installation. Some advantages of the multiprocessing approach follow.

1. Processors may often be added without the need for additional personnel.
2. If the primary benefit to be gained is more processor capacity, i.e., if storage and I/O capabilities are sufficient, then adding processors is more economical than adding completely separate systems.
3. Modularly designed symmetric multiprocessor systems make it fast and economical to add new processors.
4. The additional space required for another processor is much less than that required for a complete computer system.
5. System capacity may be increased smoothly in smaller increments.
6. Queuing theory tells us that better throughput is obtained when a single stream of arrivals is directed to a multiple server facility than when the arrivals are divided into multiple streams and routed to single server facilities (where the servers in both types of system have identical service rates).

7. The multiprocessors are more cost effective over a wide range of work loads.

There are many disadvantages to the multiprocessor approach.

1. Multiprocessing operating systems tend to be more complex than uniprocessor systems
2. Multiprocessor hardware is more complex than uniprocessor hardware
3. When the upper limit of processors on a multiprocessor system is finally reached, further expansion at the installation can be quite costly if a second multiprocessor system is obtained.

Error Recovery

One of the most important capabilities of multiprocessor operating systems is their capability to withstand equipment failures in individual processors and to continue operation. These capabilities are supported in great part by carefully designed software. Many techniques are commonly used to facilitate error recovery. These include:

1. Critical data for the system and the various processes should be maintained in multiple copies. These should reside in separate storage banks - so that failures in individual components will not completely destroy the data.
2. The operating system must be designed so that it can run the maximal configuration of hardware effectively, but it must also be able to run subsets of the hardware effectively in case of failures.
3. Hardware error detection and correction capabilities should be implemented so that extensive validation is performed but without interfering with the efficient operation of the system.
4. Idle processor capacity should be utilized to attempt to detect potential failures before they occur.
5. The operating system should direct a functioning processor to take control of a process running on a failing processor.

Symmetrical Multiprocessing in TOPS-I/O

In Digital Equipment Corporation's TOPS-10 system, master/slave restrictions of early versions have been eliminated by giving each processor full functional capabilities. The resulting organization is called Symmetrical Multiprocessing (SMP). I/O devices can be connected to each of the processors. All monitor calls, including those for I/O, can be executed on all processors.

Because monitor calls can be executed by any processor, even if a processor is running a program that requests I/O on a device connected to a different processor, the processor, the processor can continue to run the job. The I/O is queued for initiation by the processor.

SMP considers the processor running a particular job to be the executing processor. The processor connected to the various devices the job is using is called the owning processor. A running job's requests for I/O on the executing processor are entered into that processor's I/O queues. I/O requests for the other processors cause the executing processor to issue a request to the owning processor to queue the I/O request. Immediately upon making the request, the executing processor completes the monitor call and the job is resumed - the owning processor handles the I/O. One advantage of this scheme over master/slave organization is that context–switching overhead is greatly reduced. In master/slave organization, I/O requests on the slave cause a context-switch to the master, and these can be costly.

With SMP scheduling, each of the processors can execute the scheduler to seek the next job to run. This generally results in a particular job running on different processors at different times. The queued protocol used for I/O guarantees the correct handling of I/O requests regardless of which processor is currently executing a job and which I/O devices contain the users' files.

SMP utilizes a single job queue and each processor can select jobs from that queue for service. Thus SMP is able to perform load-balancing operations not ordinarily done in the other multiprocessor organizations.

SMP scheduling in a two-processor system is performed as follows: One processor concentrates on running high-priority and interactive jobs. The other processor gives priority to background work if it can find any: otherwise this processor also handles high-priority and interactive jobs. This scheduling scheme is asymmetric; it tends to force one processor to favor interactive processes and the other to favor compute-bound processes.

SMP

Dispatching occurs frequently in uniprocessor systems and even more frequently in multiprocessor systems. Because the processors execute the same routines and examine the same data when looking for processes to run, serious contention problems may develop. To help minimize this contention in SMP, the clocks on all the processors are skewed so that clock interrupts occur at different times.

When a clock interrupts a processor to run the dispatcher, the processor also examines a global I/O request queue to determine if it must perform I/O for processes running on other processors. When I/O finishes, the waiting processes are made runnable. These processes may then be run on any available processor.

One interesting problem that develops in this multiprocessing configuration is that one processor may modify a process's data in cache storage and another processor may then attempt to run that process from primary storage with stale data. To prevent this problem, a processor must cause the updated data in the cache to replace the old data in primary storage before any other attempts are made to use the data again.

Interprocessor communication is a frequent occurrence in SMP, especially because one copy of the operating system is shared by all of the processors. SMP's designers chose a software doorbell approach for interprocessor communication. One processor may not interrupt another via a hardware interrupt mechanism. Rather each processor voluntarily "listens" for a doorbell when it has nothing else to do.

To improve reliability and availability SMP has been made sensitive to the condition of the storage in which it resides. When the operating system determines that the storage is malfunctioning, it simply relocates itself into a properly functioning area of storage.

*C.MMP and CM**

Researchers at Carnegie-Mellon University have developed several significant multiprocessor systems. These include C.mmp and Cm*. C.mmp is a 16-processor system consisting of PDP-11/40 minicomputers. The processors share 16 storage modules through a crossbar-switch matrix. Accesses from any processor to any storage module have the same cost because of the symmetry of the connection scheme. Sixteen storage references can occur concurrently provided that each is directed to a different storage port. Because the complexity of the crossbar-switch matrix increases with the square of the number of processors and storages, the C.mmp architecture is not useful for constructing very large-scale multiprocessors.

Cm* consists of 50 LSI-11 microprocessors. It is constructed from processor-storage pairs called computer modules. Each of these is referred to as a Cm. Cm's are grouped into clusters. Intercluster buses connect clusters. The cost of a storage reference depends on whether it is directed to a module's local storage, to the storage of another module in the same cluster, or to the storage of a module in another cluster. These three different types of storage references have a cost ratio of 1:3:9. Thus optimal performance depends on ensuring that most storage references in an application are directed to the local storages of the modules making those references.

Both of these multiprocessor systems have been used to solve a large number of problems exhibiting a high degree of inherent parallelism.

In many cases, nearly linear improvements in performance (over the uniprocessor approach) have been achieved. A linear improvement means that with n processors the job will execute n times faster. This has occurred for example in certain mathematical applications such as integer programming and the solution of partial differential equations. The results of these efforts have demonstrated the importance of large-scale multiprocessing as a means of greatly reducing the execution times of highly parallel algorithms.

The Future of Multiprocessors

Most indications are that the use of multiprocessing systems will greatly increase in the future. There are many reasons for this optimistic forecast:

- Reliability is becoming an ever-increasing consideration in computing environments.
- The cost of processors is declining rapidly because of advances in microelectronics.
- There will be a significant increase in the use of languages that allow users to express explicit parallelism. Multiprocessors may perform highly parallel programs much faster than uniprocessors. Applications will no doubt be discovered in which the true simultaneity of multiprocessors becomes important.
- Researchers are making much progress in the automatic detection of parallelism.
- The limitations of uniprocessors are being reached. Electromagnetic signals can travel no faster than the speed of light, and some uniprocessors already work at speeds in which electromagnetic signals may move less than one foot in the computer during the processing of an operation. Size limitations will eventually force designers to use multiprocessors to achieve throughput improvements.

Various studies of trends in computer architecture point to the development of systems that will combine both symmetric and asymmetric multiprocessing to create a hierarchy of processors within a system. The term polyprocessors has been used to describe such systems. Regardless of how future multiprocessors will be structured, it is clear that operating systems of the future will be greatly influenced by multiprocessor computer architecture.

KEYWORDS

MULTIPROCESSING

SYMMETRIC MULTIPROCESSING

ASYMMETRIC MULTIPROCESSING

TIME-SHARED COMMON BUS

MULTIPORT MEMORY

CROSSBAR SWITCH

MULTISTAGE SWITCHING NETWORK

HYPERCUBE SYSTEM

LOOSELY COUPLED

TIGHTLY COUPLED

SUMMARY

Multiprocèssing is the use of two or more central processing units (CPUs) within a single computer system. The term also refers to the ability of a system to support more than one processor and/or the ability to allocate tasks between them

- In symmetric multiprocessing each processor of symmetric multiprocessing systems runs an identical copy of the operating system, and these copies communicate with one another as needed.
- In asymmetric multiprocessing, application processes are assigned to a specific CPU that has its own memory.
- By utilizing many CPU's, systems may realize many goals. Among these are very high reliability and availability, and increased computer power.
- Reliability is improved because if a processor fails, the other processes may continue functioning. The system will continue to operate although with reduced capabilities. Increased computer power is made possible by combining the processing power of several processors.
- With decreasing hardware costs it has become common to connect a large number of microprocessors to form a multiprocessor. In this way, large-scale computer power can be achieved without the use of costly ultra high-speed processors.

  The most common multiprocessor system organizations are:
- Time-shared common bus
- Multiport memory
- Crossbar switch
- Multistage switching network
- Hypercube system
- Loosely coupled multiprocessing involves connecting two or more independent computer systems via a communication link. Each system has its own operating system and storage.
- Tightly coupled multiprocessing uses a single storage shared by the various processors and a single operating system that controls all of the processors and system hardware

REVIEW QUESTIONS

1. What is multiprocessing?
2. Differentiate between symmetric and asymmetric multiprocessing
3. Explain all the multiprocessor system organizations in details
4. Differentiate between tightly coupled and loosely coupled multiprocessing systems.
5. Write short note on the future of multiprocessors.

FILL IN THE BLANKS

1. ____________is the use of two or more central processing units (CPUs) within a single computer system.
2. In ____________ each processor of symmetric multiprocessing systems runs an identical copy of the operating system, and these copies communicate with one another as needed.
3. In____________, application processes are assigned to a specific CPU that has its own memory.
4. ____________multiprocessing involves connecting two or more independent computer systems via a communication link.
5. ____________multiprocessing uses a single storage shared by the various processors and a single operating system that controls all of the processors and system hardware
6. Multiprocessing operating systems tend to be more complex than ______________.

TRUE OR FALSE

1. In multiprocessing, reliability is improved because if a processor fails, the other processes may continue functioning.
2. The cost of processors is increasing rapidly because of advances in microelectronics
3. When the upper limit of processors on a multiprocessor system is finally reached, further expansion at the installation can be quite inexpensive if a second multiprocessor system is obtained.

4. Symmetrical multiprocessing is the most complex organization to implement, and the most powerful.
5. Tree structured or hierarchical is suitable for distributed computation within a hierarchically structured organization
6. Fully connected is usually neither necessary nor feasible.

ANSWERS

FILL IN THE BLANKS

1. Multiprocessing
2. *symmetric multiprocessing*
3. asymmetric multiprocessing
4. Loosely coupled
5. Tightly coupled
6. uniprocessor systems

TRUE OR FALSE

1. TRUE
2. FALSE
3. FALSE
4. TRUE
5. TRUE
6. TRUE

❑❑❑

UNIT-7
CASE STUDIES OF OPERATING SYSTEMS

DOS OS2
UNIX
WINDOWS 98
WINDOWS NT-2000

"If you're not failing every now and again, it's a sign you're not doing anything very innovative."
—W. Allen

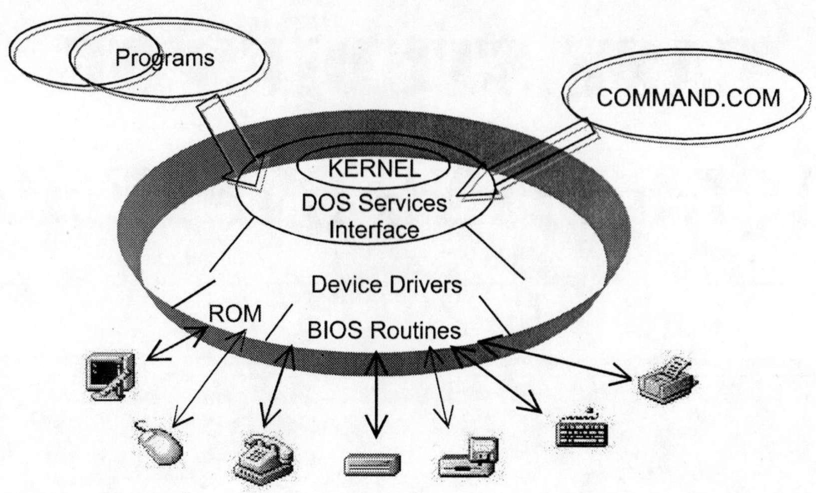

DISK OPERATING SYSTEM

INTRODUCTION

Most users today have a computer with a hard disk drive. When the computer is turned on, the operating system will be loaded from the hard drive into the computer's memory, thus making it available for use. The process of loading the operating system into memory is called bootstrapping, or booting the system. The word booting is used because, figuratively speaking, the operating system pulls itself up by its own bootstraps. When the computer is switched on, a small program (in ROM-read-only memory) automatically pulls up the basic components of the operating system from the hard disk. From now on, we will refer to MS-DOS by its commonly used abbreviated name, DOS, pronounced to rhyme with boss.

The net observable result of booting DOS is that the characters C> (or possibly C:\>) appear on the screen. The C refers to the disk drive; the > is a prompt, a signal that the system is prompting you to do something. At this point you must give some instruction to the computer. Perhaps all you need to do is key certain letters to make the application software take the lead. But it could be more complicated than that because C> is actually a signal for direct communication between the user and the operating system.

Although the prompt is the only visible result of booting the system, DOS also provides the basic software that coordinates the computer's hardware components and a set of programs that lets you perform the many computer system tasks you need to do. To execute a given DOS program, a user must issue a command, a name that invokes a specific DOS program. Whole books have been written about DOS commands, but we will consider just a few that people use for ordinary activities. Some typical tasks you can do with DOS commands are prepare (format) new diskettes for use, list the files on a disk, copy files from one disk to another, and erase files from a disk.

A short History of MS-DOS

At mid-1980 Digital Research's CP/M-80 was the operating system most commonly used on microcomputers based on the Intel 8080 and Zilog Z-80 microprocessors, and a wide range of application software was available for use with CP/M-80. At that time, Tim Paterson wrote an operating system called 86-DOS for Seattle Computer Products. To ease the process of porting 8-bit CP/M-80 applications into the new 16-bit environment, 86-DOS was designed so that it were nearly identical to those of CP/M-80.

- In October 1980, IBM designed the new line of personal computers. Microsoft paid a fee to Seattle Computer Products for the right to sell Peterson's 86-DOS.
- In July 1981, Microsoft purchased all rights to 86-DOS, and renamed it MS-DOS.
- In the fall of 1981, the first IBM PC was released, IBM offered MS-DOS as its primary operating system. IBM was the only major computer manufacturer to ship MS-DOS version 1.0 with its products.
- In June 1982, MS-DOS version 1.25 was released, and a number of bugs was fixed and it supported double-sided disks and improved hardware independence in the DOS kernel.
- In March 1983, MS-DOS version 2.0 (equivalent to PC-DOS 2.0) was released. It contained many significant innovations and enhanced features.
- MS-DOS version 2.11 was subsequently released to improve international support, and to fix a few minor bugs. Version 2.11 rapidly became the base version shipped for 8086/8088-based personal computers by every major OEM.

- In October 1985, MS-DOS version 2.25 was released. It was distributed in the Far East but was never shipped by OEMs in the United States and Europe.
- MS-DOS version 3.0 was introduced by IBM in August 1984 with the release of the 80286-based PC/AT machines. It included many new features.
- In November 1984, MS-DOS version 3.1 was released which added support for the sharing of files and printers across a network. Beginning with version 3.1, a new operating-system module called the redirection intercepts an application program's requests for I/O and filters out the requests that are directed to network devices, passing these requests to another machine for processing.
- Since version 3.1, the changes to MS-DOS have been evolutionary rather than revolutionary.
- Version 3.2, which appeared in 1986, generalized the definition of device drivers so that new media types (such as 3.5-inch floppy disks) could be supported more easily.
- Version 3.3 was released in 1987, concurrently with the new IBM line of PS/2 personal computers, and drastically expanded MS-DOS's multilanguage support for keyboard mappings, printer character sets, and display fonts.
- Version 4.0, delivered in 1988, was enhanced with a visual shell as well as support for very large file systems.
- Version 5.0, delivered in 1991, was expanded upon and improved the earlier versions with capable to work with more than one program at the same time, and with the new user interface, MS-DOS Shell.
- Version 6.0 was released in 1993 and version 6.22 was released in 1994.

While MS-DOS has been evolving, Microsoft has also put intense efforts into the areas of user interfaces and multitasking operating systems. Microsoft Windows, first shipped in 1985, provides a multitasking, graphical user "desktop" for MS-DOS systems.

What does the future hold for MS-DOS? Only the long-range planning teams at Microsoft and IBM know for sure. But it seems safe to assume that MS-DOS, with its relatively small memory requirements, adaptability to diverse hardware configurations, is still useful.

b. First Approach to MS-DOS

Recall that Operating System is a group of software tools which allow users and programmers to use the computers in the best way.

The people who use the computers have various levels of needs. They are divided into users and programmer groups:

- User needs a group of the commands for handling the data files or program files, copping the diskettes and running the applications as word processor, spreadsheet, ect ...
- The programmer needs a group of tools for developing the programs. He needs the editor, assembler, compiler, linker and debugger. Moreover, the programmer's work will be easier if he is capable of calling the subroutines of the OS to perform the tasks such as manipulation of the files, data transmission between peripheries of the computers.

Internal Structure of DOS

- The most important components of MS-DOS are as the follows:
- The BIOS module
- The DOS kernel
- The command processor.

The conceptual model for DOS as the master supervisor of resources of a computer system is shown in the following figure.

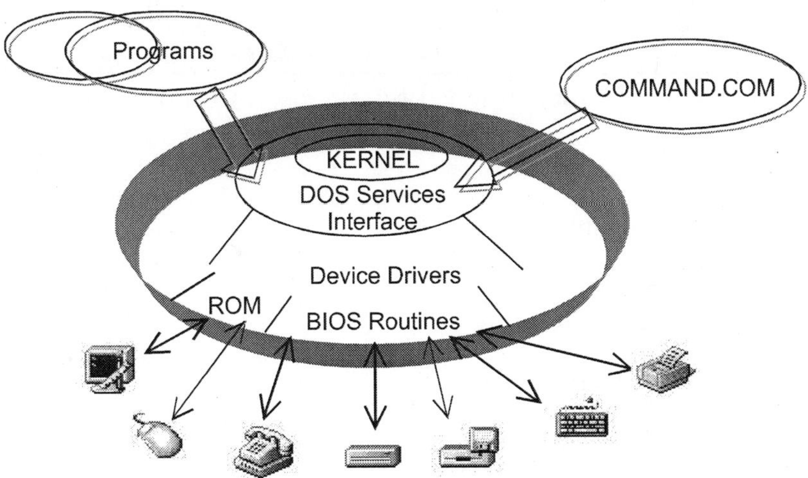

The functional parts of DOS

The BIOS Module

The BIOS is specific to the individual computer system and is provided by the manufacturer of the system. It contains the default resident hardware-dependent drivers for the following devices:

- Console display and keyboard (CON)
- Line printer (PRN)
- Auxiliary device (AUX)
- Date and time (CLOCK$)
- Boot disk device (block device)

The MS-DOS kernel communicates with these device drivers through I/O request packets; the drivers then translate these requests into the proper commands for the various hardware controllers. In many MS-DOS systems, including the IBM PC, the most primitive parts of the hardware drivers are located in read-only memory (ROM) so that they can be used by stand-alone applications, diagnostics, and the system startup program.

The terms resident and installable are used to distinguish between the drivers built into the BIOS and the drivers installed during system initialization by DEVICE commands in the CONFIG.SYS file.

The BIOS is read into random-access memory (RAM) during system initialization as part of a file named IO.SYS. (In PC-DOS, the file is called IBMBIO.COM.) This file is marked with the special attributes hidden and system.

The DOS kernel

The DOS kernel implements MS-DOS as it is seen by application programs. The kernel is a proprietary program supplied by Microsoft Corporation and provides a collection of hardware-independent services called system functions. These functions include the following:

- File and record management
- Memory management
- Character-device input/output
- Spawning of other programs
- Access to the real-time clock

Programs can access system functions by loading registers with function-specific parameters and then transferring to the operating system by means of a software interrupt.

The DOS kernel is read into memory during system initialization from the MSDOS.SYS file on the boot disk. (The file is called IBMDOS.COM in PC-DOS.) This file is marked with the attributes hidden and system.

Command processor

The command processor is contained in the file named COMMAND.COM. Its tasks are as follows:

- Displaying the "A>" or "C>" prompt on the screen,
- Accepting user input
- Controlling input execution.

Command processor is only a special program which executes under DOS control.

The command processor consists of the three following modules:

- Resident portion,
- Transient portion
- Initialization routine.
- The resident portion (the part that always stays in the computer's memory) is loaded in lower memory, above the DOS kernel and its buffers and tables. It contains various routines called critical error handlers. These allow the computer to react to deferent events, such as pressing the <Ctrl><C> or <Ctrl><Break> keys or errors during communication with external devices. This part of COMMAND.COM issues error messages and is responsible for the familiar prompt: Abort, Retry, Ignore?
- The transient portion is loaded at the high end of memory. It contains code for display prompt (C>), reading user input from the keyboard and executing the input. The name of this module is derived from fact that the RAM memory where it is located is unprotected, and can be overwritten under certain circumstances.
- The initialization portion is loaded during the booting process and initializes DOS. When its job ends, it is no longer needed and the RAM memory it occupies can be overwritten by other program. It processes the AUTOEXEC.BAT batch file (the user's list of commands to execute at system startup), if one is present, and is then discarded. The commands accepted by the transient portion of the command processor can be divided into three groups: internal commands, external commands and batch files.
- Internal commands, sometimes called intrinsic commands, lie in the resident portion of the command processor. COPY, RENAME and DIR are internal commands.
- External commands, sometimes called extrinsic commands or transient programs, must be loaded into memory from diskette or hard disk as needed.

FORMAT and CHKDSK are external commands. After execution the command processor releases the memory used by these programs. This memory can then be used for other purposes.

- A batch files is a text file containing a series of DOS commands (intrinsic, extrinsic, or batch commands). When a batch file is started, a special interpreter in the transient portion of the command processor executes the batch file commands.

Execution of batch file commands is the same as if the user entered them from the keyboard. An important batch file is the AUTOEXEC.BAT file which executes immediately after DOS is first loaded. Like all commands of a batch file, these commands are checked for internal commands, external commands or calls to other batch files. If the first is true, the command executes immediately, since the code is already in memory, in the transient portion of the command processor. If it is an external command or another batch file, the system searches the current directory for the command. If such a file doesn't exist in this directory, all directory specified in the PATH command are searched in sequence. During the search, only files with the .COM, .EXE or .BAT extension are examined. Since the command processor cannot search for all three extensions at the same time, it first searches for files with .COM extensions, the for .EXE files and finally for .BAT files. If the search is unsuccessful, the screen displays an error message and the system waits for new input.

A transient program has nearly complete control of the system's resources while it is executing. The only other tasks that are accomplished are those performed by interrupt handlers (such as the keyboard input driver and the real-time clock) and operations that the transient program requests from the operating system. MS-DOS does not support sharing of the central processor among several tasks executing concurrently, nor can it wrest control away from a program when it crashes or executes for too long. Such capabilities are the province of MS OS/2, which is a protected-mode system with preemptive multitasking (time-slicing).

The original IBM PC was constructed around an Intel 8088 microprocessor, a 16-bit processor with an 8-bit I/O bus. PC/AT and smaller PS/2 machines use the newer 80286 processor, while more powerful PS/2 computer use the 32-bit Intel 80386 and the Intel 80486 (now it is Pentium III chips).

The Shell

DOS is command driven. Users request support by typing commands in response to a system prompt (Fig. 15.3). When the return key is pressed, the shell, called COMMAND.COM, interprets the command and calls the appropriate lower level routine or program. COMMAND.COM consists of a command interpreter and a number of resident (or internal) operating system routines that remain in memory at all times.

Accessing Peripherals

The task of accessing peripheral devices is divided between two of the operating system modules (Fig. 15.4). IO.SYS (called IBMBIO.COM under PC-DOS) is a hardware-dependent module that issues physical data transfer commands. On an IBM PC, this module interacts with a proprietary, basic input/output system, or BIOS, implemented in read-only memory.

Fig. DOS is command-driven. To request support, a user types a command in response to a system prompt. The operation system then reads and interprets the command and calls the routine that carries out the command.

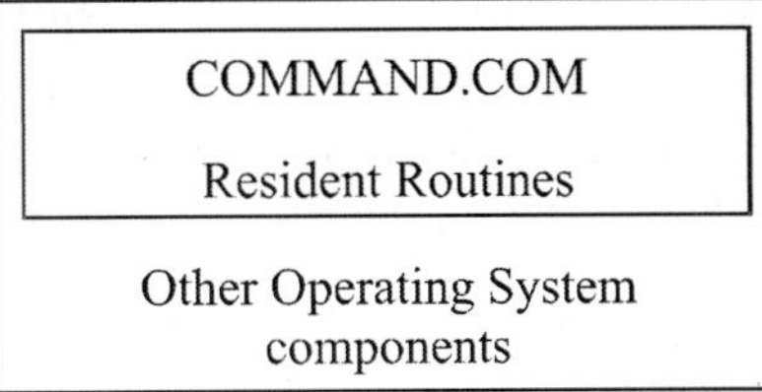

Resident Commands

BREAK PATH
CALL PAUSE
CHDIR PROMPT
CLS REM
COPY REN
CTTY RMDIR
DATE SET
DEL SHIFT
DIR TIME
ECHO TYPE
ERASE VER
EXIT VERIFY
FOR VOL
GOTO d:
IF
MKDIR

Transient Commands

APPEND LIB
APPLY LINK
ASSIGN MACHINE
ATTRIB MAP
BACKUP MODE
BOOTF MORE
CHCP NLSFUNC
CHKDSK NOSTACK
COMMAND PART
COMP PREP
COMPACT PRINT
CONFIGUR RDCPM
DEBUG RECOVER
DETECT REPLACE
DISKCOMP RESTORE
DISKCOPY SEARCH
DSKSETUP SELECT
EDLIN SHARE
EXE2BIN SHIP
FC SORT
FIND SUBST
FORMAT SYS
GDU TREE

GDUSTR	*XCOPY*
GRAFTABL	*ZCOM*
GRAPHICS	*ZSPOOL*
JOIN	
KEYB	
LABEL	

- Logical I/O and other file system functions are implemented by a hardware-independent module called MSDOS.SYS (IBM DOS.COM under PC-DOS). MSDOS.SYS accepts logical I/O requests from application programs or other operating system modules, translates them into physical I/O commands, and passes the physical commands to IO.SYS. Note that only IO.SYS, the machine-dependent module, deals directly with peripheral devices. A version of MS-DOS written for a COMPAQ computer and written for a Zenith computer will differ only in their IO.SYS; other operating system modules will be the same.

Two modules, IO.SYS and MSDOS.SYS, share responsibility for accessing peripheral devices.

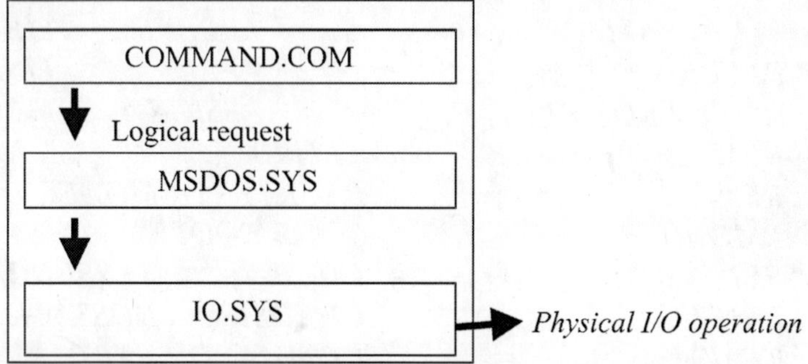

- Each physical device attached to the computer is described in a special file called a device driver (Fig. 15.5). Character drivers control such devices as the keyboard, the screen and the printer. Block drivers control disk and similar block-oriented devices, and transfer data in 512-byte blocks. The device driver is used by MSDOS.SYS to translate logical I/O requests to physical form. Certain standard device drivers are built into the operating system (Fig. 15.5). Additional devices can be defined by adding a description to a special file called CONFIG.SYS.

MSDOS.SYS uses a device driver to translate logical I/O requests to physical form.

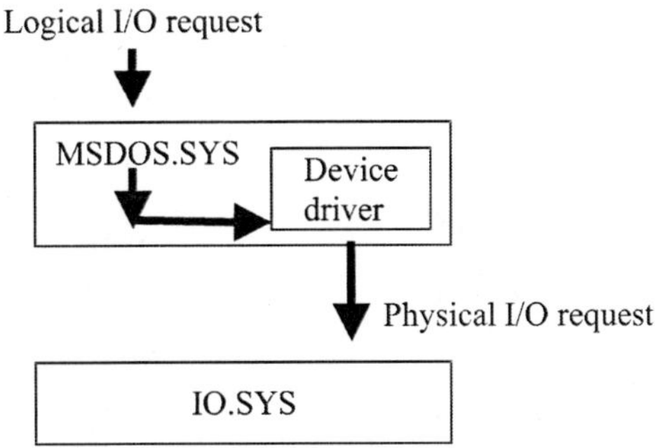

Standard Character Device Drivers

Name	*Description*
AUX	*First serial printer or modem*
COM1	*Same as AUX*
CLOCK$	*Real-time clock*
COM2	*Second serial device(printer or modem)*
CON	*Console-keyboard/display*
LPT2	*Second parallel device(usually, printer)*
LPT3	*Third parallel device*
NUL	*"Null" device-output discarded*
PRN	*First parallel printer*
LPT1	*Same as PRN*

The File System

MSDOS.SYS converts logical I/O requests to physical form. One of its responsibilities is directory management.

MSDOS.SYS is responsible for directory management

- *Commands are read and interpreted by COMMAND.COM. Following a make directory (MKDIR) command, COMMAND.COM calls MSDOS.SYS.*
- *MSDOS.SYS then asks IO.SYS to read the directory.*

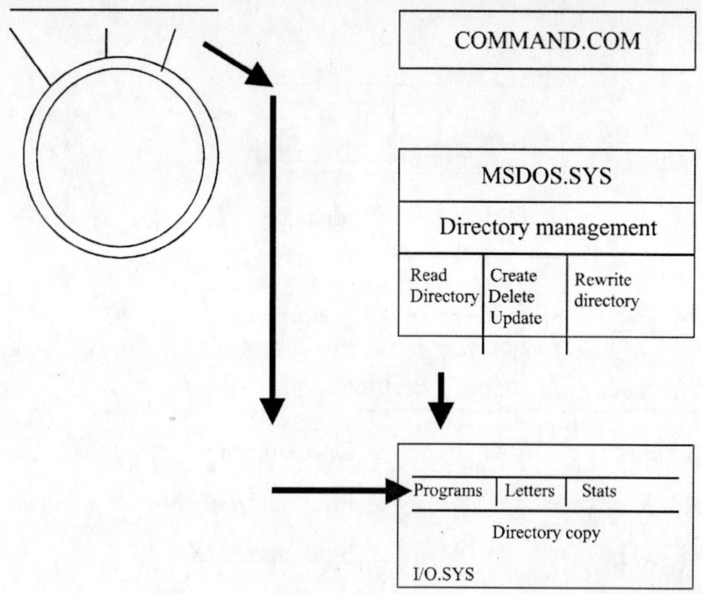

- *Once the directory is in memory, MSDOS.SYS can modify it. In this example, a new directory entry is added.*
- *Finally, MSDOS.SYS asks IO.SYS to write the directory to disk.*
- The first sector holds the boot routine. Next come two copies of the file allocation table (FAT) followed by the root directory. On system disks, the various components of the operating system follow the root directory.
- Disk space is allocated in *clusters*. On a single-sided disk, each cluster holds 512 bytes (one sector); on a double-sided disk, each cluster holds 1024 bytes (tow sectors). The clusters are numbered sequentially, and the *file allocation table* contains an entry for each cluster on the disk. The first cluster points to the second cluster following a chain of pointers. The cluster belonging to a file need not be contiguous.

This diagram shows the format of a typical DOS disk. If the disk does not contain a copy of the operating system, the space set aside for IO.SYS, MSDOS.SYS, and COMMAND.COM is used for data.

- DOS views the data stored in a disk file as a continuous stream of bytes. Logical I/O operations request data by relative byte (rather than by relative record or relative sector).

Interrupt Processing

- The Intel 8086 family relies on interrupts to establish communication with peripheral devices. Processing interrupts is an important operating systems function.
- The key to interrupt processing is an interrupt vector table that occupies the first 1K bytes of memory (Fig. 15.9). This table holds the addresses (interrupt vectors) of up to 256 different interrupt processing modules, most of which are found in MSDOS.SYS or IO.SYS.
- Two special registers are also crucial. The instruction counter is found in the IP, or instruction pointer register, also called the IC, or instruction counter register. Another register points to a memory stack.
- The interrupt itself consists of an electronic pulse and the address of an interrupt vector. When an interrupt occurs, hardware copies the contents of the IP register (along with a few other registers) to the stack (Fig. a), and loads the specified interrupt vector into the IP register (Fig. b). As the next machine cycle begins, the first instruction in the interrupt processing routine is fetched (Fig. c). Once the interrupt is processed, the contents of the stack are copied back into the IP register, and the original program resumes processing (Fig. d).

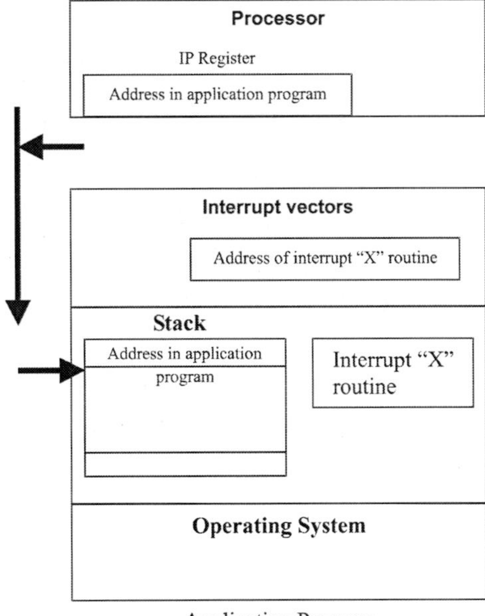

Application Program

- Interrupts are much more common than you might imagine. For example, each time you press a key on the keyboard, an interrupt is generated. In response, the operating system copies a single character into memory, and then waits for the next interrupt to herald the arrival of the next character. A few keys, such as return and escape, signal the operating system to take a different action. Interrupts also allow the printer, a disk drive, and other peripherals to communicate with the main processor.
- *When an interrupt occurs, the contents of the instruction pointer register are copied to the stack.*
- *Next, the specified interrupt vector is loaded into the instruction pointer.*
- *With the next machine cycle, the first instruction in the interrupt processing routine is fetched.*
- *Finally, the contents of the stack are loaded back into the instruction pointer register and the application program resumes processing.*

Booting DOS

- The steps of booting DOS are as follows:
- When the system is started or reset, program execution begins at address 0FFFF0H. This is a feature of the 8086/8088 family of microprocessors and has nothing to do with MS-DOS. Systems based on these processors are designed so that address 0FFFF0H lies within an area of ROM and contains a jump machine instruction to transfer control to system test code. It performs several tests on the hardware and memory and then starts to load the DOS.
- First the PC checks for a disk in the floppy disk drive. If a disk exists in the floppy disk drive, the PC checks the disk for the boot sector. If a disk is not in the drive, the PC searches for a hard disk from which to boot DOS. If a hard disk does not exist, the PC displays an error message asking the user to insert a system disk.
- The first sector on a bootable floppy disk or hard disk is called the boot sector. The program in the boot sector is read into memory and executes. First, it checks for the presence of two files: IBMBIO.COM (sometimes called IO.SYS) and IBMDOS.COM (sometimes called MSDOS.SYS). A bootable floppy disk or hard disk must contain these two files or an error message is displayed. Next, these program files are loaded into memory.
- The program file IBMIO.COM consists of two following modules:
- The basic device drivers for keyboard, display and disk.

- The initialization sequence for DOS. When the IBMIO.COM program executes it continues to initialize the system by moving the DOS kernel (loaded in the IBMDOS.COM program file) to the last available memory location.
- The DOS kernel continues to
- build several important tables and data areas,
- perform initialization procedures for individual device drivers which were loaded with the IBMIO.COM program file.
- Next, DOS searches the boot disk for a file named CONFIG.SYS. If found, the commands contained in the file are executed. These commands add device drivers to DOS, allocate disk buffers and file control blocks for DOS and initialize the standard input and output devices.
- Lastly, the command processor COMMAND.COM is loaded and control is passed to it.
- The booting process ends.

COM and EXE Programs

- DOS recognizes following three types of program files:
- File with BAT extension.
- File with COM extension. A COM program cannot exceed 64K in size. The program code, data and stack of the COM program are stored in one 64K partition. A COM program file is stored on disk as an image copy of RAM memory.
- File with EXE extension. An EXE program can be as large as the memory capacity available to DOS. The code, data and stack of EXE program may be stored in different segments, and depending on program sizes, may be distributed over several segments. An EXE program file is stored in a special format.

Keyboard and Mouse Input

- Keyboard is the fundamental means of user input under MS-DOS. This follows naturally from the MS-DOS command-line interface. During the first few years of MS-DOS's existence, when 8088/8086-based machines were the norm, nearly every popular application program used key-driven menus and text-mode displays.
- However, as high-resolution graphics adapters (and 80286/80386-based machines with enough power to drive them) have become less expensive,

programs that support windows and a graphical user interface have steadily grown more popular. Such programs typically rely on a pointing device such as a mouse, stylus, joystick, or light pen to let the user navigate in a "point-and-shoot" manner, reducing keyboard entry to a minimum.

Keyboard Input Methods

Applications running under MS-DOS on IBM PC—compatible machines can use several methods to obtain keyboard input:

- MS-DOS handle-oriented functions
- MS-DOS traditional character functions
- IBM ROM BIOS keyboard-driver functions

These methods offer different degrees of flexibility, portability, and hardware independence.

- The handle, or stream-oriented, functions are philosophically derived from UNIX and were introduced in MS-DOS. A program uses these functions by supplying a handle, or token, for the desired device, plus the address and length of a buffer. When a program begins executing, MS-DOS supplies it with predefined handles for certain commonly used character devices, including the keyboard:

Handle	*Device name*	*Opened to*
0	Standard input (stdin)	CON
1	Standard output (stdout)	CON
2	Standard error (stderr)	CON
3	Standard auxiliary (stdaux)	AUX
4	Standard printer (stdprn)	PRN

These handles can be used for read and write operations without further preliminaries. A program can also obtain a handle for a character device by explicitly opening the device for input or output using its logical name (as though it were a file). The handle functions support I/O redirection, allowing a program to take its input from another device or file instead of the keyboard, for example.

- The traditional character-input functions are a superset of the character I/O functions that were present in CP/M. Originally included in MS-DOS simply to facilitate the porting of existing applications from CP/M, they are still widely used.

The MS-DOS traditional keyboard functions offer a variety of character and line-oriented services with or without echo and Ctrl-C detection. These functions are summarized on the following page.

Int 21H Function	Action	Ctrl-C checking
01H	Keyboard input with echo	Yes
06H	Direct console I/O	No
07H	Keyboard input without echo	No
08H	Keyboard input without echo	Yes
0AH	Buffered keyboard input	Yes
0BH	Input-status check	Yes
0CH	Input-buffer reset and input	Varies

- Use of the IBM ROM BIOS keyboard functions presupposes that the program is running on an IBM PC—compatible machine. The ROM BIOS keyboard driver operates at a much more primitive level than the MS-DOS functions and allows a program to circumvent I/O redirection or MS-DOS's special handling of certain control characters. Programs that use the ROM BIOS keyboard driver are inherently less portable than those that use the MS-DOS functions and may interfere with the proper operation of other programs; many of the popular terminate-and-stay-resident (TSR) utilities fall into this category.

Ctrl-C and Ctrl-Break Handlers

During most character I/O operations, MS-DOS checks for a Ctrl-C (ASCII code 03H) waiting at the keyboard and executes an Int 23H if one is detected. If the system break flag is on, MS-DOS also checks for a Ctrl-C entry during certain other operations (such as file reads and writes). Ordinarily, the Int 23H vector points to a routine that simply terminates the currently active process and returns control to the parent process - usually the MS-DOS command interpreter.

In other words, if your program is executing and you enter a Ctrl-C, accidentally or intentionally, MS-DOS simply aborts the program. Any files the program has opened using file control blocks will not be closed properly, any interrupt vectors it has altered may not be restored correctly, and if it is performing any direct I/O operations (for example, if it contains an interrupt driver for the serial port), all kinds of unexpected events may occur.

You can use a number of partially effective methods to defeat Ctrl-C checking. But the simplest and most elegant way to defeat Ctrl-C checking is simply to substitute your own Int 23H handler, which can take some action appropriate to your program.

Pointing Devices

- Device drivers for pointing devices are supplied by the hardware manufacturer and are loaded with a DEVICE statement in the CONFIG.SYS file. Although the hardware characteristics of the available pointing devices differ greatly, nearly all of their drivers present the same software interface to application programs: the Int 33H protocol used by the Microsoft Mouse driver. Version 6 of the Microsoft Mouse driver (which was current as this was written) offers a number of functions for programmers.

2.2.3 Video Display

The visual presentation of an application program is one of its most important elements. Users frequently base their conclusions about a program's performance and "polish" on the speed and attractiveness of its displays.

Video Display Adapters

The video display adapters found in IBM PC—compatible computers have a hybrid interface to the central processor. The overall display characteristics, such as vertical and horizontal resolution, background color, and palette, are controlled by values written to I/O ports whose addresses are hardwired on the adapter, whereas the appearance of each individual character or graphics pixel on the display is controlled by a specific location within an area of memory called the regen buffer or refresh buffer. Both the CPU and the video controller access this memory; the software updates the display by simply writing character codes or bit patterns directly into the regen buffer. (This is called memory-mapped I/O.)

The following adapters are in common use:

- Monochrome/Printer Display Adapter (MDA). Introduced with the original IBM PC in 1981, this adapter supports 80-by-25 text display on a green (monochrome) screen and has no graphics capabilities at all.
- Color/Graphics Adapter (CGA). Also introduced by IBM in 1981, this adapter supports 40-by-25 and 80-by-25 text modes and 320-by-200, 4-color or 640-by-200, 2-color graphics (all-points-addressable, or APA) modes on composite or digital RGB monitors.
- Enhanced Graphics Adapter (EGA). Introduced by IBM in 1985 and upwardly compatible from the CGA, this adapter adds support for 640-by-350, 16-color

graphics modes on digital RGB monitors. It also supports an MDA-compatible text mode.

- Multi-Color Graphics Array (MCGA). Introduced by IBM in 1987 with the Personal System/2 (PS/2) models 25 and 30, this adapter is partially compatible with the CGA and EGA and supports 640-by-480, 2-color or 320-by-200, 256-color graphics on analog RGB monitors.
- Video Graphics Array (VGA). Introduced by IBM in 1987 with the PS/2 models 50, 60, and 80, this adapter is upwardly compatible from the EGA and supports 640-by-480, 16-color or 320-by-200, 256-color graphics on analog RGB monitors. It also supports an MDA-compatible text mode.
- Hercules Graphics Card, Graphics CardPlus, and InColor Cards. These are upwardly compatible from the MDA for text display but offer graphics capabilities that are incompatible with all of the IBM adapters.

Support Considerations

- MS-DOS offers several functions to transfer text to the display, to clear the screen, position the cursor and select colors and attributes with standard escape sequences embedded in the output. Programs that use only the MS-DOS functions will operate properly on any computer system that runs MS-DOS, regardless of the level of IBM hardware compatibility.
- On IBM PC - compatible machines, the ROM BIOS contains a video driver that programs can invoke directly, bypassing MS-DOS. The ROM BIOS functions allow a program to write text or individual pixels to the screen or to select display modes, video pages, palette, and foreground and background colors. These functions are relatively efficient (compared with the MS-DOS functions, at least), although the graphics support is primitive.
- Unfortunately, the display functions of both MS-DOS and the ROM BIOS were designed around the model of a cursor-addressable terminal and therefore do not fully exploit the capabilities of the memory-mapped, high-bandwidth display adapters used on IBM PC—compatible machines. As a result, nearly every popular interactive application with full-screen displays or graphics capability ignores both MS-DOS and the ROM BIOS and writes directly to the video controller's registers and regen buffer. Programs that control the hardware directly are sometimes called "ill-behaved," because they are performing operations that are normally reserved for operating-system device drivers.

Printer and Serial Port

- MS-DOS supports printers, plotters, modems, and other hard-copy output or communication devices with device drivers for parallel ports and serial ports. Parallel ports are so named because they transfer a byte - 8 bits - in parallel to the destination device over eight separate physical paths (plus additional status and handshaking signals). The serial port, on the other hand, communicates with the CPU with bytes but sends data to or receives data from its destination device serially — a bit at a time — over a single physical connection.
- Parallel ports are typically used for high-speed output devices, such as line printers, over relatively short distances (less than 50 feet). They are rarely used for devices that require two-way communication with the computer. Serial ports are used for lower-speed devices, such as modems and terminals, that require two-way communication (although some printers also have serial interfaces). A serial port can drive its device reliably over much greater distances (up to 1000 feet) over as few as three wires— transmit, receive, and ground.
- The most commonly used type of serial interface follows a standard called RS-232. This standard specifies a 25-wire interface with certain electrical characteristics, the use of various handshaking signals, and a standard DB-25 connector. Other serial-interface standards exist—for example, the RS-422, which is capable of considerably higher speeds than the RS-232— but these are rarely used in personal computers at this time.
- MS-DOS has built-in device drivers for three parallel adapters, and for two serial adapters on the PC or PC/AT and three serial adapters on the PS/2. The logical names for these devices are LPT1, LPT2, LPT3, COM1, COM2, and COM3. The standard printer (PRN) and standard auxiliary (AUX) devices are normally aliased to LPT1 and COM1, but you can redirect PRN to one of the serial ports with the MS-DOS MODE command.
- As with keyboard and video display I/O, you can manage printer and serial-port I/O at several levels that offer different degrees of flexibility and hardware independence:
- MS-DOS handle-oriented functions
- MS-DOS traditional character functions
- IBM ROM BIOS driver functions

In the case of the serial port, direct control of the hardware by application programs is also common.

Printer Output

The preferred method of printer output is to use the handle write function (Int 21H Function 40H) with the predefined standard printer handle (4).

You can write independently to several list devices (for example, LPT1, LPT2) by issuing a specific open request (Int 21H Function 3DH) for each device and using the handles returned to access the printers individually with Int 21H Function 40H.

An alternative method of printer output is to use the traditional Int 21H Function 05H.

Programs that run on IBM PC—compatible machines can obtain improved printer throughput by bypassing MS-DOS and calling the ROM BIOS printer driver directly by means of Int 17H. Use of the ROM BIOS functions also allows your program to test whether the printer is off line or out of paper, a capability that MS-DOS does not offer.

Note that the printer numbers used by the ROM BIOS are zero-based, whereas the printer numbers in MS-DOS logical-device names are one-based. For example, ROM BIOS printer 0 corresponds to LPT1.

Finally, the most hardware-dependent technique of printer output is to access the printer controller directly. Considering the functionality already provided in MS-DOS and the IBM ROM BIOS, as well as the speeds of the devices involved. The disadvantage of introducing such extreme hardware dependence for such a low-speed device would far outweigh any small performance gains that might be obtained.

The Serial Port

MS-DOS support for serial ports (often referred to as the auxiliary device in MS-DOS manuals) is weak compared with its keyboard, video-display, and printer support. This is one area where the application programmer is justified in making programs hardware dependent to extract adequate performance.

Programs that restrict themselves to MS-DOS functions to ensure portability can use the handle read and write functions (Int 21H Functions 3FH and 40H), with the predefined standard auxiliary handle (3) to access the serial port.

The standard auxiliary handle gives access to only the first serial port (COM1). If you want to read or write COM2 and COM3 using the handle calls, you must issue an open request (Int 21H Function 3DH) for the desired serial port and use the handle returned by that function with Int 21H Functions 3FH and 40H.

Some versions of MS-DOS have a bug in character-device handling that manifests itself as follows: If you issue a read request with Int 21H Function 3FH for the exact number of characters that are waiting in the driver's buffer, the length returned in the AX register is the number of characters transferred minus one. You can circumvent this problem by always requesting more characters than you expect to receive or by placing the device handle into binary mode using Int 21H Function 44H.

MS-DOS also supports two traditional functions for serial-port I/O. Int 21H Function 03H inputs a character from COM1 and returns it in the AL register; Int 21H Function 04H transmits the character in the DL register to COM1. Like the other traditional calls, these two are direct descendants of the CP/M auxiliary-device functions.

MS-DOS translates the traditional auxiliary-device functions into calls on the same device driver used by the handle calls. Therefore, it is generally preferable to use the handle functions in the first place, because they allow very long strings to be read or written in one operation, they give access to serial ports other than COM1, and they are symmetrical with the handle video-display, keyboard, printer, and file I/O methods described elsewhere in this book.

For programs that are going to run on the IBM PC or compatibles, a more flexible technique for serial-port I/O is to call the IBM ROM BIOS serial-port driver by means of Int 14H. You can use this driver to initialize the serial port to a desired configuration and baud rate, examine the status of the controller, and read or write characters.

As with the ROM BIOS printer driver, the serial-port numbers used by the ROM BIOS are zero-based, whereas the serial-port numbers in MS-DOS logical-device names are one-based. In this example, serial port 0 corresponds to COM1.

Unfortunately, like the MS-DOS auxiliary-device driver, the ROM BIOS serial-port driver is not interrupt driven. Although it will support higher transfer speeds than the MS-DOS functions, at rates greater than 2400 baud it may still lose characters. Consequently, most programmers writing high-performance applications that use a serial port (such as telecommunications programs) take complete control of the serial-port controller and provide their own interrupt driver. The built-in functions provided by MS-DOS, and by the ROM BIOS in the case of the IBM PC, are simply not adequate.

File Management

MS-DOS provides at least two distinct operating-system calls for each major file or record operation as the follows:

- ***FCB Functions:*** It refers to the set of file and record functions that are compatible with CP/M as FCB functions. These functions rely on a data structure called a file control block (hence, FCB) to maintain certain bookkeeping information about open files. This structure resides in the application program's memory space.

The FCB functions allow the programmer to create, open, close, and delete files and to read or write records of any size at any record position within such files. These functions do not support the hierarchical (treelike) file structure that was first introduced in MS-DOS version 2.0, so they can be used only to access files in the current subdirectory for a given disk drive.

- ***Unix handle functions:*** It will refer to the set of file and record functions that provide compatibility with UNIX as the handle functions. These functions allow the programmer to open or create files by passing MS-DOS a null-terminated string that describes the file's location in the hierarchical file structure (the drive and path), the file's name, and its extension. If the open or create operation is successful, MS-DOS returns a 16-bit token, or handle, that is saved by the application program and used to specify the file in subsequent operations.

When you use the handle functions, the operating system maintains the data structures that contain bookkeeping information about the file inside its own memory space, and these structures are not accessible to the application program. The handle functions fully support the hierarchical file structure, allowing the programmer to create, open, close, and delete files in any subdirectory on any disk drive and to read or write records of any size at any byte offset within such files.

a. Volumes and Directories

Each file in an MS-DOS system is uniquely identified by its name and its location.

The location, in turn, has two components: the logical drive that contains the file and the directory on that drive where the filename can be found.

Logical drives are specified by a single letter followed by a colon (for example, A:). The logical drive contains a self-sufficient file system. It contains one or more directories, zero or more complete files, and all the information needed to locate the files and directories and to determine which disk space is free and which is already in use.

Directories are simply lists or catalogs. Each *entry* in a directory consists of the name, size, starting location, attributes, and last modification date and time of a file or another directory that the disk contains. The detailed information about the location of every block of data assigned to a file or directory is in a separate control area on the disk called the *file allocation table* (FAT).

- Every disk has two following distinct kinds of directories:
- the root directory.
- all other directories.

The root directory is always present and has a maximum number of entries, determined when the disk is formatted; this number cannot be changed. The subdirectories of the root directory, which may or may not be present on a given disk, can be nested to any level and can grow to any size. This is the hierarchical, or tree, directory structure. Every directory has a name, except for the root directory, which is designated by a single backslash (\) character.

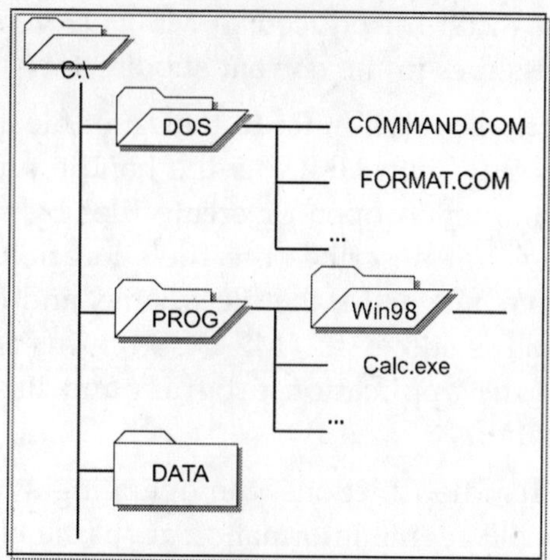

MS-DOS keeps track of a "current drive" for the system and uses this drive when a file specification does not include an explicit drive code. Similarly, MS-DOS maintains a "current directory" for each logical drive.

You can select any particular directory on a drive by naming in order - either from the root directory or relative to the current directory - the directories that lead to its location in the tree structure. Such a list of directories, separated by backslash delimiters, is called a path. When a complete path from the root directory is prefixed by a logical drive code and followed by a filename and extension, the resulting string is a fully qualified filename and unambiguously specifies a file.

b. Volume Labels

Support for volume labels was first added to MS-DOS in version 2.0. A volume label is an optional name of from 1 to 11 characters that the user assigns to a disk during a FORMAT operation. Beginning with MS-DOS version 3.0, you can use the LABEL command to add, display, or alter the label after formatting. In MS-DOS version 4, the FORMAT program also assigns a semi-random 32-bit binary ID to each disk it formats; you can display this value, but you cannot change it.

- The distinction between volumes and drives is important:
- A volume label is associated with a specific storage medium.
- A drive identifier (such as A) is associated with a physical device that a storage medium can be mounted on.

Disk Internals

Each track of the disk is divided into sections called sectors. A sector is the smallest physcial storage unit on the disk. The data size of a sector is always a power of two, and is almost always 512 bytes. The MS-DOS file systems allocate storage in clusters, where a cluster is one or more contiguous sectors. MS-DOS bases the cluster size on the size of the partition. As a file is written on the disk, the file system allocates the appropriate number of clusters to store the file's data.

If contiguous clusters (clusters that are next to each other on the disk) are not available, the data are written elsewhere on the disk, and the file is considered to be fragmented. Fragmentation is a problem when the file system must search several different locations to find all the pieces of the file you want to read. The search causes a delay before the file is retrieved. A larger cluster size reduces the potential for fragmentation, but increases the likelihood that clusters will have unused space. Using clusters larger than one sector reduces fragmentation, and reduces the amount of disk space needed to store the information about the used and unused areas on the disk.

To access the disk the computer needs to convert physical disk geometry (the number of cylinders on the disk, number of heads per cylinder, and sectors per track) to a logical configuration that is compatible with the operating system. This conversion is called translation.

Since sector translation works between the disk itself and the system BIOS or firmware, the operating system is unaware of the actual characteristics of the disk. The disk could become inaccessible if the parameters used to set up the disk are lost, which can happen if the CMOS is corrupted or modified. In this case, the controller might translate to a configuration that adds up to the same total amount of disk space, but the operating system is not able to read data from the new arrangement. The disk has to be reformatted.

Many state-of-the-art disks now have a feature called Translation Mode. The disk controller queries the system BIOS to determine the logical parameters the computer needs. If the number of cylinders, heads, and sectors per track the computer needs is within the range supported by the disk, the controller automatically configures itself to match those parameters.

MS-DOS presents disk devices as logical volumes that are associated with a drive code (A, B, C, and so on) and that have a volume name (optional), a root directory, and from zero to many additional directories and files.

MS-DOS provides battery of disk services through Int 21H. Using these services, you can create, open, read, write, close, and delete files in a uniform way, regardless of the disk drive's size, speed, number of read/write heads, number of tracks, and so on.

- Requests from an application program for file operations actually go through two levels of translation before resulting in the physical transfer of data between the disk device and random-access memory:
- MS-DOS views each logical volume, whether it is an entire physical unit such as a floppy disk or only a part of a fixed disk, as a continuous sequence of logical sectors, starting at sector 0. MS-DOS translates an application program's Int 21H file-management requests into requests for transfers of logical sectors, using the information found in the volume's directories and allocation tables.
- MS-DOS then passes the requests for logical sectors to the disk device's driver, which maps them onto actual physical addresses (head, track, and sector). Disk drivers are extremely hardware dependent. In most versions of MS-DOS, a driver for IBM-compatible floppy- and fixed-disk drives is built into the MS-DOS BIOS module (IO.SYS) and is always loaded during system initialization; you can install additional drivers for non-IBM-compatible disk devices by including the appropriate DEVICE directives in the CONFIG.SYS file.

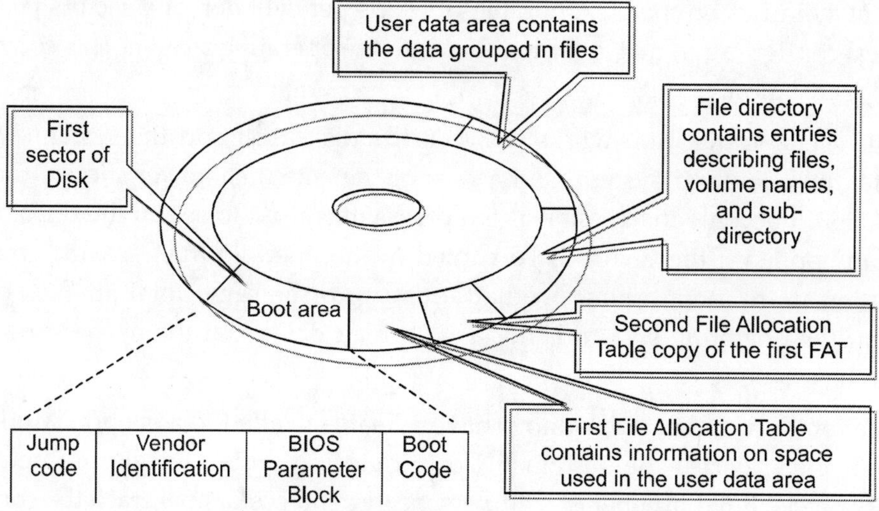

The relative positions of the components of a typical disk

- Each MS-DOS logical volume is divided into several fixed-size control areas and a files area. The size of each control area depends on several factors, but all of the information needed to interpret the structure of a particular logical volume can be found on the volume itself in the boot sector.

a. The Boot Sector

Logical sector 0, known as the boot sector, contains all of the critical information regarding the disk medium's characteristics.

➢ The first byte in the sector is always an 80x86 jump instruction (JMP). If JMP opcodes is not present, the disk has not been formatted or was not formatted for use with MS-DOS.

➢ Following the initial JMP instruction is an 8-byte field that is reserved by Microsoft for OEM identification. The disk-formatting program, which is specialized for each brand of computer, disk controller, and medium, fills in this area with the name of the computer manufacturer and the manufacturer's internal MS-DOS version number.

➢ The third component of the boot sector is the BIOS parameter block (BPB) in bytes 0BH through 17H. This data structure describes the physical disk characteristics and allows the device driver to calculate the proper physical disk address for a given logical-sector number; it also contains information that is used by MS-DOS and various system utilities to calculate the address and size of each of the disk control areas (file allocation tables and root directory).

➢ The final element of the boot sector is the disk bootstrap routine. The disk bootstrap is usually read into memory by the ROM bootstrap, which is executed automatically when the computer is turned on. The ROM bootstrap is usually just smart enough to home the head of the disk drive (move it to track 0), read the first physical sector into RAM at a predetermined location, and jump to it. The disk bootstrap calculates the physical disk address of the beginning of the files area, reads the files containing the operating system into memory, and transfers control to the BIOS module at location 0070:0000H.

b. The Reserved Area

The boot sector is actually part of a reserved area that can span from one to several sectors. The reserved-sectors word in the BPB, at offset 0EH in the boot sector, describes the size of this area.

c. The File Allocation Table

When a file is created or extended, MS-DOS assigns groups of disk sectors from the files area in powers of 2 to it. These are known as allocation units or clusters. The number of sectors per cluster for a given medium is defined in the BPB and can be found at offset 0DH in the disk's boot sector.

The file allocation table (FAT) is divided into fields that correspond directly to the assignable clusters on the disk. These fields are 12 bits in MS-DOS versions 1 and 2 and may be either 12 bits or 16 bits in versions 3.0 and later, depending on the size of the medium.

- The first two fields in the FAT are always reserved. On IBM-compatible media, the first 8 bits of the first reserved FAT entry contain a copy of the media descriptor byte, which is also found in the BPB in the boot sector.
- The second, third, and (if applicable) fourth bytes, which constitute the remainder of the first two reserved FAT fields, always contain 0FFH.

The remainder of the FAT entries describe the use of their corresponding disk clusters. The contents of the FAT fields are interpreted as follows:

Value	*Meaning*
(0)000H	Cluster available
(F)FF0—(F)FF6H	Reserved cluster
(F)FF7H	Bad cluster, if not part of chain
(F)FF8—(F)FFFH	Last cluster of file
(X)XXX	Next cluster in file

Each file's entry in a directory contains the number of the first cluster assigned to that file, which is used as an entry point into the FAT. From the entry point on, each FAT slot contains the cluster number of the next cluster in the file, until a last-cluster mark is encountered.

At the computer manufacturer's option, MS-DOS can maintain two or more identical copies of the FAT on each volume. MS-DOS updates all copies simultaneously whenever files are extended or the directory is modified. If access to a sector in a FAT fails due to a read error, MS-DOS tries the other copies until a successful disk read is obtained or all copies are exhausted. Thus, if one copy of the FAT becomes unreadable due to wear or a software accident, the other copies may still make it possible to salvage the files on the disk. As part of its procedure for checking the integrity of a disk, the CHKDSK program compares the multiple copies (usually two) of the FAT to make sure they are all readable and consistent.

d. The Root Directory

Following the file allocation tables is an area known in MS-DOS versions 2.0 and later as the root directory.

- The root directory contains 32-byte entries that describe files, other directories, and the optional volume label.
- An entry beginning with the byte value E5H is available for reuse; it represents a file or directory that has been erased. An entry beginning with a null (zero) byte is the logical end-of-directory; that entry and all subsequent entries have never been used.

The format of a single entry in a disk directory is presented in the following figure. Total length is 32 bytes (20H bytes).

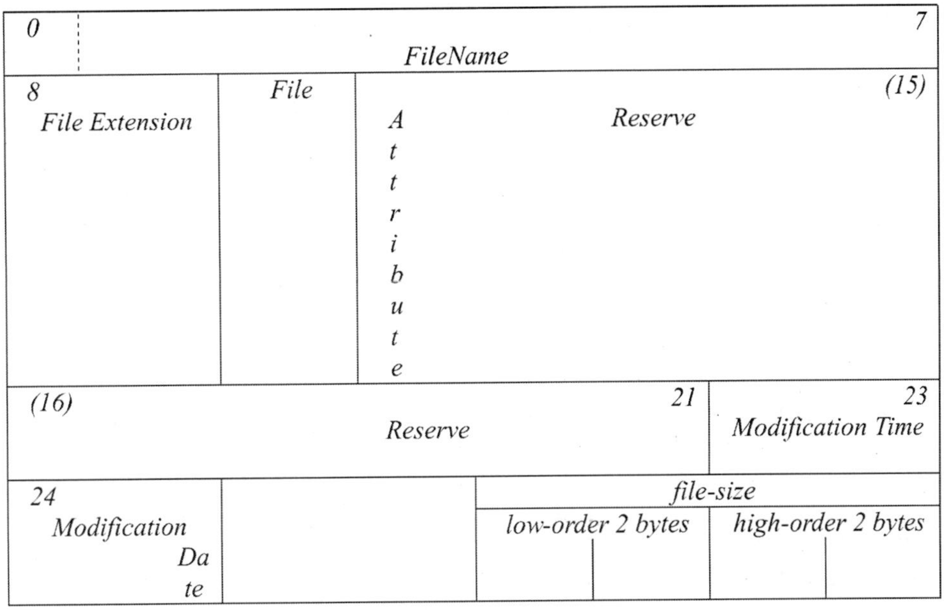

<table>
<tr><td colspan="5">0 … 7
FileName</td></tr>
<tr><td>8
File Extension</td><td>File</td><td colspan="3">Attribute   (15)
Reserve</td></tr>
<tr><td colspan="3">(16) … 21
Reserve</td><td colspan="2">23
Modification Time</td></tr>
<tr><td rowspan="2">24
Modification Date</td><td rowspan="2"></td><td colspan="3">file-size</td></tr>
<tr><td colspan="2">low-order 2 bytes</td><td>high-order 2 bytes</td></tr>
</table>

- The first byte of the filename field of a directory entry may contain the following special information:

Value	*Meaning*
00H	Directory entry has never been used; end of occupied portion of directory.
05H	First character of filename is actually E5H.
2EH	Entry is an alias for the current or parent directory. If the next byte is also 2EH, the cluster field contains the cluster number of the parent directory (zero if the parent directory is the root directory).
E5H	File has been erased.

➤ The attribute byte of the directory entry is mapped as follows:

Bit	*Meaning*
0	Read-only; attempts to open file for write or to delete file will fail.
1	Hidden file; excluded from normal searches.
2	System file; excluded from normal searches.
3	Volume label; can exist only in root directory.
4	Directory; excluded from normal searches.
5	Archive bit; set whenever file is modified.
6	Reserved.
7	Reserved.

➤ The time field is encoded as follows:

Bits	*Contents*
00H—04H	Binary number of 2-second increments (0—29, corresponding to 0—58 seconds)
05H—0AH	Binary number of minutes (0—59)
0BH—0FH	Binary number of hours (0—23)

➤ The date field is encoded as follows:

Bits	*Contents*
00H—04H	Day of month (1—31)
05H—08H	Month (1—12)
09H—0FH	Year (relative to 1980)

➢ The file-size field is interpreted as a 4-byte integer, with the low-order 2 bytes of the number stored first.

Size and position of the root directory are fixed and are determined by the FORMAT program when a disk is initialized. This information can be obtained from the boot sector's BPB. If the disk is bootable, the first two entries in the root directory always describe the files containing the MS-DOS BIOS and the MS-DOS kernel. The disk bootstrap routine uses these entries to bring the operating system into memory and start it up.

e. The Files Area

- The files area is the remainder of the volume after the root. MS-DOS views the sectors in this area as a pool of clusters, each containing one or more logical sectors, depending on the disk format.
- Each cluster has a corresponding entry in the FAT that describes its current use: available, reserved, assigned to a file, or unusable (because of defects in the medium). Because the first two fields of the FAT are reserved, the first cluster in the files area is assigned the number 2.
- Directories other than the root directory are simply a special type of file. Their storage is allocated from the files area, and their contents are 32-byte entries——in the same format as those used in the root directory——that describe files or other directories.
- Directory entries describe other directories will contain an attribute byte with bit 4 set, zero in the file-length field, and the date and time that the directory was created. The first cluster field points, of course, to the first cluster in the files area that belongs to the directory. The portion of the root directory of an MS-DOS disk, showing the entry for a subdirectory named MYDIR is as the follows:

0080 4D 59 44 49 52 20 20 20 20 20 20 10 00 00 00 00 MYDIR .....

00 00 00 00 00 00 87 9A 9B 0A 2A 00 00 00 00 00 ....*.....

- All directories except the root directory contain two special directory entries with the names . and ... MS-DOS puts these entries in place when it creates a directory, and they cannot be deleted.
- The . entry is an alias for the current directory; its cluster field points to the cluster in which it is found.
- The .. entry is an alias for the directory's parent (the directory immediately above it in the tree structure); its cluster field points to the first cluster of the parent directory. If the parent is the root directory, the cluster field of the ..

entry contains zero. The hex dump of the first block of the directory MYDIR is as follows.

```
      0  1  2  3  4  5  6  7  8  9  A  B  C  D  E  F
0000  2E 20 20 20 20 20 20 20 20 20 20 10 00 00 00 00  .          .....
0010  00 00 00 00 00 00 87 9A 9B 0A 2A 00 00 00 00 00  ..........*.....
0020  2E 2E 20 20 20 20 20 20 20 20 20 10 00 00 00 00  ..         .....
0030  00 00 00 00 00 00 87 9A 9B 0A 00 00 00 00 00 00  ................
0040  4D 59 46 49 4C 45 20 20 44 41 54 20 00 00 00 00  MYFILE  DAT ....
0050  00 00 00 00 00 00 98 9A 9B 0A 2B 00 15 00 00 00  ..........+.....
0060  00 00 00 00 00 00 00 00 00 00 00 00 00 00 00 00  ................
0070  00 00 00 00 00 00 00 00 00 00 00 00 00 00 00 00  ................
  .
  .
  .
```

This directory contains exactly one file, MYFILE.DAT.

f. Fixed-Disk Partitions

- Fixed disks have another layer of organization beyond the logical volume structure already discussed: partitions. The FDISK utility divides a fixed disk into one or more partitions consisting of an integral number of cylinders. Each partition can contain an independent file system and, for that matter, its own copy of an operating system.
- The first physical sector on a fixed disk (track 0, head 0, sector 1) contains the master boot record, which is laid out as follows:

Bytes	*Contents*
000—1BDH	Reserved
1BE—1CDH	Partition #1 descriptor
1CE—1DDH	Partition #2 descriptor
1DE—1EDH	Partition #3 descriptor
1EE—1FDH	Partition #4 descriptor
1FE—1FFH	Signature word (AA55H)

➢ The partition descriptors in the master boot record define the size, location, and type of each partition, as follows:

Byte(s)	*Contents*
00H	Active flag (0 = not bootable, 80H = bootable)
01H	Starting head
02H—03H	Starting cylinder/sector
04H	Partition type
00H	not used
01H	FAT file system, 12-bit FAT entries
04H	FAT file system, 16-bit FAT entries
05H	extended partition
06H	"huge partition" (MS-DOS versions 4.0 and later)
05H	Ending head
06H—07H	Ending cylinder/sector
08H—0BH	Starting sector for partition, relative to beginning of disk
0CH—0FH	Partition length in sectorsThe active flag, which indicates that the partition is bootable, can be set on only one partition at a time.

MS-DOS treats partition types 1, 4, and 6 as normal logical volumes and assigns them their own drive identifiers during the system boot process. Partition type 5 can contain multiple logical volumes and has a special extended boot record that describes each volume. The FORMAT utility initializes MS-DOS fixed-disk partitions, creating the file system within the partition (boot record, file allocation table, root directory, and files area) and optionally placing a bootable copy of the operating system in the file system.

Memory management

➢ Memory is required in order for computer to work.

➢ There are two types of computer memory:

➢ RAM - Random Access Memory

➢ ROM - Read-Only memory.

When a program is started, the file containing the program is loaded from diskette or hard drive into the memory area of the computer. The DOS command interpreter tells the computer where in memory to load the program file.

a. Conventional and Extended Memory

- The IBM-PC computers powered by the Intel 8088/86 CPUs are capable of referencing or addressing up to 1 Meg of memory.
- The 80286 CPU computer is able to address up to 16 Meg memory locations.
- The computer based on the next generation of the microprocessor (80386, 80486, ...) are able to address 4 gigabytes memory locations.
- The original DOS was designed around the 1 Meg limit and this range of memory has become known as conventional memory.
- The additional memory beyond the 1 Meg limit is referred to as extended memory.

  If the computer has 1 Meg of memory, a program still may not be able to use this full amount of memory. Most programs can only use up to 640K of memory.

When we load a program, DOS makes memory available to the program in a contiguous section. The maximum amount of memory that DOS can make available to a program is 640K. The other 384K is reserved by DOS. The layout of the conventional memory is presented on following figure.

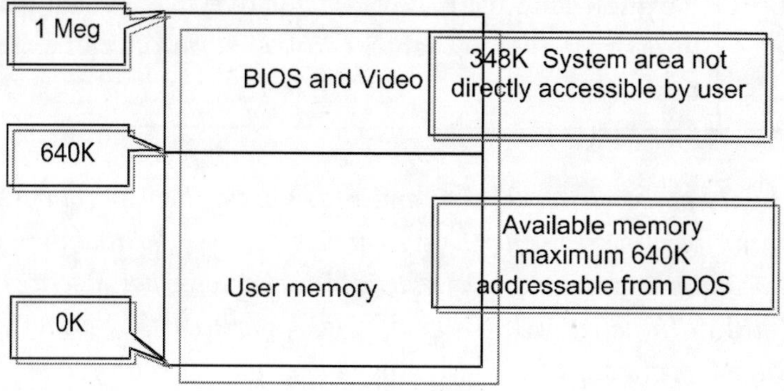

Layout of conventional memory

- Low memory ranges up to the 640 K limit. Sometimes we call it user memory. Some portions of DOS are stored within low memory. The remainder of low memory is for user programs and data.
- About the 640K limit, conventional memory ranges up to the 1 Meg limit. The additional 384K of memory is reserved by DOS and is sometimes referred to as upper memory. Within upper memory are the BIOS ROM, video memory and ROM and other hardware dependent programs (network cards, modem, hard drive controllers).

  Usually only parts of upper memory are used by the computer. This leaves unused sections of memory in this address range.

Extended memory

- The memory above the 1 Meg conventional limit is called extended memory.
- In a 80286, up to 16 Meg of memory is addressable.
- For 80386 and 80486 computers, up to 4 gigabytes of memory is addressable. Unfortunately, DOS can't automatically use this extended memory.

  The layout of a typical computers with 80286, 80386, 80486 and 80586 CPUs and 1 Meg of memory is presented in the following figure.

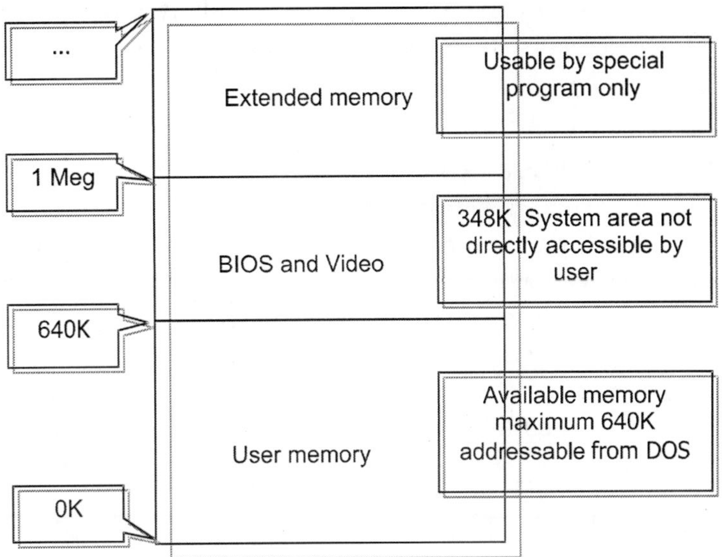

Extended memory layout

- The layout of conventional memory for new computers is identical to that for 8086 and 8088 computers. The IBM-PC has 640K of conventional memory and an area reserved for the BIOS, video and other hardware-dependent devices. The remaining 384K of memory is found in an area above the 1 Meg limit. So this 384K is part of extended memory.
- The new computers operate in what is call real mode in order to be compatible with the 8086 and 8088 computers. In this mode, the computer can address a maximum of 1 Meg of memory. So a new computer in real mode cannot use memory beyond the 1 Meg limit.
- The microprocessor can be switched to protected mode in order to use memory beyond the 1 Meg limit. In this mode, the 1 Meg memory limitation is removed. So you can store and retrieve information beyond the 1 Meg line.

Unfortunately switching to protected mode isn't easy. We can use special instruction to switch from real mode to protected mode, but there isn't an instruction for switching back to real mode.

- As long as only conventional memory is used, DOS ensures that only one program uses that area memory. DOS manages the memory by assigning or allocating parts of memory to the various programs (resident utility programs, applications, drivers).
- Different programs may not work together if they are both using extended memory. There are some DOS programs that can use extended memory. They are RAM disk, hard drive cache. However, many other programs can only use extended memory as expanded memory.

Expanded memory

- Extended memory has two disadvantages:
- It can only be used on computers with 80286 CPU and later
- Not all programs have been written to take advantage of extended memory.
- Some companies joined forces to develop a uniform method for adding and using additional memory on the PC. This method called the Expanded Memory Specification (EMS).
- Expanded memory is a combination of hardware and software. Memory that uses this scheme must be addressable below the 1 Meg limit.

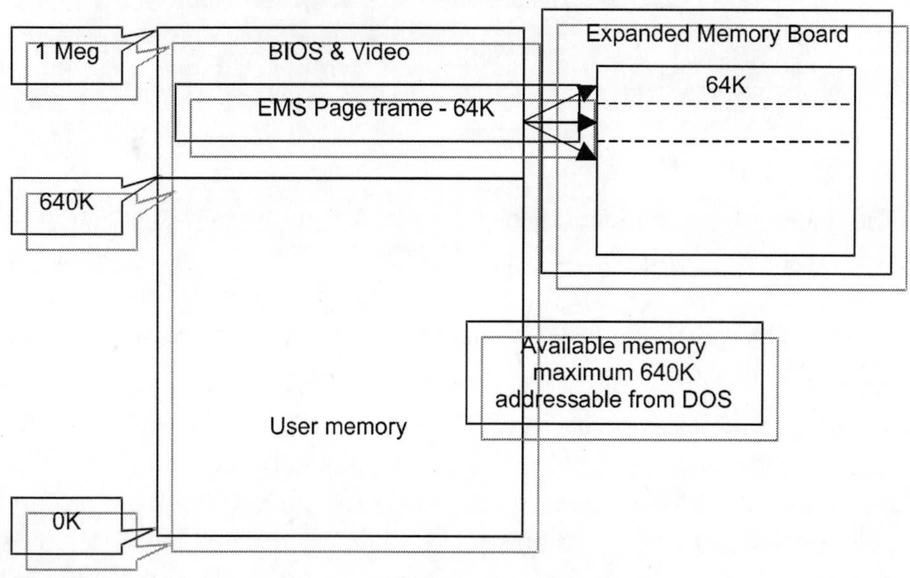

Expanded memory layout

- An area in upper memory, between 640K and 1Meg, is designed as a page frame.

- The page frame is a 64K area of memory that acts as a window to a much larger area of expanded memory. The electronic circuitry lets us select the part of expanded memory that appears in this window at any give time.
- Just as DOS manages memory up to the 640K limit, special software called an EMS driver manages the expanded memory. When a program references a section of expanded memory that isn't in the window, the EMS software/ hardware combination replaces an unneeded section of memory out of the page frame with the section that is needed.
- The expanded memory on the EMS circuit board is completely independent of the computer's conventional memory (and extended memory, if present). The electronic circuitry on the board manages the data in the EMS memory.

  Of course, a program must be especially written to be able to use expanded memory. But many programs are already set up to recognize and take advantage of a computer's expanded memory. One of them is Microsoft Windows.

  Computers with 80386, 80486 CPUs and latter are capable of converting extended memory into expanded memory without requiring additional hardware.
- The DOS driver called EMM386.EXE is used by 80386, 80486 CPUs, ... has the following capabilities:
- Conversion of the extended memory into expanded memory. The driver makes the extended memory function according to the LIM/EMS standard.
- High memory between 640K and 1 Meg that isn't being used by DOS can be used to store driver programs and many Terminate and Stay Resident (TSR) programs using the LOADHIGH command. By moving drivers into high memory, additional conventional memory is freed up for applications.

High memory

- The high memory area on the computers with 80286 CPUs or latter is a small area of memory located in the first 64K of extended memory (starting at 1 Meg). To take advantage of the high memory area, the computer must have extended memory. The high memory area is part of extended memory (extended memory begins at address 1 Meg).
- By using the high memory area to store certain parts of DOS, we can free up parts of conventional memory for the applications. While 64K may not seem like much, some applications may not work unless these are a minimum amount of conventional memory available.

- The DOS driver HIMEM.SYS is used to manage the high memory area. However, only a few applications are capable of running from the high memory area.

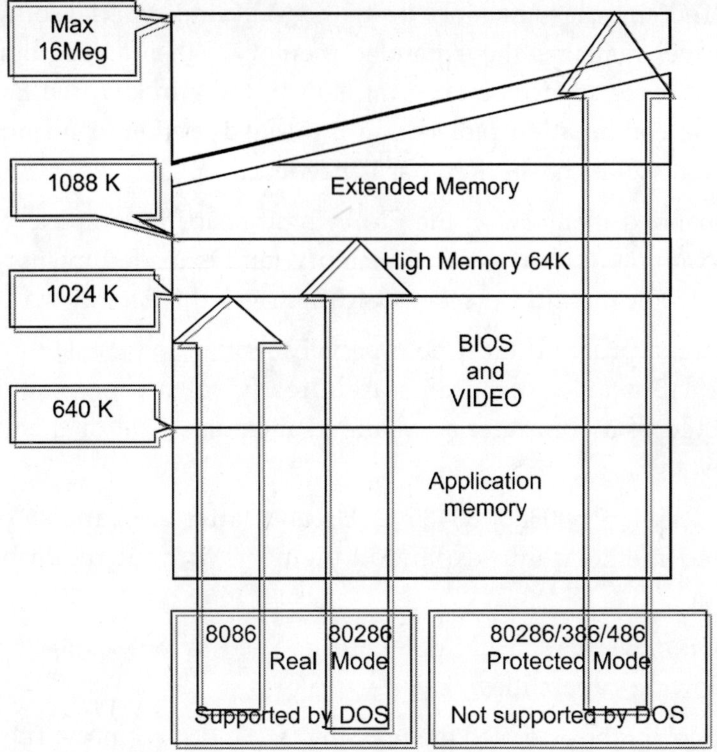

Special features of high memory

Upper memory

- The upper memory blocks or upper memory is a memory above the 640K line and below the 1 Meg. These areas are most often used for hardware-related memory requirement: video graphic cards, network adapters and specialized hard drive controllers.
- Upper memory is never completely filled. There are always "holes" in this range that are unused. The upper memory area is reserved for hardware add-ons
- The LOADHIGH command is used to load a program into upper memory.
- The DEVICEHIGH command is used to load drivers into upper memory.
- Computers with 80286 CPUs or higher: the high memory can be used and the computers can have extended memory, so upper memory isn't as readily available. To use upper memory, we must change address at which the computer begins to look for this memory.

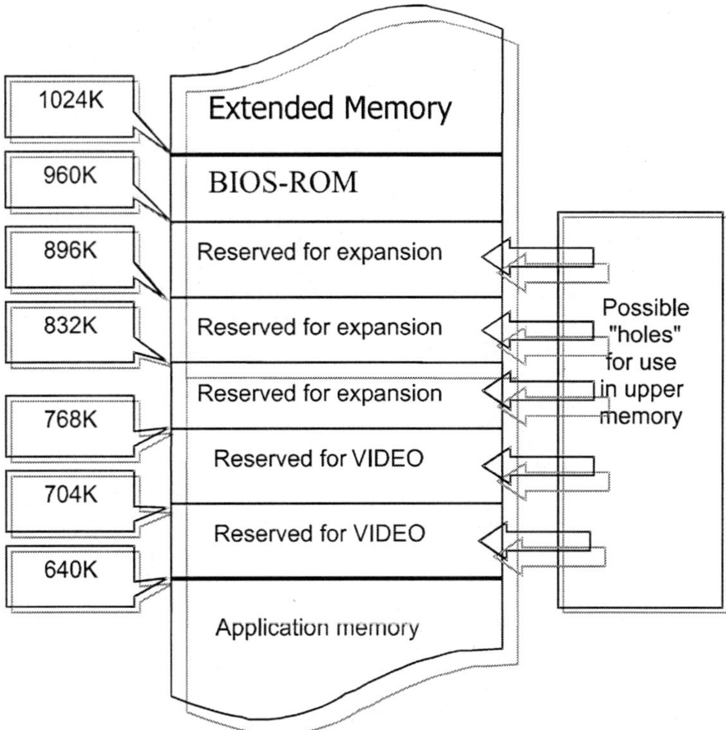

Special features of upper memory

- Three ways to use upper memory by changing address:
- On computers with 80386, 80486 or latter, we can use a virtual memory technique. Do this by using the EMM386 driver.
- On a computer that has the NEAT chip set, we can use technique similar to a 386. Do this by using the special NEAT setup program that re-maps memory above 1 Meg as upper memory.
- Some EMS boards are capable of making additional memory available at any address. By using this type of board and the special EMS driver, we can add upper memory.
- Address in upper memory are used by hardware devices. Adding more hardware devices uses more addresses in upper memory. For example, a VGA graphics card will normally use a 32K block of upper memory beginning at C0000H.
- The expanded memory limits the amount of memory available as upper memory. Since expanded memory uses a 64K block of memory in this range for its windows, 64K of the total amount of upper memory becomes unavailable.

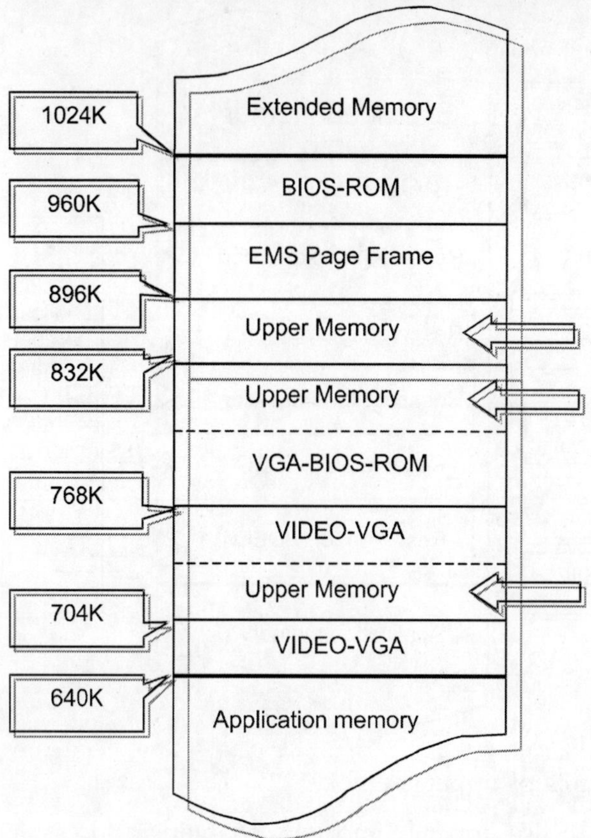

Upper memory with VGA card and EMS page frame

- Diagram of the upper memory:
- one block of memory for a VGA graphic card
- some other blocks for an EMS board.
- some blocks at the end of upper memory for the ROM BIOS.
- 128K of upper memory is unused.

Note that upper memory isn't available as a continuos block of memory.

XMS Memory

- XMS (eXtended Memory Specification) is a way to administer the use of extended memory, high memory and upper memory.
- We can divide memory administration tasks into:
- low memory (user memory) – managed by DOS
- EMS memory – managed by the EMS driver
- upper, high and extended memory – managed by the XMS driver

This means that the XMS driver is an important part of the memory scheme. Prior to XMS, different applications have used extended memory independently, which leads to program incompatibilities.

- DOS does not manage upper, high and extended memory directly. Instead, the driver program HIMEM.SYS is used to manage the memory.

Customizing Memory

- DOS 5.0 and later is capable of providing more conventional memory up to the 640K line than earlier versions of DOS. This is possible because of the skillful use of memory above 640K – either in upper memory or high memory.

Using high memory

- If extended memory – beginning at 1 Meg – is available. DOS can use the first 64K as the high memory area and store part of itself there. Insert the following lines at the start of the CONFIG.SYS file:

  DEVICE = HIMEM.SYS

  DOS = HIGH

  Then the remaining memory from 640K and above is available as XMS memory.

b. Using upper memory

- To use memory as upper memory, we must start the EMM386.EXE driver in the CONFIG.SYS file. The XMS driver must be loaded ahead of the EMM386 driver. The following is the correct order for using these drivers in the CONFIG.SYS file:

  DEVICE = HIGH

  DEVICE=EMM386.EXE

- EMM386 automatically converts all of the existing extended memory to expanded memory. Since this is not always desirable, the parameter NOEMS tells the driver not to allocate any EMS memory but still allocate upper memory. To use the extended memory as XMS memory and still use EMM386 to provide upper memory, call both driver programs as follow:

  DEVICE=HIGH.SYS

  DEVICE=EMM386.EXE NOEMS

- We must also tell DOS to reserve all of the existing upper memory and make it available as "ordinary" conventional memory.

  DOS=HIGH, UMB

  Where UMB represents the upper memory block.

- Example: to reserve upper memory and high memory for DOS on a 80386 or higher computer and use 512K for expanded memory, use the following command lines:

DEVICE=HIGH.SYS

DEVICE=EMM386.EXE 512

DOS=HIGH, UMB

REM Other lines of the CONFIG.SYS follow

We can use NOUMB instead of UMB to prevent DOS from using the upper memory area as memory.

Booting DOS

Flipping the power switch (or simultaneously pressing the control, alt, and delete keys) causes hardware to read into memory the first sector from the disk in the system drive. The boot then reads IO.SYS, which, in return, initializes key system tables, reads MSDOS.SYS, and, finally, reads COMAND.COM.

Running DOS

Once loaded, DOS controls literally everything that happens on the computer. First, COMMAND.COM gets control and, by calling IO.SYS, displays a system prompt on the screen. As the user types a command, each character generates an interrupt. Responding to the interrupt, the operating system reads the character, stores it in memory, and, again using IO.SYS echoes it to the screen.

Fig. After the system is booted, the operating system's resident components occupy memory.

Interrupt vectors (first 1K)
IO.SYS
MSDOS.SYS
COMMAND.COM (resident)
Transient Area
COMMAND.COM (overlay)

The basic work flow is simple. A prompt is displayed. The user types a command or a program name. The appropriate operating system module or application program gets control. As the program runs, the operating system supports it by processing interrupts. Eventually, it returns control to COMMAND.COM, and the process is repeated, again and again, until the machine is shut down. DOS is command driven.

❑❑❑

"Education's purpose is to replace an empty mind with an open one." —M. Forbes

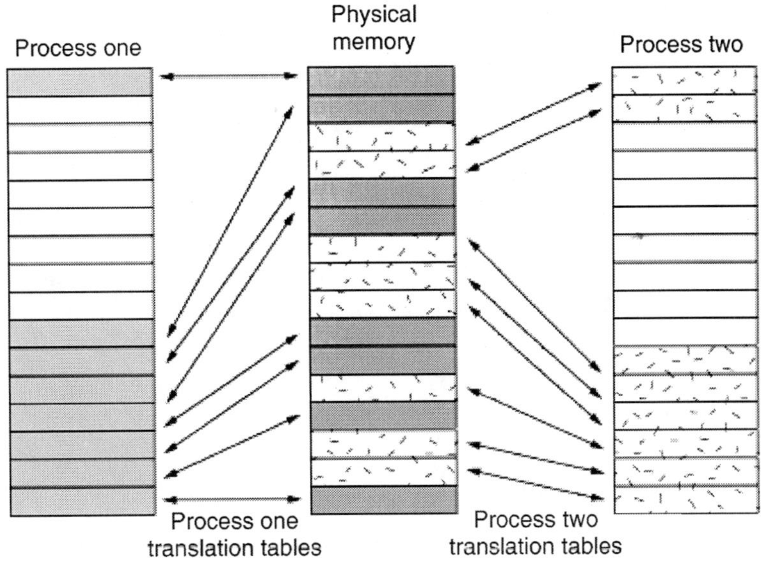

Address translation

UNIX

UNIX SYSTEM INTERNALS

UNIX is a time-sharing system, with program segments swapped in and out of memory as required. To ensure reasonable response time, processor access is limited by time-slicing. Segmentation is the most common addressing scheme, and most UNIX systems implement virtual memory techniques. Today, UNIX is a standard, particularly in the academic world, and is available on a variety of machines.

Essentially UNIX shell is a command interpreter, the shell is treated much like an application program and is technically not part of the operating system. This is an important UNIX innovation, because it allows a user to replace the standard shell with a custom shell.

Among its resident modules, UNIX contains an input/output control system, a file system, and routines to swap segments, handle interrupts, schedule the processor's time, manage memory space, and allocate peripheral devices. Additionally, the operating system maintains several tables to track the system's status.

Routines that communicate directly with the hardware are concentrated in a relatively small Kernel . The kernel is hardware dependent and varies from system to system. However, the interface to the kernel is generally consistent across implementations.

Because most operating systems are written in assembler language, they are limited to a single family of computers. UNIX on the other hand, was written primarily in a high-level language (c), making it highly portable (only a small portion of the kernel is written in assembler).

Unix user communicates with the operating system through a shell. Hardware-depended logic is concentrated in the kernel.

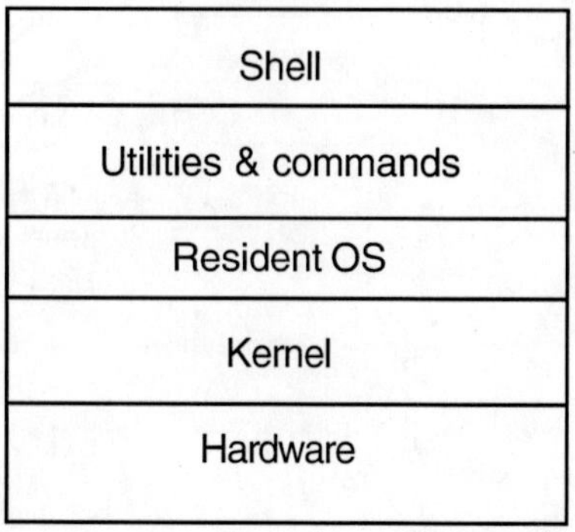

Shell
Utilities & commands
Resident OS
Kernel
Hardware

Images and Processes

The pseudo-computer concept is another important UNIX innovation. A user's routine is viewed as an image, defined by Ritchie and Thompson as an "execution environment" that consists of program and data storage, the contents of general purpose registers, the status of open files, the current directory, and other key elements. To the user, it appears that this image is executed on a private pseudocomputer under control of a command-driven operating system.

In reality, UNIX is a multiple-user, time-sharing system. An image consists of three segments (Fig. 2). First, starting at virtual address 0, is a program text segment, followed by a data segment. The image ends with a stack segment. Between data and the stack segments is a free area. As the program runs, the data segment grows toward high memory (down in Fig.2), and the stack segment grows toward low memory. The execution of an image is called a process. As a process executes, the image's text, data, and stack segments must be in memory.

Fig. 2 An image consists of a program text segment, a data segment, and a stack segment.

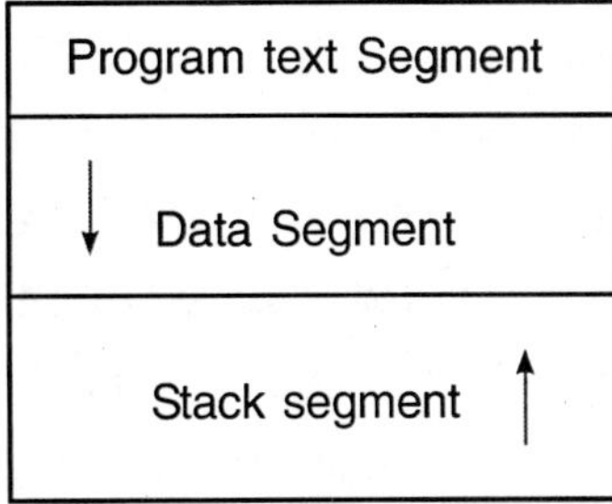

The data and stack segments, on the other hand, are private; for example, if two users are executing the same code, memory will hold one text segment, two data segments, and two stack segments. Additionally, each process has its own system data segment containing data needed by the operating system when the process is active. This system data segment is not part of the user's image; the user cannot access it. When the user calls the system (for example, to request I/O), the process switches from a user state to a system state, making the system data segments available to UNIX.

The text segment is reentrant. It two or more processes are executing the same code, only a single shared text segment is physically stored in real memory. The data and tack segments, however, are private.

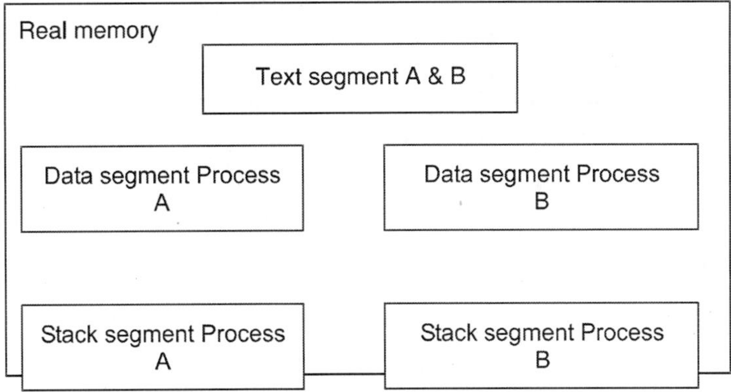

Process Creation

A process is created by a system call named fork. The fork system call, part of the operating system, is called by an executing process. In response, UNIX duplicates that process, creating two identical copies. Because both copies contain the system data segment, they share open files and other key data. The operating system distinguished between the parent and the child by giving them different return codes from the fork call. Thus, although the parent and the child are identical, they can check the return code and take different actions.

The parent starts the operation by calling fork. It's a system call, so a return address is stored in the process's system data area and UNIX gets control. After the duplicate process is created, control returns to the parent, which checks the return code. By convention, the parent gets the process number (called the process id, or pid) of the child (a positive integer), while the child gets a return code of 0 (a negative return code indicates an error). Because the return code is positive, the parent normally calls wait, and waits for the child to die/ finish processing. (Fig. a).

Fig. a) the parent calls fork. In response, the operating system creates a duplicate process (the child), and returns control to the parent. Since the return code is a positive integer, the parent drops into a wait state.

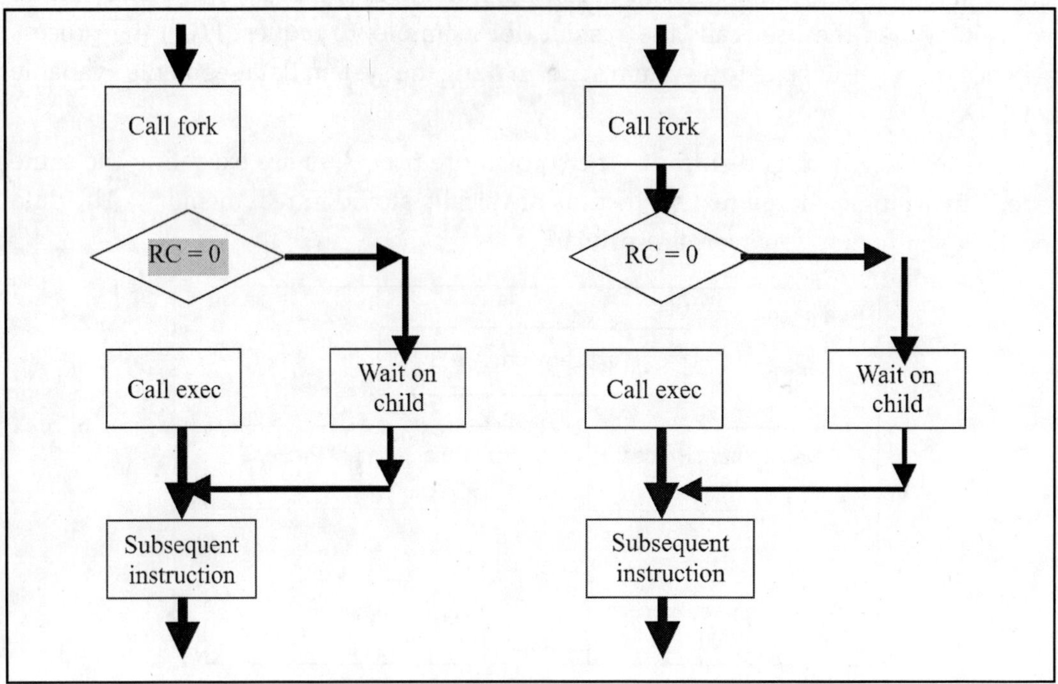

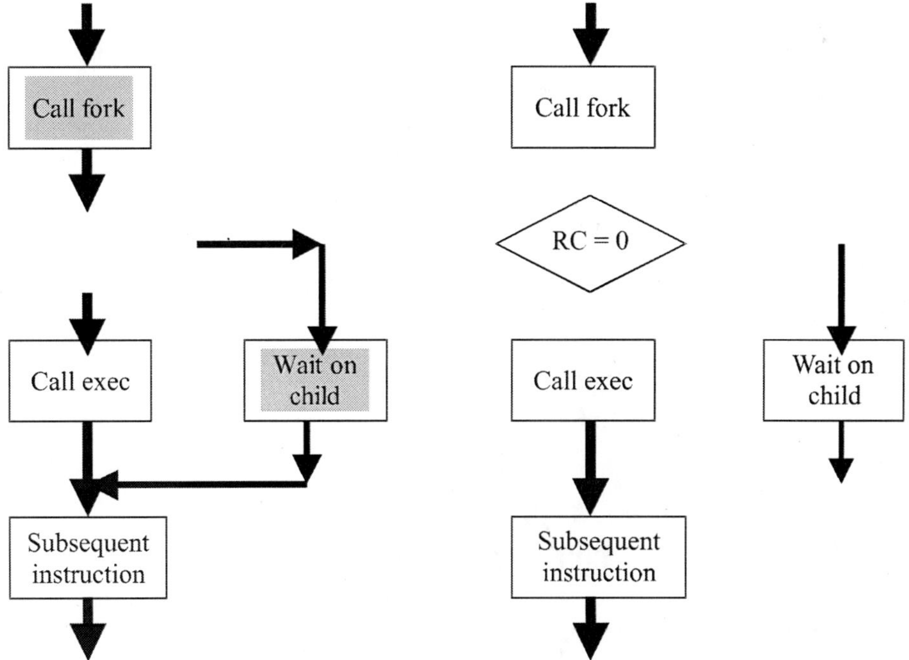

Eventually, the child begins to execute. Because it is a duplicate of the parent, the return address in its system data area points to the instruction immediately following fork (addresses are virtual). The child begins by checking the return code (Fig. 4b). It's 0, so the child calls another system call, exec.

Fig(b) the child begins by checking the return code. Because it's 0, the child calls exec.

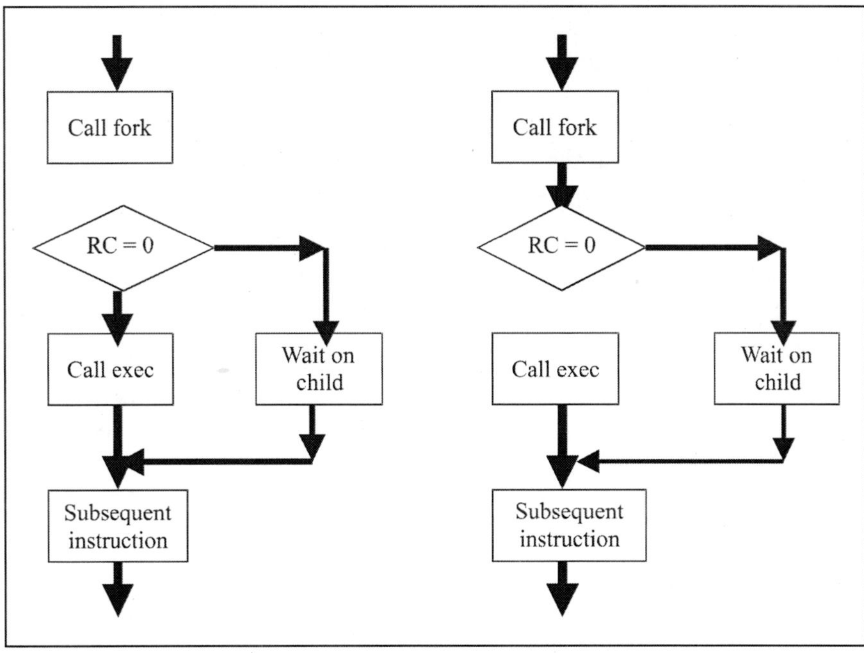

- The exec routine responds by overlaying the child's text and data segments with the contents of a new file (Fig. 4c). Technically, the resulting image is still the same process, but its contents are different, and UNIX might have to rearrange memory to accommodate the new segment. Later, when the child dies/ finish processing, the parent can resume processing.

Fig..c The exec routine overlays the child's text and data segments with the contents of a new file.

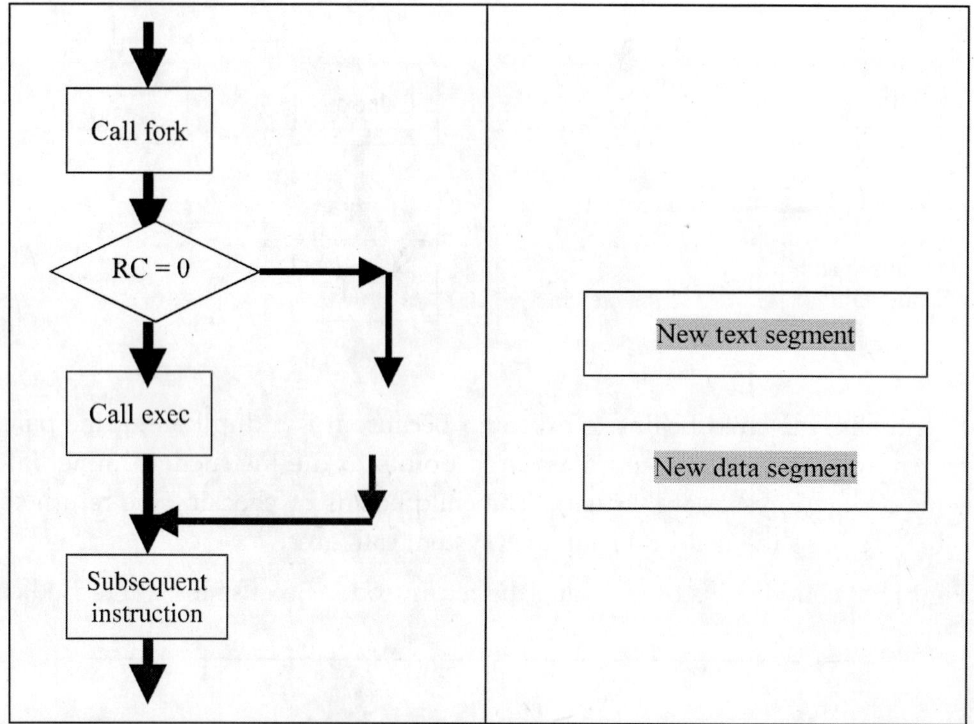

The parent calls fork. In response, UNIX duplicates the process, and returns control to the parent. Because the return code is a positive integer (the child's process number), the parent calls wait, and "goes to sleep" until the child dies/ finishes work. Eventually, the child gets control. It is a duplicate of the parent. When the parent called fork, the address of its next instruction was recorded in the system data area. The child's system data area contains the same (virtual) return address, so when the child gets control, the instruction following fork is executed. Typically, this instruction checks the return code. Because the return code is 0, exec is called, and a new program overlays the child. Following exec, the first instruction in this new program gets control. Eventually, the new program calls exit, and thus the child dies/ finishes work. Consequently, the parent is awakened, and, eventually, resumed processing.

Fig. d) When the child dies/ finishes processing, the parent resumes processing. Note that the child Process no longer exists.

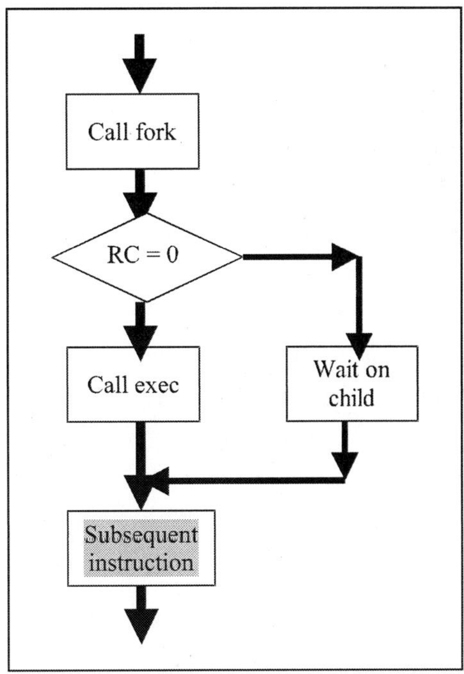

4. Initialization

When UNIX is booted, a process named init is activated. This "original ancestor" creates one process for each terminal line; for example, if the system supports eight concurrent terminals, eight processes are created. A user logs on to one of these processes. The logon process then (normally) executes (exec) the shell, and thus is overlayed. Later, when the shell dies (in other words, when the user logs off), init creates a new logon process.

When a user logs on, the logon process scans a table of login names, verifies the password, identifies the user's default shell and executes either the Bourne shell or the C shell. Because the shell is treated as a process, it's relatively easy to substitute a custom shell. Another option is no shell. In response to a particular login name, the logon process can start an application routine, effectively placing the user inside a restricted shell, thus limiting that user to commands and responses appropriate to that application routine. The logon process overlays itself with the user's primary system interface. When that interface dies, init starts another logon process, which waits for another user to log on.

5. Process Management

UNIX is a multiple-user operating system, with several concurrent programs occupying memory. It is inevitable that two or more programs will want the processor at the same time, so the operating system must carefully schedule them. Thus, UNIX contains a dispatcher.

The UNIX dispatcher relies on a process table that contains one entry for each process (Fig. 5). The entry is allocated when the process is created (fork) and freed when the process dies. Each entry contains all the data needed by UNIX when the process is not active. Among other things, the process table entry indicates whether the process is ready (awake) or waiting (asleep).

- For example, imagine the shell (the parent) has just received a command that requires a new process; and thus has called fork. In response, UNIX creates the new process, assigns it a process id (a positive integer), adds a new entity to the process table, and returns control to the shell. The shell then (typically) calls wait, and goes to sleep until the newly created child dies/ finishes work.

Fig. UNIX maintains a process table with one entry per process. The dispatcher uses this information to schedule processes.

One entry per process.
Each entry contains:
- Process number
- Process state (ready, waiting)
- Process priority
- Event number process is waiting on
- Text table address
- Data segment address
- Stack segment address
- System data segment address

- Meanwhile, the child gets control, calls exec, and carries out the command. As it finishes processing, it calls exit and dies. The death of a process generates an event that produces a signal. The event is reported to the operating system's event-wait routine as a positive integer-the event number or process number. UNIX responds by searching the process table and waking (setting to a ready state) every process waiting for that event.
- Each user process has a priority. Priorities are recomputed frequently by dividing execution time by elapsed real time; the smaller the number, the higher the priority. When an event signal is sensed, the operating system's event-wait routine gets control. First, it awakens all processes waiting for

that event. Then, it searches the process table, selects the highest priority ready process, and starts it. Imagine a process calls fork, performs some calculations, and then calls wait. What if, between fork and wait, the new process gets control and dies? By the time the parent calls wait, the event it plans to wait for has already happened.

- Because the child process has already died, it will not appear in the process table. When the UNIX wait routine gets control, it checks the process table, and, if the calling routine has no children, returns an error code. A programmer/ operator should be prepared for this sequence of events any time parallel processes are activated.

6. The Shell

- The UNIX shell is a customized command line interpreter. UNIX sees the shell as simply another process, so it is subject to change. The idea of a custom shell was an important UNIX innovation.
- When init creates a logon process, it opens the standard input, output, and error files, so the logon process can accept user input from the terminal and display both normal output and error messages. When a user logs on, the shell overlays the logon process's text and data segments, but the system data segment is not affected. Thus the shell's standard input, output, and error files are open. Consequently, the user can begin issuing commands without opening these standard files.
- In response to a command, the shell sets up an exec, calls fork, and then waits for the child process to carry out the command. If the command is followed by an ampersand (&), the shell does not wait. Instead, it starts a new process to carry out the command in parallel, and immediately displays a prompt for the next command.

Case1 What Is a Kernel?

The most fundamental level of UNIX is the kernel. User programs execute under the protection of the kernel and use its services. The kernel provides a standard interface to the system hardware and provides standard services over and above that to ease the process of developing and executing software on the hardware platform.

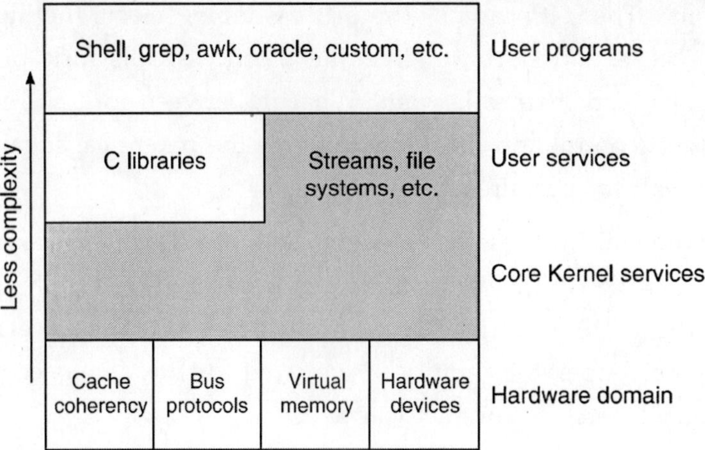

Case1.1 "That Picture"

The above diagram provides a concise view of the structure of a UNIX system, This diagram is supposed to represent the various layers in a UNIX system. Going from bottom to top, the software engineering effort becomes less complex and less shared. For example, every program in the system uses the virtual memory subsystem, although this is a very complex part of the system. It is a sharable part of the system, but each of its users is protected from the inherent complexity by the layers below it. This is the overriding mission of the kernel: to protect users from each other, and from the complexity of the system.

Starting at the lowest level, we have the platform itself, or the hardware domain. Included in this domain are all the physical attributes that need to be taken care of in order to execute software on the system. Some of these things are partially taken care of by the hardware but still require explicit action from the software on the system to instruct the hardware how it should, for example, ensure that the CPU cache reflects valid data for the next process to use.

Moving up the stack, we get to the core kernel services. This layer ensures that all layers above it are taken care of, in addition to providing standard interfaces to the hardware domain. For example, one of the overriding concepts of the UNIX model is that everything is a file. The core kernel services take care of this interface, providing the upper layers with a way of viewing (nearly) all hardware objects as a linear file.

This layer also provides the *process abstraction*. This is essentially how executing programs are handled by the system, providing each process with the illusion that it is operating independently on private hardware. It also takes care of isolation between these processes, ensuring that one process cannot corrupt the execution environment of another in any way.

In addition, the kernel also provides value-added services that can be used by the user programs. These are software modules that are not essential for the operation of the system but provide a more usable interface for the user. A prime example of this is the availability of many filesystems. A filesystem does not contribute directly to the running of the system but is more than just a simple service. It must have access to kernel memory for the sharing of the filesystem buffer cache and must have fast access to the hardware itself.

Everything else on the stack is user code. That is, it is not directly associated with the kernel. The C libraries are reusable software modules that are used to aid the rapid construction of user software. Note that Oracle is associated with the user processes at the very top of the model.

This is probably the highest-level view of what the kernel *does*; now it is time to take a look at how this is achieved from an implementation perspective.

Case1.2 Execution Modes

The UNIX operating system operates in two distinct modes: kernel and user. The kernel does not do anything mysterious; it is just software like the rest of the system:

```
$ file unix
unix: ELF 32-bit LSB executable 80386 Version 1
$ file /bin/grep
/bin/grep: ELF 32-bit LSB executable 80386 Version 1
or
$ file vmunix
vmunix: ELF-64 executable object file - PA-RISC 2.0 (LP64)
$ file iotest
iotest: ELF-64 executable object file - PA-RISC 2.0 (LP64)
```

It is executed on the same processors as the user software. However, the kernel has special duties and normally operates with a privileged status from a *hardware* perspective, able to access and modify addresses and registers that user mode cannot. This mode of execution is called *kernel mode*.

There are two distinct situations in which kernel mode is entered, excluding the boot process:

- A user process executes a system call or raises an exception (explicit kernel processing).
- System housekeeping occurs, such as time-slicing and servicing interrupts (implicit kernel processing).

Case1.3 "Explicit Kernel Processing (Process Context Kernel Mode)"

Starting with the user process, let's have a look at UNIX from a user perspective in order to see where the kernel fits in.

A user connects to the UNIX system by some mechanism, such as a login process for a shell user or an SQL*Net connection for a database user. Whichever way the user connects, the net result is a *process* on the system. This process is the executing context of a user program, and it is supported by the kernel with an operating environment. The environment for a process consists of

- A private memory map, including private stack and program counter
- A share of available processor capacity, up to 100 percent of one CPU if required and available
- The system call interface

The private memory map is a set of memory pages over which the user has exclusive rights. This memory map is actually a virtual memory map, which will be discussed in case3.2. For now, it is enough to think of this memory as a contiguous block of memory that is private to the user process. The block of memory is composed as shown in Figure case2.

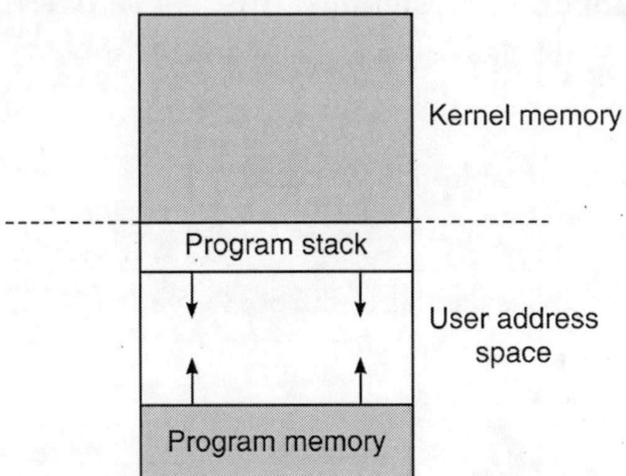

The lower portion of the memory map is accessible to the process, and the upper half of the map is a shared mapping of the kernel memory. All user processes have the kernel memory in their address spaces but cannot access it. In 32-bit UNIX implementations, it is common for the lower 2GB of the 32-bit address range to be used for user memory and the upper 2GB for kernel memory.

The "program memory" in the Figure case2 refers to all memory used to execute the user program, excluding the stack. This memory is further divided into as many as five types:

1. Text (the program itself)
2. Data (initialized variables)

3. BSS (uninitialized variables), including heap memory allocated by the malloc() family

4. Shared libraries (can include all items above for each library)

5. Shared locations (shared memory, memory mapped files)

The program stack is typically started at the top of the user address space, growing downward, while the program memory starts at the base and grows upward.

If this process is executing a program that operates only within that private memory map-that is, never requests more memory (program memory or stack), never causes an exception, and never needs to do any I/O-this process will never explicitly switch into kernel mode.

Considering that any kind of output, including screen output, is I/O, this hypothetical program would not be very useful to anybody. In order to perform I/O, however, the process needs to access the hardware of the system, which it cannot do in user mode. In this case, the process will execute a system call, which invokes a few actions on the system and results in the process running in kernel mode. This mode of execution is considered as *process context kernel mode.*

In modern systems, kernel mode is a hardware state invoked by a hardware trap on the processor. This puts the processor into kernel mode and allows the executing process to perform the required privileged operations. In order to continue, the kernel must first save the processing context of the user process-that is, program counter, general-purpose registers, memory management information, and stack pointer. It's worth noting that a switch to kernel mode usually does *not* need to perform any processor cache management, because the memory map does not change. Kernel mode and user mode both exist within the same process context, so no cache lines need to be invalidated on a switch into kernel mode. In fact, it is likely that the kernel processing will require some of the user pages, particularly the *u-area* (see Section case2.1), and any buffers required to process system calls. Once the transition to kernel mode is complete, the kernel can start to process the system call request.

While a process is in kernel mode, it has access to both kernel memory and user memory. However, no user code is executed while the process is in kernel mode. Instead, the user request is validated and, if permitted, performed on *behalf* of the user mode side (user context) of the process. Kernel execution occurs in the same process context as the user program, so all processor cycles consumed during this process are logged against the process under SYS mode

It was mentioned earlier that a process could cause an *exception*. An exception is caused by a process attempting to do something that is either impossible or prohibited.

Examples of this include segmentation violations (a process attempting to access memory that has not been allocated to it) and divide-by-zero exceptions. In this case, the kernel processes the relevant exception handler for that event, such as initiating a core dump, within the context of the process.

Case1.4 Implicit Kernel Processing (System Context Kernel Mode)

The second way that kernel code executes is when certain events occur in the system. These events basically consist of software and hardware *interrupts* and occur for various reasons. By processing these interrupts with *interrupt handlers*, the kernel ensures that

- All runnable processes receive a "fair share" of the CPU.
- All hardware interfacing is performed.

When a processor receives interrupts, it stops executing the current process and executes the *interrupt handler* for that interrupt. This happens regardless of whether the process was operating in user mode or in kernel mode, although the kernel has the ability to block interrupts selectively.

Interrupts are asynchronous with respect to the currently executing process and are caused by events that are not directly initiated by the process itself. Therefore, the handler must execute outside the context of the current process and neither logs its execution cycles against that process[1] nor accesses its address space.[2] This type of execution is considered as *system context kernel mode.*

The kinds of things that generate interrupts are I/O devices returning a completion status (including network traffic) and the hardware clock.

There are situations in the execution of the kernel code in which an interrupt handler cannot be serviced. One prime example of this would be if the kernel were already executing kernel code for a prior interrupt of that type. In this case, the kernel could corrupt its own address space by having incomplete memory updates from the first interrupt when the second is received. This situation is prevented through the use of

Interrupt Priority Levels (IPLs).

Using IPLs, the kernel can instruct the processor to ignore interrupts that it receives that have a lower priority than the specified level. Therefore, the kernel can set the interrupt level at a suitable level prior to processing a critical (i.e., protected) section of code. Any interrupts that have a lower priority than the one set are ignored by the processor, and the critical section can complete safely.

Interrupt levels are hardware-dependent entities and thus vary among processor architectures. Typically, there are several hardware interrupts, and a smaller number of software interrupts that can be programmed. The highest interrupt level is always reserved for machine exceptions: If there is a fatal problem in the hardware or the operating system, all processing must cease immediately to protect against widespread data corruption resulting from unknown states in the system. When a fault of this nature is detected, the highest-level interrupt is generated in order to generate a "panic" of the system.

The next level down is usually reserved for the hardware clock, followed by various peripheral interrupts (disk, network, etc.), and software interrupts have the lowest priority level. Below all of this comes level zero, which is the level at which user mode processing occurs. This allows *anything* to interrupt user mode processing.

The Hardware Clock

The hardware clock is a critical component of a UNIX system. It not only determines the rate at which the processor is driven (this is why it is known as *clock speed*) but also generates interrupts that the kernel uses to implement *timeslicing*.

When the system boots, the kernel programs the hardware clock to interrupt the processor at defined intervals. Each time this interval arrives, a high-priority interrupt is received that is processed by the kernel's *clock interrupt handler*. This handler runs in system context, because it has nothing to do with any user process.

The period that the clock interrupts is determined by the value for one *tick*, frequently set at *100 Hz*, or *10 milliseconds*. Every 10 milliseconds, the interrupt handler is fired and must perform several critical functions, such as incrementing the system time, updating the system and user time statistics for running processes, and posting alarm() signals to processes that have requested them. The clock handler also ensures that the illusion of concurrent execution is maintained on the system by providing the mechanism for implementing *time sharing*.

Time Sharing

Every process in the system is assigned a *quantum*, which is the maximum amount of time the process can execute on the processor, before other processes must be considered for execution. This period varies between platforms and between scheduler classes, but is typically 100 milliseconds, or ten ticks of the hardware clock.

When the quantum is used up, the kernel checks the run queue, and determines whether the process must be suspended from execution and put back onto the run queue. If there are no processes on the run queue of sufficient priority, the process is allowed to execute for another quantum. If the process is taken off the processor, it remains dormant until it is scheduled back onto the processor when it reaches the head of the queue. This period is typically very short and is weighted by the priority of processes on the run queue.

In this way, the kernel can provide the illusion to all the processes in the system that they are concurrently running on the processor. This, combined with the private memory map, provides a private environment for each process. More detail is provided on process scheduling in the next section.

Case2 Processes

In the preceding section, a level of detail was reached with regard to what a process *is* from an execution standpoint. From a high-level perspective, a process is simply the kernel's abstraction of all the attributes of a running program, in order to control its execution.

All user processes in the system have an entry in the *process table*, with the following attributes:

- A private, virtual memory map
- A runtime context (program counter, registers, stack pointer, etc.)
- System resources

Case2.1 The Process "Table"

The process table is the master reference for the process. Although the detail of the process table is not directly useful in implementing large Oracle systems, an understanding of the concepts is useful and helps when developing monitoring hooks into the system.

In physical terms, the process table exists as two structures for each process: a proc structure and a u structure (or u-area). Historically, the proc structure was a table of fixed size that was set at kernel link time and was not changeable at runtime. This is the reason for the quotation marks around the word "table" in the head-it really isn't a "table" any more.

The proc structure contains all the information that the kernel could require when the process is not running, and so exists in kernel memory that is always mapped. By contrast, the u-area contains information that usually is needed only while the process is actually running; the u-area is stored in the private memory map of the process.[4]

The reason for using two structures to maintain the process control information is that some of the information does not need to be accessible by the kernel when the process is not running. It does not make sense to tie up global kernel memory for information that is typically not required when the process is not running.

Depending on the specific implementation, the u-area can contain the following information for each process:

- File descriptor table
- Process control block (execution context of the process, including general-purpose registers, stack pointer, MMU registers, etc.)
- Per-process kernel stack
- Pointer to corresponding proc structure

Though the list above covers the major items, many other pieces of information can be stored in the u-area.

The proc structure focuses on the more globally accessed attributes of a process:

- User credentials
- Signal masks
- PID
- Active process list pointer (see case 2.2)
- Queue list pointers for run queue
- Priority information
- Indirect pointer to u-area

All of the items listed above, with the exception of the PID, can be written to by other processes in the system or the kernel, and therefore need to be globally accessible. The list pointers will be covered in more detail in case2.2.

When the process information is divided among such structures, it can complicate the retrieval of this information. UNIX commands, such as ps and fuser, use information from both of these structures and therefore require access to all of this information, even when the process in question is not active and could even be swapped out to disk. When the process is swapped out to disk, this includes the u-area, and so special access methods need to be available for gaining access to this information from the swap area. This can be achieved using special system calls or through the use of a custom API. The actual method used is implementation-dependent.

Case2.2 Process Scheduling

The subject of process scheduling is one that can have a direct bearing on the performance of your Oracle database. Although this has been touched on already in this chapter, it merits some more detail.

As previously mentioned, UNIX is a time-sharing system at heart. This means that the kernel will provide the illusion to all the processes on the system that they all have their own CPU to run on. On a large database server with 4,000 processes, it is not practical (or scalable) to provide a processor for each process, and so it is the time sharing that allows a far smaller number of processors to provide this illusion.

The key to providing this illusion is the hardware clock, as previously discussed, and *context switches*. Context switching is best covered in case3, and so for now it is safe to view context switching from the high level of just switching processes on and off processors. Also, to make this discussion simple, assume that we are referring to a uniprocessor UNIX platform.

Process Scheduling Primer: Uniprocessor Platforms

When a process has used its time quantum (i.e., when the hardware clock interrupt handler has fired) and another process is waiting to execute (the other process is termed *runnable*), it is switched off the processor and the new process is switched onto the processor. The switching of processes, and the entire clock interrupt handler, must be very efficient in order to minimize the overhead of processing small time slices. If this operation is a noticeable percentage of the quantum itself, then this is the percentage of system that is "wasted" on the task of time sharing.

This simplistic view of time sharing is useful in gaining an initial understanding of the concepts. However, the actual implementation of time sharing is a good deal more complex, having to deal with such things as different priority processes, balancing throughput against response time, managing CPU cache warmth on multiprocessor machines, and so on. The handling of this complex time-sharing requirement is called *process scheduling*.

There are several variables that affect which process will be placed on an available processor:

- Priority of process
- Recent CPU usage for process
- "Nice" value
- Machine load average
- Position in run queue

When a process becomes runnable, it is placed on a run queue-that is, a queue for the processor in order to be run. This is achieved by adding the proc structure of the process onto a linked list that makes up the run queue.

The architecture of the run queues is very platform-specific, especially when the platform supports complex hardware arrangements such as NUMA. In order to keep this discussion simple, we will refer to the Berkeley software distribution (BSD) run queue architecture.

BSD maintains several run queues, each of which queues processes of a specific priority. When a process has used its quantum on the processor, the scheduler scans the run queues in order, from highest priority to lowest priority. If a process is found on a run queue with a priority greater than or equal to that of the currently executing process, the old process is switched off the processor and the queued process is switched on. If there are no processes on queues with priority greater than or equal to that of the currently executing process, the process is permitted to continue running for up to another quantum before the queues are checked once again.

If a process of higher priority becomes runnable, the current process is preempted off the processor even if it has not used its entire quantum.

The priority of a process is governed by two factors and will be constantly adjusted by the kernel during the lifetime of the process based on the system load average. These factors are the estimated recent CPU usage by this process and the "nice" value of the process.

The nice value of a process is specified by the user at process start-up using the nice command. This value ranges from -20 to +19, with the default being 0. Superuser privileges are required to decrease the nice value, because this increases the priority of the process above the normal priority for user processes. A user can elect to put a larger nice value on the process in order to run at a lower priority and therefore be "nice" to the other users of the system.

The recent CPU usage of the process is calculated using several algorithms. It is not necessary to go into the specifics of these algorithms, because they are covered comprehensively in various other books (see _case9 at the end of this chapter). It worthwhile discussing the basics, however.

If a process is using a good deal of CPU, this will be reflected in the recent CPU counter, which in turn is used as a negative weighting factor in the algorithm that determines the priority of the process. Therefore, CPU-intensive processes cannot dominate a system unless there are only lower-priority processes in the run queue or the system is idle. Likewise, if there are two processes trying to use as much CPU as possible, they will end up on the same low-priority run queue and will compete against each other.

The recent CPU counter is incremented for every tick the process executes. This value is then weighted once a second, using the system load average and the process nice value in order to give the counter a decay over time. The load average is used as the amnesia factor in keeping track of the used CPU; if the system is very heavily loaded, the CPU counter will take a long time to forget previous CPU usage, and the priority of the process will be proportionately lower. If the load average is small, the used CPU will be forgotten relatively quickly, and the process will gain a higher priority.

If a process needs to block while it is running, such as waiting for an I/O operation to complete, it is taken off the processor and placed on a different type of queue-one of the *sleep queues*. The process stores a *wait channel* in its proc structure and puts itself onto the correct sleep queue for that resource. The wait channel is typically the address of the structure on which the process is waiting, which is hashed to obtain the correct sleep queue. When a resource becomes available, its address is hashed by the kernel to find the correct queue, and all processes waiting on it are woken and put back on a run queue.

If the process was blocked waiting for the completion of a system call, such as a read(), the process is put on a high-priority run queue until the process completes the switch back into user mode. At this point, the process priority is reduced, typically resulting in the process being switched off the processor in order to service processes of higher priority.

When processes are executing on a processor, they are neither on a run queue nor on a sleep queue. At this point, the process is active and exists on another list. In SVR4, this list is known as practive and is a linked list of all the processes currently on the processor, linked against the "active processor link" item in each proc structure.

Advanced Scheduling: Multiprocessor Process Scheduling

When multiple processors are present in a system, the scheduling algorithms become more complex. In the case of NUMA systems, this is an attempt to keep active processes close to their resident memory. In SMP machines, it is implementation-dependent: Some platforms do no extra scheduling work, whereas others do.

SMP

With multiple processors (sometimes referred to as *engines* by kernel engineers) and a relatively low number of runnable processes at any one time, some major optimizations can be made by maintaining cache warmth in the CPU caches. This is known as *cache affinity*.

An algorithm can be implemented, using the number of clock ticks since the process last ran, which determines whether the process is likely to have cache warmth on the processor on which it last ran. Waiting for the correct engine to become available may incur a delay in the execution of the process, and so this algorithm needs to be well tested with real applications.

In testing with and without affinity, OLTP Oracle workloads have been shown to exhibit as much as 15 percent more throughput when affinity is enabled.

NUMA

In NUMA configurations, it becomes more critical that the scheduler place processes on the correct engine. Although some NUMA configurations support dynamic page relocation between NUMA nodes, this is expensive at best, and the majority of memory for a given process will always reside on one node or another anyway. Therefore, it is a fair assumption that the scheduler should always attempt to schedule processes on engines on the same node as the resident set of the process.

This results in several per-node run queues, in order to ensure the locality bias in selecting processes to run. It's worth noting that the scheduler cannot factor in the location of any mapped shared memory, because this is not part of the process's private memory. In the case of all the processes in the system all running the same binary (such as oracle), the operating system may elect to store a single shared text segment local to each NUMA node in order to maximize the locality of reference.

Case2.3 Signals

Signals are the mechanism used to notify processes of asynchronous events. Even novice users are familiar with the kill command, which is used to send these signals to processes.

Most users are aware of the signal mechanism only from the user perspective-that of killing a process in order to terminate its execution. In fact, signals are very much more flexible than a simple termination mechanism, and most can be trapped and controlled in a programmable manner by the process.

Signals are passed to the process by the kernel. They can be initiated by other processes in the system or by the target process itself. The kernel passes the signal to the process by setting a bit that corresponds to the signal in the proc structure for the process, as shown in Figure case3.

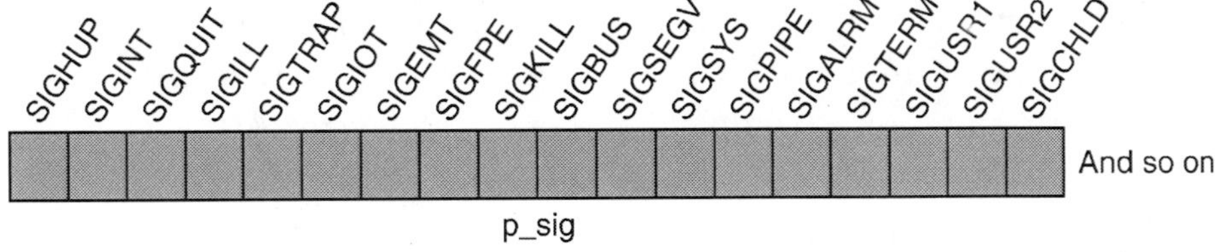

Signal bitmask in proc structure

This bitmask is called p_sig in SVR4 and p_siglist in BSD-based implementations. The bitfield is used to store *pending signals* for the process.

Before the pending signal bitmask is updated, however, the kernel checks that the signal has not been explicitly ignored by the process. If the signal has been ignored, the kernel will not even set the bit in the bitmask. Once the bit is set in the proc structure, the kernel will attempt to wake up the process in order to receive the signal (if it is not already running). After this, the processing of the signal is entirely the responsibility of the process itself.

The signal bitmask is checked

- Every time the process returns to user mode from kernel mode
- Before going to sleep in kernel mode
- On waking from an interruptible sleep

The trend here is for the bitmask to be checked prior to returning to user mode from kernel mode. The reason for this is that some signals (namely SIGKILL and SIGSTOP) cannot be processed in user mode, because their handlers are not programmable. Once the bitmask is checked, the signals that have been received are processed by the process *in kernel mode*. The first action the kernel takes is to check if the signal is SIGKILL or SIGSTOP. If so, the actions are taken in kernel mode without returning to user mode. These actions terminate the process, or suspend the process and put it to sleep, respectively.

Case3 Memory Management: The Virtual Memory System

case3.1 Introduction

In simplistic, single-tasking computer systems, programs can be compiled to locate themselves, and run, at specific memory addresses within the available physical memory. The flow of control is passed from task to task on completion, with potentially only one program in memory at any one time.

A very simple operating system, for example, has an operating system "kernel" compiled to run at a specific address and all user programs compiled to run at another specific address. The control of the system starts with the operating system, from which other programs can be executed. The other programs all locate themselves at addresses separate from that of the O/S; the O/S can remain in memory while this happens. Once the program is complete, the operating system gains control of the system once more.

There are several problems with this arrangement:

- Little or no memory protection between programs: All programs can read or write all memory locations.

- Programs are limited to an unknown, finite amount of physical memory on the system.
- Programs must execute serially and, unless compiled for physically separate memory ranges, must overlay the previously executing program.

The last problem has two serious implications:

1. The system cannot support multitasking.
2. Software development is complex and machine-dependent.

These implications go directly against two of the design goals of UNIX, and so this arrangement is a nonstarter. Another scheme must therefore be adopted-*virtual memory* and its associated *memory management*.

case3.2 Virtual Memory Introduction

UNIX systems implement virtual memory. Virtual memory separates the address space seen by a process from real physical memory addresses. This is achieved using memory address translation as an operating system function.

Address Translation

Address translation allows all processes in the system to address the same locations as if they were private, with the system ensuring that the physical address used is distinct from other processes.

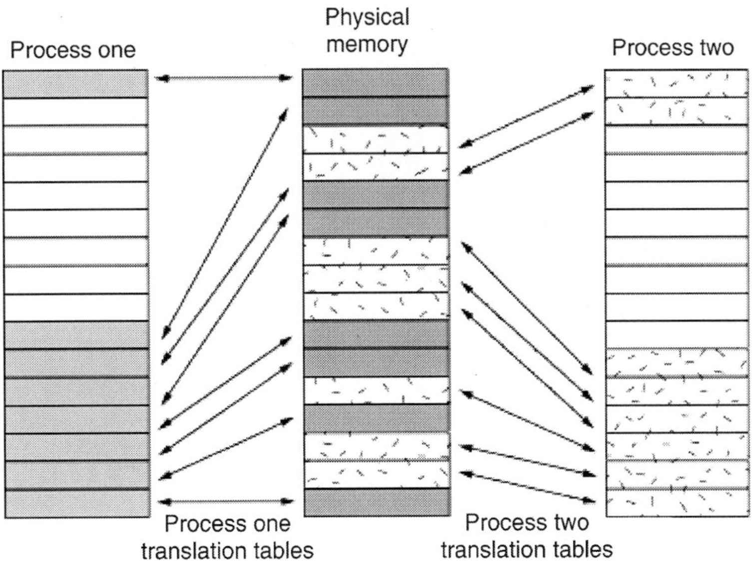

Address translation

In Figure case5, there are two processes, each using half of the physical memory in the machine (for simplicity of example). Each of the two processes has an identical address space, or memory map, that is the same size as the physical address space. Although these processes are using physically different memory locations, both are under the illusion that they start at address zero[6] and have contiguous memory allocated beyond that (plus stack).

Each of the cells in Figure case5 represents the smallest unit of granularity that the UNIX system considers from a memory management perspective-a *page*. The concept of a page is used in order to reduce the space and resource overhead of managing a large amount of memory on the system. It is common in modern systems for the page size to be set at 4KB, although some systems now support variable page sizes in order to increase the efficiency of very large memory (VLM) applications.

The glue that holds this process together is the *address translation tables*. These tables hold the mapping of virtual addresses (those that the process uses) to physical addresses (actual memory locations). In UNIX systems, these tables normally come in the form of *page tables* and, optionally, *translation lookaside buffers (TLBs)* in the processor *memory management unit* (*MMU*).

The page table consists of several *page table entries (PTEs)* for each process, arranged as an array, as shown in Figure

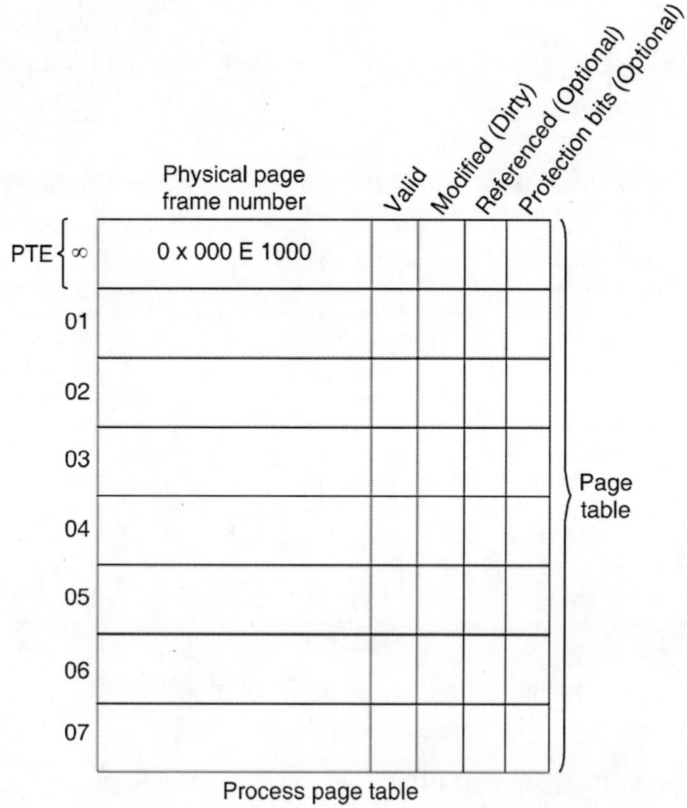

Process page table

For a given *virtual* page frame (00 to 07 in Figure case6) of a process, there is a corresponding PTE, located at the same offset in the array that makes up the page table. So, the first page that makes up the address space of the process in this example is mapped to the page starting at *physical* address 0x000E1000. The actual offset within the page remains the same as the offset within the virtual page.

It was mentioned earlier that some systems now support variable-size pages. This is a result of the overhead now imposed in managing the huge quantities of memory found in very large systems. For example, if an Oracle database server has a 4GB SGA, this typically means that each connection to the database needs to have a page table large enough to cater for every page in the SGA in addition to the process memory itself. Each PTE is typically 32 bits, and so a 4KB page size would yield a 4MB (1 million times 4 bytes) page table for each process. Not only does this size of page table mean the kernel is spending a good deal of time managing page tables, but this memory is also located in kernel memory, not user memory. If 5,000 users are due to connect to this system, this means the kernel memory needs to be greater than 20GB. When variable page sizes are used, the SGA can be assigned, say, 4MB pages, thus reducing the size of the page table for the mapping.

The actual structure of each entry in the page table is defined by the hardware architecture-specifically the MMU of the processor. Each processor family has its own structure for defining virtual to physical mappings in the MMU, and some support more functionality in the hardware than others, specifically in the area of *memory protection* and the presence of a *referenced bit*.

Although the hardware dictates the structure of the page table entries, it is the UNIX kernel that is responsible for all the manipulation of the entries in the table and for ensuring that the MMU is using the correct PTEs for the running process. At this stage, it is worth mentioning the effects of the two major variants of CPU cache architecture: *physically mapped* and *virtually mapped*.

A physically mapped architecture is laid out as shown in Figure

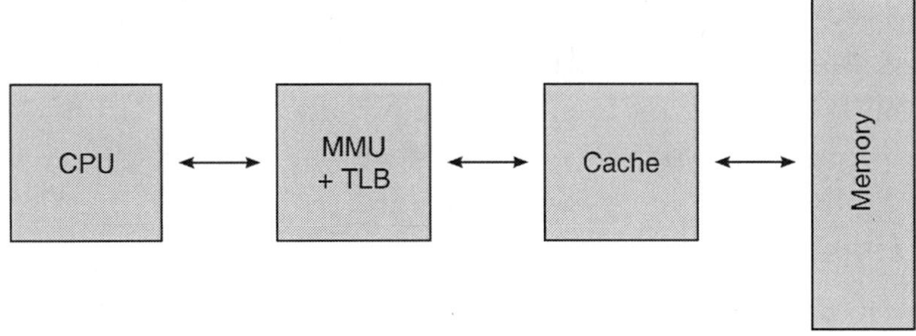

Physically mapped cache

Case7 This is the traditional approach to caching, because the operating system does not need to be aware of the operation of the cache. Whenever a request for data is made by the CPU, the address (which remains as a virtual address) is passed through to the MMU, which does a conversion of the virtual address to a physical address. It does this using the TLB, which is a *fully associative cache*. This means that it has the ability to search all the lines (fully associative access) in the TLB concurrently, to determine the physical address to search for in the cache.

The TLB contains PTEs specified by the kernel, and this is the reason why the structure of the PTE is dictated by the CPU architecture. The kernel is responsible for loading the registers of the TLB with the correct PTE information for the active process. For any given process, the kernel mappings will not change, because all processes have the kernel mapped in their address space. On the right of the MMU in Figure case7, all addresses are physical.

It is clear that having to precede even the cache access with a lookup on the TLB can impose a significant overhead. In the case that the TLB does not contain the PTE required for the operation, a reference to main memory needs to be made in order to prime the TLB. Luckily, this normally means that the page has not been accessed for a comparatively long time, and so the impact is not felt very frequently.

In some modern systems, a different approach has been taken with the cache. Instead of using the physical address to determine the correct line and tag within the cache, the virtual address is used (see Figure case8).

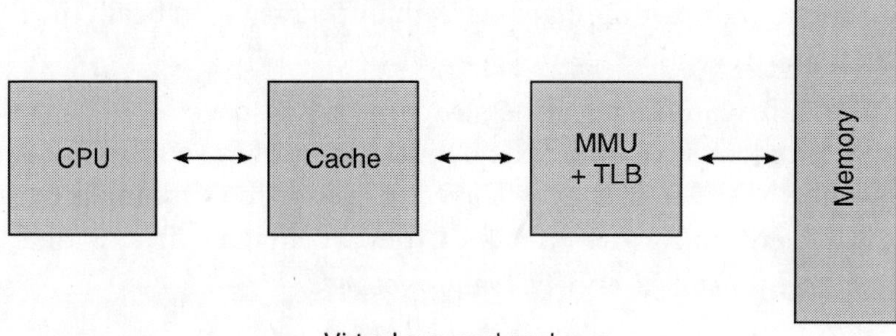

Virtual mapped cache

The effect of this is that the CPU can request data from the cache directly by virtual address. The MMU needs to be used only when a cache miss occurs and a physical memory access is required. The requirement for a TLB is less in this arrangement, because the MMU is now positioned in a slower part of the system than it is in a physically mapped architecture. This having been said, many architectures implement virtual caches with TLBs for enhanced performance.

The downside of a virtual cache is that the kernel is now required to manage much of the cache coherency, because the hardware is unaware of the differences among the many identical virtual addresses that refer to different physical memory locations. Address 0x1000 for process A is *not* the same memory location as address 0x1000 for process B.

To alleviate the ambiguity in the cache, the system typically uses the process ID of the relevant process as part of the tagging infrastructure in the cache. The hardware has no concept of process IDs,[8] and so the coherency of the cache must involve the operating system: At a minimum, the kernel must inform the processor of the identity of the current process in order for the correct tags to be checked in the cache.

Cache coherency across DMA operations is also more complex, because the majority of I/O devices have no concept of virtual addresses; they transfer to and from physical memory addresses.

Context Switch

When the operating system switches one process off the processor and puts a different one on, several actions must be taken to

- Preserve the context of the prior process.
- Restore the context of the activated process.

  These actions constitute the formal definition of a *context switch*. The context of a process typically includes the following:

- Stack pointer
- Program counter
- Other general-use registers in CPU
- Virtual address mapping

The first three attributes are referred to as the *process control block*, or PCB, and relate directly to saving the execution context of the process. The last attribute is that of the PTEs, and their presence in the TLB.

When a new process is switched onto a processor, the MMU must be informed of the new address mappings for that process. This applies whether the cache is virtual or physical. If a TLB is present, the kernel must also ensure that any mappings that are not relevant for the new process are invalidated, making the MMU reload the correct mapping from memory on access. This is necessary because the MMU does not have any concept of the process executing on the CPU, and merely changing address mappings does not mean that the process has just changed. The classic example of this would be a process issuing an exec() call, which results in all prior mappings changing to support the new program.

The kernel will load up the MMU's registers with the location of the new page table for the process, followed by a flush of the irrelevant TLB entries for the new process. The new process will keep all of the kernel TLB entries, because these addresses will continue to have the same mapping for the new process.

Once this process has been completed, the new process is allowed to run.

Further MMU Considerations

The operation of the MMU and associated TLB are somewhat complicated by the following aspects of modern UNIX systems:

· Memory protection

· Presence of swap area

· Multiprocessor (MP) architectures

The MMU determines whether or not a page can be read from or written to. This includes mapped pages with memory protection bits set in the PTE and unmapped pages that the process cannot use. In either case, the MMU raises a trap for the kernel to deal with.

The presence of the swap area is discussed in Section case4, where we complicate the virtual memory system further by using more memory than we physically have.

In multiprocessor systems, the presence of the TLB introduces further cache coherency considerations that are unrelated to the CPU cache coherency. For example, if the virtual-to-physical mapping or memory protection for a *kernel* page changes, TLBs in *all* MMUs must be updated to reflect this change. Another example would be shared memory accessed by several processes. This includes explicit shared memory segments and also *copy-on-write* data segments for a program that has executed fork() with no exec(). Copy on write will be discussed in later.

In this case, the kernel must initiate a "TLB shootdown" in order to ensure that all other TLBs are current with the new information. This is an explicit operation, for which the kernel typically maintains a set of data structures that map which PTEs are located in the various TLBs on the MP system. Using this map, the kernel can explicitly invalidate the changed PTEs in all the TLBs.

Any changes in the PTEs are typically *not* loaded into the various TLBs, because doing so would be a very expensive default operation. Instead, the entries are simply invalidated, forcing the MMU to reload the entry on the next reference. In many cases, the reload will not be required before the process is switched off the CPU, and so the work is prevented altogether.

case4 Virtual Memory Hierarchy

The preceding section concentrated on the generic attributes of virtual memory (VM), where a finite amount of memory is available on the system and is the maximum amount of memory that can be used among all the processes.

In reality, many of the pages of a given process do not need to be resident in memory all the time, and making them so would be wasteful of the valuable memory resource. A good example of this is Oracle Forms, where the size of the physical process may be 16MB or more. In a running system, experience has shown that only around 8MB of these pages need to be in memory at any one time in order to execute the Forms application with performance quite comparable to that of a fully resident image.

In order to support this optimization of real memory, the memory hierarchy needs to be extended to physical disk, the next step down in the memory hierarchy (see Figure case9).

case4.1 The Memory/Disk Hierarchy

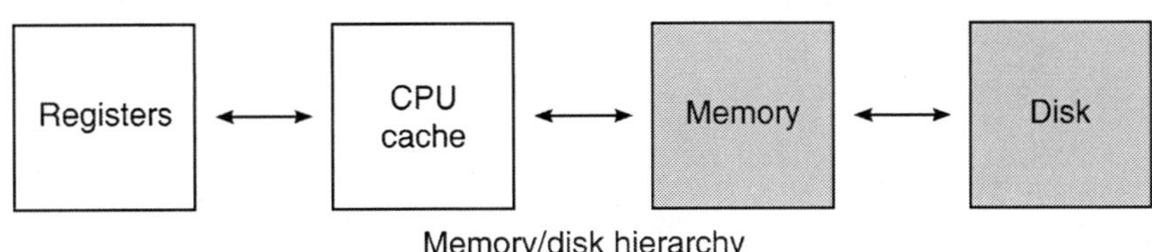

Memory/disk hierarchy

The use of physical disk spindles is a natural extension of the familiar memory hierarchy between CPU cache memory and main system memory. The next step after main system memory is physical disk, which is much cheaper and slower than system memory.

Using disk to extend memory capacity was once a larger issue than it is today. In the past, memory chips were scarce and expensive, and the system architectures were not able to address large amounts of real memory. Therefore, disk-based memory hierarchies were essential to providing the capability for many concurrent users on a UNIX system.

In modern systems, memory is a far less important issue than it used to be, in terms of both cost and addressability. In fact, in building a high-performance Oracle database server, it is preferable always to work within the confines of the physical memory on the system, and not to rely on physical disk to provide additional memory capacity.

Unlike the case of Oracle Forms cited above, Oracle Server processes share critical resources between them, meaning that one process can directly slow down all other processes in the system by holding one of the resources for an extended period. If the process needs memory that has been paged out to disk in order to complete the processing under a latch, all other processes will wait for this page-in operation before the latch is released.

The use of disk in the memory hierarchy is not limited to the sharing of physical memory, however. It also allows the rapid execution of program executables, by breaking the reliance on the entire image being in memory prior to execution. This allows the program to execute as soon as the first page is resident in memory.

case Implementing the Hierarchy

Demand Paging

Although the full detail of the hierarchy varies across implementations, all modern virtual memory systems implement a form of *demand paging*. Demand paging extends the concepts presented in the preceding section by specifying that any given page in the system can be resident or nonresident (on disk) at any one time. This does not affect the operation on that piece of memory, because the kernel intervenes if the page is nonresident and loads the page back into memory before the operation is carried out.

The implementation of demand paging is based on the operation of the MMU and PTEs. When a page is requested, the request is serviced by the MMU. If the MMU cannot resolve the request, because the page is either not resident or not yet allocated, a page fault is generated. This is serviced by the kernel, and the appropriate action is taken, based on why the page reference could not be resolved by the MMU. If the page has never been allocated, the kernel will generate an exception for the process and send the appropriate signal.

If the page has been allocated but is located on disk, the kernel will load the page back into memory and create a new map for that virtual address, pointing it to the new physical address. The operation will then be allowed to continue.

Virtual Memory Cache Analogy

Virtual memory can be considered a cache of disk storage. This does not mean that it is the same as the buffer cache, but rather a more complex affair. However, it is safe to view the primary execution object as the on-disk copy of the memory itself. In the same way that a CPU cache mirrors the contents of physical memory in order to speed access, so the physical memory of the system is mirroring the contents of the disk in order to speed access to it.

In the case of program executables, this is a very straightforward concept to grasp: The program is on disk and, on each access to the pages that make up the file, the page is loaded into some available physical memory location in order to speed the access to the instructions in that page. The analogy to CPU caches here is the loading of cache lines (analogous to pages) from physical memory (analogous to disk blocks) before execution.

In the case of other memory objects-namely, anonymous objects such as data segments, user stacks, and so on-there is initially *no* on-disk representation. In order to deal with this, an area of disk is allocated from the swap area, a special partition or series of partitions set up for this task. This then becomes the on-disk representation of the pages allocated for this process.

When a page is first allocated to an anonymous piece of memory, nothing happens; the kernel simply ensures that the disk area is available. On first access, the page is allocated a physical memory page, which would be zero-filled by the kernel on first use. The process can now use this page as required, operating as a write-back cache (see case 2.1.4). The disk version of this block becomes stale at this point.

This allocation is just the same as a CPU writing to a cache line for the first time; as soon as the CPU has written to it, the line in physical memory is stale, and the line in cache represents the current version.

Pager Objects

The implementation of the actual paging interface varies among different VM systems, so the method presented here represents one of the more common approaches-that of an object-based implementation.

The first concept of an object-based pager interface was introduced above; there are two different types of memory consumer, both of which are used by a process:

- File-based memory objects, such as program executables and mmap() files.
- Anonymous memory, such as program data segments, heap, and stack.

When segments of these types are created by the kernel, the kernel instantiates an object specific for that type of memory allocation. Both of the classes that define this object implement a standard interface that the kernel expects to be present (see Figure case10).

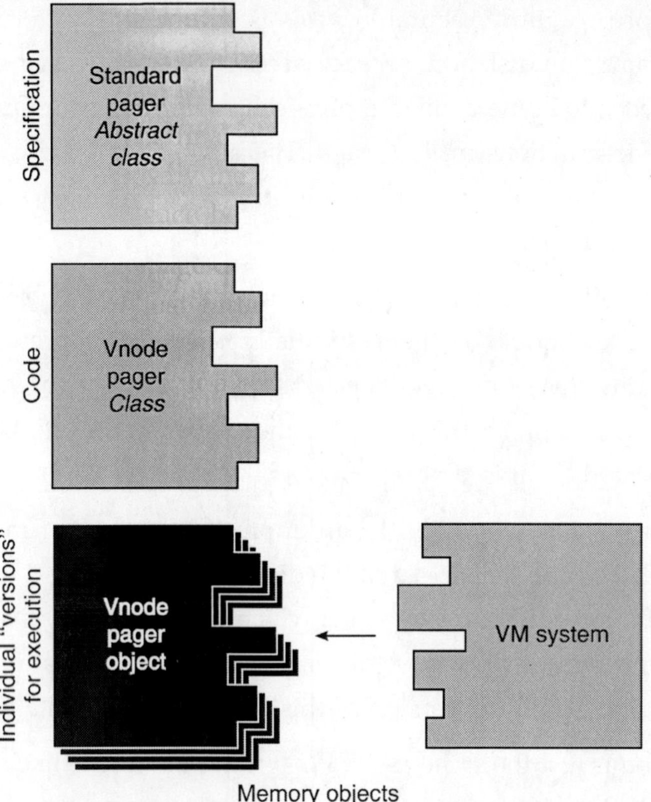

For those not familiar with object-oriented concepts, don't worry-it is not important that you fully understand these concepts at this stage. Basically, an *abstract class* is one that simply defines what is required from a class that *subclasses* it (it adopts the abstract class as its parent specification). A *class* is code that is fully inclusive from data and function perspectives. It contains all the data declarations and all the functions that operate on that data.[9] When a class is invoked, an *object* is created, which is basically a physical "version" of the class-one that exists in executable form in memory.

In the case of memory objects, the VM system is no longer concerned about the implementation or special requirements of a particular type of pager. As long as the pager subclasses the abstract class (i.e., specification) that the VM system expects, the VM system does not need to be cognizant of any of the detail.

The example in Figure case10 uses a *vnode* pager object. A vnode is an important part of the operation of modern UNIX kernels. It is the kernel's view of an active file. The "v" in vnode stands for *virtual*-that is, the vnode is an abstraction of any particular filesystem's unique file identifier. It exists in order to break the prior hard link between the kernel and a filesystem, and allows any filesystem with a vnode interface to be mounted in the same way as any other filesystem.

At the end of the vnode pointer is an actual node pointer to the physical file. Therefore, a vnode uniquely identifies a file on the system, and this is the reason that the pager object that deals with files is based on the vnode of the file.

One pager object is instantiated for every mapped file. If more than one user has the file mapped, they will share the same pager object. Whenever an operation must be performed on a page owned by this object, the VM system will call one of the standard functions on the object in order for the object to perform the operation accordingly. This includes freeing the page for another process, or reallocating physical memory for a page that has already been paged out to disk.

The problem of handling memory mapped files is different from that of anonymous memory allocations, and so this is why there are different pager routines for each.

The pager routine for anonymous objects does not have a source file in a filesystem to pass pages to and from. Instead, these objects are transient objects that exist only for the lifetime of the process that is using them. There is no on-disk representation of these objects before they exist in physical memory. When memory pages used by these objects need to be freed, the pager writes the page out to the *swap area*, which is a dedicated set of disk partitions for this task that is shared by all processes. For this reason, this pager routine is frequently termed the *swap pager*.

Although this pager is not the vnode pager, both classes present the same interface to the kernel, using vnode and offset pairs to identify the actual page. The vnode in the case of anonymous objects is that of the swap area.

A process on the system uses both types of objects and looks a little like the arrangement shown in Figure case11.

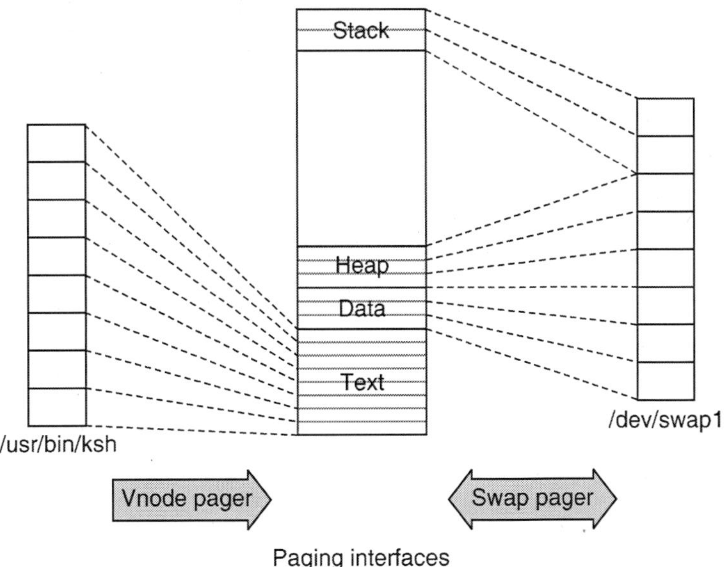

Paging interfaces

Figure case11 illustrates the pager interfaces used by a simple executable program, such as the Korn Shell (/bin/ksh). When the program starts, a vnode pager object is created to map the executable file. The program starts to execute but cannot do so until the first page of the executable[10] is in memory. The vnode pager is called on at this point to allocate a page in memory and bring in the first page of the executable.

Almost immediately after this, the first page of the data segment needs to be available, and so a pager object needs to be made. The object would be the swap pager, because the contents of this memory will be modified during use, and this should not be reflected back into any file in the filesystem. The first page of the data segment is created by the swap pager, and execution continues.

As soon as anything needs to be placed on the stack, the kernel creates the first page of the stack segment and assigns the swap pager to it. Likewise, as soon as the program needs to use any memory on the heap, another object is created to store the heap segment, which also is a swap pager object.

In Figure case11, the vnode pager is a unidirectional arrow, because the mapped file is an executable (executables never get written to by the VM system). If the process were to map another file using mmap(), the vnode pager would also be responsible for ensuring that all dirty pages were first written back to the file before freeing the page.

Paging Mechanics

Now that the actual page handlers are known, we can forget about them once again and concentrate on the VM system itself and the mechanics of its operation.

The VM system varies to a large degree across implementations, but they all have the same fundamental goal: to keep as many active (i.e., currently used) pages in physical memory at any one time. They also typically all have the same basic theory for achieving this goal.

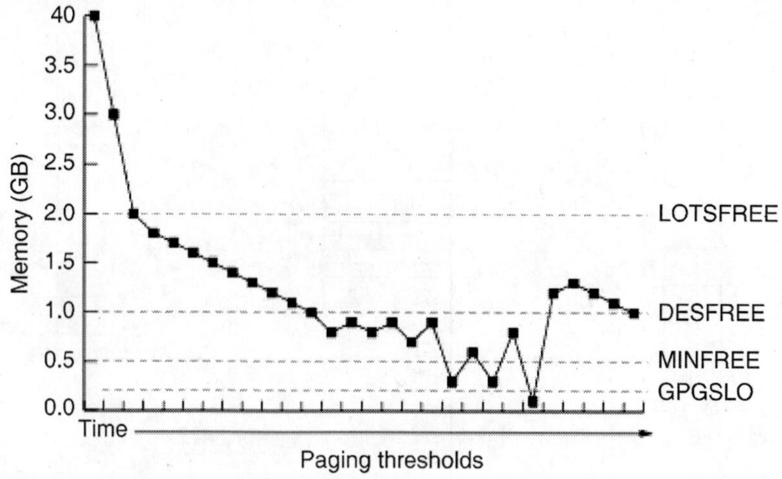

Paging thresholds

Figure case12 shows the four parameters used by the SVR4 UNIX memory management algorithms. Essentially, these four parameters define how aggressively the VM system should work toward freeing memory in the system. The first parameter, *lotsfree,* declares that if the free memory is above this point, no action needs to be taken by the VM system to free memory-there is *lots free.* When free memory falls below this threshold, the VM system starts to find pages that can be written out to disk and subsequently free the physical memory page. This *pageout* routine is run four times per second at this point. In Figure case12, the rate of memory decline is reduced because the VM system starts to free infrequently used pages.

The next threshold is *desfree.* If memory falls below this point, the VM system starts *desperation paging,* because memory is getting very low. The pageout process is executed on every clock() cycle at this point, and the VM system works hard to free up memory. In the chart, the free memory level starts to become more erratic, because the requests for memory continue and the VM system is almost managing to keep the number of free pages constant. Desfree defines the amount of memory the O/S must attempt to keep free at all times.

The next threshold is *minfree.* Serious memory starvation occurs at this point, and the system becomes far more aggressive over the selection of pages to pageout. If memory still cannot be freed, and the free memory count falls below *gpgslo,* the system has to admit defeat in using the paging algorithms.

At gpgslo, the VM system changes gear and goes into swapping mode. It is deemed that memory is so scarce at this point that VM operations will dominate the CPU on the system and start *thrashing.* Thrashing is where the system spends all of its time paging in and out in an attempt to keep active pages in memory. Swapping involves paging out entire processes to the swap area, rather than trying to work out which pages should go out.

The swapping starts with the processes that are oldest. In fact, very old, inactive processes may have been swapped out much earlier in the process, just as a housekeeping action. Then sleeping processes get swapped out, followed by processes that are at the back of the run queue. At this stage, the system is essentially unusable.

In order to implement this memory management, the VM system adopts several algorithms for identifying pages to page out. One of the common ones is the not recently used algorithm, also known as the two-handed clock (see Figure case13).

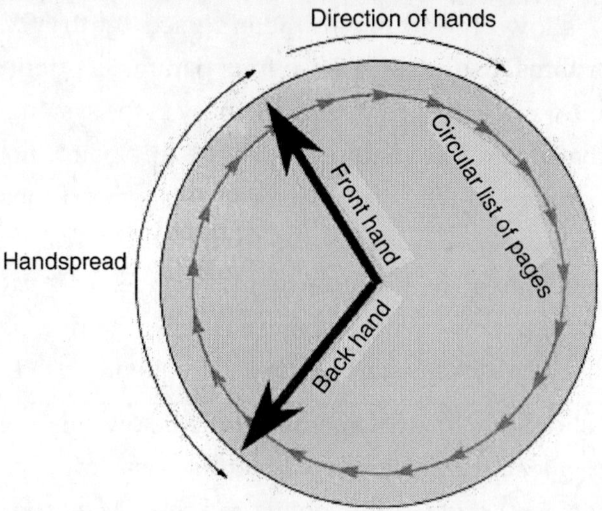

Two-handed clock algorithm

This algorithm approximates an LRU algorithm but requires significantly less management overhead. The pages of memory are arranged as a circular linked list, where the "last" element points to the first element in order to make a full loop. There are then two "hands" that are applied to searching of this list. The front hand goes through the list and turns off the referenced bit of the PTE. If the page is accessed after this, the bit is turned back on by the reference. If the bit remains off when the back hand inspects the buffer, then it is not recently used and is eligible to be freed.

The handspread is the number of buffers that separate the scans of the two hands. A small gap implies that only very frequently referenced pages will be ineligible for freeing. A large gap allows less frequently accessed pages to remain in memory. Alternatively, the speed at which the hands go around has the same effect, and this is the variable that the kernel changes depending on the amount of free memory.

When a page is to be freed, the VM system can pull the vnode and offset for the page out of the kernel structure and use this to call the correct object pager in order to carry out the procedure. The routine in the pager is called pageout(). If the page is dirty (written to but not flushed to disk), it must be written out before being freed. It is the responsibility of the relevant pager object to ensure that this occurs.

Likewise, when a page fault results in a trap, the vnode and offset for the required page are passed to the relevant pagein() routine in the pager object. This could happen for any of the following reasons:

- The page is part of an executable or mapped file and has not yet been accessed.
- The page has been paged out to swap.
- The page is a new anonymous page and needs an initial allocation.

There is a separate routine for each of these cases. In the first case, the pager simply needs to allocate a free page and fill it with the contents of the corresponding vnode and offset on disk. In the second case, the pager performs a similar operation using the swap area. The final case requires allocation of a new page, and filling of the new page with zeros by the kernel. This is defined behavior for new pages, and some programs expect such behavior.

This kind of single-page demand paging is good in theory but not very efficient in practice. In practice, just getting the required page does not make the best use of statistical facts in the way that memory is accessed. The statistic in question, of course, is the locality of reference: If a certain page is requested, it is likely that the adjacent pages will also be required in the short term. The cost of a single page fetch from disk is so huge in comparison with the time the CPU can process that page that it makes sense to get a few adjacent pages at the same time. The additional disk overhead is tiny if the next pages are also adjacent on the physical disk, and so greater efficiency can be achieved in this way.

In addition to the standard threshold-based memory management method, some implementations adopt further optimizations. Regardless of the amount of memory left free in the system, it is also desirable to prevent proactively any processes from growing beyond a reasonable[11] size. This reduces the VM work required when the thresholds are crossed. While most VM systems keep track of the *resident set size* (*RSS*) of each process, not all allow specific action to be carried out on the basis of that number. Others, such as Sequent DYNIX/ptx, compare the current RSS of the process against a tunable parameter called *maxrs*. If the process grows beyond the defined value for maxrs, the VM system starts to pageout older pages of the process's resident set until its size comes back down to the defined limit.

Case4.3 Implications of fork() and exec()

The fork() system call is used to create new processes. The kernel creates an exact copy of the process that calls fork() and gives it a new execution thread for that process. The new process has an individual PID and retains the calling process as the parent of the process. At this point, both the parent and the child continue to execute the same application code, from exactly the same point: the return of the fork() system call.

The complexity of fork() and the reason it is present in the section on memory management have to do with the way that it is typically used. It may already be evident that the kernel will do anything to avoid work that is not necessary; this is the secret of keeping operating system overhead to a minimum. In the case of fork(), it is actually unusual for the child process to continue executing the same code as the parent. Instead, the child typically calls the exec()[12] system call.

The exec() call invokes another program within the process that calls it. In order to do this, the address space for the process has to be redefined, making the previous set of memory mappings irrelevant for the child process. If the kernel has just gone to all the trouble of copying all the pages that comprise the parent to make this new process, that work would be wasted.

Therefore, when the kernel receives a fork() call, it typically makes an optimized copy of the parent process. This copy involves only copying of the PTEs for the parent process, thereby making the child an exact copy of the parent, including the physical memory that it uses. Of course, if the parent or the child were to write to one of the pages, it could corrupt the other process, and so another procedure is required to support this optimized copy.

This procedure is called *copy on write*. The kernel makes a copy of the parent's address space and sets up protection bits on the PTEs. If the parent or the child attempts to write to one of these pages, a protection exception is raised, which the kernel processes. Only at this stage does the kernel make a copy of the page and set the master and the copy to read/write. Therefore, if the child writes to only a few pages before issuing an exec() call, only the required amount of memory copying occurs.

BSD offers an alternative to copy on write in the form of a vfork() system call. Using this call, the child "borrows" the entire address space of the parent, and the parent blocks until the child issues an exec(). This is specifically designed for use in programs that know that an exec() always follows the fork().

Case4.4 Summary

The VM system is a fundamental part of the UNIX kernel. For large Oracle database servers, the VM system can be required to perform a good deal of work, even though the system should be configured to keep all the processes and SGA in real memory at all times.

The reason for this is that there are still a huge number of distinct processes on the system, and Oracle relies heavily on the operating system to manage the address spaces for these processes. Each of these processes can be very large, and certainly a great deal of PTE manipulation is required.

In the case of very large SGAs, the operating system must implement changes above and beyond the provision of the standard 4KB page size. One of these optimizations-variable page sizes-was discussed in this section. Another good optimization for the reduction of PTEs in Oracle-like systems is *shared PTEs*. Just as the operating system already shares the PTEs for text segments, it is also possible to create just one set of PTEs for the shared memory segment to which all processes refer. This reduces the memory consumption of the page tables enormously.

Although the details of the virtual memory system are not essential for building a high-performance Oracle database system, a good understanding of VM can be helpful in comprehending system operation under load and in correlating system statistics.

Case5 I/O System

Case5.1 Everything is a File

One of the fundamental design concepts of the UNIX system was to abstract all I/O operations as linear file operations. This allows the kernel to take the complexity of physical hardware devices away from programmers, and to deal with it internally instead. A good example of this would be a tape drive, which has the concept of records. A linear file has no concept of records but only of a continuous stream of bytes. Therefore, the kernel takes care of the record-based communication with the tape drive, allowing the programmer to read from and write to the tape device using standard read() and write() system calls.

This concept has mostly held true to this day, although the number of ioctl()[13] and other custom call types available has sometimes made it appear not to be so.

The rule, however, is that pretty much everything can be treated as a file. This makes I/O programming on UNIX systems very portable and straightforward as a result of the kernel (specifically the device drivers) taking the complexity away from the programmer.

Something to bear in mind when looking at system statistics is that the number of read() and write() system calls being executed does not correlate with disk I/O. Rather, these calls include logical I/O in and out of the filesystem buffer cache as well as all network and terminal I/O.

Case5.2 Filesystems

The filesystem is a user-friendly interface to the raw disk. It presents a hierarchical tree of directories and files (see Figure case14) and allows concurrent access to files and directories by all users with permission to do so.

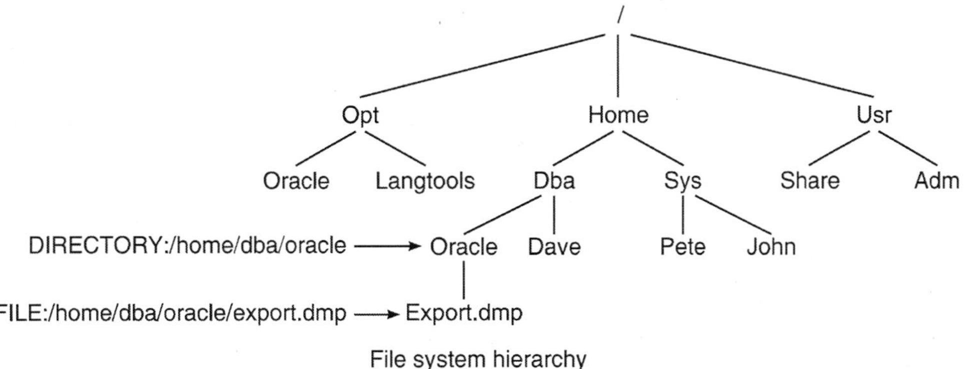

File system hierarchy

All UNIX filesystems share this common interface to the user, regardless of the implementation details of the filesystem or of whether it is local or remote.

Although the interface to the filesystem is very different from the SQL interface used by Oracle, the requirement for the filesystem is virtually identical to the Oracle database. Both are tasked with optimizing the reading and writing of data, in an organized fashion, to and from physical disk.

Just like Oracle, it would be very inefficient to make all of the I/O requests physical, requiring disk I/O for every request. Therefore, filesystems perform all I/O through a cache layer known as the *buffer cache* (see Figure case15).

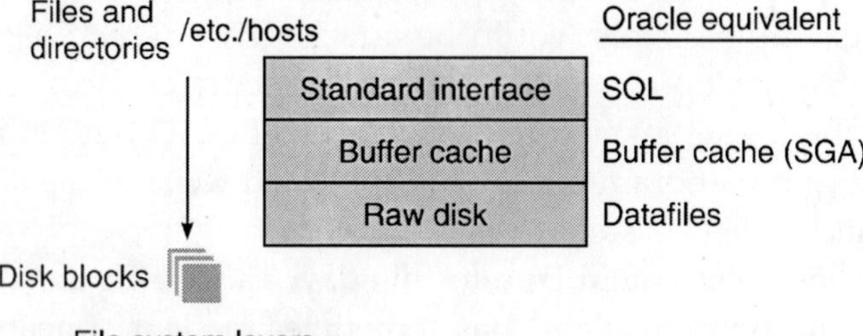

File system layers

Using the layers shown in Figure case15, the filesystem presents a familiar interface to the user, the hierarchical view, with two types of available objects: files and directories. The access to the objects is all done by means of the buffer cache, apart from special "trusted" operations. Although the logical perspective of the file is that of a contiguous file, this is not physically true. All mappings to the blocks that make up a file are maintained by the filesystem itself.

The filesystem implementation has changed a good deal over the life of the UNIX operating system. The simplest filesystem is the System V filesystem, known as the s5fs, and we will use this as an introduction to filesystem implementations.

The s5 Filesystem maintains three different areas on disk, as shown in Figure case16.

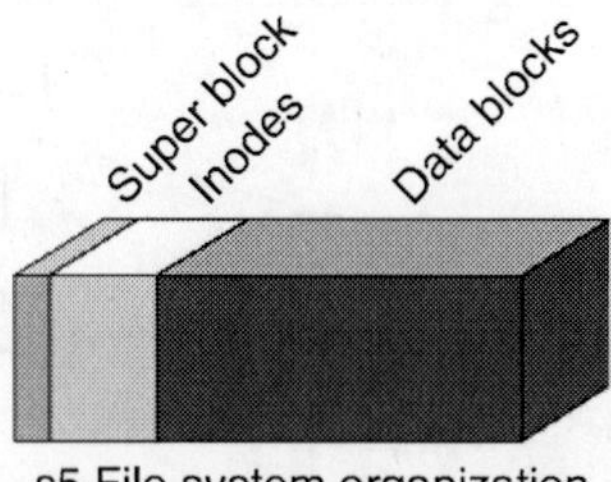

s5 File system organization

The *superblock* is the equivalent of a segment header in Oracle, in that it stores the freelist for inodes and data blocks and general information about the file. It is always stored as the first block on disk and is of fixed length. After the superblock comes the *inodes*.

Inodes are the entry points for all files. There is one inode for each file in the filesystem. Contained in the inode are pointers to actual data blocks, access information, permissions, and file owner information. The inode is read when ls -l is executed in a directory, in order to read the information above.

The inode is of fixed length so that each inode in the table can be addressed by a number*size formula. Included in this size is sufficient information to store up to ten block addresses for the actual file. For very small files (up to 10KB with 1,024 block size), this is sufficient. For larger files, the inode stores three levels of *indirect block addresses*. The first level is a pointer to a single data block that contains only further lists of block addresses. This allows for an additional 256 blocks (256KB) to be addressed. The second level of indirect block is a pointer to a block that contains only indirect block pointers. Again, 256 pointers can be stored in a single 1KB block, and so the maximum file size catered to by going to the double indirect block is 64MB (256*256*1024 bytes). Finally, there is a third level of indirection, a pointer to a block of pointers to blocks of pointers. This yields a maximum file size of 16GB (256*256*256*1024 bytes), although a 32-bit address limitation allows for only a 2GB maximum in practice, because we have to be able to lseek() forward and backward the full size of the file. Still, this is not too bad for an old, retired filesystem.

The first inode in a filesystem is reserved for the root directory of that filesystem. This is not the same as *the* root directory; it assumes the name of the directory at which it is mounted-that is, if a filesystem were mounted as /opt/oracle, the first inode would be a pointer to the "oracle" directory when the filesystem was mounted there. More precisely, the first inode is for the root directory of the filesystem.

A directory is simply another type of file. It is a file that has a format known to the filesystem, containing a list of names and inode numbers for the files within it. When ls is called without any options, only the directory is read. When a file is referred to by name, the directory is checked first to get the inode for the file. With the inode, it is just a case of going to corresponding offset in the inode table and retrieving the access information for the file.

If a directory gets too large (too many entries), its performance can be degraded. This is the equivalent of doing full table scans in Oracle; the filesystem code must go all the way through the directory "file" in order to satisfy certain requests, such as a vanilla ls. Likewise, ls -l requires a lookup of the actual inode for each entry; this is something to bear in mind when building filesystems.

Modern Filesystems

The s5fs did a reasonable job for its life span but suffered from several drawbacks, including performance. The Berkeley fast filesystem (FFS) improved on some of these drawbacks by optimizing the organization of the filesystem on disk and allowing long filenames (s5 allowed only 14 characters). However, even FFS is not suitable for commercial application, particularly if a database is to be built on the filesystem.

The drawbacks of these filesystems are

- Poor crash recovery
- Poor performance
- File size limitations

Traditional filesystems do not cope well with system crashes. Any dirty (unwritten) blocks in the filesystem buffer cache at the time of the crash will be lost, and there is no formal approach to recovering the filesystem. Instead, the filesystem must be laboriously scanned with the fsck utility in order to validate its integrity. Often the utility is not able to rationalize what it finds, and intervention is required by an operator, possibly resulting in file loss or corruption. This is bad enough in itself, but it also takes a good deal of time to get to this stage-possibly many, many minutes. It is essential for a large production system to recover more quickly than this, regardless of whether or not there is a hot standby system.

In order to get around the problem of unwritten dirty blocks, traditional filesystems have to support *synchronous writes*. This is the only way the database writer, for example, can guarantee that a block is actually going onto disk. This means that the database writer must wait for the completion of this write, potentially taking place at several locations on the physical disk, involving several lengthy seek operations. This results in poor performance for the filesystem.

The traditional filesystems are block-based in their addressing. This is not acceptable for large database systems, because there is an enormous administration and performance overhead from this scheme when very large files are used.

Modern filesystems have been engineered to overcome these problems and to support database systems more effectively. One of the most successful of these is the *journaling filesystem*, notably the *Veritas VxFS*. These filesystems operate even more like database servers than do the traditional ones.

Essentially, these filesystems rely on redo logs within the filesystem in order to increase its performance and recovery. When a write occurs, it can be written directly to the buffer cache and also to the redo log. The redo log is on a sequential portion of disk, and so this write is fast. The write to the actual redo log on disk only occurs at the commit point for the write, which is the end of the write. Until this point, the writes go into a redo log buffer, in much the same way as in Oracle. The redo log buffer scheme also supports group commits of multiple transactions.

The write to the data area of the filesystem is not required, because the redo log is capable of rebuilding the data area in the event of a crash. The crash recovery is based on the presence of a redo log, the filesystem check at start up needs only to roll forward the changes that have occurred since the last checkpoint of the data area. This makes recovery very reliable and fast.

The filesystem is designed for very large files, and so both the filesystem and the files within it can be very large. Instead of using single block references to the data area of the filesystem, the journaling filesystem uses extents (contiguous groups of blocks), in the same way as Oracle does. A new extent is allocated for the file, and the extent is referenced instead of a single block. This allows large files to be supported with less overhead than in the traditional block-based approach and to provide considerably greater performance as a result of the contiguous grouping of data blocks.

Case5.3 Raw Disk

UNIX allows direct access to raw disk. The interface to the disk is through a UNIX special file, which is opened using standard system calls and accessed using normal read, write, and seek calls. To an application using the raw disk, it just looks like one large file.

Raw disk partitions have several drawbacks:

- The unit of allocation to the database is the entire file.
- Cannot use standard file manipulation commands on datafiles.
- Cannot use bundled backup tools (cpio, tar, pax) to backup the files.
- Cannot easily determine how much space is free within a group of raw device files, or how large the files actually are.

They also have positive attributes:

- Not subject to any operating system locking
- Not subject to any operating system caching
- Can be shared between multiple systems

These advantages are very important. Essentially, using raw disk removes the operating system from the operation of the Oracle I/O process, with the exception of the device drivers that perform the actual I/O. Any number of processes can read from and write to the partition concurrently, if the partition resides on multiple physical disks (see Section case5.5). Also, raw disk is currently the only way of mounting the same Oracle database on multiple UNIX hosts for Oracle Parallel Server.[15]

In order to gain these advantages, however, it is important to work through the list of disadvantages and to produce procedures and techniques that make them operationally acceptable.

Entire File Allocations

When raw disk is used, raw partitions are supplied to Oracle as a datafile. This means that the entire file, and not just a part of it, must be allocated to Oracle at any one time. In reality, this does not present much of a problem. The physical disk can be sliced into several raw partitions of different sizes.

The size and number of these partitions will vary with database requirements, but the concept maps to all databases. It makes sense to keep the range of partition sizes fairly small in order to make the management simplistic. For example, use allocation sizes of 4GB, 2GB, 1GB, 500MB, and 100MB. This allows quite large tablespaces to be built from a relatively small number of files, and the small ones to be built from small files.

Use of Standard File Manipulation Commands

Often the hardest attributes of raw disk to get used to is the inability to use the standard UNIX file utilities such as cp and mv. In reality, a well-configured database system does not require a great deal of file manipulation once it is laid out. If a disk is found to be "hot," a file can still be physically moved by using the dd command to suck the contents out of one partition and put it into a new partition.

When raw devices are used, it also makes sense to work around the naming of typical raw devices. In fact, the naming of the files is one of the major objections most people have to using them. What does /dev/rdsk/c10t5d3s4 mean to anyone, as far as the size and location of the raw device are concerned? Logical volume managers help a little here by providing more user-definable naming conventions, but there are even better ways around this.

The first thing to do after creating all the devices is to make a directory of symbolic links (ln -s). These links should be placed in a common location *away* from the /dev directory, somewhere near the Oracle codeset. A good convention is to have a root from which all these things happen, such as /opt/oracle. Under this root you can locate the codeset (say, /opt/oracle/oracle815) and the directory containing the symbolic links to the actual raw devices.

Each symbolic link should have a descriptive name, such as "db00_1000M_10_000," which means database set 00, 1000MB slice, RAID 1+0, slice number 000. With a directory called /opt/oracle/SPARE containing all these files, it is very easy to determine the types and numbers of available datafile slices and their RAID characteristics.

At database creation time, make another directory under /opt/oracle to put the used symbolic links in, such as /opt/oracle/PRD1. Creating the database would then go a little like this (assuming that the init.ora has been created and resides in /tmp for now):

```
$ cd /opt/oracle/PRD1
$ mv /tmp/initPRD1.ora .
$ ln -s $PWD/initPRD1.ora $ORACLE_HOME/dbs/.
$ mv ../SPARE/db00_500M_10_000 system_01.dbf
$ svrmgrl
Oracle Server Manager Release 3.1.5.0.0
(c) Copyright 1997, Oracle Corporation. All Rights Reserved.
Oracle8 Enterprise Edition Release 8.1.5.0.0
With the Partitioning option
PL/SQL Release 8.1.5.0.0
SVRMGR> connect internal
Connected.
SVRMGR> create database PRD1 CONTROLFILE REUSE
2> datafile "/opt/oracle/PRD1/system_01.dbf" size 500M REUSE
etc
```

For control files, they are ideally located in small pieces of "leftover" disk allocation. These are pieces of disk that represent the 0.1GB of a 9.1GB drive, for example, or remainder disk after rounding the allocations down. It is required that these pieces be on raw disk if OPS is used. Otherwise, it is possible to put the control files in the UNIX filesystem, although it is best to keep all the datafiles in one form or the other (raw or FS).

Backup

Backup does not present a great problem in building very large database systems. The reason for this is that you can no longer adequately manage the backup of the database using cpio or tar anyway. For a large database, it is necessary to use a fully featured backup product in order to get software indexed backups, allowing more control over tape identification and faster recovery times. In addition, the bundled archivers do not support features such as parallel tape streaming, which allows much greater backup throughput. This becomes important as the database size becomes very large.

All of the third-party backup products provide the facility to backup raw disk partitions as easily as filesystems. However, you must ensure that the symbolic link directory also gets backed up on a regular basis, because this is the tie between the location of the files that Oracle expects, and the actual location in /dev.

Space Management

When the procedures laid out above are used, space management does not present any more problems than a filesystem presents. It is very clear how much space is left for allocation to the database from looking in the SPARE directory. The only thing that is not possible with raw devices is the automatic extension of datafiles, using Oracle.

Case5.4 Filesystems Versus Raw Disk

The debate over the use of filesystems versus the use of raw disk has been raging for years. There are good points and bad points on each side, and it is not clear where the balance lies. Despite this, each has several clear advantages that factor into the decision process.

Filesystems

There are two fundamental problems associated with the use of filesystems. First, the filesystem buffer cache causes slow writes. As this is all that occurs on redo logs during normal operation, this is bad. Second, the single-writer lock imposed on a per-file basis can limit write performance to datafiles.

On the plus side, the files in a filesystem are very visible and easy to interpret and administrate. Nevertheless, when you are dealing with very large datafiles, it is undesirable to be moving 4GB or 8GB files around, so the significance of this advantage is debatable.

The other advantage of using a filesystem is application-specific-the advantage of gaining additional benefit from the filesystem buffer cache. In cache theory terms, the filesystem buffer cache can be viewed as the L2 cache, with the Oracle cache being the L1. It can also be viewed from the perspective of double buffering; there is no difference in speed between the two caches, and so there is no benefit for the frequently used blocks and a fairly significant overhead in managing the same blocks in two caches. With 64-bit Oracle, this advantage is difficult to justify any more; all the memory that would have been in the filesystem cache can now be given to Oracle across all three buffer pools.

Raw Disk

Raw disk essentially puts Oracle in the driver's seat as far as I/O is concerned. With the operating system responsible only for communication with the hardware, there is no additional CPU overhead incurred from managing filesystem caches. Raw disk is not subject to any kind of operating system locking and can be used in parallel server configurations.

From a logical perspective, there is no reason why a raw disk database system should ever be slower than a file-system-based system. The only condition under which this could occur would be a deficiency in the Oracle caching algorithms. With a file-system-based database, every miss in the Oracle buffer cache results in a read() system call. This bears a finite cost, as does the subsequent searching and cache management in the filesystem buffer cache. If there still is a miss, the physical read must occur anyway, making the true overhead for the miss twice as bad as it would be in a raw disk system (ignoring the constant cost of the disk read).

If the memory used for the buffer cache were used in the Oracle buffer cache, it is likely that there would be a hit in the Oracle cache layer, eliminating the additional system call for the filesystem logical read.

Advanced filesystem implementations provide more hooks to allow Oracle to circumvent the filesystem layer itself and go straight to raw disk. This leaves the filesystem performing only an offline administration function and not participating in the actual operation of the database. This may be the best of both worlds, providing all the advantages of the filesystem (visibility, file extension capability) without the disadvantages.

Case5.5 Logical Volume Managers

In Section 2.8, we introduced I/O and RAID levels. In Chapter 2, these levels were mostly hardware concepts focused on the disks and their performance. In addition to hardware RAID, most vendors offer some kind of *logical volume manager (LVM)*.

An LVM is an addition to the kernel that provides RAID functionality from the host. No special hardware is required to do this, only standard disk drives.

There are several reasons why this is a good thing. First, if multiple controllers are used, a stripe can be set up across all the controllers. This maximizes the performance of the controllers to gain best performance. If this approach is taken, however, care must be taken that controller redundancy is preserved, because if one of the many controllers that make up the stripe were to fail, the entire stripe array would be unavailable. In the case of EMC disk arrays, the EMC does not provide a striping function. Therefore, some kind of software stripe is required in order to perform striping on this device. Although it provides the *disk* redundancy within, controller redundancy is still required.

Second, using a software volume manager allows disk devices to be given more user-friendly names than standard disk slicing offers. This will become apparent in this rapid introduction to the operation of volume managers.

There are several fairly basic concepts used in all software volume managers. The first of these concepts is the *volume group* (see Figure case17). A volume group is the largest grouping used within the volume manager and is composed of several disk objects.

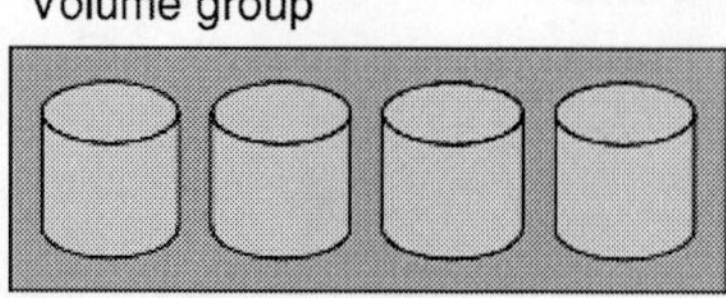

Volume group

When the disks (or disk slices) have been added to the volume group, this volume group has a capacity equal to the combined capacities of the disk devices within it.

The next stage is to create logical volumes from the volume group. These logical volumes can be called anything at all, therefore allowing meaningful naming conventions to be implemented. From the volume group in Figure case17, we could create a single volume four times larger than a physical disk. This would create a very large logical volume, but it would be practically useless because it is likely that the I/O would be concentrated within a small portion of the volume's total size.

In order to create a more useful volume, we would instruct the volume manager to create it (or, more likely, a smaller one) but to use a stripe (or chunk) width somewhat smaller than that of a physical disk. If we use a 128KB stripe width, the volume manager will go off and distribute the volume across the disks 128KB at a time, round-robin fashion.This means that a read of 512KB in the example above would include all drives in the volume group.

Logical volumes

In Figure case18, six logical volumes have been created from the "bucket" of space in the volume group. All of these volumes are striped across all the disks within the volume group.

At this point, the operation of software RAID is the same as that of hardware RAID but is calculated and initiated from the host. This has two implications on the host processing. First, the administration of the RAID subsystem is now a task that the operating system must be concerned with, increasing the cost of any given I/O operation initiated on those devices. While this is a fairly small increase, it is something that should not be overlooked.

The second implication is, for the most part, valid only when LVM-based mirroring is used. When mirroring from the host, the host must make write requests to two controllers for every write request. This increases the bus utilization on write-intensive applications. In addition, when the system crashes, the host comes up trusting only one side of the mirrored pair. The other side of the mirror is marked STALE and is in need of resilvering. Although this is a process that Oracle is now involved in,[16] the traditional approach to it was to perform a full disk-to-disk copy from the active side of the mirror to the stale side of the mirror. While this copy is in progress, all new writes must also be written to both sides, whereas all reads come only from the active side. This can have an enormous impact on the I/O throughput of the system, and an even bigger impact on the available CPU capacity on the system, because this operation is very CPU-intensive.

Case6 Interprocess Communication (IPC)

As UNIX systems became more powerful and complex, it became apparent that there was a need for some way to allow processes to communicate in order to coordinate processing of common workloads. All types of such communication are known as *interprocess communication (IPC)*. The first and most basic form of IPC comes in the form of the *pipe*.

Case6.1 Pipe Communication

A pipe is initiated by a process prior to forking a child process. The pipe() system call opens two file descriptors. One of these descriptors is open for reading, and the other is open for writing. In this preliminary state, anything written to the write descriptor will be available for reading from the other file descriptor. This is not very useful until a fork() call is made.

After the fork() call has been made, both processes retain all the open files that the parent had before the call. The parent closes the read file descriptor, and the child closes the write descriptor, and now there is a useful way to communicate between the processes. At this stage the communication is unidirectional only; if two pipe() calls had been made, bidirectional communication could be set up.

This is the mechanism used by the shell in order to enable operations such as

$ who -u | grep jeff

The shell forks once in order to continue processing with processes other than itself. This parent shell process then simply blocks (suspends) with a wait() call, waiting for the child processes to terminate execution.

The first child then initiates the pipe() sequence as above, but then takes it one step further. After the fork() of the second process, the shell (it is still just two clones of the shell; no exec() has been called yet) uses the dup() system call to reallocate the file descriptors. For the process destined to become who, the stdout descriptor is closed, and the writeable end of the pipe is associated with the usual stout descriptor using dup(). This means that this process will now send all normal output to the pipe instead of to the screen.

The process destined to become grep does the opposite-it closes the stdin file descriptor and uses dup() to make the read end of the pipe become the standard input for the process. At this stage, the two processes issue the exec() system call to become the requested processes, and the output of who is passed to grep.

This is the mechanism used by the Oracle PIPE driver for client/server communication within a common host.

Case6.2 System V IPC

System V introduced three new forms of IPC: shared memory, semaphores, and message queues.

Shared Memory

Shared memory is a simple concept: Create a piece of memory that many processes can map into their address spaces. Changes made by one user are immediately visible to the other processes, without the need for any kind of system call. Owing to the lack of required system calls once the shared memory segment has been created, this is a very fast form of IPC.

The Oracle SGA is created within a shared memory segment for providing IPC among all the processes that are connected to the Oracle database. The system call to create a shared memory segment is shmget(), which creates the segment and returns a *key* for the segment. Any number of processes can now attach the segment to their address space using the shmat() system call.

A shared memory segment, once created, is an entity in its own right. Even if no processes are attached to it, it still remains in memory. It could be created one day and only initially attached to a year later. The only thing that will clear a shared memory segment, apart from a reboot, is an explicit call to shmctl() with the remove flag set. This can be done from the command line using the ipcrm -m <key> command.

As mentioned previously, it is preferable for the operating system to provide some way of sharing page tables for shared memory regions. Otherwise, a large Oracle SGA can use a very large amount of memory in page table allocations.

Although shared memory provides no formal locking techniques, synchronization of updates can be achieved either by using the atomic operations supported in the hardware or by using semaphores. Semaphores are too slow to be used as latch mechanisms because of the required system calls, and so Oracle uses atomic memory updates with test and set to manage the synchronization of the SGA.

Semaphores

Semaphores are used for coordinating processes. They are kernel-controlled counters that support only two operations: increment and decrement. Rather confusing, for English speakers at least, is the fact that these operations are called V ops and P ops, respectively. They are referred to in this way because they were named by a Dutchman called Dijkstra, who is credited with the invention of the semaphore.

A semaphore can have any positive value, or a value of zero. Negative values are not permitted. The idea is that waiting processes attempt to decrement the semaphore, and processes that have finished running increment the semaphore. If decrementing the semaphore by the requested amount would result in a negative value, the process is blocked in the kernel until the semaphore has been incremented (by other processes) such that the operation would not result in a negative value.

Oracle uses semaphores (in non-OPS configurations) to implement slow waits such as latch *sleeps* (not latch *gets*) and enqueues. OPS configurations have to hand this task off to the DLM in order to manage enqueues between instances. In most configurations, Oracle uses semaphores to provide a communication mechanism between Oracle processes. For example, when a commit is issued, the message is sent to the log writer by way of a semaphore on which the log writer sleeps. Whenever required to perform work, the log writer is posted by incrementing the semaphore on which the log writer waits (seen in V$SESSION_WAIT as "rdbms ipc message"). The alternative mechanism for waking up processes to perform work is the *post/wait driver*. This is typically a UNIX kernel addition that allows more specific communication between the processes, through a direct posting mechanism.

Message Queues

Message queues are essentially multireader, multiwriter pipes that are implemented in the kernel. Processes can place messages on a message queue, and other processes can read these messages off the queue in a first-in, first-out order.

The reading of messages is subject to the messages meeting the criterion specified in the msgrcv() call. This criterion is a *message type*, specified as an integer. If no message meeting the criterion is found, the receiver will block (suspend) until such a message is sent to the message queue.

Message queues are not a very efficient means of communication, because a write and a subsequent read require two system calls and two copies to and from kernel memory. If the messages are large, this copying becomes prohibitively expensive in processing terms.

Message queues are sometimes useful in implementing instructions to running processes, where the message is small. Oracle does not utilize message queues.

"Any fool can write code that a computer can understand. Good programmers write code that humans can understand. " — *M. Fowler*

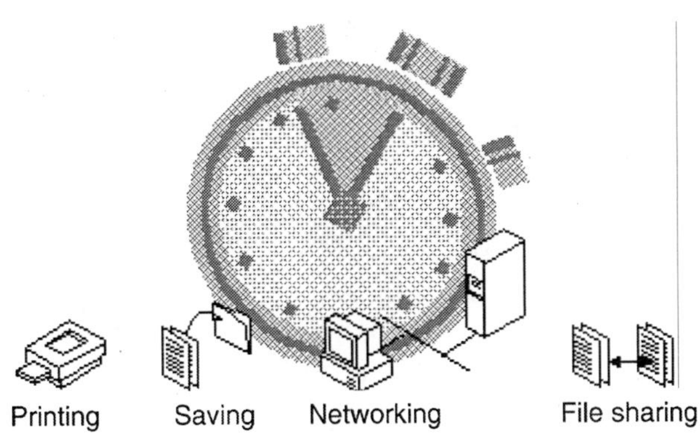

WINDOWS 98 AND OS2

INTRODUCTION

Microsoft Windows started out as a shell. Windows uses a colorful graphics interface that, among other things, eases access to the operating system. The feature that makes Windows so easy to use is a graphical user interface (GUI-pronounced "goo-ee"), in which users work with on-screen pictures called icons and with menus rather than with keyed-in. They are called *pull-down menus* because they appear to pull down like a window shade from the original selection. Some menus, in contrast, called pop-up menus originate from a selection on the bottom of the screen. Furthermore, icons and menus encourage pointing and clicking with a mouse, an approach that can make computer use both fast and easy.

To enhance ease of use, Windows is usually set up so that the colorful Windows display is the first thing a user sees when the computer is turned on. DOS is still there, under Windows, but a user need never see C> during routine activities. The user points and clicks among a series of narrowing choices until arriving at the desired software.

Although the screen presentation and user interaction are the most visible evidence of change, Windows offers changes that are even more fundamental. To understand these changes more fully, it is helpful at this point to make a comparison between traditional operating systems for large computers and Windows.

In addition to adding a friendly GUI, Windows operating systems added another important feature to DOS - *multi-tasking*. Multi-tasking occurs when the computer has several programs executing at one time. PCs that ran under DOS could only run one program at a time. Windows-based computers can have multiple programs (e.g. a browser, a word processor, and several Instant Messaging instances) running at the same time. When programs are executing at the same time, they are said to be executing *concurrently*.

As we learned, personal computers have only one CPU that handles just one instruction at a time. Computers using the MS-DOS operating system without a shell are limited not only to just one user at a time but also to just one program at a time. If, for example, a user were using a word processing program to write a financial report and wanted to access some spreadsheet figures, he or she would have to perform a series of arcane steps: exit the word processing program, enter and use and then exit the spreadsheet program, and then re-enter the word processing program to complete the report. This is wasteful in two ways: (1) the CPU is often idle because only one program is executing at a time, and (2) the user is required to move inconveniently from program to program.

Multi-tasking allows several programs to be active at the same time, although at an instant in time the CPU is doing only one instruction for one of the active programs. The Operating System manages which instructions to send to the CPU. Since computers are so fast, the operating system can switch the program that gets to execute on the CPU so quickly, the user can not tell. This is what allows your computer to be "listening" for incoming instant messages, for instance, while you use a word processor to write a paper.

Microsoft Windows 98

The Microsoft® Windows® 98 operating system is considered to be the revolutionary version of the Microsoft Windows operating system. It is the successor to MS-DOS®, Windows version 3.1, and Windows for Workgroups version 3.x, Windows 95.

GUIDED TOUR FOR ADMINISTRATORS

- Windows 98 introduces a new user interface that makes using the personal computer easier and more efficient for users, regardless of their expertise.

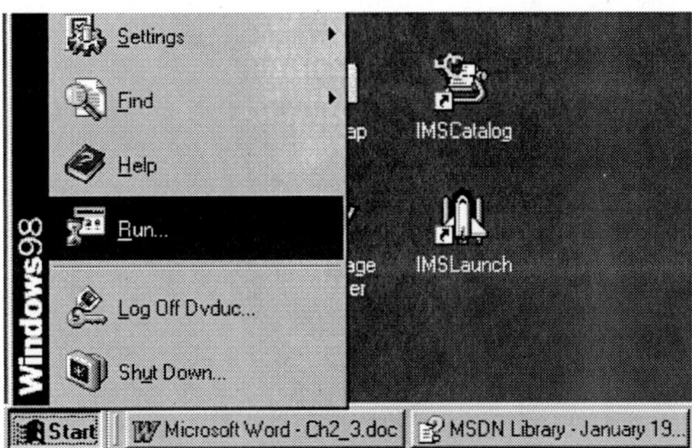

- Plug and Play: Windows 98 enables many new hardware devices to automatically configure themselves on the computer. Plug and Play devices choose settings, such as IRQs or DMA channels, without requiring you to set them. And, under Windows 98, Plug and Play devices can be added to a computer that doesn't have a Plug and Play BIOS.

  Windows 98 simplifies setup and configuration of devices that aren't Plug and Play-compliant. The Add New Hardware wizard detects legacy devices and migrates hardware settings to the Registry during installation. This ensures that legacy device settings are not overwritten when Plug and Play devices are added.

  Windows 98 supports for PCMCIA and portable "hot" docking and undocking. It means that users can add or remove a device such as a PCMCIA card while the computer is running. The computer automatically detects that the state of the hardware has changed and adjusts the system settings accordingly.

- The 32-bit architecture and superior resource handling in Windows 98 reduce downtime and support calls by providing a more stable operating system environment. Out-of-memory errors are not a practical issue in Windows 98 because the system resource constraints have been virtually eliminated. This lets your users run numerous applications without running out of memory.

Windows 98 supports for 32-bit components includes the redirector, the protocol, the network adapter, and File and Printer Sharing services. Being written to run in a multitasking environment, these components take up no real-mode memory and offer fast and stable networking. Windows 98 comes with 32-bit versions of an IPX/

SPX-compatible protocol and TCP/IP (with a DHCP client). A variety of other protocols and 16-bit network clients are also supported.

Windows 98 does a better job of tracking program resources and cleaning up after an errant application stops. The freeing of system resources after an application is closed means system performance is less likely to degrade over time.

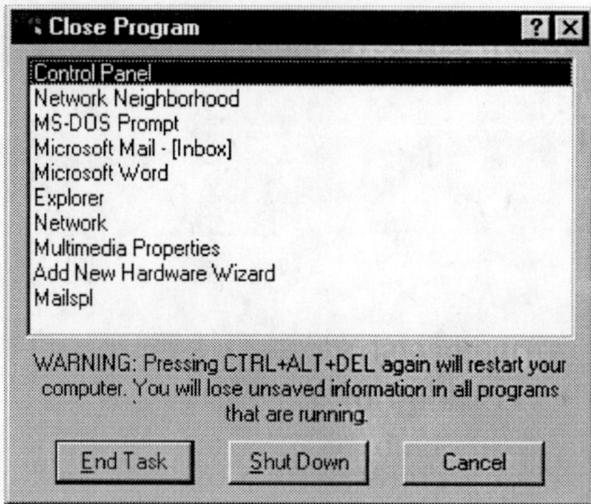

- Built-in Networking: Windows 98 comes complete with 32-bit networking components to allow it to work seamlessly with all major networks — including Novell® NetWare® and Windows NT™ Server — and other Windows 98 peer servers. Windows 98 support for 32-bit components includes the redirector, the protocol, the network adapter, and File and Printer Sharing services. Written to run in a multitasking environment, these components take up no real-mode memory and offer fast and stable networking. Windows 98 comes with 32-bit versions of an IPX/SPX-compatible protocol and TCP/IP (with a DHCP client). A variety of other protocols and 16-bit network clients are also supported.

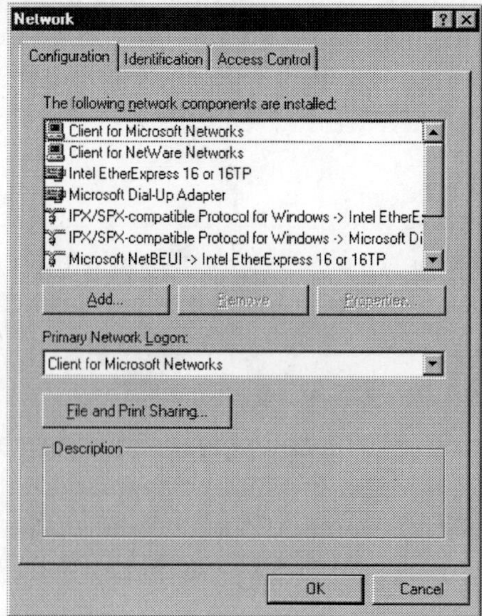

- With Network Neighborhood, users can browse network servers — even those from different network vendors — all from a single location. And, with support for universal naming convention (UNC) pathnames, it's as easy to access resources on the network as it is those on the local hard disk.
- Centralized Security: Windows 98 supports pass-through, server-based security for

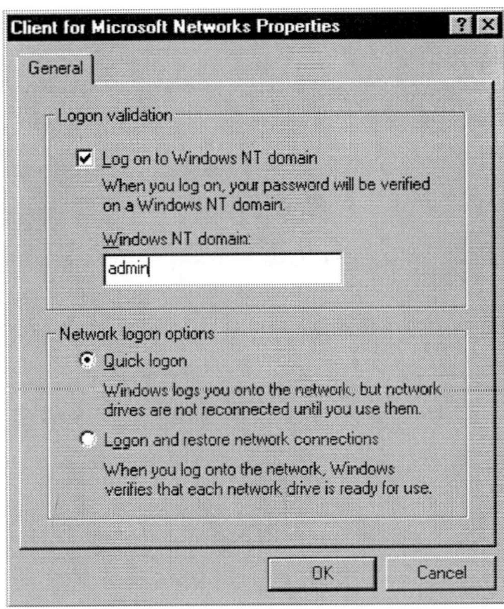

- NetWare and Windows NT networks, allowing each client computer to leverage the existing security scheme. Windows 98 supports requiring a validated logon to the server before the user can use Windows 98 in a network environment.
- User profiles describe user-specific or computer-specific information, such as software preferences and settings. Hardware profiles define current hardware settings for the computer. With profiles, users can work in a consistent and customized environment, which makes it easier to use and manage computers.
- New 32-bit printing, graphics, and other subsystems speed up operations for common tasks. Windows 98 supports and enables a whole new class of 32-bit applications with preemptive multitasking, allowing the computer to do more than one task at a time. Under Windows 98, 32-bit applications also support new capabilities such as long filenames and UNC paths in common dialog boxes.
- Preemptive Multitasking and Multithreading for 32-Bit Applications: Windows 98 supports and enables a whole new class of 32-bit applications with

preemptive multitasking, allowing the computer to do more than one task at a time. With 32-bit applications, users do not need to wait for completion of a particular task, such as downloading a large file from the network, before they can begin work on another task.

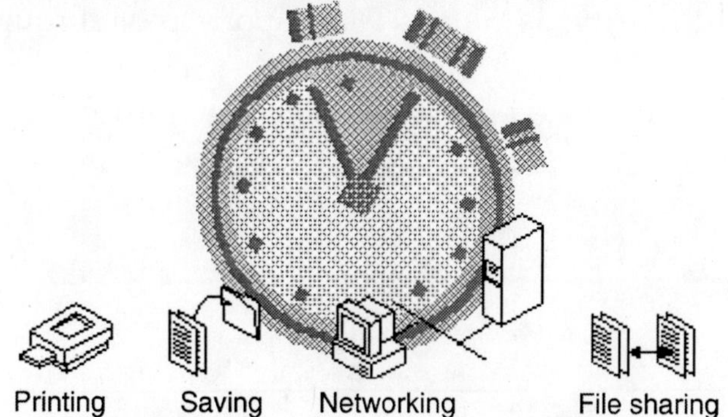

- Dial-Up Networking in Windows 98 allows the user to connect to network resources, such as files and electronic mail, using Point-to-Point Protocol or server-based dial-in packages such as NetWare Connect, Windows NT RAS, or Shiva® NetModem.

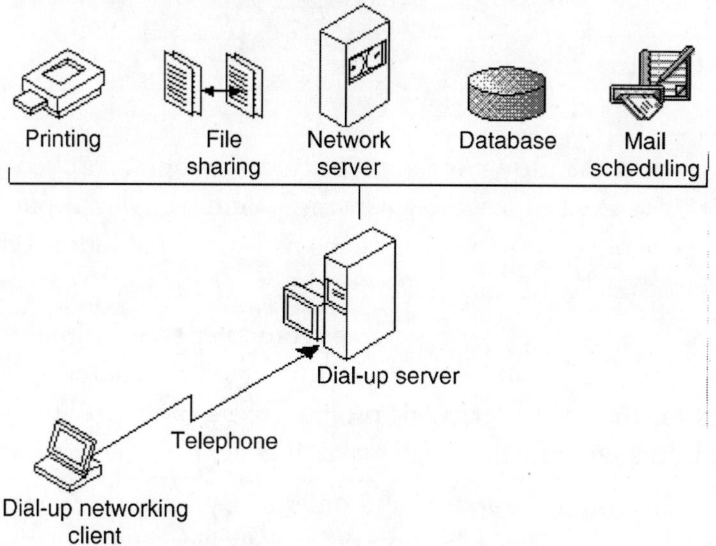

- Built-in Messaging: Windows 98 includes support for a variety of messaging services including electronic mail and fax, plus access to the Internet and online services. These services enable users to communicate more easily with others

Disks and File Systems

The new 32-bit, protected-mode file system support in Windows 98 allows optimal access to hard disks, CD-ROM drives, and network resources. The new file system support means faster, better performance for all file I/O operations than what was available under earlier version of MS-DOS or Windows

Because of enhancements to the file systems, there is no longer an eight-character limit on filenames that was imposed by the FAT file system under MS-DOS. You can use long filenames and directory names in Windows 98 and in any applications that support long filenames.

The enhanced FAT file system in Windows 98 also permits exclusive access to a disk device for file system utilities. File system utilities, such as ScanDisk, require exclusive access to the file system to ensure data integrity in a multitasking environment. Otherwise, if a file on the disk were to be saved while the utility was writing information to the disk at the same time, data corruption could occur.

Exclusive disk access means you can now run disk management and optimization utilities without quitting Windows. You can even complete tasks such as disk defragmentation without stopping work in other applications. The exclusive access support is used by the disk utilities provided with Windows 98 and can be used in Windows-based disk management utilities from any.

The file system also detects when Windows 98 shuts down improperly. If Windows 98 is shut down without going through the standard shutdown sequence, real mode Scandisk will be executed at the next startup. The purpose of running Scandisk is to correct potential errors in the file allocation table (FAT) before continuing the boot process. In the event that a Disk read/write error is encountered during normal Windows 98 operation, a flag will also be set to run real mode Scandisk with Surface Scan.

a. File Allocation Table

File allocation table (FAT) refers to a disk format, which is a way of organizing the storage space on a hard disk.

FAT organizes information about the files on the hard disk, representing each one as a chain of numbers that identifies where each part of a file is located. The operating system uses the FAT to look up a file and find which clusters that file is written to on the hard disk.

- FAT is probably the most widely recognized disk format, being read by most operating systems.

- A 12-bit FAT was first used by Microsoft for managing floppy disks and logical drives smaller than 16 MB.
- A 16-bit FAT was introduced in MS-DOS version 3.0 for larger drives.

FAT32

FAT32 provides the following enhancements over previous implementations of the FAT file system:

- FAT32 goes beyond the capabilities of FAT16.
- FAT32 supports drives of up to 2 terabytes in size.
- FAT32 decreases the cluster size on large drives, thus reducing the amount of unused space. For example, with FAT16, a 2 GB drive has a 32 KB cluster size. The same drive under FAT32 has 4 KB clusters.
- Programs load up to 50% faster. FAT32's smaller cluster size enables the new and improved Disk Defragmenter to optimally locate the portions of an application and its supporting files needed at the time it is loaded.

To maintain the greatest possible compatibility with existing programs, networks, and device drivers, FAT32 was implemented with as little change as possible to existing architecture, internal data structures APIs, and on-disk format for Windows 98.

- Many internal and on-disk data structures have been revised or expanded, because 4 bytes are now required to store cluster values. Existing tools and drivers should continue to work on FAT32 drives.
- MS-DOS block device drivers (for example, Aspidisk.sys) and disk tools must be revised to support FAT32 drives.
- Note:
- A FAT32 volume cannot be compressed using Microsoft DriveSpace 3.
- You cannot dual boot Windows 98 and Windows NT 4.0 if you use FAT32. Windows NT 4.0 cannot access or boot from a FAT32 drive

FAT16 vs. FAT32

- FAT16 is still available because of its widespread compatibility with all other non-Microsoft operating systems.
- The major benefits of FAT32 are that it is more efficient than a 16-bit FAT on larger disks (sometimes by as much as 20–30 percent), and that it can support disk drives larger than 2 GB without having to use multiple partitions.

➢ *Note*: In real-mode MS-DOS or when running Windows 98 in safe mode, FAT32 is considerably slower than FAT16.

Some older applications that were written to FAT16 specifications may be unable to display free or total disk space over 2 GB correctly. Windows 98 provides new MS-DOS and Win32 APIs that applications can use to determine free or total disk space over 2 GB.

- The following table shows a comparison of FAT16 and FAT32.

FAT16	FAT32
Most operating systems (MS-DOS, Windows 98, Windows NT, OS/2, and UNIX) are designed to implement and use it.	FAT32 can be used only in Windows 98 and Windows 95 OSR2.
It is efficient, both in speed and storage, on logical drives smaller than 256 MB.	Drives smaller that 512 MB are not supported by FAT32.
Disk compression, such as Drvspace, is supported.	Disk compression is not supported with FAT32.
The largest drive is limited to 2 GB.	The largest drive can be up to 2 terabytes.
Storing files in a FAT16 system can be inefficient in larger drives as the size of the cluster increases.	FAT32 cluster sizes are 4 KB (drives less than 800 MB).

Cluster Sizes of FAT16 and FAT32

The largest possible file for a FAT32 drive is 4 GB minus 2 bytes.

➢ Within the file allocation table :

➢ The FAT32 file system includes 4 bytes per cluster

➢ The FAT16 file system contains 2 bytes per cluster

➢ The FAT12 file system contains 1.5 bytes per cluster.

Note that the high 4 bits of the 32-bit values in the file allocation table for FAT32 are reserved and are not part of the cluster number.

➢ The following table provides a comparison of FAT16 and FAT32 cluster sizes according to drive size.

Drive size	FAT16 cluster size	FAT32 cluster size
256 MB – 511 MB	8 KB	Not supported
512 MB – 1023 MB	16 KB	4 KB
1024 MB – 2 GB	32 KB	4 KB
2 GB – 8 GB	Not supported	4 KB
8 GB – 16 GB	Not supported	8 KB
16 GB – 32 GB	Not supported	16 KB
>32 GB	Not supported	32 KB

b. File Systems

With the Windows 98 installable file system, multiple file systems can coexist on the computer. Windows 98 includes the file systems described as follows:

➢ Virtual File Allocation Table

In Windows 98, the 32-bit *virtual file allocation table* (VFAT) file system is the primary file system and cannot be disabled. VFAT can use 32-bit, protected-mode drivers or 16-bit, real-mode drivers. Although VFAT will function correctly when 16-bit disk drivers are being used by IO Supervisor (IOS), its performance is compromised. VFAT handles all hard disk drive requests, using 32-bit code for all file access for hard-disk volumes.

➢ Network Redirectors

A network redirector (such as Microsoft Client for NetWare Networks or Client for Microsoft Networks) is a file system driver that accesses the network file system. Windows 98 supports multiple network redirectors simultaneously.

➢ UDF (Universal Disk Format system)

DVD disks use UDF.

➢ CD-ROM File System

The virtual CD-ROM file system (CDFS) has the same responsibilities for a CD-ROM device as VFAT has for a standard hard disk. If a CD-ROM device is detected, the CDFS driver loads dynamically. When CDFS is installed, the standard disk type-specific device and Disk SCSI translator are replaced with CD-ROM versions. The CDFS driver is a protected-mode version of MSCDEX.EXE, providing the interface from the CD-ROM device to the operating system.

INTRODUCTION TO WINDOWS 98 NETWORKING

a. Windows 98 Networking

The Basics

The Windows 98 operating system includes built-in networking support for popular networks, plus an open, extensible networking architecture. For supported networks other than Microsoft networking, the computer must already have the networking software from another vendor installed. Windows 98 Setup adds only the client or protocols required to work with Windows 98. The following networks are supported:

- Artisoft® LANtastic® version 5.0 and greater
- Banyan® VINES® version 5.52 and greater
- DEC™ PATHWORKS™ (installed as a protocol)
- Microsoft networking — Microsoft LAN Manager, Windows for Workgroups 3.x, and Windows NT
- Novell® NetWare® version 3.11 and greater
- SunSoft™ PC-NFS® version 5.0 and greater

The built-in networking components include support for a wide range of network transports (such as TCP/IP and IPX/SPX), industry-wide communications protocols (such as RPC, NetBIOS, and named pipes), and existing network device standards (such as NDIS and ODI). Because of the extensible architecture, other network vendors can add network connectivity enhancements and application support, and you can mix and match components at every layer.

The Issues

If the real-mode network is running when you start Windows 98 Setup, the appropriate network client is installed automatically. This is the recommended method for installing networking support in all cases. When Setup detects existing network components, it installs the appropriate supporting software automatically and moves the configuration settings to the Registry, wherever possible.

If Windows 98 Setup detects that NetWare networking components are present, it installs the new protected-mode client, Microsoft Client for NetWare Networks, plus the supporting protected-mode protocol and adapter drivers. To maintain the existing real-mode client and support configuration, you must run Setup in Custom mode and manually select the NetWare client.

Microsoft recommends using the 32-bit, protected-mode networking components wherever possible. With protected-mode networking components, all configuration settings are stored in the Registry, so you do not have to maintain configuration files such as AUTOEXEC.BAT, PROTOCOL.INI, or NET.CFG.

If you must run a real-mode client, networking settings are required in AUTOEXEC.BAT, plus a NETSTART.BAT file might be required to start the network during system startup. Configuration settings are maintained in PROTOCOL.INI or a similar file, depending on the particular network.

b. Network Configuration Overview

You can install and configure all networking options for Windows 98 automatically or manually during Windows 98 Setup. You can also install and configure networking support after installing Windows 98 by using the Network option in Control Panel. In the Network option, you can set properties for:

- Configuration of network clients, adapters, protocols, and services
- Identification of the computer on the network
- Access control, to specify the security used when other users access this computer over the network

In the procedures presented in the following sections, it is assumed that Windows 98 and the appropriate networking hardware have already been installed on your computer. You might also need to install or configure various supporting components, such as security, mobile networking components, agents for backup and remote administration software, and support for user profiles and system policies.

Installing Networking Components

The recommended method for installing networking components for Windows 98 is to ensure that the existing real-mode networking components are running when you start Windows 98 Setup. In this case, Setup detects the existing components and installs corresponding support for Windows 98 automatically and, wherever possible, migrates configuration settings to the Registry.

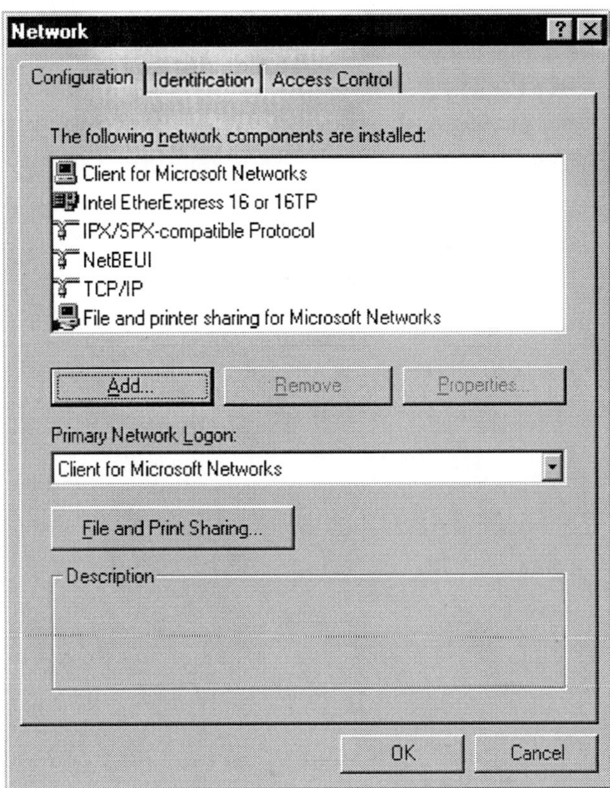

To install networking components after Windows 98 is installed, firstly click the Configuration tab, and then click Add in the Network option in Control Panel.

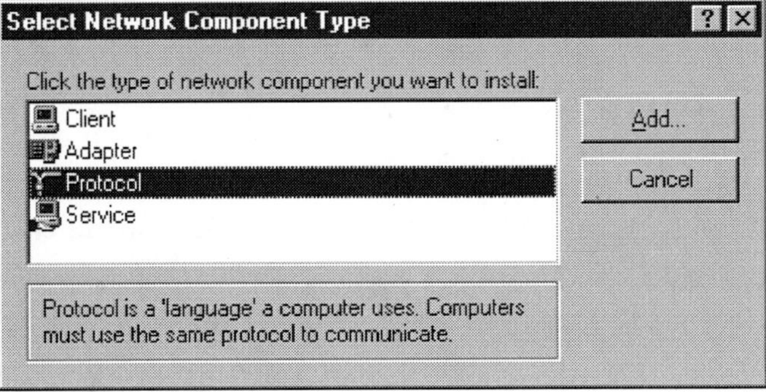

Then in the Select Network Component Type dialog box, double-click the type of component to install, as described in the following list.

Component	Description
Client	Installs client software for the types of networks the computer is connected to. You can use either a 32-bit network client (which needs no real-mode components) or older real-mode networking clients. There is no limit to the number of 32-bit network clients you can install, but you can have only one real-mode network client installed at a time. Some networks are supported only as primary networks.
Adapter	Installs drivers for the network adapters in the computer. However, the recommended method for installing a new adapter is to use the Add New Hardware option in Control Panel. You can configure the type of driver to use (such as enhanced-mode NDIS, real-mode NDIS, or ODI), specify the resources for the adapters you are using (such as I/O, IRQ, and transceiver type), and define other options for the adapter.
Protocol	Installs network protocols and sets related options.
Service	Installs peer file and printer sharing services and other types of network services, such as backup agents, additional print services, Microsoft Remote Registry, and Network Monitor.

Lastly, In the Select dialog box, select the name of the component manufacturer in the Manufacturers list, and then select the specific component in the Models list. Then click OK.

Setting Computer Name and Workgroup

Windows 98 requires that you define a workgroup and computer name for each networked computer, independent of the type of networking software you use. This information is required if you install networking software during Windows 98 Setup. You can also change the computer name or workgroup after Setup is complete.

➢ To specify the computer name, workgroup, and description for a computer

1. In the Network option in Control Panel, click the Identification tab.

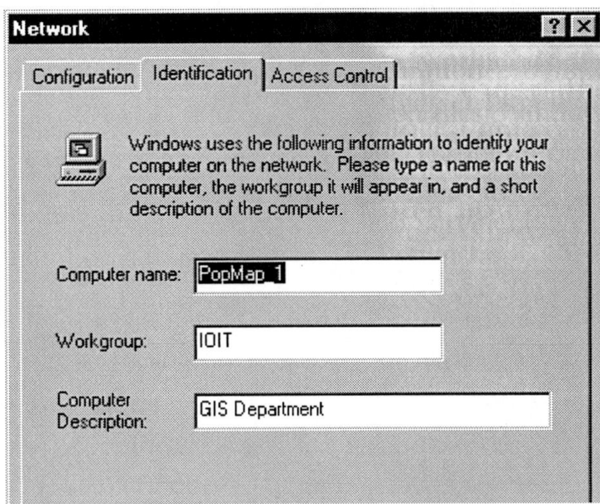

2. Type the values for the computer identification settings as described in the following list.

Setting	Description
Computer Name	The computer name must be unique on the network. It can be up to 15 characters long, with no blank spaces. The computer name can contain only alphanumeric characters, plus the following special characters: ! @ # $ % ^ & ( ) - _ ' { } . ~
Workgroup	The workgroup name does not need to be unique, but it uses the same naming conventions as the computer name.
Computer Description	This information is displayed as a comment next to the computer name when users are browsing the network.

Plug and Play Networking Overview

The networking components in Windows 98 are designed for dynamic Plug and Play operation with most ISA, EISA, PCI, IBM Micro Channel®, and PCMCIA network adapters. To take advantage of these features, the computer must be running all protected-mode networking components, including client, protocols, and network adapter drivers.

NDIS 3.1 supports adding and removing Plug and Play network adapters dynamically while the computer is running. If an event occurs such as undocking a portable computer, the Windows 98 protocols can remove themselves from memory automatically. However, the Windows 98 protocols must load information during system startup to be available. So when an event occurs such as the dynamic addition of a PCI network adapter, the operating system prompts you to restart the computer. If you are certain that the required protocol is already loaded, you can ignore this message.

Additional Plug and Play networking benefits are available when you use 32-bit sockets with PCMCIA cards. You can click the PCMCIA icon on the taskbar to remove the card without shutting down Windows 98 or turning off the computer. Using the PCMCIA icon causes the operating system to perform an orderly shutdown. Windows 98 notifies applications that the network is no longer available and automatically unloads any related drivers or protocols.

To help mobile users who might need to change adapters in their hardware, Windows 98 uses 32-bit Card and Socket Services to support hot removal and insertion of PCMCIA cards, including network adapters. Support for hot docking means that users do not have to restart their computers each time they make a change to the configuration.

Network Plug and Play support in Windows 98 includes application-level support. An application created for Windows 98 might be designed with the ability to determine whether the network is available. Therefore, if a network adapter is removed, for example, the application automatically puts itself into "offline" mode to allow the user to continue to work, or it shuts down.

c. Windows 98 on MS Networks

Computers running Windows 98 can communicate and share resources with other computers running Windows 98, Windows for Workgroups, Windows NT Server and Windows NT Workstation, and LAN Manager on Microsoft networks. This section presents procedures and technical information about using Windows 98 on Microsoft networks.

Client for Microsoft Networks is the 32-bit, protected-mode network client for Windows 98 that provides the redirector and other software components for Microsoft networking. Client for Microsoft Networks also supports limited interoperability with other Microsoft-compatible server message block-based (SMB) servers such as IBM® LAN Server, DEC™ PATHWORKS™, AT&T® StarLAN, and LAN Manager for UNIX® Systems local area network software.

You can install Client for Microsoft Networks to serve as the sole network support for Windows 98 or to coexist with Client for NetWare Networks or clients from other network vendors

On server-based networks, central servers running Windows NT Server or Microsoft LAN Manager 2.x act as file and print servers and provide support for managing network logon and security.

In the peer-to-peer networking model, at least one computer must — but each computer can — act as both a client and a server. As a client in a peer network, the computer can access the network resources shared on another computer. A peer network can be an appropriate networking solution for small offices with only five to ten users.

Any computer running Windows 98 can act as both a client and a server on peer networks. If you have the technical expertise, you can establish the wiring for a small peer network using Windows 98 yourself; otherwise, use the services of a system integrator.

Installing Client for Microsoft Networks

In Windows 98, Client for Microsoft Networks provides the redirector (VREDIR.VXD) to support all Microsoft networking products that use the SMB protocol. This includes support for connecting computers running Windows 98, LAN Manager, Windows NT, Windows for Workgroups, and Workgroup Add-on for MS-DOS networking software for personal computers running MS-DOS.

Because Windows 98 network redirectors are implemented as file system drivers, Client for Microsoft Networks provides mechanisms for locating, opening, reading, writing, and deleting files, submitting print jobs, and making available application services (such as named pipes and mailslots).

If a previous Microsoft network client is running when Windows 98 Setup is started, then Client for Microsoft Networks is installed automatically. You can also add Client for Microsoft Networks after you add network hardware to the computer.

Configuring the Primary Client for Network Logon

If you set Client for Microsoft Networks as the Primary Network Logon, the Microsoft network is used to download system policies and user profiles, and the first logon prompt that appears will be for the Windows NT network. Also, if more than one network client is installed, the last login script will be run from Windows NT (or LAN Manager, depending on your network).

Configuring Logon and Reconnection Options

In the Network option in Control Panel, you can specify network validation and resource connection options. If you enable logon validation, Windows 98 automatically attempts to validate the user by checking the specified domain. You must enable this option if you want to access user profiles and system policies on a Windows NT domain. If logon validation is required on your network and this option is not configured, you might not be able to access most network resources. If this option is configured and you (or another user) do not provide a correct password, you might not have access to network resources.

Note The user's user name and password must be specified in a user account on the specified Windows NT domain, LAN Manager domain, or Windows NT computer for logon validation to work.

You can also set logon validation by using system policies. With system policies, you can prevent the user from accessing resources on the local computer if the correct logon password is not provided.

Note Windows 98 does not support using a LAN Manager domain controller as a pass-through security provider, but LAN Manager can provide logon validation.

When you use Quick Logon (which is the default), Windows 98 can start up and return control of the user interface faster than if the physical connections are made. Because your computer might not be attached to the resource when you click a drive icon for the first time (for example, in My Computer), you might see a slight delay before the contents of that network drive are displayed. This delay is balanced against a possibly long startup time, depending on the number of persistent network connections you maintain.

Note Quick Logon requires password caching to function properly. If system policies are used to disable password caching, users cannot use Quick Logon successfully with peer servers configured with share-level security.

NETWORK TECHNICAL DISCUSSION

a. Network Adapter Drivers and Protocols: The Basics

A network adapter (sometimes called a network interface card, or NIC) is a hardware card installed in a computer so it can communicate on a network. The network adapter provides one or more ports for the network cable to connect to, and it transmits and receives data onto the network cable.

Every networked computer must also have a network adapter driver, which controls the network adapter. Each network adapter driver is configured to run with a certain type of network adapter.

A networked computer must also have one or more protocol drivers (sometimes called a transport protocol or just a protocol). The protocol driver works between the upper-level network software and the network adapter to package data to be sent on the network.

For two computers to communicate on a network, they must use identical protocols. Sometimes, a computer is configured to use multiple protocols. In this case, two computers need only one protocol in common to communicate. For example, a computer running File and Printer Sharing for Microsoft Networks that uses both NetBEUI and TCP/IP can communicate with computers using only NetBEUI or only TCP/IP.

In Windows 98, all network adapter drivers and protocols supporting protected-mode clients are configured by using the Network option in Control Panel rather than by manually editing configuration files. Configuration values are stored in the Registry.

NDIS Driver Basics

Windows 98 supports the Network Device Interface Specification (NDIS) versions 2.x and 3.1 protocol and adapter drivers, and provides an NDIS 3.1 replacement for version 3.0 drivers, which are incompatible with Windows 98.

By using NDIS 3.1 drivers, Windows 98 can support a wide range of network media, including Ethernet, token ring, and ArcNet®. The NDIS 3.1 specification accommodates Plug and Play features, so that in many cases network adapters can be added and removed dynamically while the computer is running.

Network Protocol Basics

Windows 98 network protocols are implemented as 32-bit, protected-mode VxDs that offer high performance and use no conventional memory. Windows 98 can support multiple protocols simultaneously, and protocol stacks can be shared among the installed network clients. For example, the IPX/SPX-compatible protocol can support both Client for NetWare Networks and Client for Microsoft Networks. The following protocols are included with Windows 98.

- Microsoft IPX/SPX-compatible protocol

  This protocol is compatible with the Novell NetWare Internetwork Packet Exchange/Sequential Packet Exchange (IPX/SPX) implementation. Windows 98 includes both 32-bit, protected-mode and real-mode support for this protocol. This protected-mode protocol provides the following benefits:
- Support for any Novell NetWare-compatible network client
- Support for packet-burst mode to offer improved network performance
- Support for the Windows Sockets, NetBIOS, and ECB programming interfaces
- Support for automatic detection of frame type, network address, and other configuration settings
- Connectivity with servers and workstations on NetWare or Windows NT Server 3.5 networks, and mixed networks

- Routable for connectivity across all network bridges and routers configured for IPX/SPX routing
- Microsoft TCP/IP

  This is a complete implementation of the standard, routable Transmission Control Protocol/Internet Protocol (TCP/IP) protocol. Windows 98 includes only protected-mode support for this protocol. Microsoft TCP/IP provides the following benefits:

- Support for Internet connectivity and the Point-to-Point Protocol (PPP) used for asynchronous communication
- Connectivity across interconnected networks with different operating systems and hardware platforms, including communication with many non-Microsoft systems, such as Internet hosts, Apple® Macintosh® systems, IBM® mainframes, UNIX® systems, and Open VMS™ systems
- Support for automatic TCP/IP configuration using Windows NT Dynamic Host Configuration Protocol (DHCP) servers
- Support for automatic IP-address-to-NetBIOS computer name resolution using Windows NT Windows Internet Naming Service (WINS) servers
- Support for the Windows Sockets 1.1 interface, which is used by many client-server applications and many public-domain Internet tools
- Support for the NetBIOS interface, commonly known as NetBIOS over TCP/IP
- Support for many commonly used utilities, which are installed with the protocol
- Microsoft NetBEUI

This protocol is compatible with existing networks that use NetBIOS extended user interface (NetBEUI), including Windows for Workgroups peer networks, Windows NT Server, LAN Manager, and other networks, and includes support for a NetBIOS programming interface. Windows 98 provides both protected-mode and real-mode support for this protocol.

NetBEUI was first introduced by IBM in 1985, when it was assumed that LANs would be segmented into workgroups of 20 to 200 computers and that gateways would be used to connect one LAN segment to other LAN segments or to a mainframe. NetBEUI is optimized for high performance when used in departmental LANs or LAN segments. Microsoft NetBEUI under Windows 98 is completely self-tuning and provides much better performance over slow links than did earlier versions of NetBEUI.

All three protocols are Plug and Play-compliant, so they can be loaded and unloaded automatically. For example, if a PCMCIA network adapter is removed from the computer so that the network is no longer available, the protocols are unloaded automatically after any dependent applications have been notified.

b. Network Adapters and Protocols: The Issues

Windows 98 Setup automatically configures a computer to use protocols and drivers to match network components that are running when Setup is started.

If you are setting up Windows 98 for a new networking option, you must choose which types of network adapter drivers and protocols to use. Because Windows 98 has an open architecture, you have a lot of flexibility in this decision. Windows 98 supports both NDIS and Transport Driver Interface (TDI) standards, allowing Windows 98 to communicate with many other networking products and making it possible to choose from a variety of network adapters and protocols.

Choosing adapters and drivers for best performance

Network adapters have become exceptionally reliable and inexpensive. The low cost of Ethernet adapters, including new Plug and Play hardware, means that usually the cost-effective way to improve network performance is to replace an older network adapter with a new model. The cost for the new hardware is offset almost immediately by savings in support time and improved performance. In choosing a new network adapter, you should also consider buying an adapter that matches the computer bus. For example, PCI network adapters are available for use in PCI computers.

Choosing separate protocol and adapter drivers

With some networks, each computer's network adapter driver and protocol are separate pieces of software. With other networks, a single piece of software called a monolithic protocol stack acts as both adapter driver and protocol. Microsoft recommends that you choose separate 32-bit, protected-mode protocols and drivers rather than monolithic stacks, which run only in real mode. However, Windows 98 includes mapping technology for users who must continue to use real-mode NDIS 2 or ODI drivers.

Choosing NDIS versus ODI drivers.

Windows 98 supports NDIS versions 2.x and 3.1. All network adapter drivers and protocols shipped with Windows 98 conform to NDIS. You can use any combination of protocol and network adapter drivers that conforms to NDIS. Microsoft recommends that you use NDIS 3.1 drivers whenever possible with Windows 98.

The *Open Datalink Interface* (ODI) specification was defined by Novell and Apple Computer to provide a protocol and API for communicating with network adapter drivers, and to support the use of multiple protocols by a network adapter driver. To ensure the most flexibility in Windows 98, Microsoft recommends that you use NDIS 3.1 drivers whenever possible if you are running Windows 98 with Microsoft Client for NetWare Networks. If you are using a Novell-supplied network client, Novell recommends using ODI-based client software rather than monolithic IPX drivers.

Choosing a protocol

Windows 98 can support multiple network protocols, and can share a protocol among the network providers that are installed. You might choose more than one protocol to ensure communication compatibility with all systems in the enterprise. However, choosing multiple protocols can cause more network traffic, more memory used on the local workstations, and more network delays. You probably want to choose a single protocol wherever possible. The following briefly presents some issues for each Windows 98 protocol.

For the IPX/SPX-compatible protocol:

This protocol is required and installed automatically with Microsoft Client for NetWare. When Windows 98 Setup determines that it cannot install Client for NetWare Networks on a computer running a Novell-supplied network client, Setup still tries to install this protected-mode protocol.

This protocol cannot be used to configure Windows 98 to support NetWare over ArcNet. Instead, you must use real-mode IPX drivers with NetBIOS support on ArcNet network adapters.

With this protocol, it is not necessary to load the Novell-supplied VIPX.386 driver, because the Microsoft protocol provides virtualized services to all VMs and applications.

For Microsoft TCP/IP:

TCP/IP in general has been known to require careful planning and management of the IP address space. However, this problem is vastly reduced when DHCP servers are used to manage assignment of IP addresses for computers running Microsoft TCP/IP.

If you want to take advantage of DHCP for automatic IP addressing or use WINS for name resolution on computers running Windows 98, the appropriate Windows NT servers must be in place on the network.

This protocol cannot be used on NetWare networks that require NetWare/IP.

For Microsoft NetBEUI:

NetBEUI is a nonroutable protocol that cannot cross routers, although it can cross bridges and source routing bridges.

NetBEUI is optimized for high performance only for use in departmental LANs or LAN segments.

One common method for setting up a network is to use NetBEUI plus a protocol such as TCP/IP on each computer that needs to access computers across a router. If you set NetBEUI as the default protocol, Windows 98 uses NetBEUI for communication within the LAN segment and uses TCP/IP for communication across routers to other parts of the WAN.

c. *Network Adapters and Windows 98*

Windows 98 supports up to four network adapters in a single computer. Windows 98 Setup automatically detects most network adapters, installs the appropriate driver for the adapter, and provides appropriate default settings to configure the adapter. If you add a new network adapter, its driver is bound automatically to all NDIS protocols currently running on the computer; if any protocols are added later, they will also be bound automatically to the network adapter driver.

Configuring Network Adapters

If you add a new network adapter after Windows 98 is installed, you should use the Add New Hardware option in Control Panel to install the correct driver for the adapter.

When you use the Add New Hardware option, be sure to choose Detection for determining the correct driver and resource assignment. You should configure network adapter drivers manually only after you have tried all detection and automatic configuration methods.

If you experience problems with settings for a network adapter, you should begin troubleshooting by removing the network adapter driver in the Network option in Control Panel. Then use the Add New Hardware option to reinstall support for the network adapter, using detection to ensure that Windows 98 determines the correct adapter driver and standard settings for that network adapter.

➤ Binding Network Adapter Drivers to Protocols

For a protocol to communicate with each network adapter on your computer, the network adapter driver must be bound to the protocol. The bindings define the relationships between networking software components. Windows 98 automatically binds the appropriate protocols to the network adapter.

You can change the bindings, for example, if you do not want to use a specific protocol with a particular network adapter. Or, as another example, if the computer is on a local area network and is also connected to the enterprise internetwork, you might not want the computer's shared resources to be seen on the internetwork. In that case, you can disable the binding between the related protocol and the adapter that connects the computer to the internetwork.

➤ Configuring Network Adapter Resource Settings

Windows 98 can determine hardware settings for most network adapters. For this reason, the recommended method for installing or configuring network adapter drivers is to use the Add New Hardware option in Control Panel, using detection to determine the correct driver and resource settings. You should accept the proposed settings unless you are absolutely sure they are incorrect.

Most devices cannot share IRQ settings, memory buffer addresses, or ROM addresses. Where possible, Windows 98 identifies and resolves conflicts. However, if one of the supported devices does not seem to work, the problem may be the particular hardware configuration. To make sure there are no conflicts among network adapters or other peripherals, or between the system board and adapters, check the settings in Device Manager.

Sometimes settings for network adapters are set with software, sometimes with jumpers or switches on the hardware. If settings for a network adapter can be configured through software, you can configure settings using the Network option in Control Panel.

Setting LAN Adapter Numbers

NetBIOS defines the interface between the network client and the protocol layers using a set of function calls that allow an application to use the protocol services. Because many network applications use NetBIOS to send commands to the protocol driver, the NetBIOS interface is supported by all protocols provided with Windows 98.

Each combination of a NetBIOS network protocol and a network adapter forms a logical network over which computers can communicate with each other. For example, a computer can have a token ring adapter and an Ethernet adapter, and might use NetBEUI on the token ring network and both NetBEUI and TCP/IP on the Ethernet network. In this case, the computer is connected to three logical networks, each of which is assigned a NetBIOS LAN adapter (LANA) number that Windows 98 uses for communication.

When Windows 98 uses multiple protocols, it transmits data first using one protocol, then again using the next protocol, and so on. When multiple protocols are installed on a computer, the first protocol to be used is called the primary protocol.

On a computer running Windows 98, each binding of a protocol to a network adapter has a LAN adapter number assigned to it. (For example, one protocol bound to two network adapters requires two LAN adapter numbers; two protocols each bound to two adapters requires four LAN adapter numbers.)

In Windows 98, LANA numbers are assigned dynamically in sequence of binding order for the protocols, beginning with 7 and then 0, 1, and so on. This accommodates dynamic Plug and Play events such as removing a network adapter while the computer is running. If you are running Windows 98 in such a dynamic environment, Windows 98 cannot guarantee that a given protocol will receive the same LANA number each time the system is started. Although if the computer's network hardware never changes, the LANA numbers may not change at each startup. However, the default protocol is always LANA 0.

d. TCP/IP Protocol

Microsoft TCP/IP provides communication across interconnected networks that use diverse hardware architectures and various operating systems. TCP/IP can be used to communicate with computers running Windows 98, with devices using other Microsoft networking products, or with non-Microsoft systems such as UNIX.

Microsoft TCP/IP provides all the following elements necessary for networking:

- Core TCP/IP protocols, including the Transmission Control Protocol (TCP), Internet Protocol (IP), User Datagram Protocol (UDP), Address Resolution Protocol (ARP), Internet Control Message Protocol (ICMP), and Domain Name Protocol (DNS). This suite of Internet protocols provides a set of standards for how computers communicate and how networks are interconnected.
- Support for application programming interfaces, including Windows Sockets and NetBIOS.
- TCP/IP diagnostic tools to detect and resolve TCP/IP networking problems, including **arp**, **ftp**, **nbtstat**, **netstat**, **ping**, **route**, and **tracert**, plus Windows-based Telnet and IP Configuration (WINIPCFG) utilities.

  In addition, when you install Microsoft TCP/IP under Windows 98, the following enhancements are included:
- Client for DHCP, for automatic configuration of computers running TCP/IP on networks that have DHCP servers

- Client for WINS, for dynamic resolution of IP addresses to computer names on networks that have WINS servers
- Point-to-Point Protocol for asynchronous communication.

Configuring TCP/IP with DHCP

In an effort to make implementing the TCP/IP protocol more manageable, Microsoft worked with other industry leaders to create an Internet standard called Dynamic Host Configuration Protocol (DHCP) for the automatic allocation of IP addresses. DHCP is not a Microsoft standard, but a public Request for Comments (RFC 1541) that Microsoft has implemented.

DHCP allows you to establish a range of valid IP addresses to be used per subnetwork. An individual IP address from the range is assigned dynamically to any DHCP client requesting an address. DHCP also allows you to establish a lease time that defines how long an IP address is to remain valid. Other configuration parameters can also be assigned using DHCP, such as subnet mask, DNS and WINS server identification, and so on.

A computer running Windows 98 cannot be a DHCP server. A DHCP server runs as a service on a Windows NT 3.5 Server computer. If DHCP is available company-wide, users can move from subnet to subnet and always have a valid IP address. The IP Configuration utility (WINIPCFG) allows users or administrators to examine the current IP address assigned to the computer, the IP address lease time, and other useful data about the TCP/IP configuration.

When TCP/IP is installed, Windows 98 automatically enables the option to obtain an IP address from a DHCP server. This option can be disabled using the Network option in Control Panel if you want to enter an IP address manually.

If Microsoft TCP/IP is configured to obtain an IP address from a DHCP server when a DHCP server is not available on the network, the next time Windows 98 starts, an error message announces that the DHCP client could not obtain an IP address. To solve this problem, use the procedure described in the following section to configure TCP/IP manually.

Name Resolution for Windows Networking

For TCP/IP and the Internet, the globally known system name is the computer's host name, appended with a DNS domain name (for example, rhit.microsoft.com). This defaults to the computer name (NetBIOS name) defined during Windows 98 Setup. The default name can be changed in the DNS dialog box when you are configuring TCP/IP properties.

Computers use IP addresses to identify each other, but users usually find it easier to work with computer names. A mechanism must be available on a TCP/IP network to resolve names to IP addresses. To ensure that both the name and the address are unique, the computer using Microsoft TCP/IP registers its name and IP address on the network during system startup. Computers running Microsoft TCP/IP on the network can use one or more methods for name resolution in TCP/IP internetworks, as summarized in this section.

➢ Broadcast name resolution

Computers running Microsoft TCP/IP can use broadcast name resolution, which is a NetBIOS-over-TCP/IP mode of operation defined in RFC 1001/1002 as b-node. This method relies on a computer making IP-level broadcasts to register its name by announcing it on the network. Each computer in the broadcast area is responsible for challenging attempts to register a duplicate name and for responding to name queries for its registered name.

➢ LMHOSTS or HOSTS files.

An LMHOSTS file specifies the NetBIOS computer name and IP address mappings; a HOSTS file specifies the DNS name and IP address. On a local computer, the HOSTS file (used by Windows Sockets applications to find TCP/IP host names) and LMHOSTS file (used by NetBIOS over TCP/IP to find NetBIOS computer names) can be used to list known IP addresses mapped with corresponding computer names. LMHOSTS is used for name resolution in Windows 98 for internetworks where WINS is not available.

➢ The HOSTS file is used as a local DNS equivalent to resolve host names to IP addresses.

➢ The LMHOSTS file is used as a local WINS equivalent to resolve NetBIOS computer names to IP addresses.

Each of these files is also known as a *host table*. Sample versions of LMHOSTS (called LMHOSTS.SAM) and HOSTS files are added to the Windows directory when you install Windows 98 with TCP/IP support. These files can be edited using any ASCII editor, such as WordPad or Edit. To take advantage of HOSTS or LMHOSTS, DNS must be enabled on the computer.

➢ Windows Internet Name Service

Computers running Microsoft TCP/IP can use WINS if one or more Windows NT Server computers configured as WINS servers are available, containing a dynamic database for mapping computer names to IP addresses. WINS can be used in conjunction with broadcast name resolution for an internetwork, where other name resolution methods are inadequate. WINS is a NetBIOS-over-TCP/IP mode of operation defined in RFC 1001/1002 as h-node or m-node; WINS clients default to h-node. Notice that WINS is a dynamic replacement for the LMHOSTS file.

- Domain Name System name resolution.

  DNS provides a way to look up name mappings when connecting a computer to foreign hosts using NetBIOS over TCP/IP or Windows Sockets applications such as FTP. DNS is a distributed database designed to relieve the traffic problems that arose with the first growth explosion on the Internet in the early 1980s. A DNS name server must be configured and available on the network. Notice that DNS replaces the functionality of the HOSTS file by providing a dynamic mapping of IP addresses to host names used by TCP/IP applications and utilities.

  Windows 98 provides support for multiple DNS servers and up to two WINS servers. Support for either service can be configured automatically from a DHCP server, manually in Windows 98 Setup, or after Setup by using the Network option in Control Panel.

Microsoft NetBEUI Protocol

Windows 98 provides the NetBIOS extended user interface (NetBEUI) protocol for compatibility with existing networks that use NetBEUI. Because NetBEUI is nonroutable and was designed for smaller LANs, you should use the TCP/IP or IPX/SPX-compatible protocol for enterprise-wide networks that require a routable protocol.

NetBEUI in Windows 98 supports a NetBIOS programming interface that conforms to the IBM NetBEUI specifications and includes several performance enhancements. The NetBEUI module, NETBEUI.VXD, is accessible through the NetBIOS interface.

If Windows 98 Setup detects NetBEUI during installation, it installs support for Microsoft NetBEUI automatically. You can add or configure this protocol at any time.

Device Management

Windows 98 allows you to configure and manage your system devices by using Device Manager, which you gain access to by clicking the System icon in Control Panel. Using Device Manager is recommended and is described in the sections that follow.

a. *Understanding Device and Bus Classes*

To install and manage device drivers and allocate resources, Windows 98 groups devices and buses into classes. The registry contains a subkey for every class of device supported, and the hardware tree is organized by bus type. Windows 98 uses class installers to install drivers for all hardware classes. Device Manager, for example, sends messages to the various class installers to tell them to add, remove, or configure specific hardware.

The following are some examples of class names defined in the Windows 98 registry.

Adapter	**Keyboard**	**MTD**	**Ports**
CD-ROM	Media	Net	Printer
Display	Modem	NetService	SCSI Adapter
FDC	Monitor	Nodriver	System
HDC	Mouse	PC Card	USB devices
HID			

The Hardware Tree

The Windows 98 hardware tree is a record of the current system configuration, based on the configuration information for all devices in the hardware branch of the registry. The hardware tree is created in RAM each time the system is started or whenever a dynamic change occurs to the system configuration.

Each branch in the tree defines a *device node* with the following requirements for system configuration:

- Unique identification code, or device ID.
- List of required resources, including resource type, such as interrupt request (IRQ) and memory range.
- List of allocated resources.
- Indication that the device node is a bus, if applicable (each bus device has additional device nodes under it in the tree).

Displaying Hardware Tree Information in Device Manager

Most information in the Windows 98 hardware tree can be accessed by using Device Manager. Device Manager contains a representation of the active hardware device tree, listing the system device nodes. Under each node are listed the actual devices configured for your system; double-clicking a device node exposes its device list. You can reconfigure the device driver and resource settings for a specific device from the **Device Properties** dialog box, reached by clicking the device name and then **Properties**.

- Note: You can also see the information in the hardware tree in the Windows 98 registry.

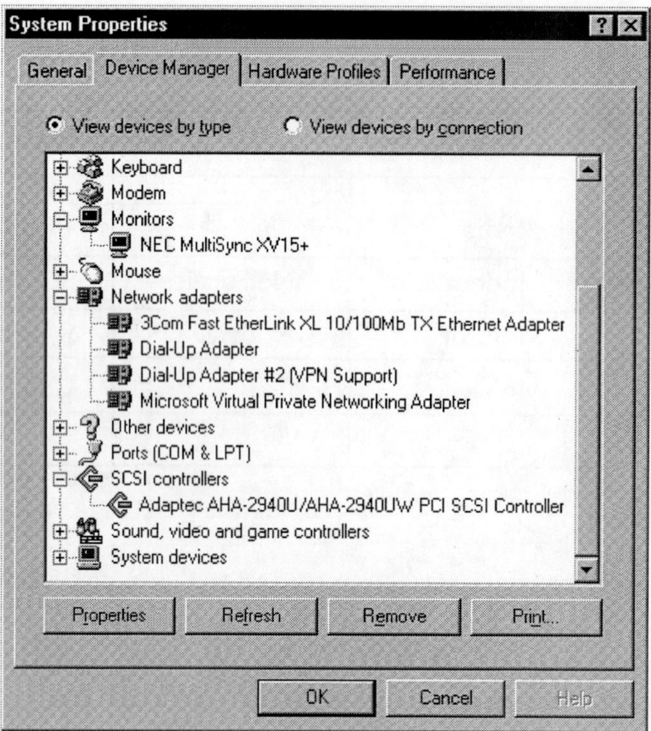

DEVICE MANAGER DIALOG BOX

b. Plug and Play Support

Plug and Play is an independent set of computer architecture specifications that hardware manufacturers use to produce computer devices that can be configured with no user intervention.

You can install hot-pluggable Plug and Play–compliant devices simply by plugging in the device. For other devices, such as Plug and Play Industry Standard Architecture (ISA) cards, you must plug in or install a device while the computer is off and then turn the computer back on to initialize the device.

- For example, a user can do the following:
- Insert and remove such Plug and Play–compliant devices as PC Cards without having to configure them.
- Connect to or disconnect from a docking station or network without restarting the computer or changing configuration parameters.
- Add a new monitor by plugging it in and turning it on.

  Windows 98 detects the presence of a Plug and Play–compliant device. This is known as *enumerating* the device. After enumeration, the device driver can be configured and then loaded dynamically, requiring little or no user input. Certain buses (for example, peripheral component interconnect [PCI] and Universal Serial Bus [USB]) are also automatically enumerated; these buses take full advantage of Plug and Play capability.

  You can add some Plug and Play functionality by adding Plug and Play–compliant devices on legacy computers. Therefore, it is best to add Plug and Play–compliant devices on legacy computers rather than adding non–Plug and Play devices.

- To be able to use *all* Plug and Play features, however, your system must also include one of the following:
- An Advanced Configuration and Power Interface (ACPI) BIOS.
- A Plug and Play BIOS (for Plug and Play devices on the system board).
- The Plug and Play–compliant hardware devices (including buses).
- The Plug and Play implementation in the Windows 98 operating system provides the following benefits:
- Dynamically loads, initializes, and unloads drivers in protected mode.
- Supports a wide range of device types (as described in "Plug and Play Device Types" later in this chapter).
- Provides enumeration of devices, which is critical for Plug and Play on legacy computers.
- Notifies other drivers and applications when a new device is available for use. Windows 98 also includes an automatic installation procedure to ensure that appropriate drivers are installed and loaded.
- Provides robust, seamless operation through the integration of all subsystems and the startup process.
- Provides an architecture with a consistent driver and bus interface for all devices.

Plug and Play Device Types

A variety of devices are compliant with Plug and Play. The following sections describe the types of devices and provide details for Plug and Play.

➢ *Note:* Windows 98 assigns resources first to ISA, EISA, and Micro Channel Architecture (MCA) devices, next to PCI devices, and finally to Accelerated Graphics Port (AGP) devices.

USB Devices

Universal Serial Bus is a bus standard that brings Plug and Play capability to external hardware devices, such as keyboards, mouse devices, speakers, and cameras. USB devices are hot pluggable. This means that they can be connected at any time, even when the computer is running. USB devices are automatically configured as soon as they are physically attached — without the need to reboot or run the setup sequence.

IEEE 1394 Devices

The IEEE 1394 bus is designed for high-bandwidth PC devices such as digital camcorders, cameras, and videodisc players. Windows 98 supports hot plugging of IEEE 1394 devices. To use an IEEE 1394 device, you must obtain the appropriate Win 32 Driver Model (WDM) driver. Windows 98 includes a driver for a digital camera; for other drivers, contact your hardware manufacturer.

SCSI Devices

Small computer system interface *(SCSI)* is a multiple-device chained interface used for many devices such as hard disks and CD-ROM drives. Plug and Play SCSI devices support dynamic changes to the adapter and automatic configuration of device ID and termination, as long as the driver supports it.

➢ Configuration of a SCSI device can be separated into two distinct processes:

➢ Configuring the SCSI bus itself, for example, by terminating both ends of the SCSI bus and setting device IDs.

➢ Configuring the SCSI host adapter, for example, by assigning an interrupt request (IRQ) channel, direct memory access (DMA) channel, and so on.

➢ Configuring a SCSI bus that is not Plug and Play–compliant is difficult for most users. The long list of issues related to configuring a SCSI bus includes the following:

➢ SCSI device ID assignment

➢ Termination

- SCSI parity
- Command sets
- Disk geometry and software

PC Card Devices and CardBus

Windows 98 supports the new features of products designed for the *PC Card* standard, also known as the Personal Computer Memory Card International Association (PCMCIA) standard. These products include multifunction cards, 3.3-V cards, and 32-bit PC Cards (CardBus). These advances add the modularity and bus-independence of Plug and Play without affecting device drivers.

Windows 98 also supports *CardBus,* a 32-bit implementation of PC Card also known as PC Card 32. CardBus brings 32-bit performance and the benefits of the PCI bus to the PC Card format. CardBus allows laptop PCs to run high-bandwidth applications such as Video Capture.

VL Devices

The Video Electronic Standards Association (VESA) Local (VL) bus standard allows high-speed connections to peripherals (compared to ISA devices). VL bus devices are not totally Plug and Play–compliant but work similarly to ISA devices.

PCI Devices

- The peripheral component interconnect *(PCI)* local bus has become the industry-standard bus and is used in most Pentium computers. It is considered the successor to the VL bus.
- Windows extracts PCI and ISA Plug and Play – compliant device resource information from the system BIOS, and the BIOS provides the PCI IRQ Steering Table for PCI devices. With the information from the PCI IRQ Steering Table, Windows 98 can reassign PCI device resource requirements dynamically, if necessary.
- Note: Windows 98 can manipulate only the ISA IRQ that is mapped to a particular PCI INT#. It cannot alter the link value for the PCI device listed in the PCI IRQ Routing Table.

ISA Devices

Industry Standard Architecture (ISA) bus design is the architecture specified for the IBM PC/AT. Plug and Play ISA devices can be used on existing computers, because the specification does not require any change to ISA buses.

- To configure Plug and Play ISA devices, the system performs the following actions:
- Isolates each card and retrieves a unique device ID and a unique serial number.
- Reads the resource requirements and capabilities stored on each card.
- Allocates resources to each card, reserving these resources so that they cannot be assigned to other Plug and Play cards in the computer.
- Activates the Plug and Play ISA cards.

EISA Devices

Extended Industry Standard Architecture (EISA) is a bus design for *x*86-based computers, specified by an industry consortium. EISA devices use cards that are upwardly compatible from ISA. EISA devices use standard software mechanisms for identification and configuration. Windows 98 includes a bus enumerator that makes configuration information from these devices accessible to the operating system. This means that Windows 98 does not reconfigure EISA cards but instead uses the information that hardware detection derives from the EISA nonvolatile RAM storage to determine which resources are used.

c. Other Device Types

Other device types can take advantage of Plug and Play if they provide mechanisms for identification and configuration. These include integrated device electronics (IDE) controllers, Extended Capability Ports (ECPs), and communications ports.

Parallel ports (ports designated as LPT) can also take advantage of Plug and Play. The most common parallel port type is the Centronics interface. Plug and Play parallel ports meet Compatibility and Nibble mode protocols defined in IEEE P1284.

For totally Plug and Play–compliant computers, the BIOS also meets Plug and Play specifications. For computers that comply with the Plug and Play BIOS specification, the file Bios.vxd provides the BIOS Plug and Play enumerator. For computers that conform to the ACPI specification, the file Acpi.sys provides the motherboard Plug and Play enumerator.

APPLICATION SUPPORT IN WINDOWS 98

- Windows 98 optimizes the performance of applications written for it, as well as existing applications created for MS-DOS and previous versions of Windows. Applications perform more smoothly than with MS-DOS, Windows for Workgroups, Windows 3.1, or Windows 95, because Windows 98 significantly increases system resources available to them and more efficiently manages how they use system memory. In addition, Windows 98 increases the number of timers, COM and LPT ports, Windows menu handles, and other resources available to applications.

- Windows 98 also supports:
- new and existing versions of COM technology (ActiveX Controls and Automation)
- Web authoring technologies HTML and JavaScript.
- Distributed Component Object Model, which lets application components work with each other across a network or across the Internet. Users can access and share information without needing to know the location of an application's components.
- The Virtual Machine Manager, an integral part of the Windows 98 architecture, manages the memory required by each application. A virtual machine (VM) is an environment in memory that functions like a separate computer for each application. All Win32-based and Win16-based applications run in the System VM, in which all system processes also run. Each MS-DOS-based application runs in its own VM.

a. Distributed Component Object Mode

- The *Distributed Component Object Model (Distributed COM)* extends the Component Object Model (COM) to allow components of a distributed application to communicate over the network securely and transparently. The existing COM applications can use Distributed COM without any modifications. In a corporate environment, Distributed COM lets application developers break down an application into a multitier design using smaller components that can communicate directly with each other across computers.
- For example: your company might deploy a distributed order entry application that uses individual components for sales tax calculations, with each component designed for a different geographic sales region. Each of these sales channel components uses the same inventory component located on a network server. As the inventory changes, you can change the inventory component without having to rewrite and recompile the sales tax components for each of the sales regions.
- Distributed COM is particularly powerful for component applications running across computers for the following reasons:

- Distributed COM is transport-neutral: Components can communicate with each other over any network transport. In Windows 98, Distributed COM supports Transmission Control Protocol/Internet Protocol (TCP/IP).
- Distributed COM is language-neutral: ActiveX controls, Java applets, and components written in many languages (such as Microsoft Visual Basic, Microsoft Visual C++®, or even COBOL or Pascal) can communicate with each other through COM.
- Distributed COM is platform-independent: Distributed COM runs on Windows 98, Windows NT, UNIX, and legacy operating systems, providing a common application infrastructure across a company's entire information systems environment.
- Distributed COM is based on open standards: Distributed COM uses the Open Group distributed computing environment (DCE) remote procedure call (RPC) mechanism for communication between clients and servers across the network. For more information about COM, go to http://www.microsoft.com/com/.

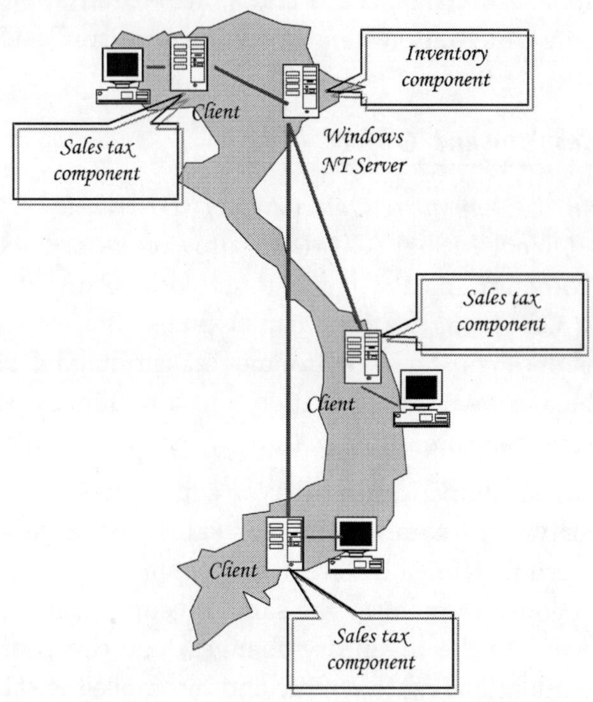

OVERVIEW OF DISTRIBUTED APPLICATIONS USING DISTRIBUTED COM

b. Win32-based Applications

Win32-based applications receive the full benefit of the performance enhancement features in Windows 98. Because each Win32-based application runs in a separate memory space, it can take complete advantage of the preemptive multitasking capabilities of Windows 98.

c. Win16-based Applications

Win16-based applications designed for Windows 3.1 run under Windows 98 without modification, but these applications run in a shared memory space and cannot take advantage of preemptive multitasking. For Win16-based applications that are known to need special parameters to run, Windows 98 includes an Apps.inf file that defines parameters for each application.

Windows 98 does not allow you to specify a working directory in the properties sheet of a Win16-based application. This is because the program file has links assigned to it that rely on unchanging data. However, you can achieve the same effect by creating a shortcut for the application and specifying a working directory in the **Start In** box in the **Properties** dialog box for the shortcut.

d. MS-DOS-based Applications

MS-DOS-based applications can take advantage of the improved memory management and increased system resources that are made possible by the system architecture used in Windows 95 and Windows 98. Most applications can now run in a window. An MS-DOS-based application that does not run well under Windows can run in exclusive MS-DOS mode, which makes all system resources available to that application.

For MS-DOS-based applications that need special parameters to run, Windows 98 includes an Apps.inf file that defines parameters for each application.

- When running under Windows 98, MS-DOS-based applications also benefit from the following:
- Improved robustness, including better virtualization for computer resources, such as support for timers and sound devices.
- Improved support for highly graphical MS-DOS-based applications. This allows you to run video-mode style applications in a window rather than in a full screen.

- Improved memory protection. Windows 98 includes a global memory-protection attribute in the **Properties** dialog box for executable files. This attribute allows the MS-DOS system area to be protected from errant MS-DOS-based applications.
- Improved printing performance and font support, including user-scalable windows with support for TrueType fonts in VMs.
- Local environment settings for VMs. You can also customize the VM environment by specifying a batch file in an executable file's properties.

WINDOWS 98 ARCHITECTURE COMPONENTS

Microsoft Windows 98 is a 32-bit operating system that provides built-in Internet connectivity, Plug and Play hardware support, high performance, robustness, and backward compatibility with Windows 95. Windows 98 enhancements to Windows 95 include more sophisticated power management, multiple video display support, and integrated support for the latest hardware. Also included is support for the new Win32 Driver Model (WDM), allowing a WDM device to run under both Windows 98 and future versions of Windows NT using the same driver.

These features are supported by the components shown in the following figure.

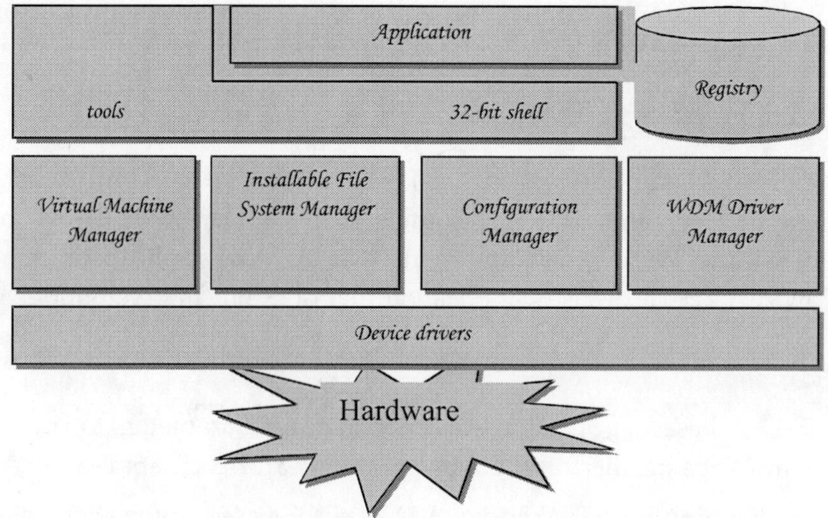

Windows 98 components

- Like Windows 95, Windows 98 is derived from the Windows 3.1 platform and includes the following features:
- A complete 32-bit kernel, including memory management, and preemptive multitasking and multithreading support.

- A fully integrated 32-bit, protected-mode file system, which eliminates the need to rely on a separate copy of MS-DOS once the system boots up.
- 32-bit installable file system drivers supporting FAT, FAT32, ISO 9660 (CD-ROM), ISO 13346 (Universal Disk Format/Digital Video Disc [UDF/DVD]), network redirection, and high performance. These file system drivers also support the use of long file names and an open, modular architecture to handle future expansion.
- WDM support, which allows a WDM-supported device to run under both Windows 98 and future versions of Windows NT using the same driver.
- Improved system-wide robustness and "cleanup" after an application or driver fails. This delivers a more stable and reliable operating environment.
- A dynamic hardware and environment configuration, which reduces the need for users to adjust and restart their systems manually.

a. Windows 98 Registry

The central information database for Windows 98 is called the *registry*. This hierarchical database both simplifies the operating system and makes it more adaptable. The registry simplifies the operating system by eliminating the need for Autoexec.bat, Config.sys, and INI files, however, Windows 98 still supports the use of these files when legacy applications require them. It makes the operating system more adaptable by storing user-specific and configuration-specific information so you can share one computer among multiple users and have more than one configuration (such as in-the-office and on-the-road configurations) for each computer.

A primary role of the registry in Windows 98 is to serve as a central repository for hardware-specific information for use by the hardware detection and Plug and Play system components. Windows 98 maintains information about hardware components and devices that have been identified through an enumeration or detection process, in the hierarchical structure of the registry. When a new device is installed, the system checks for an existing configuration in the registry. If none is found, Windows 98 then searches all available media for the driver that best matches the device. Once the driver is found, it is added to the registry alongside the settings for the device.

b. Device Drivers

Windows 98 provides improved support for hardware devices, including disk devices, display adapters, pointing devices, modems, fax machines, and printers.

In Windows 3.1, device drivers were, for the most part, monolithic and complex to develop. In this case, monolithic means that the driver had to provide all services, user interfaces, API functions, and hardware-access services to operate under Windows 3.1. Starting with Windows 95, and continuing with Windows 98, we provide a universal driver/minidriver architecture that makes driver development easier for hardware vendors. By having the operating system provide basic device services for a given hardware class natively, the vendor is required to provide only device-specific code for their particular hardware. In addition, Windows 98 uses the WDM architecture, which provides a common set of I/O services understood by both Windows 98 and future versions of Windows NT. With WDM, developers can write a single device driver for both operating systems.

c. Virtual Machine Manager

The Virtual Machine Manager manages resources needed for each application and system process running on the computer. Virtual Machine Manager creates and maintains the virtual machine environments in which applications and system processes run.

A *virtual machine* (VM) is an environment in memory that, from the application's perspective, looks as if it is a separate computer, complete with all the resources available on the physical computer that an application needs to run.

Windows 98 has a single VM called the System VM, in which all system processes run. In addition, each Win32-based application runs in its own VM, whereas Win16-based applications share a single Win16 VM. Each MS-DOS- based application runs in its own VM.

The Virtual Machine Manager is responsible for three key areas of services:

- Process scheduling.
- Memory paging.
- MS-DOS Mode support (for MS-DOS-based applications that must have exclusive access to system resources).

d. Installable File Systems

Windows 98 features a layered file system architecture that supports multiple file systems, including the virtual file allocation table (VFAT), CD-ROM file system (CDFS), and UDF.

The new file system architecture makes the computer easier to use and improves file and disk I/O performance. Features of the new file system architecture include long file name support and a dynamic system cache for file and network I/O.

Long file name support improves ease of use because users no longer need to reference files by the MS-DOS 8.3 file name. Instead, users can specify names of up to 255 characters to identify their documents. In addition, file names seem less cryptic and easier to read, because Windows 98 hides the file name extensions from users.

Windows 98 features 32-bit, protected-mode code for reading information from — and writing information to — the file system and the disk device. It also includes 32-bit dynamically sizable caching mechanisms, and a full, 32-bit code path is available from the file system to the disk device. Moreover, it includes an open file system architecture for future system support.

e. Configuration Manager

To support Plug and Play functionality, Windows 98 architecture includes a component called Configuration Manager, which orchestrates the configuration process. This process might involve many bus and device architectures coexisting on a single system, with more than one device type using the same bus architecture, yet with each device having a separate set of configuration requirements. For example, a mouse and a keyboard can both use the same keyboard controller bus; a CD-ROM drive and a hard disk drive might both use the same SCSI bus.

f. Core System Components

Windows 98 includes a core composed of three components — User, Kernel, and Graphics Device Interface (GDI). Each of these components includes a pair of dynamic-link libraries (DLLs) one 32-bit and one 16-bit) that provide services for the applications you run. Windows 98 is designed to use 32-bit code wherever it significantly improves performance without sacrificing application compatibility. Windows 98 retains existing 16-bit code where it is required to maintain compatibility or where 32-bit code would increase memory requirements without significantly improving performance. All the Windows 98 I/O subsystems (such as networking and file systems) and device drivers are 32-bit, as are all the memory management and scheduling components, including the Kernel and Virtual Memory Manager.

g. Application Support

Windows 98 supports Win32-based, Win16-based, and MS-DOS-based applications. Win32-based and Win16-based applications run in the System VM. Win32-based applications each run in a separate address space, while Win16-based applications run together in a shared address space. Each MS-DOS-based application runs in its own VM.

INRODUCTION TO OS/2

OS/2 is a computer operating system, initially created by Microsoft and IBM, then later developed by IBM exclusively. The name stands for "Operating System/2," because it was introduced as part of the same generation change release as IBM's "Personal System/2 (PS/2)" line of second-generation Personal Computers. OS/2 is no longer marketed by IBM, and IBM standard support for OS/2 was discontinued on December 31, 2006.[1] Currently, Serenity Systems sells OS/2 under the brand name eComStation.

OS/2 was intended as a protected mode successor of PC-DOS and Microsoft Windows. Notably, basic system calls were modeled after MS-DOS calls; their names even started with "Dos" and it was possible to create "Family Mode" applications: text mode applications that could work on both systems.[2] Because of this heritage, OS/2 is like Windows in many ways, but it also shares similarities with Unix and Xenix.

OS/2 is also remembered for being one of the first major operating system to have its own advocacy group. Team OS/2 was a grassroots, ad-hoc organization of volunteers, who promoted and supported the operating system and applications designed for it.

Development history

The development of OS/2 began when IBM and Microsoft signed the Joint Development Agreement in August 1985.[3] It took two years for the first product to be delivered.

OS/2 1.0 was announced in April 1987 and released in December as a text mode-only OS. However, it featured a rich API for controlling the video display (VIO) and handling keyboard and mouse events so that programmers writing for protected-mode no longer had to call the BIOS or access hardware directly. In addition, development tools included a subset of the video and keyboard APIs as linkable libraries so that family mode programs were able to run under MS-DOS. A task-switcher named Program Selector was available through the Ctrl-Esc hotkey combination, allowing the user to select among multitasked text-mode sessions (or screen groups; each could run multiple programs).[4]

Communications and database-oriented extensions were delivered in 1988, as part of OS/2 1.0 Extended Edition: SNA, X.25/APPC/LU 6.2, LAN Manager, Query Manager, SQL.

The promised GUI, Presentation Manager, was introduced with OS/2 1.1 in November 1988.It had an almost identical user interface to Windows 2.1.

The Extended Edition of 1.1 sold only through IBM sales channels introduced distributed database support to IBM database systems and SNA communications support to IBM mainframe networks.

Version 1.2 introduced Installable Filesystems and notably the HPFS filesystem. HPFS provided a number of improvements over the older FAT filesystem, including long filenames and a form of alternate data streams called Extended Attributes.[6] In addition, extended attributes were also added to the FAT filesystem.[7]

The Extended Edition of 1.2 introduced TCP/IP and Ethernet support.

OS/2 and Windows-related books of the late 1980s acknowledged the existence of both systems and promoted OS/2 as the system for the future.[8]

Breakup

The collaboration between IBM and Microsoft unraveled in 1990, between the releases of Windows 3.0 and OS/2 1.3. Initially, at least publicly, Microsoft continued to insist the future belonged to OS/2. Steve Ballmer of Microsoft even took to calling OS/2 "Windows Plus".[However, during this time, Windows 3.0 became a tremendous success, selling millions of copies in its first year.Much of its success was due to the fact that Windows 3.0 (along with MS-DOS) was bundled with most new computers. OS/2, on the other hand, was only available as an expensive stand-alone software package. In addition, OS/2 lacked device drivers for many common devices such as printers, particularly non-IBM hardware. Windows, on the other hand, supported a much larger variety of hardware. The increasing popularity of Windows prompted Microsoft to shift its development focus from cooperating on OS/2 with IBM to building a franchise based on Windows. Several technical and practical reasons contributed to this breakup:

Differences in culture and vision: Microsoft favored the open hardware system approach that contributed to its success on the PC; IBM sought to use OS/2 to drive sales of its own hardware, including systems that could not support the features Microsoft wanted. Microsoft programmers also became frustrated with IBM's bureaucracy and its use of lines of code to measure programmer productivity. IBM developers complained about the terseness and lack of comments in Microsoft's code, while Microsoft developers complained that IBM's code was bloated.

Differences in API: OS/2 was announced when Windows 1.0 was near completion, and the Windows API already defined. However, IBM requested that this API be significantly changed for OS/2.[15] Therefore, issues surrounding application compatibility appeared immediately. OS/2 designers hoped for source code conversion tools, allowing complete migration of Windows application source code to OS/2 at some point. However, OS/2 1.x did not gain enough momentum to allow vendors to avoid developing for both OS/2 and Windows in parallel. IBM's involvement was much more successful in redefining Windows' visual appearance after the 1.0 release, giving it what is today perceived as the "Windows 3.0 look".

OS/2 targeted the 80286 processor: IBM insisted on supporting the Intel 80286 processor, with its 16-bit segmented memory mode, due to commitments made to customers who had purchased many 80286-based PS/2's because of IBM's promises surrounding OS/2.[16] Until release 2.0 in April 1992, OS/2 ran in 16-bit protected mode and therefore could not benefit from the Intel 80386's much simpler 32-bit flat memory model and virtual 8086 mode features. This was especially painful in providing support for DOS applications. While, in 1988, Windows/386 2.1 could run several preemptively multitasked DOS applications, including expanded memory (EMS) emulation, OS/2 1.3, released in 1991, was still limited to one 640KB "DOS box".

Given these issues, Microsoft started to work in parallel on a version of Windows which was more future-oriented and more portable. The hiring of Dave Cutler, former VMS architect, in 1988 created an immediate competition with the OS/2 team, as Cutler did not think much of the OS/2 technology and wanted to build on his work at Digital rather than creating a "DOS plus". His "NT OS/2," was a completely new architecture.

IBM grew concerned about the delays in development of OS/2 2.0 and the diversion of IBM funds earmarked for OS/2 development towards Windows. Initially, the companies agreed that IBM would take over maintenance of OS/2 1.0 and development of OS/2 2.0, while Microsoft would continue development of OS/2 3.0. In the end, Microsoft decided to recast NT OS/2 3.0 as Windows NT, leaving all future OS/2 development to IBM. From a business perspective, it was logical to concentrate on a consumer line of operating systems based on DOS and Windows, and to prepare a new high-end system in such a way as to keep good compatibility with existing Windows applications. While waiting for this new high-end system to develop, Microsoft would still receive licensing money from Xenix and OS/2 sales. Windows NT's OS/2 heritage can be seen in its initial support for the HPFS filesystem, text mode OS/2 1.x applications, and OS/2 LAN Manager network support. Some early NT materials even included OS/2 copyright notices embedded in the software. One example of NT OS/2 1.x support is in the WIN2K resource kit. OS/2 support also includes Presentation Manager support with the addition of the Windows NT Add-On Subsystem for Presentation Manager.

32-bit era

OS/2 2.0, released in April 1992, was touted by IBM as "a better DOS than DOS and a better Windows than Windows". For the first time, OS/2 was able to run more than one DOS application at a time. This was so effective that it allowed OS/2 to actually run a modified copy of Windows 3.0, itself a DOS extender, including Windows 3.0 applications. Also new in version 2.0 was the Workplace Shell, a true object-oriented environment.

OS/2 2.0 was, unlike its predecessor, a hybrid 16-bit/32-bit operating system although performance did not notably degrade on the Pentium Pro, an Intel CPU renowned for poor 16-bit performance at the time. The graphics subsystem (Gre) and multimedia (MMPM/2) were updated in a servicepack (and bundled into OS/2 2.1), Warp 3 brought about a fully 32-bit Windowing system, whilst Warp 4 introduced the object-oriented 32-bit GRADD display driver model.

DOS compatibility

Because of the limitations of the Intel 80286 processor, OS/2 1.x could run only one DOS program at a time, and did this in a way that allowed the DOS program to have total control over the computer. A problem in DOS mode could crash the entire computer. In contrast, OS/2 2.0 could benefit from the virtual 8086 mode of the Intel 80386 processor in order to create a much safer virtual machine in which to run DOS programs. This included an extensive set of configuration options to optimize the performance and capabilities given to each DOS program. Any real mode operating system (such as Xenix) could also be made to run using OS/2's virtual machine capabilities, subject to certain direct hardware access limitations.

Like most 32-bit environments, OS/2 could however not run protected-mode DOS programs using the older VCPI interface, unlike the Standard mode of Windows 3.0 and 3.1; it only supported programs written according to DPMI.

Unlike Windows NT, OS/2 also always gave DOS programs the possibility of masking real hardware interrupts, so any DOS program could deadlock (*crash*) the machine this way. OS/2 could however use a hardware watchdog on selected machines (notably IBM machines) to break out of such a deadlock. Later, release 3.0 leveraged the enhancements of newer Intel 486 and Intel Pentium processors—the Virtual Interrupt Flag—to solve this problem.

Windows 3.x compatibility

Compatibility with Windows 3.0 (and later Windows 3.1) was achieved by adapting Windows user-mode code components to run inside a virtual DOS machine. Originally, a nearly complete version of Windows code was included with OS/2 itself: Windows 3.0 in OS/2 2.0, and Windows 3.1 in OS/2 2.1; however, IBM later developed versions of OS/2 that would use whatever Windows version the user had installed previously, patching it on the fly, and sparing the cost of an additional Windows license. It could either run full-screen, using its own set of video drivers, or "seamlessly," where Windows programs would appear directly on the OS/2 desktop. The process containing Windows was given fairly extensive access to hardware, especially video, and the result was that switching between a full-screen WinOS/2 session and the Workplace Shell could occasionally cause issues.

Because OS/2 only ran the user-mode system components of Windows, it was not compatible with Windows device drivers (VxDs) and applications needing them.

Multiple Windows applications ran in a single Windows process, just as they would under native Windows. To achieve true isolation between Windows 3.x programs, OS/2 could run multiple copies of Windows in parallel. This approach required considerable system resources, especially memory. It was possible to use DDE between OS/2 and Windows applications, and OLE between Windows applications only.

Native features

OS/2 2.0 provided a 32-bit API for native programs, though the OS itself was a mixture of 16-bit and 32-bit code. It also included a new GUI environment called the Workplace Shell. This was a fully object-oriented GUI that was a significant departure from the previous GUI. Rather than merely providing an environment for program windows (such as the Program Manager), the Workplace Shell provided an environment in which a user could manage programs, files and devices by manipulating objects on the screen.

The "Warp" years

The OS/2 Warp 3 startup screen

OS/2 version 3.0, released in 1994, was labelled as "OS/2 Warp" to highlight the new performance benefits, and generally to freshen the product image. "Warp" had originally been the internal IBM name for the release: IBM claimed that it had used Star Trek terms as internal names for past OS/2 releases, and that this one seemed appropriate for external use as well.

At the launch of OS/2 Warp in 1994, Patrick Stewart was to be the Master of Ceremonies; however Kate Mulgrew of the then-upcoming series Star Trek: Voyager was substituted at the last minute.

OS/2 Warp offered a host of benefits over OS/2 2.1, notably broader hardware support, greater multimedia capabilities, Internet-compatible networking, and it included a basic office application suite known as IBM Works. It was released in two versions: the less expensive "Red Spine" and the more expensive "Blue Spine" (named for the color of their boxes). "Red Spine" was designed to support Microsoft Windows applications by finding and using Windows already installed on the computer's hard drive. "Blue Spine" included Windows support in its own installation, and so could support Windows applications without a Windows installation. As most computers were sold with Microsoft Windows pre-installed, "Red Spine" was the far more popular product. OS/2 Warp Connect, which had full network support built-in, followed in mid-1995, again in "Red Spine" and "Blue Spine" versions.

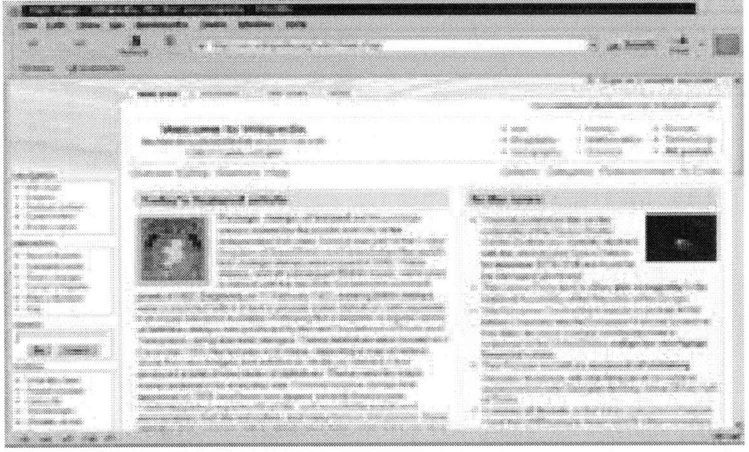

Mozilla 1.7.13 for OS/2 Warp 4.

In 1996, Warp 4 added Java and speech recognition software. IBM also released server editions of Warp 3 and Warp 4 which bundled IBM's LAN Server product directly into the operating system installation. The UK-distributed free demo CD-ROM of OS/2 Warp essentially contained the entire OS and was easily, even accidentally, cracked, meaning that even people who liked it didn't have to buy it. This was seen as a backdoor tactic to increase the number of OS/2 users, in the belief that this would increase sales and demand for third-party applications, and thus strengthen OS/2's desktop numbers. This suggestion was bolstered by the fact that this demo version had replaced another which was not so easily cracked, but which had been released with trial versions of various applications. In 2000 the July edition of Australian Personal Computer magazine bundled software CD-ROMs, included a full version of Warp 4 that required no activation and was essentially a free release.

IBM also released a version of OS/2 that ran on its PowerPC workstations, and promised to produce low-cost PC style machines with the PowerPC processor. However, the PowerPC version of OS/2 was dropped less than a month after its release, and plans for supporting machines were scuttled. Such moves were seen in the industry as indicative of IBM's lack of long-term commitment to the operating system. Ironically, Microsoft Windows NT provided support for PowerPC — a chip co-developed and promoted by IBM — for over 5 years.

Warp 4 was the last widely distributed version of OS/2, and IBM soon announced the end of marketing the operating system to individual users.

Fading out

Overall, OS/2 failed to catch on in the mass market and is today little used outside certain niches where IBM traditionally had a stronghold. For example, many bank installations, especially Automated Teller Machines, run OS/2 with a customized user interface; French SNCF national railways used OS/2 1.x in thousands of ticket selling machines. Telecom companies such as Nortel use OS/2 in some voicemail systems. Nevertheless, OS/2 still maintains a small and dedicated community of followers. IBM, unlike Microsoft, charged ISVs for the OS/2 development kit (Microsoft gave the Windows SDK away for free).

Although IBM began indicating shortly after the release of Warp 4 that OS/2 would eventually be withdrawn, the company did not end support until 2006-12-31.[25] Sales of OS/2 stopped on 2005-12-23. The latest IBM version is 4.52, which was released for both desktop and server systems in December 2001. A company called Serenity Systems has been reselling OS/2 since 2001, calling it eComStation. The latest stable version is 1.2, released in 2004. Version 2.0 was due for release early in 2007[26], but release candidate 4 for version 2.0 was not released until December 2007.

IBM is still delivering defect support for a fee.[27] IBM urges customers to migrate their often highly complex applications to e-business technologies such as Java in a platform-neutral manner. Once application migration is completed, IBM recommends migration to a different operating system, suggesting Linux as an alternative.

Virtualization

As of 2008 virtualization support for OS/2 appears to be improving in a number of third-party products. OS/2 has historically been more difficult to run in a virtual machine than most other legacy x86 operating systems because of its extensive reliance on the full set of features of the x86 CPU. During a pre-launch session (ESX3) with VMware in Oslo, Norway, December 2005, they specifically said that OS/2's use of the CPU's ring 2 was the reason that it would not run in VMware.

A side effect of this is that it is difficult to run OS/2 inside of the popular VMware software product. A beta of VMWare Workstation 2.0 released in January 2000 was the first hypervisor which could run OS/2 at all. Later, the company decided to drop official OS/2 support,[28] presumably because it would require serious work that cannot be economically justified. It is still possible to boot OS/2 by setting **guestOS = "os2experimental"** in the .vmx file of the VM (checked with VMware Workstation 3.0 and 5.5), but trying to run different versions of OS/2 leads to frustrating problems most of the time. Specifically, one can run OS/2 Warp 4 at Fixpack 5, but installing later Fixpacks will make the virtual machine unusable. Ecomstation 1.2 and 2.0 beta 4 will not install.[29] Versions 1.x will crash immediately with a "TRAP 0000". Versions 2.x are too ancient to recognize the simulated IDE CD-ROM, do not recognize the virtual SCSI hardware and can crash with "TRAP 000C" after some operations.

Version 3.0 (Red) and Version 4.0 (Warp 4) seems to work fine under VMWare Server 1.04, however the 'guestOS = "os2experimental"' will flash an error and change the vmx file to **guestOS = "other"**. This seems to work just fine for both of these versions.

The lack of official VMware support for running OS/2 created the opportunity for a new virtualization company. A large German bank needed a way to use OS/2 on newer hardware that OS/2 did not support. As virtualization software is an easy way around this, it desired to run OS/2 under a hypervisor. Once it was determined that VMware was not a possibility, it hired some Russian developers to write a host-based hypervisor that would officially support OS/2. Thus the Parallels, Inc. company and their Parallels Workstation was born.[30]

Microsoft continues to support OS/2 as a hosted operating system in its Virtual PC product. OS/2 and eComstation can both be installed in Microsoft VirtualPC (checked with VPC 2004) although a virtual machine built in VPC 2004 would not run in VPC 2007.

VirtualBox from Innotek currently supports OS/2 as a guest. Innotek also developed the "additions" code in both Virtual PC and Virtual Server which greatly improves host-guest OS interactions in OS/2.

QEMU and Bochs also support running OS/2 as they're full x86 system emulators and not virtualization software, and thus emulates the entire x86 architecture instead of relying on the host CPU, essentially allowing OS/2 unrestricted access to Ring 2, albeit an emulated one.

ATMs

ATM vendors NCR Corporation and Diebold Incorporated have both adopted Microsoft Windows XP as their migration path from OS/2.

Diebold Incorporated initially shipped XPe exclusively but following extensive pressure from customer Banks to support a common OS had them switch to support XPpro to match their primary competitor NCR Corporation.

Security niche

OS/2 has very few native computer viruses.[31] Its design possibly could have made it as vulnerable as Windows , but its reduced market share appears to have discouraged virus writers. There are, however, OS/2-based antivirus programs, dealing with DOS viruses and Windows viruses that could pass through an OS/2 server.

Future

There is a community of OS/2 users and developers, along with loyal company customers, hoping that IBM will release OS/2 or a significant part of it as open source. Petitions to that end were made in 2005 and 2007, but IBM declined, citing legal, technical and strategic reasons. It is unlikely that the entire OS will be open at some point in the future, because it contains third-party code, much of it from Microsoft.

Version 2.0 had such a long design cycle that its design started while OS/2 1.1 was still under development, and thus, portions of it were developed in conjunction with Microsoft, even though Microsoft never released a branded version of 2.0 (although they did release a beta in their name). IBM's contribution to versions 1.2 and earlier mostly resides in the GUI components; however, bug fixes and substantial performance changes to the entire system in 1.3 were made by IBM, and much more of the overall system (including the kernel) for 2.0 was developed by IBM. The aborted PowerPC port did not involve Microsoft at all, and has been proposed as the basis for an open-source 64-bit version of OS/2. Still, the community has suggested that, even if only the IBM portion of it is made open, the missing parts could be written by the same community to form a next-generation version of the OS. Code could perhaps be integrated from the Wine or ReactOS projects. Many developers believe that these missing parts include many of the legacy 16-bit components not revised since OS/2 1.x, and are exactly the parts that should be rewritten anyway. There is an ongoing petition to open parts of the OS arranged by OS2World.com.

With the possibility of an open-source future for OS/2, the OS may be given a new lease of life. IBM's current and heavy involvement with several open source projects indicate that opening parts of OS/2 will not be difficult for the company. But until then, OS/2's future remains in limbo.

Open source operating systems such as Linux have already profited from OS/2 indirectly through IBM's release of the improved JFS file system which was ported from the OS/2 code base.

OS/2 programs will eventually use emulators and compatibility layers for running programs dedicated for OS/2.

Technology

The graphic system has a layer named Presentation Manager that manages windows, fonts, and icons. This is similar in functionality to a non-networked version of X11 or the Windows GDI. On top of this lies the Workplace Shell (WPS) introduced in OS/2 2.0. WPS is an object-oriented shell allowing the user to perform traditional computing tasks such as accessing files, printers, launching legacy programs, and advanced object oriented tasks using built-in and 3rd party application objects that extended the shell in an integrated fashion not available on any other mainstream operating system. WPS follows IBM's Common User Access user interface standards.

Hardware vendors were reluctant to support device drivers for alternative operating systems including OS/2 and Linux, leaving users with few choices from a select few vendors. To relieve this issue for video cards, IBM licensed a reduced version of the Scitech display drivers, allowing users to choose from a wide selection of cards supported through Scitech's modular driver design.

WPS represents objects such as disks, folders, files, program objects, and printers using the System Object Model (SOM), which allows code to be shared among applications, possibly written in different programming languages. A distributed version called DSOM allowed objects on different computers to communicate. DSOM is based on CORBA. SOM is similar to, and a direct competitor to, Microsoft's Component Object Model. SOM and DSOM are no longer being developed.

OS/2 also includes a radical advancement in application development with compound document technology called OpenDoc, which was developed with Apple. OpenDoc proved interesting as a technology, but was not widely used or accepted by users or developers. OpenDoc is also no longer being developed.

The multimedia capabilities of OS/2 are accessible through Media Control Interface commands. The last update (bundled with the IBM version of Netscape Navigator plugins) added support for MPEG files. Support for newer formats like PNG, progressive JPEG, DivX, Ogg, MP3 comes from third parties. Sometimes it is integrated with the multimedia system, but in other offers it comes as standalone applications.

The TCP/IP stack is based on the open source BSD stack.

Problems

Some problems were classic subjects of comparison with other operating systems:

Synchronous input queue (SIQ): if a GUI application was not servicing its *window messages*, the entire GUI system could get stuck and a reboot was required. This problem was considerably reduced with later Warp 3 fixpacks and refined by Warp 4, by taking control over the application after it had not responded for several seconds.

No unified command line: OS/2 divided programs into strict categories and communication between programs of different categories was problematic: It was not possible to enter fullscreen mode from a "windowed OS/2 session"; a separate "fullscreen OS/2 session" was required, which could not be made windowed. OS/2 sessions could launch new DOS sessions, but with DOS sessions (which *could* be toggled fullscreen) it was not possible to start OS/2 programs.Therefore transparent *piping* of data was not possible. Worse, in the absence of 8.3 aliases for filenames and directories and DOS API extensions supporting long filenames, it was also problematic to give DOS programs access to files managed from OS/2 programs. Even native OS/2 programs had problems communicating: a command-line program could not fully access the system clipboard, which was reserved for "GUI" programs. Workarounds consisted in creating special helper programs (for example an invisible GUI program just for accessing the clipboard) or in using client-server setups, where the client and the server were different types of programs, but communicated using some available way. Just as OS/2 1.x, the 32-bit system was apparently designed with the idea that users would rapidly make a switch to all-native programs.

No unified object handles. The availability of threads probably led system designers to overlook mechanisms which allow a single thread to wait for different types of asynchronous events at the same time, for example the keyboard and the mouse in a "console" program. Even though *select* was added later, it only worked on network sockets. In case of a console program, dedicating a separate thread for waiting on each source of events made it difficult to properly release all the input devices before starting other programs in the same "session". As a result, console programs usually polled the keyboard and the mouse alternatively, which resulted in wasted CPU and a characteristic "jerky" reactivity to user input. In OS/2 3.0 IBM introduced a new call for this specific problem.

No unified virtual memory and disk cache. Modern operating systems can use the entire available RAM for disk caching and can map files into the address space of processes. OS/2 had a dedicated memory pool for disk caching and could not map files. This could result in decreased performance and RAM waste.

"A complex system that works in invariably found to have evolved from a simple system that worked".
— *J. Gall*

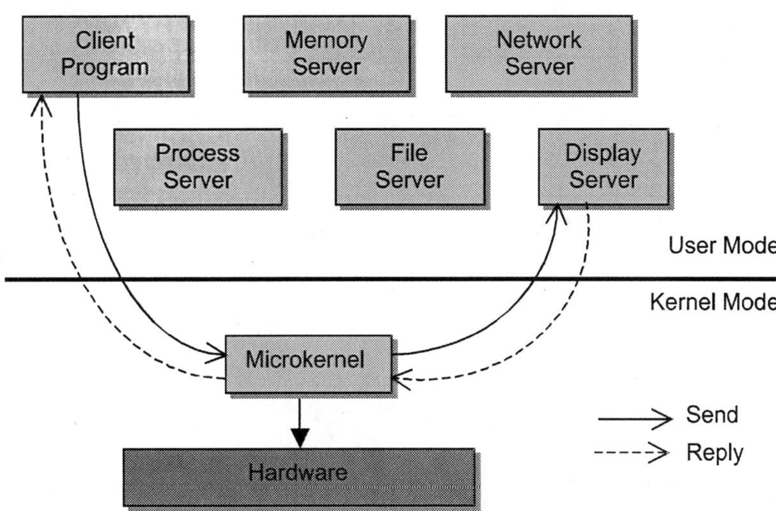

NOS WINDOWS NT 2000

INTRODUCTION

Network operating systems manage the same basic services as operating systems like printing, disks and so forth. In addition, they make it possible to share resources such as documents, printers, CD-ROMs, and other devices. The NOS enhances the reach of the client PC by making remote services available as extensions of the local native operating system. Although a number of users may have accounts on a PC, only a single account is active on the system at any given time. The NOS supports multiple user accounts at the same time and enables concurrent access to shared resources by multiple clients. It also distributes their functions over a number of networked computers. Many of the operating systems include network capabilities and therefore, in some sense, might be considered network operating systems for example Windows 3.11, Windows 95, Windows 98 etc. However, operating systems such as these have limited network capabilities. They may not protect shared documents adequately, and they may slow to a crawl when sharing or printing large documents. Network operating systems were designed especially to share network resources efficiently. The most common of these network operating systems are Windows NT, Novell NetWare, AppleShare and UNIX

Network operating systems require fast computers with large amounts of disk space and random access memory (RAM). For this reason, network operating systems usually run on servers (rather than clients). Like operating systems, each network operating systems requires unique kinds of hardware. The NOS can provide following functionality:

1. **Resource sharing**

   It then adds functions that allow access to shared resources by a number of users concurrently.

2. **Multi-user**

   A user account on the server enables the server to authenticate the user and to allocate appropriate resources the user is allowed to access. Systems that provide this capability are called multiuser systems.

3. **Multitasking**

   A NOS server is a multitasking system. Internally, the OS must be capable of executing multiple tasks or processes at the same time.

4. **Multiprocessing**

   Some systems are equipped with more than one processor, called multiprocessing systems. They are capable of executing multiple tasks in parallel by assigning each task to a different processor.

5. **Multithreading**

   The NOS can provide multithreading. The operating systems that support multithreading enable programmers to design programs whose threaded parts can execute concurrently

6. **Client server**

   Client systems contain specialized software that allows them to request shared resources that are controlled by server systems responding to a client request.

   The three most popular network operating systems are Windows NT, UNIX and Linux. In this chapter we will take a close look at Windows NT.

   The facilities provided by NOS depend on the size and type of network. For example, in a peer-to-peer network all the stations on the network have equal status. In this system one station may act as a file server and another as a print server. At the same time, all the stations are clients. A client is a computer that can be used by users of the network. A peer-to-peer network has little security so the NOS only has to handle

- communications,
- file sharing,
- printing.

If a network contains one or more servers, the NOS has to manage

- file sharing,
- file security,
- accounting,
- software sharing,
- hardware sharing (including print spooling),
- communications,
- the user interface.

File sharing allows many users to use the same file at the same time. In order to avoid corruption and inconsistency, the NOS must only allow one user write access to the file, other users must only be allowed read access. Also, the NOS must only allow users with access rights permission to use files; that is, it must prevent unauthorised access to data. It is important that users do not change system files (files that are needed by the NOS). It is common practice for the NOS to not only make these files read only, but to hide them from the users. If a user looks at the disk to see what files are present, these hidden files will not appear. To prevent users changing read only files to read write files, and to prevent users showing hidden files, the NOS does not allow ordinary users to change these attributes.

To ensure the security of data, the network manager gives users access rights. When users log onto a network they must enter their user identity and password. The NOS then looks up, in a table, the users' access rights and only allows them access to those files for which access is permitted. The NOS also keeps a note of how the users want their desktops to look. This means that when users log on they are always presented with the same screen. Users are allowed to change how their desktops look and these are stored by the NOS for future reference.

As many users may use the network and its resources, it may be necessary for the NOS to keep details of who has used the network, when and for how long and for what purpose. It may also record which files the user has accessed. This is so that the user can be charged for such things as printing, the amount of time that the network has been used and storage of files. This part of the NOS may also restrict the users' amount of storage available, the amount of paper used for printing and so on. From time to time the network manager can print out details of usage so that charges may be made.

The NOS must share the use of applications such as word processors, spreadsheets and so on. Thus when a user requests an application, the NOS must send a copy of that application to the user's station.

Several users may well wish to use the same hardware at the same time. This is particularly true of printers. When a user sends a file for printing, the file is split into packets. As many users may wish to use a printer, the packets from different users will arrive at the print server and will have to be sorted so that the data from different users are kept separate. The NOS receives these packets and stores the data in different files for different users. When a particular file is complete, it can be added to the print queue.

The NOS must also ensure that users' files are saved on the server and that they cannot be accessed by other users. To do this the network manager will allocate each user a fixed amount of disk space and the NOS will prevent a user exceeding the amount of storage allocated. If a user tries to save work when there is insufficient space left, the NOS will ask the user to delete some files before the user can save any more. In order to do this, the server's hard drive may be partitioned into many logical drives. This means that, although there may be only one hard drive, different parts of it can be treated as though they are different drives. For example, one part may be called the H drive which is where users are allowed to save their work. This drive will be divided up into folders, each of which is allocated to a different user. Users only have access to their own folders but can create sub-folders in their own folders. The NOS must provide this service as well as preventing users accessing other users' folders. Another part of the drive may be called (say) the U drive where some users can store files for other users who will be allowed to retrieve, but not alter, them unless they are saved in the user's own area. The NOS will also only allow access to certain logical drives by a restricted set of users.

For all the above to work, the NOS will have to handle communications between stations and servers. Thus, the NOS is in two parts. One part is in each station and the other is in the server(s). These two parts must be able to communicate with one another so that messages and data can be sent around the network.

Finally, the NOS must provide a user interface between the hardware, software and user, but a NOS has to offer different users different interfaces. When a user logs onto a network, the NOS looks up the needs of the user and displays the appropriate icons and menus for that user, no matter which station the user uses.

The NOS must also allow users to define their own interfaces within the restrictions laid down by the network manager.

It must be remembered that users must not need an understanding of all the tasks undertaken by the NOS. As far as users are concerned they are using a PC as if it were solely for their own use. The whole system is said to be transparent to the user. This simply means that users are unaware of the hardware and software actions. A good user interface has a high level of transparency and this should be true of all operating systems.

WINDOWS NT

The Windows NT technology operating system boasts a user-friendly software platform that has become almost universal in its compatibility with databases, programming, and Web development. Building on the Windows NT Server and Workstation platform provides a unified way to give users access to resources on a variety of operating systems. In addition, it lets organizations extend a consistent set of system services and user interfaces across the network. From rich application, communication, and advanced media and Web features, the NT server offers a complete end-to-end solution. NT servers give you the ability to exploit the popularity of compatible third-party products and such applications as Active Server Pages, for dynamic content Web pages, or SQL Server, for specialized database tasks. Windows NT is the operating system for server developed by Microsoft. The interface of the software is similar to that of Windows 95/98. It's gaining market share due to the ease of use.

What is Windows NT

Windows NT, Abbreviation of Windows New Technology, is a 32-bit, a preemptive multi-tasking Operating System technology. It supports multiple CPU's giving true multi-tasking, using symmetrical multiprocessing. Windows NT is scalable and designed for use on a broad range of platforms, including high-end workstations.

A preemptive multi-tasking Operating System means that the Operating System controls allocation of CPU time, stopping one application from hanging the OS. Symmetrical multiprocessing implies that the processors share all tasks, as opposed to asymmetrical multiprocessing, where the OS uses one CPU and the applications another. NT is also a Fault Tolerant Operating System, which means one application cannot interfere with another's memory space.

Unlike earlier version of Windows ,such as Windows 95, NT is a complete Operating System, and not an addition to DOS.NT supports different CPU's: Intel x86, IBM PowerPC and DEC Alpha. NT's other main plus is its Security with a special NT file system (NTFS) that allows permissions to be set on a file and directory basis. When you use the Windows NT operating system, you can share files, directories, and resources such as printers, in addition to using multimedia programs and connecting to the Internet.

Brief history of Windows NT

The Windows environment was created to run on the Microsoft DOS operating system in 1980's. Microsoft and IBM joined forces to create a DOS replacement that would run on the Intel platform that led to the creation of OS/2, and at the same time Microsoft was working on a more powerful operating system that would run on other processor platforms. The idea was that the new OS would be written in a high level language ,such as C, so it would be more portable. Microsoft hired Dave Cutler to head the team for the New Technology Operating System (NT). Originally the new OS was to be called OS/2 NT.

In the early 1990's Microsoft release version 3.0 of its windows OS which gained a large user base, and it was at this point that Microsoft and IBM's split started as the two companies disagreed on the future of their OS's. IBM views Windows as a stepping stone to the superior OS/2, where as Microsoft wanted to expand Windows to compete with OS/2, so they split, IBM kept OS/2 and Microsoft change OS/2 NT to Windows NT. The first version of Windows NT (3.1) was release in 1993 and had the same GUI as the normal Windows Operating System, however it was a pure 32 bit OS, but provided the ability to also run older DOS and Windows apps, as well as character mode OS/2 1.3 programs.

Windows NT Operating Systems

Windows NT technology is available in two main operating systems:

Windows NT Server 4.0

It was designed for server systems of various types: file servers, database servers, print servers, network name servers and so on. It is an operating system that runs on a server, which enables you to manage a network of computers and other devices, such as printers, scanners, video cameras, and scientific instruments.

Windows NT Workstation 4.0

It was designed for a system whose resources are used almost exclusively by a single user. It is an operating system that runs on a single computer, which enables you to run desktop programs and connect to a network.

Hardware and software requirements for Windows NT

Hardware and software requirements vary depending on how you configure your network and which add-in services of Windows NT Server you install.

Hardware requirements

The minimum hardware specification required to run each release of the professional workstation version of Windows NT has been fairly slow-moving until the 6.0 Vista releases, which requires a minimum of 15 GB of free disk space plus an additional 5 GB of extra space for 6.0, a 10-fold increase in free disk space alone over the previous version.

WINDOWS NT HARDWARE REQUIREMENTS

WINDOWS NT HARDWARE REQUIREMENT S

NT VERSION	CPU	RAM	FREE DISK SPACE
NT WORKSTATION 3.51	386, 25 MHz	8 MB	90 MB
NT 4.0 WORKSTATION	486, 33 MHz	12 MB	110 MB
2000 PROFESSIONAL	PENTIUM, 133 MHz	32 MB	650 MB
XP PROFESSIONAL [2]	PENTIUM MMX, 233 MHz	64 MB	1.5 GB
VISTA [3]	PENTIUM III, 800 MHz	512 MB	15 GB

The following peripherals are required:

- VGA display monitor
- 3.5-inch floppy disk drive
- CD-ROM drive
- Network adapter
- Mouse

Software requirements

Windows NT Server software is supplied on two CDs. The first CD contains the basic Windows NT network operating system. The second CD contains the Windows NT Server Option Pack, which includes additional features that you can choose to install.

In addition to the server software, one of the following operating systems compatible with Windows NT required:

- Windows 2000
- Windows NT Workstation
- Windows 98
- Windows 95
- Windows 3.1*x*
- MS-DOS®
- Apple Macintosh
- Novell NetWare
- OS/2
- UNIX

Features of Windows NT

The most important features of Windows NT are as follows:

Performance

Windows NT was also designed to be a high-performance operating system, as the following features demonstrate:

- **True 32-bit design**: Windows NT was written using 32-bit code exclusively, providing an inherent speed advantage over operating systems containing 16-bit technology.
- **Multitasking and multiprocessing features**: Windows NT's preemptive multitasking allows smooth and even simultaneous execution of all running processes. Its multiprocessor support lets the operating system become instantly more powerful by spreading processes and individual threads of execution within processes, across multiple CPUs.
- **RISC CPU support**: From the outset, Windows NT was designed to support several different types of high-powered RISC processors such as the PowerPC, DEC Alpha AXP, and MIPS CPUs. Windows NT can run on Intel-based PCs and high-performance workstation-level systems.

Portability

Portability in Windows NT means that it isn't tied to any single architecture or technology; it can be "ported" to different types of hardware without being completely rewritten.

Compatibility

The compatibility is the operating system's ability to work with existing applications. Microsoft designed Windows NT to run a wide variety of different applications and to interact with a number of different operating systems.

Scalability

Another important aspect of the Windows NT operating system is its scalability, which means you can use Windows NT on a wide range of systems, from personal computers to large systems with multiple processors.

- **Multiplatform support**: With its layered, microkernel architecture, Windows NT can support new and more powerful processors.
- **Multiprocessor support**: Support for multiple CPUs in a single system lets Windows NT scale to the number of available processors on the system and instantly become more efficient as the number of processors increases.
- **Scalable security model**: Windows NT's support for two different security models, the workgroup model and the domain model, enables the same product to address the needs of small as well as large businesses.

Security

Some of Windows NT's most important and touted features relate to security. From the beginning, Microsoft intended for Windows NT to be a secure operating system on which business and government users could rely to protect their data. Windows NT's security goes far beyond that of previous PC operating systems, providing security on par with many minicomputer and mainframe systems. Windows NT offers several layers of system security, including

- **Domain security model**: Windows NT's domain security model is a sophisticated network access scheme that lets administrators implement strict security for who receives access to what information and resources on the network.
- **NTFS file system**: Windows NT includes a special file system, NTFS, which complements the Windows NT security design. NTFS is tightly integrated with Windows NT's other security features, letting administrators utilize a

variety of different access levels for users and workgroups, down to the directory and file level.

- **Fault tolerance features**: Windows NT also includes significant fault tolerance features. Fault tolerance refers to a system's ability to withstand various kinds of equipment failure.

Reliability

The Windows NT operating system provides superior *reliability*, so you can use it as a foundation for mission-critical applications. This reliability makes Windows NT an ideal client workstation and network server because both types of systems need to be up and running as much as possible.

Advantages of Windows NT

- Windows NT is a 32-bit, multi-tasking, great protection, and highly portable due to the fact that, NT has micro-kernel architecture.
- NT has none of the annoying limitations of DOS, such as the 640K barrier.
- NT is much more powerful than Windows 95/98 or its predecessors.
- With greater multi-tasking and multi-threading, NT should be more responsive, efficient, and faster than other MS offerings, and perhaps even more so than UNIX.
- Windows XP was the first NT-based OS to be aimed at home users. It supports OpenGL, and numerous high-end applications, as well as standard 32-bit Windows applications, run on NT-based systems.
- Furthermore, NT 4.0 and 2000 had the same user interface as Windows 95/98, and XP's.
- Windows NT provides a more stable computing environment than Windows 95/98.

Disadvantages of Windows NT

- There is a big problem called BSOD—"**Blue Screen of Death**." NT's famed "uncrashability"—its memory protection, for example—simply isn't all that it claims to be.
- In addition, NT-based Operating systems are not an inexpensive option.
- Microsoft looks to be moving to a per-year licensing scheme; you won't buy it once and be happy, instead you'll have to "presubscribed" every year.

Windows NT 4.0

Windows NT 4.0 was the third release of Microsoft's Windows NT operating system, released onto the market in 1996. It is a 32 bit windows system available in workstation and server versions with a graphical environment similar to Windows 95. Whilst more stable than Windows 95 it is also less flexible from a desktop perspective. Much of the stability is gained by vitalizing the hardware and having software applications access the system APIs rather than the hardware directly as was done in DOS and continued with windows 95 and on. The trade off is that writing to the APIs rather than the hardware directly requires much more work be done by the computer and so hardware intensive applications such as games run much more slowly. Whilst many programs written for the Win32 API will run on both Windows 95 and Windows NT, the majority of 3d games will not. The dichotomy between the NT and '9x' lines of windows arguably only ended with the arrival of Windows XP by which time the gaming APIs- such as Open GL- and DirectX had matured sufficiently to be more efficient to write for than common PC hardware and the hardware itself had become powerful enough to handle the API processing overhead acceptably.

Windows NT 4.0 was rendered 'obsolete' with the advent of Windows 2000 but is still (2004) in widespread use despite Microsoft's many efforts to persuade customers to upgrade to more recent versions.

Specific packages

- Windows NT 4.0 Terminal Server is an NT OS that allows the user to log on to a remote machine, and operate it normally. This same functionality has been implemented as Terminal Services (in Windows 2000), and Remote Desktop (Windows XP and Server 2003).
- Windows NT 4.0 Enterprise Server is the precursor to the Datacenter line of the Windows server family. Enterprise Server was designed for high-demand, high-traffic networks.
- Windows NT 4.0 Server was designed for small-scale Business Server systems.
- Windows NT Workstation was designed for use as the general business desktop OS. Boasting a pure 32-Bit environment, with unparalleled stability, it quickly became a success.

Windows NT 4.0 offered the following new features:

- NTFS file system support
- Security model

- Remote Access Server (RAS)
- OS/2 and POSIX subsystems
- Ability to run on Intel, Alpha, MIPS, and Motorola processors

What is NTFS?

NTFS, short for NT File System, is the most secure and robust file system for Windows NT, 2000, and XP. It provides security by supporting access control and ownership privileges, meaning you can set permission for groups or individual users to access certain files.

The most important features of NTFS are:

- NTFS supports compression of individual files and folders which can be read and written to while they are compressed.
- NTFS is a recoverable file system, meaning it has the ability to undo or redo operations that failed due to such problems as system failure or power loss.
- NTFS supports Macintosh files.

  Remember if you are attempting to set up a dual-boot between Windows NT 4.0 and Windows 2000 or XP, you must have at least Service Pack 4 for Windows NT installed. When installing Windows 2000 or XP, all NTFS partitions are converted to NTFS 5.0. Without Service Pack 4, Windows NT cannot recognize NTFS 5.0, and therefore the computer would be unable to boot to Windows NT. You should also note that the additional capabilities of NTFS 5.0 are available only in Windows 2000 and XP, and these features will not work in Windows NT

Windows NT 4.0

Operating systems take years to develop. Once complete, they remain lifeless untill applications are written to exploit their capabilities. This causes that ordinary users often own and use 10- or 20-year-old operating system technology. In 1988 Microsoft started creating new technology (NT) operating system for the 1990s. The strategy of the Microsoft is to produce a family of Windows-based operating system. Windows NT, as the next-generation Windows system is named, takes its place at the high end of the Windows family. Microsoft's plans identified the following market requirements and design goals.

- The customers require the following features of the operating system:
- Portability across families of processors, such as the Intel x86 line

- Portability across different processor architectures, such as complex instruction set computing (CISC), such as the Intel x86 processors, and reduced instruction set computing (RISC), such as MIPS, DEC, and PowerPC
- Transparent support for single-processor and multiprocessor computers
- Support for distributed computing
- Built-in networking
- Industry standards compliance, such as POSIX (Portable Operating System Interface based on Unix), a standard for US government computing contracts.
- Certifiable security, such as C2, Functional C2. These class levels are defined by US Department of Defense. US government security levels extend from level D (least stringent) to level A (most stringent).
- The following are the Windows NT design goals:
- In making this operating system *compatible:* the designers provided support for existing file systems and applications, network connectivity to several existing networking environments.
- *Portability* means that Windows NT runs on both CISC (Intel® 80386 or higher) and RISC (MIPS® R4000™ or Digital Alpha AXP™) processors.
- *Scalability* means that Windows NT is not bound to single-processor architectures but takes full advantage of symmetric multiprocessing hardware. Today, Windows NT can run on computers with from 1 to 32 processors.
- Windows NT includes a uniform *security* architecture. For the corporate environment, it provides a safe environment to run mission-critical applications.
- *Distributed processing*: Windows NT is designed with networking built into the base operating system. Windows NT also allows for connectivity to a variety of host environments through its support of multiple transport protocols and high-level client-server facilities (pipes, remote procedure calls (RPCs), and Windows Sockets).
- *Reliability and robustness* refer to an architecture that protects applications from damaging each other and the operating system: a recoverable file system, NTFS, and advanced memory management techniques.
- *Localization*: Windows NT supports the International Organization for Standardization (ISO) Unicode standard.
- *Extensibility* points to the modular design of Windows NT: the flexibility of adding future modules at several levels within the operating system.

Windows NT overview

Today's operating systems provide two fundamental services for users.

- First, they make the computer hardware easier to use. They create a "virtual" machine that differs markedly from the real machine. Indeed, the computer revolution of the last two decades is due, in part, to the success that operating systems have achieved in shielding users from the obscurities of computer hardware. In addition, programmers no longer need to rewrite an application for every computer they want to run it on.
- Second, an operating system shares hardware resources among its users. One of the most important resources is the processor. A multitasking operating system, such as Windows NT, divides the work that needs to be done among processes, giving each process memory, system resources, and at least one thread of execution, an executable unit within a process. The operating system runs one thread for a short time and then switches to another, running each thread in turn. Even on a single-user system, multitasking is extremely helpful because it enables the computer to perform two tasks at once. For example, a user call edit a document while another document is printing in the background or while a compiler compiles a large program. Each process gets its work done, and to the user all the programs appear to run simultaneously.

In addition to sharing the processor, the operating system divvies up memory and regulates access to files and devices. Every operating system differs in the way it presents its virtual machine to users and in how it divides resources among them.

a. Windows NT Models

What is an operating system model? The dictionary defines model as a tentative description of a system or theory that accounts for all its known properties. An operating system model is a broad framework that unifies the many features and services the system provides and the tasks it performs.

The Windows NT design was guided by a combination of several models.

- Windows NT uses a *client/server model* to provide multiple operating system environments (initially, Windows, MS-DOS, OS/2, and POSIX) to its users.
- Windows uses an *object model* to uniformly manage operating system resources and dispense them to users.
- A third model, *symmetric multiprocessing* (SMP), allows Windows NT to achieve maximum performance from multiprocessor computers.

Client/Server model

Operating system code can be structured in a number of different ways.

➢ One approach, particularly common in smaller operating systems such as MS-DOS, organizes the operating system as a set of procedures and allows any procedure to call any other. This *monolithic structure* does not enforce data hiding in the operating system, and it embeds assumptions about how the system fits together throughout the operating system code. Extending such a system can be difficult work because modifying a procedure can introduce bugs in seemingly unrelated parts of the system.

In all but the simplest monolithic operating systems, applications are separated from the operating system itself. That is, the operating system code runs in a privileged processor mode (called kernel mode), with access to system data and to the hardware; applications run in a nonprivileged processor mode (called user mode), with a limited set of interfaces available and with limited access to system data. When a user-mode program calls a system service, the processor traps the call and then switches the calling thread to kernel mode. When the system service completes, the operating system switches the thread back to user mode and allows the caller to continue. The monolithic operating system structure with separate user and kernel processor modes is shown in the following figure.

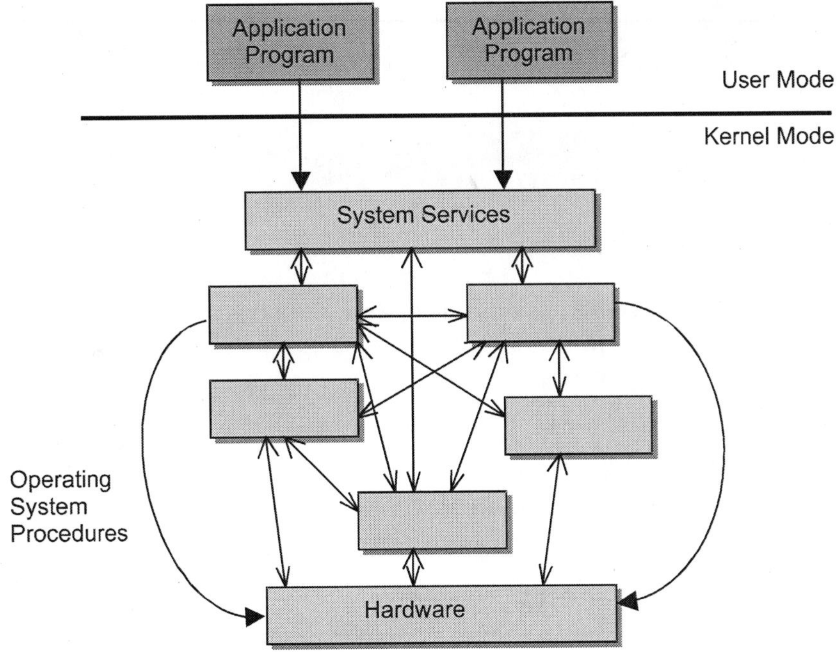

Monolithic Operating System

➢ A different structuring approach divides the operating system into modules and layers them one on top of the other. Each module provides a set of functions that other modules can call. Code in any particular layer calls code only in lower layers. On some systems, such as VAX/VMS or the old Multics operating system, hardware even enforces the layering (using multiple, hierarchical processor modes). The following figure illustrates one possible *layered structure*.

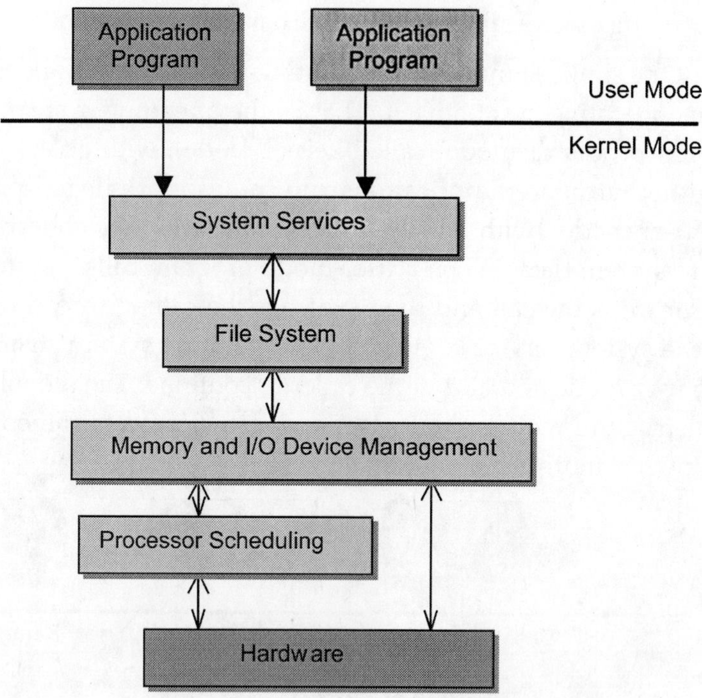

Layered Operating System

One advantage of a layered operating system structure is that each layer of code is given access to only the lower-level interfaces (and data structures) it requires, thus limiting the amount of code that wields unlimited power. This structure also allows the operating system to be debugged starting at the lowest layer, adding one layer at a time until the whole system works correctly. Layering also makes it easier to enhance the operating system; one entire layer can be replaced without affecting other parts of the system.

➢ A third approach to structuring an operating system is the *client/server model.* The idea is to divide the operating system into several processes, each of which implements a single set of services, for example, memory services, process creation services, or processor scheduling services. Each server runs in user mode, executing a loop that checks whether a client has requested one of its services. The client, which can be either another operating system component or an application program, requests a service by sending a message to the server. An operating system kernel (or microkernel) running in kernel mode delivers the message to the server; the server performs the operation; and the kernel returns the results to the client in another message, as illustrated in the following figure.

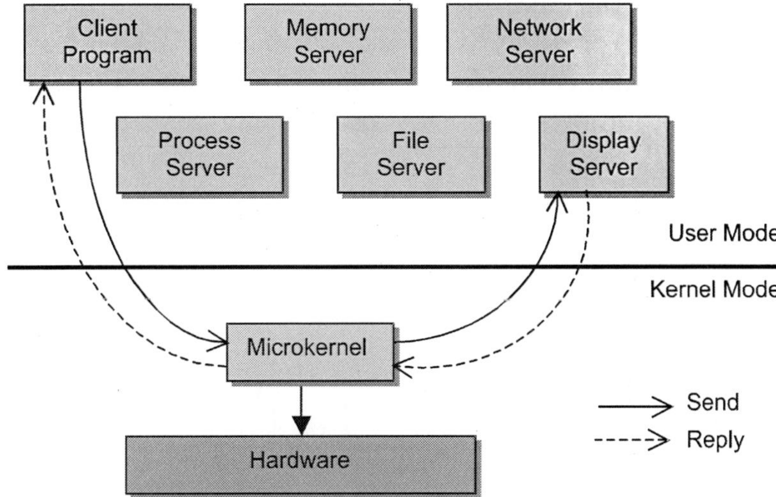

Client/Server Operating System

The client/server approach results in an operating system whose components are small and self-contained. Because each server runs in a separate user-mode process, a single server can fail (and perhaps be restarted) without crashing or corrupting the rest of the operating system. Furthermore, different servers can run on different processors in a multiprocessor computer or even on different computers, making the operating system suitable for distributed computing environments.

The structure of Windows NT borrows from both the layered model and the client/server model. The kernel-mode portion of Windows NT is called the NT executive. It comprises a series of components that implement virtual memory management, object (resource) management, I/O and file systems (including network drivers), interprocess communication, and portions of the security system. For the most part, these components interact with one another in a modular, rather than a layered, fashion. Each component calls the others through a set of carefully specified internal routines.

However, the layered operating system model comes into play in the NT executive's I/0 system, described shortly, and in the bottommost portions of the NT executive: the NTkernel and the hardware abstraction layer (HAL). All other components of the NT executive are layered on these two components. The NT kernel performs low-level operating system functions, much like those found in microkernel, client/server operating systems-for example, thread scheduling, interrupt and exception dispatching, and multiprocessor synchronization. It also provides a set of routines and basic objects that the rest of the executive uses to implement higher-level constructs. Below the kernel is the HAL dynamic-link library (DLL), a layer of code that protects the kernel and the rest of the NT executive from platform-specific hardware differences. The HAL, manipulates hardware directly. Windows NT uses the client/sierver model primarily to provide APIs and the facilities that one ordinarily regards as air operating system environment. The servers communicate with application processes through a message-passing facility provided in the NT executive.

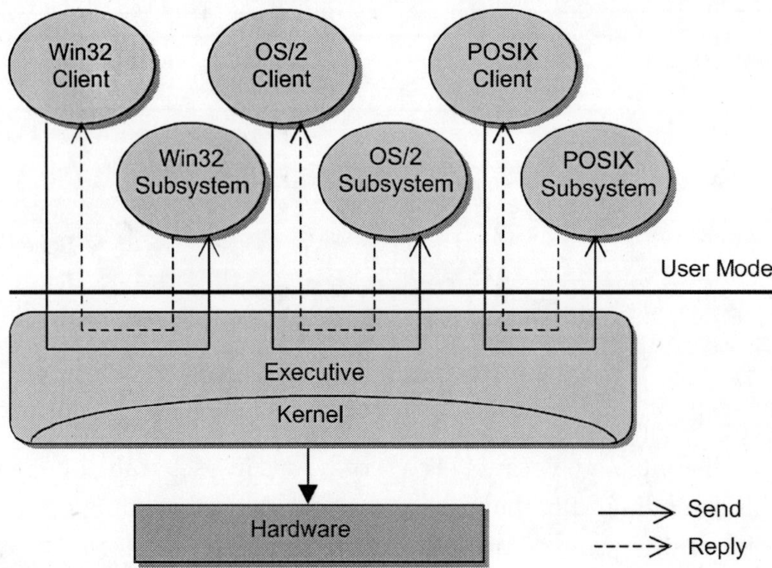

Windows NT's Client/Server Structure

Object Model

The operating systems are considered as programs that "have no top." As with other large software systems, it is difficult to identify a single "main program" that drives an operating system. Therefore, instead of attempting to design such a system from the top down, *object-oriented methodology* focuses initially on the data that the software must manipulate to do its job. For an operating system, such data takes the form of system resources - files, processes, blocks of memory, and so on. The primary goal of designing a system around data is to create software that is easy (and cheap) to change and to maintenance. Software maintenance includes changes such as adding new features, modifying data formats, fixing bugs, and accommodating new hardware.

One way in which object-oriented software minimizes change is by hiding the physical representation of data within objects. An object is a data structure whose physical format is hidden behind a type definition. It embodies a set of formal properties (called attributes) and is manipulated by a set of services.

Although not strictly an object-oriented system , Windows NT uses objects to represent system resources. Any system resource that can be shared by more than one process- including files, shared memory, and physical devices - is implemented as an object and manipulated by using object services. This approach lessens the impact of changes that will be made in the system over time. If a hardware change, for example, forces a change in the operating system, only the object that represents the hardware resource and the services that operate on the object must change; code that merely uses the object remains the same. Likewise, when the system needs to support new resources, a new object is created and added to the system without disturbing the existing code.

In addition to limiting the effects of change, building an operating system based on objects has some distinct advantages:

- The operating system accesses and manipulates its resources uniformly. It creates, deletes, and refers to an event object in the same way it does a process object: by using object handles. And because each resource is an object, tracking resource usage is done simply by monitoring the creation and use of objects.
- Security is simplified because all objects are protected in the same way. When someone tries to access an object, the security system intervenes and validates the operation, regardless of whether the object is a process, a section of shared memory, or a communication port.
- Objects provide a convenient and uniform paradigm for sharing resources between two or more processes. Object handles are used to manipulate all types of objects. Two processes share an object when they each open a handle to it. The operating system can track how many handles are open to an object to determine whether the object is still in use. The operating system can then delete the object when it is no longer in use.

Symmetric Multiprocessing

Multitasking is the operating system technique for sharing a single processor among multiple threads of execution. However, when a computer has more than one processor, the multitasking model must be upgraded to a mulli-processing model. A computer that has two processors can execute two threads simultaneously. Thus, whereas a multitasking operating system appears to execute multiple threads at the same time, a multiprocessing operating system actually does it, executing one thread on each of its processors.

Multiprocessing operating systems fall into one of two categories, suppotting either asymmetric or symmetric processing, as illustrated in the following figure.

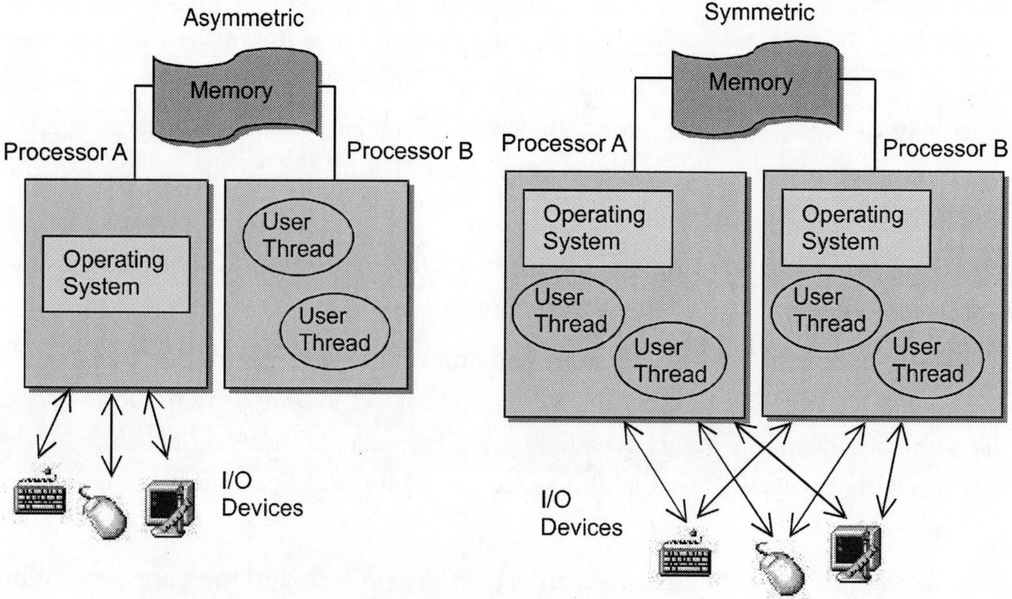

Asymmetric and Symmetric Multiprocessing

Asymmetric multiprocessing (ASMP) operating systems typically select the same processor (A, for example) to execute operating system code while other processors run only user jobs. Because operating system code runs on a single processor, ASMP operating systems are relatively easy to create by extending existing single-processor operating systems. ASMP operating systems are especially well suited to running on asymmetric hardware, such as a processor with an attached coprocessor or two processors that don't share all available memory. However, it's difficult to make ASMP operating systems portable. Hardware from different vendors tends to vary in its type and degree of asymmetry.

Symmetric multiprocessing (SMP) systems, including Windows NT, allow the operating system to run on any free processor or on all processors simultaneously, sharing memory among them. This approach better exploits the power of multiple processors because the operating system itself can use a significant percentage of a computer's processing time, depending on the applications it is running. Executing the operating system on only one processor can tax that processor, leave others idle, and decrease the system's throughput; as the number of processors on the system increases, operating system activities are more likely to become a bottleneck. In addition to balancing the system load, SMP systems reduce downtime because operating system code can execute on other processors if one processor fails. Finally, because symmetric hardware is implemented similarly from vendor to vendor, it is possible to create a portable SMP operating system.

Windows NT incorporates several features that are crucial to its success as a multiprocessing operating system:

The ability to run operating system code on any available processor and on multiple processors at one time. With the exception of its kernel component, which handles thread scheduling and interrupts, all operating system code can be preempted (forced to give up a processor) when a higher-priority thread needs attention.

- Multiple threads of execution within a single process. Threads allow one process to execute different parts of its program on different processors simultaneously.
- Server processes that use multiple threads to process requests from more than one client simultaneously.
- Convenient mechanisms for sharing objects between processes and flexible interprocess communication capabilities, including shared memory and an optimized message-passing facility.

b. Windows NT Structure

The structure of Windows NT can be divided into two parts:

- the user-mode portion of the system (the Windows NT protected subsystems)
- the kernel-mode portion (the NT executive).

A detailed illustration of Windows NT is shown in the following figure.

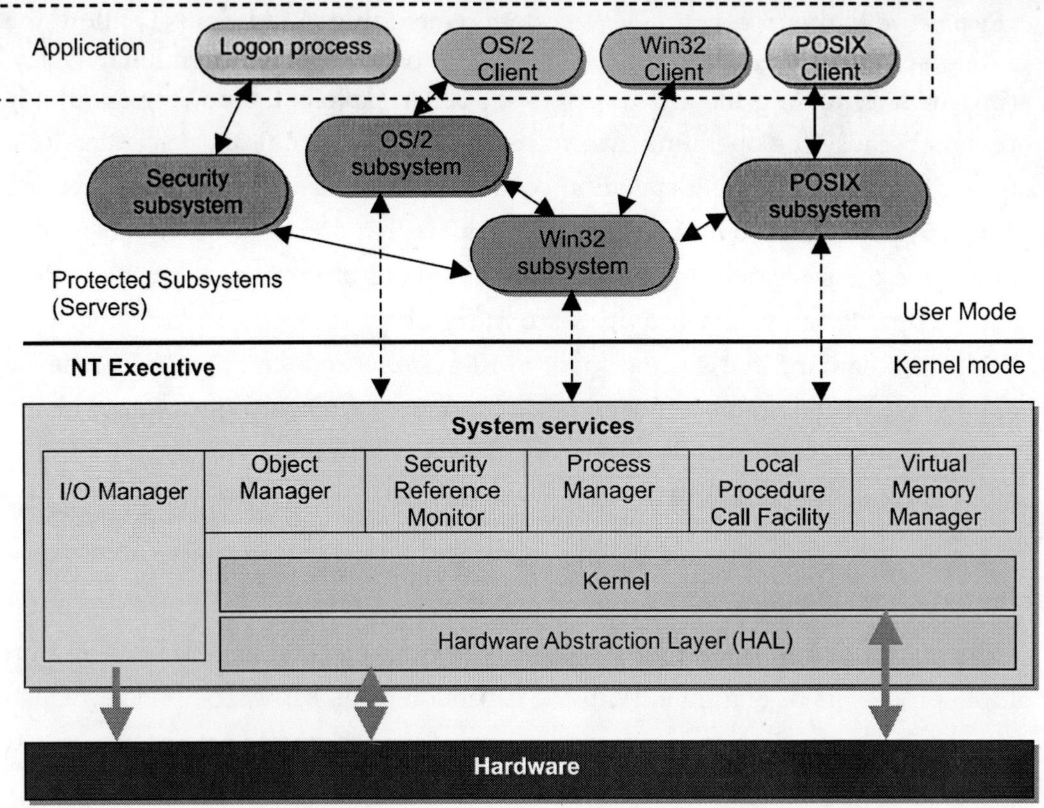

Windows NT Block Diagram

Windows NT servers are called *protected subsystems* because each one resides in a separate process whose memory is protected from other processes by the NT executive's virtual memory system. Because the subsystems do not automatically share memory, they communicate by passing messages. The solid lines in above figure represent paths that messages can take between clients and servers or between two servers. All messages pass through the executive, but for simplicity's sake, those paths are not shown in the figure.

As mentioned previously, the NT executive is an operating system engine capable of supporting any number of server processes. The servers give the NT executive its user and programming interfaces and provide execution environments for various types of applications.

Protected Subsystems

As the term "server" implies, each protected subsystem provides an API that programs can call. When an application (or another server) calls an API routine, a message is sent to the server that implements the API routine via the NT executive's *local procedure call* (LPC) facility, a locally optimized message-passing mechanism. The server replies by sending a message back to the caller.

Windows NT has two types of protected subsystems: *environment subsystems* and *integral subsysteems*.

- An environment subsystem is a user-mode server that provides an API specific to an operating system. When an application calls an API routine, the call is delivered through the LPC facility to the environment subsystem. The environment subsystem executes the API routine and returns the result to the application process by sending another LPC.

  Windows NT's most important environment subsystem is the Win32 subsystem, which makes Microsoft's 32-bit Windows API available to application programs. In addition, the Win32 environment subsystem provides Windows NT's graphical user interface and controls all user input and application output. Windows NT also supplies a POSIX environment subsystem, an OS/2 environment subsystem, a 16-bit Windows subsystem, and an MS-DOS subsystem. These subsystems provide APIs but use the Win32 subsystem to receive user input and to display output.

- The remaining protected subsystems - the integral subsystems - are servers that perform important operating system functions. Several integral subsystems have come and gone during Windows NT's development, but one has remained throughout: the security subsystem. The security subsystem runs in user mode and records the security policies in effect on the local computer. For example, it keeps track of which user accounts have special privileges, which system resources are audited for access, and whether audit alarms or audit messages should be generated. In addition, the security subsystem maintains a database of information about user accounts, including account names, passwords, any groups the user belongs to for security purposes, and any special privileges the user owns. It also accepts user logon information and initiates logon authentication.

Several components of the Windows NT networking software are also implemented as integral subsystems. Two are worth mentioning here: the workstation service and the server service. Each of these services, as networking subsystems are often called, is a user-mode process that implements an API to access and manage the LAN Manager network redirector and server, respectively. The redirector is the network component responsible for sending (redirecting) I/O requests across a network when the file or device to be accessed is not local. The server sits on the remote machine and receives such remote requests. Both the LAN Manager redirector and the LAN Manager server are implemented as file system drivers-that is, as part of the NT I/0 system, described shortly.

Executive

The NT executive is the kernel-mode portion of Windows NT and, except for a user interface, is a complete operating system unto itself. The executive consists of a series of components, each of which implements two sets of functions: system services, which environment subsystems and other executive components can call, and internal routines, which are available only to cornponents within the executive.

Although the executive provides API-like system services, it is fundamentally different from the environment subsystems. It does not run continually in a process of its own but instead runs in the context of air existing process by taking over an executing thread when important system events occur. For example, when a thread calls a system service and is trapped by the processor or when an external device interrupts the processor, the NT kernel gains control of the thread thatwas running. The kernel calls the appropriate system code to handle the event, executes it, and then returns control to the code that was executing before the interruption.

Executive components maintain independence from one another, each creating and manipulating the system data structures it requires. Because the interfaces between components are carefully controlled, it is possible to completely remove a component from the operating system and replace it with one that operates differently. As long as the new version implements all the system services and internal interfaces correctly, the operating system runs as before. Maintaining the operating system is also air easier task because the NT executive components interact in predictable ways.

The responsibilities of the executive components are listed here:

- Object manager. Creates, manages, and deletes NT executive objects, abstract data types that are used to represent operating system resources.
- Security reference monitor. Enforces security policies on the local computer. It guards operating system resources, performing run-time object protection and auditing.
- Process manager. Creates and terminates processes and threads. It also suspends and resumes the execution of threads and stores and retrieves information about NT processes and threads.
- Local procedure call (LPC) facility. Passes messages between a client process and a server process on the same computer. LPC is a flexible, optimized version of remote procedure call (RPC), an industry standard communication facility for client and server processes across a network.

- Virtual memory (VM) manager. Implements virtual memory, a memory management scheme that provides a large, private address space for each process and protects each process's address space from other processes. When memory usage is too high, the VM manager transfers selected memory contents to disk and reloads the contents when they are used again, a practice known as paging.
- Kernel. Responds to interrupts and exceptions, schedules threads for execution, synchronizes the activities of multiple processors, and supplies a set of elemental objects and interfaces that the rest of the NT executive uses to implement higher-level objects.
- I/O system. Comprises a group of components responsible for processing input from and delivering output to a variety of devices. The I/O system includes the following subcomponents:
- I/O manager. Implements device-independent input/output facilities and establishes a model for NT executive I/O
- File systems. NT drivers that accept file-oriented I/O requests and translate them into I/O requests bound for a particular device.
- Network redirector and network server. File system drivers that transmit remote I/O requests to a machine on the network and receive such requests, respectively.
- NT executive device drivers. Low-level drivers that directly manipulate hardware to write output to or retrieve input from a physical device or network.
- Cache manager. Improves the performance of file-based I/O by storing the most recently read disk information in system memory. The cache manager uses the VM manager's paging facility to automatically write modifications to the disk in the background.
- Hardware abstraction layer (HAL). Places a layer of code between the NT executive and the hardware platform on which Windows NT is running. It hides hardware-dependent details such as I/O interfaces, interrupt controllers, and multiprocessor communication mechanisms. Rather than access hardware directly, NT executive components maintain maximum portability by calling the HAL routines when they need platform-dependent information.

Windows NT is a portable operating system, designed to limit the amount of code that relies on a particular hardware architecture. Some processor-specific code (for instance, Intel 486 or MIPS R4000) is required, however, and is located in the lowest layers of the NT kernel, with smaller portions located in the VM manager. These components, particularly the NT kernel, hide processor differences from the rest of the operating system.

Platform-dependent code-that is, code that relies on a particular manufacturer's implementation of a MIPS R4000 computer, for example-is located in the HAL, and is provided by individual computer manufacturers. Device drivers contain device-specific code, of course, but they avoid processor-dependent and platform-dependent code by calling NT kernel routines and HAL routines.

Logon Session

Windows NT is a secure operating system that requires each user to establish an account and to log onto that account before access to the system is granted. Each user account has associated with it a security profile, which is a collection of security-related information stored in a system database. The security subsystem employs this information to verify that users are who they claim to be. The system components involved in logon are highlighted in the following figure.

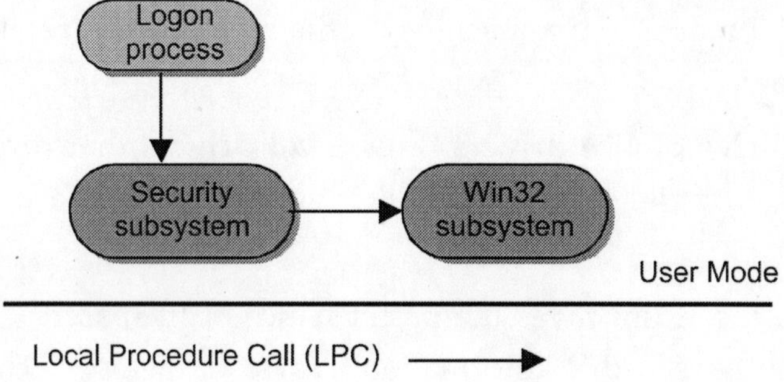

Logging On

A security system process, called a *logon process*, sits waiting for user input. Several logon processes can be active, each one monitoring a separate class of logon devices-for example, a keyboard/mouse combination or a network connection. A thread in the process detects when a user attempts to access the system and prompts the user for an account name and a password.

From there the logon process passes the user's information to the security subsystem, which checks the information against a security database. If the logon is authentic, the subsystem creates an object that uniquely identifies this user in all subsequent transactions. The object, called an *access token*, is the key to security in Windows NT: It determines which system resources the user's threads may access.

After the user's identity is established, the security subsystem creates a process, attaches the user's access token to it, and then passes the process to the Win32 subsystem, which runs the Win32 Program Manager in the process's address space. With that, the user has established a logon session. Windows NT supports both local and remote logons, and a server machine running Windows NT is likely to have numerous logon sessions active at the same time.

Environment Subsystems

The Win32 environment subsystem provides Windows NT's user interface. It controls the video display, the keyboard, the mouse, and other input devices attached to the machine. In addition, it is a server for Win32 applications, implementing the Win32 API.

Not all applications are Win32 applications, and the Win32 subsystem does not control the execution of non-Win32 applications. When the user runs air application that the Win32 subsystem does not recognize, the subsystem determines what type of application it is and then either calls another subsystem to run the application or calls code to initialize an MS-DOS environment in which to run the application.

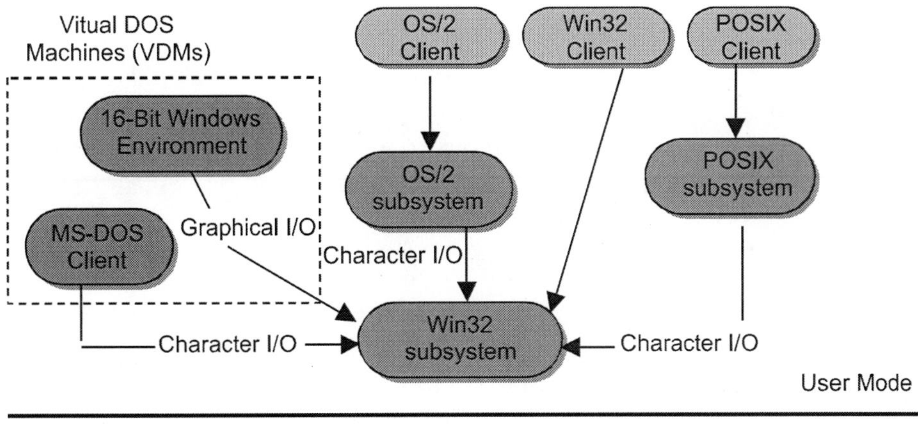

Environment Subsystems and Client Application

Each of the environment subsystems supplies an API that its client applications use. For example, the Win32 subsystem supplies 32-bit Windows API routines, and the 0S/2 subsystem supplies OS/2 API routines. Applications cannot mix and match API routines from different subsystems because each environment subsystem operates differently. A file handle created by the Win32 subsystem does not translate to the POSIX subsystem, for example. Furthermore, such hybrid applications would not run on MS-DOS/Windows, POSIX, or OS/2 operating svstems.

MS-DOS and 16-bit Windows emulation are supplied by an environment subsystem called a *virtual DOS machine* ('VDM), which provides a complete MSDOS machine environment. MS-DOS and 16-bit Windows applications run within the context of VDM processes, which are unlike other environment subsystems in that multiple VDM processes can be running at one time.

Because the Win32 subsystem handles all video output, the other environment subsystems must direct the output of their applications to the Win32 subsystem for display. The VDM running 16-bit Windows applications translates the applications' output calls into Win32 calls and sends them in a message to the Win32 subsystem for display. The OS/2 and POSIX subsystems, as well as any VDMs running MS-DOS applications, direct their applications' character-mode output to the Win32 subsystem, which displays the output in character-mode windows, called *consoles*.

An environment subsystem can support many client applications. Each subsystem keeps track of its clients and maintains any global information that all the client applications share. Although several subsystems and VDMs might be running, Win32 is the only environment subsystem that makes itself visible. To the user, it appears that Windows runs all the applications.

Native Services

Environment subsystems implement their API routines by calling NTnative services, the system services provided by individual components of the NT executive. The VM manager supplies memory allocation and deallocation services, for example, whereas the process manager provides services to create and terminate processes and threads.

Because the native services are used by different environment subsystems, they must be general-even primitive. They must be flexible, without unnecessary built-in constraints. And they must not generate side effects that might conflict with the diverse needs of the environment subsystems.

One way in which the native services are flexible is in their ability to act on any process the caller specifies. The caller supplies a handle to a process, and the service operates on that process. For example, a subsystem can call a native service to create a thread or allocate memory for one of its client processes. Of course, most normal processes cannot perform such operations on other processes. Environment subsystems have powerful access tokens that grant them control over their clients.

Protected subsystems, DLLs, and components of the NT executive are the primary users of NT native services. Applications that run on Windows NT are written to Win32, MS-DOS, 16-bit Windows, POSIX, and OS/2 programming interfaces, which are supplied by environment subsystems.

Objects

Many, perhaps most, NT native services are object services. That is, they perform some action on an object in the NT executive. A thread opens a handle to an object and then uses that handle when calling services to operate on the object.

Shareable resources, including processes, threads, files, and shared memory, are implemented as objects in the NT executive. This allows the operating system to take advantage of the similarities among resources and to use common code wherever possible in order to manage them. The NT object system is a focal point for several types of resource management tasks, such as resource naming, placing limits (called quotas) on the amount of resources each process can use, sharing resources between two processes, and securing resources against unauthorized access.

Environment subsystems frequently call object services to create, open a handle to, manipulate, or delete objects. For example, if the user starts a Win32 application -Microsoft Excel, for instance-the Win32 subsystem calls the NT process manager to create a process (the process in which Excel will run) and open a handle to it. The process manager, in turn, calls the object manager to create a process object and a thread object. Similarly, if the user saves a new Excel spreadsheet, the Win32 subsystem calls the NT I/0 manager to create a file object that represents the file in which the spreadsheet is stored and to open a handle to the object. The I/0 manager calls the object manager to do the job.

Much of NT's resource management takes place when some process creates an object and/or opens a handle to an object. For example, when a process (in this case, the Win32 subsystem) creates an object, it can optionally give the object a name. Giving an object a name makes that object available for sharing by other processes. A process that wants to share the object simply retrieves the object's name by calling the NT object manager and then opens a handle to that object.

Objects are allocated from operating system memory. To keep any one process from using too much system memory, processes are charged a set amount of their quota each time one of their threads opens a handle to a particular type of object. If a process exhausts its quota, the object manager does not allow it to open any more object handles.

In addition to managing resources and facilitating resource sharing, the NT object system serves as a focal point for resource security. When a process opens a handle to an NT object, the NT security subsystem is activated. Each object has attached to it a little database, called an access control list (ACL), contaming information regarding which processes can access the object and what they can do to it. When a process opens a handle to an object, it specifies the operations it wants to perform. For example, it might open a file for read access. The security system checks whether the process is allowed read access to the file object in question, and if so, the object manager returns an object handle containing read access. The caller can then use the handle to read from that particular file. If the caller also needs write access to the file, it can request both read and write access when it opens the first handle or it can open a second handle for write access. Because a process must open a handle to an object before it call do anything to it and because opening a handle invokes the security system, no process can bypass NT security.

Virtual Memory

Operating systems adopt different views of physical memory and require their programs to access memory in specified ways. In Windows NT, application programs run in an operating system environment that behaves like Windows, MS-DOS, POSIX, or OS/2. The challenge is to allow all the different types of applications to run without being rewritten and without bumping into each other in memory.

Each of Windows NT's environment subsystems provides a view of memory that corresponds to what its applications expect. Underneath the environment subsystems, the NT executive has its own memory structure, which the environment subsystems access by calling NT native services.

The NT memory architecture is a virtual memory system based on 32-bit addresses in a flat (linear) address space. A process's virtual address spaceis the set of addresses available for the process's threads to rise. At runtime, the VM manager, with assistance from hardware, translates, or maps, the virtual addresses into physical addresses, where the data is actually stored. By controlling the mapping, the operating system can ensure that individual processes don't bump into one another or overwrite the operating system.

Each process's virtual address space is 4 gigabytes (2^{32} bytes), with 2 gigabytes reserved for program storage and 2 gigabytes reserved for system storage. Four gigabytes (or even 2) is much larger than the amount of physical memory likely to be available on ordinary machines. When physical memory becomes full, the VM manager transfers, or pages, some of the memory contents to disk. Paging data to disk frees physical memory so that it call be used for other things. When a thread accesses a virtual address that has been paged to disk, the VM manager loads the information back into memory from disk.

In Windows NT, the operating system resides ill high virtual memory and the user's code and data reside in low virtual memory, as shown in the following figure. A user-mode thread cannot read or write to system memorv directly.

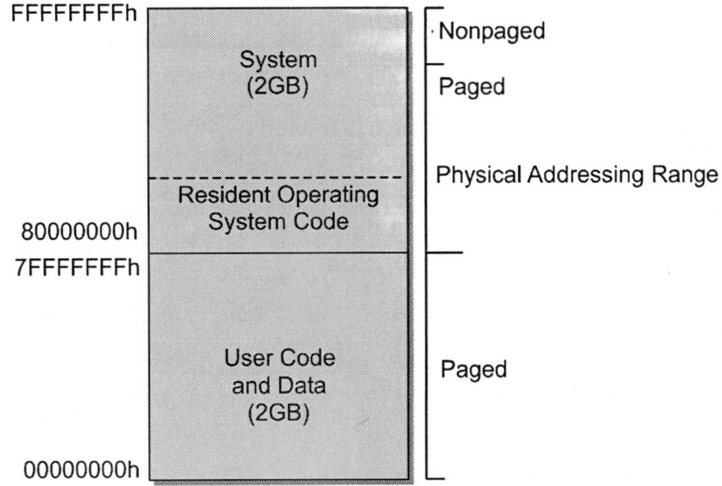

NT Address Space Layout

A portion of the system memory, called *nonpaged pool,* is never paged to disk and is used to store some NT objects and other important data structures. Another portion of system memory, called *paged pool,* is paged to disk. All of user memory can be paged.

I/O and File Systems

As with memory, environment subsystems provide whatever I/O facilities their applications expect. They implement those individual facilities by calling native NT I/O services.

The native I/O system uses an asynchronous I/O model, but it provides system services that allow environment subsystems to use either a synchronous or an asynchronous model. Asynchronous I/O allows a caller to request an I/O operation and then do other work while the device finishes transferring the data. The I/O system automatically notifies the caller when the I/O is complete so that the caller can do subsequent processing. Because I/O devices are generally much slower than processors, a program that does a lot of I/O can often improve its performance by using asynchronous I/O.

Windows NT supports multiple file systems, including the *file allocation labLe* (FAT) file system, the *high-performance file system* (HPFS), and a new file system called the *NT file system* (NTFS).

The I/O manager allows device drivers and file systems (which it views as "device" drivers) to be loaded dynamically into and out of the system, based on the needs of the user. Drivers are modular and can be layered one on top of another, which, for example, allows different file systems to call the same floppy disk driver or hard disk driver to access files, as shown in the following figure.

User Mode

NT Executive Kernel mode

System services

I/O Manager

Object Manager

Security Reference Monitor

Process Manager

Local Procedure Call Facility

Virtual Memory Manager

Kernel

Hardware Abstraction Layer (HAL)

FAT File System Driver

NTFS Driver

HPFS Driver

Floppy Disk Driver

Hard Disk Driver

Layered Drivers

The layered driver model also provides the ability to insert additional drivers in the hierarchy. For example, logical file system drivers or fault tolerant drivers can occupy intermediate levels in the driver hierarchy.

Windows NT provides access to files on the LAN Manager network through a file system driver called the Windows NT redirector. The redirector accepts requests for remote files and directs them to a LAN Manager server on another machine.

Internationalization

The goal for Windows NT is to be a truly multilingual operating system, one that provides a solid foundation for developing and using international applications.

➢ Locales

A locale consists of a language, a country, and a code set, the binary codes used to represent the characters of a particular language. (Windows ANSI is one such code set.) When installing Windows NT, the user selects a language to use and is assigned a default locale. The default locale gives the user culturally correct defaults for keyboard layout, sorting order, currency, and date and time formatting. The user can override any of these defaults.

Even more flexibility is desirable, however. In multilingual countries such as Canada, Switzerland, and Belgium, users require the ability to switch among two or more languages on a regular basis. Moreover, some companies, including Microsoft, have divisions in which several different languages are routinely spoken. Ideally, each user should be able to switch among locales at any time or to send data among locales without losing information. To accomplish this, applications (and in this case, Windows) must be separated into two pieces:

- Code, which can be used in all locales
- Data, which must be translated for different locales

In Windows, the data category consists of resources such as menus and messages. These resources are separated from the main body of the code and can be attached to or detached from Windows. When the user switches locales, the resource set changes to represent the new locale. Since the set of Windows resources is much smaller than Windows itself, many different resource sets can be loaded at installation time, allowing the user to switch between locales easily without loading new files from floppy disks. Moreover, a single Windows NT package can be shipped to all countries with localization support already built in. The only remaining task is to translate the resource files and the documentation.

To facilitate localization, Windows NT's Win32 subsystem provides a national language support (NLS) API that gives applications (and Windows NT) access to culturally correct string comparisons; collation tables for sorting the characters of different languages; date, time, and currency formatting routines; and routines for determining the locale that is in effect and the other locales present on the system. In addition, the NLS API provides routines to convert between the international code set used by Windows NT and other commonly used code sets. (More on this topic in the next section.) Both the Win32 subsystem and the C runtime library provide their own API routines based on NLS. Using these facilities allows applications to support localization without having to duplicate the substantial database (tables, code sets, and so on) required to do so.

- Unicode

The lowest layer of localization support is in the representation of individual characters, the code sets. The United States has traditionally employed the ASCII (American Standard Code for Information Interchange) standard for representing data. For European and other countries, however, ASCII is riot adequate because it lacks common symbols and punctuation. For example, the British pound sign is omitted, as are the diacritical marks used in French, German, Dutch, and Spanish.

The International Standards Organization (ISO) established a standard code set called Latin1 (ISO standard 8859-1), which defines codes for all the European characters omitted by ASCII. Microsoft Windows uses a slight modification of Latin1 called the Windows ANSI code set. Windows ANSI is a *singlebyte coding scheme* because it uses 8 bits to represent each character. The maximum number of characters that can be expressed using 8 bits is 256 (2^8).

A *script* is the set of letters required to write in a particular language. The same script is often used for several languages. Windows ANSI and other single-byte coding schemes can encode enough characters to express the letters of Western scripts. However, Eastern scripts such as Japanese and Chinese, which employ thousands of separate characters, cannot be encoded using a single-byte coding scheme. These scripts are typically stored using a double-byte coding scheme, which uses 16 bits for each character, or a multibyte coding scheme, in which some characters are represented by an 8-bit sequence and others are represented by a 16-bit, 24-bit, or 32-bit sequence.

To address the problem of multiple coding schemes and to accommodate a more comprehensive set of scripts, Windows NT employs the new Unicode standard for data representation. Unicode, a 16-bit character-coding scheme, can represent 65,536 (2^{16}) characters. This is enough to include all languages in computer commerce today. Unicode also includes representations for punctuation marks, mathematical symbols, and a set of graphical characters called dingbats, with plenty of room remaining for future expansion.

Unicode separates the "essence" of a character from the font and formatting information used to display it. Each code corresponds to one (and only one) character; font information is applied to Unicode characters to display them in various styles and shapes. The following figure illustrates the layout of scripts and symbols in Unicode.

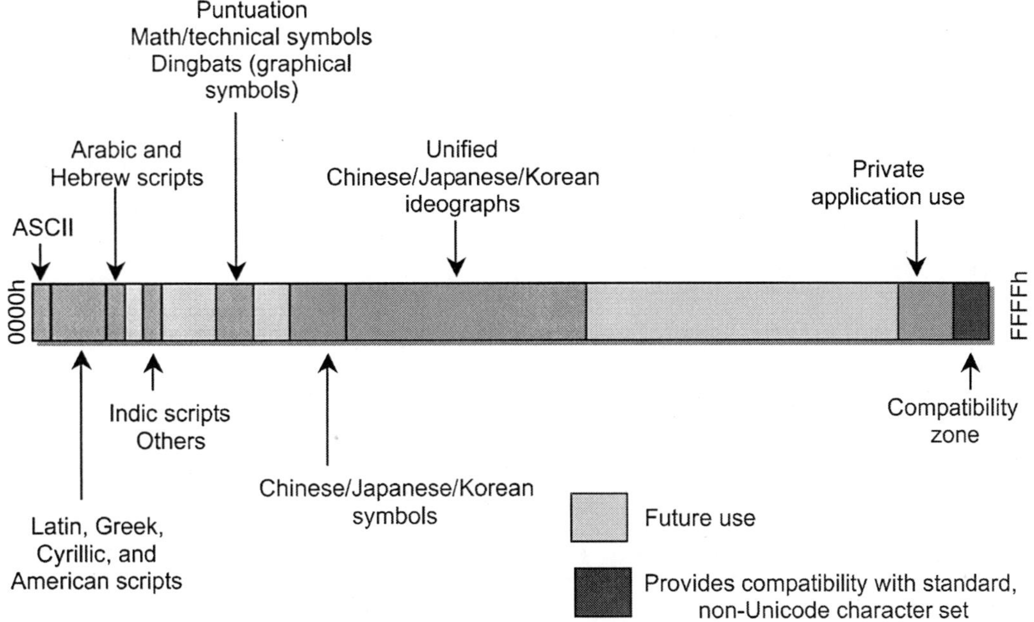

Unicode Layout

Although the Win32 subsystem provides both ANSI and Unicode string API routines, Unicode is Windows NT's native code set. All character strings in the system, including object names, pathnames, filenames, and directory names, are represented with 16-bit Unicode characters. Even the Win32 subsystem converts any ANSI characters it receives to Unicode strings before manipulating them; it converts them back to ANSI, if necessary, upon exit from the system.

Using Unicode removes all limitations on the set of characters that Windows NT can represent. Because Unicode establishes a unique code for every character of every script, Windows NT can ensure that the round-trip character translation, into and out of the system, is always accurate.

Deploying Windows NT Server

There are some issues to be considered when deploying Windows NT Server that are not a factor in deploying Windows NT Workstation. These include which licensing mode to use, whether the server is to be a domain controller, and server-specific services that you might want to install. Answer files and Uniqueness Database Files (UDFs) provide most of the tools you need for specifying options while deploying Windows NT Server.

a. Choosing a Licensing Mode

When installing Windows NT Server, you must specify whether the server is licensed in "per seat" or "per server" mode. You can provide this information in an answer file. For the installation to be completely unattended, you must supply this information in the answer file.

b. Installing a Domain Controller

When installing Windows NT Server, you can specify that the server be a member of a Workgroup or a Domain, or you can set the computer to be a domain controller. For the installation to be completely unattended, you must supply this information in the answer file. The answer file entries for adding a server to a Workgroup or Domain are the same as those for workstations.

c. Replacing a Primary Domain Controller (PDC)

If the primary domain controller (PDC) is not available, and you want to configure a new PDC rather than promoting an existing backup domain controller (BDC), a new security identifier (SID) will be created for the domain. If the old PDC is then brought back on-line, it will not be able to process logon requests because it does not know the domain SID. To use both servers on the domain, you will need to reinstall Windows NT on one of them, while the other is available as a PDC.

d. Installing Specific Services

To install network services, you will need to create one or more sections in the answer file in which you list the service you want to install. You can give these section any name you want. The sections you create must be specified with a line in the [Network] section of the answer file. The syntax is as follows:

[Network] InstallServices = *services_list_section*[, *services_list_section*] . . .

Then, in the section you create, list the services you want to install. Parameters are provided in a third section, which you also create and give any name you want, as in the following example:

[Network] InstallServices = ServiceList [ServiceList] SNMP = SNMPParameters [SNMPParameters] Accept_CommunityName = MicrosoftCommunity Send_Authentication = YES Any_Host = NO Limit_Host = HostSystem ....

The value to the left of the equals sign in the section you create to list the services is the same as the key for the service in the Registry(SNMP in the [ServiceList] section, in this example). The values for the parameters are also the same as those used in the

Registry. Registry entries are documented in the online help. The following table lists server-specific services and the key used to specify them:

Service Name	Key
Alerter	AlertNames
Browser	Browser
DHCP Server	DHCPServer
FTP Server	FTPsvc
Internet Server	InstallInternetServer
NetBIOS over TCP/IP	NetBt
NetLogon	NetLogon
Remote Access (RAS)	RemoteAccess
Server	LanmanServer
WINS	WINS

e. Fault Tolerance Issues

If you are installing Windows NT on a mirrored partition, you must disable mirroring before deployment, and then reestablish mirroring after installation is complete.

Mirrored partitions are a feature you may have implemented in an existing installation of Windows NT Server, in which a copy of a partition on one disk dr... is maintained on another disk drive. If the primary disk fails, no data is lost, sin... ve information written to the primary disk was also written to the secondary d... ce all ... isk.

Windows NT DISK, File Systems

This section describes the physical structure of hard disks and f... loppy disks, and presents an overview of ways to logically organize areas on you... r disks.

a. Two File Systems: FAT and NTFS

Windows NT supports two file systems as the follo... ws:

- File Allocation Table (FAT). The computer c... an access files on a FAT volume when it is running Windows NT, Window... s 95/98, MS-DOS, or OS/2. FAT is more efficient for smaller volumes.

- Windows NT File System (NTFS). The computer must be running Windows NT to be able to access files on an NTFS volume. NTFS is more efficient for larger volumes. NTFS provides file and folder security for your application programs and data.

  This is a general recommendation for determining which file systems to use for which volumes:

- Use a small FAT primary partition (between 250 and 500 MB, depending on the total disk space and page file size) as the C drive. Use this partition for both your system and boot partition.
- Format the rest of your disk space as NTFS, and use the NTFS volumes for application programs and data. You might want to create more than one NTFS volume.

Note: The FAT file system works the same in Windows NT as it does in MS-DOS, Windows 3.1x, and Windows 95/98. You can install Windows NT on your existing FAT primary partition. When running Windows NT, you can move or copy files between FAT and NTFS volumes. You cannot use Windows NT with any compression or partitioning software that requires disk device drivers to be loaded by MS-DOS.

With Windows NT, you can create and use long filenames as well as short filenames. Long and short filenames can be used on both NTFS or FAT volumes. A long filename can be up to 256 characters long. Short filenames are in the format xxxxxxxx.yyy, and are compatible with MS-DOS and OS/2.

b. Maximum Sizes

The maximum file size and volume size for the FAT file system is 232 bytes (4 GBs). FAT can support a maximum of 65,535 clusters per volume.

The NTFS architecture is designed to use numbers up to 264 bytes (16 exabytes, or 18,446,744,073,709,551,616 bytes). In theory, it is possible to have a volume 264 bytes in size. Even if there were hardware available to supply a logical volume of that capacity, there are other limitations to the maximum size of a volume.

Partition Tables are limited by industry standards to 232 sectors. The sector size is a function of hardware and industry standards, and is normally 512 bytes. While sector sizes might increase in the future, the current size puts a limit on a single volume of 2 terabytes (232 * 512 bytes, or 241 bytes).

Windows NT provides the capability to combine discontiguous disk areas when creating volume sets, stripe sets, and stripe sets with parity, but these volumes have the same limitations. Even if there were physical disks with 2 terabyte (TB) capacity, they could not be combined to create larger volumes without increasing the physical sector size. For the time being, 2 TB should be considered the practical limit for both physical and logical volumes using NTFS.

With the NTFS file system, you can have a maximum of 232 clusters per file. This is an implementation limitation, not a file size restriction. There is no specific limit to the number of files on an NTFS volume. However, you will not be able to create any new files when your volume is so full that Windows NT cannot allocate another entry in the MFT.

c. Disk Sectors Critical to the Startup Process

There are two sectors on the disk that are critical to starting the computer:

- Master Boot Record.

  The Master Boot Record, created when you create the first partition on the hard disk, is probably the most important data structure on the disk. It is the first sector on the disk. The location is always track (cylinder) 0, head (side) 0, and sector 1.

  The Master Boot Record contains the Partition Table for the disk and a small amount of executable code. On x86-based computers, the executable code examines the Partition Table, and identifies the system partition. The Master Boot Record then finds the system partition's starting location on the disk, and loads an copy of its Partition Boot Sector into memory. The Master Boot Record then transfers execution to executable code in the Partition Boot Sector.

- Partition Boot Sector.

  The information about primary partitions and an extended partition is contained in the Partition Table, a 64-byte data structure located in the same sector as the Master Boot Record (cylinder 0, head 0, sector 1). The Partition Table conforms to a standard layout that is independent of the operating system. Each Partition Table entry is 16 bytes long, making a maximum of four entries available. Each entry starts at a predetermined offset from the beginning of the sector, as follows:

- Partition 1 0x01BE (446)
- Partition 2 0x01CE (462)
- Partition 3 0x01DE (478)
- Partition 4 0x01EE (494)

  The last two bytes in the sector are a signature word for the sector and are always 0x55AA.

The Partition Boot Sector contains information that the file system uses to access the volume. On x86-based computers, the Master Boot Record use the Partition Boot Sector on the system partition to load the operating system Kernel files, or in the case of Windows NT, the boot loader. The Windows NT Partition Boot Sector consists of:

- A jump instruction.
- The OEM name and version.
- A data structure called the BIOS Parameter Block.
- Another data structure called the extended BIOS Parameter Block.
- The bootstrap code.

The BIOS Parameter Block (bytes 11 through 35 of the Partition Boot Sector) describes physical parameters of the volume. The extended BIOS Parameter Block begins immediately after the BIOS Parameter Block. The length of this structure is different for FAT and NTFS volumes. The information in the BIOS Parameter Block and the extended BIOS Parameter Block is used by disk device drivers to read and configure volumes.

The Partition Boot Sector is the first 512-byte sector at the beginning of the volume. The sector always ends with 0x55AA, which is a sector signature word that marks the end of the sector.

d. What Happens When You Start Your Computer

These are the steps involved when you start a computer that has a Windows NT installed as one of the operating systems.

- Power On Self Test (POST) processing: When you power on or restart a computer, it goes through its Power On Self Test (POST) routine, which determines:
- The amount of real memory.
- Whether the needed hardware components (such as the keyboard) are present.
- Initial startup process: After the POST on x86-based computers, the system BIOS attempts to locate the startup disk. If there is a floppy disk in drive A, the system BIOS uses drive A as the startup disk. If there is no disk in drive A, it then checks the first hard disk that is powered up. When the hard disk is the startup disk, the system BIOS reads the Master Boot Record, and loads it into memory. The system BIOS then transfers execution to the Master Boot Record. The code in the Master Boot Record scans the Partition Table for the system partition. When the Master Boot Record finds the system partition, it

loads sector 0 of the partition into memory, and executes the code in the sector. Sector 0 on the system partition can be a program or diagnostic program, or a Partition Boot Sector that contains startup code for an operating system. The Partition Boot Sector code starts the operating system in a manner defined by the operating system.If there is no system partition on the first hard disk, the Master Boot Record displays errors such as the following:

- Invalid partition table
- Error loading operating system
- Missing operating system
- Boot loader process: The boot loader enables you to select the operating system that you want to start and loads the operating system files from the boot partition. Boot loader processing is different on x86-based and RISC-based computers. NTLDR function controls the operating system selection process and hardware detection prior to the Windows NT Kernel initialization. NTLDR must be in the root folder. When NTLDR starts executing, it clears the screen and displays the boot loader message, which is:

OS Loader V4.0

- Selecting the operating system: The boot loader displays the screen from which you select the operating system to start. NTLDR displays a menu from which you select the operating system to start. This screen is based upon the information in the Boot.ini file. The screen looks like this:

  OS Loader V4.0 Please select the operating system to start:

  Windows NT Server Version 4.0

  Windows NT Server Version 4.0 (VGA mode)

  Use ↑ and ↓ to move the highlight to your choice. Press Enter to choose. Seconds until highlighted choice will be started automatically: 29

  If you do not select an entry before the counter reaches zero, NTLDR loads the operating system specified by the default parameter in the Boot.ini file. Windows NT Setup sets the default entry to the most recent copy of Windows NT that you installed. You can edit the Boot.ini file to change the default entry if you want to default to an operating system other than the most recently installed version of Windows NT.

- Detecting hardware: Ntdetect.com is the hardware recognizer. It collects a list of currently installed components and returns this information to NTLDR. Ntdetect.com executes after you select a Windows NT operating system on the boot loader screen (or the timer times out). When Ntdetect.com begins to execute, you see the following line on the screen:

NTDETECT V1.0 Checking Hardware . . .

Ntdetect.com detects the following components:

- Computer ID
- Bus/Adapter Type
- Video
- Keyboard
- Communication Ports
- Parallel Ports
- Floppy Disks
- Mouse/Pointing Device
- Selecting a configuration: When you have selected the version of Windows NT to start, and the boot loader has collected hardware information, you see the following screen:

  OS Loader V4.0 Press spacebar now to invoke Hardware Profile/Last Known Good menu.

  The boot loader waits a few seconds for you to press the spacebar. If you do not press the spacebar and you have only one hardware profile, the boot loader loads Windows NT by using the Default configuration.
- Loading the Kernel: When you press ENTER on the **Hardware Profile/ Configuration Recovery** menu or the boot loader automatically makes the selection for you, the computer is in the Kernel load phase of Windows NT startup. You see several dots as the boot loader loads the Windows NT Kernel (Ntoskrnl.exe) and the hardware abstraction layer (Hal.dll) into memory.
- Initializing the Kernel: You know that the Kernel is initializing when the screen turns blue, and you see text similar to the following:

  Microsoft (R) Windows NT (TM) Version 4.0 (Build 1345) 1 System Processor (64 MB Memory)

  This means that Ntoskrnl.exe has successfully initialized and that control has passed to it. During the Kernel initialization phase, the Kernel:
- Initializes the low-level device drivers that were loaded in the previous phase.
- Loads and initializes the other device drivers.
- Runs programs, such as Chkdsk, that need to be run before it loads any services.
- Load and initializes services.
- Creates the page file.

- Starts subsystems that are needed to run Windows NT.
- Logging on: When Kernel initialization finishes, you see the **Begin Logon** dialog box, which contains the text **Press Ctrl + Alt + Delete to log on**. At this time, Windows NT might still be initializing network drivers, but you can logon now.

The order and the processing is somewhat different, depending upon the hardware platform (x86-based computer or RISC-based computer). Windows NT might not start up or operate correctly if any hardware components do not initialize correctly. Startup fails if any of the files required to start Windows NT are not present in the correct folder, or if one of the files has been corrupted.

e. Contents and Purpose of Boot.ini

When you install Windows NT on an x86-based computer, Windows NT Setup puts the Boot.ini file at the root of the system partition. NTLDR uses information in the Boot.ini file to display the screen from which you select the operating system to start.

Here is a sample Boot.ini file:

[boot loader] timeout=30 default=multi(0)disk(0)rdisk(0)partition(1)\WINNT [operating systems] multi(0)disk(0)rdisk(0)partition(1)\WINNT="Windows NT Server Ver 4.0" multi(0)disk(0)rdisk(0)partition(1)\WINNT="Windows NT Server Ver 4.0 [VGA mode]" /basevideo /sos

The Boot.ini file has two sections, [boot loader] and [operating system].

[boot loader] Section

This section contains the following information:

Parameter	*Description*
timeout	The number of seconds the user has to select an operating system from the boot loader screen before NTLDR loads the default operating system. If the value is 0, NTLDR immediately starts the default operating system without displaying the boot loader screen. You can also set this value to -1, in which case NTLDR waits forever for you to make a selection. You must edit the Boot.ini file to set the value to -1 because it is an illegal value for the System option in Control Panel.
default	The path to the default operating system.

[operating systems] Section

This section contains the list of available operating systems. Each entry includes the path to the boot partition for the operating system, the string to display in the boot loader screen, and optional parameters. There is an example of the use of this section of the Boot.ini file in the above section. The Boot.ini file supports starting multiple versions of Windows NT operating systems, as well as starting one other operating system. The other operating systems that can be included in the Boot.ini file are Windows 95/98, MS-DOS, and OS/2.

Boot.ini Switches

There are several switches that you can add to the end of the Windows NT entries in the [operating system] section of the Boot.ini file. They are not case sensitive. The following table contains Boot.ini Switches.

Switch	Description
/BASEVIDEO	The computer starts up using the standard VGA video driver. If you have installed a new video driver, but it is not working correctly, selecting the Windows NT entry with this switch enables you to start the computer so you can change to a different driver.
/BAUDRATE	Specifies the baud rate to be used for debugging. If you do not set the baud rate, the default baud rate is 9600 if a modem is attached, and 19200 for a null-modem cable. This switch has a secondary effect of forcing the /DEBUG switch as well, whether or not use you use /DEBUG.
/CRASHDEBUG	The debugger is loaded when you start Windows NT, but remains inactive unless a Kernel error occurs. This mode is useful if you are experiencing random, unpredictable Kernel errors.
/DEBUG	The debugger is loaded when you start Windows NT, and can be activated at any time by a host debugger connected to the computer. This is the mode to use when you are debugging problems that are regularly reproducible.
/DEBUGPORT	Specifies the com port to use for debugging, where *x* is the communications port that you want to use. Like /BAUDRATE, this switch will also force the /DEBUG mode.
/MAXMEM:n	Specifies the maximum amount of RAM that Windows NT can use. This switch is useful if you suspect a memory chip is bad. See Chapter 6, "Troubleshooting Disk and Startup Problems," for more information.
/NODEBUG	No debugging information is being used.
/NOSERIALMICE	Disables serial mouse detection of the specified COM port(s). Use this switch if you have a component other than a mouse attached to a serial port during the startup sequence. If you use /NOSERIALMICE without specifying a COM port, serial mouse detection is disabled on all COM ports.

/SOS	Displays the driver names while they are being loaded. Use this switch if Windows NT won't start up and you think a driver is missing.

Editing Boot.ini

When you install Windows NT, the Boot.ini file has the Read Only, System, and Hidden attributes set. You can edit the timeout and default parameters in the Boot.ini file by using the System option on Control Panel, regardless of the value of these attributes.

If you want to edit the Boot.ini file by using a text editor, you need to make the file visible before you can open it, and you need to turn off the Read Only attribute to be able to make changes to it. You can change the attributes by using My Computer, Windows NT Explorer, or the command prompt.

f. Using Hard Disks With More Than 1024 Cylinders

Windows NT can take advantage of hard disks with more than 1024 cylinders if you enable extended translation. Windows NT does not have a limit to the number of cylinders it can address, but the system and boot partitions are limited to 1024 cylinders by the system BIOS, which must use INT 13 to access the disk during startup.

The following error messages might appear when extended translation is not enabled on disks larger than 1024 cylinders, and the Master Boot Record is unable to locate the Partition Boot Sector:

- o Error loading operating system.
- o Missing operating system.

If you create your system and boot partitions in Windows NT Setup, you do not have to concern yourself with these details, because Setup will not create a partition that cannot be used to start Windows NT. When Windows NT has completed startup, it does not use the values in the Starting and Ending Head, Sector, and Cylinder fields of the Partition Table. Instead, it uses the Relative Sectors and Number Of Sectors fields. These fields provide a full 32 bits to represent sectors, which results in volumes of up to 232 sectors. With a standard sector size of 512 bytes, the 32-bit fields used for the Relative Sectors and Number of Sectors result in a maximum possible volume size of:

512 bytes x 4,294,967,296 = 2,199,023,255,552 bytes, or 2 TB.

When creating primary partitions or logical drives on a disk, Windows NT writes the correct values to the Partition Table fields whenever possible. When the Ending Cylinder field for an entry in the Partition Table goes beyond cylinder 1023, Windows

NT writes the maximum permitted values to these fields in the Partition Table. This prevents the system BIOS from calculating the Starting and Ending addresses based on erroneous data.

SCSI Hard Disks

If your SCSI controller can be configured to perform translation, you can create a boot partition or system partition that is within the first 1 or 4 GB of the disk, depending upon the translation used by the controller. To create the largest possible system and boot partitions, you need to enable translation on the controller. If translation was not already enabled, you will need to low-level format the hard disk, recreate partitions, and format them. Check with your hardware manufacturer for specific advice and details.

Once Windows NT has been initialized, it uses its SCSI disk device drivers to directly interact with the disk without using the BIOS INT 13 interface. Therefore, the Starting and Ending Head, Sector, and Cylinder fields are not important after the computer has completed startup.

IDE and EIDI Hard Disks

The system and boot partitions on IDE hard disks are also limited to 1024 cylinders if the controller does not translate the disk address. Secondary disks that do not contain the system or boot partition might not be limited to 1024 cylinders, depending on the translation scheme used by the controller and disk.

IDE disks use a different data structure for representing the number of cylinders, number of heads, and number of sectors per track than the Partition Table and BIOS INT 13 interface. According to the IDE specifications, the maximum number of cylinders is 65536, the maximum number of heads is 16, and the maximum number of sectors per track is 255. The maximum size is 136.9 GB. Because the BIOS/IDE interface has been constrained to use the lowest common denominator, the result is a limit of about 504 MB for an IDE disk on an Intel-based ISA bus computer.

There are new controllers and disk device drivers that use an Enhanced Disk Parameter Table to translate between the logical sector layout internal to the IDE disk and the logical sector layout addressable by the BIOS INT 13 interface. These disk drivers and devices can support larger disks. These disks and controllers are referred to as enhanced IDE, or EIDE, devices.

ESDI Hard Disks

ESDI disks are an older type that came before the IDE disks. ESDI disks use the CHS (cylinder, head, sector) addressing and have a 1024 cylinder limitation. Some controller cards get around this limitation by implementing a translation scheme in the onboard controller BIOS.

The translation is totally transparent to Windows NT, and the standard disk device driver works without any change. ESDI disks are capable of being low-level formatted with various values of sector per track, such as 53 or 63. Here are two examples:

1024 cylinders x 15 heads x 53 sectors per track x 512 bytes per sector = 398 MB

1024 cylinders x 15 heads x 63 sectors per track x 512 bytes per sector = 472 MB

Thus, using 63 sectors per track yields 74 MB more space. Windows NT is compatible with either geometry, and, depending on the disk or controller, can access cylinders beyond 1023. You can use Windows NT to create and format the disk space beyond cylinder 1023, but it cannot be accessed by MS-DOS. However, some controllers can remap the remaining cylinders beyond 1023 so that either MS-DOS or Windows NT can use the entire capacity. For example:

1632 cylinders x 15 heads x 53 sectors per track x 512 bytes per sector = 634 MB

Removable Disks and Floppy Disks

Most types of removable media can work with Window NT. Even though removable media are assigned a floppy disk icon in My Computer and Windows NT Explorer, they are not handled by the same part of the operating system. Floppy disks are handled by Floppy.sys. All SCSI-based removable media are handled through the normal SCSI disk device drivers. Most magneto-optical, Bernoulli, Syquest, and similar removable-media disks are treated like hard disks under Windows NT, and do not require special disk device drivers. WORM and other types of "Write once" media are not supported in Windows NT.

There are several limitations that are unique to removable media in Windows NT.

- Removable media can only have a single primary partition. Extended partitions are not supported.
- Removable media devices cannot be used as part of a volume set, stripe set, mirror set, or stripe set with parity.
- It is not possible to format a floppy disk with the NTFS file system. The Windows NT operating system formats all floppy disks with the FAT file system, because the additional files required for the NTFS file system use too much space on a floppy disk.
- If you format a removable disk with the FAT file system, you can remove the disk while Windows NT is running.

- When you format any removable disk with the NTFS file system, or if the page file is located on removable media, you can only remove the disk after you shutdown Windows NT.

Windows 2000

Windows 2000 is designed to: provide a true 32-bit, preemptive, reentrant, virtual memory operating system, run on multiple hardware architectures and platforms, run and scale well on SMP systems, be a great distributed computing platform, both as a network client and as a server, run most existing 16-bit MS-DOS and Microsoft Windows 3.1 applications, meet government requirements for POSIX 1003.1 compliance, meet government and industry requirements for operating system security, and be easily adaptable to the global market by supporting Unicode. It is designed to be portable through the use of the HAL, or Hardware Abstraction Layer.

According to Richard , the HAL: "isolates the operating system from platform-specific hardware differences." (87). As of April 2001, Windows 2000 has only been implemented for the Intel x86 architecture.

The OS did use some state-of-the-art concepts in its construction, because it is written largely with an Object Oriented design in mind. Windows 2000 also uses a relatively new concept in its implementation, a hybrid microkernel.

Commercially and economically Windows 2000 has been successful. As of February 2001, a year after its introduction, over one million licenses for the Server version had been sold according to news.com.

The parts of the operating system that were done well are the hybrid kernel design and the APIs that allow applications to be compatible with newer versions of the operating system. However, there has been criticism of the weak remote administration facilities built into the operating system when compared to the available features of a UNIX operating system. Critics point to the important role of remote administration in an operating system that use used for servers.

Scheduling

Windows 2000 implements a priority-driven preemptive scheduling system.

Thread Priorities

Levels

Internally, Windows 2000 uses 32 priority levels, ranging from 0 to 31. These values are broken up into three groups, namely sixteen real-time levels (16-31), fifteen variable levels (1-15), and one system level (0), reserved for the zero page thread. The Win32 API groups these 31 priority levels into six separate classes, namely Real-time

(22-26), High (11-15), Above-normal (8-12), Normal (6-10), Below-normal (4-8), and Idle (2-6). These classes are then broken down into relative priorities: Time-critical, Highest, Above-normal, Normal, Below-normal, Lowest, and Idle. A thread's priority is based upon both the process' priority and the thread's relative priority. When threads are created they generally inherit their process base priority, which defaults to the value at the middle of each process priority range (4, 6, 8, 10, 13, or 24).

In Windows 2000, a process has one priority level, while a thread receives two values: the current priority and the base priority.

Priority Boosts

The priority of a thread can be boosted in the following cases :

- Upon completion of an I/O operation
- After waiting on executive events or semaphores
- After threads in the foreground process complete a wait operation
- When GUI threads wake up because of windowing activity
- When a thread that's ready to run hasn't been running for some time, as in the event of CPU starvation

When a thread in the dynamic priority range (0-15) is released from a wait state, the scheduler may temporarily boost the thread's priority to give it a chance to complete execution based on the new data the thread acquired. These boosts range from a single priority level for the completion of an I/O event up to eight priority levels following the completion of a sound .

Boosts applied to threads returning from a wait state receive a boost of one, but to favor interactive applications a boost of 2 is applied to threads returning from a wait state if that thread owns a window. A boost is also applied to foreground threads to improve the perceived responsiveness of interactive applications. I/O requests to devices that warrant better responsiveness have higher boost values.

The priority boost is always applied to a thread's base priority, never to its current priority. After a boost is applied, the thread will run for one quantum at the elevated priority level, after which it decays one priority level and runs another quantum, continuing until it has degraded to its base priority level. A thread with an elevated priority level may still be preempted by another thread with a higher priority level, but the interrupted thread will complete its time slice before returning to its base level. A threads priority level will never be boosted into the Real-Time priority range.

Real-Time Priority

Windows 2000 maintains 15 priority levels titled real-time. These levels are normally reserved for kernel-mode system threads. The difference between threads running at the real-time level and those running at other priority levels is that threads in the real-time range have their thread quantum reset if they are preempted. While Windows 2000 uses a set of priorities called real-time, Windows 2000 does not provide real-time operating system facilities, such as guaranteed interrupt latency.

Scheduling Queues

Windows 2000 maintains a queue for each priority level. The queues contain threads that are in the ready state and are waiting to be scheduled for execution. To speed up the selection of which thread to run or preempt, Windows 2000 maintains a 32-bit bitmask called the *ready summary*, which indicates at least one thread in the ready queue for that particular priority level ready to run . Windows 2000 also maintains a second bitmask, the *idle summary*, in which each bit that is set represents an idle processor .

Windows 2000 handles wait queues in an interesting way. When a thread enters a wait state on one or more objects (valid objects include an event, a semaphore, a mutex, and I/O completion port, a process, a thread, etc), that thread performs a synchronization of its *dispatcher state* with the object in question. A thread cannot resume its execution until the *dispatcher state* of the object in question returns from a nonsignaled state to the signaled state. A thread can wait on more than one object at a time, and can also specify that its wait should be canceled if it hasn't ended within a certain amount of time. Whenever the kernel sets a particular object to the signaled state, it checks to see whether any threads are waiting on the object. If they are, the kernel releases one or more of the threads from their waiting state so that they can continue execution. When a thread returns from the wait state 1 quantum unit is deducted from the thread's remaining quantum so that I/O bound threads are not unfairly favored.

Quantum

A quantum is defined as the amount of time a thread gets to run before Windows 2000 checks to see if another thread at the same priority should get to run. When a thread has run for its entire allotted quantum, Windows 2000 checks if there is another thread at the same priority level that is in the ready queue. If there is, the currently executing thread is moved to the back of its priority level's queue and the next thread in the ready queue is dispatched to the processor for execution.

Context Switching

In Windows 2000, a thread's context and the procedure for context switching can vary depending on the processor's architecture. The saving and reloading of this data is made possible by using a kernel-mode stack. Typically, however, a context switch involves saving and reloading the following data:

- Program counter (PC)
- Processor status register
- Other register contents
- User and kernel stack pointers
- Pointer to the thread's address space in which it runs

CPU Starvation

Windows 2000 maintains a system thread called the *balance set manager*. Once per second, this thread executes and scans 16 of the ready queues for any threads that have been in the ready state for longer than 300 clock ticks. The next second, it scans the remaining queues, continuing where it stopped the previous pass. When the *balance set manager* finds a thread that has been waiting for execution for longer than 300 clocks ticks, it will boost that threads priority to the highest non-real-time level (15) and sets its quantum to double the normal time. If the thread has not completed execution after two complete quantums its current priority level is set to the base priority level. The *balance set manager* will only boost 10 threads per execution pass.

Zero Page Thread

When there is no runnable thread for a CPU, Windows 2000 will dispatch the zero page thread. The zero page thread is reported as running at priority 0, though it really does not have a priority at all. The zero page thread polls for deferred interrupt processing. The zero page thread performs the following functions:

- Enables and disables interrupts, allowing any pending interrupts to be delivered
- Checks for any deferred procedure calls pending on any processor and delivers them, if necessary
- Checks whether a thread has been selected to run next on the CPU and, if applicable, dispatches the thread
- Performs checks for power management functions

Multiprocessor Scheduling

Windows 2000 pads each thread with two CPU numbers stored within the thread block: *Ideal processor* and *last processor*. Ideal processor is chosen randomly from the number of CPUs the system has and remains static unless specifically changed with a system call. These values drastically reduce the amount of swapping of secondary cache data that occurs when a thread is moved from one CPU to another in its next quantum.

When selecting a thread for execution, Windows 2000 attempts to perform the following steps:

1. Schedule the thread on an idle processor in order of ideal, last, and current CPU
2. Schedule the thread on any idle processor
3. Preempt a thread currently running on a processor in order of ideal, last, and current CPU

Processor affinity

Each thread contains a processor *affinity mask* that specifies the processors a thread is permitted to run. By default, a thread can run on any processor. The affinity mask is used to allow tightly coupled processes to better communicate together. Windows 2000 won't move a running thread that could run on a different CPU in order to run a thread with an affinity for the first CPU.

Thread States

Windows 2000 maintains seven thread states:

- Ready – Threads waiting to execute
- Standby – A thread that has been selected to run next on a particular processor
- Running – An executing thread
- Waiting – A thread waiting on a particular event to occur
- Transition – A thread that is ready for execution but its kernel stack is paged out of memory
- Terminated – A thread that finishes execution
- Initialized – Used when a thread is being created

State Transitions

In Windows 2000, a thread can change its state due to a variety of different events.

- Voluntary Switch – This occurs when a thread enters a wait state on an object.
- Preemption – a higher-priority thread that has become ready to run can preempt a thread. This can happen when a higher-priority thread has completed a wait or a thread's priority has been increased.
- End of Quantum – The execution of a thread will be stopped if its quantum has elapsed. If the thread has not completed execution it will be moved to the end of the ready queue.
- Termination – This occurs when a thread has completed execution or its parent's process is terminated.

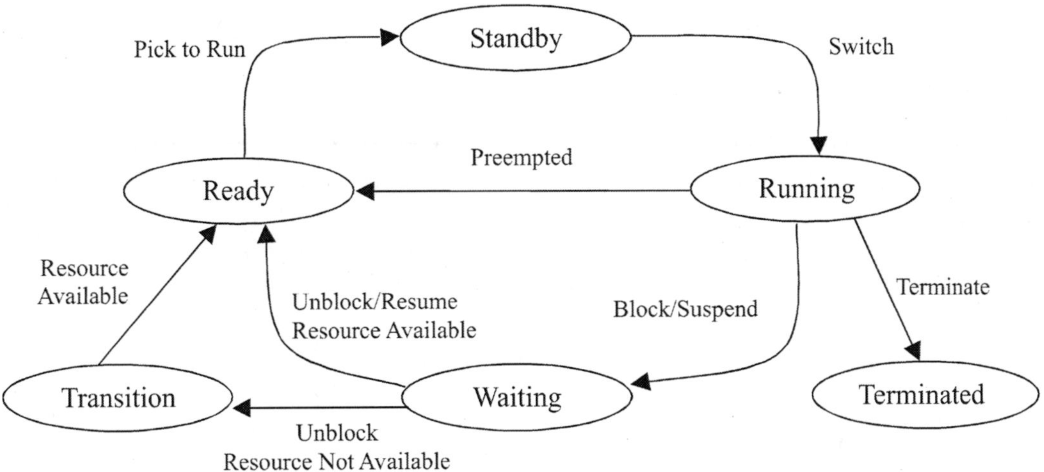

Memory Management

The memory manager in Windows 2000 provides services for virtual memory management, shared memory between processes, memory mapped files, locking memory, and protecting memory. The memory manager is intended to operate over a variety of platforms and utilize page sizes between 4 Kbytes to 64 Kbytes.

Virtual Memory Management

Each user process in Windows 2000 has a separate 32-bit address space, allowing 4 gigabytes of memory per process. However, 2 gigabytes of this address space is reserved for the operating system so that the available virtual address space for each user is 2 gigabytes .

Pages in a process address are allocated into one of three states: free, reserved, or committed. Free pages are pages that are not currently being used by the process. A reserved page is a way for a thread to set aside a range of virtual addresses that may be needed in the future. These reservations do not count against the user addressable space allotted to the process. Committed pages have been set aside in the memory manager's page file (1). Applications first reserve address space and then commit pages in that address space. Because the addresses are merely reserved, actual access of them is not possible and will result in an access violation.

Pages are written to disk by first being moved from the process working set to the modified list and finally to the disk. The handling of reserving and committing memory is efficient in that memory usage is reduced because committed pages are reserved until needed. It is also a reasonably fast and inexpensive operation under Windows 2000 because it does not consume any committed pages (Soloman 389-391).

Protecting Memory

Memory protection is provided to prevent a user processes from accidentally or purposely accessing the address space of another process or the operating system itself. There are four main ways in which memory is protected in Windows 2000. First, all system wide data structures and memory pools used by kernel-mode system components can be accessed only while in kernel mode, not user mode. Should user-mode threads attempt to access a kernel-mode system component, the memory manager will report this as an access violation. Second, each process has a separate, private address space, which cannot be accessed by any thread that belongs to another process. This assures that threads running in one process cannot access a page belonging to another process. The only exceptions are if the memory is shared or if another process has virtual memory read or write access to the process object. Third, all processes are also supported by some form of hardware-controlled memory protection. These access restrictions include read/write, read-only, no-access, execute, execute read, execute read/write, write/copy, execute write/copy, and guard. Lastly, shared memory objects have standard access-control lists that are checked when a process attempts to access a shared memory area. This serves to limit shared memory access to only processes with the proper rights. In order to create the shared memory object, the thread must have at least read access to the underlying file object or the operation will fail .

Shared Memory and Mapped Files

Shared memory can be defined as "memory that is visible to more than one process or that is present in more than one process virtual address space". Each process maintains its own private memory areas where it can store its own data, but the program instructions and unmodified data pages can be shared without harm because of hardware memory protections. This type of sharing occurs automatically because the code pages in executable images are mapped as execute-only and the writable pages are mapped as copy-on-write. Implementing shared memory involves the use of shared objects. These objects represent a block of memory that two or more processes can share and can be mapped to the paging file or to another file on a disk. When a process maps a copy-on-write view of a section object that contains read/write pages, the memory manager suspends making a copy of the pages until the page is written to. Therefore, copy-on-write page protection is used to conserve physical memory.

Locking Memory

There are two ways that pages can be locked in memory. Once a page is locked, it remains in memory until unlocked. The first method of locking a page in memory is for a device driver to call a kernel-mode function to lock the page in memory. There is no limit enforced on the number of pages a driver can lock in memory, although a driver cannot lock more pages than the resident available page count will allow. The second way to lock pages in memory is through the *VirtualLock* function. This function can be called by an application to lock pages in their process working set. "The number of pages a process can lock cannot exceed its minimum working set size minus eight pages" . If all the threads in the process are in a wait state, the memory manager is free to remove such pages from the working set if memory demands dictate. This can actually disrupt performance because when a thread wakes up to run, the memory manager must first read in all the locked pages before the thread executes. For this reason, it is generally a good idea to let the memory manager decide which pages remain in physical memory.

Page Directories

Each process has a single page directory that the memory manager creates to map the location of all page tables for that process. The physical address of the process page directory is stored in the kernel process block and is also mapped virtually. All executable code running in kernel mode uses to virtual memory addresses, not physical ones. The Central Processing Unit can determine the location of a page because a register inside the CPU contains the physical address of the page directory. The page directory is composed of page directory entries or PDEs. Each PDE is 4 bytes long and describes the state and location of all the possible page tables for that process.

Before referencing a byte within a page using an offset, the CPU first needs to be able to find the page that contains the desired byte of data. To do so, the operating system constructs another page of memory, containing the mapping information needed to find the desired page. This page of mapping information is referred to as a page table. Because Windows 2000 provides a private address space for each process, each process has its own set of process page tables to map that private address space. However, the page tables that describe the system space are shared among all processes.

File Management

"A file management system is the set of system software that provides services to users and applications in the user of files" . The only way that a user or application is able to access a file is through the file management system.

Windows 2000 includes support for these file system formats: NTFS, CDFS, UDF, FAT12, FAT16, and FAT32. CDFS or CD-ROM file system is the read-only formatting standard for CD-ROM media. UDF file system allows support for DVD media and CD-RW media. Windows 2000 supports the FAT file system primarily to enable upgrades from other versions of Microsoft Windows and for compatibility with other operating systems, and as a floppy disks .

The file system designed for Windows NT/2000 is NTFS. It is designed to meet high-end requirements for workstations and servers. Examples of such high-end applications are client/server applications, resource intensive engineering and scientific applications, and network applications for large corporate systems. NTFS uses 64-bit cluster indexes; however, Windows 2000 limits the size of an NTFS volume to those addressable using 32-bit clusters. Notable features of NTFS are recoverability, file and directory security, disk quotas, file compression, directory-based symbolic links, and encryption.

NTFS uses a simple but powerful approach to organize information into four regions on a disk volume. The layout of an NTFS volume is depicted in the figure below.

Partition boot sector	Master file table	System files	File area

The first few sectors on any volume are occupied by the partition boot sector, which contains information about the volume layout, the file system structures, and the boot information and code. The master file table contains information about the files and folders on the NTFS volume and information about available unallocated space. The system files region follows the master file table and is usually approximately 1 megabyte in length. It contains files such as the log file and the attribute definition table. The log file is a list of transaction steps used for NTFS recoverability. The attribute definition table "defines the attribute types supported on this volume and indicates whether they can be indexed and whether they can be recovered during a system recovery operation" .

Threads

Windows 2000 supports both user-level and kernel-level threads. Several types of kernel-level threads are available within Windows 2000.

Kernel-Level Threads

There are several types of kernel-level threads available in Windows 2000. A user mode kernel-level thread is created and runs in user mode and can be preempted by the scheduler.

System worker threads are created by other threads and only exist to do work for other threads . There are different types of system worker threads. Delayed worker threads are not time critical and their stack can be paged out. Critical worker threads have time critical work items and their stacks always reside in memory. Hypercritical worker threads always have their stack in main memory, and are used to free terminated threads.

Kernel mode system threads have all the attributes of a user mode thread, but can only be run in kernel mode. Objects running in kernel mode can only create this type of thread. A kernel mode system thread has no user process address space and must allocate all its storage needs dynamically from the heap; this is different than a user mode system thread .

User-Level Threads

A user-level thread or fiber is created as a normal thread, and then converted to a fiber. The scheduler does not preemptively schedule different fibers. Instead, a fiber must be switched to from another fiber in the process. The system can preempt the process controlling the fiber suspending the execution of the fiber as stated in the Windows Platform SDK documentation.

Mutual Exclusion and Synchronization

Different methods of mutual exclusion and synchronization are employed inside and outside of the kernel of Windows 2000. Within the kernel, much of the mutual exclusion is done using spinlocks. The objects providing mutual exclusion and synchronization outside the kernel rely on services provided by the kernel.

Kernel Synchronization

Synchronization in the kernel of Windows 2000 guarantees that only one processor can be executing in a critical section. To accomplish this, several methods are employed within the kernel. One way of enforcing mutual exclusion and synchronization within the kernel is by disabling certain interrupts. A different method, spinlocks, is used to protect the core data structures of the kernel.

Some areas where mutual exclusion and synchronization are needed within the kernel on a single processor machine are dealt with by modifying how interrupts are handled. When a critical section dealing with data structures that do not constitute the core of the operating system are entered on a single processor machine, interrupt handlers that use the same resource that the critical section provides are masked so that these interrupts will not execute .

Another way mutual exclusion is dealt with which is better suited to multiple processors is the use of a spinlock. A spinlock works by providing a global data structure in the kernel. Before entering a critical section, the kernel must acquire the spinlock associated with the critical section. If the spinlock is not available, the executing code employs busy waiting until the resource becomes available. When finished executing the critical section, the kernel will release the spinlock .

To improve on the performance of spinlocks, a queue is employed. When a process makes a request for the spinlock, and the spinlock has already been acquired the request is placed on a queue. When the request can be fulfilled, a flag in the processor is set . A benefit of this is that FIFO order is enforced for requests for the spinlock.

Executive Synchronization

The methods of mutual exclusion and synchronization are different outside the kernel. Instead, executive objects use dispatcher objects. Examples of these objects are mutexes, semaphores, events, and waitable timers . To use these objects, a thread will issue a wait on one of these objects. While waiting on a dispatcher object, the thread is placed into a suspended state until the dispatcher object enters a signaled state.

Types of Dispatcher Objects

- Mutex – This creates a section of code that can only be entered by a thread that posses the mutex. When the mutex is released, the mutex is passed to a waiting thread.
- Semaphore – This limits the number of times a resource can be used. A semaphore reaches a signaled state when its count drops to zero; when this happens, all waiting threads are released.
- Event – This can be used to tell a waiting thread that a specified event has happened. To do this, a wait is issued on an event and when the event occurs, and when an event is set, the waiting threads will be released.
- Waitable timer – This creates a timer object that will release its threads after a specified time interval has elapsed or when a specified time is reached.

Windows 2000 and its successors will continue to be very successful in the market place. It provides for both user and kernel processor modes, and scales from one to thirty two CPUs using SMP. Both user-mode and kernel-mode threads are supported by Windows 2000. A wide variety of synchronization mechanisms to provide mutual exclusion and synchronization, including mutexes, semaphores, events, and timers, exist to support multithreaded applications. Support for large amounts of memory is built in with a file system that can support the growing capacity of storage devices. The preemptive nature of Windows 2000 allows for it to be able to handle a wide variety of situations and applications from a workstation to a large server.

GLOSSARY

- **Access Control List** - (ACL) A list of the services available on a server, each with a list of the hosts permitted to use the service.
- **Access Control Matrix** - provides an appropriate mechanism for defining and implementing strict control for both the static and dynamic association between processes and domains
- **Address** (1) The number of a particular memory or peripheral storage location. Like post office boxes, each byte of memory and each disk sector has its own unique address. Programs are compiled into machine language, which references actual addresses in the computer. (2) As a verb, to manage or work with. For example, "the computer can address 16MB of memory."
- **Address Binding** The binding of instructions and data for a process to physical memory or absolute addresses. This can happen at compile time, load time or execution time.
- **Address space** A computer's address space is the total amount of memory that can be addressed by the computer. For example, the Pentium can address 4GB of physical memory and 64TB of virtual memory. A program's address space is the actual memory used by the program when running. It may refer to physical memory (RAM chips) or to virtual memory (disk) or to a combination of both.
- **Algorithm** A set of ordered steps for solving a problem, such as a mathematical formula or the instructions in a program. The terms algorithm and logic are synonymous. Both refer to a sequence of steps to solve a problem. However, an algorithm implies an expression that solves a complex problem rather than the overall input-process-output logic of typical business programs.
- **Allocation** To reserve a resource such as memory or disk.
- **Application** A specific use of the computer, such as for payroll, inventory and billing. For a list of major application software categories, see application software.
- **Atomic functions** Indivisible. An atomic operation, or atomicity, implies an operation that must be performed entirely or not at all. It may not be interrupted For example, if machine failure prevents a transaction to be processed to completion, the system will be rolled back to the start of the transaction.

- **Background Process** - A background process does not monopolize the shell.
- **Base** (1) A starting or reference point. (2) A multiplier in a numbering system. In a decimal system, each digit position is worth 10x the position to its right. In binary, each digit position is worth 2x the position to its right.
- **Batch** - a job with no human input, so its automatic; the batch scheduler is responsible which input jobs goes next - 1touch; cpu scheduler - infinite touches
- **Batch data entry** Entering a group of source documents into the computer.
- **Batch file** A file containing data that is processed or transmitted from beginning to end, or a file containing instructions that are executed one after the other. A .BAT file is used in DOS and a shell script in UNIX.
- **Batch scheduler** - the amount of jobs executed over time
- **BCD** Binary coded decimal: each digit of a decimal number is converted to a 4 bit binary number
- **Best fit** Leaves least space over and so minimises fragmentation.
- **Binary Semaphore** - can only assume the value 0 or 1
- **Binary** Two state system which can be On/Off etc with states represented by digits 0 (Off) or 1 (on).
- **Bios** Basic Input/ Output System: part of the OS closest to hardware. Is a program (sometimes called "firmware" (between software and hardware) contained in ROM memory on the BIOS chip.
- **Bit** Binary digit (0 or 1)
- **Block** A group of disk records that is stored and transferred as a single unit.
- **Blocked State** - process is blocked by another process
- **Boolean** Logical variable which can take values TRUE or FALSE.
- **Buffer** Area of memory provided for specialised functions: eg. To store data for a processor, to provide temporary storage for data passing between devices where there is a speed or data size mismatch.
- **Buffer Overflow Attack** - In November 1988, the Internet Worm shut down over 6,000 systems, just about cutting off all traffic on the Internet. One of the methods used to gain access to these systems was a buffer overflow exploit of a Unix service "finger." When you finger a user, the finger service returns information about the user, such as the user's real name and phone number. In the case of the Worm, the buffer overflow attack on finger replaced the server program with a Unix command interpreter, or shell. This shell was then used to copy across a program that uploaded, linked, and then executed a new copy of the Worm.
- **Buffering** - a system call that read a file to disk using an entire block of data in a region of memory

- **Burst Time** Total CPU access time required by a process before and I/O burst is required and usually measured in milliseconds. The operation of a process takes place with a series of interspersed CPU and I/O bursts.
- **Bus** Several parallel wires as on the motherboard or along a data cable which connect to more than one device. A common pathway, or channel, between multiple devices. The computer's internal bus is known as the local bus, or processor bus. It provides a parallel data transfer path between the CPU and main memory and to the peripheral buses. A 16-bit bus transfers two bytes at a time over 16 wires; a 32-bit bus uses 32 wires, etc. The bus is comprised of two parts: the address bus and the data bus. Addresses are sent over the address bus to signal a memory location, and the data is transferred over the data bus to that location.
- **Byte** 8 bits
- **Caching** - A small fast memory holding recently accessed data, designed to speed up subsequent access to the same data.
- **Caching** - saving something which will be used multiple times
- **Caching** Cache provides temporary storage memory area for high speed access such as the CPU accessing memory. Cache memory provides higher speed access, but is more expensive than ordinary RAM.
- **Capability List** - for a domain is a list of objects together with the operations allowed on those objects; the object is often represented by its physical name or address(capability)
- **Channel** - is a dedicated, special purpose CPU found in mainframes and in other high-end systems. The job of a channel is to offload I/O work from the main CPU. The idea is that the channels keep the data flowing smoothly, while the main CPU remains free to process data
- **Child Process** - A process created by another process (the parent process). Each process may create many child processes but will have only one parent process, except for the very first process, which has no parent.
- **Clock Cycle** - the clock cycle is the time between two adjacent pulses of the oscillator that sets the tempo of the computer processor. The number of these pulses per second is known as the clock speed, which is generally measured in MHz (megahertz, or millions of pulses per second) and lately even in GHz (gigahertz, or billions of pulses per second). The clock speed is determined by a quartz-crystal circuit, similar to those used in radio communications equipment. Some processors execute only one instruction per clock cycle. More advanced processors, described as superscalar, can perform more than one instruction per clock cycle.
- **Coalesce** - the term, which means combining two adjacent free partitions into a single larger partition; like water drops merging; The bottoms of the

constituent domains are coalesced into a single bottom in the sum. This may be generalised to any number of domains.

- **Compaction** - The coding of data to save storage space or transmission time. Although data is already coded in digital form for computer processing, it can often be coded more efficiently (using fewer bits)
- **Compare and Swap Instruction** - This instruction is a read-modify-write instruction
- **Concurrency** When several processes attempt to access the same data. Leads to the critical section problem.
- **Consistency** keeping the same data in several copies of the same file through processes that might be altering one or other of the copies.
- **Content Switch** - remembers state through sessionID, good across multiple servers as long as session has not timed out
- **Context Switch** - switch from one process to another process
- **Context switch** Switching by the CPU scheduler of access provision to the CPU from one process to another. Time taken typically ranges from 1 - 1000 micro (Ü) secs. See P 248. Standard Hard disk transfer rate ~ 1 MB / second. To transfer process of 100 k will then take 100/1000 = 1/10 sec = 100 ms. To swap in and out = 2 (100 + 8 (latency)) = 216 ms. For efficient CPU utilisation we need execution time for each process to be long compared to this swap time.
- **Contiguous** - back to back, will maximize, difficult to allow the file to go; when you deframent your system you basically put all files back to back
- **Contiguous File Allocation** - Each file occupies a set of contiguous blocks on the disk. Allocation using first fit / best fit. Need for compaction. Only starting block and length of file in blocks are needed to work with the file. Allows random access. Problems with files that grow
- **Control Unit** - starts process at CPU; (processor) The part of a CPU responsible for performing the machine cycle - fetch, decode, execute, store.
- **Controller** An electronic circuit board or system. In a personal computer, controllers contain the circuitry to run a peripheral device and are either contained on a plug-in expansion board or on the motherboard. Increasingly, plug-in boards for disk control, networking, sound, etc., are being replaced by built-in circuits (chips) on the motherboard. In larger computers, a controller may be contained on one or more boards or in a standalone cabinet.
- **Counting Semaphore** - can assume only non-negative integers
- **CPU Bound** - processes that perform lots of computation and do little IO. Tend to have a few long CPU bursts.

- **CPU** Central Processing Unit
- **CPU Scheduling** - figures out which active process is to run next
- **Critical Section** - a section of code that needs mutual exclusion because it is accessing a shared resource Data file which multiple processes can access and alter. Concurrency problems (race condition) arise if the file is accessed by more than one process at a time.
- **C-SCAN** - One way with fast return (Lower service variability)
- **Cycle stealing** - S. pp465. When the entire transfer is finished, the DMA controller interrupts the CPU. When the DMA controller seizes the memory bus, the CPU is momentarily prevented from accessing main memory, although it can still access data items in its primary and secondary cache.
- **Cylinder** A HDD consists of multiple platters. Each platter is divided into rings or tracks. A group of tracks on which sectors are all the same size is a cylinder. The cylinder includes vertically corresponding sectors on the platters.
- **Data** Technically, raw facts and figures, such as orders and payments, which are processed into information, such as balance due and quantity on hand. However, in common usage, the terms data and information are used synonymously. The amount of data versus information kept in the computer is a trade-off. Data can be processed into different forms of information, but it takes time to sort and sum transactions. Up-to-date information can provide instant answers. A common misconception is that software is also data. Software is executed, or run, by the computer. Data is "processed." Software is "run."
- **Data Block** - logical unit of allocation; smallest unit of allocation
- **Deadlock** - A deadlock is a situation in which two computer programs sharing the same resource are effectively preventing each other from accessing the resource, resulting in both programs ceasing to function.
- **Demand paging** Memory and processes and divided into 4K pages. Only a limited number of a process's pages are kept in memory at a time. Demand paging means that a particular page of program code is loaded into memory as required.
- **Denial of Service Attack** - so many messages that a web server seizes up; which cause networked computers to disconnect from the network or just outright crash. For example, a teenager using very simple DoS tools managed to cripple the web sites of large companies like Yahoo and Amazon during a series of attacks in February 2000 (see this CNN article). These attacks are sometimes also known as "nukes", "hacking", or "cyber-attacks", but we will use the technically correct term of DoS attacks. Often the vic-

tims are people on Internet Relay Chat (IRC), but DoS attacks do not involve IRC servers in any way, so IRC operators (IRC ops) cannot stop or punish the offenders. Denial of service should not be confused with other attacks like viruses, Trojan Horses, and cracking or "hacking"■

- **Direct Access** - IBM mainframe terminology for a disk drive, in contrast with a tape drive which is a sequential access device.
- **Directory** Data structure on a secondary storage device (FDD, HDD) which together with a second data structure, the FAT records storage and other information about stored files on the device
- **Dirty Bit - modified** bit; A bit associated with each frame. Set to 1 by hardware whenever a page is **modified**.
- **Disk** A direct access storage device. E.g. floppy disk, hard disk, magnetic disk, optical disk and videodisc.
- **Disk Map** -identifies where all the pages are on the disk
- **Dispatcher** - sets the timer and restores the state; dispatcher thread reads incoming requests for work from the network
- **Dispatching** - selecting the next program to run;
- **Distributive Operating Systems** - inheritantly more complex than non-distributive systems and should avoid OS unless you must
- **DMA** - S. pp465. Direct Memory Access, the way many computers avoid burdening the main CPU with PIO by offloading some of this work to a special-purpose processor called a DMA.
- **Driver** Also called a device driver is a program routine that links a peripheral device to the operating system. It is written by programmers who understand the detailed knowledge of the device's command language and characteristics and contains the precise machine language necessary to perform the functions requested by the application. When a new hardware device is added to the computer, such as a display adapter, sound card or CD-ROM drive, its driver must be installed in order to run it. The operating system calls the driver, and the driver "drives" the device. Routines that perform internal functions, such as memory managers and disk caches, are also called drivers. In a PC, fundamental drivers that manage such components as the keyboard, floppy and non-SCSI hard disks, are included in the system BIOS chip. Additional drivers are loaded at boot time by the operating system. In a PC, fundamental drivers that manage such components as the keyboard, floppy and non-SCSI hard disks, are included in the system BIOS chip. Additional drivers are loaded at boot time by the operating system.

- **Effective access time (EAT)** Memory access time is how long it takes for a character in memory to be transferred to or from the CPU. In a personal computer, fast RAM chips have an access time of **70 nanoseconds** (ns) or less. SDRAM chips have a burst mode that obtains the second and subsequent characters in 10 ns or less.Disk access time is an average of the time between initiating a request and obtaining the first data character. In includes command processing, seek time and latency. Fast hard disks have access times of **10 milliseconds (ms)** or less. This is a common speed measurement, but disk performance is influenced by channel speed (transfer rate), interleaving and caching. Effective access time can be significantly increased by page faulting which occurs in demand paging. The page faulting rate needs to be kept as small as possible. See Text P 297 where memory access time is ~ 100 ns, page fault service time is ~25 ms (250 000 times as slow). Note that disk access times (seek time + latency) are much slower again ~ 10 - 100 ms
- **Encryption** - UNIX uses it to save passwords, it is basically an algorithm to encode a password or whatever so it can't be hacked.
- **Environmental variable** - An environmental variable is a type of variable used in Unix and other operating systems to pass important information to running programs.
- **Exec/execvp** - executes a file
- **Execution** To run a program (follow instructions in the program). Same as run. Execution time is the time in which a single instruction is executed. It makes up the last half of the instruction cycle.
- **External Fragmentation** - space that has not been allocated but cannot be used (not used but allocated)
- **External Interrupt** - An interrupt caused by an external source such as the computer operator, external sensor or monitoring device, or another computer.
- **Fast Interrupt** - There are two separate things that a 'fast' interrupt handler seeks to achieve: reduced and constrained interrupt latency.
- **FAT** - is a linked list, problem is that it has to cache and it takes up a lot of memory
- **FAT Table** - The component of an MS-DOS or Windows 95 file system which describes the files, directories, and free space on a hard disk or floppy disk. A disk is divided into partitions. Under the FAT file system each partition is divided into clusters, each of which can be one or more sectors, depending on the size of the partition. Each cluster is either allocated to a file or directory or it is free (unused). A directory lists the name, size, modification time and starting cluster of each file or subdirectory it contains.

- **Fault rate** This refers to the rate of occurrences of faults, which occurs when the CPU requests code which is not currently stored in memory. A new page has to be swapped in and the "victim" page swapped out.
- **FCFS** - First Come First Served
- **FIFO** - First in first out (Fairest of them all)
- **File Allocation Table (FAT)** – Variation of the link list (MS/DOS and OS/2) A section of the disk at the beginning of each partition (Volume) is set aside to contain a FAT. FAT has one entry for each disk block, pointing to the next block in the file.
- **File System** - A system for organizing directories and files, generally in terms of how it is implemented in the disk operating system. The collection of files and directories stored on a given drive. As an extension of this sense, "file system" is sometimes used to refer to the representatation of the file system's organisation (e.g. its file allocation table) as opposed the actual content of the files in the file system.
- **First fit** Allocution method which allocates to a device the first available resource which is suitable, irrespective of the adverse effect of segmentation.
- **Fixed Partition** - A process using fixed partitions must fit into a predetermined number of pages.
- **Foreground Process** - A process that monopolizes the shell so that no more commands can be entered until it finishes.
- **Fork** - make a child process, exact copy of the parent
- **Formatting a Disk** - your laying out a data structure to manage the disk
- **Fragmentation** - wasted space
- **Fragmentation** (internal, external) Refers to allocated memory or storage space which is unusable. External fragmentation occurs when contiguous blocks of memory are too small to be used. Internal fragmentation refers to allocated memory which cannot be used such as a partially filled end block when memory is allocated in blocks.
- **Frame Table** - the table that keeps track of all page frames. What page frames are free and what has been allocated and to whom?; an entry for each frame. Is the frame is use, if so which process.
- **FSCAN** - N-step-SCAN with N = queue size at beginning of SCAN cycle (Load sensitive)
- **Gantt chart** A type of floating bar chart usually used in project management to show the use of resources or tasks over time.
- **General Purpose Register** - General Purpose Registers are used to perform arithmetic functions. Some computers have only 1 General Purpose Register which is called the Accumulator whereas others have up to 16.

- **Hard Link** - keeps the inode
- **Hardware** Machinery and equipment (CPU, disks, tapes, modem, cables, etc.). In operation, a computer is both hardware and software. One is useless without the other. The hardware design specifies the commands it can follow, and the instructions tell it what to do.
- **Hit Ratio** - measurement of the effctiveness of accessing a cache (percentage of time that you find what you are looking for in each cache); The Cache Hit Ratio is the ratio between the number of times 4D actually finds objects in the data cache, compared to the total number of times it tries to access objects in the data cache.
- **Huffman Codes** – a compression technique for characters
- **I/O Address** On PCs, a three-digit hexadecimal number (2AB, 2A0, etc.) used to identify and signal a peripheral device (serial port, parallel port, sound card, etc.). Address assignments must be unique, otherwise conflicts will occur. There are usually a small number of selectable addresses on each controller card.
- **I/O Bound** - processes that perform lots of IO operations. Each IO operation is followed by a short CPU burst to process the IO, then more IO happens.
- **I/O system** (Input/Output) Transferring data between the CPU and a peripheral device. Every transfer is an output from one device and an input into another.
- **IDE** Integrated Drive Electronics is a type of hardware interface widely used to connect hard disks, CD-ROMs and tape drives to a PC. IDE is very popular because it is currently the least expensive way to connect peripherals. Starting out with 40MB capacities years ago, 2GB and 4GB IDE disk drives have become entry level, costing less than five cents per megabyte.
- **Index file allocation** - Indexed allocation is bringing all the pointers together.
- **Inode** - a structure, like a record type of C++ ect...; provides booking information (i.e. owner, group, permissions, size, modification)
- **Inode/Inode List** - A data structure holding information about files in a Unix file system. There is an inode for each file and a file is uniquely identified by the file system on which it resides and its inode number on that system. Each inode contains the following information: the device where the inode resides, locking information, mode and type of file, the number of links to the file, the owner's user and group ids, the number of bytes in the file, access and modification times, the time the inode itself was last modified and the addresses of the file's blocks on disk.

- **Interactive** - a measurement of quality; A term describing a program whose input and output are interleaved, like a conversation, allowing the user's input to depend on earlier output from the same run.
- **Interactive** Back-and-forth dialog between the user and a computer.
- **Internal Fragmentation** – unusable space that has been allocated;space that has been allocated but not used
- **Inter-Process Communication** - IPC, Interprocess communication (IPC) is a set of programming interfaces that allow a programmer to create and manage individual program processes that can run concurrently in an operating system. This allows a program to handle many user requests at the same time.
- **Interrupt** - A signal informing a program that an event has occurred. When a program receives an interrupt signal, it takes a specified action (which can be to ignore the signal). Interrupt signals can cause a program to suspend itself temporarily to service the interrupt.
- **Interrupt** – An interrupt is a signal from a device attached to a computer or from a program within the computer that causes the main program that operates the computer (the operating system) to stop and figure out what to do next. A signal that gets the attention of the CPU and is usually generated when I/O is required. For example, hardware interrupts are generated when a key is pressed or when the mouse is moved. Software interrupts are generated by a program requiring disk input or output. An internal timer may continually interrupt the computer several times per second to keep the time of day current or for time-sharing purposes. When an interrupt occurs, control is transferred to the operating system, which determines the action to be taken. Interrupts are prioritised; the higher the priority, the faster the interrupt will be serviced.
- **Interrupt level** - which is a integer value defining a relative ordering for dispatching; The purpose of this is to allow certain BusMember instances to see an event before others, and in the case of Event objects, keep the event from propagating onward.
- **IOP** - have direct access to memory
- Keep track of programs
- **Kernel** - The essential part of Unix or other operating systems, responsible for resource allocation, low-level hardware interfaces, security etc.
- **Kernel** The fundamental part of a program, typically an operating system, that resides in memory at all times and provides the basic services. It is the part of the operating system that is closest to the machine and may activate the hardware directly or interface to another software layer that drives the hardware.

- **Kernel Thread** - A kernel thread is a kernel entity, like processes and interrupt handlers; it is the entity handled by the system scheduler
- **Latency** - The time it takes for a packet to cross a network connection, from sender to receiver.
- **Library Thread** - faster than kernel threads,
- **LIFO** - Last in first out (Max. locality and resource utilization)
- **Light weight process** - A single-threaded sub-process which, unlike a thread, has its own process identifier and may also differ in its inheritance and controlling features.
- **Link** - the connection between a certain accompanying directory and the shared file
- **Linked File Allocation** - Each file is a linked list of blocks.
- **Load Balancing** - Load balancing distributes traffic efficiently among network servers so that no individual server is overburdened.
- **Logical address** Logical or virtual address is the programmer's view of memory. Usually this has to be translated into a physical address which is the address of a particular byte in one of the RAM chips on the motherboard or on a peripheral interface board. This is memory from the perspective of the CPU. Available addresses which the CPU can use are determined by the size of the address bus.
- **Long-term Scheduler** - selects processes from this pool and loads them into memory for execution; likes CPU because it's slower and fair
- **Machine Check** - I think it is a register in the kernel that checks if the CPU is OK
- Manage memory
- Manage/control overall performance
- **Memory cycle** A series of operations that take place to read or write a byte of memory. Memory cycle time is the time it takes to perform one memory cycle.
- **Memory Management** - A collection of techniques for providing sufficient memory to one or more processes in a computer system, especially when the system does not have enough memory to satisfy all processes' requirements simultaneously. Techniques include swapping, paging and virtual memory. Memory management is usually performed mostly by a hardware memory management unit.
- **Memory mapping** The location of instructions and data in memory.
- **Memory** The computer's workspace (physically, a collection of RAM chips). It is an important resource, since it determines the size and number of programs that can be run at the same time, as well as the amount of data that

can be processed instantly. All program execution and data processing takes place in memory. The program's instructions are copied into memory from disk or tape and then extracted from memory into the control unit circuit for analysis and execution. The instructions direct the computer to input data into memory from a keyboard, disk, tape or communications channel. As data is entered into memory, the previous contents of that space are lost. Once the data is in memory, it can be processed (calculated, compared and copied). The results are sent to a screen, printer, disk, tape or communications channel. Memory is like an electronic checkerboard, with each square holding one byte of data or instruction. Each square has a separate address like a post office box and can be manipulated independently. As a result, the computer can break apart programs into instructions for execution and data records into fields for processing.

- **Message Queue** - In programming, message queueing is a method by which process (or program instances) can exchange or pass data using an interface to a system-managed queue of messages. Messages can vary in length and be assigned different types or usages. A message queue can be created by one process and used by multiple processes that read and/or write messages to the queue.
- **micro-** one millionth, 10^{-6} or Ü. 10^{6} micro secs in a second
- **Microcode/Firmware** - Microcode is programming that is ordinarily not program-addressable but, unlike hardwired logic, is capable of being modified. Microcode may sometimes be installed or modified by a device's user by altering programmable read-only memory (PROM) or erasable programmable read-only memory (EPROM). IBM uses this term in preference to firmware. Firmware is programming that is inserted into programmable read-only memory (programmable ROM), thus becoming a permanent part of a computing device. Firmware is created and tested like software (using microcode simulation). When ready, it can be distributed like other software and, using a special user interface, installed in the programmable read-only memory by the user. Firmware is sometimes distributed for printers, modems, and other computer devices.
- **milli-** one thousandth, 10^{-3} or m. 103 milli secs in a second
- **Mirroring** - A mirror is a Web site or set of files on a computer server that has been copied to another computer server so that the site or files are available from more than one place
- **MMU** - Memory Management Unit. maps virtual addresses to real addresses; A hardware/firmware component that assists with the mapping of virtual addresses to real addresses. A hardware device or circuit that supports vir-

tual memory and paging by translating virtual addresses into physical addresses. Simply, it has the responcibility to turn Virtual Address into Real Address.

- **Motherboard** The main printed circuit board in an electronic device, which contains sockets that accept additional boards. In a personal computer, the motherboard contains the bus, CPU and co-processor sockets, memory sockets, keyboard controller and supporting chips. Chips that control the video display, serial and parallel ports, mouse and disk drives may or may not be present on the motherboard. If not, they are independent controllers that are plugged into an expansion slot on the motherboard.
- Much more effective for direct access. Inefficient for small files
- **Multiprocessor** - operating system's that support two or more CPU's within a computer
- **Multi-programming** – the ability to run more than one process at a time; don't add any complexity to an operating system, business value is only reason to add complexity to OS2 types: privalous, non privalous
- **Multi-programming** Multiprogramming or cooperative multitasking – when a process has to wait, say for an I/O service, execution of another job in memory can begin.
- **Multi-tasking** The running of two or more programs in one computer at the same time. The number of programs that can be effectively multitasked depends on the type of multitasking performed (pre-emptive vs cooperative), CPU speed and memory and disk capacity. Programs can be run simultaneously in the computer because of the differences between I/O and processing speed. While one program is waiting for input, instructions in another can be executed. During the milliseconds one program waits for data to be read from a disk, millions of instructions in another program can be executed. In interactive programs, thousands of instructions can be executed between each keystroke on the keyboard.
- **Multi-threading** Multitasking within a single process. It allows multiple streams of execution to take place concurrently within the same process, each stream processing a different transaction or message. In order for a multithreaded program to be of any value, it must be run in a multitasking or multiprocessing environment, which allows multiple operations to take place.
- **Multi-user** A system which allows more than one user. E.g. Unix, NT.
- **Mutex** - A mutual exclusion object that allows multiple threads to synchronise access to a shared resource. A mutex has two states: locked and unlocked. Once a mutex has been locked by a thread, other threads

attempting to lock it will block. When the locking thread unlocks (releases) the mutex, one of the blocked threads will acquire (lock) it and proceed.

- **Mutual Exclusion** - A collection of techniques for sharing resources so that different uses do not conflict and cause unwanted interactions. One of the most commonly used techniques for mutual exclusion is the semaphore.
- **Mutual exclusion** When a group of processes are accessing a shared file or other resource, and they need to do this one at a time, some mechanism is needed to ensure when one process has the resource, all others are temporarily excluded.
- **Named Pipe** – A Unix pipe with a filename created using the "mknod" command. Named pipes allow unrelated processes to communicate with each other whereas the normal (un-named) kind can only be used by processes, which are parent and child or siblings (forked from the same parent).
- **Nano-** one thousand millionth, 10^{-9} or n. 10^{9} nano secs in a second
- **Nice Value** - The nice command is used to execute a command at a different scheduling priority than usual. Each process has a nice value which is used to calculate its priority. Nice values range from 0 to 39, with higher nice values resulting in lower priorities. By default, when nice is not used, commands have a nice value of 20. nice executes command with a nice value equal to 20 plus increment.
- No external fragmentation. Effective for sequential access. Problematic for direct access.
- **Non - Privileged Instruction** - I/O instructions are one example of privileged instruction, clock interrupt is another one.
- **Nonpreemptive Scheduling** – picks a process to run and then just lets it un until it blocks
- **N-step-SCAN** - SCAN of N records at a time (Service guarantee)
- **Operating system** The master control program that runs the computer. It is the first program loaded when the computer is turned on, and its main part, called the kernel, resides in memory at all times. It may be developed by the vendor of the computer it's running in or by a third party. It is an important component of the computer system, because it sets the standards for the application programs that run in it. All programs must "talk to" the operating system. The main difference between an operating system and a network operating system is its multiuser capability. Operating systems, such as Macintosh System 7, DOS and Windows, are single user, designed for one person at a desktop computer. Windows NT and UNIX on the other hand are network operating systems, because they are designed to manage multiple user requests at the same time.

- **Page** - Arbitrary division of the address space. Fixed in size. 4k is a common size
- **Page Fault** - Referencing a page which is not currently in memory
- **Page fault** A page fault occurs when the CPU asks for a page which is not actually in memory. A page has to be swapped out and the required page has to be swapped into memory. If the victim page has not been altered it may be possible just to copy the new page in over the victim page
- **Page Frame** - A place in memory (i.e. Ram) that can be used to store a Page
- **Page Slot** - the location on disk (i.e. the swap device) where a page resides; A place on the page/swap device where a page can reside
- **Page Table** - identifies which pages are in main memory, and in which page frames those pages are located
- **Page table** A table which links virtual or logical memory to physical memory locations.
- **Page/Swap device** - the logical paging/swapping disk partition
- **Paging** - A technique for increasing the memory space available by moving infrequently-used parts of a program's working memory from RAM to a secondary storage medium, usually disk. The unit of transfer is called a page. Paging allows the total memory requirements of all running tasks (possibly just one) to exceed the amount of physical memory, whereas swapping simply allows multiple processes to run concurrently, so long as each process on its own fits within physical memory.
- **Paging Scheme** - all pages have the same size, can place the new page into any free slot
- **Parent Process** - The process that invoked fork is the parent process, and the newly created process is the child process. Every process has one parent process, but can have many child processes.
- **Parity** – a concept for data communication, purpose is for data integrity, used to correct and detect errors
- **Partition** A reserved part of disk or memory that is set aside for some purpose. On a PC, new hard disks must be partitioned before they can be formatted for the operating system, and the FDISK utility is used for this task. It can make one partition, creating one drive letter for the entire disk, or it can make several partitions sized to your requirements. For example, drives C:, D: and E: could be the same physical disk, but they would act like three separate drives to the operating system and user.
- **Peripheral** Any hardware device connected to a computer, such as a monitor, keyboard, printer, disk, tape, graphics tablet, scanner, joy stick, paddle and mouse.

- **Peripheral bus** An input/output bus that connects peripherals to the computer. ISA, EISA, PCI and VL-bus are examples of peripheral buses used in a PC.
- **Peripheral Expansion Board** A printed circuit board that plugs into an expansion slot and extends the computer's ability to control another type of peripheral device. All the boards (cards) that plug into a personal computer's bus are expansion boards, such as display adapters, disk controllers and sound cards.
- **Phenomenon of locality** - A normal behavior of almost all programs. At any point in time the address reference by running a program are fairly localized. Only a small set of pages.
- **Pipe** - One of Unix's buffers which can be written to by one asynchronous process and read by another, with the kernel suspending and waking up the sender and receiver according to how full the pipe is.
- **Pre-emptive multitasking** A multitasking method that shares processing time with all running programs. Pre-emptive multitasking creates a true time-sharing environment in which all running programs get a recurring slice of time from the CPU. Depending on the operating system, the time slice may be the same for all programs or it may be adjustable to meet the current mix of programs and users. For example, background programs can be given more CPU time no matter how heavy the foreground load and vice versa.
- **Preemptive Scheduling** – picks a process and lets it run for a maximum of some fixed time
- **PRI** - Priority by process (Control outside the disk queue management)
- **Priority** Give an order of importance to a request or process.
- **Priority Aging** - a scheduling technique to avoid starvation that is used with priority scheduling; an issue of fairness, prevents starvation because priority gets higher as time passes
- **Priority Scheduling** - "Round Robin," each process is assigned a priority and the runnable process with the highest priority is allowed to run
- **Private Key Encryption** - also referred to as conventional or symmetric or single-key encryption was the only available option prior to the advent of Public Key encryption in 1976. This form of encryption was used by Julius Caesar, the Navaho Indians, German U-Boat commanders to present day military, governemnt and private sector applications. It equires all parties that are communicating to share a common key.
- **Privileged Instruction** – A machine code instruction that may only be executed when the processor is running in supervisor mode. Privileged in-

structions include operations such as I/O and memory management. A process running in privileged mode can execute all instructions from the instruction set;

- **Process** – A process is an instance of a program running in a computer. Processes can exchange information or synchronize their operation through several methods of interprocess communication (IPC). (a running program)
- **Process Alocation Algorithm** - how processes can be assigned to nodes in an effective way
- **Process Control Block** – entries of the process table that contains information about the process' state, its program counter, stack pointer, memory allocation, the status of its open files, its accounting and scheduling information, and everything else about the process that must be saved when the process is switched form running to ready or blocked state so that it can be restarted later as if it had never stopped.
- **Process Enable Message Bus** - costly; never ending; must consolidate systems
- **Process Table** - to implement the process model, the OS maintains a table (an array of structures) called the process table
- **Process Tree** - structure of your system
- **Processor** A hardware device (chip) which can read and execute program code.
- **Program** A collection of instructions that tell the computer what to do. A program is called software; hence, program, software and instructions are synonymous. A program is written in a programming language and is converted into the computer's machine language by software called assemblers, compilers and interpreters.
- **Program Check** - I think it is a check that all programs are present in their needed places
- **Program Counter** - A register in the central processing unit that contains the addresss of the next instruction to be executed. The PC is automatically incremented after each instruction is fetched to point to the following instruction.
- **Psuedo Process** – We will refer to the thread that implements this child "process" as the pseudo-process
- **Public Key Encryption** - A cryptographic system that uses two keys — a public key known to everyone and a private or secret key known only to the recipient of the message. When John wants to send a secure message to Jane, he uses Jane's public key to encrypt the message. Jane then uses her private key to decrypt it. An important element to the public key system is

that the public and private keys are related in such a way that only the public key can be used to encrypt messages and only the corresponding private key can be used to decrypt them. Moreover, it is virtually impossible to deduce the private key if you know the public key.

- **Queue** A temporary holding place for data such as message queue, print queue, ready queue.
- **Race Condition** - a logical error, usually involving incorrect use of mutual exclusion that is exposed by how events are ordered in time; ERROR - logical problem, mutual exclusion done incorrectly - exposed by how events are ordered in time (all DBMS and OS are prone to race conditions)
- **RAID** – Redundant Array of Independent Disks, to install a box full of disks next to the computer, typically a large server, replace the disk controller card with a RAID controller, copy the data over to the RAID and then continue normal operations; In RAID level 0 consists of viewing the virtual single disk simulated by the RAID as being divided up into strips of *k* sectors each, with sectors 0 to *k*-1 being strip 0, sectors *k* to 2*k* -1 as strip 1, and so on; RAID level 0 works best with large requests, the bigger the better; performance is excellent and the implmentation is straightforward
- **RAID** - redundant array of independent disks; originally redundant array of inexpensive disks) is a way of storing the same data in different places (thus, redundantly) on multiple hard disks. By placing data on multiple disks, I/O operations can overlap in a balanced way, improving performance. Since multiple disks increases the mean time between failure (MTBF), storing data redundantly also increases fault-tolerance.
- **RAM** Random Access Memory. This is volatile storage to which the CPU (and the DMA controller) have access. RAM is a group of memory chips, typically of the dynamic RAM (DRAM) type, which functions as the computer's primary workspace. The "random" in RAM means that the contents of each byte can be directly accessed without regard to the bytes before or after it. This is also true of other types of memory chips, including ROMs and PROMs. However, unlike ROMs and PROMs, RAM chips require power to maintain their content, which is why you must save your data onto disk before you turn the computer off.
- **Ready List** – The ready processes in the system are kept in a 'queue' called the ready list. This list is sorted by the priority of the processes; the lowest priority process appears at the head of the list and the highest priority process is at the tail. Processes of the same priority are sorted by the order in which they are to get service. Thus when a new process is inserted, it is inserted not at the end of the list, but at a point determined by its priority.

The current process is not on this list, its id is stored in a global integer variable called currpid.

- **Ready** Ready queue holds processes which are ready to be scheduled for access to the CPU.
- **Ready State** - ready to run, but not actually running on the CPU
- **Real Memory** - Backing each page of virtual memory is a page of real memory (called a frame) or some secondary storage, usually disk space. The disk space might be swap space or just some ordinary disk file. Actually, a page of all zeroes sometimes has nothing at all backing it - there's just a flag saying it is all zeroes.
- **Real time** An immediate response. It refers to process control and embedded systems; for example, space flight computers must respond instantly to changing conditions. It also refers to fast transaction processing systems as well as any electronic operation fast enough to keep up with its real-world counterpart (animating complex images, transmitting live video, etc.).
- **Realtime** - a measurement of correctness, based on responsiveness - most systems
- **Real-time** - a system is one In which time plays an essential role. One or more physical devices external to the computer generate stimuli and the computer must react appropriately to them within a fixed amount of time
- **Reference Bit - unmodified** bit;A bit associated with each Frame. Set to 1 by hardware whenever a page is **referenced**. Reset to 0 by hardware periodically.
- **Register** A small, high-speed computer circuit that holds values of internal operations, such as the address of the instruction being executed and the data being processed. When a program is debugged, register contents may be analysed to determine the computer's status at the time of failure.
- **Register Save Area** – The register save area is a set of consecutive quadwords in which registers that are saved and restored by the current procedure are stored. The register save area (RSA) begins at the location pointed to by the RSA offset. The contents of the return address register (R26) are always saved in the first register field (SAVED_RETURN) of the register save area.
- **Resource Manager** - A resource manager is a user-level server program that accepts messages from other programs and, optionally, communicates with hardware.
- **Resource Manager** – The Resource Manager provides routines that allow your application (and system software) to create, delete, open, read, modify, and write resources; get information about them; and alter the Resource Manager's search path.

- **Resource** The components of a system that are required by software or hardware. It refers to resources that have finite limits such as memory and disk. In a PC, it may also refer to the resources required to install a new peripheral device, namely IRQ's, DMA channels, I/O addresses and memory addresses.
- **Response time** - Time between submission of requests and first response to the request.
- **ROM** Read Only Memory is a memory chip that permanently stores instructions and data. Its contents are created at the time of manufacture and cannot be altered. ROM chips are used to store control routines in personal computers (ROM BIOS), peripheral controllers and other electronic equipment. They are also often the sole contents inside a cartridge that plugs into printers, video games and other systems.
- **Rotation Delay** - 1/3 of the time when disks rotate is lost to rotational delay for data placement
- **RSS** - Random scheduling (For analysis & simulation
- **Running State** - process is running on CPU
- **Safe sequence** A sequence for scheduling processes such that a situation will never be reached where a process could ask for more resources than it could be given thereby leading to deadlock.
- Save/restore program status
- **SCAN** - An algorithm for scheduling multiple accesses to a disk. A number of requests are ordered according to the data's position on the storage device. This reduces the disk arm movement to one "scan" or sweep across the whole disk in the worst case. The serivce time can be estimated from the disk's track-to-track seek time, maximum seek time (one scan), and maximum rotational latency.
- **Scheduling algorithms** SSTF, FCFS, SJF, RR. etc.
- **Secondary storage** External non-volatile storage, such as disk and tape.
- **Sector** - A unit of data or memory, often, but not exclusively, on a magnetic disk or magnetic tape; also called block
- **Seek Time** - The time it takes for a disk drive to move its head(s) from one track to another. The seek time depends on the power of the servo, the mass of the heads, the number of tracks traversed and the time taken to position the heads over the target track accurately enough to start data transfer.
- **Segment** - independent address spaces
- **Segment Table** - a table of segments
- **Segmentation Scheme** - placement policy that uses either: Best Fit, First Fit, Worst Fit

- **Semaphore** A shared space for inter-process communications (IPC) controlled by "wake up" and "sleep" commands. The source process fills a queue and goes to sleep until the destination process uses the data and tells the source process to wake up.
- **Sequential Access** - Refers to reading or writing data records in sequential order, that is, one record after the other. To read record 10, for example, you would first need to read records 1 through 9. This differs from random access, in which you can read and write records in any order.
- **Short-term Scheduler** - like I/O, because it is quicker
- **Signal** - Signals are a process event notification mechanism that has been part of the UNIX system from the earliest days. Signals are used to notify a process or thread of a particular event. Many engineers compare signals with hardware interrupts, which occur when a hardware subsystem such as a disk I/O interface (an SCSI host adapter, for example) generates an interrupt to a processor as a result of a completed I/O.
- **Slow Interrupt** - A simple mode 1 interrupt causes the system interrupt to run only one third of the time. Useful for studying ROM routines.
- **Smart Cards** - are a small, tamperproof computer that can engage in a discussion (called a protocol) with a central computer to authenticate the user
- **Software** Instructions for the computer. A series of instructions that performs a particular task is called a program. The two major categories of software are system software and application software. System software is made up of control programs such as the operating system and database management system (DBMS). Application software is any program that processes data for the user (inventory, payroll, spreadsheet, word processor, etc.)
- **Software Interrupt** - Interrupt signals initiated by programs are called software interrupts. A software interrupt is also called a trap or an exception
- **Spin Lock** - Spin locks are kernel-defined, kernel-mode-only synchronization mechanisms, exported as an opaque type: KSPIN_LOCK. A spin lock can be used to protect shared data or resources from simultaneous access by routines that can execute concurrently and at raised IRQL in SMP machines. Many components use spin locks, including drivers
- **Spooling** Synchronised Peripheral Operations On Line. The overlapping of low-speed operations with normal processing. It originated with mainframes in order to optimise slow operations such as reading cards and printing. Card input was read onto disk and printer output was stored on disk. In that way, the actual business data processing was done at high speed, since all I/O was on disk.

- **SSTF** – Shortest service time first (High utilization, small queues); problems are starvation and no distration for which way BOOM is going
- **Starvation** - a low priority process doesn't get access and eventually ages and never gets run
- **Starvation** - when a low priority process does not get access to an available resource, due to the fact the system is busy; a low priority process doesn't get access and eventually ages and never gets run
- **Stateful** - cookies are URL rewriting which makes the stateless HTML page Stateful
- **Status Register** - A register in most CPUs which stores additional information about the results of machine instructions, e.g. comparisons. It usually consists of several independent flags such as carry, overflow and zero. The CSR is chiefly used to determine the outcome of conditional branch instructions or other forms of conditional execution.
- **Striping** - distributing data over multiple drives
- **Super Block** - Section of computer hard disk drive that contains information about the file system.
- **Swap/Page Device** - To move a program from fast-access memory to a slow-access memory ("swap out"), or vice versa ("swap in"). The term often refers specifically to the use of a hard disk (or a swap file) as virtual memory or "swap space".
- **Swapping** - OS suspends a process by removing all pages of a process to the swap device (swap out) or un-suspends a process (swap in). Take entire process address space and take off or suspend process
- **Symbolic Link** - keep the path name its linked to in the directory
- **Synchronisation** Refers to events that are synchronised, or coordinated, in time. Causing events to occur in a particular order.
- **System Call/Supervisor Call** - (System Call)The mechanism used by an application program to request service from the operating system.
- **System mode** - where both the system level and the application level instructions can be simulated
- **Test & set** An atomic function used to provide for synchronisation.
- **Test and Set Instruction** - a hardware instruction that is used to provide for mutual exclusion
- The link list is implemented in that section. Actual file blocks contain no links.
- **Thrashing** - modern operating systems want to avoid thrashing, will use a MinMax Algorithm so at a level you will start to swap out, then at a different level you begin to swap in (contention)

- **Thrashing** - MPL is too high. Processes cannot reach their working set and there is an excessive amount of paged faults.
- **Thread** - a thread is placeholder information associated with a single use of a program that can handle multiple concurrent users.
- **Threading** - Threads are similar to processes, in that both represent a single sequence of instructions executed in parallel with sequences, either by time slicing or multiprocessing. This allows a program to split itself into two or more simultaneously running tasks. A common use of threads is having one thread paying attention to the graphical user interface, while others do a long calculation in the background. The user will see the application responsive. Threads are distinguished from traditional multi-tasking processes in that processes are typically independent, carry considerable state information, and interact only through system-provided inter-process communication mechanisms. Multiple threads, on the other hand, typically share the state information of a single process, share memory and other resources directly. On operating systems that have special facilities for threads, it is typically faster for the system to context-switch between different threads in the same process than to switch between different processes. An advantage of a multi-threaded program is that it can operate faster on machines that have multiple CPUs, or across a cluster of machines
- **Time Slice** - the time allocated to a process by the dispatcher;a time interval also called quantum. The period of time for which a process is allowed to run uninterrupted in a pre-emptive multitasking operating system.
- **Timer** - also called clocks, keep the time also keep processes from monopolizing the CPU
- **Track** - The part of a disk which passes under one read/write head while the head is stationary. The number of tracks on a disk surface therefore corresponds to the number of different radial positions of the head(s). The collection of all tracks on all surfaces at a given radial position is known a cylinder and each track is divided into sectors.
- **Track** A storage channel on disk or tape. On disks, tracks are concentric circles (hard and floppy disks) or spirals (CDs and videodiscs). On tapes, they are parallel lines. Their format is determined by the specific drive they are used in. On magnetic devices, bits are recorded as reversals of polarity in the magnetic surface. On CDs, bits are recorded as physical pits under a clear, protective layer.
- **Transaction** An activity or request. Orders, purchases, changes, additions and deletions are typical business transactions stored in the computer. Transactions update one or more master files and serve as both an audit trail and

history for future analyses. Ad hoc queries are a type of transaction as well, but are usually just acted upon and not saved. Transaction volume is a major factor in figuring computer system size and speed.

- **Translation Lookaside Buffer** - a cache, the most recent transalations for virtual address to absolute addresses
- **Trap Door** - "man in the middle" intermediary; the intermediary takes packets and corrupts them
- **Trap** To test for a particular condition in a running program; for example, to "trap an interrupt" means to wait for a particular interrupt to occur and then execute a corresponding routine. An error trap tests for an error condition and provides a recovery routine. A debugging trap waits for the execution of a particular instruction in order to stop the program and analyse the status of the system at that moment.
- **Trapdoor/Backdoor** - a secret way into someone elses machine
- **Trojan Horse** - S. 660. a code segment that misuses its environment; a Trojan horse is a program in which malicious or harmful code is contained inside apparently harmless programming or data in such a way that it can get control and do its chosen form of damage, such as ruining the file allocation table on your hard disk.
- **Turnaround time** Time elapsing between request for a service and its completion. It is the sum of wait time and service time. It could be understood as difference between arrival and departure or completion times.
- **Unix Shell** - is a command line interpreter
- **Unix Shell** - is a command line interpreter; the outermost part of an operating system that interacts with user commands
- **Unsafe state** A system is in an unsafe state when it would be possible for a process to ask for more resources than are available leading to a situation of deadlock. An unsafe state does not necessarily lead to deadlock because processes may not call upon the maximum number of required resources.
- **User mode** - where only the application level instructions can be simulated. User mode simulation is faster than system mode, but doesn't support features such as multi-threading, hence for perfect simulation accuracy, it is necessary to use system-mode
- **Variable Partition** - A process using variable partitions may allocate and deallocate pages during its execution. The use of variable partitions permits the location, size and even the number of partitions to vary dynamically. The deallocation of pages then benefits processes that need to increase their partition sizes.

- **Virtual Address** - A memory location accessed by an application program in a system with virtual memory such that intervening hardware and/or software maps the virtual address to real (physical) memory. During the course of execution of an application, the same virtual address may be mapped to many different physical addresses as data and programs are paged out and paged in to other locations.
- **Virtual Address Space** - piece of hardware that make virtual address space into virtual address
- **Virtual machine** The illusion a process has that it is the only process using the OS and hardware resources. The illusion is created by resource schedulers and memory management which allocate requested resources according to some algorithm. The CPU executes instructions so fast that all resource requests seem to be answered immediately.
- **Virtual memory** Simulating more memory than actually exists, allowing the computer to run larger programs or more programs concurrently. It breaks up the program into small segments, called pages, and brings as many pages into memory that fit into a reserved area for that program. When additional pages are required, it makes room for them by swapping them to disk. It keeps track of pages that have been modified, so that they can be retrieved when needed again.
- **Virus** - like worms are designed to spread into other programs and wreak havoc in a system, including modifying and destroying files and causing cashes and program malfunctions
- **Volatile** Volatile memory is memory which is lost once power is turned off. Whilst power is on the contents of volatile memory must be constantly refreshed.
- **Wait** - waits and blocks parent until child dies
- **Waiting State** - waiting for some event like IO to happen
- **Waiting time** Time between requesting a resource and actually receiving it.
- **Working Set** - minimum number of pages a process needs in memory to run efficiently
- **Worm** - a free standing program that are aware of the network and tried to find others on the network in a self replicating manner; a process that uses the spawn mechanism to clobber system performance
- **Worst fit** Here the largest available resource (e.g. RAM) is allocated leaving the largest amount of free space in the hope that the large available area could still remain useful.

REFRENCES

1. *Operating System Concepts* (7th Edition) by Abraham Silberschatz, Peter Baer Galvin, and Greg Gagne
2. *Modern Operating Systems* by Andrew S. Tanenbaum
3. *Operating Systems* by Stuart Madnick and John Donovan
4. *Operating Systems: AND C Programming Language* by Gary Nutt, Brian W. Kernighan, and Dennis Ritchie
5. *Introduction to Operating Systems* by Philip Avery
6. *The Architecture of Computer Hardware and System Software: An Information Technology Approach* by Irv Englander
7. *Operating Systems Design and Implementation* (3rd Edition) by Andrew S Tanenbaum and Albert S. Woodhull
8. *Understanding Operating Systems*, Fifth Edition by Ann McHoes and Ida M. Flynn
9. *Operating Systems Principles* by Lubomir F. Bic and Alan C. Shaw
10. *Operating Systems: Internals and Design Principles* (6th Edition) (GOAL Series) by William Stallings
11. *Guide To Operating Systems*, Enhanced Edition by Michael Palmer
12. *Survey of Operating Systems* (Mike Meyers' Computer Skills) by Charles Holcombe and Jane Holcombe
13. *Operating Systems: A Systematic View* (6th Edition) by William S. Davis and T.M. Rajkumar
14. *Developing Your Own 32-bit Operating System* by Richard Burgess
15. *Operating System Design-Internetworking with Xinu: v. 1* by Douglas E. Comer
16. *Introduction to Operating Systems and Networks* by Ruth A. Watson
17. *Schaum's Outline of Operating Systems* by J. Archer Harris
18. *Operating Systems* by C. Ritchie

19. *The Integral Operating System* by Ken Wilber

20. *The Design and Implementation of the FreeBSD Operating System* by Marshall Kirk McKusick and George V. Neville-Neil

21. *Design of the UNIX Operating System* (Prentice Hall Software Series) by Maurice J. Bach

22. *Learning the Unix Operating System: A Concise Guide for the New User* by Jerry Peek, Grace Todino, and John Strang

23. IT Essentials 2: Network Operating Systems Companion Guide

24. *Mac OS X V10.5 Advanced System Administration* by Edward R. Marczak

25. *Operating System Design-Internetworking with Xinu: v. 1* by Douglas E. Comer

26. *Mike Meyers' A+ Guide to Operating Systems* by Michael Meyers